The Monograph and its Chapters

This is one of five volumes that make up the Monograph on the Planning and Design of Tall Buildings. For reference purposes the broad outline of the material contained in the five volumes is as follows:

PC PLANNING AND ENVIRONMENTAL CRITERIA FOR TALL BUILDINGS

1. Philosophy of Tall Buildings
2. History of Tall Buildings
3. Social Effects of the Environment
4. Sociopolitical Influences
5. Economics
6. Architecture
7. Interference and Environmental Effects
8. Urban Planning
9. External Transportation
10. Parking
11. Operation, Maintenance, and Ownership
12. Energy Conservation
13. Motion Perception and Tolerance
14. Project Management
15. Application of Systems Methodology

SC TALL BUILDING SYSTEMS AND CONCEPTS

1. Structural Systems
2. Mechanical and Service Systems
3. Electrical Systems
4. Vertical and Horizontal Transportation
5. Cladding
6. Partitions, Walls, and Ceilings
7. Foundation Systems
8. Construction Systems

CL TALL BUILDING CRITERIA AND LOADING

1. Gravity Loads and Temperature Effects
2. Earthquake Loading and Response
3. Wind Loading and Wind Effects
4. Fire
5. Accidental Loading
6. Quality Criteria
7. Structural Safety and Probabilistic Methods

SB STRUCTURAL DESIGN OF TALL STEEL BUILDINGS

1. Commentary on Structural Steel Design
2. Elastic Analysis and Design
3. Plastic Analysis and Design
4. Stability
5. Stiffness
6. Fatigue and Fracture
7. Connections
8. Load and Resistance Factor Design (Limit States Design)
9. Mixed Construction

CB STRUCTURAL DESIGN OF TALL CONCRETE AND MASONRY BUILDINGS

1. Characteristics of Concrete and Masonry Tall Buildings
2. Design Criteria and Safety Provisions
3. Concrete Framing Systems for Tall Buildings
4. Optimization of Tall Concrete Buildings
5. Elastic Analysis
6. Nonlinear Behavior and Analysis
7. Model Analysis
8. Stability
9. Stiffness, Deflections, and Cracking
10. Creep, Shrinkage, and Temperature Effects
11. Design of Cast-in-place Concrete
12. Design of Structures with Precast Concrete Elements
13. Design of Masonry Structures

This Monograph is a major focus of the Council on Tall Buildings and Urban Habitat. The objective is to document the state of art relative to the planning and design of tall buildings and to indicate possible future advances and areas of further research. Please inform the Headquarters of any significant omissions or of additions that should be made.

The opinions expressed are those of the committees and do not necessarily reflect those of the publisher, the professional society sponsors, or the U.S. National Science Foundation which partially supported the work that led to this Monograph.

Published by
American Society of Civil Engineers
345 East 47th Street
New York, N.Y. 10017

Council Headquarters
Fritz Engineering Laboratory—13
Lehigh University
Bethlehem, Pennsylvania 18015

Tall Building
Criteria and Loading

Library of Congress Catalog card number: 79-56002
ISBN 0-87262-237-1

Printed in the United States of America

Monograph on
Planning and Design of Tall Buildings

Volume CL

Tall Building
Criteria and Loading

Group Coordinators

Leslie E. Robertson
Takeo Naka

Group Editors

Edwin H. Gaylord
Rowland J. Mainstone

Group Secretary

Le-Wu Lu

Council on Tall Buildings and Urban Habitat

Steering Group

D. Sfintesco*	Chairman	C.T.I.C.M.	Paris
F. R. Khan*	Vice-Chairman	Skidmore, Owings & Merrill	Chicago
L. S. Beedle*	Director	Lehigh University	Bethlehem
G. W. Schulz*	Secretary	Universität Innsbruck	Innsbruck
L. W. Lu	Research Advisor	Lehigh University	Bethlehem

F. L. Codella*	Tower International	Cleveland
H. J. Cowan*	University of Sydney	Sydney
B. M. Dornblatt	B. M. Dornblatt and Associates, Inc.	New Orleans
P. Dubas	Swiss Federal Institute of Technology	Zürich
G. F. Fox	Howard, Needles, Tammen, & Bergendoff	New York
Y. Friedman	Architect	Paris
B. Frommes*	IFHP	Luxembourg
J. M. Garrelts	Columbia University	New York
M. P. Gaus	National Science Foundation	Washington
J.A. Gilligan	United States Steel Corporation	Pittsburgh
T. R. Higgins	Consulting Engineer	New York
B. G. Johnston	University of Arizona	Tucson
T. C. Kavanagh	Iffland Kavanagh Waterbury	Hastings-on-Hudson
H. R. Lane	H. R. Lane AIA Assoc. Architects	Los Angeles
I. Martin	Capacete-Martin & Assoc.	San Juan
C. Massonnet	Universite de Liege	Liege
W. A. Milek	American Institute of Steel Construction	New York
T. Naka	University of Tokyo	Tokyo
E. O. Pfrang	National Bureau of Standards	Washington
J. Rankine	Rankine & Hill Engineering Consultants	Sydney
R. C. Reese	Consulting Engineer	Toledo
L. E. Robertson	Skilling, Helle, Christiansen, Robertson	New York
P. H. Sedway	Sedway/Cooke	San Francisco
R. Thoma	Hentrich, Petschnigg & Partners	Dusseldorf
E. K. Timby	Howard, Needles, Tammen & Bergendoff	New York
A. W. Turchick	American Society of Civil Engineers	New York
B. Thürlimann	Swiss Federal Institute of Technology	Zürich
I. M. Viest	Bethlehem Steel Corporation	Bethlehem
G. Wästlund	Kungliga Tekniska Hogskolan	Stockholm

*Member of Executive Committee

Editorial Committee

L. S. Beedle (Ch.), D. Sfintesco, F. R. Khan, L. W. Lu, G. W. Schulz, R. Kowalczyk, M. P. Gaus, J. I. Moyer, P. A. Parisi

Group PC: T. C. Kavanagh, Y. Friedman, R. Thoma, R. C. Herrenkohl, W. Henn, C. Norberg-Schulz

Group SC: F. R. Khan, J. Rankine, W. P. Moore, H. D. Eberhart, H. J. Cowan

Group CL: L. E. Robertson, T. Naka, R. J. Mainstone, E. H. Gaylord, L. W. Lu

Group SB: T. R. Higgins, P. Dubas, C. N. Gaylord, M. Watabe, L. W. Lu

Group CB: R. C. Reese, I. Martin, B. Thürliman, G. Wästlund, J. G. MacGregor, I. Lyse, T. Huang

Chairman, Vice-Chairman, and Editors of each committee (identified in each chapter), affiliates representing sponsors, and selected national representatives.

Professional Society Sponsors

International Association for Bridge and Structural Engineering (IABSE)
American Society of Civil Engineers (ASCE)
American Institute of Architects (AIA)
American Planners Association (APA)
International Federation for Housing and Planning (IFHP)
International Union of Architects (UIA)

Foreword

This is one volume of a multivolume Monograph bringing together current knowledge about tall buildings themselves and about their interactions with the urban environment. Topics covered include structural and service systems, foundations, loadings and structural safety, structural design methods, architecture and urban planning, related cultural, social, and political factors, and the management and operation of buildings in use. The whole Monograph consists of 52 chapters arranged in the following five volumes:

Volume PC: Planning and Environmental Criteria for Tall Buildings
Volume SC: Tall Building Systems and Concepts
Volume CL: Tall Building Criteria and Loading
Volume SB: Structural Design of Tall Steel Buildings
Volume CB: Structural Design of Tall Concrete and Masonry Buildings

This volume deals with the loads to which tall buildings are subjected, and with the precise definition of the related structural requirements that are necessary before a client's basic needs can be translated into a safe design. The basic needs and associated architectural, planning, and engineering concepts are dealt with in Volumes PC and SC. Detailed aspects of structural design are dealt with in Volumes SB and CB.

It is important to take into account all possible loadings, whatever the height of building, but even more particular care is needed in the case of *tall* buildings. Steel buildings at present hold the record for height and tax the designer's ingenuity in providing adequate resistance to lateral loadings. Concrete buildings are more numerous and widely distributed. Vertical gravity loads may, for them, present the main problem. Both these types of loads are among those considered in this volume.

The title "Criteria and Loading" has been chosen to reflect the fact that the discussion does not stop short at the description of the loads to be expected, but includes a chapter on safety and the probabilistic basis of rational design criteria. Reference is also made, as appropriate, to current Codes and Specifications. The contents, the over-all purpose, and the special contributions of the volume are described more fully in the Preface which follows this Foreword.

The Monograph as a whole should be of value to all those with major responsibilities for planning and design practice. A more detailed statement concerning its objective and its development is described in the Foreword to the concrete volume (Volume CB), to which reference is here made. In addition to the function of the Monograph to communicate to knowledgeable persons the state-of-the-art and the most advanced knowledge in the field, the text on a given topic may well be most useful to those in *other* disciplines. The Council has seen considerable benefit accrue from the mix of professions, and this is no less true in the Monograph itself.

To afford such benefit to all appropriate professionals, every effort has been made to make the glossary a comprehensive one.

In the same vein, where more than one point of view was appropriate, those views were set forth. Since there are several instances in which there is no final answer, there are numerous points of controversy; and such controversy has not been avoided.

Tall Buildings

A full definition of the term "tall building" as used in the Monograph is given in the Foreword to Volume CB, but is worth repeating here in condensed form: A building is a structure designed for residential, commercial, or industrial purposes. A *tall* building is one in which "tallness" strongly influences planning, design, or use.

The Council

This Monograph has been prepared by the various topical committees of the Council on Tall Buildings and Urban Habitat. The Council is an activity sponsored by engineering, architectural, and planning professionals throughout the world, and was established to study and report on all aspects of the planning, design, construction, and operation of tall buildings.

The Professional Society sponsors are the International Association for Bridge and Structural Engineering (IABSE), the American Society of Civil Engineers (ASCE), the American Institute of Architects (AIA), the American Planning Association (APA), the International Federation for Housing and Planning (IFHP), and the International Union of Architects (UIA).

Some of the Professional Society sponsors have contributed further to the Council's work through closely related activities. The American Society of Civil Engineers has been one of these. A committee of its Structural Division has arranged highly relevant technical sessions as part of the Society's National Meetings. Since 1970, 15 of these have been held in major cities of the United States. One of the keys to this involvement has been the interest of the "contact member" of the ASCE Structural Division Executive Committee. Those who have served in this role have been: William J. Hall, Barney Dornblatt, Fred Sterbenz, Fred Palmer, and Donald Strand.

Direct contributions to the Monograph have come from many countries and many people. One further notable characteristic is that much of the material has been prepared by practicing designers. Members of design and industrial firms accounted for nearly two-thirds of the 175-member editorial team. The wide mix of disciplines has also been notable—right from the initial planning phase to the final reviews of the written contributions. To this the Monograph owes its unusually broad perspective.

In addition to the editorial committee, more than 800 individuals made specific contributions. All told, about thirteen hundred committee members from 78 countries had opportunity to review at least one chapter.

Units, Symbols, References

With regard to the units, it will be evident to the reader that complete uniformity in the text was not achieved. The general guideline was to use SI units first, followed by American units in parentheses and metric when necessary. A conversion table for units is supplied at the end of the volume. Because of the extensive amount of new artwork that otherwise would have been involved, and the consequent delay, many previously existing drawings and tables remain with their original units. However, enough conversions are given throughout to enable a proper interpretation.

A list of symbols appears at the end of the volume. Because variations between chapters (and variations from Draft ISO/1015 3898 of December 1975), the chapter number is identified with each citation.

The spelling was agreed at the outset to be "American" English.

The arrangement of the references (alphabetical, followed by date) serves the following purposes:

1. In the text the articles can be cited without later having to change the numbers if additional references are added.
2. The reference list can be conveniently collected alphabetically and, similarly, does not have to be rearranged.
3. The purely bibliographic items (those documents not cited in the text but which relate to the chapter) can be included in the same list without detracting from its function as a reference list.

A condensation of the relevant references and bibliography will be found at the end of each chapter. On the one hand, it is for convenience; and on the other hand, it will be necessary in those cases where reprints are made of the chapter. Full citations are given only in a composite list at the end of the volume with an indication of the committee that has used the reference in its work.

The following format is suggested for those who wish to refer to a chapter, to a volume, or to the Monograph as a whole in their own publications:

To refer to a *chapter*:

> Council on Tall Buildings, Committee 9, 1980
> QUALITY CRITERIA, Chapter CL-6, Vol. CL of Monograph on
> Planning and Design of Tall Buildings, ASCE, New York.

To refer to a *volume*:

> Council on Tall Buildings, Group CL, 1980
> TALL BUILDING CRITERIA AND LOADING, Vol.CL of Monograph
> on Planning and Design of Tall Buildings, ASCE, New York.

To refer to the *Monograph*:

> Council on Tall Buildings, 1978–1981
> PLANNING AND DESIGN OF TALL BUILDINGS, a Monograph in
> 5 volumes, ASCE, New York.

The Monograph has been, from the start, the prime focus of the Council's activity, and it is intended that its periodic revision and the implementation of its ideas and recommendations should be a continuing activity on both national and international levels. Readers who find that some topic is inadequately treated or calls for further thought, are invited to bring it to our attention. Perhaps also they can draw our attention to publications or recent research results that have been overlooked. It is planned that periodically "new information about tall buildings and the urban habitat" will be collected and disseminated. Your contributions should be submitted. Each committee will get a chance to update its material.

As one of the Committee leaders said, "We never can reach the 'perfect' Monograph. A Monograph as it is at this moment, published as soon as possible, is much better than the perfect Monograph never published at all."

Acknowledgment

This work would not have been possible but for the financial support of the National Science Foundation and the American Iron and Steel Institute, who supported the program out of which the Monograph developed. The understanding and support of Dr. Michael Gaus of NSF has been most appreciated.

Acknowledgment is next due the staff at the Fritz Engineering Laboratory with whom it has been my pleasure to be associated. Special mention is due Dr. Le-Wu Lu who has been co-director of the project from which this effort has evolved; he has given particular attention to Volume CL as "Group Secretary," providing not only a technical review, but maintaining contact with the editorial committee for this volume. François Cheong-Siat-Moy assisted in this phase as well. Other staff members involved were: Jack Gera (Draftsman), Richard Sopko (Photographer), Mary Snyder (Secretary), Perry Green (Research Assistant), and Pat McHugh, Suzanne Gimson, and Edward Beedle, Student Assistants.

Special acknowledgment is due Jamie Moyer, who since 1975 has served as my associate responsible for all of the processing and production phases of the Monograph effort at Lehigh. She performed outstanding service not only to us on the headquarters staff but to each member of the editorial committee.

We are indebted to Paul Parisi, Richard Torrens, and Irving Amron (ASCE) for guidance and direction during the publication phases of the work. Janet Davis served notably as editorial consultant to ASCE. Her attention to editorial detail was remarkable.

Next, tribute is due the Chairmen and Vice-Chairmen who provided leadership to the committees. To the Committee Editors fell the major burden of writing, editing, adjusting, and rewriting. Their contributions have been most significant. All of these are identified on the title page of the respective chapters.

The true "authors" of the Monograph were sometimes the committee editors, but in most cases they were the contributors and reporters whose papers formed the essential first drafts—the starting point. These are identified in the acknowledgment page that follows the title page for each chapter.

The coordinating and editing effort on the volume as a whole has been the work of the Group Coordinators, Leslie E. Robertson and Takeo Naka, and the Group Editors, Rowland Mainstone and Edwin Gaylord. Rowland Mainstone, the non-USA Editor of the volume, diligently contributed not only the insights gained from his personal researches, but also the wider point of view of one associated with one of the world's principal government-supported Building Research Establishments. Edwin Gaylord applied his skills not only from the background of the field of education, in which he is a leader, and from his significant experience as an author, but also as a member of active specification-writing groups and councils interested therein.

The Council has been most fortunate to have the leadership of Leslie Robertson who has been responsible for the structural design of some of the world's tallest buildings and of innovations therein. The Council is equally indebted to Takeo Naka whose role as an educator has kept knowledge into the forefront and who has continued, in so-called retirement, as a contributor to the commentary and specification-writing groups that are so important to the actual *use* of the new data. The Council acknowledges, with sincere gratitude, the contributions of both of these leaders.

Lehigh University   *Lynn S. Beedle*
Bethlehem, Pennsylvania   *Editor-in-Chief*
1980

Preface

Structural safety and serviceability become increasingly important considerations in the choice of over-all form of a building as its height increases. The design criteria by which they are assured should therefore be of interest not only to structural designers but also to all others concerned with over-all planning.

These criteria stem, on the one hand, from the loads that must be carried and, on the other, from general considerations of safety that recognize the inherent variabilities both of the loads themselves and of such things as material strengths and workmanship. They are largely, though not wholly, independent of the materials chosen. Where they are affected by the choice of material they are discussed further in Volumes SB and CB.

For structural specialists, and for code writers, these chapters are essential basic reading for the further discussions in Volumes SB and CB. Also, it is hoped that they will give designers other than structural specialists all the basic understanding they need of the requirements to be met if the client is to be given a structurally adequate building at reasonable cost.

The first five chapters deal with different classes of load—gravity loads and temperature effects, earthquake loads, wind, fire, and accidental loads. We then turn to quality control—control of the variations of material strengths and workmanship—and to over-all safety considerations.

Gravity Loads and Temperature Effects

The weight of the building and of its contents is the principal load due to gravity. The contents of the building, the live loads, depend on the occupancy of the building; the accuracy of their assessment has been increased by sample surveys in several countries and by considering the probability of various load combinations. Additional gravity loads may occur during the construction of the building, and these loads require special consideration. Changes in temperature cause expansion or contraction of structural members, and these impose stresses that may be appreciable.

Earthquake Loading and Response

The reliability of earthquake-resistant design has been improved greatly by obtaining more accurate information on ground motion and on the dynamic response of the building.

It is advisable to make seismic-resistant structures light, symmetric, and ductile. Structural discontinuities should be avoided. Connections should be made large enough to assure that they are not highly stressed. Special consideration must be given to the possibility of stress reversal and to assuring the continued functioning of essential building services.

Wind Loading and Wind Effects

Although the effect of wind is particularly important in the design of tall buildings, very few high-rise structures have suffered damage from wind. This is due largely to improved statistical prediction of extreme wind loads and to the use of wind tunnels to examine the response of tall structures.

While human comfort is adversely affected by excessive sway of a tall building and by windiness in pedestrian precincts, these conditions can be avoided with proper design.

Fire

Modern design procedures consider the spread of fire, the removal of smoke, and the development of areas of refuge. If this is done correctly, as described in this chapter, the risk of loss of life from fire in a tall building is greatly reduced.

Accidental Loading

Although it is unlikely that a building will be damaged by an explosion or by an impact from an airplane, the result could be so catastrophic that the possibility must be considered. The design must assure that progressive collapse is prevented.

Quality Criteria

A system of quality control is necessary to make certain that the materials used in the building attain the specified characteristics. Separate consideration is given to structural steel, concrete, concrete block, brick, and glass. Material selection, shop fabrication, field construction, and tolerances are discussed in detail.

Structural Safety and Probabilistic Methods

Just as loads are subject to statistical variation, so also are the properties of the materials used. The idealizations and approximations of analysis and design introduce variable errors in predicted performance. Probabilistic methods of analysis are required to assure adequate safety of the completed structure.

The chapter discusses failure criteria and the methodologies for establishing consistent safety, for evaluating uncertainty, and for establishing appropriate safety levels.

The volumes *Planning and Environmental Criteria for Tall Buildings* and *Systems and Concepts*, along with this volume, are devoted to general principles which have broad application to tall buildings, regardless of the material of construction. Designers of tall buildings will find a wealth of useful information in these volumes and it is hoped that architects and engineers, not specializing in the structural disciplines, will find the reading both rewarding and interesting.

Leslie E. Robertson
Takeo Naka
Edwin H. Gaylord
Rowland J. Mainstone
Le-Wu Lu

Contents

Contents

CL-3   Wind Loading and Wind Effects

Contents

CL-5 Accidental Loading

Contents

CL-7 Structural Safety and Probabilistic Methods

Tall Building Criteria and Loading

Chapter CL-1

Gravity Loads and Temperature Effects

Prepared by Committee 5 (Gravity Loads and Temperature Effects) of the Council on Tall Buildings and Urban Habitat as part of the Monograph on the Planning and Design of Tall Buildings.

Raymond C. Reese Chairman
G. Bernard Godfrey Vice-Chairman
G. Robert Fuller Editor

AUTHOR ACKNOWLEDGMENT

Special acknowledgment is due those individuals whose contributions and papers formed the substantial first drafts of the various sections of this chapter. First are the state-of-art reporters from the 1972 International Conference whose material was published in the Lehigh Proceedings. These individuals are:

R.C. Reese, Sections 1.1, 1.2, 1.3, and 1.7
G. R. Mitchell, Sections 1.2, 1.3, 1.5, and 1.8
S. M. Johnson, Sections 1.2, 1.3, 1.6, and 1.8
K. Apeland, Sections 1.3, 1.7, and 1.8
M. Izumi, Section 1.4
L. Y. Huang, Section 1.5
W. E. Greene, Jr., Section 1.8.

In addition to this, other sections were based on special contributions prepared by:

E. Rosenblueth, Section 1.2
R. J. Wheen, Section 1.6
G. R. Fuller, Section 1.3.

CONTRIBUTORS

The following is a complete list of those who have submitted written material for possible use in the chapter, whether or not that material was used in the final version. The Committee Chairman and Editor were given quite complete latitude. Frequently length limitations precluded the inclusion of much valuable material. The Bibliography contains all contributions. The contributors are: D.E. Allen, K. Apeland, F.D. Beresford, F. A. Blakey, R. A. Crist, G. R. Fuller, T. V. Galambos, G. B. Godfrey, W. E. Greene, Jr., P. Grundy, M. M. Guttero, L. Y. Huang, M. Izumi, S. M. Johnson, A. P. Kabaila, G. F. König, C. K. Lalwani, J. A. P. Laurie, H. S. Lew, R. J. Mainstone, M. Marosszeky, G. R. Mitchell, K. Muto, V. Navaratnarajah, M. K. Ravindra, R. C. Reese, E. Rosenblueth, Y. Saillard, L. M. Schneider, W. R. Schriever, J. R. Shaver, B. H. Spratt, P. J. Taylor, B. F. Thomas, M. Wakabayashi, R. J. Wheen, R. W. Woodgate, R. N. Wright.

COMMITTEE MEMBERS

K. Apeland, F. D. Beresford, F. A. Blakey, A. Bohac, G. R. Fuller, G. B. Godfrey, W. E. Greene, Jr., P. Grundy, M. M. Guttero, L. Y. Huang, M. Izumi, A. Johnson, S. M. Johnson, A. P. Kabaila, H. Kaupa, C. K. Lalwani, J. M. Leigh, M. Marosszeky, E. Paloheimo, A. Picardi, E. M. Poulsen, R. C. Reese, E. Rosenblueth, L. M. Schneider, W. R. Schriever, S. Shore, A. G. Sokolov, P. J. Taylor, R. J. Wheen, J. Witteveen.

Gravity Loads and Temperature Effects

1.1 INTRODUCTION

This chapter considers the magnitudes of dead, live, and construction loads, and meteorologic loadings of snow and temperature effects.

With the increasing tendency to combine load effects probabilistically it becomes increasingly important to distinguish clearly each category of load. Some attention is given to the reduction of live loads in high-rise structures because of the unlikely situation that all floors will be simultaneously loaded. Attention is also given to the combination of load effects, not only live, dead, and temperature, but wind, earthquake, blast and the like, as well. A review of load surveys and associated load prediction is covered in this chapter (Reese, 1973).

1 Classification

Dead Loads. Dead loads can be defined as including every element of weight in the structure itself. Dead load includes all parts of the structural frame, floor finishes and underfill, ceilings and their supports, permanent partitions, casework, exterior walls and cladding, interior walls, and permanent equipment.

Live Loads. Live load can be defined as the weight superimposed on the structure by the use and occupancy of the building. It is that portion of gravity load which is not climatologically dependent and not considered as dead load. Live loads include the allowance for all occupants, furniture, fixtures, books and cases (as in a library), automobiles, delivery carts, desks, safes, filing cabinets, loose book cases, mechanical equipment (to which impact factors may have to be applied), lateral thrust of earth against walls, weight of earth fill, hydrostatic pressure, etc.

While snow is a gravity load, it is common to separate it from other live loads, to appraise it climatologically and then incorporate the results into the live-load effects (Portland Cement Association, 1974). Snow loads are considered under Snow Loads and Temperature Effects.

Impact and Dynamic Loads. Impact and dynamic loads, as covered herein, refer to impact and vibrational aspects of mechanical equipment, transportation devices, and machinery. Exterior dynamic forces such as earthquake and wind are covered in other chapters. Elevator loadings are a good example of impact and dynamic loads. Ventilating fans, powered trolleys, air compressors, printing presses, and similar equipment cause dynamic loads.

Temperature Effects. Temperature effects are here limited to those resulting from normal weather cycles. Temperature differentials as related to fire, explosion, blast, and the like are considered in Chapters CL-4 and CL-5.

Construction Loads. Overloading of structures during construction is a problem that must be considered by designers. Storage of materials, shoring, bracing, and connections during construction are some of the factors discussed in this chapter.

2   Significance of Load Intensities

Load intensities for design purposes are usually stated in mean values of weight per unit of area. This is often supplemented with a requirement of a considerably higher intensity of weight over a relatively small area of floor to account for possible concentrations. These values as specified in codes are regarded in three different ways.

The deterministic approach relies on experience and engineering judgment to derive unique values. It recognizes these as somewhat arbitrary. But it regards them as sufficiently realistic to give reasonable assurance of structural safety when they are matched by strengths calculated according to approved procedures.

The probabilistic approach uses probability theory and statistical methods to derive less arbitrary and more realistic values with stated coefficients of variation to denote levels of confidence to be placed in the recommendation. It calls for a similar approach in the estimation of strengths to permit safe matching.

The position taken by the Comité Européen du Béton (CEB) (and, to a less formalized degree, by ANSI A58.1) is called semiprobabilistic. The CEB endorses the idea of statistical determinations and establishes the "characteristic load" as one that has a 5% chance of being exceeded once in the life of the structure.

Whichever method is used, if different load factors are to be applied to various loadings (dead, live, or other), it becomes necessary that each type of loading be carefully defined and that the loading variability be considered.

1.2   DEAD LOAD

1   Computation of Dead Load

Calculation of dead weights is not a complex problem once the plans approach completion. However, large variations in both density and dimension can exist and only approximate values can be derived in some cases. Inclusion of all items also requires careful attention.

The main concerns during analysis should be to differentiate properly between types of loading, to use each with the appropriate load factor, and to consider the probable variation in such computed values.

When the plans are in the formative stages and many decisions have not yet been made, some degree of visualization and imagination is required. As designs progress, early estimates of dead load can be (and should be) reviewed and revised if necessary.

Building codes from most countries are similar in specifying dead-load provisions. Usually tables are presented listing materials for walls, partitions, and slabs, and floor, roof, and wall coverings, with applicable densities or weights per unit of area.

2 Variations in Computation of Dead Load

There is a tendency among structural engineers to regard dead loads as almost deterministically known. However, when dead loads have been measured in actual structures, they have almost always been substantially higher than expected. Differences between computed and actual values as high as 20% have been common. It seems, therefore, appropriate to recognize the state of affairs and compute dead loads in a more realistic manner than has been customary. On the other hand the difference between actual and nominal dead loads is a random variable.

It is impractical to have to consider checkerboard and other patterns of part of the dead load. A convenient, approximate way of dealing with dead-load variability is to use relatively low magnitudes, assumed deterministic, and to treat the variable excess as a live load (Rosenblueth, 1973).

Generally speaking, the weight of the structure itself is considered to be known to the designer and relatively constant in comparison with the imposed loads. In reality, variations in the self-weight of the structure may be caused by:

1. Changes in the moisture content of the materials due to drying out, rain, condensation, and flooding, and even chemical changes.

2. Structural alterations such as adding stories or replacing parts of the original structure, such changes being normally under the control of a designer.

3. Changes in floor, wall, and ceiling surfaces, and use of partitions to subdivide rooms (Mitchell, 1973).

In addition there are other sources of variation that need to be taken into account as inaccuracies in the design process:

1. Exact volumes are not known. They must be estimated. For example, there is a tolerance in building concrete forms. Variations of 6 mm (1/4 in.) to 13 mm (1/2 in.) from plan dimensions are common, and calculated loads are based on plan dimensions. This problem is usually considered when deriving appropriate load factors. The load factor for dead load includes an allowance for probable undersize (and, therefore, understrength). But part of this allowance already is duplicated because the calculated load is too high. In the case of an oversized member, the strength (at least in some aspects) is increased. This strength increase offsets the underestimate of weight. Again, there is a duplication of effect in the applicable load factor. There is little the designer can do other than base calculations on nominal sizes. Design load factors must continue to reflect effects of tolerance in size, while recognizing that a tolerance in size reflects an offsetting tolerance in strength.

2. The unit weights are not known. They too must be estimated. The usual procedure is to use tables promulgated either by code or by recognized authorities. Completed plans, except in the case of review of a failure, are seldom available at the design stage. A provision must be made for probable sizes of members not yet designed with a note to verify them at a later stage of design (Reese, 1973).

3. Another problem concerns items specified after the design period. Masonry walls may be of hollow tile, concrete block (heavy or lightweight), or brick. Structural concrete may be lightweight or normal aggregate, or floor finishes may be ceramic tile with or without a concrete underlay, or concrete topping, or vinyl tile. Often selections are not made until alternate bids aid in a decision. In such cases, the designer usually assumes the heaviest of the choices, or a value slightly below that. If the difference is significant, the designer may instruct bidders to deduct a calculated percentage for certain alternatives, with the provision to revise the original design, if warranted.

4. Finally, estimates of the dead loads effectively supported by structural elements are also approximations. In the first place, we normally calculate them on the basis of tributary areas appropriate to simply supported framing (extending, for example, halfway to the next supporting element). Effects of continuity in the framing are ignored except in cases of gross disparity in span lengths or end conditions, or both. Secondly, we tacitly make two further assumptions that are never fully justified. We assume that there is a clear distinction between elements that carry loads of a certain kind (primary beams carrying floor loads to the supporting columns) and secondary elements (secondary beams or floor slabs) that merely pass loads, including their own dead weights, to the primary ones. And we assume that the load-bearing elements are complete and have achieved their final stiffnesses before the secondary elements are added to apply their loads. In fact, there is rarely such a clear distinction of structural function and construction rarely proceeds in quite this way—particularly in the case of cast-in-place concrete and composite construction. Where loads are progressively applied to such a structure that is, at the same time, increasing in stiffness, they may well produce stresses different from those estimated —indeed, this very possibility is deliberately exploited in some prestressing techniques. In one instance Mainstone (1960) has shown the effect of increasing stiffness of the load-bearing elements of a composite floor system to be so great that the major "dead load" stresses in some beams were a frozen "memory" of the constructional live loads rather than stresses directly induced by the final dead load.

The net result of all of the items listed is that, in a capably executed and conventional design, an estimate of the dead load supported by a member might be off by 15% to 20%, or more, which is a large variation (Johnson, 1973), and that estimates of resulting stresses might further be in error. Thus, contrary to popular belief, dead loads cannot be accurately forecast. The problems of takeoff of volumes from an incomplete and ever-changing set of plans, and of guessing at the weights of elements not yet designed, have no ready solution.

However, most designers are aware of these problems and tend to be conservative in estimating the weights of trial members, with such methods as scaling (or using) center lines instead of clear dimensions in estimating volumes. Further, code writers usually consider the problem when deriving appropriate load factors.

1.3 LIVE LOAD

1 Live-load Determination

Live loads are the result of human actions. This sets them apart from natural forces that may be presumed to conform to physical laws and to be predictable (or potentially predictable) within specifiable limits on the basis of past experience. Human actions will never be predictable in the same way. Past experience can therefore be no more than a partial guide to a likely future, and the only limits that we can confidently place on future loads are those determined by the extremes of what is physically possible. These are not usually of much practical interest. Live loads as specified in current codes are the result of judgments based on broad and largely unquantified experience (including the absence of structural failures directly attributable to underspecification) or, more recently, on load surveys. The extent to which, particularly in the former case, they may be excessive is still a matter of debate.

Because buildings are usually designed for a particular kind of usage it is traditional to base recommended floor loadings on the type of occupancy, for example (Mitchell, 1973):

1. Residential (houses, apartments, hotels).

2. Institutional (hospitals, prisons).

3. Educational (schools, colleges).

4. Public assembly (halls, auditoriums, restaurants).

5. Offices (including banks).

6. Retail (shops, department stores, supermarkets).

7. Storage (warehouses, libraries).

8. Industrial (workshops, factories).

9. Garages.

However, it is sometimes difficult for the designer in the initial stages of design to predict the loading conditions that will be imposed during the life of the structure. Accordingly, it has been found incumbent in building codes to establish live loads to be used for design, and engineers generally follow these regulations. Most regulations take two forms—equivalent uniform loads and prescribed concentrations.

Equivalent Uniform Loads. Prescribed equivalent uniform loads are intended to represent the effects of the varying live load in the building. The values are established by review and approximation of actual loads. They are conservative judgments, producing designs which stand up and which have sufficient rigidity for occupancy use.

Concentrated Loads. Concentrated loads are prescribed for certain cases such as parking garages, office floors, stair treads, roof scuttles, and elevator machine room floors. In general, the values prescribed seem reasonable and the locations prescribed cover most critical areas. However, one problem is that, with the current trend toward thin slabs, metal decks, and pan construction, the load is of limited use without also indicating the area to which it is applied. Many building codes are deficient in this regard.

Another deficiency is that many codes do not specify when, or to what degree, the stipulated uniform and concentrated live loads are concurrent or nonconcurrent. For example, if the concentration to be used in the design of a garage floor represents the jack holding up one end of the automobile, the equivalent uniform load representing one half of the automobile would not be additive to the jack reaction (Johnson, 1973).

2   Live-load Magnitudes

Codes from most countries are similar in specifying live-load conditions. Generally tables are presented listing types of occupancy or usage with applicable live loads in terms of weight per unit of area. A tabulation of code live-load values from numerous countries is contained in Table 1.1.

Although major changes in occupancy during the life of the structure have been considered by some to be a problem, it is not considered important herein. It is assumed that any such change would induce the owner and the building official to require a report by a competent structural engineer that the structure has the necessary capacity for the occupancy contemplated.

Loads given in codes are usually a minimum required for public safety. An owner or his design team may find it desirable to design for a greater load than the minimum, either because the code loading is not high enough for their use or because economics dictate a greater capacity to assure flexibility in occupancy.

Various structural systems may have different responses to the same load. For example, a safe rolled across an open web joist floor may successively impose its entire weight on an individual member, but rolled across a reinforced concrete flat plate floor the load would be automatically distributed by the floor system. Hence, it is customary to supplement a uniform load over the floor surface with a substantially greater concentrated load spread over a very limited area. Other methods of dealing with nonuniform loads are also available. Generally, code writers prefer, as far as possible, to establish loading values typical of the occupancy and independent of the response of the structure. They prefer to incorporate any variations in response in the methods of calculating that response (Reese, 1973).

For further discussion of magnitudes of occupancy loads see Article 2 of Section 1.8, Survey Results.

3   Variations in Live Loads

While dead loads can be forecast with some degree of precision, live loads are not as easily predicted. First, the owner may be planning rentable floor space while seeking tenants. It can, for instance, be assumed that the occupancy will largely be offices, stores, stores/garages, or garages, but it cannot readily be foreseen which offices will be private, general work rooms, computer rooms, file rooms, or storage

Table 1.1 Typical recommended live loads

Occupancy (1)	Australia (AS1170, Part 1-1971)			Britain (CP3: Chap. V Part 1: 1967)		
	kPa (2)	psf (3)	kfg/m² (4)	kPa (5)	psf (6)	kgf/m² (7)
Assembly Halls				(Note 1)		
fixed seat	4.0	84	408	4.0	84	408
movable seat	5.0	104	510	5.0	104	510
platform	5.0	104	510	5.0	104	510
Balcony (exterior)						
public	4.0	84	408	(Note 3)		
Corridors		(Note 1)				
first floor	4.0	84	408	(Note 4)		
apartments	3.0	63	306	(Note 4)		
hospitals	3.0	63	306	(Note 4)		
offices	3.0	63	306	(Note 4)		
theaters	4.0	84	408	(Note 4)		
Dance Halls and Ballrooms	4.0	84	408	5.0	104	510
Dining Rooms and						
Restaurants	2.0	42	204	2.0	42	204
Fire Escapes						
general						
multifamily residential						
Garages						
passenger cars only	3.0	63	306	2.5	52	255
approach ramps	5.0	104	510	2.5	52	255
Hospitals						
operating rooms, labs	3.0	63	306	2.0	42	204
private rooms, wards	2.0	42	204	2.0	42	204
Libraries						
reading rooms	2.5	52	255	2.5	52	255
book stacks		(Note 2)			(Note 13)	
Office Buildings						
offices	3.0	63	306	2.5	52	255
lobbies	4.0	84	408	2.5	52	255
corridors	3.0	63	306	(Note 3)		
Residential						
apartments	2.0	42	204	1.5	31	153
hotels	2.0	42	204	2.0	42	204
public rooms	2.0	42	204	2.0	42	204
stairs	4.0	84	408	(Note 7)		
corridors	3.0	63	306	(Note 3)		
Stairs						
buildings over						
three stories	4.0	84	408	(Note 7)		
Stores						
first floor	5.0	104	510	4.0	84	408
upper floors	5.0	104	510	4.0	84	408
wholesale	5.0	104	510	4.0	84	408
Theaters						
aisles, corridors, lobbies	4.0	84	408	(Note 9)		
orchestra floor	4.0	84	408	(Note 9)		
balconies	4.0	84	408	(Note 9)		
stage floors	7.5	156	765	7.5	156	765

Table 1.1 (continued)

Occupancy	Canada (NBC 4:1)			CIB (Bulletin No. 4)			France (NF PO6.001)		
	kPa (8)	psf (9)	kfg/m² (10)	kPa (11)	psf (12)	kgf/m² (13)	kPa (14)	psf (15)	kfg/m² (16)
Assembly Halls				(Note 10)					
fixed seat	2.4	50	244	4.0	84	408	4.9	102	500
movable seat	4.8	100	488	4.0	84	408	4.9	102	500
platform	4.8	100	488				4.9	102	500
Balcony (exterior)									
public	4.8	100	488				4.9	102	500
Corridors	(Note 5)			(Note 11)					
first floor	4.8	100	488	3.0	63	306	3.4	71	350
	(Note 12)								
apartments	1.9	40	195	3.0	63	306	1.7	35	175
hospitals	4.8	100	488	3.0	63	306			
offices	4.8	100	488	3.0	63	306			
theaters	4.8	100	488	3.0	63	306	4.9	102	500
Dance Halls and									
Ballrooms	4.8	100	488				4.9	102	500
Dining Rooms and									
Restaurants	4.8	100	488				4.9	102	500
Fire Escapes									
general	4.8	100	488						
multifamily residential	4.8	100	488						
Garages									
passenger cars only	2.4	50	244				(Note 6)		
approach ramps									
Hospitals									
operating rooms, labs	3.6	75	366						
private rooms, wards	1.9	40	195						
Libraries									
reading rooms	2.9	60	293						
book stacks	7.2	150	732						
Office Buildings									
offices	2.4	50	244				2.0	41	200
lobbies	4.8	100	488				2.5	51	250
corridors	4.8	100	488	(Note 10)					
	(Note 5)								
Residential									
apartments	1.9	40	195	1.5	31	153	1.7	35	175
hotels	1.9	40	195	1.5	31	153	1.7	35	175
public rooms	same as assembly halls						4.9	102	500
stairs	1.9	40	195				2.5	50	250
corridors	1.9	40	195	(Note 11)			1.7	35	175
	(Note 12)								
Stairs									
buildings over three stories	same as corridors						3.9	82	400
Stores				(Note 10)					
first floor	4.8	100	488	4.0	84	408	4.9	102	500
upper floors	4.8	100	488	4.0	84	408	3.9	82	400
wholesale	4.8	100	488				(Note 8)		
Theaters									
aisles, corridors, lobbies	(Note 9)						4.9	102	500
orchestra floor	(Note 9)						4.9	102	500
balconies	(Note 9)						4.9	102	500
stage floors							4.9	102	500

Table 1.1 (continued)

Occupancy	Germany (DIN 1055, 61.3)			Italy (C.N.R. UNI 10012-67)			Japan (AIJ Standard)		
	kPa (17)	psf (18)	kgf/m² (19)	kPa (20)	psf (21)	kgf/m² (22)	kPa (23)	psf (24)	kgf/m² (25)
Assembly Halls							(Note 14)		
fixed seat	4.9	102	500	4.9	102	500	2.9	61	300
movable seat	4.9	102	500	4.9	102	500	3.5	74	360
platform	4.9	102	500	4.9	102	500			
Balcony (exterior)									
public	4.9	102	500	4.9	102	500	2.9	61	300
Corridors									
first floor				4.9	102	500			
apartments	2.0	41	200	2.0	41	200	1.8	37	180
hospitals	3.4	72	350				1.8	37	180
offices	2.0	41	200	3.4	72	350	2.9	61	300
theaters	4.9	102	500	4.9	102	500	3.5	74	360
Dance Halls and Ballrooms	4.9	102	500	5.9	122	600	3.5	74	360
Dining Rooms and Restaurants	4.9	102	500	3.4	72	350	2.9	61	300
Fire Escapes									
general									
multifamily residential									
Garages									
passenger cars only	3.4	72	350	2.9	61	300	5.4	113	550
approach ramps	4.9	102	500				5.4	113	550
Hospitals									
operating rooms, labs									
private rooms, wards							1.8	37	180
Libraries							(Note 18)		
reading rooms									
book stacks									
Office Buildings									
offices	2.0	41	200	3.4	72	350	2.9	61	300
lobbies				3.4	72	350			
corridors	2.0	41	200	3.4	72	350	2.9	61	300
Residential									
apartments	1.5	31	150	2.0	41	200	1.8	37	180
hotels	1.5	31	150	2.0	41	200	1.8	37	180
public rooms				3.4	72	350	3.5	74	360
stairs				3.9	82	400	1.8	37	180
corridors	2.0	41	200	2.0	41	200	1.8	37	180
Stairs									
buildings over three stories				4.9	102	500			
Stores									
first floor	4.9	102	500	4.9	102	500	2.9	61	300
upper floors	4.9	102	500	4.9	102	500	2.9	61	300
wholesale	4.9	102	500	4.9	102	500			
Theaters									
aisles, corridors, lobbies	4.9	102	500	4.9	102	500	3.5	74	360
orchestra floor	4.9	102	500	4.9	102	500			
balconies	4.9	102	500	4.9	102	500	3.5	74	360
stage floors	4.9	102	500	4.9	102	500			

Table 1.1 (continued)

Occupancy	South Africa (SBR: Ch. 3–1970)			U.S.A. (ANSI A58.1–1972)			U.S.S.R. (SN & P II-A.11-62)		
	kPa (26)	psf (27)	kgf/m² (28)	kPa (29)	psf (30)	kgf/m² (31)	kPa (32)	psf (33)	kgf/m² (34)
Assembly Halls							(Note 16)		
fixed seat	3.8	80	391	2.9	60	293	3.9	82	400
movable seat	4.8	100	488	4.8	100	488	4.9	102	500
platform				4.8	100	488	4.9	102	500
Balcony (exterior)									
public				4.8	100	488	3.9	82	400
Corridors									
first floor	4.8	100	488	4.8	100	488	2.9	61	300
apartments	1.9	40	195	3.8	80	391	2.9	61	300
hospitals	4.8	100	488	3.8	80	391	2.9	61	300
offices	2.4	50	244	3.8	80	391	2.9	61	300
theaters	4.8	100	488	4.8	100	488	3.9	82	400
Dance Halls and Ballrooms				4.8	100	488	3.9	82	400
Dining Rooms and Restaurants				4.8	100	488	2.9	61	300
Fire Escapes									
general				4.8	100	488			
multifamily residential				1.9	40	195			
Garages	(Note 15)								
passenger cars only	1.4	30	143	2.4	50	244			
approach ramps									
Hospitals									
operating rooms, labs				2.9	60	293	2.0	41	200
private rooms, wards				1.9	40	195	1.5	31	150
Libraries				(Note 17)					
reading rooms				2.9	60	293	2.0	41	200
book stacks				7.2	150	732	4.9	102	500
Office Buildings									
offices	2.4	50	244	2.4	50	244	2.0	41	200
lobbies	3.8	80	391	4.8	100	488	2.9	61	300
corridors	2.4	50	244	3.8	80	391	2.9	61	300
Residential									
apartments	1.9	40	195	1.9	40	195	1.5	31	150
hotels	1.9	40	195	1.9	40	195	2.0	41	200
public rooms				4.8	100	488	2.0	41	200
stairs				4.8	100	488	2.9	61	300
corridors	1.9	40	195	3.8	80	391	2.9	61	300
				(Note 3)					
Stairs									
buildings over three stories				4.8	100	488	2.9	61	300
Stores									
first floor	3.8	80	391	4.8	100	488	3.9	82	400
upper floors	3.8	80	391	3.6	75	366	3.9	82	400
wholesale				6.0	125	610	3.9	82	400
Theaters									
aisles, corridors, lobbies				4.8	100	488	3.9	82	400
orchestra floor				2.9	60	293	3.9	82	400
balconies				2.9	60	293	3.9	82	400
stage floors				7.2	150	732	4.9	102	500

Table 1.1 (continued)

Notes

1. Additional concentrated design loads are specified.
2. Libraries: stack rooms 3.3 kPa (69 psf, 337 kgf/m²) per clear meter of room height.
3. Same as occupancy served.
4. Subject to crowd loading (except grandstands): 4.0 kPa (84 psf, 408 kgf/m²). Subject to loads greater than crowds (trolleys, etc.): to be determined, but not less than 5.0 kPa (104 psf, 510 kgf/m²). All others: same as occupancy served.
5. For corridors less than 1.2 m (4 ft) wide, use design load for occupancy served.
6. To suit occupancy.
7. Same as floors to which they give access, but not less than 3.0 kPa (63 psf, 306 kgf/m²) nor more than 5.0 kPa (104 psf, 510 kgf/m²).
8. Stores: heavier than listed loads, if required. Boutiques: same as listed for upper floors.
9. See "Assembly Halls" and "Corridors" for loads.
10. Higher design loads specified for "more important structures."
11. Corridors, exits, and foyers: shall not be less than 3.0 kPa (63 psf, 306 kgf/m²) but 1.0 kPa higher than area served.
12. Corridors above first floor in apartments, hotels, and motels: 4.8 kPa (100 psf) on first floor.
13. Libraries: stack rooms 2.4 kPa (15 psf per ft) per meter of stack height; minimum 6.5 kPa (136 psf, 663 kgf/m²).
14. Load values for design of beams and slabs; values are reduced for girders and for earthquake design.
15. For columns: 1.4 kPa (30 psf) with no reduction; floors: alternating live load of 4.1 kN/m (281 psf, 418 kgf/m²) and 6.1 kN/m² (418 psf, 622 kgf/m²) spaced alternately at 1.7-m (5.6-ft) and 2.6-m (8.5-ft) intervals.
16. Coefficient of overloading of 1.2 to 1.4 is multiplied times each particular live-load value.
17. Stack rooms: books and shelving at 10.2 kN/m³ (65 pcf) but not less than listed load.
18. Live load for reading room of library is to be determined corresponding to actual circumstances. Live load for book stacks is not stipulated in law, but specified in AIJ Standard for Design Load as: Bookroom with single floor, not less than 550 kgf/m²; bookroom with mezzanine (two floors), not less than 1000 kgf/m².

rooms. In light occupancy structures, some floors may have to be reinforced for a tenant with severe loading requirements.

In addition, types of equipment, such as computers and files, alter with time and as needs change. Also, as mentioned, the normal pattern can be upset by a sudden short-lived change. If one starts with the statistical principle of comparing similar items, loads would have to be broken into a great number of categories just to cover the various types encountered in most tall buildings. All the uncertainties of loads throughout the life of the structure make too many such classifications impractical.

With regard to precise numerical values for each load assumption, the size of a member results from not only the assumed magnitude of load, but also the method of analysis used and the strength levels considered acceptable. Since all of these are involved in computations, it is not vitally important that each have a value with a high degree of precision if reasonable assumptions are made and if the final result is an acceptably good design.

Now that we prepare more sophisticated designs and multiply different types of loads by different load factors, it becomes desirable to consider each load requirement as a reliable appraisal of the occupancy which it represents. Not only should it be a reliable appraisal, but there should be some measure of possible variation to see what the likely low and high values might be.

In an ordinary high-rise office building, not intended for a specialized occupancy, the likely loads are probably consistent from office to office (tables, desks, chairs, filing cases, and a limited number of people with private offices less heavily populated than large, congested work rooms). Detailed surveys have been made to determine weights of people and furniture at a given moment in typical offices. By selecting those considered typical, a fair degree of uniformity is obtained in the results and standard deviations are small. The loads resulting from a statistical analysis of the weights obtained are also rather small. These data, however, cannot be entered into design calculations. They were the values at the moment of observation, and for some time before and after. Yet it is not hard to visualize circumstances under which the measured load can be greatly increased (Reese, 1973).

In the case of gravitational loadings due to imposed immobile loads in a particular type of occupancy, there is variation not only from zone to zone, but also from time to time. The time-variability may be considered to consist of a short-term variation (caused by rearrangement of loads that are typical of the occupancy) and a long-term variation (caused by changes in the general character of the loads normally found in that occupancy) (Mitchell, 1973).

Short-term random variations in loading which might occur on particular floor zones will probably not affect the frequency-distribution of loadings. The resulting modified loadings will almost certainly have been found already on other zones. In this case variation with time can be assumed to be the same as variation with location.

Karman (1966, 1969) has shown that on this basis an application of probability theory leads to a simple formula for assessing the revised probabilities. If a load occurs with probability P in any one population of loaded floor slabs, it will occur with cumulative probability P^n after n rearrangements. Long-term trends, however, cannot be treated in this way and inevitably there will be a need for new surveys of certain occupancies.

Turning now to the gravitational loads produced by people and by mobile equipment, there is a short-term variation with time which may be considered to be adequately covered by observed spatial variations. There is, however, in certain occupancies a medium-term variation, due to increased stocks of goods or to crowding of people on certain occasions, which may be of overriding importance (Mitchell, 1973).

The foregoing is intended to suggest that, while unique figures for load and possible variation in that load are desirable for each occupancy, there are sizable obstacles to the accomplishment of these goals.

As noted earlier, characteristic loads are defined as that level of load which has a selected probability (say, 5 in 100, that is 1:20) of being exceeded once during the useful life of the structure. While this is a clear-cut definition, it is extremely difficult to apply for lack of accumulated data to treat statistically. Even with a good collection of data, carefully segregated into groupings of similar situations, there are questions about unusual load conditions. Long-term observations of some selected areas should indicate likely changes with time even if a complete mathematical determination does not result (see Figs. 1.1 and 1.2).

Until a strong body of statistical evidence to the contrary is collected, live loads specified in codes should be considered as having been established by consensus through experience and judgment as the characteristic load level (Reese, 1973).

4 Live-load Reductions

Accumulation of loads on a column or any other supporting structure depends on a number of parameters. In particular, the following variables are of primary importance (Apeland, 1973): (1) Character of live load; (2) tributary area on a single floor; (3) number of supported floors; and (4) coincidence of loadings from different floor levels.

Additionally, the problem of reduction of loads will depend on parameters and decisions that are not of a purely probabilistic nature, such as: (1) Special requirements to avoid progressive collapse; (2) ratio of dead load to live load; and (3) individual choice of characteristic live loads irrespective of initial function of building.

It is widely recognized that the live load on a building floor is not uniform, as assumed for design. Actual loading consists of different areas having different loading intensities. In general, the smaller the area surveyed, the larger the loading intensity. Design engineers take account of this fact by use of "live-load

Fig. 1.1 Failure of warehouse slab *(Courtesy: John Leigh, Broken Hill Proprietary, Ltd.)*

reductions." There are three common forms to these reductions, described as follows (Johnson, 1973).

Percentage Method. This method is applied as follows:

1. In structures intended for storage purposes, all columns, piers, or walls and foundations may be designed for 85% of the full assumed live load. In structures intended for other uses, the assumed live load used in designing columns, piers or walls, and foundations may be as follows: 100% of live load on roof; 85% of live load on top floor; 80% of live load on next floor; and 75% of live load on next floor below. On each successive lower floor, there may be a corresponding decrease in percentage, provided that at least 50% of the live load is assumed.

2. Girder members, except in roofs and as specified herein, carrying a designed floor load on 18 m² (200 ft²) or more of floor area may be designed for 85% of the specified live loads.

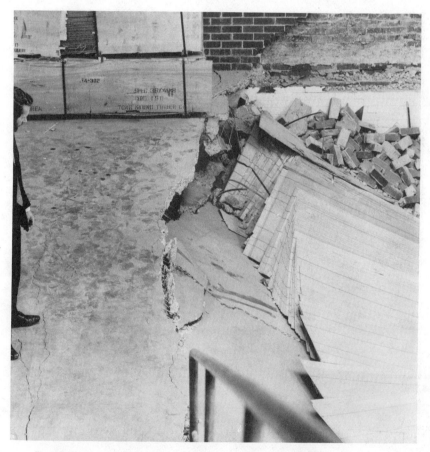

Fig. 1.2 Warehouse slab overload *(Courtesy: John Leigh, Broken Hill Proprietary, Ltd.)*

3. In designing trusses and girders which support columns, and in determining the area of footings, full dead loads plus live loads may be taken with reductions as permitted above.

The essence of this method is that main members (those supporting large floor areas) may be designed for something less than the stipulated uniform live-load intensity. The larger the area supported, the less the intensity of the distributed load for which the supporting element must be designed. This does not mean that there will be no areas supported by the element that are fully loaded to the basic design intensity before reduction. It does mean that the average load over the entire area supported has a value less than the maximum value. This is simple and obvious. The problems are to derive a proper numerical evaluation of the reduction, and to consider the moments and torsions resulting from asymmetry of the load application. The latter must be considered by a separate computation.

For storage occupancy (which sometimes is extended to include commercial occupancies) designed for a basic uniform load intensity of more than 4.8 kPa (100 psf, 488 kgf/m²), a smaller reduction is permitted. This is because the floor in such an area of occupancy is more likely to be fully loaded.

Dead Load to Live Load Ratio Method. The second form of live-load reduction is exemplified by the following (Johnson, 1973):

1. Live loads of 4.8 kPa (100 psi, 488 kgf/m²) or less: the design live load on any member supporting 14 m² (150 ft²) or more may be reduced at the rate of 0.08% per 0.09 m² (1.0 ft²) of area supported by the members, except that no reduction shall be made for areas to be occupied as places of public assembly. The reduction shall exceed neither 60% nor R as determined by

$$R = 100 \times \frac{D + L}{4.33L} \qquad (1.1)$$

in which R = reduction (%); D = dead load (load per unit of area of the area supported by the member); and L = design live load (load per unit of area of the area supported by the member).

2. Live loads more than 4.8 kPa (100 psf, 488 kgf/m²): no reduction shall be made, except that the design live loads on columns may be reduced 20%.

Note the increased reduction with increased contributory area (floor area supported by the element) and lesser, limited reduction for storage and commercial areas. Also note that certain limits have been added—no reduction on members supporting contributory areas less than a certain value, and an upper limit value of 60%, or R (Eq. 1.1). This formula, which represents a "fail-safe" philosophy, was developed by Dunham (1947). It is derived to assure that, should full live load happen to occur over the entire area supported by a structural element, even though said element had been designed on the basis of reduced live load, the element will not fail or be stressed to the yield point.

Tributary Area Method. The third form of live-load reduction is exemplified by the following:

1. Where a structural member supports a tributary area of floor, roof, or combination of these greater than 83.5 m² (900 ft²) used for storage,

manufacturing, retail stores, garage, or assembly, the design live load due to occupancy (excluding snow) is the basic live load multiplied by

$$0.5 + \frac{15}{\sqrt{A}} \tag{1.2}$$

in which A = accumulated tributary area in 0.09 m² (1.0 ft²).

2. Where a structural member supports a tributary area of floor, roof, or combination of these greater than 18.5 m² (200 ft²) for any use or occupancy other than those indicated above, the design live load due to occupancy (excluding snow) is the basic live load multiplied by

$$0.3 + \frac{10}{\sqrt{B}} \tag{1.3}$$

in which B = accumulated tributary area in 0.09 m² (1.0 ft²).

This form of live-load reduction provides for: (1) Increased reduction with increased tributary area; (2) lesser rate and reduction for storage and commercial areas than for, say, office and residential areas; (3) an upper limit to the reduction (the formulas become asymptotic for large tributary areas, see Fig. 1.3); and (4) the exclusion of certain loads of probable full contribution, such as snow loads.

The over-all effect of these provisions is similar to that of the regulations previously quoted. It reflects the current trend toward probabilistic analysis and is based on the concept that the influence of area on equally probable loadings can be expressed by a distribution function.

Live-load Reduction Problems.   The three approaches to evaluating live-load reductions have several common faults. Perhaps most important is that they have little basis of quantification. Hopefully, load surveys will improve this situation. Presumably, statistical analysis will enable designers to refine their application of the basic principles described. However, there are two other, albeit lesser, factors which have received little attention in the past and which merit consideration.

The first is that live-load reduction effects are not independent of the type of structural frame selected or the material of which it is constructed.

If we accept the live load as a variable load, concentrated in some areas and of less magnitude in others, it follows that the ability of the structure to support such a load depends on its ability to "smooth out" the peaks in loading intensity by bridging the loads in the high-intensity areas to the framing supporting the areas of less intensity. This ability depends on the type of framing, the materials, type of connections, continuity, etc.

The second factor is that the load in a building is a function of the age of the building. Observe a building in construction. First the foundation is completed; then the structure; next comes the cladding; the piping and ductwork go in; followed by the finishes. Only then does the occupant (live) load occur. By this time the floor structure may be three to four months old. The foundation and lower tiers of columns are even older before they receive the full load which they ultimately must support (Johnson, 1973).

Some of the supporting structural elements of the building (foundations, for example) will be of concrete, which gains strength with age. The designer proportions these structural elements based on the strength of specimens at a prescribed age (for concrete, 28 days). The strength gain in concrete after the 28-day period, particularly in elements like footings and piers which exist in conditions conducive to curing, can increase by 20% to 30% in the four-month to one-year period postulated above. Should the structural elements be designed for strength consistent with the time at which the full load is applied? The load factors or the live-load reduction factors should reflect this and should differentiate between floors, columns, and foundation elements.

Some typical reduction formulas are illustrated in Fig. 1.3 (Apeland, 1973). Load reductions are illustrated by the accumulated column load (live-load portion) as a function of the number of floors. Load intensity and tributary areas are assumed equal for all floors. The column load is $W = nW_L A$. The tributary area $A = 20$ m^2 (215 ft^2) is used for the Norwegian Code and Dunham's proposition. The wide scatter indicates that this problem deserves more attention in order to establish reliable criteria for the code writer as well as the designer.

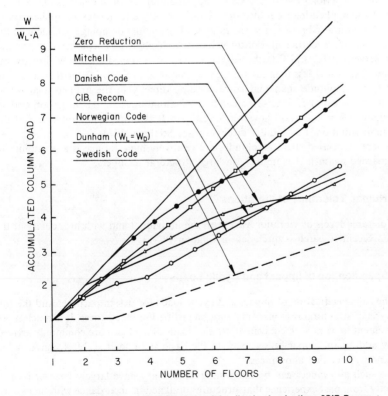

Fig. 1.3 Comparison of various methods for determining live-load reductions [CIB Recom.: percentage method; Norwegian Code: tributary area method; Dunham ($W_L = W_D$): dead/live load ratio method]

1.4 IMPACT AND CYCLIC LOADS

There are two classes of normal live loads that are dynamic rather than static in their action: impact loads and cyclic loads. The structural response depends on the masses set in motion and on stiffness and damping characteristics.

True mass impacts are unlikely to be of significant magnitude unless they fall within the category of "accidental" loads discussed in Chapter CL-5. The much smaller impacts associated, for instance, with people walking and with the moving of furniture may generally be assumed to be provided for in the specified static live loads. A possible exception (relevant chiefly to component design) is occasional impact by elevator cars being brought to rest.

Cyclic loads are usually associated with machinery and may call for special provisions in design to isolate the main structure from them. Possibilities of resonant vibrations of the supporting structure must be considered.

1 Structural Response

The analysis of structural response to true mass impact is discussed in Chapter CL-5.

Under cyclic load the amplitude of the structural response depends not only on that of the applied load but also on the ratio R of the frequency of application to that of a natural vibration, and the ratio D of the actual damping coefficient to the critical damping coefficient. For the values of D likely to be encountered in practice (say between 0.02 and 0.1) the response may be assumed to follow directly the applied load for R less than say 0.25, to be amplified in the $1/2D$ for $R = 1$, and to be less in amplitude than that corresponding directly to the applied load for R greater than say 1.5. Precise calculation of amplitudes in the neighborhood of resonance ($R = 1$) is not, however, called for. It is more important to avoid the resonant situation. For a fuller discussion see Steffens (1974).

Where associated stress amplitudes are relatively high, fatigue is a possibility to be guarded against. It is unlikely in large structural members.

2 Human Tolerance of Vibrations

Tolerable levels of vibration vary with the individual and with his activity at the time. Recent research is discussed in Chapter PC-13.

3 Specification of Impact and Cyclic Loads

The full specification of impact and cyclic loads for design purposes and the full analysis of structural responses may not be justified in many cases. It is much more convenient to work with equivalent "static" loads. Such loads are commonly arrived at by adding an "impact allowance" to the basic static load. Table 1.2 gives some commonly specified allowances.

No such allowances can be universally valid. They have largely been arrived at directly from past experience that structures designed in accordance with them have given satisfactory service. This does not guarantee that they will be equally valid when structural forms change.

Table 1.2 Impact allowance

Load (1)	Amount of increase, as a percentage (2)
Elevator supports and machinery	100
Traveling crane support girders and connections	25
Slow crane (less than 1.0 m/s)	10
Fast crane (more than 1.0 m/s)	20
Light machinery supports, shaft or motor driven	not less than 20
Reciprocating machinery or power-driven unit	not less than 50
Hangers supporting floors and balconies	33

4 Noise and Vibration Problems

All buildings are vibrated by traffic, wind, equipment, and other sources. When the motion exceeds a certain level, occupants feel unpleasant movement. Many studies have been made concerning tolerable levels of vibration, and Fig. 1.4 shows an example.

Reactions of individuals to the same motion are different, and are also related to the position of the person—standing, resting, or sitting. Usually people feel vibrations of high frequency, although low frequencies may cause feelings similar to seasickness. This should directly concern the designer of high-rise buildings, but little information is available. Fig. 1.5 shows one suggested measure of tolerable vibration (Izumi, 1973).

Unpleasant vibrations are a serviceability limit state, separate from failure caused by resonance, which should be considered by designers of tall buildings. For example, reducing the mass of a floor system can jeopardize the comfort factor for the occupants. Therefore, a dynamic analysis will be required for many innovative floor systems. For further discussion of drift and stiffness requirements, refer to Chapters SB-5 and CB-9.

1.5 SNOW LOADS AND TEMPERATURE EFFECTS

Snow loads and temperature effects are considered as meteorological loadings. Meteorological loading means the loads that arise because of atmospheric conditions outside and inside a building. These include loads from wind (both steady and gusty), snow and ice, rain and hailstones, dust, and the effect of restraint of materials used in construction to thermal and moisture movements. Only snow loads and temperature effects are considered in this chapter; wind is covered in Chapter CL-3.

Thermal and moisture movements and wind loadings depend on internal as well as external atmospheric conditions. But since conditions inside the building are usually controlled by man, only variations in the external atmosphere need be considered. These thermal and moisture movements also depend on the type, size, shape, and location of the building and are, with minor exceptions, independent of occupancy. There is usually a variation in intensity with the size of the area being considered.

The level of meteorological loadings is inherently variable with time as well as with the locality being considered. For each such locality the usual pattern consists of a series of fairly regular cyclical variations, together with less regular variations due to immediate, local, regional, and world meteorological conditions (Mitchell, 1973).

1 Snow Loading

Because of climatic variations between and within countries, there is little point in direct comparison of snow loadings given in national codes. It is more important to study the known phenomena of snow distribution on roofs.

The snow load on a roof depends on the climatological ground snow load and on the type, size, proportions, site, and orientation of the building, and heat loss through the roof. The climatological ground snow load is defined as the maximum expected snow load (weight per unit of area) in a specified average return period (typically 25 yr, 50 yr, or 100 yr). These loads are usually obtained from maps

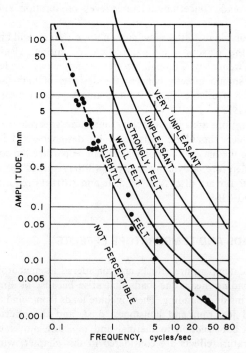

Fig. 1.4 Tolerable sinusoidal vibration

containing isolines of ground snow load. Regions where unusually high accumulations of snow may occur are marked on maps for special consideration in determination of design loads (Mitchell, 1973).

Snow on the Ground.   In any given major climatic area (of which there may be several in a large country), the heaviest snow loads on the ground may vary according to region, district, or site. Regional variations and some district variations (those due to altitude, proximity to the sea, or existence of a large conurbation) may be considerable and it may prove desirable to specify the resulting snow loads separately. Clearly there is need to limit the number of such zones used in codes, and local variations would therefore be ignored except for their contribution to the regional average. When determining the latter, the safety/economy basis for assessing snow loads implies that observations of ground snow load within a code region ought to be statistically weighted according to the number of new buildings expected, particularly those of low rise or large span, in the part of the region where the observations are made. The existing population level may often be a sufficient index of this.

Conditions of greatest snow load may occur as a result of a single heavy fall or accumulation of several falls of snow, or of snow followed by rain. At a given location, observations of snow depth and density, or of the equivalent depth of

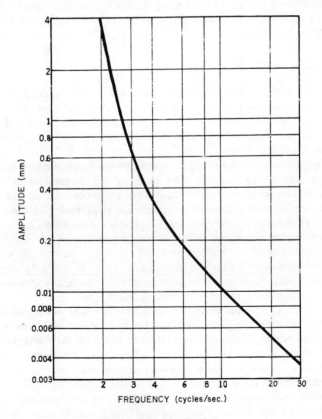

Fig. 1.5 Tolerable vibration

water, are made over a period of years and the maximum value for each year determined. This period may be fairly limited, but in view of the need to attempt to estimate the maximum load for a period approximating the life of a building, a statistical analysis using an extreme value distribution is sometimes used. This yields the expected maximum snow load on the ground in a specified "average return period" (Mitchell, 1973).

Snow on Roofs. Except in windless or very sheltered conditions the total load on a roof tends to be less than that on the same area of ground, because some snow is removed by wind. The wind may also remove parts of individual deposits later, and there may be evaporation and melting due to a diurnal rise in air temperature or to heat loss through the roof. On the other hand, melting followed by nocturnal fall of temperature and consequent refreezing may tend to prevent removal by winds.

Drifting and melting, and the receipt of snow blowing from, or sliding from, higher roofs affect not only the total load on the roof but also its distribution. Where the shape of the roof produces a local decrease in wind speed, the intensity of snow load on the roof may be greater than that on the ground. The ratio of roof load to load on the ground is sensitive to wind speed and direction, and particularly to its duration. It appears unlikely at present that the resulting variations from building to building will be calculable specifically. A more generally applicable statistical approach is therefore called for, in which the loads on a large number of buildings of a given type are observed and related to the regional average snow load on the ground (Mitchell, 1973).

2   Temperature Effects

The effect of environmental temperature changes, as manifested by differential expansion or contraction of building members, on structural frame stability, serviceability, and response is the main subject of this section. Specifically, the problems and approaches to tall building planning and design and the nature of temperature loads are considered (Huang, 1973).

The first decades of this century witnessed the construction of tall buildings and structures that approached and then exceeded the magnitudes of height and configuration for which temperature loads were a significant factor. The controlled, constant temperatures achieved for the interior environment of these buildings, however, eliminated the problem of temperature differential movements. Tall offices or related occupancy buildings had the protection of a fully insulated complete enclosure of the building structure, as well as increasingly sophisticated mechanical systems for guaranteed temperature control to assure the comfort of the occupants. These conditions kept column lengths constant, and stresses due to temperature changes were not considered a design factor.

The problem of seasonal movement of the exterior skin was solved by jointing, such as curtain wall slip joints, and attachment to the stable enclosed structure. During construction, effects of temperature variation on the temporarily exposed structure were compensated for and corrected by staged construction, and reduced by the limited areas and volumes that were actually exposed.

Innovative trends in architecture and structural engineering during the creative 1960s made environmental problems and effects on tall buildings a significant factor in design. The generator for these innovations was the economic pressure to provide: (1) Greater amounts of enclosed space in the face of rising costs for centrally located, serviced land; and (2) the products of an increasingly sophisticated technology in an era of discernible material scarcity. The pressure to reduce building cost resulted in reduced mass and consequently reduced building stiffness, but without compromising safety. Evolution of increasingly more sophisticated approaches to evaluating the cause and effects of stress have generally been equal to the challenge.

Another area of concern with temperature effects is brought about by tall building innovations such as exposure or partial exposure of exterior building frames, primarily vertical load-bearing elements, and the breakthrough in height limitations. Seasonal temperature variations can have a drastic effect on frame stresses and deformations.

The paramount structural innovation was a change in concept that broke the pattern of high-rise framing. The traditional masonry bearing wall formed a new expression in both reinforced concrete and structural steel. The result was an economical, functional, and esthetic solution which achieved greater heights by conceptualizing a tall building as a vertical tube or series of tubes. Closely spaced exterior columns, spandrel beams, and bracing redistribute vertical loads uniformly along the perimeter, resist lateral loads, and replace mullions for the support of glass. Advantages of exposed columns include increased floor area, reduced interior wall area cladding and exterior column cladding, and a distinctive contemporary appearance.

In buildings up to ten stories high, enclosed and not greater than about 60 m (200 ft) long in any horizontal direction, thermal-change action can usually be disregarded. Frame temperature stresses are negligible, and there is no effect on interior partitions and wall cladding due to the resulting imperceptible frame racking or movement. However, good engineering practice may dictate that buildings not in moderate climates, or buildings with fully exposed exterior columns, be considered for analysis at the discretion of the design engineer.

Buildings between 10 and 30 stories in height experience a vertical movement due to temperature change which may require temperature load consideration. For example, a concrete structure up to 30 stories with nonexposed columns will not usually be affected by temperature, although differential creep and shrinkage between exterior and interior vertical supporting elements may need attention.

Generally, for buildings up to 20 stories, temperature effects are disregarded. However, buildings with exposed columns and that exceed 15 to 18 stories will have perceptible temperature effects on the structure, depending on degree of exposure, floor stiffness, and height. Investigation is recommended to consider the inclusion of thermal stresses or thermal stress relief in design and analysis and the potential racking of partitions.

Buildings greater than 30 stories in height usually require an extensive analysis of temperature-induced vertical action to prevent potential serious distortion and failure of both structural and nonstructural elements.

The major concern is with high-rise and ultrahigh-rise building applications under the action of ambient temperature on vertical load-carrying elements (Huang, 1973).

Nature of Temperature Loads. Changes in the temperature of a structure (including particularly changes in temperature differentials) are not in themselves considered loads. But they do give rise to internal stresses as a result of restraints to free expansion and contraction. It is to these stresses, aggregated across a section, that we give the name "temperature load."

The structural response to a change in temperature is seen in its deformations, expansion or contraction of building materials in all directions, the change in dimension being a function of that dimension. The general equation for deformation is the familiar equation combining length, temperature change, and a constant. In general, slender building elements experience pronounced effects from a temperature change more than membranes or plates, for which Poisson's ratio has a compensating effect. These effects occur in the longitudinal direction, with insignificant or no effect on the perpendicular dimension.

A structure responds to the free expansion of an element by distortion, increased stresses, and secondary effects on nonstructural elements. In some cases failure occurs whereby the structure is torn apart under combined effects of creep, shrinkage, and temperature.

Generally, for buildings over about 30 stories in height and 60 m (200 ft) in length, vertical and horizontal temperature action must be considered. The characteristic ambient temperatures should be determined and the change in temperature from a chosen datum should be applied to the structural elements. The response of the material and the frame to temperature, and the combination of this action with all others in the building, completes the cycle of load determination and application.

If a material of some defined shape is allowed to respond to the influence of its ambient temperature, the internal stress generated is a function of the change in length allowed. The boundary conditions are:

1. Complete, uninhibited, unrestricted expansion for which the internal stresses are zero.

2. Total restraint with a change in length unable to take place, for which the internal stresses are maximum.

3. Some condition between (1) and (2) in which restraint is involved but is not absolutely rigid.

The range of problems involved in a consideration of temperature effects can be identified as follows:

1. Comparatively small uniform change in temperature.

2. Large variation in temperature and thermal dilations.

3. Time-dependent flow and fracture occurring in addition to usual elastic effects.

4. Brittle materials.

Most building applications can be identified by the first item, with the other items relegated to the areas of cryogenics and elevated temperatures. Consequently, the approach can be considerably simplified. In addition, since the lateral dimensions of building elements are small compared to the longitudinal (for example, columns, beams, walls), a rigorous approach is unnecessary. However, when the mass of the building element is large, as in some concrete columns, thermal gradient can become a significant factor in reducing the elastic constants; although the modulus of elasticity or the coefficient of expansion can be considered as average constants in a great many practical situations. Still, in specialized or complicated cases where resulting magnitudes are prohibitive, experiments should be required in support of theory or to furnish direct data.

For the useful life of the building, indoor design conditions for an optimum comfort range will dictate about a 25°C (77°F) temperature level. This can be used as the interior design temperature assuming long-term occupancy and reasonable maintenance.

The lowest and highest effective temperature of all exterior columns during the full seasonal cycle must be determined. Since weather conditions rarely remain constant over a long period of time, the chance of attaining a true steady state of heat conduction through a section is remote. Consequently, an equivalent steady state of heat conduction must be derived. Studies reveal that the factors controlling heat transfer are time lag and attenuation of exterior temperature amplitudes, a kind of thermal inertia. The time lag and attenuation of amplitudes depend on the frequency of temperature change and the thermal properties of the member. Materials with high thermal conductivity, such as steel, will respond more quickly to a temperature change and require consideration of hourly temperature. Concrete on the other hand has a high thermal inertia and, based upon studies made in the United States, it is considered adequate to use minimum mean daily temperature, with a frequency of recurrence in 40 years on a regional basis, as the equivalent steady state of exterior temperature for design purposes. The local weather bureau is the best source for mean temperatures.

The design temperature differential is taken to be the difference between inside air and outside air temperatures. Winter differentials are more severe than summer in most cases. When the resulting contraction due to temperature drop is combined with shrinkage in exterior concrete columns, for example, the frame distortion is even more severe. The differential is then applied to a particular structural element for gradient analysis. Direct radiation and wind each have an effect on surface temperature and exterior design temperature which cannot be ignored in major structures (Huang, 1973).

In contemporary architecture, exterior columns can be partially or fully exposed. In partial exposure, the exterior columns project beyond the glass line. For structural steel construction, metallic or nonmetallic cladding is provided to protect the column from thermal influences. In recent years, weathering steel was developed and the projected portion of column exposed to the weather was not cladded. For reinforced concrete construction, the exterior column may or may not be covered, depending on the architectural expression desired.

In full exposure, the exterior column is completely clear of the glass line. For structural steel construction, normal insulation and light metallic or nonmetallic cladding will have very little effect on the column temperature. The average ambient temperature may be used for the average column temperature.

After the equivalent steady-state temperature is selected, the isotherms and temperature gradient through the column must be determined. The gradient depends on the shape of the section and the boundary conditions. The problem is to determine the lowest and highest temperatures and calculate the average temperature through the section. The steady-state heat flow through the column can be determined by either a numerical analysis using the relaxation method or by graphical solution. Each method offers a solution of the integral equation for nonuniform thermal stress distribution. In the numerical method, the two-dimensional or three-dimensional steady-state heat flow is replaced by a grid network and a successive approximation procedure is utilized to estimate temperature at each node of the grid. This method of analysis is cumbersome unless a computer is available. The graphical method is quite simple to apply. For a given section with known boundary temperatures, the isotherms and heat flow lines can be readily drawn. The graphical method is accomplished by drawing two sets of intersecting lines. One set represents the heat flow, and perpendicular to that set are the isothermal lines. The two sets of curves intersect at right angles, forming curvilinear squares. From this information, the mean gradient and average temperature of the column can be determined (Huang, 1973).

Design and Analysis. When dealing with thermal action, in general, the designer has the following options for solution:

1. Allow free movement (use joint and slip details).

2. Proportion material for induced stress (assume full restraint against thermal action reduced to partial restraint under influence of building stiffness).

3. Counteract dilation by neutralizing the thermal generator.

4. Some combination of the above approaches.

Longitudinal and horizontal thermal effects have been, for the most part, accommodated by allowing free movement within intervals based on past experience and in such a way as to maintain structural integrity.

The following is a recommended procedure for the design and analysis of tall buildings under the action of temperature on vertical structural elements for the purpose of proportioning structural material for induced stress.

1. Proceed if planned height greater than 10 stories.

2. Preliminary Analysis:
   (a) Schematic treatment of exposed columns.
   (b) Simplifying assumptions for frame analysis: (i) one-bay or two-bay model; (ii) ignore stiffnesses imparted by nonstructural elements; (iii) simplified floor and column stiffnesses; (iv) uniform column temperature; (v) general coefficients of expansion.
   (c) Frame analysis to determine order of magnitude of upper-floor distortion.

3. Compare Order of Magnitudes:
   (a) Proceed with final design if upper-floor distortion exceeds a rationally determined criterion based on the particular situation.
   (b) Neglect correction for temperature effects if distortion is less than a minimum established criterion.
   (c) Preliminary analysis is sufficient between these two criteria.

4. Evaluate treatment of exposed structural elements, floor stiffness relationships, etc.:
   (a) Proportion structural elements.

5. Final Design:
   (a) Determine structural and nonstructural element stiffnesses.

(b) Prepare two-bay or complete frame model.

(c) Determine column temperature distribution and gradient effects; test for accurate coefficient of expansion.

(d) Combine results with building loads.

(e) Proportion and detail structural elements.

(f) Detail nonstructural elements; confirm assumptions regarding cladding, air conditioning, etc.

Nonloadbearing interior partitions have in recent years displayed a consistent pattern of cracking in tall buildings, which can be related to temperature movements. These cracks were originally attributed to shrinkage restraint in the partition material, until observations confirmed that corner and peripheral cracks occurred most often in partitions located perpendicular to exposed columns in exterior bays of upper floors of tall buildings, and seemed due to a racking and distortion of the partition plate as the surrounding frame moved from a rectangular shape to that of a parallelogram.

Partitions are usually susceptible to damage from the slightest movement. Deflections of structural elements have always been carefully controlled when in contact with partitions. The recent increased magnitudes of building height combined with the use of higher-strength structural materials and avoidance of heavy cladding or facing material (both of which reduced frame mass and stiffness)—as well as increased pressure to economize on partitions and curtain walls—have created this additional condition of racking cracks.

The partitions themselves (especially those of nonmetallic materials) are responsible for a degree of the noted response, because of their reaction to thermal and moisture volume changes, and their assembly strength and tightness. Other factors influencing the potential cracking include the frame elastic and time-dependent deflection under load, volume changes due to drying shrinkage, humidity change, or chemical reaction such as corrosion, and differential support settlement. Careful observations of the nature and location of cracking will determine the degree and type of influence in effect. Only varying temperature volume changes in frame movements will cause racking in upper floors.

The most serious cracking has been observed in partitions tightly connected to the structural frame. This suggests a number of solutions to partition manufacturers and architectural detailers, such as:

1. Create a load-bearing partition to resist stresses imposed upon it. Many tall buildings are framed vertically by structural shear walls that are quite capable of doing just this. However, the need for small interior enclosed space and the fact that stresses accumulate in elements of greater resistance, such that the partition will collect loading as it approaches the foundation, have rendered this approach uneconomical in most applications.

2. Provide a control joint which allows sufficient movement along the periphery of the partition. Buildings greater than six to ten stories in height and with exposed concrete columns will create some distress in most nonloadbearing partitions. A peripheral control joint is recommended. For a partition whose length is twice its height, the end wall control joint will be one-half of the thickness of the ceiling control joint (considering the simple geometry of distortion of a rectangle within a parallelogram) with the base considered tight at the floor. The anticipated movement of the frame must be

determined during the design stage and used in the specification of partitions and details. Most partition manufacturers provide recommendations for control joint thickness and details including some provision for frame racking due to wind. The introduction of peripheral joints is considered by partition manufacturers to have little or no effect on fire ratings, and to have a tendency to improve sound isolation if properly detailed and constructed.

Note that partition jointing renders the frame considerably less stiff. This is a welcome addition to frame movement analysis since, in the absence of measurements of actual behavior, the contribution of partitions to stiffness has been heretofore crudely estimated. With this assumption, residual frame movement can be more accurately determined although the resulting movements will be more severe. Restrictions of building movement as a result of building stiffness have been estimated to be from 20% to 50% of the free vertical movement calculated by differential temperatures (partition contribution to stiffness not specified). One manufacturer recommends partition control joints of 22.2 mm (7/8 in.) at the ceiling and 11.1 mm (7/16 in.) at the end wall for a 40-story concrete building, using a multiplier of 0.30 to account for building stiffness. The engineer should utilize the latest information on field measurement data and methods of analysis in determining movement for tall buildings rather than accept any general recommendations regarding partition distress avoidance (Huang, 1973).

Please refer to Chapter CB-10 for the design of concrete buildings for temperature loads.

1.6 CONSTRUCTION LOADS

Overloading of structures during construction is a notorious abuse. By far, most of the failures occur during construction. Hardy Cross stated to his students that "if the structure can be built, it probably will be safe for use." This may undoubtedly be true for the majority of buildings, but it is not a philosophy to be followed by the prudent engineer. It does not account for the probability of abnormal or excessive loads such as earthquake, severe wind, or explosions (Johnson, 1973). Feld (1964) cites some 50 pages of examples of failures occurring during construction.

The design of the structure must provide a margin of safety so that construction can proceed without danger of collapse. Construction proceeds according to tried and proven methods which have been found to result in maximum economy. Any restraints on these methods must result in increased cost, which is likely to be more than the value of including a reasonable margin of extra strength in the original design. Design live loads or stresses should be conservatively established.

A contrary position is that, while all of the foregoing is true, the problem of overloads occurring during construction is one of policing and that it is incumbent on the contractor to plan and police his operations to avoid excessive overloads. The design should not bear the penalty for the contractor's convenience. The latter point of view (that is, design the structure for the loads incident to the occupancy and provide adequate policing) certainly is an ideal. The practical difficulty of policing and enforcement of: (1) Construction practice; (2) postconstruction alteration; and (3) tenant practices is no simple matter. The problem is one of organization of the building industry and the legal responsibilities involved.

One of the most insidious of construction overloads is that which occurs in the construction of concrete buildings using conventional and apparently safe techniques. In the field of reinforced concrete flat plate and slab construction, particularly where these are used in multistory structures, several methods of shoring have been devised to form the floors and to support them until the concrete has gained sufficient strength to bear the dead load and loads which may be superimposed by construction at higher levels. Formwork is an appreciable proportion of the cost of such floors, and its reuse at higher levels is desirable as soon as possible. Access to the area occupied by formwork so that other building operations may proceed freely is another reason why it is desirable to strip formwork early. However, there is a risk of damage or collapse if the forms are removed too soon. Damage may be cracking of the floors, which can result in both immediate and creep deflections that can lead in turn to other defects in partition walls and finishes (Beresford, 1964). An example of such a failure is shown in Figs. 1.6 and 1.7, a failure that took place at Bailey's Crossroads, Virginia, in March 1973.

It is a common practice in multistory construction to support a freshly placed floor on a number of lower floors through vertical props between them. Each floor in such a system then shares in carrying the weight of all floors in the system plus the formwork. Basically the intention is that higher floors will be relieved of loads, while lower floors will carry loads greater than their self-weight. When a floor is freshly placed there will be one floor more than the number of supporting floors in such a system, and it is possible that some floors will be overloaded. A knowledge of the current load conditions on each floor is therefore desirable.

In addition, if freshly placed floors are supported by propping from a number of previously placed floors in a regular cycle, loads of more than twice the dead load of one slab are imposed on lower floors at ages earlier than that at which the design strength of the concrete is attained. The existence of these dangerously excessive loads is well documented in papers such as that by Agarwal and Gardiner (1974).

In conventional construction the problem is either ignored or a technique of reshoring is used which reduces the peak loading, but at the cost of additional loading on more recently cast slabs. A new system devised by Wheen (1974) puts the positive control of construction loadings in the hands of the builder and is capable of completely eliminating this slab overload problem. The system depends for its functioning on the incorporation into the shoring props of small devices having an elastic/plastic load-deformation characteristic. The importance of the new system will be realized as longer floor spans and faster construction cycles are demanded.

In the normal type of construction it is difficult to eliminate overloading of slabs without expensive additions in design or procedure. Increased flexural and shear capacity cannot be readily obtained without an increase in dimensions, which brings about a corresponding increase in construction loads. It is important that the current conditions of slabs under construction are appreciated by those in charge of the work, and that additional loads are not applied during this period (Beresford, 1964). It is necessary, therefore, to carry out analyses of the procedure, so that floor loads are determined for each level of construction at all significant times, and to arrange the building schedule accordingly so that the floors perform well in service.

The end result of an analysis of a proposed construction sequence is a value for the load carried by each floor and by each set of shores for every operation. Normally two basic operations are relevant, casting a new floor and removing a set of shores.

Shore loads do not present many decision-making problems since details of the shoring system can readily be adjusted to give the required degree of security. The actual form of the shores, by virtue of their separate and temporary nature, does not influence the basic structural design. Floor loadings need to be compared with estimated properties of the concrete floors to determine whether or not the construction procedure or, in rare cases, the basic structural design has to be adjusted to provide safety or security against failure.

Fig. 1.6 Bailey's Crossroads—an example of failure during construction *(Courtesy: National Bureau of Standards)*

Since concrete floor slabs usually sustain construction loads before they have attained their design strength, their flexural and shear characteristics at ages of only a few days need to be considered. It is acknowledged that these properties depend primarily upon the tensile concrete strength rather than compressive strength, and, indeed, it has been pointed out that the flexural strength of a reinforced concrete member becomes substantially independent of the concrete strength within two or three days. This is to the advantage of the designer seeking faster construction, and many codes allow use of the tensile concrete strength in the assessment of safe construction loading.

For most practical cases the calculated floor loadings exceed the allowable values when estimated as a proportion of the service design loadings. A loading in construction more severe than service loadings requires decisions regarding the seriousness of this situation (Beresford, 1971).

Of more consequence is the consideration of excessive deflection. Overstressing in the construction phase may cause extensive cracking of the member, resulting in reduced stiffness and high elastic deformations, plus long-term deflections due to concrete creep. Analysis also reveals that cracking of a concrete floor slab, at least at restrained edges, is inevitable under service loads. Therefore, the "no-cracking" criterion is generally unattainable. In flat slabs it can be shown that cracking and deflection at midspan constitute a more severe condition which provides a convenient cut-off point for allowable loading. However, quite often midspan cracking cannot be avoided, and it is necessary to analyze each individual case using

Fig. 1.7 Bailey's Crossroads (Courtesy: National Bureau of Standards)

methods that take account of the cracked state of the members. Where deflections are found to be excessive, the solution is more likely to stiffen the structural unit than to modify the shoring procedure.

The analysis of construction loadings for shoring and reshoring procedures in the construction of multistory buildings is sufficiently documented and simplified so that any proposed shoring system can be readily analyzed and risk of damage to floors assessed. Measurements indicate that these systems will yield results that can be confidently used in design. The failure of the analyses to account for creep in floors during construction generally causes an error which is on the conservative side. Designers should, however, be aware of this deficiency and make due allowance in extremely fast construction. Whether or not unsatisfactory long-term behavior results from construction stresses is a question that must be resolved by analysis of individual cases (Beresford, 1971).

1.7 COMBINED LOADING

1 General

The loading conditions to which a tall building may be subjected during its useful life are many and varied. In considering them, each exposure is a limit state, and designing for all likely exposures is considered as a Limit State Design. There can be limit states of ultimate strength, service load, deflection, cracking, or any other state that needs investigation. The effect of a load on a structure is called an "action," and actions can be divided into many causes, as illustrated in Fig. 1.8. Any and all possible combinations must be considered. This does not necessarily imply elaborate calculations.

The combination of load effects was more easily visualized under the straight-line, working-stress method, where the stresses at service load were often half the ultimate capacity. If wind effects were added, the stresses were then raised 33-1/3% because of the infrequency of simultaneous full loads. Similarly, as other effects were added, the stresses could be further increased, the upper limit being the desirability of remaining enough below the ultimate capacity even under the worst combinations of load effects to provide some reserve strength and some margin for inaccuracies.

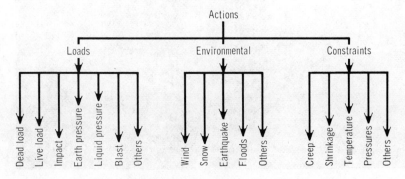

Fig. 1.8 Sources of "action" on a structure

With current load factor design, similar results can be reached by weighting each load effect with a factor selected to express probabilistically its contribution to the total result. There is, of course, only one ultimate capacity, but as more actions are evaluated numerically, the need for a margin to cover actions that have not been evaluated is reduced. This is sometimes hard to visualize because if sufficiently many actions are combined simultaneously, they require weightings that become decimal fractions. This does not mean that only a portion of one effect is to be combined with a portion of another, but that there are relative weightings of different actions (Reese, 1973).

In general, the probability of a combination of two independent sources of load acting simultaneously on a structure will be less than the probability of either of the two loads acting separately. For the design problem, however, statistical properties of the loads are only one aspect. The response of the structure to a particular load combination is equally important. It follows that the problem of combination of loads should be classified as a subproblem of the more general problem of principles of design (Apeland, 1973).

One method of combining loads is to assign a probability factor to various combinations of load. An example using this system follows.

Combining Loads.   Except when applicable codes make other provisions, all loads listed herein shall be considered to act in the following combinations, whichever produces the most unfavorable effects in the building, foundation, or structural member concerned, reduced when appropriate. The most unfavorable effect may occur when one or more of the contributing loads are not acting.

The combinations are:

1. D
2. $D + L$
3. $D + (W$ or $E)$
4. $D + T$
5. $D + L + (W$ or $E)$
6. $D + L + T$
7. $D + (W$ or $E) + T$
8. $D + L + (W$ or $E) + T$.

In this list, D = dead load consisting of: (1) The weight of the member itself; (2) the weight of all materials of construction incorporated into the building to be permanently supported by the member, including built-in partitions; (3) the weight of permanent equipment; and (4) forces due to prestressing.

Also, L = live loads due to intended use and occupancy (including loads due to movable partitions and traveling cranes), snow, ice, or rain, earth and hydrostatic pressure, and horizontal components of static or inertial forces; W = wind load; E = earthquake load; and T = loads, forces, and effects due to contraction or expansion resulting from temperature changes, shrinkage, moisture changes, creep in component materials, movement due to differential settlement, or any combination thereof.

Probability Factor.   The total of the combined load effects may be multiplied by the following load combination probability factors (an increase in the allowable stresses in conjunction with a decrease due to the above load combinations is not allowed): (1) 1.00 for combinations 1 through 4; (2) 0.75 for combinations 5 through 7; and (3) 0.66 for combination 8.

Live Load Counteracting Dead Load.   When live loads counteract dead loads in a structural member or joint, special care shall be exercised by the designer to assure adequate safety for possible stress reversals.

2   Limit States Design Method

Since the limit state method appears to be the only realistic approach to the general problem of treatment of safety of structures, the problem of combination of loads will be reviewed in connection with the limit state method.

If a structure is subject to the effects of two loadings, which separately have the probabilities p_a and p_b respectively, the probability $p = p_a \times p_b$ for the loadings acting simultaneously will be less than either of the probabilities p_a, p_b.

Joint probabilities are essentially dependent on two types of variation, spatial and temporal. For combinations of snow and wind loads with gravity loads, both types of variation exist for wind as well as snow. However, because sufficient statistical data are not available for snow and wind loads, an exact probabilistic combination cannot be made. The probability of combinations must be estimated in relation to the methods for the specification of snow and wind loadings.

Recently, proposals have been made to add a progressive failure limit state to ultimate limit states and serviceability limit states (Apeland, 1973).

The selection of limit states is dependent upon an evaluation of representative load levels as compared to corresponding load and material parameters which are significant at that particular load level. In combining these parameters the characteristic values are multiplied by weight coefficients in order to derive the closest fit to actual conditions. Thus, the limit state method will be determined at the following levels of approximation: (1) Selection of limit states; (2) selection of representative parameters; and (3) selection or determination of load coefficients (weighting factors) or coefficients for other parameters.

In general, only effects of loads can be combined, not load coefficients, and loads can only be combined directly when their effects are colinear and superimposable. However, this does not mean that load coefficients should always be associated with load effects. For second-order problems this can easily be comprehended. Assume that an eccentric buckling problem is formally solved by a moment formula

$$M = Fe \left(\frac{1}{\dfrac{F_c}{F - 1}} \right) \qquad (1.4)$$

in which F and F_c = axial and Euler load, respectively, and e = eccentricity. It is obvious that if the weighting coefficient is put on the load effect M instead of on the load F, the result will be unsafe. The safest way is to associate the load coefficient formally with the loads. The characteristic values of a particular load should then be determined by evaluating the load intensities on a specific area for a defined probability.

It still remains to find a definition of characteristic loads for all types and specific useful lives of structures. For external loads, characteristic loads are by definition those that have an agreed probability of not being exceeded during the expected life of the structure. Where a reduction in load is more dangerous for the stability of the structure, the minimum values should be taken as the more unfavorable.

For loadings that may be considered random, a characteristic load Q_k may be defined by

$$Q_k = Q_m (1 + k\delta) \tag{1.5}$$

in which Q_m = value of the most unfavorable loading, with a 50% probability of not being exceeded in the expected life of the structure; δ = relative mean quadratic deviation of distribution of maximum loading; and k = coefficient depending on the probability of loadings greater than Q_k. The value of the average loading Q_m is derived from a statistical analysis of a number of structures of the same function as the one under consideration, designed for the same service life.

Recently, a complete revision of load specifications and codes of practice for aluminum, steel, reinforced and prestressed concrete, and wood was carried out in Norway. The revision was based on a semiprobabilistic method using CEB/FIP Recommendations as a guide. Through this method, coordination and uniformity of regulations for the various materials have been obtained. This is mainly due to the fact that the design problem has been subdivided into a load portion and a material property portion.

However, some problems still remain to be solved, particularly for load combinations in connection with special material phenomena such as fatigue and brittle fracture. These phenomena require special care in the selection of the appropriate limit state and the definition of the characteristic load value. A considerable amount of research still remains to be done in the field of selection of limit states, characteristic values, and combinations of loadings as well as combinations of load effects (Apeland, 1973).

1.8 LOAD SURVEYS AND STATISTICAL EVALUATION

In order to be able to develop methods of design based on probability, it is necessary to obtain a sufficient amount of data for the various parameters of the problem. For material properties data are easily obtained, and statistical evaluation is the normal procedure for the determination of characteristic values. Additionally, material properties usually have a normal distribution, which facilitates statistical treatment (Apeland, 1973). For loadings on buildings, however, the situation is quite different. Load surveys require extensive investigations in order to yield reliable results.

Computerized methods of analysis allow the structural engineer to use more realistic models to predict structural behavior with an ever-increasing level of confidence. However, the codified loading requirements that are used to implement these models remain, at best, a coarse estimate of the occupancy live loads. These codified live loads, determined by professional consensus, have proved satisfactory to date, in that virtually no failures have occurred which can be directly attributed to inadequately specified live loads. This might suggest that live-load requirements in current use are too stringent, or, on the other hand, might suggest that near-critical failure conditions may exist in many buildings. The response to these suggestions, of course, is that the degree of safety for buildings simply cannot be identified either deterministically or probabilistically. It is also recognized that most live-load data (usually collected with fire-load data) are outdated and insufficient for an accurate determination of live loads (Greene, 1973).

The major occupancy live loads are: (1) Ordinary everyday loads, including load buildup with time and change of occupancy, and (2) unusual or extraordinary loads associated with people crowding or furniture stacking. Two major gains should result from an improved understanding of occupancy live loads: (1) More consistent structural safety analysis can be performed and a realistic margin of safety can thereby be established, and (2) if it can be verified that current design loads exceed the loads needed for adequate design, a second benefit of reduced material cost would result.

Major live-load surveys of buildings have been conducted in Mexico, Hungary, Great Britain, and just recently in the United States (Culver, 1976). In Great Britain nearly two million square feet of office space were surveyed for fire loads and live loads. The procedures employed in this survey required the accurate location and weight of all furniture and equipment. The surveys conducted in Hungary and Mexico also required the accurate location and weight of furniture and equipment. The bookkeeping required for these data constitute the most costly operations of load surveys. Therefore, the United States study involved the use of "average" weights established from manufacturers' data for items of similar size and construction. No direct weighing was used, which made the inventory process less time-consuming.

Results of most past surveys were expressed primarily in statistics of the data collected, which reflect the observed "single point-in-time" condition. The British and Hungarians, by use of a stochastic model, did study the dependence of statistics of the maximum-in-time (sustained) load on age and change of occupancy in their study of office buildings. In Mexico, a model developed by Horne was used to predict design loads for areas of various sizes and to review load reduction versus area characteristics. The use of stochastic models during the planning and execution of fire-load and live-load surveys has been extremely limited. Successful use of stochastic models can produce, from limited surveys, the basic data needed to study the fire-loads and live-loads phenomena. These kinds of models for use with stratified sampling techniques were used by the U.S. National Bureau of Standards for office buildings. The objective was to produce the information needed to predict fire and live loads with a high level of confidence from relatively small samples.

It should be noted that an important aspect of live-load surveys is the accumulation of fire-load data. The gathering of very little extra information such as floor covering, finishes of room surfaces, estimates of free and confined contents of rooms, and the size and location of wall penetrations provide the fire engineer with the load data needed to evaluate fire safety requirements. Fire protection code specifications are primarily based on 100% burn-out of room or building contents. The building-contents or fire-loads information used to develop these specifications is usually based on load data that were collected over thirty years ago. The character of furniture and equipment for office buildings has changed over the years; the increased use of movable partitions, etc., has caused further departures due to the use of fire test procedures based on old and inadequate data. Fire-load and live-load surveys should be combined, as they have been in most of the major occupancy-loads surveys (Greene, 1973).

1 Survey Results

Domestic Occupancy Loadings. Johnson, reporting on load surveys of 139 apartments, notes that the maximum load intensity measured in a 10-yr period was about 1.2 kPa (26 psf, 127 kgf/m²). The mean value on an area of about 28 m² (300 ft²) was only 0.3 kPa (6 psf, 29 kgf/m²). The usual value used for design is 1.9 kPa (40 psf, 195 kgf/m²), that is, 50% more than the maximum intensity measured (Johnson, 1973).

Johnson considered loadings from furniture and persons separately. For that reason the results cannot easily be analyzed for the purpose of studying load versus room size and tributary area (Apeland, 1973).

Karman made surveys of 183 dwellings having a total area of 12 585 m² (135 000 ft²) in Hungary. He studied the intensity (load/area of room) of long-term loadings from furniture and persons and the effects of size of room and size of dwelling. The results of Karman's investigations clearly show the relationship between load intensity and room size. The smaller the room, the greater the load intensity.

It is of particular interest to observe how the statistically determined load intensities increase with rearrangement of families among the dwellings. The mean long-term loading increased from 0.4 kPa (8.7 psf, 42.5 kgf/m²) for a single occupancy to 0.7 kPa (15.2 psf, 74.2 kgf/m²) for 20 rearrangements of occupants.

Office Occupancy Loading. A number of load surveys in office buildings had been carried out before the probabilistic approach to the treatment of safety of structures was generally accepted. Investigations were centered on surveying actual live loads in office buildings, with the dual purpose of obtaining more realistic design loads to reduce live loads for building members (Apeland, 1973).

The first, by White in 1930 for the Steel Structures Research Committee, was on eight such tenancies in Britain totalling 15 000 m² (161 000 ft²). The maximum load occurring on each of certain sizes of floor zone was given for each tenancy as a maximum load intensity. Examination of these showed that, if safes were excluded (dealt with separately as concentrated loads), there was a consistent decrease in the maximum load intensity as the area was increased. Unfortunately the published results do not include the frequency distribution of the load intensities within any one of the tenancies (Mitchell, 1973).

The second survey was made by Dunham around 1945 and was of two buildings in Washington, D.C. of 42 000 m² (452 000 ft²) total area. Here again, frequency distributions of the loading intensity on specific sizes of floor zone are not given, but only the maxima observed (with undefined probability) on certain such sizes on each floor. These maximum values show in general a decrease with area, a ten to one range on different floors of the same building, and no great difference between the absolute maxima observed in the two buildings. On the basis of these observations Dunham proposed a method for the reduction of loads based on the size of the tributary area (see Article 4 of Section 1.3). However, the reduction is limited by the ratio of total load to live load (Apeland, 1973).

Dunham et al. reporting on surveys of two buildings show floor loads of 1.9 kPa (40 psf, 195 kgf/m²) in 88% of the area of one building and 97.5% of another building. Maximum load intensities were 4.3 kPa (90 psf, 439 kgf/m²) and 5.0 kPa (106 psf, 518 kgf/m²) on areas of about 90 m² (1000 ft²). Reporting on ten buildings, they show the highest load to be 1.9 kPa (40.2 psf, 195 kgf/m²) with 1.2 kPa (25 psf, 122 kgf/m²) or less on 87.6% of the area (Johnson, 1973).

An extremely useful survey is reported by Mitchell and Woodgate in 1971. The Building Research Station in Britain, in conjunction with the Construction Industry Research and Information Association, made a survey of floor loadings on 200 000 m² (2 152 000 ft²) of office accommodation involving 32 buildings and 119 occupying firms. This was not a specially selected sample, but a random sample of office buildings built between four and 14 years prior to the survey, in three different areas of London. Analysis was based on a statistical approach to design and on the requirement of complete flexibility of use within the office type of occupancy. The frequency distributions and the variously probable loading intensities are given for nine different sizes of floor zone from 1.0 m² to 192 m² (10.8 ft² to 2065 ft²), together with the load concentration factors required to convert these intensities into equivalent uniformly distributed loads for a number of structural parameters (such as moments in slabs and shears in beams) and various slab boundary conditions (Mitchell, 1973).

The Mitchell and Woodgate report showed a 99% probable level of load intensity for floors above ground floor as 2.0 kPa to 3.0 kPa (42 psf to 63 psf, 205 kgf/m² to 308 kgf/m²) for areas of 5.2 m² (56 ft²), and 1.6 kPa to 2.0 kPa (33 psf to 42 psf, 161 kgf/m² to 205 kgf/m²) for areas of 31 m² (336 ft²), and 1.1 kPa to 1.6 kPa (22 psf to 33 psf, 107 kgf/m² to 161 kgf/m²) for areas of 110 m² (1174 ft²) (Johnson, 1973).

Based on the assumption of interdependence of loads on different floors, column load reductions were computed for two probabilities. Since the assumption about interdependence will not be correct in many cases, the reductions of loadings were also determined from the histograms of the actual loadings, which were examined. From these results Mitchell and Woodgate concluded that a consistent reduction of loading intensity of about 25% on all floors after the first supported floor appeared to be a reasonable figure (Apeland, 1973).

Bryson and Gross reported in 1967 preliminary results on 11 650 m² (125 000 ft²) of floor area in two buildings in the United States. They give histograms of load intensities on room-sized areas [areas of from 10 m² to 42 m² (108 ft² to 450 ft²) lumped together] separately for each building. Also given are percentage occupied floor space and proportions of floor space loaded to certain levels (Mitchell, 1973).

The U.S. National Bureau of Standards (NBS) initiated a limited load-survey program for the evaluation of both floor live load and fire loads in the mid-1960s. This resulted in the survey of all rooms in two government office buildings, the Administration Building at NBS and a Federal Office Building in Washington, D.C. In the survey report published in December 1967, extensive statistical data reduction procedures were employed. As an initial step, these investigators limited the survey to collecting data related to the total effects of live loads in rooms and on entire floors. Statistical data reduction accomplished through extensive computer programming culminated in the presentation of results in the form of numerous tables and frequency distribution plots. One of the most interesting of the latter, not previously reported, reveals that occupants on the average retain about 60% of an office room floor as free space, that is, unoccupied by furniture or equipment. For predicting extraordinary personnel load effects, the potential area of occupancy becomes an important limiting factor, since people cannot crowd into areas already occupied by furniture and equipment. No attempt was made during this survey to evaluate maximum sustained or extraordinary loads (Greene, 1973).

In 1973, the U.S. General Services Administration (GSA), National Academy of Sciences, and NBS initiated a survey to determine fire loads and live loads in office buildings. Twenty-three buildings were surveyed, from four geographical areas of the United States: northeast, north-central, south, and west. Buildings ranged in age from two to 73 years, in height from two stories to 49 stories, and consisted of both private (16) and government (7) occupancy. The survey was designed to identify factors such as building height, building age, and geographical location, which affect the magnitude of fire loads and live loads. A special survey technique and data processing procedure were developed to collect data economically and efficiently from a large number of buildings. The total number of rooms surveyed was 2433, of which 74% were general and clerical offices (Culver, 1976). Survey results were presented evaluating the influence of building characteristics (height, age, location), occupant characteristics (type of firm), and room characteristics (room size and use) on the magnitude of fire loads and live loads. The data were utilized to develop mathematical models for predicting load magnitudes.

Some conclusions of the survey are as follows:

1. Magnitude of room fire loads and live loads is not affected by geographic location of building, building height, or building age.

2. There does not seem to be a significant difference between loads in government and private office buildings.

3. There is a definite tendency for loads to be concentrated around the perimeter of rooms.

4. The mean number of discrete concentrated floor loads in the rooms surveyed was 18.

5. The 99% fractile for the heaviest load in a room is quite close to the value currently used for designing office buildings.

6. In the majority of offices surveyed, between 20% and 40% of floor area was occupied by furniture and equipment.

Educational Occupancy. The principal subtypes of educational occupancy are schools, colleges, and universities. There may be similarities between the occupancies of some parts of the buildings used for these various purposes and this may reduce the total number of variables in this category. Some parts of educational establishments may be considered to be assembly occupancy, with the attendant problems of loading from persons. Some surveys in technical colleges have been made in Britain and results will be published (Mitchell, 1973).

According to investigations by Stineman, average weight of furniture is 0.48 kPa (10 psf, 49 kgf/m^2). Maximum possible occupant load (2 adults per seat plus crowding along walls) is 0.86 kPa (18 psf, 88 kgf/m^2); total = 1.34 kPa (28 psf, 137 kgf/m^2).

In loading tests for schoolhouse floors by the Milwaukee Board of Education, 258 pupils crowded into a 72.5 m^2 (780 ft^2) classroom normally intended to accommodate 48 pupils plus teacher (filling all seats double and all aisles and open spaces). The resultant load, including furnishings, was 2.0 kPa (42 psf, 205 kgf/m^2). Under normal conditions, estimated total load was 0.53 kPa to 0.62 kPa (11 psf to 13 psf, 54 kgf/m^2 to 63 kgf/m^2).

Usual design values are 1.9 kPa to 2.4 kPa (40 psf to 50 psf, 195 kgf/m^2 to 204 kgf/m²), that is, the physically possible maxima are far above what reasonably might be expected (Johnson, 1973).

Institutional Occupancy. Of the institutional occupancies, hospitals are clearly the most important at the present time. Apart from a survey of wards in three hospitals in New York State in 1924 (not on a statistical basis) and some work by Karman, little factual information appears to be published. In any case current attention to space planning, provision of greater privacy and soundproofing of wards, centralization of services, and air conditioning is likely to produce a completely different pattern of loading from that which has existed in the past. The British Building Research Station plans to undertake a survey on this type of occupancy (Mitchell, 1973).

Retail Occupancy. Dunham reports some sampling surveys of parts of two department stores in the United States which were carried out just before 1950. In both cases the sample areas on which the loads were assessed were fairly large (usually larger than bay sizes and forming part, or the whole, of departments), but the actual areas varied from sample to sample and parts of the buildings were ignored. On the basis of certain assumptions regarding the crowding of aisles, the results showed that in each of the departments this latter condition was likely to be the ruling loading by quite a large margin, but no evidence was given of the incidence of actual crowding and its fall-off with increasing footage. From the loads present in the normal (uncrowded) condition it is possible by grouping departments of roughly similar areas to obtain some idea of the range (if not the frequency distribution) of load intensities on such areas within each building. It is also possible to show how the buildings compare with each other in respect to the mean loads and the way in which this changes with increasing area.

Storage Occupancy. Dunham (1947) gives the results of a survey of two warehouses, one in New York and one in Washington. In the first case the results are given in terms of the load intensities on structural bays, which were mostly about 40 m² (430 ft²). They are given in such a manner that, together with the structural plan of a typical floor, it is possible to derive useful information about the load intensities on areas of bay size, and multiples thereof, in this one building. In the second survey the results are not given in sufficient detail for this to be done.

Garages and Car Park Occupancy. The multistory car park or garage is a common feature of many cities. Fortunately there are limitations on the types of vehicle required to be accommodated and, given certain basic information, it would be relatively simple to carry out a statistical survey without disturbing users and without weighing on site. A survey of this type of occupancy is currently being made by the British Building Research Station (Mitchell, 1973).

2 Conclusions on Load Surveys

If codes gave an indication of the way in which recommended loads were derived and the basic data on which they were based this would be very useful. It would help designers to identify any possible abnormal loads that were not allowed for; it would help those responsible for enforcing regulations; and it might almost be considered essential for committees charged with revising the codes.

It should be noted that all occupancies for which surveys have so far been made show a decrease in the load with increase in the size of floor zone considered. It would seem desirable that recommended loadings should be expressed either directly, or by implication, in terms of the area of the floor zone considered. This point needs emphasis because, while in the past it may have been adequate to assume an average bay size when recommending imposed loads for floors, with some reductions for beams and columns, the surveys that have so far been made show a fairly rapid decrease in loading with increase in area at the sizes of bay formerly used. It is possible that for some of the larger bays that can now be built with modern construction systems the recommended loadings might be unnecessarily heavy and therefore restrict development. Moreover, the use of prefabricated floor units, and the problem of possible load concentration on other structurally significant areas smaller than normal bay size, mean that load specification independent of area may result in lowered safety factors.

It will be seen that in many of the surveys reported, only the load intensity (that is, total load/area considered) has been examined, and it has apparently been assumed that the loads are uniformly distributed insofar as their effects are concerned. While this is justifiable in some cases, it is not always so, and the effects of load concentration have to be taken into account by the use of equivalent uniformly distributed loads, or other appropriate measures (Mitchell, 1973).

1.9 CONDENSED REFERENCES/BIBLIOGRAPHY

The following is a condensed bibliography for this chapter. Not only does it include all articles referred to or cited in the text, but it also contains bibliography for further reading. The full citations will be found at the end of the Volume. What is given here should be sufficient information to lead the reader to the correct article: the author, date, and title. In case of multiple authors, only the first named is listed.

Agarwal 1974, *Form and Shore Requirements for Multistorey Flat Slab Type Buildings*
Allen 1973, *Summary Report: Gravity Loads and Temperature Effects*
Apeland 1973, *Reduction of Live Loads and Combinations of Loads*

Beresford 1964, *An Analytical Examination of Propped Floors in Multi-Storey Flat Plate*
Beresford 1971, *Shoring and Reshoring of Floors in Multistorey Buildings*
Blakey 1965, *Stripping of Formwork for Concrete in Buildings in Relation to Structural Design*
Bohac 1968, *Life Loads Reduction in the Main Elements Design of the Multistorey Industrial*
Bohac 1971, *Floor Loadings in Retail Premises—The Results of a Survey*
Bohac 1973, *The Uniform Live Load Reduction for the Design of the Main Structural Elements*
Bohac 1976, *Floor Loadings in Domestic Buildings—The Results of a Survey*

Crist 1976, *Deflection Performance Criteria for Floors*
Culver 1976, *Survey Results for Fire Loads and Live Loads in Office Buildings*

Dunham 1947, *Design Live Loads in Buildings*

Feld 1964, *Lessons from Failures of Concrete Structures*

Galambos 1973, *Load Factor Design for Combination of Loads*
Glauser 1973, *Loadings*
Godfrey 1971, *Gravity Loads and Temperature Effects*
Greene 1973, *Stochastic Models and Live Load Surveys*
Grundy 1963, *Construction Loads on Slabs with Shored Formwork in Multistory Buildings*
Guttero 1970, *Provisional Proposal Concerning Overloads in Offices*
Guttero 1971a, *Study of Overloads in Offices Done in 1960*
Guttero 1971b, *Pilot Investigation of Overloads in Garages*
Guttero 1975, *Pilot Investigation of Overloads in Proposed Halls*

Huang 1973, *Temperature Loads*

Izumi 1973, *Impact and Dynamic Load Effects*

Jain 1973, *Effect of Construction Stages on the Stresses in Multi-Storied Frames*
Johnson 1973, *Dead, Live and Construction Loads*

Karman 1966, *Investigations of Occupancy Loadings on Floors of Dwellings*
Karman 1969, *Statistical Investigations on Live Loads on Floors*
Kostem 1972, *Thermal Stresses and Deformations in Pneumatic Cushion Roofs*
Kostem 1976, *Load Carrying Capacity of Ribbed Prestressed Concrete Roof Panels*
Kwiatkowski 1974, *Load Distribution on Vertical Braces in a Multi-Storey Frame*

Lalwani 1973, *Design Assumptions*
Laurie 1975, *Design Loads for Tall Buildings*
Lew 1976, *Safety During Construction of Concrete Buildings—A Status Report*

Mainstone 1960, *Studies in Composite Construction, Part III—Tests on New Government*
Marosszeky 1972, *Construction Loads Imposed in Multi-Storey Structures*
Mitchell 1973, *Loadings on Buildings*
Mitchell 1971a, *Floor Loadings in Office Buildings—The Results of a Survey*
Mitchell 1971b, *Floor Loading in Retail Premises—The Results of a Survey*
Mitchell 1977, *Floor Loadings in Domestic Buildings—The Results of a Survey*
Murzewski 1972, *A Stochastic Model for Live Loads in Tall Buildings*

Navaratnarajah 1974, *A Comparative Study of Codes of Practice in Design of Tall Buildings*
Nutt 1973, *Superimposed Loads*

PCA 1974, *Report of Task 1—Loading Conditions*

Reese 1973, *Theme Report: Gravity Loads and Temperature Effects*
Robertson 1976, *Unpublished Communication to the Council*
Rosenblueth 1973b, *Floor Loads*

SAA 1971–1975, *Rules for Minimum Design Loads on Structures (Metric Units)—Dead and Live*
SNiP II-6-74 1976, *Design Loads*
Salleras 1971, *Pilot Investigation of Overloads on Dwellings*
Salleras 1974, *Investigation of Overloads in Dormitories*
Salleras 1975, *Determination of Overloads Equivalents in Dormitories*
Selvaraj 1974, *Influence of Construction Sequence on the Stresses in Tall Building Frames*
Shaver 1976, *Correlation of Floor Vibration to Human Response*
Steffens 1974,*Structural Vibration and Damage*

Taylor 1967, *Effects of Formwork Stripping Time on Deflections of Flat Slabs and Plates*
Thomas 1973, *Measurement of Glass Temperatures at Level 42 of BHP House*
Tichý 1974a, *Combinations of Structural Actions (Level I Approach)*
Tichý 1974b, *A Probabilistic Model for Structural Actions*

Vorlíček 1969, *Distribution of Extreme Values in Structural Theory*

Wheen 1973a, *Positive Control of Construction Floor Loads in Multi-Storey Concrete Buildings*
Wheen 1973b, *Positive Control of Construction Floor Loads,*
Wheen 1974, *Practical Aspects of the Control of Construction Loads in Tall Buildings*
Wright 1973, *Survey of Fire and Live Loads*

Tall Building Criteria and Loading

Chapter CL-2

Earthquake Loading and Response

Prepared by Committee 6 (Earthquake Loading and Response) of the Council on Tall Buildings and Urban Habitat as part of the Monograph on the Planning and Design of Tall Buildings.

Kiyoshi Muto	Chairman
Ray W. Clough	Co-Vice-Chairman
Gary C. Hart	Co-Vice-Chairman and Editor

AUTHOR ACKNOWLEDGMENT

Special acknowledgment is due those individuals whose contributions and papers formed the substantial first drafts of the various sections of this chapter. First are the state-of-art reporters from the 1972 International Conference whose material was published in the Lehigh Proceedings. These individuals are:

K. Muto, Section 2.1
G. W. Housner, Section 2.2
H. B. Seed, Section 2.3
J. A. Blume, Section 2.4
Y. Osawa, Section 2.5
C. W. Pinkham, Section 2.6
C. M. Duke, Section 2.7
J. Monge, Section 2.7
R. V. Whitman, Section 2.7
K. Nakagawa, Section 2.7
T. Hisada, Section 2.8.

CONTRIBUTORS

The following is a complete list of those who have submitted written material for possible use in the chapter, whether or not that material was used in the final version. The Committee Chairman and Editor were given quite complete latitude. Frequently length limitations precluded the inclusion of much valuable material. The Bibliography contains all contributions. The contributors are: A. Arias, V. V. Bertero, J. A. Blume, S. Bubnov, J. S. Carmona, R. W. Clough, C. M. Duke, T. V. Galambos, M. Gellert, J. Glück, G. C. Hart, T. Hisada, G. W. Housner, J. Krishna, J. Lord, R. L. Mayes, P. Mazilu, J. E. Monge, K. Muto, K. Nakagawa, Y. Osawa, J. Penzien, C. W. Pinkham, H. Sandi, G. R. Saragoni, H. A. Sawyer, Jr., H. B. Seed, R. Shepherd, A. R. Tamboli, R. V. Whitman.

COMMITTEE MEMBERS

A. S. Arya, L. G. Aycardi, G. V. Berg, V. V. Bertero, J. A. Blume, S. Bubnov, J. S. Carmona, P. Carydis, R. W. Clough, H. J. Degenkolb, E. Del Valle Calderon, J. Despeyroux, C. M. Duke, H. Ehm, G. Estrada-Uribe, D. G. Eyre, M. Gellert, A. Gerich, E. Giangreco, J. Glück, G. B. Godfrey, B. Goschy, Z. B. Gregorian, R. D. Hanson, G. C. Hart, T. Hisada, G. W. Housner, M. Izumi, P. Karasudhi, H. S. Kellam, T. Kobori, J. Krishna, J. Lord, P. Mazilu, J. Munoz-Duque, K. Muto, A. Negoita, N. M. Newmark, N. Nielsen, Y. Osawa, T. Paulay, J. Penzien, C. W. Pinkham, E. P. Popov, R. Rios, E. Rosenblueth, H. Sandi, H. A. Sawyer, Jr., H. B. Seed, R. Shepherd, M. A. Sozen, K. V. Steinbrugge, C. A. Syrmakezis, A. R. Tamboli, S. Tezcan, R. V. Whitman.

CL-2

Earthquake Loading and Response

2.1 INTRODUCTION

The problem of earthquake loading and response may be unique among the design criteria applied to tall buildings, as it is related to the nonstationary characteristics of strong motion earthquakes with a small probability of occurrence, as well as to the dynamic properties of the structure—including the interaction of the structure and subsoil in the elastic and inelastic ranges.

The most common method of analysis used in seismic design replaces the dynamic action upon the structure by so-called equivalent static seismic forces. The forces prescribed in typical codes are recognized to be much less than the maximum effective inertia forces which might be induced during a major earthquake if the building remained elastic. Thus it should be expected that a structure designed in accordance with these equivalent forces will be strained beyond the elastic limit by a major earthquake loading, and it is essential that the yield capacity and ductility of the structure be considered carefully during the design process, which should be based on the philosophy of adequate damage control.

With this critical factor in mind, the earthquake problem has been divided into seven phases, and statements on the scope of these phases, in the light of recent developments of engineering seismology and earthquake engineering, are presented in the following paragraphs.

1 Earthquake Ground Motion

An earthquake is defined as the ground vibration induced by a sudden release of strain energy accumulated in the crust and upper mantle. Due to the various types of mechanisms of energy release and to the complexity of the constitution of the ground, observed earthquakes on and near the ground surface show apparently random, complicated motions. The characteristics of earthquake waves change along the time axis: P waves come first, and S waves next, then surface waves follow.

Seismicity maps, including zoning maps, are provided in many earthquake countries based on statistical data accumulated from ancient times, recent activities of faults, average energy release in some areas, etc. It is also becoming possible to estimate roughly the magnitude and location of future earthquakes using such data as the results of geodetic surveys, energy calculations, and observations of microearthquakes. However, it still is not feasible to predict the time, location, and magnitude of strong earthquakes.

Considering the seismic history and ground conditions of a given site, dynamic analyses of structures are carried out through various methods. One is to apply a set of observed typical earthquake motions. El Centro Earthquake (N-S), of maximum acceleration of 0.33 g recorded in 1940, has been used often for dynamic analyses. Standardized spectra are also used.

Another method is to follow the characteristic changes in earthquake motion when it propagates from the origin to the structure via crusts and surface layers. To simplify the analytical steps, the existence of a so-called base rock is sometimes assumed. Some empirical and theoretical formulas have been developed to get the maximum velocity of base-rock motions from the magnitude, focal depth, and epicentral distance of an earthquake.

Idealized artificial motions, calculated from white noise and harmonic functions in combination with various types of filtering and weighting functions, also may be assumed to represent the base-rock motion.

The earthquake motion of the base rock is modified and amplified by surface soil layers, and the predominant vibration of the ground is sometimes clearly observed, affecting the dynamic behavior of structures. It should be noted that long-period and long-duration motions caused by certain seismological and geological conditions particularly influence tall buildings.

In addition to ground shaking during an earthquake, disruptions of the ground surface by faulting and other associated permanent deformations of rock and soil are important causes of structural failure which should be considered carefully in the seismic design.

2 Dynamic Characteristics of Soil-Structure Systems

Surface layers significantly modify earthquake effects on structures. For example, distribution of earthquake damage in afflicted areas is influenced closely by the characteristics of subsoil layers. The influence of the soil layers is sometimes included in mathematical models in the form of soil-structure systems; in other cases, input earthquake motions to be applied to structures are modified in consideration of the surface layers.

In both cases, detailed investigations to determine appropriate soil characteristics are required. Shear wave velocity measurements are recommended, but other types of seismic prospecting are sometimes required. Some convenient soil-test methods, such as penetration tests and microtremor measurements at the ground surface, may also be effectively used. Through field and laboratory studies, the elastic and inelastic properties of soils including the thickness of layers, their densities, and wave velocities are obtained. These properties may be utilized in formulating mathematical models of the dynamic soil-structure system considering the interaction effect of structure and subsoil.

In many cases, the effects of soils are represented by combinations of springs and dash-pots in vertical and horizontal directions: the result is a model with sway and rocking motion. When matrices are formed including soil layers (by the finite element method, for example), the interaction problem is included, but great care must be exercised in determining the positions of the soil boundaries in the mathematical model.

Some structures, like those with pile foundations, do not have a clearly defined boundary between soil and structure. However, some analyses show that for normal types of piles the relative movements between piles and soil can be small, and often the influence of the piles on the ground motions may be disregarded.

When a building is supported by relatively rigid foundations like concrete piers or caissons, soil-structure interaction should be considered for the evaluation of the earthquake response of the building.

Wave propagation and reflection theories are also used for estimating the dynamic response of the ground and structures.

3 Analysis of Dynamic Response

Techniques for computing structural behavior under a specified excitation have been established and proven through comparison of the measured and calculated

Redwood tree 6 feet in diameter on line of fault split to height of 35 feet (Photo by: Richard L. Humphrey)

response of structures. Such comparisons, however, require a proper mathematical model that can represent the dynamic characteristics of the real structure and, at the same time, a complete description of the excitation.

The formation of an appropriate mathematical model of a tall building itself is possible, even if it is a special type of structure, provided that the deformation of the structure during the vibrational motion remains in the elastic range. In this linear analysis, the mode superposition method is frequently used, and approximate maximum values are sometimes calculated by the so-called "square root of sum of squares" method, when the possibility of significant errors in the result is small. In this method, an arbitrary small damping coefficient can be assigned to each vibration mode, if necessary. To analyze a structure composed of several kinds of materials, a method which assumes a different viscous damping ratio for each material can be applied. When the soil-structure system is considered, the formation of the model poses many problems. Nonlinear, nonhomogeneous characteristics of the soil, together with large damping effects, etc., are subjects which require further study.

It is at present and will continue to be impossible to predict exactly the earthquake ground motions to be expected in the future, and stochastic treatments, therefore, are very useful.

From economic considerations, partial damage of structures caused by a very strong motion having a small occurrence probability generally is allowed. As loss of life should be prevented insofar as possible, structures should usually be ductile, and not be allowed to collapse. Therefore, nonlinear analysis may sometimes be required in seismic design. Ductile structures are generally checked by linear analysis, as they should not be damaged in a moderate earthquake. Moreover, the behavior of structures in the linear range gives the structural designers important data on their dynamic characteristics, and complex structural systems can be investigated in this way.

4   Observation of Structural Behavior

In order to calibrate analytical models, predicted earthquake response must be supported by experimental evidence. Laboratory studies are needed in checking both the static and dynamic behavior of structures.

In static tests, stiffness, strength, and hysteretic characteristics of structures are checked. Based on these test results, mathematical models for dynamic analysis should be properly defined. Repeated cyclic straining behavior is one of the important factors to be considered in seismic design, as it is related directly to the collapse of structures in major earthquake motions of long duration. The stiffening effects of nonstructural elements can also be checked with static tests.

Methods of repairing damaged structures also should be evaluated using model tests, so that knowledge and experience can be gained regarding the structural and economic problems associated with the repair of the buildings.

In dynamic tests, shaking tables and dynamic pulsators are usually used. When shaking tables are used, one may have to use miniature models, and similarity is one of the problems to be carefully considered.

Field studies, through free and forced vibration tests using exciters, pulsators, and so forth, as well as observations of the structural response to both microtremors and actual earthquakes, are quite significant. Improvements in accuracy and sensitivity of exciters have made it possible to perform detailed field tests concerning frequencies, dampings, soil effects, etc., but the loading level developed is very low compared to that which occurs during actual severe earthquakes. Microtremor measurement is a convenient method to check the dynamic response characteristics of a structure to small-amplitude vibration.

Strong earthquake measurements are useful for checking whether the assumed mathematical model used in analyses is appropriate, and such measurements contribute much to the development of nonlinear dynamic analysis procedures. In typical tall buildings it is desirable that measurements be made at the base, a middle story, and the top of the buildings. Also it is desirable to install instruments on the ground at an appropriate distance from the structure to determine the effects of interaction between the soil and structure.

5 Evaluation of Earthquake Damage

The study of earthquake damage to structures provides a great deal of information concerning both earthquake effects and structural behavior. In some areas of severe and frequent earthquakes, lessons from the past should be utilized, but, generally, the recurrence period of earthquakes in any one region is so long that economic considerations are more powerful than the bitter lessons; thus the disasters are repeated. In many countries and cities, however, the lessons are crystallized into "structural regulations" and "seismic load requirements."

When earthquake damage has taken place, inspections should be made quickly so that one may observe and record the real state of damaged buildings before they are altered, removed, or repaired. Aftershock measurements are important, and, if possible, the response of some structures to aftershocks should be obtained.

Effect of ground slip, Mission Street, San Francisco, California *(Photo by: Richard L. Humphrey)*

Evaluation of the effects of local earthquake motions, in both damaged and undamaged buildings, correlated with analytic studies, is necessary for improving the seismic design of future buildings.

If pre-earthquake preparations are made, such as testing of dynamic properties of the structure, detailed investigation of soil characteristics, and installation of strong motion measuring instruments, the scientific value of the postearthquake investigations will be significantly improved.

6 Economic and Social Aspects

During the period between 1926 and 1960, about 350 000 people were killed by earthquakes throughout the world. This corresponds to the loss of 10 000 lives yearly. The protection of human lives should be one of the principal goals of seismic design of structures. After this goal is satisfied, economic considerations will have a primary effect on the design. To minimize life hazard, important facilities, such as those especially used to serve and house people in the case of disasters and those necessary for the continued functioning of society, should be constructed with extra strength to keep their functions operable during and after earthquakes. Examples are hospitals, fire stations, police stations, military stations, and other public buildings which serve as rescue and emergency activity centers. Broadcasting centers, telephone and telegram stations, and other communication centers also should be able to retain their functions in order to give people exact and correct information. Otherwise confusion and panic may be spread, and coordinated postearthquake operations would be inhibited.

Special buildings for disabled persons should be constructed to survive earthquake with small amounts of damage because their occupants cannot escape from severely damaged structures. Infant accommodations, such as nursery schools, kindergartens, and elementary schools, and protective institution asylums are in a similar category. The level of damage in nuclear power stations, gas and oil tanks, chemical factories, and gasoline stations, should be minimized and they should have higher resistance than ordinary buildings. Structures like large-scale high-rise buildings which house many people may also require a high level of earthquake resistance.

Psychological effects of earthquakes on people in tall buildings should be carefully considered. To avoid panic, emergency instructions should be given to the occupants ahead of time. Some important facilities such as elevators, stairways, electric and water supplies, should be designed to continue their functions during and after the earthquakes.

As the probability of a severe earthquake occurrence is very small, it usually is not economically justifiable to provide complete elastic resistance to this maximum earthquake. Thus the safety and economy of the structure should be well balanced.

The cost-benefit ratio for earthquake protection can be analyzed including the probability of occurrence of various degrees of earthquake, the initial cost, initial strength, running cost, aging effect, repair cost, interest, etc. These analyses are directly connected to the permissible damage related to the earthquake intensities and to the earthquake insurance problems.

7 Code Requirements

The aims of earthquake resistant design of building structures are: (1) To prevent loss of human life and personal injury; (2) to assure continuity of vital services; and (3) to minimize damage to property in the event of earthquakes, at minimum cost.

It is a well recognized fact, however, that to give complete protection against the maximum possible earthquake shaking is not usually financially feasible. It is generally accepted that earthquake design force levels should be set large enough: (1) To prevent structural damage and minimize other damage in moderate earthquakes, which occasionally occur; and (2) to have a negligible probability of collapse or serious damage in severe earthquakes, which very seldom occur.

The seismic design of buildings usually is carried out by one of the following methods: (1) By using equivalent static loading to give a suitable strength distribution throughout the structure, which when combined with inbuilt ductility will give satisfactory performance during dynamic excitation; or (2) by a dynamic analysis based on appropriate earthquake motions for the site and soil conditions.

In the first method, the value of the base shear coefficient or the lateral seismic coefficient used to define the equivalent static loading depends on many factors, including the dynamic properties of the structure, the type of construction, the importance of the structure, the seismicity of the region, and the subsoil conditions. The force induced by an earthquake on a structure may act in any direction. However, it is usual to consider only horizontal components of the earthquake forces, and these are taken to act nonconcurrently along the two main axes of the structure. Appropriate vertical seismic forces are assumed to act in the unfavorable direction in the design of a structure or portions of a structure when it is considered necessary.

Earthquake forces larger than the usual values are considered for the design of parts or portions of buildings such as cantilever parapets, structures projecting from the roofs (towers, tanks, penthouses, chimneys), ornamentations, appendages, etc. Other provisions of seismic codes include distribution of horizontal shear, evaluation of overturning moments and horizontal torsional moments, drift limitations, separation of buildings, setbacks, and structural design requirements including the problems of necessary ductility.

In the second approach to earthquake resistant design, the design loading due to earthquake motion is determined by a dynamic analysis. This method, which is based upon earthquake response spectra or response to time-history accelerograms, is frequently recommended, and may be required for specific structures such as slender high-rise buildings. Appropriate selection of input data and damping characteristics is required.

It is generally considered that the design static earthquake loading and associated response criteria provide the practical form for seismic design of standard types of structures; however, rational analysis should not only be permitted but encouraged, and in some countries, dynamic design based on time-dependent dynamic analysis is permitted or encouraged in the design of important high-rise buildings. This is the most reliable method for performing seismic design of structures.

2.2 EARTHQUAKE GROUND MOTION

The shaking of the ground during a tectonic earthquake is caused by the passage of seismic waves generated by the release of stored up stress in the earth's crust when sudden slip takes place on a geologic fault (Wiegel, 1970; Newmark and Rosenblueth, 1971; Richter, 1958). Three main types of faults have generated significant destructive ground shaking: (1) Strike-slip faults; (2) normal thrust faults; and (3) shallow-angle thrust faults. It is thought that the characteristics of surface ground shaking very close to the fault differ somewhat for the three types of fault. A strike-slip fault, such as the famous San Andreas fault in California, lies in an essentially vertical plane and the slip is mainly a relative horizontal displacement across the fault plane. The normal thrust fault which generated the 9 February 1971 San Fernando, California earthquake, had a fault plane making an angle of approximately 45° with the ground surface, and the slip reflected a horizontal compression in the earth's crust so that during the earthquake the upper rock mass moved uphill over the lower rock mass. A relative horizontal component of displacement across the fault plane also occurred (Gutenberg and Richter, 1954; Rothé, 1969). A normal thrust fault can be thought of as a plane of shear failure resulting from horizontal compression in the rock forming the earth's crust. The 1964 Alaska earthquake was generated on a shallow-angle thrust fault making an

Panoramic view of portion of San Francisco burned district containing fireproof buildings: 1 Pacific States Telephone and Telegraph Company's Main Office; 2 Union Trust Building; 3 Wells Fargo Building; 4 Crocker Building; 5 Sloane Building; 6 Shreve Building; 7 Chronicle Building; 8 Monadnock Building; 9 Mutual Savings Bank; 10 Spreckels or Call Building; 11 Aronson Building; 12 Kamm Building; 13 Whitehall Building; 14 Spring Valley Building; 15 The Dewey Building; 16 Butler Building *(Photo by: R. J. Waters & Co.)*

Newspaper Square (Market Street). Call Building, at far right, survived earthquake, though gutted by fire. Chronicle Building at left *(Courtesy: California Historical Society Library)*

Panoramic view of portion of San Francisco burned district containing fireproof buildings: 17 Hotel St. Francis; 18 Hotel Alexander; 19 James Flood Building; 20 Hotel Hamilton; 21 United States Mint; 22 California Casket Company's Building *(Photo by: R. J. Waters & Co.)*

angle of approximately 15° to 20° with respect to the ground surface, and the slip was one which predominantly represented movement of the lower rock mass into and beneath the upper rock mass. This fault displacement is attributed to the relative motion of two large crystal plates moving into each other with the result that the oceanic plate is thrust under the continental plate, deep into the earth's mantle. Because a point on the ground surface close to the fault is in a different relation to the fault plane for each of the foregoing types of faulting, the ground shaking close to the fault may have different characteristics for these three kinds of earthquake generation, but the number of recorded ground motions is not yet sufficient to define the differences. At a distance of several miles or more from the fault, the ground shaking generated by these three types of faulting appears to have very similar characteristics during the phase of large accelerations. Following this phase, long-period motion is observed and a normal thrust fault appears to generate stronger long-period motion (surface waves). The precise nature of these relatively long-period waves is not well understood, but their occurrence is significant for tall buildings which have relatively long natural periods of vibration and may, therefore, be excited into strong vibrations by the long-period waves.

1   Nature of Ground Shaking Generated by Fault

The seismic waves generated by a fault are dilational (compression) and rotational (shear) stress waves produced by the sudden drop in stress level when slip occurs on the fault (Wiegel, 1970; Newmark and Rosenblueth, 1971; Richter, 1958). Under appropriate circumstances, when reflecting from the surface of the earth, these waves produce surface waves whose amplitude of motion decreases exponentially with depth. The velocity of a compression wave in rock is about 1.8 times the shear wave velocity, and the surface wave velocity is about 0.9 times the shear wave velocity. Because of these differences in wave speeds, the three types of waves tend to separate as they travel away from the fault. In addition, of course, the amplitudes of the waves attenuate as they propagate. It is observed that the compression waves tend to have higher frequencies and lower acceleration amplitudes than the shear waves, and the surface waves tend to have much longer periods and larger displacement amplitudes. However, in the usual accelerogram recorded within about 30 miles of the causative fault, the contribution of the compression waves is not readily distinguishable from that of the shear waves.

During an earthquake, Love waves can be excited in softer, surface sedimentary deposits. This is a type of shear wave in which a north traveling wave has east-west particle motion which decreases to essentially zero amplitude at the rock surface underlying the soft deposit.

Presumably the state of stress across a fault before slip is not uniform and the stress drop during slip is not uniform. These nonuniformities affect the character of the seismic waves generated. Slip on the fault is initiated at a point and the boundary of the slipped surface propagates outward from this point at a velocity estimated to be approximately equal to the velocity of a shear wave [about 3.2 km (2 miles) per sec]. If slip propagates over a relatively small area, an earthquake of relatively small magnitude is generated; and if the slip propagates over a relatively large area, an earthquake of relatively large magnitude is generated. The magnitude 5.3 March 1957 San Francisco earthquake was generated on the San Andreas fault by slip over an area estimated to be roughly 4.8 km (3 miles) in diameter. The 1906

San Francisco earthquake was also generated on the San Andreas fault; its assigned magnitude was 8-1/4 and the slipped area was approximately 400 km (250 miles) in length and extended from the surface of the ground to a depth of approximately 8 km to 16 km (5 to 10 miles). The size and shape of the slipped area will influence the stress waves that are generated. For example, the seismic waves generated by a small area of slip will be relatively weak in the longer period waves, for the duration of slipping on the fault may be only one second or less. The character of the seismic waves is also affected by the nature of the slip, for it has been observed that some large earthquakes are composed of a time sequence of separate slips, while others appear to be composed of a number of earthquakes occurring successively along a fault. This is just saying that the propagation of the slip front and the slipping itself is not a smooth, uniform process, and this influences the seismic waves that are generated. The approximate length of fault slip observed with earthquakes at various magnitudes is listed in Table 2.1.

2 Intensity, Epicenter, Magnitude

Seismologists commonly describe the size of an earthquake by the Richter magnitude number, locate an earthquake by specifying its epicenter, and indicate the severity of ground shaking at a point by giving a Modified-Mercalli Intensity number (Richter, 1958). Each of these three terms is used in a special sense by seismologists, and consequently they are frequently misunderstood by engineers. The best measure of intensity, for engineering purposes, is a recorded accelerogram that gives the time history of ground shaking. An inexpensive seismoscope is also used to measure the intensity of ground shaking. In the United States, this is a two-dimensional pendulum having a natural period of vibration of 0.75 sec and about 10% of critical damping (National Oceanic and Atmospheric Agency). Its excursions are traced on a smoked watchglass which thus gives a record of the amplitude of the motion, but does not give information on the time at which different portions of the motion occurred. The seismoscope record indicates the amplitude of motion that a building with 0.75 sec period and about 10% damping would have during the earthquake and, hence, the amplitude of the seismoscope record is a measure of the intensity of ground shaking in terms of the response of structures having periods of vibration about 0.75 sec.

Seismological papers usually describe the severity of ground shaking by giving the Modified-Mercalli Intensity number. The Modified-Mercalli Scale is a concise

Table 2.1 Relation between magnitude and fault slip length

Magnitude of earthquake (1)	Approximate length of fault slip, in miles (2)
3	0.3
4	0.8
5	2
6	5
7	25
8	190
8.5	530

tabular description of the commonly observed effects of ground shaking on the works of man, on nature, and on the senses of man (Richter, 1958). Hence, the MM number is a rather crude, subjective estimate of the ground shaking which is useful in the absence of any instrumental records.

Seismologists can use seismographic records to locate the point on the fault where slip began. This is called the focus, center, or hypocenter, and the point on the surface of the ground directly above is called the epicenter. The center of energy release is, in general, never the center of the slipped fault area.

To provide a more reliable measure of the size of an earthquake, Richter (1958) utilized comparative seismograph readings. The peak amplitude of a seismograph record depends mainly on the size of the earthquake S, the distance to the center of energy release d, the character of the faulting f, and the nature of the local geology at the seismograph site lg, and can be expressed as

$$A = A(S,d,f,lg) \tag{2.1}$$

If some A_0 is taken as a reference, the ratio of A to A_0 is a measure of the relative size of the two earthquakes, that is

$$\frac{A}{A_0} = \frac{A(S,d,f,lg)}{A(S_0,d_0,f_0,lg_0)} \tag{2.2}$$

If all measurements are made at distances large compared to the dimensions of the slipped fault area and these are converted to a standard distance d_0, the influence of both d and f can reasonably be disregarded. (The orientation of the fault with respect to the instrument site can less reasonably be disregarded, but the effect of orientation is usually averaged out by using several readings at different orientations.) If all seismographs are sited on bedrock, the influence of local geology can be reasonably neglected, and $A/A_0 = A(S)/A(S_0)$. Richter defined the magnitude M of the earthquake so that $M = \log_{10}(A/A_0)$ with the seismograph having a period of 0.8 sec and critical damping. For engineering purposes, M is an indication of the size of the slipped fault area and, hence, is an indication of the area affected by strong shaking. The magnitude M is not a good direct measure of the peak accelerations generated by an earthquake, for this information cannot be retrieved from an amplitude measurement made at a relatively large distance from the causative fault. Having recorded the ground accelerations produced by a number of earthquakes having the same M, it is, of course, possible to use M as an indicator of accelerations to be expected.

Lists of earthquakes and their magnitudes are given by Gutenberg and Richter (1954) and Rothé (1969).

3 Influence of Geology on Seismic Waves

The reflections and refractions caused by inhomogeneities in the material through which the seismic waves travel have an influence on the waves and, hence, on the ground shaking at a point. Although, in principle, these could produce wide variation in the characteristics of ground shaking, it appears that in the United States these influences are normally not especially pronounced. For example, strong ground motions recorded at El Centro, California, Taft, California, and Olympia,

Washington (Fig. 2.1) are very similar in characteristics even though these widely separated sites are on quite different geologic formations (International Association for Earthquake Engineering, 1969). In Fig. 2.1, the Tehachapi earthquake (A) was of magnitude = 7.7, distance to fault break = 25 miles; the El Centro earthquake (B)

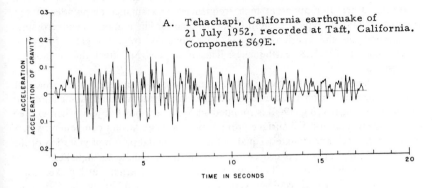

A. Tehachapi, California earthquake of
    21 July 1952, recorded at Taft, California.
    Component S69E.

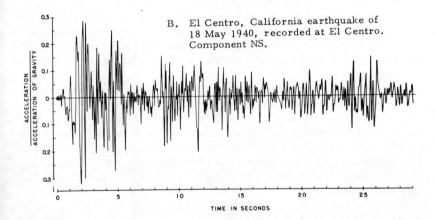

B. El Centro, California earthquake of
    18 May 1940, recorded at El Centro.
    Component NS.

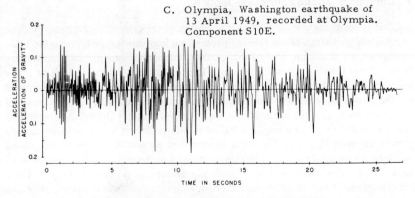

C. Olympia, Washington earthquake of
    13 April 1949, recorded at Olympia.
    Component S10E.

Fig. 2.1 Accelerograms of typical strong ground shaking

was of magnitude = 7.1, distance to fault break = 5 miles; and the Olympia earthquake (C) was of magnitude = 7.5, distance to fault break = 15 miles.

In some locations the influence of the geological formations on the seismic waves is very pronounced. Ground motions recorded in Lima, Peru, Santiago, Chile, and Koyna, India (International Association for Earthquake Engineering, 1965) exhibit relatively larger amplitudes at high frequencies and smaller amplitudes at low frequencies than do typical western U.S. earthquakes. The number of zero crossings per second on the accelerograms is approximately twice as great for these earthquakes as for U.S. earthquakes. This is a geologic effect that is not yet understood.

The influence of local geology is also sometimes pronounced. For example, the old lake bed on which the center of Mexico City (International Association for Earthquake Engineering, 1960) is founded shakes like a bowl of jelly when excited by seismic waves, and the surface ground motion has a strong component with a period of 2.5 sec approximately equal to the fundamental period of vibration of the lake bed. Similar effects have been reported during Japanese earthquakes.

During the 9 February 1971 San Fernando, California earthquake, some influences of travel path geology were observed on the campus of the California Institute of Technology, where two accelerographs separated by about 305 m (1000 ft) recorded ground motions approximately 50% stronger at one site than the other, both having the same local geology [270 m (900 ft) of alluvium] (Gutenberg and Richter, 1954; Rothé, 1969). Also, the motion recorded at the Seismological Laboratory on granite differed appreciably from and had a higher acceleration than the instrument 4.8 km (3 miles) away in the Faculty Club on the campus (900 ft of alluvium).

The nature of the seismic waves that combine to produce the particle motion on the surface of the ground is very complex and not well understood. Many waves affect the particle simultaneously and these can have directions of propagation ranging from horizontal to vertical. They may combine in such a fashion that the shaking at one point differs appreciably from that at a nearby point. This introduces a probabilistic aspect, for it indicates that two earthquakes of the same magnitude and at the same distance from a site can produce ground motions that may have appreciable differences.

4   Duration of Strong Earthquake Motion

Close to the causative fault the characteristics of the ground shaking may depend strongly on the details of the faulting process, such as shortest distance to the fault, orientation of the fault, the nature of the fault displacements, local subsidiary faulting, etc. However, at a horizontal distance from the causative fault of a few miles the details of the faulting process do not appear to have a significant influence on the strong acceleration phase of the ground shaking. The recorded ground accelerations at El Centro, California, Taft, California, and Olympia, Washington, are representative of what might be called standard United States large earthquake ground motions (Fig 2.1). During a short initial portion the intensity of ground acceleration increases to strong shaking, followed by a strong acceleration phase of shaking, and this is followed by a gradually decreasing portion of motion. These accelerograms have spectral characteristics similar to "white noise" over the approximate period range 0.3 sec to 10 sec. The strong shaking durations of earthquakes of different magnitudes are presented in Table 2.2 for locations in the vicinity of the causative fault. Accelerograms of strong shaking are published by several agencies (International Association for Earthquake Engineering, 1960, 1965, 1969; Jennings, 1971; Hudson, 1971; Earthquake Engineering Research Laboratory, 1969-1971; Housner, 1963).

5   Response Spectra of Ground Motions

It is customary to portray the influence of the ground shaking on structures by means of the response spectrum (Wiegel, 1970). The response spectrum is a plot of the peak response of a one-degree-of-freedom oscillator, of period T and damping ratios n, that is subjected to the ground acceleration (Figs. 2.2 to 2.9). Fig. 2.2 shows the relative velocity spectrum S_v computed for the NS component of motion recorded in the basement of the Millikan Library building, with damping 0, 2%, 5%, 10%, and 20% of critical. The dotted line is the Fourier amplitude spectrum. For very long periods S_v approaches the maximum ground velocity. The large hump in the spectrum at 1.8-sec period is apparently fortuitous, as it does not appear in the other component of motion.

The peak response quantity plotted is either relative displacement S_d, relative velocity S_v, or absolute acceleration S_a, of the oscillator mass. Often the pseudovelocity is plotted, which is related to the other quantities by

$$S_{ps} = \frac{2\pi}{T} S_d = \frac{T}{2\pi} S_a \qquad (2.3)$$

The response spectra are computed over a range of periods and for a number of different values of damping. The spectrum curves indicate how severely each mode of the building may vibrate, but do not give information on the times of occurrence of the peak values, which usually are different for different modes. The response spectrum gives a concise and informative description of the vibratory effect of the ground acceleration on buildings; but it must be recognized that the structure is assumed to respond elastically, thus damage effects cannot be inferred directly from response spectra.

The spectra shown in Figs. 2.2 through 2.9 are for the lateral component of ground motion. Fig. 2.5 shows component N81W of the magnitude 7 earthquake approximately 242 km (150 miles) to the south of Mexico City. The accelerogram was recorded in the basement of the 43-story Latino-Americana tower. The hump in the spectrum at 2.5-sec period represents the fundamental mode vibration of the soft clay that was formerly a lake bed. A standardized curve of El Centro, 1940, intensity for such lateral motions is shown in Fig. 2.10 (Housner, 1963).

Vertical ground motion records have been analyzed using response spectrum techniques. Fig. 2.11 shows one such spectrum (California Institute of Technology, 1972). It refers to the earthquake of May 18, 1940; damping values are 0, 2%, 5%, 10% and 20% of critical.

Torsional or twisting ground motion can be approximately estimated from the lateral components of ground motion. Fig. 2.12 shows a torsional spectrum for the 1940 El Centro earthquake (Hart et al., 1975).

6 Estimating Future Ground Motions

It is not possible to predict accurately when and where earthquakes will occur, how strong they will be, and what characteristics the ground motions will have. Therefore, the engineer must estimate the ground shaking his building is likely to experience. Various methods having different levels of sophistication are used to accomplish this. The most commonly used methods are described as follows.

The simplest method is to construct a seismic risk map such as those used in conjunction with most building codes (International Conference of Building Officials, 1976). Different zones indicate different intensities of ground shaking to be considered in the design. Seismic risk maps usually have very little detail; for example, the building code map of California has all of southern California in the same seismic zone. The construction of a risk map is based mainly on the seismic history from a probabilistic point of view. Different methods of constructing seismic

Table 2.2 Relation between duration of strong shaking and earthquake magnitude

Magnitude of nearby earthquake (1)	Approximate duration of strong shaking, in seconds (2)
5	1
6	8
7	20
8	35

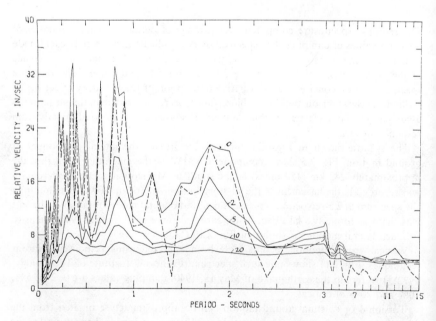

Fig. 2.2 Velocity response spectra, Millikan Library, California Institute of Technology, 9 February 1971

risk maps lead to different results. For example, the United States and Canadian building code zoning maps are in marked disagreement along the border between the two countries, especially in the eastern portion (Zone 3 contiguous to Zone 1). Since the seismicity on both sides of the border is the same it must be concluded that the method used to arrive at Zone 3 on the U.S. side of the border involves approximations different from those used to arrive at Zone 1 on the Canadian map.

Seismic zoning and microregionalization refer to more refined methods of constructing detailed seismic risk maps (Richter, 1958). In addition to the seismic history, the geologic formations are taken into account. Different techniques are used by different schools of seismic zoning but most methods place special emphasis on the quality of the surface layers of ground and very detailed seismic zones are constructed; however, the reliability of such detailed zoning methods has not been completely verified by observations in the field.

There is great practical benefit to be gained from having reliable and detailed maps that indicate seismic hazards in a form useful for planning and design. It is, therefore, desirable to continue research on this problem. The most important element of such research is ample instrumental data that include recorded ground motions at a variety of locations and for earthquakes of different magnitudes.

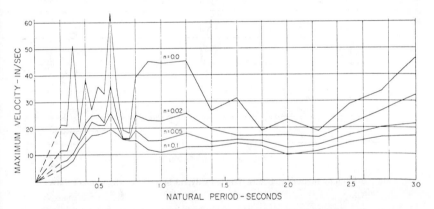

Fig. 2.3 **Velocity response spectra, Taft, California, 21 July 1952—Component N21E**

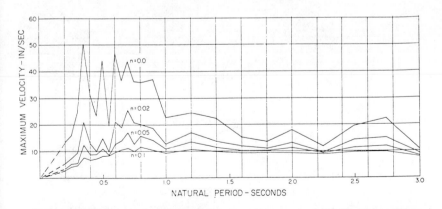

Fig. 2.4 **Velocity response spectra, Olympia, Washington, 13 April 1949—Component N80E**

A Seismic Site Evaluation is the most detailed (and costly) method of establishing a design earthquake and takes into account seismic history, active faults in the vicinity, and stress-strain properties of the materials through which the seismic waves travel. In one approach, the magnitude and distance of future earthquakes are estimated, and an estimate is made of the nature of the seismic waves generated (usually white noise), and the modification of the waves as they travel along a prescribed path to the ground surface at the site. These methods use simplifying assumptions and model the actual complex physical situation crudely.

An alternate approach to establishing a design earthquake ground motion for a building site utilizes the theory of probability to construct simulated accelerograms (Jennings et al., 1969; Amin and Ang, 1966; Ruiz and Penzien, 1969; Saragoni and Hart, 1974). This approach is based on the observation that in the region of strong shaking in the general vicinity of the causative fault a component of recorded ground acceleration usually appears to be a random function having the following characteristics:

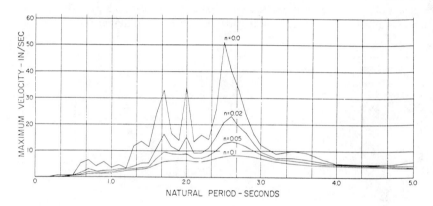

Fig. 2.5 Velocity response spectra, Mexico City, 19 May 1962—Component N8IW

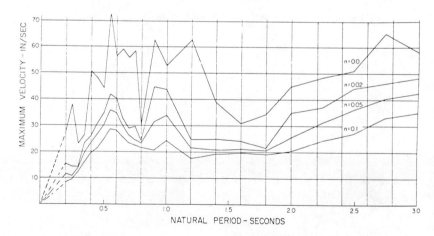

Fig. 2.6 Velocity response spectra, El Centro, California, 18 May 1940—Component NS

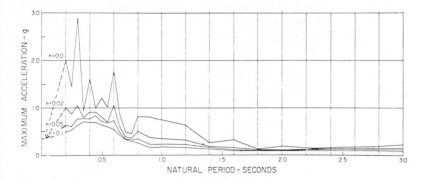

Fig. 2.7 Acceleration spectra, Taft, California, 21 July 1952—Component N21E

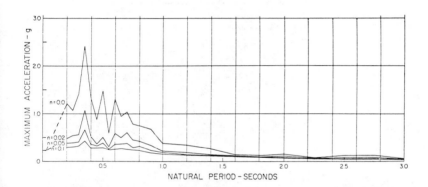

Fig. 2.8 Acceleration spectra, Olympia, Washington, 13 April 1949—Component N80E

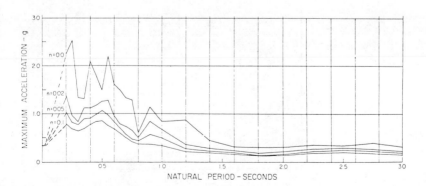

Fig. 2.9 Acceleration spectra, El Centro, California, 18 May 1940—Component NS

1. The energy in the ground acceleration rises quickly to a high value, and is more or less uniformly strong for a certain duration, which is followed by an attenuating final portion of the motion.

2. The frequency content of the motion as described by a smoothed Fourier amplitude spectrum indicates the frequency ranges in which the major part of the energy resides.

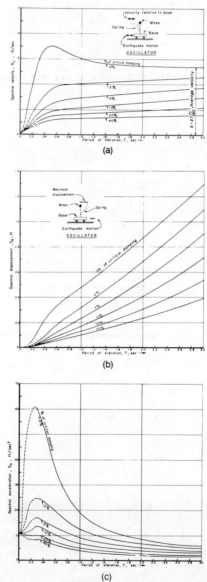

Fig. 2.10 (a) Average velocity response spectra, 1940 El Centro intensity; (b) Average displacement response spectra, 1940 El Centro intensity; (c) Average acceleration response spectra, 1940 El Centro intensity *(Housner, 1963)*

3. As exhibited by digital computation, the ground acceleration excites the modes of vibration of a building. Each mode has a response in which the amplitude of vibration initially rises, then has a certain duration of strong vibrations, and this is followed by gradually attenuating vibration.

Random functions can be generated which have properties similar to those of recorded accelerograms. This is usually done by first generating a random function that is "white" over an appropriate frequency interval and has a duration consistent with the magnitude and distance of the earthquake supposed to generate the ground shaking. This random function is filtered so as to produce the desired frequency content as specified by a prescribed ensemble average spectrum curve. The filtered

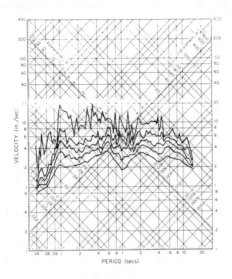

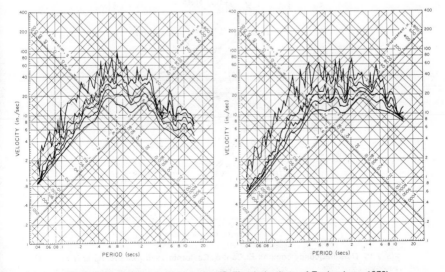

Fig. 2.11 Vertical response spectra *(California Institute of Technology, 1972)*

function is then shaped by multiplying by an amplitude shaping function that produces an initial rise in the accelerogram, an attenuating tail, and a central strong portion. The advantage of this approach is that it constructs directly a time-history ground acceleration incorporating what is known about recorded ground motions, and incorporating properties that analysis indicates the motion should have. Each simulated accelerogram is a sample from a population whose ensemble average properties are specified, and the statistical properties of the response can be examined.

The spectral content of the earthquake motion may be a function of time (Saragoni and Hart, 1974). Fig. 2.13 shows the average spectral content for each of three time regions of the El Centro, 1940 earthquake accelerogram. Variation of frequency content can be incorporated into simulated earthquakes.

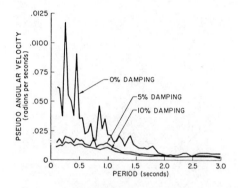

Fig. 2.12 **Pseudo angular velocity spectra for El Centro 1940 earthquake** *(Hart et al., 1975)*

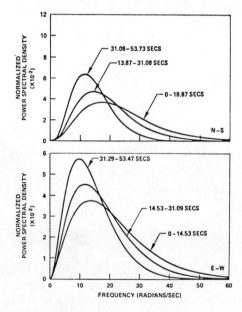

Fig. 2.13 **Time-frequency content: El Centro, California 1940** *(Saragoni and Hart, 1974)*

The intensity of shaking generally decreases with distance from the causative fault so that the contour lines of equal intensity are roughly elliptical in shape (Wiegel, 1970). It is observed that the rate of attenuation with distance of higher frequency components of the ground motion is greater than the attenuation of longer period components. This is a significant factor in the design of tall buildings, for it means that the exposure of tall buildings to shaking is greater than the exposure of low (short period) buildings. For example, the causative fault of the 1952 Tehachapi earthquake ($M = 7.7$) was 113 km (70 miles) north of the center of Los Angeles, and at this distance the higher frequency components in the ground motion had attenuated so that the peak acceleration was 5%g and no damage was done to low buildings. However, buildings whose fundamental periods were in the range of 1 sec to 3 sec vibrated strongly and received nonstructural damage. The fault that generated the 1964 Alaska earthquake ($M = 8.4$) was also approximately 113 km (70 miles) from the city of Anchorage, where buildings of 6 to 14 stories received significant structural damage but one-story and two-story buildings had comparatively little damage. For a given large earthquake, therefore, the area covered by ground shaking potentially damaging to a 50-story building is much greater than the area covered by ground shaking potentially damaging to one-story buildings. On the other hand, small earthquakes are potentially more damaging to low buildings than to high buildings. For example, the March 1957 San Francisco earthquake ($M = 5.3$) had accelerations exceeding 15%g in the epicentral region but the duration of strong shaking was less than 2 sec, so that the long period components in the motion were very weak. This earthquake excited the second and third modes of tall buildings in San Francisco much more than the fundamental mode.

The attenuation of ground shaking with distance from the causative fault is frequency-dependent (see Fig. 2.14, in which Curve A = 25 miles from center of large earthquake; Curve B = 70 miles from center of large shock; and Curve C = 8 miles from center of small, $M = 5.3$, shock), magnitude-dependent, and dependent on orientation with respect to the fault. It also depends on the geology of the region. For example, in the United States the attenuation is greatest in California, less in the midwestern part of the country, and least in the east; hence the felt area of

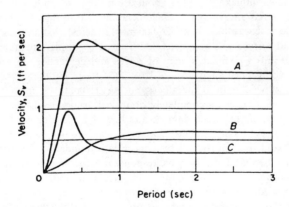

Fig. 2.14 Idealized undamped velocity spectrum curves that illustrate effect of magnitude and distance *(Wiegel, 1970)*

magnitude 7 earthquake is much larger in the eastern part of the country than in the western part. These differences in attenuation reflect differences in energy absorption and dispersion; the geometric attenuation is the same everywhere and thus the predominant influence in the near-field. Because of insufficient recorded data, the attenuation of strong ground motions is only approximately understood.

2.3   DYNAMIC CHARACTERISTICS OF SOIL-STRUCTURE SYSTEMS

Building damage resulting from earthquakes may be influenced in a number of ways by the characteristics of the soils in the affected area. In some cases damage is caused by a gross instability of the soil, resulting in large permanent movements of the ground surface, and associated distortion of a structure. For example, deposits of loose granular soils may be compacted by the ground vibrations induced by the earthquake, resulting in large settlements and differential settlements of the ground surface. An island near Valdivia, Chile was partially submerged as a result of the combined effects of tectonic land movements and ground settlement due to compaction in the Chilean earthquake of 1960, while parts of Niigata, Japan were inundated when settlement of ground adjacent to a river occurred in the Niigata earthquake of 1964.

In cases where the soil consists of loose saturated granular materials, the tendency to compact may result in the development of excess hydrostatic pressures of sufficient magnitude to cause liquefaction of the soil, resulting in settlements and tilting of structures. Liquefaction of loose saturated sand deposits resulted in major damage to thousands of buildings in Niigata, Japan in the earthquake of 1964 (Ohsaki, 1966).

The combination of dynamic stresses and induced pore water pressures in deposits of soft clay and sands may result in major landslides such as that which developed in the Turnagain Heights area of Anchorage, Alaska in the earthquake of March 27, 1964 (Seed et al., 1974). The coastline in this area was marked by bluffs some 21 m (70 ft) high sloping at about 1 on 1-1/2 down to the bay. The slide induced by the earthquake extended about 3 km (almost 2 miles) along the coast and extended inland an average distance of about 270 m (900 ft). The total area within the slide zone was thus about 526 000 m² (130 acres). Within the slide area the original ground surface was completely devastated by displacements which broke up the ground into a complex system of ridges and depression. In the depressed areas the ground dropped an average of 10.6 m (35 ft) during the sliding. Houses in the area, some of which moved laterally as much as 150 m to 180 m (500 ft to 600 ft) as the slide progressed, were completely destroyed. Major landslides of this type have been responsible for much damage and loss of life during earthquakes.

While these types of soil instability may cause catastrophic damage to buildings, they can be avoided or prevented by appropriate foundation investigations and design. On the other hand, the dynamic response of structures to ground vibrations, which also depends to a large extent on the soil conditions at the building site, cannot be avoided. Accordingly the following discussion will be limited to a consideration of building and ground response during earthquakes under conditions where no soil instability or permanent deformations are involved.

1 Effects of Soil on Dynamic Response of Buildings

The major effects that variations in local soil conditions can have on the dynamic response of structures is illustrated by building response effects in two recent earthquakes.

In the 1957 San Francisco earthquake, recordings of ground motions were made at several locations within the city. The variations in soil conditions along a 6.4-km (4-mile) section through the city and corresponding variations in recorded ground shaking characteristics are shown in Fig. 2.15. It is readily apparent that significant variations occurred both in the peak accelerations developed and in the frequency characteristics, as illustrated by the response spectra for the recorded motion. Using the recorded motions as a basis for analysis, computations have been made of the maximum base shear for a typical 10-story building located at each of the recording stations. The results are shown in Fig. 2.16. It may be seen that for the same building, the base shear would vary from a low value of about 0.9 MN (200 kips) for sites underlain by rock to values as high as 4 MN (900 kips) at a site underlain by about 91 m (300 ft) of clay and sand. Clearly it is necessary to be able to anticipate variations of this magnitude at the design stage.

Again, there was a clear relationship between building damage due to shaking and soil depth in Caracas, Venezuela in the earthquake of 1967. Although the magnitude of the earthquake was only about 6.4 and its epicenter was located about 56 km (35 miles) from Caracas, the shaking caused the collapse of four 10-story to 12-story apartment buildings with the loss of over 200 lives. Many other structures suffered structural damage and severe architectural damage.

A detailed study of the relationship between structural damage to buildings and

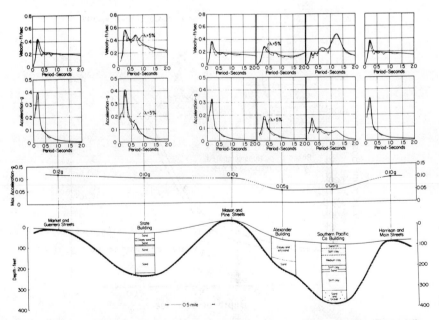

Fig. 2.15 Soil conditions and characteristics of recorded ground motions—San Francisco earthquake, 1957

the depth of the underlying soils has been reported (Seed et al., 1970; Seed and Wilson, 1967). For 5-story to 9-story buildings the structural damage intensity was slightly higher for soil depths of 50 m to 70 m (170 ft to 230 ft) than for other depths of soil, but for buildings over 10 stories high, the structural damage intensity was several hundred percent higher where soil depths exceeded 160 m (520 ft) than for soil depths below 140 m (460 ft). Again it is apparent that for tall buildings, the depth and characteristics of the underlying soil deposits had a large effect on the severity of ground motions and the resulting building damage, even in the same city and for the same earthquake.

The large magnitude of the potential effect of soil conditions on building response merits its careful consideration in evaluating the response of tall buildings during earthquakes.

2 Evaluation of Soil-Structure Interaction Effects

The interaction effects between a tall building and the foundation soils on which it rests may be divided into two parts:

1. Physical interaction effects which involve the effects of stresses and deformations at the contact boundaries between structure and soil. Potential consequences of such effects include a change in ground response adjacent to the building, changes in period of the building or in deformations of the upper floors of the building resulting from rocking deformations of the underlying soil, and changes in response of the building due to soil deformations.

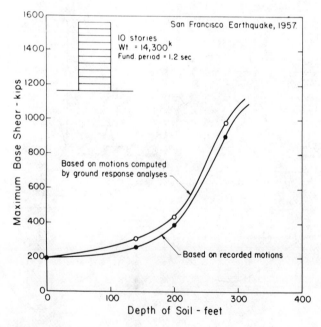

Fig. 2.16 Computed values of maximum base shear for 10-story building in San Francisco earthquake of 1957

2. Response interaction, involving changes in response of a given type of structure as a result of changes in the response of different soil deposits to earthquake-induced motions in the underlying rock.

In effect, both the soil deposit and the structure at a given site respond to the motions in the underlying rock, and analytical models have been developed for evaluating these responses. The most sophisticated of these is the finite element representation shown in Fig. 2.17(a), which permits a 2- or 3-dimensional analysis of the complete soil-structure system. A somewhat simplified analytical model, requiring some judgment in the selection of component characteristics, is the lumped mass representation for a building on a base supported by springs and dashpots to represent the foundation soils, shown in Fig. 2.17(b).

Using models of this type, some studies have been made to evaluate soil-structure interaction effects. A typical example of the results obtained in the three-dimensional analysis of an axisymmetric structure, having a period of 1.2 sec, resting on a soil deposit 61 m (200 ft) thick, is shown in Fig. 2.18. The computed values of maximum ground acceleration along the base of the structure and at the same depth in the free field adjacent to the structure are shown in the upper part of Fig. 2.18. It may be seen that for this flexible structure, representative of a building 10 to 12 stories high, the presence of the structure has no significant effect on the ground motions. A similar result was noted by Blume (1969a) on the basis of measurements of ground motions at the base of buildings and in adjacent areas during the firing of large-scale nuclear shots at the Nevada Testing Ground.

Analyses of the influence of the deformability of the ground on the period, base shear, and story deflections of tall buildings have been made by a number of investigators (Merritt and Housner, 1954; Bertero et al., 1970; Minami et al., 1970; Bielak, 1971; Chakravorty et al., 1971). In general these have shown that the deformations of the soil may influence the period, base shear, or deflections of a flexible structure by about 10% to 30% but effects rarely exceed these values. In contrast it should be noted that deformability of the soil can have large effects on the response characteristics of very heavy, stiff structures such as nuclear power plants.

An illustration of the minor influence of foundation soil compressibility on the response of flexible structures is provided by a recent study by Finn et al. (1971). Analyses were made of the response of a 10-story building on a soil foundation 30.5

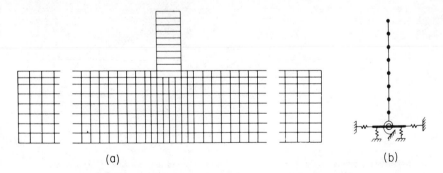

(a)   (b)

Fig. 2.17 Analytical models for soil-structure systems: (a) Finite element model; (b) Lumped mass-spring model

m (100 ft) deep, treating the soil and structure as a coupled system. The building response was then computed by decoupling the soil and structure; that is, by determining the surface motions of the ground alone and using these as base motions (under rigid base conditions) to compute the building response. A comparison of the maximum base shear for the coupled and uncoupled system analyses is shown in Fig. 2.19. For a wide range of soil stiffnesses the computed values of maximum base shear did not differ by more than 5% to 10%. While coupling may have somewhat larger effects on response in some cases, its effects are not likely to exceed several tens of percent.

However, as shown in Fig. 2.16, variations in ground shaking characteristics due to variations in soil conditions and the associated effects of response interaction between a building and the underlying soil deposits may cause variations in maximum base shear of several hundred percent. It would seem reasonable to conclude therefore that for flexible or tall buildings, the effects of physical interaction between structure and soil are of minor significance compared with the effects of the local soil conditions on the characteristics of ground surface motions. Significant improvements in design are therefore dependent on the development of techniques for determining the influence of local soil conditions on the ground motions.

3 Methods of Determining the Effect of Soil Conditions on Ground Motion Characteristics

There are three main methods by which the effect of soil conditions on ground motions may be predicted.

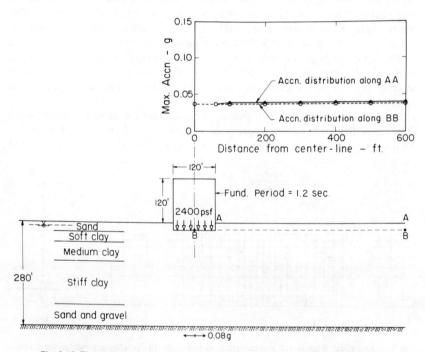

Fig. 2.18 Three-dimensional analysis of axisymmetric structure and soil foundation

By Analysis of Data from Previous Earthquakes. By analyzing the records of ground response at a large number of sites with a wide range of soil conditions, due to different magnitudes of earthquakes at different epicentral distances, it is possible to anticipate the nature of ground motions likely to be developed during future earthquakes. The over-all effects of soil and geologic conditions may be considered in two parts: (1) The influence of regional and local geology on the characteristics of the motions developed in rock formations underlying or adjacent to any given site; and (2) the effects of the local soil conditions in modifying these rock motions as they propagate to the ground surface.

Since it is unlikely that a knowledge of the geologic conditions along the travel path for earthquake waves or of the local rock conditions at large depths will ever be known in sufficient detail to assess the nature of these effects at a potential building site, it would seem that probabilistic approaches will provide the most rational method of assessing the nature of earthquake motions likely to be developed in rock at any given site. Past records must be used to provide a guide to the general characteristics of the motions and the probability of their occurrence, leading to envelopes of motion characteristics such as that shown in Fig. 2.20 (Schnabel and

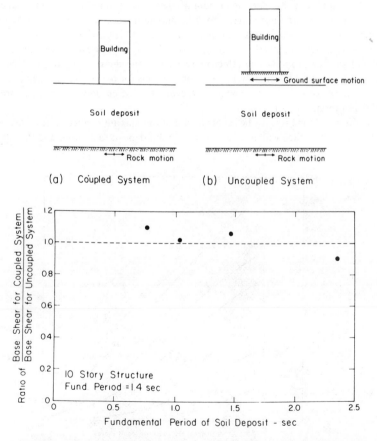

Fig. 2.19 **Influence of decoupling soil structure system on base shear for 10-story building** *(Finn et al., 1971)*

Seed, 1972), and a set of motions having the desired characteristics will be necessary to anticipate the full range of shaking effects which might develop for any given site. Such a set of motions may be obtained either by appropriate modification of existing records or by generation of artificial records using random process theory. Both procedures have been used successfully for analytical purposes. Depending on the importance of the structure, an engineer may wish to choose a maximum rock acceleration near the mean or near the upper bound as a basis for design.

Superimposed on these variations in rock motions, variations in soil conditions in any local area will also be responsible for marked differences in ground motion characteristics. The local soil deposits may modify both the intensity of the motion as measured by the maximum acceleration developed and the frequency characteristics of the motion as measured by its response spectrum. For example, a statistical analysis of over 100 recorded strong earthquake motions having peak accelerations greater than about 0.05 g (Seed et al., 1974) shows that by dividing them into four groups according to the soil conditions underlying the recording station—(1) Rock sites; (2) stiff soil conditions with soil depths less than about 45 m (150 ft); (3) deep cohesionless soil sites with depths greater than 76 m (250 ft); and (4) sites underlain by soft to medium clay and sands—the mean shapes of acceleration spectra, normalized to 1 g maximum acceleration for purposes of comparison, have the forms shown in Fig. 2.21. It is readily apparent that soils introduce a significantly larger proportion of longer period components into the ground surface motions, the effect increasing as the depth or softness of the soils increases, and that failure to recognize these effects for periods larger than about 0.5 sec could lead to major discrepancies in evaluation of ground response spectra and design criteria.

At the same time it must be recognized that the maximum acceleration developed at the ground surface will also vary from one soil deposit to another and that there is

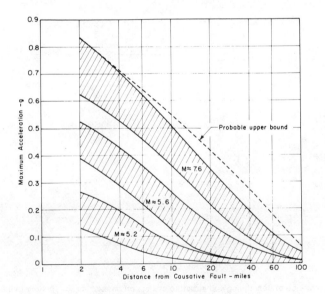

Fig. 2.20 Ranges of maximum accelerations in rock

necessarily a physical limit to the peak acceleration which any soil formation can transmit. A review of peak acceleration data observed in a number of earthquakes indicates the following general trends:

1. For low intensity motions, virtually all soil deposits tend to amplify underlying or adjacent rock accelerations.

2. For extremely high intensity motions, many soil deposits tend to attenuate the peak accelerations in underlying or adjacent rock formations.

3. Deep and soft soil deposits are more effective in attenuating peak rock accelerations than very shallow stiff soils, which may tend to amplify adjacent rock accelerations under all conditions.

Based on these considerations it seems likely that typical average relationships between peak accelerations developed in rock and those developed at the surface of different types of soil deposits will have the general form shown in Fig. 2.22 (Seed et al., 1975). With the aid of these results and those shown in Figs. 2.20 and 2.21, it becomes possible to assess the relative characteristics of motions likely to develop at different sites in any given earthquake, and thereby to assess potential differential damage patterns or modify design procedures to provide a reasonable degree of uniformity of damage intensity for all types of structures.

By Use of Microtremor or Small Earthquake Records. It might appear that the influence of soil conditions on ground motion characteristics at any site could be determined if use could be made of small earthquakes and microtremors to provide a basis for evaluating site effects. In this event mobile installations could be used to record the effects directly, since the frequency of occurrence of small earthquakes and microtremors would permit recordings to be made at frequent intervals. Unfortunately, because of the nonlinear stress-strain characteristics of soils, the behavior at small strain levels during very small earthquakes cannot be used as a direct basis for evaluating behavior at high strain levels during major earthquakes without the aid of an appropriate analytical procedure for extrapolating microtremor effects to strong motion conditions. Thus while microtremor effects can

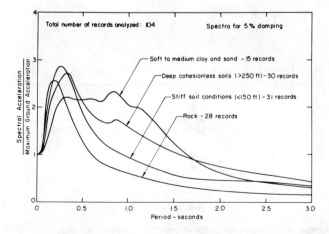

Fig. 2.21 Average acceleration spectra for different site conditions

serve an extremely useful purpose in establishing one bound on the range of possible behavior patterns and in checking the applicability of a proposed analytical procedure, they do not appear to provide, in themselves, a full predictive capability for engineering purposes.

By Analytical Procedures.   In many cases the ground motions developed near the surface of a soil deposit during an earthquake may be attributed primarily to the upward propagation of waves from an underlying rock formation. Analytical procedures have been developed in recent years for determining ground response under these conditions. The methods of analysis depend on the configuration of the soil deposit.

For cases where all boundaries of a stratified or homogeneous deposit are essentially horizontal the soil may usually be treated as a series of semi-infinite layers, and the analysis reduces to a one-dimensional problem. Two methods of approach have been used to analyze ground response under these conditions:

1. An analysis based on the use of the wave equation (Kanai, 1951; Matthiesen et al., 1964; Herrera and Rosenblueth, 1965; Kobayashi and Kagami, 1966; Roesset and Whitman, 1969; Lysmer et al., 1971). In this approach the soil comprising each layer is considered to have uniform viscoelastic properties and the motion in the underlying bedrock is considered to consist of a series of sinusoidal motions of different frequencies. The response at the surface of the deposit is then computed for a range of base rock frequencies providing a response amplification spectrum. The surface motions at a site resulting from a given base motion can then be evaluated by multiplying the Fourier spectrum of the base motion by the amplification spectrum, and inverting the resulting Fourier spectrum to determine the motions at the ground surface.

2. An analysis in which the soil deposit is represented by a series of lumped masses connected by shear springs whose characteristics are determined by

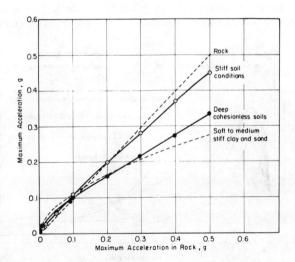

Fig. 2.22 Approximate relationships between maximum accelerations on rock and other local site conditions

the stress-strain relationships of the soils in the various layers. Similarly the damping characteristics of the system are determined by the soil properties. The response of the system to a motion generated at the base can then be made by conventional dynamic analysis procedures (Penzien, 1964; Idriss and Seed, 1968, 1970).

Both probabilistic and deterministic approaches may be used in conjunction with either method of analysis.

Whether the analysis is made by the wave propagation or the lumped mass approach, meaningful results can be obtained only if the soil characteristics are correctly represented in the analytical procedure. In this respect it is important to recognize that soils have nonlinear stress-strain characteristics, which for analysis purposes may be represented by bilinear relationships (Penzien, 1964) or multilayer relationships (Valera, 1968). However it has been found that essentially similar results can be obtained using an equivalent linear viscoelastic analysis in which the soil moduli and damping characteristics are selected to be compatible with the strains developed in the deposit (Idriss and Seed, 1968). Thus the equivalent shear moduli and damping characteristics of the soils are treated as strain-dependent properties and their values for high intensity motions are significantly different from those applicable to low intensity motions.

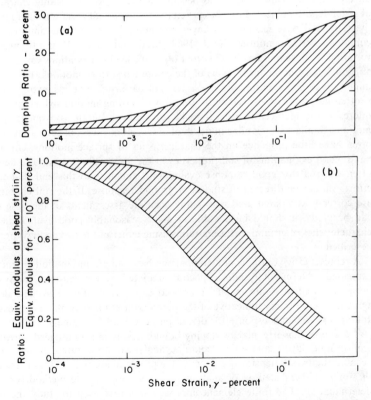

Fig. 2.23 Influence of shear strain on equivalent modulus and damping ratios for soils

Typical ranges for the variation of shear moduli and damping ratios with strain are shown in Fig. 2.23. For analysis of specific sites shear moduli are usually best determined at low strain levels by measuring the velocity of wave propagation through the soils at the site and reducing the values for response conditions involving higher strain levels in accordance with the values shown in Fig. 2.23. Damping ratios are best determined by laboratory tests, by measuring either the stress-strain relationship for the soils under cyclic load conditions or the decay in response in free vibration tests.

Analyses of simple soil profiles having the same soil characteristics and the same boundary conditions have shown that wave propagation and lumped mass analyses give the same results. Furthermore, both methods have been applied to soil profiles at locations for which records of the ground motions developed during earthquakes are available and shown to give results in reasonable agreement with the recorded values (see, for example, Idriss and Seed, 1968; Seed and Idriss, 1969, 1970; Esteva et al., 1969).

In making response analyses, it is of course important that the characteristics of the base rock motions be determined with reasonable accuracy, with regard to both amplitude and frequency characteristics. In this connection it should be noted that the amplitudes of the motions developed in the rock at the base of a soil layer are somewhat less than those developed in an adjacent rock outcrop. However, such differences are usually small, and because of the self-compensating characteristics of a soil deposit subjected to a base excitation, substantial variations in amplitude of the estimated base motion will have only minor effects on the amplitude of the computed surface motions (Seed, 1969; Seed and Idriss, 1970). In many cases variations in base motions on the order of $\pm 50\%$ lead to deviations varying between 5% and 25% from the mean value of the computed surface motions. Thus while it is important to make reasonable assessments of base rock motions, extreme accuracy is often not required, especially in dealing with strong motions which are of major interest to the engineer, in order to make reasonably accurate assessments of surface motions. Similarly, variations in depth of a deposit in excess of several hundred feet often have little influence on the characteristics of surface motions. On the other hand, good evaluations of soil properties in the upper 200 ft or so of a deposit are often essential for good response evaluations, and it is to this end that the main efforts should be directed in studies of ground response. If the soil characteristics are correctly evaluated, and reasonably accurate assessments of the base motions can be made, it should be possible to make reasonably good evaluations of the characteristics of ground surface motions using either of the two analysis procedures described.

A representative example of a comparison between ground motion characteristics expressed in terms of response spectra, predicted by lumped-mass analyses, and those recorded at a site in San Francisco is shown in Fig. 2.24. The degree of agreement is certainly indicative of the potential usefulness of these approaches for anticipating ground response for design purpose and for damage analysis studies.

If a deposit has irregular or sloping boundaries, it can no longer be treated as a semi-infinite layer, and more complex analytical procedures, which take into account the two-dimensional aspects of the problem, are required. For this purpose the finite element method of analysis proves an appropriate method for response determination. The finite element approach was first used to study the dynamic response of embankments by Clough and Chopra (1966); it has subsequently been applied to evaluate the response of earth banks and soil deposits underlain by sloping rock surfaces.

In applying the finite element method of analysis to any given field problem, it is again necessary to take into account the nonlinear stress-deformation and damping characteristics of the soils comprising the deposit. This may be done either by using multilinear representations of the actual stress-strain properties of the soil or by utilizing strain-dependent material characteristics in an equivalent linear analysis procedure.

The method has been used to investigate the response of embankments (Clough and Chopra, 1966), earth banks (Idriss and Seed, 1967; Finn, 1967) and soil deposits underlain by sloping rock surfaces (Dezfulian and Seed, 1969); solutions have been developed for linear viscoelastic materials (Clough and Chopra, 1966), nonlinear materials (Valera, 1968; Dibaj and Penzien, 1969), and nonlinear materials which may be represented by strain-compatible equivalent linear materials (Idriss et al., 1969). In addition, studies have been conducted for rigid base motions with horizontal and vertical components and for traveling wave base motions (Dibaj and Penzien, 1969; Dezfulian and Seed, 1969).

Unfortunately there has been no opportunity to date to compare the response of soil deposits computed by the finite element approach with those observed in the field. However, comparisons with the observed performance of small-scale embankments subjected to base motions on shaking tables show good agreement between computed and measured response (Kovacs et al., 1971). Furthermore, the method gives results in excellent accord with those computed by semi-infinite layer theories for deposits with horizontal boundaries, and these have been shown to be in reasonably good agreement with observed ground motions. Thus it seems likely that finite element analyses can provide reasonably good determinations of two-dimensional problems of ground response.

4   Conclusion

Analyses of building response and damage patterns in recent earthquakes have shown that ground response analyses of the type described can provide a basis for understanding and predicting the observed behavior.

Analyses of ground response in the San Francisco earthquake of 1957, for example, lead to the computed values of maximum base shear for a 10-story building located at sites having different depths of soil shown in Fig. 2.16. Values of maximum base shear for the same building determined from the recorded ground motions are also shown. It may be seen that in spite of the wide range of values at different sites, the values based on ground response analyses are in reasonable agreement with those determined from the actual ground motion records.

Again, in the Caracas earthquake of 1967, the average values of maximum base shear for buildings with different story height ranges, computed from the results of ground response analyses for the soil conditions in Caracas, are shown in Fig. 2.25, in which V_{max} = maximum base shear of building; T = natural period of vibration of building; W = weight of building; and C = design lateral force used in earthquake resistant design of building. The variation of structural damage intensity with soil depth for buildings in the same story height categories is shown in Fig. 2.25. Again it may be seen that the general pattern of damage intensity is very similar in form to that indicated by the values of base shear for different soil depths.

In the light of these and similar results, ground response analyses are now being used to some extent, particularly for tall buildings, for evaluating the response of structures to earthquake excitation. In view of the large effects of local soil conditions on the characteristics of ground surface motions and the resulting seismic response of structures, some consideration of these effects in design is clearly desirable.

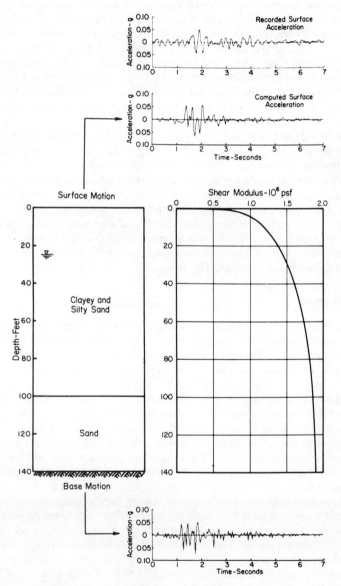

Fig. 2.24 Analysis of ground motions—Alexander Building, San Francisco, California

2.4 ANALYSIS OF DYNAMIC RESPONSE

The analysis of the dynamic response of tall buildings to earthquake motion could be done accurately if: (1) The elastic and inelastic properties of buildings were completely understood and could be idealized as tractable models; and (2) the ground motion could be accurately defined over its entire time history. Large, high-speed computers are, of course, needed to carry out the extensive and complex computations. It is common, especially in Japan and the United States, to subject idealized models of tall buildings and other special structures to either specific recorded earthquake motions or to idealized models of earthquake motions and then to obtain the responses. The reliability of the results depends upon how well

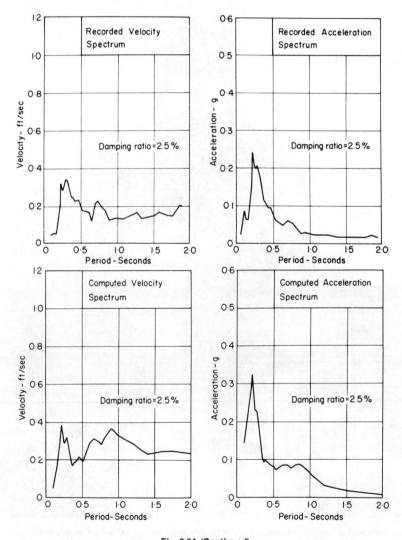

Fig. 2.24 (Continued)

the models represent the real buildings and the real motions to which the buildings will be subjected. There is increasing recognition that buildings and ground motion are more complex than has often been assumed in the past, and that more refined models should be used, the structures should be designed to perform more like the idealized models used in their design, or inelastic analysis and design procedures should be employed.

In spite of these complications, applications of basic theory and careful modeling based upon experience and good judgment generally produce results much more realistic than those of static-type seismic codes, most of which are being recognized as lagging behind current knowledge. In addition, there are useful approximate

San Francisco Chronicle Building, about 1890. The most distinctive feature of this building, the tower, was destroyed by fire in 1894 *(Courtesy: California Historical Society Library)*

techniques of analysis which can produce results well beyond the state-of-the-art as shown in current building codes. Much knowledge about the real properties of buildings and the real characteristics of earthquakes, as well as about analysis techniques, has been available in the technical literature for many years but has not generally been applied. This is unfortunate because in the interim new buildings

Chronicle Building and Annex. The original building is on right. The brown stone of the first story was badly damaged, but the pressed red brick above was uninjured. The facade of the new annex, consisting of gray sandstone and terra cotta for the first story and pressed red brick and terra cotta above, sustained little fire damage, but was considerably injured by characteristic X earthquake cracks from the seventh to the 13th stories. The steel frame was undamaged, excepting one column between the two buildings, which was unprotected at the time of the fire *(Photo by: R. J. Waters & Co.)*

have been, and are being, created without desirable properties. Although some time is, of course, required to consider and to test new concepts and procedures, many believe that actual exposure to real earthquake motion is needed to demonstrate

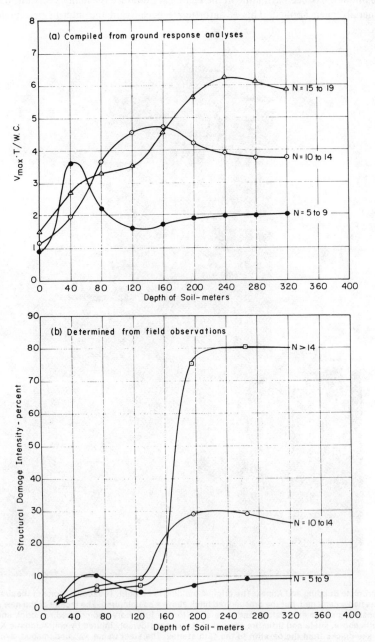

Fig. 2.25 Comparison of values of damage potential index and observed damage intensities in Caracas earthquake of 1967

validity. This approach delays progress, perhaps for many decades, and yet still does not constitute proof because of the random nature of the variables in the problem and probable sparse sampling even in the long-awaited earthquakes. Current knowledge should be applied without further delay and with or without the "test" of actual earthquakes which can be replaced by proper research and analysis. The problem of analysis, at least of a specific system subjected to a specific perturbation,

Claus Spreckels (or Call) Building. The facades made of Colusa sandstone were badly damaged on two sides. The foundations remained level, and the walls plumb. The steel skeleton frame suffered no damage. This, the tallest and most celebrated building in San Francisco, was structurally uninjured *(Photo by: R. J. Waters & Co.)*

differs from the problem of design, which should consider the fact that the building properties and the ground motion characteristics are random variables which may have values quite different from those used in a single deterministic analysis. One approach to this problem is to conduct several analyses with parameter variations. Another is to employ probabilistic theory and statistical data to estimate the degrees of risk, to evaluate the consequences, and finally to reach optimum design decisions. Design can be considered the art of creating the optimum building based upon analysis that, at least implicitly, considers the probabilistic aspects of the problem.

Dynamic analysis of tall buildings depends upon proper modeling of the building systems and of the ground motions. The building system should include everything that is subject to motion and not just a frame which may not be able to deform without causing damage. The models may be lumped mass, distributed mass, or pseudosystems with equivalent properties. They may be elastic or inelastic. The most common model for tall buildings is lumped mass with elastic springs. However, by one means or another the results must be transformed into the inelastic realm. Ground motion has been represented by peak amplitude (essentially meaningless for tall buildings), by response spectra, and by time histories. These in turn may be actual or idealized, and on a single (deterministic) basis or on a probabilistic basis by various means. Dynamic analyses may be conducted by direct integration of the general equations of motion, by normal mode theory, by the use of response spectra, or by approximate techniques. Although direct computation of the properties and responses of inelastic systems is feasible and often desirable, there are complications in modeling realistically and the required computer capacity may be unavailable. If one computes the elastic response of tall buildings to realistic strong earthquake perturbation there is almost always an output of pseudo-"elastic" shears, moments, axial forces and stresses well beyond the elastic capacities of typical buildings. Thus, one way or another, inelastic response must be recognized and treated. One approximate but most useful tool in this problem is the Reserve Energy Technique that converts readily obtained elastic output from time history or response spectra analyses and adjusts these false elastic results with simple procedures in code terms to what the results would have been if obtained with more realistic but less tractable inelastic models (Blume, 1960a; Blume et al., 1961).

1　Types of Tall Buildings

There are great variations in the types of tall buildings, and these variations affect not only their dynamic properties in the elastic range but to a much greater extent the properties in the inelastic range. Many of the traditional type buildings that have been subjected to earthquakes and the performance of which has, at least implicitly, had its effect on current earthquake code requirements are no longer being constructed, although several of them are still in existence in major cities. In the 1906 San Francisco earthquake, as an example, the tall buildings had steel frames designed either for wind forces or for no particular lateral forces, but these buildings had massive and numerous "noncalculated" masonry walls and partitions. It has been shown that not only are earthquakes much stronger than the lateral force provisions of seismic codes, but that the traditional type buildings had a great deal more resistance, especially in the damaging range, than the frames alone (Blume, 1960b). The problem exists today that seismic codes with rather low lateral force requirements permit the construction of tall buildings of a totally different character from these traditional buildings. It thus becomes important that the frames of the contemporary buildings which may have little or no assistance from nonstructural elements be designed very carefully and with realistic lateral forces in order to have satisfactory performance (Blume, 1960b).

Contemporary tall buildings are generally built with frames which may or may not be entirely moment-resisting, and there may or may not be shear walls in addition to the frames. There is also a difference in materials of the framing, which for tall buildings generally resolves itself to structural steel, reinforced concrete, or combinations of the two. Other variations in contemporary buildings involve the questions of whether the moment-resisting frame extends throughout the structure or is confined to certain localities such as the perimeter, and whether or not there is a so-called tube concept of design, a central core, or other elements or framing methods. Bracing instead of moment resistance, or combinations of bracing and moment resistance, should be used cautiously in order to assure that the structure either has strength considerably greater than the codes now require, or has adequate reserve energy and work capacity beyond the yield point deformation which is almost certain to be exceeded. A closely related problem, especially with moment-resisting frames, is the allowable drift or story distortion. It should be recognized that distortion under severe earthquake disturbance may be several times that which would prevail under code lateral forces. The results of this distortion must be evaluated. The structure must remain stable at all times, even under all the P-Δ and other secondary effects. In addition, there must be provision for the framing to distort relative to the nonstructural cladding, or costly damage to nonstructural materials must be expected.

2 Behavior of Tall Buildings

There have been relatively few failures of tall buildings under strong earthquake motion. It must be recognized, however, that there has been very little sampling of exposure of tall buildings to severe earthquake motion. Four tall buildings and a portion of another building collapsed in Caracas. No other tall buildings have collapsed although some have been damaged to a minor extent in Japan and in the Los Angeles area. San Francisco has not had a severe earthquake since 1906. Although no tall buildings collapsed there in 1906, some were damaged considerably, and essentially all had much more total strength and reserve energy and work capacity than would be provided by many contemporary structures.

On February 9, 1971, the San Fernando earthquake of magnitude 6.6 caused strong response in many tall buildings in the Los Angeles area at distances ranging from about 21 km to 48 km (13 miles to 30 miles) from the epicenter. Although this was not a large earthquake, the motion was quite severe and some damage was caused, especially to the closer buildings of moderate height without planned ductile framing. One building, for example, required repairs costing 11% of its original construction cost a few years earlier. Another lesson that has been learned from other sources is that tall buildings having long natural fundamental modes of vibration are subject to considerable response to ground shocks originating at some distance (Blume, 1972). In general, the behavior of tall buildings has, with some exceptions, been good, but they have not yet been tested under extremely severe conditions.

3 Idealized Linear Models

The dynamic system consists of every part of the building superstructure, basement stories, foundations and surrounding soil, that tends to move under

Aronson Building. The facades for the three lower stories consist of Colusa sandstone, which was badly spalled and damaged. The upper stories of terra cotta pressed brick were but slightly injured, the terra cotta being spalled and cracked in a few places. Columns in the basement, first, fifth, eighth, and tenth stories had buckled on account of the failure of the hollow tile protection *(Photo by: R. J. Waters & Co.)*

Aronson Building in San Francisco, California *(Courtesy: H. J. Degenkolb)*

Crocker Building. The facades were of granite for the first and second stories and buff terra cotta above. With the exception of the second-story windows, which were slightly spalled, the facades are comparatively little injured by the fire; but the earthquake caused considerable damage to the walls in the upper stories. A column on the ninth floor buckled on account of the failure of the hollow tile protection *(Photo by: R. J. Waters & Co.)*

ground motion disturbance. Every particle of mass, whether structural or non-structural, affects the properties and the response in some degree. In general, mass in the upper regions of the building is more important to the system's properties than mass at the lower levels. Conversely, stiffness at the lower levels is more important than stiffness at upper levels. It is customary to include all the dead weight of the structure in the computation of mass but to omit temporary live loading except for heavy warehouse type loading. Objects on the floors of buildings tend to move under severe motion as static friction is overcome. This movement relieves the mass effect on the system and probably absorbs energy in friction.

Although it is theoretically true that foundation-soil compliance should be considered, the effects of compliance versus assuming a fixed base are generally quite small for tall, flexible buildings (Merritt and Housner, 1954; Blume, 1969a).

There is much in the literature about the so-called shear system, which can be defined as a system in which the floor or diaphragm remains level and does not distort locally about horizontal axes. In other words, it is infinitely rigid in all planes and about all axes. Many traditional buildings had floor systems of such rigidity that this shear system assumption was acceptable (Blume, 1956). However, in contemporary tall buildings, joint rotation is an important contribution to the freedom of the system and in many cases column axial deformation is also a significant contribution (Blume, 1968; Rubinstein, 1964). Thus, the so-called shear system is not applicable to modern tall buildings. Means have been developed for estimating the contribution of joint rotation and column distortion to natural periods relative to that of a shear system with readily computed parameters (Blume, 1968). With adequate computer programs, of course, the exact stiffnesses can be determined in accordance with the model assumptions (Clough et al., 1963, 1964).

Distributed mass models have been used to represent tall buildings (Jacobsen, 1939). Since the mass of a typical tall building does not vary greatly with height, these models are sometimes useful, especially if corrections are made for variations of stiffness with height. In general, the modeling assumes a fixed end vertical cantilever with properties of mass, stiffness, and damping intended to represent the real structure. Progress is being made with pseudo distributed mass systems, which for purposes of estimating response of some types of buildings offer acceptable reliability and are time-saving (Blume, 1969b). Periods of buildings may be estimated by empirical equations (Housner and Brady, 1963; International Conference of Building Officials, 1976).

It has been found that contemporary buildings in the United States and South America have a wide range of framing characteristics with particular reference to the stiffness of horizontal framing as compared to that of vertical framing. Buildings with stiff vertical elements and flexible horizontal elements, for example, behave almost as a series of connected vertical cantilevers. If the floor or spandrel elements are quite rigid compared to the columns, the building is essentially a shear system. Fig. 2.26 indicates the range of natural period ratios with relative stiffness measured by an index ρ for an 8-story and a 16-story building (Blume, 1969b). In Fig. 2.26, p = ratio of horizontal to vertical stiffness; I_G = girder inertia; I_C = column inertia; L_C = column length; and L_G = girder length. If the period ratios are known or can be estimated the building can be categorized as shown. This in turn leads to valuable information about dynamic properties and behavior and stress patterns. Fig. 2.27 indicates mode shapes and participation factors for extreme values of the stiffness index ρ in a 16-story building model. Cantilever type buildings have high values of over-all moment at the lower stories (Blume, 1969b).

4 Components of Motion

Earthquake motion is three-dimensional and generally highly chaotic. Tall building response, however, after the first few seconds, at peak response levels tends to become harmonic in nature with the structure generally responding in or near one or more of its natural modes of vibration. It has been found that the greatest

The walls of the Butler Building were taken down in places because of earthquake damage, although damage to street by earthquake and fire was nominal *(Photo by: John S. Sewell)*

responses to distant energy sources are in the fundamental mode with its great importance to the lower and often critical regions of the buildings (Blume, 1969a, 1972). Fig. 2.28 shows the absolute peak modal responses to ground motion from an underground nuclear explosion about 160 km (100 miles) away (Blume, 1969a).

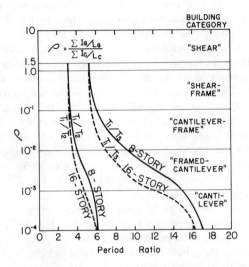

Fig. 2.26 Period ratios versus ρ, ratio of horizontal to vertical stiffness

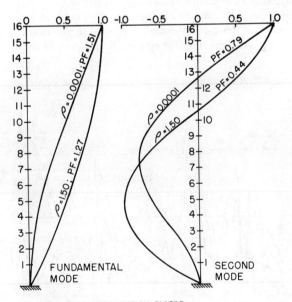

PF REFERS TO PARTICIPATION FACTOR,
TOP LEVEL DEFLECTION = 1.0

Fig. 2.27 Mode shapes, 16-story frame

It has been customary in analysis to disregard the vertical motion in tall buildings and to consider only one horizontal component at a time. If the center of mass coincides with the center of rigidity at all story levels, it has generally been considered that the motion along one major horizontal axis is independent of the motion along the other axis, and that there is no tendency for rotation (torsion) about the vertical axis. It is known from experimentation with models that even so-called symmetrical structures tend to respond along both horizontal axes under stimulation along only one axis, and that torsion may also develop. Since true ground motion is three-dimensional, with time lags and focusing effects, and materials and elements may vary from what is specified—and in view of inelastic response—it becomes evident that more consideration should be given to biaxial response than in the past, especially for tall buildings of rather slender profile. Corner colums may be significantly affected (Blume, 1971). It has been found in detailed studies of the response of tall buildings to ground motion that the motion is biaxial and tends to follow an irregular pattern even with apparent symmetry of construction and without torsion. Buildings have been shown to respond in patterns that involve high percentages of the maximum motion in each translational direction occurring simultaneously. This is illustrated in Fig. 2.29 wherein the dots are 0.1 sec apart (Blume, 1969a).

With the further complication of some buildings having planned asymmetry, there is not only a torsional response to be considered, but also the coupling of the two translational modes. Thus, perturbation in any horizontal direction can cause translational response along both horizontal axes and torsion about a vertical axis as well. In addition to the coupling, some natural modes of vibration may have periods very close to each other, making the maximum response greater than when periods are widely spaced (Rosenblueth and Elorduy, 1969).

Seismic codes generally provide for "accidental" torsion of a nominal amount even for symmetrical systems. Although this is a step forward, there is some evidence that the amount provided for may not be adequate in all cases (Newmark,

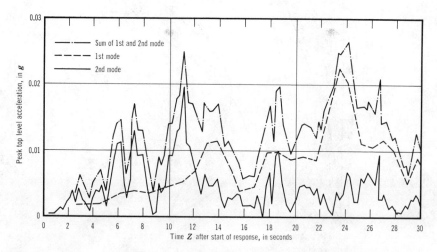

Fig. 2.28 History of peak modal acceleration, Building A longitudinal, event BENHAM *(Blume, 1969a)*

1969). Torsion as a mode of response must be considered, because even where perfect symmetry might apply in the linear range, the probabilities are great that symmetry would not be retained as the building enters the inelastic range in response to strong ground motion.

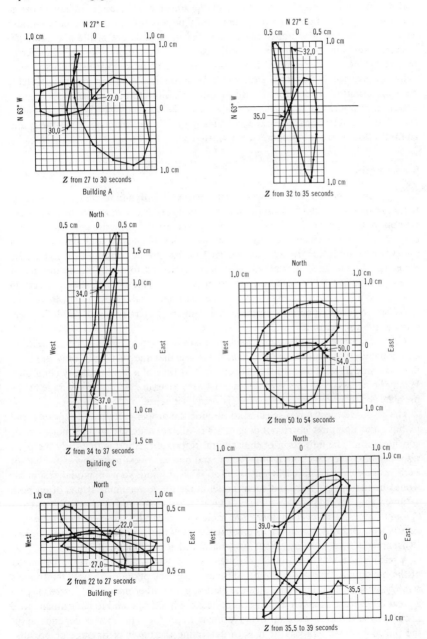

Fig. 2.29 Horizontal plan displacements at top levels, event BENHAM *(Blume, 1969a)*

5   Idealized Inelastic Systems

Essentially all existing tall buildings will respond to strong ground motion with energy content near a fundamental or high natural mode or modes to such an extent that strains will be greater than those of the linear elastic range. Behavior in the inelastic range is difficult to model realistically because of the various materials and elements, structural and nonstructural, the fact that some are brittle and some are ductile, some vary with the extent and history of prior motion or the number of reverse cycles, etc. A popular idealization because of its simplicity is elastoplastic behavior, essentially flat from yield to strain hardening. Another inelastic model is bilinear softening. There are also many other possible idealizations.

Building models in the inelastic range must be assigned yield levels and then tractable characteristics beyond yield. To do this with changes in stiffness and strength (deterioration) becomes complicated.

6   Analysis

The ground motion is, of course, a vital part of the dynamic analysis. Basically, there are two methods of dynamic response analysis, one with a time history of the ground motion, generally of acceleration, and the other a response spectrum. Either can be a single deterministic case, a series of events to explore parameters or possible exposures, or probabilistic modeling—discrete or continuous. In addition, either can be idealized, smoothed, or otherwise treated to avoid discontinuities or severe fluctuations. The response spectrum can be elastic or inelastic with certain characteristics, and for any appropriate damping value. Although a single-degree-of-freedom spectral response diagram is generally used, multifreedom spectra are also feasible.

The advantage of the time history method is that modal responses are automatically combined. The disadvantages are that the responses only apply to that one time history, and it may take significant time of a large capacity computer. It may be necessary to use several time histories to assure adequate coverage of the problem, or to use probabilistic models or adjustments.

The response spectrum is selected to provide the proper earthquake exposure and to have the damping corresponding to that of the structure in the mode under consideration. The limitation of the spectral response method is that only the peak responses are given, without a time factor, and one has to estimate how the values of each mode might combine at any instant. The absolute sum of modal responses would be the upper limit, and each model alone the lower limit. It has often been assumed that the root-mean-square value is reasonable, and it no doubt often is (Clough, 1955). However, if there are modes of generally close periods (and this occurs with coupled translational modes) the root-mean-square may be inadequate (Rosenblueth and Elorduy, 1969; Newmark and Rosenblueth, 1971).

A serious question arises in all analyses, or it should—namely, what is the period of the building to be used in the response analysis: the period with only the frame's rigidity, or that with the frame plus the cladding and other materials? There may be a great difference, as much as a 2:1 ratio, because buildings tend to have much more initial stiffness than most analysts give them credit for. The answer depends upon the purpose of the analysis. If it is to determine the onset of damage or possible damage the virgin period should no doubt be used. If it is to determine survival, the longer "structural" period should be used. However, it is no doubt no more logical to say there is a progressive lengthening of period from the start of the strong motion to its end, and thus the shorter period is more applicable at the start and the longer one near the peak or end of the strong response. Inelastic modeling would be desirable if it could be realistically done.

7 The Reserve Energy Technique

An approximate but very useful technique for inelastic analysis, design, and damage estimation called the Reserve Energy Technique (RET) has been available for many years (Blume, 1960a, 1960b; Blume et al., 1961, Appendix B). What it lacks in rigor it makes up for in simplicity (one does not require a computer) and the fact that it incorporates dynamic response to actual ground motion, energy demands, ductility, work capacity in the inelastic range, damping, and story distortion in terms with which the design engineer is familiar. There are increasing indications, especially from the 1971 San Fernando, California earthquake, that RET produces reasonable results (Blume, 1960a).

In design, RET is intended to be an additional step to, rather than a supplement for, basic seismic code requirements. The concept is to provide enough work capacity in the inelastic range of the structure to equal (or exceed) the kinetic energy demands of the earthquake ground motion that cannot be met within the elastic capacity of the system. This may be achieved by providing more ductility or more strength or, preferably, by an optimum combination of ductility and strength. In analysis, RET provides an estimation of the maximum story distortions under any specified earthquake response spectrum and also of the amount and nature of the damage, if any. The strength and energy absorption value of all materials and elements, whether or not considered as "structural," are generally considered, with allowances for deterioration. It is necessary to know the story shear-distortion (V-Δ) characteristics through the elastic range to failure which is defined here as the distortion beyond which the V-Δ curve never again becomes horizontal or slopes upward. It is necessary to limit such curves to the distortion value at which instability of the structure as a whole (including buckling or P-Δ effects) would prevail. It is to be noted that unless such V-Δ characteristics are known, or can be estimated or idealized, no procedure—no matter how rigorous—is meaningful. A common assumption, sometimes slightly conservative, is that static or slow-loading test data can be used for the development of V-Δ plots if dynamic test data are not available. If test data are not available at all, member ductility or system ductility may be derived from curvature ductility of each cross section.

The Reserve Energy Technique is general in the sense that all elements and materials are to be considered, even those that may not come into action until some distortion has occurred and those that may tend to deteriorate or fail under repeated cycles and reversals of stress. Deterioration factors are assigned to allow for any reduction of strength and stiffness, and for continuing response period changes are also made (Blume, 1960a; Blume et al., 1961, Appendix B).

8 Vertical Motion

There is no doubt that vertical vibration occurs as a result of earthquake disturbance. The peak vertical ground motion is often considered to be about 2/3 or

3/4 of the peak horizontal motion. However, there have been cases, especially at short epicentral distances, where the peak vertical motion equals or exceeds the horizontal. The vertical motion tends to have greater frequencies; on the other hand, natural vertical modes are also of greater frequency than the horizontal modes. Most codes do not require vertical motion analysis, although wherever gravity is beneficial in reducing stress the temporary change in the net vertical effect must be considered in design. One reason for the neglect of vertical effects is the fact that framing generally has a much greater reserve capacity for vertical forces than for horizontal. Another reason is that people are generally less concerned with the higher frequency vertical motion.

Indications are that natural fundamental vertical periods can be fairly long in tall buildings and have important higher modes. It would seem that as buildings become taller and have less nonstructural weight to be supported than the older buildings, the vertical response should be considered, especially where columns may be subject to combined uplift effects of over-all flexure and vertical response. This could have a significant effect on interaction diagrams. The vertical effects could also have a bearing on stability and P-Δ problems.

The modeling for vertical motion should include the axial (PL/AE) deformations of the columns and also the flexural effects of the floor systems.

9 Probabilistic Models

When performing a time history analysis during design, it is desirable that the prescribed ground motions properly characterize the expected future earthquake motions at the site under consideration. This is, however, a most difficult task to perform with reasonable reliability due to the unpredictable nature of ground motion characteristics. These uncertainties suggest that it would be most appropriate to model future strong ground motions using stochastic (or random) processes having statistical characteristics similar to those of past recorded ground motions. Earthquake motions were simulated some time ago as a superposition of random pulses of fixed amplitudes arriving randomly in time. Numerous investigators have since advanced this general approach to simulating strong ground motions (Housner and Jennings, 1964; Ruiz and Penzien, 1969).

A common stochastic model used for generating artificial ground accelerations is Gaussian nonstationary filtered white noise (Housner and Jennings, 1964; Ruiz and Penzien, 1969). To be more specific, stationary Gaussian white noise is first generated; that is, a family of accelerograms is generated, each containing a full spectrum of frequencies having the same amplitude but with phase angles that are uniformly random. It is this random character of the phase angles that makes any one accelerogram different from another. The stationary white noise is then multiplied by a deterministic time function to convert the process to an appropriate nonstationary form. This deterministic time function is obtained from a statistical analysis of past recorded accelerograms. Finally, the nonstationary process is passed through a second-order filter which attenuates the higher frequency components and amplifies components in the vicinity of the expected predominant ground frequency. The last two steps—converting to nonstationary form and filtering—may be carried out in reverse order.

The frequency and damping parameters in the filter (one setting the predominant frequency and one controlling the degree of attenuation and amplification of frequencies) are selected so that the final stochastic model will simulate free surface ground motions which properly reflect the influence of local soil conditions. The predominant frequency is decreased appropriately for the softer and deeper soil layers, and is increased for the harder and shallower layers. The damping parameter is increased with intensity of ground motion to properly reflect the increased energy dissipation due to nonlinear strain effects. These changes should, of course, be consistent with observed characteristics of past recorded accelerograms for different soil conditions, intensity levels, epicentral distance, etc.

It is important to recognize that once a stochastic ground motion model has been fully defined, any number of accelerograms can be generated from this single model and each one will differ from any other. Likewise, differences can be observed when comparing their individual response spectrum curves. Averaging these response spectrum curves yields the response spectrum curves for the entire process. It is important to remember that this latter set of curves represent the expected (or mean) values of peak response and that for each expected value of response there is a corresponding variance.

Having established an appropriate stochastic model for future strong ground motions at a given site, a family of accelerograms can easily be generated using a digital computer. Deterministic dynamic analyses can then be carried out for a particular structure using each accelerogram separately as the prescribed excitation. If the mathematical model of the structure is linear, one can use either a time history or a response spectrum method of analysis. If the model is nonlinear, one must use the time history method of analysis. In either case, peak structural response will be obtained for each accelerogram. From these results one should then compute the mean values and standard deviations of response. Previous studies have shown that standard deviations of response are relatively small for linear structures but can be quite large for elastoplastic structures (Housner and Jennings, 1964) or stiffness degrading structures (Saragoni and Hart, 1972).

It is important to recognize the degree of uncertainty involved when making design decisions based on predictions of structural response to only a single ground motion accelerogram, whether it be artificial or real. The peak response in such a case might be considerably below the mean value obtained using a family of accelerograms all of similar intensity level. Therefore the probabilistic approach to predicting structural response using a stochastic model for ground motions should be encouraged.

2.5 OBSERVATION OF STRUCTURAL BEHAVIOR

Analytical studies of earthquake response must be supported by experimental studies both in the laboratory and in the field. The main items to be observed or to be checked are: (1) Rigidity, strength, and hysteretic characteristics of structures and structural components against lateral forces; and (2) the natural periods and damping characteristics of buildings. The first group of items can be obtained by static laboratory tests using either reduced-scale or full-size models, and checked by static field tests after completion of construction. The second group can be obtained by dynamic tests using shaking tables, dynamic pulsators, and other equipment, and checked by field vibration tests using vibration excitors, earthquake observations or microtremor measurements using various kinds of seismometers installed after completion of construction.

This section is concerned primarily with dynamic tests.

1 Static Laboratory Studies

For aseismic design of tall buildings, it is essential to know the ductility and yield capacity of the structure because deformations developed during major earthquakes can be larger than those produced by the load specified for aseismic design of buildings. The main objective of static laboratory tests is to investigate the hysteretic characteristics of the load-deflection curves by applying repeated alternating loadings to a test specimen. This specimen should represent an essential part of a structure, such as a girder-to-column connection or a portal frame.

A good deal of work has been done on various types of test specimens made of steel, reinforced concrete, and other materials. These were scheduled either to investigate the general characteristics of a structural member or frame without any particular design purpose, or to check whether the member or frame behaves

James Flood Building. The facades are of Colusa sandstone, with a pink granite base to the water table. The damage to the exterior consists of spalling around a number of the window openings and earthquake cracks where the corner tower joins the side walls. The hollow tile column protection was badly damaged in many places, but fulfilled its purpose and prevented the failure of the columns *(Photo by: R. J. Waters & Co.)*

satisfactorily under the loading conditions anticipated in the aseismic design of the building.

Load-deflection curves are of the following four types: (1) Spindle-shape; (2) slip; (3) degrading stiffness; and (4) elastic nonlinear.

Type 1 is mostly seen in reinforced concrete flexural members; type 2 in reinforced concrete or prestressed reinforced concrete members under large axial stress, or in bolted joint connections of steel members; type 3 in reinforced concrete members exhibiting shear failure; and type 4 in prestressed or post-tensioned members subjected to flexural stresses less than the compressive strength of the concrete. For further details, see Chapters SB-2, SB-5, and CB-9.

2 Dynamic Laboratory Studies

Shaking tables, dynamic pulsators, and vibrating excitors are usually used for dynamic laboratory studies. With this equipment it is possible to obtain or check the dynamic characteristics—natural periods, mode shapes, and damping coefficients —of buildings or parts of buildings. Furthermore, such test procedures may make it possible to check building response to earthquake ground motion by applying simulated ground motion as an input using an automatic control system. This

James Flood Building, San Francisco, California, at Market and Powell, about 1915 *(Courtesy: California Historical Society Library)*

technique is currently under development and does not always produce satisfactory results at present, especially for a specimen with a nonlinear restoring force-displacement system.

One of the most serious problems encountered in these tests is "model-similitude" because in most cases a reduced-scale model must be used. Although the general principles of similitude are known, an appropriate interpretation from model test results to the aseismic design of a prototype building may be difficult to derive.

Recent developments and improvements in shaking tables and measuring instruments make it possible to test large-scale models with adequate accuracy. The main types of shaking tables and other equipment are:

1. Electrohydraulic system (sinusoidal, random, shock).

2. Electromagnetic system (sinusoidal, random, shock, particularly for high frequencies).

3. Mechanical gear system (sinusoidal).

4. Shock excitation system (shock).

There are few instances in which the results of dynamic laboratory tests have been taken into account directly in aseismic design procedure. The following are examples of shaking tables and their use in dynamic laboratory tests whose results were applied either directly to the aseismic design of a building or to the fundamental study of dynamic characteristics of the structure.

1. A large shaking table 3 m × 2.5 m in plan, having four hydraulic actuators each of 4535 kg (5 tons) capacity, was used to test a 1.25 scale model made of steel frames and asbestos plates. This model represents a 17-story hospital building of the Japan National Railways Z-shaped in plan (Ueda, 1969). The table acceleration was proportional to the recorded acceleration of El Centro 1940 NS component. It was applied by means of an electrohydraulic driving force system. The specimen was vibrated to failure. The natural period of the specimen changed as the failure progressed, becoming 1.5 to 2.0 times that in the elastic range.

2. A shaking table with an actuator of 1270 kg (1.4 ton) capacity has its driving force automatically controlled by an analog computer (Tajimi et al., 1966). Two perpendicular horizontal components of input ground motion can be applied to the table simultaneously. Using this shaking table, fundamental research has been carried out on a building supported by piles. A similar single component shaking table, named "University of Illinois Earthquake Simulator," has been used to study the earthquake response of reinforced concrete members in the plastic deformation range (Takeda et al., 1970).

3. A shaking table with a mechanical driving system of large capacity has been used to test a series of reinforced concrete portal frames with an applied sinusoidal input motion (Shiga and Ogawa, 1969). Good results were obtained, especially on the dynamic hysteretic loop of the frame.

4. A shock type shaking table composed of a hanging table, a damper and a pendulum has relatively large capacity (Omote et al., 1970). The input shock movement of the table can be controlled to some extent. Using this

equipment some specimens made of steel and reinforced concrete have been tested up to the plastic range and the restoring force characteristics have been investigated.

Recently a giant shaking table with large capacity has become available in Japan; it is 15 m × 15 m, having an electrohydraulic servo system and capable of producing maximum horizontal acceleration of 1.0 g (Japan National Committee of the International Association for Earthquake Engineering, 1968). Another large earthquake simulator has been developed recently at the University of California, Berkeley. It is 6.1 m (20 ft) square and has a test load capacity of 54420 kg (60 tons). The simulator can apply simultaneously one horizontal component and the vertical component of any arbitrary earthquake motion; peak acceleration in the two directions under full load are 0.67 g and 0.40 g, respectively.

3 Static Field Studies

A static test after completion of construction can provide useful data to check the structural behavior of a building as a whole, which cannot be evaluated by laboratory tests. A test to failure is of great value because the structural behavior beyond the elastic limit is most important in the aseismic design of buildings, but can be carried out only on buildings which are to be demolished.

A set of oil jacks is used to apply horizontal forces at various specified positions to the test building. The deflections and strains are measured to determine horizontal rigidity and to construct load-deflection curves of each story of the building. This kind of test has been performed on a considerable number of buildings in Japan. The first group was tested at or soon after the completion of the building. The maximum load level was less than twice the design load. This group is limited in number and also in size of the building because of the difficulty in applying the load on the building, which requires a suitable reaction apparatus. The second group involved tests to failure of buildings to be demolished. In this case, a part of the building usually is cut out from the whole building as a specimen to be tested, the remaining part being used as a reaction. The test results of several such specimens, from a one-span one-story frame to a three-span seven-story frame, have been reported. Two typical examples are mentioned below.

The first example was a static test of a three-span seven-story frame which was cut from a steel framed brick building when the building was being demolished (Funabashi et al., 1969). This building was built in 1918 and survived the big 1923 Kanto earthquake. The test results showed that the frame had a yield strength and ductility high enough to withstand severe earthquakes of that intensity.

The second example is a three-story reinforced concrete building which suffered serious damage during the 1968 Tokachi-Oki earthquake (Aoyama et al., 1970). Two two-span two-story frames with minor damage were cut from the original building and tested by applying alternating loads. As a result, the yield strength, mode of failure, and hysteretic characteristics were obtained. From various investigations, including response analysis of a properly assumed model of the damaged building which takes into account the mode of failure and other factors obtained by the experiments, it was concluded that although the response is greatly influenced by the specific characteristics of the earthquake input, damage to the building can be closely estimated.

4   Dynamic Field Studies

Field Vibration Tests.   Field vibration tests of buildings are usually made to determine the natural periods, mode shapes, and damping properties of buildings. Several methods employed in these tests are described as follows.

   1. Free vibration test. A horizontal force is applied statically by means of a wire
      cable or other device with a quick release mechanism. The sudden release of

Hotel St. Francis. The facades, consisting of a granite base and gray sandstone above, were in good condition; a few window openings were only slightly spalled by fire. With the exception of two columns in the mezzanine story, which are deflected out of plumb, the steel skeleton frame was uninjured. The good quality of the materials and workmanship were shown to good advantage, this being one of the least injured buildings structurally that passed through the earthquake and fire *(Photo by: R. J. Waters & Co.)*

the force sets the structure into free vibration. Utilizing appropriate instrumentation, the vibrational characteristics of the building can be determined. This method is simple and quick for comparatively small structures.

2. Vibration excitor or vibration generator. The vibration excitor is the most popular apparatus used in the forced vibration tests of the buildings. Usually the rotor speed is increased in a step-by-step manner. At each speed level, the amplitude is recorded. From the resonance curves and the distribution of the resonant amplitude, the dynamic characteristics of the building can be determined. An alternative method is the so-called "run-down" test. In this method, the rotor speed is continuously increased beyond the resonant frequency, and then decreased in a similar manner. The amplitudes are recorded concurrently. From the resonance curves thus obtained, the natural period and damping are determined. However, it may be shown that these curves do not represent true resonance curves in a strict sense because the input frequency changes too rapidly.

3. Manpower. When the damping of a building is small and its natural periods are moderately long, vibrations may sometimes be generated by manpower; men moving in unison at the natural frequency can supply enough energy to produce measurable motions.

4. Application of propulsive agent. Progress in astronautical sciences makes it possible to apply a rocket propellant as the excitation source for vibration tests. This method seems to be promising for the testing of tall buildings by intermittent applications of a properly controlled thrust, but would be quite expensive and has not yet been tried.

5. Another method of testing a building in the field is to produce a ground motion at the site by explosion. Such testing has been done in the elastic (Hudson et al., 1954) and also in the plastic range of the building (Polyakov et al., 1969). The former tests gave information on the ground motion input characteristics to the building; the latter gave some information on the strength of large-panel buildings subjected to a shock type ground motion.

A good deal of work has been done on tall buildings with dynamic field studies. Results of such work have been used to study the relationships between building heights and natural periods or damping ratios. However, it is still difficult to establish general formulas which would be appropriate for the aseismic design of tall buildings.

Comparisons between the measured and calculated natural periods of several high-rise buildings show that in some buildings the measured period is somewhat smaller than calculated, suggesting the effect of rigidity contributed by non-structural elements which are not taken into account for design purposes.

Microtremor Measurements.   As is well known, the ground is always vibrating with a very minute amplitude on the order of 1 micron. This motion is caused by traffic, wind, or other vibration sources and is called "microtremors." These microtremors produce vibrations of buildings. By measuring the microtremor at the top of a building, the natural periods and damping can be determined conveniently, although the dynamic properties thus determined represent those associated with very small amplitudes. By measuring the building motions of several levels, the shapes of the vibration modes can be evaluated.

Microtremor measurements are suitable for determining the natural period of buildings in large groups such as apartment houses, as the records can be taken comparatively easily and quickly. In one instance the natural periods of about 800 buildings were determined by this method.

The natural periods of several tall buildings determined by microtremor measurements have been compared with those determined using strong motion earthquake records (Tanaka et al., 1969). The results show that the latter are on the average 20% longer than the former. This suggests that the change in natural period of the buildings with increasing amplitude of motion may be considerable.

Pruitt Igoe in St. Louis, Missouri, in 1973 (Note: Project was abandoned; demolition in 1976) *(Courtesy: T. V. Galambos)*

Pruitt Igoe test building and its surroundings *(Courtesy: T. V. Galambos)*

Because of the ease with which microtremor measurements of buildings can be made, it is desirable that a method of routine analysis, including a sampling method of sufficient accuracy, be established.

Earthquake Observation.   Earthquake observation of buildings may be divided into two categories: (1) Observation of the behavior during strong motion earthquakes which rarely occur, in which the structure sometimes is stressed beyond elastic limit; and (2) observation during minor or moderate earthquakes, which occur relatively more often, and in which the structure is stressed only in the elastic range.

The observation of strong motion earthquake response in tall buildings has been carried out with special types of accelerographs since the 1930s in the United States and since the 1950s in Japan. In both countries some hundreds of accelerographs have been installed. Other countries also have similar types of strong motion recorders. The Japanese accelerographs, for example, start automatically to record earthquake motions greater than 0.01 g or 0.005 g. The record is made by scratching a roll of stylus paper by a sapphire needle, but this is to be changed to a magnetic tape recording system so that the analysis can be made more easily and quickly.

Many records of strong earthquake motions have been taken with these accelerographs, including some where buildings were damaged by accelerations with maximum values of 0.2 g to 0.5 g. Such records are available through NOAA or the California Institute of Technology in the United States, and are published in Japan as *Strong-Motion Earthquake Records in Japan*, Vols. 1 to 11. The analysis of the records has been made by the aid of either response analysis technique or

Eleven-story reinforced concrete structure subjected to dynamic shaking. With in-fill panels in place, the applied base shear was 1.2 times 1974 SEAOC Zone 4 equivalent value. With in-fill panels removed, the applied value was 3 times SEAOC value *(Galambos and Mayes, 1978)*

multiple reflection theory of waves. With both methods, satisfactory results were obtained providing the rigidity of the building was properly assumed. As expected, contribution of nonstructural elements to the rigidity of a building has been shown to be considerable.

As an example of comparative studies of observed and calculated accelerations, the results for a 16-story steel building are shown by Muto (1971). The observed records were obtained during the San Fernando, California earthquake in 1971. The dynamic model of the building includes the effect of subsoils represented as rotation and sway constraints. Good agreement is seen between the observed and calculated accelerations.

The observation of earthquake response of buildings with relatively small amplitude has been carried out in a few buildings in Japan. In a six-story reinforced concrete building, various instruments were installed to detect the accelerations, strains of frame members, earth pressure at the base of the building, etc. (Ohsawa, 1969). The records were analyzed to check and improve the method of response analyses currently used in the seismic design of buildings.

2.6   EVALUATION OF EARTHQUAKE DAMAGE

The basic philosophy usually used in building design, either explicit or implied, requires that little structural damage occur during moderate intensity earthquake ground motion; however, some damage to other elements in the building is acceptable (Seismology Committee of the Structural Engineers Association of California, 1975; Wiegel, 1970; Newmark and Rosenblueth, 1971). Also, for very high intensity earthquake ground motion, some structural damage is acceptable but the possibility of structural collapse must be minimal. For the purpose of this section, these two levels of ground motion intensity will be designated Types A and B, respectively. If the structure performs within these criteria, the duration of shaking should have little influence on the extent of damage for Type A intensity. For Type B, however, the duration of intense shaking will greatly affect the degree and extent of damage.

When an earthquake occurs every possible effort should be made to assemble and analyze the data on damage so that repetition of the errors of the past can be reduced to a minimum in the future. A study of the damage will also be necessary if there are no strong motion instruments in the area, so that estimates of the intensity of shaking can be approximated. After each earthquake, a statistical review of the structural, social, and economic factors should be compiled. The information obtained in this manner is frequently very helpful in the evaluation of earthquake damage. A thorough cataloging of damage data frequently can point the direction of analytical studies, and often will serve as a basis for confirmation of computed results.

Earthquake damage can best be evaluated shortly after the earthquake when emergency operations are still proceeding. Thus, organized teams should be established and arrangements made so that a team can have access to the damaged area immediately after the event. A later visit to the area also should be made, after the debris has been cleared, so that items initially hidden can be reviewed. The final review and evaluation of repair procedures would be made after the rehabilitation has been essentially completed.

To some extent, the study of earthquake damage to tall buildings built prior to the use of modern seismic code provisions has been reduced in importance for structurally evaluating earthquake damage and for establishing design requirements. This is because the methods, materials, and configurations of construction have changed considerably. A study of the damage in older buildings is important, however, to determine their suitability for continued occupancy. Also, the study of past earthquakes, particularly the San Francisco Earthquake of 1906, has demonstrated the general good behavior in strong earthquakes of buildings with structural steel frameworks, particularly those with the massive masonry walls and partitions in vogue at the time.

A few specific instances of damage evaluation will be cited. The items selected are those which have led to code changes, have suggested code changes, or have indicated the direction of design practice. The intent is to show the importance of damage evaluation and its relationship to the over-all process of earthquake resistant design.

1 Performance of Buildings During Earthquakes

Mexico City Earthquake of 1957.   The earthquake of July 28, 1957 in Mexico City affected tall building construction under modern earthquake design principles (Zeevaert, 1957; Rosenblueth, 1960). The main conclusion that was reached from this earthquake was the relatively large amount of damage to tall buildings in comparison to that found in short, rigid buildings. Some of the specific items noticed in relation to damage are as follows:

1. Some damage resulted because the relative rigidity of resisting elements was not considered in the design.

2. Reinforcement in reinforced concrete beams was often inadequate in the center portion of the span.

3. Pounding between adjacent elements was a cause of damage.

4. Some damage was a propagation of previous cracking resulting from differential settlements.

5. Resonance between structure and ground motion caused some damage.

6. Panic was caused by the excessive swaying of some structures.

7. Some damage in upper stories indicated that whipping action from higher modes of vibration occurred. Later studies indicate that this damage can be ascribed to the fact that a constant horizontal force factor was used in design, which relatively overdesigned the lower stories, that the penthouse period coincided with the building fundamental period, or that poor detailing prevailed.

Tall buildings designed according to modern procedures for earthquake-resistant design suffered relatively little damage. This earthquake clearly indicated the effect of distance from the epicentral region and foundation conditions on the response of tall buildings. It should be considered as having ground motion of Type A intensity.

Chilean Earthquakes of 1960. As a result of the Chilean earthquakes of May 1960, several conclusions were reached which have had an effect on tall building design (Steinbrugge and Flores, 1963):

1. Shear walls of reinforced concrete were adequate for resisting seismic forces when carefully designed and constructed. Some problems were encountered in shear wall rotation on soft soils and in walls with complex stress distributions.

2. Some damage was found as a result of torsion on L-shaped and T-shaped buildings in which torsion had not been adequately considered in design.

3. The omission of some rigid elements in calculating the distribution of lateral forces caused high local stresses in important structural members to be overlooked.

4. Extensive damage was found as a result of adjacent buildings pounding against each other.

5. Inattention to the influence of the supporting soils on structural response resulted in major damage.

6. Most damage in major structures resulted from poor construction practices, particularly the lack of quality control of concrete mix and placing of reinforcing.

This was one of the largest series of earthquakes that has been recorded. Numerous destructive shocks occurred in many regions. In most areas surveyed, the earthquake ground motion could be considered as exhibiting Type B intensity.

Acapulco Earthquakes of 1962. The earthquakes of May 11 and 19, 1962, in Acapulco, Mexico, were not locally recorded on strong motion instruments, but the intensities should be considered as Type A shaking (Binder, 1964). There were many concrete column failures indicating insufficient column ties, high vertical accelerations, or poor concrete quality. Soil conditions apparently contributed to the definition of the areas which suffered damage.

Skopje Earthquake of 1963. The Skopje, Yugoslavia, earthquake of July 26, 1963, was of moderate magnitude with severe Type B ground motions occurring over only a limited area (Berg, 1964a, 1964b). This area can be estimated based only on the extent and degree of damage. The lessons to be learned for design of tall structures from an examination of the damage are: (1) The need for ductility as well as strength in structures; and (2) the need to consider the distribution of earthquake forces in proportion to the rigidities of elements.

Alaska Earthquake of 1964. The Alaska earthquake of March 27, 1964, exhibited very high intensity ground motions in several inhabited areas (Wiegel, 1970; Berg and Stratta, 1964; Kunze et al., 1965; Wood et al., 1967; National Research Council, 1973). In most of these areas, structures had been built under modern earthquake resistant codes. As the intensity of shaking was very severe, most areas with major structures can be said to have undergone Type B intensity shaking. The lessons relating to the design of tall buildings that can be learned from this earthquake are summarized as follows:

1. Many instances of damage pointed to the fact that the more rigid elements attract the greater lateral force on buildings. If the more rigid elements are brittle, failures involving a high life hazard can result. Often the more rigid elements will impose excessive forces on the structural frame. Stairways may fail if they are more rigid than the main building.

2. Axial shear and flexural forces, including those caused by torsional effects, need to be provided for in seismic design.

3. Provisions to eliminate pounding of adjacent structures should be adequately incorporated into the design.

4. Connection details require close attention in design in regard to both strength and ductile behavior. There were numerous deficiencies of this type.

5. The efficacy of providing continuity of structural elements and multiple systems of resistance was clearly demonstrated.

6. Quality control deficiencies in damaged buildings emphasized the importance of good construction.

The effects of the earthquake on the areas of Turnagain, L Street, Fourth Avenue, and Government Hill also pointed to the importance of evaluating the presence of soils which may become unstable during the shaking.

Niigata Earthquake of 1964.   The June 16, 1964, earthquake at Niigata, Japan, demonstrated dramatically the effects of liquefaction of soils. The earthquake can be considered to have Type A intensity shaking. Most of the damage can be attributed to the earthquake effect on the foundation soils. One item of interest is the set of strong motion records with which reconciliation has been obtained.

Venezuelan Earthquake of 1967.   The damage caused by the July 29, 1967, earthquake in Venezuela has received attention from many investigators (Hanson and Degenkolb, 1967; Fintel et al., 1967; Sozen et al., 1968; Degenkolb and Hanson, 1969; Esteva et al., 1969; Seed and Idriss, 1970b). Many of the more important lessons are as follows:

1. Nonstructural elements, and those elements assumed to be not part of the lateral load resisting system, can profoundly alter the performance of the structure. These elements can also be hazardous if they are brittle.

2. Overturning forces greatly in excess of those anticipated in previous studies, research, or observations can occur.

3. The efficacy of providing continuous reinforcing on all faces of concrete, the need for providing confinement to critical compression areas, and the need to avoid shear failures were demonstrated.

4. Any single zone of weakness in the resisting system or a sudden localized change of stiffness is a zone of danger.

5. Tie requirements for concrete columns should be more stringent in buildings in earthquake areas than in buildings not requiring seismic design.

6. Connections, in general, should be as strong as the members they connect.

7. Shear transfer at columns supporting wide flat concrete beams or slabs should be adequately provided for in seismic designs.

8. Adequate interconnection of shear walls and diaphragms should not be overlooked.

9. Some pounding of adjacent buildings indicates the need to provide adequate separation.

10. Miscellaneous conclusions include the need for considering torsional effects, adequate design of roof tanks, and provisions to keep stairs operative after an earthquake.

11. The distribution of damage indicates that geologic and foundation considerations were important parameters in this earthquake and resulted in some areas of Type B shaking.

12. Design of buildings that exhibit dynamic irregularities should recognize the potential for dynamic response greater than that which a dynamically regular building would undergo. This is particularly the case when the structure is excited by Type B intensity shaking. In the case of a flexible first floor, energy absorption by inelastic deformations could occur at one level which could create an unstable condition for the building as a whole, or could require very large ductile behavior in the framing members.

Tokachi-Oki Earthquake of 1968. This affected primarily the island of Hokkaido, Japan, and had horizontal earthquake ground motions on the order of 0.18 g to 0.23 g. Many strong motion accelerograph records were obtained. The shaking lasted for two or three minutes. Most of the reinforced concrete buildings in the affected area were designed elastically for 0.18 g. The extent of damage, however, indicates that the response of some of the buildings was of Type B shaking. The damage from this earthquake as related to framing types in reinforced concrete buildings can be categorized as follows:

1. Buildings with many walls exhibiting great rigidity suffered little damage.

2. Buildings with fewer walls exhibited many shear cracks in walls but frame members had only slight cracking.

3. Some buildings with a frame but not walls collapsed by column shear failure. Torsional motions were also evident.

The types of damage from this earthquake can be described as follows:

1. Some damage as a result of whipping action was observed.

2. Damage was observed at expansion joints.

3. Some concrete stairs collapsed.

4. Few failures of column to girder joints were found.

5. Some corner columns failed.

6. Some failures resulted from arrangements of wall which were not considered in design.

7. Few beam flexural failures occurred.

8. Some damage resulted from poor quality of concrete.

9. Some damage resulted from short anchorage hooks or incorrect placement of reinforcement.

The performance of the damaged buildings would have been greatly improved by confinement of critical compression areas and by avoiding shear failures.

Mexico City Earthquake of 1968.   Observation of the damage resulting from the earthquake in Mexico City on August 2, 1968, resulted in the following conclusions (Driskell, 1968):

1. The earthquake was of moderate intensity (Type A).

2. Shear walls should have adequate strength, with properly anchored reinforcement, and should be disposed as symmetrically as possible.

3. Relatively flexible horizontal or vertical shear resisting systems will result in large displacements during earthquakes. This will result in much damage to nonstructural elements, which can be hazardous to life as well as monetarily costly.

4. Infill walls should be analyzed as to the effects they will have on the frame during an earthquake.

Santa Rosa Earthquake of 1969.   The earthquake of October 1, 1969, at Santa Rosa, California, while not affecting structures which can be termed "tall buildings," did lead to the conclusion that even in earthquakes of Type A intensity, the dynamic effects on buildings can be important, particularly on those using a flexible frame (Steinbrugge et al., 1969). The design of buildings using static design principles alone was inadequate.

San Fernando Earthquake of 1971.   The San Fernando earthquake of February 9, 1971, has provided much data which when fully compiled and analyzed will lead to important conclusions (U.S. Dept. of Commerce, NOAA and EERI, 1973; Jennings, 1971; Muto, 1971; Structural Engineers Association of Southern California, 1972; Murphy, 1973; Steinbrugge et al., 1971; Lew et al., 1971). Even though the earthquake was of moderate magnitude, there was high intensity, Type B, ground motion in an area having modern structures. The ground motion in many instances had maximum accelerations of 0.4 g or greater. No buildings over seven stories were in this area. Among the main items of interest are the more than 200 strong motion accelerograph records obtained. Many of these instruments were placed in sets of three per building—one in the basement, another at midheight, and the last at the top. The reconciliation and analyses of these data are under way and some results are available (Muto, 1971; Structural Engineers Association of Southern California, 1972; Murphy, 1973). Except for the record on Pacoima Dam, all the records of ground motion could be considered moderate shaking. It is hoped that these records will assist in selecting appropriate ground motions for use as a design Type A earthquake. The Pacoima Dam record will be of use for research as a high intensity ground motion of short duration (10 sec).

Following are the conclusions and recommendations resulting from the San

Fernando earthquake which are applicable to tall building design considerations (Murphy, 1973).

General recommendations concerning seismic loading and its distribution.

1. The destruction and serious damage to many of the hospitals in this earthquake indicates that, in most cases, the basic tenet of design was met, namely that collapse did not occur, but the buildings were rendered inoperative. This indicates a need for a change in design criteria for emergency structures.

2. An in-depth review is needed so that the appropriate types and levels of design load more closely simulate anticipated horizontal and vertical accelerations.

3. The effects of high intensity ground motion and inelastic deformation must be considered in design. In particular, the effects of elastic and inelastic drift on the capability of framing members to support vertical loads must be considered. This would apply to members which may or may not be part of the lateral load resisting system.

4. Torsional effects on buildings must be carefully assessed in design.

5. The effects of overturning forces must be closely considered in design, particularly for buildings with low damping characteristics.

6. Particular attention should be given to corner columns of frames, with consideration given to simultaneous motions in the vertical and both horizontal directions. Corner columns should be designed conservatively.

7. Consideration must be given in the design of the lateral load resisting system of the stiffening effects of elements not considered as part of the system, such as floor slabs, stairs, nonstructural infill walls, etc.

8. Major items of storage or building equipment can be injurious to the structural frame and occupants if not properly stored or anchored.

9. Effective models can be determined for use in design of major structures by dynamic analysis.

10. The usual static design of buildings with large dynamic irregularities can produce insufficient resistance to shaking of both Types A and B.

General conclusions and recommendations concerning considerations of general building layout and construction.

1. The difference in behavior between buildings designed to be earthquake resistant and those that were not was clearly demonstrated, indicating the need for an orderly review of old schools and other old buildings so that hazardous buildings can be eliminated or strengthened.

2. The importance of assuring that the actual construction conforms to the construction documents was pointed out in many instances. Periodic observation of construction by the design engineer is essential to assure an earthquake resistant structure.

3. The consequence of differing dynamic characteristics of adjoining building portions must be considered in design layouts.

4. Consideration must be given to the effects of pounding if the separation joints between building segments are inadequate to account for inelastic deformations.

5. Complex lines of resistance should be avoided. If they cannot, very careful design and detailing must be employed to avoid "weak links."

General conclusions and recommendations concerning seismic resistance of building components and materials.

1. Consideration should be given to a requirement that all concrete and masonry columns be designed for the shear resulting from the maximum possible column end moment, and that confinement at column ends be provided to resist the effect of inelastic shear wall behavior on vertical load-carrying frame members.

2. Buildings with several lateral force resisting systems should be analyzed to determine the consequence of the failure of the more rigid systems before a more flexible primary resisting system can function.

3. All lateral force moment-resisting frames should be able to perform in a ductile manner; that is, to assure confinement of critical compression and avoidance of shear failures.

4. The strength, stiffness, and inelastic behavior of shear walls and diaphragms of all construction materials should be reviewed.

5. Items such as equipment, light fixtures, ceilings, and glass can be detailed to provide adequate response to earthquakes at little additional cost.

6. Adequate securing of component parts of elevator systems to the structure should be provided. As a result of this earthquake, 674 counterweights were out of their guides and 109 of these rammed cabs traveling in the opposite directions. In addition to damage to many other elevator parts, 286 counterweight roller guides were broken or loose.

7. Hazardous materials must be stored so that earthquake motions will not dislodge them.

8. Adequate continuity (splice requirements) of the chord reinforcement for both shear walls and diaphragms must be provided. In concrete and masonry shear walls, the lap splice requirements should be reviewed to determine if confinement is required.

9. Confinement of concrete beam-column joints and columns is an important detail for design of moment-resisting frames.

10. Effectiveness of closely spaced rectangular hoops in providing confinement to concrete columns was not tested by this earthquake.

11. Slab-column joints must be analyzed to provide adequate shear transfer when frame distortions are considered.

12. The effect of incomplete development of reinforcing should be considered, particularly at the top of columns.

13. The numerous recurrences of failures at construction joints, particularly those in which comparatively low strength lightweight concrete was placed between sections of higher strength stone concrete, indicates that research should be conducted of the mechanism of failure, strength capacity, quality control, and methods to assure better performance of this construction detail.

14. Control by the design of the locations of openings in concrete and masonry walls and floors is essential so that adequate continuity and reinforcement can be provided.

15. Diaphragm stress collector members (drag ties or struts) should extend across and be well connected to diaphragms and shear walls.

16. A review of the behavior of braced elements should be made to determine inelastic behavior.

The results of the reconciliation of strong motion records in the buildings should be to increase somewhat the static values found in the Recommendations of the Seismology Committee of the Structural Engineers Association of California (1975). The recent changes to these Recommendations, requiring ductile provisions in all concrete moment resisting frames, are shown by the analyses to be in the right direction.

Managua Earthquake of 1972. The Managua, Nicaragua, earthquake of December 23, 1972, provided a demonstration of the effects of strong earthquake motions on two moderately tall buildings (EERI Reconnaissance Report, 1973; EERI Conference Proceedings, 1973; Wright and Kramer, 1973; Sozen and Matthiesen, 1975). The earthquake was of moderate magnitude but the epicenter was located close to the center of the city so that there was ground motion of high intensity, Type B. The general conclusions and recommendations that are applicable to tall building design are (EERI Reconnaissance Report, 1973; Wright and Kramer, 1973; Sozen and Matthiesen, 1975):

1. Good building practices can provide resistance to strong earth shaking at moderate cost.

2. Most damage appeared to result from deficiencies in building practices.

3. The influence of the stiffness of all elements should be considered in analyzing moment frames.

4. Torsional effects need to be considered in design.

5. Horizontal diaphragms should be designed and reinforced to transfer all loads to shear walls.

6. Masonry must be adequately reinforced in both directions and positively anchored to adjacent structural members.

7. The effects of structural setbacks should be carefully considered in design.

8. Improvement in methods of design and bracing of nonstructural items,

including elevators, is needed to reduce the hazard to life, financial loss, and continued post-earthquake use of building.

9. Emergency utilities should be provided for those buildings whose continued post-earthquake usage is most critical.

10. Nonstructural damage was much greater in the more flexible buildings (exemplified by moment-frame buildings) than in the more rigid buildings (exemplified by shear-wall buildings).

2 Conclusions

It should be remembered that an adequately designed building will not be earthquake resistant unless the design is realized through appropriate construction.

The data obtained from the network of strong motion accelerographs indicate the value of this type of instrumentation. Every effort should be made to establish and maintain effective networks in earthquake areas, so that data from future earthquakes can establish more firmly the engineering principles of earthquake resistant design.

The evaluation of the damage to buildings indicates that a review should be made of the appropriate ground motion to use as the limit of Type A motion. This may lead to some change in code base shear provisions. Also, continued adjustment of design concepts and methods is necessary so that the appropriate ductility can be provided to adequately resist Type B earthquake ground motions.

A change in the basic design criteria for some types of buildings is also indicated. Those buildings which are necessary for continued emergency operations immediately after earthquake ground motions should remain operative. This goal can be achieved by appropriate limitations on elastic and inelastic deformations resulting from Type B ground motions.

2.7 ECONOMIC AND SOCIAL ASPECTS

Investigation of the economic and social implications and desiderata of the seismic protection of tall buildings has hitherto lagged behind the study of the engineering aspects. Thus it is not possible to be completely explicit. This section attempts to state the problem, to itemize and discuss some of the relevant elements, and to treat some selected subtopics to the extent possible.

The central problem may be stated in two parts: (1) Given a proposed tall building to be designed, what incremental investment of funds should be applied to what ends in order to cooptimize seismic safety with respect to the variables of function, cost, and esthetics? (2) Given a municipality planning its future growth with an eye on seismic hazard due to tall buildings, what public policies should be established relative to acceptable seismic risk, land-use planning, and building ordinances? Part (1) is the concern of the building owner and of the structural engineer and his professional colleagues. Part (2) involves the community at large and requires initiative from the professional subcommunity. The problem in both parts is solved daily around the world, but usually without much access to organized factual information, established professional methods, or the results of research.

The policies and attitudes of the public toward the seismic hazard establish the acceptable levels of risk of death and of economic loss. For example, Los Angeles voters, shortly after the San Fernando earthquake, defeated a bond proposition to rebuild unsafe schools, thus tacitly accepting the risk extant of one death per year per 400 000 population due to earthquakes. California homeowners generally decline to purchase earthquake insurance, implying that they are willing to accept the associated risk of destruction of their homes. On the other hand, owners and financiers of tall buildings usually provide for earthquake insurance. Public attitude on economic loss is complicated by a variety of disaster relief legislation. The engineering and architectural professions should work to sustain a good level of understanding in the public mind of the consequences of the public's decisions on acceptable risk.

Two other public policies affecting high-rise buildings with regard to earthquakes are those of land-use planning and building regulations. The former may limit construction in fault zones. The latter dictate requirements of strength and flexibility, and thus strongly influence the structural materials and hence the building esthetics.

Given a regime of public policy and attitude, the professions must establish criteria of tall building design which are consistent therewith. These criteria may be classified as:

1. Protection of human activity: Life protection; continuity of work; physical comfort; mental security.

2. Continuance of building functions in and after an earthquake: Intended function continuity (for example, hospital); access and egress; services (communication, energy); facilities (elevators, air conditioning).

3. Protection of capital investment: Tolerable structural damage; tolerable nonstructural damage; tolerable damage to building contents, services, and facilities.

4. Building's role in disaster response: Evacuation and rescue of occupants; emergency services and facilities; panic prevention; role of functional building in regional disaster relief.

The paramount criterion is the avoidance of actual or near calamity of the type experienced in certain buildings in recent earthquakes in Anchorage, Tokachi-Oki, Caracas, Mexico City, and San Fernando.

Such criteria, properly established and implemented, will broadly determine what the additional cost of protecting a particular building will be, though the whole additional cost should not be set against the possible loss due to a future earthquake alone, because the protection will also improve resistance to wind and other nonseismic loads. In general the limited amount of information now available suggests that it need not exceed a minor percentage of the total building cost, the actual percentage depending not only on the level of damage tolerated but also on primary structural decisions, such as that between a rigid or flexible response of the primary resisting elements. Estimates of losses in the event of earthquake should include the losses due to loss of production, rent, etc.

1 Seismic Risk

It is generally agreed that a tall building must not collapse during the largest earthquake that is realistically imaginable. In addition, earthquakes which can be expected to occur during the lifetime of the building must not cause damage that is economically unacceptable either to an owner or to a community. This implies a balancing of risks of future losses against the initial cost of providing a stronger building, and, for conservatism in design, these risks and losses should include those from nonseismic loads.

2 Establishing Design Criteria

For many years, engineers have juggled the available facts so as to recommend a reasonable balance between initial cost and future risk, although seldom has the actual balance been stated in an explicit way. Today, it is beginning to be possible to face this balance openly and realistically. In fact, the City of Long Beach, California, has recently adopted a new code that is explicitly based upon balance risk (Wiggins and Moran, 1971).

Fig. 2.30 outlines, by means of a flow chart, a possible methodology for analyzing the costs and risks associated with designing tall buildings against earthquakes. This methodology cannot be a substitute for judgment and experience, but rather provides for a systematic organization of it. As outlined in Fig. 2.30, it is aimed at selecting seismic design requirements for a specific project or for use in a building code. However, the same general method can be used as a basis for insurance considerations or for federal disaster relief laws. A similar method has already been applied to estimating possible future losses to residential dwellings in California (ESSA, 1969).

The heart of the method is examination, in probabilistic terms, of the damage that one earthquake will cause to a particular building system built with a particular design strategy. This evaluation is repeated for different levels of earthquake, different design strategies and, where appropriate, different building systems. For each different design strategy, the initial cost required by that strategy is added to the present value of possible future losses.

In simplest terms, a particular building system might be defined as: all buildings having 8 to 13 stories. In a more refined study, a building system might be: 8-story to 13-story reinforced concrete buildings with ductile moment resisting frames. Other building systems are then defined by different ranges of stories, different construction materials, and different lateral force resisting systems. The soil conditions upon which the building is to be built also form part of the definition of the building system.

The simplest statement of design strategy is: design in accordance with the Uniform Building Code for Zone 2 (or 0, 1, or 3). More refined variations on the design requirements might also be considered. The initial cost is a function of the design strategy. This cost might be expressed as the extra cost to design for Zone 2 requirements, as compared to making no provision for earthquake resistance.

One key step is determining the earthquake occurrence probability. This is the probability that a ground motion of some given intensity will occur during, say, one year, at the site of interest. Intensity may be expressed by the Modified Mercalli scale, or better yet by the spectral acceleration for the periods appropriate to the building system. Methods now exist for making reasonable estimates for the earthquake intensity probability for any location, by appropriate analysis of the historical record and of geological information (Cornell, 1970).

The effect of various levels of ground motion upon the building system is expressed by a family of damage probability matrices. Each matrix applies to a particular building system and design strategy, and gives the probability that various levels of damage will result from earthquakes of various intensities. Table 2.4 shows one possible categorization of levels of damage. These levels of damage are described both by words and by the ratio, to replacement cost, of physical damage to the building and its contents. Table 2.3 illustrates a damage probability matrix based on the categories of damage in Table 2.4. For example, the numbers in the column labeled Intensity 8 (Modified Mercalli) show the fraction of all buildings

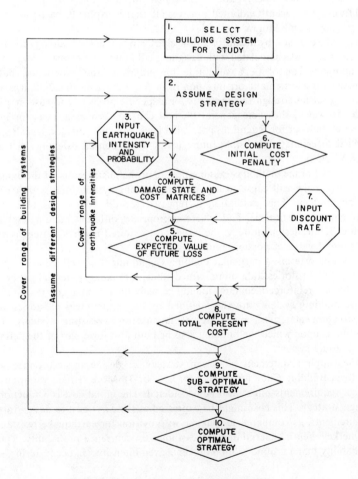

Fig. 2.30 Flow diagram for general methodology

Table 2.3 Example of damage probability matrix

Damage state	Earthquake intensity[a]					
	4	5	6	6.5	7	8
0	1.00	0.99	0.90	0.85	0.80	0.25
1	0	0.01	0.09	0.10	0.12	0.25
2	0	0	0.01	0.04	0.05	0.20
3	0	0	0	0.01	0.02	0.15
4	0	0	0	0	0.01	0.10
5	0	0	0	0	0	0.04
6	0	0	0	0	0	0.01
7	0	0	0	0	0	0
8	0	0	0	0	0	0

[a]Expressed in terms of the Modified Mercalli Intensity Scale.

Table 2.4 Damage states

Level of damage (1)	Description of level of damage (2)	Ratio to replacement cost[a] (3)
0	No damage	0
1	Minor nonstructural damage—a few walls and partitions cracked, incidental mechanical and electrical damage	0.001
2	Localized nonstructural damage—more extensive cracking (but still not widespread); possibly damage to elevators and/or other mechanical/electrical components	0.005
3	Widespread nonstructural damage—possibly a few beams and columns cracked, although not noticeable	0.02
4	Minor structural damage—obvious cracking or yielding in a few structural members; substantial nonstructural damage with widespread cracking	0.05
5	Substantial structural damage requiring repair or replacement of some structural members; associated extensive nonstructural damage	0.10
6	Major structural damage requiring repair or replacement of many structural members; associated nonstructural damage requiring repairs to major portion of interior; building vacated during repairs	0.30
7	Building condemned	1.0
8	Collapse	1.0

[a]Note that it is possible that the total loss incurred can exceed the total building replacement cost.

expected to experience each of the levels of damage should an earthquake of Intensity 8 occur.

With each damage state, there is an associated cost. These are different from the costs shown in Table 2.4, which are intended only to identify the level of damage. The total associated cost for each damage state includes, in addition to repair of structural and nonstructural damage, loss of function or lost time during repairs and, in extreme cases, injury and loss of life and impact on community. Not all of the factors can be readily expressed in dollars, and many engineers and politicians find it difficult to accept the notion of placing any sort of value on life. Yet today communities already make such judgments implicitly. For example, how do we decide that it is better to make a building owner pay extra for added resistance to earthquakes, instead of contributing the same sum toward a transit system which would reduce highway deaths?

If it were possible to express all losses in dollars, then the criterion for optimization would be minimum present total cost. Actually, future losses will be only partly expressible in dollars, and multivariate objectives must be considered. Nonetheless, the approach here outlined will serve to make clear the considerations that must be balanced to achieve an optimum design.

Note that the validity and conservatism of the optimization are enhanced if *all* losses which are sensitive to the level of seismic design strength are included. A designed increase in resistance to seismic effects would certainly reduce expected losses from wind and tornado loads, internal and external blast loads, accidental impact loads, and even gravity overloads. Thus the probabilities of these occurrences should be added to block 3 of the flow diagram of Fig. 2.30; damage probability matrices should be added to block 4; and computation of the corresponding losses should be added to block 5.

3 Damage Probabilities

The damage probability matrices are at the heart of the optimization study. A family of such matrices is required. At a minimum, different design strategies and soil conditions must be represented. It would be desirable to have data for several ranges of story heights and for different types of construction.

By assembling experience during actual earthquakes and using results from theoretical studies, it now is possible to provide tentative estimates for damage probabilities for various building systems with different levels of earthquake resistance. Table 2.3, for example, represents a first guess at the probabilities applying to modern buildings having eight or more stories, founded on firm ground, and designed approximately in accordance with the requirements of the Uniform Building Code for Zone 3. This Table was assembled by analyzing preliminary data from the San Fernando, California, earthquake of 9 February 1971. Steinbrugge et al. (1971) have prepared an excellent summary of damage to some multistory buildings. Their main conclusions concerning high-rise buildings are:

1. Steel frame and reinforced concrete (earthquake resistive) high-rise buildings performed equally well, with some exceptions, when located 24 km to 40 km (15 to 25 miles) from the epicenter. Where exceptions occurred, they were usually adverse with regard to reinforced concrete construction.

2. From a percentage loss standpoint, completed steel frame buildings never

exceeded about 1% of value. A total of five reinforced concrete structures had losses over 1%, and two of these had losses over 5%.

3. Older high-rise buildings that were not earthquake resistive performed quite badly when compared to modern high-rise construction. A limited selection of older structures in the downtown Los Angeles area all had losses over 5%.

Collection and analysis of the performance of high-rise buildings during the San Fernando earthquake is continuing (Whitman et al., 1975).

4 Vibration Hazard and Perception

In 1959, after more than a year of study, the vibration hazard subcommittee in the Architectural Institute of Japan presented the following first draft proposal (Structural Standard Committee, 1959) to the building engineering profession in Japan. Design standard value on vibration elimination in buildings:

1. Scope of application: This standard should be applied to vibrations in the living (office) space of buildings caused by equipment or other machinery in the building. Vibration in other parts of buildings, or vibration transmitted from outside the building, should not be included in this standard.

2. Amplitude of both vertical and horizontal vibration in the living (office) space should be less in principle than the value indicated on Curve B in Fig. 2.31. This limiting value was based on Meister's curves (Meister, 1937), after several additional field investigations of the relation between vibration intensity and the discontent of people living near a factory where vibration hazard was observed. The standard value is near the middle part of the

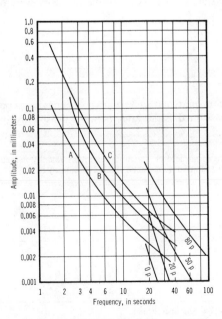

Fig. 2.31 Proposed standard: B (Meister's slightly perceptible zone: A – C)

"slightly perceptible" zone over most of the frequency range, except at low frequencies, where the proposed value is raised a little, considering the technical difficulty of vibration elimination methods.

In recent years, several prefectures or cities have established vibration limits from the standpoint of public hazard. These are given as constant velocity values of vibration, independent of frequency, and are applied for machine vibration in factories. An example for the Osaka prefecture is indicated in Table 2.5.

Several buildings of more than 25 stories have been built in Japan, following the first high-rise Kasumigaseki Building, which was completed in 1968. These tall buildings have not thus far suffered vibration problems from the standpoint of human perception.

From the human and social point of view, vibrations of a tall building as a result of earthquake are important chiefly as a possible cause of panic. A preliminary paper (Nakagawa, 1964) on the human panic problem of tall buildings was published before actual tall buildings appeared in Japan. The basic assumptions were:

1. The acceleration spectrum S_A in g units is given in hyperbolic shape as $S_A = A_G/T$, in which A_G = maximum ground acceleration in g units.

2. The fundamental natural period of tall buildings is proportional to the number of stories N, as $T = CN$. The constant C is assumed as 0.11 for steel and 0.07 for reinforced concrete structures.

3. The fundamental mode of vibration is predominant in earthquake response, and this mode is assumed as straight.

   From these assumptions, the response displacement amplitude X_N and response seismic coefficient k_N of the top story were obtained as

$$X_N = 37.2 \ C \ NA_G \tag{2.4}$$

$$k_N = \frac{1.5A_G}{CN} \tag{2.5}$$

4. The vibration limit that gives uneasy feelings to people at the top of the building is assumed as the value between the slightly and clearly perceptible

Table 2.5 Larger value of vertical or horizontal vibration velocity measured at boundary line of factory area (adopted as a Public Hazard Standard)[a]

Zone	Time of day			
	0600-0800	0800-1800	1800-2100	2100-0600
(1)	(2)	(3)	(4)	(5)
Dwelling area	0.3	0.3	0.3	0.1
Unzoned area	0.3	0.5	0.3	0.3
Commercial, semi-industrial area	1.0	1.0	1.0	0.5
Industrial area	1.5	1.5	1.5	0.7

[a]Velocity measured in millimeters per second.

limits which are extrapolated from Meister's curves to the long period range. The result is indicated in Fig. 2.32. The assumption adopted in this analysis—that the fundamental mode is predominant in earthquake response—seems not to be always true. It is reported that the response of the Kasumigaseki Building in Tokyo to the Tokachi-Oki earthquake, epicentral distance about 600 km (375 miles), was the combined vibration of its first and second modes. In a 70 km (43 miles) distant earthquake in the same year, the response acceleration was 30 gal to 40 gal at the 23rd floor level of this building, against 25 gal ground acceleration in the combined second and higher modes.

Yamada and Goto (1969) have recently conducted extensive experimental studies of human mental and physiological response to long period vibration. Male and female students were put in a test room which vibrated in sinusoidal horizontal motion of constant amplitude of 0.5, 1.0, 1.5...25 cm, while the period was changed in the sequence of 8, 7, 6,...1, 2, 3,...8 sec, step by step, of 30 sec duration each. Body positions were of four kinds: standing, sitting on a chair, sitting on the floor, and sleeping on the floor with body axis parallel or perpendicular to the direction of vibration. Fig. 2.33 is an example of results for the position of sitting on a chair. The five curves at the right are for the present studies at long period range; the other five curves were given in Ohshima's older study (1953) in the short period range (a = no feeling; b = not sure; c = slightly perceptible; d = clearly perceptible; e = strongly perceptible; f = unpleasant; g = very unpleasant).

Yamada and Goto pointed out that if the result is written as a relation between acceleration and vibrational period over the range from short to long period, the curves have the form of

$$a = \pm 4\pi^2 \left(A T + B + \frac{C}{T} \right) \tag{2.6}$$

in which A, B, C = parameters, and a very sensitive range for acceleration a is

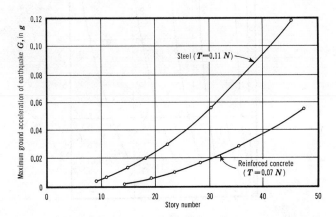

Fig. 2.32 Relation between number of stories and maximum ground acceleration of earthquake which gives some human response at top of building

found at around a 1-sec period. In the long period range, a slight change of period strongly affects the human sensitivity to both amplitude and acceleration.

For a wider discussion of problems of vibration, see Chapter PC-13.

5 Present Needs

The optimization of investment in a seismic design has hitherto received only scattered attention. We are at a stage where first attempts can be made to undertake a systematic risk analysis and to learn how such analyses can be used to make decisions. More study and research, of course, will be required before such analyses can be applied widely. Particular needs are:

1. Additional data concerning damage probability. In future earthquakes, the type and magnitude of damage in all buildings (including buildings with little or no damage) must be documented accurately. Cities located in seismic areas should prepare and maintain a list of all buildings having five or more stories, listing location of building, over-all dimensions, type of construction, type of foundation, and earthquake design criteria. Immediately following an earthquake, each such building should be visited to ascertain the general level of damage. Regulations should also be enacted now that will give building officials access to information concerning the total actual cost of repairs necessitated by future earthquakes.

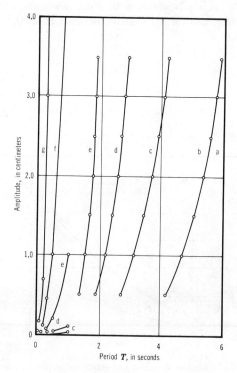

Fig. 2.33 Human response to vibration

2. Good methods must be developed for evaluating costs in addition to those of physical damage.

3. Clearer information must be obtained as to the additional initial cost of providing additional resistance to earthquakes.

2.8 CODE REQUIREMENTS

The broad objectives of current codes are: (1) To minimize loss of human life and personal injury; (2) to assure continuity of vital services; and (3) to minimize damage to property in the event of an earthquake. Since it is recognized that it is not economically feasible to give complete protection to all buildings in the event of the worst earthquake, it is generally accepted that structural damage should be prevented and other damage minimized in the occasional moderate earthquake, and that serious damage or collapse should be prevented in the much rarer severe earthquake.

In some countries dynamic analyses are recommended, based on appropriate earthquake motions for the relevant site and soil conditions. Such analyses may be required for specific types of structure, such as slender high-rise buildings and especially important structures where there are unusual risks.

More commonly static analyses are permitted, using equivalent static loadings to represent the dynamic actions of the earthquake on the structure. These loadings incorporate modifying factors to cover local variations in seismicity, type of construction, soil conditions, use of building, etc. Though they lead to smaller deformations than may be expected to result in practice from a major earthquake, they have some empirical justification in the performance of well constructed buildings in past earthquakes. But it should be remembered that this good performance may have been due to other factors that have been ignored and may not always be present—such as structural ductility and contributions to over-all response by nonstructural elements. Special care is called for in the case of tall buildings with many occupants if there is any doubt in relation to these factors.

The essential items to be covered in such codes include: (1) Distribution of horizontal shear; (2) evaluation of overturning moments and horizontal torsional moments; (3) drift limitation; (4) separation of buildings; (5) setbacks; and (6) structural design requirements, including the provision of adequate ductility.

Lateral seismic forces over the height of the building may be determined by either of the following methods (which should give similar results):

1. The total seismic force on a structure is determined by the so-called base shear coefficient. It is distributed over the height of the structure, by considering the response of the structure during earthquakes.

2. The lateral seismic force at each floor level is directly determined by so-called lateral seismic coefficients. These coefficients are generally varied over the height of the building, in consideration of the response of the structure during earthquakes.

The base shear coefficient or lateral seismic coefficient is evaluated in terms of:

1. Dynamic properties of the structure (natural periods of vibration, modal shapes, damping).

2. Type of construction (ductility or energy-absorptive capacity of the structure).

3. Importance of the structure as related to its use.

4. Seismicity of the region.

5. Subsoil conditions.

6. Allowable stresses and load factors.

Only horizontal components of the seismic forces are considered usually, and they are assumed to act nonconcurrently along the two main structural axes. Vertical seismic forces should, however, be considered also in some cases, the vertical load being taken otherwise as the total dead load plus the probable live load and (in areas subject to heavy snow) the probable snow load. Forces larger than those applicable to the building as a whole are commonly specified for certain parts of the building such as cantilevered parapets, structures projecting above the roof (tanks, penthouses, chimneys, etc.), and ornamental excrescences.

1   Base Shear Coefficients and Lateral Seismic Coefficients

The earthquake loading prescribed in most current seismic codes in the world may be represented as

$$F = C(Z,I,S,K,T)W = \Sigma f_i \qquad (2.7)$$

or

$$f_i = k_i(Z,T,S,K,T)w_i \qquad (2.8)$$

in which F = total earthquake force or shear at the base of the structure; f_i = lateral seismic force applied to the level designated i; C = seismic base shear coefficient which is determined in consideration of Z,I,S,K and T; k_i = lateral seismic coefficient assigned to level i which is determined in consideration of Z,I,S,K and T; W = total vertical load used for seismic calculations; W_i = portion of W which is located at or assigned to level i; Z = seismicity of the region (seismic zoning factor); I = importance of the structure as related to its use (importance factor); S = subsoil condition (soil factor); K = type of construction, damping, ductility or energy-absorptive capacity of the structure (construction factor); and T = fundamental natural period of vibration of the structure in the direction under consideration.

The horizontal earthquake force, summarized in Fig. 2.34, and its distribution prescribed in some typical seismic codes are as follows.

Canada.   The National Building Code of Canada (1970) prescribes

$$F = C(Z,I,S,K,T)W = Z \, I \, S \, K \, \frac{0.05}{\sqrt{T}} W \qquad (2.9)$$

in which Z = 1, 0.5, 0.25; I = 1.3, 1.0; S = 1.5, 1.0; K = 1.33, 1.0, 0.8, 0.67; and

f_i = same as that of the United States Uniform Building Code.

The design earthquake loading may be determined by a dynamic analysis.

United States of America. The Uniform Building Code (1976) prescribes

$$F = C(Z,I,S,K,T)W = Z\,I\,S\,K\,\frac{1}{15\sqrt{T}}\,W \tag{2.10}$$

in which Z = 1.0, 3/4, 3/8, 3/16; I = 1.5, 1.25, 1.0;

$$\left.\begin{array}{l} S = 1.0 + \dfrac{T}{T_s} - 0.5\left(\dfrac{T}{T_s}\right)^2 \text{ for } \dfrac{T}{T_s} \leq 1.0 \\[3mm] S = 1.2 + 0.6\dfrac{T}{T_s} - 0.3\left(\dfrac{T}{T_s}\right)^2 \text{ for } \dfrac{T}{T_s} > 1.0 \end{array}\right\} \; S \geq 1.0$$

$T \leq 0.3$ sec; T_S = characteristic site period (sec) ($0.5 \leq T_S \leq 2.5$); K = 1.33, 1.0, 0.8, 0.67; $1/(15\sqrt{T}) \leq 0.12$; $1/(15\sqrt{T})S \leq 0.14$; and

$$f_i = \frac{(F - f_t)w_i h_i}{\displaystyle\sum_{x=1}^{n} w_x h_x} \tag{2.11}$$

in which $F = \Sigma_{i=1}^{n} f_i + f_t$; $f_t = 0.07TF < 0.25F$; and $f_t = 0$ for $T \leq 0.7$ sec, where f_t = concentrated load at the top of a slender structure.

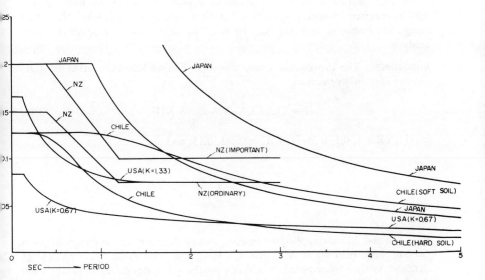

Fig. 2.34 Comparison of base shear coefficients for structural steel buildings (values adopted to correspond with the Japanese allowable stress)

New Zealand. The New Zealand Standard Code of Practice for general structural design and design loadings (NZS 4203, 1976) prescribes

$$F = C(Z,T,R,S,K,T)W = [Z,S,T] \, I \, R \, K \, W \tag{2.12a}$$

$$F = C_0 \, I \, R \, K \, W \tag{2.12b}$$

The C_0 values are given as follows: No parentheses, Zone A; (   ) Zone B; and [ ] Zone C. For rigid and intermediate soils

$$C_0 = 0.15, \, (0.125), \, [0.1] \quad T \leq 0.45 \text{ sec}$$

$$C_0 = 0.075, \, (0.0625), \, [0.05] \, T \geq 1.2 \text{ sec}$$

Linear variation for $0.45 < T < 1.2$. For flexible soil

$$C_0 = 0.15, \, (0.125), \, [0.1] \quad T \leq 0.6, \, (0.7), \, [0.8]$$

$$C_0 = 0.0825, \, (0.075), \, [0.065] \, T \geq 1.2$$

Linear variation for $0.6, \, (0.7), \, [0.08] \, T < 1.2$. Also, in Eqs. 2.12, $I = 1.0, \, 1.3, \, 1.6$; R = risk factor = $1.0, \, 1.1, \, 2.0, \, 3.0$; $K = K'M$; K' = structural type factor = $0.8, \, 1.0, \, 1.2, \, 1.6, \, 2.0, \, 2.5$; M = structural material factor = $0.8, \, 1.0, \, 1.2$; and

$$f_i = \frac{(F - f_t)w_i h_i}{\sum\limits_{x=1}^{n} w_x h_x} \tag{2.13}$$

in which $F = \sum_{i=1}^{n} f_i + f_t$; and $f_t = 0.1F$ for slender structures.

Dynamic analysis using spectral modal analysis is allowed for any building, and may be required for special structures. The base shear is scaled to $0.9F$. Numerical integration response analysis may be used to supplement the spectral modal analysis.

Venezuela. The Provisional Standard for Earthquake-Resistant Structures (December 26, 1967) prescribes

$$F = C(Z,I,S,K)W = Z[I \, S \, K]W \tag{2.14}$$

in which $Z = 1, \, 0.5, \, 0.25$; $[I \, S \, K] = 0.045, \, 0.15$; and

$$f_i = F \frac{w_i h_i}{\sum\limits_{x=1}^{n} w_x h_x} \tag{2.15}$$

Eqs. 2.14 and 2.15 are applied for buildings which do not have more than 20 floors nor are more than 60 m in height. For designing taller buildings, a method of dynamic analysis is required in addition to the static design method. The final stresses to be used for design shall not be less than 60% of those resulting from the application of the static design method.

Union of Soviet Socialist Republics. The Standards and Regulations for Buildings in Seismic Regions (1970) prescribe

$$f_{ki} = k_{ki}(Z,I,T_k)w_i \tag{2.16a}$$

$$f_{ki} = [Z \ I] \ \beta_k \ \eta_{ki} \ w_i \tag{2.16b}$$

in which f_{ki} = design seismic force acting at i in kth vibrational mode; T_λ = natural period of kth vibration; $[Z \ I]$ = 0.1, 0.05, 0.025; β_λ = $1/T_\lambda$, 0.8 $\leq \beta_k \leq 3$ (β_k increased for very slender structures); and

$$\eta_{ki} = \frac{x_{ki} \sum_1^n w_j x_{kj}}{\sum_1^n w_j x_{kj}^2}$$

in which x_{kj}, x_{ki} = deflection at j and i in kth free vibration.

In designing most structures, only the fundamental mode of vibration of the structure need be considered. For towerlike structures (height × width $\geq$ 5) and flexible frame structures ($T_1 > 0.5$ sec), higher modes (up to the third mode) of vibration should be considered. In this case, the stresses (moments, axial and shear forces) of the structure are computed by

$$N = \sqrt{N_{\max} + 0.5 \sum_1^n N_i^2} \tag{2.17}$$

in which N = value under consideration; $N_{\max}$ = maximum value among all modes of vibration; and N_i = value other than $N_{\max}$.

The seismic stress induced in buildings higher than five stories should be multiplied by the factor

$$\alpha = 1 + 0.1(n - 5) \leq 1.5$$

in which n = number of stories.

Japan. The Building Standard Law (1950) prescribes

$$f_i = k_i(Z,S,K)w_i \tag{2.18a}$$
$$f_i = Z[S \ K] \ 0.2w_i \qquad 0 < H \leq 16 \text{ m} \tag{2.18b}$$
$$f_i = Z[S \ K] \ (0.2 + \Delta)w_i \qquad 16 \text{ m} < H \tag{2.18c}$$

in which H = building height; Z = 1, 0.9, 0.8; $[S \ K]$ = 0.6, 0.8, 1.0, 1.5; $Z[S \ K] \geq 0.5$; and Δ = increment, 0.01 every 4 m over 16 m.

These formulas are usually applied for buildings up to 45 m (148 ft) in height. For the aseismic design of tall buildings whose height is over 45 m, a method using dynamic analysis based on time-history accelerograms is commonly employed.

A comparison of base shear coefficients including those of the United States and Japan is shown in Fig. 2.34.

Turkey. The Specifications for Structures to be Built in Disaster Areas (July 1975) prescribe

$$F = Z'K'S \, I \, W \tag{2.19}$$

in which $Z = 0.10, 0.08, 0.06, 0.03$; $K = 0.6$ min, 1.6 max; and

$$S = \frac{1}{|0.8 + T - T_0|}, \, S \leq 1, \, K \, S \, I \geq 0.5 \tag{2.20}$$

Also in Eq. 2.20, $I = 1.0, 1.5$; T_0 = predominant period of soil (0.2 min, 0.9 max); and

$$f_i = \frac{(F - f_t)w_i h_i}{\sum_{i=1}^{n} w_x h_x} \tag{2.21}$$

in which $F = \sum_{i=1}^{n} f_i + f_t$; and $f_i \leq 0.15F$.

These formulas are applied for buildings which do not exceed 75 m (246 ft) in height. For designing taller buildings, dynamic analysis should be made. The total lateral force calculated as a result of such dynamic analysis shall be not less than 70% of F.

India. The Criteria for Earthquake Resistant Design of Structures (January 1970) (IS: 1893–1970, second revision) prescribe

$$F = C(Z,I,S,K,T)W = \alpha_h \, I \, S \, K \, \frac{0.5}{\sqrt[3]{T}} \tag{2.22}$$

in which $\alpha_h = 0.08, 0.05, 0.04$; $I = 1.0, 1.5$; $S = 1.0, 1.2, 1.5$; $K = 1.33$ max and 0.33 min; and

$$f_i = \frac{Fw_i h_i^2}{\sum_{i=1}^{n} w_i h_i^2}$$

These formulas are applied for buildings which do not exceed 40 m (131 ft) in height. For buildings greater than 40 m in height and up to 90 m (295 ft) in height, modal analysis is recommended. For buildings taller than 90 m, detailed dynamic analysis shall be made based on expected ground motion.

Seismicity of the region where a structure is to be built is usually indicated by a seismic zoning map, which may be based on the seismic history of the region or seismotectonic factors, or on a combination of these approaches.

The maximum intensity of earthquakes to be expected in a region in a given period of time, say about 100 yr, is sometimes considered as the basis of the local seismicity. The intensities are given in terms of the Modified Mercalli Intensity Scale (1931) in some seismic countries such as the United States and the USSR. The intensity of the most seismically severe zone is usually IX of the MM Scale, which may correspond to 0.3 g to 0.5 g in ground acceleration.

Some seismic codes include classifications of structures depending upon the importance of the structure. Larger static forces are frequently required for: (1) Buildings which are essential for public well-being in the case of earthquakes; and (2) buildings where large numbers of people assemble.

The first category includes hospitals, emergency relief stores, fire stations, telephone exchanges, broadcasting and television buildings, and electrical distribution stations. These structures should remain in operation after the earthquake. The second category includes assembly buildings, schools, theaters, etc., where many lives in each structure may be endangered.

The value of the importance factor employed in seismic codes is usually in the range of 1.2 to 1.5. In the USSR and other seismic countries in eastern Europe, much larger values (2 and 4) are used in the aseismic design of more important structures.

It should be noted that this factor is not intended to cover the design considerations associated with special structures such as nuclear power stations located in seismic regions.

In some seismic codes, the effects of subsoil conditions are taken into account independently or in combination with the type of construction of the building in evaluating earthquake forces. It is recognized that some components of the seismic ground motion are magnified on soft subsoil layers, and that buildings constructed on soft soil in general suffer greater damage than those on hard layers. On the other hand, it is generally recognized that the motion of the ground at a particular site during an earthquake has a predominant period of vibration which is in general short on firm ground and long on soft ground. Therefore, attention should be paid to the problem of the resonance of a structure with the ground motion, together with the complex interaction between them.

In the evaluation of earthquake forces, the ratio of soil factor for soft soil to that for hard soil is generally taken in the range of 1.5 to 2. In some countries, such as Chile and Mexico, the soil factors are given in combination with the type of construction, taking their dynamic properties into consideration.

The over-all ductility of a structure is an important attribute of its earthquake resistance. The capability of absorbing a large amount of energy in the inelastic range is essential to avoid catastrophic failure.

Moment-resisting frames of ductile materials such as structural steel and ductile reinforced concrete have shown good earthquake resistant characteristics. In the case of reinforced concrete buildings, however, structures in which failures are due to shear cannot absorb much energy in the inelastic range under repeated cyclic loadings, and they sometimes suffer destructive damage due to brittle failures. Provisions to avoid shear failures in such buildings should be followed.

In some seismic codes, such as those of the United States, Canada, and Turkey, the coefficient K is assigned to different types of structural systems. The ratio of the maximum value of K to the minimum is in the range of 2 to 2.7 as shown in these codes.

It is interesting to note that the construction factors are considered in relation to the damping of the structure in the Romanian seismic code.

2 Vertical Forces

In most seismic countries the vertical seismic forces due to earthquakes are not considered for the design of structures except for the effect of uplift forces and for very important structures such as reactor buildings in nuclear power stations. It should be noted, however, that the vertical seismic coefficients of 1.2 to 1.4 are usually considered for seismic design of buildings in Italy and France.

3   Control of Lateral Deflections and Separation of Buildings

Control of lateral deflection or drift of a story relative to its adjacent stories is considered to deal with the problems of: (1) Restriction of damage to the nonstructural components, such as glass panels, curtain wall panels, plaster walls, and other partitions; and (2) protection from motion sickness or discomfort.

It should be noted that realistic interstory drifts during earthquakes are best estimated by computations using a method of dynamic analysis. However, drift limitations using design static earthquake loading are given in some seismic codes. The values of the interstory drift are limited to 0.002 of the story height under the design seismic loadings in Mexico.

In the United States Uniform Building Code, no definite value is given for the drift, but 0.005 of the story height is recommended in the Commentary. In Japan there is also no provision on drift in the Building Standard Law, but the value of 20 mm (0.8 in.) per story is usually taken as the limit of drift for high-rise buildings when computed by an elastic dynamic analysis.

In connection with the problem of drift, there are provisions on the separation of buildings in some seismic codes such as those of the USSR, Venezuela, Mexico, and Portugal, to avoid contact under deflections due to earthquakes.

4   Torsional Effects

The torsional effects of earthquake forces are considered in the aseismic design of a structure when the center of mass and center of rigidity do not coincide. However, possible additional torsional response should be expected due to errors in the estimation of relative rigidities of structural elements, errors in the estimation of distribution of dead and live loads at floor level, and the torsional input motions of the ground. Considering these accidental effects, the seismic codes of some countries such as Mexico, Canada, and the United States consider larger eccentricities than the computed ones. When the eccentricity thus increased is relatively large in comparison with the corresponding plan dimension, the effect of torsion is doubled, or a dynamic analysis is required in the Canadian seismic code.

5   Overturning Moments

Since a building (especially a tall building) oscillates with the participation of not only the fundamental but also higher modes of vibration, the evaluation of the *overturning moment* at a given level of the building should be made by a method of dynamic analysis.

The distribution of earthquake forces prescribed in the seismic codes primarily reflects the forces that may be developed by the dominant fundamental mode. Therefore it has been considered that the overturning moments computed by the distributed earthquake forces prescribed in the code may be conservative for the calculation of the axial loads from earthquake forces on vertical elements and footings.

In the seismic code of Canada, reduction factors of the overturning moment at any given level are prescribed. The value of the reduction increases with the increase of the fundamental period of vibration of the building, and also with the distance from the top of the building to the lower level under consideration.

6   Allowable Stress

When an elastic analysis is used, the allowable stresses of structural materials for combined dead, live, and earthquake loads are usually taken to be larger than the allowable stresses for dead and live loads alone. In most seismic codes the allowable stresses of structural materials are increased from 1/3 to 1/2. In some codes, allowable stresses are near the yield point.

In some countries, the ultimate strength design method may be used for seismic design of buildings. In this case an appropriate load factor (usually 1.3 to 1.5) is applied to the design earthquake forces.

7   Dynamic Analyses

The usual practice of dynamic analyses is to use either the earthquake response spectrum or time-history accelerograms as the basis of design.

Modal analysis procedures based on earthquake response spectra are prescribed in the seismic codes of India, France, Mexico, New Zealand, Peru, Romania, USSR, and Yugoslavia. In the modal analysis the maximum dynamic response is usually obtained by the method of "square root of sum of squares," taking the first three vibrational modes into consideration.

Dynamic analyses based on the time-history accelerograms of appropriate earthquakes are recommended for aseismic design of tall buildings in the seismic codes of India and Canada. In Japan dynamic analyses are commonly used for aseismic design of tall buildings over 45 m (148 ft) in height. The analyses are performed on a vibrational model simulating the actual system, using appropriate earthquake ground motions selected in consideration of the seismicity and ground condition of the site.

When the structural response obtained by the dynamic analysis is not satisfactory, the assumed structural model is modified and a revised response is computed. This procedure is repeated until a sound structural design of the building is accomplished. The seismic design criteria commonly applied for tall buildings in Japan are as follows.

The design base shear coefficient of tall buildings is usually in the range of $0.36T$ to $0.18T$, in which T = fundamental period of vibration of the building.

The main structural frame of the building is generally designed to remain in the elastic range considering earthquake motions with the maximum acceleration of 2.0 m/sec^2 to 3.5 m/sec^2 (6.5 ft/sec^2 to 11.5 ft/sec^2) in the Tokyo area. In this case, the maximum interstory drift is usually limited to 20 mm (0.8 in.). However, if seismic shear walls are provided in the frame, they are sometimes permitted to yield into the plastic range with a ductility factor of 2 or less. The elastoplastic response of the structure is sometimes examined by considering the maximum ground acceleration of 4.0 m/sec^2 to 5.0 m/sec^2 (13.1 ft/sec^2 to 16.4 ft/sec^2), and the shear force response in each story of the building should, in general, be kept below the ultimate story shear capacity.

2.9 CONDENSED REFERENCES/BIBLIOGRAPHY

The following is a condensed bibliography for this chapter. Not only does it include all articles referred to or cited in the text, but it also contains bibliography for further reading. The full citations will be found at the end of the Volume. What is given here should be sufficient information to lead the reader to the correct article: the author, date, and title. In case of multiple authors, only the first named is listed.

Amariei 1975, *Comparative Aspects with Regard to Earthquake Response of Structures*
Amin 1966, *A Nonstationary Stochastic Model for Strong-Motion Earthquakes*
Aoyama 1970, *A Study on the Cause of Damage to the Hachinohe Technical College*
Applied Technology Council 1978, *Tentative Provisions for the Development of Seismic*
Arias 1973, *Rating of Ground Motion*
Arya 1973, *Seismic Behavior and Design of Multi-Storied Steel Buildings*
Aycardi 1973, *Structural Behavior Under Seismic Load*

Berg 1964a, *The 1963 Skopje Earthquake*
Berg 1964b, *The Skopje, Yugoslavia Earthquake, July 26, 1963*
Berg 1964, *Anchorage and the Alaska Earthquake of March 27, 1964*
Bertero 1970, *Seismic Analysis of the Charaima Building Caraballeda, Venezuela*
Bertero 1973, *Ductility and Seismic Responses*
Bielak 1971, *Earthquake Response of Building-Foundation Systems*
Binder 1964, *The Acapulco, Mexico, Earthquakes of May 11 and May 19, 1962*
Blume 1960a, *A Reserve Energy Technique for the Design and Rating of Structures*
Blume 1960b, *Structural Dynamics in Earthquake Resistant Design*
Blume 1961, *Design of Multistory Reinforced Concrete Buildings for Earthquake Motions*
Blume 1967, *A Structural Dynamic Analysis of an Earthquake Damaged Fourteen-Story Building*
Blume 1968, *Dynamic Characteristics of Multistory Buildings*
Blume 1969a, *Response of Highrise Buildings to Ground Motion From Underground Nuclear*
Blume 1969b, *Structural Dynamics of Cantilever-Type Buildings*
Blume 1970, *The Motion and Damping of Buildings Relative to Seismic Response Spectra*
Blume 1971, *Building Columns Under Strong Earthquake Exposure*
Blume 1972, *Highrise Building Characteristics and Responses Determined from Nuclear*
Blume 1973, *Elements of a Dynamics-Inelastic Design Code*
Bubnov 1973, *Damage Evaluation*

California Institute of Technology 1972, *Analysis of Strong Motion Earthquake Accelerograms*
Carmona 1973, *Earthquake Effects on the Masonry of Multistory Buildings*
Carydis 1975, *Influence of the Discontinuity Along the Height of Multistory Frames*
Carydis 1975, *Response Spectra of Greek Strong Motion*
Castellani 1973, *Oscillations of a Tall Building, Due to Out of Phase Seismic Motions Along*
Chakravorty 1971, *Approximate Analysis of 3-DOF Model for Soil-Structure Interaction*
Ciesielski 1972, *Dynamical Problems in the Design of Tall Buildings*
Ciongradi 1975, *The Effect of Interaction Between Structure, Foundation and Soil*
Clough 1955, *On the Importance of Higher Modes of Vibration in the Earthquake Response*
Clough 1963, *Large Capacity Multistory Frame Analysis Programs*
Clough 1964, *Structural Analysis of Multistory Buildings*
Clough 1966, *Earthquake Stress Analysis in Earth Dams*
Clough 1974, *Earthquake Simulator Test of a Three Story Steel Frame Structure*
Cornell 1970, *Probabilistic Analysis of Damage to Structures Under Seismic Loads*

Degenkolb 1969, *The July 29, 1967, Venezuela Earthquake, Lessons for the Structural Engineer*
Del Corro Gutierrez 1973, *Calculations of the Earthquake Action According to the NTE ECS-1973*
Dezfulian 1969a, *Seismic Response of Soil Deposits Underlain by Sloping Rock Boundaries*
Dezfulian 1969b, *Response of Non-Uniform Soil Deposits to Travelling Seismic Waves*
Dibaj 1969a, *Nonlinear Seismic Response of Earth Structures*
Dibaj 1969b, *Response of Earth Dams to Travelling Seismic Waves*
Dimarogonas 1975, *A Transfer Matrix Approach for the Response of Tall Buildings to Real*
Dorwick 1977, *Earthquake Resistant Design*
Driskell 1968, *Mexico City Earthquake of 2nd August, 1968*
Duke 1973, *Economic and Social Aspects*

Earthquake Engineering Research Laboratory 1969–1971, *Strong-Motion Earthquake*
EERI Conference Proceedings 1973, *Managua, Nicaragua Earthquake of December 23, 1972*

EERI Reconnaissance Report 1973, *Managua, Nicaragua, Earthquake of December 23, 1972*
ESSA 1969, *Studies in Seismicity and Earthquake Damage Statistics, 1969*
Esteva 1969, *Lessons From Some Recent Earthquakes in Latin America*

Ferrante 1973, *Earthquake Loading*
Finn 1967, *Static and Seismic Analysis of Slopes*
Finn 1971, *The Effect of Foundation Soils on Seismic Response of Structures*
Fintel 1967, *Preliminary Report—Behavior of Reinforced Concrete Structures in the Caracas*
Funabashi 1969, *Vibration Tests and Test to Failure of a 7 Storied Building Survived a Severe*

Gellert 1972, *The Influence of Axial Load on Eigen-Frequencies of a Vibrating Lateral Restraint*
Giangreco 1974, *On the Seismic Behavior of Tall Buildings and Other Related Structural Types*
Glück 1973, *Torsional-Flexural Vibration of Multi-Story Structures*
Greco 1972, *The Seismic Response of Plane Framed Structures of Any Shape*
Greco 1973, *Trends in the Modern Code*
Group for Dynamic Tests of High-Rise Buildings 1969, *Summarized Report on Dynamic Tests*
Gutenberg 1954, *Seismicity of the Earth*

Hanson 1967, *The Venezuela Earthquake, July 29, 1967*
Hart 1974, *High-Rise Building Response: Damping and Period Nonlinearities*
Hart 1975, *Torsional Response and Design of Buildings*
Herrera 1965, *Response Spectra on Stratified Soil*
Higashi 1974, *Synthetic Research on Earthquake Resistant Characteristics of Reinforced*
Hisada 1971a, *Earthquake Loading and Response Criteria*
Hisada 1971b, *Earthquake Loading and Response Criteria*
Hisada 1971c, *Earthquake Resistant Design of High-Rise Buildings in Japan*
Hisada 1973, *Loading and Response Criteria and Code Requirements*
Housner 1947, *Characteristics of Strong-Motion Earthquakes*
Housner 1956, *Limit Design of Structures to Resist Earthquakes*
Housner 1963, *U.S. Atomic Energy Commission Report TID-7024*
Housner 1963, *Natural Periods of Vibration of Buildings*
Housner 1964, *Generation of Artificial Earthquakes*
Housner 1973, *Earthquake Ground Motion*
Hudson 1954, *Measured Response of a Structure to an Explosive-Generated Ground Shock*
Hudson 1971, *Strong-Motion Instrumental Data on the San Fernando Earthquake of February 9*
Husid 1974, *Earthquake Response Reduction in Buildings with an Elastoplastic Story*

IAEE 1960, *Proceedings of Second World Conference on Earthquake Engineering*
IAEE 1965, *Proceedings of Third World Conference on Earthquake Engineering*
IAEE 1969, *Proceedings of Fourth World Conference on Earthquake Engineering, Santiago*
IAEE 1973, 1976, *Earthquake Resistant Regulations—A World List*
ICBO 1970, *Uniform Building Code*
ICBO 1976, *Uniform Building Code*
ISO 1970, *Methods of Evaluating Design Earthquake Forces on Structures*
Idriss 1967, *Response of Earth Banks During Earthquakes*
Idriss 1968a, *Seismic Response of Horizontal Soil Layers*
Idriss 1968b, *An Analysis of Ground Motions During the 1957 San Francisco Earthquake*
Idriss 1969, *Computer Programs for Evaluating the Seismic Response of Soil Deposits*
Idriss 1970, *Seismic Response of Soil Deposits*
Izumi 1971, *Impact and Dynamic Load Effects*

Jacobsen 1939, *Natural Periods of Uniform Cantilever Beams*
Japan National Committee of IAEE 1965, *Niigata Earthquake of 1964*
Japan National Commitee of IAEE 1968, *Some Recent Earthquake Engineering Research*
Jennings 1969, *Earthquake Motions for Design Purposes*
Jennings 1971, *Engineering Features of the San Fernando Earthquake, February 9, 1971*
Juhasova 1973, *Dynamic Properties of Some Types of Framed Tall Buildings*

Kanai 1951, *Relation Between the Nature of Surface Layer and the Amplitudes of Earthquake Motions*
Kawasumi 1968, *General Report on the Niigata Earthquake of June 16, 1964*
Keintzel 1975, *Ductility and Safety of Shear Wall Tall Buildings in Seismic Regions*
Kenya Government Ministry of Works 1973, *Code of Practice for the Design and Construction*
Kobayashi 1966, *A Numerical Analysis of the Propagation of Shear Waves in Multi-Layered Ground*
Korenev 1973, *Dynamical Vibration Absorbers of Tall Buildings and Towers*
Kovacs 1971, *Studies of Seismic Response of Clay Banks*
Krishna 1973, *Aseismic Design of Buildings*

Krishna 1973, *Suitability of Tall Buildings in Seismic Zones*
Kunze 1965, *The March 27, 1964, Alaskan Earthquake*

Lew 1971, *Engineering Aspects of the 1971 San Fernando Earthquake*
Lord 1973, *Inelastic Dynamic Behavior of Tall Buildings*
Lysmer 1971, *Influence of Base-Rock Characteristics on Ground Response*

Matsumoto 1975, *The Sensitivity of Response Spectra for Dynamic Analyses of Tall Buildings*
Matthiesen 1964, *Site Characteristics of Southern California Strong-Motion Earthquake Stations*
Mazilu 1973, *Aseismic Design in Romania*
Meister 1937, *The Physiological Evaluation of Vibration Measurement*
Merritt 1954, *Effect of Foundation Compliance on Earthquake Stresses in Multistory Buildings*
Minami 1970, *Some Effects of Substructure Proportions and Adjacent Soil Interaction on the Seismic*
Murphy 1973, *San Fernando, California, Earthquake of February 9, 1971*
Muto 1971, *Strong Motion Records and Simulation Analysis of KII Building in San Fernando*
Muto 1974, *Aseismic Design and Post Construction Study*
Muto 1974, *Aseismic Design and Study of Tall Reinforced Concrete Buildings*
Muto 1974, *The Earthquake Resistant Installing Method of Telecommunication Instruments in High*

NOAA 1928–1977, *United States Earthquakes*
Nakagawa 1964, *Simple Consideration on Human Panic Problem in Case of Small Earthquake*
Narita 1974, *The Structural Design of Kaijo Building (Tokyo Marine and Fire Insurance Building)*
National Research Center for Disaster Prevention 1970, *Strong-Motion Earthquake Records in Japan*
National Research Council Committee on Alaska Earthquake 1973, *The Great Alaska Earthquake*
Nejman 1974, *Gravi-Stability of Tall Buildings*
Newmark 1969, *Torsion In Symmetrical Buildings*
Newmark 1971, *Fundamentals of Earthquake Engineering*
New Zealand Standard 1976, *Code of Practice for General Structural Design and Design Loadings*

Ogura 1971, *Part 1: Shear Design in New Recommendation of AIJ for Structural Design*
Ohsaki 1966, *Niigata Earthquakes, 1964 Building Damage and Soil Condition*
Ohsawa 1969, *Earthquake Measurements in and Around a Reinforced Concrete Building*
Ohsawa 1971, *Observation of Structural Behavior*
Ohsawa 1971, *Experimental Study of Structural Behavior*
Ohshima 1953, *Vibration and Human Beings*
Omote 1970, *Experiment and Research on the Response of the Model Structure Under Impact*

Penzien 1964, *Seismic Analysis of Bridges on Long Piles*
Pinkham 1973, *Evaluation of Earthquake Damage*
Polyakov 1969, *Investigations into Earthquake Resistance of Large-Panel Buildings*
Port and Harbor Research Institute 1978, *Annual Report on Strong-Motion Earthquake Records*

Rainer 1971, *Dynamic Ground Compliance in Multi-Story Buildings*
Rao 1974, *Stability of Foundations of Tall Structures Under Earthquakes*
Richter 1958, *Elementary Seismology*
Roesset 1969, *Theoretical Background for Amplification Studies*
Rosenblueth 1960, *The Earthquake of 28 July 1957, in Mexico City*
Rosenblueth 1969, *Response of Linear Systems to Certain Transient Disturbances*
Rothé 1969, *The Seismicity of the Earth*
Rubinstein 1964, *Effect of Axial Deformation on the Periods of a Tall Building*
Ruiz 1969, *Probabilistic Study of the Behavior of Structures During Earthquakes*
Ruscheweyh 1973, *Empirical Values of Natural Frequencies of Tall Buildings*

Sandi 1973, *Non-Synchronous Ground Motion*
Sara 1972, *Dimensioning of Framed Structure for Reinforced Concrete Buildings in Seismic Area*
Saragoni 1972, *Nonstationary Analysis and Simulation of Earthquake Ground Motion*
Saragoni 1973, *A New Kind of Ground Motion*
Saragoni 1974, *Simulation of Artificial Earthquakes*
Sarria Molina 1973, *Seismic History and Research*
Sawyer 1973, *Economic Basis for Seismic Resistance*
Schnabel 1972, *Accelerations in Rock for Earthquakes in the Western United States*
Seed 1967, *The Turnagain Heights Landslide, Anchorage, Alaska*
Seed 1969, *The Influence of Local Soil Conditions on Earthquake Damage*
Seed 1969, *Influence of Soil Conditions on Ground Motions During Earthquakes*
Seed 1969, *Characteristics of Rock Motions During Earthquakes*
Seed 1970a, *Analyses of Ground Motions at Union Bay, Seattle During Earthquakes and Distant*

Seed 1970b, *Relationships Between Soil Conditions and Building Damage in Caracas Earthquake*
Seed 1974, *Site Dependent Spectra for Earthquake-Resistant Design*
Seed 1975, *Relationships Between Maximum Acceleration, Maximum Velocity Distance*
Seismology Committee of the Structural Engineers Association of California 1975, *Recommended*
Shepherd 1973, *New Zealand Earthquake Provisions*
Shibata 1969, *Observation of Damages of Industrial Firms in Niigata Earthquake*
Shiga 1969, *The Experimental Study on the Dynamic Behavior of Reinforced Concrete Frames*
Sozen 1968, *Engineering Report on the Caracas Earthquake of 29 July 1967*
Sozen 1975, *Engineering Report on the Managua Earthquake of 23 December 1972*
Steinbrugge 1963, *A Structural Engineering Viewpoint (Chilean Earthquakes of May 1960)*
Steinbrugge 1969, *The Santa Rosa, California, Earthquakes of October 1, 1969*
Steinbrugge 1971, *San Fernando Earthquake, February 9, 1971*
Structural Engineers Association of Southern California 1972, *Post Earthquake Analysis*
Structural Standard Committee 1959, *Design Standard Value on Vibration Elimination of Building*
Suzuki 1971, *General Report on the Tokachi-Oki Earthquake of 1968*

Tajimi 1966, *New Type Two Axes Electrohydraulic Shaking Table by Seromechanism and Earthquake*
Tajimi 1974, *Aseismic Problems on a Tall Building Erected at a Site Underlain by an Inclined Base*
Takeda 1970, *Reinforced Concrete Response to Simulated Earthquakes*
Tamboli 1973, *Soil-Structure Systems*
Trigario 1973, *Some of the Problems Faced in the Design of a Multi-Floor Building*

U.S. Department of Commerce, NOAA, and EERI 1973, *The San Fernando, California Earthquake*
Ueda 1969, *Study on the Large Scale Displacement Vibration Test for the 1/25 Scale Model*

Valera 1968, *Seismic Interaction of Granular Soils and Rigid Retaining Structures*
Vanmarcke 1972, *Properties of Special Moments With Application to Random Vibration*

Wakabayashi 1973, *Core Design*
Wargon 1975, *Application of Post-Tensioning Techniques and Other Uses of Cables in High Rise*
Watabe 1975, *Seismic Loading and Response of Tall Buildings*
Whitman 1969, *Effect of Soil Conditions Upon Damage to Structures: Caracas Earthquake*
Whitman 1975, *Seismic Design Decision Analysis*
Wiegel 1970, *Earthquake Engineering*
Wiggins 1971, *Earthquake Safety in the City of Long Beach Based on the Concept*
Wong 1974, *Evaluation of Settlement Under Earthquake Loading of Buildings Founded in Granular*
Wood 1967, *The Prince William Sound, Alaska, Earthquake of 1964 and Aftershocks*
Wright 1973, *Building Performance in the 1972 Managua Earthquake*

Yamada 1971, *Effect of Cyclic Loading on Buildings*
Yamada 1974, *Aseismic Safety of Reinforced Concrete Buildings*
Yerlici 1974, *A Comparison of Earthquake Loads for a Tall Building Determined by Different*

Zeevaert 1957, *Latino Americana Building*
Zilch 1974, *Design of Structures for Earthquake Loads—A State of the Art Report*

Tall Building Criteria and Loading

Chapter CL-3

Wind Loading and Wind Effects

Prepared by Committee 7 (Wind Loading and Wind Effects) of the Council on Tall Buildings and Urban Habitat as part of the Monograph on the Planning and Design of Tall Buildings.

Alan G. Davenport   Committee Chairman
Sean Mackey   Vice-Chairman
William H. Melbourne   Editor

AUTHOR ACKNOWLEDGMENT

The essential first draft of this chapter is the work of A. G. Davenport and W. H. Melbourne. Its starting point was the set of the state-of-art reports from the 1972 International Conference, held at Lehigh University, prepared by:

J. E. Cermak	R. D. Marshall
P. W. Chen	W. H. Melbourne
W. A. Dalgliesh	J. Springfield
A. G. Davenport	L. K. Stevens
H. Ishizaki	H. van Koten
S. Mackey	T. A. Wyatt

CONTRIBUTORS

The following is a complete list of those who have submitted written material for possible use in the chapter, whether or not that material was used in the final version. The Committee Chairman and Editor were given quite complete latitude. Frequently length limitations precluded the inclusion of much valuable material. The Bibliography contains all contributions. The contributors are: J. Blessmann, J. E. Cermak, P. W. Chen, W. A. Dalgliesh, A. G. Davenport, K. J. Eaton, H. Ishizaki, M. Ito, S. Mackey, R. D. Marshall, J. R. Mayne, W. H. Melbourne, C. Scruton, J. Springfield, C. Spyropoulos, L. K. Stevens, B. F. Thomas, H. van Koten, B. J. Vickery, R. E. Whitbread, T. A. Wyatt.

COMMITTEE MEMBERS

S. B. Barnes, M. R. Barstein, J. Blessmann, M. Castanheta, J. E. Cermak, A. L. Chasteau, P. W. Chen, A. N. Chiu, R. Ciesielski, C. Ciray, A. P. Colin, W. A. Dalgliesh, A. G. Davenport, R. G. Dean, C. L. Dym, R. Estrada, B. H. Hellers, I. W. Huisman, H. Ishizaki, M. Ito, J. Kozak, B. M. Leadon, G. Macchi, S. Mackey, R. J. Mainstone, C. Manuzio, R. D. Marshall, J. R. Mayne, W. H. Melbourne, A. Negoita, N. M. Newmark, D. Olivari, R. A. Parmelee, H. Paschen, D. C. Perry, M. Pirner, H. Ruehle, G. I. Schueller, C. Scruton, D. Sfintesco, A. G. Sokolov, J. Springfield, C. Spyropoulos, L. K. Stevens, T. N. Subba Rao, A Tedesko, H. van Koten, B. J. Vickery, R. E. Whitbread, T. A. Wyatt, E. Zeller, J. Zielinski.

Wind Loading and Wind Effects

3.1 INTRODUCTION

The purpose of this chapter is to survey the significant features of the interaction of a tall building with the wind. Such a survey will identify design problems and some criteria, and indicate the approaches available for making quantitative estimates of key design parameters. Reasons for requiring a more rational and refined approach to the wind loading of tall buildings have recently become more compelling. The new opportunities for more carefully tailored design afforded by: (1) Development of new architectural forms and structural systems; (2) the introduction of a broader range of materials, especially higher strength steels and concrete; (3) the formulation of new methods of analysis; and (4) last but not least, the application of the computer to both the design and analytical processes, have created a demand for a more exact description of the wind loading, which more traditional approaches cannot always supply.

The traditional approach to wind loading that has been used in conjunction with the design of tall buildings and other structures assumes the wind pressure to act in a steady fashion. This is convenient in that it allows the appropriate coefficients of pressure to be estimated from wind tunnel tests carried out in a uniform steady velocity in a wind tunnel. The velocity used in design has been variously determined from maximum gust speeds, or from average velocities measured over a minute or a "mile of wind," depending on the nature of the routine meteorological measurements. There is usually an adjustment for the variation of velocity with height which is sometimes based on the maximum gust variation with height and sometimes on the mean speed variation with height. The resulting pressures usually are in the range 1.0 kPa to 2.5 kPa (20 lb/ft² to 50 lb/ft²) and are applied to various elements of the structure such as the main frame and the glass. For many types of structures higher stresses are normally permitted when combining wind with other loads.

Although convenient, this quasi-steady approach to wind loading is unrealistic in several respects. Furthermore, there is a need for broadening the basis of design against wind to include more explicitly such factors as allowable deflections, comfort of occupants, and fatigue of the frame, as well as strength. The diversity of

145

structures now being built makes the problem of formulating wind loads using simplified umbrella loadings more and more difficult if at the same time they are to be economical and satisfactory from a performance standpoint.

It should be noted that a full description of the wind loading process crosses several scientific disciplines. In the first place it relies on an adequate description of the wind climate from meteorological records. It requires an understanding of the atmospheric boundary layers, turbulence properties and the variation of wind speed with height; of the aerodynamic forces produced by the interaction of the body with the turbulent boundary layer; and of the dynamic response of the structure to wind forces, which in certain instances may involve problems of aerodynamic instability. Finally, the response of each element has to be gaged in the light of the measures and criteria of acceptable performance, and this analysis requires a probabilistic approach.

There have been four International Conferences on Wind Effects on Buildings and Structures, in 1963, 1967, 1971, and 1975. Their Proceedings can serve to provide a background to this chapter. In addition, two review papers are particularly relevant, the Theme Report at the Lehigh Conference by Davenport (1973) and the Freeman Scholar Lecture by Cermak (1975).

3.2   DESIGN PROBLEMS AND CRITERIA

1   Early Studies

Although the first studies of wind action of tall buildings date back to at least the turn of the century, the most substantial studies, it appears, were made around 1930 coinciding with a boom in skyscraper construction. These studies and their discussion in the technical literature identified many of the major problems and

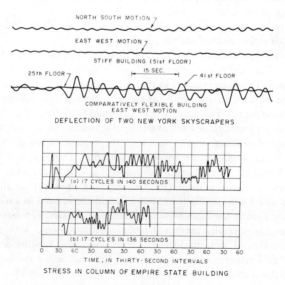

Fig. 3.1 Response of tall buildings *(Coyle, 1931)*

resulted in static design methods similar to those referred to previously.

Dynamic sway and vibration in taller buildings were discussed at length and measured in several buildings by Coyle (1931) and later Rathbun (1940) using horizontal pendulums and vertical plumb bobs hung down vertical shafts. A selection of these measurements is shown in Fig. 3.1. In describing the observations on the Empire State Building, Rathbun (1940) states that the "building tended to vibrate continuously like the tines of a tuning fork." All the traces show that the sway motion occurs primarily in what turns out to be the fundamental frequency of the building, with little evidence of the higher harmonics. The importance of stiffness in controlling this motion was recognized and, during the 1930s, various empirical deflection limits—such as 1/500 of the building height—were proposed. Spurr in his influential treatise on "Wind Bracing" stated somewhat pessimistically, however, that "the whole question of vibration in buildings from the effect of variable wind pressures is complicated by the indeterminate nature of the pressures themselves as well as by the great variation in size, shape, weight, height and location of buildings." Today this crucial problem of predicting vibration is more tractable, as indicated here.

2 Response to Wind Action

Contrary to the traditional notions of static wind pressure, the wind pressure actually measured on buildings fluctuates with significant energy. The windward pressures are generally positive and the amplitude of fluctuating pressures large. The leeward wake pressures in contrast are negative and relatively calm. The pressures on the side walls, measured in the wake just to the rear of the separation points, are negative with large amplitude fluctuations. These pressure fluctuations vary randomly not only in time but also in space, over the faces of the building. Examples of pressure fluctuations are given in Fig. 3.2 taken from full-scale measurements on the CIBC Building in Montréal by Dalgleish (1971).

While the design of cladding may be strongly influenced by local pressures, the response of the building as a whole is dependent on the integrated effect of the pressures over the various faces. The nature of these integrated responses is discussed in detail in Section 3.4. It is concluded there that the prediction of response can be divided into: (1) The response to mean wind speeds and their

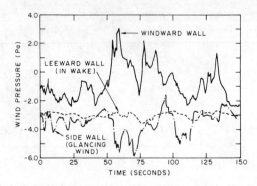

Fig. 3.2 Typical wind pressures on cladding of CIBC building, Montréal, Canada *(Dalgleish, 1971)*

associated directions; and (2) the maximum dynamic response of the structure due to a given mean wind, which will usually be related to an oscillation in the fundamental mode. Wind is responsible for a variety of design problems to be enumerated in the following Articles.

3 Progression Towards Collapse of Structural Frame in Wind

It is significant that there appear to be no reports of completed tall buildings having collapsed due to wind action. A few have collapsed during erection, and an example is shown in Fig. 3.3. One of the few cases of severe damage is the Meyer-Kiser Building shown in Figs. 3.4 and 3.5. This occurred during the Miami hurricane of 1926. The cladding was severely damaged and the steel frame deformed plastically; occupants reported severe swaying throughout the storm. More recently the Great Plains Life Building in Lubbock, Texas, of similar proportions to the Meyer-Kiser Building, suffered similarly in a tornado; cladding was damaged, the frame distorted, and swaying reported, but the building did not collapse.

The progression towards a state of complete collapse is a complicated process.

To describe the process fully, account must be taken of the static and dynamic character of the loading in the torsional and two transverse directions, the load deformation characteristics of the building including both the ductility and second-order axial effects, the participation and eventual breakdown of archi-

Fig. 3.3 Collapse of steel frame building under construction, Toronto, Canada; August 9, 1958
(Photo by J. Lynch, Federal News Photos Canada, Ltd.)

Fig. 3.4 Damage to Meyer-Kiser building in 1926 hurricane at Miami, Florida *(Schmitt, 1926)*

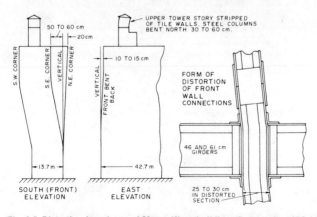

Fig. 3.5 Distortion in column of Meyer-Kiser building *(Davenport, 1972a)*

tectural finishes and cladding, the fatigue behavior of the joints, and the "feedback" of all these effects on the dynamic nature of the loading itself. In the final analysis, a tall building under the action of wind will reach a state of collapse by the action of the axial dead load. As the wind strength increases, the deflection produced increases the eccentricity of the dead loads to the point at which the so-called P-Δ effect topples the building. On the way, architectural finishes will have either cracked or yielded, losing their capacity to sustain load, plastic hinges will have progressively formed at column beam connections throughout the structure, and the low-cycle fatigue may have damaged some members.

Hence, an important criterion in the wind loading of tall buildings is that predicted wind loads will lie well below the value of the load corresponding to the limit of stability (Stevens, 1967). It is also important to know the structure stiffness, indicated by the slope of the load-drift curve shown in Fig. 3.6.

For a given building it generally turns out that while the mean moment due to wind effects is dependent only on the square of the wind speed, $\bar{u}^2$, the fluctuating moment tends to increase more rapidly than $\bar{u}^2$; it increases somewhat with a power of the period ($T_0 = 1/n_0$) generally in the range 0 to 2, and decreases with increase in the damping, roughly proportional to (damping)$^{-1/2}$.

Returning to Fig. 3.6, as the wind load increases so also the stiffness tends to "soften" and the period increases; at the same time the damping increases. Vickery (1970) has suggested that the damping increases from the range 0.005 to 0.02 for small amplitudes to 0.04 to 0.10 for amplitudes close to yield. It turns out that these two effects more or less compensate each other and the response can be more or less predicted by the line assuming constant period and constant damping.

It is important to note that for predicting the collapse performance of a structure, the axial dead load can have a vital effect. Not only does it supply the final coup de grace, but it can significantly reduce the period of vibration. The latter in turn has the effect of increasing the effective dynamic loading and reducing the stiffness. In short, once a certain flexibility is reached, the trend towards impending instability may be quite rapid.

There are various other characteristics of the progression to collapse. In many

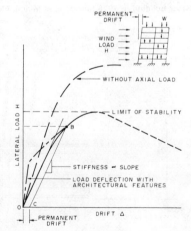

Fig. 3.6 Failure under wind action *(Davenport, 1975a)*

buildings architectural finishes provide a significant source of stiffness if not of strength. This is on the whole not desirable, because the more rigid these finishes, the more resistance they "attract," and the earlier they will crack and crumble. While it is difficult to estimate the degree of participation of the architectural finishes, the effect is unmistakable. Measurements of vibration periods made before, during, and following the San Fernando earthquake in California on buildings subject to severe shaking indicate periods substantially longer during the earthquake than before; the period after is shorter than during the earthquake, but the recovery is far from complete. Representative periods for these three conditions are 0.90 sec, 1.40 sec, and 1.05 sec.

The implication is that, following moderate shaking, as might be the case in a windstorm, little reliance should be placed on any stiffness which at small amplitudes may accrue from the architectural finishes and secondary components of the structure. The permanent set which can result if a structure only deflects to point B in Fig. 3.6 is shown by the columns in Fig. 3.5.

In those cases where the structure is fairly rigid, the structure may then appear to behave in an idealized elastoplastic manner. Vickery (1970) has examined this problem and has concluded that, to produce significant cumulative permanent set, the mean wind speed needs to be about 20% greater than that needed to produce yielding.

Wyatt and May (1971) studied wind-induced plastic deformation in some inelastic structures by numerical simulation methods, and concluded "that the expectation of plastic damage can in many cases be predicted from the results given, and a ductile structure can thus be designed for a lower strength than would be safe in an otherwise brittle structure, provided other criteria are still satisfied."

Rough estimates indicate that current design procedures correspond to a failure rate, for the building as a whole, on the order of 1/100 000 in a 100-yr life.

4 Excessive Deflections and Damage to Architectural Finishes

Excessive deflections are directly related to several problems, in particular the damage to architectural finishes and partitions, and distortion of mechanical equipment such as elevator rails. In those cases where no deliberate care is taken to isolate the architectural finishes from the structural frame (by expansion joints or gaps) there is fairly adequate experience to suggest that most masonry cannot take

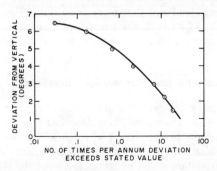

Fig. 3.7 Specification for performance of antenna *(Davenport, 1975a)*

racking shear distortions greater than about 1/500 without showing some distress; this rule has been used in New York for many years and seems to have proved satisfactory. Behavior which might result in distortions greater than this might therefore usefully be limited to roughly a 1/100 to 1/10 chance of recurrence in a 10-yr "maintenance cycle."

In another context, deflections (or more precisely rotation) can be a serious limitation on the performance of television and radio antennas now commonly mounted on tall buildings. The performance criteria for these structures is occasionally defined in terms of the number of recurrences allowed as a function of amplitude. A typical curve is shown in Fig. 3.7. This is representative of a variety of response-recurrence curves.

5   Cladding and Glass Design—Stack Effect Internal Pressures

In recent years glass and cladding design have been a source of major concern. Although of less consequence than collapse of the main structure, damage to glass nevertheless has its hazards and costs, as exemplified by the Great Plains Life Building, Fig. 3.8(a). A less expensive example of cladding failure is the Travelodge in Darwin, Australia, after Cyclone Tracy [Fig. 3.8(b)]. Use of very large window lights and panels incurs greater danger to pedestrians when breakage does occur (see Fig. 3.9).

The actual mechanism of breakage can be complicated. Some types of glass are susceptible to both solar radiation and wind pressure. Sealing and mullion detailing can be influential, as can the tempering and the glazing, whether double glazed or single. Repeated loading can produce a form of fatigue due to an accumulation of very high stress. Failure in glass usually starts at nicks or scratches in the glass: these can be caused by carelessly handled debris during construction or, during a wind storm, by flying gravel from roofs or even by broken glass from other floors.

It seems appropriate to suggest that damage of more than one window in 1000 in a 10-yr period would be a desirable expectation—although this will depend greatly on the building type and the size of the window.

An associated problem in the prediction of pressures for cladding design is the stack effect and the effect of air handling equipment and leakage on the internal pressures. As well as being important for cladding design itself, these additional pressures can be significant in the design of certain partitions, roofing, fire and smoke control, and air conditioning.

The Wind Loading Handbook (Newberry and Eaton, 1974), written as a guide to the British Wind Code CP3 1972, has a wealth of illustrations identifying cladding failures and a commentary on many of the causes, as also has Saffir (1975).

6   Comfort of Occupants and Acceleration Threshold

Comfort of occupants has been a major source of concern in the design of tall buildings. Robertson and Chen (1967) have described experiments to determine the threshold of perception to the very low frequency movements found in tall buildings; the results are shown in Fig. 3.10. Yamada and Goto (1975) have also discussed criteria in motion in tall buildings, including the effect of head motion. Reference should also be made to Chapters SB-5, CB-9, and PC-13.

It appears unavoidable that these thresholds will be exceeded during the life of a

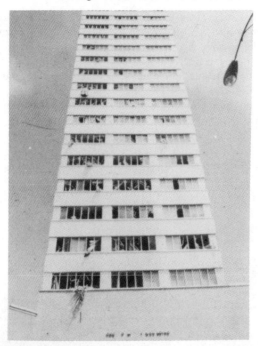

Fig. 3.8a South elevation of Great Plains Life Building, Lubbock, Texas. Glazing damage was particularly severe on southwest corner of building *(Somes et al., 1971)*

Fig. 3.8b Failure of brick facade on the Travelodge in Darwin, Australia after Cyclone Tracy

structure. The questions then arise, what response will be tolerated, and how frequently? Robertson (1973) has suggested the use of an "Occupant Sensitivity Quotient" to define the comfort limitation. This is the ratio of the expected acceleration to the mean threshold acceleration at the particular frequency of the structure. This can be related to the full-scale observations by Hansen et al. (1973) as indicated in Fig.3.11.

From these results some indication can be derived of the profile of structural response which is acceptable from the viewpoint of occupant comfort.

Fig. 3.9 Falling cladding panel during storm at Brighton, England, 1974 *(Photo by Brighton Evening Argus)*

7   Wind in Pedestrian Areas

It is now recognized that unpleasantly strong wind conditions at pedestrian levels in built-up urban areas can result from a variety of phenomena. The obstruction to the wind flow caused by buildings significantly taller than their surroundings can deflect faster moving air at greater heights down to street level. Narrow streets and "slots" between adjacent tall buildings can produce Venturi effects causing acceleration and focusing of wind currents. The fast flow of air past flat surfaces can generate roller-type vortices at breaks in the surface, such as those occurring at the leeward corners of buildings; these vortices with their axes vertical can produce strong eddies extending down to street level. These aerodynamic phenomena are frequently very sensitive to wind direction. The street level wind climate can be adversely affected if these sensitive directions are alined with the prevailing wind direction.

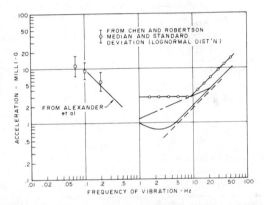

Fig. 3.10 Threshold of perception to horizontal motion *(Chen and Robertson, 1972)*

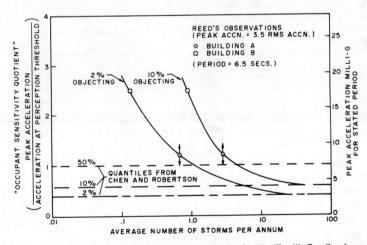

Fig. 3.11 Comparison of Robertson's "Occupant Sensitivity Quotient" with Reed's observations *(Davenport, 1975a)*

While in recent years progress has been made in the development of methodologies for both prediction and alleviation, there are, unfortunately, no simple methods presently available for reliably predicting the likely ensuing wind climate. Furthermore, realistic criteria of acceptability are still developing. There is, nevertheless, sufficient information to give positive indications of what appears to be generally workable.

The most reliable method of assessing wind climate is organized around testing in an appropriate wind tunnel. It is, however, a necessary step that such tests be combined with meteorological information, so that the important influence of the prevailing wind direction in exacerbating the problem can be assessed. (Conversely, if these "sensitive" directions are alined with wind direction for which the incidence of stronger wind is infrequent, the results may not be serious.) The wind tunnel

Table 3.1 (a) Tentative comfort criteria for windiness (*Davenport, 1972b; Aynsley et al., 1976*)[a]

Activity (1)	Areas applicable (2)	Relative comfort			
		Perceptible (3)	Tolerable (4)	Unpleasant (5)	Dangerous (6)
Walking fast	sidewalks	5	6	7	8
Strolling, skating	parks, entrances, skating rinks	4	5	6	8
Standing, sitting —short exposure	parks, plaza areas	3	4	5	8
Standing, sitting —long exposure	outdoor restaurants, bandshells, theaters	2	3	4	8
Representative criteria for acceptability			<1 occasion per week	<1 occasion per month	<1 occasion per year

[a]Units: Beaufort Number. Temperatures > 10°C (48°F).

At lower temperatures relative comfort level might be expected to be reduced by one unit for every 20°C reduction in temperature.

Table 3.1 (b) Relationship between Beaufort Number and wind speed in meters per second

Beaufort Number	1	2	3	4	5	6	7	8
Mean wind speed in range at 10 m height in open country	0.9	2.4	4.4	6.7	9.3	12.4	15.5	18.9
Gust speed at 2 m height from $\hat{V}_2 = \bar{V}_{10}\,1.5 \times 0.8$	1	3	5	8	11	15	19	23
Mean wind speed in range at 2 m height in city area from $\bar{V}_2 = 0.5\,\hat{V}_2$	0.5	1.5	2.5	4	5.5	7.5	9.5	11.5

study should be carried out in a wind tunnel capable of reflecting certain qualities of the natural wind, including its turbulence and variation of velocity with height. The procedures used for wind tunnel testing of environmental conditions are discussed in Section 3.8.

In any study of wind conditions, it follows that a set of criteria for wind conditions must be adopted. Previous research by Wise (1971), Melbourne (1971a), Davenport (1972b), and others has given us some indications. These are summarized in Table 3.1 and provide a framework of limits within which to operate. Valuable psychological experiments on human response to wind have been described by Hunt et al. (1976). With reference to Table 3.1(b), note that the relationship between mean wind speeds and peak gust speeds is discussed further in Article 3 of Section 3.8.

8 Other Problems

The designer must take into account many other problems partly associated with wind, which will be covered in later sections. The most significant of these are: (1) Combined effects of wind and temperature; (2) the aerodynamic contribution to noise; (3) the erosion, scouring, and penetration of wind-driven rain; and (4) the disposal of effluents and intake pollution.

9 Statistical Description of Design Criteria

The objective of any design approach to wind loading must be the prediction of those modes of structural performance which in one way or another impair the serviceability of the structure. It is emphasized that the prediction of the effects of wind can only be expressed statistically. While it is not possible to predict the exact time or severity of a storm, it is possible nevertheless to estimate the average rate of occurrence—assuming that the past climatic processes are representative of the future. It is possible to estimate the average rate at which specific levels of response recur. Conceptually the situation can be summarized in a response-recurrence diagram such as Fig. 3.12.

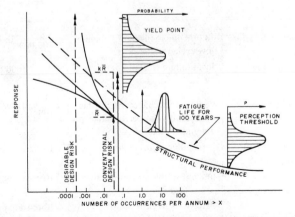

Fig. 3.12 **Response recurrence diagram and structural criteria** *(Davenport, 1972d)*

It follows that any criteria governing the performance must also be expressed in terms of acceptable ratio of recurrence, even if these are extremely small. Ideally these will be explicitly defined (by the client or alternatively by the code). The tentative recurrence ratios suggested are summarized in Table 3.2 (Davenport, 1972a). In most situations prediction of final performance intimately involves other statistics, such as those governing the strength of materials or the perception of people to movement; these features are indicated in Fig. 3.11. Basic to this prediction, however, is a description of the response recurrence to wind, which will be dealt with in much greater detail in the following sections.

Summarizing, the prediction of the response of tall buildings can be subdivided into: (1) The prediction of the occurrence of various mean wind speeds and their associated directions; and (2) given the occurrence of that wind, the prediction of the maximum dynamic response of the structure. The first constitutes a climatological problem; the second is an aerodynamic or aeroelastic problem involving both the steady and fluctuating response to the turbulent wind.

The dominant problems in the design of tall buildings are concerned with the following phases:

1. (a) The assessment of the wind climate of the region.

    (b) The adjustment of the wind climate to take account of the local topography of the site; the assessment of local wind structure (mean velocity profile and turbulence structure).

2. (a) The determination of the steady pressures and forces due to the mean wind.

    (b) The determination of the dynamic response of the structure.

Table 3.2 Effects of wind on tall buildings and tentative design criteria (*Davenport, 1972a*)

Effect (1)	Nature of Unserviceability (2)	Recurrence Rate (3)
Stresses in primary structure	failure due to instability, high or low cycle fatigue	$< \dfrac{1}{100,000}$ in 100-yr life
Forces on exterior skin	local failure of cladding or glass	< 1 per 1000 panes in 10-yr period
Deflection of structure	damage to architectural finishes, deterioration of performance of antenna structures	$< \dfrac{1}{100}$ in 10-yr period
Dynamic sway of structure	perceptible to occupants	< 1 occasion per 10 yr
Windiness in pedestrian precincts	uncomfortable to pedestrians	< 10 occasions per 1 yr
Windiness in pedestrian precincts	dangerous to pedestrians	< 1 occasion per 1 yr

(c) The determination of the fluctuating pressures on the exterior of the building.

(d) The evaluation of environmental problems.

3.3   METEOROLOGICAL FACTORS IN THE DESIGN OF TALL BUILDINGS

1   Scales of Motion

The motion of the atmosphere, as it is manifested by the wind, is compounded of air movements of a wide range of scales. On the very large scale there are seasonal fluctuations in the wind. On a scale comparable with the weather maps seen in the press or used by airlines there are large-scale synoptic fluctuations identified by the patterns of isobars moving across the country. On a still smaller scale are fluctuations which are best observed on high-speed anemometer records. Such a record is shown in Fig. 3.13, which was obtained from three instruments mounted on a tall mast.

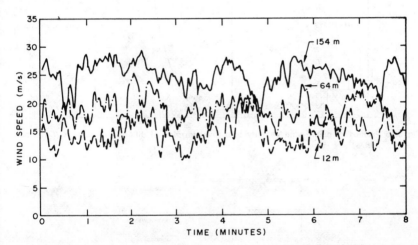

Fig. 3.13 Record of wind speed at three heights on a mast in open terrain, East Scale, Australia *(Deacon, 1955)*

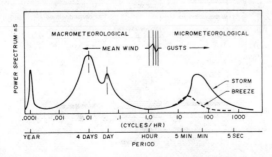

Fig. 3.14 Idealization of the wind speed spectrum over an extended frequency range *(Van der Hoven, 1957)*

It is convenient for analytical purposes to separate the widely different scales of fluctuations into two categories. The large-scale fluctuations, down to the scale of weather map fluctuations, will be referred to as fluctuations in the mean velocity. Fluctuations of a much smaller character, such as those appearing in the anemometer record, will be referred to as gusts.

It has been shown by Van der Hoven's (1957) analysis of the wind speed spectrum that a region of low energy exists between these two major energy containing scales, as shown in Fig. 3.14. The existence of a spectral gap centered about a period of approximately half an hour, discussed in some detail by Davenport (1967a), has provided a convenient period to which a mean wind speed can be referenced which reflects only synoptic variations. The period chosen should be long enough to minimize nonstationarities within the period, and if possible short enough to reflect

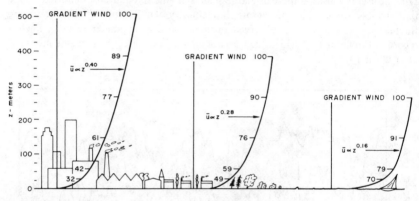

Fig. 3.15 Profiles of mean wind velocity over level terrains of differing roughness *(Davenport, 1967a)*

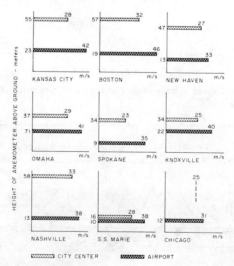

Fig. 3.16 Comparison of 1-in-50-year wind speeds at airports and city meteorological stations in United States *(Davenport 1967d)*

short-term storm activity like thunderstorms. A period from ten minutes to one hour seems to represent a suitable period to define the mean wind speed and other variables, such as the response of a tall building, so that they can be classified into two main groupings: (1) Those associated with the mean wind speed, which are conveniently described as static, time-averaged loads; and (2) those associated with the gustiness or turbulence of the wind, which are predominantly dynamic in character. The properties of the mean flow and gusts are now described separately.

2 Properties of the Mean Wind

Reference to Fig. 3.13 suggests that the mean wind speed at each of the three heights remains more or less constant throughout the period of record and gust fluctuations take place about this mean. A further feature revealed by this record is that the magnitude of the mean velocity increases with height. This increase of the mean velocity with height is a fairly well understood phenomenon, along with the influence of the roughness of the terrain. It has been discussed in detail by Davenport (1960, 1963) and is summarized here.

This variation of velocity with height is best considered as a gradual retardation of the wind nearer the ground due to surface friction. At heights great enough for the wind to be virtually independent of surface friction the wind moves freely under the influence of the pressure gradient and attains the so-called gradient velocity. The height at which this occurs is the gradient height. Fig. 3.15 suggests typical mean velocity profiles for a nominal gradient wind speed of 100. This shows that the wind speed at 30 m (98 ft) in a city is less than half of that in open country. This reduction in velocity in a city is well confirmed by the values in Fig. 3.16, which compares the wind speeds in cities and their local airports in the United States. Although anemometers in the city are generally mounted higher above ground than at the airport, the mean wind speed is seen to be invariably lower.

The classical fluid mechanics representation of the change of velocity $\bar{u}$ with height z uses a logarithmic profile which can be written in the alternative forms

$$\frac{\bar{u}_z}{u_*} = \frac{1}{k} \ln\left(\frac{z}{z_o}\right) \tag{3.1}$$

or

$$\frac{\bar{u}_z}{\bar{u}_{\text{ref}}} = \frac{1}{k} \sqrt{\kappa} \ln\left(\frac{z}{z_o}\right) \tag{3.2}$$

or

$$\frac{\bar{u}_z}{\bar{u}_g} = \frac{1}{k} C_g \ln\left(\frac{z}{z_o}\right) \tag{3.3}$$

in which $u_* = \sqrt{\tau_o/\rho}$ = friction velocity; τ_o = surface shear stress; ρ = air density; z_o = roughness length of the surface; k = von Kármán's constant (≈ 0.4 when using natural logarithms); $\varkappa = \tau_o/\rho\bar{u}_{\text{ref}}^2 = (u_*/\bar{u}_{\text{ref}})^2$ is the surface drag coefficient based on a mean velocity at a reference height, $\bar{u}_{\text{ref}}$, usually 10 m (33 ft); and C_g = geostrophic drag coefficient. The value of C_g can be estimated from

$$C_g \approx 0.16 \left(\frac{\bar{u}_g}{f_c z_o} \right)^{-0.09}$$

in which $f_c = 1.452 \times 10^{-4} \sin \lambda \ sec^{-1}$ = the Coriolis parameter, and λ = latitude.

Alternatively, the variation of velocity with height can be expressed as a power law of the form

$$\frac{\bar{u}_z}{\bar{u}_g} = \left(\frac{z}{z_g} \right)^a$$

in which $\bar{u}_z$ = mean velocity at height z; $\bar{u}_g$ = mean velocity at the gradient height z_g; and a = exponent depending on surface roughness as shown in Fig. 3.15.

Although the logarithmic profile is the more rigorously based and generally accepted description of the mean velocity profile of rough wall turbulent boundary layers, it lacks the simple convenience of the empirical power law where the essential information is carried in the value of the exponent a. It should be noted in this context that a value of the roughness length z_o, while having typical values for given full-scale situations as shown in Table 3.3, does not uniquely define a boundary layer mean velocity profile in the absence of a definition of the geometry of the roughness elements (including density) and shear stress information such as that given by the friction velocity or surface drag coefficient. A further discussion on the power law-logarithmic law relationship is given by Ishizaki (1971a) and Simiu (1973a).

Table 3.3 Typical properties of mean velocity profiles in atmospheric boundary layer

Terrain (1)	Gradient height z_g, in meters (2)	Power law exponent a (3)	Surface drag coefficient based on $\bar{u}_{10m}$ $\varkappa$ (4)	Roughness length z_o, in millimeters (5)
Rough sea	250	0.12	0.001	5 to 10
Open grassland	300	0.16	0.005	10 to 100
Forest and suburban areas	400	0.28	0.015	300 to 1000
City centers	500	0.40	0.050	1000 to 5000

Table 3.4 Depth of internal boundary layer at a transition in roughness

Transition (1)	z_{o_1}, in meters (2)	z_{o_2}, in meters (3)	Fetch distance		
			50 meters	500 meters	5000 meters
Open country—suburb	0.02	0.20	11	70	450
Suburb—city center	0.20	2.0	19	110	700
Suburb—open country	0.20	0.02	9	55	350
City center—suburb	2.0	0.20	13	90	500

3   Change of Terrain Roughness

If the roughness of the terrain changes abruptly—as for example from open prairie to suburban development, or vice versa—the flow in the boundary layer goes through a gradual transition. The upstream velocity profile gradually adjusts to the downstream profile. Near the ground the situation is much as is shown in Fig. 3.17, in which, as indicated, the roughness length of the surface changes from upstream z_{o_1} to z_{o_2} downstream. At the edge of the two surfaces an internal boundary layer develops. This separates the flow regime whose profile has adjusted to the downstream surface from the outer flow, which up to that point has not been affected by the new surface.

Elliott (1958) has developed a general approach to the transition problem and has given a relationship between the thickness of the internal boundary layer δ and the downstream fetch distance x as

$$\frac{\delta}{z_{o_2}} = A \left(\frac{x}{z_{o_2}}\right)^{0.8} \tag{3.4}$$

in which A = a slowly varying function of the roughness length ratio z_{o_2}/z_{o_1}

$$A = 0.75 - 0.03 \log_e \frac{z_{o_2}}{z_{o_1}} \tag{3.5}$$

Typical values of the depth of the internal boundary layer δ as a function of the fetch distance x are given in Table 3.4. These suggest the full depth of the boundary layer is reached in less than 5 km (3.1 miles).

More recent work has been reviewed and extended by Plate (1971) and Pasquill (1972).

4   Cyclones, Tropical Cyclones, Tornadoes, and Thunderstorms

The description of boundary layer winds has in meteorological terms been generally applicable to storms whose origin is an extensive mature pressure system or cyclone, as they are loosely described. Other storm origins are worth noting at this stage.

Tropical cyclones or hurricanes (as they are known in American regions), and typhoons (as they are known in Asian regions), are mature pressure systems with a difference in that they originate over large warm bodies of water and derive their

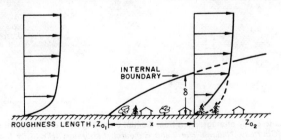

Fig. 3.17 Development of internal boundary at roughness discontinuity

energy from latent heat released by the condensing of water vapor. They are a cyclonic low pressure system with strong vertical vorticity rotating counterclockwise in the northern hemisphere and clockwise in the southern hemisphere, when viewed from above. The entire system (up to several hundred kilometers in radius) translates in a random fashion with speeds in the range 0 to 10 m/s. As they approach the coast they bring strong winds, heavy rain and tidal surges, and in many regions of the world between the 10th and 30th parallels, north and south, are responsible for the extreme wind speeds. Once over land, the cyclone is deprived of the warm water energy source, and wind speeds begin to decay, reducing generally by about 30% to 40% in the first 150 km (94 miles) travel over land (Cermak, 1974). A photograph of the cloud formation identifying Hurricane Betsy is shown in Fig. 3.18.

Tornadoes are a most intense atmospheric singularity with highly concentrated vertical vorticity, and lesser forms are known as waterspouts and dust-devils. They range up to 3000 m (10 000 ft) in diameter, and have maximum wind speeds up to 150 m/s (500 ft/sec). A review of tornadoes is given by Cermak (1974) in which he included Figs. 3.19 and 3.20 to illustrate the characteristics of tornadoes.

Thunderstorms have their genesis in the local initial uplift of warm, moisture-

Fig. 3.18 Hurricane Betsy photographed from Gemini 5 at 18 km (11 mi) elevation on 3 September 1965 *(Courtesy: National Hurricane Research Laboratory; Photo by U.S. Air Force Air Weather Service)*

Fig. 3.19 Tornado of 5 June 1966 at Enid, Oklahoma *(Courtesy: National Severe Storms Laboratory; Photo by Leo Ainsworth)*

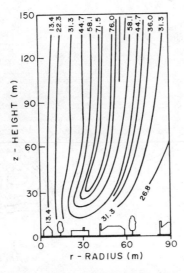

Fig. 3.20 Isotachs for tangential wind speeds in Dallas, Texas, tornado of 2 April 1957, derived from motion picture of debris *(Hoecker, 1961)*

laden air. If the surrounding air is cooler than the uplifted air, the elevation continues and the system is said to be unstable, and strong updraughts with associated strong ground level inflow result. The initial uplift may arise through excessive heating near the ground, a cold front, or mechanical uplift by mountains. A study of the characteristics of thunderstorms along with a statistical analysis has been given by Gomes and Vickery (1976a).

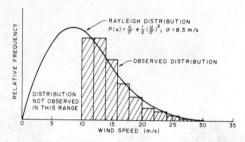

Fig. 3.21 Rayleigh distribution of wind speed at 500 m at John F. Kennedy Airport, New York City *(Davenport, 1967a)*

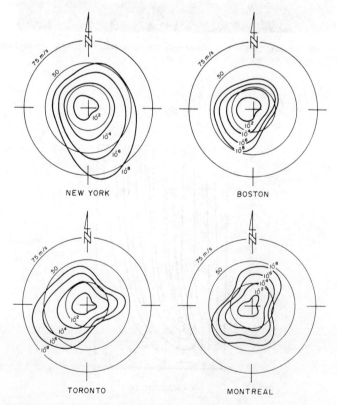

Fig. 3.22 Probability distributions of mean gradient wind speeds over North American cities for full year (probability per 22.5 sector wind speed exceeds u_{mph}**)** *(Davenport, 1972a)*

Both tornadoes and thunderstorms are very small-scale in nature and are responsible for the highest wind speeds recorded in many parts of the world. In particular, they differ from the extensive mature pressure systems in that the fetch over which a boundary layer can develop is often very short, hence vertical profiles such as those given in Fig. 3.15 do not apply except at relatively low levels.

5 Climatological Properties of Wind

The properties of the mean wind can only be conveniently expressed statistically. Several statistical properties are of value in structural engineering design. One is the over-all distribution of wind speed, not taking direction into account. This generally follows a Rayleigh distribution or a curve having similar characteristics, as shown in Fig. 3.21. From this curve the total proportion of time during which the mean velocity is in excess of certain values may be determined.

The Rayleigh distribution is a member of a general class of distributions known as Weibull distributions having a cumulative distribution

$$\text{Probability (velocity} < u) = F_u(u) = e^{-(u/c)^k} \tag{3.6}$$

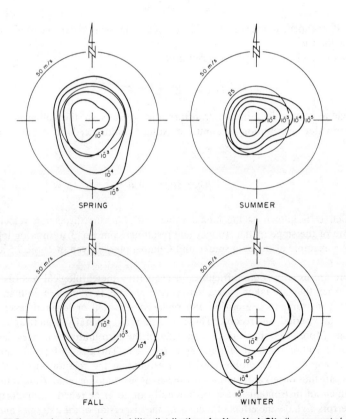

Fig. 3.23 Seasonal variation of probability distributions for New York City *(Isyumov et al., 1974)*

in which c = scale factor, and k = exponent. This distribution is found to give good correspondence with observations; invariably k is found to be close to 2, the value for the "exact" Rayleigh.

The same distribution can be used to describe the joint distribution of wind speed and direction in the form

Probability (velocity $< u, \theta <$ wind direction $< \theta + d\theta$)

$$= F_{u\theta}(u,\theta)\, d\theta = A(\theta)e^{-[u/c(\theta)]^{k(\theta)}} \qquad (3.7)$$

in which $A(\theta)$ = the conditional probability density that the wind lies in a sector centered on θ; c and k are now functions of θ. Various distributions corresponding to this description are shown in Fig. 3.22, and for New York a typical seasonal variation is shown in Fig. 3.23.

A second statistical distribution of use derives from the extreme value methods of Gumbel (1954) applied to annual maximum wind speeds. The annual probability P of u being exceeded is sometimes expressed in terms of the return period R, using the definition

$$P_{(>u)} = \frac{1}{R} \qquad (3.8)$$

Thus R = expected average number of years between recurrences of velocities greater than u.

The Fisher Tippett Type 1 distribution

$$P(u_{\text{extreme}} > u) = 1 - e^{-e^{-a(u-U)}} \qquad (3.9)$$

through a double logarithmic transformation results in the following form of extreme value distribution of annual maximum wind speeds in common use, for $R > 5$

$$u_R = U + \frac{1}{a}\ln R \qquad (3.10)$$

in which U is known as the modal value, and $1/a$, the dispersion velocity, is a measure of the slope of the straight line resulting from Eq. 3.10 in a log log-linear plot. An example of the data source and Gumbel plot is given in Table 3.5 and Fig. 3.24.

There are usually some difficulties in evaluating meteorological records, particularly when they are taken over a long period of time. It is more often than not the case that instruments are moved and replaced, elevated or lowered several times during the period of record. These translations generally significantly affect readings. More often than not the character of the surroundings changes due to the encroachment or removal of buildings, trees, etc. This also affects the indicated wind speed. A further problem exists in estimating the relationship of the wind speeds at the observing station to those at a building site. Calibration and adjustment of instruments are uncertain and can never be relied on. Unfortunately these errors all have the effect of increasing the dispersion of the extremes and hence exaggerating the long return period winds.

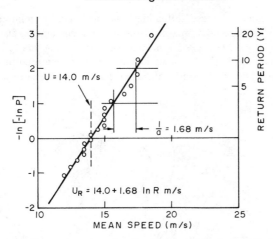

Fig. 3.24 Gumbel plot of annual maximum hourly mean speeds, Sydney, Australia *(Vickery, 1974)*

Table 3.5 Annual maximum hourly wind speeds at Observatory Hill, Sydney, Australia (*Vickery, 1974*)

Rank, n (1)	Speed in meters per second (2)	Year (3)	$P = \dfrac{n}{N+1}$ (4)	$-\ln(-\ln P)$ (5)
1	12.0	1954	0.050	−1.10
2	12.5	1958	0.100	−0.83
3	13.0	1950	0.15	−0.64
4	13.5	1953	0.02	−0.48
5	13.5	1959	0.25	−0.33
6	13.5	1962	0.30	−0.19
7	14.0	1963	0.35	−0.05
8	14.0	1955	0.40	+0.09
9	14.5	1960	0.45	+0.23
10	15.0	1969	0.50	+0.37
11	15.0	1966	0.55	+0.51
12	15.0	1956	0.60	+0.67
13	15.0	1952	0.65	+0.84
14	15.5	1951	0.70	+1.03
15	16.5	1961	0.75	+1.25
16	17.0	1957	0.80	+1.50
17	17.5	1966	0.85	+1.82
18	17.5	1967	0.90	+2.25
19	18.5	1968	0.95	+2.97

To obviate some of these difficulties and in order to minimize the errors associated with using records obtained from single anemometers, Davenport (1961) proposed using a gradient speed wind map, as for example that given by Baynes (1974) for Canada in Fig. 3.25. A similar method has been used in the Australian Wind Code (AS 1170-Pt 2), where all actual gust wind speed readings have been

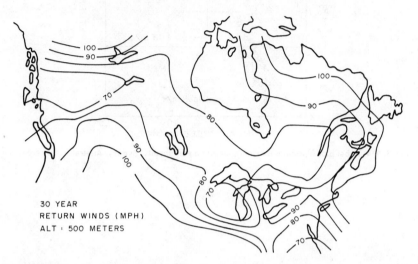

Fig. 3.25 Gradient mean wind speeds at 500 m over Canada for 30-year return period *(Baynes, 1971)*

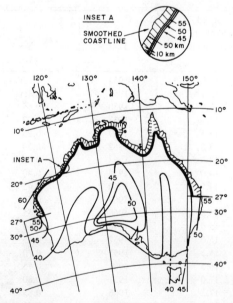

Fig. 3.26 Regional basic design 3-second maximum gust wind velocity, from Australian Wind Code *(Australian Standardizing Body, 1975),* **referred to height of 10 m in open country terrain (airfield sites)**

corrected to a standard reference to account for variations in height, local terrain roughness, and position errors caused by nearby structures as given in Fig. 3.26.

Although it would seem that many of the problems of determining and representing design wind speeds have been solved, some real difficulties yet remain. A few of these are:

1. The Gumbel method uses only the maximum values and discards the bulk of the observed data. It therefore requires long records of data (typically 20 yr or more) and demands great confidence in the maximum annual values recorded. Methods based on the parent distribution can overcome some of these problems (Gomes and Vickery, 1974).

2. Extreme values predicted from annual maximum wind data, which are a mixture of several phenomena—such as fully developed mature storms of cyclonic origin and thunderstorms or tropical cyclones (hurricanes or typhoons)—are usually not valid. Methods are required which treat each of the different mechanisms separately and represent them correctly. For example, tropical cyclones have to be analyzed for the joint probability of occurrence and of crossing given regions (Russell, 1971; Gomes and Vickery, 1976b); and for tornadoes, see Thom (1963) and Wen and Ang (1975). A critical look at probabilistic models of extreme wind speeds has recently been given by Simiu and Filliben (1975).

3. Extreme values predicted on an hourly mean maximum basis can virtually submerge the effect of short duration storms such as thunderstorms and for long return periods underestimate the design wind speeds (Melbourne, 1975b). A method of analyzing thunderstorm data has been given by Gomes and Vickery (1976a).

4. Any design wind speed based on a specific return period and applied using allowable stress techniques can produce greatly varying risks of failure where there are differing values of the dispersion. In Australia, for example, it is

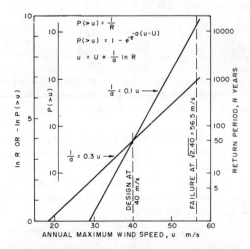

Fig. 3.27 Variation of risk failure for $1/a = 0.1$ **and** $1/a = 0.3$ *(Melbourne, 1975b)*

found that $1/a$ varies between 10% of U in the south where annual maximum values are caused by fully developed mature storms of cyclonic origin, through values of 20% of U for the regions dominated by thunderstorms, to 30% of U for the northern coastal areas dominated by tropical cyclones, the effect of which can be illustrated by the ratios of extreme wind speeds given in Fig. 3.27. This has also been recently discussed by Schueller and Panggabean (1976).

6   Turbulence Structure

A study of Fig. 3.13 reveals some characteristics of gusts that are significant from the viewpoint of wind loading. As remarked previously, the mean velocity at each height remains effectively constant throughout the period of record but increases with height. The amplitude of gust fluctuations is more or less constant with height with approximately the same rate of fluctuation, but the turbulence intensity $\sigma_u/\bar{u}$ decreases with height, as shown in Fig. 3.24. The similarity in the fluctuations at different heights is slight in the case of the rapid changes, but slower variations of a minute or so are detectable at all heights.

The character of turbulence is most conveniently and succinctly expressed in statistical terms. For a full discussion see Lumley and Panofsky (1964) and Davenport (1963). The fluctuation characteristics of turbulence can be expressed in terms of the power spectrum of turbulence and the associated probability distributions. (A procedure to obtain the spectrum is to represent the fluctuating velocities shown in Fig. 3.13 by an electrical voltage, record this voltage on magnetic tape, and play the tape through filters which suppress all fluctuations except those having a frequency close to a chosen frequency. If this filtered signal is fed to a wattmeter measuring power, the resulting level on the meter indicates the power at the chosen frequency. The plot of the power for various selected frequencies gives the power spectrum.)

The spectra of the various components of turbulence near the ground in strong winds can, it appears, be represented satisfactorily by universal functions of the type suggested by Davenport (1961) and the von Kármán type suggested by Harris (1968), which take the form

$$\frac{nSu(n)}{\bar{u}'^2} = f\left(\frac{nL}{\bar{u}}\right) \tag{3.11}$$

in which $Su(n)$ = power per unit interval of the frequency n of the velocity component u; $\bar{u}'^2$ = variance or mean square value of the fluctuating component of the velocity component u; $\bar{u}$ = mean of velocity component u; and L = length scale.

The length scale L, it appears, may vary slowly with height near the ground, but may be expected to be of the same order as the total boundary layer thickness. Hino (1971) discusses this aspect when he derives a form for the spectrum using Kolmogorov's hypothesis and energy balance approach. He found that the spectral peak frequency (n_{peak}) decreases according to the power law exponent a as height from the ground z is increased, that is

$$n_{peak} \propto \left(\frac{z}{z_1}\right)^{4a-1} \tag{3.12}$$

Illustrations of the longitudinal velocity spectrum are shown in Figs. 3.28 and 3.29.

Generally the turbulent energy is much greater in city areas than in smooth open terrain. The spectrum of vertical velocity is similar in form but of slightly smaller magnitude, and the length scale is more or less proportional to height. The lateral

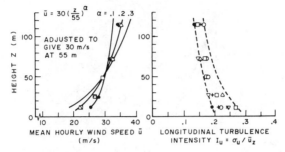

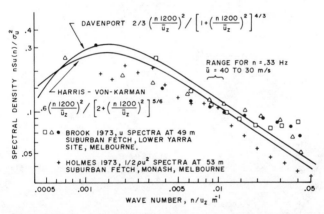

Fig. 3.28 Characteristics of full-scale wind flow over suburban roughness for neutral stability conditions *(Melbourne, 1973)*

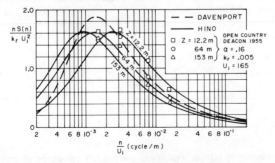

Fig. 3.29 Comparison of gust spectral formulas with experimental data *(Hino, 1971)*

velocity spectrum appears to be similar to the longitudinal spectrum but the power is about two-thirds.

The similarity of the fluctuations at different heights can be expressed by the narrow band correlation (or coherence) function. The correlation coefficient varies between $+1$ and -1. A value of $+1$ indicates complete correlation between velocities, -1 a complete antiphasal correlation, and 0 a random association. It has

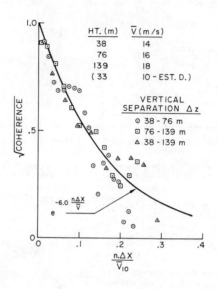

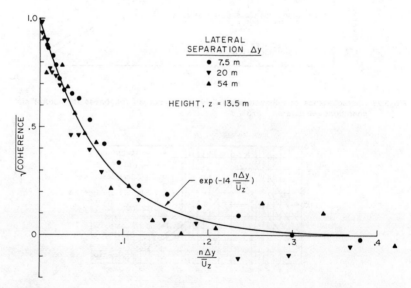

Fig. 3.30 Measurements of vertical and lateral (horizontal) coherence of longitudinal velocity fluctuations

been shown that the coherence in the velocity fluctuations of frequency n at two heights separated by a distance ΔZ is given closely by

$$\sqrt{\text{coherence}} = \exp\left(-C_z\frac{n\Delta Z}{\bar{u}}\right) \tag{3.13}$$

Similarly, the correlation between longitudinal velocity fluctuations at points separated laterally, Δy, can be expressed by

Fig. 3.31 John Hancock Center in Chicago, Illinois, on the shoreline of Lake Michigan

$$\sqrt{\text{coherence}} = \exp\left(-C_y \frac{n\Delta y}{\bar{u}_z}\right) \qquad (3.14)$$

Where C_z and C_y are constants, and in the case of the vertical coherence, the height of the reference velocity $\bar{u}$ must be defined. The values of C_z vary between 6 and 14 (Pielke and Panofsky, 1970); values of C_y tend to be a little greater and to vary with height approximately with $1/\sqrt{z}$ (Choi, 1971; Shiotani and Iwatani, 1971). Examples of these are given in Fig. 3.30.

Fig. 3.32 Apartment building, Delft, The Netherlands

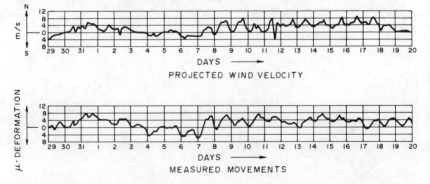

Fig. 3.33 Long period record of deformation in columns of Delft apartment building *(Davenport, 1972a)*

The third property that is required to define the turbulence characteristics is the probability distribution. (Perhaps the term relative frequency is more apt, but this requires the word frequency to do double duty in describing the rate of fluctuation as well.) It appears, on both theoretical and experimental grounds, that turbulence has a probability distribution which is approximately "normal" or "Gaussian."

This probability distribution can be written

$$P(u) = \frac{1}{\sqrt{\pi}\sigma} \int_{-\infty}^{u} \exp - \frac{(u - \bar{u})^2}{2\sigma^2} \, du \qquad (3.15)$$

which expresses the probability that a velocity less than u is obtained. The parameters needed to define this distribution are the mean velocity $\bar{u}$ and the standard deviation or root mean square fluctuation σ_u, both of which are found straightforwardly. An important fact is that the mean square fluctuation is in fact a measure of the total "power" of the turbulence, and is, therefore, related to the spectrum by

$$\sigma^2 = \int_{0}^{\infty} S(n) \, dn \qquad (3.16)$$

that is, the area under the spectrum.

One particularly important characteristic obtained from the probability distribution is the ratio between the maximum peak gusts and the hourly mean value. Shellard (1963) and Durst (1960) have presented some full-scale data and work by Hino (1964), and Brooks and Spillane (1968) have discussed the effect of averaging time and sample duration on the estimation and measurement of maximum wind gusts. For practical purposes it has been found convenient to express a maximum gust value $\hat{u}$ as

$$\hat{u} = \bar{u} + g\sigma_u \qquad (3.17)$$

in which g = peak factor; if $\hat{u}$ is a 2-sec to 3-sec maximum gust and $\bar{u}$ = the hourly mean, a value of $g = 3.5$ is appropriate.

If the spectra, correlation functions, and probability distributions are known, all of the turbulence properties that are significant from the viewpoint of wind loading are defined.

The theoretical relationships by which this framework can be extended have been discussed by Harris (1971) and compared with real wind measurements.

3.4   WIND LOADING MECHANISM AND FULL-SCALE EXAMPLES

1   Response of Tall Buildings to Wind

Davenport (1973) illustrated the response of tall buildings by full-scale column strain measurements made on an apartment building in Delft by Van Koten (1968), and on the John Hancock Center in Chicago by Davenport et al. (1970), shown in Figs. 3.31, 3.32, 3.33, and 3.34.

It is noted that the records in Figs. 3.33 and 3.34 are at two widely differing time scales. Fig. 3.33 shows simultaneous traces of the wind velocity component normal to the building and the deformation in the same direction. It is seen over this very slow time scale, on the order of days, that the deformation tends to follow the wind velocity. In Fig. 3.34, at B, a much faster chart speed is used, and it can be seen that significant dynamic deformations occur with suggestions of resonant response at the natural frequency. In this respect the character of the response of the taller, more slender John Hancock Center is dissimilar and reveals a far stronger resonant character with somewhat less evidence of the slower variations. In Fig. 3.35 the power spectral densities for the two fluctuations are sketched. These reveal the distinct differences in the energy distribution with frequency of the response.

It turns out that the fluctuations in the response of a tall building can be classified into two main groupings as described in Section 3.3: those associated with fluctuations in the mean wind speed, conveniently described as static, time-averaged loads, and those associated with the gustiness or turbulence of the wind which are predominantly dynamic in character. Power spectral densities of wind speed and

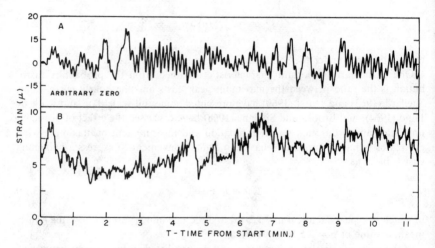

Fig. 3.34 Comparison of wind induced column strains on John Hancock Center, Chicago (A) and apartment building, Delft (B) *(Davenport, 1972a)*

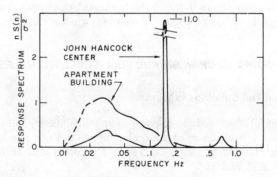

Fig. 3.35 Comparison of spectra of response of buildings A and B *(Davenport, 1972a)*

response are exemplified in Fig. 3.36. As noted in Section 3.3, there is a distinct break in both power spectra at a frequency of approximately 1 cycle per half hour; there are plausible physical reasons for this. It suggests that a suitable separation between "mean wind speed" and "gusts," and also between the "mean response" and the "dynamic response," can be made using this gap; it also implies that "mean values" averaged over approximately half-hour intervals are reasonable for station-arity. For the purposes of this chapter this averaging time convention is adopted.

Summarizing, the prediction of the response of tall buildings can be subdivided into: (1) The prediction of the occurrence of various mean wind speeds, and their associated directions; and (2) given the occurrence of that wind, the prediction of the maximum dynamic response of the structure. The first constitutes a climato-logical problem; the second is an aerodynamic or aeroelastic problem involving the steady and fluctuating response to the turbulent wind.

2   Along-Wind and Cross-Wind Response

It has proved convenient to divide the response of tall buildings to wind action into those motions that are along-wind and those that are cross-wind. This distinction of convenience really relates to the forcing mechanisms rather than the response, because in many cases the along-wind and cross-wind motions are of similar magnitude resulting in a response along an elliptical path with major and minor axes of similar length. This can be illustrated by plotting the continuous path of the motion of the top of a tall building as given by a trace taken from the rectangular 151 m (495 ft) high BHP House by Melbourne in Fig. 3.37(a), and a response dominated by cross-wind motion as shown by a trace of the circular London Post Office Tower in Fig. 3.37(b).

To justify any separate analysis of along-wind and cross-wind motions, it is necessary to establish that these motions are effectively uncorrelated. If in the case of a tall symmetrical building there was significant correlation between these motions, the extremes would tend to lie along some preferred axes other than the

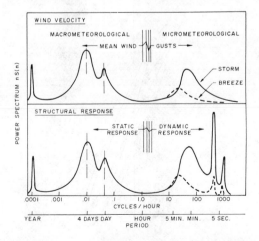

Fig. 3.36 Power spectra of wind velocity and structural response over an extended frequency range
(Davenport, 1972a)

wind axes; if independent, that is uncorrelated, the extremes would be symmetrically distributed about the wind axes.

The lack of correlation between along-wind and cross-wind motions has been observed in many model studies; and the joint probability distribution of accelerations measured at the top of the full-scale 151 m high BHP House by Melbourne (1974, 1975c), given in Table 3.6, illustrates the symmetry which tends to confirm the independence of these motions and consequently the independence of the excitation mechanisms. It can also be seen that this joint probability distribution is similar to a bivariate normal distribution in which the probability of exceeding a displacement of four standard deviations in one direction is similar to the probability of exceeding a combined displacement of three standard deviations in both directions.

Along-Wind Response. Since the early 1960s from the work primarily of Davenport (1967) and Vickery (1966) it can be concluded that the along-wind

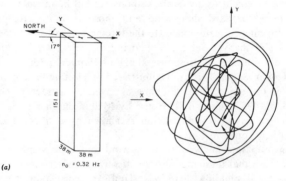

Fig. 3.37(a) Trace of path of top of BHP House in a strong wind *(Melbourne, 1975c)*

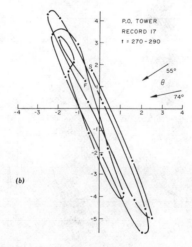

Fig. 3.37(b) Trace of path of top of London Post Office Tower (dots at 1-sec intervals) *(Newberry et al., 1973; Courtesy: Building Research Establishment—Crown copyright reserved)*

response of most structures originates almost entirely from the action of the incident turbulence of the longitudinal component of the wind velocity (superimposed on a mean displacement due to the mean drag). Their analytical methods, using spectral and spatial correlation considerations to predict the along-wind response of many structures, have become highly developed, to the point at which the gust factor approach is included in a number of wind loading codes.

To predict the response of a structure to a gusting wind it is necessary to define the spectrum of the loads induced by gusts. To appreciate the relationship between the spectrum of the over-all loads on a building and the spectrum of velocity fluctuations it is convenient to think in terms of wavelengths (or the inverse-wavenumbers) rather than frequencies. If the mean wind speed at a given height is $\bar{u}(z)$ then we can associate a wavelength $\lambda = \bar{u}(z)/n$ with a frequency component n; λ is then a linear measure of the size of gusts or eddies producing load fluctuations at frequency n.

The effectiveness of a gust in terms of producing a load on a large structure will depend largely on the gust size in relation to the size of the structure, that is, the ratio λ/h or $\bar{u}/nh$. In the case of high frequency components, the ratio $\lambda/h \ll 1$ and the pressures produced are well organized or correlated only over quite small areas of the building; their total effect is small since in some areas they will tend to produce increased loads while simultaneously, at other parts of the structure, there will be a decrease in load. The pressures due to the high frequency components of the wind spectrum are poorly correlated over the building as a whole. On the other hand, the very low frequency components of gustiness are associated with values of $\lambda/h \gg 1$, and in this case their influence is felt over the whole, or at least large areas, of the building simultaneously.

Cross-Wind Response.   By comparison with the along-wind forcing mechanisms the cross-wind forcing mechanisms have proved to be so complex that as yet there is

Table 3.6 Joint probability distributions[a] *(Melbourne, 1975c)*

	Cross-Wind					
	$2\sigma_y \to 3\sigma_y$	$\sigma_y \to 2\sigma_y$	$0 \to \sigma_y$	$0 \to -\sigma_y$	$-\sigma_y \to -2\sigma_y$	$-2\sigma_y \to -3\sigma_y$
$2\sigma_x \to 3\sigma_x$			0.006	0.008		
$\sigma_x \to 2\sigma_x$		0.02	0.05	0.05	0.02	
$0 \to \sigma_x$	0.007	0.04	0.12	0.14	0.05	0.007
$0 \to -\sigma_x$	0.004	0.03	0.11	0.12 (0.116)	0.06 (0.046)	0.007 (0.007)
$-\sigma_x \to -2\sigma_x$		0.01	0.04	0.04 (0.046)	0.02 (0.018)	(0.003)
$-2\sigma_x \to -3\sigma_x$			0.007	0.006 (0.007)	(0.003)	

[a]Values in brackets are for a bivariate normal distribution

$$p_{(xy)} = \frac{1}{2\pi\sigma_x\sigma_y} e^{-\frac{1}{2}\left(\frac{x^2}{\sigma_x^2} + \frac{y^2}{\sigma_y^2}\right)}$$

no generalized analytical method available to calculate cross-wind response of buildings. In many cases the major criterion for the design of tall buildings is the cross-wind response. This has meant that the only recourse left has been to determine this response from aeroelastic model tests conducted in a wind tunnel model of the natural wind. Unfortunately this has meant that much of the work done in this area has been directed towards specific projects, and much proprietary information which could be of general use has not been published.

Probably the main reason why theoretical methods for predicting cross-wind response of structures generally have proved so intractable is that there are several quite separately identifiable excitation mechanisms which are frequently super-imposed. Melbourne (1975a) has identified the excitation mechanisms as being associated with: (1) The wake; (2) the incident turbulence; and (3) the cross-wind displacement. The main aerodynamic variables on which all three mechanisms depend arise from the characteristics of the incident freestream turbulence structure and the mean wind speed.

Fortunately in the case of tall buildings it has been concluded by Saunders and Melbourne (1975) that:

1. The cross-wind motion of most, if not all tall buildings of constant rectangular cross section, under strong-wind action, standing clear of the upstream roughness, is primarily due to the energy available in the high frequency side-band of the mechanism of vortex shedding. That is, the cross-wind motion of these buildings is predominantly due to wake-excitation.

2. The nondimensional cross-wind force spectral densities of the tall prismatic model buildings studied are insensitive to the level of motion of the model buildings up to a reduced velocity of at least 10. Therefore, the effect of the level of motion of most rectangular-sectioned buildings on the cross-wind aerodynamic input can be neglected.

From these conclusions Saunders and Melbourne have proposed a semiempirical method of calculating the cross-wind response of tall rectangular prism buildings which will be summarized in Section 3.5.

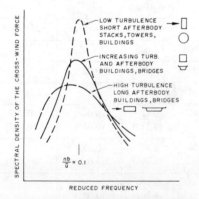

Fig. 3.38 Trend of frequency distribution of forces originating from wake which are available to excite cross-wind motions for various structures and freestream turbulence (Melbourne, 1975a)

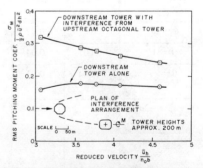

Fig. 3.39 Effect of interference excitation on cross-wind response of downstream building (Melbourne 1975a)

Using a large amount of background information, Melbourne (1975a) has suggested a diagrammatic representation of the forces originating from the wake available to cause cross-wind excitation of various structures as a function of reduced frequency ($nb/\bar{u}$) as given in Fig. 3.38.

The implication of Fig. 3.38 is that all bluff bodied structures get some cross-wind excitation originating from the wake. In practice it seems that for a majority of structures the wake excitation is dominant. It is only when the afterbody becomes long enough to cause significant flow reattachment (that is, becomes a more efficient lifting body) that the incident turbulence excitation becomes first significant and then dominant, or at very low values of reduced frequency for certain sections when the rate of displacement (galloping) excitation becomes dominant.

Also included under wake excitation is the interference effect of the wake shed by an upstream structure, which could equally well be described as excitation due to incident turbulence for the structure affected. A rather significant example of this has been given by Melbourne (1975a) in Fig. 3.39 where model studies predicted an increase in response of between 50% and 100% of a tall building due to the upstream interference of a building of similar size. Further generalized measurements on interference effects between buildings have been given by Melbourne and Sharp (1976).

3 Torsional Response

Significant torsional response has been noticed in some buildings. A particular case where the torsional response caused occupancy discomfort was recorded by Hansen et al. (1973). Durgin and Tong (1972) demonstrated torsional instabilities of

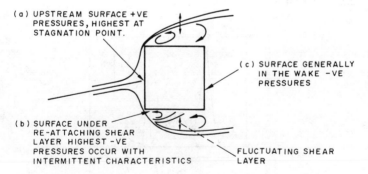

Fig. 3.40 Three pressure areas of bluff body in turbulent flow *(Melbourne, 1975b)*

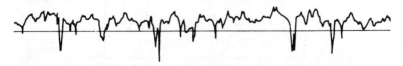

Fig. 3.41 Pressure trace on model tall building taken on streamwise surface near leading edge to illustrate the intermittent pressure fluctuation characteristics of this region *(Melbourne, 1975b)*

a building model, particularly when the torsional and bending mode frequencies are very close and there are asymmetries of the axial mass distribution at the shear center. Saunders (1971) extended a quasi-steady theory on one degree of freedom galloping instability of three-dimensional square prisms to include the torsional mode, and discussed the magnitude of parameters such as rate of change of aerodynamic moment with rate of change of angle on the torsional response of the prism.

It has been the practice for many years at some wind tunnel establishments to model torsional modes on aeroelastic building models, but little or no information is available in the open literature, implying that it has rarely been a significant design consideration for conventional buildings, although the possibility is being kept under observation.

4 Cladding Pressures on Tall Buildings

The determination of design pressures for cladding and glazing has proved particularly difficult because of the difficulty of establishing the effective aero-dynamic pressures and the variability of the glazed panel. There are three distinct pressure areas on a bluff body shown diagrammatically in Fig. 3.40:

1. The upstream face where pressures are positive. The RMS fluctuations relate to the incident turbulence with an approximately normal distribution.

2. The streamwise faces (including roofs) near an upstream corner under the reattaching shear layer, where the highest negative pressures occur. The RMS fluctuations relate to wake pressure fluctuations, but the distribution is far from normal due to intermittency which, it is suggested, is related to the curvature of the shear layer, and this in turn is dependent on the fluctuating reattachment point.

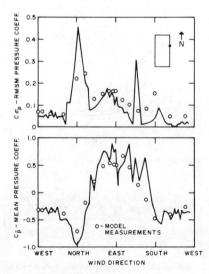

Fig. 3.42 Mean and RMS pressure fluctuations measured on the 260-m Commerce Court Building in Toronto, Canada *(Dalgliesh, 1975)*

3. The rear faces well downstream of any reattachment in the wake where the pressures are negative. The RMS fluctuations relate to wake pressures and are relatively low with distributions showing moderate intermittency. The pressures in these areas are not normally critical for cladding design.

Full-scale examples of these pressure fluctuations were given in Fig. 3.2 taken from measurements on the CIBC Building in Montréal by Dalgleish (1971). Cermak and Sadeh (1971) have given model examples of the relationship between upstream face pressures and the incident turbulence noted in (1), and further examples illustrating the intermittency characteristic noted in (2) are given in Fig. 3.41 from model tests by Melbourne (1975b). In Fig. 3.41, the trace was measured at Location (b) for $\beta = 350$, for which the probability distributions and model configuration are given in Fig. 3.73.

As it is the high negative pressure areas under reattaching shear layers which tend to determine cladding design and the turbulence characteristics, leading edge shape and corner angle (and in some cases Reynolds number) are significant. For this reason modeling of this phenomenon has been difficult, and some widely differing pressures are offered throughout the general literature which need careful interpretation. Unfortunately some of the more extreme pressures (associated with a vortex sheet originating from a corner inclined to the local flow coupled with a fluctuating reattachment line), which have been measured on wind tunnel models, do seem to occur in full scale. Hence for design purposes it is necessary to be relatively conservative at this time. Knowledge of realistic internal pressures, particularly in large structures, is also very limited.

An example of full-scale measurements of mean and RMS pressure fluctuations on the 260-m (853-ft) Commerce Court Building in Toronto by Dalgleish (1975) is given in Fig. 3.42. These are compared with model measurements made at the University of Western Ontario. In the upper part of Fig. 3.42, $C\sigma_p = p/(\frac{1}{2}\sigma\bar{u}^2_{top})$; in the lower part $C_{\bar{p}} = (p - p_o)/(\frac{1}{2}\sigma\bar{u}^2_{top})$.

For design purposes the intermittent nature of the highest peak suctions seems to be best described by using a peak factor g, defined as being the number of standard deviations by which the average hourly maximum exceeds the mean, that is

$$g = \frac{\text{average maximum hourly value—mean}}{\text{RMS value of the fluctuating component}} \tag{3.18}$$

hence $\hat{p} = \bar{p} + g\sigma_p$, or in coefficient form $C_{\hat{p}} = C_{\bar{p}} + gC\sigma_p$.

An example illustrating the random nature from short records to the variations of the peak factor, and the intermittent nature of some of the pressure fluctuations, is given in Table 3.7 of full-scale pressure measurements made on the 120-m (394-ft) high Asahi-Tokai Building in Tokyo by Fujii et al. (1974).

Melbourne (1975b) has suggested that for design purposes the peak factor g should be related to a probability level, or crossing rate, and Davenport (1975) has commented further, in discussion on Peterka and Cermak (1975), that the design load must be related to load-time capacity of glass. This problem and the problem of model response times will be discussed in detail in Section 3.7 on the Prediction of Cladding Loads.

Some of the largest negative pressure values observed in model and full scale have been associated with vortex formation following separation from discontinuities on

Table 3.7 Pressure measurements on the Asahi-Tokai Building
(Fujii et al., 1974)

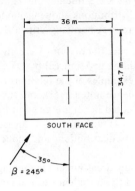

SOUTH FACE

$35°$

$\beta = 245°$

ALL NUMBER 4 PRESSURE
TAPS ARE ON FACE CENTER
LINE.

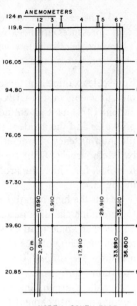

NORTH , SOUTH FACE

Location (1)	$\bar{P}$, in kilograms per square meter (2)	$\hat{P}_{max}$, in kilograms per square meter (3)	Root mean square (4)	$C_{\bar{P}}$ (5)	$C\sigma_{\dot{P}}$ (6)	$C_{\hat{P}}$ (7)	g (8)
			Record 1[a]				
W4a	−2.51	−20.38	3.45	−0.10	0.14	−0.83	5.2
W4b	−3.89	−18.82	4.04	−0.16	0.17	−0.77	3.7
W4c	−5.46	−21.95	4.27	−0.22	0.17	−0.90	3.9
W4d	−2.74	−23.91	3.86	−0.11	0.16	−0.98	5.5
W4e							
W4f	0.60	−18.42	1.90	−0.02	0.08	−0.75	9.4
N4a							
N4b	−4.93	−12.15	1.15	−0.20	0.05	−0.50	6.3
N4c	−7.57	−16.07	1.36	−0.30	0.06	−0.66	6.3
N4d	−6.04	−18.42	2.01	−0.25	0.08	−0.75	6.2
N4e	−6.12	−20.38	2.81	−0.25	0.11	−0.83	5.1
N4f	−3.69	−16.86	3.54	−0.15	0.14	−0.69	3.7
E4a	−6.21	−13.33	1.78	−0.25	0.07	−0.54	4.0
E4b	−8.81	−19.21	1.67	−0.36	0.07	−0.78	6.2
E4c	−8.74	−18.42	1.95	−0.36	0.08	−0.75	5.0
E4d	−10.76	−24.70	2.61	−0.44	0.11	−1.0	5.8
E4e	−10.54	−27.79	3.44	−0.43	0.14	−1.13	5.0
E4f	−6.25	−24.70	4.50	−0.26	0.18	−1.0	4.1
S4a	8.50	27.83	3.28	0.34	0.13	1.14	5.9
S4b	10.42	26.66	3.53	0.43	0.14	1.09	4.6
S4c	11.89	25.48	3.52	0.49	0.14	1.04	3.9
S4d	9.35	21.17	3.38	0.38	0.14	0.86	3.5
S4e	9.62	21.17	3.10	0.39	0.13	0.86	3.7
S4f	5.04	14.90	2.34	0.21	0.10	0.61	4.2

the face of buildings; an example of this was given by Ostrowski et al. (1967) from model studies on the Bank of America Headquarters Building.

A well illustrated paper on full-scale failure of cladding has been prepared by Eaton (1975). Although they are concerned with low-rise structures, the full-scale measurements of cladding pressures reported by Eaton and Mayne (1975) and Marshall (1975) are particularly relevant to this area of study.

3.5 ANALYTICAL APPROACHES TO ESTIMATION OF LOAD AND RESPONSE

In Section 3.2, several design problems were identified, and in Article 9 of Section 3.2 objectives of the design approach were set out in two phases, and the statistical description of design criteria was introduced. In this section the analytical

Table 3.7 (continued)

Location (1)	$\bar{P}$, in kilograms per square meter (2)	$\hat{P}_{max}$, in kilograms per square meter (3)	Root mean square (4)	$C_{\bar{P}}$ (5)	$C_{\sigma P}$ (6)	$C_{\hat{P}}$ (7)	g (8)
			Record 2[b]				
W4a	−4.43	−16.36	2.55	−0.27	0.15	−1.01	4.9
W4b	−5.63	−20.38	2.95	−0.34	0.18	−1.23	5.0
W4c	−4.70	−16.07	3.19	−0.28	0.19	−0.97	3.6
W4d	−4.43	−23.52	3.60	−0.27	0.22	−1.42	5.3
W4e							
W4f	0.64	−12.15	1.62	0.04	0.10	−0.73	7.1
N4a							
N4b	−2.65	−7.45	1.33	−0.16	0.08	−0.45	3.6
N4c	−6.93	−14.50	1.36	−0.42	0.08	−0.87	5.6
N4d	−4.32	−16.86	1.41	−0.26	0.08	−1.02	8.9
N4e	−4.31	−14.11	1.79	−0.26	0.11	−0.85	5.5
N4f	−3.62	−12.15	1.31	−0.22	0.11	−0.73	4.7
E4a	−6.01	−15.29	1.93	−0.36	0.12	−0.92	4.8
E4b	−6.27	−14.90	1.95	−0.38	0.14	−0.90	4.4
E4c	−6.91	−16.07	2.33	−0.41	0.14	−0.97	3.9
E4d	−7.53	−19.21	2.94	−0.45	0.18	−1.16	4.0
E4e	−6.18	−23.13	4.04	−0.37	0.24	−1.39	4.2
E4f	−2.76	−18.42	4.24				
S4a	5.71	18.03	3.41	0.34	0.21	1.09	3.6
S4b	7.22	18.82		0.43		1.18	
S4c	7.76	19.60	3.34	0.47	0.20	1.18	3.5
S4d	6.48	18.82	3.97	0.39	0.18	1.18	4.0
S4e	5.61	17.25	2.90	0.34	0.18	1.04	3.9
S4f	3.97	11.37		0.24		0.68	

[a]Date: 12/4/73; record duration = 512 sec; wind direction, $\bar{\beta} = 245°$; wind speed $\bar{U}_h$ = 19.8 m/s; reference dynamic pressure, $\bar{q}_h$ = 24.5 kg/m². Peak pressures measured for 0.3 sec.

[b]Date: 12/4/73; record duration = 256 sec; wind direction, $\bar{\beta} = 245°$; wind speed $\bar{U}_h$ = 16.3 m/s; reference dynamic pressure, $\bar{q}_h$ = 16.6 kg/m². Peak pressures measured for 0.3 sec.

approaches available to the designer for the second phase of the design process, that of determining pressures, forces, and response for a particular building, will be set out. In Section 3.6, which follows, the experimental approaches will be described. Then in Section 3.7 methods of combining phase one estimates of the wind climate with the phase two analytical or experimental response data will be presented.

The mechanisms associated with wind loading on a tall building were introduced in Section 3.4, partly to validate the separation of the along-wind and cross-wind components. This separation is particularly important when it comes to developing analytical methods of predicting wind loading on tall buildings and the resultant response.

At this time (1979) the analytical methods available still rely on empirical data; many of the data have been obtained from wind tunnel tests on models and still require considerable full-scale validation, particularly in relation to the cross-wind component. This section will describe what empirically based analytical methods are available for the designer of tall buildings for both total loading of the frame and local loading of cladding or glazing. The quasi-steady approach used by many wind loading codes will not be admitted here as being a satisfactory approach for this purpose for tall buildings, even in cases where many factors have been admitted to try and make the quasi-steady approach workable for larger buildings. The reason is simply that none of these methods can be used for cross-wind loading, and in most cases they tend to be conservative for the along-wind loading.

1   Along-Wind

A method of determining the along-wind loading and response of isolated structures was developed in a series of papers by Davenport (1961, 1962, 1964, 1967) and Vickery (1966, 1969). These methods essentially considered that the along-wind response of a structure resulted from the action of the spectrum of forces produced by the fluctuating longitudinal velocity components of the turbulent incident wind stream. This led to the development of the "Gust Factor Approach" for the prediction of the response and loading of tall buildings (Davenport, 1967b; Vickery,

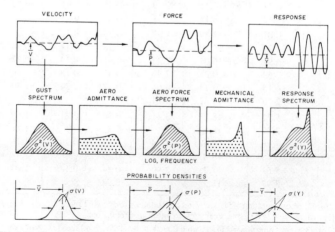

Fig. 3.43 Elements of the statistical approach to gust loading *(Davenport, 1967b)*

1966, 1969; Velozzi and Cohen, 1968). In essence, the aim of the method is to produce a gust factor G, which relates the peak to mean response in terms of an equivalent design static load, distribution, or load effect Q, as is becoming widespread in European codification, that is

$$\text{design value } Q = G\bar{Q} \tag{3.19}$$

Note that this gust factor G is not to be confused with the peak factor g.

The theory behind this approach, which is expressed graphically in Fig. 3.43, can be summarized as follows. The force spectrum on a plate or prism could be shown to be

$$S_F(n) = \frac{\bar{F}^2}{\bar{u}^2} \chi^2 S u(n) \tag{3.20}$$

in which $\bar{F}$ = mean drag; $\bar{u}$ = mean longitudinal velocity; n = frequency; $Su(n)$ = spectrum of the longitudinal velocity component averaged for 1-hr period; and χ^2 = an aerodynamic admittance function relating the size of the gust disturbance to the size of the structure, which can be expressed as a function of $n\sqrt{A}/\bar{u}$, where A = frontal area of the building such that $\sqrt{A}$ becomes a typical length dimension.

The aerodynamic admittance function as measured experimentally in wind tunnels, and as determined theoretically by Vickery and Davenport (1967), is given in Fig. 3.44.

Eq. 3.20 gives the relationship between the spectrum of the load fluctuations on a simple structure and the spectrum of the longitudinal component of turbulence in

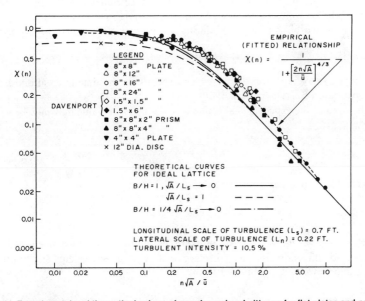

Fig. 3.44 Experimental and theoretical values of aerodynamic admittance for flat plates and prisms normal to the flow (Re $\simeq 2 \times 10^4$) (*Vickery, 1969*)

the uniform turbulent flow in which the structure is placed. If the structure is regarded as a single degree of freedom system with an undamped fundamental natural frequency n_o, a damping ζ (as a fraction of critical), and a spring constant k, then the spectrum of the displacement $(x = \bar{x} + x')$ of the structure can be expressed in its simplest normal modal form as

$$S_x(n) = \frac{1}{k^2} |H(n)|^2 S_F(n)$$

$$= 4 \frac{\bar{F}^2}{\bar{u}^2} \frac{1}{k^2} \chi^2 |H(n)|^2 Su(n) \qquad (3.21)$$

in which

$$|H(n)|^2 = \frac{1}{\left[1 - \left(\dfrac{n}{n_o}\right)^2\right]^2 + 4\zeta^2 \left(\dfrac{n}{n_o}\right)^2}$$

is the mechanical admittance function, which accounts for the dynamic resonant response arising from inertial effects, but the mean square value $\sigma_x^2 = \int S_x(n)$, and $\bar{x} = \bar{F}/k$. When these substitutions are made in Eq. 3.21, it can reduce to the form

$$\frac{\sigma_x}{\bar{x}} = 2 \frac{\sigma_u}{\bar{u}} \sqrt{B + \frac{SE}{\zeta}} \qquad (3.22)$$

in which B and SE/ζ are related to the integrals of the background (or low-frequency) part and resonance peak of the response spectrum. The background or low-frequency part relates to that part of the spectrum where the response of the structure follows the low-frequency change in wind speed (squared).

The expected peak value of x' during an interval of time may be expressed as

$$\hat{x} = \bar{x} + g\sigma_x \qquad (3.23)$$

in which g = average peak factor which depends on the time interval and form of the spectrum of x (Davenport, 1964).

The ratio of the expected peak value of x' to the mean value may now be written

$$\frac{\hat{x}}{\bar{x}} G = 1 + gr \sqrt{B + \frac{SE}{\zeta}} \qquad (3.24)$$

in which G = gust response factor, and

$$r = \frac{2\sigma_u}{\bar{u}} \qquad (3.25)$$

From a knowledge of the mean pressure distribution and hence mean load in the along-wind direction to give displacement $\bar{x}$, the equivalent static pressure distribution to give $\hat{x}$ is obtained from

$$\hat{p}_z = G\bar{p}_z \qquad (3.26)$$

or in terms of a generalized design load $Q = G\bar{Q}$ (Eq.3.19).

Codification of Gust Factor Approach. Davenport originally developed the gust factor approach for the Danish Wind Code. It was later published in a revised form by Davenport (1967) and then further used in the Canadian Structural Design Manual. This development differed from a similar approach by Vickery (1966) in that it employed a theoretical rather than an experimental expression for the aerodynamic admittance function. The assumptions necessary in the theoretical approach have been discussed in detail by Vickery (1968). Velozzi and Cohen (1968) presented a development which attempted to account for not only the limited size of gusts in directions normal to wind but also the influence of gust length. While the along-wind extent of a gust is undoubtedly of significance, there is no doubt that this attempt to include length effects led to significant underestimates of the gust response factor. More recently Simiu (1973, 1975) has attempted to differentiate betwen the correlation of loads on the front and loads on the rear face of a building and the variation with height of the spectrum of the longitudinal velocity fluctuations, and Vickery (1972) has suggested a minor modification that permits the use of the gust factor in situations where the turbulence levels are high and the second-order effects (such as mode shape), disregarded in earlier developments, become significant. Vickery (1973b) presented a form for the various parameters involved in the computation of gust response factors for tall buildings, along with an

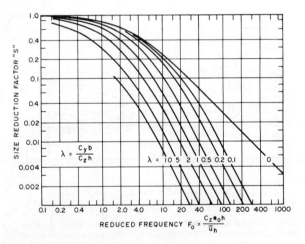

Fig. 3.45 Size reduction factor S (Vickery, 1973)

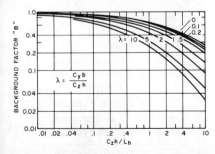

Fig. 3.46 Background factor B (Vickery, 1973)

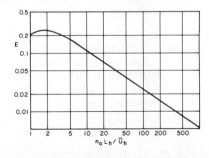

Fig. 3.47 Gust energy factor E (Vickery, 1973)

example reproduced here in Figs. 3.45 through 3.48 and Tables 3.8 and 3.9.

The size reduction factor S is shown in Fig. 3.45 as a function of the modified aspect ratio $C_y b/C_z h$ and a reduced frequency $C_z n_o h/U_h$. The latter parameter is, physically, the ratio of the height of the building to the average vertical extent of disturbances with the wavelength $U(h)/n_o$ which excites the structure at its natural frequency. Where b = breadth of the building normal to the stream direction, the coefficient C_z is obtained by fitting an exponential curve

$$\exp\left\{ -\frac{C_z|\Delta z|n}{\bar{U}_z} \right\} \tag{3.27}$$

to the normalized co-spectra discussed in Section 3.3, and similarly for C_y (see suggested values in Table 3.8). The factor $\lambda = C_y b/C_z h$ is the aspect ratio modified to take account of the difference between the lateral and vertical extent of gusts.

The factor B is presented in Fig. 3.46 as a function of the modified aspect ratio and the parameter $C_z h/L_h$, which is proportional to the ratio of the building height to the across-wind scale of turbulence L_h given in Fig. 3.48.

The energy factor E is equal to the normalized spectrum of the longitudinal component of turbulence and is shown in Fig. 3.47 as a function of $n_o L_h/\bar{U}_h$. The

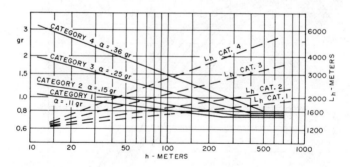

Fig. 3.48 Values of gr and L_h (Vickery, 1973)

Table 3.8 Data for use with gust factor approach (Vickery, 1973)

Quantity (1)	Value (2)
C_z	10
C_Y	15
L_h	see Fig. 3.48
Damping (ζ, fraction of critical):	
Low stress levels—steel frame	0.005 to 0.010
reinforced or prestressed concrete	0.005 to 0.010
Working stress levels—steel frame	0.01 to 0.02
reinforced concrete	0.015 to 0.03
Near yield—steel frame	0.04 to 0.06
reinforced concrete	0.05 to 0.10

parameter $n_o L_h/U_h$ is proportional to the ratio of the wavelength $\bar{U}_h/n_o$ to the wavelength at which the energy spectrum is a maximum.

The product gr is shown in Fig. 3.48. The factor r is closely related to the intensity of turbulence, which is related to terrain category (surface roughness) and height. In plotting gr the peak factor g has been taken as equal to 3.5, and the terrain categories are defined by the power law exponent a of the mean velocity profile.

The peak factor g can be evaluated theoretically (Davenport, 1964). If the distribution of the response is Gaussian we have

$$g = \sqrt{2 \log_e \nu T} + \frac{0.577}{\sqrt{2 \log_e \nu T}} \tag{3.28}$$

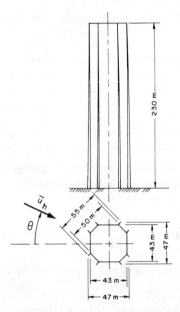

Fig. 3.49 Major dimensions of building used for calculation in Table 3.9

Table 3.9 Characteristics of a sample tall reinforced concrete building[a] (Vickery, 1973b)

Characteristics (1)	Value (2)
Natural frequency, in fundamental mode	0.2 Hz
Height	230 m
Characteristic dimension $(\sqrt{A})$	45 m
Bulk density	280 kg.m^{-3}
Damping: working stress levels	$\zeta = 0.02$
Design mean wind speed at gradient height (500 m)	45.8 m/s
Terrain category 4	$a = 0.36$

[a]The major dimensions of the building are shown in Fig. 3.49.

in which $g = \hat{x}/\sigma_x$; $\hat{x}$ = expected peak value of the response x in a time period T; σ_x = standard deviation of RMS value of the response; and ν = average "cycling" rate of the response, that is

$$\nu \simeq n_o \sqrt{\frac{\dfrac{SE}{\zeta}}{B + \dfrac{SE}{\zeta}}}$$

For most buildings Eq. 3.28 yields values of g quite close to 3.5, and in view of the over-all accuracy of the gust factor approach (typically $\pm 15\%$) the adoption of a constant value for g is acceptable. A value of 3.5, or a value defined by Eq. 3.28, is not acceptable in all situations since both estimates depend upon the response being normally distributed. This is close to the truth if the response in question is the over-all along-wind deflection of a building, and since the gust factor approach is concerned with this type of response a value of about 3.5 can be justified. Departures from a normal distribution are, however, likely in other circumstances. In the separated flow region of a building the local pressure fluctuations and roof response commonly exhibit extreme intermittency and peak factors of up to 10 have been measured in both model and full-scale situations (see Article 4 of Section 3.4). In other circumstances, particularly where extreme cross-wind motions are induced by vortex shedding, the distribution tends to move from normal to sinusoidal, and peak factors of 2 or less can occur (Melbourne, 1974, 1976).

Sample calculations for tall reinforced concrete building. For dimensions and specifications, refer to Fig. 3.49 and Table 3.9.
Mean wind loads.   The mean wind speed profile is

$$\bar{U}_z = \bar{U}_g \left(\frac{z}{h}\right)^{0.36}$$

$$= 45.8 \left(\frac{z}{h}\right)^{0.36}$$

$$\bar{U}(h) = 45.8 \left(\frac{230}{500}\right)^{0.36} = 34.5 \text{ m/s}$$

The mean loads per unit height above 20 m are, using Australian Wind Code AS1170 Part 2 (Australian Standardizing Body, 1975) at $\theta = 0°$

$$\bar{w}_z = 12.9 + 25.8 \left(\frac{z}{h}\right)^{0.72} \text{ kN/m}$$

and at $\theta = 45°$

$$\bar{w}_z = 14.9 + 29.8 \left(\frac{z}{h}\right)^{0.72} \text{ kN/m}.$$

The corresponding base bending moments are 850 MN $\cdot$ m and 980 MN $\cdot$ m for $\theta = 0°$ and $\theta = 45°$, respectively.

Gust factor computations.   For Category 4 and $h = 230$ m we have, from Fig. 3.48, $L_h = 3700$ m and $gr = 1.05$

$$\lambda = \frac{C_y b}{C_z h} = \frac{15 \times 45}{10 \times 230} = 0.29$$

$$\frac{C_z h}{L_h} = \frac{10 \times 230}{3700} = 0.62$$

from Fig. 3.46, $B = 0.68$

$$\frac{C_z n_o h}{\bar{U}_h} = \frac{10 \times 0.20 \times 230}{34.5} = 13.3$$

from Fig. 3.45, $S = 0.085$

$$\frac{n_o L_h}{\bar{U}_h} = \frac{0.20 \times 3700}{34.5} = 21.5$$

and from Fig. 3.47, $E = 0.07$

$$G = 1 + gr \sqrt{B + \frac{S E}{\zeta}}$$

$$= 1 + 1.05 \sqrt{0.68 + \frac{0.085 \times 0.07}{0.02}} = 1 + 1.05\sqrt{0.98}$$

$$= 2.04 \text{ for } \theta = 0° \text{ and } 45°, \ \zeta = 0.02.$$

The design base moments are then 1730 MN·m for $\theta = 0°$ and 2000 MN·m for $\theta = 45°$. The corresponding values determined by the more conventional quasi-steady "peak gust" approach (as per AS1170) are 2000 MN·m and 2300 MN·m, respectively.

The European Convention for Constructional Steelwork (ECCS) is developing proposals for a code of practice suitable for wide application. These proposals have been discussed by Sfintesco and Wyatt (1975). Wyatt (1971) also discussed alternative static analysis using correlations of wind speed without frequency decomposition, as expressed by cross-wind integral scales, with corresponding uncertainty in values thereof.

Along-Wind Response Evaluation.   Wyatt has prepared the following comments on the gust factor approaches and evaluation of the along-wind response.

The key to analysis is the evaluation of the admittance function χ^2. This requires double integration to sum the products for all possible pairings of infinitesimal elements of area of the structure and of the tendency of gust action at each point to excite the natural mode, multiplied by the correlation of the gust components at those points (in the static analysis, a similar summation of the effect of gusts on the load effect in question). This is tedious, especially in respect of the broad band of frequencies (background effect) where the calculation must be repeated to allow the spectrum to be drawn. Various simplifications are given in the references. The method of determining χ^2 experimentally (Fig. 3.44) using the combined effect of the correlations of the upstream face and downstream face pressures is a simplification which Simiu (1973, 1975) has tried to overcome. However, it is worth noting that the Royex House full-scale measurements (Newberry et al., 1973), as well as showing poor correlation of small fluctuations between upstream face and downstream face, also show higher upstream face correlations than were determined experimentally on a complete body. This is not at all surprising, but highlights the known errors and indicates that they are to some extent self-compensatory within the accuracy of the gust factor approach.

Results in Fig. 3.44 refer to the total effect, as if the structural mode were a uniform displacement. As has already been implied, the strict solution should take account of the mode shape. Wyatt (1971, 1975a) has suggested a method of evaluating the equivalent size of idealized structure for any actual shape. A further simplification had already been developed by Davenport (1968), whereby results for both the background and resonant effects are tabulated on the assumption that both the natural mode shape function and the structural influence function are directly proportional to the height above ground. The former is sufficiently accurate for most tall buildings of roughly uniform mass and stiffness distribution, and the latter (strictly correct for the base moment of a uniform building) leads to a satisfactory approximation for most load effects near the base of buildings, excepting the effects of over-all torsion on the structure. Such procedures have been incorporated in national codes of practice or design manuals, or both. The root-mean-square load effect obtained by integrating the response spectrum (Fig. 3.43 and Eq. 3.20) is expressed as

$$\frac{\sigma_Q}{Q} = 2 \frac{\sigma_u}{\bar{u}} \sqrt{B + \frac{SE}{\zeta}} \qquad (3.29)$$

in which B and SE/ζ are related to the integrals of the background and resonance parts of the response spectrum, respectively. In the example given in Figs. 3.45 through 3.48 and in the presentation given in the Canadian Structural Design Manual, S depends on the area affected by a "resonant gust" by comparison with the size of the structure, and E (F in the Canadian Manual) expresses the relative strength of the resonant gust component at a point. The gust intensity $\sigma_u/\bar{u}$ is incorporated in the exposure factor gr; in this (as in most similar presentations) the turbulence RMS σ_u has been assumed invariant with height. As current opinion suggests lower values for σ_u with increasing height, the load effect may be overestimated.

The evaluation of the dynamic augmentation of the load effect is thus straightforward. Much less straightforward is the determination of appropriate discount of the design load factor (factor of safety). Conventional design load factors are essentially the outcome of experience obtained with static design procedures but in all cases some dynamic response has been inevitable, and in many cases it is by no means negligible. An appropriate reduction of design load factors is entirely justified when using the methods outlined here, and is indeed essential if economy is to be realized.

To summarize the applicability of the methods described:

1. The methods are based on rational simplification of complex phenomena, and in particular assume that the wind load fluctuations are dominated by the fluctuations in the incident wind speed.

2. Existing data permit only a generalized input of incident wind speed, thus excluding cases where the input will be dominated by the effect of discrete structures of similar size in the incident flow region.

3. The procedure as summarized by Fig. 3.43 makes clear the delicate sensitivity of the dynamic response on the relative alinement in terms of frequency of the input spectrum and the two admittances, which incorporate all the governing variables referred to in Article 2 of Section 3.2. The analysis of the resonant contribution is straightforward and involves relatively well-established data (apart from uncertainty over structural dynamic properties, notably damping and "nonstructural" supplementation of stiffness, which affect equally the wind tunnel procedures in Section 3.6). This analysis is therefore a major advance over earlier methods, and is at the very least a guide to the need for further studies.

4. The background (alternative terminology "broad-band" or "quasi-static") effect is for simple cases analogous to the size reduction factor in some earlier methods whereby large structures were designed for effective speeds less than the peak gust speed. The effect involves less well established data, but the result for such cases is not generally very sensitive. Simple generalized chart presentations are usually sufficient.

5. The background effect becomes a more significant design factor when load effects arise which are especially sensitive to loads on a limited section of the structure, most conspicuously so when the mean pressure on some parts are subtractive from the net design value. For such special cases evaluation of the admittance functions for the specific case is justified; relation to a standard result, probably by an "equivalent size" approach, is usually sufficient.

6. The basic assumptions do not justify excessive refinement of calculation, but in view of the rapid extension of knowledge of input wind data it may be valuable to check or to recalculate quoted results with more up-to-date input.*

7. The design load factor must be modified in accordance with the degree of detail in the analysis.

---

* For example, see the following Engineering Science Data Unit (ESDU) Data Items:

72026 Characteristics of Wind Speed in the Lower Layers of the Atmosphere near the Ground: strong wind (neutral atmosphere).

74030 Characteristics of Atmospheric Turbulence near the Ground. Pt. I Definitions & General Information.

74031 Characteristics of Atmospheric Turbulence near the Ground. Pt. II Single Point Data for Strong Winds (neutral atmosphere).

75001 Characteristics of Atmospheric Turbulence near the Ground. Pt III Variations in Space and Time for Strong Winds (neutral atmosphere).

2 Analysis of Acceleration (Comfort) Criteria

The accelerations of the structure due to wind are dominated by the resonant components of response. The RMS acceleration $\sigma_{\ddot{x}}$ contribution from response in the lowest mode is $(2\pi n_o)^2$ times the RMS displacement of the resonant component (and correspondingly in any other mode). The expected peak value is $g\sigma_{\ddot{x}}$ as before. The lowest mode is generally dominant but other modes should be checked if there is reason to suppose that there are natural frequencies not much greater than the lowest value, for example in the case of structure of low torsional stiffness. The net RMS value is obtained by adding the squares (variances) of the individual modal contributions.

It was pointed out in Section 3.4 that the cross-wind motion is likely to be of major importance in acceleration response. This is discussed further in the following Article.

3 Cross-Wind

The cross-wind excitation of tall buildings was introduced in Section 3.4, where the conclusions of Saunders and Melbourne (1975) that the cross-wind motion of tall buildings is predominantly due to wake excitation were reproduced in full. Generalized empirical methods of predicting the cross-wind response of tall buildings have been difficult to formulate, even assuming total dependence on wake excitation, because of the effects of turbulence, building geometry, operating reduced frequency range, density, structural damping, and upstream interference.

Vickery (1973) and Melbourne (1975a) have presented formulas based on series of wind tunnel measurements which allow a rough approximation to be made of the cross-wind response of a tall building. They are useful in deciding whether there is likely to be a problem sufficient to warrant further investigation with an aeroelastic model test.

A more comprehensive approach, still based on empirical wind tunnel data, and which can take into account the variables of turbulence, building geometry, operating reduced frequency range, structural stiffness, density, and damping has been given by Saunders and Melbourne (1975). The method has been given with data for isolated rectangular buildings and is based on a generalized cross-wind force spectrum from which the response spectra and hence RMS response may be calculated as

$$S_y(n) = \frac{S_F(n)\,H^2(n)}{K^2} \tag{3.30}$$

$$\sigma_y = \sqrt{\int S_y(n)\,dn} \tag{3.31}$$

in which $S_F(n)$ = the "power" spectral density of the cross-wind aerodynamic force; K = effective stiffness of the model building, defined by Eq. 3.33; $S_y(n)$ = the "power" spectral density of the cross-wind displacement of the top of the model building; and $H^2(n)$ = the mechanical admittance of the model building, which is expressed as

$$H^2(n) = \frac{1}{\left[1 - \left(\dfrac{n}{n_o}\right)^2\right]^2 + 4\zeta^2\left(\dfrac{n}{n_o}\right)^2} \tag{3.32}$$

in which n_o = natural frequency; and ζ = fraction of critical damping (equivalent viscous damping). The effective stiffness is defined by

$$K = (2\pi n_o)^2 M \qquad (3.33)$$

in which M = effective mass of the building, which is equal to the total mass of the building divided by 3 for a building that can be approximated by a straight-line pivoting about the base and that can be assumed to have a uniform density over the building.

The procedure for determining force spectra analytically is shown diagrammatically in Fig. 3.50, and examples of cross-wind force spectra for some rectangular buildings are given in Fig. 3.51.

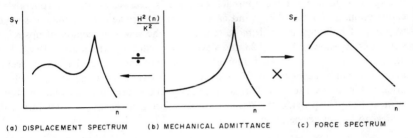

(a) DISPLACEMENT SPECTRUM   (b) MECHANICAL ADMITTANCE   (c) FORCE SPECTRUM

Fig. 3.50 Determination of displacement spectrum from force spectrum and mechanical admittance (*Saunders and Melbourne, 1975*)

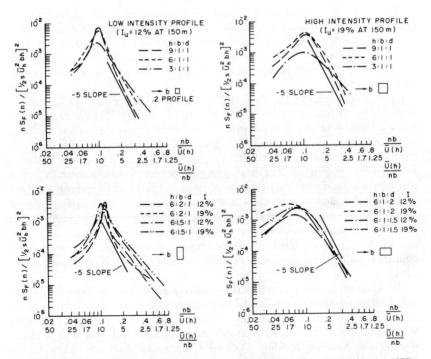

Fig. 3.51 Cross-wind force spectra of rectangular buildings (*Saunders and Melbourne, 1975*)

Whitbread (1975) has shown that the generalized force spectra can be obtained simply and directly from a rigidly mounted model rather than from model response spectra as used by Saunders and Melbourne (1975). This method is quite satisfactory provided it is known that displacement effects on the force spectra are negligible, which Saunders and Melbourne demonstrated was the case for a large range of rectangular buildings. However, the assumption becomes invalid for buildings and towers that are very lightly damped and operating at reduced frequencies at around or below 0.1. Ellis (1975) has presented a technique for obtaining force spectra from accelerometers mounted in an aeroelastic model which can also take account of mode shape, should this ever become a significant parameter.

The acquisition of much more experimental data than those available, and given in Fig. 3.51, to support the approach outlined is necessary before a generalized codification, as for the along-wind case, can be undertaken. Also, the cross-wind response of buildings is much more sensitive to the wake interaction of upstream structures, as shown in Fig. 3.38 and developed further by Melbourne (1976). For most tall buildings in the environment of other buildings of similar size, it seems that it will still be necessary to obtain data from specific wind tunnel tests, as will be discussed in the next section. This is particularly so because the cross-wind response is most likely to provide the design criteria relating to occupancy comfort with respect to lateral acceleration.

4   Design Pressure for Glass and Cladding

The aerodynamic origin of local pressures on the surface of a tall building has been discussed in Section 3.4 in relation to three distinct areas, the upstream face, the streamwise face under reattaching shear layers, and the rear faces in a fully developed wake region. The description of design pressure loading on cladding in terms of mean plus peak fluctuating component $\hat{p} = \bar{p} + g\sigma_p$, was also introduced, with examples.

Some recent papers by Dalgliesh (1971), Allen and Dalgliesh (1973), Tryggvasen et al. (1975), Melbourne (1975b), and Peterka and Cermak (1975) have discussed the statistical treatment and determination of design pressures for glass and cladding. Allen and Dalgliesh (1973) and Davenport (1975c), in particular, discussed rate effects on ductile (steel) and brittle (glass) panels which will be discussed further in Section 3.7. They conclude that the cladding can be considered as a statically loaded structure because the natural frequency of metal and glass panels varies from about 5 Hz to 50 Hz, and in most cases this frequency is higher than significant wind turbulence frequencies. During elastic deformations a panel can be represented as a statically loaded structure and dynamic amplification can be disregarded. Only for unusual, high-frequency wind turbulence, created locally by building corners or by significant surface irregularities, is dynamic magnification likely to become significant.

Unfortunately, none of these papers gives any direction as to the determination of actual design pressures except by wind tunnel testing. This will be discussed in detail in Sections 3.6 and 3.7. As yet, there is no generalized analytical approach available for the determination of design pressures on cladding. Several wind loading codes, such as the National Building Code of Canada and recent additions to the Australian Wind Code AS1170, do give limited guidance on the determination of cladding pressures on tall buildings. There have been some ad hoc tests on models of particular building projects to determine cladding loads, and although it is proprietary, much of the information is accessible, particularly those tests conducted at the Boundary Layer Wind Tunnel Laboratory, University of Western Ontario, which could provide guidance.

It would be unreasonable to leave this area without making some comment on the problem of the large coefficient of variation associated with the strength of glass. One summary of the problem is given in the Australian Standard 1288-1973, Installation of Glass in Buildings. The recommended glass thicknesses in this code are based on a 50-yr return design wind pressure, a cofficient of variation of glass strength of 25%, and a probability of failure of 0.2%. The design stress for glass for these conditions is equal to the mean breaking stress divided by 3.5, the latter figure sometimes being referred to as a "safety factor."

3.6 WIND TUNNEL MODELING APPROACHES TO DESIGN

Engineers concerned with the effects of wind on buildings and structures have in the past often turned to experimental model methods to provide design data. Documented wind tunnel experiments on bluff bodies by Eiffel, Prandtl, Irminger and others date back to the eve of the 20th century. With the intense interest in aeronautics precipitated by the First World War, however, relatively little progress was made in structural or building aerodynamics. A resurgence of interest among engineers in the effects of wind on buildings and structures was brought about by the collapse of the first Tacoma Narrows Suspension Bridge in 1940. Structural engineers naturally turned to the well-established body of theoretical and experimental aeronautical aerodynamics.

Aeronautical wind tunnels with relatively short working sections, designed to produce uniform low turbulence flows, were used to investigate wind-induced effects on buildings and structures. Although use was made of established aeroelastic and aerodynamic similarity theory to model the properties of particular structures, little attention was usually given to achieving wind tunnel flow conditions representative of natural wind. It is not too surprising, therefore, that generally there was disagreement between wind tunnel results and available full-scale measurements. Not until Jensen (1958) presented his "Model Law for Phenomena in Natural Wind" did the need for modeling the turbulent shear flow properties of natural wind become fully recognized.

Techniques for the modeling of wind effects on buildings and structures have improved considerably since the 1960s with the advent of several large wind tunnels designed to produce turbulent boundary layer models of the natural wind. The need to model structures and the turbulent characteristics of the natural wind more accurately has increased as structures have become more competitively designed, often very tall and slender and with low damping.

The requirements for the modeling of buildings to measure wind effects are generally agreed among workers in the field. However for a number of reasons the techniques used and assumptions made to achieve these requirements vary considerably. Probably the main reason for this is not so much lack of agreement as variations in the capabilities of the various wind tunnel facilities and associated equipment. This section will outline the model scaling requirements, describe modeling techniques, and give examples of model measurements.

1   Types of Wind Tunnel Tests

Wind tunnel tests currently being conducted on buildings can be divided into two types. The first is concerned with the determination of wind loading effects to enable the design of a wind resistant structure. The second is concerned with the flow fields induced around the structure—for example, as it affects pedestrian comfort and safety at ground level, or the rise of a plume from a chimney stack—and ground level or air intake concentration levels of exhaust pollutants.

The types of tests used to determine wind loading effects can be divided further into those which are quasi-steady and those which model the dynamics of both the wind and the structure.

The quasi-steady type of tests usually involves the measurement of mean (sometimes called static) pressure distributions or force on on a building in a nominally steady wind speed. The pressure or force coefficients so determined are then used to calculate full-scale loadings by means of a maximum gust wind speed usually called the design wind speed. This approach is relatively simple and quite satisfactory for many structures, and is the approach used in most of the wind loading codes. However, even mean measurements depend on the turbulence characteristics of the incident air flow, and so the turbulence must be modeled.

The limitations of the quasi-steady approach occur when the wind loading on the building is significantly increased or decreased by the response of the building to the energy available at resonant frequencies, or when it is due to cross-wind excitation. When this occurs, a full dynamic test is usually required to determine the wind loading. A dynamic test to cover the effects of structural response requires that the velocity profile and turbulent properties of the natural wind be modeled correctly, along with such structural modes as could be expected to be excited and the damping of the structure.

Tests for modeling flow fields and diffusion rates also generally require that the velocity profile and turbulent properties of the natural wind be modeled correctly. The velocity gradient is most important as the upstream face pressure gradients and hence flow fields are directly related to the local incident dynamic pressure. In some cases the turbulent properties in detail are not quite so important as, for example, the entrainment, and hence diffusion rate of a buoyant plume in the initial phases is more dependent on internal plume turbulence which is dominated by buoyant motions. In this section reference to modeling of plumes and dispersion of pollutants is restricted to tests in a neutral atmosphere where the local flow fields around structures cause significant entrainment of pollutants into wake regions. Modeling of thermal effects on atmospheric motions and hence large-scale diffusion studies have been undertaken (Cermak, 1971), but it is considered outside the scope of this field as few wind tunnels are equipped with wall heating (or cooling).

2   Model Scaling Requirements

The modeling of wind effects on buildings requires first that a satisfactory model of the natural wind be produced and then that a similarly scaled structural model be tested in this model wind environment. Criteria and techniques for achieving a model of the natural wind have been discussed in various depths by Jensen (1958), Davenport and Isyumov (1967), Cermak et al. (1966, 1971), Templin (1969), McVehil et al. (1967), Nemoto (1968), Armitt and Counihan (1968, 1969),

Melbourne (1971), and Cook (1973). The principles of aeroelastic modeling of structures have been discussed in many papers. In the area of buildings such principles and requirements have been discussed by Scruton (1963), Whitbread (1963), Melbourne (1972), and Vickery (1972).

The most direct and reliable method of predicting the response of a building to wind action while in the design stage is to construct and test an aeroelastic model. The similarity requirements to be satisfied to assure similarity of behavior between model and full-scale prototype may be determined by dimensional analysis or similarity arguments (Pankhurst, 1964; Langhaar, 1951). A summary of the main points in the development of criteria for modeling the response of a building to wind action is as follows.

Main Properties on which the Process Depends—Properties of the Fluid.

Mean wind speed at a reference height $\bar{u}$ ($\bar{u}_{10}$ or $\bar{u}_g$).

Density ρ.

Dynamic viscosity μ.

The vertical mean wind speed profile $u_z/\bar{u}_g$.

The turbulence characteristics of the wind, in particular for the longitudinal component as represented by the turbulence intensity $\sigma_u/\bar{u}$, the normalized power spectral density $nSu(n)/\sigma_u^2$, and the normalized cross-spectral density (or coherence), and to a lesser extent the same for the other components.

Properties of the Building.

Aerodynamic (external) shape, that is, linear dimension L.

Distribution of elastic stiffness with typical elastic modulus E.

Distribution of mass with typical structural density ρ_s.

Distribution of structural damping, characterized by an over-all logarithmic decrement for decaying oscillations δ or critical damping ratio ζ, $[\zeta = (\delta/2\pi)]$.

With correctly scaled external shape, distribution of mass and stiffness, and correctly scaled turbulence and mean wind profile properties (as will be discussed in Article 3, which follows), the model will be dynamically similar to the full scale if the following nondimensional parameters have the same values on the model as on full scale: density ratio ρ_s/ρ; stiffness parameter $E/\rho\bar{u}^2$; viscosity parameter (Reynolds number) $\rho\bar{u}L/\mu$; and damping parameter ζ.

It is rarely possible to construct a model as a replica of the prototype in materials with the physical properties prescribed by these similarity requirements, and acceptable compromises must be sought by ignoring parameters that have little influence on the structural response to wind action.

For tall buildings with sharp corners, the Reynolds number has little effect on the air flow pattern and hence pressure field around the building and is usually ignored. Also, in many cases the fundamental mode of oscillation in bending may be approximated by a straight line. The model may therefore be constructed as a rigid replica of the correct external shape but spring mounted on gimbals at its base, as will be discussed in Article 4 of this section.

3 Natural Wind Models

If the natural wind is to be modeled at all accurately, the minimum requirements are similarity of: (1) Velocity profile $\bar{u}_z/\bar{u}_g$; (2) turbulence intensity $\sigma_u/\bar{u}_z$; and (3) power spectral density of the longitudinal component $nSu(n)(\sigma_u)^2$.

Various techniques have been used to achieve these minimum requirements. Basically the natural wind, for strong wind, neutral conditions, is a rough wall turbulent boundary layer with some larger scales superimposed, and hence is best modeled in the same way. Unfortunately, the development of a rough wall boundary layer requires very long wind tunnel working sections, and it is only in the last decade that special wind tunnels with this requirement have been built. Most of these boundary layer wind tunnels have been of the open circuit type and descriptions of the development of the natural wind models by the augmented growth of a rough wall boundary layer have been given in numerous references (see preceding Article 2). The techniques for developing a natural wind model in a straight section, such as an open circuit wind tunnel, are illustrated by the wind tunnel at Colorado State University shown in Fig. 3.52 (Cermak, 1975). A

Fig. 3.52 View of model and boundary layer development in the 2 ½-m square working section wind tunnel at Colorado State University *(Cermak, 1975)*

diagrammatic view of a relatively short tunnel for part depth boundary layer simulation at the Building Research Establishement in England is shown in Fig. 3.53 (Cook, 1975). (In Fig. 3.53, length of flow processing section = 5 m; test section = 3 m; $\bar{x}$ section = 2 m $\times$ 1 m; over-all length = 14 m.) A novel method of producing a natural wind model shear flow, using a system of jets, has been developed by Teunissen (1975) at the U.T.I.A.S. Toronto, shown in Fig. 3.54. Other systems using cross jets have been developed by Gorecki and Blessmann. The main advantage of using jets is that the turbulence and shear characteristics can be quickly changed. A Euromech 50 meeting on wind tunnel simulation of the atmosphere boundary layer, listing some facilities, was reported by Hunt and Fernholz (1975).

At Monash University, Australia, wind models are developed in two working sections of a closed circuit wind tunnel as shown in Figs. 3.55 and 3.56 (Melbourne, 1972, 1975a). In the 4 m $\times$ 3 m working section, model scales of between 1/100 and 1/300 for a range of terrain conditions are developed by superimposing a large two-dimensional separation bubble on a rough wall boundary layer growing along three legs of the wind tunnel circuit. In the 2 m $\times$ 2 m working section, another shear layer is initiated with triangular vorticity generators, which is again

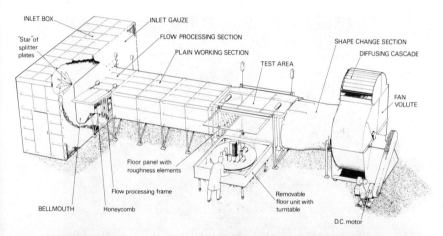

Fig. 3.53 BRE Boundary Layer Wind Tunnel, example of relatively short tunnel for part-depth boundary layer simulation *(Cook, 1975; Courtesy: Building Research Establishment —Crown copyright reserved)*

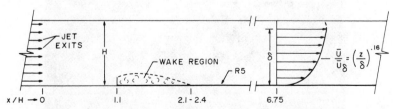

Fig. 3.54 Wind tunnel configuration at UTIAS Toronto, Canada, using jets, barrier, and roughness to develop a model wind shear flow—designation R5 denotes surface roughness *(Teunissen, 1975)*

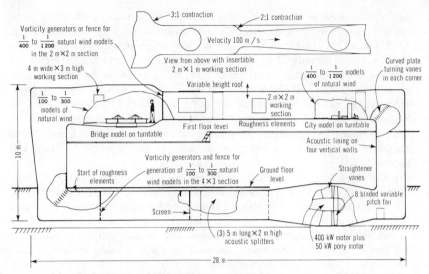

Fig. 3.55 Layout of 400 kW wind tunnel at Monash University in which natural wind models are developed *(Melbourne, 1975a)*

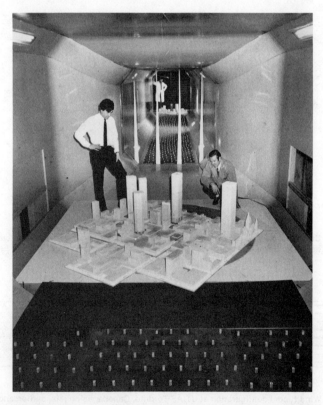

Fig. 3.56 Model buildings in 4 m × 3 m and 2 m × 2 m working sections of Monash University 400 kW wind tunnel set up to produce scale models of natural wind in each section, for alternate use *(Melbourne, 1975a)*

superimposed on an inner developing rough wall boundary layer. Model scales of between 1/400 and 1/1200 are developed in this working section, again for a variety of terrain conditions obtained by varying the size of the roughness elements and the vorticity generators.

An example is shown in Fig. 3.57 of the minimum natural wind characteristics which it is suggested are required to be modeled reasonably accurately for model tests of wind effects on structures.

4 Aeroelastic Models

The wind loading on a structure is only truly modeled when the wind and the structure are both fully modeled, that is, the model structure can respond to the loading system in the same way as the full-scale structure.

In terms of the scaling requirements it is essential that the structure length scale, time scale, and inertia force scale are the same as the model of the natural wind. Then with respect to the stiffness requirements, the ratio between model and full-scale inertia and elastic forces, as can be expressed by the stiffness parameter $E/\rho\bar{u}^2$, must be kept constant. Last, but not least, the damping ratio (or energy dissipation ratio) must be the same for model and full scale.

In many cases some distortion of these specific criteria can be permitted without causing significant violation of the over-all modeling criteria. The simplest way to illustrate this is to quote several examples. It is convenient to refer to scaling ratios of model over full scale with a subscript r, for example

$$L_r = \frac{\text{model length}}{\text{full-scale length}}.$$

1. The derivation of time or velocity scales is important. In the simplest form

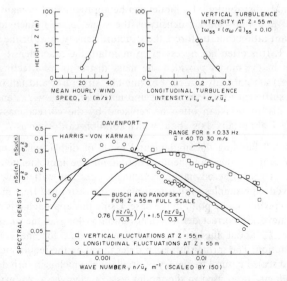

Fig. 3.57 Characteristic of 1/150 scale model of wind flow over suburban-factory fetch *(Melbourne, 1973)*

the Strouhal number (or Reduced Frequency) must be equal in model and prototype, that is

$$\left(\frac{nL}{\bar{u}}\right) \text{model} = \left(\frac{nL}{\bar{u}}\right) \text{full scale} \qquad (3.34)$$

$$\frac{n_r L_r}{\bar{u}_r} = 1 \qquad (3.35)$$

therefore

$$\bar{u}_r = n_r L_r \qquad (3.36)$$

or $\bar{u}_r = L_r / T_r$, in which T_r = time scale ratio, giving $T_r = L_r / \bar{u}_r$.

2. For a tower, building, or part of a structure where the mode of resistance is pure bending (flexural) or torsion, the Stiffness Parameter criterion can be modified from $E/\rho\bar{u}^2$ = Const. to $EI/\rho\bar{u}^2L^4$ = Const., or $GJ/\rho\bar{u}^2L^4$ = Const., in which EI and GJ = sectional flexural and torsional stiffnesses. For $\rho_r = 1$ this gives

$$(EI)_r = (GJ)_r = L_r^4 \bar{u}_r^2 \qquad (3.37)$$

3. For cables or members where the mode of resistance is purely axial the Stiffness Parameter criterion can be modified from $E/\rho\bar{u}^2$ = Const. to $EA/\rho\bar{u}^2L^2$ = Const., in which EA = force per unit strain. For $\rho_r = 1$ this gives

$$(EI)_r = L_r^2 \bar{u}_r^2 \qquad (3.38)$$

4. The mass distribution of a model can be approximated in many ways. If the model and full-scale air density is the same, $\rho_r = 1$, then to maintain a constant ratio of inertia forces the structure density must be the same, that is, $\rho_{s_r} = 1$. It is often not necessary to maintain the exact density at all scaled points in the model provided the mass distributions affecting the motion (modes) are correctly scaled. For line-like structures and tall buildings it is often sufficient to scale mass per unit length m as $m_r = L_r^2$, and the correct mass distribution can often be replaced by the correct mass moment of inertia I about any axis about which rotation can occur as $I_{m_r} = L_r^5$.

5. For a tall building the fundamental mode of displacement, made up of a combination of shear and bending action, may be approximated by a straight line. In terms of aerodynamic modeling it does not matter how this mode is achieved. The simplest way is to use a spring restrained rigid model which is free to pivot about a point in the base. Using this approach it is not necessary to achieve the correct density distribution as long as the mass moment of inertia I_m about the base is the same as that for the correct density distribution. The spring stiffness is determined by the requirement to achieve a fixed scaled natural frequency of oscillation, which is in turn determined by the velocity ratio used in the model tests or vice versa. An example of this

(a)

(b)

Fig. 3.58 Composite photograph of rigid element model mounted on flexure pivots to allow
along-wind and cross-wind displacements pivoting about base of building at University of
Western Ontario Boundary Layer Wind Tunnel Laboratory *(Photo by Ron Nelson
Photography)*

type of model at the University of Western Ontario is shown in Fig. 3.58. For this model the scaling ratios of model over full scale are

moment of inertia

$$I_{m_r} = L_r^5 \text{ for } \rho_r = \rho_{s_r} = 1 \tag{3.39}$$

moment about base (stiffness)

$$H_r = \bar{u}_r^2 L_r^3 \tag{3.40}$$

and time scale given by period

$$T_r = \frac{I_{m_r}}{H_r} = \frac{L_r}{\bar{u}_r} \tag{3.41}$$

as it must.

6. A more detailed representation of a tall building can be achieved using a physical model analogous to the familiar mathematical "lumped-mass" model. A five-mass model with 15 degrees of freedom is shown in Fig. 3.59. The modeling parameters for this type of model are best described with

Fig. 3.59 University of Western Ontario Boundary Layer Wind Tunnel exploded view of five-element aeroelastic model building with sway and torsion modes modeled *(Davenport et al., 1970a; Photo by Ron Nelson Photography)*

reference to the mass and stiffness matrices of the real structure and those of the model, that is

$$\mathbf{K_M} = \mathbf{K_p} \times L_r^3 T_r^{-2} \rho_{s_r} \qquad (3.42)$$

$$\mathbf{M_M} = \mathbf{M_p} \times L_r^3 \rho_{s_r} \qquad (3.43)$$

The prototype mass and stiffness matrices $(\mathbf{M_p}, \mathbf{K_p})$ must of course be reduced to the same number of degrees of freedom as in the model.

5   Pressure Measurements on Models

Static pressure measurements can be made through flush surface pressure taps on the face of a model.

The scaling requirement with respect to bluff bodies with sharp corners is essentially maintenance of the natural wind parameters of velocity profile, turbulence intensity profile, and spectra. Probably the most important parameter is the achievement of turbulence scales and intensities which dominate the radius of curvature of the shear layers (see Section 3.4), as for design purposes the highest (negative) pressures often occur in regions under the shear layer near the leading

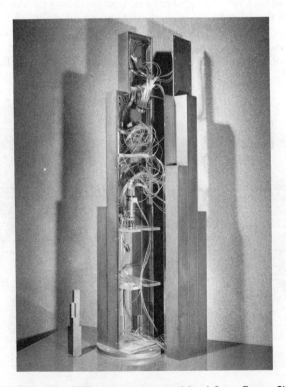

Fig. 3.60 View of 1:400 and 1:2000 scale pressure models of Sears Tower, Chicago, Illinois
(Davenport et al., 1971; Photo by Ron Nelson Photography)

edge. The intermittent behavior of the radius of curvature of these shear layers seems to be responsible for the very high negative peak pressures which occur in these regions for critical angle of attack conditions.

It is essential that measurements be made of mean, RMS, and peak pressures or probability distributions of pressures from which the peak factor g can be evaluated. This means that pressure transducers with a frequency response of 1 kHz to 2 kHz are required for model scales on the order of 1/400. It also means that tubes from pressure taps have to be very short, or transducers flush mounted, to maintain the required frequency response. Alternatively, when using digital data reduction systems, a probability distribution can easily be obtained each time and extrapolated to the desired probability level (frequency response) as suggested by Melbourne (1975b). An example of a pressure tapped model for making the range of pressure measurements required is given in Fig. 3.60 of the Sears Tower models tested at the Boundary Layer Wind Tunnel Laboratory at the University of Western Ontario by Davenport et al. (1971). Examples of pressure measurements made on this model will be given in Section 3.7, along with further discussion on frequency response and design loads.

6   Ground Level Wind Distributions

Model studies to determine the distribution of wind flow at ground level have been employed for a variety of applications. Most commonly the aim of such studies is to evaluate the ground level wind climate around buildings, which is discussed separately in Section 3.8. Other applications include the use of small-scale topographic models such as that shown in Fig. 3.61 to examine wind speed profiles and to transfer meteorological data from a measuring station in the field to the site

Fig. 3.61 Topographical model of Pittsburgh in University of Western Ontario Boundary Layer Wind Tunnel (*Robertson and Chen, 1967; Photo by Ron Nelson Photography*)

of a major structure. Similar studies have been used to map ground level wind speeds.

An example of a wind map prepared as part of a study of ground level winds near a proposed building is shown in Fig. 3.62 (Vickery, 1974). The contours shown are the ratios of the ground level gust speed to the mean speed at an anemometer site for which long-term records were available. The gust speed is the "95%" speed, that is, the speed which is exceeded for about 5% of the time during which the mean speed at the airport is constant. Maps of this type obtained for a number of wind directions can be integrated with the anemometer records to yield an estimate of the ground wind climate. In this instance very high speeds were observed in the vicinity of the northern corner, and it would therefore be desirable to arrange pedestrian access ways in such a manner that this area was avoided.

7 Dispersal of Gaseous Pollutants

The dispersal of gaseous pollutants in the environment of tall buildings is closely dependent on the wind flow about the buildings. There are two types of problems of current interest to building designers:

1. The height of a chimney stack, carrying boiler or other types of gaseous exhaust, must be sufficient to assure that the exhaust plume clears the immediate buildings, otherwise there is no point in having a chimney stack.

2. Where pollutants are exhausted into wake regions of buildings, it is necessary to determine the resultant concentrations that occur at air-conditioning intakes and at street level.

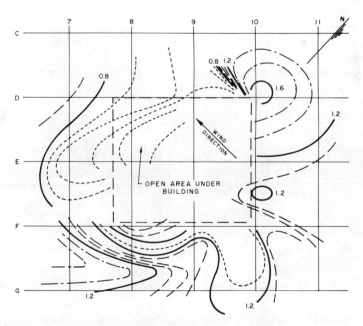

Fig. 3.62 Map of ground level wind speeds in vicinity of a building *(Vickery, 1974b)*

In recent years, both of these problems have been the subjects of model testing on an ad hoc basis. Model scaling criteria for the full turbulent diffusion process have been discussed by Cermak et al. (1966), including the problems of modeling thermal stratification of the atmosphere, which is very important for large-scale diffusion studies. For problems where only the near field to the building is involved, it is usually adequate to model a neutrally stable atmospheric wind. In this case the problem is reduced to that of a stream of buoyant contaminating fluid entering either a boundary layer stream or a wake region. The path and spread of the contaminating plume in the initial phases are dependent primarily on exit buoyancy and momentum conditions in relation to the freestream momentum, as described by Csanady (1973). To achieve dynamic similarity for these types of model studies, it is necessary to keep the following nondimensional scaling parameters equal in both scales (Melbourne, 1968; Snyder, 1972)

$$\text{plume buoyancy} \quad \frac{\Delta \rho g D}{\rho \bar{u}^2}$$

$$\text{initial plume momentum} \quad \frac{\rho_p w^2 D^2}{\rho \bar{u}^2 L^2}$$

$$\text{plume mass flow rate} \quad \frac{\rho_p w D^2}{\rho \bar{u} L^2}$$

in which $\bar{u}$, L, and ρ = freestream velocity at building height, building width dimension, and freestream density, respectively; D, W, $\Delta \rho$, and ρ_p = initial plume diameter, vertical velocity, density defect ($\rho - \rho_p$), and density, respectively; and g = gravitational acceleration.

It is usual to use helium as the buoyant exhaust gas in model studies to achieve as high a model velocity as possible (even so, model freestream velocities are mostly on the order of 1 m/s).

In Fig. 3.63 an example is given of the way in which a plume path can be influenced by the flow field around a building. The plume path is traced visibly by introducing smoke (vaporized oil) into the exhaust gas. For given wind conditions it is then possible to determine a suitable stack location and height to avoid direct

(a)   *(b)*

Fig. 3.63 Downwash visualization by smoke emission from small-scale: (a) Stack downwind of building; (b) Stack upwind of building (*Cermak, 1974*)

entrainment of the plume into the building wake or premature ground strike of part of the plume. Examples of tests measuring ground level concentrations from chimney stack plume and car part exhaust discharge are given by Cermak (1974).

A description of a model study of the contamination of air-conditioning intakes by flue gas exhausted into the wake region at the top of a tall building has been given by Melbourne and Gartshore (1975a). This type of study involves the measurement of pollutant concentrations, and one of the most satisfactory ways to do this is to use a helium plume, or a plume with a helium tracer, and measure the very low levels of helium concentrations at various locations with a mass spectrometer tuned to helium. An example of this type of measurement is given in Fig. 3.64. A similar test using carbon dioxide as the tracer has been described by Whitbread (1974).

McCormick (1971) has discussed air pollution in the locality of buildings, and in particular refers to Halitsky (1965) who gave a general equation to express the distribution of gas concentration in the flow field around a building

$$C = \frac{K\dot{Q}}{AV} \tag{3.44}$$

in which C = concentration; $\dot{Q}$ = gas release rate; A = maximum frontal projected area of building; V = wind speed at roof level; and K = nondimensional coefficient that is a function of space coordinates. It is "approximately unity on the

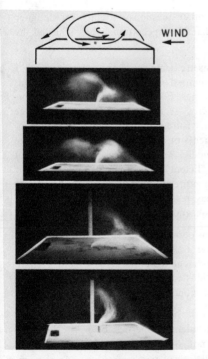

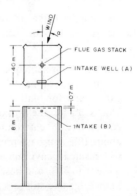

Test description	Mean wind speed (m/s)	Wind direction (α)	% of flue gas in intake air
Intakes at A	5–17	0°	0.25 – 0.40
Intakes at A	5	0° – 180°	0.25 – 0.40
Intakes at B	5	0°	0.15

Fig. 3.64 Example of model measurements of intake contamination by flue gas exhaust using helium in buoyant exhaust and as tracer *(Melbourne and Gartshore, 1975)*

side walls" where the gas is released within the cavity (wake region) on the roof. Rummerfield et al. (1967) reported these comparisons of full-scale measurements with Eq. 3.44 for concentrations within the immediate wake region.

8 Wind Tunnel Test Expectations

A note by Melbourne (1973) with the above title was written for the Tall Buildings Conference held at Lehigh University. It contains several summarized observations which may be of some help to a structural designer when embarking on a wind tunnel test program. In particular it was noted that the designer can expect to get reasonably satisfactory predictions of full-scale wind loading and building response only if:

1. Complete and reliable meteorological data are available.

2. Natural wind has been modeled to account for distributions of scale and intensity of turbulence.

3. The structure is modeled to account for length scale (which must be the same as that of the natural wind model), mass and stiffness distribution, modes that affect aerodynamic characteristics and, last but not least, damping.

4. The measurements are made and analyzed on a probabilistic basis which includes correlation of load and response in two perpendicular directions in the case of a tall building.

It was also suggested that there were a few other questions on which the designer should get satisfactory answers to assure that his expectations were achieved, as follows:

1. What wind tunnel blockage corrections are being used? This question is valid for all types of model tests in a bounded wind tunnel working section, particularly for bluff bodies like buildings. For example, even a model that blocks 3% of the working section cross-sectional area requires blockage corrections to environmental flow measurements of velocity pressure of about 10% and base pressure coefficients of about 0.1; while 10% blockage will result in environmental flow velocity pressure measurement errors of more than 30%, and base pressure coefficient errors of about 0.5. Despite this knowledge one still sees models and pictures of models which fill up to 20% of working section cross-sectional areas, results from which must be virtually useless. Reference is made to McKeon and Melbourne (1971).

2. Have the meteorological data been corrected for original anemometer position errors, height, and type of terrain? In Australia it has been found necessary to correct many of the basic meteorological data, and even to reject records from a number of stations where anemometers have become shielded. Topographical modeling occasionally becomes necessary to resolve this problem.

3. Has the fetch of roughness or turbulent properties been satisfactorily modeled for all wind directions? If not, there is not much point in using probabilistic approaches for the prediction of response.

4. Does the model correctly permit all modes which might influence aero-dynamic input, particularly cross-wind?

5. Are the maximum wind loads likely to occur in thunderstorm conditions? If so, then there may be reason to be conservative because less is known about thunderstorms and short period meteorological records may not permit satisfactory extreme value estimates. A similar comment could apply to tropical cyclones (hurricanes, typhoons).

3.7 INTEGRATION OF RESPONSE AND WIND DATA FOR DESIGN PURPOSES

Any combination of mean wind speed and direction will possess a wind structure that is conditioned by the surface over which the wind has passed, and it will have a probability of occurrence. To determine the design parameters relating to wind loading, it is necessary to combine the statistical wind data with response or pressure estimates for various wind conditions obtained either analytically or from wind tunnel tests. The aim of this process is to predict the response or load history of the building or components of the building during its likely lifetime, and to determine extreme values of the wind loading for use in either limit state or allowable stress design methods.

1   Prediction of Extreme Response

The word "response" is used generally here to cover any response functions that are linearly related, such as deflection, acceleration, base overturning moment, bending moment in a particular column, etc. Note that, contrary to conventional design assumptions, the response in this exercise is always considered to be bidirectional and can be resolved along x and y axes. the general response variable will be designated s.

Different methods in detail can be used. The one described here and illustrated in

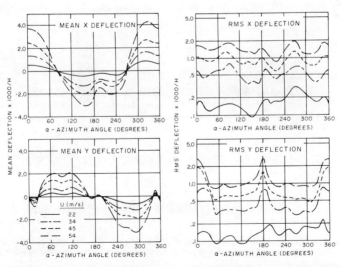

Fig. 3.65 Mapping of mean and RMS deflection of tall rectangular building from aeroelastic model (Davenport, 1972a)

Fig. 3.67 is based on the concept of having hourly mean and RMS response data, such as those shown in Fig. 3.65 after Davenport (1972), from which the average hourly peak value can be identified by means of a peak factor obtained from the probability distribution of the variable as introduced in Sections 3.4 and 3.5, that is

$$\hat{s} = \bar{s} + g\sigma_s \qquad (3.45)$$

in which $\hat{s}$ = average hourly peak value; $\bar{s}$ = hourly mean value; σ_s = standard deviation or RMS of the fluctuating component; and g = peak factor defined as the number of standard deviations by which the average hourly peak (maximum) value exceeds the mean.

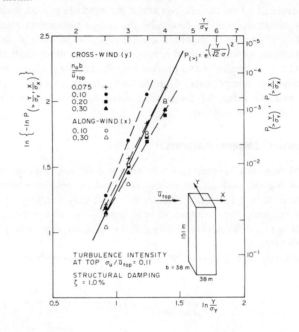

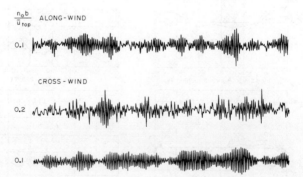

Fig. 3.66 Cumulative probability distribution of upcrossings for displacement of top of tall building model in suburban boundary layer as function of reduced frequency *(Melbourne, 1975a and 1977)*

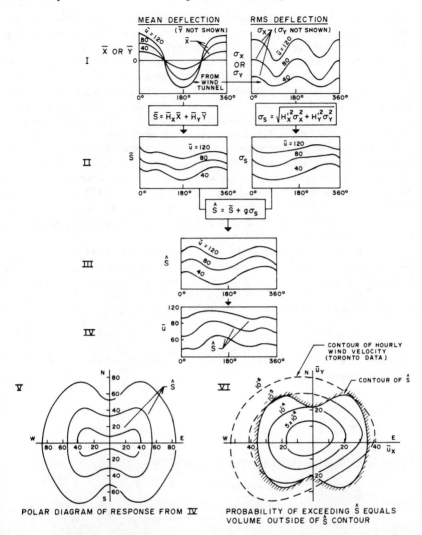

POLAR DIAGRAM OF RESPONSE FROM IV

PROBABILITY OF EXCEEDING $\hat{S}$ EQUALS VOLUME OUTSIDE OF $\hat{S}$ CONTOUR

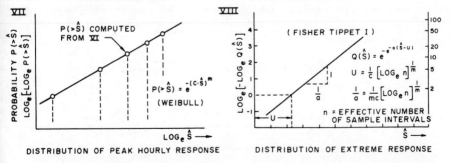

DISTRIBUTION OF PEAK HOURLY RESPONSE

DISTRIBUTION OF EXTREME RESPONSE

Fig. 3.67 Procedure for predicting probability of maximum response *(Davenport, 1972a)*

If the peak factor cannot be satisfactorily treated as a constant, the procedure is somewhat more lengthy but in principle no more difficult. When using data from wind tunnel tests the peak factor is usually established from response probability distributions measured at the time. When using partly analytical techniques an assumption that the process is normally distributed allows the use of the method given by Davenport (1964). However, the cross-wind response of a building cannot always be considered to be normally distributed, and Melbourne (1974) has given a number of probability distributions (upcrossing rates) for various operating reduced frequencies, reproduced in Fig. 3.66, from which peak factors can be obtained.

The peak response is a function of both wind speed and wind direction, and either functional or tabular relationships must be established for $\hat{s}(\theta, \bar{u})$. This also implies recognition of the effects of changes in approach terrain (affecting turbulence intensity and velocity profile), shielding, and upstream wake interference effects as noted in Section 3.4. These effects or peak response must be taken into account either analytically or from wind tunnel model studies before the prediction of extreme response can be undertaken.

The wind data are required in the form of a probability distribution of hourly mean wind speed at the height to which the response estimates are referred, usually the top of the building, such as is given in Fig. 3.67. These data may be expressed as a cumulative probability distribution, as a function of wind direction θ, or $22\text{-}1/2°$ segments as in Fig. 3.67, in terms of a Weibull distribution

$$P(\theta)_{(>\bar{u})} = A(\theta)e^{-[\bar{u}/c(\theta)]^{k(\theta)}} \tag{3.46}$$

The values of $A(\theta)$, $c(\theta)$, and $k(\theta)$ are, as indicated, functions of wind direction. It is, of course, necessary that

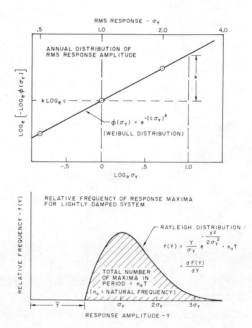

Fig. 3.68 Analysis of number of occurrences of cyclic response to wind (Davenport, 1972a)

$$\int_0^{2\pi} A(\theta)d\theta = 1 \tag{3.47}$$

With the base information of $\hat{s}(\theta,\bar{u})$ and $P(\theta)_{(>\bar{u})}$ the procedure for the prediction of extreme response can be outlined graphically as shown in Fig. 3.67 from Davenport (1971), and functionally for the two directions separately as follows:

1. The variation of the hourly peak values of response can usually be represented by a functional relationship of the form

$$\hat{s}(\theta,\bar{u}) = B(\theta)\bar{u}^{C(\theta)} \tag{3.48}$$

in which $B(\theta)$ and $C(\theta)$ = functions of wind direction.

2. The response functions are inverted to give $\bar{u}$ as a function of $\hat{s}(\theta)$

$$\bar{u} = \left[\frac{\hat{s}}{B(\theta)} \right]^{1/C(\theta)} \tag{3.49}$$

3. Then, as a function of response, the probability of exceeding the related value of $\bar{u}$ as a function of wind direction from the cumulative wind speed probability distribution (Eq. 3.46) can be integrated to give the total cumulative probability of exceeding a given value of response.

4. The return period for $R \gg 1$ can be obtained from

$$P(>\hat{s}) = \frac{1}{nR} \tag{3.50}$$

in which n = number of independent observations per yr, which can be taken to be about 1000 on the basis of the typical Van der Hoven spectrum for storms resulting from fully developed cyclonic phenomena (Vickery and Davenport, 1970).

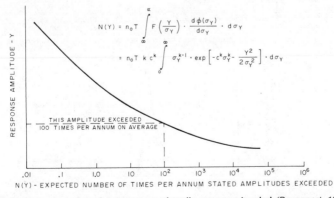

$$N(Y) = n_0 T \int_{-\infty}^{\infty} F\left(\frac{Y}{\sigma_Y}\right) \cdot \frac{d\phi(\sigma_Y)}{d\sigma_Y} \cdot d\sigma_Y$$

$$= n_0 T \, k \, c^k \int_0^{\infty} \sigma_Y^{k-1} \cdot \exp\left[-c^k\sigma_Y^k - \frac{Y^2}{2\sigma_Y^2}\right] \cdot d\sigma_Y$$

RESPONSE AMPLITUDE – Y

THIS AMPLITUDE EXCEEDED
100 TIMES PER ANNUM ON AVERAGE

.01   .1   1.0   10 10^2 10^3 10^4 10^5 10^6
N(Y) - EXPECTED NUMBER OF TIMES PER ANNUM STATED AMPLITUDES EXCEEDED

Fig. 3.69 Analysis of number of occurrences of cyclic response to wind *(Davenport, 1972a)*

5. The resulting distributions of the peak hourly response can usually be fitted by a Weibull distribution as shown in Fig. 3.67.

6. At this point the procedure has continued all the way separately for the response resolved in two directions. The determination of the probability of combinations of response can be complex. However, this can be achieved by assuming that for each wind direction the along-wind and cross-wind responses are independent, and that the joint probability of the combined responses is a bivariate normal distribution as demonstrated in Section 3.4.

This procedure attempts to integrate the salient meteorological, aerodynamic, and structural factors in a form that is readily amenable to design decisions. It has been used in one form or another over the past few years in the design of a number of tall buildings.

2 Prediction of Numbers of Occurrences

Another procedure which may be of importance is the prediction of the load occurrence diagram. The procedure has been defined in detail by Davenport (1966). Briefly, the first step is to establish the distribution of the various RMS values to be expected during quasi-stationary intervals of appropriate duration, such as 1 hr. This procedure takes the same form as that illustrated in Fig. 3.67, resulting, for example, in the distribution of RMS responses as shown in the upper diagram of Fig. 3.68. At this point it is possible to apply Rice's (1944) formula for the distribution of maxima, which follow a Rayleigh distribution as indicated in the

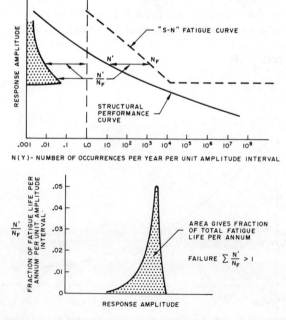

Fig. 3.70 Estimation of cumulative fatigue damage due to wind according to Palmgren-Miner Law (Davenport, 1975a)

lower diagram of Fig. 3.68. The integral defined in Fig. 3.69 then yields the distribution of expected number of times per year that given response amplitudes are exceeded. In fact, the left-hand end of this curve should correspond closely to the extreme value distribution already determined.

From this estimate of the number of load occurrences it is possible to compute the expected rate of damage due to fatigue action. The procedure is shown in Fig. 3.70. The model used here is the Miner damage law, which appears to give estimates that are as reasonable as other models. A more sophisticated procedure, based on a Goodman diagram approach, which also incorporates the influence of the mean response, could be performed without excessive additional complexity.

3 Prediction of Horizontal Accelerations Affecting Human Comfort

As described in Section 3.2, the motion of tall buildings under wind action has long been a source of annoyance. The prediction of horizontal accelerations in terms of frequency of occurrence can be achieved following the same processes outlined in Articles 1 and 2 of this section. Robertson and Chen (1967) and Chen and Robertson (1972) have discussed these processes with examples, such as are given in Fig. 3.71.

4 Prediction of Cladding Loads

To obtain data for the design of cladding elements, and glazing in particular, it is necessary to combine pressure estimates with meteorological data to establish extreme pressures for various probabilities of occurrence. There is virtually no method of estimating pressures not based on wind tunnel model tests; hence it is assumed that this is the source of pressure data, and that they are available in the coefficient form of $C_{\hat{p}}$, $C_{\bar{p}}$, and $C\sigma_p$ as introduced in Section 3.4. That is, for each wind direction the average hourly maximum pressure in coefficient form is known all over the surface of the building, or at least at a number of chosen pressure tap locations. Examples of pressure distributions and associated peak factors measured on a model of the Sears Tower in Chicago by Davenport et al. (1971) are given in Fig. 3.72.

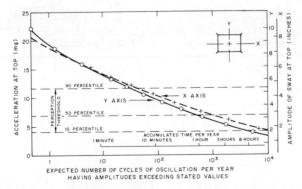

Fig. 3.71 Expected number of cycles of oscillation per year having amplitudes exceeding stated values *(Chen and Robertson, 1972)*

The problem of determining the maximum pressures on a building—testing at enough stations, for fine enough increments of wind direction (and increments of 1° to 2° are commonly needed to get maximum values in critical situations), and for adequate ranges of turbulence and effect of possible nearby buildings—is extremely time consuming. However, a still greater problem remains, and that is defining a design maximum pressure. The range of peak factors relevant to cladding loads has been illustrated in Sections 3.2 and 3.6, and it is essential that these be evaluated for every reading or a conservative value be used for different pressure areas. It is not sufficient to rely on the maximum value recorded during a pressure measurement unless the response characteristics of the pressure measuring system are well known. This is because there can be a frequency at which there will be an increase due to resonant response followed by a cutoff at higher frequencies, or alternatively there can be sufficient viscous damping for the frequency response to roll off slowly (Iberall, 1950; Gomes and Cermak, 1967). It has been suggested by Melbourne (1975b) that the probability of exceeding a certain pressure, even for intermittent pressure fluctuations, can be represented by a Weibull distribution as shown in Fig. 3.73. If digital data reduction systems are being used, it is just as easy to get this Weibull output which can be extrapolated to overcome frequency response cutoff, or to ignore amplifications due to resonant response characteristics. The peak factor can then be more rationally selected as being that associated with a given probability level, and Melbourne (1975) has suggested that a peak factor based on a probability of exceeding 10^{-5}, which in relation to 1 hr is approximately 1/30 sec, would cover most cladding and glazing elements. However Davenport (1975), in his discussion on Peterka and Cermak (1975), has pointed out that it would be quite incorrect to apply loads determined for such short durations of time to glazing elements whose "design strength" has been determined from loads applied for a longer time when the material is known to have effectively increased strength for

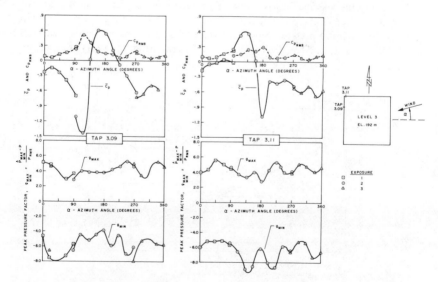

Fig. 3.72 Variation of mean and RMS pressure coefficients and peak pressure factors at selected taps (Davenport et al., 1971)

short durations. This effect of load duration on glass strength is shown in Fig. 3.73(a), which gives maximum stress at break origin for various durations of sustained loading. Hence, the problem is not so much that the loads predicted for short duration from wind tunnel tests do not actually occur [full-scale measurements support their existence (Dalgliesh, 1974, 1975; Eaton and Mayne, 1975; Fujii et al., 1974)], but that the design loads used must match the known load performance characteristics of the cladding. With respect to glazing, Allen and Dalgliesh (1973) have proposed a

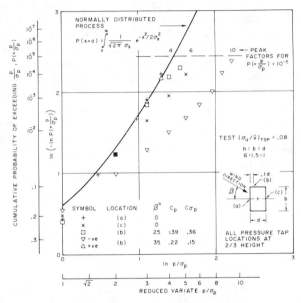

Fig. 3.73 Cumulative probability distributions of pressure measurements on surface of 1/400 model of 151-m high rectangular building *(Melbourne, 1975b)*

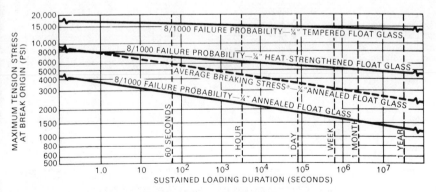

*Based on ¼″ annealed float glass, 60 second MOR of 6000 psi.

Fig. 3.73(a) Relationship of breaking stress to duration of uniform load *(PPG Industries, 1979)*

"wind on glass factor" based on the stress corrosion theory of Brown (1969) related to load duration theory for glass design.

Assuming that a rational peak pressure has been established, then for a given wind direction, or band of wind directions, the probability of exceeding a given pressure level at a given point can be directly related to the probability of exceeding the mean wind speed required to produce that pressure. The wind speed cumulative probability distribution information required is the same as that for the prediction of extreme response and number of occurrences referred to in Articles 1 and 2 of this section.

The probability of exceeding a given pressure level at a given point can then be summed for all wind directions. These total probability distributions can be fitted to a Weibull distribution in the same way as the response was fitted in Article 1 of this section. [It should be noted that this process has to be done separately for the maximum positive and maximum negative (suction) pressures.]

These data can then be used directly in design for a nominated probability level, or the maximum pressures can be related to return period again in the same way as response was related in Article 1.

An example of contours of maximum pressures and suctions for a return period of 100 yr is presented in Fig. 3.74 for the Sears Tower in Chicago following on from the previous example of wind tunnel data for the same building measured by Davenport et al. (1971).

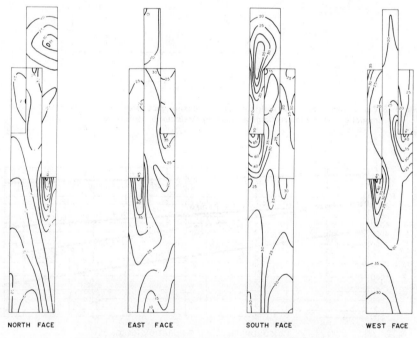

NORTH FACE   EAST FACE   SOUTH FACE   WEST FACE

CONTOURS OF MAXIMUM SUCTIONS (PSF) FOR 100 YEAR RETURN PERIOD

Fig. 3.74 Contours of maximum negative pressures (in pounds per square foot) on surface of Sears Tower, Chicago, predicted from model measurements *(Davenport et al., 1971)*

3.8   ENVIRONMENTAL WIND FLOWS AROUND BUILDINGS

The study of flow fields induced around buildings has increased in recent years mainly because some large buildings have been erected which, because of combinations of shape, height, and isolation, have induced wind flows in public accessways and recreational areas much higher than could be reasonably tolerated. Hence, it has become common practice now to submit building design proposals to wind tunnel testing to determine the likely wind environment around the buildings, and to modify and add protection to achieve acceptable conditions. One result of these studies is an accumulation of expertise in means of avoiding high induced wind speeds. Most of this section will describe flow mechanisms, good design practice for the avoidance of high induced wind speeds around buildings, and the criteria involved.

1   Wind Flow Around a Building

There are two quite separate flow fields causing high induced wind speeds at ground level, which have been described by Melbourne and Joubert (1971) with the aid of Fig. 3.75, as follows:

1. The first type of flow is caused by the pressure distribution on the windward face of a building. It tends to be directly related to the local wind dynamic pressure, which increases with height. This pressure gradient induces flow vertically down the face below the stagnation point (which can be as high as 80% of the building height). This flow rolls up into a standing vortex system at the base of the building, causing high wind velocities in this region. Buildings of near circular planform, which promote lateral flow, do not produce strong vertical flows. Conversely, rectangular and concave buildings do produce strong vertical flows with consequent high wind conditions in the standing vortex system. The configuration of upstream buildings can be critical for this flow because under certain conditions the vortex flow behind a lower upstream building can augment the vortex in front of the larger building, further increasing the high wind velocities at the base.

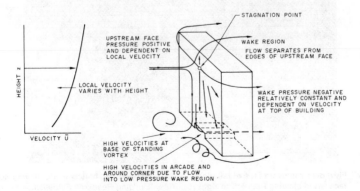

Fig. 3.75 Flow field around building *(Melbourne and Joubert, 1971)*

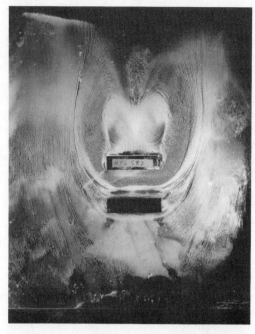

Fig. 3.76 Example of pattern of flow at ground level around tall building, with low building at small distance to windward *(Penwarden and Wise, 1975; Courtesy: Building Research Establishment—Crown copyright reserved; Photo by Building Research Station)*

Fig. 3.77 Flow over windward face of tall block—smoke pumped into hollow model having holes in face, wind blowing from left to right *(Courtesy: Building Research Establishment—Crown copyright reserved; Photo by Building Research Station)*

2. The second type of flow is caused by the pressure difference between the low pressure wake regions (leeward and side faces) and the relatively high pressure regions at the base of the windward face. Flow directly between these two regions through arcades or around corners can cause very high local wind velocities. The low wake pressure tends to be dependent on the velocity along the top free boundary, that is, the freestream velocity at the top of the building. Hence, the taller the building the lower the wake pressure and the higher the velocities which are induced through arcades and around corners for a given aspect ratio. In general, this problem is much harder to control because the wake pressure cannot easily be modified.

These flow fields have been illustrated beautifully by Penwarden and Wise (1975) (in relation to the adverse effect of a lower upstream building), and are reproduced in Figs. 3.76 and 3.77. In Fig. 3.76, solid line shows approximate position and maximum speed in vortex flow; broken line shows approximate position and maximum speed in corner streams.

There are literally hundreds of proprietary reports which discuss particular building and flow situations, and a few have been summarized in the general literature. Wise (1971) discussed the effects of groups of buildings, and many full-scale examples in the United Kingdom have been given by Penwarden and Wise (1975). Gandemer (1975) has described a number of studies in France and in particular some funneling effects. Isyumov and Davenport (1975) discussed some studies in North America, and Cermak (1974) has also referred to a number of studies carried out at the Colorado State University. Melbourne and Joubert (1971) and Apperley and Vickery (1974) have presented some model and full-scale studies in Australia.

2 Environmental Wind Speed Criteria

Before discussing techniques for predicting, avoiding, or ameliorating environmental wind conditions, it is necessary to establish some criteria as to the acceptability or unacceptability of certain wind speeds. That is, to form some assessment of the effects of wind on people as they use main pedestrian accessways near buildings, recreational areas, or just go window shopping.

The Environmental Problem. Isyumov and Davenport (1975) have discussed the background as follows.

The most significant problem caused by ground level wind speeds is the effect on people. There is a multitude of other effects: for example, increased convective heat transfer; greater rain penetration through the building skin and accelerated weathering; increased noise levels; flying dust, sand, paper, leaves, and other debris; increased snow drifting; malfunctions of fountains; and damage to plants and trees. Although these are important for total design, the effect of wind on people is the foremost consideration. In evaluating the acceptability of a ground level wind environment, the questions of safety and the impediment of movement are paramount. However, a successful utilization of an outdoor precinct further requires a comfortable environment to gain public acceptance of the area, not just as a thoroughfare, but as a pleasant place to be. This is largely an economic consideration, as uncomfortable wind conditions would discourage people from frequenting outdoor shops, cafes, etc.

Concern for safety and severe impediment of movement around tall buildings, even in otherwise moderate wind conditions, are not exaggerated. Many reports of injuries received in falls attributed to windy conditions can be found in the literature and the press. Melbourne and Joubert (1971) report people having great difficulties with balance at wind speeds gusting up to 10 m/s (45 mph) around an exposed slab type building 140 m wide, 13 m deep, and 50 m high (460 ft × 43 ft × 164 ft) at Monash University. Furthermore they report people being blown over around the same building at a gust speed of 23 m/s (51.5 mph). Penwarden (1974) reports the deaths of two elderly ladies in Great Britain as a result of skull injuries received when they were blown over by wind around tall buildings. The gust speed in one of these cases was estimated at 25 m/s (56 mph). Similarly, reports of people blown over by winds around skyscrapers in the U.S.A are provided by MacGregor (1971). North American plazas are particularly hazardous during winter when icing further reduces balance. Criteria for severe impediment of movement with resulting loss of balance and even toppling can be based on purely mechanical and aerodynamic considerations. Although the wind force required to topple a person varies with surface area, weight, physical fitness, body position, and wind direction, it is generally accepted that wind speeds around 20 m/s (45 mph) are threshold conditions for physical danger.

Evaluation of wind speeds below this physical danger threshold is far more difficult because it entails considering the highly subjective question of human comfort. Comfort in this sense is not used to describe complete mental and physical satisfaction with the environment but rather its acceptance. Wind speed influences not only physical comfort—namely the acceptance of wind induced forces and their effect on apparel and freedom of movement—but it also affects thermal comfort, namely the heat balance of the body and the physiological and sensory response to a lowering or raising of the body temperature. Both physical and thermal comfort are highly subjective. Also both become important considerations only for nonessential activities. For example, windy conditions below the danger threshold may not unduly distress a seasonally dressed individual walking to work. The same conditions, on the other hand, may discourage him or her from lunching or relaxing outdoors. In general, comfort or discomfort for particular wind conditions depends on the type of activity and dress; climatic differences, the season and specific weather conditions (namely the air temperature, relative humidity, solar radiation and the presence of precipitation); and the physical, physiological, and psychological state of the individual. Seasonal variations are of particular importance as the same breeze, refreshing on a hot summer day, may increase the chill factor in winter. Similarly, although man in cold climates generally seeks shelter from wind, the reverse is true in hot climates where windy conditions tend to improve the thermal comfort either through a greater convective heat loss or by increasing the rate of evaporation.

Environmental Wind Speed Criteria. Table 3.1 presented tentative comfort criteria based on research by Wise (1971), Melbourne and Joubert (1971), and Davenport (1972). This table provides a general summary of wind speed criteria ranging from perceptible to dangerous, and the acceptability in terms of frequency of occurrence. Because it is based on mean wind speed some interpretation with respect to gust speeds is required, examples of which are given in Table 3.1(b).

It is worth commenting further on the relationship between the peak gust and mean wind speeds (see Eq. 3.17) because it has an important bearing on the prediction of wind environment by means of wind tunnel testing to be discussed in the next Article. It seems reasonable to conclude that it is the peak gust wind speeds and associated gradients which people feel most, and as such it is of interest to know under what conditions they occur.

The observations of Melbourne and Joubert (1971) indicate that the areas in full scale which have been classed as having unpleasant or unacceptably high wind speeds were all associated with high mean wind speeds. Later, model and full-scale measurements by Isyumov and Davenport (1975) and Melbourne (1974) continued to show that the windiest areas were associated with high mean wind speeds, but that the turbulence intensity was important in determining the peak gust wind speeds. In the case of the former, the ratio of peak gust wind speed over mean wind speed $\hat{u}/\bar{u}$ for the three windiest conditions, respectively, was 1.5, 2.7, and 2.8, and for the latter 1.9, 1.9, and 2.4; for areas and wind directions with lower wind conditions, and obviously for much greater turbulence intensities, this ratio was typically as high as 5.0. This means that to get an accurate prediction of peak gust

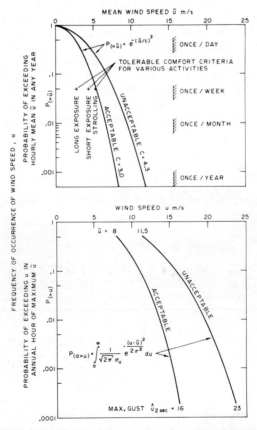

Fig. 3.78 Probability distributions of criteria for ground level wind speeds in public accessways, for $\hat{u} = 2.0\ \bar{u}$ and $\sigma_u = 0.3\ \bar{u}$, in terms of daylight time per year for which given wind speed is exceeded *(Melbourne, 1975d)*

wind speeds from wind tunnel model tests, it is essential that mean and RMS or peak values for a given probability level be accurately measured.

Although it is possible to have unpleasant areas with low mean wind speeds and high turbulence intensities, the evidence to date does seem to indicate that in areas likely to have unacceptably high wind conditions, such as near corners, in narrow alleys and in arcades, the turbulence intensity is relatively low and that in these areas it would be reasonable to assume that the peak gust wind speeds will be about twice the mean wind speed. This means that wind tunnel investigations in terms of establishing and improving likely areas of unacceptably high wind conditions can be reasonably based on very simple and inexpensive model measurements of mean wind speed. However, it does not mean that the need to model the turbulence characteristics of the incident wind stream can be overlooked, as a low turbulence stream would produce quite different flow fields and erroneous information.

It is possible to look at the environment wind criteria over a full probability range against which model measurements, properly integrated with wind data, can be compared. In Fig. 3.78, the criteria from Melbourne (1971) are shown developed in terms of probability distributions for daylight time per year. Similar distributions can be prepared for various seasons and different time blocks in the day if required. In the lower part of Fig. 3.78 the distribution of the maximum gust speeds per year, of 23 m/s and 16 m/s, are shown as a normal distribution back to the maximum hourly mean wind speed per year, for $\hat{u} = 2.0\,\bar{u}$ and $\sigma_u = 0.3\,\bar{u}$. In the upper part of Fig. 3.78 the cumulative distribution of hourly mean wind speeds has been shown as a Weibull distribution with $k = 2$, that is a Rayleigh distribution.

As well as knowing the total number of hours per year that a mean wind speed is exceeded $[P_{(>u)}]$ it is useful to know the number of storms per year during which a mean wind speed is exceeded, or alternatively the magnitude of storms with average

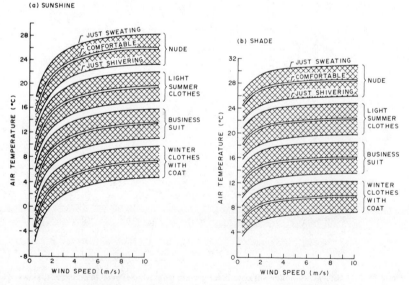

Fig. 3.79 Examples of comfort conditions for strolling *(Penwarden, 1973; Courtesy: Building Research Establishment—Crown copyright reserved)*

frequencies of occurrence of 1/year, 1/month, 1/week, and 1/day. Davenport (1971) has given a method for doing this and these average frequencies of occurrence have been added to Fig. 3.78.

In relation to the criteria presented in Fig. 3.78, it is interesting to note a procedure used by the Building Research Establishment in England in determining likely "User Satisfaction" based on full-scale experience as reported by Penwarden and Wise (1975). They have found that if the frequency of exceeding a mean wind speed of 5 m/s (16.4 ft/sec) exceeds 20% (876 daylight hr per yr) protective measures are likely to be needed; between 10% and 20% complaint is likely but may be insufficient to provoke action; and below 10% (438 daylight hr per yr) conditions are likely to be satisfactory.

Penwarden (1973) has added examples of comfort for strolling given in Fig. 3.79.

Lawson (1973) discussed the variation of wind speed with averaging time and related these to a Beaufort number system suggested by Penwarden (1973). The combination of this approach has been more recently discussed by Lawson and Penwarden (1975).

3　Prediction of Wind Environment Around a Building

Although some experience has been gained from assessing full-scale wind conditions about a variety of buildings, it is necessary to turn to wind tunnel model testing if a confident prediction of the wind environment induced around a specific building proposal is required. In a model test the wind speeds at a number of locations can be measured for different wind directions and combined with local wind data, to permit the frequency of occurrence of wind speeds at those locations to be calculated and compared with environmental wind speed criteria.

To model the turbulent flow conditions induced by buildings, it is necessary to place the model building in a model of the natural wind, which as a minimum must reproduce the correct mean velocity and turbulence intensity profiles as described in Section 3.6.

A model of the specific building complex along with adjacent buildings is required in sufficient detail to assure that the aerodynamic flow fields are satisfactorily modeled. In general, surface features up to a meter in depth do not need to be modeled, as they have little effect on the flow field around a building; however, details of this size can be significant locally, that is at ground level, and should be included. In addition to the specific building complex and adjacent buildings, it is essential to model all major buildings for at least 800 m (2600 ft) radius as the shielding effect of single buildings can be significant. It is not usually possible to mount these additional buildings on a wind tunnel turntable and it is normal practice to have them as single block models which can be placed upstream for the relevant wind directions. An example of such a model arrangement was shown in Fig. 3.53.

There are varying degrees of sophistication in the techniques which can now be used to measure the effect of wind on people at the model scale. A person feels the wind as a force or pressure distribution which varies as the square of the wind speed. The ideal way to measure this effect then is to measure the forces on a model person. Unfortunately at most model scales this is a very small target and although it has been attempted, it is a difficult instrumentation problem and cannot be generally recommended. There are two simple alternatives: to measure either pressure with a total head and static tube, or velocity with a hot wire (or hot film) probe. In both cases the velocity pressure or velocity measured has to be referenced to a velocity pressure or velocity measured in the freestream at some height or distance that is free from the influence of the buildings. It is convenient to make this reference at or near gradient height, or alternatively at a known anemometer site. The main aim is to have the reference at a point where the meteorological data of wind speed frequency of occurrence can be established, which then allows frequency of occurrence of wind speeds at each station under test to be established by virtue of a simple ratio.

The velocity pressure and hot wire velocity measuring techniques both have advantages and disadvantages. The hot wire technique has problems in that hot wire measurements in turbulence intensities over 20% become increasingly suspect. In particular, the hot wire is insensitive to wind direction in the plane normal to the wire, hence reverse flows appear as a positive addition to the mean velocity measured by this technique. As most environmental wind flows involve turbulence intensities above 20% and frequently about 30%, the mean velocity measured by a hot wire anemometer is quite unreliable. However, if only peak velocities are used, in particular those obtained from a probability analysis for a fixed low probability level, then the problem is to a large extent overcome because there is no dependence on a mean velocity measurement. On the advantage side the hot wire, used with the wire vertical, records velocity independent of wind direction; hence, once the probe has been placed at a measuring station, the model can be rotated for different wind directions without any further adjustment of the probe. For the same reason there is a disadvantage in not gaining some knowledge of the local flow direction. Hot wire and associated equipment is relatively expensive.

The velocity pressure can be simply measured by using a length of small diameter tube (1 mm to 2 mm diam), bent into the horizontal plane to measure total pressure,

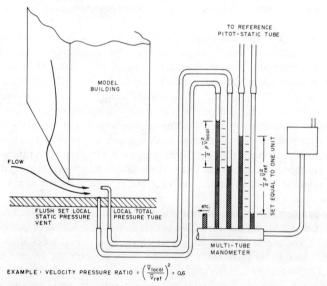

EXAMPLE: VELOCITY PRESSURE RATIO $= \left(\dfrac{\overline{V}_{local}}{\overline{V}_{ref}}\right)^2 = 0.6$

Fig. 3.80 Arrangement for measuring mean velocity pressure ratios in model environmental wind flow investigation (Melbourne, 1971a)

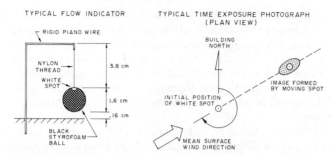

Fig. 3.81 Styrofoam ball used as wind speed indicator for model ground wind speed measurements *(Isyumov and Davenport, 1975b)*

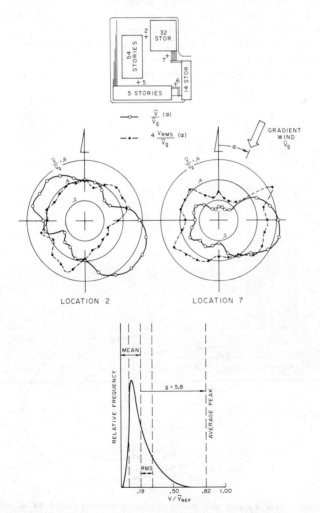

Fig. 3.82 Typical mean, RMS, and probability distribution of wind speed measurements as ratio with mean gradient wind speed *(Isyumov and Davenport, 1975a and 1977)*

and a surface static vent can be provided with a similar tube as shown in Fig. 3.80. If only mean velocity pressures (dynamic pressures) are being measured, then the local static and total pressures from a number of stations can be displayed on a multitube manometer and the difference, which is the dynamic pressure, can be compared directly as a ratio with the reference dynamic pressure, as shown in Fig. 3.80. This method requires little expensive equipment, and measurements at a number of stations can be made at the same time. The disadvantage is that the total pressure tubes have to be adjusted to point into the local flow direction for every change of total wind direction. The further disadvantage is that to get fluctuating or peak values, a pressure transducer and associated electronic equipment must be used, which is about as expensive as using the hot wire equipment.

Isyumov and Davenport (1975b) described a technique, in use for some time at the University of Western Ontario, which used a styrofoam ball hanging on a thread (Fig. 3.81). Time exposure photographs of the horizontal movement of the ball were calibrated to indicate mean wind speed and direction and flow fluctuations. Typical results of mean and RMS wind speeds measured with a hot film probe and probability distribution and peak factors are shown in Fig. 3.82.

Another method of presenting velocity ratio data is shown in Fig. 3.83 from

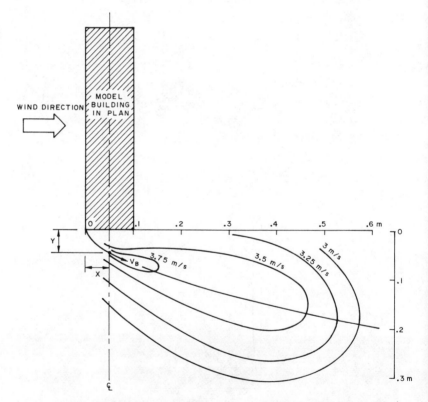

Fig. 3.83 Corner stream mapped from model studies for building height 0.4 m, width 0.4 m (Penwarden and Wise, 1975; Courtesy: Building Research Establishment—Crown copyright reserved)

Penwarden and Wise which maps the velocity field in plan for one wind direction. A similar but more extensive plan was shown in Fig. 3.62 from Apperley and Vickery (1974).

These wind tunnel data can be integrated with the climatological gradient wind speed data as described in Section 3.7 to give predictions of wind speed frequency of occurrence over a year or longer, as shown in Fig. 3.84.

4   Guidelines for Avoiding High Induced Wind Speeds at Ground Level

With a knowledge of the wind flow fields induced around buildings, it is possible for the architect to create designs that avoid causing high induced wind speeds at ground level. The following notes have been set down by Melbourne (1971) to provide some guidance.

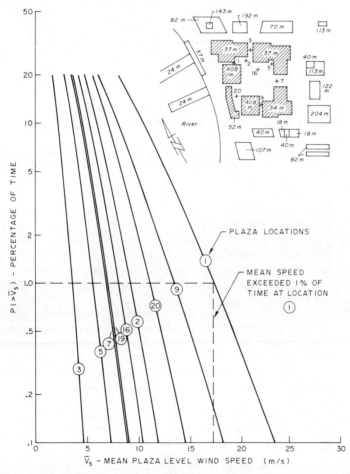

Fig. 3.84 Typical prediction of mean wind exceeded at several plaza locations over an entire year (*Isyumov and Davenport, 1975a and 1977*)

1. Buildings will only induce high ground level wind speeds if a significant part of the building is exposed to direct wind flows. It is in fact the direct exposure of a building face to high speed wind flows, rather than building height alone, which causes the problem. For example, a 20-m (65-ft) high building at an airport site can induce higher wind speeds at a corner than a 100-m (330-ft) high building in a city center. If a building has to be built on an exposed site, then much more attention to some of the following guidelines is needed.

2. In what situation can a proposed building be regarded as being either exposed or adequately shielded? A general rule is that a building should be regarded as potentially exposed for any particular direction if half of the building height is clearly above upstream buildings which can provide shielding. An upstream building of half height is reckoned to shed a wake region of low wind speeds which will cover about three-quarters of the downstream building under consideration, and the direct wind flow striking the building above this wake will tend to be deflected up and around rather than downwards. The shielding effect of upstream buildings is one of the most significant factors to be taken into account when an assessment of environmental wind conditions is being made, and the shielding provided by single buildings can be effective for between 500 m and 1000 m (1640 ft to 3280 ft) downstream.

3. If a building is regarded as being exposed for some or all wind directions, then there are some fundamental configuration factors which can be taken into account.
   (a) Rectangular buildings with a main face rising clearly from ground level, normal to any of the unshielded prevailing wind directions, should be avoided as these are the most common cause of environmental wind problems.
   (b) Rectangular buildings placed on a podium or lower stage building complex which deflects the downward wind flow before it reaches ground level, can be satisfactorily used in many cases. Canopies (preferably with parapets) can also be used to deflect this flow and lift a standing vortex above pedestrian level. However, canopies (unless very extensive) do little to ameliorate high wind speeds induced at the corners of buildings or in colonnades.
   (c) Buildings with circular or near circular planform promote lateral flow and induce little downward vertical flow, and hence they are to be preferred in exposed situations. Circular buildings do induce high wind speeds at the maximum width normal to the wind direction, similar to that induced at the corners of rectangular buildings. However, in the case of circular buildings, this is caused by acceleration of the local flow around the circle which can be reduced to a large extent by relatively low height upstream shielding; this is not so for rectangular buildings, because much of the flow around the corners originates from flow induced down the windward face from higher levels.

4. Arcades and colonnades at the base of exposed buildings can provide openings between the high upstream face pressures and low base pressures through which high wind speeds can be induced. In the case of arcades, it is

usually necessary to provide means of sealing them with revolving doors or mechanically operated sliding doors on strong windy days. Colonnades should not be designed as main public accessways or as window shopping precincts unless adequate upstream shielding is assured.

5. There seems to be no reason why high wind speeds cannot be accepted in certain areas, such as near corners, in narrow passages between buildings, or on tops of podiums, provided such areas do not have to be used for general public access. For example, gardens and architectural features can be placed at a corner to prevent pedestrian access close to the corner and to provide a local wind break for areas immediately downstream of the corner. An open podium area set up for recreational purposes would only be used when weather conditions (including wind) are pleasant. Narrow passages between buildings are often used only for vehicular access, and as such can tolerate much higher wind conditions.

6. The architect is mostly concerned with the wind environment in the immediate vicinity of the particular building being designed. In most cases, even when buildings are exposed, it is usually possible to provide canopies, local wind breaks, sealed arcades, etc., to achieve satisfactory wind conditions in adjacent areas (even after the event). However, it is important to realize that one of the worst features of exposed rectangular buildings is the increased wind flow induced at ground level generally, and particularly on the opposite side of the street. This type of problem is by far the most difficult to deal with, because much of it is caused by pressure and flow fields well away from the face of the building concerned, and consequently local changes within the site boundaries have little effect. To overcome this problem it is often necessary to undertake major configuration changes, such as reducing height, changing planform, or setting a tower well back on a podium. It is obvious that this type of problem cannot be solved easily after a building has been constructed, and must be taken into account in the very early design stages.

3.9 CODE DESIGN

The rapid developments in understanding wind action have been reflected also in the development of new code approaches. These are so diverse that it is not possible to be more than highly selective in discussing them. At least some general trends can be suggested. Excellent discussion of the then current trends were offered by Stevens (1973), Wyatt (1973), and Chen (1973) in papers presented at the Lehigh Conference.

In principle the development of a design wind loading can be formalistically expressed as

$$p = \bar{q}\, C_p\, C_g\, C_e \tag{3.51}$$

in which p = effective design pressure; $\bar{q}$ = effective mean reference velocity pressure; C_p = aerodynamic shape factor or pressure coefficient; C_g = effective gust effect factor; and C_e = exposure factor allowing for the height and siting of the structure.

Some discussion of these components is in order. The effective design pressure p, is generally most conveniently a static pressure although, as the presence of C_g implies, it may be derived from a pressure which is fluctuating in time as well as over the surface of the structure. It is therefore necessary to relate this pressure to the application, whether for the design of the main structural frame or for cladding, and also to the criteria used. If it is for the main structural frame it is generally an integrated pressure and recognizes the feedback effect of any dynamic response. It is necessary to reflect the level of loading risk associated with the application.

The reference velocity pressure $\bar{q}$ is perhaps most rationally (but not always in practice) thought of as a mean value, average over 10 min to 1 hr, at some reference height in some representative exposure such as flat open country. The latter consideration is often dictated by the convenience of using airport data at a standard reference height of 10 m as the climatic base for wind speed. Some expression of the risk level can be obtained by using different return periods. A commonly used return period is 50 yr, which expresses a load level close to the average largest load to be expected in that period of time. It does not necessarily exclude the possibility of larger loads, and to guard against this some additional load or safety factoring is needed.

The aerodynamic pressure coefficient C_p takes several forms. Most generally they are mean pressure coefficients. They should be derived in representative flow conditions reflecting, in particular, the velocity profile and turbulence in the atmosphere. They should be integrated values (or drag coefficients) for design of the structural frame. For cladding design special treatment of local conditions may be needed.

The gust factor C_g expresses the additional loading, if any, due to the effect of gusts. This can in principle accommodate both the reduction in load due to the lack of spatial correlation of gusts and the additional loading due to resonance of the structure. Both these effects will be present to some smaller extent in cladding response, for which the unfactored local pressure peak may in fact be a suitable design load.

The exposure factor allows for the variation of the pressure with height above ground as well as the modification of the velocity or pressure with the change in topography, whether this is due to the roughness of the terrain or its contours in hilly regions.

Clearly there are many variants on Eq. 3.51. In older codes it was common to base wind pressures on the force on a flat plate. Drag coefficients in steady flow were obtained and associated with maximum gust speeds.

The magnitude of this maximum gust speed depends partly on the response time of the instrument, which is not a particularly desirable feature. This gives a formula of the type $p = kV^2$. The velocity variation with height was commonly based on gust speed variations, usually describing a slower rate of increase of velocity with height. This approach, if the size of the structure is large and the resonance small, may present a useful upper bound. Other codes, recognizing the spatial averaging effects of gusts and perhaps the inertial resistance of some structures, have based the wind speed over a short term average. The United States Code has for example used a "fastest mile," a wind speed averaged roughly over a half-minute to a minute. It is however still significantly higher than the mean over a stable averaging time of 10 min to 1 hr, perhaps by 20% to 30%. If such a reference wind speed is used some additional allowance for intense local gust action or resonant response may be necessary.

Pressure coefficients are generally mean pressure coefficients, but for some purposes such as cladding design they may be based on local gust pressure coefficients, that is, the ratio of peak measured pressure to the mean reference velocity pressure. The necessity to use pressure coefficients measured in the turbulent boundary layer has been stressed earlier. The first code to do this was the Danish Code based on the work of Jensen.

Dynamic gust effect factors, first introduced by Davenport for the Danish Code, have been adopted elsewhere in a number of other codes, such as the Canadian, Australian, and ANSI, with some slight modification. These are applicable primarily to the design of the whole structure and take account of resonant effects and spatial averaging of gusts as well as variations in terrain roughness.

3.10   CONCLUDING REMARKS

This chapter has attempted to identify various problems associated with wind action which affect the successful outcome of a tall building. These range from factors affecting human comfort, such as windiness in the surrounding streets, discomfort due to motion, and sounds induced by groaning of the frame or whistling around protrusions, to those factors affecting the integrity of the over-all structure or the cladding.

Reviewing the developments in recent years in the engineering treatment and solution of these problems, it is apparent that the physical descriptions of the phenomena have come significantly closer to the physical reality. Two essential characteristics of wind action have been recognized: (1) The importance of the dynamic components of the wind actions; and (2) the statistical characteristics of the wind and climate. Recognition of these aspects of the wind brings us closer to rational treatment in design. Complementary to the improvement in the wind loading is the refinement of criteria. There is an inherent danger in mismatching more refined descriptions of wind action with criteria which evolved through more empirical notions of how the wind acted. This chapter has attempted to suggest, at least qualitatively, how these criteria might be expressed.

To aid the designer there are now at least two avenues that can be explored. For very tall structures wind tunnel methods using simulated boundary layer flow provide a detailed insight into the mechanism of response to wind. When combined with a description of the wind climate these can provide a detailed prognosis of wind response applicable to a wide variety of issues—among others, the subtle interactions that take place between the directional characteristics of the wind and the directional response sensitivity of the structure can be evaluated, if required. The wind tunnel can be treated as an analog computer accepting straightforwardly many of the complexities of the wind structure, brought about by the particular urban topography which surrounds the building, and many of the complexities of the response of the structure itself.

On an analytical plane the gust response factor approach allows a somewhat more idealized estimate to be made of the structural response. This method exposes to view many parameters, such as the natural frequency, damping, and geometric shape, which conventional static approaches had formerly concealed. This in itself is a step forward.

Codes for wind loading have an important role to play in safeguarding against poor design for wind. Since developments in the structural composition can produce surprisingly swift changes in response to wind it is important that codes at least reflect the sensitivities to key parameters. This they do not always do. However, in an account of design developments given by Stevens (1973), Wyatt (1973), and Chen (1973) at the Lehigh Conference it was clear that some codes are moving forward. Calibration of some of the newer dynamic modeling methods by reference to full-scale measurements has provided a satisfactory level of confidence in these. This allows the further development of structural analysis and synthesis to follow from a sound description of how the wind acts.

3.11 CONDENSED REFERENCES/BIBLIOGRAPHY

The following is a condensed bibliography for this chapter. Not only does it include all articles referred to or cited in the text, but it also contains bibliography for further reading. The full citations will be found at the end of the Volume. What is given here should be sufficient information to lead the reader to the correct article: the author, date, and title. In case of multiple authors, only the first named is listed.

Allen 1973, *Dynamic Wind Loads and Cladding Design*
Amaral 1973, *Commentaries on the Proposal for the Revision of the Brazilian Standard*
Ang 1971, *Formulation of Wind-Resistant Design Based on Acceptable Risk*
Anthony 1970, *The Background to the Statistical Approach*
Anthony 1974, *The Wind Environment of Buildings with Particular Reference to the Penang*
Anthony 1975, *Wind Engineering—The Personal View of a Practising Engineer*
Apperley 1974, *The Prediction and Evaluation of the Ground Level Wind Environment*
Arakawa 1974, *Strong Gusts in the Lowest 250-m Layer over the City of Tokyo*
Armitt 1968, *The Simulation of the Atmospheric Boundary Layer in a Wind Tunnel*
Australian Standardizing Body 1975, *Rules for Minimum Design Loads*
Aynsley 1973, *Wind Effects on High and Low Rise Housing*
Aynsley 1974, *Environmental Wind Problems Around Buildings*
Aynsley 1976, *Architectural Aerodynamics*

Baines 1963, *Effects of Velocity Distribution on Wind Loads and Flow Patterns on Buildings*
Bandrabur 1975, *An Experimental Study on the Effect of Wind in Determining the Heat*
Barstein 1971, *Some Problems of Design of Tall Structures for Wind Effect*
Baynes 1974, *The Statistics of Strong Winds for Engineering Applications*
Bearman 1970, *Wind Loads on Structures in Turbulent Flow*
Bearman 1971, *Wind Loads on Structures in Turbulent Flow*
Bearman 1975, *The Flow about Oscillating Bluff Structures*
Botizan 1971, *Computation by Takebaya Method of Irregular Building Frames with Variable*
Briggs 1969, *Plume Rise*
Brooks 1968, *The Effect of Averaging Time and Sample Duration on Estimation*
Brooks 1973, *A Study of Wind Structures in an Urban Environment*
Brown 1969, *A Load Duration Theory for Glass Design*
Brown 1975, *The Tall Buildings Experience: Perception of Wind Movements*
Button 1975, *Considerations of Energy, Environment and Structure in Window Design*

Cartwright 1956, *The Statistical Distribution of the Maxima of a Random Function*
Cermak 1965, *Simulation of Atmospheric Motion by Wind Tunnel Flow*
Cermak 1969, *Fluctuating Moments on Tall Buildings Produced by Wind Loading*
Cermak 1970, *Separation-Induced Pressure Fluctuations on Buildings*
Cermak 1971, *Pressure Fluctuations on Buildings*
Cermak 1971a, *Laboratory Simulation of Atmospheric Boundary Layer*
Cermak 1971b, *Wind Loading and Wind Effects*
Cermak 1973, *Wind Effects on Tall Buildings—Areas for Research*
Cermak 1974, *Wind Pressures on a House Roof*
Cermak 1975, *Application of Fluid Mechanics to Wind Engineering*
Cham 1974, *Wind Tunnel Investigation on the Flood-lit Tower of the Singapore National*
Chang 1971a, *Tornado Wind Effects on Buildings and Structures with Laboratory Simulation*
Chang 1971b, *What We Learned from the Tornado of Lubbock, Texas, USA, May 11, 1970*

Chang 1974, *Solutions to the Wind Motion Problem in Tall Building Design*
Chen 1972, *Human Perception Thresholds of Horizontal Motion*
Chen 1973, *Design Developments—North and South America*
Cheng 1974, *Topographical Effects on Wind Patterns*
Chiu 1974, *Wind Effects on Tall Buildings*
Chiu 1974, *Wind Forces on High-Rise Buildings and Comments*
Chiu 1974, *Simulating Wind Records for Dynamic Response Analysis*
Chiu 1974, *Structure Response to Wind Forces*
Choi 1971, *Correlation and Spectral Functions of Atmospheric Turbulence*
Choi 1976, *Estimation of Design Wind Speeds in Hong Kong*
Ciesielski 1972a, *Dynamical Problems in the Design of Tall Buildings*
Ciesielski 1972b, *Dynamic Characteristics of Tall Buildings as Determined by the Measurements*
CIRIA 1971, *The Modern Design of Wind Sensitive Structures*
Cohen 1967, *Proposed American Standard Building Code Requirements for Minimum Design*
Colin 1963, *Execution of Tests on Models of Buildings Carried Out in an Aerodynamic Tunnel*
Cook 1973, *On Simulating the Lower Third of the Urban Adiabatic Boundary Layer in a Wind*
Cook 1975, *A Boundary Layer Wind Tunnel for Building Aerodynamics*
Cook 1975, *Calibration and Use of Hot-Wire Probe for Highly Turbulent and Reversing Flows*
Corke 1975, *Flow Near Model of Building in Simulated Atmospheric Surface Layers Generated*
Coull 1971, *Hull-Core Structures Subjected to Lateral Forces*
Counihan 1969, *An Improved Method of Simulating an Atmospheric Boundary Layer in a Wind*
Counihan 1975, *Adiabatic Atmospheric Boundary Layers: A Review and Analysis of Data*
Coyle 1931, *Measuring the Behaviour of Tall Buildings*
Csanady 1973, *Turbulent Diffusion in the Environment*

Dalgliesh 1967, *Wind Pressure Measurements on a Full-Scale High-Rise Office Building*
Dalgliesh 1969a, *Digital Data Acquisition System for Measuring Wind Effects of Tall Buildings*
Dalgliesh 1969b, *Experience with Wind Pressure Measurements on a Full-Scale Building*
Dalgliesh 1970, *Wind Pressure Measurements on Full Scale Buildings*
Dalgliesh 1971, *Statistical Treatment of Peak Gusts on Cladding*
Dalgliesh 1973, *Research Review—North and South America*
Dalgliesh 1974, *Wind Loads for Glass Design*
Dalgliesh 1975, *Comparison of Mode/Full-Scale Wind Pressures on a High-Rise Building*
Da Rocha 1973, *Ultimate Strength Analysis of Tall Buildings*
Davenport 1960, *A Rationale for the Determination of Basic Design Wind Velocities*
Davenport 1961a, *The Application of Statistical Concepts to the Wind Loading of Structures*
Davenport 1961b, *The Spectrum of Horizontal Gustiness near the Ground in High Winds*
Davenport 1962, *The Response of Slender Line-like Structures to Gusty Wind*
Davenport 1963a, *The Relationship of Wind Structure to Wind Loading*
Davenport 1963b, *Buffet of Structures by Gusts*
Davenport 1964, *Note on Distribution of Largest Value of Random Function with Application*
Davenport 1966a, *Estimation of Repeated Loads on Structures with Application to Wind*
Davenport 1966b, *The Treatment of Wind Loading on Tall Buildings*
Davenport 1967a, *The Dependence of Wind Loads on Meteorological Parameters*
Davenport 1967b, *Gust Loading Factors*
Davenport 1967c, *The Application of the Boundary Layer Wind Tunnel to the Prediction*
Davenport 1967d, *The Relationship of Meteorological Factors to Wind Loading*
Davenport 1970, *Analysis of Wind Induced Building Movement and Column Strain*
Davenport 1970, *A Study of Wind Effects on the Commerce Court Project—Part II*
Davenport 1970a, *A Study of Wind Effects for the Theme Towers, Century City, Los Angeles*
Davenport 1970b, *Study of Wind Effects on the World Trade Center, New York: Exterior*
Davenport 1971, *Wind Loads*
Davenport 1971, *A Study of Wind Effects for the Sears Project*
Davenport 1971, *A Preliminary Appraisal of Wind Loading Concepts of the 1970 Canadian*
Davenport 1971a, *On the Statistical Prediction of Structural Performance in the Wind Environment*
Davenport 1971b, *Wind Loading and Wind Effects*
Davenport 1972a, *An Approach to Human Comfort Criteria for Environmental Wind Conditions*
Davenport 1972b, *Wind Loading and Wind Effects*
Davenport 1972c, *Structural Safety and Reliability Under Wind Action*
Davenport 1973, *Theme Report: Wind Loading and Wind Effects*
Davenport 1973, *Wind Loads and Safety of Tall Buildings*
Davenport 1975, *The Ground Level Wind Environment in Built-up Areas*
Davenport 1975a, *Criteria for Design Against Wind Action*
Davenport 1975b, *Perspectives on the Full-Scale Measurement of Wind Effects*
Davenport 1975c, *The Design of Tall Buildings for Wind Forces: International Developments*
Davenport 1976, *Discussion of "Wind Pressures on Buildings—Probability Densities"*
Deacon 1955, *Gust Variation with Height up to 150 m*
Drakatos 1975, *The Noise in Tall Buildings*
Duchene-Marullaz 1975, *Full Scale Measurements of Atmospheric Turbulence in a Suburban Area*

Durgin 1972, *The Effect of Twist Motion on the Dynamic Multimode Response of a Building*
Durst 1960, *Wind Speeds over Short Periods of Time*
Dutt 1974a, *An Investigation of the Wind Pressure Distribution on the M.I.T. Tower, Shah Alam*
Dutt 1974b, *An Approach to the Simplification of the Dynamic Characteristics of Wind Loading*

Eaton 1975, *Cladding and the Wind*
Eaton 1975, *The Measurement of Wind Pressures on Two-Storey Houses at Aylesbury*
Elliott 1958, *The Growth of the Atmospheric Internal Boundary Layer*
Ellis 1975, *A New Technique for Evaluating the Fluctuating Lift and Drag Force Distribution*
Esquillan 1963, *The 1963 French Regulations Defining the Effect of Wind on Buildings*

Ferry Borges 1971, *Design Criteria for Wind Loads on Statistical Basis*
Fichtl 1969, *The Characteristics of Atmospheric Turbulence as Related to Wind Loads on Tall*
Finzi 1967, *The New Italian Regulations for Wind Loads on Structures*
Fleming 1971, *Structural Framing for Drift Limitation in Highrise Buildings*
Focsa 1975, *Some Aspects Concerning the Effect of Wind on the Thermal Conditions in Tall*
Franck 1963, *Model Law and Experimental Techniques for the Determination of Wind Loads*
Fujii 1974, *Wind Pressure Measurements on a Tall Building—Further Results from the Asahi-Tokai*
Fujimoto 1975, *Dynamic Model Tests of a High-Rise Building in Wind Tunnel Flow and in Natural*
Fujita 1974, *Recent Concepts of Tornado Winds*
Funakawa 1971, *Vibration of a Cylinder Caused by Wake Force*

Galambos 1973, *Structural Deflections—A Literature and State of the Art Survey*
Gandemer 1975, *Wind Environment around Buildings: Aerodynamic Concepts*
Gill 1969, *Guidelines in Selecting Wind Measuring Instruments and their Locations for Wind Loading*
Gilling 1971, *The Influence of a Wind-Tunnel Study on the Design for the Qantas Centre*
Givoni 1972, *Air Flow Around High Rise Buildings*
Goldman 1974, *Time-Dependent Variations of Vertical Storm Wind Profiles*
Gomes 1974, *On the Prediction of Extreme Wind Speeds from the Parent Distribution*
Gomes 1976a, *On Thunderstorm Wind Gusts in Australia*
Gomes 1976b, *On the Prediction of Tropical Cyclone Gust Speeds along the Northern Australian*
Gorove 1967, *Dynamic Response of Pressure Transmission Lines to Pulse Input*
Goto 1975, *Research on Vibration Criteria from the Viewpoint of People Living in High-Rise*
Gumbel 1954, *Statistical Theory of Extreme Values and some Practical Applications*

Halitsky 1965, *Extensions on Stack Height Required to Limit Contamination of Building Air*
Hanafusa 1974, *Structure of the Planetary Boundary Layer in High Winds Observed from a 0.5-km TV*
Hansen 1973, *Human Response to Wind Induced Motions of Buildings*
Harris 1963, *The Response of Structures to Gusts*
Harris 1968, *On the Spectrum and Autocorrelation Function of Gustiness in High Winds*
Harris 1970, *The Nature of the Wind*
Harris 1971, *The Nature of the Wind*
Harris 1975, *The Relevance of Wind Structure to Design*
Hart 1969, *Combining a Wind Tunnel Analysis with a Three-Dimensional Analytic Building Analysis*
Hino 1964, *On the Gust Factor Relationship Between the Instantaneous Maxima and Averaging*
Hino 1971, *Spectrum of Gusty Wind*
Hirsch 1971, *Newer Investigations of Non-steady Wind Loadings and the Dynamic Response of Tall*
Hirsch 1975, *Vibration Measurements on a Cable-Stayed Bridge under Construction*
Hoecker 1961, *Wind Speed and Air Flow Patterns in the Dallas Tornado of April 2, 1957*
Holley 1975, *Use of Dynamically Responding Manometers to Monitor Structural Wind Pressure Loads*
Hollister 1969, *The Engineering Interpretation of Weather Bureau Records for Wind Loading on*
Holmes 1973, *Wind Pressure Fluctuations on a Large Building*
Holmes 1975, *Pressure Fluctuations on a Large Building and Along-Wind Structural Loading*
Huh 1971, *The Behaviour of Lift Fluctuations on the Square Cylinders in the Wind Tunnel Test*
Hunt 1975a, *Wind Tunnel Simulation of the Atmospheric Boundary Layer: A Report on Euromech 50*
Hunt 1975b, *Turbulent Velocities Near and Fluctuating Surface Pressures on Structures in Turbulent*
Hunt 1976, *The Effects of Wind on People; New Criteria Based on Wind Tunnel Experiments*

Iberall 1950, *Attenuation of Oscillatory Pressures in Instrument Lines*
Ishizaki 1967, *Effects of Wind Pressure Fluctuations on Structures*
Ishizaki 1971, *Influence of Adjacent Buildings to Wind*
Ishizaki 1971a, *Storm Frequencies and Wind Load Problems*
Ishizaki 1971b, *Current Studies on Wind Loads in Japan*
Ishizaki 1973, *Research Review—Asia and Australia*
Ishizaki 1974a, *Problems in Designing Window Glass Against Wind Pressure*
Ishizaki 1974b, *On the Wind Resistant Design of Exterior Cladding*
Ishizaki 1975, *On the Design of Glass Pane Against Wind Loading*
Isyumov 1974, *Model Studies and the Prediction of Full Scale Levels of Stack Gas Concentration*
Isyumov 1975, *Some Full Scale Measurements of Wind Induced Response of the CN Tower, Toronto*

Isyumov 1975a, *The Ground Level Wind Environment in Built-Up Areas*
Isyumov 1975b, *Comparison of Full Scale and Wind Tunnel Wind Speed Measurements*

Jackson 1975, *A Theory for Wind Flow over Escarpments*
Jensen 1958, *The Model Law for Phenomena in the Natural Wind*
Jensen 1963, *Proposed Code of Practice for Wind Loads for Denmark*
Jensen 1965, *Model Scale Tests in Turbulent Wind*
Jensen 1967, *Some Lessons Learned in Building Aerodynamic Research*
Jensen 1967, *Maximum Wind Velocities in Denmark*
Joubert 1967, *The Drag of Bluff Bodies Immersed in a Turbulent Boundary Layer*
Joubert 1971, *Drag of a Bluff Body Immersed in a Roughwall Boundary Layer*
Juhasova 1973, *Dynamic Properties of some Types of Framed Tall Buildings*

Kamei 1971, *Application to Design of Research on Tall Building Wind Effects*
Kato 1974, *Experimental Study on Buffeting Vibrations of Tall Buildings*
Kato 1971, *Wind Tunnel Test for Dynamic Response of Tall Buildings*
Kato 1976, *Wind Loading Studies on Tall Buildings at Model Scale*
Katsura 1974, *Fluctuating Wind Pressure on the Side Surfaces of Models with Long Rectangular*
Kawai 1975, *On the Relation Between the Fluctuations of Wind Speed and Pressure on the Windward*
Kawai 1976, *Local Wind Pressure Characteristics on a Full-Scale Tall Building*
Kawatani 1971, *Characteristics of the Mean Flow over a Simulated Urban Area*
Khan 1971, *Service Criteria for Tall Buildings for Wind Loading*
Kobayashi 1971, *Measurement and Analysis of Vibration of High-Rise Building in Strong Wind*
Kochle 1974, *Measuring the Oscillations of Tall Buildings with a Laser-interferometer*
Koenig 1970, *A Contribution to the Analysis in a Gusty Wind*
Kolousek 1973, *Vibration of Structures of Tall Buildings*
Kolousek 1975, *Wind Effects on Tall Buildings*
Koppes 1969, *Design Wind Loads for Building Wall Elements*
Korenev 1971, *Some Problems of Dynamic Design of Elastic Structures, Equipped with Dampers*
Korenev 1973, *Dynamical Vibration Absorbers of Tall Buildings and Towers*
Korenev 1975, *On Damping Wind Induced Vibrations of Flexible Structures*
Kozak 1971, *Statical Systems of Tall Buildings with Core Structures*
Krishnaswamy 1971, *Recent Wind Tunnel Investigations on Aerodynamic Stability of Engineering*
Kulkarni 1973, *Effects of Winds on Tall Buildings*
Kus 1971, *The New Polish Code of Practice for Wind Loads in Comparison with Other Actual*

Lam 1973, *Wind Effects on Tall Buildings in Hong Kong*
Lam 1975, *Wind Load for Cladding Design*
Laneville 1971, *Effects of Turbulence on Galloping of Bluff Cylinders*
Laneville 1975, *An Explanation of Some Effects of Turbulence on Bluff Bodies*
Langhaar 1951, *Dimensional Analysis and Theory of Models*
Laurie 1975, *Design Loads for Tall Buildings*
Lawson 1973, *The Wind Environment of Buildings: A Logical Approach to the Establishment*
Lawson 1974, *The Measurement of Short Term Average Pressures in a Wind Tunnel Investigation*
Lawson 1975, *The Effects of Wind on People in the Vicinity of Buildings*
Leadon 1974, *Terrain and Wind Climate Description and Wind Profile Instrumentation*
Leutheusser 1969, *Influence of Architectural Features on the Static Wind Loading of Buildings*
Lin 1967, *Probabilistic Theory of Structural Dynamics*
Lumley 1964, *The Structure of Atmospheric Turbulence*

MacDonald 1971, *A Method for Calculating the Vibration Amplitudes of Slender Structures*
MacGregor 1971, *Why the Wind Howls Around Those Plazas Close to Skyscrapers*
Mackey 1973, *Summary Report: Wind Loading and Wind Effects*
Mackey 1974, *A Full Scale and Wind Tunnel Study of Wind Loading on a Building*
Mackey 1975, *Some Aspects of High Rise, High Density Urban Development in Hong Kong*
Mackey 1975, *Spatial Configuration of Gusts*
Makino 1971, *Some Field Test Results of Wind Pressures on a Tall Building*
Malinowski 1971, *Wind Effect on the Air Movement Inside Building*
Marshall 1975, *A Study of Wind Pressures on a Single Family Dwelling in Model and Full Scale*
Martin 1976, *Modal Control of Multi-Story Structures*
Maugh 1969, *Design and Construction for What Wind Loads and Why*
McCormick 1971, *Air Pollution in the Locality of Buildings*
McDonald 1970, *Structural Response of a Twenty Story Building to the Lubbock Tornado*
McKeon 1971, *Wind Tunnel Blockage Effects and Drag on Bluff Bodies in a Rough Wall*
McVehil 1967, *On the Feasibility of Modelling Small Scale*
Melbourne 1968, *Wind Tunnel Modelling of Buoyant Chimney Plumes*
Melbourne 1971, *Problems of Wind Flow at the Base of Tall Buildings*
Melbourne 1971a, *Ground Level Winds Caused by Large Buildings*
Melbourne 1971b, *Comparison of Pressure Measurements Made on a Large Isolated Building*
Melbourne 1972, *Modelling of Structures to Measure Wind Effects*

Melbourne 1973a, *West Gate Bridge Wind Tunnel Tests*
Melbourne 1973b, *Wind Tunnel Test Expectations*
Melbourne 1974, *Peak Factors for Structures Oscillating Under Wind Action*
Melbourne 1975, *A Wind Tunnel Model Study of Air Conditioning Contamination by Intake of*
Melbourne 1975a, *Cross-Wind Response of Structures to Wind Action*
Melbourne 1975b, *The Relevance of Codification to Design*
Melbourne 1975c, *Probability Distributions of Response of BHP House to Wind Action and*
Melbourne 1975d, *Discussion on Session (7)—Practical Application*
Melbourne 1976, *Effects of Upwind Buildings on the Response of Tall Buildings*
Melbourne 1977, *Probability Distributions Associated with the Wind Loading of Structures*
Mehta 1974, *Tornadic Loads on Structures*
Mihalache 1975, *Some Aspects Concerning the Dynamic Response of Tall Buildings*
Miller 1972, *Model Analysis of the Qantas Centre*
Miller 1973, *Qantas Centre, Sydney, Design and Construction Planning*
Minor 1974, *Window Glass in Windstorms*
Mitsuta 1974, *Preliminary Results of Typhoon Wind Observation at Tarama Island, Okinawa*
Miyoshi 1971, *Wind Pressure Coefficients on Exterior Wall Elements of Tall Buildings*
Mori 1974, *Wind Tunnel Studies of Wind Excited Oscillations of Tall Buildings*
Muller 1975, *Measurements of Wind-Induced Vibrations on a Concrete Chimney*
Murakami 1975, *Wind Effects on Air Flows in Half Enclosed Spaces*
Murota 1974, *An Experimental Study on the Drag Coefficient of Screens for Building Use*
Murzewski 1972, *Maximum Wind Load for a Prescribed Situation of a Building*
Muto 1971, *Fluttering Design of Keio Plaza Hotel*

Naudascher 1974, *Fluid-Induced Structural Vibrations*
Negoita 1975, *Framed Tall Buildings Subjected to Lateral Forces*
Nejman 1974, *Gravi-stability of Tall Buildings*
Nemoto 1968, *Similarity Between Natural Local Wind in the Atmosphere and Model Wind*
Newberry 1963, *The Measurement of Wind Pressures on Tall Buildings*
Newberry 1967, *The Nature of Gust Loading on Tall Buildings*
Newberry 1971, *Wind Pressures on the Post Office Tower, London*
Newberry 1973, *Wind Loading on Tall Buildings—Further Results from Royex House*
Newberry 1973, *Wind Pressure and Strain Measurements at the Post Office Tower*
Newberry 1974, *Wind Loading Handbook*
Novak 1971, *Galloping and Vortex Induced Oscillations of Structures*
Novak 1971, *Research of Wind Effect on High Buildings and Structures in the Czechoslovak*

O'Bryne 1974, *Wind Loading in Nairobi—Plan—East Africa*
Olmer 1973, *Measurements of Tall Buildings Oscillations*
O'Rourke 1975, *Serviceability Analysis for Wind Loads on Buildings*
Orczykowski 1972, *The Problems of Tall Concrete Buildings Realization*
Ostrowski 1967, *Vortex Formation and Pressure Fluctuations on Buildings*
Otsuki 1971, *Wind Excited Vibrations of a Tower of Nearly Square Cross Section*

Page 1974, *Five Meteorological Facets of the Design of Tall Buildings*
Panggabean 1974, *A Contribution to the Statistical Analysis of the Design Wind Velocity*
Panggabean 1975, *Reliability Based Design of Slender Structures Under Wind Action*
Panggabean 1976, *On the Dependence of the Frequency Density of the Wind on the Height*
Pankhurst 1964, *Dimensional Analysis and Scale Factors*
Pasquill 1972, *Some Aspects of Boundary Layer Description*
Penwarden 1972, *Wind Environment Around Tall Buildings*
Penwarden 1973, *Acceptable Wind Speeds in Towns*
Penwarden 1975, *Wind Environment Around Buildings*
Peterka 1974a, *Probability Distributions of Wind Pressure Fluctuations on Buildings*
Peterka 1974b, *Peak Pressure Duration in Separated Regions on a Structure*
Peterka 1975a, *Wind Pressures on Buildings—Probability Densities*
Peterka 1975b, *Turbulence in Building Wakes*
Peyrot 1974, *Multi-degree Dynamic Analysis of Tall Buildings Subjected to Wind*
Pielke 1970, *Turbulence Characteristics along Several Towers*
Pirner 1973, *The Verification of Dynamic Response of Tall Buildings Under Wind Loading*
Pittsburgh Plate Glass Company 1965, *Glass Product Recommendations—Structural*
Plate 1971, *Aerodynamic Characteristics of Atmospheric Boundary Layers*
Poestkoke 1976, *Comparison of Full Scale Wind Climate Around a High-Rise Building*
Prahbu 1975, *Design Criteria for Stability of Cylindrical Shells Subjected to Wind Loading*
Pris 1963a, *Determination of the Action of Turbulent Wind on Buildings and Structures*
Pris 1963b, *Preparation of Tests on Models of Buildings in Aerodynamic Laboratory*

Ramesh 1973, *Wind Forces on Tall Buildings—Evaluation to Design*
Ranga Raju 1975, *Blockage Effects on Drag of Sharp-Edged Bodies*
Rathbun 1940, *Wind Forces on Tall Buildings*
Reardon 1973, *Brisbane Wind Storm*

Reese 1973, *A Method to Determine the Sensitivity of Mathematical Models in Deterministic*
Reeves 1974, *Development and Application of a Non-Gaussian Atmospheric Turbulence Model*
Rice 1944, *Mathematical Analysis of Random Noise*
Riera 1973, *Direct Wind*
Robertson 1967, *Application to Design of Research on Wind Effects*
Robertson 1969, *The Treatment of Wind in the Design of Very Tall Buildings*
Robertson 1973a, *Limitations on Swaying Motion of Tall Buildings Imposed by Human Response*
Robertson 1973b, *Design Criteria for Very Tall Buildings*
Rummerfield 1967, *Estimation of Local Diffusion of Pollutants*
Ruscheweyh 1973, *Empirical Values of Natural Frequencies of Tall Buildings*
Russell 1971, *Probability Distribution of Hurricane Effects*

Sae-Ung 1975, *Active Control of Building Structures Subjected to Wind Loads*
Sae-Ung 1976, *Active Control of Building Structures Subjected to Wind Loads*
Sadeh 1972, *Turbulence Effects on Wall Pressure Fluctuations*
Saffir 1974, *Effects of High Wind on Glazing and Curtain Walls, and Rational Design Methods*
Saffir 1975, *Glass and Curtain Wall Effects of High Winds: Required Design Criteria*
Saul 1974, *Effect and Calculation of Damping on the Response of Tall Buildings*
Saunders 1971, *Flutter Instability of Rectangular Buildings*
Saunders 1975, *Tall Rectangular Building Response to Cross-Wind Excitation*
Scanlon 1977, *Flow-Induced Vibrations of Civil Structures*
Schiff 1974, *A Measuring System for Determining Wind Loads and the Resulting Response*
Schmitt 1926, *The Florida Hurricane and Some of Its Effects*
Schneider 1975, *Wind and Stress Measurements at the Munich Olympic Tower*
Schneider 1975, *An Investigation of Wind Excited Transversal Oscillations of Slender Structures*
Schneider 1976, *On the Calculation of Probability of Failure of Slender Structures Using the Monte*
Schriever 1968, *Recent Research on Wind Forces on Tall Buildings*
Schriever 1976, *Ground Level Winds Around Tall Buildings*
Schueller 1974, *Reliability of Tall Buildings Under Wind Action*
Schueller 1974, *Some Aspects of Reliability Assessments of Structures Under Wind Action*
Schueller 1975, *The Calculation of the Design Wind Velocity Based on a Reliability Concept*
Schueller 1975, *Spectral and Time History Approach for the Prediction of the Behaviour of Slender*
Schueller 1976, *Probabilistic Determination of Design Wind Velocity in Germany*
Schueller 1976, *Reliability Considerations Based on Measurements of Wind Effects Taken*
Scruton 1963, *On the Wind-excited Oscillations of Stacks, Towers and Masts*
Scruton 1967, *Aerodynamics of Structures*
Sfintesco 1975, *Proposed European Code of Practice: Current Work of the ECCS Towards*
Shears 1970, *Problems in the Application of Statistical Design Methods*
Shears 1975, *Report on Wind and Vibration Measurements Taken at the Emley Moor Television*
Shellard 1963, *The Estimation of Design Wind Speeds*
Shellard 1967, *Results of Some Recent Special Measurements in the United Kingdom Relevant*
Shinozuka 1977, *Active/Passive Control of Civil Engineering Structures*
Shiotani 1967, *Lateral Structures of Gusts in High Winds*
Shiotani 1971, *Correlations of Wind Velocities in Relation to Gust Loadings*
Shiotani 1974, *A Study of Wind Flow at the Base of Buildings*
Simha 1973, *Wind Effect on Buildings*
Simiu 1973a, *Logarithmic Profiles and Design Wind Speeds*
Simiu 1973b, *Gust Factors and Alongwind Pressure Correlations*
Simiu 1974, *Improved Methods for Determining Wind Profiles and Dynamic Structural Response*
Simiu 1975a, *Probabilistic Models of Extreme Wind Speeds: Uncertainties and Limitations*
Simiu 1975b, *Equivalent Static Wind-Loads for Tall Building Design*
Simiu 1975, *The Buffeting of Tall Structures by Strong Winds*
Singer 1967, *The Micrometeorology of the Turbulent Flow Field in the Atmospheric Surface*
Singer 1969, *The Adequacy of Existing Meteorological Data for Evaluating Structural Problems*
Smart 1967, *Dynamic Structural Response to Natural Wind*
Snyder 1972, *Similarity Criteria for the Application of Fluid Models to the Study of Air Pollution*
Society of Steel Construction of Japan 1975, *Wind Resistant Design Regulations—A World List*
Somes 1971, *Lubbock Tornado: A Survey of Building Damage in an Urban Area*
Soon 1974, *Wind Tunnel Investigation on the Flood-lit Tower of the Singapore National Stadium*
Springfield 1973, *Codes and Model Testing*
Standen 1971, *A Wind Tunnel and Full-Scale Study of Turbulent Wind Pressures on a Tall*
Stansby 1975, *The Value of Wind Research to Civil Engineering*
Stevens 1967, *Elastic Stability of Practical Multi-Storey Frames*
Stevens 1973, *Design Developments—Asia and Australasia*
Surry 1967, *Turbulence in a Wind Tunnel and its Use in Studying the Turbulence Effects*
Surry 1975, *Fluctuating Pressures on Tall Buildings*

Takahashi 1971, *A Study of the Return Period and Design Load by means of the Monte-Carlo*
Takeuchi 1971, *Actual Fluctuating Wind Pressure on a Tall Building and its Response*
Tamura 1968, *Pressure Differences Caused By Wind on Two Tall Buildings*

Tanaka 1971, *Vibrations of Bluff-Sectional Structures under Wind Action*
Taoka 1974, *Vibrations of Tall Reinforced Concrete Buildings to Wind Forces*
Taylor 1970, *The Relevance to a Constructor*
Templin 1969, *Interim Progress Note on Simulation of Earth's Surface Winds by Artificially*
Teunissen 1975, *Simulation of the Planetary Boundary Layer in a Multiple-Jet Wind Tunnel*
Thom 1963, *Tornado Probabilities U.S.A.*
Thom 1967, *Toward a Universal Climatological Extreme Wind Distribution*
Thomann 1973, *Wind Action on Tall Buildings*
Thomas 1972, *Mounting of Anemometers in the Victoria Dock Area*
Thomas 1973, *The Structural Instrumentation of BHP House*
Tichy 1974a, *Combinations of Structural Actions (Level I Approach)*
Tichy 1974b, *A Probabilistic Model for Structural Actions*
Trigario 1973, *Some of the Problems Faced in the Design of a Multi-floor Building*
Tryggvasen 1975, *On the Prediction of Design Pressures for Glass and Cladding with Particular*

Van Der Hoven 1957, *Power Spectrum of Horizontal Wind Speed in the Frequency Range*
Van Koten 1967, *Wind Measurements on High Buildings in the Netherlands*
Van Koten 1971, *The Comparison of Measured and Calculated Amplitudes of Some Buildings,*
Van Koten 1973, *Research Review—Europe and Africa*
Velozzi 1968, *Gust Response Factors*
Vickery 1966, *On the Assessment of Wind Effects on Elastic Structure*
Vickery 1967, *A Comparison of Theoretical and Experimental Determination of the Response*
Vickery 1969, *On the Reliability of Gust Loading Factors*
Vickery 1970, *Wind Action on Single Yielding Structures*
Vickery 1970, *An Investigation of the Behaviour in Wind of the Proposed Centre Point Tower*
Vickery 1971a, *On the Assessment of Wind Effects on Elastic Structures*
Vickery 1971b, *Wind Induced Vibrations of Towers, Stacks and Masts*
Vickery 1972, *On the Aeroelastic Modelling of Structures in Wind*
Vickery 1973, *On the Prediction of the Ground Level Wind Environment*
Vickery 1973a, *Notes on Wind Forces on Tall Buildings*
Vickery 1973b, *On the Provisions and Limitations of the Australian Wind Loading Code*
Vickery 1973c, *On the Use of Balloon Data to Define Wind Speeds for Tall Buildings*
Vickery 1974a, *The Structural and Environmental Effects of Wind on Buildings and Structures*
Vickery 1974b, *The Design and Performance of a Low-Cost Boundary Layer Wind Tunnel*
Vorliček 1969, *Distribution of Extreme Values in Structural Theory*
Vorliček 1974, *Theoretical Models of Yearly Snow Load Maxima*

Walker 1975, *Investigations of Wind Design Criteria Using a Statistical Simulation Model*
Ward 1972, *Experimental Determination of Structure and Foundation Parameters Using*
Wardlaw 1972, *Wind Tunnel Investigations in Industrial Aerodynamics*
Wargon 1973, *Centerpoint Project, Sydney*
Wargon 1975, *Application of Post-Tensioning Techniques and Other Uses of Cables in High*
Wen 1971, *Monte Carlo Solution of Structural Response to Wind Load*
Wen 1975, *Tornado Risk and Wind Effect on Structures*
Whitbread 1963, *Model Simulation of Wind Effects on Structures*
Whitbread 1974, *Wind Load and Environmental Studies for the 183 m National Westminster*
Whitbread 1975, *The Measurement of Non-steady Wind Forces on Small-scale Building Models*
Wianecki 1971, *Aerodynamic Studies on Aeroelastic Models of Towers and Tall Buildings*
Wiren 1975, *A Wind Tunnel Study of Wind Velocities in Passage Between and Through*
Wise 1965, *Studies of Air Flow Around Buildings*
Wise 1971, *Effects Due to Groups of Buildings*
Wittmann 1976, *On the Damping of Slender Reinforced Concrete Structures*
Wootton 1970, *Aerodynamic Stability*
Wyatt 1970, *The Calculation of Structural Response*
Wyatt 1971, *The Ultimate Load Behaviour of Structures under Wind Loading*
Wyatt 1971, *A Review of Wind Loading Specifications*
Wyatt 1973, *Design Developments—Europe, Africa*
Wyatt 1975a, *A Proposed European Code of Practice*
Wyatt 1975b, *The Relevance of Probabilistic Analysis to Design*

Yamada 1975, *Criteria for Motion in Tall Buildings*
Yang 1975, *Application of Optimal Control Theory*
Yang 1977, *Active Tendon Control of Slender Structures*
Yoshikawa 1974, *On the Wind Pressure and the Wind Flow Around a Tall Building*

Zeller 1971, *Wind-induced Vibration of Real Building and Aerodynamic Pressure Acting on It*
Zuk 1968, *Kinectic Structures*
Zuk 1970, *Kinectic Architecture*

Tall Building Criteria and Loading

Chapter CL-4

Fire

Prepared by Committee 8A (Fire) of the Council on Tall Buildings and Urban Habitat as part of the Monograph on the Planning and Design of Tall Buildings.

Duiliu Sfintesco   Chairman
Joseph F. Fitzgerald   Vice-Chairman and Co-Editor
Margaret Law   Editor

AUTHOR ACKNOWLEDGMENT

Special acknowledgment is due those individuals whose contributions and papers formed the substantial first drafts of the various sections of this chapter. First are the state-of-art reporters from the 1972 International Conference whose material was published in the Lehigh Proceedings. These individuals are:

P. Arnault III, Section 4.1

M. Law, Section 4.1

H. Ehm, Section 4.2

R. H. Jensen, Section 4.3

G. R. Claiborne, Section 4.4

L. Wahl, Section 4.4

K. Kawagoe, Section 4.5.

In addition to this, the contents of this chapter were based on special contributions prepared by the following individuals:

M. Law, Sections 4.2 and 4.11

B. Barthelemy, Section 4.3

A. H. Gustaferro, Section 4.3

J. Kruppa, Section 4.3

L. G. Seigel, Section 4.4

J. F. Fitzgerald, Section 4.5

J. H. McGuire, Section 4.5

D. J. Rasbash, Section 4.5

J. J. Keough, Section 4.7

R. J. Thompson, Section 4.8

H. E. Nelson, Section 4.10

R. C. Elstner, Section 4.11

R. H. Wildt, Section 4.11

K. Kawagoe, Section 4.12

F. Jackson, Section 4.14.

CONTRIBUTORS

The following is a complete list of those who have submitted written material for possible use in the chapter, whether or not that material was used in the final version. The Committee Chairman and Editor were given quite complete latitude. Frequently length limitations precluded the inclusion of much valuable material. The Bibliography contains all contributions. The contributors are: D. E. Allen, P. Arnault III, B. Barthelemy, H. Bizri, B. Bresler, G. R. Claiborne, J. G. Degenkolb, E. Dore, H. Ehm, R. C. Elstner, J. F. Fitzgerald, G. Freeman, M. Galbreath, A. H. Gustaferro, G. A. Harrison, F. Jackson, Cdt. Jaunet, R. H. Jensen, S. Kajfasz, K. Kawagoe, J. J. Keough, R. F. Kill, D. Knight, K. Kordina, F. W. C. Kotze, J. Kruppa, M. Law, M. G. Lay, T. T. Lie, R. J. Mainstone, A. F. Margarido, H. W. Marryatt, J. H. McGuire, J. Milner, H. E. Nelson, O. Pettersson, E. Prendergast, D. J. Rasbash, W. R. Schriever, L. G. Seigel, D. Sfintesco, N. F. Somes, R. J. Thompson, J. Uribe, C. W. Volkamer, L. Wahl, R. A. Wheatley, R. H. Wildt, J. Witteveen, C. H. Yuill.

COMMITTEE MEMBERS

P. Arnault III, G. N. Badami, M. Badr. B. Barthelemy, H. Bizri, R. W. Bletzacker, J. A. Bono, B. Bresler, J. Brozzetti, S. Bryl, A. Cabret, J. G. Degenkolb, S. Eggwertz, H. Ehm, R. Estrada, General Ferauge, J. F. Fitzgerald, G. Freeman, G. R. Fuller, M. Galbreath, R. G. Gewain, P. K. Heilstedt, M. Holley, R. H. Jensen, S. Kajfasz, K. Kawagoe, J. J. Keough, D. Knight, K. Kordina, C. N. Kostem, J. Kruppa, M. Law, M. G. Lay, E. V. Leyendecker, J. Lindner, R. J. Mainstone, A. F. Margarido, H. W. Marryatt, M. M. Maxwell, J. Milner, C. S. Morgan, A. F. Nassetta, H. E. Nelson, O. Pettersson, D. J. Rasbash, V. Reichel, L. E. Robertson, F. Rosati, J. B. Scalzi, L. G. Seigel, D. Sfintesco, D. A. Simha, R. G. Slutter, N. F. Somes, P. S. Symonds, H. D. Taylor, P. H. Thomas, J. Uribe, E. H. Vanmarcke, L. Wahl, R. A. Wheatley, R. H. Wildt, R. B. Williamson, J. Witteveen, C. H. Yuill.

CL-4 Fire

4.1 INTRODUCTION

The essential function of a building is to provide a safe, comfortable space for human life and various activities and situations. This implies, as a primary role, protection of its users from climatic and other external influences as well as from natural or man-produced hazards. However, certain risks are inherent in the building itself, the most characteristic one being the fire risk. Therefore it is of the utmost importance to keep this risk and its consequences as small as possible.

Obviously, some important aspects of the fire risk are directly related to the size, design, equipment, and use of the building. Consideration of these factors leads to an adequate series of provisions for fire safety. This means that fire protection, like any other part of the building project, must be commensurate with the importance, complexity, and type of the building concerned. In particular, tall buildings require special, carefully observed provisions in order to cope with the fire risk implicitly resulting from their height, architectural and constructional features, and type of occupancy.

Therefore it would not be correct to say that the risks for the users grow directly with the height of the building or the number of stories, as in fact additional or increased risks for them result rather from a discrepancy between the actual provisions for fire protection and the building characteristics, irrespective of the height or type of the building. In other words, a well designed, well equipped, and well protected tall building can and must be as safe as a low one. Eventually it may be even safer, due to greater care exercised and to the recourse to equipment and other means which cannot be reasonably afforded for a small building.

Of course, there have been some spectacular, catastrophic fires in tall buildings. They have been the subject of comment far beyond the professional area. The objective analysis of such fire incidents represents a most useful source of information for fire-engineering science and results in practical lessons for all those concerned with fire safety. It demonstrates, moreover, that such events have been possible only as a consequence of simple nonobservance of elementary requirements for fire protection. Therefore tall buildings definitely do not deserve to be quoted as

251

necessarily implying greater risks for the occupants than low buildings; they rather imply the need for adequate treatment and consideration at their own scale. This fact is quite clearly confirmed by statistics reflecting facts, not comments or subjective, sometimes biased, opinions. As an example, let us examine some data from three countries for a given period, 1971 to 1973, shown in Table 4.1.

It can reasonably be assumed that the lower figures for tall buildings in Table 4.1 are due in part to their better condition as compared with low buildings and thus reflect the actual situation. These figures speak for themselves. They seem to deny the emotionally formulated arguments against tall buildings with regard to fire safety, but plead for careful, adequate design and fire protection. The purpose of this chapter is to provide information on safe design and correct equipment for the fire protection of tall buildings.

Another consideration is the acceptable risk and the resulting requirements for tall buildings as compared with low ones. In fact, the primary objective of general codes or regulations is to protect human life and safety, which includes the users and the fire fighting team: structural integrity is required to the extent commanded by this objective only, while additional fire resistance needed for economic considerations is generally left to the discretion of the building owner or the insurance company. The situation is different for tall buildings: their serviceability after fire is not only a more critical economic question but also a social and employment problem, and last but not least, it affects the normal course of activities in the urban context. The collapse or major damage of a tall building is not acceptable for many reasons. This results in special requirements and the need to find means to meet them.

Fire safety is always the result of various elements. It is particularly complex for tall buildings. Therefore it must be the concern of all participants in the design, construction, and equipping of the building, in consultation with professional fire

Table 4.1 Evidence of fires and fatalities *(Courtesy: Duiliu Sfintesco)*

Type of data (1)	France (2)	United Kingdom (3)	Australia (4)
Criterion of tall building	$h > 30$ m (for office) $h > 50$ m (for apartments)	$h > 24$ m	$h > 25$ m
Number of tall buildings	~400	~5000[a]	~600
Fires in tall buildings	225	3882	638
Persons killed by fire in tall office buildings	1[b]	0	0
Persons killed per 100 fires in tall buildings (all occupancies)	0.44[b]	0.13	0.78
Persons killed per 100 fires in low buildings	0.85	1.35	1.50

[a]Personal estimate.

[b]This single victim had deliberately returned to the fire area for some purpose.

fighters. This multiprofessional operation must be assured from the very beginning of the project and maintained during the operations, in order to achieve efficient and economic fire protection through a system approach.

This chapter is intended to describe the various aspects of the problem and to suggest a well-balanced, efficient combination of all necessary provisions and expertise.

4.2 NATURAL FIRES, STANDARD FIRES, AND FIRE LOADS

When a fire begins in a room or compartment the main hazard is to the people within the compartment, who will be exposed to smoke, toxic gases, and flames. Once the fire has become fully developed, human survival will no longer be possible and the main hazard is to the structure containing the fire. Beyond the compartment, there will be a risk of spread of fire, smoke, and toxic gases to the rest of the building and, through the windows, radiation will present an exposure hazard to nearby buildings.

Because of the many people at risk in a tall building, it is particularly important to try to reduce the risk of ignition and rapid spread of fire during the early stages of fire growth. Tests have been developed in many countries to assess the ease of ignition of materials used as inner surface coverings to line walls and ceilings—and to determine their subsequent behavior during the early stages of a fire. It is now recognized that there is poor correlation between these tests, which do not necessarily represent practical conditions. Resistance to structural collapse and the containment of fire in one compartment are also particularly important for tall buildings. The standard fire used to assess the ability of a structure to withstand the effects of a fully developed fire—the fire resistance test (ISO, 1975)—is virtually the same throughout the world. While it is recognized that this test, too, does not necessarily represent natural fire conditions, it is fair to say that where there has been major loss of life from a fire in a modern tall building, this has been caused mainly by the contents of the building, not the structure.

The degree of fire resistance required for the structure is related to, among other things, the fire load, and some assessments of the amounts of fire loads in different occupancies have been made. Fire resistant compartment walls and floors are a basic provision for the containment of a fire, but the many service ducts and other shafts found in tall buildings penetrate these compartments and can spread fire throughout, unless special measures are taken to prevent this. These measures are dealt with in Section 4.6.

1 Ignition and Spread of Fire

In an attempt to reduce the risk of ignition and spread of fire it is usual to place some restrictions on the type of wall and ceiling surfaces, the degree of control depending on the size and use of the room or compartment, and the number of people at risk. For example, an escape route will have noncombustible wall and ceiling surfaces, while a small living room might be permitted to have combustible surfaces provided they had a rate of flame spread within a specified limit. The increasing use of plastic materials, in particular, has led to suggestions that there should also be a control of furnishings and fittings in tall buildings, or even a

Powerful street stream reaching fire *(Courtesy: Chicago Fire Department)*

Heavy hose stream in use at high-rise fire *(Courtesy: Chicago Fire Department)*

complete ban on some materials. The problem is that the hazard presented by a particular material or combination of materials can vary with circumstances.

The spread of fire from an ignition source will depend on the geometry and spacing of the adjacent combustible materials and on their thermal properties; it is not normally possible to establish a unique critical temperature or a threshold rate of heating for ignition of a material, although models have been developed which have proved useful, for example, in assessing the risk of fire spread between buildings by radiation (Law, 1963). This model is related to the ignition of vertical surfaces and is not necessarily applicable to the geometrical situations found in rooms. It is clear, however, that thin materials are more likely to be ignited than thick ones, because less heat is needed to raise their temperature, and a foamed material with low density and low thermal conductivity will more rapidly attain a high surface temperature.

A research program being carried out under the auspices of the CIB (Thomas, 1973) has been designed to investigate some of the factors affecting the early growth of a fire in a room. The position and size of the ignition source (at the center or corner of the room), the position and size of the window opening, the amount and dispersion of the fuel (wood cribs), and the type of lining (noncombustible or hardboard), have been varied. The time for all the upper surfaces of the cribs to be involved in fire was measured, and a preliminary analysis has indicated that the effect of adding the hardboard lining was sometimes no more than could be obtained by certain changes in other variables.

It is because the significance of the behavior of the lining material depends so much on the circumstances that the many "flame spread" tests which have been developed, although normally distinguishing between the best and worst materials, have appeared unsatisfactory in practice. For this reason a working group of the International Standards Organization, ISO/TC92, has been working on tests for "reaction to fire," which would assess the key properties of ignitability, flame spread, rate of heat release, and smoke production which could be related to particular situations (Malhotra, 1974). Parallel investigations are being carried out to assess ways of using new furnishing materials so that they do not present a significantly worse hazard than those they replace. It has been found, for example, that for sustained ignition the type of fabric covering and the size of the ignition source can be as important as the type of padding material used (Palmer and Taylor, 1974).

Pending further guidance, as the results of the research are assessed, it would seem prudent to use noncombustible materials on exposed surfaces of the building structures, wherever possible, since this would be expected to reduce the chance of a fire developing from a small ignition source. Unless cavities can be fire stopped, any nonexposed surfaces should also be noncombustible, to reduce the risk of unseen fire spread. As will be shown later, such measures, by reducing the fire load, can also reduce both the risk of structural damage and the risk of large flames emerging from the windows.

2 Fully Developed Building Fires

Rate of Burning and Temperature. It is important to be able to estimate the rate of burning, the temperatures attained, and the fire duration so that the following hazards can be assessed:

1. Damage to the internal structure containing the fire.

2. Radiation exposure to nearby buildings, from the windows and emerging flames.

3. Radiation and flame exposure to any external structure of the building on fire.

4. External fire spread from floor to floor caused by flames emerging from windows.

The fire duration can be determined from the total fire load, and assessments of fire loads are reviewed in Article 3 of this section. To assess the rate of burning and temperature, considerable effort has been expended on calculations of a heat balance for a fire in a compartment, various simplifying assumptions being necessary.

Heat balance for a natural fire in a compartment.   When the fire becomes fully developed inside the compartment, the heat produced will be transferred partly to the enclosing walls and ceiling, and partly to the unburnt fuel, while the rest will be lost through the windows by radiation and in the outflowing stream of flames and hot gases. A heat balance measured for a fire in a room of dimensions 8 m × 4 m (26 ft × 13 ft) on plan showed, for example, that the heat loss in the effluent gases was on the order of 50% and feedback to the unburnt fuel on the order of 10% (Heselden, 1968). The rate of weight loss, or rate of burning, of the fuel will depend on the rate of heating it receives, its configuration, and its composition.

Models which have been developed to calculate the heat balance in a compartment are based on an assumption of a uniform temperature distribution (not likely to be found in deep compartments), and a ventilation controlled burning rate R (in kilograms per second) of the form

$$R = k A_W h_W^{\frac{1}{2}} \tag{4.1}$$

in which A_W and h_W = window area and height, respectively, measured in meters. The value of k originally derived was about 0.09, although more recently it has been shown that it can vary. A research program carried out under the auspices of the CIB (Thomas, 1974) gives comprehensive data on the effects of variations in the amount, spacing, and thickness of fire load, ventilation, and shape of compartment on the value of k and on fire temperature, which can reach values on the order of 1200°C (2192°F).

Effect of type of fire load.   Nearly all experiments are based on wood as the fire load, because until recently this has been assumed to be representative of most furniture commonly found in buildings. To estimate the effects of other combustible materials adjustment has been made by relating their calorific values to that of wood, or expressing all fire loads in megajoules rather than kilograms. This is an approximation since it cannot be assumed that the rate of burning is related to the rate of heating in the same way as wood; the rate of burning of polyurethane foam, for example, is much more sensitive to the value of irradiance than is wood (Roberts, 1974). Most experiments have used wood in the form of cribs, since these are easily reproduced, and the burning of a crib has been analyzed so that it can be related to the behavior of actual fire loads of furniture.

Experiments with domestic furniture in well ventilated rooms indicate that with ample ventilation the effective fire duration would be about 20 min (Theobald and

Heselden, 1968). Experiments with office furniture containing closely packed papers showed that not all the papers were consumed (ECCS, 1974a): the amount burnt would depend on the rate of heating from the surrounding fire, which for offices is likely to be low, and it has been suggested that in these circumstances the effective fire load is significantly less than the total. When some of the fire load is dispersed on the walls and ceilings in the form of combustible inner surface materials this can produce large flames from the windows. Little study has been made of the effects of an increasing amount of plastics on the behavior of a fully developed fire, but one effect, for low fire load, well ventilated conditions, could be a significantly shorter but hotter fire with more flames from the windows. In general, the use of plastics could lead to larger flames being produced.

Effects of Fire on Structure—The Standard Fire.   Where the thermal properties of the structural materials are known and failure can be defined in terms of a critical temperature, it is possible to calculate heat flow and hence the possibility of failure for a calculated or given temperature-time fire condition (Petterson, 1973). For structures with a significant heat capacity, errors in estimation of the variation of fire temperature with time will be smoothed, but care is needed if the behavior of the materials of the structure is sensitive to the actual fire temperatures attained, particularly if the thermal properties of the materials have been measured in the standard test which does not necessarily represent natural fire conditions. Because this test forms the basis of most legislation for fire resistance, and the results of the test are the main sources of data for material properties, efforts have been made to relate the effects of natural fires to the effects of the standard fire. (This has been considered an improvement on earlier relationships based on equal areas under temperature-time curves.) The relationship depends to some extent on the test specimen considered (ECCS, 1974a), but an approximate relationship has been derived (Law, 1973b) as

$$t_f = \frac{L}{\sqrt{A_W A_T}} \tag{4.2}$$

in which t_f = fire resistance as measured in the standard test, in minutes; A_W = window area, in square meters; A_T = surface area of the enclosing walls and ceiling of the compartment or room containing the fire, in square meters; and L = total weight of fire load, in kilograms. Whatever the shortcoming of the various methods being developed, they mark a significant advance towards the achievement of a fire engineering design for building structures.

Radiation and Flames from Windows.   The radiation or exposure hazard to nearby buildings will depend on the radiating temperature of the compartment on fire, which can be assumed to be a black body (Law, 1968), the extent of openings which are radiating, and the area and radiating intensity of the emerging flames. Models to determine safe separation distances have been developed (Law, 1963; McGuire, 1965), based on geometrical relationships and simplified assumptions about radiating intensity.

External structural elements close to the windows can be heated by radiation from the openings and by radiation and convection from the flames. An analysis by Thomas and Law (1974) of Yokoi (1960), Seigel (1969), and others shows that the height of the flame tip L above the base of the fire is proportional to $(R/W)^{2/3}$, in which R = rate of burning, and W = window width.

In general, the shape of the flame trajectory varies with the shape of the window, wide flame fronts being closer to the wall than narrow ones. Long flames may be expected if flammable linings are used, if there is a fire on more than one floor, or if there is a wind across the fire. Projections and upstands can provide useful shields to external structural members but offer little protection against the risk of external fire spread from floor to floor (Ashton and Malhotra, 1968). For this reason, among others, large areas of combustible materials on walls, ceilings, and partitions should not be permitted.

3 Fire Loads

The amount of fuel—the fire load—has always been regarded as the most important factor affecting fire behavior and, traditionally, the fire grading of buildings has been directly related to fire load per unit floor area, following the work of Ingberg (1928). It is interesting to note that although the effect of ventilation has not been taken into account in most building codes, Ingberg himself pointed out that it altered the fire behavior.

Domestic, office, hospital, and school fire loads are generally considered as low, shops and department stores as medium, and storage buildings as high fire loads (Law and Arnault, 1973). For modern buildings, the most recent surveys have tended to be in office buildings, giving an average of about 20 kg/m² (about 4-1/2 lb per sq ft), but with a long tail to the distribution for high values such as record rooms (Law and Arnault, 1973; ECCS, 1974a). Domestic fire loads are usually considered to be on the order of 25 kg/m² (5-3/4 lb per sq ft) and this has been confirmed by measurements of furniture used in experimental simulation of domestic fires. A somewhat unexpected result was obtained for the fire load in car parks, which was found to be so low that, combined with a lack of propensity to spread fire from one car to the next, little or no structural fire resistance is required if the park is well ventilated (Butcher et al., 1968; Gewain, 1974). Recent surveys inside buildings have tended to distinguish between "fixed" and "movable" fire load, the fixed being part of the structure and the fittings, and under the control of the building designer, and the movable being the furniture and contents provided by the tenant. The designer should take the opportunity to keep the fixed fire load to the minimum.

4.3 STRUCTURAL BEHAVIOR

1 Concrete Structures

Behavior of Simply Supported Slabs and Beams during Fire Exposure. Fig. 4.1 shows a simply supported reinforced concrete slab. The rocker and roller supports indicate that the ends of the slab are free to rotate and expansion can occur without resistance. The reinforcement consists of straight bars located near the bottom of the slab. If the underside of the slab is exposed to fire, the bottom of the slab will expand more than the top, resulting in a deflection of the slab. The strength of the concrete and steel near the bottom of the slab will decrease as the temperature increases. When the strength of the steel reduces to that of the stress in the steel, flexural collapse will occur.

Fig. 4.2 illustrates the behavior of a simply supported slab exposed to fire from beneath. In Fig. 4.2, M_t and $M_{t\theta}$ = ultimate moment capacity at normal and fire temperatures, respectively; and M = working moment.

It is generally assumed that during a fire the dead and live loads remain constant, while the strengths of the heated materials are reduced, so that flexural failure can be assumed to occur when $M_{t\theta}$ is reduced to M. From this, it can be noted that the critical temperature and hence the fire resistance depends on the load intensity and the strength-temperature characteristics of steel. In turn, the duration of the fire until the critical steel temperature is reached depends for the most part upon the protection afforded to the reinforcement. Usually the protection consists of the concrete cover, that is, the thickness of concrete between the fire-exposed surface and the reinforcement. In some cases additional protective layers of insulation or membrane ceilings might be present.

Behavior of Statically Indeterminate Slabs and Beams during Fire Exposure. Structures that are continuous or otherwise statically indeterminate undergo changes in stress when subjected to fire. Such changes in stress result from temperature gradients within structural members, or changes in strength of structural materials at high temperatures, or both.

Fig. 4.3 shows a two-span continuous beam whose underside is exposed to fire. The bottom of the beam becomes hotter than the top and tends to expand more than the top. This differential heating causes the ends of the beam to tend to lift from their supports, thus increasing the reaction at the interior support. This action results in a redistribution of moments, that is, the negative moment at the interior support increases while the positive moments decrease.

During the course of a fire, the negative moment reinforcement (Fig. 4.3) remains cooler than the positive moment reinforcement because it is better protected from the fire. Thus, the fire resistance of a continuous reinforced concrete beam is generally significantly longer than that of a simply supported beam having the same cover and loaded to the same moment intensity. Since, by increasing the amount of negative moment reinforcement, a greater negative moment will be attained, care must be exercised in designing the member to assure that a secondary type of failure will not occur. Furthermore, the negative moment reinforcing bars must be long enough to accommodate the complete redistributed moment and change in the

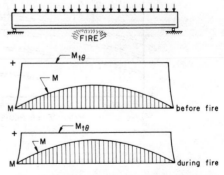

Fig. 4.1 Simply supported reinforced concrete slab subjected to fire from below.

Fig. 4.2 Moment diagram for simply supported beam or slab before and during fire exposure.

location of inflection points. It is recommended that at least 20% of the maximum negative moment reinforcement in the span extend throughout the span.

Estimating Fire Resistance (ISO R834).   Fig. 4.4 can be used to estimate the fire resistance of continuous reinforced concrete (normal weight) beams and slabs. [In Fig. 4.4, $\omega = \rho f_y / f_c'$. See ACI 318-77, Chapter 18.] To use the chart, first estimate the negative moment at the supports, taking into account the temperatures of the negative moment reinforcement and of the concrete in the compressive zone near the supports. Then estimate the maximum positive moment after redistribution. Entering the appropriate chart with the ratio of that positive moment to the

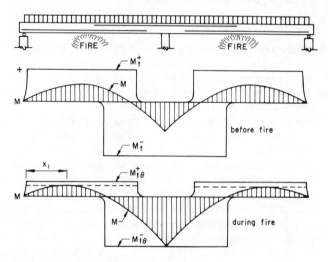

Fig. 4.3 Moment diagrams for continuous two-span beam before and during fire exposure

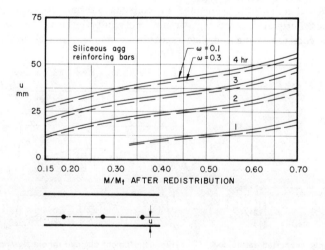

Fig. 4.4 Fire resistance of reinforced concrete slabs as influenced by moment intensity and redistribution

initial positive moment capacity, the fire resistance for the appropriate cover (positive moment region) can be estimated. If the resulting fire resistance is considerably different from that originally assumed in estimating the steel and concrete temperatures, a more accurate estimate can be made by trial and error. Usually such refinement is unnecessary.

It is also possible to design the reinforcement in a continuous beam or slab for a particular fire resistance period. From the lowermost diagram of Fig. 4.3, the beam can be expected to collapse when the positive moment capacity $M_{i\theta}^+$ is reduced to the value indicated by the dashed horizontal line, that is, when the applied moment at a point x_1 from the outer support $M_{x1} = M_{i\theta}$.

Behavior of Floors and Roofs in Which Restraint to Thermal Expansion Occurs during Fire Exposure.   If a fire occurs beneath a small interior portion of a large reinforced concrete slab, the heated portion will tend to expand and push against the surrounding part of the slab. In turn, the unheated part of the slab exerts compressive forces on the heated portion. The compressive force, or thrust, acts near the bottom of the slab when the fire first occurs, but as the fire progresses the line of action of the thrust rises as the heated concrete deteriorates. If the surrounding slab is thick and heavily reinforced, the thrust forces that occur can be quite large, although at high temperatures, creep can relax stress to some extent. The thrust is generally great enough to increase the fire resistance significantly. In most fire tests of restrained assemblies, the fire resistance is determined by temperature rise of the unexposed surface rather than by structural considerations, even though the temperature of the reinforcing steel often exceeds 800°C (1472°F).

The effects of restraint to thermal expansion can be characterized as shown in Fig. 4.5. The thermal thrust acts in a manner similar to an external prestressing force, which, in effect, increases the positive moment capacity. (In Fig. 4.5, note that if $M_t < M$ the effects of axial restraint permit beams to continue to support load.) It is possible to determine the magnitude and location of the required thrust to provide a given fire resistance, provided the temperature distribution at the required fire test duration can be determined.

The guidelines in ASTM E119-74 (1974) given for determining conditions of

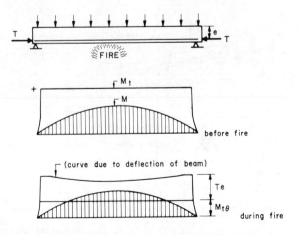

Fig. 4.5 Moment diagrams for axially restrained beam during fire exposure

restraint are useful for preliminary design purposes. Basically, interior bays of
multibay floors or roofs can be considered to be restrained, and the magnitude and
location of the thrust are generally of academic interest only. A review of the effects
of fire in big concrete buildings is given by Kordina and Krampf (1972), together
with design guidance.

2 Steel Structures

Strength of Steel. As far as mild steel is concerned, variations with the
temperature of yield point and Young's modulus are given by Figs. 4.6 and 4.7. The
scatter on these figures is due both to the variability of measurement at high

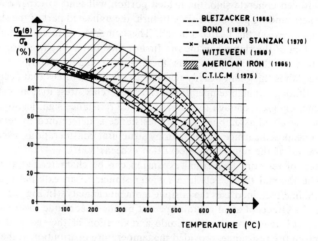

Fig. 4.6 Yield point at elevated temperatures, or 0.2% proof stress, of mild structural steels, as
percentage of yield point at room temperature, represented as function of temperature T

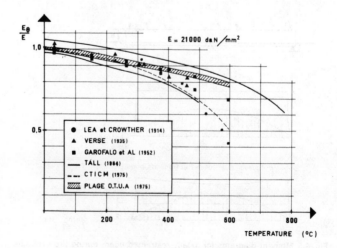

Fig. 4.7 Young's modulus variation with temperature

temperatures and to creep, which becomes noticeable above 350°C (662°F) and in building fires is important for temperatures above 600°C (1112°F).

Effects of creep. The exact determination of the fire resistance of a steel structure taking into account the change in steel properties with temperature, including creep, is very complicated. The approach of Dorn (1962) is simpler, and assumes that creep strain ϵ_t depends only on stress σ and a variable θ (in hours) defined by

$$\theta = \int_0^t e^{-\Delta H/RT} dt \qquad (4.3)$$

in which ΔH = energy of activation of creep (in joules per mole); R = general gas constant (in joules per mole per degree Kelvin); T = temperature, in degrees Kelvin; and t = time, in hours.

Fig. 4.8 shows the curves of strain ϵ_t against θ. The linear portion (secondary period of creep) has a slope $d\epsilon_t/d\theta$ denoted by Z, the Zener-Hollomon parameter (hr^{-1}). Both Z and the ordinate at the origin $\epsilon_{t,o}$ are assumed to depend only on stress σ.

As a relation between these parameters, Harmathy gives

$$\epsilon_t = \frac{\epsilon_{t,o}}{ln2} \cosh^{-1}\left(2\,\frac{Z\theta}{\epsilon_{t,o}}\right) \qquad (4.4)$$

With Eq. 4.4, creep strain ϵ_t can be calculated for any θ value, if $\Delta H/R$ is known, which depends on the type of steel and the variation of Z and $\epsilon_{t,o}$ *with stress* σ. These data can be obtained with conventional creep tests.

Choice of critical temperature. Critical temperature has generally been taken close to 500°C (932°F), but calculations and tests show that it varies considerably with the type of structure and its load.

Statically Determinate Beams. From these creep relationships and using one of the failure criteria proposed by Ryan and Robertson (1959), Harmathy (1967b)

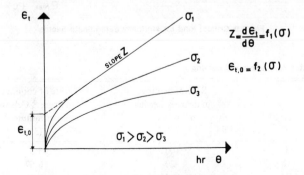

Fig. 4.8 Creep strain versus time

gives, for the critical temperature of statically determinate beams for allowable stresses of 14 daN, for joist or truss

$$\theta_r = \frac{70\ 000}{46.52 - 2.3\log\dfrac{L}{l} - 4.23\dfrac{I_d}{I}} - 460 \tag{4.5}$$

and for beam

$$\theta_r = \frac{70\ 000}{45.62 - 4.23\dfrac{I_d}{I}} - 460 \tag{4.6}$$

in which θ_r = critical temperature, in degrees Fahrenheit; L = beam span; l = distance between connections of two successive diagonals of joist or truss; and I_d = moment of inertia of the supported slab.

Statically Indeterminate Beams.   A more general method can be used, which is based on plasticity calculation. In this case, creep is necessarily disregarded; but the resultant error is not of great significance (Thor, 1973). For example, for a uniformly loaded statically determinate beam (see Fig. 4.9), creep effects on critical

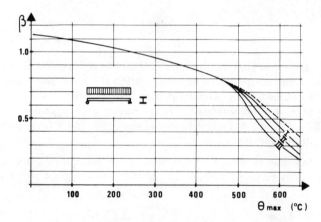

Fig. 4.9 Critical load for statically determinate beams

Table 4.2 Rates of heating and cooling

Curve (1)	Rate of heating, in degrees Celsius per minute (2)	Rate of cooling, in degrees Celsius per minute (3)
I	100	33.3
II	20	6.67
III	4	1.33

temperature are less than 10%. Fig. 4.9 presents the coefficient ß for calculation of the critical load q_{cr} for a simply supported I section beam of "mild" steel with a uniformly distributed load, as a function of the maximum steel temperature θ_{max} for three different rates of heating and cooling (I, II, III). Details of the three rates are given in Table 4.2. Fig. 4.9 also shows the value of β for infinitely fast rates of heating and cooling for purposes of comparison. It is assumed that the temperature is the same all over the beam and that there is no restraint on longitudinal expansion of the beam.

The following example illustrates this general method. Suppose a restrained beam, supported in its middle, is subjected to evenly distributed load p, as shown in Fig. 4.10. The failure of this beam occurs by the formation of five plastic hinges with a plastic moment capacity of M_p

$$M_p = Z_p \sigma_e \tag{4.7}$$

in which Z_p = plastic modulus. Failure load P_u is connected to plastic moment M_p by

$$P_u = \frac{16M_p}{l^2} = \frac{16Z_p}{l^2} \sigma_e. \tag{4.8}$$

Yield stress σ_e decreases with temperature as indicated in Fig. 4.6, until it is the same as for failure load P_u. Thus there is a beam temperature for which applied load is equal to failure load, which can be derived from

$$\sigma_e(\theta_r) = \frac{pl^2}{16Z_p} \tag{4.9}$$

Or, expressing maximal stress σ in the beam in terms of load p

$$\sigma_e(\theta_r) = \frac{12S_e\sigma}{16Z_p} = \frac{\sigma}{f\chi} \tag{4.10}$$

in which $f = Z_p/S_e$ = shape factor; and $\chi = 16/12$ = statically indeterminate factor. In other terms

$$\frac{\sigma_e(\theta_r)}{\sigma_e} = \frac{12S_e\sigma}{16Z_p\sigma_e} = \frac{P}{P_u(\theta_o)} \tag{4.11}$$

By this approach (Kruppa, 1976), critical temperature calculation of an evenly heated structure is reduced to failure load calculation at room temperature $P_u(\theta_o)$.

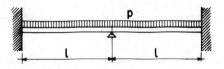

Fig. 4.10 Restrained beam with center support

In fact, a structure exposed to fire rarely has a homogeneous temperature. For section temperature variations, Fig. 4.11 (Kruppa, 1975) shows that a highest temperature assumption is safer than a medium temperature assumption, although there is little difference in real behavior.

Differences in temperature along the profiles can be taken into account by this method. At the extreme, some parts of the structure, if protected, can almost be at normal temperatures, and prevent longitudinal expansion of heated members (in steel or in concrete) and introduce supplementary forces. This phenomenon can be considered for a steel member axially loaded, including forces and displacements in the two parts of the structure, as shown by Fig. 4.12. In Fig. 4.12, θ = temperature; α_θ = free unitary expansion; ϵ_θ = real unitary expansion; and ϵ_κ = restrained unitary expansion.

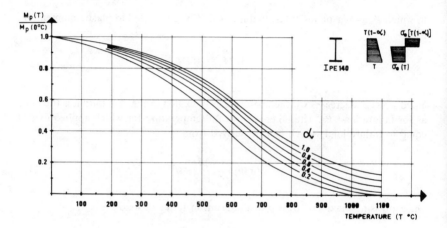

Fig. 4.11 Variation of plastic moment related to different temperature distributions

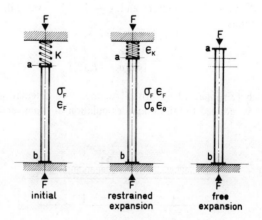

Fig. 4.12 Unitary expansion

Forces in the member and surrounding structure which prevent its thermal expansion are equal and respectively proportional to ϵ_κ and ϵ_θ. Consequently, supplementary stress in the profile is

$$\sigma_\theta = \frac{\alpha_\theta\,E(\theta)}{\dfrac{E(\theta)}{R} + 1} \tag{4.12}$$

in which R = structural rigidity with respect to the restraining member.

Whatever way is used to determine the critical temperature of a structure, it is necessary to know how the structure will be heated under fire exposure, related to its fire protection.

Unprotected Steel. There are no great problems with calculating the heat flow to unprotected rolled profiles, and the expression

$$\Delta\theta_a = K\frac{S}{V}\frac{1}{Cp_a\rho_a}[\theta_f - \theta_a(t)]\Delta t \tag{4.13}$$

can generally be used, in which $\Delta\theta_\alpha$ = increase in steel temperature between time interval t and $t + \Delta t$; and K = heat transfer coefficient (radiation and convection) given for standardized fire (ISO F 834) by the formula (in kW/m^2 °C)

$$K = 0.023 + 3.48 \times 10^{-11}(T_f^2 + T_a^2)(T_f + T_a) \tag{4.14}$$

in which $T_f = \theta_f + 273$, in degrees Kelvin; $T_a = \theta_a + 273$, in degrees Kelvin; S/V = size and shape factor (massivity coefficient), ratio of heated area to volume (m^{-1}); Cp_a = specific heat of steel (kJ/kg · C); ρ_a = density of steel (kg/m³); θ_f = medium temperature of fire between the time interval t and $t + \Delta t$, in degrees Celsius; $\theta_a(t)$ = temperature at time t, in degrees Celsius; and t = time, in seconds. Eq. 4.14 supposes an instantaneous heat transfer through the steel and is only valid for profiles which are not too massive.

This limitation has been evaluated by making a comparison between the simplified model and a two-dimensional theoretical analysis. It has been found that this assumption leads to results in agreement (within a tolerance of 10%) with the two-dimensional finite differences analysis when S/V is greater than 30 m⁻¹ (Fig. 4.13) (CTICM, 1975). This limitation has no great practical consequence, because members having S/V lower than 30 m⁻¹ are not currently used in practice.

Protected Steel. Heat flow calculations, and fire tests, show that to maintain stability during fires in buildings steel must normally be protected, using materials with either a high thermal capacity or a low thermal conductivity. Heat flow calculations take account not only of heat transfer by radiation or convection from the fire, but also of heat conduction through the protective material, governed by Fourier's law

$$\frac{\partial\theta}{\partial t} = a\left(\frac{\partial^2\theta}{\partial x^2} + \frac{\partial^2\theta}{\partial y^2} + \frac{\partial^2\theta}{\partial z^2}\right) \tag{4.15}$$

in which $a = \lambda/C_p\rho$ = thermal diffusivity of protective material.

The diffusivity components are not well known, as they vary with temperature. Moreover, Wakamatsu (1972) showed that heating depends on the member strain. Thus, thermal characteristics and methods of use of a protective material cannot be dissociated (see Section 4.4).

For these reasons, research engineers have developed calculation methods based on test results. Most of these methods contain the following assumptions:

1. The outside temperature of the insulation is equal to the fire temperature.

2. Transfer is unidirectional through the insulation.

3. There is no temperature gradient in the steel.

In these methods, thermal capacity of the insulation is considered either directly, or indirectly by adding part of it to the thermal capacity of the steel.

In order to avoid complicated calculations (step by step methods), simplified formulas or charts have been proposed, giving directly stability time reached versus a certain insulation (Law, 1972; Lie and Stanzak, 1974).

Only the heating calculation can be simplified in this method, by deriving a coefficient that characterizes the average thermal properties of the protective material over the duration of an actual fire test.

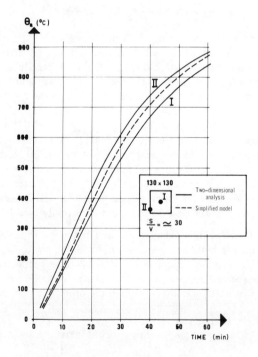

Fig. 4.13 Comparison between simplified model (Eq. 4.13) and two-dimensional analysis

Heating of a protected member can also be calculated in a step by step calculation using

$$\Delta\theta_a = \frac{1}{\frac{1}{K} + \frac{e}{\gamma}} \frac{S}{V} \frac{1}{Cp_a\rho_a}[\theta_f - \theta_a(t)]\Delta t \qquad (4.16)$$

in which the coefficient γ = insulation, whose thickness is represented by e. Variations of γ with the temperature are obtained from heating curves of highly loaded protected profiles, using Eq. 4.16. Then it is possible to establish flow charts for stability times giving necessary thickness versus the critical temperature and S/V (see Fig. 4.14).

Other methods of protection.   Less conventional methods of protecting steel are the use of water or concrete to fill hollow sections. In the first case, water circulates either by natural convection or by pumping, and very long stability ratings can then be achieved. In the second case, the concrete may or may not be load bearing, but the steel will still reach very high temperatures unless it has an outer layer of protective material (CIDECT, 1970).

Composite beams.   With composite beams there is the same difficulty as for concrete-filled sections (Fig. 4.15). However, for statically determinate beams, one can get an idea of the profile temperature when the beam failure occurs, owing to the plasticity calculation (Arnault et al., 1976).

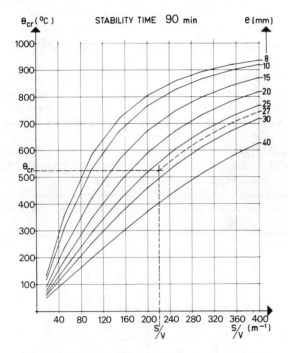

Fig. 4.14 Necessary thickness versus critical temperature and S/V

Two assumptions are necessary: a medium temperature in the profile, and a temperature lower than 200°C (392°F) in the compressed concrete. This last assumption, justified by the insulation rating generally required for the slab, permits the use of constant thermal properties for the concrete. Plastic moment in a section is then obtained, for a profile temperature of θ_a, as

$$M_p(\theta_a) = \sigma_e(\theta_a)Am - \frac{\sigma_e(\theta_a)^2 A^2}{2 R_u b} \qquad (4.17)$$

For a statically determinate beam, failure occurs when the maximum moment in the span becomes equal to the plastic moment, whence the critical temperature may be determined.

Research must be undertaken on heating of continuous composite beams and calculation of their stability.

External Fire Exposure. The calculation methods of the preceding paragraphs are not suitable for external structures where the fire exposure is different. The fire resistance of these elements has received limited study. Seigel's theoretical studies (1964) can be quoted, as well as experimental research conducted in Germany, Switzerland (Bongard, 1963), and France (Arnault et al., 1974).

In these studies, only the heat transfer to the elements has been estimated. The determination of their stability under load is theoretically complicated because of significant temperature variations in the elements (Fig. 4.16) and horizontal thrust induced by the thermal expansion of supported internal beams.

Concluding Remarks. All the calculation methods for the stability of steel structures presuppose a suitable resistance of connections. Recent experimental research has shown that bolted connections have a fire resistance at least equal to that of structural parts they join. This is especially due to the connection's higher mass and to the increase of its strain capacity with temperature.

To conclude, it seems difficult to propose a calculation method for the fire resistance of a steel structure that is simple as well as complete. For instance, the Swedish method (Pettersson et al., 1976) takes into account creep and real fires, to the prejudice of its simplicity. On the other hand, the French method (CTICM, 1975) is simpler but uses more simplifying assumptions.

Nevertheless, existing knowledge allows the appraisal of numerous steel structures for fire resistance and thus to obtain, for this type of construction, a safety degree at least similar to other materials.

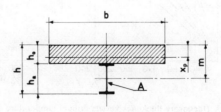

Fig. 4.15 Composite beam

4.4 STRUCTURAL PROTECTION: REQUIREMENTS AND QUALITY CONTROL

Fire resistance requirements for structural protection are specified in building codes for particular classes and occupancies of buildings. They are usually expressed in terms of the time that building elements must withstand the effects of the standard fire exposure. They are based primarily on the size and height of the structure and on the expected combustible content associated with the occupancy or use of the building. But other factors, such as the effectiveness of fire fighting facilities, may also be given consideration in arriving at fire resistance requirements. As a result, specific requirements vary from one to four hours, depending on the country or code body setting the regulations.

1 Fire Resistance Standards

Although the standard of fire protection required by regulations may vary from country to country, the test used to demonstrate compliance is essentially the same

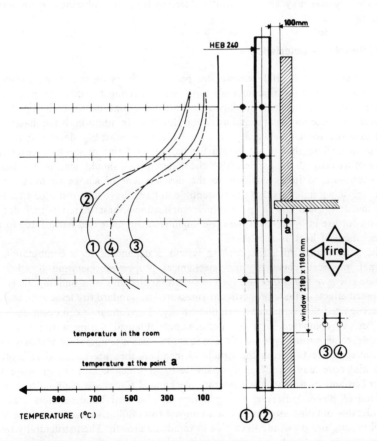

Fig. 4.16 Maximum temperature around (1,2) and inside (3,4) an external unprotected column placed at 100 mm from window of room containing fire *(Arnault et al., 1974)*

in nearly all countries. The International Standard fire exposure defined by ISO Recommendation R834 is similar to many individual national standards which have endurance reported from tests in one country may be used in another with little error.

However, standard test procedures are seldom representative of conditions encountered in actual building fires, because the test specimens must be of limited size and often are only portions of a complete structure. Therefore, interest has developed in the use of analytical methods in addition to test data to predict the performance of structural elements of buildings during fire exposure. These methods, discussed in Sections 4.2 and 4.3, generally involve a combined structural and thermal analysis to determine the effect of any specified fire exposure on the stability of the structure. But the methods can be complex and do not take into account such things as surface spalling of concrete, or cracking and separation of fire protective coatings. For most assemblies, analytical methods are not sufficiently reliable, and therefore the fire test is essential. Consequently, the standard fire test remains the most generally accepted measure of performance of building constructions during fire exposure, even though it is recognized that the performance indicated by test may be significantly different from that obtained in an actual building.

2 Material Characteristics

To assure effective and reliable fire protection for structural components in buildings, a material (or combination of materials) must remain in place and provide adequate thermal insulation for the structural member during a fire exposure of some anticipated intensity and duration. In addition, if the material is used as a fire barrier between parts of a building, it must not develop cracks or serious distortions that might permit the passage of flame or smoke or excessive temperature through the barrier. Also, the material itself should, whenever possible, not contribute to fire growth or to the development of smoke or toxic gases. Although some materials that are susceptible to flame have demonstrated excellent heat-shielding capability in space-vehicle applications, these materials may not be suitable for use in buildings if their use might result in increased hazard due to the development of heat and smoke.

The performance of a fireproofing system is dependent on a combination of thermal, physical, chemical, and mechanical properties operating together to provide effective fire protection for the structural elements of a building. Only the combined effects of these properties are measured in standard fire tests, even though it is recognized that significant variations in actual performance can occur during a real fire, as compared with the performance obtained during a fire test. For example, some insulating materials lose strength at high temperature and may tend to disintegrate or fall from the structural members they are intended to protect. Such materials may be effective in fire tests, in which conditions are carefully controlled and in which only minimum mechanical forces are required to hold a material in place. However, during a fire in an actual building there may be considerable building movement due to impact from falling objects, and there may be vibrations and pressure effects due to rapid fire growth. Then structurally weak fire-protective materials may fail mechanically early in the fire and leave the structure of the building unprotected. If such a situation should occur, it is conceivable that a system of structural fire protection that has demonstrated excellent fire endurance in a standard test might provide little protection in an actual building fire.

Similar situations may be anticipated with regard to nonmechanical properties of materials. Even though a material may remain in place during fire exposure, its effectiveness may not be readily obtained from a single fire test because fire endurance does not depend uniquely on material properties. Fire intensity may also be important. For example, in the case of materials that contain water or that depend on material transformations (such as sublimation or intumescence) to retard heat flow to a protected member, the performance measured during a standard fire test may bear little relation to performance obtained during exposures of higher or lower intensity because the processes of sublimation, intumescence, and vapor diffusion are strongly affected by the energy available from the fire. Yet reliable fire-endurance ratings must be established if the satisfactory design of fire-resistive buildings is to be accomplished. It appears necessary to establish some form of quality control for structural fire protection to accomplish this purpose.

3 Suggestions for Improved Reliability of Protection

Two methods of establishing reliable ratings appear possible. One is a highly analytical approach dependent on complete knowledge of all thermal, physical, chemical, and mechanical properties of the fire-protection materials, and on a thorough understanding of all theoretical and mathematical relationships for the unsteady-state processes encountered during any fire exposure. But even if all these property values could be made available (for the complete temperature range anticipated), this approach would be exceedingly complex and would certainly require verification by carefully developed test methods. Therefore, a second approach based on empirically determined properties related to thermal and mechanical performance in special, well-defined tests is essential. If this approach is followed, empirical "performance properties" could be obtained from simple tests requiring limited facilities. Then these properties could be used to design fire-protective systems for any type of construction. Such properties could be established by new standardized procedures, and a basis for acceptance by building officials could be developed.

These special tests would measure unsteady-state heat transfer, combustibility, smoke and toxic-gas generation, and factors related to the reliability and durability of the protective material. Table 4.3 shows examples of the type of data that might be collected at both normal and elevated temperatures. But it should be recognized that it may not be necessary to collect all the data indicated for all materials. Many fireproofing materials are inorganic and do not burn, and for such materials tests of combustibility would not be necessary. Also, the durability of some materials at normal temperature may be known from the results of existing standard tests run for other purposes, and for such materials, durability would need to be studied only at high temperatures. No specific test methods or limiting property values have been indicated in Table 4.3 and these matters will require careful consideration. In some cases it may be possible to use existing standards, but in others it may be necessary to develop new methods.

However, regardless of the test methods used, the data obtained should be basic and design oriented so that they may be applied generally to the development of reliable systems of structural fire protection. For example, the strength of gypsum board at elevated temperature has been related to its ability to remain in place as a fire-protective membrane, and a method of computing the fire endurance based on this limiting temperature has been described by Magnusson and Pettersson (1969). The temperature limit proposed for the unexposed surface of fiber-reinforced gypsum board was 550°C (1022°F), which was reported as the temperature at which gypsum boards disintegrate. Therefore, the fire endurance calculated by the method proposed by Magnusson and Pettersson would be the maximum that should be expected for an unstressed-gypsum-board fire-protection system. If stresses are developed in the gypsum because of the method of fastening or because of distortion or other effects during fire exposure, a lower temperature limit would seem appropriate and a decreased fire endurance would be calculated. Although the reliability and the performance of a fire-protective material are clearly dependent on the temperature of the material, it is interesting to note that standard fire-test procedures in use today do not require that such temperatures even be measured or recorded. Establishing appropriate temperature limits may be difficult, but such limits appear necessary.

In addition to developing test methods and acceptance criteria to evaluate the reliability of fire-protective materials, it is also important to develop improved methods for measuring heat-transfer effects. Although the calculation of heat transfer and temperature distribution may be possible for columns and other simple structural elements, complex assemblies such as floor systems may be studied more easily with the aid of observations made during carefully planned fire tests. Since the purpose of the tests would be to evaluate thermal effects only, provision for structural loading of the specimen would not be necessary, and the test facility could be considerably smaller and simpler than that prescribed by existing standards. If the test facility is designed carefully, it would appear possible to evaluate the behavior of fire-protective materials at high temperature and to obtain reliable heat-transfer data from a single test.

If improved methods are developed to assure the quality of structural fire protection, it may be possible in some cases to reduce fire protection requirements

Table 4.3 Required properties of fireproofing materials *(ECCS, 1974a)*

Use of data (1)	Property to be measured (2)		
Durability at normal temperature [0 to 38 °C (0 to 100 °F)]	density impact cohesion adhesion	cracking shrinking weathering corrosion	compression expansion hardness spalling
Durability at elevated temperature [319 °C to 1370 °C (600 °F to 2500 °F)]	impact distortion shrinking	cohesion adhesion expansion	spalling cracking compression
Smoke and toxic gas hazard[a]	rate of heat release total heat release	gas analysis smoke generated	
Fire spread and structural stability[a]	basic tests of protected solid steel specimens special tests of representative constructions		

[a]Measurements to be made with heat flux exposures ranging to 50 kW/m^2 (4.76 kW/ft^2).

to more realistic values, because large safety factors are often applied in current regulations to compensate for unpredictable performance. Also, if reliability can be improved, more confidence may be developed in fire protection design methods and it may be possible to eliminate much expensive large-scale testing for structural fire endurance (Magnusson and Pettersson, 1969).

4.5 NONSTRUCTURAL PROTECTION

1 Chemical Aspects

Although over the past 10 to 20 years the numbers of fatalities and casualties due to fire have remained fairly constant, there is a major shift in the cause of death from burns and scalds on the one hand to smoke and toxic gases on the other. Deaths from the latter cause now form the majority of fatalities. There has, of course, over the years, been specific legislation directed at the prevention of those types of fires that would be expected to cause burns—for example, requirements for fire retardant materials in clothing. It is only in recent years that the importance of smoke and toxic gases has been appreciated so that thoughts on possible ways of controlling these aspects of fires are beginning to be formulated. Reviews of the problem have been presented by Dufour (1963), Rasbash (1967), and Wagner (1972). It is vital, of course, that before control can be put into effect substantial information should be obtained on the nature and amount of the smoke and gases that may be produced from the wide variety of materials found in the structure and contents of buildings. A question that needs answering in this context is, do the newer synthetic materials found in buildings contribute an undue share towards these undesirable effects? Clear information is also needed on the way the various chemical species might affect people and the way people are actually affected by fires as a result of the combined effect of smoke, toxic gases, temperature, and change in the oxygen concentration of the atmosphere.

Smoke. Smoke is formed by the condensation of the less volatile products of decomposition and incomplete combustion of organic materials. The amount of smoke produced depends upon the chemical nature of the material and the conditions of the fire. As far as the chemical nature is concerned, in general the smaller the molecule that is fed into the vapor phase and the more oxygenated it is, the less will be the tendency to produce smoke.

Most materials tend to produce more smoke when they are burning under conditions of restricted air supply or when they are smoldering (Gross et al., 1967; Bowes and Field, 1969). Some organic materials may produce more smoke, however, under free air supply conditions, particularly if the materials are plastics containing a substantial fraction of aromatics. Also, the longer the time the vapor is in the vapor zone and subjected to preheating, the greater the amount of smoke that is produced (Stark, 1972), and as the scale of the fire increases, more smoke tends to be produced.

Several methods have been developed in the 1970s for measuring the propensity of materials to form smoke under laboratory conditions. These methods have in common the accumulation of smoke in a chamber and the operation of a certain degree of dilution before the measurement of optical density. There is only limited agreement among the tests on the order of ranking materials for smoke-producing propensity. There are differences of opinion concerning correlation of the amount of smoke produced in small-scale bench tests and in full-scale test fires.

Two major ways are coming into use for expressing the amount of smoke produced by materials. In the United States (Gross et al., 1967), smoke densities are often expressed in the form of specific optical density, which is the obscuration over a path of unit length produced when the smoke evolved from a surface of unit area is stirred into the space of a unit volume. This allows a prediction of the amount of smoke that may be evolved in a fire if the area exposed to the heating process in the fire is known. In the United Kingdom there has been a tendency to use the "standard" optical density (Heselden, 1971), which is defined as the optical density per meter obtained when the combustion products from 1 gram of burning material are stirred into a volume of 1 cubic meter. On this basis, wood and cellulosic materials tend to produce, under free burning conditions, standard optical densities of between 0.01 and 0.05 in small-scale tests and between 0.01 and 0.10 in large-scale tests; polyurethane foam about 0.1 to 0.2 in both full-scale tests and laboratory tests. Polystyrene, however, gives much larger values in large-scale fires (0.6 to 0.9) than in small-scale fires (0.1 to 0.2) (Heselden, 1971).

Toxic Gas. Complete combustion of cellulosic materials produces carbon dioxide and water vapor. However, it is only under conditions of very effective and intimate ventilation that such combustion is obtained in real fires. It is normal for certain amounts of carbon monoxide to be produced, and over the years it has been traditionally accepted that carbon monoxide is the main toxic component of combustion gases. In general, the amount of carbon monoxide produced increases as the ventilation to the fire decreases, and as the fire load increases (Stark, 1972; Rasbash and Stark, 1966): first because of the tendency to give imperfect combustion, and second because of the tendency of the unburned decomposition products to be evolved, these decomposition products containing a substantial amount of carbon monoxide. However, Tewerson (1971) has shown that the relationship with these variables is not monotonic, and that there are peaks in the carbon monoxide as the ventilation is varied for different scales.

For reasonably free burning in full-scale fires of room size, the ratio of carbon monoxide to carbon dioxide is approximately 1 to 10, and although hundreds of other volatile components are evolved during the combustion of cellulosic materials, there is no evidence so far that any of them has an effect comparable to carbon monoxide. Broadly speaking, this is also the case for organic materials containing only carbon, hydrogen, and oxygen. Although phenol resins produce substantial amounts of phenol and related compounds under laboratory conditions, and these compounds can be highly toxic (Woolley and Wadley, 1970), full-scale tests have not so far indicated that substantial quantities may be produced in real fires.

Atoms other than carbon, hydrogen, and oxygen in the molecule of the organic material can give rise, of course, to the production of a wide range of compounds, many of which can be highly toxic. Thus the presence of nitrogen often gives rise to hydrogen cyanide; it may also give rise to oxides of nitrogen in significant quantities, but this has not been fully checked. Polyurethane foams have been found to decompose in fires by the production of a yellow smoke at about 300°C (572°F). This yellow smoke contains almost all the nitrogen in the molecule and decomposes or reacts at higher temperatures to produce hydrogen cyanide at a temperature of about 1000°C (1832°F). Most of the original nitrogen in the resin is obtained in the form of hydrogen cyanide (Stark, 1972; Woolley, 1972), and full-scale trials with a sufficient amount of fuel present to allow these high temperatures to be produced have confirmed that large quantities of hydrogen cyanide are formed (Stark, 1972). Polyurethane foam may also form significant quantities of tolylene diisocyanate at temperatures around 300°C (572°F), that is, it accompanies the formation of the yellow smoke (Woolley and Wadley, 1972). In addition, under some conditions, more carbon monoxide may be obtained with polyurethane than with cellulosic materials (Stark, 1972). For plastics containing halogens, it is likely that the bulk of the halogen is evolved as the hydrogen halide. This is certainly the case for polyvinyl chloride, although a detailed investigation of this material has indicated that no significant amounts of phosgene are produced (Wagner, 1972; Stark, 1972).

There is a substantial gap in the information concerning combustion products of materials containing phosphorus and antimony as fire retardant additives. The possibility that these materials might give significant quantities of volatile toxic materials cannot be ruled out.

Effects of Smoke and Toxic Gases in Practice.   Broadly speaking, smoke traps people and toxic gases kill or injure them. Experiments of full-scale fires have shown that people away from the origin of the fire are usually threatened by smoke before toxic gas or temperature (Shorter et al., 1960; Kingman et al., 1953). However, people in rooms directly above a fire may be threatened by carbon monoxide first (Kingman et al., 1953). Evidence indicates that the most important way in which people are trapped by smoke is, as one would expect, by a reduction of visibility. However, smoke can also cause confusion and difficulty by lachrymatory and other eye irritation, by irritation to the lungs and breathing channels, and, in some cases, as a result of psychological aversion. In general, people are killed by the toxic effects of carbon monoxide with the possible addition of other gases as indicated previously. However, one cannot rule out the effect of anoxia resulting from the depletion of oxygen, the damage to respiratory tracts caused by hot gases, and the action of smoke particles in the respiratory tract as contributing factors to these effects.

There is as a first approximation a reasonable correlation between visibility in smoke and the optical density. (Optical density in this case is defined as the negative of the logarithm to the base ten of the fraction of a light beam penetrating the smoke.) Thus an optical density of 0.07 per meter corresponds to a visibility of about 10 m assuming irritant effect on the eye. An investigation carried out at Loughborough University (Wood, 1972) has indicated that a significant percentage of people turned back from within a smoke laden area if the visibility was less than about 3 m. This gives an indication of the visibility to design for when control of smoke is being considered. Until quite recently, little systematic work had been done on why people die in smoke laden atmospheres in fires. Autopsies certainly show that in the majority of cases there was sufficient carbon monoxide (Rasbash, 1967) to account for unconsciousness, but other possible intoxicants have not been examined. This is now being rectified at Johns Hopkins University (Halpin, 1973) by systematic and detailed investigation on fatalities caused by fire. The results of this investigation so far have confirmed that carbon monoxide is the main toxic constituent. However, it has also been found that alcohol was present in the blood of a high proportion of the fatalities, and there might be synergistic effects between different constituents.

Corrosion. Special corrosive effects have been attributed to the hydrogen chloride that may be evolved from polyvinyl chloride during a fire (Swedish FPA, 1969). It would be expected that metallic materials with exposed surfaces would be directly attacked by the hydrogen chloride, and it has been suggested that the hydrogen chloride may permeate through concrete to the reinforcing steel, but experiments in the United Kingdom have not confirmed this (Morris and Hopkinson, 1974).

2 Smoke Control

In the first half of this century, high-rise buildings were not particularly noted for smoke problems other than those customarily encountered in many building fires. This has resulted from strict enforcement of measures aimed, in general, at fire limitation. Extensive compartmentation and sharp restriction on the use of flammable lining materials on walls and ceilings have probably been the two most effective measures taken.

Equally good performance cannot be expected from high-rise buildings constructed around the middle of this century. Some are in areas where building codes and enforcement are loose and there have been instances of disastrous fire propagation. Fire propagation is not, however, the concern of this article, which is confined to large-scale smoke problems and their avoidance, always assuming that the associated fire is confined to a single compartment. The following are the principal reasons why this category of smoke problem is more probable in high-rise buildings constructed around the middle of this century:

1. Reduced utilization of compartmentation. It is now quite common for the whole of one story to constitute a single office space. Later in this article it will be shown that the density of smoke in the upper half of a building, resulting from stack action and fire in a lower story, is highly dependent (inversely) on the number of compartments into which the fire story is divided—assuming that the fire is confined to one compartment.

2. Increased use of flammable interior lining materials.

3. General use (interior finish, insulation, furnishings) of materials that have a propensity for generating dense smoke.

4. Greater use of recirculating ventilation systems in which the supply air is largely taken from the return system, with only a small percentage of fresh air.

Nature of the Problem. The life safety philosophy underlying the design of most buildings, so far as the avoidance of a disaster is concerned, has hitherto been to provide for the complete evacuation of all occupants before untenable conditions become widespread. Thus, although large areas of a conventional (low) building might become smoke-logged, the length of time before this takes place is likely to be longer than the few minutes required for complete evacuation. High life loss is not, therefore, to be expected unless some unfortunate architectural arrangement gives rise to simultaneous contamination of all escape routes.

In high-rise buildings such an unfortunate architectural arrangement is almost sure to be present, for the escape routes are vertical stair shafts that tend to communicate with common areas at all levels of the building. By the mechanisms of expansion or stack action of a heated building, smoke from a fire at a low level can at a very early stage contaminate all the elevator and stair shafts and halt further evacuation. If conditions for the general dispersal of smoke throughout the building are present, the potential for disastrous life loss exists. Considerable time might elapse before untenable conditions would become widespread throughout the building, but this delay would be of little help to the occupants.

Measure of smoke contamination.   To indicate how conditions tending to create disastrous life loss might arise, a review of the mechanisms responsible for dispersal of contamination throughout a building is desirable. It must be prefaced, however, by a discussion of the levels of contamination that can be tolerated in an atmosphere.

In the context of fire and the high-rise building, where a specification of a continuously acceptable level of contamination is necessary, it is convenient to express contamination in terms of the percentage of the atmosphere in a fire area that is tolerable in an atmosphere intended to be tenable. Assuming particularly adverse conditions in a fire area, the differing considerations of carbon monoxide toxicity and visibility suggest that an atmosphere will remain tenable if it contains no more than about 1% by volume of the contaminated air from the fire region.

Although the combustion and pyrolysis of certain plastics can generate gases of such high toxicity and in such quantities that percentages lower than those quoted could be intolerable, this does not immediately imply that the 1% value should be regarded as invalid, since virtually all materials produce smoke and carbon monoxide, but the "exotic" gases are usually specific to a particular material. As it is unlikely that one such material would be the only one involved in a fire, the specific gas would be diluted below the maximum possible level even within the fire area. As an upper limit of acceptability, the 1% figure may thus be taken as virtually universally valid.

Smoke Control Mechanisms

Expansion.   During the course of a fire, the compartment temperature will rise from about 300°K (25°C, 77°F) to at least 900°K (625°C, 1157°F). The volume occupied by the gases originally in the compartment will thus multiply by three, so that two-thirds will be displaced, much of it to other parts of the building.

With optimum distribution (that is, the most undesirable), a volume of the building equal to about 50 times the fire space volume could be rendered untenable. Such fortuitous, widespread dispersal is very unlikely, however, and the probable principal effect would be fouling of the escape shafts. Where the fire has broken out at a low level in the building such fouling can completely obstruct evacuation of all the occupants at higher levels. Expansion unfortunately complements stack action caused by heating the building, which will be discussed later. Expansion maximizes the flow of contaminants to the shafts; stack action gives upward flows through the shafts to the upper floors.

Recirculating air-handling fans.   If an air-handling system includes a recirculation feature, as most do, it is bound to disperse contamination. However, the process involving the fans as a driving force can be readily terminated by switching off the system. This can be achieved automatically by monitoring the return air with one or more sensitive smoke detectors judiciously located. However it is questionable whether shutting down an air-handling system will stop smoke leakages. An air-handling system that has been shut down will of course serve as ready paths for the transfer of contamination by other mechanisms, such as stack action, to be discussed later.

Wind. The pressures generated within a building by exterior winds can be significant, but their effect will almost invariably be confined to moving pollutant laterally within a building. In a high-rise tower, lateral smoke movement will have a lower potential for disastrous life loss than will vertical movement.

Stack action. This is the name given to the familiar chimney effect that occurs when the temperature within an enclosure is higher than that outside; it is manifested by flow into the enclosure at a low level and out at higher levels. Two sources of stack action are likely: (1) The fire itself; and (2) the heating of the building in cold weather, or cooling in very hot weather.

The stack effect generated by a fire is not likely, of itself, to be responsible for polluting a large building, provided the fire is confined to a single story. Over a height of 3 m (10 ft), the total pressure head generated will be no more than 25 Pa (0.1 in. WG). Assuming that leakage areas linking the fire region and its surroundings consist of cracks around doors, etc., and not of open doors or the like, such a head will serve to pollute directly only immediately adjacent areas.

Stack action resulting from building heating, on the other hand, can be a major mechanism of air movement. Operating as it does over the whole height of the building, far greater pressure differences can be created despite the fact that the temperature differential involved is much lower than that resulting from a fire. Temperature difference proves to be a much less significant factor than total height of heated compartments.

Always assuming that smoke dispersal by way of recirculating air-handling systems is avoided, combating building heating stack action in cold weather is a most useful basis for the development of smoke control methods for most tall buildings. It must always be borne in mind, however, that the expansion mechanism is also important and that fire in a shaft can create even greater pressure differences than building heating stack action. The mechanism of stack action, particularly as it relates to building heating, will be discussed in more detail.

Building-Heating Stack Action. In a simple compartment [Fig. 4.17(a)] the influence of stack action can be completely analyzed: where the atmosphere in a compartment such as that shown is warmer than outside, air enters at the bottom levels and leaves at the top—in other words, the pressure difference across an opening is directed inwards at lower levels and outwards at higher levels. As no discontinuities should exist, it follows that at some level between the two no pressure difference exists. It is convenient to refer to this level as the neutral pressure plane.

The analysis commences by postulating a location for the neutral pressure plane; a statement of its actual level is one of the results of the analysis. Referring to Fig. 4.17, consider the lower opening: a pressure difference across it results from the fact that the column of cold gas outside the enclosure, between the levels of the neutral plane and the lower opening, weighs more than the corresponding column inside the enclosure.

By the same argument, there is a pressure difference across the upper opening. The level of the neutral plane is given by

$$\frac{h_2}{h_1} = \left(\frac{A_1}{A_2}\right)^2 \frac{T_\theta}{T_o} \qquad (4.18)$$

in which A_1 and A_2 = areas of the lower and upper openings, respectively; and T_θ and T_o = absolute temperatures. Thus, h_2/h_1 is inversely proportional to the square of the ratio of the opening areas and, if either is large compared to the other, the neutral plane will lie at that level.

Where a tall multistory building is considered, the number of available flow paths is so great that analysis requires a computer. Fig. 4.17(b) gives the computer analysis results for a hypothetical 20-story building in which exterior wall leakage was taken as 0.23 m² (2.5 sq ft) per story; interior leakage to shafts as 0.47 m² (5 sq ft) per

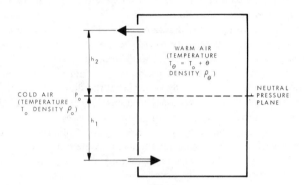

Fig. 4.17(a) Stack action

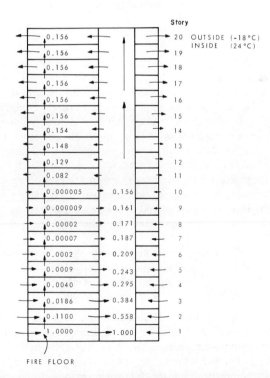

Fig. 4.17(b) Conditions in hypothetical 20-story building (numbers denote steady state proportion of gases from fire floor)

story; and leakage through each floor as 0.35 m² (3.75 sq ft). It must be kept in mind that this is a hypothetical 20-story building. However, in a real building the leakage between the floors and through the shafts usually exceeds that of the computer's determinant results on permeability.

The arrows in Fig. 4.17(b) indicate the direction of air flow at each opening, and those on the exterior wall suggest, as was the case, that flows into and out of the building at top and bottom are much greater than those at other levels. For example, flow into the ground floor was 101 kg/min (223 lb/min); it had become about half this [59 kg/min (129 lb/min)] at the seventh floor, and was down to 17 kg/min (37 lb/min) at the 10th floor.

The numerals appearing in the diagram relate to the steady-state proportion, in the region in which the number appears, of the gases that migrated there from the ground floor. Assuming a fire on the ground floor, it has already been suggested that to maintain tenability an atmosphere should contain no more than 1% of that of the fire floor. In Fig. 4.17(b) it may be seen that the shafts and the floor spaces in the upper half of a building have concentrations greatly exceeding this criterion.

A factor not recorded in Fig. 4.17(b) is that over 96% of the gas that moved vertically in the building did so by way of the shafts. In other words, flow through the floors may be neglected (except for the local problem it creates on one or two floors immediately above the fire). For conditions no more complex than those of Fig. 4.17(a), this feature actually permits a simple analytical resolution of the problem to quite a close approximation. One useful formula that can be developed on this basis is

$$C = \frac{3C_o}{Nn} \tag{4.19}$$

in which C = contaminant concentration in the upper half of a building; C_o = contaminant concentration on the grade level fire floor; N = number of stories in the building; and n = number of similar compartments into which the fire floor is divided. Eq. 4.19 gives the prediction that, where the product Nn exceeds 300, major smoke problems should not develop throughout a building, which means that tall buildings are more fire safe. This conclusion, however, is highly hedged with qualifications, for the formula applies to conditions of complete symmetry. One significant and likely departure is window breakage on the fire (ground) floor. It would raise the pressure there and hence increase the flow of contaminants to the shafts. An interesting corollary of this observation is that, under the same conditions, the opening of a window and door in a compartment adjacent to one on fire would reduce contaminant concentrations (where the fire is at a low level in a building).

The finding that 96% of the gas that moved vertically in the hypothetical building did so by way of the shafts is of great importance. It leads to the conclusion that smoke movement resulting from building heating stack action should be combated by eliminating flow of smoke by way of vertical shafts.

Approaches to Smoke Control in High Buildings. Having identified the nature of the problem and quantified some of the variables involved, the practicality of various possible solutions can be discussed. An obvious approach would be to limit the amount of material with a propensity for generating smoke and toxic gases but this is normally impractical for the following reasons. Considering again the hypothetical 20-story building discussed previously, a simple calculation indicates that once unacceptable pollution becomes established, steady destruction of only 6 kg/hr (0.2 lb/min) of any materials would be sufficient to maintain it continuously throughout the shafts and top half of the building. Although substantially higher rates of destruction would usually be called for to create such disastrous conditions initially, the fact remains that the quantities of material available in a building are orders of magnitude greater than would be required. It is thus not practical, under all but the most exceptional circumstances, to eliminate this hazard by limiting the quantity of the offending materials.

However, control of the hazard is still possible without the virtual banning of the materials from the building; their involvement in fire can be suitably limited by full sprinklering and, in fact, many fire authorities are convinced that such an approach is the most practical and reliable. A sprinkler system also has the merit of countering the fire problem generally, not merely the smoke aspect of it.

Another possible solution is to dilute smoke and toxic gases to acceptable levels as they issue from a region involved in fire and flow to adjacent regions. The required diluent flow rates can be deduced from a knowledge of the rate of pollutant flow and of the criterion of tenability. In the hypothetical 20-story building under the conditions previously outlined, about 1.3 m³/sec (2 800 cfm) of pollutant would be expected to flow from a grade level fire floor into the shafts. The diluent air requirement to maintain tenable conditions (dilution by 100) could thus be as high as 130 m³/sec (280 000 cfm) for this particular example. In general, the dilution approach on its own is unlikely to be the most economical.

Of the approaches involving control of air movement, the most practical is that in which favorable pressure differences are created across various partitions within a building. It can be achieved by either natural venting or mechanical pressurization, and in developing suitable techniques the most appropriate objective, as specified earlier, is combating building heating stack action. At the same time, the significance of the initial expansion mechanism must always be borne in mind.

To appreciate the pressure pattern within a building—an essential prerequisite to modifying it—it is convenient to utilize pressure characteristic diagrams. These are not, precisely, simple graphs of pressure and some explanation is called for.

Pressure Characteristic Diagrams.   The right side of Fig. 4.18 is a pressure characteristic diagram representing the conditions prevailing in the enclosure illustrated on the left, the latter being a reproduction of Fig. 4.17(a). At first sight the

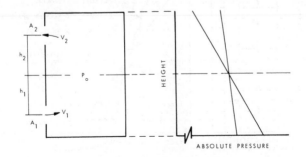

Fig. 4.18 Pressure characteristic

diagram appears to be a simple graph of pressure against height, the latter being used as ordinate for convenience. One minor departure can be seen in that a break in the scale of the abscissa is shown. This is called for on the grounds that the pressure differences to be represented amount to little more than 500 Pa (2 in. WG), whereas the absolute pressures involved are in the region of 100 kPa (400 in. WG).

A second feature is not apparent, but is much more important. It is that the slopes of the lines do not represent, quantitatively, pressure change with height. The presentation represents, quantitatively, pressure difference between two regions at the same height. The scales must not be used to determine from a single characteristic the change in pressure from, say, one floor to another two stories above it.

The need for adjustment of the slopes is clarified by reference to Fig. 4.19, which shows characteristics of a typical building. If the slopes of the three characteristics illustrated were made to conform to the scale, they would be very similar, and delineating the floor space characteristic between those of the interior and exterior would prove very difficult. In a typical building the pressure variation from top to bottom compared with the total stack action associated with a temperature difference θ will be T_θ/θ (absolute interior temperature/temperature difference). Were the interior temperature very high, the ratio would approach unity and the interior characteristic be almost vertical, representing virtually no variation of pressure with height. For interior and exterior temperatures of 24°C and −18°C (75°F and 0°F), the ratio of pressure difference, top to bottom of the building, to total stack action would be about 7, and the use of "true" slopes would give presentation problems.

Given any set of characteristics, as in Fig. 4.19, the important feature is that, at any level to be considered, gas flow from one region to another will be towards the region whose characteristic is more to the left. In the typical building whose characteristics are illustrated, smoke generated in a lower story will flow into shafts and, at higher levels, from the shafts to the floor spaces.

An important concept of smoke control is that if a shaft characteristic is entirely to one side (left or right) of the characteristics of all the other parts of the building, the shaft will not serve to transfer smoke from one story to another. If the characteristic is to the extreme right, the shaft itself will remain unpolluted; but if it is to the extreme left it will probably become contaminated. In order to better

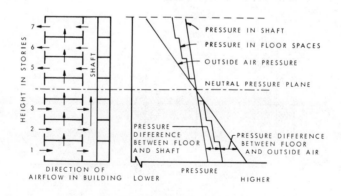

Fig. 4.19 Typical building pressure characteristics

understand these conditions and how they can be achieved, it is useful to consider various conditions in a simple, heated shaft with no adjoining building components.

Fig. 4.20 shows the pressure differences that will prevail in a simple shaft under three different conditions. Fig. 4.20(a) is intended to represent the case where openings of equal area exist at the top and bottom of the shaft. With this symmetrical arrangement the neutral pressure plane is substantially at midheight, air flowing into the bottom of the shaft and out at the top.

Fig. 4.20(b) represents a shaft vented only at the top, where the neutral pressure plane is therefore located. Looking ahead to the application of top venting to control smoke, the important feature here is that through any leakage that might exist at any level in the shaft (except the top) flow will be inward.

Fig. 4.20(c) represents a bottom-vented shaft, with the neutral pressure plane at the lowest level. Analogously (but conversely to the top-vented case), the interesting feature of the bottom-vented shaft is that flow will be outward through any leakage that might exist at any level other than at the very bottom.

Utilization of Pressure Characteristic Diagrams. The development of smoke control techniques aimed at combating flow of smoke in shafts owing to stack action is usually based on either divorcing the shafts from the building or applying the principles discussed in relation to Fig. 4.20 to building pressure characteristics such as those of Fig. 4.19.

Fig. 4.21 shows the characteristics of a vented shaft in addition to those of Fig. 4.19. In fact, if the leakage from the building to the shaft were substantial, the top venting could have a general influence on the pressure distribution within the

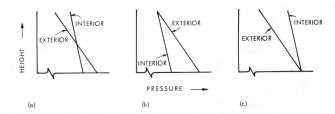

Fig. 4.20 Shaft characteristics: (a) Vented top and bottom; (b) Top vented; (c) Bottom vented

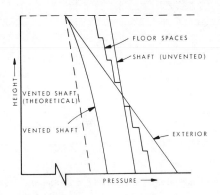

Fig. 4.21 Top-vented shaft

building. The effect would be a shift to the left of the pressure characteristics relating to the remaining regions. If all the shafts were top vented, the floor space characteristic would move to the left to the extent that, at the top, it would approach coincidence with the exterior characteristic.

The dashed line in Fig. 4.21 illustrates the location of the vented shaft characteristic predicted by the most elementary theory. In fact, the characteristic tends to be curved as shown. In general, the slope of a characteristic is uniquely determined by temperature conditions, the atmosphere involved being substantially static. In this particular case, however, the curvature is associated with pressure losses up the shaft owing to heavy flow.

Figs. 4.22 and 4.23 are included in the National Building Code of Canada to provide guidelines for the top venting of shafts. In Figs. 4.22 and 4.23, curve A applies to shafts enclosed by unplastered unit masonry or by plaster and steel stud construction with all openings reasonably sealed; curve B applies to shafts enclosed by monolithic concrete or by plastered unit masonry with all openings tightly sealed. They are based on assumed shaft leakage areas of 1 m² per 400 m² (1/4 sq ft per 100 sq ft) for curve A and half this value for curve B. Fig. 4.23 is less stringent than Fig. 4.22 because widespread air injection will move characteristics to the right, facilitating the maintenance of a vented shaft characteristic to the left of all others. Upper limiting heights prevail, above which top venting based·on the graphs will not be completely effective. To extend the upper limiting heights, shaft leakage must be reduced.

Although top venting can assure that a shaft does not transfer smoke from one story to another, it actually promotes contamination of the shaft. Where this is to be avoided, the shaft characteristic should be moved to the extreme right, by either air injection or bottom venting.

The dashed line on the extreme right of Fig. 4.24 shows the idealized location of the characteristic for a bottom-vented shaft. By injecting warm air into it, in addition to bottom venting, this condition can be readily established. Without air injection, the flow of fresh air into the bottom of the shaft, making up losses to the

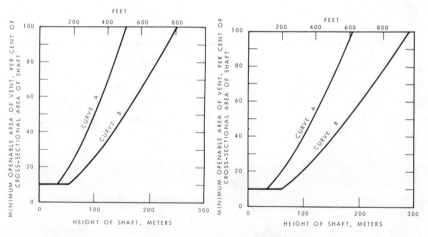

Fig. 4.22 Required area of top vent (no shaft pressurization)   Fig. 4.23 Required area of top vent (several other shafts pressurized)

building at all other levels, will give considerable cooling and hence curvature of the bottom part of the characteristic, as is also shown in Fig. 4.24.

The protected shaft characteristics shown in Fig. 4.24 are coincident with the exterior characteristic at grade level. To avoid smoke transfer from floor spaces in the absence of window breakage, the shaft characteristic need be no further to the right than the floor space characteristic. Coincidence with the exterior characteristic at grade level is desirable for two reasons, however. First, a floor space characteristic would coincide with the exterior characteristic in the event of window breakage, a likely development during a fire. Thus, to maintain adequately high pressure in the shaft, the characteristic must not lie to the left of the exterior characteristic. At higher levels it must also be to the right of the unvented shaft characteristic.

The second reason for maintaining coincidence of the exterior and shaft characteristics at grade level is the avoidance of undesirable pressure differences across doors; it relates particularly to stairwells. Maintaining ideal conditions in a stairshaft is best achieved by opening the grade level door to the exterior and injecting air at a rate of up to 7 m³/sec (15 000 cfm) to maintain a slight, positive differential across the doorway, together with a further 0.05 m³/sec or 0.1 m³/sec (100 cfm or 200 cfm) for each door into the stair, depending on whether it is weatherstripped.

An advantage of a large basic flow of up to 7 m³/sec (15 000 cfm) is that it can act as a diluent to reestablish a satisfactory atmosphere rapidly, following any untoward event that permits contamination. Failure to initiate smoke control measures at the outbreak of fire or the simultaneous opening of too many doors are circumstances that could give rise to contamination and call for a high diluent air flow.

Leakage between an elevator shaft and adjacent spaces is much greater than that of a stairshaft. Consequently, an injection rate that will not establish too great a pressure differential and yet be sufficient to serve as a diluent does not necessarily call for venting. Typical required air flow rates are specified by the National Building Code of Canada (Assoc. Com. on the National Building Code of Canada, 1973) through use of the formula $F(0.023d + 0.0014a)$ m³/sec, or $F(0.25d + 0.0014a)$ cfm, in which d = number of small single doors to the shaft; a = area of enclosing walls of the shaft, in meters squared or square feet; and F = factor which varies with height and the lowest exterior design temperature [F ranges between 3.5 and 4.3(700

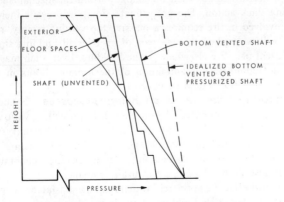

Fig. 4.24 Bottom-vented or pressurized shafts

and 850) for low buildings, and between 10 and 15(2000 and 3000) for extremely high buildings].

Smoke Control Systems in Buildings.   To develop satisfactory smoke control measures it is almost invariably necessary to consider a building as an entity. Some particularly important features will be briefly referred to.

The primary object of a smoke control system in a high-rise building is the avoidance of a disaster involving substantial life loss. This alone is so difficult to assure that it may not be possible, with the same measures, to offer substantial protection to building occupants in the immediate vicinity of fire, and protection of these people may best be considered as a separate issue. Usually the most practical approach is to arrange for immediate evacuation of an area following early warning provided by fire detectors. Sprinklers may also reduce the smoke generation sufficiently to avoid undue hazard.

A second premise is that the building basically conforms to all currently accepted fire protection concepts and that, following an outbreak of fire, all essential doors are closed. Attention should also have been paid to the flammability of interior finish materials and contents to assure that fire development is not so rapid as to create disastrous conditions before remedial measures (for example, the closing of doors) can be taken. Probably the most important feature is that the building should be adequately compartmented by fire resistant construction.

It is also assumed that the aim in developing the system is to combat smoke migration resulting from building heating stack action together with the initial expansion process. The transfer of smoke from one story to another by way of shafts is thus the mechanism to be countered.

One other factor that must be borne in mind is the possibility of fire in a shaft. This could completely change the perspective of smoke control measures. To inject air into an elevator shaft to maintain it smoke-free during the course of a fire in a floor space is sound practice; but should the fire actually occur in the shaft itself (for example, in goods loaded into an elevator car), air injection would be most undesirable and would serve only to disperse smoke throughout the building. Substantial top venting is probably the best means of attempting to create a favorable pressure pattern in the building if there is fire in the shaft.

To avoid contamination of an upper story, a shaft requires a greater top vent area when there is a fire in it than when the smoke movement mechanism involved is building heating stack action. The unfortunate situation prevails therefore that a shaft heavily involved in fire requires a massive top venting facility, regardless of measures that will be applied to it as part of an over-all building smoke control system in the event of a fire elsewhere in the building. Even such massive venting will probably not eliminate contamination of the topmost floors in a very high building, where evacuation would be called for.

Smoke control systems based on natural processes.   Numerous, quite different, smoke control systems can be developed. In presenting various examples, it is convenient to divide them into two categories: (1) Natural systems, not involving the use of air-handling systems; and (2) mechanical systems. The division is of interest in the context of reliability, although the reliability of other components will also be involved in an over-all assessment.

Probably the most effective approach to maintaining satisfactory conditions in a substantial portion of a high building is to divide it vertically into two in an appropriate manner, providing horizontal access from one half to the other, preferably at every story. Smoke flow in the shafts of one half is avoided by assuring that smoke is entirely excluded from all that portion of the building.

It would not be wise merely to subdivide a building into two by way of a wall and close-fitting doors, as illustrated in Fig. 4.25, relying on symmetry of pressure between the two halves, since such asymmetrical influences as wind tend to promote unacceptable smoke transfer, and breakage of a window on a low level fire floor could have a most unfortunate effect.

Referring back to Fig. 4.19, it may be seen that the pressure in a low-level floor space is usually much lower than the exterior value, although it will rise in the event of substantial window breakage. So far as compartment B in Fig. 4.25 is concerned, all four walls will be at exterior pressure and gases will flow in through them. Three will deliver fresh air and one contaminated air. The steady-state conditions finally established in compartment B will thus be about one quarter as bad as those in compartment A, which is still an intolerable situation.

An intriguing remedial measure would be to assure large window openings in compartment B should fire develop in the adjacent compartment A. This approach could only be considered acceptable so far as the tightly constructed common wall is concerned. To avoid transfer as a result of miscellaneous asymmetrical pressure disturbances such as wind, access from one portion of the building to the other should be by way of a vented lobby (shown in Fig. 4.26).

The foregoing discussion of how to divide a building effectively into two leads to other approaches, but these will be mentioned only briefly because development details are usually specific to a particular building design.

As shafts constitute the principal path by which smoke migrates throughout a building, their removal would be an effective measure. Thus, stair and elevator shafts could be located alongside a building, with access by open bridges. Certain

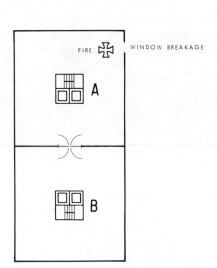

Fig. 4.25 Unsatisfactory divided building

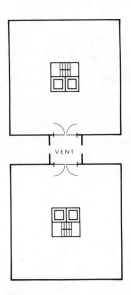

Fig. 4.26 Ideal divided building

service shafts that are too closely associated with the building to permit spatial separation could be provided with top venting, which would probably prove to be quite satisfactory.

To avoid the unfortunate feature of unenclosed access to stair and elevator shafts given by the arrangement just described, a largely satisfactory measure of separation can be achieved by using lobbies at every point of access to a stair or elevator shaft, venting them on the outbreak of fire. With most such arrangements some of the walls bounding the shafts will be common to the building. Such walls must be made tight to avoid seepage of pollutant through them from fire in a floor space. This could also be minimized in winter conditions by bottom venting of the shafts.

Complete protection of a building against catastrophic life loss would, at first sight, seem possible by top and bottom venting of various shafts. Top venting has, in fact, been suggested as complementary to some of the "natural" methods so far discussed. Total dependence on bottom venting of a shaft as a means of avoiding smoke transfer from story to story and of contamination of the shaft is, however, open to question.

It would seem quite likely that undesirable conditions could arise in summer. Assuming air-handling systems switched off and no wind prevailing, the single straight line shown in Fig. 4.27 could represent the characteristics of all the spaces in a building in summer. Neither top nor bottom venting of a shaft would displace its characteristic.

Following the outbreak of a fire on a floor space at the level indicated, expansion would force heated gases into the shafts primarily through leakage around doors, heating at least the upper portions and causing rotation of the characteristics. Top and bottom venting would assure minimum pressure differences at these respective levels and thus give rise to characteristics of the nature indicated. Conditions in the top-vented shaft would be satisfactory, contaminant entering from the fire floor being discharged from the top.

The characteristic of the upper portion of the bottom-vented shaft would, however, be well to the right of all others, and hence contaminant flow from the shaft to upper floor spaces would be promoted. This being so, it is generally desirable, when wishing to maintain a shaft characteristic well to the right of all others, to inject air into the shaft.

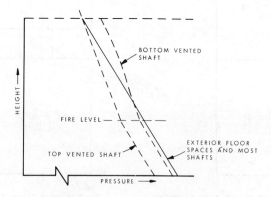

Fig. 4.27 Summer fire conditions: vented shafts

Mechanical smoke control systems. The first type of system to be discussed under this heading is, once again, the use of vestibules for separation, but pressurized instead of vented. This approach is of particular value where no convenient exterior wall is available for provision of a vent.

It would not be sufficient merely to assure that the pressure in such a vestibule is a little higher than those in the two adjacent areas it is serving to separate. At low levels in winter (see Fig. 4.19) the pressure in the area involved in fire could rise to the exterior value as a result of window breakage. Under these conditions vestibule pressure should be slightly higher still. In the upper parts of the building this precise effect will not occur. In general, air flows of between 0.1 m³/sec and 0.2 m³/sec (200 cfm and 400 cfm) per door (less for weatherstripped doors) will prove adequate.

Probably the most useful application of a mechanical system will be to pressurize elevator and stair shafts to establish the (dotted) pressure characteristic furthest to the right in Fig. 4.24. The air flow requirements called for in stair and elevator shafts were discussed earlier when the merits of moving shaft characteristics to the right and left were outlined. Should the outer skin of a building be unusually tight, injection of air into all the shafts could move the floor space characteristics quite heavily to the right. Basically, this is perfectly acceptable, but in practice asymmetries in air deliveries could give problems. If the air supply to an elevator shaft with a substantial top leakage were low, the characteristic could be to the left of a floor space characteristic, giving flow from the floor space to the shaft.

To avoid problems of this nature it is desirable that some of the shafts should be top vented, and fortunately this is usually the most convenient approach for service shafts. Such top venting tends to move the floor space characteristics to the left. A further advantage is that it is essential in the event of fire in a shaft.

The tendency of floor space characteristics to move to the right when air is injected into most shafts has led to the development of a further smoke control approach, that of pressurizing a whole building and venting the fire floor. Fig. 4.28 shows the idealized characteristic of such a building. The basic idea is that if the building characteristic is to the right of the exterior then venting of a fire floor, regardless of its level, will assure that its pressure is lower than that in all adjacent spaces. If the method is considered as an extension of the pressurized shafts concept and air injection is largely confined to shafts, it can serve as a satisfactory smoke

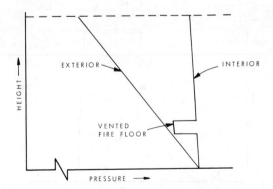

Fig. 4.28 Idealized pressurized building characteristic

control method, always assuming that the fire is in a floor space that can be vented. Where air injection is confined to floor spaces, however, various deficiencies can arise. The principal problem concerns the symmetry of the distribution of the air and the different conditions demanded in summer and in winter. In winter, assuming for convenience a uniform building, Fig. 4.28 indicates that the air flow requirement would be high at the top of the building and zero at the bottom. During the summer, however, the exterior and building interior characteristics will be more nearly parallel (see Fig. 4.29), and air flow requirements will be the same all the way up the building. A poor situation exists where a large shopping complex forms the base of a tower structure with a common elevator system. At higher levels summertime flows between a fire floor and the shafts will probably be in the wrong direction unless venting of the fire floor is massive.

So far there has been no discussion of the means of venting that might be adopted as part of a building pressurization/vented fire floor approach to smoke control. If exterior wall venting is chosen, a required vent area can reasonably be taken as a function only of the sum of the leakage from the space concerned to all adjacent spaces. Adoption of a vent area appreciably larger than the total leakage to other areas of the building will usually be adequate. It must also be borne in mind, the building being pressurized, that flaming from the vent will probably be extensive. Exterior cladding for several stories above the vent must therefore be capable of withstanding exposure to heat.

Smoke shafts are a popular means of venting a fire area, regardless of whether a building is pressurized, and this topic is deserving of discussion under a separate heading.

Venting by Smoke Shafts. The pressure characteristic of a smoke shaft can be so substantially to the left of those of the remainder of a building that the potential for creating a much reduced pressure in a fire region would appear to be great. Fig. 4.30 shows the conditions that can prevail in winter in an unpressurized building in which provision of a smoke shaft constitutes the only smoke control measure. In summer also, substantially similar conditions will develop once the shaft has been heated by hot gases forced into it by the initial expansion process.

The feature that makes complete reliance on a smoke shaft (as the total smoke control system) impractical for all but windowless areas and regions above the neutral pressure plane of a building is the possibility of window breakage. Referring

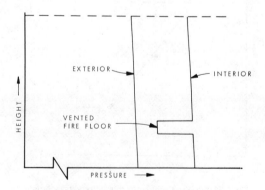

Fig. 4.29 Pressurized building: summertime

to Fig. 4.30, it may be seen that at the level postulated for the fire floor the exterior characteristic is well to the right. If the area of windows that break appreciably exceeds the cross-sectional area of the flow path via the smoke shaft, the effect of the smoke shaft will be negated and the pressure in the fire area may rise above that of adjacent areas.

A further caution regarding smoke shafts concerns their tightness. Even a well-constructed steel damper might have a leakage of 2% of its open area, so that a smoke shaft having such a damper at every floor is unlikely to be effective for buildings higher than 200 m (650 ft). For still higher buildings, smoke shafts serving lower stories would need to have tight imperforate walls over much of the height, precluding their capability to serve all the stories in the building.

An eventuality worth discussing, although currently only hypothetical, is the possibility of an explosion in a smoke shaft. In North America, smoke explosions occur in buildings approximately once a year and very occasionally, perhaps once in 5 yr, they cause serious damage and sometimes casualties. Theoretically, such explosions are as likely to occur in smoke shafts as in floor spaces. The question thus arises as to whether the adoption of explosion relief measures for smoke shafts is warranted.

Any hazard associated with an explosion in a smoke shaft could be eliminated by providing explosion reliefs at various levels in the shaft. Vent areas equal to the cross-sectional area of the shaft would assure, according to a British report (Ministry of Labour, 1965), that overpressures would not exceed a value $p = 0.276$ length/diameter kPa $[p = 0.04$ length/diameter (psi)] up to a limiting value of L/D of 60 (giving $p = 16.5$ kPa or 2.4 psi). In view of the fact that only the gases in a portion of a shaft would usually be within the flammability limits at the time of an incident, design to this overpressure would probably be satisfactory.

Unreinforced concrete or cinder block walls [200 mm to 300 mm (8 in. to 12 in.)] are said to be capable of withstanding overpressures of 14 kPa to 20 kPa (2 psi to 3 psi) (Glasstone, 1962), and unreinforced brick wall panels of a similar thickness can withstand about 50 kPa (7 psi to 8 psi). Blast resistant construction can be designed to contain overpressures of at least 70 kPa (10 psi). In most cases, therefore, sturdy construction of a smoke shaft would, of itself, provide adequate protection against a

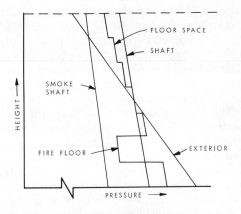

Fig. 4.30 Smoke shaft

smoke explosion, and the provision of vents other than at the top of the shaft would not be necessary. Should a vent prove to be desirable at some location up the height of the shaft and the shaft to have no exterior wall, venting could be effected by way of a service area unlikely to be occupied. The service area itself would then, in turn, require some measure of venting.

Although the likelihood of a smoke explosion in a smoke shaft is remote, it seems unwise to use the shaft walls as load-bearing elements unless they have been designed to withstand an explosion either by virtue of venting or because of robust construction.

Miscellaneous Considerations. The principal ancillary problem to be avoided in devising smoke control measures is the development of undesirably high adverse pressure differences across doors. It is difficult to open a conventional door against a pressure differential exceeding 50 Pa (0.2 in. WG), and at this pressure elevator doors tend to malfunction.

With one or two exceptions undesirable pressure differentials arise when a door communicates with an atmosphere that is, substantially, at exterior pressure. The circumstances under which this condition prevails fall into two categories: (1) Where, by design (for example, venting), the atmosphere is automatically at exterior pressure; and (2) where the atmosphere is inadvertently brought to the exterior value by window breakage.

Examples of the first category include grade-level access doors of numerous high buildings in regions experiencing low temperatures. Conventional doors in these locations are often difficult to open and a common solution to the problem is to provide revolving doors, which are unaffected by pressure differentials. A less common solution is to provide "balanced doors." Initially, these rotate about the center point and hence offer no net opposing force dependent on pressure.

Certain types of smoke control measure tend to give rise to pressure differentials across doors, usually at the extreme upper and lower levels. One example is the protection of shafts by the use of vented vestibules. Assuming that the shafts are heated, substantial pressure differences appear across doors well removed from the neutral pressure plane. In every case such as this, a form of balanced door should theoretically be used where an adverse differential exceeding 100 Pa (0.4 in. WG) can exist.

The second category of door problem, where the atmosphere is inadvertently brought to the exterior value following window breakage, can occur during fires at high levels in existing high-rise buildings. One virtually never hears of this, however, and hence it is difficult to assess the emphasis that should be placed on avoiding such a problem in new buildings. The following is a possible argument for paying more attention to it in buildings incorporating certain smoke control measures. The door problem on the fire floor of older buildings will only arise after the fire has attained an intensity sufficient to break windows, and by this time all occupants of that floor will probably have vacated it. In new buildings that include certain smoke control methods, however, the fire floor may be vented to the exterior as soon as the alarm sounds and before evacuation is complete. Some means of countering door problems is desirable under these circumstances.

Although it does not, at first sight, appear to be a closely related aspect of the subject, the influence of exterior temperature on the performance of smoke control measures can be conveniently discussed in the same context because it has great bearing on door problems. Smoke infiltration into certain critical shafts and smoke transfer from one story to another, by vertical shafts generally, are to be combated regardless of season and mechanism involved (for example, stack action or expansion). By preventing these movements, control measures continue to be effective in summer as well as winter.

The distribution of door problems is likely to be quite different in summer, however. With natural control measures, involving venting, there will probably be no door problem. With mechanical control methods, however, care must still be exercised. The pressurized building/vented fire floor approach gives a clear example of the type of effect that is likely. In summer, the exterior characteristic will not be as in Fig. 4.28 but will have about the same slope as that of the interior, giving the conditions shown (idealized) in Fig. 4.29. Door problems may occur at any level in the event of window breakage; opening exterior doors at grade level will obviously give the same effect, and operation of the elevator doors might be impaired. The most convenient means of eliminating all possible door problems during the summer season would be to modulate the pressurizing air supply, reducing flows substantially.

Where smoke control in a very high building involves air injection into elevator shafts, modulation (with exterior temperature) might also be necessary to avoid summertime door problems.

Conclusions.   The principal conclusions may be summarized as follows:

1. It is not feasible to avoid a smoke disaster in a tall building by attempting to limit the quantity of smoke-producing materials it contains. The equivalent, however, of limiting the quantity that can be involved in a single fire, by the installation of a complete sprinkler system, is generally practical.

2. A smoke control system designed to avoid major disaster in a building will generally not enhance the life safety of occupants in the immediate vicinity of the origin of a fire. With some exceptions this question is best treated separately, the most practical approach usually being to arrange for immediate evacuation following early warning.

3. Assuming that recirculating air-handling systems are immediately inoperative at the outbreak of fire, it is pollution of critical shafts and smoke transfer from one story to another by way of vertical shafts that are to be guarded against if a major disaster is to be avoided. The mechanisms likely to create the greatest problems are expansion and building heating stack action.

4. Where a smoke control system is intended to combat the effects of fire in a floor space the possibility of a fire in a shaft should be considered. In this event, top venting is probably the only smoke control measure likely to be of much value. Fire in a shaft can pose such a substantial threat to life safety that any shaft in which much risk of fire exists should be sprinklered or include some alternative means of extinguishing fire.

5. Smoke control systems will often involve architectural design (for example, divided building, provision of vestibule protection) and can be conveniently divided into two classifications, those based on natural processes and those using mechanical systems.

One of the main concerns during an actual fire is the transfer of contaminant gases throughout the building. This has been a fire safety hazard in *all* types of building structures. Tall buildings can be made as safe as any other buildings provided that the fire protection design provides for the control of smoke and its movement throughout the structure.

3 Panic Reaction

Panic is a term commonly and often incorrectly used when dramatically describing the actions of people subject to stress caused by a disaster, crisis or accident. According to those who have done in-depth analytical research on the subject, panic is a reality and does occur; however, the occurrence of panic is less frequent than most people believe. Normally, when people are under severe stress, they can and do react intelligently to severe stress without panic.

Definitions.   The following are various definitions of the term "panic" used by the researchers studying human reactions.

1. A demoralizing terror with or without clear cause.

2. Sudden destruction of self control leading to frantic action.

3. Highly emotional behavior which is excited by the presence of an immediate severe threat and which results in increasing the danger for the self and for others.

4. The state of an individual who has lost control over fear.

To achieve a true panic situation specific conditions must be present, according to Rubin and Cohen (1974). These would be, for example: (1) A real or perceived imminent threat; (2) a limited route to escape the threat; (3) imminent blockage of that escape route; and (4) a lack of or breakdown in communication with others. These elements may not be enough in themselves to cause panic, but would have to be present in this or similar form before true panic would ensue.

According to Schultz (1964) the three essential components of panic are: (1) Fear; (2) flight; and (3) limited access to escape routes.

Misconceptions about Panic Behavior.   Contrary to popular belief, panic is relatively rare, and, in general, people cope remarkably well not only with fire emergencies but also with a wide variety of disaster situations. Research on behavior in a range of actual emergencies should assist greatly in the transition from findings about movement in nonemergency or drill situations to hypotheses about evacuation in cases of actual fire in buildings. (It should be noted that communication systems, increasingly being provided in high-rise buildings for use in fire emergencies, have a considerable influence on how people perceive an emergency or a drill situation.)

The limited information available suggests that people do cope well in fire emergencies. Quarantelli (1977) and others support this contention and point out that where panic has occurred this behavior was confined to a small proportion of the people present. Although mass panic does occur it is not typical and only a few instances have been documented. This conclusion includes the experiences gained during the bombings and attacks on civilian populations during World War II. Normally, when panic does occur, it occurs with individuals or small groups, although there are obvious exceptions which are noted later.

Many commonly held notions about panic and human behavior under extreme stress conditions are incorrect. Listed herewith are the corrected versions:

1. Mass panic is a phenomenon that occurs rarely and only under certain circumstances.

2. Few actual cases of looting can be discovered.

3. Stricken populations are not a "dazed, helpless mass" but help themselves and perform rescue and welfare tasks.

4. The social group organization does not break down but is strengthened.

5. There are only isolated examples of breakdown of moral codes.

6. There is no significant increase in psychosis and psychoneurosis.

7. Emotional aftereffects are widespread but relatively mild and transitory.

8. Morale and optimism soon rebound and are abnormally high in some respects.

9. The big problem of crowd control is not flight of the victims from the disaster area, but a convergence of people to the disaster area from the outside (Pauls, 1958).

Nature of Panic Behavior. Quarantelli (1977) notes three covert panic features: an acute fear reaction, anticipation, and a focus on a specific threat. He also notes three overt panic features: its flight nature, its nonsocial aspect, and its nonrational (rather than irrational) aspects. Following are excerpts from Quarantelli (1977).

Covert Features. Covertly, panic involves (1) fear, not anxiety, (2) a projection into the future rather than a view of the past, and (3) a perceived place of danger rather than a generalized threat.

Fear. In panic the physical self is seen as seriously threatened, thus the panicky reaction is characterized not so much by the presence of fear as by unchecked fear. Persons may feel extreme fear for their actual physical safety and yet maintain a high degree of control over their activities. This is well illustrated by soldiers involved in combat. Usually they maintain control over their fears. Conversely, in panic there is a collapse of existing curbs on the impulse to flee. The participant is the individual who has lost control over fear.

Projection to the Future. The orientation of attention of panic participants is always to the future, to what subsequently may be endangering to the physical self. It is the anticipatory rather than retrospective perceptions of danger that accompany panic activity. Furthermore the potential threat is seen as having immediate consequences, at most within the time span of several minutes. A rapid reaction of some sort is viewed as necessary in order to survive the quickly anticipated perilous effects. However, that panicky individuals react toward very immediately rising threats rather than retrospective dangers does not mean that there necessarily exists an objective peril. In fact, the realness or illusoriness of the threat is, as far as a panicky reaction is concerned, of little import. Thus, panicky reactions will occur in situations involving no real threat simply because a danger is perceived as possible. This often happens after an explosion.

Specific Threat. Panic participants are not only aware of what they are immediately afraid for (which is their own physical survival) but they also know what they are afraid of. The covert response of the person in panic is never in regard to the unknown or the incomprehensible as such. The reaction is always regarding a specific threat. Consequently flight continues only to the extent people believe themselves well within the danger area. Fleeing stops when there is the belief that one is no longer exposed to the consequences of the threat. The characteristically short duration of panic flight stems from this fact that panicky persons run only as far as necessary to get outside of the perceived zone of danger.

Overt Features. Overtly, panic involves (1) directional rather than purely random flight, (2) nonsocial rather than antisocial activities, (3) and nonrational rather than irrational behavior.

Flight. Flight is the outstanding feature of panic insofar as outward manifestation is concerned. . . . The loss of control over fear and the focalization of thought on escaping does not mean a panicky person is completely unresponsive to other aspects of the situation or that there is just blind fleeing. On the contrary, a panicky individual orients the fleeing and modifies the flight behavior in terms of the perceived circumstances. Thus, a panic participant does not blindly run into objects; if possible, an attempt is made to go around obstacles in one's path. An attempt is made to go through a door before an effort is made to flee through a window, etc.

Panic flight is not a random or headlong stampede; it is directed towards the goal of getting away from the area of danger. Thus, the flight behavior is always oriented with reference to a location of danger; that is, panicky people flee from particular locales, such as a collapsing building or a gas-filled house. Usually this involves movement away from specific points of danger: panic participants thus run away from, for example, the flaming section of a building. However, if some danger lies between presumed safety and the endangered persons, the flight may be in the direction of that specific peril. Thus, panicky persons may run toward dangerous objects if escape from the threat lies in that direction (e.g., toward sheets of flame if the only known exit from a building is on the other side). Much panic fleeing which appears to an outside observer as blind fleeing into danger is of this nature. The behavior is not, as some have asserted, characterized by blindness to reality. Instead as one person who fled in panic observed: "Since my escape through the door was cut off, I shielded my face with my hands and crashed head first through a window. It was my only hope of getting out."

Nonsocial. The Flight Behavior in Panic always takes on a nonsocial character; however, such behavior is not necessarily antisocial. This is more than a play on words. The panicky person acts in a nonsocial rather than antisocial way by disregarding the usual social relationship and expectations. Even the strongest primary group ties may be shattered and the most socially expected behavior patterns may be ignored. It is only in the very rare instance that panic takes the form of a mass of individuals trampling over one another in a wild stampede.

The nonsocial aspect of panic behavior tends to be short-lived; but it is this feature which, even at an overt level, distinguishes many cases of panic from controlled withdrawal behavior. People acted in an erratic and partially unorganized fashion, but unlike when persons are panicky, most of their behavior was in terms of the group norms that ordinarily guided their activities. Such excited flight should not be confused with panic flight.

In panic there is no unity of action, no cooperation with others, no joint activity; there is a total breakdown of corporate or concerted behavior. In short, panic flight is the very antithesis of organized group behavior, it is the manifestation of nonsocial behavior at its zenith.

Nonrational. Just as panic is nonsocial rather than antisocial, so it is nonrational rather than irrational behavior. Moreover, when fleeing in a collective panic, participants are at least partially aware of the presence of others although they do not respond to these other individuals in terms of their usual social roles. However, to state that panic flight involves a degree of awareness on the part of participants is not to suggest in any way that it is a highly rational activity. It certainly does not involve the weighing of alternative courses of action that might be followed in the situation.

Rather than being rational or irrational, the behavior of a panic participant is nonrational. The panicky person just thinks of escaping, making no attempt to cope with the threat other than to flee from it. Furthermore, there is no account taken of the possible consequences of the fleeing behavior. In certain infrequent circumstances this may be even more dangerous than the panic-inciting threat itself. The behavior of the panicky person thus is nonrational in the sense of not considering alternative courses of behavior to fleeing and of not foreseeing the possible consequences of panic flight. In fact, it is only rarely and almost always because of the presence of physical barriers, that panicky individuals may proceed to knock one another down and to trample over each other. Such collectively maladaptive activity, however, is definitely not a common characteristic of the behavior of panicky persons.

Summary of Panic Features. In summary, panic is an acute fear reaction marked by flight behavior. Subjectively, there is an intense fear reaction, i.e., a strong impulse to flee from a threatening danger. Panic participants are seized by fear of a specific object perceived as involving an immediate and extreme threat to physical survival. Overtly, the flight behavior always involves an attempt to remove one's self physically from the endangered area. In fleeing, the participants do not weigh the social consequences of their action and are highly individualistic and self-centered in their flight with with regard to one another; thus, the behavior is nonrational and nonsocial, although not necessarily nonfunctional or maladaptive. Since there is no consideration of alternative courses of action to flight, the thought being focused on the removal of one's self from danger, usual social relationships and role patterns are ignored and there is no possibility of group action.

Social interaction. Of utmost importance, however, is the nature of the interaction with others that occurs prior to and during panic flight. In the case of collective panic, it is through individuals interacting with one another that there occurs a cognitive clarification of what the situation is and what can or cannot be done about it. Social interaction is basic in bringing about the definition of the crisis situation as a threatening one. It plays a major part in reinforcing the definition of the situation as one in which only flight is possible. Finally, panic flight frequently terminates as a result of the interaction among the participants, leading them to perceive themselves as out of the danger area. And possibly most important of all, it is frequently the presence and response of other persons that motivates individuals to control their fears, consequently diminishing the possibility of panicky reaction.

Others have described the nature of panic behavior in less scientific terms than Quarantelli. Panic behavior, however, can be summarized by saying that it is a condition of abnormal fear in individuals who then violently react to escape a perceived dangerous situation without regard to others but only to save themselves. The normal cooperative ties between individuals disappear and the selfish personal needs are of paramount importance.

Conditions Necessary for Panic to Occur. It is apparent from the various studies made on the subject of panic that there is no universal agreement on all the factors which might produce panic. Those who studied examples of panic in military units mention lack of confidence in the leader and the lack of group identification in the case of individuals who panicked shortly after joining a front line unit. Also, fatigue or other weakening physical conditions and lack of training or pre-thought to cope with the particular threat encountered are held to be factors that contribute to panic in some cases.

Quarantelli (1977) suggests that there are two definite conditions, present before a crisis situation arises, which are important in facilitating the possible development of a panic when the crisis does occur:

1. Fear and the thought that there may be a panic if something should go wrong. People have mentally considered this as a possibility, perhaps because they have heard of other panics in similar situations.

2. The people in the crisis situation are not connected socially. Families therefore would not be as subject to panic behavior as individuals alone. This has significant ramifications in apartment occupancies.

Quarantelli also suggests that there are three conditions necessary for panic to occur:

1. The person feels he is going to be trapped—is not actually trapped as yet but will be trapped unless he does something about it.

2. A sense of inability to do something about getting out. He feels that he is not going to be able to make it to a place of safety.

3. He feels completely alone in resolving his dilemma. He cannot count on help from others; he must cope with the crisis on his own.

To use Quarantelli's two preconditions to panic and three conditions for panic in an example, consider a stair crowded with people exiting a high-rise building because of the sounding of a fire alarm. The crowd is stopped at the upper levels because of the influx of more people from the floors below; suddenly, the people stopped at the upper level smell smoke. What's the possibility of a panic?

First, if they or any of them wondered themselves of the possibility of a panic occurring before the smell of smoke, they meet the first condition. No doubt some of them considered this because of the popular misconceptions of panic and their jammed condition on the blocked stair.

Secondly, assume that this high-rise building is occupied by many independent offices and businesses; therefore, the people on the stair have no social contact with one another for the most part. If they make no social contacts or collectively organize some plan of action before the smell of smoke, they fulfill the second precondition.

Now, with the introduction of the smell of smoke, a person unable to go either up or down the stair and jammed between people on the stair will certainly feel trapped but not necessarily hopeless. He will very likely feel alone in the solid mass of humanity and therefore feel the necessity to save himself.

It can be seen that the various conditions for panic as described by Quarantelli can be met, but that there are naturally degrees of meeting most of the conditions. Also, even though one individual may panic in the situation described, it does not follow that a general panic will ensue. The one individual may be forcibly controlled rather easily and may even give moral fortitude to the others. On the other hand, the interaction of the group may tend to incite a general panic or it may tend to help the group collectively control their fears.

There are so many variables that one can see that panic prediction is far from an exact science. Its rarity indicates that special blending of the ingredients is necessary for it to ever occur. Quarantelli's analysis, however, may make it possible to design a structure to eliminate the possible occurrence of one of the essential elements of panic.

Examples of Panic Behavior.   Panics do occur, and with tragic results. However, as previously noted, very few cases of mass panic have been authenticated in the last fifty years. This is in spite of the fact that there have been extensive wartime attacks on civilian populations. Another factor noted by the researchers was the apparent lack of objective reporting of disasters. Panic was assumed on the part of the writer and descriptions were couched to impart appropriate emotional feelings to the reader.

Following are excerpts from *Newsweek* (December 7, 1942, pages 43–44) describing the Coconut Grove fire of 1942:

> Every available table was taken ... a girl, her hair ablaze, hurtled across the floor screaming 'Fire'!

That shriek heralded catastrophe. Some 800 guests, insane with panic, [Ed: Notice the terminology] lunged in a wild scramble to get out the only way they knew ... the revolving door exit. Flames flashed with incredible swiftness ... smoke swirled in choking masses through hallways. The revolving doors jammed as the terror-stricken mob pushed them in both directions at the same time. Blazing draperies fell setting women's evening gowns and hair on fire.

Patrons were hurled under tables and trampled to death. Others tripped and choked the six foot wide stairway up from the Melody Lounge. Those behind swarmed over them and piled up in layers—layers of corpses ... the fire was quickly brought under control, but the fatal damage was done.

Quarantelli's (1977) studies indicate no more than one third of the patrons truly panicked.

Another well known panic situation, the infamous Iroquois Theater fire in 1903, has been described by Foy and Harlow (1928):

Somebody had of course yelled 'Fire!'—there is almost always a fool of that species in an audience; and there are always hundreds of people who go crazy the moment they hear the word ...

The horror in the auditorium was beyond all description. There were thirty exits, but few of them were marked by lights, some had heavy portieres over the doors, and some of the doors were locked or fastened with levers which no one knew how to work.

It was said that some of the exit doors ... were either rusted or frozen. They were finally burst open, but precious moments had been lost—moments which meant death for many behind those doors. The fire escape ladders could not accommodate the crowd, and many fell or jumped to death on the pavement below. Some were not killed only because they landed on the cushion of bodies of those who had gone before.

But it was inside the house that the greatest loss of life occurred, especially on the stairways leading down from the second balcony. Here most of the dead were trampled or smothered, though many jumped or fell over the balustrade to the floor of the foyer. In places on the stairways, particularly where a turn caused a jam, bodies were piled seven or eight feet deep ...

An occasional living person was found in the heaps, but most of these were terribly injured. The heel prints on the dead faces mutely testified to the cruel fact that human animals stricken by terror are as mad and ruthless as stampeding cattle. Many bodies had the clothes torn from them, and some had the flesh trodden from their bones.

More recent examples of panic situations with large groups can be found in accounts of the Saõ Paulo, Brazil, high-rise fire (Willey, 1972b):

For a time the situation seemed hopeless for those trapped on the heliport. Many did not expect to be rescued and were on the verge of panic. One man jumped to his death from the roof. Another attempted to slide down the south wall on a lightning cable. The cable ended some distance down; he fell to his death.

A chief rescue officer learned that two helicopters were available for service. He and another fire fighter boarded one, located at a heliport on a nearby high rise building. Three other fire fighters boarded the other helicopter and proceeded to the Andraus Building. By that time (approximately 5:15 P.M.) the fires on various floors had consumed much of the available fuel and the massive flame front had subsided. The helicopters were able to approach the building and the rescue officer attempted to land. However, the people on the heliport were so desperate to be rescued they surged toward the aircraft and attempted to pull it down, and, fearing an accident, the pilot flew off. The second helicopter with the three fire fighters hovered just above the crowd, and the fire fighters dropped to the roof. A landing site was cleared and the rescue officer landed.

The primary task for the rescue officer was to gain control of the crowd and prevent panic. This was accomplished with the aid of volunteers from the crowd. A television antenna was dismantled for use as a landing site barricade. Reassurance of rescue and the leadership of fire fighters established order and prevented further casualties.

The scene was to change again when fire fighters discovered the closed door to the stairway. When it was opened they found a mass of people below crushed up against the horizontal sliding door, many of them seriously injured by those pushing from below. Fire fighters then brought another 100 persons to the roof. Some were unconscious from smoke inhalation; others had suffered broken bones and lacerations. The most serious cases were laid out on the roof ready for evacuation.

The roof crowd began to despair again when they saw the injured brought to the heliport. They thought that the injured would be evacuated first, delaying their rescue, and some presented self-inflicted injuries, hoping to be among the first. Nevertheless, the fire fighters were able to maintain control and organize evacuation. . .

. . .At the top of the stairway, below the closed heliport access door, frantic crowding and pushing by people attempting to reach the heliport caused many injuries. (Willey, 1972b)

Note that panic by definition requires flight, either on foot or by other means. Individuals jumped, lowered themselves on lightning cables, pushed their way up stairs and attempted to overrun the rescue helicopters. Flight alone is not necessarily panic, but it would appear that true panic existed at times in this disaster.

Panic as a Design Consideration. Knowledge of basic occupant behavior is necessary to successfully plan and design a building to eliminate the possibility of an occurrence of a panic-producing situation. Actually with the present state of the art this cannot be assured; however, with proper thought the possibility can be substantially reduced.

To better understand the mental processes that a person uses in evaluating a threat situation that could eventually result in panic, Withey (1962) has identified the following elements:

1. *Recognition.* The individual must become aware of the warning stimulus. The threat cues in a fire are usually continuous in nature with an increasing intensity due to the dynamics of flame, heat and smoke. Two factors tend to obscure these warning signals. First, there is an attempt to pattern and structure cues in familiar terms, thereby discounting the threat. Second, people are less likely to predict unfavorable events than favorable ones. Therefore, a harmless plausible explanation is often accepted as the truth in spite of evidence to the contrary.

2. *Validation.* Validation consists of efforts to verify the information previously received. In most threat situations individuals communicate with neighbors to help assess whether the perceived threat is a valid one.

3. *Definition of the Situation.* The individual attempts to obtain information better describing the magnitude, timing and possible losses threatened by the event. The *role* concept adopted by the individual is a very important factor. The fire officer in a threat situation with his entire family may react very differently from his expected professional role. In many instances, roles may conflict thereby making it difficult to even define the appropriate one for the situation.

4. *Evaluation.* Evaluation is the preparation phase for action. It is the step in the decision process where a decision is made to behave in a particular manner. The behavior of others is often a determining factor.

5. *Commitment.* Commitment is the action taken in response to the threat and results in success or failure in alleviating the threat.

6. *Reassessment and Overcommitment.* After the failure of a previous action to alleviate the threat, more intense effort is often expended. At this stage the individual is more susceptible to nonadaptive behavior. As successive failures are encountered, frustation increases and adaptive behavior is more difficult to achieve.

Besides these basic elements of threat evaluation we also have a wide range of ability and speed of perception, comprehension, and action in a group of individuals. Glass (1969) states that

> ... behavior under emergency conditions is dependent upon such variables as the perceived nature and intensity of the traumatic agent, the preset attitude of the individual, variations in individual ability and speed of perception, comprehension and action, and the composition of the group presented with the emergency condition. A state of emergency is subject to differential perception. While the threat is common its perception is relative. Threats which are seen as mild to moderate by one individual may be deemed severe to another and will produce corresponding degrees of apprehension, concern or tension. It is the degree of arousal produced by the perception which motivates response.
>
> Individuals may be categorized within this frequency distribution to predict group responsiveness:
>
> 1. Trained or Emergent Leaders—15% to 20% of the population—quickly grasp available environmental information, integrate the situation with past experience, and make decisions which are realized in effective action.
>
> 2. The Easily Led—approximately 50% of the population—have adequate environmental perception, but are not able to produce adequate solutions or action. While unable to produce actions they are highly suggestible and will respond to either effective leadership or join others in mass flight.
>
> 3. The Poorly Effective or Dependent—10% to 15% of the population—have imperfect perception and difficulty in responding. They require more direct external structuring of their responses.
>
> 4. The Ineffective and Stunned—10% to 25% of the population—have impaired perceptions and give inadequate or irrational responses.
>
> 5. The Withdrawn from Reality—no more than 1% of the population—show primitive behavior with illogical responses or no response. Unable to cope in any manner, they manifest complete psychological withdrawal.
>
> Two factors will greatly affect the proportions of individuals within these categories for a specific occasion:
>
> 1. The Adaptive Time Factor: At the onset of the emergency stress approximately 100% of the population may be noneffective; with the passage of time the ability of the majority of individuals to react effectively shows dramatic increase.
>
> 2. The Group Composition Factor: An untrained heterogeneous group will contain a larger proportion of individuals producing less effective behaviors. A trained and homogeneous group will produce a higher proportion of effective and adaptive behavior. (Meisen, 1977)

If the proper threat definition, evaluation, and action is taken by the "trained and emergent leaders" described by Glass as comprising 15% to 20% of the population, the possibility of panic is substantially reduced or eliminated.

As was noted earlier, intense fear and the feeling of immediately impending entrapment are essential elements in panic. In examining the initial threat evaluation elements described by Withey (1962) it appears that the individual's "Definition of the Situation, Evaluation, and Commitment" can be influenced by design elements of the building ultimately to reduce the possibility of intense fear and the feeling of impending entrapment. This is especially true of the high-rise building which is more adaptive to a controlled environment. If the individual can be kept informed of the problem, is aware of the safety features built into the structure, knows or feels that there are alternate escape routes, and has some preplanning for an emergency, we can greatly increase the possibility that his definition, evaluation and finally his commitment of action will not result in panic. He will not be faced with intense uncontrollable fear, nor feel that he is faced with immediately impending entrapment, two essential conditions of panic.

Recognition of the importance of these items in recent years, especially in high-rise buildings, has resulted in various design features and requirements specifically addressed to not only increasing the actual fire safety of the building but to influencing the reaction of the humans involved, in other words, to enabling the occupants to react properly in order to assist themselves in the emergency and thereby prevent any potential panic from occurring.

The techniques that can be incorporated into our designs may include the following items to improve the individual's response to an emergency:

1. The individual can be kept informed of an emergency and given assurance and instructions through communication systems of various types.

2. The individual can better evaluate his predicament and the course of action he may follow by being made aware of the safety features in the building. Training programs have already been made mandatory by many building managers and by some governmental jurisdictions. Instructional information can also be made available to the building occupants and displayed along with the normal exit signs.

3. A reduction in the possibility of entrapment either actual or perceived can be facilitated by use of compartmentation concepts, smokeproof stairs and elevators, smoke control systems, horizontal exiting techniques, and heliports, to name a few. Special note should be made of the relatively small stair capacities allowed under present regulations. Stairs quickly fill to capacity and become blocked when multiple floors are evacuated at the same time. Recognition must be made of this fact and emergency exiting planned accordingly.

4. Preplanning for an emergency can be handled in many ways including drills for occupants, "floor captains," fire wardens, building managers, and engineers. The local fire department should also be familiar with the emergency systems of a building including the use of communication systems, smoke control systems, and fireman's control features of elevators, among others.

Obviously, the more such features are either designed into the building or made part of the operational requirements by management or by mandatory regulations, the less chance there is that a person will make the wrong decision in his initial threat evaluation; an evaluation that could result in extreme fear. In addition, these features will greatly lessen the possibility of perceived or actual entrapment, an ingredient of true panic.

The Future. Unfortunately, the incidence of panic-producing situations will undoubtedly rise in the future. The general increase in world population coupled with the added sophistication of buildings, equipment, and the increased energy consumption needed to sustain that population, will result in a future increase in disasters of various types and magnitudes. Ideally, the environmental and safety concerns of a more informed and intelligent population will reduce the incidence of disasters; however, past experience indicates that the common course of action is apathy towards a potential hazard until a tragedy of some kind motivates a change.

As we have noted, human behavior in stress situations has received a great deal of attention, but it is also commonly agreed that much is unknown. High stress and panic situations are difficult to evaluate or reproduce. Rubin and Cohen (1974) relate the difficulties:

> The conduct of field studies poses another problem for the investigator —a human one, somewhat akin to the moral one noted earlier. The researcher in a dangerous situation is not immune to the threat that the subjects of the study are exposed to. Under these circumstances, how is it possible to maintain objectivity and not be subject to the stress encountered by everyone sharing the experience? How valid are data collected even by highly trained scientists under these conditions?
>
> The laboratory approach also faces criticism. One can never be certain that a situation is truly stressful for the subjects because this evaluation is highly subjective.
>
> In formulating a systematic program of research in fire safety, an investigator concerned with human responses to emergencies operates under a number of formidable constraints. Unlike the engineer, the social scientist cannot produce destructive experiments at will. Sociologists and psychologists fortunately must stop short of inducing experiences that constitute a real threat to the existence and health of the subjects. Real fires do not stop short.

Obviously, difficult as it may be, answers must eventually be found to the many questions that remain unanswered relative to human behavior under stress conditions. Panic is but one facet of furtive human behavior. Humans are very complex organisms compared to the relatively simple mechanics of fire and the building environment. Some of the more obvious human behavior questions that need additional research follow.

1. Will people perceive "areas of refuge" in a building to be safe environments? Will they attempt to leave the building instead?

2. Will people move up to an area of refuge without being forced by smoke or flame?

3. What messages should be transmitted to people, and in what form, to achieve the best results?

Future research must include the continued study of human behavior, but we should immediately consider features that may be incorporated into our designs based on the present state of the art. This assumes that, given a conscious informed analysis of present human behavior knowledge combined with the technical abilities of our designers, we can develop safer buildings in the near future.

Through an analysis of the superior capabilities of men and machines we may be able to combine the best features of both to develop a system of safety best geared to handle emergencies properly. This does not suggest an answer but a method of development. The following summary comparison of the capabilities of men and machines was made by McCormick (1957).

> Human beings appear to surpass existing machines in their ability to:
> 1. Detect small amounts of sound or light.
> 2. Receive and organize patterns of light or sound.
> 3. Improvise and use flexible procedures.
> 4. Store information and recall relevant facts at the appropriate time.
> 5. Reason inductively.
> 6. Exercise judgment.
> 7. Develop concepts and create methods.
> Existing machines appear to surpass humans in their ability to:
> 1. Respond quickly and dependably to control signals.
> 2. Apply great force smoothly and precisely.

3. Perform repetitive tasks accurately.
4. Store vast amounts of information and then reproduce, summarize or analyze
   that information in a predetermined manner.
5. Perform intricate computations rapidly and accurately.
6. Perform many different functions simultaneously.

An imaginative designer should in the future be able to incorporate the best of
both machine and human systems to achieve a far better end product dealing with
the safety of the humans in a building environment, which, of course, is our prime
concern.

4.6 ARCHITECTURAL LAYOUT AND DETAILS

The architect will be concerned to design the layout of his building in relation to
others to allow for such features as daylighting and views over the city, but the
hazard of fire spread will also be taken into account. Provision of roads and
entrances for occupants and visitors, and for service and other vehicles is another
important feature. The same routes will also be used for fire fighting and
evacuation, and as far as possible the fire safety patterns of movement should
exploit the natural circulation patterns of the building. It is essential to take into
account how the building will be used when it is occupied, since fire safety measures
which interfere with the normal running of the building are likely to be rendered
ineffective by the occupants. The most obvious example is the provision of doors,
intended to restrict smoke and fire spread, which will be wedged open if they
interfere with day to day movement. Therefore such doors should normally be held
open by a device which will operate to close them automatically when a smoke or
heat detector gives a signal. Escape routes will not be kept clear and unobstructed if
there is inadequate storage space or there is no proper provision for removal of
rubbish.

1 Space Around Building

Exposure Hazard.   Radiation from windows of burning rooms and from emerging flames can present an exposure hazard to nearby buildings unless there is
adequate separation (Law, 1963). The amount of space required obviously depends
on the area of facade that is assumed to be burning at any one time. If the building
has effective compartmentation at each floor, then the space required for
daylighting is likely to be more than enough to allow for the exposure hazard. The
use of noncombustible materials for both internal and external surfaces of the
building reduces the external flaming and hence the exposure.

Fire Brigade and Ambulance Access.   A plan for dealing with fires will be
worked out with the local fire brigade. This will take into account fire fighting
access, routes taken by the people escaping from the building, and space for
ambulances to arrive, to provide first aid, and to depart with any casualties. The
layout should be designed to keep these activities separate and to facilitate control
of crowds of sightseers.

2 Space Within Building

Compartment Size.   The traditional method of containing a fire is to provide
compartments of a limited size bounded by fire-resistant walls and floors. This

assists fire fighters, gives less severe fires, and reduces the maximum likely loss. However, as discussed earlier, in modern tall buildings compartmentation may be less effective. The most extreme example is the atrium building where it could be said that most of the building is one single compartment. An alternative method of restricting the size of a fire is a sprinkler installation, but if this is used to compensate for loss of compartmentation, then smoke control measures and means of escape must be very carefully designed. Notwithstanding these active methods of protection, the enclosures of escape routes, places of safety, and fire-fighting access routes (discussed below) must still provide effective compartments. For normal use, a number of floors may be connected by open staircases or escalators, for example in department stores and hotels. Automatic rolling shutters or doors can be used to seal off these separate floors in the event of fire.

Fires in basements tend to be more severe and to present smoke and fire-fighting problems. For these reasons it is particularly important to separate a basement from the rest of the building by an effective compartment floor.

Means of Escape.

General principles. The design of means of escape is a feature which can only be carried out effectively by carefully identifying the potential sources of outbreak

Firemen in action *(Courtesy: Chicago Fire Department)*

of a fire and then predicting the routes which the smoke and hot gases are likely to take. A detailed understanding of the way in which the building is to be used is therefore essential. It is not possible to make comprehensive recommendations to cover every possible risk, but certain principles can be understood and applied.

The basic assumption is that a person should be able to reach a place of safety without assistance, and without using elevators. People are reluctant to move through quite low concentrations of smoke and it is usually assumed that everyone should be able to reach an exit within two to three minutes. The travel distance to an exit is therefore limited. The exit should be to a protected route which leads directly to a place of safety, which may be the open air for the lower floors or a compartment within the building for the upper floors. It need not be assumed that the whole building must be evacuated.

Design of escape route.   A person confronted by a fire should be able to turn his back and make his way unaided to an exit within the given time. In practice this means that there should always be at least two exits in substantially different directions and that exits should be provided at regular intervals. "Dead end" situations should only be permitted where there is a small distance to travel, of under 10 m (33 ft).

The width of corridors and the width, number, and spacing of exits depend on the number of people and the speed of travel, and are always calculated on the assumption that one exit is blocked by fire. Normally there is a lower limit to the width, on the order of 1 m, to allow at least two persons to move shoulder to shoulder. A review of evacuation times (Melinek, 1975) suggests that flow rate is a maximum for population densities between 1 person and 5 persons/m^2. Average measured flow rates, given as persons per meter per sec, are: Level passage, 1.5; stairs up, 1.1; and stairs down, 1.15.

To restrict smoke travel, smoke doors can be provided at regular intervals. Pressurization may also be used. Measures should be provided to ventilate the protected route or otherwise keep it smoke-free. Escape from the roof by helicopter should not be relied on. Wind, heat, and smoke may prevent the helicopter from landing, and it can carry only a limited number of people at a time.

Readily visible, well illuminated signs for exit routes and exit doors should be provided and emergency lighting is essential.

Different occupancies.   Population densities and behavior patterns will vary with the type of occupancy. Where it is not possible to predict the maximum number of people likely to be present, figures based on surveys for the particular locality should be used. Problems for particular types of occupancy are outlined in Section 4.8.

Materials and construction.   It is important to provide noncombustible wall and ceiling surfaces for escape corridors and protected routes. The enclosure of the protected route should have the appropriate level of fire resistance and should not have any openings to storage cupboard, refuse chute, or other fire risks. The whole of an escape route should be clear of obstruction.

3 Construction Details

Materials.   It is probable that most fires start in the contents of a building rather than the structure, so that the main objective in controlling the materials used in construction of the building is to reduce the rate of flame spread and the amount of smoke and toxic gases produced, and to minimize the contribution to the fully developed fire, particularly where external flaming is concerned. (See following paragraphs.) In addition, noncombustible materials should be used for the main elements of structure to avoid problems of the unseen smoldering fire and of reinstatement.

Construction. The details at junctions of elements of structure are important features of safe design. Serious fire spread has occurred, for example, where walls did not continue to meet the underside of the floor slab but stopped at the level of a suspended ceiling, or where a floor slab did not extend as far as the external cladding. All such voids are potential paths for fire and smoke spread.

Services and trunking passing through walls and floors should be protected by fire resisting enclosures. Small pipes may not need such protection; one code of practice, for example (British Standards Institution, 1968), suggests limiting values of 25-mm (1-in.) diam for pipes of combustible material, and 150-mm (6-in.) diam for noncombustible material, provided the pipe is adequately fire stopped where it passes through.

Doors can play an important part in fire safety precautions. Failure of doors usually occurs between the door and the frame or in the ironmongery such as at hinges, latch, or lock rather than in the main body of the door itself. The whole door assembly must therefore be tested. Vision panels of fire-resistant glazing can be provided for fire-resistance periods up to 1 hr.

All methods of fixing must be appropriate to the type of element and proved by test to perform satisfactorily.

4   Security Considerations

The need for ready access under fire conditions often conflicts with the need to keep doors locked for security reasons under normal working conditions. Locked doors can hinder escape and hamper fire fighting. One solution is automatic lock release operated by smoke or heat detectors. Another is the provision of exit door alarms or alarmed panic hardware monitored by a central surveillance unit.

4.7   SAFETY DEVICES

It is generally agreed that the fire safety of occupants, contents, and structure of the modern high-rise building is best achieved by employing a total systems approach in the design of the building and its services. Such a systems approach relies upon the efficient interplay of a number of safety devices. The systems design is dealt with in Section 4.11. This section includes discussion of the safety devices to be employed for: (1) Early detection of fire; (2) communications for exchange of information; (3) containment of the fire; (4) movement of the occupants to safe areas; (5) control of the flow of smoke and hot gases; and (6) the fire-fighting operation. This listing is not necessarily in the order of priority.

1   Fire Detection

Research has developed a family of devices designed to detect one or more symptoms of the incipient stages of a fire. A particular objective is to achieve reasonable sensitivity without a high incidence of false alarms.

Typical symptoms monitored by warning devices are: (1) High air temperature; (2) rapid increase in air temperature; (3) flow of hot-air currents; (4) airborne solids and condensed vapors; (5) airborne ionized matter; (6) radiation from flames; and (7) noises generated by the combustion process.

Thermal Detectors. The better of these detectors give signals only when two criteria are satisfied: the air reaches a predetermined temperature, but at a preset rate of temperature increase. The sensitivity of the devices depends upon the principle of operation, but more particularly upon the thermal lag represented by the heat capacity of the sensing element and its location in the air currents flowing in the compartment. An efficient detection system requires flexibility to permit relocation of point detectors to take account of projections at ceiling level and to conform to subsequent rearrangements of the partitioning layout.

Optical Detectors. The three basic types detect either obscuration or reflection, or they monitor light in the infrared and ultraviolet wavebands.

1. Obscuration detectors give an alarm when the proportion of light received from a standard light source falls below a predetermined value; interruption being caused by airborne particles or refraction by heated air currents. The better devices have a dual photocell arrangement whereby the light output from the source is continually monitored and any alarm signal is based on an out-of-balance between the two photocells. While the latter type overcomes troubles caused by progressive fall-off in lamp efficiency, the inherent liability to false alarms remains as the instruments are unable to differentiate between interruptions to the beam caused by solid bodies, dust in the air stream, or dust accumulated on the reflector or the lens systems.

2. Nephelometer units are designed to measure the amount of light reflected to a receiver by solid particles carried in the air stream. Basically these are a reversal of the principle employed in the type just described, as they monitor the scattered light rather than the direct light. A unit (Gibson and Packham, 1972) has been developed which draws samples of air from selected compartments or from different positions in the return-air system and compares the light scatter with that from an air sample drawn simultaneously from outside the building. The unit can be adjusted to give signals of different urgencies according to the degree of difference in light scatter between the samples.

3. Radiometers having wide angles of view are used to monitor the radiation in either the infrared or ultraviolet wavebands emitted in the compartment under surveillance. The infrared detectors are more commonly used as they can react to the presence of a heat source before the flaming stage of combustion develops. The units are too costly for monitoring small individual offices, but are ideal for the surveillance of large unsubdivided areas, such as landscaped offices. They can be mechanized to scan a large field of view, and one type can distinguish between radiation from, say, an electric room heater and flames of a fire.

Combustion Gas Detectors. Units that monitor the presence of airborne particles in the size range 0.01 μm to 1.0 μm are popularly referred to as combustion detectors. They usually comprise an open chamber and a semisealed reference chamber in which the flows of ionized matter produced by a radioactive source are compared. The presence of very small particles reduces the ion mobility in the open chamber and an alarm is given when the imbalance between the chambers exceeds a preset limit. The units are widely used and do give early warning of most fires, but they have shortcomings. They can give false alarms if the gas velocity increases, and they are insensitive to cold smoke and to the products of pyrolysis of some materials such as PVC.

Superior detectors are available that have both an optical and a combustion detection function incorporated in the one point unit.

Others. Other detection devices exist, ranging from sonic detectors that detect the minor crackling noises emitted when materials burn, to closed-circuit television that allows a single operator to monitor a number of large areas.

2 Communications

If a building is equipped with an efficient fire-detection system connected by landline to a fire station, the fire brigade is automatically summoned and the appropriate person in the building is notified of a fire and its approximate location. If no detection system is installed, the person first discovering the fire has the responsibility of initiating the appropriate action. If the housekeeping of the building has been good, that person will have been instructed and will immediately call the fire brigade and then notify the person responsible for emergency control within the building before taking action to attempt to control the fire.

A central command post for the emergency controller should be located in a position where it will remain safe and accessible during a fire. It should be equipped with mimic panels to read out operation of the detector system, the sprinkler system, the settings of the air-handling system, the stair pressurizing system, and the emergency lighting system so that the controller is aware of conditions throughout the building during any fire. The control post should have a communication systems allowing public address to all stories of the building and permitting the selection of individual stories at will. The system should permit the controller to converse privately with wardens on all stories and the playing of the evacuation signal on any selected story, and the occupants of the building should be familiar with the purpose of those signals. They should be distinctive sounds reserved only for fire emergency use.

3 Containment of the Fire

To contain a fire within the area of its origin it is necessary to isolate the fire in a structural compartment and to take steps to extinguish the fire or retard its development so that it will remain within the compartment until the arrival of the fire brigade.

Fire Doors. Structural compartmentation has been discussed earlier, and it is clear that the effectiveness of such subdivision is weakest at the openings for access by occupants and services. Fire doors have been developed to protect these openings and their effectiveness is rated according to their performance in standard fire-resistance tests (ISO, 1974). A fire door is a compatible assembly comprising one or more leaves, a frame, and operating hardware. Special doors may include features such as glass vision panels.

The reliability of a fire door to resist a fire after years of everyday service as a normal door depends largely upon the quality of hardware items fitted, and upon regular maintenance or replacement of these items. A survey of the condition of fire doors in buildings occupied by Australian Government departments has revealed that the majority of cases of faulty operation of doors result from misalinement of the three hinges commonly used to swing the doors. (United States standards do not permit the use of only two hinges on fire doors.) Another major cause of trouble is the selection of light-duty domestic hardware items such as closers and latchsets for commercial applications where heavy-duty units are necessary.

Fire doors subdividing stories and protecting entrances to stair shafts and elevator shafts should be doors that close automatically as soon as traffic has passed. If for some reason, such as convenience in the everyday operation of the building, it is required to hold a fire door in the open position for extended periods, this should not be done by stays incorporating a thermally released link. Such devices can permit the passage of considerable smoke and hot gas before they release and permit the door to close. The preferred hold-open device is an electromagnet that releases automatically if power fails and if a fire-detection or sprinkler system operates. Hold-open devices are now available that incorporate a smoke detector mounted in the stream of air flowing beneath the door head so that the door closes automatically when smoke arrives at the door. Another advantage of such a hold-open device is that the position of all fire doors can be monitored from

Moving in for overhauling operations *(Courtesy: Chicago Fire Department)*

the central control station and can be released by disconnecting power in an emergency.

Fire Dampers and Fire Stopping. Fire dampers are incorporated at the terminations of air-handling ducts or at the points where ducts pass through walls or ceilings that are required to penetrate a floor that is required to be fire resisting.

Fire dampers must demonstrate their effectiveness in standard fire-resistance tests (ISO, 1968), but at least one national code (SAA, 1974) specifies performance requirements for resistance to cold-air leakage to assure that dampers can be used to impede the passage of cold smoke. Such dampers may be motorized or held open by an electromagnet so that they may be brought to the closed position by operation of a smoke detector monitoring the condition of the air flowing within the duct.

While fire dampers are traditionally constructed of steel, some novel dampers are in course of development including one patented unit (Fire, 1972) that relies upon an intumescent-paint coating to seal the openings in a honeycomb section when the air passing along the duct becomes sufficiently hot. Such a unit does not, however, react to the flow of cool smoke along a duct.

Fire stopping should be employed to seal superfluous openings where services pass through fire-resisting members or to seal gaps in construction, such as spaces between concrete floor slabs and exterior curtain walls. Such fire stopping is intended to prevent the formation of flues that would permit the flow of smoke and hot gases and may take the form of cement grouts, gypsum-vermiculite plaster, or high-temperature mineral wool or batts of ceramic fiber packed solid or otherwise suitably supported to block the opening.

Automatic Water Sprinklers. The record of performance of automatic water-sprinkler systems in high-rise buildings (Marryatt, 1971) shows that these systems are the most effective means of confining a fire to its area of origin until the arrival of the fire brigade. In past years owners have voluntarily equipped many tall buildings in the United States with sprinklers, and since 1960 authorities have demanded that sprinklers be installed throughout buildings exceeding 42 m (135 ft) in height in certain cities of Australia. In the United States, the General Services Administration decided that sprinklers will in future be installed in all government buildings exceeding five stories in height, and several municipal and state authorities require the fitting of sprinklers in tall buildings.

While there are many national codes setting forth rules for the design and installation of automatic water-sprinkler systems, they all have similar formats and are based upon data produced by a few insurance-sponsored research laboratories. Some of these codes have been modified to introduce an extra-light-hazard system for the protection of tall buildings housing low-fire-load occupancies such as offices and domestic apartments. A group of building officials has published a code designed specifically to reduce life hazards rather than property loss. The code requires the mandatory installation of a suppression system essentially designed to contain a fire and to control the total smoke produced [The Building Officials and Code Administrators Life-Hazard Suppression System (BOCA, 1973)].

Economies claimed (Claiborne, 1971) to be possible with a life-hazard suppression system are reduced water supplies, small-bore copper piping with soldered connections, and better water distribution from newly designed heads. It is also hoped that a reduction in the hydraulic pressure of the acceptance test will reduce the mass of the heat-sensing element and thus reduce the considerable thermal lag of the present heads.

Hosereels and Portable Extinguishers. Even in buildings equipped with automatic water sprinkler installations having direct line connection to warn the fire brigade of water flow in the system, it is advisable to have some equipment to permit occupants to combat fire at its incipient stage. The duration and severity of fire that can develop before conventional sprinkler heads are brought into operation is not generally appreciated. A fire may burn at low severity and develop considerable volume of smoke over a period of several minutes before the first sprinkler head operates. The United States building codes generally exempt a sprinklered building from installing wet standpipes hose and spray-control nozzles for use by the occupants. If the fire is more severe than an extinguisher can control, people should evacuate and leave fire extinguishing to the professionals and the sprinklers.

Over the years various portable fire extinguishers have been developed, and efforts are being made to achieve uniformity in their method of operation, to assist the general public.

4 Movement of Occupants to Safe Areas

If a standard fire-evacuation sound were to be adopted internationally, all occupants, whether regular occupants or casual visitors, would know that on hearing the sound they should proceed to the emergency fire stairs, where they would be instructed by floor wardens as to whether they should proceed upwards or downwards, and to what level. So that such an operation will be carried out calmly and in an orderly manner, without having individuals wishing to return to their work stations to carry out some overlooked operation or to collect some forgotten property, regular fire drills are necessary. It may be necessary to include a covenant for fire drills in the tenancy agreement. Regular drills will impress upon occupants that the stairs are the means of emergency vertical movement, and that the elevators will have been automatically taken out of normal service and will be reserved for use at the discretion of the fire brigade.

Emergency Lighting of Exits. Tall buildings are generally equipped with standby diesel generating sets to supply electric power to essential services should there be interruption to the local main supply. During the early stage of a fire such a system can be relied on to provide normal corridor and stair-shaft lighting. However, as fire develops and damages circuit wiring on the fire-involved story, the normal lighting system may fail and essential lighting, such as that identifying exit signs and illuminating stair shafts, should be maintained independently.

Elevators. Experience has demonstrated that elevators may become unsafe during fires in buildings and in general their capacity for evacuation is limited (the NFPA states that elevators shall not constitute required means of egress). They may be necessary for moving handicapped people, and at the present stage of technology the best method of providing reliable and safe vertical transportation during a severe fire is to install the elevator in a fire-resisting shaft having a lobby that is structurally fire-isolated, and in addition has an independent supply of both air and electricity.

The record shows that the principal hazards are: (1) Smoke and heat pollution of the elevator shaft; (2) stopping of cars between floors; (3) thermal and smoke damage to the control panels in the main motor room; (4) thermal distortion of the doors, safety-interlocking devices, and guide runners at the story involved in the fire; and (5) malfunctioning of the elevator car.

The record of elevator performance under fire conditions is such that many building codes now require that warning notices be displayed prominently near call buttons warning people against attempting to use an elevator during a fire in the building.

Many buildings now have independent elevator systems serving different height stages of the building. Such systems can be designed so that a fire may affect the elevators in one height stage only, and thus leave the remaining elevators available for normal operation throughout the emergency. An additional requirement is that selected cars be available for use by firemen, with an overriding manual control from within the car. The emergency telephone within the car can provide a valuable means of communication between the main lobby and firemen on the fire-affected story.

Stair Shafts. Because of the hazards associated with the use of elevators, stair shafts are the means by which occupants can move vertically upward or downward during fires in tall buildings. For a stair shaft to provide safety under severe fire conditions, several ancillary safety devices should be provided:

1. The location of the entrance to stair shafts should be defined by well displayed illuminated signs within the story.

2. The interior of the stair shaft should be clearly illuminated by lighting supplied from a reliable power source.

3. Access opening to the shaft should be fitted with self-closing fire doors.

4. If the stair shaft is not automatically pressurized, entry should be made through a ventilated lobby so as to minimize the amount of smoke that may enter the shaft at each opening of the access door.

A major conflict arises between safety and security considerations in tall buildings that house multiple tenancies. For security reasons it has become accepted that, provided doors provide free access from each story to a stair shaft, they may be locked to prevent entry from the stair shaft to the story. This means that if a person enters a stair shaft and allows the door to close it may be necessary to descend the full height of the shaft before reentry to the building can be gained at street level. Such an arrangement must create a reluctance to use stair shafts under normal conditions and could contribute to panic under fire conditions. The New York Fire Brigade has proposed a compromise by which reentry to the building should be possible within four stories above and below any point of entry to a stair shaft, and the nearest point of reentry should be indicated clearly on every locked door. Another possible compromise is to have all stair shaft doors openable from within the stair shaft, but to have the doors monitored electrically so that upon each opening an audible warning sounds within the story and an alarm signal is indicated at the central control point or security station for the building. Unless some such compromise is reached it could be necessary to require that all latches securing entrance doors to stair shafts in tall buildings be fitted with electrically operated fail-safe swivel strike mechanisms that are de-energized under fire conditions so that they may be forcibly opened from within the shaft when required. Such electrically controlled and monitored security latches are currently available but not universally accepted for fire doors.

5   Control of Flow of Smoke and Hot Gases

Air-Handling Systems. Most tall buildings incorporate air-handling systems which vary considerably according to the climate, the type of occupancy, and the proportion of the day during which the building is occupied.

Opinion has been divided as to the technique that should be used to minimize the contribution of air-handling systems to fire spread. The original technique was to fit dampers at each point of entry to a vertical shaft and to rely upon the heat from the fire to trigger thermally released devices to close the damper when the fire reached a sufficient severity. This technique permitted "cold" smoke to be freely circulated by the recycle system during the early stages of a fire, and caused the hot gases to travel up stair shafts and elevator shafts when eventually the dampers sealed off the air-handling system.

Research and full-scale experiments in buildings equipped with recycle and air-handling systems are leading to general agreement that by incorporating certain safety devices the air-handling system may be used to ease the fire problem rather than to increase it. The Institution of Heating and Ventilating Engineers (1973) has published an excellent summary of the state of the art.

One feature that requires careful consideration is the optimum location of discharge and intake points for air-handling systems. The selection should take into account the effect of prevailing winds and surrounding buildings on the possible intake of smoke discharged from the building or from surrounding buildings.

Local Smoke Venting. Modern furnishings and fittings produce considerable quantities of dense and acrid smoke, and in almost every fire situation some smoke extraction will be needed. While the normal air-handling system may assist in preventing smoke pollution of other stories, it is not likely to have sufficient capacity to purge smoke from the fire-affected story. Accordingly, in most fires, firemen will have to open windows to discharge smoke. Degenkolb (1974) has discussed desirable areas of openable window for cross ventilation to discharge smoke, but there are no firm rules as area-perimeter ratios, potential smoke load, and prevailing wind conditions are important variables. It is clear that the breaking of fixed windows in tall buildings is a public danger if the glass is not annealed so that it shatters into very fine pieces on impact. For this reason, consideration should be given to installation of latch mechanisms to permit firemen to open windows from the story below in cases where the building is heavily heat and smoke logged by the time firemen reach the level of the fire in the building.

Pressurizing Escape Routes. The air pressures developed in compartments during building fires will vary widely according to the severity of the fire, the volume of the compartment, and the degree of inlet and outlet ventilation. Measurements made during experimental fires (Butcher et al., 1968) indicate that with well developed fires pressures on the order of 5 Pa (0.000725 psi) can develop. Experiments in a 3-story building in Australia and in a department store in the United Kingdom (Malhotra and Milbank, 1964) have demonstrated that a pressure differential of 7.5 Pa (0.001088 psi) and higher is sufficient to prevent smoke from a well developed fire leaking past a door. It has been further demonstrated that smoke will not flow through an open door against an air flow on the order of 0.8 m/sec (2.7 fps).

In Australia (SAA, 1974) some local government authorities will waive the requirement for a ventilated lobby approach to stairs in tall buildings provided the stair is equipped with fans and sensors that will automatically, when fire is detected in the building, cause the stair to be positively pressurized with respect to each story. The first building to be tested for these requirements was a 22-story apartment building officially approved in 1962, and since then over 100 buildings exceeding 42 m (135 ft) in height have been so approved in the city of Sydney. The requirements assure that even when firemen lay a hosepipe from story to story via the stair shaft, the opening of at least one other door will not permit smoke to enter the shaft, and even under adverse conditions women and children may gain access to the stair.

The design difficulties will vary according to the height of the building and the difference between the indoor and outdoor temperatures, and will depend on whether the building has a balanced air-handling system. It is not possible to formulate a simple design procedure, but the present state of the art has been summarized (Hobson and Stewart, 1972; JFRO, 1969), and full-scale tests have demonstrated the effectiveness of the system (Moulen, 1973; Butcher and Hall, 1971; Building Services Engineer, 1971). It is most important that the performance be achieved when all other building systems are operating in the fire mode, and that the air-handling systems for smoke control in buildings are brought into action automatically when fire is detected, even at those times when the comfort air-handling system may be shut down for economy or for maintenance.

6   Concluding Remarks

The effectiveness of most of the devices described is dependent upon a continuing supply of either electricity or water. While these may be supplied from standby diesel generators and from holding tanks, respectively, the continuing delivery to the particular apparatus needs to be assured. This is particularly the case with electrical supply to vital emergency equipment, such as exhaust fans and stairwell pressurizing fans, firemen's elevators, emergency lighting, and communications systems. Attention must be given to design detail, and the use should be considered of both independent parallel circuitry and copper-sheathed, mineral-insulated-copper conductors for supply to vital equipment.

4.8   PARTICULAR TYPES OF OCCUPANCY

Among the most significant characteristics determining the degree of fire safety problem in any building is the occupancy, which is usually defined in terms of the people, processes, and things confined within the space of the building. These usually form the basis for major fire safety code criteria. There is little wonder why occupancy plays such an important role, because it is the differences among the activities in a building that most clearly distinguish fire hazards and exposures between one activity and the next.

Most people concerned with fire safety recognize the tremendous overlap between the consideration given to protecting people and property, but here, too, the differences that do exist are based on occupancy characteristic differences.

The matter of protecting property adequately is usually viewed as secondary to the responsibility to provide adequate life safety. Through satisfactory provisions for life safety, a suitable degree of property protection can be achieved. However, continuity of operations may be important for business reasons—for example, furnishing automatic data processing support for vital company-wide information systems—or for social reasons, for example, reinstating a hospital or a medical supplies center to full working order, and a higher standard of protection would therefore be required.

The following articles will briefly review some of the differences among the several occupancy classifications most commonly used.

1   Assembly Occupancies

Assembly occupancies include all buildings or portions of buildings used for gathering together a number of persons for such purposes as deliberation, worship, entertainment, amusement, or awaiting transportation. They are characterized by high concentrations of people who frequently are unfamiliar with the environment. The "processes" include everything from performing, religion, and dining, to exhibiting products, concepts, and the arts. Contents can range from nothing more than the people observing an oral presentation to elaborate furnishings and decorations and large quantities of materials being displayed. Ignition sources introduced into these environments can include smoking materials (often prohibited), and open flames for magical fetes and demonstrations such as cooking, glass blowing, metal sculpturing, etc.

The principal concern in assembly occupancies with respect to life safety is to furnish adequate relief from congestion at the time of an emergency, thereby avoiding panic. Therefore, adequate means of escape, including the access to exits, the exits from the fire area, and the discharge from the exits to a safe location, must be of sufficient capacity to preclude jamming. With high-rise buildings a common desire is to place conference facilities and restaurants on the top floor to take advantage of the scenery from the top of the building or to capitalize on the psychological rewards of "reaching the top." This poses particular problems in terms of life safety, since there is a tendency for the adverse effects of fire to "seek" the upper portions of a building (Juillerat and Gaudet, 1967).

Another important factor in emergency evacuation is that the layout contributes to efficient movement of people. Heavy reliance on the occupants being familiar with the location is usually unreasonable, and due consideration must be given to the ability to furnish inherent understanding by means of the layout, symbolic instructions (exit signs, etc.) and, if necessary, local instructions responsive to the confusion and noise during the emergency itself.

2   Educational Occupancies

Generally, this occupancy classification is limited to those parts of a building in which direct instruction is given and presents the characteristics of assembly occupancies. Peripheral activities, such as laboratories and library facilities, may be considered to be under other occupancy classifications.

Pupils range from very small children through post-college graduate work into the later years of life in industrial and adult educational programs. Therefore, the characteristics of the people range from the very young, who must be highly trained and led in an emergency, to the generally self-reliant and able adult occupant. The people involved are usually familiar with the environment after a few classes of instruction. Contents in these facilities are usually limited to chairs and tables or desks, and the characteristic fuel loading is almost universally light to moderate, depending on the construction of furniture used.

The most important concerns for life safety have to do with controlling the environment in which the student is placed, his ease of evacuation, and his awareness of and confidence in the means for evacuation. Children are usually well trained in the proper procedures for following instructions and leaving schools during fire alarms. One of the most common characteristics for dealing with very young children is not to permit them above the ground floor, as they have difficulty negotiating stairs. On the other hand, college students are seldom drilled in evacuation procedures, but are generally quite capable of negotiating stairs and of appraising the best means for escape and locating the necessary escape routes.

Consideration must be given to protection of educational occupants from exposure to subordinate occupancies, such as cooking and industrial arts.

3 Health Care (Institutional) Occupancies

These facilities are used for treatment or care of people suffering from physical or mental illness, disease, or infirmity; for the care of infants, convalescents or aged persons; and for penal or corrective purposes. They provide sleeping facilities and are occupied by persons who are mostly incapable of self-preservation because of age, physical or mental disability, or because of security measures not under the occupants' control. The processes in institutional facilities are many and varied in terms of occupancy process hazards. However, they are frequently associated with flammable gases, in combination with electrical equipment, serious hazards, and problems of control associated with smoking, etc. The contents range in terms of fuel loading from light to moderate, with a moderate to high degree of ignitability.

High-rise buildings have been used for health care facilities and penal institutions for a number of years. Hospitals have experienced significant fires (Juillerat, 1962) which have led to valuable improvements in fire protection in general. The characteristics already described for these types of facilities demand a life safety system which depends on a minimum of movement of the occupants.

The structural isolation of occupants from fire is a major characteristic of the most commonly employed fire protection systems. The value of the defense afforded by automatic extinguishment, which carries with it early control of fires before they become serious, has received well justified growing recognition, and entire hospitals and nursing homes are more commonly being designed to incorporate and rely upon these systems.

Penal institutions, which generally represent a mixture of many occupancy types, have found difficulty in employing automatic extinguishment in view of the tendency for the inmates themselves to incapacitate the systems. Subsequently, various schemes are being sought to counter these sabotage activities, and it is hoped that the near future will offer acceptable solutions to dealing with the problem.

Life safety in health care and penal institutions depends heavily on minimizing the combustibility of the environment. Isolation or automatic extinguishment protection (or both) for higher hazard areas is necessary. A well-trained, competent staff must be prepared to play a necessary role in the protection and rescue system of the institution. These system needs and protection considerations for institutional occupancies are common to low and high-rise buildings, but the further limitations imposed by high-rise buildings require further compensation for and better recognition of all these factors.

4 Residential Occupancies

A residential building is one in which sleeping accommodation is provided for normal residential purposes and includes all such buildings except institutional occupancies.

In terms of high-rise design, they are generally limited to apartments, hotels, and dormitories. The primary differences among these are that in apartment and dormitory buildings the occupants are generally quite familiar with their surroundings and the emergency facilities, whereas in hotels people generally stay for a short period and seldom bother to familiarize themselves with either the hazards or the emergency facilities available to them. On the other hand, hotel guests do not cook meals or do other household tasks.

The basic living spaces in all these subclasses are characterized by a light to moderate fuel loading represented by the furnishings that accompany dining, lounging, conversing, and study. Apartments also contain the equipment associated with domestic cooking. All of these facilities can carry with them various allied occupancy activities such as storage, and centralized building equipment; hotels in particular include dining, centralized restaurant facilities (cooking and dining), laundries, and exhibit, meeting, and administrative facilities. Therefore, mixed occupancy is usual in hotel buildings, and this can have a significant fire exposure impact on the residents.

In both hotels and apartment buildings, the living units should be individual compartments. Because of the traditional, social, and political aspects of residential occupancies ("a man's home is his castle"), there is a longstanding concept of "insulating" one dwelling unit from others through fire resistive separations. This concept recognizes the responsibility of the community to assure that a neighbor is not unduly exposed by a neighbor's carelessness with fire. Where there is a high degree of compartmentation within residential occupancies there is little risk of a holocaust. Nevertheless, there have been incidents of apartment fires in which corridors and even other apartments were filled with smoke and heat without the fire itself leaving the room of fire origin, primarily as a result of breakdown in the compartmentation of the building (Peterson, 1969; Watrous, 1969). Despite the greater control that can be exercised over the contents of hotel rooms, the same principles still apply. Therefore, it continues to be highly important that occupants of all residential buildings be furnished with early warning of their danger when fire occurs, and that they expedite their departure before the conditions become intolerable within the escape routes.

Because of the relatively low density of people in high-rise hotel and apartment occupancies, the adequacy of exit capacity has seldom been a problem. However, failure to enclose stairwells, eliminate dead-end corridors, and properly control elevators during emergencies has been the cause of recurring incidents of life loss.

5 Mercantile Occupancies

Mercantile occupancies include stores (shops), markets, and other rooms, buildings, or structures for the display and sale of merchandise. The customers are frequently in high concentrations, in an unfamiliar environment. The buildings usually contain a moderate to high fuel load which can significantly expose other tenants as well as other parts of the building. High-rise buildings may contain only mercantile occupancies, but more often mercantile occupants use only a number of lower floors, thereby presenting a relatively high fuel loading of relatively easily ignitible contents located beneath floors used for other (residential or office) occupancies.

Although sprinkler protection is probably the most effective available and reliable single life safety system component in any high-rise occupancy, it is an essential mechanism for the control of fire and protection of life where mercantile occupancies are on multiple floors. Characteristic of mercantile occupancies are a combination of relatively high fuel loading in relatively large undivided areas, frequently crowded conditions, and unenclosed floor openings furnishing stair and escalator access between floors. Major disasters have occurred in high-rise buildings containing retail department stores on the first several floors with neither sprinkler protection nor enclosed floor openings (Watrous, 1973; Willey, 1972b). Other important features to prevent confusion and ensuing panic are that all exit facilities and signs be clearly distinguishable from other visual displays, and that the method of evacuation to safety be inherently explicit within the arrangement of the space layout and the marking of the exit facilities.

6 Office Occupancies

Office occupancies are used for the transaction of business other than mercantile, for the keeping of accounts and records, and similar purposes. They may include small doctors' clinics for outpatient service and libraries. Offices usually contain a mixture of people both familiar and unfamiliar with the locality, although the highest concentration is usually of those who frequent the space daily and therefore know the layout. Processes are service oriented. Fuel loadings are light to moderate, depending on construction of furniture and the configuration of materials (paper) being handled and stored, as well as the containers for those materials. Ignition sources are generally very limited and well controlled. Office occupancies frequently are exposed by other occupancies, such as mercantile or light industrial activities in the same building.

As in all high-rise buildings, the dependence on adequate structural support systems and an adequate degree of compartmentation between floors is necessary. But lack of enclosure of floor openings, excessive fuel loading through the misuse of combustible materials in interior finishes and decorations, and failure to isolate floors from each other through poor workmanship enclosing construction openings and perimeter floor and wall panel joints, have proved catastrophic in several fires including some widely publicized fires in the United States (Powers, 1971a, 1971b; Willey, 1973). While the crowding conditions experienced in assembly and other occupancies do not prevail in offices, large numbers of people can become exposed to a single fire, and the potential for disaster is equally serious in a high-rise office building (Sharry, 1974). Therefore, the provision of a suitable personnel movement system (which may be not evacuation but relocation of occupants) is imperative. The orientation of the occupants with that system and how it is designed to protect them is essential to success in furnishing life safety to office occupants. A high degree of success can be expected through the provision of automatic sprinker protection, and this approach offers the maximum degree of flexibility in office layout throughout the life of a building.

7 Industrial Occupancies

Industrial occupancies include factories making products of all kinds and properties devoted to operations such as processing, assembling, mixing, packaging, finishing or decorating, and repair, but also including laboratories and laundries. High-rise industrial buildings are not common in new construction, but there is every reason to expect that the value of land and its conservation will be recognized in the future construction of buildings for industrial use, just as it is for office and other occupancies.

They are characterized by people, equipment, and facilities involved in the processes of converting materials to more usable forms. People are generally able-bodied and self-sustaining in terms of protecting themselves during emergencies; they are also familiar with at least the environment and area in which they perform their duties. Industrial occupancies probably have the greatest variety of hazards in terms of ignition sources and fuel loads among the many different industries. Variety is found in both the processes and the contents, which may range from light to very high fuel loading. Life safety for these facilities must therefore be designed on a systems approach. Most industrial facilities incorporate a relatively high degree of property protection afforded by automatic sprinkler protection in view of the favorable insurance rate treatment or local code mandate. This should not be the basis for complacency in considering life safety at every opportunity to assure that layouts and exposures are in accord with good life safety fundamentals, and that potential for entrapment through inaccessibility to exits is not overlooked.

In those industries incorporating industrial processes and production lines, the problems of compartmentation can seldom be adequately met through conventional methods (fire walls and floors), and automatic suppression becomes a critical response to the need to minimize the spread of fire through unavoidable vertical openings serving production processes.

8 Storage Occupancies

Storage portions of tall buildings are primarily for the storage or shelter of goods, merchandise, products, and vehicles. They are characterized by high concentrations of value and a wide variety of combustible contents ranging from low hazard to very high hazard materials. Storage facilities can house critical materials, particularly when continuity of production or of supplying markets depends on the materials stored. Highly active storage facilities, such as in mail order catalog operations, take on the characteristics of industrial operations in terms of both staffing (life safety) and exposure to ignition sources from the higher level of traffic.

Though important regardless of occupancy, life safety is not such a problem in storage facilities because they usually contain few people, and ignition during occupancy can normally be detected by employees early enough for escape. As automated materials handling equipment becomes more common, the life safety risk will possibly be reduced further. Nevertheless, it is important that favorable experience not breed complacency among those responsible for life safety in storage facilities. It is important to avoid dead ends in the layout and to assure that high hazard materials are properly isolated so personnel are not exposed to fire risk.

Like industrial properties, designated warehousing facilities are usually protected by automatic sprinklers because of: (1) Higher probability of maintaining continuity of critical activities dependent on warehouse support; and (2) the advantages of lower insurance costs. However, it must be recognized that tall buildings tend to have deep basements, which may become filled over the years with discarded goods, often under inadequate supervision.

9 Buildings under Construction

An important fire safety consideration of buildings under construction is the following: at no time during the life of a building will it be exposed to a higher level of fire threat than during its construction or alteration. The physical capabilities of people in a building during construction are perhaps most favorable—construction workers are among the most rugged and able-bodied of individuals. However, the building contains a greater number of ignition sources, such as those accompanying welding, smoking, and temporary wiring. There are relatively uncontrolled fuel loads in the form of building materials, concrete forms, and cartons and wrappings; structural steel supports of the building are unprotected; fire protection facilities and equipment are in varying degrees of readiness; the building and fires within it are exposed to high winds; and housekeeping is difficult to control. Beyond this, portions of the building may be occupied prior to completion of construction, thereby adding to those exposed by the construction work. Exit facilities may not be entirely under control.

Life safety is dependent on the application of the same principles during the construction period that apply upon completion and full occupancy of the building. Exit facilities must be complete and maintained clear of obstructions. The relationships and configuration of uncompleted facilities must not expose the occupants to fire risk in the occupied areas, and the means of egress must be protected from the fuel load imposed by construction materials. Fire protection systems must be installed and working. Housekeeping must be maintained throughout the process. Packing materials of both construction and moving operations must be kept cleared from the building to minimize the potential for easily ignited fires. Usually it is necessary to assign one or more individuals specifically to the responsibility of surveillance over these conditions, since the demands of completing construction and contracts frequently distract responsible supervision from these important duties.

4.9 PROVISIONS FOR FIRE FIGHTING

The height and architectural configuration of modern tall buildings has required a significant change in the traditional fire-fighting techniques that were developed and used to cope with fires in conventional lower buildings. These unique characteristics of tall buildings result in special concerns to the fire service which involve, among other things, the problems they encounter in attempting to gain access to the upper floors in emergency situations, and the communication equipment malfunctions they routinely experience from these massive steel and reinforced concrete structures. The fire services are also concerned with the difficulties encountered in attempting to vent smoke or control smoke movement due to the tremendous stack effects and high wind conditions normally found at the upper elevations. In addition, the need to protect occupants in place rather than attempt mass evacuation, and the operational limitations of an exclusively interior attack on the fire, also complicate their successful fire-fighting effort.

These problems and others must be offset by special architectural design provisions and by the inclusion of additional mechanical features which specifically address the problem areas.

1 Preplanning

Architectural design varies from building to building, as do the location and operation of equipment vital to fire-fighting operations; therefore, one important

Cleaning out glass fragments to protect citizens on street below (Courtesy: Chicago Fire Department)

aspect of any successful rescue and fire-fighting operation in a tall building is the need for the fire service to know the building and its equipment prior to an actual emergency. The officers from the first responding station should have a thorough knowledge of the architectural and mechanical features of all tall buildings in their area. They should also have a working arrangement with the building management on procedures to be followed by both the fire service and building management in an emergency. This preplanning can reduce delays and confusion and substantially affect the success of both rescue and fire-fighting efforts.

However, although preplanning is a normal function of a professional metropolitan fire service, several practical considerations greatly limit the extent to which it can be relied upon for fire system design purposes. First, there may be a large number of tall buildings within a congested central area, and it is not possible for fire fighters to have a detailed knowledge of each. Secondly, over the life span of a typical building a certain amount of renovation and remodeling can be expected so that the configuration of a building will change periodically, complicating preplanning by the fire service. Thirdly, the rotating shift arrangements and normal turnover of personnel result in a fairly large number of people who would have to become familiar with a given building. Finally, it is possible that when a fire does occur in a given building, the normal first responding unit would be unavailable and another unit would have to respond to the emergency. In view of these facts, two principles should be adhered to in fire systems design:

1. Within a given fire department jurisdiction, fire system components must be fairly uniform from building to building in their operation, location, and general arrangement.

2. A fire system design cannot include as a requirement for its successful use a complex or unique operating procedure for the fire service. It is the obligation of the designer to make the building system compatible with the local fire service's operating procedure.

These considerations may be significant constraints to the designer; however, they provide for more efficient and effective operations by the fire service.

2 Access to Fire

First priority for arriving fire fighters is the evaluation of the fire, that is, to establish its exact location, its size and potential for spread, its impact on the occupants, and the means necessary to contain and extinguish the fire. This is most often done by a firsthand observation of the fire by fire service personnel using the elevators when possible to reach the scene of the fire.

Unless the elevators can be made available immediately to the fire fighters, dangerous delays may result. To facilitate this evaluation and subsequent fire fighting at least one elevator and preferably all elevators should be controllable by use of a fireman's switch at the ground floor level. When operated the switch immediately returns the elevator to ground floor; thereafter, and until the switch is cancelled, the elevator is controllable only from within the car. Again, at least one fireman's elevator must have an independent electrical supply through an emergency circuit and be capable of operation on the emergency electrical power system. In theory this elevator should provide a safe and reliable method whereby men and equipment could be vertically transported to the scene of a fire with a minimum of delay.

There have been, however, many accidents throughout the world involving both firemen and building occupants in elevators which have engendered an inherent distrust of their safety in the early stages of a fire. It is normal standard practice for fire personnel to travel by elevator to a point one or two floors below the lowest known fire floor for safety reasons, and then to carry their equipment the remaining one or two floors. Through misunderstanding or error, elevators have, in certain instances, proceeded directly to a fire floor, the doors have opened and the occupants have been incinerated or suffocated. Manual control of the car doors by the fire fighters is essential; however, door warping from heat on the fire floor has in various cases jammed the door in the open position.

Also the electrical supply is subject to failure and may trap personnel in hazardous situations. The electrical supply to the elevator is susceptible to short circuits caused by the water used in fire-fighting operations. Elevator electrical equipment is very difficult and expensive to make waterproof, although it would certainly be desirable to incorporate this feature.

There is a certain amount of risk taken when using an elevator in a fire emergency; however, in many cases the elevator is the only practical means to transport men and equipment to the upper portions of a tall building. As many reliability features as possible should be built into the elevator systems to minimize these risk factors.

An ideally safe elevator arrangement would have the elevator in a separate tower or separated from the main portion of the building with a smokeproof and fireproof enclosure, mechanically or naturally vented to the outside. Exterior elevators must be protected from fire on each floor by appropriate fire shields if they are to be used in emergencies.

3 Communications

After the first arriving crews have reached the fire area, they must communicate their evaluation of conditions to Fire Command in order to properly coordinate rescue and fire-fighting operations. Because of the unreliability of the fire service radios in buildings, a built-in communication system must be available for use by the fire fighters. Communication devices should ideally be located in the stairwells, near standpipes, and in elevator cars for contact with Fire Command on the ground floor. In addition, a selective communication system should be available for use by Fire Command to issue appropriate instructions to the building occupants.

4 Central Control Stations

These communication systems should be controlled by Fire Command at a Central Control Station on the ground level. This station should also be capable of monitoring elevators, water and electrical supplies, and all mechanical equipment in the building which could affect smoke movement, as well as control any stair door unlocking systems. The over-all fire-fighting and life-saving operations would be controlled from this station.

5 Sprinklers and Compartmentation

Due to the height of many modern tall buildings it is impractical to evacuate the occupants in an emergency. It then becomes necessary to provide protection for these people while they remain in the building. This may be accomplished through the use of areas of refuge or by automatic extinguishing systems.

Sprinkler systems, when properly designed, installed, and maintained, provide a very good first stage fire-fighting capability. Ideally, the system should be provided with a two-source water supply, emergency electric power for pumps, and a value monitoring system. Earthquake-prone areas must consider the potential damage problems. Consideration should also be given to the possibilities of explosion damage either accidental or otherwise.

Adequately designed safe areas of refuge (compartmentation) may also be used. They represent a more passive system for fire protection, but still would require mechanical equipment to maintain differential air pressures in adjacent compartments, smoke exhaust capabilities, and door closing devices.

Both sprinklers and areas of refuge (compartmentation) have their strong and weak points in providing safety to the fire fighters and building occupants, and as a means of facilitating the fire-fighting operations. They represent different approaches to the same problem. Both can be effective when properly designed and maintained. The communication system is a very important element in the successful use of a compartmentation or sprinkler concept as it relates to the proper protection of building occupants. Communication with occupants is essential.

6 Standpipes

The basic objective of fire fighting is to reach the seat of the fire with sufficient extinguishing agents to put it out. In other words, a fire emergency cannot be ended until a fire fighter brings a hose to bear upon it, or in the case of a sprinklered building, completes extinguishment. Here the distinguishing characteristic of a tall building—its height—works against the fire fighter in two ways: (1) It is difficult to advance hose lines manually up many flights of stairs; and (2) considerable pressure is needed to deliver water to the level of the fire. Consequently, provision for the operation of hose lines must be included within the structure. This takes the form of standpipes.

Standpipe systems and their associated pumping equipment can be simple or complex depending on building height. However, in every case they should be located within the fire-resistive stairwell enclosures to give fire fighters a protected point from which to begin their attack and to provide a reliable means of escape should that be necessary. In buildings with large floor areas additional standpipes may be provided in the tenant spaces some distance from the stairwell to provide flexibility, but the stairwell standpipes should never be omitted. Standpipe hose connections should obviously be standardized and be compatible with fire service hose sizes. The water may be pumped from below or it may be supplied from gravity tanks at the top of the building. The use of gravity tanks is a more reliable means of supply in the event of a power failure. Pressure, however, may not be adequate at the top of the building with a gravity tank and the tank weight increases the structural cost of the building frame. Pumping water from below permits a more compact system with adequate pressure but requires that provisions be made to assure reliability.

Motor fire apparatus can be used to supply standpipes through street level connections and may be the only sources of supply to a building height of approximately 107 m (350 ft) [based on an engine discharge pressure of 1724 kPa (250 psi)].

When the building height exceeds 107 m (350 ft), depending upon engine discharge pressure, it is usually not possible for street level pumpers to supply water to the top of the building. The fire service is then totally dependent on the building's water supply system to fight the fire. In these cases, the reliability of the standpipe system is critical. Reliability is accomplished in two ways: simplicity of design and duplication of components. All mechanical and electrical components must be kept as simple as possible to reduce the possibility of malfunction and to ease maintenance. The fire system is not used on a daily basis and will stand by idle for long periods of time. When needed, however, it must be instantly available.

The operation of the standpipe system must be automatic and that requires various pressure-sensing switches, flow indicators, and supervisory devices. However, elaborate control systems with numerous delicate components, or systems with sensing devices operating in series, should be avoided.

In very tall buildings all components and power supplies must be duplicated so that if one component fails the other can provide at least partial service. Two independent sources of power should be provided for fire pumps. There should be two separate pumps serving each separate portion of the standpipe system. If one pump fails or is out of service for repairs, then the other pump can be placed on line. One of the pumps should be directly powered by its own diesel engine or be supplied power from the emergency generator operated by the diesel engine. The fire pumps should discharge into separately controllable standpipe risers. Duplicate water supplies must be provided either through separate supply mains or through the use of an on-site reservoir. Reliability is essential.

7 Stair Door Unlocking Systems

Fire-fighting operations normally start below the fire floor and progress up through the stairwells to the fire floor. When stair doors are locked from the stair side for security reasons, provisions must be made for an automatic unlocking capability controllable from the Fire Command Station, or else adequate equipment must be available to the fire fighters to gain access through the stair fire doors. Such stair use by the fire fighters will quite often make egress by that stair impractical for occupants above the fire floor and reinforces the need for areas of safe refuge for the occupants or a reliable sprinkler system to contain the fire at its onset.

8 Emergency Electric Power

Emergency generators should be available to operate at least one elevator which serves all floors of the building, all fire pumps as previously mentioned, any mechanical equipment necessary for smoke control or smoke exhaust, and the emergency lighting and exit and instruction signs. Diesel driven generators have a better reliability record and are preferred. In addition, the main electric vaults, emergency generators, and main electric risers, should be in locations protected from fire or water damage.

9 Smoke Control

Because of the normally fixed window design of many tall buildings, fire-fighting personnel must be prepared to operate in blinding smoke and noxious and toxic gas conditions. Self-contained breathing apparatus must be available along with adequate supplies of reserve air. Ideally, the mechanical air-handling equipment should be available for use to exhaust smoke or to provide differential pressures to control smoke movement. The introduction of fresh air, if available, must be at the discretion of the officer in charge. An adequate communication system is mandatory for these types of operations.

If the safety of civilians and fire personnel on the ground can be assured, the fire might be vented by breaking windows. This is, however, potentially dangerous in tall buildings because of the normally ever-present wind. Ideally, windows or panels that can be opened at the discretion of the fire-fighting personnel should be provided. Mechanical or natural draft smoke shafts operable by the fire personnel at the scene of the fire would also be of benefit.

10   Use of Helicopters

Experimental work has been done using specially equipped fire service helicopters to hoist and direct hoses for exterior attacks on fires at heights above the reach of ground-based hoses. Hose capacities are as yet limited, and obviously building configuration, site, and weather conditions are factors in the success of such operations.

Although fires should, whenever possible, be approached from below, there are times, especially with buildings providing safe areas of refuge, when an approach from above may be necessary or desirable. There may also be instances when rescue or the removal of casualties would best be accomplished from the top of the structure. To accommodate such possibilities a clear area should be provided at the roof level suitable for an emergency landing by a helicopter. These areas need not be designed as heliports. Roof design loads need not be increased. All that is needed is a conscious awareness on the part of the designer and building manager that emergency operations by helicopter from the roof should be considered.

11   Conclusion

The possibility of a fire in a tall building over the life of the building is quite high, especially in residential occupancies. However, the probability of a very serious fire occurring is small, depending, of course, on the adequacy of the design features and equipment mentioned. The fire service must have a built-in advantage in all fire emergency situations in tall buildings in order to adequately protect the occupants and control the fire. They can only achieve this advantage with the cooperation of the designer and building management.

4.10   SYSTEMS DESIGN

1   Goal-Oriented Approach

The goal-oriented systems approach to fire safety will be an important part in future design of buildings. It is a system that is responsive to operational goals established for protection of life or property, or both.

The goals as they apply to a particular building become design parameters, or performance requirements. These parameters establish the actual quality level to be met by the designer. The parameters lead to an over-all qualitative view of the various elements and subsystems that influence the achievement of the parametric requirements. The system is based on an axiom that there is no state of absolute safety and no way of providing absolute assurance of fulfillment of any individual parameter. It is probabilistic. The system demonstrates the interrelationship of system elements and the basic protocol of element arrangement. The more exact the available data for numerical probability the more exact the results. Where probability data cannot be firmly developed, prudence will require the type of conservative position traditionally taken in the establishment of fire-safety requirements. Therefore, the more exact the data the more flexible the system.

The system output is visualized in the form of specific design requirements developed by the designer. These requirements are to be individually unregulated but collectively responsive and valid to the system parameters.

There are four main areas of value in this approach:

1. It provides a system that will more correctly and with a greater surety provide for the safety of the occupants, visitors, and users of the buildings, better assure the preservation of the investment in those buildings, and better provide for the continuance of the operations and services housed within them. It provides a mechanism of avoiding underdesigned facilities, with the expectation of periodic disastrous consequences, while simultaneously breaking away from elements of gross overdesign of safety, with the resultant interference with operations and limitations on progress in design innovation.

2. The system approach provides the maximum degree of flexibility that will allow the designer the widest possible range in meeting all his client's objectives within the safety parameters established. Innovation and trade-off within the system are distinctly possible.

3. Cost effectiveness. The approach is particularly worth while in those considerations where the protection of life needs have been satisfied, and the prime consideration is the degree of protection to be provided to property or to the continuity of an operation.

4. Systems manageability. Since the system is goal-oriented, a change in goals reflects itself in a change in parameters that permeate through the entire system or the portion of a system affected by a particular parameter. This provides management with capability of executing its goals with confidence without having to attempt to rationalize the individual impact of a specific design requirement.

The parameter level constitutes the interface between management direction and design execution. In this analogy management controls the inputs to the parameters and design controls the fulfillment of parameters.

The expectations are outlined in matrix form, shown in Fig. 4.31. It compares the expected performance from a goal-oriented systems approach with the predecessor types of fire-safety control systems typified by the specification code of former years and the component performance code approach generally in current use. This matrix uses relatively simplistic approaches, and the labels are generalizations.

The first consideration is Level of Safety. Both the specification code and the component performance code are public safety oriented and they do not consider the proprietary or business and operational interest of the building owner, nor do they state their objective level of safety. In the case of the goal-oriented system it is essential to state the actual level of safety requirements.

The next column in the matrix considers Flexibility. In the specification code, flexibility was limited to a few carefully detailed alternate building systems. Today's component performance code is much broader than this old specification code in its flexibility, but although permitting a wide degree of flexibility for the specific component or subsystems, it allows no trade-off between component systems. In the goal-oriented system the degree of flexibility is potentially total, limited only by the capability of meeting the system parameters.

The third column in the matrix considers Cost Effectiveness. Obviously, the specification type code had little capability for cost effective development due to the rigidity of the requirements. In the component performance system there is a limited range of options, and basically no methodology of accounting for the worth of an option that is better than the minimum legal requirement. In the goal-oriented system, broad responsiveness to cost effective efforts is executed in consort with the fire safety parameters.

The fourth column is headed Responsiveness to Goals. If we were talking about the goal-oriented system only we would call it manageability. In the specification or component code approach, the goals have not been expressed and the codes only recognize conforming or nonconforming. This technically makes one violation of the code as serious as another and provides no mechanism for counterbalancing such by increased protection in some other area.

The next consideration, related to responsiveness, is headed Measurement of

	LEVEL OF SAFETY	FLEXIBILITY	COST/ EFFECTIVENESS	RESPONSIVENESS TO GOALS	MEASURABILITY OF RESULTS	RESPONSIVENESS TO BUILDING TECHNICAL ADVANCES (& INNOVATION)	IMPLEMENTATION EFFORT AND TALENT LEVEL
SPECIFICATION CODE	CAN FUNCTION WITHOUT ACTUAL LEVEL STATED EXPERIENCE BASED PUBLIC SAFETY ORIENTED	STRICTLY LIMITED TO DETAILED ALTERNATIVES	VERY LITTLE CAPABILITY DUE TO RIGIDITY OF REQUIREMENTS	UNDETER- MINABLE	GO-NO-GO NO DEVIATION ACCEPTABLE	NON-REACTIVE RESISTIVE	SIMPLE (COOK BOOK) APPLICATION
COMPONENT PERFORMANCE CODE	NO ANALYTIC MEASUREMENT PROPRIETARY INTERESTS NOT CONSIDERED FALLS SHORT IN HIGH-RISE	RIGID IN ARRANGEMENT VARYING FLEXIBILITY ALLOWED FOR SPECIFIC COMPONENTS	LIMITED RANGE OF OPTIONS		BASICALLY GO-NO-GO DEVIATIONS OR ADJUSTMENT CONSIDERED NON- COMPLIANCE	ACCEPTS ITEM DEVELOPMENT RESTRICTS MOST SYSTEM CONCEPTS	SPECIALIZED TECHNICIANS AND INFORMATION DESIRABLE
GOAL ORIENTED SYSTEM PERFORMANCE	ANALYTICALLY BASED NECESSARY TO STATE ACTUAL LEVEL CAN BE SET TO INCLUDE ALL DESIRED OBJECTIVES	POTENTIALLY TOTAL (SUBJECT TO SYSTEM PARAMETERS)	BROAD RE- SPONSIVENESS TO COST EFFECTIVE EFFORTS IN CONSORT WITH FIRESAFETY PARAMETERS	AS GOOD AS MEASUREMENTS AND DATA USED	RECOGNIZES IMPOSSIBILITY OF ABSOLUTE ASSURANCE OF ANY GOAL MEASURES PERFORMANCE PROBABILITY	READILY REACTIVE ACCEPTS NEW CONCEPTS BASED ON THE ESTABLISHED CAPABILITIES	PROFESSIONAL TECHNOLOGY

Fig. 4.31 Comparison of various approaches

Results. In the code approach the only measurement that can legitimately be made is conforming or nonconforming. Deviations or adjustments are considered a form of noncompliance. The degree of noncompliance is not a recognized factor or measurement. The goal-oriented system recognizes the impossibility of absolute compliance with a rigid goal. It registers its performance in a probabilistic manner. This probabilistic measurement is the key to the versatility of the goal-oriented approach.

The next to last column in the matrix considers Responsiveness to Technological Advances and Innovations. The specification code is absolutely nonresponsive and could accept a technological advance only by rewriting of the code. The performance concept code is much more receptive to technological advances so long as the scope of technology is limited to one individual component at a time. It accepts item development but restricts most systems concepts. It is this capability of accepting item development that has permitted much of today's innovation in construction.

The systems approach is readily reactive to technological advances, accepting them based on their ability to establish their fire safety capabilities and reactions. The systems then can interrelate the worth of any element with the other building components and thereby develop an over-all system quality.

The final entry in the matrix is entitled Implementation Effort and Talent Level. This is one measurement of the price tag to the designer. Specification type codes were simple cookbook rules. They forced specific requirements on the designer and required little if any talent in their application. The effort requirements were limited to knowing the short list of alternatives allowed and designing with them as absolute restrictions on the design.

The component performance approach has generated a group of specialized technicians and special information. There are currently engineers and designers who are experts in designing to meet the restrictions of the code or determining whether a specific design meets the code requirements. Often such technicians are not competent in determining whether a specific conforming or nonconforming design is actually safe or unsafe.

The goal-oriented systems performance visualizes a professional technology. Its application will not be easy and will require good professional engineering input. The development and application of this technology will remove real control of fire safety from the hands of the few who write the codes and standards and move it toward the direction of a technology that is no more owned or controlled than arithmetic. This is not a mechanism for destroying codes or conscientious standards bodies. However, the advancement of this type of system will change, and upgrade, the mission of these organizations, making them an integral participant rather than an outside limiter of the design team.

2 How the System Operates

Let us now take a look at the system and how it operates, visualized as in Fig. 4.32. The important point is the central position called "Designed Fire," which is designed limitations of the fire potentials. In the development of the systems approach some of these elements merge, and the overview becomes somewhat simplified and revised as shown in Fig. 4.33. Here the core is still the designed fire, but the integral components have been redefined. Fire energy input integrates the interactions of fuel load and its environment in determining the fire characteristics. The item previously labeled compartmentation has been renamed physical confinement to emphasize that not only the surfaces of the compartment but also the over-all structural rigidity of the building are involved. Extinguishment has been revised to suppression, as this seems to better connote both the automatic and manual application of extinguishing agents.

More important are the changes in the external or subordinate systems. In this, the key elements are life support, primarily involved in smoke control to maintain life tolerable conditions; the people movement system, that is, the arrangement for relocation of people from areas of danger to areas of safety; the emergency communications; and, finally, the emergency preparedness of the occupants. All of the elements related to property damage are in the core; the external elements all are items necessary in addition to consideration of the fire itself in order to assure the protection of people. The arrows interconnecting the external subsystems with the designed fire core indicate the interdependence and interrelationship of all of these items.

With the key items of these diagrams in mind, let us now see how these relate to each other and to over-all goals. First, the goals, which are divided into two areas. The first group is of sociologically focused goals. These are goals that represent both the legal and ethical responsibility of the designer, the manager, or the political authority establishing the requirements for the protection of life and of the community.

In the development of the goal-oriented system it is desirable to fix the level of safety that will be achieved. At this stage, it is possible to identify the areas of safety involved and develop the parametric description of what is expected in a normal

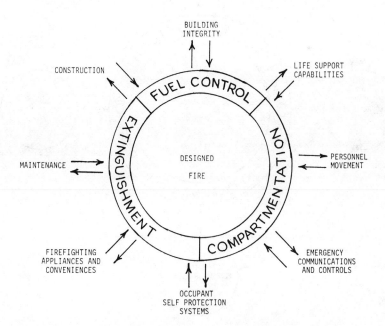

Fig. 4.32 Interrelation of system elements

building, but not to fix the degree of risk to life that citizens will tolerate, or conversely the degree of safety they are willing to pay for in building costs, taxes, and other impositions.

In the meantime, typical performance parameters on a time and tolerance basis can be simplified as shown in Fig. 4.34 for an office. Note that these parametric requirements do not state anything regarding numbers of units of exits, exit travel distances, or even that evacuation is a necessary objective. Rather, the conditions necessary to meet the goals are given. The time allowed in the initial or immediate area of fire origin actually is a representation of the risk tolerated by current practice. Unfortunately, the numerical probability of harm is not known. If it were, there would be a valid measurement of what the political authorities today believe is acceptable by their electorate. With this, trade-off adjustments could be developed as compensation for extra risk or to credit for extra protection.

The second group of goals and resultant parameters is mission-focused. This is that management-determined level of fire safety necessary to meet its own mission-focused responsibilities to protect its investments and its ability to continue in business or operation. The establishment of these is based totally on good

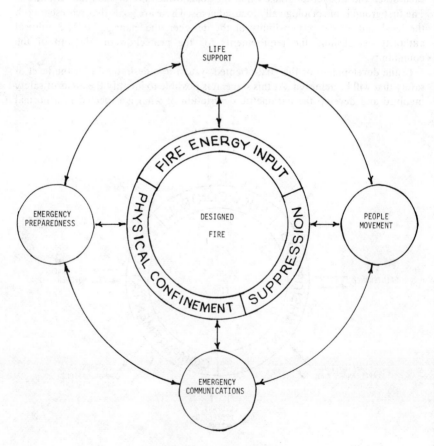

Fig. 4.33 Simplified relation

management, whether this management is by self-insured determiner as it is with the government, or by the joint consideration of the owner and his fire insurance underwriter as is commonly done in private enterprise. These can be best determined in terms of probability measurements. The methodology of measurement may well vary from one situation to another. In the design of buildings where it is not practical to establish money as a parameter, because the actual occupancy of the space is not known at the time of building design, it is quite suitable to use modular terms which relate the probability of success in limiting the degree of fire involvement to a modular delineation of the building, with the smallest unit usually considered being a work station and the largest unit being the building in its entirety. In situations such as warehousing, where it is possible to establish an economic basis, value can readily be used as the item of determination. Whenever this is possible it of course produces the most meaningful results.

Analytical evaluation, however, is not the only use of the system and it is not necessary that every use be as sophisticated or numerically oriented as the analytical approach would indicate. The system develops a decision tree.

An example extracted from the decision tree is shown in Fig. 4.35. Here the success of a barrier is dependent on the barrier being complete. It is also equally dependent on its structural integrity if exposed to fire; and finally, it is dependent

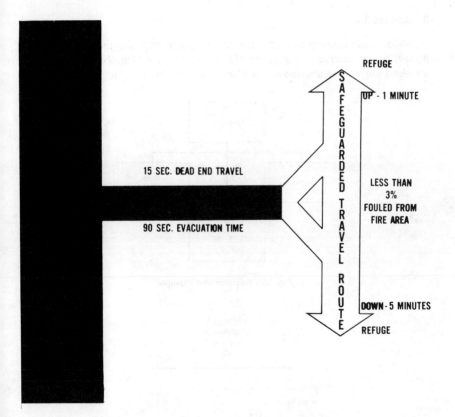

Fig. 4.34 Performance parameters for office facility

upon thermal resistance in preventing the passage of ignition temperatures to the unexposed side of the wall, even though it may be complete and structurally intact.

An example from the fire safety decision tree is the impact of construction and occupancy versus suppression, as shown in Fig. 4.36. To the degree that construction and occupancy limit fire, success in the limitation of the fire characteristics has been achieved. To the degree that this is reinforced by a suppression system, additional safety has been provided. On this basis, a direct relevance in trade-off between elements of construction or elements of occupancy can be made with manual suppression capability or automatic suppression systems such as automatic sprinkler systems, or both.

Fig. 4.37 shows the major breakdowns of the system and provides for the entry of working parameters for the designer. Most of the decision capability relates to the control of the building fire. Each of the terminal boxes in Fig. 4.37 represents the start of a major branch of the tree. Of all the branches of the decision tree the one which most affects the total outcome is "Limitation of Fire Characteristics," as shown in Fig. 4.38. For each of the elements shown in the "Limitation of Fire Characteristics" branch, probability prediction graphs will be necessary to develop the analytical results. A typical expression would be as shown in Fig. 4.39, predicting the structural integrity of various elements and systems.

3 Application

In the actual development of a fire safety system by a designer, he or his fire protection engineering consultant would submit this type of probability prediction for the elements, arrangements, and conditions of his specific design. The first

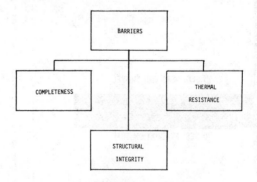

Fig. 4.35 Decision tree example

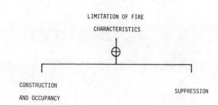

Fig. 4.36 Application of fire safety decision tree

example of an application of this goal-oriented approach by the U. S. Government's General Services Administration is the 24-story Federal Building in Atlanta, Georgia (GSA, 1974).

It is recognized that the systems approach is not completely established and will need field experience, and will be self-improving through such experience. However, it is sufficiently developed to have been placed in use; it offers the capability of better designs and better meeting of safety obligations and objectives.

In an actual design project the designer would be provided with the system concept document and would consult with his fire protection engineering consultant, giving him examples and typical input curves. The designer, with the

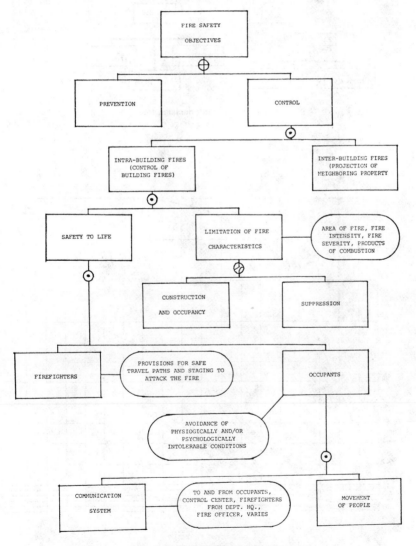

Fig. 4.37 Overview of decision tree

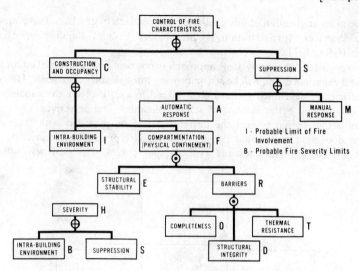

Fig. 4.38 Branch of decision tree

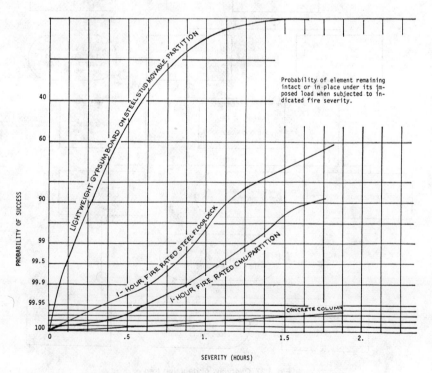

Probability of element remaining intact or in place under its imposed load when subjected to indicated fire severity.

Fig. 4.39 Typical probability prediction graph—structural integrity

assistance of his fire protection engineering consultant, would develop the actual expected performance and determine the validity of the performance curves provided. He would, as part of the design, fully delineate and annotate the total systems concept and the results expected from it. This could be done in the form of an annotated decision tree. His presentation would include a full description, for the building operators, of how the system works, how they are expected to use it, what sort of emergency preparedness reaction will have to be developed in order to react successfully to the system, and how the system elements are to be maintained to assure the integrity of the over-all system.

Within these parameters the traditional fire safety restrictions and limitations placed on the designer will be reduced or even eliminated.

4.11   ANALYSIS AND REPAIR OF FIRE DAMAGE

1   Concrete Structures

Research into the behavior of structural concrete when exposed to fire has been attained almost entirely from laboratory work employing a standard fire test similar to the ISO 834 test. Allied work has included studies of the thermal properties of concrete and the strength-temperature relationships of reinforcing steels, conventional and prestressed.

This work has established not only an appreciation for, but also a rational understanding of the cause and effect of surface spalling, the importance of cover on reinforcement, the loss of load-carrying capacity, and the function of end restraint upon the load-carrying capacity of the member. There is presently sufficient knowledge to calculate the required proportions of a concrete beam or slab system with adequate cover and adequate reinforcement to withstand, without failure, a standard fire of a given duration.

On the other hand, relatively few standardized procedures have been evolved for finding the load-carrying capacity of concrete elements following fire exposure, although it is reasonable to deduce residual strength on the basis of the normal deterioration of laboratory-heated materials subjected to similar temperatures. In addition, the effects of rapid cooling by fire hoses are not reproduced in the standard test.

Structural concrete can never look worse than after it has been exposed to a major fire. There will be extensive spalling of concrete surfaces, often exposing reinforcement. (The degree of spalling depends on the aggregate and whether secondary reinforcement is incorporated in the cover.) Some reinforcement may be displaced. Thin slabs may have large deflections. The surface will be covered with soot which will reveal even the finest of hairline cracks. At first sight, it is difficult to believe that the concrete members could again be made to carry their intended loads with adequate safety.

On the other hand, extensive surface damage is not necessarily an indication of damage through the cross section. Damage to the concrete itself is generally confined to spalling and that which has clearly changed in appearance. Much of the strength may be expected to recover.

Recovery of Strength.   Concrete heated by a building fire loses compressive strength and continues to lose it on cooling. However, where the temperature has not exceeded 300°C (572°F) most of the strength will eventually be recovered (Lie, 1972; Green, 1971). While the exposed surface of concrete can reach 1000°C (1832°F) or more, the comparatively low thermal diffusivity means that the 300°C contour may be at only a small depth below the heated surface. Reinforcing steel recovers virtually all its strength on cooling (see the following paragraphs). Cold drawn prestressing wire loses part of its strength permanently if heated above 300°C, and it may suffer substantial relaxation losses.

Assessment of Damage. Once the shock of visual appearance has abated, several factors must be considered in judging the future load-carrying and behavioral capabilities of the structural concrete elements. These are:

1. Effective cross section which remains after spalling and heating above 300°C.

2. Effect of cracks due to differential heating and cooling of the structure as a whole (as it affects properties of the cross section and continuity).

3. Residual yield strength of the steel reinforcement.

4. In prestressed members, residual prestress force. The temperature history of the fire can often be estimated by careful examination of the debris, noting changes in appearance of plumbing fixtures, glass objects, and other hardware.

Reduction of cross section. To assess the effective remaining cross section requires the removal of all surface material by chisel, and careful measurement. Calculations can assume an additional 1/4-in. of damage, or petrographic examination of cores can establish the exact depth of damage. There may be a permanent change in color after heating to about 300°C (Bessey, 1950), and thermogrammetry and dilatometry may be used to assess temperatures attained (Harmathy, 1968). Compression tests of cores can indicate the strength of the concrete to be assumed in calculations, rather than the strength originally specified by the designer. Due to even slight surface damage, results obtained by a Swiss hammer are meaningless. On the other hand, ultrasonic measurements can be employed to determine the soundness and strength of the remaining concrete.

Cracks. Most fine cracks are confined to the surface of the concrete and are probably caused by the rapid cooling of the surface. Major cracks which could influence future behavior and load-carrying capability are generally self-evident from visual examination. Very wide cracks near supports may indicate loss of anchorage of reinforcement.

Reinforcement. Reinforcement is, in many cases, manufactured as a hot-rolled steel product. Consequently, if the steel cools slowly following exposure to heat from fire, all physical properties will return to original values. Sudden cooling, if it is hit by water from a fire hose, can induce partial tempering and an undesirable brittleness. This rarely happens but, if suspected, possible tempering can be detected by means of a portable hardness tester. Also, test coupons can be removed from regions of low stress for metallurgical analysis and for physical testing. Unless the hot-rolled reinforcement has been exposed for any length of time to temperatures exceeding 600°C (1112°F) due to early spalling of its concrete cover, the possibility of permanent reduction in strength is remote. Cold worked reinforcement heated above 400°C(752°F) will, however, lose a measurable proportion of the strength obtained due to cold working.

Prestressed reinforcement. Prestressing tendons, even more than high strength reinforcement, attain their full strength by means of the cold working of the steel. Upon cooling, therefore, some but not all of the strength loss is regained. The final strength can be determined in three ways. First, the exposed temperature can be determined by petrographic examination of the concrete in the vicinity of the strand, and the strength reduction upon cooling can be estimated on the basis of test data specially determined or obtained from the manufacturer. Second, the strength can be determined by measurement of the microhardness of the steel. Third, a coupon can be removed from a low-stress area of the member for physical testing. The third method is the most accurate.

The prestress force in a member following fire can be determined by "tuning" a strand; that is, by exposing a length of strand for several feet and measuring the frequency of vibration over a finite length between supports. An alternate method is the "bow string" approach which utilizes measurement of transverse deflection for a given load applied midspan between supports at a given distance. Both methods are difficult to perform accurately because they require previous calibration utilizing similar strand or wire with identical conditions of support.

Remedial Measures. In some situations, replacement of a damaged member may be the most practical and economic solution. Elsewhere, reinstatement will be justified in order to avoid inconvenience and loss or damage to other structural members.

Where new members are connected to existing ones, monolithic action must be assured; this calls for careful preparation of the concrete surfaces and continuity of steel. For reinstatement, the removal of loose friable concrete is essential, to assure adequate bonding. Extra reinforcement should be fixed by experienced welders.

New concrete may be placed either by casting with formwork or by the gunite method (Green and Long, 1971); with the latter it may be possible to avoid increasing the original dimensions of the member. The choice of method will depend on the thickness of the new concrete, the surface finish required, the possibility of placing and compacting concrete in the formwork, and the degree of importance attached to an increase in size of section.

Large cracks can be sealed by injection of a latex solution or resin. Various washes or paints are available to restore the appearance of finely cracked or crazed surfaces.

Test Loading. Although the previous discussion presents a means of analyzing fire-damaged concrete structures and assessing the value of repairs within a reasonable degree of accuracy, final acceptance may require proof by load test. Performance should be judged in terms of recovery of deflection after removal of the load. If the remedial methods have been carried out with care and have been well supervised, the fire resistance of the repaired member will normally exceed the standard required.

2   Steel Structures

The postfire repair of a steel-framed structure is a situation that few designers have confronted. Unfortunately, damaging fires do occur occasionally; the problem has arisen in the past. The following brief discussion of the subject provides some general recommendations, as well as an appraisal of the conditions under which structural damage can be expected.

There is little in the technical literature about the principles of repairing fire-damaged structural steel frames. Fires are unique; their effect on a building and the extent of required repairs is a special situation that has to be considered and handled for each particular circumstance. The following checklist outlines several, but not necessarily all, of the parameters that should be investigated by any designer contemplating the repair of a steel-framed structure.

1. An appraisal should be made of those members that have been subjected to potential damage. For convenience, this appraisal should be conducted on members grouped as to their importance to the structure: (i) Columns; (ii) primary horizontal members, such as girders and trusses; and (iii) secondary floor members, such as beams, fillers and floor deck.

2. After identifying those members of potential damage, each structural member in the fire-damaged area should be evaluated for individual damage. This evaluation should include not only the member itself, but the connections of that member to other members within the structure. Damaged members should be divided into three categories: (i) Members having nominal damage and adequate structural capacity for continued service without further repair; (ii) members having light damage that can be repaired in place; and (iii) members with severe damage that should be replaced. When the manner of repair has been determined for each member, a plan of repair sequence should be developed. This is usually quite simple and can be handled by the steel fabricator. However, in rare cases where main structural members have to be replaced, the temporary stability of the structure will have to be taken into consideration.

3. Throughout all of these steps, the designer must recognize that expediency will often dictate his approach. Fires usually mean a temporary loss of business and rental income; owners and occupants will insist on a rapid restoration of building service and availability, a situation that may lead to costly, but quick, solutions.

Fortunately, steel is a material with a very high tolerance for fire. In fact, it is itself a product of fire. All the processes of its manufacture, from smelting the ore to rolling the structural shape, are done at temperatures above those that are likely to occur in an accidental building fire and, of equal importance, the material's properties at elevated temperatures are well known.

At this point, the designer needs only some guidance on evaluating the degree of structural damage. Fortunately, in steel, the rule is simple: any steel member which has been distorted by fire so that it has a permanent deflection, crippled web or flange area, or damaged end connections should be considered for either in-place repair or replacement.

In practice, it may be easier to apply the corollary: any structural steel member remaining in place, with negligible or minor distortions to the web, flanges, or end connections, shall usually be considered satisfactory for further service.

There are only two exceptions which should be considered by the designer. Quenched and tempered structural steels, of which relatively small tonnages have been used, may undergo a change in properties during the heating and cooling cycle of a fire. A second area of possible departure from the rule stated previously pertains to high strength fasteners. Under certain conditions it is possible that their properties may be altered by prolonged fire exposure; but, should there be any question, it is relatively easy to remove individual fasteners for test purposes and, should replacement be necessary, to replace those that are suspected of damage.

In conclusion, structural repair after a major fire in a steel-framed building is to be expected. The standard fire tests, by which the assemblies are rated, do not preclude the possibility of damage short of structural collapse and other limiting end point criteria. But fortunately, in steel construction, the evaluation of damage is relatively straightforward and, for the most part, can be done by visual inspection. Furthermore, because a structural steel frame is essentially an interconnected construction made up of individual, relatively small pieces, the removal and replacement of members can be undertaken expeditiously, relatively economically, and with a minimum of disruption to the remainder of the structure.

4.12 EXAMPLES OF FIRES IN TALL BUILDINGS

In comparison with low-rise buildings, fires in tall buildings present different problems related to fire and smoke spread, evacuation, occupant safety, and fire fighting.

Recently, there has been an increase in the number of large fires in tall buildings in which occupants were trapped by smoke. This is especially noticeable in countries having little experience in the design of multistory buildings. The traditional basic fire safety features must of course be incorporated in the design of tall buildings —but more than that, experience with fires in tall buildings indicates that additional fire safety provisions must also be provided.

In many of the recent disasters, the compartmentation (the passive fire protection system) was inadequate and there were no active fire protection systems (automatic alarms or automatic sprinkler systems). Even where adequate compartmentation is provided, its effectiveness may be reduced if insufficient attention is paid to the detailing of service ducts and other voids. Automatic detection and alarm systems should take account of how the building will be used over the whole 24-hr period.

The fire examples that follow point out the very real possibilities of a major disaster occurring *when fundamental fire safety design precepts are not followed*, and also illustrate the various problems that occur under different fire conditions even when the structure is designed to contemporary safety standards. The examples are by no means all-inclusive of high-rise fires but merely representative, and are included to illustrate the weaknesses in our present design, material use, and construction techniques. They can therefore be used to improve the fire safety of our future creations. Hopefully, we learn from experience.

Additional information and details on these and other examples can be obtained from the National Fire Protection Association, 60 Batterymarch Street, Boston, Mass. 02110, USA.

1   Occidental Center Tower, Los Angeles, USA

This 32-story steel-framed office building built in 1964 suffered an arson fire on the 20th floor on November 19, 1976 (Fig. 4.40). The building was equipped with combination fixed temperature-rate of rise detectors. There was no sprinkler system. Stairwells contained appropriate 6-in. standpipes supplied by a 750-gpm pump in

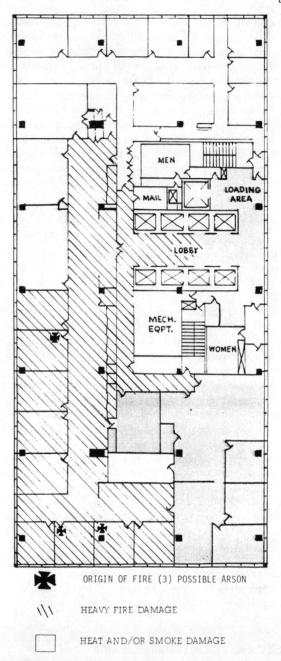

ORIGIN OF FIRE (3) POSSIBLE ARSON

HEAVY FIRE DAMAGE

HEAT AND/OR SMOKE DAMAGE

Fig. 4.40 Occidental Tower, Los Angeles, California—20th floor plan *(Lathrop, 1977)*

the basement. Siamese connections were also provided for fire department pumper augmentation.

The fire was immediately detected and the fire department was on the scene shortly thereafter. The fire department was able to use the elevators to reach the scene of the fire; however, by that time the fire had spread through the outside windows to the floor above. The fire was knocked down approximately 1-1/2 hr after the initial alarm. In all, approximately 300 fire fighters and 17 engines were used to combat it. Various slab-to-slab partitions with solid core doors and the lack of interior means of vertical firespread helped contain the fire.

An automatic suppression system would have greatly reduced the approximately $3 600 000 in damage and would have been essential had the building been located in an area which could not have supplied the massive fire-fighting force necessary to bring a fire of this type under control.

2   World Trade Center, New York, USA

This 110-story steel-framed office building suffered a fire on the 11th floor on February 23, 1975. The loss was estimated at over $2 000 000. The building is one of a pair of towers, 412 m in height.

The fire started at approximately 11:45 P.M. in a furnished office on the 11th floor and spread through the corridors toward the main open office area. A porter saw flames under the door and sounded the alarm. It was later that the smoke detector in the air-conditioning plenum on the 11th floor was activated. The delay was probably because the air-conditioning system was turned off at night.

The building engineers placed the ventilation system in the purge mode, to blow fresh air into the core area and to draw air from all the offices on the 11th floor so as to prevent further smoke spread.

The fire department on arrival found a very intense fire. It was not immediately known that the fire was spreading vertically from floor to floor through openings in the floor slab. These 300-mm × 450-mm (12-in. × 18-in.) openings in the slab provided access for telephone cables. Subsidiary fires on the 9th to the 19th floors were discovered and readily extinguished.

The only occupants of the building at the time of fire were cleaning and service personnel. They were evacuated without any fatalities. However, there were 125 firemen involved in fighting this fire and 28 sustained injuries from the intense heat and smoke. The cause of the fire is unknown.

3   Tae Yon Kak Hotel, Seoul, Korea

This 21-story reinforced concrete office and hotel building, built in 1970, burned completely on December 25, 1971 killing 163 and injuring 60 others. The building was separated vertically, offices on one side and the hotel on the other. Each half was served by a stair. The stair on the hotel side was open at the lobby level and at the three floors just above the lobby. The doors at the other floors were hollow core with closers. The office stairs were protected with rolling steel doors at floor openings; however, both stairs exited into the lobby. Although there was access to the hotel stairs from the various office floor levels, there was not access to the office stairs from the hotel side of the building. The plans and sections are shown in Figs. 4.41, 4.42, and 4.43.

The building had vertical shafts for mechanical equipment which opened into the ceiling space at the floor levels. The ceilings throughout the building were plywood on wood framing and there were openings through the room partitions above this combustible ceiling in the hotel portion. The partitions in the office portion were of combustible material. There was a liberal use of rice paper and wood paneling.

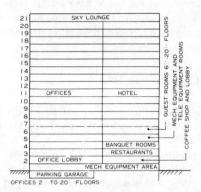

Fig. 4.41 Tae Yon Kak Hotel, Seoul, Korea—elevation *(Willey, 1972a)*

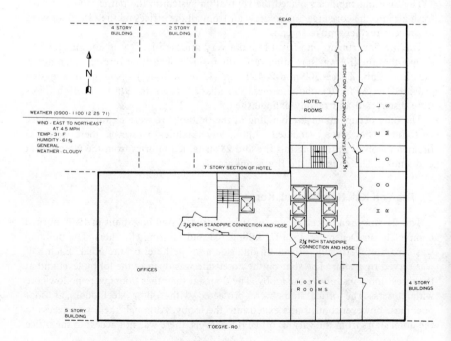

Fig. 4.42 Tae Yon Kak Hotel Building, Seoul, Korea—typical floor plan *(Willey, 1972a)*

There were three 64-mm (2-1/2-in.) standpipes, one adjacent to each stair and the elevators. The standpipe system was supplied by a tank at the 22nd floor which in turn was supplied by an electric pump. There was also a manually started emergency generator available to supply power to the pump, the elevators, and some lighting circuits and exit signs. The building had an automatic fire alarm system. The sleeping rooms had fixed-temperature heat detectors.

The exact details of the fire are not known. The fire started at approximately 10:00 A.M. in the 2nd floor coffee shop. The ignition was believed to have been due to a liquefied petroleum (LP) gas cylinder supplying a small cooking stove, or from a defective spare LP gas cylinder in the vicinity of the stove.

Fed by LP gas the fire immediately engulfed the coffee shop, and spread throughout the lobby and over the combustible interior wall finishes, cutting off the escape routes down the hotel stairs. The fire then spread up the unenclosed stairway to the 3rd and 4th floors. The smoke entered the ventilating system to the main vertical ventilation ducts. Smoke and toxic gases were spread throughout the office and hotel portions of the building through the ventilating ducts.

The fire burned progressively through the building for several hours and was not extinguished until 5:30 P.M. The hotel occupants were first aware of the fire by the smell of smoke. Over 100 occupants escaped the burning building by using either sheet ropes, jumping from lower floors, or by aerial ladders. Six occupants were

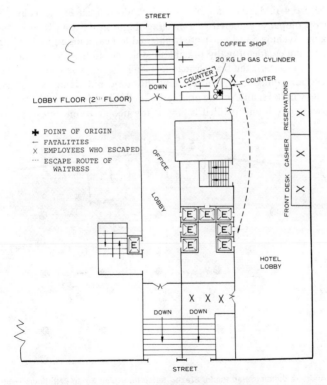

Fig. 4.43 Tae Yon Kak Hotel, Seoul, Korea—lobby floor plan *(Willey, 1972a)*

rescued from the roof by helicopters. Thirty-eight people jumped to their deaths and 121 perished in the fire.

The basic fire safety elements were lacking in this building. Open stairs, open shafts, highly combustible ceilings, the use of Liquefied Petroleum Gas, inadequate method of eliminating toxic gases, and the lack of a proper water supply—all contributed to the inevitable high losses incurred when dangerous combinations of inadequacies are allowed to exist, especially in high-rise buildings.

4 Andraus Building, Saõ Paulo, Brazil

This 31-story reinforced concrete department store and office building built in 1961 burned completely and spectacularly on February 24, 1972, killing 16 and injuring over 375 others. The office building had only one stair which for the most part was not properly enclosed. The department store which occupied the lower 7 stories had 4 unenclosed stairwells. The upper floors were occupied by more than 40 different companies. Ceilings were of combustible fiber tile and partitions and flooring were of wood. The wood forms used in construction had also been left in place above the combustible ceilings. There were no manual or automatic detection or suppression systems. The one stairwell contained a 64-mm (2-1/2-in.) standpipe supplied by a tank at the 31st floor. The tank was in turn supplied by an electric pump in the basement. There were no siamese connections. A typical plan is shown in Fig. 4.44

Just before 4 P.M., the staff of the Saõ Paulo branch of the Tokyo Kaijo Fire Insurance Company, gathered in a meeting room on the 24th floor of the 31-story building on Avenida Saõ Joaõ, were frightened to hear a loud shout of "Fire." After supervising the escape of many Brazilian employees to the roof by the stair, guided by the Japanese staff, the branch manager and the vice-manager searched for any employees remaining in the offices. By this time red flame was already visible outside the windows, and smoke gradually filled the office area. When they reached the stairway they found it filled by the many people trying to escape to the roof,

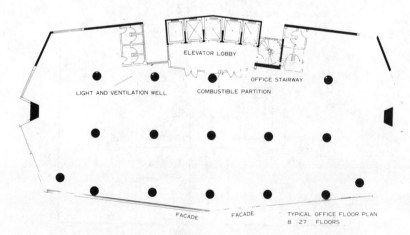

Fig. 4.44 Andraus Building, Saõ Paulo, Brazil—office floor plan 8th to 27th floors (Note: combustible subdivision walls not shown—load bearing columns and walls are shaded.) (Willey, 1972b)

who found that the door in the roof slab had been closed from the outside. The people who were trapped inside the stairway used the fire hydrant to cool down the environment and to wet their clothes. The people who reached the roof also suffered from heavy smoke and heat.

In spite of the rapid spread of fire, most people in the building escaped to the ground level by the stairs or other routes, and about 400 people who were trapped inside the staircase and on the roof were rescued by helicopters between 5:45 P.M. and 9:30 P.M. The total death toll was only 16, a miraculously low number.

The cause of fire was not clear, but it started on the 3rd or 4th floor of the department store, in which a large number of low-pressure gas cylinders were used for heating instead of the town gas which was supplied to the building. The fire was completely out of control by the time the fire department arrived on the scene. The fire communicated from floor to floor on the outside of the building aided by a brisk wind, and spread so rapidly that at one point the entire building was engulfed in flames with fire reaching far above the roof and projecting 15 m (50 ft) into the street.

Luckily the wind protected the one stairwell which allowed approximately 300 people to reach the roof and another 200 to survive in the upper portion of that stairwell. They were eventually removed by helicopter. The death toll was remarkably small considering the extent of the fire which virtually destroyed all but the concrete frame of the building. The 27-km/hr (17-mph) wind, luckily from the right direction, saved hundreds from certain death.

This building lacked all of the basic fire safety features normally required in any building let alone a 31-story high-rise structure. A fire department, no matter how well equipped and trained, would have an impossible task in combating fires in buildings of this type.

5 One New York Plaza, New York, USA

This 50-story reinforced concrete core building with steel floor and column framing suffered an extensive fire on August 5, 1970, starting at 5:45 P.M. and lasting 5 hours, destroying the 33rd, 34th, and 35th floors, killing 2, injuring 30, and doing approximately $10 000 000 in damage. The building had been completed in early 1970 and tenant improvements were just being completed.

The building had 152-mm (6-in.) standpipes in each stairwell supplied by 50-m³ (13,000-gallon) tanks. There were 2 manual 0.047-m³/s (745-gpm) fire pumps and a manual fire alarm system with one pull box on each floor that sounded an alarm in the elevator lobby, at every 10th floor level, in the 1st floor lobby control console, and at various machine rooms throughout the building. Operation of the fire alarm automatically shuts off supply fans.

The vertical shafts were protected with fire dampers; however, the exterior curtain walls for all practical purposes were vertical flues lined with polystyrene foam board and were open to the ceiling space at the floor levels (Fig 4.45). In addition there were openings between floors around cable and duct penetrations. The furnishings contained a large amount of combustible material including foamed polyurethane and rubber cushions.

The fire started in a ceiling space and eventually ignited the polyurethane foam board insulation which dropped flaming plastic droplets. The fire involved the overstuffed furniture which accelerated the combustion process with the large amounts of fuel and flammable gases given off by the foamed polyurethane.

Floor openings negated the horizontal fire separation necessary to prevent vertical fire communication, and the use of polyurethane insulation and large amounts of plastic coated cable in a manner that allows direct exposure to fire permitted the building structure itself to initiate the beginning of this significant fire. The highly combustible contents then took over to produce a very serious fire-fighting problem for the fire department. This fire highlights the fact that our new fireproof buildings are anything but that. Almost everything used in these buildings but the basic frame is combustible to some extent, and that fact must be considered in designing and planning for a fire emergency. Note should also be taken that the two people were killed when their elevator stopped at the fire floor.

6   919 Third Avenue Building, New York, USA

This 47-story reinforced concrete core building with steel floor and column framing suffered a fire on the 5th floor on December 4, 1970, destroying a portion of that floor, killing 3, and injuring 20. The building had been completed that year and tenant work was still in progress at the time of the fire.

The building was occupied principally by carpet manufacturers and carpet wholesalers and the fire started in occupancy of this type. The fire was confined for the most part to a specific area by the fire partitions required and the unpierced horizontal separations. The fire did warp the exterior skin allowing a small amount

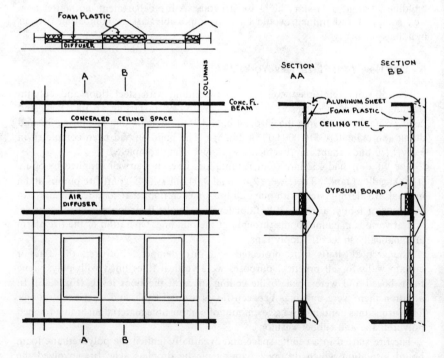

Fig. 4.45 One New York Plaza, New York, USA—sketch of outer wall arrangement showing vertical flues, aluminum flashing, and foamed plastic insulation *(Powers, 1971a)*

of fire penetration to the floor above, but for the most part it was contained by the building structure. The fire, though contained, was very intense and did structural damage to the floor system above. Total property damage to the building and its contents was estimated at $2 500 000.

This fire being at the 5th floor level was fought to a major extent from the outside of the building. Obviously, if it had occurred on an upper floor the fire-fighting problems would have been much more severe.

Although vertical air handling ducts were protected at each floor with fire dampers, smoke spread to the upper portions of the building was a major problem. Air-handling equipment was manipulated by the building engineers at the direction of the fire department, which assisted in the control of smoke movement. However, at least some occupants on upper floors were compelled to break the unoperable windows for fresh air. Stairs became unattainable because of smoke entry at the fire floor due to the use of standpipes in the stair shafts.

The use of the elevators resulted in the 3 fire deaths when the car inadvertently stopped at the fire floor. Others were almost killed in the same way but were rescued by fire fighters (Powers, 1971b).

Recommendations were made at the time of this fire that smokeproof stairs, vertical fire separations at the exterior walls between windows, sprinkler protection for certain highly combustible occupancies, smoke venting capabilities at individual floors, and prefire plans be required in high-rise buildings, in addition to present requirements. Note was also made that elevator call buttons should not be responsive to heat or smoke.

7   Hawthorne House, Chicago, USA

This 39-story reinforced concrete apartment building built in 1967 suffered a fire in an apartment on the 36th floor at approximately 1:30 A.M. on January 24, 1969, killing 4, one from an apparent heart attack. The building had two enclosed stairwells, one being a smokeproof stair (Fig 4.46). Each stairwell contained a standpipe with a 64-mm (2-1/2-in.) fire department connection and a 36-mm (1-1/2-in.) connection with a hose attached at each floor.

Corridors were of one hour construction with the exception of a vertical 254-mm

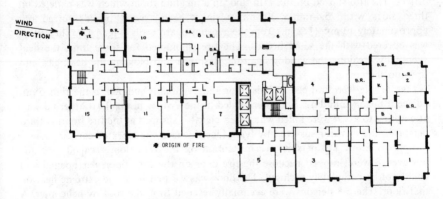

Fig. 4.46   Hawthorne House, Chicago, Illinois—floor plan of 28th to 39th stories *(Watrous, 1969)*

(10-in.) strip adjacent to each corridor door that was particle board on the corridor side used to facilitate the installation of a light fixture. Corridor doors were 43-mm (1-3/4-in.) solid core but were cut to provide a 381-mm (15-in.) high immovable transom. The transom-door connection was rabbeted; however, there was no frame to help prevent warping in the event of a fire. The corridor doors were not required to be self closing.

The fire was thought to have started in a sofa and smoldered for some time before windows broke and flashover occurred. One occupant of the involved apartment, though severely burned, was able to open the corridor door and make his way down the corridor to another apartment where he died.

The high winds now blowing through the apartment created a blowtorch effect and pushed the flames down the corridor. The fire department fought the corridor fire from the stairwells and was eventually able to gain access to the apartment. The fire consumed virtually all combustibles in the apartment of origin.

The corridor walls and doors held in spite of the deficiencies and there was a minimal amount of smoke spread to the upper floors of the building, However, the apartment of origin was close to the top of the building. The smokeproof stair tower was used to vent much of the smoke forced down the corridor.

Many occupants of apartments on the fire floor remained in their apartments and did not suffer any ill effects. One person who attempted to leave his apartment and use the stairs died in the corridor. One other occupant died in the apartment involved in the fire, and another resident of the building died of a heart attack after using the stairs. Occupants above the fire floor had no trouble using the smokeproof stairs.

Because the fire department had a great deal of trouble using the elevator to gain access to the fire because of occupant evacuation, a requirement for firemen's automatic control of elevators was passed on a retroactive basis. In addition, door closers on apartment corridor doors were also made a requirement on a retroactive basis.

8   Rault Center, New Orleans, USA

This 16-story-plus-penthouse reinforced concrete building built in 1968 suffered a fire on November 29, 1972, killing 6. The structure is half apartments and half offices. The fire started on the 15th floor in a meeting room which was paneled on three sides with 25.4-mm × 305-mm (1-in. × 12-in.) wood boards furred out approximately 13 mm (1/2 in.) from the gypsum board walls (Fig. 4.47). The ceiling was covered with the same boards. The fire smoldered for some time, the heat eventually breaking the windows causing flashover and blowing the heat, gas, and fire into the corridor.

Five people were trapped on this floor and eventually jumped to the roof of an adjacent 8-story building. Four were killed in the 7-story jump. Two other persons attempting to assist were killed when their elevator stopped at the fire floor. A third person in the elevator survived by lying face down in the elevator car.

Approximately 140 persons in a restaurant on the 16th floor escaped by stair; however, 8 were trapped because the fire door on the 15th floor was opened and could not be completely reclosed. The door was warped from the extreme heat on that floor. These 8 persons were eventually rescued from the roof by helicopter. A similar helicopter rescue attempt of the 5 persons trapped on the 15th floor was unsuccessful.

This fire generated a great deal of interest in mandating sprinkler systems in this type of occupancy.

9   Baptist Towers (Housing for the Elderly), Atlanta, USA

An 11-story reinforced concrete apartment building completed in April, 1972 suffered a fire on the 7th floor on November 30, 1972, killing 10 (Fig. 4.48). The building contained 300 apartments, with 30 apartments on the fire floor. Each floor is served by 3 stairwells located at the ends of the corridors in the tee-shaped structure. The elevator lobby is at the intersection of the tee. Each stairwell contained a 152-mm (6-in.) standpipe with a 64-mm (2-1/2-in.) fire department hose connection. A fourth 6-in. standpipe was located in the elevator lobby. Nearly 23 m (75 ft) of 36-mm (1-1/2-in.) hose was also provided at each standpipe. A 0.063-m³/s (1 000-gpm) fire pump supplied the system.

A manual local fire alarm system was provided with pull stations at each stairwell and the elevator lobby. A fire alarm annunciator panel also handled an emergency call system activated by a switch in each apartment bathroom.

Corridors supplied make-up air to apartments to compensate for the 0.047-m³/s (100-cfm) exhaust from the apartment kitchens and baths. Corridor door undercuts up to 38 mm (1-1/2 in.) had been provided to accommodate the airflow requirements. This same undercutting was done to the labeled stair doors for some reason. Corridor doors were 43-mm (1-3/4-in.) solid core with wood frames. The corridor carpeting had an unusually high fire hazard characteristic, being made of 100% polypropylene bonded to foam rubber and cemented to the floor slab.

The fire started at 2:00 A.M. in one of the 7th floor apartments, #710. The first indication of trouble came from Apartment #710 through the emergency call system at the 2nd floor annunciator panel. (The staff member investigating the trouble light was later found dead in the elevator at the 7th floor level.) The occupant then left the apartment, but did not reshut the corridor door or activate

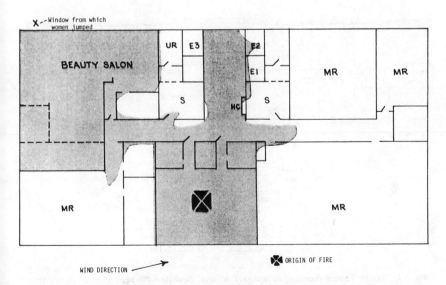

Fig. 4.47 Rault Center Building, New Orleans, Louisiana—floor plan of 15th story *(Watrous, 1973)*

the fire alarm. The 16-km/hr (10-mph) wind blowing through the apartment pushed the fire into the corridor and blocked egress for many of the other residents of that floor. The highly combustible carpeting contributed to the corridor fire spread and generated enough heat, gas, and smoke to penetrate the apartments on that floor through the door undercuts, and in some instances through door failure. Many who remained in their apartments were killed, and some while attempting to escape down the corridors.

Smoke spread through upper floors and was especially severe on the 10th floor where another elevator car was located with the car and hatch door open. Large quantities of smoke flowed up the shaft openings at the 7th and 10th floors due to the open doors, which may have been held open by their photoelectric cell safety devices. One person died on the 10th floor from smoke inhalation.

Many people were rescued with aerial ladders, and had the fire occurred at a higher level there would have been many more deaths.

10   Joelma Building, Saõ Paulo, Brazil

A 25-story reinforced concrete office building burned completely from the 12th floor to the roof on February 1, 1974 killing 179 and injuring 300 (Fig. 4.49). The building had been completed in 1973 but, like the Andraus Building which had been completely consumed by fire in 1972, contained only one open stair, and combustible partitioning and ceilings. The only concession to fire safety was a 64-mm (2-1/2-in.) standpipe with 36-mm (1-1/2-in.) hose on each floor. The water supply, both domestic and fire, was from a roof storage tank.

The building was occupied by approximately 750 people at the time of the fire, which began in a defective air conditioning unit in a 12th-floor window. The fire quickly spread up the drapes to the combustible ceiling and then throughout the floor. The fire then proceeded vertically up the stair and on the outside of the

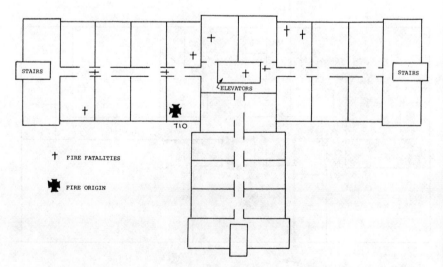

Fig. 4.48 Baptist Towers (housing for elderly), Atlanta, Georgia—7th floor plan *(Willey, 1973)*

structure. The fire burned itself out in approximately 1-1/2 hr, consuming all combustibles above the 11th floor level.

Most of the people who escaped from the upper portions of the building (approximately 300) used the manually operated elevators. Though certainly not recommended for evacuation they were functional until the heat and smoke at the 12th and 13th floors became untenable and their use was discontinued.

Approximately 160 people sought refuge on the roof of the building expecting rescue by helicopter. Helicopters were not able to effect rescue and only 81 survived by seeking refuge under corrugated cement roof panels. Note should be made that of the 179 fatalities, 40 jumped to their deaths, 30 having jumped after the fire had burned itself out.

This tragedy is another example of a complete lack of any thought given to the possibility of a fire.

11   Sennichi Building, Osaka, Japan

Fire broke out on the 3rd floor, a clothing sales floor, of the Sennichi Department Store Building (7 floors) in Osaka at 10:30 P.M., on May 13, 1972. Among the 179 persons who were at the amusement bar "Play Town" on the 7th floor, 118 persons were killed.

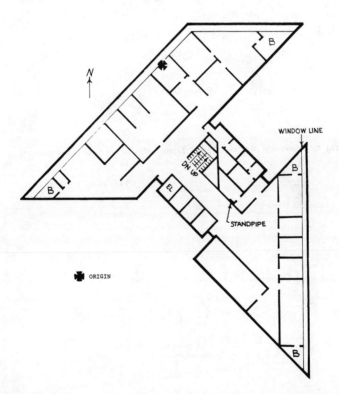

Fig. 4.49 Joelma Building, Saõ Paulo, Brazil—12th floor plan, typical of all floors *(Willey, 1974)*

The plan of the 3rd and 7th (Play Town) floors are shown in Figs. 4.50 and 4.51, respectively. Fire broke out at the bedding sales area in front of an elevator on the 3rd floor. It is reported that a smoker's match was thrown down on bedding by a repairman and caused the fire. The horizontal fire separation shutters of the two escalator pits had been left open, allowing fire spread from the 3rd floor to the 4th floor in 16 minutes and to the 7th floor in 19 minutes. The smoke that was generated on the 2nd to 4th floors passed through the vertical shafts, such as staircases, elevators, and air-conditioning ducts, and entered Play Town on the 7th floor.

Analysis of Sennichi Building Fire.   To clarify the smoke movement in this fire, some analysis on the basis of data prepared by the Osaka Fire Department Bureau, Osaka Building Bureau, and Osaka Police was made by Wakamatsu (1971). The results of the analysis should be quite reliable in view of the fact that this calculation system was verified by field experiment in the Building of the Ministry of Welfare,

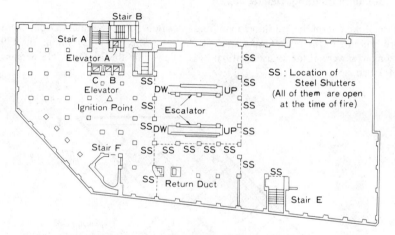

Fig. 4.50 Sennichi Building, Osaka, Japan—plan of 3rd floor (fire breakout)

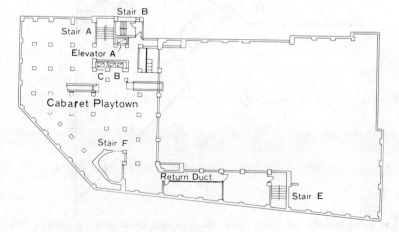

Fig. 4.51 Sennichi Building, Osaka, Japan—plan of 7th floor (Play Town)

scheduled for demolition. Naturally some variation would be expected, since the conditions used for calculations may be different from the real conditions.

Fig. 4.52 briefly shows the calculation procedures, and Fig. 4.53 shows the network of calculation. A computer (TOSBAC-3400) was used as follows.

1. Various conditions (combustibles, fire compartment, openings, the outside conditions) are prepared as input data on the basis of the drawings of the building and the report of the investigation.

2. A simulated network (somewhat simplified), showing the composition of openings and flow paths of the building, is prepared on the basis of this network.

3. The fire room temperature is calculated as a function of the time elapsed on the basis of the relevant data of (1).

4. The data of (1) and (3) are fed into the calculation system of (2) to calculate the mass rate of air or smoke flowing at individual parts, concentration of gases or smoke, temperature and pressure, etc., for each compartment (including shafts) at 3-minute intervals.

Results of Calculation: Temperature in Fire Compartment. It is difficult to estimate the transient process of combustion at the early stages of a large compartment fire. In this instance the combustion rate at the early stage was estimated on the basis of Thomas' (1967) method. Next, the temperature in the fire compartment was calculated by using the calculation system based on Kawagoe and Sekine's theory (1963).

It was estimated that the combustion on the 2nd floor was about 80% of the combustion on the 3rd floor on the basis of the report of the Building Research Institute (1972) as well as the record of maximum temperature of the 2nd floor. Fig. 4.54 shows calculated results of the temperature in the fire compartments on the three floors.

Smoke Passage. Fig. 4.55 shows an example of calculated results concerning the flow rate and the concentration ratio of smoke (ratio of concentration to that of fire

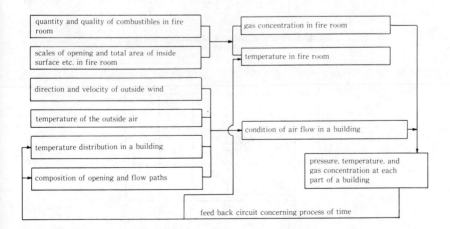

Fig. 4.52 Outline of calculation procedure

compartment 18 minutes after the outbreak of the fire). This shows that the smoke generated in the fire compartment flowed up into the Play Town bar on the 7th floor mainly through the return duct for air conditioning, the elevator A, and the

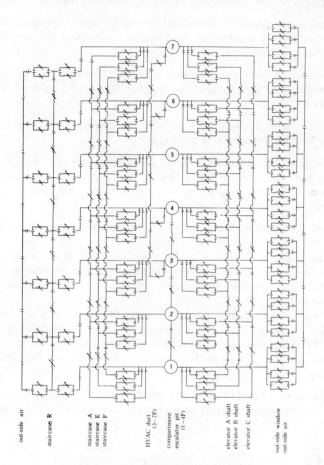

Fig. 4.53 Simulated network of Sennichi Building

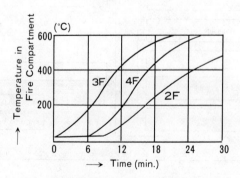

Fig. 4.54 Average temperature

stairs F. The return duct had three fire dampers, but none of them could be closed because of the seized hinges.

Elevator A became one of the main passages of smoke because the shaft was not completely enclosed and the doors in the shaft were opened at the 7th floor. Staircase F became a passage of smoke because the steel rolling shutter for fire separation on the 2nd floor was not closed. It became the largest passage when a shutter of the staircase at the Play Town part (7th floor) was opened after 15 minutes to enable occupants to escape from Play Town through the staircase.

Figs. 4.56 and 4.57 show the temperature and the flow rate of the smoke that entered the 7th floor through the three shafts.

The temperature of the smoke passing through the return duct exceeded 400°C (752°F) at the opening of the duct on the 7th floor after the fire fully developed. It is supposed that the tip of flame came out of the return duct grille on the 7th floor. Therefore, if there had been combustibles near the grille, fire would have spread to the 7th floor through this duct.

Smoke did not flow to the 7th floor through staircase F during the first 10 minutes. It is estimated that air probably flowed down the staircase from the 7th floor during this period. After 15 minutes, the shutter of staircase F was opened, and the external windows of Play Town were gradually broken. Then, much smoke began to flow into Play Town through stairway F.

Conditions in Play Town. Fig. 4.58 shows the change of average temperature in Play Town. It can be seen that the people in Play Town were exposed to considerable heat even though the temperature at the lower level was probably considerably lower than at the upper level.

Fig. 4.59 shows the smoke (gas) concentration in Play Town as a ratio to the concentration in the fire compartments. Therefore, the absolute concentration in Play Town can be easily obtained if the gas concentrations in the fire compartments

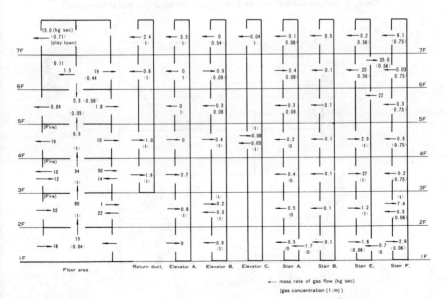

Fig. 4.55 Condition of mass rate and concentration at each part of building at 18 minutes after fire breakout

are given. The gas concentration in the fire compartment was estimated as the following values on the basis of Rasbash's method (1967), gas content, and using $AH^{1/2}W^{-1}$ (in which A = opening area; H = height of opening; and W = amount of combustible material in fire compartment): O_2 concentration, 10%; CO_2 concentration, 9%; CO concentration, 2%.

Fig. 4.60 shows the concentration of O_2 and CO and the time to reach lethal conditions in Play Town. The lethal condition was assumed as the following:

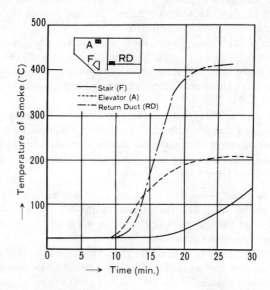

Fig. 4.56 Temperature of smoke flowing into 7th floor (by major passages)

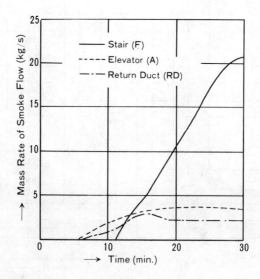

Fig. 4.57 Mass rate of smoke flowing into 7th floor (by major passages)

CO = 0.5% (upper limit), or O_2 = 13% (lower limit), or $(CO)(t)$ = 10% min (product of the concentration of CO and the duration of exposure).

According to Fig. 4.60, it took 17.5 minutes to reach the lethal limit. In other

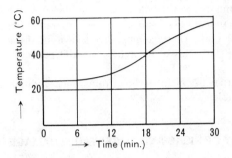

Fig. 4.58 Average temperature in Play Town on 7th floor

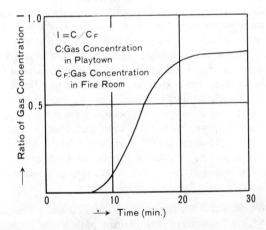

Fig. 4.59 Relative concentration of gas in Play Town (by concentration in fire compartment)

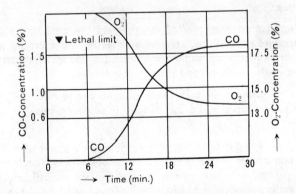

Fig. 4.60 Concentration of CO and O_2 and lethal limit in Play Town

words, the lethal limit was reached 10 minutes after smoke began to enter the 7th floor. This shows that human survival in Play Town became impossible within an extremely short period.

There are many more examples of fires in tall buildings which could be detailed. An evaluation of numerous fires that occurred between 1961 and 1971 was undertaken by the National Loss Control Service Corporation under contract to the City of Chicago, Illinois. Their summary is shown in Table 4.4. Additional information from the study may be secured from the Department of Buildings, City of Chicago.

Table 4.5 is a partial list of other fires from which additional fire experience information is available.

4.13 PHILOSOPHY OF RISKS AND ACCEPTABLE DAMAGE

The design of a structure must allow for features such as collisions by vehicles, explosions, and fire. As both the resistance of the structure and the occurrence and degree of these features mentioned are basically stochastic, there will always be some risk that damage will be caused by extreme situations. Accepting the fact that no full statistical information is available, it appears that fire is by far the most important extreme situation that will cause damage in structures (Ligtenberg, 1971). The present design against risks is based mainly on the assessment of the structural behavior under the factored loads at room temperature together with additional provisions based on experience and intuition, if risks other than overloading are involved. It is now clear that this approach does not provide a homogeneous design that takes into account the possible fire risks. As buildings become larger, it must be assumed that potentially the damage due to fire will increase.

All this has led to a growing conviction that the problem of fire protection of buildings can be solved satisfactorily only by other means besides experience and intuition. The principal aspects of this approach are:

1. Characteristic features of a fire, such as duration and temperature, can be estimated with a number of well-defined parameters. Important aspects include the quantity and nature of combustible material, possibility of ventilation, and the geometrical and thermal properties of the fire compartment.

2. The mechanical properties of the structural materials will change as the temperature rises. If the temperature rises beyond a certain level ϑ_{cr} the structure will collapse, and ϑ_{cr} will depend on the material that is used, the nature of the structure, and the way it is loaded.

3. The temperature in the parts of the structure can be calculated from the gas temperature curve, while the danger to adjoining premises can also be defined.

The approach indicated in these points makes it basically possible by mathematical means to obtain information on the structural behavior during fire, bearing in mind that all the parameters which govern the problem are basically stochastic. This means that the fire resistances which are to be found as a result of the calculation can in fact only be given in terms of probability. These concepts lead to the modern theories of structural safety in which fire is considered as a risk together with other risks like overloading, extreme wind loads, explosions, and so on. This aim is to achieve a homogeneous design in which the risks due to the several extreme situations are comparable.

Making such calculations in the field of fire engineering necessitates, however, a large amount of basic data on fire itself and on the structural behavior under fire conditions. Their collection is the object of an extensive research activity over the whole world.

The standard of precautions must take into account that: (1) Too low a standard may involve unacceptable risks for persons in the building or result in excessive fire damage, or both; and (2) too high a standard will mean incurring unnecessary expense. In the following articles the principles on which to base a decision are summarized and discussed.

1 Basic Principles

The basic principle of fire engineering must be to find safety standards that lead to an optimal solution from the socioeconomic point of view. This calls for a well-defined parameter by which the socioeconomic and economic costs and benefits can be expressed. For this purpose the concept of "fire-cost-expectation" can be introduced. This is the probable cost that will be caused by fire during a certain period. In this concept, "cost" must be taken very generally. It comprises the cost of losses and expenditure on safety measures. The following main components must be considered:

1. Loss. Loss of lives; direct economic losses (structure and content); and indirect economic losses (effect of disturbances or interruption in production).

2. Expenditure. Cost of fire prevention measures; cost of alarm systems, extinguishing systems and other fire-fighting and safety devices; and cost to the community of providing insurance.

The objective must be, with respect to the total investment in fire protection:

1. To balance the fire prevention measures, fire-fighting and safety devices to give the optimum effect (so-called suboptimization).

2. To choose such a level of suboptimized total investment that the sum of loss plus expenditure will be a minimum (see Fig. 4.61).

This principle, unmodified, is valid on a community level for a fire brigade district, or for an industrial area, or for a large industry with its own fire brigade resources.

Applied to a single building it must be modified because investment for fire prevention and fire-fighting measures is already provided by the community.

To make Fig. 4.61 operational, the relationship between the costs of precautions and the costs of probable losses must be known. This implies knowledge of: (1) The probability of occurrence of fire; (2) structural behavior under fire conditions expressed in probabilistic terms; and (3) value of the possible damage at the moment of fire outbreak.

Unfortunately, the data that are at present available, in particular the statistical data, are still inadequate. Nevertheless, in the literature several approaches have

Table 4.4(a) Summary of high-rise fire experience (Courtesy: National Loss Control Service Corporation)

Reference number[a] (1)	Number of stories (2)	Fire floor (3)	Fire spread		Extent (6)	Shafts and chutes (7)
			Interior (4)	Exterior (5)		
1	36	B	*		B-36	*
2	12	B	*		B-12	
3	14	1			1-14	*
4	29	3			3-10	
5	47	5	*		5-33	
6	6	6			6	
7	13	B	*		9-13	*
8	11	11			11	
9	5	3			3-5	
10	12	7		*	7-12	
11	19	9			9	
12	30	6			6	
13	21	12			12	
14	16	11		*	11-16	
15	16	4			4-13	
16	31	9			9-13	
17	52	35			35-38	*
18	18	4			4	
19	38	1			1	
20	16	B	*		B-6	
21	12	9	*	*	N.R.[b]	
22	7	4	*		4-6	
23	37	6			N.R.	
24	21	B	*		21	*
25	22	B	*		N.R.	*
26	14	11			N.R.	
27	102	20	*		N.R.	*
28	31	22	*		N.R.	*
29	18	8	*		N.R.	
30	36	34			34-36	
31	7	2	*		2-7	
32	12	2	*		2-12	
33	24	13		*	N.R.	
34	24	11			N.R.	
35	28	6			6-28	
36	27	20	*		N.R.	
37	12	B				
38	12	N.R.	*		N.R.	
39	21	1		*	1-21	
40	20	16				
41	16	6				
42	14	B			B-14	
43	12	B			N.R.	*
44	26	2			2-26	
45	9	5			5-9	

Table 4.4(a) Summary of high-rise fire experience

Smoke spread					
Elevators (8)	Stairs (9)	Ventilation system (10)	Other (11)	Evacuation required (12)	Number of deaths (13)
	*	*		*	
*	*			*	3
	*			*	21
	*			*	
*	*	*		*	3
				*	4
*				*	16
				*	25
*	*			*	10
*	*			*	4
					1
*	*			*	
*	*				
*	*			*	2
*		*		*	
			*		
				N.R.[b]	
	*				
	*			*	1
				*	
				N.R.	
				N.R.	
				N.R.	
				N.R.	
	*			*	
				*	
			*		
	*	*		*	4
					2
*	*			*	
				N.R.	
				N.R.	
				*	
*				*	
*					
*	*			*	
				*	

Table 4.4(a) (continued)

Reference number[a] (1)	Number of stories (2)	Fire floor (3)	Fire spread		Extent (6)	Shafts and chutes (7)
			Interior (4)	Exterior (5)		
46	40	36			32–40	
47	43	B			30–47	*
48	50	43	*		33–50	
49	50	45			45–50	
50	38	1			29–38	
51	95	66				
Totals			17	5	38	10

[a]See Table 4.4(b) for key to reference numbers.
[b]N.R. = Not Reported.

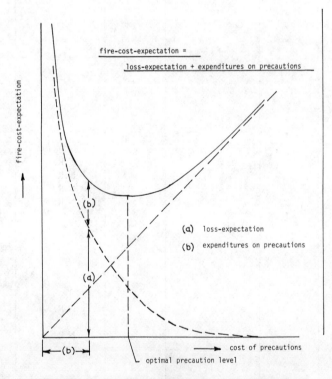

Fig. 4.61 Principle of cost-benefit comparison *(ECCS, 1974b)*

been attempted which provide a rough idea of the influence of the several parameters that determine the fire-cost-expectation. The results will be discussed in more detail in the next sections.

In evaluation, another basic difficulty will arise concerning socioeconomic

Table 4.4(a) (continued)

Smoke spread				Evacuation required (12)	Number of deaths (13)
Elevators (8)	Stairs (9)	Ventilation system (10)	Other (11)		
*				*	4
*				*	
*	*	*		*	2
				N.R.	
*	*			*	1
17	18	5	2	35	103

considerations, such as loss of life. To make this comparable with the other factors involved it must be expressed in money terms. This appears to be hardly possible because the "value" of human life will be influenced strongly by ethical, psychological, and political considerations. Moreover, as far as fire is concerned, the measures necessary to save human lives may be quite different in kind or degree from those necessary to reduce economic losses. This means that for practical reasons, a distinction is made between primary and secondary fire prevention (Witteveen and Twilt, 1971).

Primary fire prevention covers the complex of precautions taken to serve socioeconomic interests. The costs cannot be weighed against the benefits by means of economic disciplines only. Primary requirements are concerned with human safety, human values, and public interest. Secondary fire prevention covers the complex of fire precautions taken to serve economic interests. The costs can and must be weighed against their benefits. In other words, their costs must not exceed the prospective abatement of the losses. Secondary fire precautions are concerned solely with material values. Precautions concerned with safeguarding of lives, etc., are excluded.

2 Evaluation

Primary Fire Prevention.   Besides situations in which people are killed directly by the fire, a fire in a building may endanger its occupants:

1. If timely and safe evacuation is impossible owing to the lack of adequate, effective escape routes and exits.

2. If the possibility of safe evacuation is forestalled by smoke production or a very rapidly spreading fire.

3. If the structure collapses before the occupants can vacate it (as will be discussed later, this point is of minor importance).

In practice, no absolute guarantee can be given that there will be no personal

Table 4.4(b) High-rise fire reports surveyed *(Courtesy: National Loss Control Service Corporation)*

Reference number (1)	Building and location (2)	Date (3)
1	Office Building, Montréal, Canada	Dec. 21, 1962
2	Beacon Arms Hotel, Ottawa, Canada	July 31, 1964
3	Hotel Roosevelt, Jacksonville, Florida	Dec. 29, 1963
4	Apartment Building, Chicago, Illinois	Apr. 7, 1969
5	Office Building, New York, N.Y.	Dec. 4, 1970
6	Sherry Biltmore Hotel, Boston, Mass.	March 29, 1963
7	Hartford Hospital, Hartford, Conn.	Dec. 8, 1961
8	Apartment Building, Montgomery, Ala.	Feb. 7, 1967
9	Office Building, New York, N.Y.	Feb. 25, 1969
10	Apartment Building, Atlantic City, N.J.	Apr. 18, 1969
11	Apartment Building, Chicago, Illinois	Nov. 5, 1969
12	Apartment Building, Chicago, Illinois	Nov. 16, 1969
13	La Salle Hotel, Chicago, Illinois	Feb. 26, 1970
14	Apartment Building, Chicago, Illinois	Apr. 11, 1970
15	Apartment Building, Chicago, Illinois	Apr. 19, 1970
16	Conrad Hilton Hotel, Chicago, Illinois	Jan. 25, 1970
17	Bank of America Building, San Francisco, California	Nov. 18, 1970
18	Seneca Hotel, Chicago, Illinois	March 20, 1970
19	Office Building, Columbus, Ohio	Dec. 24, 1965
20	Department Store, Newark, N.J.	March 18, 1964
21	Office Building, Lincoln, Nebraska	Dec. 9, 1965
22	College Classroom Building, New Haven, Conn.	June 14, 1969
23	Hotel New Yorker, New York, N.Y.	Nov. 7, 1963
24	Penn-Sheraton Hotel, Pittsburgh, Pa.	Nov. 18, 1963
25	Hotel, St. Louis, Mo.	Jan. 11, 1964
26	Office Building, Wilmington, Del.	June 16, 1964
27	Empire State Building, New York, N.Y.	Jan. 9, 1963
28	Office Building, San Antonio, Tex.	July 31, 1965
29	Hotel, Detroit, Michigan	May 21, 1965
30	Office Building, Dallas, Tex.	June 3, 1969
31	Neiman-Marcus Dept. Store, Dallas, Tex.	Dec. 19, 1964
32	Military Park Hotel, Newark, N.J.	Dec. 24, 1965
33	Office Building, New Orleans, La.	Jan. 8, 1966
34	College Dormitory, Columbus, Ohio	May 27, 1968
35	College Administration Building, Chicago, Illinois	May 5, 1970
36	College Library, Austin, Tex.	Aug. 10, 1965
37	College Dormitory, Stillwater, Okla.	Oct. 3, 1966
38	Theological Library, New York, N.Y.	Apr. 18, 1966
39	Hartford Plaza Building, Chicago, Illinois	Apr. 3, 1968
40	Apartment Building, Chicago, Illinois	Apr. 25, 1968
41	Apartment Building, Chicago, Illinois	Feb. 15, 1969
42	Apartment Hotel, Chicago, Illinois	Jan. 7, 1971
43	Commonwealth Hotel, Chicago, Illinois	March 13, 1968
44	Thorndale Beach Condominium, Chicago, Illinois	Jan. 8, 1968
45	Apartment Building, Chicago, Illinois	Feb. 3, 1971
46	Hawthorne House Apartment Building, Chicago, Illinois	Jan. 24, 1969
47	Hotel New Yorker, New York, N.Y.	July 30, 1969
48	One New York Plaza Office Building, New York, N.Y.	Aug. 5, 1970

Table 4.4(b) (continued)

Reference number (1)	Building and location (2)	Date (3)
49	Chemical Bank Building, New York, N.Y.	Sept. 4, 1968
50	Chateau Champlain Hotel, Montréal, Canada	Dec. 30, 1967
51	John Hancock Center, Chicago, Illinois	Apr. 8, 1971

accidents. It is more important to provide such a standard of precautions that the risk of personal injury is acceptably low. The difficulty, however, is to find useful standards concerning what is acceptable and what is not.

One solution that has been tried is to express the value of a human life in terms of production and consumption (Abraham and Thedié, undated). However, on this basis the value of children and old people turns out to be negative. Another attempt to estimate a monetary value of human life (Melinek, 1972) analyzes risks that people are willing to take in daily life. Some examples are worked out concerning introduction of speed limits, use of pedestrian subways, smoking, and employment. This is reasonable, however, only if people are aware of the consequences of the risks they take. Moreover, political and psychological reaction of the community will have a great influence on the decision making. The death of, say, 50 people due to one or two big fires will alarm the community much more than the same number of victims spread over several incidents and in not too short a time. In the first case it is distinctly possible that the provision for fire prevention must be increased, and so the value of life, due to political pressure.

Summarizing, it can be stated that expressing the value of human life only in economic terms will not result in a reliable cost-benefit comparison in respect of primary fire prevention. Certainly ethical and political considerations are to be taken into account. It is thought that the total number of victims in a certain period and the way in which they are spread over the several incidents will be an important parameter.

Up to the present (1980) it is thought that a more realistic approach is to distribute the money society is willing to spend over the several risks involved, proportionally to the values of those risks. This leads to a comparison of the risk of loss of life due to fire with other risks. As an example road traffic is chosen. Table 4.6 gives over-all figures showing the number of road users killed per 100 000 inhabitants valid for some Western European countries for the year 1967. It also shows the average accident risk assuming a life expectancy of 75 yr. In Table 4.7, the number of persons killed due to fire in some Western European countries is presented. Also figures are given concerning the average accident risk based on a life expectancy of 75 yr.

Although there is considerable scatter, which will partly be caused by the fact that the given figures are only rather rough estimates, it appears that, on the average, accident risk due to fire is about 1:1500 during a lifetime. This risk is about one-thirtieth that of a fatal road accident.

Looking at the measures to reduce loss of life it must be kept in mind that in the case of a structure, fire can be regarded as causing the material properties to deteriorate fairly slowly. The structure's fire resistance is generally adequate to allow the occupants to escape from the building. Experience shows that people other than fire fighters are hardly ever killed or severely injured by collapse of fire-damaged structures.

Primary fire prevention thus puts the emphasis on escape routes, and limiting the production and propagation of smoke and toxic gases and spread of fire; the load-bearing capacity of the structure is of secondary importance.

Most of the important fires in which people have died were concentrated in only a comparatively small number of incidents in places of public resort such as hotels, nightclubs, or medical institutes such as hospitals or mental homes.

A complication in deriving conclusions from the existing statistical data is the tendency to build more high-rise structures. Obviously the difficulty in providing sufficient escape will increase, as well as the probability of occurrence of a fire. The last point will be elucidated in more detail. Of the fires now occurring in the home in the Netherlands, for example, it is estimated that in about 10% of these incidents there is a real risk of progressive damage to the building. A statistical survey carried out in the United Kingdom concerning industrial and storage buildings (Baldwin and Allen, 1970) tends to show a probability of structural damage of 14%, which is in fairly good agreement with the percentage just mentioned. Based on a useful life of 75 yr and a total of 3 000 000 homes, the risk of such a disaster is approximately (400 × 75)/3 000 000 or 1:100 per home in the Netherlands.

For a high-rise block, the risk will obviously increase with the number of apartments. In such a block, therefore, there is a real risk of such a fire occurring in the course of its useful lifetime. In view of this risk and its social importance, the directives for high-rise blocks require precautions to be taken against the entire building or part of it collapsing.

Table 4.5 Additional high-rise fire reports *(Courtesy: National Loss Control Service Corporation)*

Type of building (1)	Location (2)	Number of stories (3)	Date (4)	Number of deaths (5)
Office	Rio de Janeiro, Brazil	22	June 29, 1963	5
Office	New York, N.Y., USA	25	Nov. 22, 1961	3
Dormitory	Columbus, Ohio, USA	24	May 10 and 22, 1968	2
Office	Mexico City, Mexico	11	Dec. 9, 1964	1
Hotel	New Orleans, La., USA	17	July 23, 1971	6
Bank	Dallas, Tex., USA	36	Nov. 18, 1961	
Office	Los Angeles, Calif., USA	13	Jan. 28, 1966	
Office	Chicago, Ill., USA	22	May 27, 1965	4
Office	Bogotá, Colombia	24	July 23, 1973	4
Office	Atlanta, Ga., USA	24	Dec. 5, 1968	
Hotel	Rosemont, Ill., USA	10	April 2, 1973	
Department store	Kumamoto, Japan	9	Nov. 28, 1973	103
Office	Tucson, Ariz., USA	11	June 25, 1973	
Office and apartments	Chicago, Ill., USA	100	Nov. 15, 1972	
Office	New York, N.Y., USA	34	July 11, 1975	
Office	New York, N.Y., USA	110	April 17, 1975	

Another important factor, which is closely related to the scale-enlargement, is the increasing risk of casualties for fire brigade and salvage personnel. Considerations of this kind also lead to special precautions to assure structural integrity under fire conditions.

Summarizing, it can be stated that in making cost-benefit calculations concerning primary fire prevention, the main difficulty is making allowance for ethical and political factors. It is thought that the most realistic way to solve this problem is to distribute the money available for reducing the several public risks, in proportion to their magnitude.

On average, the risk of loss of life due to fire is comparatively small compared with that due to road traffic. However, special attention must be paid to buildings like hospitals, hotels, and warehouses. Also high-rise buildings will in general induce extra risk.

Concerning the necessary measures, emphasis is on escape routes, and control of the production and propagation of smoke and toxic gases and spreading of fire. The structure's load-bearing capacity is, with the exception of high-rise buildings and other buildings for which evacuation of people is difficult or impossible, of secondary importance.

Secondary Fire Prevention.   Secondary fire prevention covers the complex of fire precautions whose cost ought to be weighed against their value. In order to do this, it is necessary to be able to evaluate fire-cost-expectation (FCE) in money terms. (The fire-cost-expectation is the probable cost that will be caused by fire during a certain period.) If measures are taken in order to diminish the FCE, the cost of the

Table 4.6 Number of persons killed as result of traffic accidents in 1967 per 100 000 inhabitants
(ECCS, 1974a)

Country (1)	Number of persons killed per 100 000 inhabitants (2)	Average accident risk if life expectancy is 75 years (3)
United Kingdom	16	1:83
West Germany	28	1:48
France	27	1:49
The Netherlands	23	1:58

Table 4.7 Number of persons killed by fire in 1967 per 100 000 inhabitants

Country (1)	Number of persons killed per 100 000 inhabitants (2)	Average risk if life expectancy is 75 years (3)
United Kingdom	1.38	1:966
Sweden	1.68[a]	1:794
France	0.57[b]	1:2339
The Netherlands	0.51[a]	1:2614

[a]Caution is required in interpreting the figures, especially in the case of countries with a small population, like Sweden and The Netherlands. One or two severe fires can have a strong influence on the results.
[b]Because no 1967 values were available for France, 1971 values are given.

measures ought to be smaller than the decrease of the FCE, otherwise the measures cause a loss instead of a gain (shown schematically in Fig. 4.61).

The FCE is influenced by three independent factors:

1. The probability of flashover in any one room. Flashover is a stage in the development of a fire in an enclosure at which the speed of propagation of flame increases significantly and the whole enclosure becomes involved in fire. It is assumed that there is some structural damage only in cases where flashover occurs.

2. The consequences of such a fire causing structural damage, the spread of fire to adjacent rooms, and the production and propagation of gases damaging the contents.

3. The direct and indirect economic consequences of the phenomena considered in (2). The problem can be approached from two angles: (a) That of the national economy; and (b) that of business economics. These two aspects will be discussed in succession.

Fire prevention at national level.   Looking at fire prevention at the national level, a complex of risks of different types is involved. Therefore it will be difficult to make use of a statistical or a deterministic description of the factors determining the expected damage by fire and mentioned earlier. Examining the losses due to fire and the costs of the precautions to reduce these losses is thought to be a more realistic approach. For this purpose, Table 4.8 gives the direct losses due to fire as a percentage of the gross national product for the year 1965.

It is seen that the direct losses for most of the countries amount to 0.20% to 0.30% of GNP. A fire, however, causes not only direct damage, such as loss of buildings, machinery and stocks, but often indirect damage as well. Indirect damage is that caused by stoppages in production, sales, etc. No figures are available showing the extent of such indirect damage.

Based on random sampling in the Netherlands, indirect damage of about one-half the direct damage on the total seems a fair estimate (Witteveen, 1969). The fact that such an important component of the total losses is missing in most of the available data means that one has to be very careful in analyzing these data. Therefore we will limit ourselves to a broad discussion concerning some tendencies.

From loss statistics it becomes clear that in several countries the direct annual losses related to GNP have tended to increase in recent years. This increase in fire damage is due mainly to upscaling of industry. As a result of the increase in losses, in some countries a growing tendency can be detected to increase also the level of precautions.

Insurance companies in particular sometimes urge further efforts by the authorities to limit material damage. Reducing fire damage is of course a laudable endeavor in itself, but it is often overlooked that the necessary precautions may involve heavy expense. If, for instance, all industrial buildings were to be equipped with automatic fire extinguishing installations, fire loss would undoubtedly be reduced, but the cost of the installations would certainly be bigger than the abatement in damage. On the other hand, some precautions, such as information and research, cost little by comparison. It must be kept in mind that the fire costs in fact are composed of the sum total of the damage itself and the cost of precautions taken to limit it. To give a rough idea of the present situation, Table 4.9 gives estimates of the annual fire costs in a number of countries.

Somewhat surprisingly it appears that the proportions of the different components of the fire cost are about the same for the countries mentioned.

The figures available are insufficient to indicate the most favorable distribution of the cost, but it can be concluded from Table 4.9 that only about 40% of the total fire costs are due to losses. This means that in the present situation already 60% of the total fire costs are assigned to precautions. Comparing the presented figures with those of Table 4.9 it appears that on the average, the total annual fire costs amount to about 1% of the GNP.

As stated before, increasing the cost of precautions is justified only if the sum total of cost of damage and of precautions is not increased. In principle, losses and expenditures should be allocated so that their sum total is a minimum. This is shown qualitatively in Fig. 4.62. The lower curve gives the relationship between cost of damage and precautions, and the upper curve that between cost of precautions and total national fire cost (that is, losses plus expenditures). The second curve can thus be derived from the first. The minimum standard of precautions necessary for primary fire prevention is also shown. It is by no means certain that the present allocation of losses and expenditures is the optimum (point A on the curve). If the

Table 4.8 Direct losses due to fire as percentage of gross national product of several countries for 1965

Country (1)	Direct losses due to fire, as a percentage of gross national product (2)
United Kingdom	0.24
West Germany	0.14
France	0.33
The Netherlands	0.21
Canada	0.28
Denmark	0.23
Finland	0.16
Norway	0.29
Sweden	0.20

Table 4.9 Estimates of annual fire costs in some countries as percentage of total fire costs

Source of cost (1)	United Kingdom (2)	The Netherlands (3)	United States of America (4)	Canada (5)
Losses:				
direct economic loss	30.0	26.3	29.5	30.3
indirect economic loss	—	12.3	—	—
loss by injury	0.2	—	4.7	0.3
Expenditures:				
suppression	26.8	15.4	32.2	34.3
prevention and protection	16.0	15.4	13.7	14.8
costs of providing insurance	26.8	30.8	19.5	20.2
research and development	0.2	0.3	0.4	0.1

present position corresponds to point C there is no justification for increasing cost-incurring precautions; they could more appropriately be reduced. Only if the present position corresponds, say, to point B is an increase in precautions economically justified. The problem is, however, that the relationship between costs of damage and precautions is not known (lower curve in Fig 4.62) and decisions therefore have to be based on qualitative considerations. The same applies to allocation of individual cost items. It is quite possible in principle to obtain a more effective cost allocation by increasing fire brigade capacity and at the same time reducing precautions in buildings, or vice versa. So far, no serious effort has been made to obtain greater knowledge regarding the cost-benefit ratio of fire prevention, yet this will be essential before sound measures can be taken.

Fire prevention at commercial level. For fire prevention at the commercial level, it can be stated that in general there is more detailed information, and in principle a more detailed estimate of the relationship between cost of precaution and damage expectation is possible. A condition, of course, is that the physical and statistical laws involved can be described with sufficient accuracy.

Besides physical and statistical influences, however, human factors also are involved (for example, psychological reaction and discipline). In this discussion we will limit ourselves to the structural fire engineering design, and damage due to smoke production and so on will be omitted.

Probability of occurrence of fire and flashover. The probability of occurrence of a fire and subsequently the probability of flashover occurring in any room will be strongly influenced by human factors. (Structural damage before flashover will be slight.) A rough estimate of both risks in dwellings has already been made in discussing the primary fire prevention. The risk of flashover appears to be 10^{-2} during an expected useful life of a dwelling, the risk of occurrence of fire being 10 times greater.

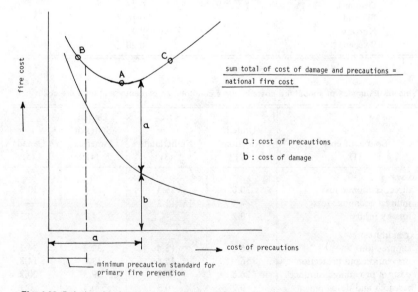

Fig. 4.62 Relationship between cost of precautions and national fire cost *(ECCS, 1974b)*

The "over-all" risk of flashover occurring in a building constituting a number of apartments can be derived from the probability mentioned previously. For a high-rise dwelling block with apartments which are equal in size, equally equipped and used in the same way, this risk will obviously increase proportionately to the number of apartments.

According to Lie (1972), the probability of occurrence of flashover is related to a risk per year and per unit floor area. He makes two extreme estimates based on existing data: for high fire risk, $P_f = 10 \times 10^{-7}$ per m² per yr; and for low fire risk, $P_f = 0.5 \times 10^{-7}$ per m² per yr.

Assuming a dwelling with a floor surface of 130 m² and a useful life of 75 yr, a risk of flashover during lifetime will be found of about 1% in case of high fire risk and about 0.05% in case of low fire risk. It is seen that the value for high fire risk is of the same order as that calculated for family houses according to Dutch circumstances.

Somewhat different figures for the United Kingdom are derived according to Thomas and Baldwin (1971). They suggest that, assuming an economic lifetime of 75 yr, the number of fires occurring during such period would be: 3.3 for industrial buildings; 0.4 for offices; and 0.2 for houses.

Using a small sample, Baldwin and Allen (1970) estimated the chance of structural damage, in case of a fire, to be 14%. Assuming that flashover has occurred only in those cases, the following rough estimates of the chance of flashover during a lifetime can be given: 0.46 for industrial buildings; 0.06 for offices; and 0.03 for houses.

It is emphasized once more that the given risks are very much dependent on human factors and can, as far as the ignition is concerned, be influenced only to a small degree by technical measures. The probability of flashover, however, can be influenced strongly by technical precautions (for example, applying sprinkler installation, reducing the time of calling the fire brigade, supervision, etc.). These facts will to some extent be responsible for the considerable scatter in the figures given in the preceding paragraphs. Besides this it must be kept in mind that all the information is based on fairly rough estimates.

Structural consequences of fire.   The structural behavior under fire conditions is described traditionally in terms of fire resistance time. The fire resistance is correlated to criteria concerning either temperature conditions occurring at certain places in the structural member or collapse of the member.

From a statistical point of view it must be emphasized that only the probability can be given that the named criteria will be reached. This probability will depend on the chosen fire resistance criteria and the stochastic properties of both the load function S and the response function R. A limit state occurs if $S > R$. In Fig. 4.63 the stochastic approach is given in a schematic way. Subsequently several items given in this scheme will be discussed.

Load function S.   At the moment a flashover occurs in a compartment the loads will be random choices of varying loads during lifetime. The value of these loads will be much lower than the maximum loads that can be expected during lifetime (Fig 4.64). This is in contradiction with the present design methods for fire.

Response function R.   The load-bearing capacity of a structure is influenced by the structural dimensions and the material properties. In the case of fire the material properties are substantially influenced by the temperature rise.

Some data are available on material properties at elevated temperatures, but little is known about the scatter in these properties. The ambient temperature in case of a fully developed fire is a stochastic quantity. Taking into account the heat flow properties of the fire and the heat flow properties of the structure, which are also of a stochastic nature, the temperature in the relevant parts of the structure can be predicted. Finally the bearing capacity of the construction during a fire can be calculated. Of course this bearing capacity R is again a stochastic quantity.

Determination of probability of reaching limit state p_f. Knowing the stochastic properties of the S and R the probability of reaching a limit state can be calculated. Cornell (1969) enunciated the principles of this approach using analytical methods. Based on such methods Lie (1972) has investigated the influence of factors like floor area, building size, and stochastic properties of fire load density. Due to lack of reliable basic data however, the results can only be used in a qualitative way. The same holds true for other studies in which, given flashover, some detailed calculations are performed concerning the chance of failure for specific structural

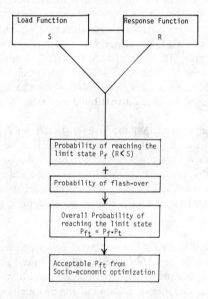

Fig. 4.63 Probabilistic approach toward fire engineering design (skeleton) *(ECCS, 1974b)*

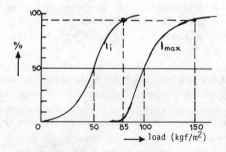

Fig. 4.64 Comparison between instantaneous floor-load I_i and maximum floor-load I_{max} during lifetime according to Arne Johnson *(ECCS, 1974b)*

elements like steel beams and concrete slabs. In these studies, instead of analytical methods, use is made of Monte Carlo simulations. The work done by Magnusson (1973) attracts particular attention because it is based on the most realistic assumptions made so far.

Economic consequences.   The aim of this subsection is to analyze what probability is acceptable in a pure economic sense. When the limit state has been reached for a structural element, there will also be consequential losses.

Obviously this depends on the function of the structural element involved. The failure, for example, of a window pane by fire will not cause so much damage as failure of a column which provides stability to a whole structure. In the first case, besides damage to the contents of the room only a pane has to be replaced. In the second case the whole building including the contents will be lost.

Ligtenberg (1971) introduced a method by which the influence of the function of a structural element on the consequential damage can be indicated. For this purpose the consequential damage C is expressed as a fraction of the cost of the structural element involved K thus

$$C = nK \hspace{3cm} ' \hspace{0.3cm} (4.20)$$

in which n = parameter giving information about the functional importance.

A broken window pane will cause a damage $\sim 1K$ to $2K$. If a floor fails and causes extensive damage n may well be on the order of magnitude of 1000. If the failure of a column in a high-rise building causes a total collapse the damage may be many millions of times as great as the initial cost of the column. Limit states, however, do not always mean collapse—for reaching, say, a certain specified deflection, n may be only 0.1 or 1.0.

The cost-expectation due to the consequential damage may be approximated now by the product of the probability of flashover p_i, the probability of reaching the limit state p_f, and the consequential damage when the limit state has been reached (nK). Thus

$$\text{cost-expectation due to consequential damage} = p_i p_f nK \hspace{1cm} (4.21)$$

The total fire-cost-expectation (FCE) is the sum total of costs of structural element involved and the consequential damage, that is

$$\text{FCE} = K + p_i p_f nK \hspace{2cm} (4.22)$$

Obviously the probability of reaching the limit state p_f can be decreased by taking protective measures. This means that the initial costs of the structural element will increase, but a small increase in the quality of the fire protection will lead to a considerable decrease of p_f, and in general the cost of fire protection will increase less than what would be proportional to the effectiveness. As a result of these two facts, the additional cost to reduce the probability of reaching a limit state will be comparatively small.

However, up to the present all studies performed to quantify cost-benefit calculations in the field of fire engineering must be considered as pilot studies. The final aim, that is the possibility of a fire engineering design fully based on the principles described, is still far from being achieved. Therefore we will continue the discussion in a qualitative sense. As can be understood and demonstrated, precautions must be taken in accordance with the functional importance of the structural members under consideration. In practice this means, for example, that more attention has to be paid to the columns of the first floor of a high-rise building than to the beams bearing its roof. Generally speaking, designs in which failure of one single structural member causes the whole structure to be lost (in other words n-value is high) must be avoided.

Reduction of n can be achieved by:

1. Statically indeterminate design. The fact that the load-bearing capacity is provided by only one or a few structural elements will obviously result in a high value of n. From the point of view of fire engineering, designing multiple statically indeterminate structures is preferable.

2. Compartmentation. Even in a statically indeterminate structure the value of n will be high if it can be expected that the fire will spread easily all through the structure. Therefore, in addition to the statically indeterminate design it will be advisable to supply fire resistant compartmentation.

Of course it must be kept in mind that possible extra cost in realizing the factors mentioned above must be weighed against their benefit. This means that for the

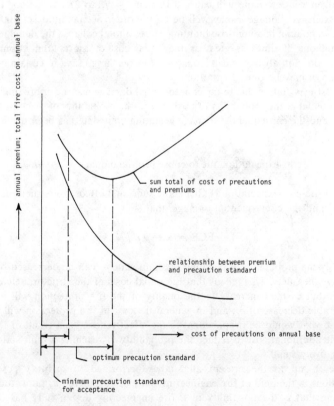

Fig. 4.65 Cost-benefit comparison on business level *(ECCS, 1974b)*

construction as a whole also, a cost-benefit comparison has to be made. Doing this, the approach discussed previously can be used as a base. Considering the construction as a whole, there is an important item which was not discussed in detail so far: the influence of insurance.

The optimum standard of precautions is reached when the total of the costs of precautions and damage expectancy relative to the insurance premium is a minimum. Fig. 4.65 shows this qualitatively, by analogy with Fig. 4.62.

In order to make this model operational, the insurer must know the ratio between precaution standard and damage expectancy. From this he can determine the relationship between precaution standard and premium. By calculating the cost of the precaution standard, the owner can relate cost and premium (lower curve in Fig. 4.65). Owing to lack of statistics, the relationship between precautions and premium incorporated in the rates is thus determined qualitatively and is often unclear. With the possibilities now available and outlined earlier, a better adjustment should certainly be feasible in future.

A final point, and an aspect of some importance, is the following: in taking measures to improve fire prevention for a building, their ultimate effect will have to be carefully considered.

Experience has shown that a fire often damages the structure so badly that the building has to be demolished even though it has not collapsed. The cost of protecting it against collapse can then be regarded as lost. In such a case, precautions would better have been limited to a standard at which evacuation is guaranteed. On the other hand, examples are conceivable where it is important to be able to use the building after a fire: for instance, high-rise apartments and multistory industrial buildings. In such cases it seems advisable to switch the limit state criterion from the failure criterion to a reserviceability criterion with the possibility of replacement or repair. This will generally result in higher requirements.

4.14 APPENDIX: FIRE DRILL

The following photographs are the record of an actual fire drill carried out by the fire brigade in Hong Kong. The captions with each photograph provide the story of this dramatic simulation. The photographs and captions are courtesy of Fred Jackson, President, Hong Kong Branch, Institution of Fire Engineers, Hong Kong.

Fig. 4.66 The 32-story apartment building "Tower Louisa" in Hong Kong was selected for the fire drill. Fire "reported" on 28th floor. Persons on roof waving for help. (Time: 16:59)

Fig. 4.67 Firemen on the scene, en route to elevator in which they will ascend to the 26th floor. (A floor, two below that of the known or suspect floor on fire, was selected for safety.) Fire station was 3/4 miles away. (17:04)

Fig. 4.68 Fireman actuates switch adjacent to elevator. Operation of the switch brings the elevator to the ground floor immediately neutralizing all other landing call buttons, and the electrical supply to the elevator bypasses the input and cannot be turned off accidentally. (17:05)

Fig. 4.69 In attendance at 26th floor. Line from riser goes up stairs to 28th floor and roof. (17:07)

Fig. 4.70 Brought up in the elevator by the first attending crews, hose, dividing breeching, and branches are being connected and advanced from 26th floor to roof. (17:07)

Fig. 4.71 Breathing apparatus, compressed air open circuits, duration about 40 minutes. Entry control was established on floor. It has been checked and found to be free of fire and smoke. Information already transmitted to control center. (17:09)

Fig. 4.72 Lines from 26th floor to the upper floors already charged. (17:10)

Fig. 4.73 Jets (fire streams) on roof (32nd floor). The roof was chosen in the drill to eliminate the possibility of water damage to the apartments on the 28th floor. (17:10)

Fig. 4.74 Light portable pump taken up in elevator or carried by hand to best level to boost high level jets. (17:39)

Fig. 4.75 A different exercise. This action is to lift firefighting equipment from the nearest helipad to the roofs of buildings, offshore islands, and inaccessible locations.

Fig. 4.76 Fireman en route to join his colleagues and equipment (already "dropped" at fire site). Helicopters of the Royal Air Force and the Auxiliary Air Force (as shown) are available round the clock for these duties and on call. Loading and size govern men and equipment at any one time. At one bus crash rescue on an offshore island at least six helicopters were in use for casualty evacuation.

4.15 CONDENSED REFERENCES/BIBLIOGRAPHY

The following is a condensed bibliography for this chapter. Not only does it include all articles referred to or cited in the text, but it also contains bibliography for further reading. The full citations will be found at the end of the Volume. What is given here should be sufficient information to lead the reader to the correct article: the author, date, and title. In case of multiple authors, only the first named is listed.

AISI 1965, *Structural Properties of High Strength Steels at Elevated Temperature*
ANSI 1969, *Operation of Elevators Under Fire or Other Emergency Conditions*
ASCE 1973, *Planning and Design of Tall Buildings: Bibliography of Tall Buildings*
ASHRAE 1972, *Infiltration and Natural Ventilation*
ASHRAE 1973a, *Fire and Smoke Control*
ASHRAE 1973b, *Symposium on Experience and Applications on Smoke and Fire Control*
ASTM 1974, *Standard Methods of Fire Test of Building Construction and Materials*
Abraham undated, *The Cost of Human Life in Economic Decisions*
Alpert 1972, *Calculation of Response Time of Ceiling-Mounted Fire Detectors*
Arnault 1974, *Heating Behavior of External Columns Under Fire Exposure*
Arnault 1976, *Resistance in Fires of Structures Made of Steel and Concrete*
Ashton 1964, *Curtain Walling and Fire Protection*
Assoc. Com. on the National Building Code of Canada 1973, *Measures for Fire Safety in High*

BOCA 1973, *Proposed Standard for the Design and Installation of the Suppression Systems*
BRI 1972, *Strength of Sennichi Department Building After Fire*
BSI 1968, *Precautions Against Fire: Office Buildings*
BSI 1970, 1974, *Automatic Fire Alarm Systems in Buildings*
Badami 1973, *Hi-Rise Building Construction in India and Problems of Fire*
Baldwin 1970, *Some Statistics of Damage to Buildings in Fires*
Barrett 1969, *A Computer Technique for Predicting Smoke Movement in Tall Buildings*
Bessey 1950, *Investigation on Building Fires: Visible Changes in Concrete or Mortar Exposed*
Birman 1973, *Fire and Safety*
Bletzacker 1966, *Effect of Structural Restraint on the Fire Resistance of Protected Steel Beams*
Boner 1973, *Fire Protection in Tall Buildings*
Bongard 1963, *Burning Test for Protected Steel Structures*
Bono 1969, *New Criteria for Fire Endurance Test*
Bowes 1969, *The Assessment of Smoke Production by Building Materials in Fires*
British Fire Protection Systems Association Ltd. 1973, *Report on the Performance of Fire Alarm*
Building Services Engineer 1971, *Smoke Tests in the Pressurized Stairs and Lobbies*
Butcher 1966, *The Temperature Attained by Steel in Building Fires*
Butcher 1968, *Pressurisation as a Means of Controlling the Movement of Smoke and Toxic*
Butcher 1968, *Fire and Car-Park Buildings*
Butcher 1971, *Smoke Tests in the Law Courts Building*

CIDECT 1970, *Concrete Filled Hollow Sections*
CTICM 1975, *Forecasting Fire Effects on Steel Structures*
Cavoulakos 1975, *Fire Protection of Tall Buildings*
Christian 1970, *Fire Behavior of Interior Finish Materials*
Claiborne 1971, *Automatic Sprinkler—It Is, It Isn't*
Claiborne 1973, *Requirement for Fire Protection and Safety in Tall Buildings*
Colell 1973, *Some Safety Measures Against Fires in Very High Buildings*
Concrete and Masonry Industry 1975, *Fire Safety in High-Rise Buildings*
Cornell 1969, *A Probability-Based Structural Code*
Correale 1973, *Stair Pressurization for Fire Protection*

De Cicco 1972, *Report of Fire Tests, Analyses and Evaluation of Stair Pressurization*
Degenkolb 1971, *Smoke-Proof Enclosures*
Degenkolb 1974, *The Evolution of High Rise Fire Protection*
Devaty 1973, *Fireproof Floors with Metal Panels*
Dick 1953, *Air Infiltration Through Gaps Around Windows*
Dorn 1962, *Progress in Understanding High Temperature Creep*
Dufour 1963, *Survey of Available Information on the Toxicity of the Combustion and Thermal*

ECCS 1974a, *Research Into the Fire Resistance of Steel Structures*
ECCS 1974b, *Fire Safety in Constructional Steelwork*

Ehm 1973, *Behavior of the Structure Under Fire*
Elevator World 1971, *Editorial, Speaking of Issues*
Emmons 1967, *Fire Research Abroad*

FOC 1968, *Rules for Automatic Sprinkler Installation*
Fire 1972, *Intumescent Honeycomb Fire Barriers now Available*
Fitzgerald 1973, *Building Code Changes and Hi-Rise Safety*
Fitzgerald 1976, *Bibliography on Panic Reaction*
Foy 1928, *Clowning Through Life*
Freeman 1974, *Problems Associated with Fire in Tall Buildings*
Fujita undated, *Characteristics of Fire Inside a Non-Combustible Room and Prevention of Fire*

GSA 1971a, *Public Buildings Service International Conference of Fire Safety in High-Rise*
GSA 1971b, *Reconvened International Conference on Fire-Safety in High-Rise Buildings*
GSA 1973, *Research Practice Needs*
GSA 1974, *Fire Safety Systems—Richard B. Russell Courthouse and Federal Office Building*
GSA 1975, *Building Fire Safety Criteria*
Galbreath 1968a, *Fire in High Buildings*
Galbreath 1968b, *A Survey of Exit Facilities in High Office Buildings*
Galbreath 1969, *Time of Evacuation by Stairs in High Buildings*
Garofolo 1952, *The Influence of Temperature on the Elastic Constants of Some Commercial*
Gewain 1974, *Fire Experience and Fire Tests in Automobile Parking Structures*
Gibson 1972, *A Very Early Warning Smoke Detector*
Glass 1969, *Mass Psychology—The Determinants of Behavior Under Emergency Conditions*
Glasstone 1962, *The Effects of Nuclear Weapons*
Green 1971, *Reinstatement of Concrete Structures After Fire*
Green 1971, *Unit Repairs to Fire Damaged Concrete Structure*
Gross 1962, *Experiments on Burning of Cross Piles of Wood*
Gross 1965, *Experimental Fire in Enclosures*
Gross 1967, *American Society of Testing and Materials STP 422*
Gustaferro 1975, *How Fire Considerations Affects the Design of Tall Buildings*

Halpin 1973, *An In Depth Fire Casualty Study*
Hamzah 1974, *Fire Protection of High Rise Buildings in Kuala Lumpur*
Harmathy 1967, *Deflection and Failure of Steel Supported Floors and Beams in Fire*
Harmathy 1968, *Determining the Temperature History of Concrete Construction During Fire*
Harmathy 1970, *Elevated Temperature Tensile and Creep Properties of Some Structural*
Harrison 1974, *The High-Rise Fire Problem*
Heselden 1968, *Parameters Determining the Severity of Fire*
Heselden 1971, *Fire Problems of Pedestrian Precincts Part 1: The Smoke Production of Various*
Hobsen 1972, *Pressurization of Escape Routes in Buildings*
Humphreys 1973, *The Alarming Problem*
Hutcheon 1968, *Smoke Problems in High-Rise Buildings*

IHVE 1973, *Recommendations Relating the Design of Air-handling Systems to Fire and Smoke*
ISO 1974, *Fire Resistance Tests on Door and Shutter Assemblies*
ISO 1975, *Fire Resistance Test of Structures*
ISO 1976, *Fire Resistance Test on Door and Shutter Assemblies (Revised)*
Ingberg 1928, *Test of the Severity of Building Fires*

JFRO 1969, *Movement of Smoke on Escape Routes in Buildings*
Japanese Association of Fire Science and Engineering 1972, *Fire*
Japanese Association of Fire Science and Engineering 1974, *Occasional Report*
Jensen 1973, *Means of Fire Fighting and Safety Devices*
Jerus 1972, *Fire Safety in Tall Buildings*
Juillerat 1962, *The Hartford Hospital Fire*
Juillerat 1967, *Fire at Dale's Penthouse Restaurant*

Kawagoe 1963, *Estimation of Fire Temperature-Time Curve in Rooms*
Kawagoe 1967, *Estimation of Fire Temperature-Time Curve in Rooms*
Kawagoe 1971, *Factors Influencing Natural Fires and Their Development*
Kawagoe 1973, *System Design for Fire Safety*
Kimura 1957, *Basic Theory of Building Plan*
Kingman 1953, *The Products of Combustion in Burning Buildings*
Kordina 1972, *An Examination of the Effects of a Big Fire in Some Concrete Buildings*
Kotze 1975, *Fire Fighting, Education and Evacuation Problems in Tall Buildings*
Kruppa 1975, *Determination of the Critical Temperature of a Statically Indeterminate Structure*
Kruppa 1976, *Study of Temperatures and Criteria of Steel Structures*

Kulkarni 1973, *Fire Protection in High-Rise Buildings*

Lathrop 1975, *In Oseola, A Matter of Contents*
Lathrop 1977, *300 Fire Fighters Save Los Angeles High-Rise Office Building*
Law 1963, *Heat Radiation From Fires and Building Separation*
Law 1968, *Radiation from Fires in a Compartment*
Law 1972, *Nomograms for the Fire Protection of Structural Steel Work*
Law 1973a, *Fire Loads, Natural Fires and Standard Fires*
Law 1973b, *The Prediction of Fire Resistance*
Law 1974, *Fire—The Risks and the Precautions*
Lay 1973, *A Rational Approach to Fire Resistant Design*
Lea 1914, *The Change of the Modulus of Elasticity and of Other Properties of Metal*
Lie 1972, *Fire and Buildings*
Lie 1974, *Fire Resistance on Reinforced Concrete Columns*
Lie 1974, *Empirical Method for Calculating Fire Resistance of Steel Columns*
Lie 1975, *Control of Smoke in High-Rise Buildings*
Ligtenberg 1971, *What Safety Margin is Necessary in a Structure?*
Lowman 1973, *Problems of Fire Prevention and Means of Escape in the Case of Fire*
Lyalin 1973, *Structural Fire Precautions in the Soviet Union*

Magnusson 1969, *A Qualified Fire Protection Design of Structural Steel Members*
Magnusson 1969, *Fire Engineering Dimensioning of Insulated Steel Structures*
Magnusson 1971, *Comments on the Rate of Gas Flow and Rate of Burning for Fires in Enclosures*
Magnusson 1973, *Probabilistic Analysis of Fire Safety*
Mak 1975, *Ultimate Strength Design of Multi-Story Steel Building Columns for Fire*
Malhotra 1964, *Movement of Smoke in Escape Routes and Effect of Pressurization*
Malhotra 1974, *Determination of Flame Spread and Fire Resistance*
Margarido 1974, *The Fire and Restoration of the "Edificio Andraus" in Saõ Paulo, Brazil*
Marryatt 1971, *Automatic Sprinkler Performance in Australia and New Zealand*
Marryatt 1974, *Significant Fire Cases in Australia*
Martin 1965, *Diffusion Controlled Ignition of Cellulosic Materials by Intense Radiant Energy*
McCormick 1957, *Human Engineer*
McGuire 1965, *Fire and the Spatial Separation of Buildings*
McGuire 1970, *Factors in Controlling Smoke in High Buildings*
McGuire 1971a, *Smoke Control in High-Rise Buildings*
McGuire 1971b, *Smoke Control in High-Rise Buildings*
McGuire 1975, *Simple Analysis of Smoke-Flow Problems in High Buildings*
McHale 1974, *Life Support Without Combustion Hazards*
Meisen 1977, *Emergencies in Tall Buildings: The Designers Respond to Human Response*
Melinek 1972, *A Method of Evaluating Human Life for Economic Purposes*
Melinek 1975, *CIB Symposium on the Control of Smoke Movement in Building Fires*
Ministry of Labour 1965, *Guide to the Use of Flame Arresters and Explosion Reliefs*
Morris 1974, *Fire Research Note No. 995*
Motta 1973, *Complementary and Protection Works in Steel Structures*
Moulen 1973, *Control of Smoke From Fire in an Air-Conditioned Building*

NFPA 1967, *Life Safety Code*
NFPA 1971, *Installation of Sprinkler Systems*
NFPA 1972, *Fire Journal*
NFPA 1973a, *Code for Safety to Life from Fire in Buildings and Structures*
NFPA 1973b, *Life Safety Code*
NFPA 1974a, *Standard for Automatic Fire Detectors*
NFPA 1974b, *Taiyo Department Store Fire, Dumamoto, Japan*
NFPA 1975a, *Standard for Installation of Sprinkler Systems*
NFPA 1975b, *Standard for the Installation, Maintenance and Use of Portable Fire Extinguisher*
NFPA 1975c, *Standard for Fire Doors and Windows*
Newsweek 1942, *Catastrophe: Coconut Grove, Boston's Oldest Nightclub*
Nikai 1971, *Method of Fireproofing Steel Framed Building in Japan*
Nilsson 1971, *The Effect of Porosity and Air Flow Factor on the Rate of Burning for Fire*

OTUA 1975, *Data on Some Currently Used Steels*
O'Hagan 1972, *New York Fire Department Conducts Fire Tests in High-Rise*

Palmer 1974, *Fire Hazards of Plastics in Furniture and Furnishings; Ignition Studies*
Patton 1971, *Life Safety System*
Pauls 1958, *Movement of People in Buildings*
Pauls 1975, *Evacuation and Other Fire Safety Measures in High Buildings*

Peterson 1969, *Ohio State University Fires*
Pettersson 1973, *Fire Engineering Design of Tall Buildings*
Pettersson 1976, *Fire Engineering Design of Steel Structures*
Powers 1971a, *New York Office Building Fire*
Powers 1971b, *Office Building Fire, 919 Third Avenue, New York City*

QMC-IMR 1973, *Smoke from Burning Plastics*
Quarantelli 1977, *Panic Behavior: Some Empirical Observations*

Rasbash 1966, *The Generation of Carbon Monoxide by Fires in Compartment*
Rasbash 1967, **Smoke and Toxic Products Produced at Fires**
Roberts 1974, *The Behaviour of Polyurethane Foam in Fire*
Robertson 1959, *Proposed Criteria for Defining Load Failure of Beams, Floors and Roof*
Rubin 1974, *Occupant Behavior in Building Fires*

SAA 1971, *Code for Automatic Sprinkler Installations*
SAA 1972, *Use of Lifts in Emergencies*
SAA 1973-1975, *Methods for Fire Tests on Building Materials and Structures*
SAA 1974, *Australian Specification for Fire Dampers*
SAA 1974, *SAA Mechanical Ventilation and Air Conditioning Code, Part I—Fire Precautions*
SAA 1974, *Rules for Automatic Fire Alarm Installations*
SAA 1976, *Fire Door Code: Fire Doors*
Sampson 1972, *The General Services Administrations's Systems Approach to Life Safety*
Sander 1973, *A Fortran IV Program to Simulate Air Movement in Multi-Storey Buildings*
Sarto 1966, *Behavior of End Restrained Steel Members Under Fire*
Sasaki 1965, *Air Leakage Value for Residential Windows*
Schultz 1964, *Panic Behavior: Discussion and Readings*
Seigel 1969, *The Projection of Flames from Burning Buildings*
Sfintesco 1971, *Fire and Blast*
Sfintesco 1973a, *Fire and Blast*
Sfintesco 1973b, *Fire Safety Criteria for the Design of Tall Buildings*
Sfintesco 1973c, *Theme Report: Fire and Blast*
Sfintesco 1976, *Towering Haven—Condensed Story of a Fire*
Sharry 1973, *An Atrium Fire*
Sharry 1974, *South America Burning*
Sharry 1975, *High-Rise Hotel Fire, Virginia Beach*
Shaw 1973, *Fortran IV Programs for Calculating Sizes and Venting Capacities of Smoke Shafts*
Shaw 1973, *Air Leakage Measurements of the Exterior Walls of Tall Buildings*
Shaw 1974, *Program to Simulate Stair-Shaft Pressurization System in Multi-Storey Buildings*
Shorter 1960, *The St. Lawrence Burns*
Shorter 1967, *Fire in Tall Buildings*
Simha 1973, *Fire Safety in Tall Buildings*
Simms 1960, *Ignition of Cellulosic Materials by Radiation*
Smith 1970, *The Rate of Burning of Wood Cribs*
Stark 1972, *Smoke and Toxic Gases from Burning Plastics*
Stone 1974, *Office Building*
Stramdahl 1973, *The Tranas Fire Tests*
Swayne 1975, *Fire Protection at the National Archives*
Swedish FPA 1969, *International Symposium: Plastic-Fire-Corrosion*

Tall 1961, *Residual Stresses in Welded Plates. A Theoretical Study*
Tamura 1969, *Computer Analysis of Smoke Movement in Tall Buildings*
Tamura 1970, *Analysis of Smoke Shafts for Control of Smoke Movement in Buildings*
Tamura 1970, *Natural Venting to Control Smoke Movement in Buildings Via Vertical Shafts*
Tamura 1970, *Air-Handling Systems for Control of Smoke Movement*
Tamura 1971, *Smoke Movement in High-Rise Buildings*
Tamura 1972, *Computer Analysis of Smoke Control With Building Air Handling System*
Tamura 1973, *The Pressurized Building Method of Controlling Smoke in High-Rise Buildings*
Tamura 1973, *Basis for the Design of Smoke Shafts*
Tamura 1974, *Experimental Studies on Pressurized Escape Routes*
Tewerson 1971, *Some Observations on Experimental Fires in Enclosures Part 1: Cellulosic*
Theobald 1968, *Fully Developed Fires with Furniture in a Compartment*
Thomas 1967, *Theoretical Considerations of the Growth to Flashover of Compartment Fires*
Thomas 1967, *Fully Developed Compartment Fires—Two Kinds of Behaviour*
Thomas 1970, *Burning Rate of Ventilation Controlled Fires in Compartments*
Thomas 1971, *Some Comments on the Choice of Failure Probabilities in Fires*
Thomas 1973, *Effects of Fuel Geometry in Fires*

Thomas 1974, *Fires in Model Rooms: CIB Research Programmes*
Thomas 1974, *The Projection of Flames From Buildings on Fire*
Thompson 1975, *The Decision Tree for Fire Safety Systems Analysis: What It Is and How to Use*
Thor 1973, *Deformations and Critical Loads of Steel Beams Under Fire Exposure Conditions*

Underwriters Laboratories, Inc. 1971, *Smoke Detectors, Photoelectric Type, for Fire-Protective*
Underwriters Laboratories, Inc. 1974, *Smoke Detectors, Combustion Products Type*
Underwriters Laboratories, Inc. 1974, *Thermostats, Fire Detection*
Uribe 1973, *The Avianca Fire*

Verse 1935, *The Elastic Properties of Steel at High Temperatures*
Vinnakota 1974, *Fire Resistance of Steel Structures*
Vinnakota 1975, *Behavior of Steel Structures in Fire*

Wagner 1972, *Survey of Toxic Species Evolved in the Pyrolysis and Combustion of Polymers*
Wakamatsu 1969, *Calculation of Smoke Movement and Measures Controlling Smoke*
Wakamatsu 1969, *Field Experiment on Smoke Control (Smoke Stopping Experiment)*
Wakamatsu 1971, *Calculation of Smoke Movement in Buildings*
Wakamatsu 1972, *Design of Fire Cover on Steel Structure*
Watrous 1969, *Fire in High-Rise Apartment Building, Hawthorne House, Chicago*
Watrous 1973, *High-Rise Fire in New Orleans*
Wheatley 1973, *Fire Temperature and Toxic Effects on Structures and Occupants*
Wheatley 1974, *Fire and Smoke Problems in Tall Buildings*
Willey 1972a, *Tae Yon Kak Hotel Fire, Seoul Korea*
Willey 1972b, *High-Rise Building Fire, Saõ Paulo, Brazil*
Willey 1973, *Baptist Towers Housing for the Elderly, Atlanta, Georgia*
Wilson 1968a, *Stack Effect in Buildings*
Wilson 1968b, *Stack Effect and Building Design*
Wilson 1970, *Fire and High Buildings*
Wilson 1971, *The Smoke Problem and Its Control in High-Rise Building*
Withey 1962, *Reaction to Uncertain Threat*
Witteveen 1966, *Fire-Resistant Construction in Steel Buildings*
Witteveen 1969, *Basic Principles of Fire Prevention in Buildings and the Theoretical Determination*
Witteveen 1971, *Basic Principles of Fire Prevention*
Witteveen 1972, *Fire and Blast*
Wood 1972, *The Behavior of People in Fires*
Woolley 1972, *The Thermal Decomposition Products of Phenol-Formaldehyde*
Wooley 1972, *Nitrogen-Containing Products from the Thermal Decomposition of Flexible*
Wu 1974, *Modeling and Simulation of a Fire Protection Probability Decision Tree on*

Yokoi 1960, *Study on the Prevention of Fire-Spread by Hot Upward Current*
Yuill 1975, *Fire Safety in Tall Buildings—Design Factors*

Tall Building Criteria and Loading

Chapter CL-5

Accidental Loading

Prepared by Committee 8B (Accidental Loading) of the Council on Tall Buildings and Urban Habitat as part of the Monograph on the Planning and Design of Tall Buildings.

Duiliu Sfintesco   Chairman
Joseph F. Fitzgerald   Vice-Chairman
Rowland J. Mainstone   Editor

AUTHOR ACKNOWLEDGMENT

Special acknowledgment is due those individuals whose contributions and papers formed the substantial first drafts of the various sections of this chapter. First are the state-of-art reporters from the 1972 International Conference whose material was published in the Lehigh Proceedings. These individuals are:

R. J. Mainstone, Sections 5.2, 5.4, 5.5, 5.6, and 5.7
N. M. Newmark, Sections 5.2, 5.4, and 5.5.

In addition to this, the Editor has drawn extensively on other publications of these reporters and of other authors as indicated by references in the text.

CONTRIBUTORS

The following is a complete list of those who have submitted written material for possible use in the chapter, whether or not that material was used in the final version. The Committee Chairman and Editor were given quite complete latitude. Frequently length limitations precluded the inclusion of much valuable material. The Bibliography contains all contributions. The contributors are: S. Granstrom, S. Kajfasz, R. J. Mainstone, S. N. Mandy, N. M. Newmark, N. F. Somes.

COMMITTEE MEMBERS

J. F. Fitzgerald, S. Granstrom, E. V. Leyendecker, R. J. Mainstone, N. M. Newmark, L. E. Robertson, D. Sfintesco, N. F. Somes, J. Witteveen.

CL-5

Accidental Loading

5.1 INTRODUCTION

This chapter deals with the principal types of loads to which buildings may be subjected in addition to those considered in the preceding chapters. Gravity loads, loads due to temperature change, and wind loads are experienced by all buildings. Earthquake loads are experienced by all buildings from time to time in earthquake-prone areas. But, as with fire, only some buildings, wherever they are, will experience the loads to be considered here to a degree that, with hindsight, would have called for special provisions in design for the avoidance of damage. Tall buildings, simply by virtue of their greater size, will be more likely to suffer than most others. But, even so, some 95% or more may be expected to reach their design lives without so suffering. It is in this sense that the loads may all be referred to as "accidental," irrespective of the fact that some—like some fires—are the result of deliberate acts, because even these acts are unforeseeable in relation to particular buildings at the time of design. This unforeseeable character of the loads sets them apart and calls for a different sort of recognition in design.

The commonest such loads, even in peacetime, are explosive blast loads. These may act internally or externally. Internally, they may result from the detonation of high explosives, usually placed deliberately, or from the slower deflagration of low explosives, usually accidental accumulations of flammable gas/air mixtures. Externally, they may again result from one or other of these causes, but there is the added possibility of loads acting over the entire building as a result of distant atomic explosions.

Impact loads are the other main category. They can be of many kinds, ranging from minor loads that are a hazard only for windows, partitions, and the like, to much greater loads due to collisions of large vehicles or aircraft with the building. They may also arise from the mishandling of structural elements during construction, or from the fall of elements broken or deprived of support by a primary blast loading.

A further possibility is the shock load associated with a sonic boom—though, as will be seen, this is no more of a hazard than minor impacts.

393

All these loads are transient and evoke essentially dynamic responses in the structural elements on which they act. Where the effective durations of the loads are short in relation to the fundamental natural periods of vibration of the elements, the impulse due to the load is more important than the peak value, and loads exceeding the normal static strength may be comfortably withstood. Where, in addition, the postelastic response is ductile, peak loads still more in excess of the static strength may be withstood without loss of load-bearing capacity, though at the expense of some permanent deformation and possible local damage. Some attention will therefore be given to these responses.

In view however of the low probability of occurrence of the loads and the impossibility of predicting where and with what force they will act, it is generally recognized as being more important to assure that local damage will be safely contained wherever it occurs than to predict and place limits on its magnitude. Some local damage, commensurate with the immediate cause, is usually tolerable provided that it does not result in more extensive collapse. The aim in design might then be described as structural "robustness." This has the merit of giving also a structure that will be less prone to serious failure in the event of other unforeseeable hazards, such as badly misplaced or missing reinforcement, local gross weaknesses in materials, and undetected local weaknesses in foundations—all of which, though they are not in themselves loads, may throw other unforeseen loads on the structure.

Experience has shown that tall buildings with frames of steel or reinforced concrete that have been well designed to carry normal loads and that have a good measure of flexural and tensile continuity at joints are, without further special provision, well able to bridge over considerable local damage (see, for instance, Baker et al., 1948). Similar buildings of cast-in-place reinforced concrete bearing-wall construction designed to act as box frames may also be expected to have this capacity. But continued improvements in analytical techniques leading to structural forms that are more efficient in terms of the primary design criteria, coupled with the increasing use of lightweight claddings, partitions, and fireproofing, are continually reducing the hidden bonuses of strength available to resist unforeseen extreme loads. Even for these forms it is therefore becoming more desirable to formulate explicit criteria to assure the safety of the structure as a whole in the event of major accidental loading. There are also forms which past experience has shown to be more at risk because they do not automatically possess comparable hidden bonuses of strength. One such form is the bearing-wall structure in either masonry or precast concrete which relies largely on gravity to maintain continuity at wall-to-floor joints and in which the floor slabs are not fully continuous over intermediate supports. Another is the beamless flat-slab form in which there is a possible risk of punching shear failures at the column heads when the slabs are subjected to upward blast pressures or to the impact loads of falling debris. Explicit consideration of the risks is all the more necessary for these forms. Finally it should be noted that there is evidence that the basic risks are increasing. On the one hand, sabotage bombings are becoming more frequent and widespread; on the other hand, other changes are taking place which must increase the risks of other loadings.

We shall consider first the characteristics of the different loads and their likely frequencies of occurrence. We shall then turn to structural responses and their prediction, and to other relevant aspects of design. Here we shall deal only in broad outline with the prediction of responses, for the reason given previously, but shall include some discussion of measures that may usefully be taken to reduce some of the basic hazards. We shall deal finally with the codification of design criteria.

5.2 LOADS

1 Explosive Blast Pressures

The detonation of high explosives, including atomic warheads, is independent of atmospheric oxygen and occurs very rapidly within a very small space. Within this small space large quantities of very high temperature gas are produced with a consequent very high local pressure rise. A shock wave is thus generated which spreads away from the source at a speed well in excess of that of sound. Behind the shock front is a blast "wind." In the case of low explosives like flammable gases, atmospheric oxygen is required to support combustion. The flammable mixture is thus necessarily much more dispersed, and it is necessary for a flame front to travel

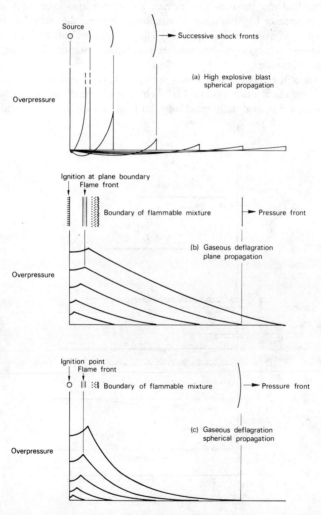

Fig. 5.1 Pressure distributions (above atmospheric) at successive instants for high-explosive and low-explosive blasts (pressure scales not comparable)

a considerable distance before it is all burnt. This takes much longer than the detonation of a high explosive and is normally referred to as a deflagration. Pressure builds up much more slowly and travels ahead of the flame front at the speed of sound without any shock wave. Actual flame speeds depend both on the nature of the flammable mixture and on the source of ignition and manner and extent of confinement (if any). Commonly they are only a few meters per second rising to within the range 10 m/sec to 100 m/sec, though detonation speeds may exceptionally be reached in the later stages of deflagrations in long ducts or tunnel-like spaces as a result of acceleration of the flame front by the buildup of pressure behind it. There is also some evidence that they may sometimes be reached in large unconfined vapor clouds when there is a powerful source of ignition.

The pressures typically associated with the two types of explosion (excluding the special cases of gaseous detonations) are illustrated schematically in Fig. 5.1. The pressures plotted are those in the moving air stream associated with the blast. (Pressures experienced by buildings or structural elements that stand in the way of the blast will be considered subsequently.) They are plotted at successive instants as the shock front or pressure front reaches increasing distances from the point of detonation or ignition.

In the case of the high-explosive blast there is always an abrupt rise in pressure at the shock front and a much less rapid fall behind it to a small negative pressure that never exceeds 1 bar, is usually much less, and can usually be safely ignored. The

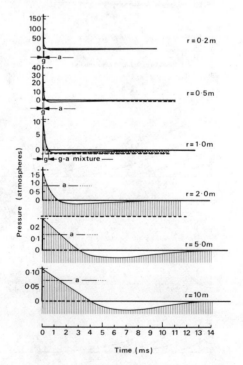

Fig. 5.2 Pressure-time curves at selected distances r from a 1-kg charge of TNT

peak pressure falls rapidly with increasing distance, though the duration of the positive pressure, and hence its spatial distribution at any instant, increase.

In the case of the gaseous deflagration the pattern is almost reversed. Since pressure builds up only slowly at the moving flame front the pressure front is ill-defined and associated with a pressure only slightly above atmospheric. The peak pressure at any instant is at the flame front itself. Behind it the pressure is slightly lower and ahead of it there is a continuous fall. The rate of this fall depends on both the geometry of propagation and the flame speed. Some acceleration of the flame was assumed in plotting and two different geometries: plane [Fig. 5.1(b)] and spherical [Fig. 5.1(c)]. It was also assumed that the mean flame speed was on the order of 1/10 the speed of sound.

Quantitative data on the shock waves generated by high-explosive blasts and on associated spatial and temporal pressure distributions are readily available in numerous publications, such as Norris et al. (1959), Kinney (1962), Newmark (1963), Glasstone (1964), and Brode (1968). Selected pressure-time and pressure-distance curves for a 1 kg charge of TNT are reproduced in Figs. 5.2 and 5.3 from Granstrom (1956). In Fig. 5.2, the ordinates give the pressures above atmospheric. In Fig. 5.3, the instants t_i are those at which the shock wave passes through the points of observation of Fig. 5.1, and the vertical dash-dot-dash line marks the position of the center of the charge. In both Figs. 5.2 and 5.3, g = gas; a = air. These curves relate to spherical propagation in free air [like Fig. 5.1(a)]. Most

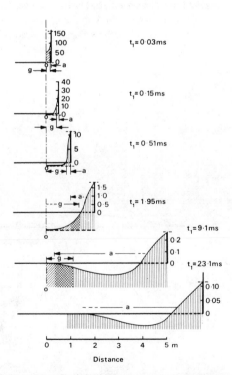

Fig. 5.3 Pressure-distance curves at selected instants t_i after detonation of same charge as in Fig. 5.1

authors (including Granstrom) also give scaling laws which enable the effects of larger charges or equivalent atomic charges to be derived from such curves. Some also give analytic expressions for the pressures, and for the associated drag pressures due to the blast "wind." Such expressions are summarized in Newmark (1973).

Corresponding data on pressure variations with time for gaseous deflagrations may be found in Cubbage and Simmonds (1955), Astbury et al. (1970, 1973), Rasbash et al. (1970), Dragosavic (1972), Yao (1973), Van Uchelen and Menzel (1973), and Butlin and Tonkin (1974). A few measured pressure-time curves for explosions in domestic-sized rooms are reproduced in Fig. 5.4. These cannot however be regarded as typical in the same way as the curves in Figs. 5.2 and 5.3. Indeed, no two gaseous deflagrations, even if the same quantities of the same gas are involved, are likely to have the same pressure-time characteristics except in closely controlled laboratory tests. Manner and extent of confinement, initial distribution of the gas, and source of ignition may all have marked effects on the progress of combustion.

The maximum possible pressure that can be reached is that which results from a reaction between all the gas and all the atmospheric oxygen in an enclosure that is strong enough to withstand the pressure. This pressure is about 700 kPa (101.5 psi) whatever the gas, though the requisite proportion of gas and air—the stoichiometric mixture—varies from one gas to another. All flammable gases will also burn at somewhat higher or lower concentrations, but the maximum attainable pressures will then be less.

Pressures actually reached are almost invariably one or two orders of magnitude less than the absolute maximum because the volume of gas actually burnt within a given total volume is that much less than the volume required for a stoichiometric

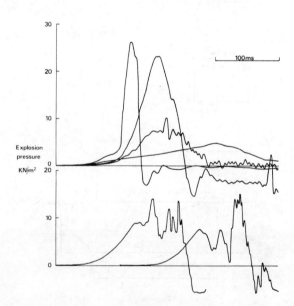

Fig. 5.4 Measured pressure-time curves for experimental ignitions of layers of natural gas and air or manufactured gas and air in domestic-sized rooms

mixture throughout. In part this is because the volume of gas initially present is usually considerably less. In part, also, it is because much of the gas that is initially present is dispersed more widely by the pressure developed in the early stages of the explosion. When the explosion occurs in the open (usually as a result of the ignition of a large unconfined cloud of vapor resulting from a spillage or other escape of a flammable liquid) there is little to prevent this wider dispersal. When the explosion is an internal one, dispersal is initially prevented beyond the confines of the room or other space involved. But the enclosure is usually, in part at least, relatively weak. Windows are broken and doors, partitions, and light claddings are blown aside at pressures of only a few kilopascals and dispersal of the remaining unburnt gas in the enclosure becomes possible through the vents so created.

The sequence of events is shown schematically in Fig. 5.5 for the commonest type of internal explosion (upper and lower curves are for large and small vents, respectively). During the initial stage the pressure rises slowly (because the initial flame front is small) to a value P_v at which the primary vent (usually a window) fails. Expulsion of unburnt gas then commences and the rate of pressure rise begins to drop below that which would otherwise have occurred as shown by the broken line A. If the vent is large, a peak pressure is fairly soon reached and the pressure then falls continuously to a value a little below atmospheric. If the vent is small, there is likely to be a further rise in pressure after an initial fall from the first peak and this may result in a higher second peak. There is also a possibility of minor shock waves being generated by the breaking of the vent, with consequent small high-frequency fluctuations in pressure, as shown by the dotted line in the lower sketch. An unconfined explosion probably resembles one in a confined space with a large and very weak vent. Fig. 5.6 shows the venting process.

The time scale in Fig. 5.5 is, as noted, only approximate. It will be influenced both by the size of the enclosure (and hence the distance the flame has to travel) and the speed of the flame front. A domestic-sized room was assumed; for a larger room the scale would be extended. The speed of the flame front will be affected by the

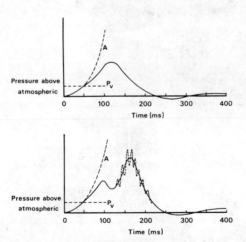

Fig. 5.5 Pressure-time curves for vented internal gas explosions (time scale only approximate and indicative of typical explosions in small rooms)

characteristic burning velocity of the gas and, often more significantly, by turbulence and acceleration of the gas-air mixture through which the flame is traveling. Turbulence is likely to have a predominant influence where there are numerous obstacles, such as furniture, to the expansion of the compressed gases behind the flame front. Acceleration of the gas-air mixture will be predominant in

Fig. 5.6 Stages in venting of internal gas explosions in three-story experimental brick building
(Courtesy: British Ceramic Research Association)

explosions in long ducts and similar spaces. The speed is important not only in determining the duration of loading but also in determining the magnitude of the peak pressure, since even the lightest vents take time to move out of the way after breaking, and it takes time for unburnt gas to be expelled through them. The faster the flame front travels, therefore, the less effective they will be and the higher the peak pressure.

Partly because so many factors influence the pressure-time curve, much less progress has been made in deriving analytic expressions for it than in the case of high-explosive blast pressures. The most useful work to date is probably that of Yao (1973), though Yao's expressions call for machine computation, take into account only the turbulence that results from the breaking or bursting of vents, and do so only by means of a turbulence correction factor that must be determined empirically for the particular situation. They cannot yet be regarded as a design tool. Less ambitiously, several other investigators have suggested purely empirical formulas for the peak pressure alone, notably Rasbash (1969), Dragosavic (1973), and Cubbage and Marshall (1973). Principal parameters in all these formulas are the pressure at which the vent breaks or bursts, and the area of the vent in relation to the cross-sectional area of the enclosure or its volume. Mainstone (1971) used the first of these formulas in a comprehensive nomogram presentation of data on the breakage of glass windows and associated explosion peak pressures. At best, however, all the formulas have limited ranges of validity and their practical usefulness is considerably restricted by their disregard of the time scale.

2 Resulting Loads on Buildings and Structural Elements

In the case of gaseous deflagrations there is usually little difference between the pressures in the moving air stream and those experienced by a building or structural element exposed to the blast. For design purposes any difference can be ignored. Local variations in pressure over the face of an element are also small in relation to the mean pressure experienced at any instant as indicated by Figs. 5.1 (b) and (c). This is probably also true of the pressures on complete buildings due to a major external gaseous deflagration with a source some distance away, since the increased distances over which the pressure wave has to travel will be matched by an increased time scale of the pressure-time curve. As a rough guide, based on limited present data, pressures on structural elements due to accidental internal explosions are unlikely to exceed 25 kPa to 50 kPa (3.5 psi to 7 psi) except in situations of unfavorable geometry (long tunnel-like spaces), high turbulence (which may also arise when a flame front moves from room to room), or poor venting. In small to medium sized rooms the peak pressure will be reached in a few tenths of a second and the pressure will fall to slightly below atmospheric in a similar or slightly longer time. In large rooms such as open-plan offices, the time scale may be doubled. Pressures on complete buildings due to external explosions will depend on distance from the source, but may reach similar values at distances on the order of 100 m (330 ft) from a major source. The time scale is likely then to be still longer.

In the case of high explosive blast the pressures experienced by buildings or structural elements that stand in the way do, on the contrary, considerably exceed the pressures that would have existed in an unobstructed moving air stream, and they are highly nonuniform at any instant partly because the basic pressure itself is highly nonuniform in the vicinity of the shock front, as indicated by Fig. 5.1 (a). The basic pressures are magnified by reflection of the shock front from the face or faces directly exposed to it, and additional drag pressures are superimposed as a result of the blast "wind." The final net loading can be very different from the basic "free field" or "side on" overpressure, very different for different elements of a structure, and different again for the complete building in the case of an external blast.

Fig. 5.7 (from Popplewell, 1975) illustrates predominantly diffraction-type loading (due to the diffraction of the shock front) in the simplest case of a solid boxlike building standing square to a vertical incident shock front from a fairly distant source. Pressure-time curves are plotted for two different basic peak pressures. The lower diagrams show pressure-time variations of P_s (= basic "free field" or "side on" overpressure) and $\bar{P}$ (= pressure on building) as multiples of P_{s0} (= P_s at time 0) for two values of P_{s0}; P_{s0} = 7 kPa (1 psi) for the full lines and 35 kPa (5 psi) for the dashed lines. The magnification of the basic pressure on initial reflection increases with increase in this pressure. Close to the source it may reach twelve times, but it is between two and three times at the pressure levels for which it is likely to be feasible to design tall buildings for external blast. The net translational loading on the building as a whole is, of course, the difference between the total front and rear loads.

Fig. 5.8 (a) shows this summation, the rear load being plotted here as a negative pressure in the direction of blast propagation. Fig. 5.8 (b) shows similarly the loads at front and rear and the net load on an idealized open framed structure. Diffraction loading here is short-lived since the individual members of the frame are soon enveloped by the blast. Drag loading due to the blast "wind" therefore predominates for most of the time. The net translational loading on buildings with extensive

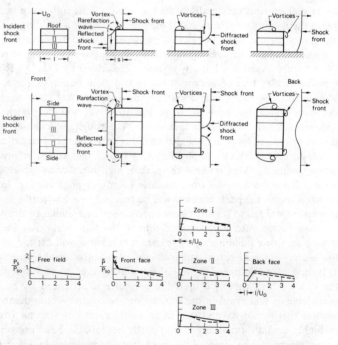

Fig. 5.7 Diffraction of blast wave around closed boxlike building

glazing or other light cladding will be intermediate between those represented in
Fig. 5.8, since much of the glazing or cladding may be expected to fail if the peak
pressure exceeds, say, 10 kPa (1.5 psi). In Fig. 5.8, the dashed lines represent the
basic free field overpressure on the front face multiplied by the area of this face.

Quantitative data and analytical expressions relevant to the estimation, for design
purposes, of pressures due to distant large explosions may be found in the
publications of Norris et al., Kinney, Newmark, Glasstone, and Brode cited
previously. Granstrom (1956) gives graphs which may be used for the estimation of
pressures due to closer detonations of conventional explosives, though again only
for external explosions. A publication of the United States Army, Navy, and Air
Force Departments (1969) gives graphs relevant also to internal explosions.

As compared with the loads due to gaseous deflagrations, the resultant loads are
always of very short duration. For buildings as a whole, and for all but small, light
elements with high frequencies of vibration, the total impulse (given by the area
under the curve of net load against time) is therefore more important than the
precise manner in which the load varies and its peak value.

3 Impact Loads

Accidental impacts give rise to highly localized impulses of durations varying
from those typical of high-explosive blast to those typical of gaseous deflagrations.
The shorter durations arise only in the case of impacts by small concentrated masses
with elements of a structure that are strong and stiff enough to bring them to rest
with little deformation. The longer durations are much more usual, chiefly because
most impacting masses are of considerable size in relation to their initial velocity
and are brought to rest progressively as they themselves break up (or bounce from
edge to edge in the case, for instance, of a falling slab).

Some measured and estimated impact loads are reproduced in Fig. 5.9. Loads are
plotted nondimensionally as reaction/static weight (from Popp, 1965; Mainstone,
1966; and Riera, 1968. For aircraft impacts, see also Dietrich and Fürste, 1973;
Lange and Laue, 1973). Peaks in the load-time curves correspond here to contacts
with the more rigid and heavy parts of the impacting body, such as an engine. They

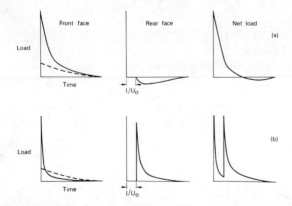

Fig. 5.8 Load-time curves for closed boxlike building (a) compared with similar curves for idealized
open framed structure (b)

are most numerous for the road-vehicle impacts because the test vehicle had a heavy load which was thrown forward on impact. They are least numerous for the aircraft impact because the method of estimation made no allowance for minor hard contacts and none for the possible partial disintegration of the aircraft after the initial impact. It should however be noted that the measured loads were measured as total support reactions for the column or slab that was hit. The actual impacts had a spatial as well as a temporal spread, and this is averaged out. In addition, the slab hit by the helicopter responded elastically, so there was some dynamic amplification of the basic impact load.

A feature that distinguishes impact loads from the blast loads considered previously is their direct dependence on the deformational response of the structure that is hit. This is seen, for instance, in the two curves for road-vehicle impacts. The velocities of impact did not differ much, but the resulting loads differed greatly chiefly because the reinforced concrete columns that received the impacts were of different strengths and stiffnesses. Where the impacted structure deforms readily the impacting body will be brought to rest more slowly, and the impulse will be of longer duration with a counterbalancing reduction in the peak force. Where there is considerable local plastic deformation at the point or points of impact, there will also be correspondingly less energy to be absorbed by general deformation, which means another reduction in the forces transmitted further away. Since the loads estimated for the aircraft impact assumed an impact with a completely rigid body, they will overestimate the peak loads to be expected in an impact with a typical tall building.

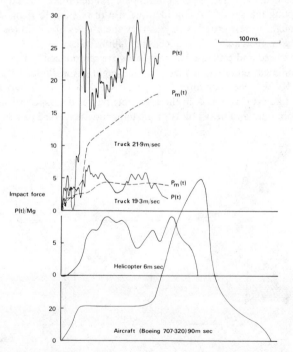

Fig. 5.9 Measured (upper curves) and estimated (bottom curve) loads due to horizontal impacts by heavily laden truck and aircraft and vertical impact by helicopter

It will be apparent that, even if it is possible for design purposes to assign appropriate values to the mass and velocity of an impacting body, the resulting loads on the structure that is hit cannot be estimated independently of some of the characteristics of this structure. Momentum and energy must both be conserved in the impact and calculations may be based on these two principles. Use of the first calls, however, for an estimate of the proportion of the total mass that may be assumed to be set in motion by the impact. Use of the second calls for some assumption of the proportion of the total energy that is dissipated in local plastic deformation in the contact zone and, usually, for the further assumption that general deformations and corresponding energy absorptions are the same under static and impact loading. This last assumption will always be somewhat in error.

The simple theory of perfectly elastic and perfectly plastic rigid-body impacts is given in Norris et al. (1959), Section 6.5. Possible approaches to the analysis of impacts of practical interest have been reviewed recently by Sahlin and Nilsson (1975) and by Kavyrchine and Struck (1975). A parallel review paper by Struck and Voggenreiter (1975) gives further examples of possible loads.

4 Sonic Boom

A sonic boom is another air shock, but a very weak one by comparison with the blast loads considered previously. The simple shock wave is of N-form, as shown in Fig. 5.10, with a total duration of 1/10 sec up to a few tenths of a second but peak positive and negative overpressures of the order of only 0.1 kPa (0.07 psi). Exceptionally the pressures might rise to about 1 kPa (0.7 psi), but they will still only be comparable with wind loads and hardly seem to call for any special provisions in the design of tall buildings. Multiple shocks may sometimes be experienced as a result of reflections. Sharpe and Kost (1971), Clarkson and Mayes (1972), and Warren (1972) may be consulted for more details of the boom itself and of observed structural responses, including comparisons with wind and other loads.

5 Other Accidental Loads

Two other types of load may be mentioned finally that are not amenable to quantification in the same way as those considered hitherto. These are a gross overloading of a part of the structure either during construction or as a result of subsequent misuse by the occupants, and the loading that may result, as mentioned

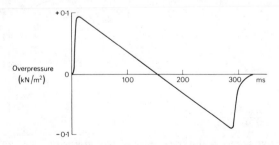

Fig. 5.10 Typical basic sonic-boom shock wave

in the introduction, from local faults in construction or unanticipated and undetected local weaknesses in foundations.

5.3 FREQUENCIES OF OCCURRENCE OF LOADS

Since all the loads are, in some way, man-made, frequencies or probabilities of occurrence can, at best, be considered only in the same way as for man-made gravity loads. They are not inherent characteristics of the physical world we live in, but always susceptible to change by human action. The statistics we can gather by looking back at recent experience can thus never be more than a guide for making judgments about future risks.

1 High-Explosive Blast

This is particularly true of high-explosive blast loads on tall buildings. Except in rare instances such loads will always result from deliberate hostile acts, either in open warfare or in more limited and usually clandestine sabotage. This is not the place for speculation under the first of these heads. Recent experience probably has more validity under the second head. Here it points unmistakably to a progressive increase in the risk since the late 1960s and to its becoming more and more a worldwide phenomenon. Fortunately hitherto nearly all attacks have been made with relatively small charges of conventional explosives, sufficient only to cause local damage in the first instance to the structures of modern tall buildings. The most representative available statistics are probably those for the United States, where the risk of attack in 1972 was comparable with and slightly greater than the risk of an accidental internal gas explosion. In areas where a state verging on open hostilities exists, the risk must of course be higher.

2 Internal Blast due to Gaseous Explosions

The Ronan Point incident in 1968 directed attention in Great Britain to the frequency of accidental gas explosions in dwellings. The only data available at the

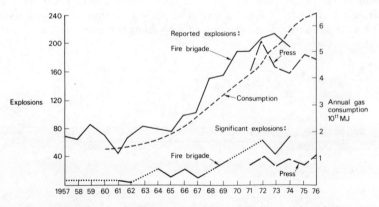

Fig. 5.11 Gas consumption in dwellings, reported gas explosions, and explosions causing significant structural damage in Great Britain 1957–1976

time were the reports submitted by fire brigades to the Fire Research Station since 1957. These were primarily concerned with fires but also covered other incidents when attended by a brigade. Analysis of these reports showed a steadily rising number of incidents in which an explosion was recorded, but a fairly constant rate of 5 per 10^{10}MJ in terms of gas consumption (which had also steadily risen). Rather less than a fifth of the explosions were thought to have been of sufficient force to have caused significant structural damage (Fry, 1971).

In 1971 (after an earlier pilot study) a detailed survey specifically of accidental explosions was started. Mainstone et al. (1978) give results for the first six years. Press reports were used here as the primary source of information, supplemented by inspection or inquiry, or both, in cases of doubt or particular interest. Fig. 5.11 shows the over-all picture presented by both these data and the earlier data, plus that abstracted from subsequent fire brigade reports. Inspections were much more numerous during the first two years and included assessments, on the basis of the damage caused, of the peak pressures reached. Fig. 5.12 shows expectations of different peak pressures on the basis of these assessments. Figs. 5.11 and 5.12 are not directly comparable because the survey covered all accidental explosions in nonindustrial buildings and not merely those in dwellings. Fig. 5.12 therefore covers a wider range of incidents.

Detailed analysis of the survey results showed, in fact, that there were some significant differences in risk for different uses of a building. The average risk for all nonresidential uses was, for instance, more than three times the average risk for all residential uses. The units of accommodation in terms of which the risk was

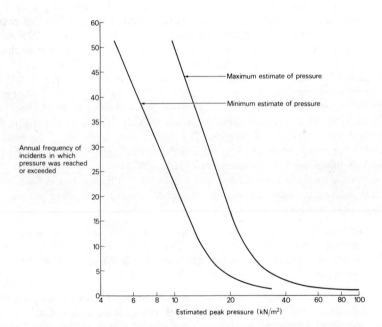

Fig. 5.12 Frequencies of occurrence of internal gas explosions of different severities in nonindustrial buildings in Great Britain between April 1971 and March 1973 (annual gas consumption approximately 5.8×10^{11}MJ)

expressed were, however, larger on average than for residential uses, and for office use—the most likely nonresidential use in a tall building—the sample was too small for a meaningful figure to be obtained. The most important conclusion from the point of view of the design of tall buildings was possibly that the risk for apartments was about twice those for detached and semidetached houses and bungalows. Between 1971 and 1977, an average of 4.3 apartments per year per million in purely residential buildings suffered significant structural damage (costing more than £800 for structural reinstatement at 1977 United Kingdom prices). Three times this number were damaged in multiuse buildings. Excluding the latter, this means a risk of damage to an individual apartment of about 1 in 4000 for a 60-yr life. This leads to a risk of about 1 in 40 of damage within a block of 100 flats, as compared with the risk of 1 in 50 assessed by the Ronan Point Tribunal (Griffiths et al., 1968). The increase is fairly directly related to an increase in the consumption of gas, and further increase may be expected if consumption continues to rise or if a larger proportion of the more hazardous bottled gas is used. The true risk is probably a little higher because it is unlikely that the press reports received indicated its full extent.

Few comparable data are available from other countries. Ligtenberg (1969) gives brief details of a survey of press reports of all kinds of accidental structural damage in the Netherlands in 1967. There were 200 instances of damage by explosions of all kinds (including external blast) for a total building stock of about 3×10^6. This suggests a much higher basic risk (1 in 250 for a 60-yr life) than in Great Britain, but the figure is probably inflated in comparison with the British figure of 1 in 4000 by a broader criterion of structural damage, as well as by the inclusion of incidents involving external blast. Burnett et al. (1973) summarize two collections of data for the United States. The more reliable data are taken from Little (1967) which covers explosions of piped gas only during the years 1957 to 1966. On the basis of these data it is estimated that 0.42 structurally significant explosions occurred in dwellings for every 10^{10}MJ of natural gas sold. This is lower than both Fry's estimate for the same period for Great Britain and the more precise estimate of 0.50 per 10^{10}MJ for all nonindustrial buildings for the years 1971-77. Different criteria of damage may again be responsible for part of the difference. Since there is no breakdown into different types of dwelling, a direct comparison with the British risk figure for individual apartments is not possible. The over-all risk figure of 2.2 per million dwellings per year is however comparable with the over-all British figure of 2.1 per million dwellings per year for the years 1971 to 1977.

Generalization from these limited and somewhat conflicting data is hazardous, but the following guidelines may be suggested for the assessment of risks to particular tall buildings:

1. The British data clearly show an almost proportionate increase in risk with increase in consumption of gas, but no merit in replacing piped gas as a fuel by bottled (liquefied petroleum) gas. The latter is indeed more than twice as hazardous.

2. Taking present British conditions as a standard, the risk of a structurally significant explosion in a single unit of accommodation (such as an individual apartment) is about 0.5 per 10^{10}MJ of natural gas sold. "Structurally significant" may be roughly equated with a peak dynamic pressure of at least 5 kPa (0.9 psi). In about 25% of these incidents the peak dynamic

pressure is likely to be at least 10 kPa (1.7 psi), and in about 5% it may exceed 25 kPa (3.6 psi).

3. There is no clear evidence of any major difference in risk in other highly developed countries with similar building practices and standards of accommodation, and little reason to expect such a difference. Elsewhere the risk may be greater on account of greater crowding, restricted window areas providing reduced venting, less inherent safety in gas installations, a proportionately greater use of more hazardous fuels such as bottled liquefied petroleum gas, or multiple use of buildings (especially the admission of light industry, food processing, etc., into predominantly residential buildings).

4. Though the risk will vary with the factors just mentioned, it should not be assumed that it can be reduced in a particular building by the exclusion of a piped gas supply. Such exclusion does not preclude its subsequent provision, does not guarantee that bottled gas or other hazardous substances will not be used, and does not guarantee either that gas will not leak into the building from a nearby fault in the piped gas distribution system. Some of the most serious recent internal explosions have been caused in this way.

5. As a much rougher guide, the risk of a "structurally significant" explosion on any floor of a tall building is probably between 1 in 10^5 and 1 in 10^4 per year in most cases. The lower risk will be more typical in highly developed and safety conscious countries.

3 External Blast due to Gaseous Explosions

To produce damaging external explosions, rather than damaging internal ones, much larger leakages of flammable gases or spillages of volatile flammable liquids are required on account of the lack of confinement. Damaging external blast is therefore much rarer, and there are correspondingly fewer data on which to base the prediction of future risks. The risks are, in addition, almost certainly much less uniform. Buildings sited close to chemical plants, oil refineries, and large storage facilities will be subject to much more than the average risk. Buildings sited close to major distribution routes (by road, rail, water, or pipeline) will also be subject to above-average risk, though probably not quite as high. For most other buildings the risk is probably insignificant in relation to that of internal blast.

The assessment of risk for tall buildings in particular situations can best be made on the basis of past experience of the particular hazard, bearing in mind that there has been an unmistakable increase in the number and damage potential of such explosions in recent years. Strehlow (1973) has reviewed and analyzed 108 accidental explosions of unconfined vapor clouds reported over the years 1930 to 1972, mostly in the United States and Germany. A wider review is that of Steele et al. (1973). This notes the concern of the United States National Transport Safety Board (1969) over the construction of tall buildings immediately over expressways.

4 Impact

If impacts arising in the course of construction or as a consequence of local failures due to other causes are excluded, the main risks are from heavy vehicles and aircraft, and will obviously vary widely with the location of the building. British data for the years 1971 to 1977 (Mainstone et al., 1978) show that the number of vehicle impacts that caused significant structural damage was less than the corresponding number of accidental internal explosions, that there was a much smaller incidence of severe damage, and that there was no instance of significant damage to a building of more than three stories. This last observation probably reflects partly the fact that the most hazardously sited buildings were usually low ones and partly the greater strength, at ground level, of most higher buildings: a heavier impact is required to cause similar damage. No comparable data are known for other countries. On the basis of much less adequate data, Fribush et al. (1973) have attempted to deduce the risk for multistory residential buildings in the United States, and have arrived at a figure comparable with the risk of a damaging internal explosion. This conflicting conclusion is based, however, on the arbitrary assumption (among others) that the incidence of damage to multistory buildings is proportional to the number of such buildings in the total building stock, and must be rejected for the reasons just given. The true risk is probably, on average, at least an order of magnitude less than the explosion risk, though there may be individual buildings for which it is higher. Somes (1973) has estimated, on the basis of data supplied by the United States Federal Aviation Authority, that the risk of impact by an aircraft for buildings located more than 5 km (3.1 miles) from the end of an airport runway is on the order of 1 in 10^8 per building per year. He makes no distinction between buildings of different shapes and sizes, so this is presumably an average risk for the United States. For tall buildings in some city centers the risk may be expected to be well above average, and may be between 1 in 10^6 and 1 in 10^4 for a 60-yr life, depending on size and location.

5 General

If we set aside the relatively trivial sonic boom, we are left with predominantly an explosion risk. For most tall buildings the present total risk, in the course of a 60-yr life excluding a major war, is probably between 1 in 10^3 and 1 in 10^2 per floor. Only loads capable of causing significant local damage to the main structure are considered here.

5.4 STRUCTURAL RESPONSES AND INSTANCES OF DAMAGE

This total risk may be an order of magnitude less than the risk of a damaging fire. Against this fact we must set the further fact that any of the loads could lead to disaster within a fraction of a second, leaving no opportunity for human intervention to mitigate the damage once the explosive has been detonated or ignited or the building has been hit. Some instances of damage will now be described, prefaced by a general discussion of the nature of the structural responses.

1 Structural Responses

The very short duration of the loading, whatever its cause, means that the response will usually be a dynamic one in which the inertia of the resisting structure or structural element plays a significant role. On account of the high magnitudes of the loads, the response will usually also extend into the postelastic range of deformations if the structure or element has some effective ductility. Most structures and structural elements used in tall buildings do have the ability to deform beyond the elastic range without much or without any loss of strength, either by virtue of inherent ductility (as in the case of steel beams) or by virtue of edge restraints (as in the case of many inherently brittle masonry walls restrained against gross deformation by the surrounding structure).

Fig. 5.13 shows a slightly idealized picture of the responses of typical structural elements, the chief idealization being the replacement of the distributed mass of each element by a single concentrated mass and the associated assumption that the element responds with only a single degree of freedom. The responses are shown for different relative durations of the load (t_d/T) and for the load-deformation relationships indicated at the right. A further idealization is the replacement of the actual resistance-displacement relationship (shown by the full line at the upper right) by an equivalent linearly elastic and perfectly plastic relationship (as shown by the superimposed broken line). The responses are discussed further in Mainstone (1974). It is sufficient to note here that initially the deformational response and associated resistance lag behind the imposed load (as shown by the left-hand shaded area for one response curve), and that loads well in excess of the static strength can be safely resisted at the expense of some permanent deformation for the shorter load durations (relative to the natural period of the element) and the higher ductilities.

As noted in the caption, the load assumed here is broadly representative of that due to an internal gas explosion or an impact. For high-explosive blast, the much steeper rise in the load and the very short duration of the peak mean that much higher peak loads in relation to static strengths can be sustained without loss of load-carrying capacity.

2 Damage by High-Explosive Blast

The chief published source for the effects of over-all external blast loading is Glasstone (1964). The effects on several multistory reinforced concrete framed

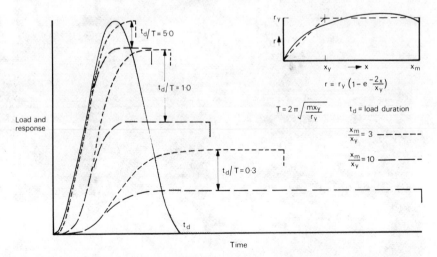

Fig. 5.13 Calculated elastoplastic responses (broken lines) of simple sprung mass to dynamic load (full line) such as might be imposed in internal gas explosion or impact

Fig. 5.14 Failure of facade columns and beams 0.58 km from ground zero at Nagasaki, Japan
(Glasstone, 1964; Courtesy: Department of Energy)

Fig. 5.15 Damage to reinforced concrete building 0.16 km from ground zero at Hiroshima, Japan
(Glasstone, 1964; Courtesy: Department of Energy)

buildings of the atomic air bursts over Hiroshima and Nagasaki are described. Figs. 5.14 and 5.15 illustrate two instances of damage. In the first case the building was almost 1 km (0.62 mile) from ground zero and experienced predominantly side load as shown in Figs. 5.7 and 5.8. In the second case the burst was more nearly overhead and the load predominantly vertical. It thus caused considerable dishing of the roof slab. Glasstone points out that, though the best constructed buildings suffered remarkably little damage to the main structure, there was considerable damage to the interiors by blast that entered through the doors and windows and by subsequent fire.

A parallel source for the effects of more localized high-explosive blast is Baker et al. (1948). This describes numerous instances of damage to multistory framed buildings by aerial bombing between 1940 and 1945. Though some damage was commonly done by impact and initial penetration of the bomb, the major damage was due to the explosive blast. When the bomb exploded within the building, as in Fig. 5.16, considerable damage was sometimes caused by uplift on floor slabs and beams above the explosion, on account of the reversals of moments which reinforced concrete is usually ill equipped to resist. In the instance shown, the slabs and beams have failed upwards then fallen downwards under their own weight. There were also numerous instances of failures of column-beam connections under such loading. Direct damage to columns and beams—that is, damage by the blast loads acting directly on them—was however usually slight except when the explosion was very close. Where such damage did occur, most multistory structures,

Fig. 5.16 Wartime damage in England to a reinforced concrete building by local high-explosive blast; the bomb exploded internally (Courtesy: Building Research Establishment— Crown copyright reserved)

whether steel framed or reinforced concrete framed, also possessed considerable ability to bridge over the local damage by virtue of continuities in the frame and the strengthening and stiffening effects of adjacent infills to the frame. Fig. 5.17 illustrates one spectacular instance of this. A corner stanchion was severed and a large brick-faced plate girder supporting all upper stanchions of the gable end of the seven-story building then fell. But the upper stories successfully cantilevered over the void that was left.

The precise locations of the explosions discussed by Baker et al. must be considered fortuitous. Bombs planted by saboteurs may sometimes be carefully sited to cause maximum damage, so that there is probably a proportionately greater risk of local damage to critical members of a structure. The known available evidence to date is, however, in no way inconsistent with earlier wartime experience of aerial bombing. Three instances may be cited as examples. In the first (Griffiths et al., 1968) there was detonation of explosives stored in a ground-floor apartment of a 12-story apartment block of large-panel construction in Algeria. The explosion destroyed the end bay of the spine wall and much of the gable wall, and badly damaged the first internal load-bearing cross wall at ground and first floor levels; but the upper stories again successfully cantilevered over the damage. In the second, a car bomb exploded alongside a four-story reinforced concrete framed building at Stanhope Barracks, Aldershot, England. It severely damaged and rendered largely ineffective one of four ground floor columns on one side, but the damage was bridged over with some local permanent deflections and other damage at first floor

Fig. 5.17 Wartime bomb damage to a steel-framed building by local high-explosive blast; the bomb exploded against external column at near end of gable wall (Courtesy: Building Research Establishment—Crown copyright reserved)

Fig. 5.18 Damage to West German Embassy, Stockholm, Sweden, by terrorist bomb *(Granstrom and Carlsson, 1976)*

Fig. 5.19 Interior of building shown in Fig. 5.18 *(Granstrom and Carlsson, 1976)*

level. In the third (Granstrom and Carlsson, 1976), a terrorist bomb was exploded on the top floor of the four-story West German Embassy in Stockholm, Sweden. The charge was estimated as being equivalent to about 10 kg (22 lb) of TNT. It largely destroyed the floor and roof slabs and severely damaged the walls of the room in which it was placed, but there was no consequential collapse and the damage at greater distances from the charge decreased rapidly with distance (Figs. 5.18, 5.19). The bomb was exploded in the room in which the photograph of Fig.

Fig. 5.20 Collapse of entire corner of 23-story block of apartments in east London, England as result of gas explosion on 18th floor (Courtesy: Building Research Establishment—Crown copyright reserved)

5.19 was taken, the room which is on the extreme right of Fig. 5.18. It is estimated that the blast effects were an order of magnitude less in adjacent rooms, and that they were an order of magnitude less again in rooms beyond these.

3   Damage by Internal Blast due to Gaseous Explosions

Damage by gaseous explosions has been reviewed by Granstrom and Carlsson (1974) and by Mainstone (1976, 1978). For fuller accounts of particular incidents that involved tall buildings, reference may also be made to Griffiths et al. (1968) and Mainstone and Butlin (1976).

The most notable and disquieting feature has been the frequency with which local damage directly attributable to the explosion has precipitated a much more extensive collapse. The buildings involved have all been residential, which may point to lower standards of structural integrity having been adopted for such buildings than, say, for tall commercial buildings. The fact that gaseous explosions were the cause, rather than high explosives, is possibly no more than a reflection of the fact that gaseous explosions have been commoner in such buildings in recent years. In all these incidents the structure above the local damage has collapsed as a result of the deprivation of direct support. In some, where the local damage has occurred at some upper level, the collapse has also progressed downwards under the impact of falling debris.

The best known instance is the Ronan Point collapse in 1968 illustrated in Fig.

Fig. 5.21 Explosion at Perpignan, France in 1973 *(Courtesy: Building Research Establishment —Crown copyright reserved)*

5.20 (Griffiths et al., 1968). Considerable turbulence was probably generated as the flame passed from the presumed point of ignition of the gas in the kitchen of one of the corner apartments into the hallway and other rooms of the apartment. The peak pressure in the hall was estimated to have been about 80 kPa (11.7 psi). The net outward pressure on the heavy flank wall of the living room was, in any case, sufficient to blow this wall out. Deprived of direct support, the walls above then also fell and the floor slabs previously supported by them fell with them. The collapse then progressed downwards as far as the cast-in-place reinforced concrete podium. A major contributory factor to both the initial failure of the flank wall and the ensuing more general collapse was undoubtedly the inadequate tying together of the large-panel elements of the main structure. These were adequately held together by the friction induced by gravity loads under normal conditions. But the blast uplift pressures must have nullified the gravity loads at the crucial time. Other similar incidents were those at Buenos Aires in 1962 and Barcelona in 1972, though much less is known about these. An explosion at Perpignan, France in 1973 (Fig. 5.21) differed chiefly in that it occurred nearer the top of the building (one floor down) and in an internal rather than an end apartment. There was thus less debris impact

Fig. 5.22 Explosion at Skovlunde, Copenhagen, Denmark in 1973 *(Courtesy: Building Research Establishment—Crown copyright reserved)*

load to cause a downward progression of the collapse and there were abutment restraints at both ends of the floor slabs subjected to this load.

Figs. 5.22 through 5.25 illustrate three instances of the effects of gas explosions at ground level. In such cases there is no risk of downward progression of a collapse as a result of debris impact loads, and there is less likelihood of the loss of frictional restraints to the ejection of walls or columns through the nullification of gravity loads. In the five-story block at Skovlunde, Denmark it is just possible that the uplift pressure generated was sufficient momentarily to accomplish this and thereby make it easier for the external load-bearing brick walls of the semibasement at the end of the block to be blown out. In the 14-story and 15-story blocks at Argenteuil, France and Bootle, England however, the uplift pressure (though clearly evident from the upward yielding of the first-floor slab whose soffit is seen in Fig. 5.25) was insufficient to do so. At Argenteuil, some of the radial cast-in-place reinforced concrete walls that were the main load-bearing elements were badly distorted by the blast, and at Bootle the gable wall with integral reinforced concrete columns seen in Fig. 5.24 was similarly distorted with a maximum outward displacement at first-floor level. But in both cases the damaged walls continued to provide some

Fig. 5.23 Explosion at Argenteuil, near Paris, France in 1971 *(Courtesy: Building Research Establishment—Crown copyright reserved)*

Fig. 5.24 Explosion on ground floor of 16-story block of apartments, Mersey House, Bootle, near Liverpool, England in 1975, exterior and interior details *(Courtesy: Building Research Establishment—Crown copyright reserved)*

Fig. 5.25 Mersey House explosion, interior *(Courtesy: Building Research Establishment—Crown copyright reserved)*

support for the superincumbent load until shores were inserted—something they would have been unlikely to have done if the peak loads had been sustained. In further incidents at Godthab (Greenland), Auch (France), and Tachov (Czechoslovakia) there were again more catastrophic collapses. In the first (Utne, 1971) and last, entire four-story buildings collapsed. In the second, about half of a seven-story building collapsed over its full height. The first three floors of this were framed in reinforced concrete and the upper floors were of load-bearing masonry with concrete slab floors. Both here (Granstrom and Carlsson, 1974) and at Godthab, a

Fig. 5.26 Explosion damage to 25-story commercial building at 312 East 46th Street, New York City in 1974 (Larry Morris/The New York Times)

contributory factor to the collapse seems to have been poor continuity reinforcement in the reinforced concrete framing. In at least four of these six incidents,
gas leaked from a main supply pipe into a closed or semiclosed service floor or crawl
space at the foot of the building and it is worth noting that in two of them
(Skovlunde and Tachov) the fault in the pipe was external to the building and the
gas leaked through loose earth into a heating duct that entered the building. At
Auch, the explosion may have been of gasoline vapor from a spill on one of two
garage floors.

The most serious known instance of damage to a tall commercial building
occurred in New York City (Fig. 5.26). The cladding was blown off almost the
whole of one face of the building and lesser damage was done to neighboring
buildings, but there appears to have been little if any damage to the structural
frame. Natural gas leaking from a main supply pipe in the basement was
responsible, this pipe having been torn away at a substandard threaded joint as the
bizarre result of being hit by a jet from a ruptured overpressurized water tank. The
gas then entered the elevator shafts and was drawn up them by the moving cars
before being ignited. This, presumably, was the reason for the great extent of the
damage.

4 Damage by External Blast due to Gaseous Explosions

Though explosions of unconfined vapor clouds have, on several occasions, led to
damage estimated at several million dollars, there are no known reports of damage

Fig. 5.27 Damage to three-story office building by external blast of unconfined gaseous explosion
(Courtesy: Building Research Establishment—Crown copyright reserved)

to tall buildings. Fig. 5.27 illustrates, however, the sort of damage that might occur if a tall building were sited near the center of such an explosion. The structure here was a three-story office building with a reinforced concrete frame sited about 70 m (230 ft) from the apparent center of the explosion at the Nypro works, Flixborough, England in 1974.

5 Damage by Impact and Other Accidents

There have been cases of major collapse due to impacts by road vehicles with older buildings of load-bearing brick construction, including one in New York City in which the entire corner of a five-story building fell (Granstrom and Carlsson, 1974), but none is yet known of similar damage to tall modern buildings. One case of impact by an aircraft is recorded. In 1945 a B-25 bomber with a mass of about 10^4 kg flew into the Empire State Building in New York City at a little over 100 m/s (328 ft/sec). It struck almost on one of the main columns between the 78th and 79th floors, but left the main frame unimpaired. Structural damage was limited to the tearing out of two spandrel beams (Fig. 5.28). A collision by a modern jumbo jet or similar aircraft might, however, be far more damaging, particularly to a lighter and somewhat lower building of recent construction.

The commonest cause of severe impact damage to tall buildings is, almost certainly, one that was passed over in Article 4 of Section 5.3—the impact of parts of the structure that have failed or broken away as a result of some other primary cause. All instances referred to of the downward progression of a collapse initiated by an explosion at some upper level are examples of it, though there is evidence that the progression of the collapse has been assisted, in some cases, by the successive pulling-away of wall panels at lower levels by those above. Another relevant primary cause of damage has been the overloading (in relation to age and strength of concrete) of recently cast flat-slab floors in reinforced concrete structures under construction. One recent and spectacular instance of this is illustrated in Fig. 5.29 and has been described by Leyendecker and Fattal (1973). The collapse of the missing center section of the building began at the 23rd floor shortly after the casting of the 24th floor and primarily as a result of premature removal of shoring. The collapse extended also to most of the parking garage as a progression of initial damage due to the impact load from above. In Boston (USA) there was a similar collapse of a whole corner of a 16-story block of flats while the top floor slab was being poured early in 1971, and earlier examples are referred to by McKaig (1962).

5.5 SIMPLIFIED ANALYSIS OF STRUCTURAL RESPONSES

Since this chapter is concerned with criteria for design rather than with design itself, it seems inappropriate to consider the analysis of structural responses in detail. A brief outline of some simple procedures that are available may, on the other hand, help the reader to assess the importance of the various loads considered here in relation to normal static loads such as those considered in Chapter CL-1. The procedure to be described first is applicable chiefly to explosive blast loads, since it calls for a prior knowledge of the variation of load with time. In the case of impact loads, this variation is usually unknown. A different procedure must therefore be adopted.

1   Responses to Loads Varying in a Known Manner

Where the variation of load with time is known, the structural response can usually be estimated with sufficient accuracy (in relation to the inevitable uncertainties in the data) in terms of the idealizations introduced in Section 5.4. The procedures are outlined more fully, with reference to high-explosive blast loads, in Newmark (1973). The summary given here is based on that outline, but is extended

Fig. 5.28 Structural damage between 78th and 79th floors of Empire State Building, New York, New York, caused when B-25 Mitchell Bomber crashed into it during heavy fog on July 18, 1945 *(Courtesy: World Wide Photos)*

to cover also the response to the loads imposed by gaseous explosions. For further detail reference should be made to Newmark (1973); also to Newmark (1956), Norris et al. (1959), ASCE (1961), and US Army, Navy, and Air Force Departments (1969).

The idealizations are illustrated in Figs. 5.30 and 5.31. The actual structure or structural element is replaced by a single mass and a spring, and the spring characteristics are assumed to be the simple equivalent of the actual resistance-

Empire State Building damage area due to bomber crash—view looking down *(Courtesy: The New York Times)*

displacement relationship shown in the lower figure. The structural response to an imposed load is governed by the following parameters of the system:

1. The effective resistance, r_y, of the system to general yielding, measured in terms of a pseudostatic load applied in the same manner as the actual load.

2. The effective period of vibration, T, of the system, corresponding to the stiffness indicated by the straight-line equivalent in Fig. 5.31 of the actual resistance-displacement relationship prior to general yielding.

3. The ductility ratio, x_m/x_y, namely the ratio between the maximum displacement or deflection (actual or allowable) and the displacement or deflection at the transition from linearly elastic to perfectly plastic response in the idealized resistance-displacement relationship.

The corresponding loading parameters for a particular pressure-time or load-time relationship are:

1. The peak magnitude of the load, p_m, measured in the same terms as the resistance r_y.

2. The effective duration of the load pulse, t_d, measured in the same units as T. This is the actual duration if the basic analysis has been performed for the actual pressure-time or load-time relationship. Otherwise it is the duration of

Fig. 5.29 Partial collapse of 26-story block of apartments (with four-story basement and adjacent parking garage) at Bailey's Crossroads, Virginia in 1973 *(Courtesy: Building Research Establishment—Crown copyright reserved)*

a dynamically equivalent load-pulse of the assumed form and with the same peak magnitude, p_m.

Responses are most conveniently represented in terms of the ductility ratio and two other dimensionless ratios derived from the remaining parameters: a duration ratio, t_d/T, and a load ratio, p_m/r_y. Fig. 5.32 presents in these terms a wide range of responses to three forms of load pulse typical of those that have been observed in vented gaseous explosions and including the displaced-cosine pulse already considered in Fig. 5.13. The impulse ($\int pd\,t$) is the same for pulses (2) and (3) and somewhat greater for pulse (1) for given values of p_m and t_d. If allowance is made for this, it will be seen that the shape of pulse makes virtually no difference to the response for values of t_d less than half of T: the response is then determined almost wholly by the value of the impulse and by the need to absorb the associated energy by structural deformation. For long durations also, the response becomes insensitive to the shape of the pulse: the value of p_m tends then to equal the static strength, r_y, though it does so more rapidly for the lower values of the ductility ratio.

In Fig. 5.33 the same response data are replotted in a manner more suitable for use in design for the load pulse numbered (3) in Fig. 5.32. Corresponding data for responses to a triangular load pulse with the instantaneous rise to p_m typical of high-explosive (including atomic) blast are similarly plotted (from Newmark, 1973) in Fig. 5.34, and some of the curves in this figure are added, as broken lines, to Fig. 5.33 for purposes of comparison [see also Struck et al. (1973)].

It will be seen that for values of t_d less than half of T, where the impulse of the load controls, the curves in the two charts are almost identical, and that major divergences occur only for values of t_d greater than T and particularly for low ductilities. In this region the effective strength is always greater, for given values of x_m/x_y and t_d/T, for the gaseous type of explosion, though the difference is unlikely to exceed 30% for the values of x_m/x_y admissible in practice for structural elements. Admissible values may generally be assumed, for design purposes, to be within the range 3 to 5 except for some compression members and other elements with a fairly brittle response, for which a value of 1.5 would be safer. Actual ductilities, even of seemingly brittle masonry walls, may however be up to 20 or 30 for individual elements with adequate end or edge restraints. Periods of vibration T for individual elements will usually be within the range 50 ms to 200 ms (somewhat longer than natural low-amplitude periods).

The possibility of elastic rebound from the position of maximum deflection must also be considered, since elastic strain energy will be stored in this position even if there is still some load acting in the direction of the deflection. The rebound may involve some reverse inelastic deformation and may also be limited by damping, but it is conservative to assume that it is completely elastic with no damping. A chart giving the ratio of the required rebound resistance r_r to the yield resistance r_y is reproduced (from Newmark, 1973) in Fig. 5.35. It should be noted that for the lower values of t_d/T there is 100% rebound, with $r_r/r_y = -1.0$.

In general, nonstructural elements like window glass and light claddings will be blown out by the sort of loads considered here that pose a threat to the main structure. Most glass will fail, for instance, at pressures below 10 kPa (1.7 psi), the actual failing pressure being dependent on the duration of the load. Mainstone (1971) gives charts relative to gaseous explosion loads. Peak pressures required to cause failure in the case of high-explosive blasts will be somewhat higher. Such failures will reduce the areas exposed to the blast in the case of external blast and should therefore be taken into account in estimating the blast loads. In the case of internal gaseous explosions they will directly reduce the peak pressures developed, as explained in Article 1 of Section 5.2.

2 Responses to Loads Whose Variation with Time Is Unknown

The analytical and design procedures outlined in the preceding Article are inapplicable where the manner of variation of the load with time and the duration of the load cannot easily be predicted with reasonable confidence. This is usually the case with impact loads. Structural responses in such cases can most readily be predicted in terms of impulse and energy, and similar procedures may be used to predict the over-all responses of tall buildings to local blast loads.

It should normally be conservatively assumed that impacts are plastic—in other words, that the impacting mass fuses after impact with the structure that is hit (with attendant loss of energy in local plastic deformation) rather than rebounding from it. This means that the energy to be absorbed in general structural deformation will be reduced, in relation to the initial energy of the impacting mass, in the ratio of the impacting mass to the combined mass set in motion by the impact. In the case of impulsive blast loads, the energy to be absorbed will be given by the momentum transmitted to the mass that is set in motion by the blast.

The chief practical difficulty lies in the correct estimation of the relevant structural mass or masses and, as a corollary of this, of the mode or modes of response. For detailed analysis, numerical methods may be most useful (Newmark and Rosenblueth, 1971). See also the reviews by Sahlin and Nilsson (1975) and Kavyrchine and Struck (1975) already referred to in Article 3 of Section 5.2.

3 Further Aspects

Two further aspects, which may be relevant in either of the cases just considered, are worth noting. One is that both steel and concrete have enhanced strengths under very rapidly applied and short-lived loading. These enhanced material strengths may further increase the dynamic strengths of structural elements as compared with their static strengths. Mainstone (1975) has recently reviewed the relevant data.

The second aspect is that the structural response may not end with the over-all response to the initial load in the fairly narrow sense in which that was interpreted. Attention has already been drawn in Article 3 of Section 5.4 to the possibilities of extensive consequential collapses after local primary damage—either as a result of deprivation of support leading to increased load being thrown on parts of the

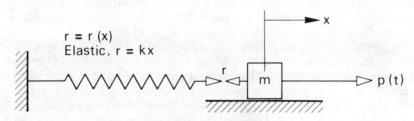

Fig. 5.30 Idealized simple spring-mass system

remaining structure so deprived, or as a result of impact loading by falling debris. Full analysis of structural response to local blast or impact loads should consider also these secondary possibilities. Secondary collapse due to deprivation of support

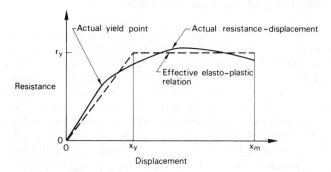

Fig. 5.31 Actual and assumed resistance-displacement relationships

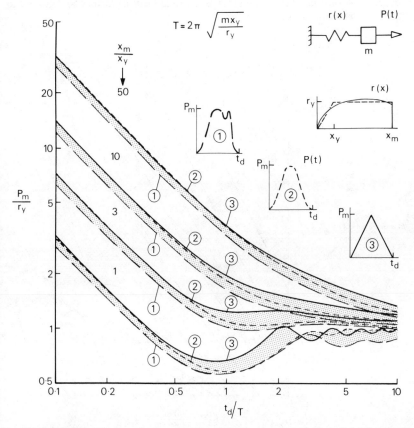

Fig. 5.32 Calculated responses to three shapes of load pulse typical of vented internal gas explosions

is probably the more important one to guard against since, if it can be avoided, debris loading will thereby be reduced.

5.6 POSSIBILITIES OF REDUCING HAZARDS

It was pointed out in the introduction to Section 5.3 that the loads are all, in some way, man-made. It follows that, in principle at least, there are two possible strategies for achieving safety. Either one can passively accept the hazards of the different types of load as they now appear, on average, to exist or as simple forward extrapolation suggests they might become during the life of a building, and then seek safety by purely structural measures. Or one can recognize that, being man-made, the loads are themselves susceptible in varying degrees to control, and seek also to reduce the risk of their occurrence or the violence of their action if they do occur. The possibility of reducing the risk of secondary impact loads after local damage, as referred to in the previous paragraph, may be regarded as one instance of the latter strategy, though the measures are, in this case, purely structural. We shall now consider some possible nonstructural measures for reducing the basic loading hazards for the different types of accidental loads as further background to a final discussion of criteria for design.

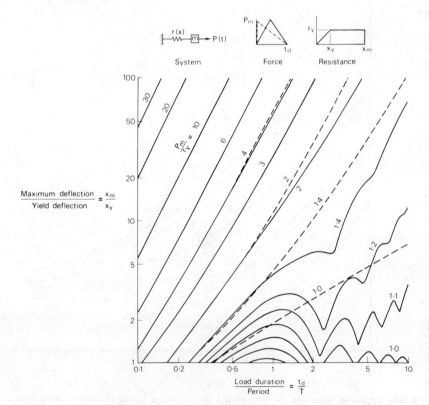

Fig. 5.33 Design chart for triangular load pulse with p_m at 0.5 t_d

1   High-Explosive Blast

It may be assumed that high-explosive blast on tall buildings will always be the result of deliberate hostile action or, if accidental in the normal sense, the result of illicit manufacture, storage, or possession of explosives within the building. To this extent there is nothing that the building designer can do to reduce the risk of explosions, though building management may have a part to play in reducing the risk of internal explosions. This apart, the building designer can exercise some control over the loads that will be experienced as a result of exposure to an external blast wave by, for instance, the choice of fenestration. But the blast wave itself will not be reduced in intensity, and it seems best to take it as the primary design criterion. For high-explosive blast it therefore seems that the basic risks, however assessed, must simply be accepted by the designer.

2   Internal Blast due to Gaseous Explosions

With internal gaseous explosions, the position is different. Various measures can be taken both to reduce the risk of hazardous accumulations of flammable gases and to reduce the pressures developed if such accumulations are ignited.

To reduce the risk of hazardous accumulations of gas, it is tempting simply to ban

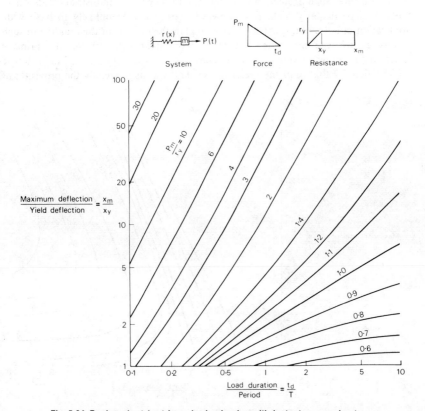

Fig. 5.34 Design chart for triangular load pulse with instantaneous rise to p_m

piped gas from tall buildings; but, as pointed out in Section 5.3, this might not achieve the desired end. It is preferable to assume that gas will be present in the building and to concentrate on the avoidance of large accumulations from leaks. There are several ways of doing this apart from the most obvious one of assuring that the whole gas installation in the building is as safe as possible. The two chief ways are the provision of ventilation and the avoidance, as far as possible, of closed spaces in which gas could most readily accumulate undetected and in which it is likely to cause the worst explosions if ignited. Where such spaces are unavoidable (as in the case of ducts and service spaces over suspended ceilings) there is all the more need for adequate ventilation, though the need may be reduced by the provision of warning devices if provision is also made for their regular maintenance and to assure that warnings will be acted upon. The evidence of recent serious explosions suggests that there is a special risk of leaks from faulty external mains into basements at the points where services enter a building, so these entry points should receive special attention.

Because of the different character of gaseous explosions as compared with high-explosive detonations, there are two ways of reducing the pressures developed if an explosive accumulation of gas nevertheless occurs and is ignited (as it almost inevitably will be). One is to suppress the explosion at an early stage by the automatic injection of an inerting substance. Injection is triggered off by the initial rise in pressure. Such protection is common in those parts of industrial plants where the risk is particularly high. It is, however, costly and is unlikely to have wide application in tall buildings. The other is to plan the interior of the building in such a way as to take maximum advantage (consistent with serving the primary functional requirements) of those characteristics of enclosures referred to in Article 1 of Section 5.2 that limit the pressure rise. This means especially the provision of

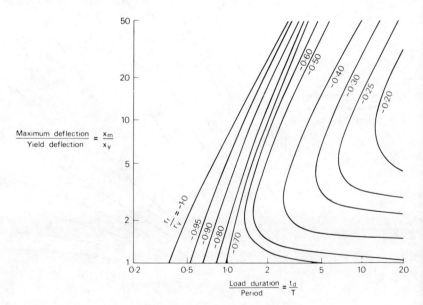

Fig. 5.35 Design chart for elastic rebound

adequate light vents (such as windows) to blow out at pressures well below the strengths of essential load-bearing elements.

Quantitative guidance on the design of ventilation systems to cope with given rates of leakage and prevent excessive accumulations of gas is now available (Leach and Bloomfield, 1973). It remains difficult, however, to set the right levels for possible or probable maximum rates of leakage and to quantify "excessive" accumulations. The studies of vented explosions referred to in the last paragraph of Article 1, Section 5.2, give some guidance in relation to the latter and to the associated choice of vents. But it is still difficult, without further such studies, to do much more than rank alternatives in order of desirability. It must also be remembered that there are practical limitations both on provisions for ventilation and the design of vents. These are partly economic and partly, in the latter case, a result of the need to assure, in tall buildings particularly, that vents will not be blown out by the wind.

3   External Blast due to Gaseous Explosions

Though the hazard of large external gaseous explosions is obviously amenable to some control, the designer of a tall building can do no more about it than about the hazard of external high-explosive blast. The one significant difference between the two from the present point of view is that the hazard of the gaseous explosion is much more dependent on the location of the building. It can therefore be greatly reduced by avoiding hazardous locations.

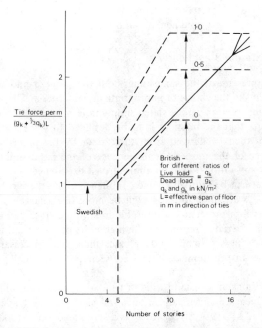

Fig. 5.36 Comparison of United Kingdom and Swedish requirements for internal floor ties in main spanning direction

4 Impact

The risks of impact from vehicles and aircraft are similarly dependent on location and can be reduced in the same way. The risk of vehicle impact can be further reduced by the designer of a building on a given site by such measures as raising the building on a plinth or protecting otherwise vulnerable columns or walls by bollards. The further possibility of reducing the risk of impact by falling debris has already been mentioned. Alongside this might be mentioned the value of adhering to safe practices in construction, particularly in the lifting and fixing of heavy components, and in the maintenance at all times of adequate shores, braces, and other necessary temporary supports.

5.7 CRITERIA FOR DESIGN: GUIDELINES FOR CODE REQUIREMENTS

With such a wide diversity of possible loads, and with alternative strategies available, in some cases at least, for the achievement of safety, it is not possible to suggest a single criterion of universal validity. Even if safety is sought by purely structural means, one type of criterion is appropriate for loads that act simultaneously over the whole height of a building and another is required for loads that act only locally but have been shown to be capable of producing far-reaching effects. Some distinction also seems desirable between loads with a relatively high probability of occurrence during the life of a typical tall building in normal circumstances (say a probability that would now be assessed at greater than 1 in 10^2) and loads that are likely to arise only in special circumstances (such as nuclear warfare) or in certain locations (such as the vicinities of major airports). We shall consider first external blast loads from distant sources—the only loads that act simultaneously over the whole height—and then all local loads.

1 Over-All External Blast Loads

These loads present, at the same time, both the simplest and one of the most difficult problems in the choice of appropriate design criteria. The simplest because the basic loading criterion can be stated simply in terms of the height, distance, and strength of burst that the building is to be designed to withstand. Other loading parameters can then be derived from these data by the procedures outlined in Section 5.2. One of the most difficult because of the impossibility of predicting future risks by any rational extrapolation of past experience.

The most that can be said with some confidence about these risks is that, in the event of nuclear war, some localities will be more likely targets than others. But where a high level of protection is desirable in such localities, tall buildings would seem to be inappropriate. Because of the high costs of giving tall buildings lateral strengths and stiffnesses significantly greater than those necessary to withstand wind and (if relevant) earthquake, it does not seem possible to call generally for any further provision.

Normal provisions to withstand wind or wind and earthquake will, in fact, confer a considerable measure of resistance to over-all blast loading. Under a design wind pressure of, say, 2 kPa (0.3 psi) regarded as a static load, only working stresses will be developed. About twice this pressure will be required to produce static yielding, and a pressure considerably higher will be required to produce yielding when it is applied as a very short-term dynamic load. If, in addition, it is assumed that much of the cladding fails in the blast, there will be a reduction in the drag forces and the free-field or side-on overpressure needed to cause serious structural distress will be still further increased. When a building is designed to resist earthquakes, an estimate of the resistance to over-all external blast can be made by considering the effective seismic coefficient which it is capable of surviving and the mass. Newmark (1966) gives a relevant comparison of responses to wind and earthquake. In drawing comparisons between these types of loading and external blast it should, however, be remembered that the enhanced resistance of the main structure to blast loads may be achieved only at the price of extensive internal damage, probably made worse by ensuing fire. Thus the main structure may survive, but not its occupants.

2 Local Loads

In the case of local loads, the chief problems are presented by their diversity and by the need to consider more than just the immediate (local) response to the primary load.

The diversity of possible loads makes it difficult, in choosing simple practicable design criteria, to take full advantage of the possibilities of reducing some of the basic hazards as discussed in Section 5.6. This is because a reduction in one hazard will usually have little, if any, effect on others. There will obviously be some over-all gain, but the statistical data on most of the risks are far from adequate to quantify it. The only exception arises where, in the absence of any measures to reduce it, one hazard might be much greater than the others. On present evidence this would be the case with the internal gaseous explosion hazard in the absence of normal venting and ventilation. Here it does seem reasonable to assume that these will be available (assuring this by a specific requirement where it cannot be taken for granted) and to take advantage of them in selecting design loadings. But it does not seem possible to go further in allowing any general relaxations of design loadings in recognition of the provision of additional venting or ventilation or other measures to reduce further this particular hazard.

The internal gaseous explosion hazard has the advantage as a possible norm for the quantification of accidental local loads that, as well as being one of the commonest causes of significant local damage, it is the one on which limits can most reasonably be placed. Some relevant figures have been given in Section 5.3. The somewhat arbitrary choice of 34 kPa (4.9 psi) as an equivalent static design load in the first British reaction to the Ronan Point incident (Ministry of Housing and Local Government, 1968) was not, in retrospect, unreasonable—though the specification of an equivalent static load rather than a dynamic pressure pulse meant that the criterion results in different levels of safety for structures with different dynamic response characteristics. The present evidence of actual recent damage to tall buildings suggests that the risks of more damaging local accidental loads from other causes are relatively slight in most cases.

The criterion just referred to (now incorporated in regulation D17 of the UK Building Regulations, 1976) was aimed specifically at the prevention of progressive collapse. It called for elements that were essential to over-all structural integrity to be capable of withstanding the loads transmitted to them by the specified pressure, and other loads considered to act simultaneously, "without structural failure." But, as an alternative to treating all primary load-bearing elements as "essential" in this way, the designer was allowed to envisage the removal of some by the accident, provided that the remaining structure could then take over part of their role by bridging over the damage. To guide him in this case, notional extents of damage to be bridged over were also specified and some guidance was given on desirable tensile continuity between elements.

As stated in the introduction, some types of structure—notably many steel frames and frames of cast-in-place reinforced concrete—are well able to bridge over local damage without special provision. The provision of specified amounts of rein-forcement to give tensile continuity between elements in other types may be regarded as the most logical means of making them equally "robust" in the face of accidental loads. As also stated in the introduction, this approach also has the merit of providing for other unforeseeable situations which are tantamount to accidental loadings without actually being loads in themselves.

Perhaps partly as a result of different initial experience, the Scandinavian countries emphasized from the start the wide range of possible accidental or unforeseeable causes of local damage (Granstrom, 1974). It is also explicitly recognized in, for instance, the Commentaries on Part 4 of the National Building Code of Canada (1975); and, whether it is so recognized or not, the recent tendency has been to call primarily for adequate tensile continuity between elements when detailed guidance is given on achieving the over-all objective of assuring that damage remains confined to the immediate locality of the initial accident. Following the lead of the CEB Recommendations for the design and construction of large-panel structures (1966), the procedure has been to specify tie forces that are to be resisted at yield stress by the reinforcement at joints. Fig. 5.36 shows diagrammatically, for purpose of comparison, the tie forces in the main load-bearing direction of floor slabs as specified in the relevant current United Kingdom and Swedish codes. Unlike the original United Kingdom guidance on desirable tensile continuity that was referred to above and was directly related to the equivalent static explosion pressure to be used in the alternative design approach, both these later specifications introduce variations according to the number of stories on the basis of judgments of the relative risks, including the potentially greater seriousness of damage to taller buildings. For the further guidance of future code writers, there are now available reports on several series of tests on the bridging of local damage and the residual stability of partly damaged structures: see particularly Sinha and Hendry (1970); Granstrom (1971); Odgaard and Olesen (1972); Wilford and Yu (1973); Yu (1974); and Armer (1977a, 1977b). The reports on damage in actual incidents that were referred to in Section 5.4 are also obviously relevant.

Whatever detailed guidance is given, it seems desirable that prime emphasis should be given to the risks to be considered and the designer's responsibilities for making adequate provision to assure that any damage will be commensurate with its cause. The Canadian Code referred to earlier does this as follows:

> Buildings and structural systems shall provide such structural integrity, strength, or other defences, that the hazards associated with progressive collapse due to local failure caused by severe overloads or abnormal events ... are reduced to a level commensurate with good engineering practice. (Clause 4.1.1.8)

The British Code on which Fig. 5.36 is partly based (CP 110: Part 1: 1972) similarly states the basic requirement:

The layout of the structure on plan, and the interaction between the structural members, should be such as to ensure a robust and stable design: the structure should be designed to support loads caused by normal function, but there should be a reasonable probability that it will not collapse catastrophically under the effect of misuse or accident. No structure can be expected to be resistant to the excessive loads or forces that could arise due to an extreme cause, but it should not be damaged to an extent disproportionate to the original cause.

The Commentary on the Canadian Code emphasizes, in addition, the value of good ductility and energy absorption capacity and the importance of structural layout.

A somewhat different approach to detailed design may be necessary when, due to the location of a particular building, extreme local loads such as those likely to result from an impact by a jumbo jet may occur. However, it is no more desirable for codes to provide for these special cases than to call generally for resistance to large nuclear blasts. "De minimis non curat lex; de maximis non debent curare normae" (The law does not concern itself with the minutiae of individual cases; nor should codes concern themselves with special extreme situations).

5.8   CONDENSED REFERENCES/BIBLIOGRAPHY

The following is a condensed bibliography for this chapter. Not only does it include all articles referred to or cited in the text, but it also contains bibliography for further reading. The full citations will be found at the end of the Volume. What is given here should be sufficient information to lead the reader to the correct article: the author, date, and abbreviated title. In case of multiple authors, only the first named is listed.

ASCE 1961, *Design of Structures to Resist Nuclear Weapons Effects*
Alexander 1970, *The Design of Structures to Withstand Gaseous Explosions*
Allen 1972, *Progressive Collapse, Abnormal Loads, and Building Codes*
Allgood 1970, *Design of Flexural Members for Static and Blast Loading*
Armer 1977a, *The Performance of Damaged Large Panel Structures*
Armer 1977b, *The Response of a Model 18-Storey Panel Structure to Impact*
Astbury 1970, *Gas Explosions in Load-Bearing Brick Structures*
Astbury 1973, *Experimental Gas Explosions—Report of Further Tests*

Baker 1948, *The Design of Framed Buildings Against High Explosive Bombs*
Brode 1968, *Review of Nuclear Weapons Effects*
Burnett 1973, *Residential Buildings and Gas-Related Explosions*
Butlin 1975, *A Review of Information on Experiments Concerning the Venting*
Butlin 1974, *Pressures Produced by Gas Explosions in a Vented Compartment*

Clarkson 1972, *Sonic-Boom-Induced Building Structure Responses Including Damage*
Cubbage 1955, *An Investigation of Explosion Reliefs for Industrial Drying Ovens*
Cubbage 1973, *Pressures Generated by Explosions of Gas-Air Mixtures*

Dept. of Employment 1975, *The Flixborough Disaster: Report of Court of Inquiry*
Dietrich 1973, *Methods for Analysing the Loading and Limiting Structural Response of Nuclear*
Dragosavic 1973, *Structural Measures Against Natural-Gas Explosions in High-Rise Blocks*

Ferahian 1972, *Buildings: Design for Prevention of Progressive Collapse*
Fribush 1973, *Estimates of Vehicular Collisions with Multistorey Buildings*
Fry 1971, *Gas Explosions Attended by Fire Brigades in Dwellings*

Geiger 1974, *Generation and Propagation of Pressure Waves Due to Unconfined Chemical*
Glasstone 1964, *The Effects of Nuclear Weapons*
Granstrom 1956, *Loading Characteristics of Air Blasts from Detonating Charges*
Granstrom 1971, *Stability of Buildings After Accidental Damage*

Granstrom 1974, *The Behaviour of Buildings Under Extreme Loads*
Granstrom 1976, *Terrorist Explosion in the German Embassy, Stockholm, 1975*
Griffiths 1968, *Report of the Inquiry into the Collapse of Flats at Ronan Point*

ISE 1969, *The Implications of the Report of the Inquiry into the Collapse of Flats at Ronan Point*

Kajfasz 1973, *External Blast*
Kavyrchine 1975, *The Effect of Impact Loading on Building: Practical Application*
Kinney 1962, *Explosive Shocks in Air*

Lange 1973, *Dynamic Loading of a Reactor Building by an Airplane Crash*
Leach 1973, *Ventilation in Relation to Toxic and Flammable Gases in Buildings*
Lewis 1961, *Combustion, Flames and Explosions of Gases*
Leyendecker 1973, *Investigation of the Skyline Plaza Collapse in Fairfax County*
Leyendecker 1976, *Abnormal Loads on Buildings and Progressive Collapse*
Ligtenberg 1969, *Structural Safety and Catastrophic Events*
Little 1967, *Public Safety and Gas Distribution*

Mainstone 1966, *Structural Tests on an Experimental Helicopter Platform*
Mainstone 1971, *The Breakage of Glass Windows by Gas Explosions*
Mainstone 1973, *Internal Blast*
Mainstone 1974a, *The Hazards of Explosion, Impact, and Other Random Loadings*
Mainstone 1974b, *Buildings and the Hazard of Explosion*
Mainstone 1975, *The Effect of Impact Loading on Building: Properties of Materials*
Mainstone 1976, *The Response of Buildings to Accidental Explosions*
Mainstone 1976, *Report on an Explosion at Mersey House, Bootle, Lancs.*
Mainstone 1978, *Structural Damage in Buildings Caused by Gaseous Explosions*
Mainstone 1978, *Accidental Explosions and Impacts: Some Lessons from Recent Incidents*
McKaig 1962, *Building Failures: Case Studies in Construction and Design*
Morton 1970, *Report of the Inquiry Into the Safety of Natural Gas as a Fuel*
Morton 1971, *The Stability of Load-Bearing Brickwork Structures*

Newmark 1956, *An Engineering Approach to Blast Resistant Design*
Newmark 1963, *Design of Structures for Dynamic Loads Including the Effects of Vibration*
Newmark 1966, *Relation Between Wind and Earthquake Response of Tall Buildings*
Newmark 1973, *External Blast*
Newmark 1971, *Fundamentals of Earthquake Engineering*
Norris 1959, *Structural Design for Dynamic Loads*

Odgaard 1972, *Local Failure in Panel Buildings: A Discussion Illustrated by a Model Test*

Palmer 1973, *Dust Explosions and Fires*
Popp 1965, *Investigations on the Impact of Vehicles on Reinforced Concrete Columns*
Popplewell 1975, *The Response of Box-Like Structures to Weak Explosions*

Rasbash 1969, *Explosions in Domestic Structures: The Relief of Gas and Vapour Explosions*
Rasbash 1970, *Gas Explosions in Multiple Compartments*
Riera 1968, *On the Stress Analysis of Structures Subjected to Aircraft Impact Forces*
Rodin 1969, *Safety in Large Panel Construction*

Sahlin 1975, *The Effect of Impact Loading on Building*
Sharpe 1971, *Structural Response to Sonic Booms*
Sinha 1970, *The Stability of a Five-Storey Brickwork Cross Wall*
Slack 1971, *Explosions in Buildings*
Somes 1973, *Abnormal Loading on Buildings and Progressive Collapse*
Steele 1973, *The Incidence of Hazardous Material Accidents During Transportation*
Strehlow 1973, *Unconfined Vapour-Cloud Explosions—An Overview*
Struck 1973, *Problems and Gaps of Knowledge in the Assessment of the Response*
Struck 1975, *The Effect of Impact Loading on Building: Examples of Impact*

US Army, Navy and Air Force 1969, *Structures to Resist the Effects of Accidental Explosions*
US National Transport Safety Board 1969, *A Study of Safety*
Utne 1971, *Explosion Disaster, Store Slette, Greenland*
Van Uchelen 1973, *Natural Gas Explosions and Building Construction*
Warren 1972, *Recent Sonic Bang Studies in the United Kingdom*
Wilford 1973, *Catenary Action in Damaged Structures*
Yao 1973, *Explosion Venting of Low Strength Equipment and Structures*
Yu 1974, *Research on Horizontal Joints in Large Panel Construction*

Tall Building Criteria and Loading

Chapter CL-6

Quality Criteria

Prepared by Committee 9 (Quality Criteria) of the Council on Tall Buildings and Urban Habitat as part of the Monograph on the Planning and Design of Tall Buildings.

Werner Quasebarth   Chairman
I. Gramolin   Vice-Chairman
E. James White, Jr.   Editor

AUTHOR ACKNOWLEDGMENT

Special acknowledgment is due those individuals whose contributions and papers formed the substantial first drafts of the various sections of this chapter. First are the state-of-art reporters from the 1972 International Conference whose material was published in the Lehigh Proceedings. These individuals are:

I. Gramolin, Section 6.1

R. L'Hermite, Sections 6.1, 6.7

E. J. White, Jr., Section 6.1

G. A. Alpsten, Section 6.2

J. T. Biskup, Section 6.2

N. Jackson, Section 6.2

T. Kamei, Section 6.2

S. Miki, Section 6.2

L. A. Napper, Section 6.2

H. Oba, Section 6.2

K. Tomonaga, Section 6.2

F. R. Preece, Sections 6.2, 6.3

P. W. Birkeland, Section 6.3

F. J. Principe, Section 6.3

R. Reznik, Section 6.3

L. J. Westhoff, Section 6.3

In addition to this, other sections were based on special contributions prepared by the following individuals:

V. Anzalone, Section 6.1

W. Quasebarth, Sections 6.2, 6.5

A. A. Anderson, Section 6.3

R. L. Blick, Section 6.3

C. W. Massie, Section 6.3

T. A. Holm, Section 6.4

E. J. White, Jr., Sections 6.5, 6.7

J. A. Millen, Section 6.6.

CONTRIBUTORS

The following is a complete list of those who have submitted written material for possible use in the chapter, whether or not that material was used in the final version. The Committee Chairman and Editor were given quite complete latitude. Frequently length limitations precluded the inclusion of much valuable material. The Bibliography contains all contributions. The contributors are: G. A. Alpsten, A. A. Anderson, V. Anzalone, P. W. Birkeland, J. T. Biskup, R. L. Blick, D. D. Calegari, B. J. Ferguson, A. E. Fiorato, F. P. Golden, B. Goschy, I. Gramolin, R. C. Heun, T. A. Holm, N. Jackson, T. Kamei, R. L'Hermite, W. H. Levelius, I. Martin, C. W. Massie, S. Miki, J. A. Millen, J. Morris, L. A. Napper, H. Oba, F. R. Preece, F. J. Principe, W. Quasebarth, S. Reznik, S. Sahlin, M. Stiller, K. Tomonaga, C. Urbano, J. H. P. Van Aardt, L. J. Westhoff, E. J. White, Jr.

COMMITTEE MEMBERS

G. A. Alpsten, V. Anzalone, P. W. Birkeland, J. T. Biskup, O. W. Blodgett, K. D. Cummins, L. H. Daniels, H. Ehm, R. Estrada, F. Faltus, A. E. Fiorato, G. F. Fox, I. Gramolin, R. C. Heun, N. Jackson, F. C. Jarrard, T. Kamei, H. A. Krentz, R. L'Hermite, W. H. Levelius, S. Miki, L. A. Napper, J. Novotny, H. Oba, A. Pousset, F. R. Preece, F. J. Principe, W. Quasebarth, R. Reznik, M. Stiller, L. Tall, N. Tebedge, L. J. Westhoff, E. J. White, Jr.

CL-6

Quality Criteria

6.1 INTRODUCTION

A system of control combining detailed planning, specifying, follow-up, and documentation which is rigorously employed to assure an intended result is generally referred to as Quality Control or Quality Assurance. The effectiveness of such a system depends upon the selection of appropriate criteria and the assignment of qualified personnel. Quality control and the need for appropriate control criteria apply to all phases of a tall building project, beginning with planning, continuing through the design, contracting, and construction phases, and culminating with execution of the final checklist, final acceptance, and the owner's unrestricted beneficial occupancy of the project.

The purpose of this chapter is to identify various functions subject to, or forming part of, quality control and to assemble and present a base of applicable criteria suitable for establishing control systems which assure both satisfactory and efficient outcome of the project.

1 Quality Control and Construction Management

The subject of construction management (or project management) is also treated in Chapter PC-14.

The quality of a material is defined by those characteristics which make the material best suited for its use. Workmanship produces the finished product and provides the product with its final character, function, and quality. Most famous examples of architecture are "quality" structures, and the raw materials used in the component parts were the very best of their time. Because these structures were quality products by master craftsmen, many of them still stand structurally sound.

In the case of enduring architectural monuments, the master builder-architect set forth criteria in his drawings and then personally monitored and supervised the efforts of master craftsmen. Each craftsman was an expert in his own material —masonry, stone, wood, iron, bronze, or other available material appropriate for the intended purpose. In current practice, the design team (consulting architects and

441

engineers), manufacturers, contractors, and various testing agencies all participate in establishing and carrying out the quality control standards for a given project. This system permits wide variation in the degree of quality control achieved because ultimate responsibility tends to be divided among many parties. For example, the architect may select and specify a particular finish. If the specification is not sufficiently definitive, the contractor's interpretation of the specification may result in a price quotation which does not accurately reflect the consultant's desire or intent. When sample material is submitted to the architect for review, it may be disapproved and the architect may view many samples before approving the one he believes to be representative of the material originally selected and specified. Quality control, after the architect's approval, passes to a material supply or manufacturing plant, and the degree of control over quality can vary dramatically from plant to plant. Even with an approved sample to match, the production material may not be fabricated and finished properly, and after delivery to the jobsite, adequate protection may not be provided. Careless work, handling, or storage procedures may damage or cause inferior installation of otherwise satisfactory material. These and other potential pitfalls dictate the scope of needed quality control and demand clear assignment of responsibility at each stage of the work.

In order to provide reliable quality, effective controls must be identified during the planning stage so they may be applied to the work at the very beginning of each fabrication and construction stage. Many owners, to an extent consistent with their understanding of the construction process, will actively convey their expectations to their consultants. This communication will usually reflect what the owner expects to see in the finished building from a cost standpoint but may also include functional and esthetic requirements. Cost considerations are primary in defining quality; not only are configuration and functional aspects of the building affected, but material selection is often dictated by price considerations. Material selection is of fundamental importance due to the direct influence the quality of component parts has on the over-all quality of the finished building. It is essential to appreciate that acceptable quality is required in structural work and foundations as well as architectural finish materials exposed to view. The importance of good structural design and quality construction of foundation and structure cannot be overemphasized. Not only must building codes and laws be satisfied, but failure to control quality can easily result in an unsatisfactory structure, which, in turn, can lead to continuing degeneration in architectural quality and reduced serviceability and usefulness of the entire building.

The size of a building should not dictate quality level required and achieved, but it does have a profound impact on construction and quality control techniques employed. For smaller buildings, control techniques are often nominal and standardized by building code, since the cost of specialized procedures cannot be justified within the project budget. This does not imply that the quality of materials in smaller structures should not be monitored—only that budgetary considerations must be respected. Larger buildings pose greater quality control demands because of material savings through design refinements, the need for more control of construction tolerances, and the repetitive nature of such construction. Poor control, whether in design or construction, can be costly to an owner not only due to increased costs during the construction period, but also due to possible accelerated degeneration which can lead to ever increasing maintenance costs and annoyances to occupants throughout the service life of the project.

While the design consultants are obligated to advise the owner of possible quality alternatives and related costs, they must also identify and assure adherence to minimum standards established by local, state or province, and national building codes. These codes contain quality control provisions for construction and, through the media of professional licensing, endeavor to provide for quality control in design. Without question, these codified features help to establish minimum standards of construction. In any event, plans and specifications must be drawn to satisfy the minimum provisions of building codes as well as owner-accepted quality standards. Additionally, and not to be ignored, plans and specifications must recognize environmental conditions, especially the effects of wind and earthquake.

Product associations as well as manufacturers of construction products can help in improving the reliability of construction. Assistance can be in the form of design standards (for example, in the USA the AISC Specification and ACI Code) as well as by direct assistance to consultants in the preparation of project specifications. An industry or a manufacturer's own quality assurance program can be issued or referenced as a part of the project specifications. One shortcoming of this system is that manufacturing quality control programs tend to be used for fabrication only, leaving installation or erection procedures subject to less well defined controls. Some local building codes require the manufacturer to certify that individual materials conform to the applicable code, the contract drawings, and the project specifications, or to one or more specifications or standards published by the American Society for Testing and Materials (ASTM), Deutsche Industrie Normen (DIN), or other nationally or internationally recognized standards organization.

The Construction Manager and other experts in contracting and construction can provide a powerful input into the over-all quality assurance program. When brought into the construction team during the design phase, the Construction Manager can bring additional perspective and experience to bear on the development of economical building systems and material selections, as well as appropriate quality control procedures to assure fulfillment of the design intent. Alternatively, through an overzealous desire to achieve minimum budget coupled with a failure to appreciate true value, the Construction Manager could force an undesirable or unacceptable lowering of quality in either the project planning or the execution stage. Ideally, the Construction Manager will thoroughly review all drawings, specifications, and contract provisions prepared for the project. He can point out areas of difficulty or success experienced in other projects, thereby assisting the owner and the consultants to establish realistic construction goals accompanied by effective quality standards.

A good example of the need for a documented quality control program before commencement of fabrication and erection is the exterior curtain wall system for any major building. After preparation by the manufacturer of a comprehensive quality control program, the detailed documentation must be submitted to and reviewed by the architect, design consultants, and the Construction Manager to assure that the program includes clear and concise steps which will result in execution of work of the desired quality, both in shop fabrication and field installation.

Exterior curtain or window wall construction is doubly important because, until it is virtually complete, the interior finish trades cannot effectively perform large portions of their work, thereby affecting the date of occupancy. When complete, the exterior wall must withstand the full range of exterior weather conditions while allowing uniform temperature and humidity within the building. Window wall design criteria and quality control procedures must recognize that negative pressures maximize at building corners.

Installation and caulking procedures alone cannot solve field problems caused by poor planning or quality control. All window wall systems for large projects should be built in mock-up form for both the typical building face exposure and corner exposure conditions. Mock-up tests should include measurements of deflection, water infiltration, and glass safety at test air pressures which are determined using the best available data for the actual building. The need for good dimensional control and good workmanship during fabrication and erection is obvious, but for all important projects the quality control program must also stipulate the required performance criteria and include provisions for verifying by actual testing that the window wall system will perform correctly when installed in the field. A well written quality control document which fails to identify all needs and conditions of the work requiring verification by test or production line monitoring is worthless.

Quality control concepts must be applied to all work at the construction site in order to minimize the occurrence of construction errors. The need for quality control personnel at the jobsite is a cost item which should be included in the total budget cost of the project.

Quality control in field operations is more difficult than for shop fabrication because of the number of materials to be installed concurrently. Additionally, even highly skilled manpower generally requires closer supervision in the field than in the shop. All types of personnel with varying levels of competence and motivation will work on a project from time to time. Where an operation may be standard in shop practice, the field craftsmen may elect one or more of a number of different ways to install a material. Close supervision must be maintained by foremen who are capable of communicating the correct requirements to the field craftsmen and laborers. Above all, the contractor must be diligent in his efforts to obtain the best field crew possible.

In conclusion, quality concepts must be introduced into a project at the time the owner initiates the master planning of a new building project. Quality requirements must be identified, defined, and refined by both owner and architect at the earliest possible date to allow the design professionals to prepare construction documents consistent with the project concepts. When the contract documents are issued for bid or negotiations, the contract language must reflect all desired and mandatory quality requirements and must require strict adherence to quality control programs developed in specific response to the actual project requirements. The Quality Control Program must realistically relate to both shop fabrication and field construction phases of the work. Construction contracts must be both technically and legally correct in their text. It is essential that costs associated with the selected quality level be understood and appreciated by all concerned, so that the finished project will fulfill the concept and expectations initially conceived by the owner.

2 Contract Documents, Criteria, and Quality Control

Quality control cannot be allowed to be a last-minute happening—rather it must be considered and planned throughout the engineering, esthetic, and environmental development of each building system. During the planning stages of projects, schematic drawings are prepared to show proposed architectural layouts and alternative structural systems. Simultaneously, outline specifications are prepared to describe all facets of the building project in brief form. These specifications describe the foundation system including soil or rock materials upon which the project is to be founded, concrete and reinforcing materials, masonry materials and mortar types, structural steel by strength and grade, welding and bolting materials, mechanical and electrical systems, elevator systems, window or curtain wall systems, fire ratings required as well as fireproofing designs intended for use, and all else necessary to describe accurately the general features of the building system planned. To achieve effective quality control consistent with the scope and the requirements of the project, special attention must be paid to those materials, service conditions, and geometries which demand special or unusual criteria. These criteria must be clearly identified in the outline specifications and thoroughly described in the final project specifications and drawings, so that quality control and inspection performed during the construction phases will assure that each building system or material is suitable in all respects for its intended use and service conditions. It is highly desirable to include quality control concepts and procedure requirements in the contract drawings and specifications for all construction projects. Detailed quality control programs, carefully prepared and thoroughly documented, are essential for tall buildings.

Project drawings and specifications for tall buildings must include the design solutions to material quality, material identification, dimensional tolerances, and quality of workmanship, as well as testing techniques and frequency of testing required. Acceptable dimensional tolerances, both for individual components and for the assembled relationship of components, must be clearly stated. With complete information, the contractor can be expected to provide the necessary construction of the desired quality without extra cost. When quality control tasks and standards are specific and applied by informed, trained personnel, questions and arguments regarding requirements can be held to a minimum. A lack of necessary information will compromise quality control efforts and will generally increase the cost of construction. There is great repetition of construction details and operations. Only by organizing quality requirements and verification procedures into a comprehensive formal program can one be sure that the quality of the construction is properly evaluated.

3　Quality Control Personnel

The source of quality control personnel will depend on contractual agreements and may be from the staff of the contractor, subcontractor, owner, design professional, or independent testing agencies. Regardless of source, quality control technicians and supervisory personnel must be thoroughly qualified to perform their assigned tasks including the keeping of meaningful, accurate, and readily understandable records. Whether in the fabrication shop or at the field construction site, quality control technicians must be in possession of all appropriate project specifications, drawings, codes, and standards, and must understand their meaning as well as why and where they apply. Nondestructive testing (NDT) personnel must be thoroughly trained and knowledgeable in their field. Visual inspectors should be carefully screened to verify that their experience, knowledge, and training qualify them for the type of work required. The professional responsible for quality control must set up standards of qualification for quality control technicians. Supervising personnel must be well versed in project requirements and standards, must be capable of making decisions regarding adequacy of quality achieved, and must carefully coordinate the efforts of quality control technicians. Scheduled briefing and instruction sessions are strongly advised at regular intervals throughout the work.

4 Material Selection

Selection of materials is a function of quality control. To a large extent, this facet of quality control will be practiced by the design professional during the design stage. In the case of structural steel, the exact material selected may be left up to the fabricator. If the designer selects no more than a minimum yield point, the AISC or other controlling specification or code may allow selection from a group of listed specifications. Also, if the designer does not place special restrictions or requirements on welding, the fabricator and erector may select one of several welding processes, not to mention the various wire and shielding mediums available. In structural concrete, conformance of concrete ingredients to ASTM standards allows selection from a wide range of materials. If the designer has special requirements for a given material, characteristics more restrictive than those described in current standard material specifications must be carefully documented in the drawings and specifications during the design phase. Where structural steel will be subjected to cold temperatures or to thickness direction tensile stresses from welded moment connections, specially selected materials or special fabrication procedures may be essential to the safety of the structure. All materials must be suitable for their intended use under all potential conditions which can be reasonably predicted. Either the design consultant must specify the correct material for each location or the service conditions must be explicitly documented to provide the contractor with the data needed to select materials with the correct properties. Suitability of material for use in actual service conditions, fundamental to the success of most structures, is essential for tall buildings.

5 Shop Fabrication

Shop fabrication of components for tall buildings generally applies to structural steel members and assemblies, and to mechanical, electrical, air conditioning, and elevator components. Where precast concrete elements are used, they also will generally be shop fabricated. Shop fabrication lends itself very well to assurance of specified quality through the contractor's own internal efforts. There is excellent opportunity to save money in fabrication costs by including in the project specifications the requirement that the fabricator monitor his own work and document achievement of the required quality through a comprehensive quality control program developed, documented, and implemented by the fabricator's own personnel. It is important for the designing professional to have the authority to review, demand upgrading if necessary, and finally approve the fabricator's quality control program, procedures, and personnel as well as to be provided free access to the fabricator's shop to view the work and free access to all quality control records both during and after completion of the work. Rigorous checking of fabricated items for soundness and dimensional conformance prior to shipment from the fabricating plant is essential to the success of any but the smallest of construction projects.

6 Field Construction

Construction at the building site is generally less subject to formally organized contractor's quality control than any other facet of the work. (Construction systems for tall buildings are treated in Chapter SC-8.) This can lead to the assignment of large numbers of surveillance personnel to monitor and verify the quality of the work. However, regardless of the number of surveillance personnel present at the site, the contractor's own quality control efforts at the construction site are extremely important. Delivery of concrete into the formwork within the specified parameters (slump, air content, unit weight, vibration) requires careful control which only the contractor's construction personnel can effect. Welding of structural steel requires continuous control, and must be promptly verified visually or by NDT

Typical programmable multiple drilling machine for steel sections *(Courtesy: Atlas Machine & Iron Works, Inc.)*

because the work often is quickly covered by following work or made inaccessible due to removal of staging. Bolting of members must be verified for both correct count and correct tightening, particularly for high-strength bolts. Reinforcing steel must be checked for correct installation. Electrical ducts and raceways, mechanical openings, and innumerable other details must be promptly verified. In addition to the foregoing, careful control of plumbness, column to column, and over-all building dimensions must be maintained by the erector. Prompt analysis of the erector's survey results or those of an independent surveyor is essential to keeping the over-all structure within specified tolerances. Access to the work and timeliness serve to emphasize the importance of effective and organized quality control by the contractor.

World Trade Center under construction *(Courtesy: The Port Authority of New York and New Jersey; photograph by A. Belva)*

7 Record Keeping

Assignment of qualified personnel, specification and selection of actual materials, the fabricated condition of each material, the condition of components and systems as installed, the tolerances to which the construction is built, and the assignment of contractual responsibilities and relationships, all must receive continuous consideration from the inception of the project and must be systematically and accurately recorded. Good record keeping of the quality of all portions of the work is essential; otherwise no one can state with certainty the condition, suitability, or correctness of items or systems previously installed.

6.2 STRUCTURAL STEEL

1 Properties of Structural Steel

The use of steel members composed of thick plate is characteristic to tall steel buildings. Heavy columns, especially in the lower levels of the building, heavy beams, and heavy transfer girders or trusses are common. Thin-plate elements, such as cladding or thin-gage slab decking, and members of normal thickness are also found in unusually large quantities. Extreme variety in material thicknesses is a distinctive feature of tall buildings. In addition, the selection and use of multiple grades and types suited to individual parts of the structure is quite common in tall buildings. (Discussion of the various structural systems for tall steel buildings will be found in Chapter SC-1. The structural design of steel buildings is the subject of Volume SB.)

Both the magnitude and the variation in mechanical properties of steel are affected by geometry, thickness, cross-sectional area, and length. Manufacturing and fabrication procedures will also affect the behavior and strength of steel structures for tall buildings. This fact may place greater significance on the *absolute* value of the actual yield strength (or any other strength characteristic of interest) than the industry standard *relative* value, should structural behavior be confirmed by full-scale tests or loading.

2 Steel Grades Used in Tall Buildings

Table 6.1 lists some common steel grades used in a few countries. Structural steel subdivides into four groups: Type 1, structural carbon steels; Type 2, high-strength and high-strength low-alloy steels; Type 3, heat-treated carbon steels; and Type 4, heat-treated alloy steels (Task Group 5, CRC, 1971). This classification has been applied to all steels listed in Table 6.1.

A detailed survey of steel grades used in tall buildings throughout the world is not available. However, in 1968, Lehigh University made a survey of steel grades used primarily in compression members in high-rise buildings in the design or erection stage in the United States (Bjørhovde and Tall, 1970). Table 6.2 summarizes some of the findings. Whereas structural carbon steel was used in almost all structures, higher yield strength steels were used in roughly 50%, and heat-treated alloy steels in 6% of the structures. This demonstrates the frequent use of multiple steel grades in building structures.

Table 6.1 Some steel grades used in different countries *(Alpsten, 1973)*

	Steel			Tensile Requirements[a]				
				σ_y[d]		σ_u		δ, as a percentage
Country (1)	Designation (2)	Type[g] (3)	Thickness range, in millimeters (inches) (4)	MN/m² (5)	ksi (6)	MN/m² (7)	ksi (8)	(9)
England	40B	1	up to 16 (5/8)	240	35			
			(16)− 25 (1)	230	33			
			(25)− 40 (1 1/2)	225	33	400−480	58− 70	22
			(40)− 63 (2 1/2)	220	32			
			(63)−100 (4)	210	30			
	43B	1	up to 16 (5/8)	255	37			
			(16)− 25 (1)	245	36			
			(25)− 40 (1 1/2)	240	35	430−510	62−74	20
			(40)− 63 (2 1/2)	230	34			
			(63)−100 (4)	225	33			
	50B	2	up to 16 (5/8)	355	51			
			(16)− 25 (1)	345	50			
			(25)− 40 (1 1/2)	345	50	500−600	72− 90	18
			(40)− 63 (2 1/2)	340	49			
			(63)−100 (4)	325	47			
	55C	2	up to 16 (5/8)	450	65			
			(16)− 25 (1)	430	62	550−700	80−101	17
			(25)− 40 (1 1/2)	415	60			
France[h]	E 24 (A 37)	1	up to 30 (1.18)	235	34	363−441	53− 64	28
			(30)−100 (3.94)	216	31			27
	E 26 (A 42)	1	up to 30 (1.18)	255	37	412−490	60− 71	26
			(30)−100 (3.94)	235	34			24
	E 30 (A 47)	1	up to 30 (1.18)	274	40	461−559	67− 81	23
			(30)−100 (3.94)	255	37			22
	E 36 (A 52)	2	up to 30 (1.18)	353	51	510−608	74− 88	22
			(30)−100 (3.94)	333	48			21
Germany	St 37-2	1	up to 16 (0.63)	240	34			
			(16)− 40 (1.58)	230	33	360−440	52− 64	25
			(40)−100 (3.94)	220	31			
	St 42-2	1	up to 16 (0.63)	260	37			
			(16)− 40 (1.58)	250	35	410−490	60− 71	22
			(40)−100 (3.94)	240	34			
	St 52-3	2	up to 16 (0.63)	350	51			
			(16)− 30 (1.18)	340	50	510−610	74− 88	22
			(40)− 50 (1.97)	330	48			

(Values in parentheses applicable only to certain products or dimensions)

[a]Minimum values when single value is given

[b]Ladle; maximum values except where marked "c"

[c]Minimum value

[d]Upper yield point where it exists, except where marked "e"

[e]Yield stress level

[f]32 ksi (221 MN/mm²) for t > 8 in.

Table 6.1 (continued)

Chemical Requirements, as a percentage[b]							
C (10)	Mn (11)	P (12)	S (13)	Si (14)	Cu (15)	N (16)	Notes (17)
0.20	1.5	0.05	0.05				semikilled
0.22	1.5	0.05	0.05				semikilled
0.20	1.5	0.05	0.05	0.5			semikilled + Nb; Nb max 0.10
0.22	1.6	0.04	0.04	0.6			semikilled + Nb + fine grain Nb max 0.10
0.18		0.05	0.05			0.007	
0.20		0.05	0.05			0.007	
0.24	(1.3)	0.05	0.05	(0.4)			
0.24	(1.5)	0.05	0.05	(0.55)			Nb + V + Ti < 0.20
0.18		0.05	0.05			0.007	
0.25		0.05	0.05			0.007	
0.20 0.22 0.22	1.5	0.045	0.045			0.009	

[g]Type 1—structural carbon steels
Type 2—high-strength and high-strength low-alloy steels
Type 3—heat-treated carbon steels
Type 4—heat-treated alloy steels
[h]Quality "2" when values differ between different subgrades

Table 6.1 Some steel grades used in different countries (Alpsten, 1973)

				Tensile Requirements[a]				
	Steel			σ_y^d		σ_u		δ, as a percentage
Country (1)	Designation (2)	Type[g] (3)	Thickness range, in millimeters (inches) (4)	MN/m² (5)	ksi (6)	MN/m² (7)	ksi (8)	(9)
Sweden	SIS 1312	1	up to 40 (1.58) (40)−100 (3.94)	220ᵉ 210ᵉ	31ᵉ 30ᵉ	360−440	52− 64	24
	SIS 1412	1	up to 40 (1.58) (40)−100 (3.94)	260ᵉ 250ᵉ	37ᵉ 35ᵉ	430−510	62− 73	23
	SIS 2172	2	up to 16 (0.63) (16)− 40 (1.58) (40)− 60 (2.36)	310ᵉ 300ᵉ 290ᵉ	47ᵉ 45ᵉ 43.5ᵉ	490−590	71− 85	21
	SIS 2132	2	up to 60 (2.36)	350ᵉ	51ᵉ	510	74	22
	SIS 2142	2	up to 60 (2.36)	390ᵉ	57ᵉ	530	77	20
USA	ASTM A 36	1		240	36ᶠ	400−552	58− 80	23
	ASTM A 242	2	19 (up to 3/4) 38 [(3/4)−1 1/2] 102 [(1 1/2)−4]	340 320 290	50 46 42	480 460 430	70 67 63	21
	ASTM A 441	2	19 (up to 3/4) 38 [(3/4)−1 1/2] 102 [(1 1/2)−4] 203 [(4) −8]	340 320 290 270	50 46 42 40	480 460 430 410	70 67 63 60	21
	ASTM A 588	2	102 (up to 4) 127 [(4) −5] 203 [(5) −8]	340 320 290	50 46 42	480 460 430	70 67 63	19
	ASTM A 572 Grade 42 45 50 55 60 65	2	 102 (up to 4) 38 (up to 1 1/2) 38 (up to 1 1/2) 38 (up to 1 1/2) 25 (up to 1) 13 (up to 1/2)	 290 310 340 380 410 450	 42 45 50 55 60 65	 410 410 450 480 520 550	 60 60 65 70 75 80	 24 22 21 20 18 —
	ASTM A 514	4	19 (up to 3/4) 63 [(3/4)−2 1/2] 102 [(2 1/2)−4]	690 690 621	100 100 90	790−930 790−930 720−930	115−135 115−135 105−135	18 18 17

(Values in parentheses applicable only to certain products or dimensions)

[a]Minimum values when single value is given

[b]Ladle; maximum values except where marked "c"

[c]Minimum value

[d]Upper yield point where it exists, except where marked "e"

[e]Yield stress level

[f]32 ksi (221 MN/mm²) for t > 8 in.

Table 6.1. (continued)

Chemical Requirements, as a percentage[b]							
C (10)	Mn (11)	P (12)	S (13)	Si (14)	Cu (15)	N (16)	Notes (17)
0.20	(0.4–0.7)	0.06	0.05	(0.05–0.25)		0.009	
0.20	(0.4–1.1)	0.05	0.05	0.5	0.4	0.009	
0.18	1.4	0.05	0.05	0.5	0.4	0.009	
0.20	1.6	0.035	0.035	0.5		0.02	several other elements prescribed
0.20	1.8	0.035	0.035	0.5		0.02	
0.26	(0.8–1.2)	0.04	0.05	(0.15–0.30)	(0.20[c])		
0.15-0.20	1.00–1.35	0.04–0.15	0.05		0.20[c]		
0.22	0.85–1.25		0.05	0.30	0.20[c]		V min 0.02
0.10-0.19	0.9–1.25	0.04	0.05	0.15–0.30	0.25–0.40		Cr 0.40–0.65 V 0.02–0.10 "Weathering Steel"
(Analysis for Grade A given; several subgrades available)							
0.21 0.22 0.23 0.25 0.26 0.26	1.35	0.04	0.05	0.30		0.015	several other elements prescribed (Nb and/or V, N)
0.15-0.21	0.80–1.10	0.035	0.4	0.4–0.8			several other elements prescribed
(Analysis for "Type A" given; several types available)							

[g]Type 1—structural carbon steels
Type 2—high-strength and high-strength low-alloy steels
Type 3—heat-treated carbon steels
Type 4—heat-treated alloy steels
[h]Quality "2" when values differ between different subgrades

In Europe, structural carbon steels are the predominant grade of steel used in tall buildings.

3   Tension Test Properties

The characteristics normally prescribed in material standards are: (1) Yield point or yield strength; (2) tensile strength; (3) elongation; and (4) reduction of area. Of these values, the yield value is of primary interest in determining the strength of structures.

Definition of Testing Terms and Symbols.   Several definitions of "yield point" or "yield strength" are commonly used in specifications. Therefore, in evaluating the results for yield strength and strain-hardening properties reported in the literature, the method of testing and definitions applied in the particular case should be given due consideration. Two terms often used have no physical significance for material behavior. These are the proportional limit and lower yield point. The proportional limit is strongly influenced by residual stresses in the test specimen and accidental load eccentricities. The lower yield point results from the flow that develops suddenly at the upper yield point, and is somewhat below the yield-stress level (the constant stress that accompanies the yielding of materials which have this property). Furthermore, the lower yield point sometimes results from a dynamic reaction in the testing machine, thus reflecting the behavior of the machine rather than of the material in the test specimen.

Yield Strength.   The definition of yield point or yield strength for the acceptance test used in mill testing in most countries is based upon the upper yield strength, if an identifiable upper yield exists. By very accurate alining and slow straining of the

Table 6.2 Some results from a survey of steel in high-rise buildings *(Bjørhovde and Tall, 1970)*

Factor surveyed (1)		Number of projects (2)
Column sections:	rolled H	59
	welded H	34
	welded □	27
	other	14
Steel grade, ASTM[a]:	A7	2
	A36	84
	A242	8
	A441	26
	A514	6
	A572	12
	other	10
Number of steel grades within project:	one grade	57
	two grades	24
	three grades	10
	more	3
Total number of projects in survey		94

[a]See Table 6.1 for strength data.

tension specimen, it may be possible to obtain an upper yield point up to 100% higher than the yield stress level, depending upon strain rate, shape and dimensional accuracy of specimen, and centricity in loading. It has also been observed that the yielding is time dependent; a specimen left with a stress between the upper and lower yield may deform plastically after a time lag of several hours. It is therefore recommended that the 0.2% offset value be adopted for all steels, including those displaying an upper yield point.

Variation of Yield Strength.   Since most standards specify a minimum rather than an average value, steel makers apply measures to assure that each heat will fulfill the predetermined requirements. Control measures will be based on the difference between predicted and nominal strengths based on mechanical tests of each cast or heat rolled into one or more specific products. This situation should lead to an unsymmetrical frequency distribution, as observed in the histograms of Fig. 6.1 (Alpsten, undated a).

Variation with Thickness.   There is variation of yield strength with plate thickness. In general, for given chemistry, the thicker the material, the lower the yield strength will be. This behavior should be expected; thicker material cools more slowly in the mill, leading to coarser grain microstructure and lower yield strength. The fact that this behavior is not always observed is due to mill control of chemical composition. A heat designated for thick plate or heavy shapes will be adjusted to contain alloying chemicals toward the maximum of the specified allowable range. This control is not 100% effective, so thick material will generally provide a smaller margin between actual and specified minimum strength than is common for thinner plates. Several commonly used steel specifications vary specified strength characteristics with thickness. However, there is a trend in modern steel specifications to alter chemistry in order to maintain constant strength requirements throughout the specified available thickness range (see examples in Table 6.1).

Effects of Straightening Operations.   From theoretical considerations, one could expect straightening operations in the rolling mill to change the tension test properties of rolled shapes. Such straightening operations are normally performed

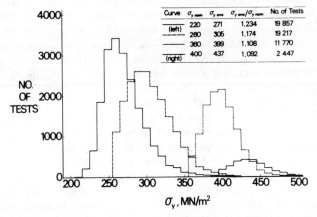

Curve	$\sigma_{y\,nom}$	$\sigma_{y\,ave}$	$\sigma_{y\,ave}/\sigma_{y\,nom}$	No. of Tests
(left)	220	271	1.234	19 857
	280	305	1.174	19 217
	360	399	1.108	11 770
(right)	400	437	1.092	2 447

Fig. 6.1   Histograms for yield strength of some 53 000 test specimens grouped according to steel grade *(Alpsten, undated a)*

by roller-straightening (rotorizing) for small to medium-size shapes, and in a gag press for deep shapes. In the first case, the action is more or less uniform along the length of the member, but in gagging, the yielding is confined to discrete lengths of the member. Results of tension tests on four H-shapes similar to W8 × 31 with each shape roller-straightened in a different manner (Alpsten, 1970a) showed no increase in yield strength for the shape straightened in production. Straightening deformations about 2.5 times larger than normally found used in production were necessary to cause a significant increase in yield strength (about 10%). No reduction in yield strength at flange tips was noted even though such a reduction could have been expected from the Bauschinger effect. However, elongation values decreased greatly as straightening work was increased, and the decreases were much more than could be predicted from the strains induced by straightening. It can be seen that ductility requirements pose a limit to straightening work allowable in normal practice.

Effects of Welding. Welding will normally increase the yield strength in the weld area. The yield strength in the weld itself will be influenced by the properties of the electrode material, and by weld-metal mixing with the melted base metal. The yield strength of the weld metal and the base metal in the heat-affected zone will be determined by the temperature cycle. For standard carbon steel such as ASTM A36, yield strength in welds will normally be about 50% greater than the parent material yield strength. These effects will be confined to the weld zone and heat affected zones, and will produce decreased elongation of the order of 25% in the weld affected zones.

Thickness Direction Mechanical Properties. Structural connections that apply load in the thickness direction are often found in welded structures. In tall buildings, this condition is often associated with the use of thick material. Such connections include beam-to-column connections, Fig. 6.2, or column base and splice plates with bending moments. Under such conditions, discontinuities parallel to the rolled surfaces may cause lamellar tearing. Thick plate material is especially prone to lamellar tearing effects.

Several investigations have been concerned with the through-thickness strength and lamellar tearing, most of them from a metallurgical point of view (Heuschkel, 1971; Burdekin, 1971). Fig. 6.3, taken from an early investigation (Brearley and Brearley, 1918), shows the variation of maximum strength, impact, reduction of area, and elongation as the orientation of test specimens is changed from parallel to perpendicular to the direction of rolling. The variation in mechanical properties is due to the numerous small and thin inclusions always present in steel. These inclusions appear in varying quantities, type, size, shape, and distribution throughout the plate thickness.

In most cases, inclusions do not affect the structural behavior of a welded joint. However, in some cases, ductility may drop to an unacceptably low value and the base metal may crack in a steplike manner during or after welding or in service. The risk of lamellar tearing tends to increase with increased weld size and increased restraint due to thick material. The problem is especially serious in heavy T-butt connections where the plates joined are thick and the restraint is severe.

Large inclusions and laminated plate, defects which appear mostly at the center of thick plate, may affect welded joint behavior adversely. However, such serious gross defects are easily located by ultrasonic inspection from the plate surfaces and visual inspection of plate edges.

4 Residual Stresses

Residual stresses in heavy members result from a superposition of stresses developed in the various phases of manufacture and fabrication. Generally, thermal residual stresses resulting from cooling after rolling increase with increasing material thickness. Results of residual stress measurements on small shapes cannot be extrapolated to the heavy members often employed in tall buildings. Residual stresses may be of importance to the designer of a tall building. The 1968 Lehigh tall building survey (Bjórhovde and Tall, 1970) noted that residual stresses were deemed of sufficient importance to make special residual stress measurements in two

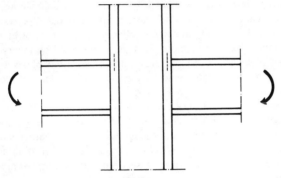

Fig. 6.2 Beam to column connection with loading in column flange thickness direction *(Alpsten, 1973)*

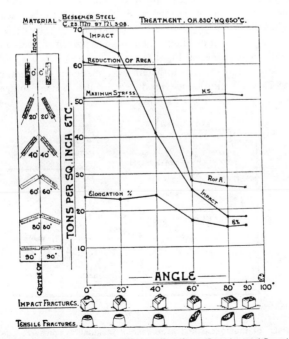

Fig. 6.3 Mechanical properties in different directions *(Brearley and Brearley, 1918)*

projects. In one of these projects, the John Hancock Center in Chicago, residual stress measurements showed that postweld stress-relieving was necessary for large welded connections in the structural frame.

Residual Stresses in Hot-Rolled Members. Numerous tests and theoretical investigations have indicated that residual stresses in rolled plates and shapes increase with member size because cooling behavior after rolling is related to the combined effects of surface heat transfer and internal heat conductivity. Surface heat transfer rate is proportional to surface area and internal conductivity to volume. Residual stresses vary across the thickness of the member. Residual stresses in thick plates, while basically similar in distribution pattern to that of thinner plates, are two to three times greater in magnitude. Reasonable agreement exists between theoretical calculations and experimental test data for residual stresses. Experimental results generally indicate smaller compressive stress at member edges and wider compressive stress regions than those predicted by theory.

The effect of geometry on residual stresses in universal-mill plates is shown in Fig. 6.4. Residual stresses in plates tend to increase with large b/t values and small values of size factor a defined on Fig. 6.4.

Fig. 6.5 shows the theoretically predicted two-dimensional variation of residual stresses in a 610-mm × 89-mm (24-in. × 3-1/2-in.) plate. The variation across the thickness is almost of the same order of magnitude as the variation across the width. Experimental measurements of two-dimensional stress variation are extremely tedious as well as very expensive because sectioning the specimens in slices over the width as well as over the thickness is required to make meaningful measurements.

Fig. 6.6 summarizes results of theoretical computations and experimental residual stress measurements on some H-shapes (Alpsten, 1968). A further comparison including the two-dimensional stress distribution for the heaviest shape (W14 × 730) being rolled at the present time [1086 kg/m (730 lb/ft)] is given in Fig. 6.7 (Brozzetti et al., 1970). For plates, there is good agreement between the theory and experiments on H-shapes in Fig. 6.6.

All residual stress tests referred to herein were made on structural carbon steels similar to ASTM A7 (no longer produced in the United States) and A36.

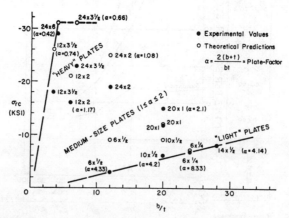

Fig. 6.4 Comparison of theoretical and experimental residual compressive stress values in universal mill plates with as-rolled edges *(Alpsten, 1968; Beer and Tall, 1970)*

Complementary tests on high-strength hot-rolled steels shapes show that the yield strength of the steel does not appear to significantly affect residual stresses. However, steels which are heat treated after rolling can be expected to exhibit considerably different residual stress patterns (Odar et al., 1967).

Residual Stresses in Welded Members. Several series of residual stress measurements have shown that the distributions of residual stresses in welded shapes and in separate plates with simulated welds are very similar (Kishima et al., 1969; Nagaraja Rao and Tall, 1961; Alpsten and Tall, 1970; Bjørhovde et al., 1971). Thus the residual stress distribution in any welded shape may be deduced from a knowledge of the residual stress distribution in corresponding component plates with simulated welds. For heavy shapes, the influence of welding on residual stress is normally quite small, except in the weld zone itself. Therefore, residual stress distributions in nonwelded and welded plates are of great interest. Stresses in thick universal-mill plates with as-rolled edges were discussed briefly and illustrated in Fig. 6.5.

Comparison between residual stresses in plates with simulated welds and heavy welded members built up from the same plates proves that residual stresses in built-up shapes may be accurately estimated from a knowledge of residual stresses measured in the welded component plates. Also proved is the fact that additional residual stresses due to welding in heavy plates and shapes are small.

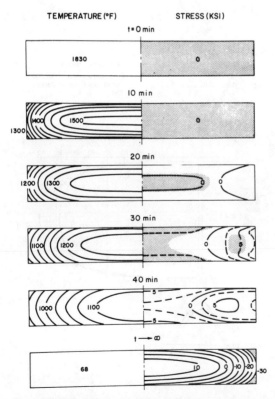

Fig. 6.5 Predicted two-dimensional variation of residual stress *(Alpsten, 1968)*

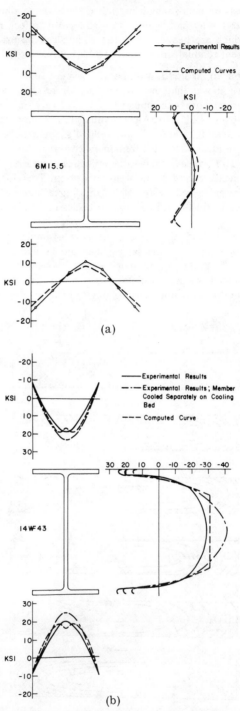

Fig. 6.6 Residual stresses in selected rolled H-shapes *(Alpsten, 1968)*

Results from residual stress studies of hot-rolled thick steel plates show that neither steel grade nor weld geometry is a major parameter affecting residual stress distribution. In spite of quite drastic changes in fabrication procedure, only small differences in residual stress distribution after welding have been noted except where annealed plate has been used. Theoretical calculations and actual tests verify that it is possible to predict residual stresses in heavy welded shapes with reasonable accuracy (Alpsten, 1972). All residual stress predictions must be based on initial

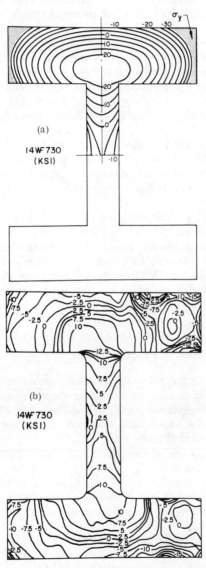

Fig. 6.7 Residual stresses in a heavy rolled W14 × 730 shape: (a) Theoretical calculation of cooling residual stresses; free heat transfer at surfaces assumed (Alpsten, 1968); **(b) Experimental results** (Brozzetti et al., 1970)

residual stresses in component plates. Tests have shown initial residual stress distribution to be the single factor of prime importance. The manufacturing process for hot-rolled plates and shapes is therefore the most important factor controlling residual stresses in heavy welded cross sections.

5   Cross-Sectional Properties

When members are rolled, shaping rollers gradually wear, resulting in variations in the cross-sectional dimensions of the rolled shapes actually produced. Production costs dictate the need to accept some dimensional variations. Underrun limits have been set to assure safe structures. Fabrication, assembly, and erection consid-erations also limit the permissible variation from theoretical dimensions. For instance, splices between two members of the same nominal size require that cross section dimensions fall within established limits to minimize or eliminate deviations in alinement leading to corrective welding or shimming. Industry accepted and established allowable tolerances for cross-sectional dimensions are given in speci-fications.

The specified tolerances for rolled H-shapes in American (ASTM A6, 1971a, 1971b), European (Euronorm 34-62, 1962), and Japanese (Tomonaga, 1971) standards are given in Table 6.3. In addition to the requirements included in Table 6.3, deviations such as web skewness, flanges out-of-square, camber, and sweep are limited by specification.

Variations measured in dimensions of approximately 5000 cross sections of light, medium-size, and some heavy rolled H-shapes (Alpsten, 1970a; Alpsten, undated b) show that variation in height and flange width is small compared to variation in thickness. Of particular interest is the tendency of flanges to be thinner and web to be thicker than the specified thickness. Variation in flange thickness appears to be the most important factor influencing the cross-sectional properties. However, the range of variation in cross-sectional properties is small compared to variation in yield strength.

6   Quality of Fabrication of Structural Steel

Plan for Quality. Traditionally, the quality or correctness of fabricated steel products has been verified in the fabricating shops by outside or independent inspectors. The concept of independent inspection has also been applied to structural steel erected in final position, and is occasionally applied to acceptance of the raw material at the steel mill.

Some owners and design professionals have come to believe that the greatest assurance of quality and fulfillment of design intent can be achieved through well planned and executed quality control procedures carried out by the fabricators' own work forces. Both the over-all quality control program and the results of individual checks or inspections throughout the course of the fabrication process must be formally documented in writing or figures. Currently, in the United States, the American Institute of Steel Construction (AISC) is conducting a program of fabricating plant certification. AISC certification is for I (simple steel structures), II (complex steel building structures), or III (major steel bridges), depending upon the level of difficulty and variety of types of fabrication that the plant wishes to undertake. AISC certification indicates that the subject plant has a fully documented quality control procedure starting with engineering, shop drawings, and material purchasing, and culminating in verification that the finished product meets all contract requirements. AISC certification also indicates that all plant quality control personnel are qualified for their functions and are responsible and report to plant management rather than to production personnel. All acceptable quality

Table 6.3 Tolerances for rolled H-shapes in American *(Adams, 1966),* **European** *(Bjørhovde et al., 1972),* **and Japanese** *(Beer and Tall, 1970)* **standards**

Type of section, with h in millimeters (inches) (1)	Tolerances				
	b, in millimeters (inches) (2)	h, in millimeters (inches) (3)	t, in millimeters (inches) (4)	d, in millimeters (inches) (5)	Area, as a percentage (6)
ASTM (1979)					
Wide flange shapes	+6.4 (0.25) −4.8 (0.19)	±3.2 (0.125)	not specified	not specified	±2.5
EURONORM[a] (1962)					
Wide-flange shapes type HEA and HEB:					
0 to 160 (6.3)	±3	{+4 (0.16) −2 (0.08)	±1.5 (0.06) ±1.5 (0.06)	±1 (0.04) ±1 (0.04)	±6
160 to 220 (8.7)	(0.12)	±3 (0.12)	±1.5 (0.06)	±1 (0.04)	(4 for
220 to 260 (10.2)		±3 (0.12)	±2 (0.08)	±1 (0.04)	Lot)
260 to 300 (11.8)		±3 (0.12)	±2 (0.08)	±1.5 (0.06)	
300 to 400 (15.7)		±3 (0.12)	±2 (0.08)	±1.5 (0.06)	
400 to 500 (19.7)		±4 (0.16)	±2 (0.08)	±1.5 (0.06)	
500 to 700 (27.6)		±5 (0.20)	±2 (0.08)	±1.5 (0.06)	
700 to 1000 (39.4)		±5 (0.20)	±2 (0.08)	±2 (0.08)	
JIS G-3192 (Tomonaga, 1971)					
Wide-flange shapes:	+3		$t < 16$ mm, ±1.5 (0.06)	$d < 16$ mm, ±1 (0.04)	
0 to 400 (15.7)	(0.12)	±3 (0.12)	$16 \leq t < 25$, ±2 (0.08)	$16 \leq d < 25$, ±1.5 (0.06)	
400 to 600 (23.6)		±4 (0.16)	$25 \leq t < 40$, ±2.5 (0.1)	$25 \leq d < 40$, ±2 (0.08)	not specified
over 600		±5 (0.20)	$t \geq 40$, ±3 (0.12)	$d > 40$, ±2.5 (0.1)	

[a]EURONORM specifications are contained in several European national codes.

control programs, whether AISC certified or not, must provide complete records demonstrating that all parts of the steel fabricated meet contract requirements.

For fabricating plants which do not operate on a formal quality control program implemented by a quality control department, a quality assurance program can be developed and committed to writing for individual projects. Such programs must be developed in direct communication with and in cooperation with the project manager, affected design professionals, and possibly the owner. To be effective and acceptable, the program must provide for detailed production checks by qualified personnel, and orderly, permanent record keeping traceable back to the specific item or operation checked.

The key to reliable and effective quality control is for the fabricating plant management and production personnel to plan for quality. Of benefit to all is the fact that effective planning for quality can create production economies by eliminating lost steps and production errors. Effective quality control organization assists the plant management and production personnel to identify the industry standard specifications, the specific project specifications, and the intended end result required, including allowable production tolerances.

Quality Assurance System. The fabricating plant quality control or assurance system must be committed to an orderly step-by-step written procedure for each department and each identifiable operation. This document must be prepared in a manner which makes it readily understandable to and usable by the purchaser as well as the fabricator's management and production personnel, including affected mechanics on the work floor.

Each element to be controlled must be identified, beginning with shop drawing and material input. Dimensional requirements including tolerances, production processes required, means of inspection (including nondestructive testing and allowable corrective procedures available or employed, if any) must be included in the production checklist for the element. In some instances, it is possible that the only allowable corrective procedure may be replacement. Acceptance for shipment must occur only when all required quality checks are performed and recorded as acceptable in the element's control document.

Depending upon contract quality requirements and industry standards, a quality feedback system may allow certain quality functions to be monitored on a random or statistical basis. For instance, the percentage of full penetration welds subjected to ultrasonic inspection may be reduced from an initial 100% to 33%, 20%, or even 10% if production testing indicates the reduced percentages are warranted. On the other hand, if an incidence of unacceptable production results occurs, production management will be alerted to the need to give certain mechanics instruction in correct performance or, possibly, to the need to redesign work methods or production processes to achieve reliably the required results. All effective quality control programs must provide feedback to management regarding production problems as well as the quality and effectiveness of production procedures, processes, and results. A well organized quality control program based on explicit work orders and feedback reports will identify responsibility and accountability of personnel for the success or need for improvement in each production operation.

Control of Material. Modern steel construction, and especially tall building construction, requires the fabrication shop to control several grades or strengths of steel, often including heat treated products. The correct material must be purchased, identified upon receipt at the fabricating plant, and placed into stock. During the fabrication process, specific identification procedures for each piece of material must assure that the correct material is provided in each location in the completed structure. Certified mill test reports may be accepted as adequate documentation of steel quality, so long as heat numbers or other unique identifying marks traceable to the original heat number are maintained. Regardless of the means of material control, the fabricator must provide documented assurance that each part of each fabricated element is the correct strength and grade.

When placing material into stock, each grade and strength of material may be color coded as well as marked with its heat number. For rolled shapes, it may be necessary to verify that the heat number is on each piece for steels purchased to specifications other than the basic specification. Some caution is necessary if, for convenience, higher strength steels are used for members or parts for which lower strengths are specified. Where considerable mixing of steel grades is required, especially when heat-treated steels are involved, permanent identification and traceability of each heat number may be advisable. In some instances, steel stencilling of heat number or other traceable code into each component part of the element may be advisable. In less demanding instances, such as unpainted steel or absence of heat treated steels, indelible ink or painted markings may be used. Special means of identification obviously must be developed for architectural exposed weathering steels. Of equal importance to steel identification is the identification of welding materials for joining steels of elevated yield points.

7 Lamellar Tearing

The subject of lamellar tearing is of particular interest in tall buildings and other large structures due to the use of heavy welded steel members or heavy rolled shapes and welded connections. Susceptibility to lamellar tearing generally increases with increased thickness; however, the problem can be experienced in steel of any thickness used in welded structural steel components.

Definition. Lamellar tearing is associated with welded steel structures in which residual stress equals or exceeds the yield strength of the steel base metal in the through-thickness (Z) direction. Fractures due to lamellar tearing have a woody appearance caused by the fracture jumping from inclusion to inclusion on different longitudinal planes within the steel. The transitions between inclusions exhibit normal ductile shear failure. The failure can be described as a series of failure planes connecting the optimum series of weakest links, normally providing the classic appearance of short steps (Fig. 6.8).

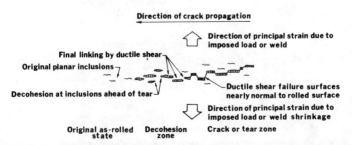

Fig. 6.8 Mechanism of initiation and propagation of lamellar tearing *(Chapeau, 1978)*

Occurrence. Whereas lamellar tearing should be anticipated near the middepth of the steel, because the frequency of inclusions is normally maximum at middepth and minimum near the rolled surfaces, it can occur at any location where inclusions are of sufficient number and orientation to reduce through-thickness ductility below the critical level for the weld joint configuration in question.

Evaluation. The common tendency is to designate through-thickness failures associated with welding as lamellar tears. When making welds which rely upon the through-thickness strength and ductility of the base metal, attention to and correct execution of each detail of welding procedure and joint design is essential, regardless of whether fillet welds, full penetration butt welds, or other weld geometry is involved.

Investigation and Identification. The most effective procedure for finding lamellar tears after welding is the ultrasonic testing procedure (see Fig. 6.9). However, identification of a defect does not automatically mean that a lamellar tear has occurred. Both the defect location and the exact weld geometry must be ascertained. A lamellar tear will not occur in the isotropic weld metal volume which, in some cases, may penetrate deep into the base metal. A lamellar tear could occur at the weld fusion line, but a defect in this location would more likely be merely lack of fusion, a different type of potentially serious defect.

Prevention. While ultrasonic testing can find inclusions and laminations prior to welding, procedures available to date cannot reliably predict or prevent lamellar tearing because small inclusions grouped near the plate surface (unlikely) or near the middepth of the base metal (more likely) often do not give sufficient signal response for accurate interpretation. On the other hand, the use of more expensive "clean" steel manufactured especially to minimize potential inclusions, may prove uneconomical and still allow joint failure due to clusters of small inclusions.

Joint Design and Execution. Where through-thickness joints are required, careful attention to weld joint geometry is essential. Elimination of unnecessary restraint and high residual stress will minimize or eliminate the danger of lamellar tearing. Additionally, careful attention to selection of weld metal, weld bead placement sequence, base metal preparation, preheat and postheat temperatures, and postweld treatment such as slow cooling or stress relieving are essential checklist items. Where major through-thickness joints must be used in the structure, ultrasonic weld examination must be part of the quality control process. If

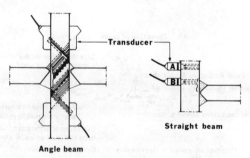

Fig. 6.9 Detection of lamellar tearing using ultrasonics *(Chapeau, 1978)*

radiography is used to provide a permanent record, this work should be preceded by meticulously thorough visual and ultrasonic examination.

6.3 CONCRETE

1 Compressive Strength Control

For tall buildings and other important construction, the capability of the hardened concrete to provide acceptable strength and unit weight at 28 days or other specified age must be verified by sampling at the time the concrete is manufactured and placed. Control of concrete quality is essentially a three-stage process. The first concern is the quality of the constituent materials delivered to the mixing plant and their proper storage before use. The second is the batching and mixing of the materials and transportation of the concrete mixture to the point of usage. The third is the sampling and testing of the concrete in its plastic and hardened states. At all stages, the rapid assessment of control test results and prompt initiation of remedial action, if required, is essential to good quality control.

Prevailing Practice. Concrete acceptance is judged by the average strength of groups of two or three standard (152-mm × 305-mm) (6-in. × 12-in.) cylinders fabricated from each sample of plastic concrete selected at the jobsite immediately prior to incorporating the concrete into the structure. When 28-day test cylinders exceed the specified strength, test reports generally receive only casual attention. But when test strengths below those specified occur, wide ranging activity involving many persons is almost always suddenly initiated.

Action by Concrete Producer. ASTM Specifications for cement, aggregates, admixtures, and ready mixed concrete contain requirements for each material and allowable tolerances for batching weights. Nevertheless, to achieve consistently uniform results, the concrete producer must know in detail the characteristics of each material and its performance when combined with other constituent materials throughout the range of practical design mix proportions. Data on material performance can be developed only by keeping comprehensive records of the performance of each mix design under actual production conditions. Chronological tabulation of mix design data and corresponding strength test results is essential to provide a continuous history of actual field performance. The data must be indexed by material indentification and by strength. Then, when a specific material must be used, the producer can refer to his files to identify mix proportions proved satisfactory in actual construction.

Statistical Quality Techniques Applied to Concrete. Statistical procedures provide a powerful tool for predicting potential quality of concrete and for documenting test results in their most useful form. In 1957, ACI Committee 214 issued a report titled "Recommended Practice for Evaluation of Compression Test Results of Field Concrete". In intervening years, this report has been updated and adopted as an ACI Standard. This document includes standardized methods for evaluating both concrete strength and reliability of testing laboratory work. Fig. 6.10 shows the distribution of 46 test results from one concrete mix. Plots of test cylinder results can be used to demonstrate the uniformity of concrete produced for a given building project or during a selected period of time. The coefficient of variation V is the uniformity indicator most often mentioned in conversation, although standard deviations are currently specified in ACI 318 (1977a). Fig. 6.11 shows the difference in required average strength for $V = 10$, $V = 15$, and $V = 20$. (In Fig. 6.11, required average strength fcr is based on the probability of 1 in 10 that a test will fall below f'_c 3000 psi specified strength.) Note that when test results have a small range of values, V is small and the frequency curve becomes tall and narrow. Clearly, concrete with $V = 10$ is more uniform and indicates better control than concrete with higher V values. Note that the base of the chart forms an asymptote for all distribution curves, indicating that an individual test result may deviate considerably from the average value. Fig. 6.11 demonstrates why the average test strength must be increased when quality control is poor, in order to limit the number of test results falling below the specified strength. For a specific project and specified concrete strength, design mix proportions and required average strength fcr must be selected on the basis of the

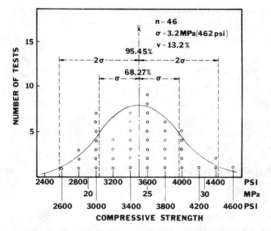

Fig. 6.10 Normal frequency distribution of strength data from 46 tests *(Principe, 1973)*

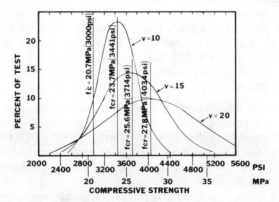

Fig. 6.11 Normal frequency curves for V = 10%, V = 15%, V = 20% *(Principe, 1973)*

concrete producer's coefficient of variation. The ratio of fcr to f'_c is often called the overdesign or overstrength factor. While use of high fcr/f'_c ratios can be used to reduce the probability of a test below f'_c to less than one test in 200, this practice is wasteful of cement, uneconomical, and generally impractical.

Figs. 6.11 and 6.12 demonstrate the effect of control on the average strength needed to reliably provide concrete of the specified strength. Fig. 6.12 (in which f'_c = specified design strength at 28 days) also shows the number of tests predicted to fall below f'_c for different combinations of V and fcr/f'_c. Note that with $V = 15$, the upper limit of good field control per ACI 214 (1977), an average strength of 1.46 times f'_c provides the possibility that one test in 50 will fall below f'_c. Clearly, the requirement that concrete always exceed a minimum specified strength leads to both excessively expensive concrete and the unenforceable requirement that no tests fall below f'_c.

Establishing Mix Proportions.   The procedures of ACI 214 (1977) may be readily applied with the use of electronic hand calculators. Based on good judgment, experienced concrete manufacturers can furnish economical mix designs that will meet specified requirements. Test data from prior production, when tabulated and plotted in accord with these recommendations, provide the basis for evaluating and determining proposed mix proportions. The adequacy of or improvement needed in production plant and jobsite quality control can be determined at the same time as the fcr/f'_c ratio is selected using the plant's demonstrated ability to control the concrete it produces as the prime criterion.

Inspection at the Site.   Inspection by qualified technicians at the batch plant, mixer truck, and actual location of concrete placement is important. Inspection provides direct means for verifying correctness of materials and workmanship, in

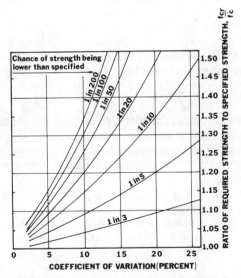

Fig. 6.12 Ratio of required average strength fcr **to specified strength** $f'c$ **for various coefficients of variation and chances of falling below specified strength** (*Principe, 1973*)

addition to giving a valuable guard against construction errors. Some building laws require filing of all inspection and test reports with the local building department as one of the prerequisites to receiving a certificate of occupancy. Large projects are often staffed with two or more technicians at the jobsite to allow frequent sampling of plastic concrete as well as detailed inspection of reinforcing steel as-installed and concrete placement procedures.

Inspection at Batch Plant. Many jurisdictions require that a qualified technician be present at the batch plant for the full duration of concrete batching and mixing operations. While assignment of a technician to the batch plant is not intended to reduce the contractor's responsibility, the mere presence of the technician can lead to the presumption that each truckload of concrete is confirmed acceptable by departure from the plant.

Recording Test Results. Early indication of sudden or excessive variations in test results is essential to good control. Accordingly, 7-day and 28-day test results must be promptly entered into a master log maintained at the jobsite construction office. This log should be readily available upon request to all responsible parties in the construction team including the concrete supplier and authorized inspecting technicians. A full-time jobsite employee experienced in concrete construction work should be assigned to log all test results and to maintain and monitor charts and graphs similar to those illustrated in ACI 214 (1977). Continuous and alert monitoring of test data is the only effective judge of concrete quality.

Quality of Testing. The foundation of all quality control is accuracy and dependability. It is vital to monitor sampling and testing procedures continuously. Test results can and should be used to evaluate uniformity of testing laboratory procedures and technician performance. Because all meaningful test results are the average of results from individual specimens made from the same sample, test value differences within each group provide direct indication of the uniformity and reliability of sampling, preparation, and testing techniques. Testing accuracy can be evaluated using the methods and test range values recommended in ACI 214-77. When the range of values within individual test groups is excessive, field sampling and laboratory procedures must and can be corrected to obtain test results indicative of the quality of concrete tested instead of careless nonuniformity in sampling and testing procedures.

Statistical Quality Control by CUSUM. Cumulative sum techniques are used for quality control in the concrete industry in Great Britain (Gage and Newman, 1972). Cumulative sum (CUSUM) control charts have been shown to be more sensitive to changes in quality than the more conventional charts (Van Dobben de Bruyn, 1968; Woodward and Goldsmith, 1964). The use of V-masks with cusum charts enables rapid quantitative estimates of significant changes in, for example, mean concrete strength. A method for choosing suitable design parameters for V-masks is given. This discussion is limited to cusum charts for mean strength and standard deviation, although similar charts could be applied to other parameters.

Specifications usually refer to concrete strengths at 28 days, but for quality control purposes it is essential to obtain much earlier indications of concrete strength if the possibility of costly remedial work is to be avoided. Accelerated curing techniques offer advantages in this respect. Whatever curing techniques and age are adopted for acceptance tests, the relationship between the early and the

28-day strengths must be reliably determined. The control and acceptance process should include a continual assessment of this relationship and should be of sufficient scope to minimize the probability of substandard concrete.

The frequency distribution of concrete test strengths for a typical concrete produced with adequate control is represented by either a Gaussian or a normal distribution curve such as that shown in Fig. 6.11. Because the two distributions are nearly identical for concrete with the same mean strength and standard deviation, it has been generally accepted that the normal distribution curve closely approximates the true distribution of concrete strengths. This forms the basis of all statistical procedures for controlling or evaluating concrete quality. The standard deviation s can be calculated using

$$s = \sqrt{\frac{\Sigma(f_c - f_{cm})^2}{n - 1}} \qquad (6.1)$$

in which f_c = an individual test strength result; f_{cm} = average or mean of all test results; and n = total number of individual test strengths.

The properties of the normal distribution curve permit calculation of the mean strength f_{cm} required to limit the number of results that fall below the specified or characteristic strength f_{cu} (British Standard CP110, 1972). When not more than 1 in 20 test results should fall below f_{cu}, the required mean strength f_{cm} can be calculated as

$$f_{cm} = f_{cu} + 1.64s \qquad (6.2)$$

Using Eq. 6.2, f_{cm} can be selected using either a standard deviation value known from previous data or an initial value based on a conservative estimate. Changes in mix proportions can be made whenever significant differences from the initial values of f_{cm} or s are detected. These changes may be necessary to assure that specified concrete strength is achieved, or may be used to effect economy if more favorable combinations of f_{cm} and s permit reduction in cement content. Control tables and charts are invariably used to present the statistical data in useful form.

The basic control chart was introduced in the United States by Shewhart in the late 1920s and was a running plot of individual test results (Bell System Technical Journal, 1926). A modified chart in which the moving average of five immediately previous results is plotted has proved more sensitive to changes in control because each point is based on more information. Control charts which maximize the amount of available information used in decision making are an improvement over Shewhart charts. Cusum charts fulfill this requirement and have demonstrated increased effectiveness in quality control work.

Mean strength (CUSUM M). To construct a cusum chart for mean concrete strength, the cumulative sum of the algebraic differences between the assumed or design mean strength and each test result is plotted against the current sample number as successive results become available. Typical calculations are shown in Table 6.4, columns 3 and 4. The associated control chart is shown in Fig. 6.13.

Where the actual mean strength, f_{cm}, of say n results differs from the design mean strength, the mean line drawn through these points will be at an angle to the horizontal. The slope of this line will be proportional to the difference between design and actual mean strength. Refer to Fig. 6.13: it is apparent that a change in mean concrete strength has occurred, probably after sample 26. The change in CUSUM M from samples 26 to 38 is -40 N/mm^2. From Eq. 6.3 the mean strength f_{cm} over this period is 29.7 N/mm^2 compared with the design mean strength of 33 N/mm^2

$$\underline{f_{cm}} = f_{cm} + \frac{(\text{change in CUSUM M over } n \text{ results})}{n} \tag{6.3}$$

In practice the reason for reduction in strength should be sought. Knowing that the change in quality probably occurred after sample 26 could prove helpful, should an investigation be necessary.

An immediate change in the concrete mix proportions seems to be indicated to restore the mean strength to design value. However, before this is done, the current standard deviation should be checked. If a significant change from the value used to calculate f_{cm} has occurred, the problem could be in batching, mixing, sampling, or testing procedures, rather than in mix proportions or ingredient materials. In the event mix proportions are changed, the CUSUM M plot must be restarted from zero as shown in Table 6.5 and Fig. 6.13.

Table 6.4 Sample data for plotting CUSUM M and CUSUM SD *(Jackson, 1974)*

Sample number (1)	Estimated 28-day strength f_c (2)	$f_c - f_{cm}$ (3)	Cumulative sum of $f_c - f_{cm}$, CUSUM M (4)	Range of adjacent results in Col. 2 (5)	Col. 5 minus design mean range (6)	Cumulative sum of Col. 6, CUSUM SD (7)
1	35.5	+2.5	+2.5			
2	32.0	−1.0	+1.5	3.5	−2.0	−2.0
3	36.5	+3.5	+5.0	4.5	−1.0	−3.0
4	35.0	+2.0	+7.0	1.5	−4.0	−7.0
5	31.0	−2.0	+5.0	4.0	−1.5	−8.5
6	30.0	−3.0	+2.0	1.0	−4.5	−13.0
7	34.5	+1.5	+3.5	4.5	−1.0	−14.0
8	27.5	−5.5	−2.0	7.0	+1.5	−12.5
9	36.0	+3.0	+1.0	8.5	+3.0	−9.5
10	42.5	+9.5	+10.5	6.5	+1.0	−8.5
11	34.5	+1.5	+12.0	8.0	+2.5	−6.0
12	32.5	−0.5	+11.5	2.0	−3.5	−9.5
13	28.5	−4.5	+7.0	4.0	−1.5	−11.0
14	35.5	+2.5	+9.5	7.0	+1.5	−9.5
15	30.0	−3.0	+6.5	5.5	0	−9.5
16	33.5	+0.5	+7.0	3.5	−2.0	−11.5
17	24.5	−8.5	−1.5	9.0	+3.5	−8.0
18	36.5	+3.5	+2.0	12.0	+6.5	−1.5
19	31.0	−2.0	0	5.5	0	0
20	26.0	−7.0	−7.0	5.0	−0.5	−2.0
21	28.0	−5.0	−12.0	2.0	−3.5	−5.5
22	40.5	+7.5	−4.5	12.5	+7.0	+1.5
23	32.0	−1.0	−5.5	8.5	+3.0	+4.5
24	33.0	0	−5.5	1.0	−4.5	0
25	37.0	+4.0	−1.5	4.0	−1.5	−1.5

***Standard deviation* (CUSUM SD).** The cusum chart for standard deviation is obtained by plotting the cumulative sum of the differences between the observed range of adjacent test results and the design mean range. For samples of two results drawn from a normal population the latter is equal to $1.13s$. Typical calculations are shown in Table 6.4, columns 5, 6, and 7. The associated control chart is shown in Fig. 6.13. An estimate of the actual standard deviation s of say n consecutive results may be obtained, in a similar manner to mean strength, from

$$\underline{s} = s + \frac{(\text{change in CUSUM SD over } n \text{ results})}{1.13\,n} \tag{6.4}$$

When a change in mix proportions is necessary to restore f_{cm} to design value without change in the standard deviation, the CUSUM SD plot can be continued as though no change had occurred with but one minor modification—the addition of the expected change in mean strength to the test result obtained immediately before the change. This is illustrated in Table 6.4 sample number 38, for the expected increase

Table 6.4 (continued)

Sample number (1)	Estimated 28-day strength, f_c (2)	$f_c - f_{cm}$ (3)	Cumulative sum of $f_c - f_{cm}$, CUSUM M (4)	Range of adjacent results in Col. 2 (5)	Col. 5 minus design mean range (6)	Cumulative sum of Col. 6, CUSUM SD (7)
26	33.5	+0.5	−1.0	3.5	−2.0	−2.0
27	26.0	−6.5	−7.5	7.0	+1.5	−0.5
28	33.0	0	−7.5	6.5	+1.0	+0.5
29	28.0	−5.0	−12.0	5.0	−0.5	0
30	35.5	+2.5	−9.5	7.5	+2.0	+2.0
31	28.0	−5.0	−14.5	7.5	+2.0	+4.0
32	25.5	−7.5	−22.0	2.5	−3.0	−1.0
33	30.0	−3.0	−25.0	4.5	−1.0	0
34	37.0	+4.0	−21.0	7.0	+1.5	+1.5
35	26.5	−6.5	−27.5	10.5	+5.0	+6.5
36	32.0	−1.0	−28.5	5.5	0	+6.5
37	29.5	−3.5	−32.0	2.5	−3.0	+3.5
38	24.0	−9.0	−41.0	5.5	0	+3.5
	(27.5)					
39	32.5	−0.5	−0.5	5.0	−0.5	+3.0
40	35.0	+2.0	+1.5	2.5	−3.0	0
41	40.5	+7.5	+9.0	5.5	0	0
42	31.5	−1.5	+7.5	9.0	+3.5	+3.5
43	26.0	−7.0	+0.5	5.5	0	+3.5
44	27.5	−5.5	−5.0	1.5	−4.0	−0.5
45	39.0	+6.0	+1.0	11.5	+6.0	+5.5
46	32.5	−0.5	+0.5	6.5	+1.0	+6.5
47	29.0	−4.0	−3.5	3.5	−2.0	+4.5
48	35.0	+2.0	−1.5	6.0	+0.5	+5.0

[a]Characteristic strength, f_{cu} = MPa; design standard deviation, s = 5 MPa; design mean strength, f_{cm} = 33 MPa; design mean range, $1.13s$ = 5.5 MPa.

in mean strength of 3.5 MPa. If a change in standard deviation occurs, the CUSUM SD plot is restarted from zero in a manner similar to the restart of the CUSUM M plot.

V-Masks. Local variations in the slope of the cusum plot are caused by random variations in the test results and may be expected even with no real change in the associated control parameter. Such local variations are illustrated in Fig. 6.14.

V-masks prepared on transparent overlays provide a convenient means for making decisions when using cusum charts. V-masks are constructed using an angle of 2ϕ bisected by a horizontal line upon which a point P is located a distance d from the angle apex (Fig. 6.14). The values ϕ and d are selected to effect the required degree of control using data developed by a number of investigators (Van Dobben de Bruyn, 1968, and others). Since control changes require correction only when the cusum plot intersects a V-mask line, the chance of unnecessary corrective action is minimized by the V-mask characteristic which allows larger deviations from f_{cm} for small values of n than when more tests are available.

V-Mask design parameters. The number of results between a change in control and the point where the cusum plot intersects the V-mask is called the run length. This, like an individual test result, is a random variable. The mean value of run lengths is called the average run length (ARL).

The departure from design f_{cm} is usually denoted by θ, expressed in terms of the actual standard deviation s of the test values. For example, a departure of 4 MPa from design f_{cm} when the standard deviation is 7 MPa gives $\theta = 0.57$. For given values of the V-mask parameters, d and ϕ, relationships between θ and the ARL have been developed by a number of investigators. It is convenient to express these established relationships between θ and ARL in terms of the numerical cusum

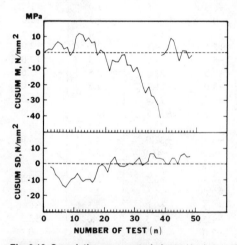

Fig. 6.13 Cumulative sum control charts *(Jackson, 1974)*

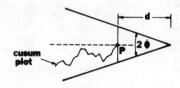

Fig. 6.14 V-mask *(Jackson, 1974)*

parameters h and k. Fig. 6.15 depicts curves based on previously reported data (Van Dobben de Bruyn, 1968) for a limited range of h and k values. These h and k values are related to the V-mask parameters d and ϕ by

$$h = dk \qquad (6.5)$$

and

$$k = W \tan \phi \qquad (6.6)$$

in which W = ratio of the horizontal length between sample numbers and vertical length of one standard deviation as measured on the cusum chart. Using the information in Fig. 6.15, suitable design parameters for a V-mask may be obtained.

The first step is to select requirements; for instance, the cusum plot must intersect the V-mask when the actual mean strength f_{cm} departs from f_{cm} by one standard deviation in 8 or fewer tests; and also when $\underline{f_{cm}}$ departs by 0.4s in 22 or fewer tests. Using Fig. 6.15, this can be expressed by

$\theta = 1.0$	$k = 0.10$	$k = 0.15$	$k = 0.20$
$\theta - k$	0.90	0.85	0.80
ARL ($h = 6$)	7.0	8.0	8.5
ARL ($h = 8$)	9.5	10.0	12.5
ARL ($h = 10$)	14.0	16.0	18.0

and

$\theta = 0.4$	$k = 0.10$	$k = 0.15$	$k = 0.20$
$\theta - k$	0.30	0.25	0.20
ARL ($h = 6$)	18.5	21.0	24.0
ARL ($h = 8$)	25.5	29.0	33.0
ARL ($h = 10$)	33.0	39.0	45.0

Only $h = 6$ with $k = 0.10$ or 0.15 provides ARL values meeting the established criteria. Noting that the ARL values for $k = 0.10$ and $k = 0.15$ with $\theta = 0$ are 45

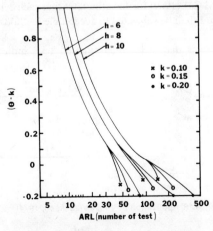

Fig. 6.15 V-mask design parameters *(Jackson, 1974)*

and 60, a k value of 0.15 is selected because it has been determined in practice that the set of V-mask parameters providing the maximum ARL value with $\theta = 0$ is preferred.

Application of V-mask to CUSUM plot. A V-mask prepared for a standard deviation of 5 MPa using the parameters $h = 6$ and $k = 0.15$ is shown in Fig. 6.16 superimposed on part of the CUSUM M plot of Fig. 6.13. When result 38 is plotted, but not before, it is found that the cusum plot intersects the V-mask just beyond sample 26. The run length is 12, therefore, and from the appropriate curve in Fig. 6.15 $(\theta - k) = 0.52$ or $\theta = 0.67$, and the associated deviation from f_{cm} is -3.35 MPa.

Field Cylinders—Handle with Care. Strength of concrete placed in most structures is accepted or rejected on the basis of 28-day tests of standard specimens cast at the construction site, generally by inspection or construction personnel. When test strengths are less than specified, additional investigation is often necessary and required. Often, actual in-place strength is determined by testing core specimens extracted from the hardened concrete in the structure. Because core samples are generally 50-mm, 75-mm, or 100-mm (2-in., 3-in., or 4-in.) diam cylinders and of varying lengths, correction factors must be used to approximate strengths obtained from standard test cylinders or cubes. When core tests or other tests of hardened concrete are required, there is always reduced confidence in the quality of concrete in the structure, regardless of the outcome of the emergency test program.

Concrete construction involves many factors: raw materials, mixing, placement, and curing. Failure to observe correct procedures can result in substandard concrete. Because the test cylinder is normally the single indicator used to accept material in the structure, it is of prime importance that cylinder tests provide a true picture of concrete in place.

Cylinder testing involves sampling, molding, job curing, transportation, laboratory moist-curing, and compression testing, all subject to human error or carelessness. Yet failure to follow correct procedures during these steps can dramatically reduce test strengths and lead to erroneous impressions regarding actual concrete quality. At the typical construction site, proper job curing of cylinders and adequate, timely transportation to the laboratory are the two items most prone to improper execution. ASTM C31 stipulates that the curing temperature for the first 24 hr after cylinder fabrication shall be between 16°C and 27°C (60°F and 80°F). ASTM C31 (1969) further stipulates that each cylinder be protected against moisture loss and shall be subjected to acceptable methods of job curing and storage.

In view of the problems that arise when cylinder tests indicate low strengths,

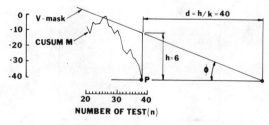

Fig. 6.16 Application of V-mask *(Jackson, 1974)*

special care to enforce correct procedures of cylinder preparation, handling and storage at the jobsite, and proper transportation to the laboratory, is extremely important. When low test results are reported on a previously satisfactory mix design, special attention should be directed to ascertain the correctness of all test cylinder procedures, especially at the jobsite.

2 Quality of Pumped Concrete

Pumping of concrete has become a sophisticated and dependable construction procedure. Dramatic savings in construction time and cost are often achieved by concrete pumping. A wide choice of pump types, carriers, and pumping capacities is available. Contractors who understand the basics of concrete pumping can employ concrete pumping techniques with confidence. Adherence to the following common sense principles should result in concrete good both for pumping and structural value.

Aggregate Size. Maximum aggregate size, based on ASTM standard sieves with no material retained, should not exceed 40% of the minimum clearance in the pump system. Properly graded sand and good size distribution in the coarse aggregate are desirable. Gap-graded harsh mixes are generally undesirable.

Amount of Cement. A cement content of 308.5 kg/m^3 (520 lb/cu yd) is desirable with 249.2 kg/m^3 (420 lb/cu yd) of cement representing a reasonable minimum; cement contents of 335.2 kg/m^3 (565 lb/cu yd) or more are not uncommon. High-early and expansive cement mixes can be readily pumped. When considering adding cement to a mix with a high cement factor, addition of fine sand or inert mineral additives may be a preferable alternative. Adding cement is expensive and can also increase creep, shrinkage and cracking potentials (ASTM STP 169a, 1966). Many pumpable mixes incorporate water-reducing and cement-dispersing additives. Excellent results have been experienced with water-reducing retarding admixtures. Admixtures which simultaneously improve workability and strength characteristics also improve the pumping characteristics of a concrete mix design.

60/40 Mix. Good dense concrete with a uniform blend of particle sizes providing minimum voids is best for pumping. Mixes with 60% coarse angular aggregate content (40% sand) are routinely pumped. Pumpable mixes will generally accommodate 65% smooth, round gravel compared to 60% rough, angular crushed aggregate.

Screen Tests. The screen test is the most important guide to suitability of both fine and coarse aggregate. Sand should conform to ASTM C33 (1978) limits except that 15% to 25% by weight should be retained on the #50 sieve, 13% on the #100 sieve, and 3% to 6% should pass the #100 sieve. Often, gradation deficiencies in sand may be corrected by adding small amounts of blend sand. Blend sand may also be used to improve strength, to reduce cement demand, or increase workability. Coarse aggregate predominantly of one size and gap-graded aggregate should be tempered by size blending whenever possible. Pumpability depends on uniformity of gradation, batching, and mixing. Most pumps cannot avoid blockage by portions of a batch that are too harsh, too lean, or too wet; the pump delivery line simply cannot accommodate wide variations in uniformity of mix proportions.

55/45 at the Outset. When beginning a pumping program, good structural mixes can be attained with 55% crushed rock and 45% C33 sand or 60% gravel and 40% C33 sand. As experience is gained, the percentage of coarse aggregate can be increased, if desirable, provided effective controls are established.

Lightweight and Porous Aggregate. Mixes with porous aggregate must be proportioned to compensate for cement paste and mixing water loss into the coarse aggregate. In the case of lightweight aggregates, mix corrections may be required to compensate for water forced into aggregate pores by pressures in excess of atmospheric pressure developed within the pump. During curing, water moves slowly out of the porous aggregate, which provides improved curing conditions and strength.

Slump and Loss of Slump Causes. Most positive displacement pumps perform well with 50-mm to 100-mm (2-in. to 4-in.) slump and will easily handle well designed mixes from 50 mm to 150 mm (2 in. to 6 in.) of measured slump. Segregation is likely with slumps exceeding 180 mm (7 in.). Concrete with slump as low as 25 mm (1 in.) has been pumped at various rates of delivery, but requires considerable knowledge and experience in mix design to pump successfully. In concrete with porous aggregates, pumping pressures drive mixing water into the aggregate with attendant slump loss unless the aggregate is saturated before batching. Lubrication within the mix and on the pumpline is required for pumping. Due to the variety of concrete mixtures pumped and their variable potentials for loss in slump during pumping, knowledgeable inspectors will always take slump tests at the point of discharge into the work. Slump tests taken at the point of delivery to the pump are useful for evaluating mix characteristics, but must not be used for acceptance of concrete placed in the work.

Improvement with Pumping. Due to better mixing, proved blending, greater density, and the beneficial effects of pump transit, concrete has been consistently improved by pumping. The harsher the mix at pump input, the greater the potential gain. Test strengths for pumped concrete have been observed to be as much as 15% higher than for the same concrete mixture sampled prior to pumping or from conventional placement.

Designing Pumpable Mixes. Use of Table 6.5 in conjunction with design procedures given by Goldbeck and Gray (1942, Rev. 1971), ACI 211.1 (1977), and ACI 211.2 (1969, R. 1977) will enable the design of standard trial mixes with assurance that pumpable normal weight concrete with the desired strength, soundness, and economy will result. Lightweight concrete mixes for pumping should be designed in consultation with the lightweight aggregate producer.

Evaluation of Quality of Pumped Concrete. Experienced pumping contractors served by experienced batch plants can place quality structural concrete mixes meeting all specification requirements without problems. In most cases, normal weight concrete mixes with good pumpability are available at no additional cost over standard mixes. Modern pumps do not require high-slump, over-sanded mixes. However, when working with a new mix design, actual performance of the mix as well as mix improvement due to pumping must be demonstrated by concrete testing and sampling at both the pump inlet hopper and the pump hose outlet. In some cases, increased strength and uniformity may justify a reduction in cement content, particularly where extra cement is included in the initial mix design to cover variations. For concrete acceptance testing, inspectors must make slump tests and test cylinders from concrete sampled at the pump hose discharge point. Inspectors new to pumping must be specifically instructed to perform all structural acceptance tests using concrete samples taken from the outlet end of the pump line.

3 Factors Influencing Quality of High-Strength Concrete

High-strength ready-mix concrete is currently available to contractors in several areas of the United States. In Chicago, concrete suppliers have been supplying high-strength concrete with conventional transit-mix equipment since 1964.

The definition of high-strength concrete varies from location to location. For the purpose of this discussion, high-strength concrete is defined as concrete providing a minimum compressive strength of 41.4 MPa (6000 psi). Concrete specified to provide 62 MPa (9000 psi) compressive strength at 56 days has been used in the Chicago area.

Delivery of High-Strength Concrete. Successful and dependable delivery of high-strength concrete requires optimum mixture proportions and modern equipment in good condition. Close attention to each facet of concrete production is mandatory. The producer must ascertain and understand the factors that can increase or decrease compressive strength and know how to control variations to achieve optimum results.

Cement. Selection of type and source of portland cement has been found to be of prime importance. Some cements produce very high early strengths with little additional strength gain at extended ages. Cement selection should be based on 28-day, 56-day, and 90-day strength test results. Fig. 6.17 shows the strength performance data of three brands and three types of portland cement used in trial mixtures. Fig. 6.18 represents the compressive strength of corresponding ASTM C109

Table 6.5   Recommended *B/Bo* ratios for normal-weight coarse-aggregate mixes proportioned by absolute volume methods *(Massie, 1971; Courtesy: New York Concrete Construction Institute)*

Square sieve rock sizes, in millimeters (inches)	Fineness Modulus of Sand								
	Fine sand			Medium sand			Coarse sand		
	2.30	2.40	2.50	2.60	2.70	2.80	2.90	3.00	3.10
(1)	(2)	(3)	(4)	(5)	(6)	(7)	(8)	(9)	(10)
#4 to 12.7 (0.5)	0.55	0.54	0.53	0.52	0.51	0.50	0.49	0.48	0.47
#4 to 19.05 (0.75)	0.62	0.61	0.60	0.59	0.58	0.57	0.56	0.55	0.54
#4 to 25.4 (1.0)	0.67	0.66	0.65	0.64	0.63	0.62	0.61	0.60	0.59
#4 to 38.1 (1.5)	0.71	0.70	0.69	0.68	0.67	0.66	0.65	0.64	0.63

[a] B = solid volume of coarse aggregate per unit volume of concrete. Bo = solid volume of coarse aggregate per unit volume of coarse aggregate. B/Bo = dry, rodded volume of coarse aggregate per unit volume of concrete.

(1977) mortar cubes. The relationship between cement mortar cube strength and concrete compressive strength is important. For Type I and II cements, the cements with higher cube strengths yielded higher concrete strengths. But for Type III cement, this pattern did not prevail. Fig. 6.19 represents further investigation of the relationship of mortar cube strength and trial batch strengths with Type I cement. The slump of the concrete mixtures was maintained in the range of 63 mm to 89 mm (2-1/2 in. to 3-1/2 in.). While these data indicate good correlation between mortar cube and concrete strengths for the Type I cements, some data have failed to indicate a reliable relationship for all cements. Therefore, it is not wise to select cement solely on the basis of mortar cube test results.

After selection of cement, the optimum cement content should be determined by a series of trial mixtures using identical aggregates from the same source. Mixtures should include different cement contents mixed to a single slump. The maximum cement content selected should be great enough to clearly demonstrate the maximum useful cement content. Because cement content in excess of the useful maximum will not produce additional strength, other materials with strength

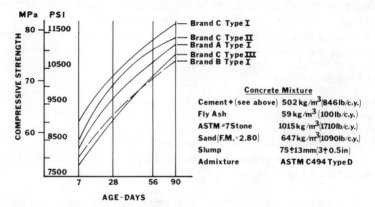

Fig. 6.17   Effect of various cements on concrete compressive strength *(Blick, 1974; Courtesy: Concrete Industry Board)*

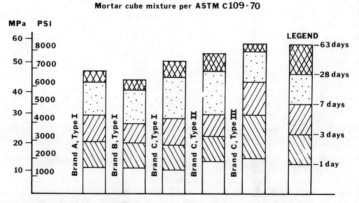

Fig. 6.18   Effect of various cements on mortar cube compressive strength *(Blick, 1974; Courtesy: Concrete Industry Board)*

producing properties should be evaluated. Pozzolans have proved useful in the manufacture of high-strength concrete.

Admixtures. There are basically three classes of chemical admixtures suitable for use in high-strength concrete: lignosulfonates, hydroxycarboxylic acids, and hydroxylated polymers. The compatibility of each available brand and type of cement should be evaluated with several different admixtures to determine the most efficient combination as well as the most beneficial quantity of admixture. Properties such as setting time, workability, water reduction, and rate of strength gain should be determined and recorded. The specific effects of chemical admixtures on concrete properties will vary between the different formulations commercially available and may also vary dramatically with different dosage rates using the same chemical admixture. Caution is required when using lignosulfonate based admixture because an overdose could lead to excessive air-entrainment.

The use of good quality fly ash may assist in the production of high-strength concrete. Fly ash with an ignition loss of 3% or less is preferable. Other pozzolans may have similar beneficial effects. The strength gain achieved in mixes using a weight of fly ash equal to 10% to 15% of the weight of cement may not be possible using cement alone.

Air-entraining agents are generally not recommended for high-strength concrete because of the potential strength loss. The primary applications for high-strength concrete such as caissons, interior columns, and shear walls do not require air-entrained concrete for durability in service.

Aggregate. Careful consideration should be given to the shape, surface texture, and mineralogy of the aggregates. Aggregate shape and surface texture affect total mixing water requirements. Mineralogy of the aggregate, mixing water, and air content control the bond strength of the cement paste to the aggregate.

Coarse aggregate. The optimum size and shape of coarse aggregate can be determined by trial batches. The optimum size aggregate will yield the greatest compressive strength per pound of cement. Trial batches should be made with several cement contents and aggregate sizes and types of less than 25-mm (1-in.) maximum size.

Initial investigation of aggregate for high-strength concrete mixtures centered around the 51.7 MPa (7500 psi) strength level. These tests revealed that gravel concrete produced lower compressive strength and modulus of elasticity (Fig. 6.20)

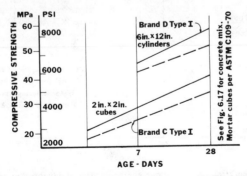

Fig. 6.19 Mortar cube strength versus concrete cylinder strength *(Blick, 1974; Courtesy: Concrete Industry Board)*

than stone concrete using the same aggregate size and cement content. The results of another study to determine optimum aggregate size for 62 MPa (9000 psi) concrete demonstrated clear distinction between ASTM#7 and #8 size stone and ASTM #7 size gravel (see Fig. 6.21). Mixtures with ASTM #8 gradation produced the greatest strength at later ages, but also produced mixtures that were sticky and difficult to work and place. Because workability is a major factor in concrete placement, ASTM #7 size stone was selected for use.

Fine aggregate. A primary function of fine aggregate in normal strength concrete is to provide workability. Because of the unusually high quantity of cement plus pozzolan in high-strength concrete, sands with a fineness modulus near 3.0

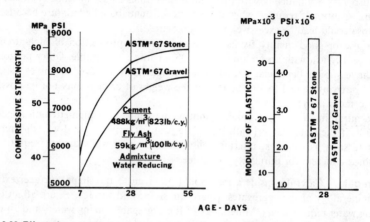

Fig. 6.20 Effect of coarse aggregate type on strength and modulus of elasticity of 51.7 MPa (7500 psi) concrete *(Blick, 1974; Courtesy: Concrete Industry Board)*

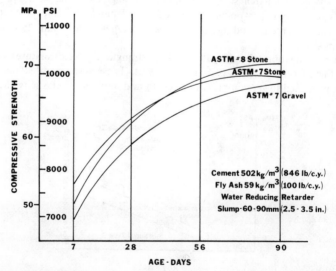

Fig. 6.21 Compressive strengths for various aggregate sizes and types of coarse aggregate for 62 MPa (9000 psi) concrete *(Blick, 1974; Courtesy: Concrete Industry Board)*

(considered coarse under normal conditions) provide the best workability and highest compressive strength. Sands with fineness modulus approaching 2.5 produced very sticky mixtures, resulting in loss of workability and increased water demand. Particle shape and surface texture of fine aggregate appear to affect mixing water demand and compressive strength as significantly as does coarse aggregate selection.

Mix Proportions. Trial mix tests have demonstrated that the optimum coarse aggregate content for high-strength concrete exceeds the values recommended in Table 6 of ACI 613 (1964). [ACI 613 (1964) has been superseded by the following documents: (1) "Recommended Practices for Selecting Proportions for Normal and Heavyweight Concrete (ACI 211.1-77)"; and (2) "Recommended Practices for Selecting Proportions for Structural Lightweight Concrete (ACI 211.2, 1969)" (Revised 1977). The figures herein represent results from trial mixes prepared using ACI 613 (1964).] This variation is due to the unusually high percentage of cementitious materials. Mixtures were very sticky when proportioned in accord with ACI 211.1 (1970) recommendations, providing less than optimum workability. Various percentages of ASTM#7 size stone aggregate were used in trial mixtures (see Fig. 6.22). Note that the optimum proportion of coarse aggregate is not limited to a narrow range.

Over the years, many researchers have stated that water-cement ratio is the most important factor affecting the strength of concrete. For high-strength concrete, this is true only after selection of the optimum coarse aggregate size and percentage.

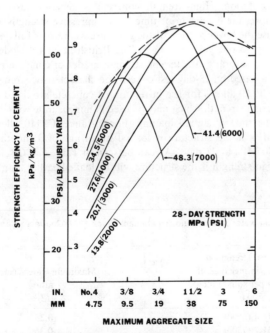

Fig. 6.22 Effects of coarse aggregate size on cement efficiency and concrete strength *(Blick, 1974; Courtesy: Concrete Industry Board)*

Experience has shown that the maximum water-cement ratios shown in Table 6.6 are required to produce concrete in the 40 MPa to 65 MPa (6000 psi to 9000 psi) strength range. For this purpose, total cement content is taken as weight of cement plus 0.67 of the weight of fly ash.

Strength loss is normally associated with increased mixing water. When using small size and angular coarse aggregate, increased cement-aggregate bond due to greater surface texture overcomes the detrimental effects of added mixing water.

Normal variations in slump cannot be tolerated in high-strength concrete. The practical slump limits for high-strength concrete delivered by conventional ready mix trucks appears to be 60 mm to 90 mm (2-1/2 in. to 3-1/2 in.).

Design and Control of Mixes. To design a concrete mixture that will reliably provide acceptable strength, the probable standard deviation in strength must be known so that an average design strength can be selected. Special consideration should be given to the overdesign factors needed for the various strength levels. The necessary magnitude of the mix-design strength is governed by the degree of control over the variables which can affect the compressive strength of concrete placed in the work. A coefficient of variation less than 10% is desirable when producing high-strength concrete. Greater variation in test strength will require uneconomical mixtures and may indicate mix design requirements which cannot be met.

Considerable strength gain after 28 days is achieved in high-strength concrete. To take advantage of this fact, high-strength concrete specifications should be based on compressive strength at either 56 days or 90 days. Extension of acceptance test age would allow, for example, the use of 48.3 MPa (7000 psi) concrete at 56 days instead of 41.4 MPa (6000 psi) at 28 days. In this case, the same design mixture could be used for either criterion. High-strength concrete is generally used in high-rise structures; therefore, the extension of time for compressive strength test results is reasonable because the lower portion of the structure will receive full dead load only after periods of up to one year or longer. The British Standard Code of Practice CP110 provides for several characteristic strength grades of concrete ranging from 7 MPa to 60 MPa based on 28-day test cubes. The characteristic strength grades of concrete which CP110 allows for use in reinforced concrete are listed in Table 6.7 along with the design strength which may be used commensurate with different ages of concrete at the time of actual loading. For instance, CP110 allows a design strength of 35 MPa if the structure is loaded at an age of 3 months versus the standard $f_{cu} = 30$ MPa at 28 days. As can be seen in Table 6.7, CP110 calls for a reduction in design strength if the structure will be loaded earlier than 28-days age of concrete.

Table 6.6 **Maximum water-cement ratio requirement** *(Blick 1974; Courtesy: Concrete Industry Board)*

Specified strength of concrete, in megapascals (pounds per square inch) (1)	Maximum water-cement ratio (2)
41.4 (6000)	0.38
51.7 (7500)	0.36
62.0 (9000)	0.34

Once the mixture proportions are selected, the strength attained in actual production should be evaluated in accordance with ACI 214 (1977). The high-strength concrete supplier should have full jurisdiction over slump, time on job, and use of additional water. Concrete should be rejected if delivery time exceeds 90 min unless it can be placed without the addition of retempering water. The maximum concrete temperature as delivered should not exceed 32 °C (90 °F). As-delivered concrete temperature is extremely important (Capacete and Martin. 1972; ACI, 1977; ACI, 1966 Rev. 1972), as are curing conditions and techniques (ACI, 1971 Rev. 1978).

An especially well qualified concrete testing laboratory must be hired for testing high-strength concrete delivered to the jobsite. A minimum of one set of test cylinders should be made for each 75 m³ (100 cu yd) of concrete placed, with each set including at least two cylinders for each test age (7, 28, 56, and 90 days). Ninety-day cylinders should be made for backup data. Cylinders must be cast and cured in strict accordance with ASTM C31 (1969), Section 7.3.

Molds for Test Cylinders.   In the program for evaluation of compressive strength, both cardboard and single-use sheet metal molds (ASTM C470, 1976) were used. Significant improvement in compressive strength was noted for specimens fabricated in single-use sheet metal molds. Table 6.8 shows the comparison for both field and laboratory cylinders using 51.7-MPa (7500-psi) concrete. Cylinders must be

Table 6.7 Allowable design strength of concrete at various ages [a] *(BSI, 1972)*

Grade (1)	Characteristic strength, fcu, in megapascals[b] (2)	Cube strength, in megapascals, at age of loading				
		7 days (3)	2 months (4)	3 months (5)	6 months (6)	1 year (7)
20	20.0	13.5	22	23	24	25
25	25.0	16.5	27.5	29	30	31
30	30.0	20	33	35	36	37
40	40.0	28	44	45.5	47.5	50
50	50.0	36	54	55.5	57.5	60

[a]BS CP 110: Part 1: 1972 (amended February, 1976).

[b]Design strength may be based on fcu or, if appropriate, the corresponding strength tabulated for the age of loading; fcu = cube strength at 28 days.

Table 6.8 Compressive strength results using cardboard versus metal molds *(Blick, 1974; Courtesy: Concrete Industry Board)*

Procedure (1)	28-day Compressive Strength, in megapascals (pounds per square inch)		Difference, as a percentage (4)
	Metal molds (2)	Cardboard molds (3)	
Laboratory molded	59.5 (8630)	54.8 (7950)	−7.9
Field molded	56.4 (8182)	52.0 (7537)	−7.9
Coefficient of variation when field molded, as a percentage	7.0	8.0	+14.3

capped with accurately alined high-strength capping compound which is allowed to develop adequate strength prior to testing—the time required is dependent on the capping compound. Selection of capping compound is important for all concrete in the 51.7 MPa to 62 MPa (7500 psi to 9000 psi) range; selection of capping compound is critical to obtaining accurate test results, regardless of concrete strength.

4   Quality of Precast Concrete

Quality control for precast concrete construction involves all the usual problems of making and placing concrete of required strength and durability, plus a great number of additional problems related to the manufacture of structural or architectural concrete elements in one location (generally a factory) and erection of the prefabricated components at a second location, the construction site. Precast concrete construction should be approached with the attitude that each member will be accurately cast and formed to produce the design dimensions, and also that all surfaces exposed to view will provide the finished appearance intended by the designer. Design aspects of precast concrete are dealt with in Chapter CB-12.

Causes of substandard products in precast construction include: (1) Inadequate planning; (2) incomplete preparation of contract drawings; (3) failure of architect/engineer to fully identify and effectively communicate to bidders the contractor's responsibility for complete and thorough planning and execution of the fabrication and erection of all precast elements and systems, along with the accommodation of, coordination with, and protection of related systems; and (4) lack of uniform quality-control practices among precast concrete suppliers.

Responsibility. The identity of both the contractor and the precast concrete manufacturer are usually unknown prior to completion of contract specifications and drawings. This places the full burden of adequate communication during the bid period upon project drawings and specifications plus addenda, if any, addressed to groups of persons with varying backgrounds, goals, and perceptions. The architect/engineer must therefore be meticulous in describing and depicting the quality of materials, workmanship, architectural appearance requirements, and latitude of options in, or specific requirements for, reinforcement, seating, and connection details.

The designer should incorporate in the contract documents all basic ground rules and required planning procedures which must be followed during the shop drawing, the manufacturing, and the erection stages of each precast concrete structure. Examples of specific topics which should be stated in the specifications or explicitly noted and shown in the contract drawings are:

1. Responsibility for assembling and coordinating all information needed to prepare complete shop drawings.

2. Verification by contractor that shop drawings are complete in all respects.

3. Checking shop drawings for dimensional accuracy.

4. Inclusion in shop drawings of applicable and correct tolerances.

5. Preparation of complete formwork drawings.

6. Preparation of complete reinforcement, embedded item, and concrete placing drawings.

7. Preparation of complete erection drawings showing each precast member and temporary bracing plans. It is essential that these plans include specific handling procedures for each erection stage.

8. Requiring each affected trade to check shop drawings and erection drawings for accuracy in number, location, and type of embedded items, sleeves, openings, and architectural details which affect timeliness, completeness, and quality in performance of the affected trade's work.

9. Schedules, procedures, and obligations for submitting shop drawings and erection plans to the architect/engineer for review prior to manufacture of precast elements.

10. Submission of concrete mix design data.

11. Submission of proposed accelerated curing procedures for precast elements or test specimens or both, if applicable.

12. Submission of manufacturing plant and field control procedures and results.

Experience has shown that relatively few designers have required constructors (usually general contractors) to perform the planning and coordinating functions listed. It is only natural for constructors to avoid the responsibility for quality control work and reporting unless they are contractually obligated and administratively reminded to perform. For large projects, these requirements can easily demand full-time attention of a competent project engineer and could require additional staff assistance.

Contracting and Precasting. For most precast-concrete construction projects, the general contractor purchases the precast concrete members from a precast and prestressed concrete supplier. Product quality often is subordinated to price due to the severe competitive bidding that normally prevails in both the general contracting and the precast concrete industries.

Quality a Policy of Management. Quality control in manufacturing industries rarely originates with workers on production lines. The industrial union has virtually eliminated the traditional pride in craftsmanship gained through training in apprenticeship programs. Thus, pride in workmanship and promotion of high-quality products must emanate from policy developed by top management.

Many precast concrete plants have grown from older concerns producing other concrete products, such as concrete block and pipe or ready-mix concrete. The Prestressed Concrete Institute (PCI) has for years been concerned with the need for quality control in plant-produced precast and prestressed concrete and has published many articles and manuals on the subject. PCI operates a plant certification program in the United States. To be certified and to maintain certification, individual plants are evaluated annually by a nationally recognized consulting engineering and inspection firm retained by PCI. Certification is based on rigorous and comprehensive plant inspection based and graded on a weighted check list (Lishamer, 1977). Additionally, spot inspections of production and shop drawing functions are performed three times during the year. Failure to maintain acceptable standards makes decertification mandatory. In 1979, 42 companies and 60 plants held PCI certification. The PCI plant certification program is nationally accepted in the United States by three model building code groups, ICBO, BOCA, and SBCC.

Structural, dimensional, and architectural-appearance objectives must be identified and developed through communication with the designing architect/engineer. Procedures to achieve the established objectives must then be implemented by engineers and trained quality-control technicians on the precast plant management team. Consistent success in producing precast concrete of high quality can be achieved only with continued dedication and determination of the plant top management team and the permeation of an attitude of discipline throughout the entire organization.

High Quality Can Be Achieved. To achieve the desired quality in each precast concrete element manufactured, the plant production forces must have technical support. Shop drawings must be complete in every respect, plant production equipment must be adequate, and a fully informed and trained quality control group must function effectively. Finally, the quality control group must report directly to top management, not to the production department.

Quality control of factory-produced concrete has several key check points, the more important of which are:

1. Rigidity, tightness, and dimensional accuracy of the forms or molds.

2. Accurate and secure placement in the formwork of all reinforcement and embedded items.

3. Accurate alinement and tensioning of prestressing steel within closely controlled tolerances.

4. Manufacture of no-slump or low-slump concrete with optimum gradation, accurate weighing or metering of each ingredient, and correct mixing time.

5. Correct, knowledgeable use of admixtures.

6. Workmanlike transportation, placement, and compaction of concrete in the formwork in strict accord with correct procedures.

7. Correct and effective curing, storage and transportation of products.

Comprehensive guidelines for production and quality control of precast concrete can be found in the PCI publications "Manual for Quality Control for Plants and Production of Precast Prestressed Concrete Products" (MNL-116, 1977a), and "Manual for Quality Control for Plants and Production of Architectural Precast Concrete Products" (MNL-117, 1977b).

5 Quality of Cast-in-Place Concrete

Final quality of concrete structural elements is dependent upon several aspects of field construction: (1) Quality and uniformity of concrete brought to the forms for placement; (2) concrete placing techniques; (3) curing techniques; (4) quality of reinforcing steel fabrication; (5) quality of reinforcing steel placement in the formwork; (6) quality of formwork construction and support; and (7) thoroughness of project coordination and supervision.

Concrete Mixtures. Design of appropriately proportioned concrete mixtures is essential to successful cast-in-place construction. (Design aspects are covered in Chapter CB-11.) Good concrete must be cohesive, yet uniformly workable when vibrated in order to fill all corners, restricted dimensions, and congested locations. Crossing reinforcing bars and embedded items act to restrict and may often prevent direct filling of the formwork by plastic concrete under gravity alone. Even where concrete can be freely placed in the forms, vibration is essential to achieve a single continuous, thoroughly consolidated, homogeneous mass uniformly bonded with the reinforcing steel.

Construction of tall buildings implies the need for large volumes of rigid and often massive concrete in the foundations as well as selective use of high-strength normal weight, lightweight structural, and, sometimes, high-strength lightweight concrete in the superstructure. Comprehensive and orderly mix design procedures combined with prudent selection of aggregate, cement, and water reducing admixture is good practice for all concrete and strongly recommended for concrete with unit weights below 1840 kg/m³ (115 lb/ft³) or compressive strengths of 34.5 MPa (5000 psi) or greater.

For lightweight structural concrete, a daily check each morning before beginning mixing and delivery operations should include actual testing at the batch plant to determine:

1. Sieve analysis of lightweight aggregate.

2. Loose unit weight of lightweight aggregate from the pile (compare with oven dry loose unit weight of same lightweight aggregate sample).

3. Percentage of moisture and free water in lightweight aggregate.

4. Sieve analysis of sand.

5. Moisture content of sand.

Mix proportions and batching weight adjustments should be made as needed based on these results.

At the jobsite, lightweight concrete should be checked for correct slump, range of entrained air content, fresh unit weight, and temperature of concrete mixture. For normal weight concrete, moisture content of fine and coarse aggregate should be checked at the batch plant, and air content and slump of the concrete mixture must be checked at the jobsite. Thoroughness of mixing and total water added must be checked for each batch of concrete. Control of lightweight concrete must be based on mixing to correct slump range, verifying or adjusting to the correct entrained air content when measured in strict accord with ASTM C173 (1978), and assuring that the fresh unit weight does not exceed the maximum consistent with achieving the 28-day air-dry weight specified for structural considerations or stipulated in fire resistance rating requirements, such as published by Underwriters Laboratories, Incorporated (ULI, 1978).

Concrete Placing Techniques. Concrete placement techniques consist of conveyance from the mixer to the point of deposit and proper consolidation techniques, including screeding, floating, and troweling for slab work. Means of conveyance are generally left to the contractor's choice, although the use of concrete pumps may be controlled or restricted by the project specifications. For tall buildings, concrete pumps, conveyor belts, and concrete hoists (elevators) are commonly used. For buildings of large floor area, motorized concrete dump buggies are often used. Concrete placement techniques for tall buildings do not vary significantly from other concrete construction except in scale and distance of conveyance, particularly vertical distance. Where concrete is placed on steel deck, consolidation by screeding and tamping is often substituted for vibration except where local spots demand vibration. Quality control considerations are primarily: (1) Avoidance of segregation; (2) slump control; (3) prevention of free-fall and flowing of concrete; (4) uniform and thorough consolidation, preferably by mechanical vibration; (5) complete filling of forms including corners, articulations, and voids between embedded items such as block-outs, anchors, and reinforcing steel; and (6) accurate and complete control of correct finish lines and elevations.

Curing Techniques.   For tall building slabwork, impermeable liquid membranes are often used in lieu of moist curing. This technique facilitates early access to the work by electrical, mechanical, and finish trades. For most other concrete work, means are adopted to prevent premature drying of the concrete. Moist curing techniques dependent upon frequent addition of wetting water are avoided wherever possible. Almost all concrete in tall buildings serves a structural purpose and, therefore, must be assured proper curing. Where absolutely needed, moist curing is provided. ACI 308-71 (Rev. 1978) gives a comprehensive discussion of curing methods and their application. BS CP110 stipulates specific curing requirements and discusses the effects of accelerated curing techniques in Appendix C.

Quality of Reinforcing Steel Fabrication.   Correctness of reinforcing bar fabrication is dependent upon thorough and accurate shop drawing (bending list), preparation, and correct execution in cutting and bending. Reinforcing steel can be provided to correct dimensions only if the detailer depicts and schedules the cutting, bending, and arrangement of reinforcing bars in numbers and sizes responsive to the full intent of the structural, architectural, and related contract drawings showing embedded items and required penetrations. Both the detailer and the inspector must be aware of the following reinforcing steel fabrication tolerances:

1. Sheared length, ±25 mm (1 in.).

2. Depth of truss bars, +0; −13 mm (+0; −1/2 in.).

3. Out to out dimensions of stirrups, spirals, ties, ±13 mm (±1/2 in.).

4. All other bend locations, ±25 mm (±1 in.).

These tolerances are commensurate with United States practice for general construction requirements and designs conforming to ACI 318 (1977b) and constructed in accordance with ACI 301-72 (Rev. 1975), "Specifications for Structural Concrete for Buildings." Detailers should apprise themselves of trade association or industry standard tolerances that could affect placement of shop cut and bent reinforcing bars. Structural designers must assess the function of the structural elements involved and must include in the project drawings or specifications all special tolerances or other data affecting the detailing and fabrication of reinforcing steel and associated accessories.

6   Quality of Reinforcing Steel Placement

Fabricated reinforcing steel and stock lengths of straight bars delivered to the construction site must be stored properly, securely, and free from contact with the ground in order to prevent contamination and rust. Jobsite personnel must assure that all material placed in the work is free from excessive rust as well as contamination by deleterious substances. Lack of uniform bonding to concrete or continuing corrosion is unacceptable. Reinforcing steel must be of correct size and dimension as well as securely supported and tied into place in the formwork. Reinforcing steel supports and separators must be adequate to withstand placement of fresh concrete without displacement of the reinforcing steel, both with regard to concrete cover between steel and formwork and with regard to bar spacing. Post-tensioning strands must be placed to accurate profile throughout each tendon length, with each tendon rigidly wired into position and anchor plates rigidly attached to formwork or other support in the correct angular and dimensional orientation. Reinforcing bars must be placed within the following location tolerances as stated in ACI 301 (1972):

1. Clear distance to formwork, ±6 mm (±1/4 in.).

2. Minimum spacing between bars, −6 mm (−1/4 in.).

3. Top bars in slabs and beams:
   Up to 200 mm (8 in.) deep, ±6 mm (±1/4 in.).
   Over 200 mm to 610 mm (8 in. to 24 in.), ±13 mm (±1/2 in.).
   Over 610 mm (24 in.), ±25 mm (±1 in.).

4. Lengthwise location, ±50 mm (±2 in.).

5. Additional applicable tolerances may be found in ACI 318 (1977b), applicable building codes, industry standards, project specifications, and project drawings.

Both ACI 318 (1977b) and BS CP110 require that specific placement tolerances needed for individual projects be stated in the contract drawings or specifications. BS CP110 relates the tolerance in concrete coverage for bars placed relative to a single concrete surface as follows: Bar size up to 12 mm (1/2 in.) + 5 mm (3/16 in.): over 12 mm to 25 mm (1/2 in. to 1 in.) + 10 mm (7/17 in.): bar size over 25 mm (1 in.) + 15 mm (5/8 in.).

Final location of reinforcement in the completed concrete work is dependent upon the clarity of the reinforcing steel detail and placing drawings, the precision with which the steel is placed, the means by which the bars are tied into place and supported in the forms, and upon the concrete placing techniques. Whatever reinforcing steel system is used, it is of prime importance to provide all reinforcement in the position required by the design documents.

In tall buildings, composite acting fluted steel deck units are often used as part of the structural system. At other times, smooth fluted steel deck units may be used as permanent formwork. Either type of deck unit may be blended with cellular deck units or raceways for electrical, telephone, and other wire-connected services. Welded steel wire fabric (WWF) is often selected for reinforcing the structural concrete slab because large areas of reinforcement can be quickly and economically installed by rolling the WWF flat from the coiled shipping unit. Position of WWF reinforcement in the slab is very likely to be important for structural reasons and must conform to fire rated construction details such as those published by Underwriters Laboratories, Incorporated or other authorities. All too often, in striving for reduced construction cost, the contractor elects to leave the WWF in contact with the steel deck until the concrete is placed, at which time the construction crew is assigned to pull it up into its final position in the plastic concrete. This very poor practice gives no assurance of correct WWF location in the finished product. Even when WWF, reinforcing bars and prestressing tendons are securely tied and supported in final position, concrete distribution and placing procedures must be carefully controlled. Motorized or hand propelled concrete buggies must travel on runways supported independently from the steel. Concrete placing crews must work with sufficient caution to avoid damaging or displacing reinforcing steel from its correct location. In order to assure the correct final location of reinforcing steel in the floor slabs of high-rise buildings, the contractor must develop and enforce proper and effective controls of reinforcing steel placement and compatible concrete placement procedures.

7 Formwork

Many systems of formwork may be economically justified for tall buildings, with the widest selection applicable to the foundation and base structure. For tall reinforced concrete buildings, reusable forms are obviously desirable and great benefits can be derived from standardization of construction details. For tall steel buildings, steel floor deck systems are often used due to the economy resulting from use of the deck as a working surface instead of standard timber planking, the structural value of the deck, and electrical system considerations (cellular deck units, preset floor inserts, integrated trench header systems).

For all forming systems, concrete sections with surfaces and cross sections within required dimensional tolerances are required. For steel deck systems, the acceptability of floor surfaces for levelness and minimum acceptable thickness may be affected by the camber of supporting structural steel, screeding procedures employed by the contractor, and deflections of structural steel and steel deck units. Rigorous control must be exercised to assure correct cambers, screeding procedures that take into account actual field measured conditions, and screeding methods which achieve the correct levelness tolerances. For most work, the traditional tolerance of 3 mm (1/8 in.) in 3 m (10 ft) is often unnecessarily strict while, over long runs, permitting excessive deviation from reference floor elevation. A more reasonable tolerance would be 6 mm (1/4 in.) in 3 m (10 ft) plus a maximum allowable deviation of ± 12 mm (1/2 in.) from the reference floor level.

8 Effects of Dimensional Variations

Real-Life Considerations.   The variations in as-built dimensions which occur in construction can be substantially greater than designers and researchers normally expect. Published tolerances (ACI 347, 1978; 301, 1975) are not always realistic or practical, while tighter tolerances specified in contract documents may prove to be wishful thinking. These considerations have been documented from field measurements and experiences (Birkeland and Westhoff, 1971).

Ordinary dimensional variations can reduce the calculated strength of slabs and beams by 25% to 50% and of columns by 25%. Probability considerations regarding concrete strength predict that a large building may have one or more columns containing concrete 50% below the specified strength. Designers should recognize that dimensional variations can cause actual structural strength to deviate greatly from values determined by precise calculation. Where slabs and beams are shallow, or columns small in cross section, the increased sensitivity of small sections to strength reduction due to dimensional deviations or understrength material is very real. Probabilistic theories of design must recognize that many significant, real-life variations cannot, in practice, be adequately anticipated.

Effect of Dimensional Variations on Structural Strength. The following examples all assume concrete with $f_c' = 25.9$ MPa (3750 psi) and ASTM A615 (1977), Grade 60 reinforcing steel.

Example 1—slab strength. Alarming stories regarding the effect of dimensional variation on slab strength are common. The following example involves both construction tolerances and a lack of coordination of mechanical inserts. Fig. 6.23 depicts a design in which a 115-mm (4-1/2 in.) thick continuous one-way slab spans 3 m (10 ft). Reinforcing steel is 12-mm (#4) deformed bars spaced 330 mm (13 in.) center to center with 19-mm (3/4-in.) clearance between bars and slab bottom. This example considers slab strength in positive moment (bottom steel in tension) near midspan. The following conditions could easily occur. After the carpenters construct the soffit formwork 10 mm (3/8 in.) high, the plumbing subcontractor places long, channel-shaped inserts flush with the slab soffit. The bottom slab steel is supported 32 mm (1-1/4 in.) clear atop the inserts, 12 mm (1/2 in.) higher than intended. Finally, the cement finishers screed the slab surface 12 mm (1/2 in.) low (not an unusual variation). These variations mean that the slab is 10 + 12 = 22 mm (3/8 + 1/2 = 7/8 in.) thinner than intended, and that the distance d for the bottom steel is 22 + 13 = 35 mm (7/8 + 1/2 = 1-3/8 in.) less than intended. The effect of the above variations is to reduce the ultimate slab strength in positive moment flexure to 50% of that intended. Probably more important is the reduced stiffness, which leads to increased deflection. In any event, proper coordination could and should readily avoid such problems.

Example 2—beam strength. Two identical 305-mm (12-in.) deep beams intersect over a column as depicted in Fig. 6.24. The project drawings show a framing plan and a beam reinforcing schedule, but no details. Assume beam top steel is 22-mm (#7) deformed bars, with actual outside diameter 25 mm (1 in.), stirrups are 9.5-mm (#3) deformed bars with outside diameter of 12 mm (1/2 in.).

In this example, the moment arm for the top steel is not affected by formwork tolerances. Because the project drawings show no specific details for intersecting beams, the stirrups are detailed the same depth. Assume the stirrups are shop fabricated 13 mm (1/2 in.) less than the detailed depth. At the building site, the ironworkers often prefabricate top and bottom beam steel into an assembly with the

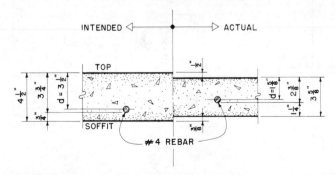

Fig. 6.23 Example of slab dimension variations *(Birkeland and Westhoff, 1973)*

stirrups and then place the assembly into the beam form, resting the bottom bars on bolsters or chairs. Assuming that the bolsters were manufactured 3 mm (1/8 in.) less than design height and are deformed downward an additional 3 mm (1/8 in.), the stirrups fall $3 + 3 = 6$ mm ($1/8 + 1/8 = 1/4$ in.) closer to the beam soffit than intended. Combined with the shortened stirrups, this causes the top steel to be $6 + 13 = 19$ mm ($1/4 + 1/2 = 3/4$ in.) lower relative to the beam soffit, than intended. After placing the reinforcing steel assembly for the first beam, the ironworkers discover the interference with the top steel for the second intersecting beam. Because the use of closed stirrups prevents upward displacement of top steel, the ironworkers elect to displace the 22-mm (#7) top bars downward, to pass under the top steel of the first beam. This top steel is now $19 + 25 = 44$ mm ($3/4 + 1 = 1\text{-}3/4$ in.) lower than intended relative to the beam soffit. This causes the as-constructed distance d to be 197 mm (7-3/4 in.) rather than 241 mm (9-1/2 in.) as intended. The ultimate strength of the beam in negative moment flexure is thus reduced to about 74% of that intended. Careful attention to the construction process should foresee and prevent problems similar to this illustration.

Example 3—column strength. The following example is simplified considerably for the purposes of illustration; actual construction conditions can be far more complex.

Consider a 305-mm (12-in.) square, tied column, with 9.5-mm (#3) ties [13 mm (1/2 in.) actual OD] and four 22-mm (#7) vertical bars [25 mm (1 in.) actual OD] as depicted in Fig. 6.25. Assume the column forms to be constructed perfectly and the reinforcing steel to be dimensionally correct in both fabrication and assembly. The only tolerances considered in this example are the locations of the formwork and the steel cage within the formwork.

In the as-built structure at the floor level in question, assume the column in the story below to be perfect except that its top deviates 25 mm (1 in.) north and 25 mm (1 in.) west from theoretical [Fig. 6.25(a)]. This by no means represents the maximum which could occur (Birkeland and Westhoff, 1971). The floor slab is placed as shown in Fig. 6.25(b). The dowels for the column above (solid circles) are

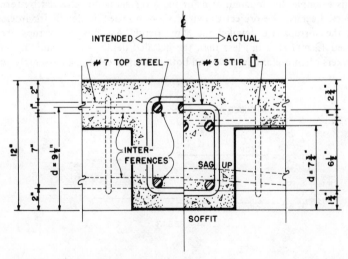

Fig. 6.24 Example of beam dimension variations *(Birkeland and Westhoff, 1973)*

the offset ends of the vertical steel from the column below. The layout crew mislocates the base of the column above 25 mm (1 in.) south and 25 mm (1 in.) east from theoretical. The ironworkers prefabricate the reinforcing steel ties and vertical bars into an assembly with correct dimensions for the column above. Therefore the upper column steel cannot be placed with the specified 38-mm (1-1/2-in.) cover unless three of four column dowels are cut, probably by gas burning. The northwest column bar still must be displaced to miss the corresponding dowel.

Fig. 6.25(c) depicts a column with a core 25 mm (1 in.) eccentric to each column axis, thereby reducing the concrete cover to 13 mm (1/2 in.) on the north and west sides. The performance of this column is questionable because of the eccentricity and the fact that the bar at the northwest corner is not in the corner of the ties. One simple way of looking at the strength of this column is to consider 51 mm (2 in.) of the cover on the south and east sides as "architectural" concrete. This leaves a 254-mm (10-in.) square "effective" column, 51 mm (2 in.) less than intended. This means the strength is reduced to about 75% of that intended.

The preceding discussion demonstrates that columns can be significantly reduced in strength due to construction tolerances alone. If additional deviations are considered (mislocated steel in column below, ties fabricated to incorrect dimensions, and understrength concrete), the potential reduction from intended column capacity could be serious.

Effect of Concrete Strength Variations on Column Strength.   A large building may include several thousand columns. The number of concrete placements required is sufficient to raise a question regarding the minimum strength of concrete which could occur in a given column.

Consider the following possible situation for columns proportioned in accord with ultimate strength design, ACI 318 (1977b). Using a 15% coefficient of variation based on field experience, the concrete mix is designed for an average strength one standard deviation above the specified strength, f'_c. In the field, due to unusual conditions, the coefficient of variation for the concrete actually produced is found to be 20%. ACI 214 (1965) statistical theory predicts that one test in 741 will fall three standard deviations (60%) below average. On this basis, a large building could have several columns with concrete strengths less than one half of that specified $(0.40 \times 1.15 f'_c = 0.46 f'_c)$. There is a good chance that one of these understrength columns will be lightly reinforced and, consequently, will be drastically understrength. In fact, such a column could easily be stressed to ultimate capacity by

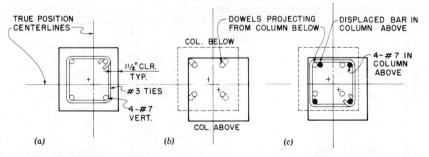

Fig. 6.25 Example of column dimension variations: (a) Column below; (b) Floor poured; (c) Column above (Birkeland and Westhoff, 1973)

dead load alone. Based on design criteria and potential field results, buildings should collapse much more frequently than they do. Actually, few columns show any sign of distress. This may occur because the bottom portion of the Poisson distribution curve is truncated by field rejections of obviously bad concrete before the bad concrete is placed in the formwork.

Actual Field Data. Field measurements in Sweden of concrete slab thicknesses and reinforcing steel depths (Johnson, 1971; Johansson and Warris, 1968) are summarized in Table 6.9. In most cases, measurements of the position of the reinforcing steel were made after concrete placement. The data indicate the magnitude of variations that can occur in floor slabs. Most of the slabs measured were thicker than intended, while the deviation of the depth of most reinforcement is negative, indicating a systematic reduction in effective depth. The measurements by

Table 6.9 Variations in cast-in-place slab thickness and effective depth of reinforcement *(Fiorato and Sahlin, 1973)*

			Slab Thickness, in millimeters				Depth of Bottom Reinforcements, in millimeters	
Site	Nominal dimension	Sample size, n	Mean value of deviations from nominal, $\overline{X}$	Standard deviation, s	Nominal dimension	Sample size, n	Mean value of deviations from nominal, $\overline{X}$	Standard deviation, s
(1)	(2)	(3)	(4)	(5)	(6)	(7)	(8)	(9)
				Johnson (1971)				
2	140	196	+5	8	122	181	−1	9
7	150	201	+2	8	130	199	−4	10
3	160	275	+3	9	141	258	−4	13
5	160	256	−15	13	141	252	−33	14
6	160	183	+1	9	141	183	−5	12
8	160	151	+9	9	142	141	−2	13
10	160	335	−1	10	141	337	−5	12
11	160	289	+5	10	142	290	−4	12
12	160	247	+3	6	142	247	−2	8
4	170	155	+14	11	150	153	−10	13
1	200	204	+5	10	180	201	−1	11
9	200	219	−14	10	182	219	−24	11
				Johansson and Warris (1969)				
1	160	42	+8	6	144	12	+3	6
2	160	84	−2	6	144	12	−3	4
3	160	51	−3	7	144	12	0	6
4	160	36	+1	5	144	12	−1	4
5	160	72	+7	5	144	12	−1	5
6	160	42	+10	7	144	12	−3	9
7	160	81	0	4	144	12	−10	5
8	160	51	−16	6	144	12	−23	5
9	160	45	+1	5	144	12	−5	4
10	160	42	+4	5	144	12	+1	4
11	160	48	+6	5	144	12	+1	5
12	160	39	+7	7	124	12	0	7

Johnson shown in Table 6.9 were made 15 years prior to those by Johansson and Warris (1969). The small deviations reported by Johansson and Warris may reflect an improvement in construction techniques and site supervision. Systematic field measurements can help to provide a basis for judging the magnitude and dispersion of actual field variations. Field data will also provide information assisting the establishment of realistic tolerances.

The present practice of specifying permissible deviations needs to be critically reviewed. Definitive data on the tolerances required to assure satisfactory structures, as well as information on tolerances which can be economically attained with given structural systems and construction techniques, are lacking. The specification of tolerances is, by itself, not sufficient to assure geometric quality in building. Field control must also be exercised to check compliance with the specifications. With no inspection or control, the resulting field variations are essentially independent of the tolerances specified. It does not help to know that specified tolerances limit the variation in reinforcement depth without the additional assurance that specification values will be achieved in practice. With regard to control of quality, the primary emphasis to date has been on materials. There is a need to develop effective quality assurance systems for geometric variations as well.

9   Project Supervision and Coordination

Reinforced concrete construction includes both cast-in-place and precast concrete. Both systems depend on formwork systems and correct placement of all elements of the reinforcing steel. Sleeves, box-outs, and embedded items are required for installing the necessary building systems and finishes to the concrete work, whether cast-in-place structural, precast structural, or architectural exposed concrete is involved. The formwork and concrete mixtures must be suitable to provide required surface appearance and dimensional accuracy. Structural concrete reinforcement is composed of reinforcing steel bars, welded wire fabric (WWF) and, possibly, pretensioning tendons or post-tensioning tendons with anchorage systems. Reinforcement must be installed in or over the formwork with the correct clearances and spacing to achieve the correct thickness of protective concrete cover, as well as the designed structural action.

All this can only be accomplished through effective project management techniques. The General Contractor or Project Manager must effectively coordinate all aspects of the concrete work to accommodate all interfacing work; this effort must start immediately upon beginning the work. Expedited scheduling is typical of major building work, meaning that failure to coordinate work or perform quality control functions is unacceptable. Control implies not only engineering sampling and verification of quality materials and work, but also contractor coordination and control of each trade, beginning immediately with shop drawings and including planning of forming systems and scheduling of work dates.

The contractor must supervise the preparation of all shop drawings to assure completeness of detailing and timeliness of preparation. Shop drawings must be submitted to the reviewing authority in a timed sequence with appropriate lead times with regard to the building schedule. Inclusion of all needed embedded items, block-outs, and sleeves must be verified so that unanticipated effects on reinforcing steel are avoided.

The contractor must develop specific control procedures to assure accuracy and correctness of form construction. Early preparation of concrete design mixes is essential to allow adjustments to mix proportions, if needed. Direction and follow-up on correct and complete placement of all required reinforcing steel and embedded items, utilization of proper concrete placing procedures including proper consolidation and screeding techniques, verifying effective curing techniques, and verifying correct form stripping times combined with reshoring (if needed) are all part of quality control. These activities and results should be documented by orderly, accurate, and frequent reports of jobsite inspections and quality control activities.

6.4 QUALITY OF CONCRETE MASONRY CONSTRUCTION

1 Production of Structural Concrete Masonry Units

Concrete masonry structural elements of tall buildings must be of predictable and high quality. Assurance of satisfactory quality must start with production and testing of concrete masonry units, mortar, and grout, and continue with carefully supervised workmanship to achieve masonry assemblages of the required strength and alinement.

Before the publication of recent engineered masonry standards (NCMA, 1968; ACI Committee 531, 1970, 1978a), existing empirical requirements frequently made the use of masonry in high-rise load-bearing construction prohibitive due to unnecessary construction costs and dimensional encroachment upon living areas by excessive, mandated wall thicknesses.

Precedents for the use of high-strength masonry of 24.1 MPa (3500 psi) existed, but the higher strengths often provided in architectural units were primarily to remedy and resist moisture penetration until new developments in design methodology presented the possibility for increased concrete strengths to be structurally useful, a subject dealt with in Chapter CB-13. The availability of engineering criteria for masonry design made masonry a structural material worthy of the close attention of structural engineers, architects, and building officials, comparable to that given to structural concrete. This development encouraged the concrete masonry industry to perform a total review of the physical properties of masonry units. While there is no consensus definition for the term "high strength block," the majority of marketing areas throughout the United States consider high-strength masonry units to provide a net-area compressive strength of 24.1 MPa (3500 psi) or greater (Holm, 1972). Several projects have been designed and built with strength levels higher than 24.1 MPa (3500 psi), but they are the exception. Strength levels greater than 24.1 MPa (3500 psi) contrast with the existing implied net compressive strength levels of approximately 13.8 MPa (2000 psi) for ASTM C90 (1975) units and 16.6 MPa (2400 psi) for ASTM C145 (1975) units. Traditionally, minimum compressive strength for concrete masonry units has been specified based on gross area, such as in ASTM C90 which calls for a compressive strength of 6.9 MPa (1000 psi). Now, however, ultimate compressive strength should always be based on the net area of the face shells and webs, disregarding the area of the voids.

Materials. Only structural-grade materials are suitable for production of high quality concrete masonry units, commonly referred to as concrete block (Holm, 1972). Correct gradation of aggregate for high-strength concrete block mixes is crucial because of the dramatic influence particle size and distribution have on porosity and compactive effort. Porosity, cement content, and aggregate particle strength are the primary factors affecting the achievement of high-strength masonry concrete (Fig. 6.26). Type I, IA, III, and IIIA cements are commonly used, although another cement, commonly called "Block Cement," has been widely used and is capable of producing high-strength block concrete. Portland-pozzolan cements may also be combined with aggregates that do not possess reactive fine fractions in order to enhance strength. Many block producers have found in-plant research beneficial to fully evaluate the strength making properties of the various combinations of cement and high-quality pozzolans available. An investigation of numerous "block cements" (Allen and Freedman, 1964) revealed the following:

1. A majority of the cements tested met all the requirements for Type III or Type IIA, ASTM C150 (1978).

2. Several "block cements" tested could not be classified within ASTM cement specification criteria. ASTM C150 (1978) stipulates an air content of 12% maximum, while the specification for air-entraining portland cement stipulates a minimum air content of 16%. "Block cements" producing an air content above 12% but less than 16% do not qualify for either specification. This fact does not indicate cement of deficient quality, but rather that existing ASTM specifications for portland cement simply do not include all cements appropriate and available for the production of concrete block.

Proportioning of Mixes.   Concrete mixtures for masonry units differ dramatically from structural cast-in-place concrete in one significant aspect: the prime goal is to incorporate sufficient mix water to maximize consolidation during machine-feed and finish cycles. Due to the open texture of concrete masonry, the usual rules regarding water-cement ratio do not apply directly to block concrete, which is placed as a nonplastic, no-slump mixture. The manufacturing and curing environment in automated block plants provides the opportunity for full mobilization of the binder. Maximum compaction is achieved in block mixes when the mix is as wet as possible without slumping after molding. Because water is the least expensive ingredient in the mix, economy demands detailed attention to maintaining the optimum water content. In the manufacture of highly compacted concrete masonry units, the wetter the concrete mixture, the lower the interstitial porosity and the

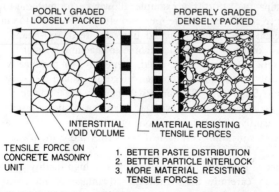

Fig. 6.26 Factors affecting strength of concrete masonry units (Holm, 1976)

higher the strength. Many other properties of concrete masonry units, such as tensile strength, elastic modulus, and resistance to the penetration of sound, are also increased by reduction of the interstitial void structure. Producers who cure concrete masonry units by the autoclave method may change the optimum ratio of cement to pozzolanic fractions when going from normal to high-strength mixes. This decision depends entirely upon the reactive nature of the pozzolanic materials used in the mix. With some material, pozzolanic material is contained within the fine fractions of the aggregate (for example with expanded shales), a fact to be taken into account in maximizing the efficiency of the binder.

Batching and Mixing. There are no special batching requirements for high-strength concrete mixes. The usual techniques provide efficient distribution of cementitious materials within the mass of aggregate. For dense aggregate mixes, the usual procedure is for aggregate and cementitious materials to be dry mixed about one minute, after which all water is added and mixed for four minutes. For lightweight aggregates with sufficient moisture content within the particle, the normal procedure is to add approximately two-thirds of the total mixing water immediately after the aggregate is charged into the mixer. After pre-wet mixing, the cementitious materials are added, and then the remaining water, after which mixing continues for a minimum of four minutes. Most plants that manufacture block for engineered masonry utilize automated weighing and batching equipment, electronic moisture controls, and mix timers in order to assure consistency of results.

Compaction and Porosity. High-strength concrete masonry units have been successfully produced by a large increase of cementitious materials, or by a moderate increase in cementitious materials combined with increased compacting effort. The properties of concrete block are significantly improved by adopting the latter procedure. Increased compactive effort (longer machine time) will produce a decrease in porosity from the $\pm15\%$ typical of commercial C90 units to the $\pm7\%$ typical of high-strength units. Interstitial porosity may be defined as the interstitial void volume divided by the absolute volume of concrete.

Total compactive effort may be divided between the time the feed drawer is over the mold box feeding material, the finish time when the stripper head compacts the fresh concrete to the desired height, and the delay time (generally 1/2 sec) immediately preceding release of the freshly molded block. These three time elements are interrelated, and it is difficult to separate the influences of the three portions of compactive effort. For example, allowing extra material to feed into the mold will require considerably more time and effort to compact the material to the appropriate height. Assigning stipulated times for feed, finish and delay time is difficult because of variations from machine to machine, primarily in the way in which the material flows into the mold. Generally, to produce units with low interstitial porosity, a minimum increase in feed and finish times used to produce regular strength ASTM C90 (1975) units will increase the total cycle time 2 sec to 3 sec. Increasing compactive effort without changing binder content will increase strength significantly. The combination of additional cement and increased compactive effort will improve physical properties more than additional cement alone.

Block producers manufacturing large volumes of high quality concrete masonry units must weigh carefully the significant advantage of increased compaction against the disadvantage of longer cycle time and lower production rate. As the total of all fixed and variable costs must be divided by the production rate to determine unit costs, block producers generally assess the financial aspects of production costs and the improved technological aspects of high quality concrete block on an individual project basis.

In-Plant Quality Control. There are several ways that quality conscious producers can approach quality control within the automated atmosphere of a concrete block plant. The first item to control is the moisture content and damp loose density of the aggregate in order to minimize variations in yield per batch. Aggregate producers should effectively control moisture content and unit weight of aggregate shipped to concrete block manufacturers in order to minimize the need for corrective adjustments during production.

It is advisable to establish regular time intervals for weighing green block sampled fresh from production in order to control the wet density of units produced. Variations in green weight will signal the need to adjust mix proportions, feed rate, and finish time. Maintenance of uniform density will lead to uniform compressive strengths and other physical properties. Periodic checks on the number of blocks produced per batch is also a valuable production check, but requires stopping the mixer and emptying the hopper.

When starting a high-strength concrete masonry job, it is advisable to develop an accurate relationship between early and 28-day strengths. Many plants test block at one or three days to determine the relationship between the early and 28-day test strengths. Gross variations in production performance can then be quickly identified and necessary corrections made promptly.

Identification of Units. High-strength block units must be differentiated from commercial ASTM C90 (1975) units. Mixing high-strength and regular commercial units in construction engineered for high-strength block is intolerable without effective control procedures at the construction site. Identification of high-strength units can be accomplished by molding a special mark into each unit or by adding a small amount of pigment to the block mix to slightly alter the color of the finished block, thereby making high-strength units readily visible. Mixing of several strength levels in individual projects is not recommended.

Physical Properties

Density. Extra compactive effort and rich binder content will produce a 5% to 10% increase in the density of concrete masonry units (Holm, 1972). Actual increase in weight depends upon aggregate gradation characteristics, particle shape, and machine compacting efficiency. The weight of standard lightweight concrete 200-mm × 200-mm × 400-mm (8-in. × 8-in. × 16-in.) two-cell hollow units may increase from 4.4N to 15.6N (1 lbf to 3-1/2 lbf) per unit. Specifications and labor restrictions affected by concrete density must reflect these changes. In many instances, the usual 1520 kg/m³ (95 lb/ft³) specified for ASTM C90 (1975) units has been increased to 1680 kg/m³ (105 lb/ft³) for high-strength units to reflect the increased density resulting from increased binder and higher compaction.

Absorption. Decrease in absorption (approximately 25%) generally parallels the increase in density. This reduction is directly attributable to the reduction in interstitial voids.

Shrinkage. The linear drying shrinkage of high-strength units when compared to ASTM C90 (1975) units may increase as little as zero to as much as 100 microstrains. The increased shrinkage is due to the increased paste content of the high-strength mixes and occurs over a longer time period due to the reduced opportunity for water to escape from highly compacted mixes. The increased shrinkage has proved to be no problem in practice because of the offsetting effect of the increased tensile strength of high-strength concrete. Most high-strength masonry load-bearing projects have utilized cross walls with lengths of only 6.1 m to 9.1 m (20 ft to 30 ft) normal to the longitudinal axis of the building. In projects where longitudinal load bearing walls run the length of the building, it is important to allow for movement by providing joints to relieve strains without reducing structural integrity of the building.

2 Testing of Masonry Units, Mortar, Grout, and Assemblages

Sampling. ASTM C140 (1975) (Sampling and Testing of Concrete Masonry Units) is cited in almost every block specification, but it appears that it is rarely enforced. Five samples should be tested in compression for every 10 000 units (or fraction thereof) used in a project. Furthermore, units should be tested periodically for the related properties of moisture content and concrete density. These data will yield other information, including net area and net volume. On a load bearing wall job, testing frequency may be modified to five units (or prisms) in compression for every 465 m^2 (5000 sq ft) of wall area, or once per floor.

It is important to recognize that consistent control of production variables has allowed careful manufacturers to reduce the overdesign factor in concrete block mixes to a statistically acceptable minimum. Block producers are cognizant of this fact and make significant in-plant efforts to produce economical, quality units conforming to the project specifications. Characteristically, however, concrete masonry units are tested without an equivalent degree of care and attention. There is widespread lack of recognition that concrete masonry units have either a specific or indirect structural role and should receive at least comparable attention to that given compression test specimen cylinders for structural concrete. Table 6.10 depicts and describes the more important testing variables that may cause indicated test strengths to vary from (normally fall below) the actual strengths provided through the producer's diligent efforts.

These variables are:

1. Capping techniques. For economy and convenience, fiber board is often used for in-plant quality control of commercial units. While producers generally recognize that fiberboard capping procedures reduce indicated test strength 10% to 15% below actual strength for normal commercial units, few recognize that the percentage of loss increases for high-strength units.

2. Moisture content. Concrete block producers should provide units with appropriately low moisture contents for acceptance testing. High moisture decreases the compressive test strength (NCMA, 1966; Self, 1975; Roberts, 1973). Load bearing walls are generally protected from the weather, and laboratory testing procedures should recognize the lower equilibrium moisture contents of protected masonry construction.

3. Rigidity of load platens. Various investigators (California Concrete Masonry Technical Committee, 1975) have determined that the ASTM thickness requirement for compression test plates is not sufficient. Thicker plates are required to develop uniform distribution of test load from the spherical test

head of the testing machine to the outer corners of the concrete block units and prisms.

4. Precision of vertical and horizontal alinement. Colinearity of the geometric axis of the specimen relative to the centroid of the loading thrust is vital in the testing of high-strength masonry. Misalinements and lack of perpendicularity can cause premature failure due to biaxial bending and horizontal

Table 6.10 Influence of major testing variables on the indicated compressive strength of concrete masonry units *(Holm, 1976)*

Variable	Cause of Variation	Effect on Indicated Strength	Reference (Remarks)
Capping Material	In-plant use of fibre board in place of lab prepared thin cap of high-strength gypsum, sulfur, mortar etc. Soft fibre board spreads, causing lateral tension.		(A) Holm (C.O.B) (B) Roberts. (C) Self 1. Solid block tend to have smaller loss of indicated strength when tested with fibre board. 2. Irregularly surfaced blocks produce wide scatter and greater loss.
Moisture Content of Concrete Masonry Unit at Time of Test	Axial loading causes secondary hydrostatic pressures due to moisture content resulting in additive lateral tensile forces.		(B) Roberts (C) Self (D) NCMA (Concrete Masonry Units should be delivered to lab at moisture contents comparable to intended use)
Thickness of Loading Platen		Considerable loss of indicated compressive strength CMU's if ASTM C140 is followed ($t = l/3$ to furthest corner). California Concrete Masonry Tech. Comm. recommends $t = l$ to minimize bending of platen—thus developing uniform deformations and stresses.	(E) C.C.M.T.C.
Center of Thrust Not Co-Linear With Geometric Centroid			(A) Holm (H) Failure is precipitated by excessively loaded corner or face resulting in false, low indicated strength.
Non-Uniform Thickness of Capping		15% loss of indicated strength from tests on units sampled from same cube sent to second lab for re-testing. (Actual high rise project).	(A) Holm (F) ASTM C140 stipulates planeness within 0.003 inches in 16 inches. Max. thickness of cap ¼" with sulfur, ⅛" with gypsum plaster.
Shape Effect			(A) Holm (S) Indicated relationship applies to one type and strength of unit. Strength ratio varies with aggregate type, block strength, etc.

(A) Holm, unreported data from experimental block runs in various plants (C, O, B, H, F, S), undated.
(B) Roberts, 1973.
(C) Self, 1975.
(D) NCMA, 1966.
(E) CCMTC, 1975.

shearing forces. In some instances, investigators have noticed horizontal tensile cracks opposite to the heavily loaded side of a specimen after initial failure, thus indicating misleading test strengths.

5. Nonuniform cap thickness (out-of-plane). Another area of poor practice is the occasional failure to provide planar capped surfaces within a flatness tolerance of 1 mm/m (0.003 in. in 16 in.). In one instance, capped surfaces were so poorly alined that the lack of alinement could be seen from over 3 m (10 ft) away. Measurement revealed almost 6 mm (1/4 in.) misalinement. This problem generally occurs with high-strength capping plasters where the high-strength gypsum paste is made too stiff and the average thickness of the cap exceeds 3 mm (1/8 in.). It is vitally important that capping be thin and uniform to assure that the unit, not the cap, is tested. Parallelism of capped surfaces is also important.

6. Shape factor. When comparing strength levels of various types of specimens with different height-to-width ratios, it is important to recognize that the indicated test strength may require adjustment by a correction factor relating the slenderness ratio of the test specimen and the restraining influence of the test machine platens. A brick sized unit may show an indicated compressive strength as much as 40% higher than a much larger concrete block shape made from the same concrete mix with equivalent machine time. The increased test strength is due to the influence on the failure mechanism of frictional restraint by the loading platens as well as the reduction of bending moment magnification caused by the slenderness ratio (Kesler, 1959).

7. Testing age. Concrete masonry units increase in strength with time somewhat less than structural cast-in-place concrete. The rate of strength increase is significantly modified by curing parameters (curing time, pressure, and temperature) and type of unit. Solid units show a greater increase in strength than hollow units. This is because moisture used in molding is released slowly due to the high compaction of high-strength mixes.

Engineered masonry codes generally provide two alternative methods for determining the allowable masonry compressive strength f'_m. One method is based on selection from a table of an empirical value for the strength of the walls (f'_m) based on the compressive strength of the individual units (f'_c). The other method allows use of a value for f'_m determined by testing small samples of walls called prisms. ASTM E447 (1974), "Standard Methods of Test for Compressive Strength of Masonry Assemblages," describes the procedure for testing small wallets of masonry incorporating typical units, mortar, and workmanship to determine data for a given project. When project specifications call for f'_m to be verified by prism testing, the usual requirement of one series of tests per floor or 465 m² (5000 sq ft) of wall area governs. The obvious purpose is to closely represent the masonry assembly actually constructed. Individual concrete masonry units should be tested concurrently with the prism tests to allow determination of responsibility should prism test results fall below the specified value of f'_m. The need for prism testing is growing due to widespread use of load bearing masonry in high-rise building construction. Prism testing is also used to justify greater f'_m/f'_c ratios through more exacting testing and controls. Economical construction of large buildings requires valid strength information in order to permit structural engineers to utilize the higher design stresses needed to achieve more efficient use of material. Problems confronted in prism testing are similar to the problems experienced in testing individual units (Dickey, 1973), and include the following:

1. Low-strength concrete masonry units.

2. Improper curing and handling, such as dropping or bumping during transportation.

3. Improper caps are more detrimental to accurate prism tests than for individual units due to increased magnification of eccentric and nonuniform loads.

4. Poor workmanship in placement of units on mortar courses will cause decreased f'_m values. High quality workmanship is needed in both prism testing and field construction.

5. Inadequate strength of grout and mortar.

Mortar Testing.   Mortar strength requirements and testing procedures are documented in ASTM C270 (1973) for nonreinforced masonry and ASTM C476 (1971) for reinforced masonry. There is great promise for systematic determination of the plastic and hardened properties of mortar using methods described in ASTM C780 (1974), "Standard Method for Preconstruction and Construction Evaluation of Mortars for Plain and Reinforced Unit Masonry." An important consideration for designers to recognize is that, in most masonry construction, the relative significance of mortar quality is minimized due to the intermittent location of joints [9.5-mm joint in 203 mm (3/8-in. joint in 8 in.)], the shape factor of joints [9.5 mm high $\times$ 32 mm plus in width (3/8 in. $\times$ 1-1/4 in.)], and the similarity in modulus of elasticity of the hardened mortar to the units joined. Self (1975) demonstrated that, beyond a certain critical strength level, a 200% increase in mortar strength will produce only an 11% strength increase in otherwise similar test prisms. Other researchers (Isberner, 1974) have reached similar conclusions. Furthermore, mortar must provide other physical properties equal in importance to compressive strength such as bond, workability, and resistance to weather and rain (Fishburn, 1961). Type S mortar proportioned and mixed in accord with ASTM Specifications seems to provide an effective balance of all important physical property requirements.

Grout Testing.   Grout should be proportioned and mixed to meet the requirements of ASTM C476 (1971). For in-place strength testing, field methods differing from ASTM have been devised to correlate grout test strengths with in-the-wall grout characteristics.

Tensile Testing of Concrete Masonry Units.   Investigators have made considerable progress in evaluating the tensile strength of concrete masonry units. At present, there is no current ASTM standard that can be used as a guide, and several different methods are used. In one method, 100% solid concrete masonry units are tested by indirect tensile splitting methods similar to those used for structural concrete (Fig. 6.27). Concrete masonry units may also be tested in tension by proprietary techniques, one being a patented method (U.S. Patent No. 3,792,608, 1973) called the "Blockbuster." Tensile versus compressive strength for various types of concrete masonry units tested by tensile splitting and by blockbuster methods are shown in Fig. 6.28. The tensile versus compressive strength relationship for block concrete is similar to that for cast-in-place concrete (Holm, 1976).

Reporting. It is important that engineers, architects, and code authorities state in project specifications and building codes the net compressive strength(s) which must be demonstrated by physical testing. This plus regular performance of strength tests and submission of test reports will indicate to all concerned that block concrete is a

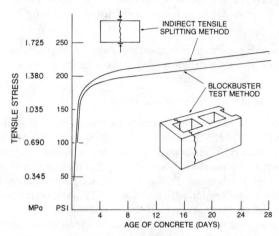

Fig. 6.27 Tensile strength of concrete block *(Holm, 1976)*

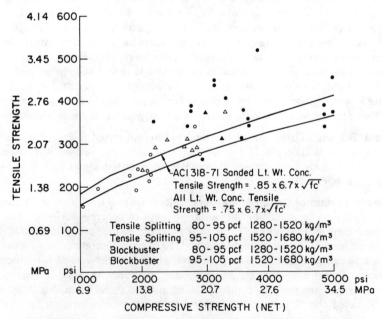

Fig. 6.28 Tensile versus compressive strength of concrete block *(Holm, 1976)*

structural concrete material. The concrete density calculated from testing in accord with ASTM C140 (1975) should be included in all strength test reports. Through proper reports, physical properties and compressive strength can be correlated and trends of interest or concern can be called to the attention of the responsible structural-design personnel.

3 Field Inspection

Inspection versus No Inspection. Because load bearing concrete masonry is an assemblage of concrete block units and mortar, fully dependent upon workmanship in the field, it is imperative to provide on-site inspection. To encourage inspection, some codes recommend reduction of allowable stresses by as much as 50% where inspection is omitted. With such reductions, the load capacity of walls designed by modern engineering methods approaches that of walls proportioned using earlier empirical codes, and provides no incentive to construct economical masonry buildings. On some projects, full-time inspection is provided for highly stressed lower floors, with limited inspection for upper story walls carrying smaller loads.

Construction Tolerance. With load-bearing masonry walls assuming the function of structural members, it is important that tolerances be more exacting than otherwise would be required. Bearing walls must be kept level and plumb (Milner and Thorogood, 1971), and in multistory construction must line up accurately story to story. Allowable tolerances for concrete masonry construction are recommended in the proposed ACI Standard 531 (1978a).

Field Inspection of Units. Visual examination of concrete masonry includes verifying that units are sound, and free of cracks and other defects. Occasional minor chipping is not cause for rejection unless the wall is exposed to view and has esthetic value. The inspector should select units for laboratory testing randomly so that the samples are representative of all units delivered to the jobsite.

Field Inspection of Grout. Nonstandard field methods for sampling jobsite mortar and grout have developed in some regions. These methods have been developed to assure owners, engineers, and building officials of the probable in-place strength and performance of field mixed materials. Use of methods deviating from ASTM standards is predicated on the fact that the high moisture loss of the grout to the surrounding absorbent masonry is not considered in the standard ASTM concrete-type cylinder approach. Lowering of the effective water-cement ratio due to absorption of mixing water by masonry units develops mortar and grout strengths significantly higher than those indicated from tests of specimens prepared using plastic lined molds. Recommendations outlining these methods are listed in the proposed Standard and commentary prepared by ACI Committee 531 (1970) as well as in certain model codes.

Field Inspection of Mortar. Field control of mortar is generally managed by following the proportioning stipulations of ASTM C270 (1973) and C476 (1971). On important masonry projects, it may be useful to measure the batch-to-batch variation of plastic and hardened mortar properties through the methods promulgated in ASTM C780 (1974). Mortar proportions, once properly established, must be closely controlled throughout the course of the project. Mortar batch sizes should be related to multiples of whole sacks of masonry cement for simplicity, convenience, and accuracy. Sand must also be batched by an accurate method. The most practical field approach is normally to use a box of one cubic foot volume (Stockbridge, 1969). In this way, the mixing man will be able, through daily repetition, to verify the number of shovelfuls required to provide one cubic foot of sand in the box, allowing the number of shovelfuls for each batch of mortar to be readily determined. For mixing both mortar and grout, correction must be made for the effect of moisture content on the bulking characteristics of sand.

6.5 ENGINEERED BRICK MASONRY

Brick masonry is a system of construction widely used throughout history dating back to ancient eras. Masonry construction enjoys frequent and varied usage in present day construction, but is often thought of as an architectural veneer or economical means of providing soundproof or fireproof partitions rather than a viable, useful, and economically competitive (though heavy) structural system.

Although the majority of design professionals may view structural design of masonry more as an art than as a science, rational design means and material properties have been increasingly well documented and codified, especially in the years since 1950 (ANSI A41.2, 1960; BIA, 1969; BS CP111, 1976; BS 5628, Part 1, 1978). As early as 1920, the Government of India sponsored extensive research of the structural strength of reinforced brick masonry members (Brebner, 1923) with the hope of escaping the high cost of structural steel and reinforced concrete construction. This work led to the extensive use of reinforced brick masonry construction in India and Japan, countries where earthquake considerations are important. Between 1922 and 1950, extensive research was performed on both reinforced and unreinforced brick masonry by the National Bureau of Standards and virtually every important engineering university in the United States. That reinforced brick masonry is indeed a material suited to engineered application, even where seismic forces, blast forces, and high wind forces must be considered, has been documented by Plummer and Blume (1953).

In the United States, both the Basic Building Code (BOCA, 1978) and the Uniform Building Code (ICBO, 1979) differentiate between engineered masonry construction with inspection and without inspection. For construction performed without inspection, ICBO permits only 50% of the design stress allowed for construction performed with inspection. This applies to both reinforced and unreinforced construction, solid or hollow units, with the exception that the allowable axial compressive stress f_m and tensile stress f_t may be increased to two-thirds the "with inspection" values when prism test values are provided. The ultimate compressive strength f'_m is the basis for determining allowable compressive shear and bearing stresses as well as the design values for the moduli of elasticity and rigidity. The value of f'_m may be determined either by using compressive strength values obtained from brick compression test specimens and tabulated presumptive values of f'_m, or by performing compression tests of prisms to obtain direct f'_m values representative of the actual construction. BOCA takes the same approach as ICBO in determining f'_m by brick tests or prism tests, but reduces design values only to two-thirds for construction performed without inspection.

1 Prism Tests Versus Brick Tests

For engineered masonry work, prism testing is the preferred method for establishing design values and evaluating work in the field. This is because the data obtained best represent actual construction quality, thereby allowing conservative assumed values based on strength of individual bricks to be replaced with realistic values obtained from brick-mortar assemblages. A minimum of five prism tests are required in each preliminary test group used to establish f'_m. Three prisms are required in each field constructed prism group tested to confirm that the design f'_m is provided in the work. Controlling codes and standards place limitations on the dimensions, construction, procedure, number, and reporting of prism tests (Fig. 6.29). The thickness of each prism specimen must duplicate the masonry wall part represented. The length of the prism must equal or exceed the prism thickness, be at least 100 mm (4 in.) long, or be the full length of a hollow masonry unit. The basic (and maximum allowable) prism height for engineered brick construction is 5 times the thickness. Minimum allowed height is 305 mm (12 in.), but not less than 2 times the thickness. For height/thickness ratios less than 5, correction factors must be applied to the actual test strengths to obtain f'_m (Table 6.11).

Prisms must be built with the same materials and the same workmanship, moisture content, production speed, joint thickness, mortar proportions, and mortar consistency intended for or provided in the actual construction. While stack bond may be permitted, care must be exercised to assure that the bond pattern and joint thickness is truly representative of the engineered brick system. Prisms constructed for reinforced brickwork must contain no structural reinforcement, but may contain metal wall ties. Where brick cells, cores, and cavities will not be completely grout filled to achieve solid-filled construction, prisms shall contain no grout. Preliminary test prisms, whether constructed in the laboratory or the field, should be constructed with the same workmanship (preferably by the same workmen) which will be provided in the structure. ICBO requires one test of field constructed prisms for each 465 m² (5000 sq ft) of wall, or three tests minimum per building. Field constructed prisms must be built and stored in locations where the ambient conditions simulate those for the walls which they represent. It is essential to protect each specimen from damage. After 48 hr of jobsite curing, stiff plywood shall be tightly wired or strapped to the top and bottom of each prism to help prevent damage to bond between brick and mortar during transportation to the laboratory. At the laboratory, prisms should be stored at $24 \pm 8°C$ and $50\% \pm 20\%$ relative humidity until 28 days old. Prior to testing, each prism must be accurately capped with material providing unit strength in excess of that of the prism. The actual f'_m value reported should be the average value obtained from the test group as modified by requirements of the controlling code, if any. For instance, ICBO (1979) limits f'_m for engineered brick to 125% of the minimum test value or the average value, whichever is less, with a maximum of 41.4 MPa (6000 psi). BOCA (1978) requires a correction factor to the average prism strength if the coefficient of variation v of the test sample equals or exceeds 10%, as

$$C_{vp} = 1 - 1.5\left(\frac{v}{100} - 0.10\right) \qquad (6.7)$$

$$f'_m = C_{vp}(\bar{X})$$ (6.8)

$$V = \frac{100S}{\bar{X}}$$ (6.9)

and

$$S = \sqrt{\sum_{i=1}^{n} \frac{(X_i - \bar{X})^2}{n - 1}}$$ (6.10)

in which C_{vp} = prism strength correction factor; f'_m = compressive strength at 28 days (or other specified age) using gross area for solid masonry, net area for hollow

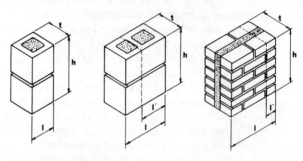

t = thickness of wall   h ≥ 2t ≤ 5t
h = height of prism   l' ≥ t ≥ 100 mm (4 in.)
l = length of prism   l ≤ 2t

Fig. 6.29 Masonry prism test specimens *(Amrhein, 1973)*

Table 6.11 Physical requirements for mortar tests *(BIA, 1972)*

Mortar type (1)	Compressive strength[a]		Minimum water retention[c] (4)	Maximum air content, as a percentage (5)	Efflorescence (6)
	Mininum[b] 7 days, in megapascals (pounds per square inch) (2)	Minimum 28 days, in megapascals (pounds per square inch) (3)			
M[d]	11.0 (1600)	17.2 (2500)			
S	7.6 (1100)	12.4 (1800)			
N	3.1 (450)	5.2 (750)	70	12	none
O[e]	1.4 (200)	2.4 (350)			
K[e]	0.3 (45)	0.5 (75)			

[a] Average of three 50-mm (2-in.) cubes per ASTM C109 (1977).

[b] If the mortar fails to meet the 7-day compressive strength requirement, but meets the 28-day compressive strength requirement, it shall be acceptable.

[c] Flow after suction, as a percentage of original flow per ASTM C91 (1978) and C270 (1973).

[d] Applies also to PL and PM mortar, ASTM C476 (1971), with 130 ± 5 flow.

[e] Not allowed for making grout.

masonry; V = coefficient of variation, as a percentage; S = standard deviation; X = individual compressive strength; $\overline{X}$ = average compressive strength; and n = number of tests in sample. BOCA (1978) similarly requires a correction factor to be applied to brick test compressive values if the coefficient of variation within the test sample exceeds 12%, as

$$C_{vb} = 1 - 1.5\left(\frac{v}{100} - 0.12\right) \qquad (6.11)$$

and

$$f'_b = C_{vb}(\overline{X}) \qquad (6.12)$$

in which C_{vb} = brick strength correction factor; and f'_b = average compressive strength of brick.

Brick testing is performed to determine modulus of rupture, compressive strength, absorption, saturation coefficient, initial rate of absorption, effect of freezing and thawing, and various other brick characteristics. When f'_m is based on brick tests, the average compressive strength of the brick sample is used to select an assumed f'_m value stipulated by the controlling code. Generally, a sample of 10 brick specimens is selected from a lot of 250 000 or fewer brick. Five bricks may be selected from each 500 000 brick, but not less than 10 brick shall be used for each test, except that hollow brick may be tested as structural clay tile, requiring only five specimens for compression testing. For solid brick, five are tested for modulus of rupture and five for compressive strength. Before testing, brick specimens must be dried at least 24 hr at 110°C to 115°C (212°F to 230°F) or until the increment of weight loss in 2 hr is less than 0.2%. Test pieces may be obtained from original brick specimens by any means providing sound, unshattered, crackfree pieces of brick with length equal to brick width ± 25.4 mm (1 in.). For standard brick with bedding width (wall or wythe thickness) of 88 mm to 95 mm (3-1/2 in. to 3-3/4 in.), the typical laboratory testing machine can crush all but exceptionally strong specimens. Only when specimen strengths exceed 100 MPa (14 500 psi) is it likely that machine capacity will become a problem.

2 Compression Testing Large Size Structural Brick

Increased production and use of larger bricks with widths of 152 mm, 203 mm, and 254 mm (6 in., 8 in., and 10 in.) necessitate special compressive testing methods, especially when specimens from 203-mm (8-in.) or wider units must be tested. Unless unusually low in strength, the size of standard test pieces will preclude crushing to failure in a 1.33-MN machine. Obviously, currently published requirements for size of brick compressive strength specimens need revision for large size bricks. Until such revisions are officially adopted, an interim procedure must be followed if high capacity testing machines are not readily available or accessible.

Presuming that reasonable correlation exists between the net or gross area compressive strength and the strength of various sizes of test specimens cut from the whole unit, certain interim procedures appear reasonable. Standard bricks made from the same clay and fired to the same degree of maturity as the large bricks can be used by the manufacturer to estimate the probable upper limit of the gross area compressive strength of large units. With this information, the testing laboratory can calculate the area of test specimens which can be crushed in a given testing machine. For units with an estimated maximum compressive strength of 82.4 MPa (12 000 psi), the test specimen should have a gross area 161 cm² (25 sq in.) or less if it is to be tested in a 1.33-MN machine. Specimens should preferably be cut from the more uniform midportion of the sample brick in order to best represent the over-all unit strength. If the actual width of the unit is 190 mm (7-1/2 in.), the specimen length cannot exceed 84.7 mm (3-1/4 in.), violating the rule that specimen length must equal brick width ± 25 mm (1 in.). Specimens may be carefully cut using a masonry saw to assure plane and parallel sides. Although bricks may include cylindrical voids called cores formed during manufacture, test specimens should be as symmetrical as possible about both horizontal axes of the original brick.

Volume of Voids. A simple but accurate method of determining the volume of voids in whole or cut brick specimens is as follows:

1. Place the unit on a sealed surface.

2. Fill all voids level with dry sand.

3. Pour the fill sand into a volumetric glass graduate.

4. Divide the volume of sand by the height of the specimen to obtain area of voids.

5. Subtract void area from gross area to obtain net area of the specimen.

6. Using the average net area compressive strengths of five specimens cut from whole brick, an accurate estimate of gross area strength of whole units can be calculated using

$$C_g = 0.95 \left(\frac{A_n}{A_g}\right) C_{ns} \qquad (6.13)$$

in which C_g = gross area compressive strength of whole unit; A_n = net area of whole unit; A_g = gross area of whole unit; and C_{ns} = average net area compressive strength of five cut specimens.

Testing Precautions. To be useful, test results must be reliable and reproducible. To this end, tests must be made on comparable specimens subjected to uniform testing conditions. In the event that oven drying of brick specimens is not possible, samples must be cured in laboratory air until all specimens have both a similar and steady moisture content. Specimens must always be capped to fill bearing surface irregularities and provide parallel and uniform contact with the testing machine bearing surfaces, thereby eliminating inaccurate results due to stress concentrations caused by irregular, out-of-plane, or point bearing conditions. Care must also be taken to aline the center of gravity of the specimen accurately with the axis of the testing machine. These precautions should assure the uniformity and meaningfulness of brick test results.

3   Absorption

The 24-hr cold water submersion and 5-hr boiling tests are two standard means for testing the water absorption capacity of brick. Tests are performed by submerging standard half-brick compression specimens in water. The results are reported in percentage gain in weight from oven-dry to saturated weight. The cold water absorption percentage divided by the boiling water absorption percentage yields the saturation coefficient, a measure of probable durability of units subjected to freezing and thawing cycles.

A second type of absorption test is performed to determine the initial rate of absorption (IRA), also called suction. This characteristic is especially important and indicates whether the moisture content of brick must be controlled at the jobsite in order to assure good bond of mortar to the brickwork. Tests are conducted using five specimens of whole brick starting in the oven-dry, cool (24 ± 8°C) condition. Specimens are immersed in 3.18 ± 0.25 mm (1/8 ± 0.01 in.) water for 1 min ± 1 sec, after which the weight gain in grams is determined. IRA is reported as weight gain in grams per standard area of 193.6 cm² (30 sq in.). Should the bearing area of the brick specimens vary more than 2.5%, whether solid or cored brick, the weight gain shall be corrected to the standard area using

$$X = \frac{193.6W}{LB} \tag{6.14}$$

in SI units, and

$$X = \frac{30W}{LB} \tag{6.15}$$

in American units, in which X = gain in weight corrected to standard area; W = weight gain; L = length of specimen; and B = width of specimen.

4   Mortar Testing

Laboratory mixing, testing, and evaluation of each mortar proposed for use in a given project is advisable prior to beginning work. Each mortar tested must be mixed using materials sampled from those which will be used in the actual work. Laboratory test batches must be mixed with proportions of each ingredient, including admixtures (if any) identical to those that will be mixed in the field. Brands of cementitious material and source of sand should remain the same throughout each project. The method of mixing materials during construction may be controlled either by volume or by weight, but must assure the correct proportion of each constituent material in each batch of mortar. Mortar types, when tested in the laboratory, must produce the physical properties shown in Table 6.12. Current standards for mortar tests are intended for samples prepared from laboratory mixed batches with initial flow within the range of 100% to 115% (130% ± 5% for reinforced masonry construction). Because mortars are mixed in the field to provide

Table 6.12 Correction factors to compressive strength of prisms

Correction factor (1)	Ratio of height to thickness (h/t)						
	2.0 (2)	2.5 (3)	3.0 (4)	3.5 (5)	4.0 (6)	4.5 (7)	5.0 (8)
BOCA, 1978	0.73	0.80	0.86	0.91	0.95	0.98	1.00
ICBO, 1979	0.82	0.85	0.88	0.91	0.94	0.98	1.00

optimum workability and water content (120-150 initial flow), test samples secured from field mixed mortar can provide meaningful and useful data only if secured at the specified laboratory testing consistency before the optimum consistency for workability is achieved or if ASTM C780 (1974) tests are correlated with laboratory obtained data. ASTM C780 (1974) tests can be extremely useful to verify the level of quality control in field masonry work.

Tests involving the tensile bond strength of mortar to brick are considered important because bond strength seems to be the single most important factor affecting the performance of engineered masonry structures. Tensile bond strength may be determined using crossed brick couplets (Fig. 6.30) assembled and tested following procedures set forth in ASTM E149 (1976). These tests can be used to evaluate the following aspects of bond strength: (1) Bond between a given brick type and a specified mortar mixture; (2) relative bond between different brick types and a specified mortar; or (3) relative bond between a given brick type and different mortars.

Bond tests are not useful for acceptance testing of mortar because of the potential for wide variation in results, but they have great value for comparing relative bond values with different combinations of mortar, grout, brick, and construction procedures. The failure mode can be adhesion between brick and mortar, brick failure, or mortar failure. With structural brick, the failure will generally be in the adhesion of mortar to the brick surface due to the high strength of both brick and mortar.

5 Flexural Bond Strength

Transverse strength of brick masonry is related to the strength of bed joints in tension. Failure normally occurs by loss of adhesion between mortar and brick. Incompletely filled joints are unacceptable where flexural stresses must be resisted. One measure of lateral or flexural resistance can be obtained through modulus of rupture or flexure testing of small beam specimens in accord with ASTM E518 (1976). Larger wall segments can be constructed to simulate actual construction and can be tested in accord with ASTM E72 (1977) in those instances where the expense

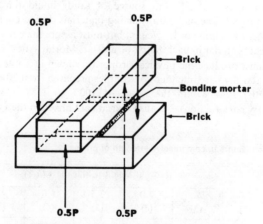

Fig. 6.30 Crossed brick couplet for tensile bond test

is warranted and adequate laboratory facilities are available. Small flexure test specimens can be constructed using solid brick and mortar and tested in accord with Fig. 6.31 for point loads or Fig. 6.32 for uniform loading, usually accomplished by use of a polyvinylchloride or rubberized cloth air bag. In the event design stresses are determined by flexure testing, it is essential that the actual construction be limited to inspected workmanship. ASTM E518 (1976) states that tests of small flexure prisms are intended as an economical means of performing comparative material evaluation tests or for quality control testing of jobsite materials and workmanship. [Wall panel tests per ASTM E72 (1977) are preferred for determining design stresses.] Each test should consist of at least five specimens with joints tooled to simulate the finished face. In the test arrangement, tooled joints should be on the bottom face. For point load tests, results from specimens that fail outside the central third should be disregarded. Modulus of rupture is calculated as

$$R_g = \frac{(P + 0.75P_s)l}{bd^2} \tag{6.16}$$

for Fig. 6.31 and

$$R_g = \frac{0.75(P + P_s)l}{bd^2} \tag{6.17}$$

for Fig. 6.32, in which R_g = gross area modulus of rupture; P = maximum applied test load; P_s = weight of specimen; l = span of specimen; b = width of specimen (length of one masonry unit); and d = depth of specimen (width of one masonry unit).

For specimens built from hollow brick units, the net modulus of rupture is calculated as

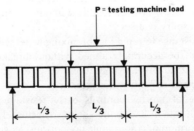

Fig. 6.31 Flexural test prism with 1/3 point loads *(ASTM E518, 1976)*

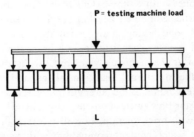

Fig. 6.32 Flexural test prism with uniform load *(Courtesy: Atlas Machine & Iron Works, Inc.)*

$$R_n = \frac{(0.167P + 0.125P_s)l}{S_n} \qquad (6.18)$$

for Fig. 6.31 and

$$R_n = \frac{0.125(P + P_s)l}{S_n} \qquad (6.19)$$

for Fig. 6.32, in which R_n = net modulus of rupture; and S_n = section modulus of actual brick surface area bedded by mortar.

6   Quality of Mortar and Grout

Mortar joins masonry units into a continuous structure with known properties and provides bond for steel joint reinforcement, metal ties, and anchor bolts, if any, to perform integrally with the masonry. Mortar may also provide architectural quality to exposed masonry through color contrasts or shadow lines from various joint tooling procedures and integral coloring admixtures.

Grout is essential to reinforced masonry and is produced by adding more water to mortar containing some lime. In reinforced masonry walls, grout bonds the masonry units and steel reinforcement together. Grout is sometimes used in nonreinforced load-bearing masonry walls to give added strength. Some or all voids may be filled in either system.

The most important quality of a given mortar or grout is workability because of its influence on both plastic and hardened mortar properties and, hence, structural performance. The interrelated mortar properties with greatest influence on workability are consistency, water retention, and setting time. Experienced workmen judge workability by good trowelability (lack of stickiness). Good mortar should spread easily, cling to vertical faces, extrude readily without dropping, and resist settling under one or more masonry courses.

Water retention (resistance to rapid loss of mixing water while remaining soft and plastic) allows units to be accurately alined without breaking adhesion between mortar and masonry. Under some conditions, low absorption units may float, showing the possible need to limit water retention.

The hardening rate of mortar controls early resistance to applied load. A well-defined, consistent rate of hardening assists in accurately laying each unit and in tooling joints. Uniform joint color, while not conclusive, generally reflects proper hardening and consistent tooling times.

The term bond applies both to the extent of bonded area and to tensile bond strength. These properties combined develop the force required to separate joined units. Good extent of bond is important to watertightness. Incomplete mortar to unit contact can allow moisture penetration and destroy tensile bond strength, the essential hardened mortar characteristic which must withstand tensile forces caused by structural action due to external loads, shrinkage, and temperature variations.

Many variables affect bond. Bond strength increases with cement content, is directly related to mortar flow (water content), is vitally affected by workmanship, and can vary widely with brick suction. For all mortars, optimum bond strength occurs at the highest water content compatible with workability, even though compressive strength decreases. Time lapse between spreading mortar and placing masonry units should be minimum because brick suction reduces mortar water content due to suction. Repositioning or inadvertent jarring of units after initial alinement will break or weaken bond, and mortar will not readhere to reestablish lost bond. Brick suction should be greater than 10 but less than 30 grams (ASTM C67, 1978) for best results. Units with 30 grams to 60 grams suction must be soaked with water to reduce suction to acceptable value.

Masonry mortars and grouts contain portland cement and require the presence of moisture to develop full strength potential. Mortar should contain the maximum mixing water consistent with workability in order to best enhance curing conditions. Freshly laid masonry should be protected from sun and drying winds. Special curing techniques are advised for severe drying conditions.

Principal factors affecting compressive strength of masonry structures are compressive strength of masonry units, mortar proportions, workmanship, and curing. Increase in compressive strength of masonry due to increase in mortar strength approximates the increase in the cube root of compressive strength. Mortar strength is a function of the type and quantity of cementitious material, and increases with cement content while decreasing with air-entrainment, lime content, if any, and water content. Contrary to concrete mixing where water-cement ratio is strictly controlled, the correct amount of water in mortar mixed at the construction site is the amount required to produce best workability. Mortar shrinkage is normally not a problem because shrinkage across joints is minuscule. With weaker mortars, the larger creep factors allow greater extensibility, better accommodating shrinkage.

Grout for use in engineered masonry walls should conform to ASTM C476 (1971). A grouting aid admixture may be desirable with high suction masonry units to prevent early water loss, thereby enhancing development of good bond and assisting complete filling of all voids. Use of admixtures containing calcium chloride is ill advised due to potential corrosion. Even though compression test specimens of field mixed grout generally produce low values, actual in-place grout generally exceeds 2500 psi because surrounding masonry reduces the water-cement ratio by absorption and then provides the absorbed moisture during the curing period, enhancing moist curing conditions.

Grout should be fluid in consistency (avoiding segregation due to excess fluidity) in order to flow around all reinforcement and into all voids. Grout consistency should be measured by the slump test. While not specified in codes, slump measured using the standard slump cone for concrete should be approximately 200 mm (8 in.) for low absorption masonry and 255 mm (10 in.) for high absorption units. Grout not placed within 1.5 hr after mixing should be discarded.

Field testing to establish grout quality is advisable. The number of specimens and frequency of testing should be specified in advance. Generally, four specimens should be cast for each 23 m³ (30 yd ³) of grout, for each day's work, or for each change in mix proportions or constituent ingredients. Grout specimens should be cast in molds formed with masonry units with the same absorption as the units in the actual construction (ACI Committee 531, 1970). The masonry mold should be lined with paper towels to prevent bond of the grout sample while at the same time allowing absorption of water by the masonry mold units. Tops of grout samples should be struck (leveled) with a trowel and immediately covered with wet burlap to assure moist curing. Testing should be by standard procedures, including proper capping and testing in damp condition.

7 Summary

Engineered brick masonry can be constructed from designs using conservative assumed design values, but is best utilized when design values are based on tests of actual brick, mortar, and grout available for use in construction. Use of the more realistic values should economize on all materials but does demand inspected quality work. Sometimes field results may appear marginal or fall below established quality requirements. In such instances, actual stresses at the points of reduced quality should be checked. If necessary, test prisms may be cut from the construction with necessary safety precautions, but only after making careful assessment of mortar proportions, mortar constituent materials, grout proportions and constituent materials (if any), possible damage to test specimens, correctness of specimen preparation, and completeness and correctness of test procedures. Obviously, all masonry units must conform to project specification and moisture control requirements, as must ties, reinforcement, and other accessories. If test results plus evaluation of affected work so indicate, unacceptable work must be removed and replaced.

6.6 GLASS FOR BUILDING WINDOWS AND CURTAIN WALLS

With the increased scope and varieties of glass usage in modern major and tall buildings, failures of various characteristics involving both glass and glazing systems have, in some cases, become widely publicized by the media. While only in rare instances has glass breakage endangered human life, this possibility, plus the potential for damage or loss of valuable building contents, the fact that broken or missing glass can render building space unusable, the probable vivid and negative publicity associated with glass breakage, and the ever-increasing likelihood of extended, costly litigation have all worked together to highlight the need for rapid improvement in the scientific understanding of all factors which can cause glass failure. Some dramatic instances of glass failure have been given wide coverage in the technical literature, while several others remain basically undiscussed. The subject is complicated by the inherent characteristics and behavior of glass itself, wind effects, glazing details, airborne missiles, scratches and abrasions, impact loadings, and other environmental factors. It is essential, once design objectives have been established, for the window-wall designer to study carefully all applicable manufacturer-furnished data so that the designer may prepare complete and appropriate specifications for both the selected glass and its mounting system. The architectural-structural interactions involving glass as a part of the cladding are treated in Chapter SC-5.

1 Structural Considerations

Assessment of failure stress for glass is made difficult because glass is a brittle material. Tensile failure occurs abruptly without plastic flow, providing glass with perfectly elastic stress-strain properties but no yield point. Rational understanding of glass under stress is further complicated by the extremely low measured values of failure stress as compared with the theoretical strength of glass which exceeds 10 000 MPa (1 420 000 psi). The actual failure stress for glass in service or in test specimens is variable for a given grade of glass and is related to surface defects or flaws, which are normally undetectable to the unassisted eye and often are undetectable in un-fractured glass, even using an electron microscope. Griffith (1920) has presented a theory relating flaw size and failure stress. Further complicating the determination of glass failure stress is the fact that glass is subject to the phenomenon of static fatigue which causes the failure stress to vary with the duration of the applied load as well as the rate of loading. Due to the variability of failure stress caused by the random occurrence and size of flaws, glass strength must be stated as an average strength with the accompanying coefficient of variation. ASTM C158 (1972) provides specific requirements for determining the modulus of rupture of flat glass using specimens of standard size with consideration to edge condition of samples, and it requires that the modulus of rupture be stated as the average value of 30 or more specimens along with the standard deviation.

Failure strength of individual lights (single panels of glass) is affected by surface area, thickness, and aspect ratio (length divided by width). The probability of failure

"River of Glass" describes the clear flow of this continuous float glass ribbon. Hundreds of conveyor rolls carry the ribbon through the 300-foot-long cooling section to bring the glass to room temperature before inspection and cutting operations (Courtesy: PPG Industries, Inc.)

at a low stress increases with an increase in surface area due to the greater probability that a defect of sufficient severity to cause failure will be included in the surface of an individual light. Deflection under load is generally minimal for small and very thick lights. For lights in which deflection divided by thickness is 0.5 or less, pure bending generally prevails; where deflection divided by thickness exceeds 0.5, such as for thin and for very large lights supported on four sides, membrane behavior combines with bending behavior to produce tension regions on both glass surfaces. When tensile stress at the glass surface equals the critical level for a surface flaw, a fracture will occur. Apparent average breaking stress levels for large lights are generally lower than for smaller lights of the same grade of glass. The stress required to break a light of glass is related to thermal history or temper, fabrication, surface quality, edge quality, support conditions, and type and rate of loading.

Striped for action—reflecting striped test pattern, a clear flat glass sample from a manufacturing line is checked for flatness by quality control technician (*Courtesy: PPG Industries, Inc.*)

2 Effect of Support Conditions

In practical glazing systems, plate edges generally rotate with negligible restraint. It is also generally agreed that glass edges can translate freely in the plane of the glass, reducing the membrane contribution to stiffness below that indicated by the solution for simply supported and uniformly loaded plates (Timoshenko, 1940). Nevertheless, lights with aspect ratios below 3 and approaching 1 demonstrate significant increase in stiffness with increasing load due to membrane action. For aspect ratios greater than 3, deflection and stress at the center of lights can be determined with reasonable accuracy using formulas for a uniformly loaded strip. For rectangular lights supported on four sides, variations in structural performance caused by differences in support stiffness are much less important than glass surface characteristics, provided that support deflection does not exceed support span divided by 175.

Variations in weathertight glazing details or in structurally adequate sash appear to have relatively small influence on surface tension stresses of glass under wind load. Generally, the stiffer the sash, the more weathertight the glazing. However, lights glazed in lock-strip type gaskets may be subject to "blow-out." Lights acceptable structurally and for weathertightness may still be sufficiently flexible to be architecturally unacceptable for visual reasons. Edge movements associated with notably flexible lights may cause displacements and stresses in thin sealant cross sections, causing rapid seal failure, which in turn can permit both leakage and glass failure. Quality of cut or factory treated edges is important if edges are free spanning and can experience bending stresses. Different edge support details can contribute to or can minimize edge tensile stresses in tinted glass and insulating glass installations. Rabbets inset into material which changes temperature slowly, such as concrete and light colored glazing materials, can have a cooling effect on glass perimeters, while dark colored glazing gaskets and thin aluminum frames can warm quickly and minimize differential temperatures in glass caused by solar energy.

Glass support systems must accommodate both curtain wall temperature movements and differential movements of the supporting structure, while also providing adequate resistance to loadings perpendicular to the glass surface as well as horizontal and vertical edge support. At least 4 mm (1/8 in.) movement per 4 m (12 ft) of mullion must be accommodated to allow for temperature change effects. Glazing members must provide for at least 12-mm (1/2-in.) deep glazing rabbets. Depth clearance for glass edges must be at least 2.5 mm (3/32 in.) to prevent metal or mounting screws from bearing on glass edges. Width clearance in the rabbet must be not less than 3 mm (1/8 in.) on both glass faces, and bite must be at least 6 mm (1/4 in.) for flexible sealing strips or 10 mm (3/8 in.) for sealant applications. Special attention must be given to mounting details for double glazed and insulating units. Only two 80 to 90 durometer (ASTM C542, 1976) neoprene setting blocks of 100 mm (4 in.) minimum length must symmetrically support lights between their 1/4 points and points at least 150 mm (6 in.) from corners. Forty to 50 durometer centering shims of 50 mm (2 in.) minimum length spaced at 750 ± 150 mm (30 ± 6 in.) centers (or continuous shims) must provide at least 3 mm (1/8 in.) bite, each face, each edge. Twenty to 30 durometer spacer blocks should be placed at midheight of both vertical glass edges and at the center of the top edge. Intermittently spaced centering shims must be placed directly opposite each other to avoid bending stresses in glass edges caused by clamping action or glass surface loadings. For double glazed or insulating glass units, pressure greater than 1.75 N/mm (10 lb/in.) should not be applied to glass edge faces by clamping action on centering shims or glazing details. Edge pressure greater than 0.17 N/mm (1 lb/in.) should be avoided at spacer blocks. Pressure of 0.70 N/mm (4 lb/in.) is required to make glazing wedges or glazing strips watertight. The goal is to have each light float in its mounting securely enclosed, supported and cushioned within its sash with adequate bite to accept maximum wind loads, while also having all mounting materials and details properly arranged to prevent delivery of point loads or twisting action to the glass. It is imperative that the glass designer carefully study and provide for the effects of mounting details on glass.

3 Effect of Impact and Other Accidental Loads

Glass thickness adequate to resist uniform wind loads may not be sufficient to resist concentrated impact loads applied by such common items as spike heels, dropped tools, rifle pellets, balls, roof gravel, shopping carts, and the like. Even when such objects have relatively low velocity, mass, and momentum, stress due to point loading may exceed the failure level. Tempered glass is especially vulnerable to point loading stresses. Cuts or scratches by diamond rings, spike heels, and other hard, sharp objects may be equally damaging. Point loads from window washers, fire hose streams, and pressure changes due to missing lights may be worthy of consideration. Minor (1974) has prepared a comprehensive study of the effects of windborne missiles. With the possible exception of sonic boom and blast loadings, resonance effects appear to be unimportant because the natural frequency of glass in place in buildings generally exceeds 10 Hz, whereas the maximum frequency of glass deflection and strain response may never exceed 2 Hz (Mayne and Walker, 1976; Ishizaki et al., 1977).

The "saw-tooth" facade of high performance glass on the R. J. Reynolds Industries, Inc., world headquarters in Winston-Salem, N.C., mirrors passing clouds and reflects the sun's heat to help reduce cooling costs (*Courtesy: PPG Industries, Inc.*)

Glass in certain locations in most buildings, such as in doors and ground level lights, is subject to potential impact loading from human beings or from inadvertently propelled objects. To minimize the hazard of cutting and piercing injuries from sharp-edged, pointed or daggerlike pieces of glass, glazed openings in selected locations may be best fitted with safety-glazing material. ANSI Committee Z97 has prepared Standard Z97.1-1972 to assist in evaluating safety glazing materials and to provide a standardized test method. The committee selected a 445-N (100-lb) boy as the typical glass breakage victim and estimated that a reasonable potential impact energy is represented by a running speed of 6.7 m/sec (22 ft/sec). It was considered unlikely that such a person would deliver the full available kinetic energy of 1020 N-m (755 ft-lb) to a sheet of glass instantaneously due either to an angular approach or the reduction of energy delivered to a point by absorbing a portion of the shock with outstretched arms or sequential contact by different parts of the body. A standard testing energy of 540 N-m (400 ft-lb) was therefore selected to represent conditions of free access, while energies of 135 N-m (100 ft-lb) and 200 N-m (150 ft-lb) were selected as testing energies representative of locations where persons cannot develop their full velocity potential. The standard requires four specimens to be tested under the impact of a freely swinging lead-shot-filled leather punching bag weighing 445 N (100 lb) with successive pendulum falls of 305 mm (12 in.), 460 mm (18 in.), and 1220 mm (48 in.) until breakage, displacement of glass intact from the test jig, or survival intact occurs. Breakage or disintegration and the drop height are reported, or the fact that the test specimen remained intact after being struck from all three drop heights. Evaluation of broken specimens is made, as detailed in the standard, to determine the presence or absence of dangerous and accessible pieces of glass or glass edges, the point being to assure that glass in service does not present cutting and piercing hazards to the public. The United States Federal Safety Standard 16 CFR 1201 (1977) requires installation of safety glazing in doors and glazed panels in building spaces accessible to the public, to prevent or reduce injuries or death caused by walking into glazed doors or glazed panels mistaken for open doors or from pushing against glazing material in the attempt to open a door. The federal standard rates glazing as Category I or Category II, based on one-time drop heights of either 460 mm (18 in.) or 1220 mm (48 in.), respectively. Of course, the need for safety glazing may be eliminated in many instances by the provision of safety rails or effective visual barriers.

4 Effect of Surface Conditions

Abrasion of glass surfaces in open areas, abrasive cleaning, weld splatter, wind-blown roof gravel, hail, and flying debris may cause surface damage, thereby reducing basic in-place strength and leading to failure under subsequent impact or wind loads. Breaking strength reduction due to normal aging combined with surface degradation due to scratching and abrasion can be expected to be on the order of 20% to 30%. Local point crushes can be more severe. Sandblasting uniformly over the entire glass surface can cause a strength reduction on the order of 50%.

Area is also a significant variable affecting surface condition. As the area of individual lights is increased, the probability that a flaw of increased severity will be contained within a region of tensile stress is also increased; consequently, average breaking stresses tend to decrease with increased surface area. In the United States, charts published by manufacturers to show recommended glass thickness as a function of lateral pressure and of glass surface area take into account the flaw severity probability density factor. In the event theoretical stress analysis is used in design, allowable working stress should be adjusted downward in inverse relationship to relative glass area.

5 Probability Concepts

The structural behavior of glass is such that the risk of breakage must be evaluated statistically. By selecting an appropriate safety factor, risk of breakage based on a normal distribution can be reduced to an acceptably small or insignificant level, but cannot be eliminated. For this reason, glass is not guaranteed against breakage. Insurance against breakage is carried by most building owners. Table 6.13 gives the relationship of safety factors to the statistical probability of failure for a large number of lights. The safety factor must be selected carefully to assure public safety and desirable performance, while at the same time considering initial and long time economy. The New York Building Code (1975) responds to this concept by specifying allowable breakage probability versus glass area and height above grade. The performance of groups containing small numbers of lights may not be as reliable as indicated in Table 6.13. For test purposes, a sample lot of 30 test specimens usually will provide suitable data.

Glass strength is variable with the variability dependent mainly on the random distribution of surface flaws. Coefficients of variation of glass strength are commonly on the order of 25% for ordinary annealed glass, 20% for heat-strengthened glass, and 15% for fully tempered glass. Manufacturers' charts for stated coefficients of variation and mean breaking stress typically include a factor to assure that breakage probability does not exceed 8 lights per 1000. Failure probability tables may or may not account for variability in wind loads and in other in-service effects which may degrade glass surfaces and, hence, strength.

Table 6.13 Relationship of coefficient of variation and statistical probability of failure[a] (*PPG Industries, 1979*)

Probability of breakage[b] at initial occurrence of 60-second design load (breaks per 1000 loaded) (1)	Maximum stress, in pounds per square inch		
	Annealed glass (coefficient of variation = 22%) (2)	Heat-strengthened glass (coefficient of variation = 15%) (3)	Tempered glass (coefficient of variation = 10%) (4)
500	6,000	11,000	23,000
50	3,800	8,300	19,000
8	2,800	7,000	17,200
4	2,500	6,600	16,600
2	2,200	6,200	16,000
1	1,900	5,900	15,500

[a]Manufacturer's published data should be checked for manufacturer's latest design information and recommendations.
[b]For a large number of lights with a statistically normal strength distribution; individual specimens will break at higher and lower levels.

By use of Table 6.13, the designer may select any probability of breakage or the related factor of safety between design stress and average breaking or failure strength. By use of the following equations, the glass designer can select a design glass stress or an assumed safety factor and, by trial and error methods, calculate the related probability of failure. The equations are

$$p(\chi) = 1 - \frac{1}{2\sqrt{\pi}} \int_{-\infty}^{x=1} e^{-1/2t^2} dt \tag{6.20}$$

and

$$t = \frac{\bar{S} - S_d}{C_g \bar{S}} \tag{6.21}$$

or

$$t = \frac{F.S. - 1}{C_g(F.S.)} \tag{6.22}$$

in which p = probability of breakage; χ = probability density function; e = natural logarithmic base; t = standard variable; $\bar{S}$ = average breaking stress; S_d = selected design stress; $F.S. = \bar{S}/S_d$, and C_g = coefficient of variation in breaking stress for glass.

Upon deciding that a failure rate of 8 lights per 1000 lights installed is acceptable, and using S = 4000 psi (27.58 MPa, 2 812 280 kgf/m²) for regular float-glass with C_g = 25%, the designer can select S_d = 1600 psi (11.03 MPa, 1 124 912 kgf/m²) (F.S. = 2.5) and demonstrate that the probability of breakage at the first design load occurrence is

$$t = \frac{4000 - 1600}{0.25 \times 4000} = 2.40$$

$$p(\chi) = 1 - \frac{1}{2\sqrt{\pi}} \int_{-\infty}^{x=1} e^{-1/2(2.40)^2} dt = 1 - 0.992 = 0.008$$

Accordingly, tension stresses in annealed float glass must not exceed 11.03 MPa (1600 psi, 1 124 912 kgf/m²) in order to provide a breakage probability of 8 or fewer lights per 1000. This can often be accomplished by selecting an appropriate glass thickness.

Missing from this analysis are two important factors: (1) The actual glass loading and its duration; and (2) the relationship between load and maximum stress in a light of glass.

6 Engineering Considerations

The stress required to break a large light of glass is related to the fabrication process, surface quality, support conditions, type of load, and load duration. A major responsibility of the designer is the determination of expected wind loads on glass surfaces. (Wind loads and effects are treated in chapter CL-3.) Building codes usually specify wind loads as an equivalent static load. Glass strength is usually based on one minute static pressure, even though high gust pressures may last less than 3 seconds. Air moves at velocities and in directions which vary with elevation and with building shape. Local velocity is best evaluated by boundary layer wind tunnel studies designed to indicate significant parapet, corner, vertical, and stack effects, particularly in urban tall buildings.

Data given in ANSI Standard A58.1-1972, "Building Code Requirements for Minimum Design Loads in Buildings and Other Structures," provide useful design information. Fig. 6.33 shows the relationship of some typical loading conditions to glass breaking stresses. Special attention must be given to high suction forces, such as at building corners. Designers often require the additional strength of heat-strengthened or tempered glass to resist wind and solar loads, impact, and other design considerations. Compared to annealed glass, heat-strengthening doubles the uniform load required to cause failure, and full tempering increases it four times. Large deflections, however, must be accepted to utilize these high loads. Also, tempered glass is more vulnerable than float glass to point loading.

The South Florida Building Code (1974) controls glass area based on ordinary annealed glass, thickness, 193 km/hr (120 mph) wind speed at 9 m (30 ft) above grade, and maximum allowable area versus height above grade with glass area multiplier factors for tempered and other types of glass. The New York Building Code (1975), although somewhat less demanding, also specifies maximum area versus thickness and height above grade, and provides area multiplier factors for full-tempered, heat strengthened, and other types of glass.

Since glass failure is a function of surface stress, a relationship between applied load and stress is needed. If glass sizes and deflections were small, with tension stresses induced by bending alone, beam and plate formulas could be used. However, due to functional considerations, such as solar heating and provision of daylight as well as esthetic considerations, architects often select window sizes and thicknesses which result in a combination of bending and membrane stresses, thereby ruling out the use of standard small deflection formulae. To overcome this problem, glass manufacturers have conducted numerous tests in order to correlate glass area and thickness to expected breakage probabilities under uniform load.

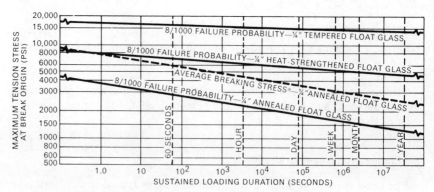

*Based on ¼" annealed float glass, 60 second MOR of 6000 psi.

Fig. 6.33 Relationship of breaking stress to duration of uniform load *(PPG Industries, 1979)*

To assure long-term satisfactory service, wind-load charts are factored to compensate for in-service weathering, cleaning, scratches, abrasion, and other environmental variables which degrade the glass surface and its resistance to wind loads. Generally, a 20% to 30% compensating factor is used, although studies indicate that glass exposed to severe abrasion can experience reduction in breaking strength of as much as 50%. Deterioration of exterior glass surfaces will reduce resistance to suction pressures (indoors to out) but will have far less or negligible effect on positive pressure loads on building facades.

Because of the large number of variables which affect the strength of glass such as area, aspect ratio, type and duration of load, and surface flaws, no single design formula has received universal agreement. One manufacturer's chart for several thicknesses of annealed float glass is shown in Fig. 6.34.

This chart is based on a computer program that employs finite element analysis to predict the maximum principal stress. Curves shown are for a probability of breakage of 8/1000 lights loaded, and a uniform wind load duration of 60 sec.

A load-stress formula has wide application in glass engineering. One such empirical formula, developed by a major manufacturer, correlates reasonably well with destructive-test values. While it involves most of the major variables that affect wind-load stress in glass plates, other factors may limit its general application. The

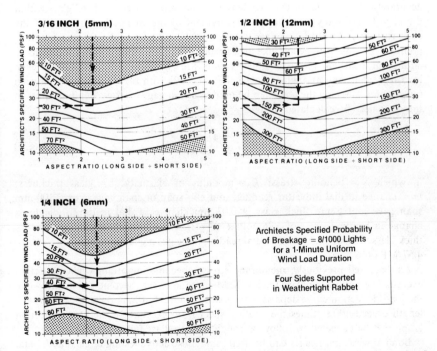

Fig. 6.34 Recommended maximum wind loading for annealed float glass *(PPG Industries, undated)*

formula is generally used where a low probability of failure is desired—that is, where a design stress less than 22 MPa (3200 psi) is acceptable. Maximum stress in a given light may be computed using

$$\alpha = 0.234 \frac{A^{0.54}L^{0.71}R^{0.18}}{t^{0.83}} \qquad (6.23)$$

in SI units, or

$$\alpha = 10 \frac{A^{0.54}L^{0.71}R^{0.18}}{t^{0.83}} \qquad (6.24)$$

in American units, in which α = maximum stress, in megapascals (pounds per square inch); A = glass area, in square meters (square feet); L = uniform applied load, in newtons per square meter (pounds per square foot); R = aspect ratio (length of long side divided by short side length); and t = glass thickness, in millimeters (inches).

Bending stress may be measured in a light subjected to experimental test loads by means of a span gage which measures change in curvature. Such a gage is composed of a rigid bar or beam with support points accurately installed at the preselected gage length, for example, 100 mm (4 in.). A sensitive dial indicator gage is mounted accurately at the center of the gage length to measure deflection of the glass within the gage length, thus providing a measurement of the change in curvature of the glass surface under load. Span gages are portable and may be moved from point to point on the glass surface to make measurements at preselected indexed locations or additional locations selected by observation. Measurements can be made for each load increment and at angles of zero, 45°, and 90° with the reference line at each index point, allowing the results to be used as strain-gage rosettes. Bending stress in the glass may be calculated using

$$S = \frac{4Etm}{c^2} \qquad (6.25)$$

in which S = bending stress; E = modulus of elasticity; t = glass thickness; m = change in dial indicator reading; and c = span of span gage. For a 100-mm span gage and 6-mm thick glass, a 0.03-mm change in dial reading indicates a change in bending stress of 5.26 MPa (763 psi). For a 4-in. span gage and 1/4-in. thick glass, a 0.001-in. change in dial reading indicates a change in bending stress of 4.57 MPa (662 psi).

As discussed previously, membrane stresses become important when deflection exceeds one-half of the glass thickness. Membrane effects become significant when the load-deflection curve departs from a straight line. For long rectangles where the length exceeds three times the width (aspect ratio exceeds 3), the load deflection graph can be expected to follow a straight line to glass failure load.

Bonded wire strain gages can be used in nondestructive testing of glass and metal framing in the laboratory and in mock-up test programs. This technique is superior to span gage application because the combined bending and membrane stresses are measured. Locations of the gages on the glass specimen are critical because the point of maximum stress moves from center of the plate to points along the diagonals nearer and nearer the corners as the load is increased. ASTM E330 (1972) provides valuable data and criteria regarding testing procedure, measurements, test chamber, safety, and reporting of results.

For economy, most testing of glass must be nondestructive. As such, most available data on load versus stress relationships do not confirm breaking stress levels or modulus of rupture (MOR). Since in-service MOR values are significantly lower than those determined at the manufacturing plant, glass strength formulas are most important in developing the MOR of glass. Glass professionals and manufacturers are continuing to research the interdependence of the effects of area, aspect ratio, and stress distribution on MOR in order to provide more comprehensive evaluation data for designers.

7   Solar Considerations

The second common in-service source of glass stress is solar loading which acts independently from wind loading. While not important for ordinary glass, tinted and reflective glass absorbs considerable heat. Tension stresses are developed at the glass edges due to temperature differentials between the solar heated central glass area and the cooler glass volume along the glazed. perimeter. Stress severity is maximum when vertical lights face bright sun 33° above the horizon with still air contacting the glass both indoors and outdoors. Regardless of thickness, 0.6°C (1°F) temperature difference between the center of the light and the glass edges produces ±0.34 MPa (50 psi) tensile stress in the central portion of the glass edges. Near each corner, edge tensile stress reduces rapidly from values near the maximum occurring at the glass center line to zero at the corners of the light. Edge stresses are affected by glass absorptivity, glass thickness and edge area, shading effects, light size, bite depth, and thermal properties of the glazing rabbet and adjacent materials.

Resistance to solar heat induced breakage is greatly enhanced by best quality cut edges, thus minimizing the opportunity of an edge break to start at a serration, spall, or point of edge damage. Because of its brittle nature, glass is extremely notch-sensitive, and factory fabrication of edges may be advisable. Designers often require the additional strength of heat-strengthened or tempered glass to resist wind and solar loads.

8   Computer Analysis

Answers to the complex behavior aspects of glass may be solved by computer analysis. Developments in finite-element methodology offer a powerful numerical approximation for nonlinear analysis of plates. This method, combined with probabilistic failure analysis of brittle materials, can improve (and has improved) engineering information on glass plate behavior. Correlation of finite-element analysis with experimental results employing bonded strain gages provides an excellent information base for dealing with stress distributions in glass plates under uniform loading (Tsai and Stewart, 1976).

9 Conclusion

Quality control considerations demand that all environmental factors affecting glass stress and strength values be determined carefully and documented prior to final design so that appropriate contract documents may be prepared in advance of construction. These factors include wind loading values, temperature effects, glazing details, impact loadings, potential for damage from scratching and abrasion, and weathering effects. In view of in-service glass breakage in today's buildings, the correct choice of glass type, thickness, and support details is essential.

6.7 SUMMARY

The preceding sections of this chapter have discussed concepts for achieving over-all project quality as well as quality considerations relating specifically to structural steel, concrete, concrete masonry, brick masonry, and glass. Although the greater part of this discussion has focused on structural materials, it is recognized that quality control considerations apply virtually to all facets of building construction, from architectural materials and finishes to mechanical, electrical, air-conditioning, elevator, communications, and all other building service and environmental systems. The term quality can be applied to a given material, device, system, or the completed building system; and criteria can be stated to describe and define the meaning of quality, explicitly or loosely. Quality control is the discipline and system of controls which determines as-produced or acceptance quality and is definition (specification or criteria) and function dependent. Quality assurance will generally include all of the features of quality control, plus administrative procedures to assure that the quality control program is effective or to assure that quality control procedures, equipment, or personnel are corrected or upgraded to achieve the desired result.

It can be seen that quality control is product or task related, whereas quality assurance, in addition, depends upon and represents management policy, whether that of an individual product manufacturer, a specialty skill or trade contractor, or a construction manager in charge of all aspects of a major construction project. Quality control depends upon defined material characteristics, specific tolerances, accurate measuring and testing devices, appropriate sampling procedures, and stipulated personnel qualifications and capabilities. Quality assurance includes the additional dimension of informed management including monitoring the performance quotient of quality control personnel and evaluating the completeness, appropriateness, and effectiveness of each quality control function, subprogram, and program as related to the over-all set of goals.

Discussion of quality control without examples quickly becomes trivial; discussion of quality considerations for individual materials necessarily restricts discussion to a few concepts and materials, forcing exclusion from consideration of many other materials and concepts worthy of discussion. Such is the case in this chapter; however, many quality control criteria and concepts can be gleaned from other parts of the Monograph.

One of the problems in assembling information on Quality Criteria is that it is much easier to be restrictive and specific than it is to provide a broad, useful, reasonably concise discussion of quality control of tall buildings, major construction undertakings, or environmental impact. Certainly given materials and product qualities can be controlled using statistical concepts, as can certain design criteria such as human perception of motion or acceleration, or the probable return period of a given design wind. Other phenomena can be evaluated on the basis of "go-no go" criteria such as acceptance or rejection of weld joint defects based on standard test blocks, calibration, and allowable oscilloscope readings on an ultrasonic testing machine. Multistory steel column and spandrel assemblies can be accepted for shipment or rejected for rework by placement in an inspection fixture built to gage over-all length, trueness of milled bearing surfaces, locational accuracy of spandrel index bolt holes, straightness, planeness, and degree of camber. Everything from precision infinitesimal tolerance techniques to experienced visual evaluation can form part of the quality criteria and impact on the design of quality control programs. While many considerations remain reasonably constant from project to project, others affected by intended use, environmental influences, and architectural intent may cause wide variations in quality criteria.

It is hoped that the items and concepts discussed in this chapter will provide insights into selection of criteria and assist in developing control procedures for materials, products, and assemblies not discussed. The key to quality control and quality assurance is the ability to discern and define that which is required, and then to document reasonable and appropriate procedures and techniques which will assure economical attainment of the predetermined goals.

6.8 CONDENSED REFERENCES/BIBLIOGRAPHY

The following is a condensed bibliography for this chapter. Not only does it include all articles referred to or cited in the text, but it also contains bibliography for further reading. The full citations will also be found at the end of the Volume. What is given here should be sufficient information to lead the reader to the correct article: the author, date, and title. In case of multiple authors, only the first name is listed.

AAMA 1971, *Aluminum Curtainwalls # 4*
ACI Committee 211 1969, *Recommended Practice for Selecting Proportions*
ACI Committee 211 1977, *Recommended Practice for Selecting Proportions for Normal*
ACI Committee 213 1979, *Guide for Structural Lightweight Aggregate Concrete*
ACI Committee 214 1957, *Recommended Practice for Evaluation of Compression Test Results*
ACI Committee 214 1965, *Recommended Practice for Evaluation of Compression Test Results*
ACI Committee 217 1977, *Recommended Practice for Evaluation of Strength Tests of Concrete*
ACI Committee 301 1975, *ACI Standard Specifications for Structural Concrete for Buildings*
ACI Committee 305 1977, *Hot Weather Concreting*
ACI Committee 306, 1972, *ACI Standard—Recommended Practice for Cold Weather Concreting*
ACI Committee 308 1971, *ACI Standard—Recommended Practice for Curing Concrete*
ACI Committee 318 1977a, *Building Code Requirements for Reinforced Concrete*
ACI Committee 318 1977b, *ACI Standard Building Code Requirements for Reinforced Concrete*
ACI Committee 318 1977c, *Commentary on Building Code Requirements for Reinforced*
ACI Committee 318 1977d, *Proposed Revisions: Building Code Requirements*
ACI Committee 347 1977, *ACI Standard Recommended Practice for Concrete Formwork*
ACI Committee 531 1970, *Concrete Masonry Structures—Design and Construction*
ACI Committee 531 1978a, *Proposed ACI Standard Building Code Requirements for Concrete*
ACI Committee 531 1978b, *Commentary on Building Code Requirements for Concrete Masonry*
ACI Committee 613 1954, *Recommended Practice for Selecting Proportions for Concrete*
ACI Committee 613 1959, *Recommended Practice for Selecting Proportions for Structural*
AISC 1978, *Specification for the Design, Fabrication and Erection of Structural Steel*
ANSI A41.1 1953, *American Standard Building Code Requirements for Masonry*
ANSI A41.2 1960, *Building Code Requirements for Concrete Masonry*
ANSI A58.1 1972, *American National Standard Building Code Requirments for Minimum*
ANSI Z97.1 1972, *Performance Specifications and Methods of Test for Safety Glazing*
ASTM 1971a, *Standard Methods of Tension Testing of Metallic Materials*
ASTM 1971b, *Standard Specification for General Requirements*

ASTM 1979, *Annual Book of Standards*
ASTM A615-78 1978, *Standard Specification for Deformed and Plain Billet-Steel Bars*
ASTM C31-69 1969, *Standard Method of Making and Curing Concrete Test Specimens*
ASTM C33-78 1978, *Standard Specification for Concrete Aggregates*
ASTM C67-78 1978, *Standard Methods of Sampling and Testing Brick and Structural Clay*
ASTM C90-75 1975, *Standard Specification for Hollow Load-Bearing Concrete Masonry Units*
ASTM C91-78 1978, *Standard Specification for Masonry Cement*
ASTM C109-77 1977, *Standard Test Method for Compressive Strength of Hydraulic Cement*
ASTM C136-76 1976, *Test for Sieve or Screen Analysis of Fine and Coarse Aggregates*
ASTM C140-75 1975, *Standard Methods of Testing Concrete Masonry Units*
ASTM C143-74 1974, *Test for Slump of Portland Cement Concrete*
ASTM C145-75 1975, *Standard Specification for Solid Load-Bearing Concrete Masonry Units*
ASTM C150-78a 1978, *Standard Specification for Portland Cement*
ASTM C158-72 1972, *Standard Methods of Flexure Testing of Glass*
ASTM C173-78 1978, *Standard Test Method for Air Content of Freshly Mixed Concrete*
ASTM C270-73 1973, *Standard Specification for Mortar for Unit Masonry*
ASTM, C336-76 1976, *Test for Annealing Point and Strain Point of Glass*
ASTM C338-73 1973, *Test for Softening Point of Glass*
ASTM C470-76 1976, *Standard Specification for Molds for Forming Concrete Test Cylinders*
ASTM C476-71 1971, *Standard Specification for Mortar and Grout for Reinforced Masonry*
ASTM C542-76 1976, *Standard Specification for Lock-Strip Gaskets*
ASTM C595-76 1976, *Specification for Blended Hydraulic Cements*
ASTM C780-74 1974, *Standard Method for Preconstruction and Construction Evaluation of*
ASTM E72-77 1977, *Standard Methods of Conducting Strength Tests of Panels for Building*
ASTM E149-76 1976, *Standard Test Method for Bond Strength of Mortar to Masonry Units*
ASTM E330-72 1972, *Standard Test Method for Structural Performance of Exterior Windows*
ASTM E447-74 1974, *Standard Test Methods for Compressive Strength of Masonry Prisms*
ASTM E518-76 1976, *Standard Test Methods for Flexural Bond Strength of Masonry*
ASTM STP 169-A 1966, *Significance of Tests and Properties of Concrete and*
Adams 1966, *Plastic Design in High Strength Steel*
Allen 1964, *A Review of Block Cements—1964*
Alpsten 1968, *Thermal Residual Stresses in Hot-Rolled Steel Members*
Alpsten 1970a, *Residual Stresses and Mechanical Properties of Cold-Straightened H-Shapes*
Alpsten 1970b, *Variations in Strength and Cross-Sectional Dimension of Structural Shapes*
Alpsten 1972, *Prediction of Residual Stresses in Medium-Size to Heavy Welded Steel Shapes*
Alpsten 1973, *Variations in Mechanical and Cross-Sectional Properties of Steel*
Alpsten undated a, *Variations in the Strength of Structural Steel*
Alpsten undated b, *Statistical Investigation of the Strength of Rolled and Welded*
Alpsten 1970, *Residual Stresses in Heavy Welded Shapes*
Amrhein 1972, *Masonry Design Manual*
Amrhein 1973, *Reinforced Masonry Engineering Handbook, Clay and Concrete Masonry*

BIA 1969, *Building Code Requirements for Engineered Brick Masonry*
BIA 1972, *BIA Technical Notes on Brick Construction*
BOCA 1978, *The BOCA Basic Building Code/1978*
BSI 1969, *Specification for Weldable Structural Steels*
BSI 1972, *Code of Practice for the Structural Use of Concrete, Part 1, Design Materials*
BSI 1976, *Structural Recommendations for Load Bearing Walls*
BSI 1978, *Structural Use of Masonry, Part 1: Reinforced Masonry*
Beckett 1974, *Windows, Performance, Design and Installation*
Beer 1970, *The Strength of Heavy Welded Box Columns*
Birkeland 1971, *Dimensional Tolerances in a Tall Concrete Building*
Birkeland 1973, *Dimensional Tolerance—Concrete*
Bjorhovde 1970, *Survey of Utilization and Manufacture of Heavy Columns*
Bjorhovde 1972, *Residual Stresses in Thick Welded Plates*
Blick 1974, *Proportioning and Controlling High-Strength Concrete*
Board of County Commissioners 1974, *The South Florida Building Code*
Bob 1975, *Quality of Lightweight Aggregates Concrete for the Walls of 11-Storied Buildings*
Bradley 1964, *Effects of Porosity on Quenched and Tempered Steel*
Brearley 1918, *Ingots and Ingot Moulds*
Brozzetti 1970, *Residual Stresses in a Heavy Rolled Shape*
Brozzetti 1971, *Welding Parameters, Thick Plates, and Column Strength*
Burdekin 1971, *Lamellar Tearing in Bridge Girders—A Case History*

CABO 1978, *PCI Plant Certification Program*
CCMTC 1975, *Recommended Testing Procedures for Concrete Masonry Units Prisms, Grout*
Cahn 1973, *Durability of Fiber Glass-Portland Cement Composites*

Calavera 1975, *Influence of Strength Variations of Materials and Dimensional Variations of*
Calegari 1973, *Electrolytic Corrosion in Steel Frames of Reinforced and Prestressed*
Capacete 1972, *Proposed Revision of ACl605-69: Recommended Practice for Hot*
Chapeau 1978, *Lamellar Tearing*
Chen 1975, *Structural Use of Sulfur for Impregnation of Building Materials*
Coe 1971, *Confidence in Welded Construction*
Concrete Construction 1976, *Water Tower Place—High Strength Concrete*

DIN 1966, *Structural Steels—Quality Specifications*
DIN 1973a, *Tensile Testing—Concepts, Symbols*
DIN 1973b, *Testing of Metallic Materials*
Daddi 1972, *Experimental Determination of Structural Imperfections in Steel H-Shapes*
Dahlin 1976, *Dimensional Deviations of Multi-Story Steel Frames*
Dickey 1973, *Masonry Stresses by Prism Testing*
Drysdale 1975, *Placement Errors for Reinforcing in Concrete Columns*
Drysdale 1979, *Behavior of Concrete Block Masonry Under Axial Compression*
Duncan 1965, *Quality Control and Industrial Statistics*

Estuar 1966, *Welding Residual Stresses and the Strength of Heavy Column Shapes*
Euronorm 34–62 1962, *Hot-Rolled Wide-Flange H-Shapes with Parallel Flange Sides*

Ferguson 1974, *The Inter-Relationship of International Material Specifications and Design Codes*
Fiorato 1973a, *Geometric Imperfections in Concrete Structures*
Fiorato 1973b, *Geometric Variations in the Columns of a Precast Concrete Industrial Building*
Fiorato 1973, *Dimensional Tolerance in Concrete*
Fishburn 1961, *Effect of Mortar Properties in Strength of Masonry*

Gage 1972, *Specifications and Use of Ready Mixed Concrete*
Goldbeck 1942, *A Method of Proportioning Concrete for Strength, Workability, and Durability*
Goschy 1974, *Geometric Imperfections*
Gramolin 1972, *Quality Control Criteria*
Green 1958, *The Effects of Porosity on Mild Steel Welds*
Griffith 1920, *The Phenomena of Rupture and Flow in Solids*

Haris, 1972, *Minimum Eccentricity Requirements in the Design of Reinforced Concrete*
Heuschkel 1971, *Anisotropy and Weldablity*
Hinkle 1963, *An Evaluation of Weld Quality as a Cost Factor*
Holm 1972, *Engineered Masonry with High Strength Lightweight Concrete Masonry Units*
Holm 1976, *Block Concrete is a Structural Material*
Holm undated, *Unpublished Data from Experimental Block Runs*
Holm 1973, *Tension Testing of Building Units*

ICBO 1979, *Uniform Building Code*
Isberner 1974, *Properties of Masonry Cement Mortars*
Ishizaki 1977, *On the Design of Glass Pane Against Wind Loading*

Jackson 1973, *Concrete Quality*
Jackson 1974, *Concrete Quality Control*
Janele 1973, *The Check of Alignment of Plane Vertical Elevation Walls*
Johansson 1969, *Deviations of the Location of Reinforcement*
Johnson 1971, *Strength, Safety and Economical Dimensions of Structures*

Kavanagh 1971, *Quality Control*
Kebo 1973, *Some Experience Acquired by Assembly of Steel Structures*
Kesler 1959, *Effect of Length to Diameter Ratio on Compressive Strength*
Kihara 1960, *Relation Between Results of Nondestructive Testing of Materials and Their*
Kishima 1969, *Residual Stresses in Welded Shapes of Flame-Cut Plates in ASTM A572 (50)*

Levelius 1971, *Quality Control*
Lishamer 1977, *Prestressed Concrete Institute Plant Certification Program*
Lorentsen 1971, *Consideration of Imperfections in the Design of Prefabricated Buildings*

Massie 1971, *If You Have Good Concrete, You Can Pump It*
Mayne 1976, *The Response of Glazing to Wind Pressure*
Miki 1971, *Quality Assurance System in Steel Frame Fabrication of Tall Building*
Milner 1971, *Accuracy and its Structural Implications for Load-Bearing Brick Construction*
Minor 1974, *Window Glass in Windstorms*

Morris 1975, *Tall Buildings: Considerations Governing the Choice of Materials and Finishes*

NCMA 1966, *Moisture Content vs. Compressive Strength of Concrete Block*
NCMA 1968, *Specification for the Design and Construction of Load Bearing Concrete*
NCMA 1971, *Special Considerations for Manufacturing High Strength Concrete Masonry*
Nagaraja Rao 1961, *Residual Stresses in Welded Plates*
Nakayama 1970, *Restraint Forces of Welding Joints on Steel Frame Fabrication*
Napper 1973, *Inspection Practices for Tall Buildings*
New York City 1975, *Building Code of the City of New York*
Newman 1959, *Effect on Fatigue Strength of Internal Defects in Welded Joints*
Newman 1965, *Exploratory Fatigue Tests on Transverse Butt Welds Containing Lack of*
Nichols 1940, *Tolerances in Building Construction*

Odar 1967, *Residual Stresses in Rolled Heat-Treated "T-1" Shapes*
Ohba 1971, *A New Concept of Building Frame Production System Intended for Mass Production*
Ohba 1968, *Automation of Manufacturing Process for Steel Structure*

PCI 1977a, *Manual for Quality Control for Plants and Production of Precast Prestressed Concrete*
PCI 1977b, *Manual for Quality Control for Plants and Production of Architectural Precast*
PPG 1979, *Glass Thickness Recommendations to Meet Architects' Specified 1-Minute Wind*
PPG TSR undated a, *Installation Recommendations—Window*
PPG TSR undated b, *Installation Recommendations—Tinted Glass*
Plummer 1953, *Reinforced Brick Masonry and Lateral Force Design*

Randall 1976, *Concrete Masonry Handbook for Architects, Engineers, Builders*
Roberts 1973, *The Effect of Different Test Procedures Upon The Indicated Strength of Concrete*
Rozlivka 1973, *Main Problems of Application of New Steels with Increased Resistance Against*

SAA 1971, *Method of Measurement of Civil Engineering Quantities (Metric Units)*
SAA 1972, *Preferred Sizes of Building Components (Metric Units)*
SAA 1973, *Code of Practice for Installation of Glass in Buildings*
SAA 1974a, *Rules for Brickwork in Buildings (Metric Units)*
SAA 1974b, *Rules for the Design and Application of Metal Arc Welding in Steel Building*
Sahlin 1971, *Imperfections in Structures Constructed with Prefabricated Elements*
Sahlin 1971, *Structural Masonry*
Sakaguchi 1971, *Effect of Weld Thermal Cycles and Stress on Friction Bolts and Surfaces*
Scholes 1975, *Modern Glass Practice*
Self M. W. 1975, *Structural Properties of Load Bearing Concrete Masonry*
Shand 1958, *Glass Engineering Handbook*
Shewhart 1926, *Quality Control Charts*
Stiller 1973, *Quality Control of Concrete in Germany*
Stockbridge 1969, *Quality Control Methods for Masonry Strength*
Szoke 1973, *Quality Control of Buildings of Large Precast Concrete Panels*

Tanaka 1970, *How to Make Production System Effective*
Taneja 1973, *Development of Light Weight Concrete for Multistoried Construction*
Task Group 5, CRC 1971, *Classification of Steel for Structures*
Taylor 1974, *Joints in Multi-Story Steel Framed Buildings*
Timoshenko 1940, *Theory of Plates and Shells*
Tomonaga 1971, *Actually Measured Errors in Fabrication of Kasumigaseki Building*
Tooley 1974, *The Handbook of Glass Manufacture*
Tsai 1976, *Stress Analysis of Large Deflection Glass Plates by the Finite Element Method*

ULI 1978, *Fire Resistance Directory*
USA Federal Safety Standard 16 CFR 1201 1977, *Architectural Glazing Materials*
Urbano 1973, *Load Tests (Gravity Loads) on Buildings*

Van Dobben De Bruyn 1968, *Cumulative Sum Tests: Theory and Practice*
Vorlíček 1976, *Statistical Design of Tolerances of Assembled Structures*

Woodward 1964, *Cumulative Sum Techniques*
Wolovits 1975, *Technical and Economic Considerations Concerning the Influence of Concrete*

Yamaguchi 1968, *Future Prospects for Steel Skeleton Fabrication*
Yokel 1971, *Strength of Masonry Walls Under Compressive and Transverse Loads*

Tall Building Criteria and Loading

Chapter CL-7

Structural Safety and Probabilistic Methods

Prepared by Committee 10 (Structural Safety and Probabilistic Methods) of the Council on Tall Buildings and Urban Habitat as part of the Monograph on the Planning and Design of Tall Buildings.

C. Allin Cornell   Chairman
Luis Esteva   Vice-Chairman
Roberto Meli   Editor

AUTHOR ACKNOWLEDGMENT

Special acknowledgment is due those individuals whose contributions and papers formed the substantial first drafts of the various sections of this chapter. First are the state-of-art reporters from the 1972 International Conference whose material was published in the Lehigh Proceedings. These individuals are:

C. A. Cornell, Section 7.1
H. C. Shah, Section 7.2
C. J. Turkstra, Section 7.2
E. Rosenblueth, Section 7.3
E. Basler, Section 7.4
N. C. Lind, Section 7.4
H. Sandi, Section 7.5
F. Moses, Section 7.6
M. Tichý, Section 7.6
L. Esteva, Section 7.7.

In addition to this, other sections were based on special contributions prepared by the following individuals:

J. R. Benjamin, Section 7.8
L. Esteva, Section 7.8.

CONTRIBUTORS

The following is a complete list of those who have submitted written material for possible use in the chapter, whether or not that material was used in the final version. The Committee Chairman and Editor were given quite complete latitude. Frequently length limitations precluded the inclusion of much valuable material. The Bibliography contains all contributions. The contributors are : A. H-S Ang, A. Baratta, E. Basler, J. R. Benjamin, C. A. Cornell, L. Esteva, G. F. König, A. C. Liebenberg, F. K. Ligtenberg, N. C. Lind, S. E. Magnusson, R. Meli, F. Moses, E. Rosenblueth, H. Sandi, H. C. Shah, M. Tichý, C. J. Turkstra.

COMMITTEE MEMBERS

D. E. Allen, A. H-S Ang, G. Augusti, J. C. Badoux, A. Baratta, E. Basler, J. R. Benjamin, A. Bignoli, J. A. Blume, M. Castanheta, C. A. Cornell, A. G. Davenport, O. De Buen, O. Ditlevsen, L. Esteva, R. Estrada, J. Ferry Borges, T. V. Galambos, J. M. Garrelts, A. M. Hasofer, G. F. König, W. J. LeMessurier, F. Levi, F. K. Ligtenberg, N. C. Lind, S. E. Magnusson, C. Manuzio, R. Meli, F. Moses, J. Murzewski, T. Naka, L. Östlund, J. Parker, L. E. Robertson, E. Rosenblueth, A. R. Rzhanitzyn, H. Sandi, R. G. Sexsmith, H. C. Shah, M. Shinozuka, H. Siebke, J. K. Sridhar Rao, K. Tal (deceased), M. Tichý, J. A. Torroja, C. J. Turkstra, A. A. Van Douwen, E. H. Vanmarcke, J. Witteveen, T. H. Wu, F. Y. Yokel.

CL-7

Structural Safety and Probabilistic Methods

7.1 SCOPE AND OBJECTIVES

1 Guide to this Chapter

This chapter is written to provide an introduction to the probabilistic methodology which is a fast growing part of structural engineering. In some cases probability has been used in detail for years; such specific discussions are left to the appropriate individual chapters elsewhere in this monograph. The most rapidly expanding subject area, however, is the use of probability and statistics in generalized approaches to structural safety. The present growth rate has made it impossible and undesirable to attempt a long-term consensus view of the field; in fact, throughout the process of preparing this chapter, meritorious proposals have continued to arise, and various specific safety checking schemes have found adoption. None can be said to have addressed the tall building uniquely, however.

The chapter is intended primarily to lead the interested engineer into this safety field, guided by a small set of its contemporary contributors. As such, it intentionally retains both the content and style of the individual authors.

Many readers may find a great number of the notions, terminology, and mathematics unfamiliar and challenging (which is not to say inherently difficult). Section 7.2 is specifically designed, however, to introduce some of the elementary tools (all of these concepts are used in other chapters of this monograph). Section 7.3 goes immediately to the issue of code specifications of structural safety, both fundamental questions and practical schemes (schemes which form the bases for many national and international code-making exercises going on in the 1970s). Section 7.4 places engineering safety decisions in the broader economic context that is possible once explicit probabilities have been estimated. Section 7.5 discusses the basic problems underlying load and load combination analysis; specific recommendations for simplified load combination treatment are under widespread development. Section 7.6 introduces system reliability theory as applied to building frames.

Some readers may wish to pass directly to Section 7.7, which provides a more

537

concise summary of the foregoing material plus some added insights. Still others may prefer to jump directly to Section 7.8, which presents in qualitative terms some of the design recommendations and implications that can be anticipated from a thorough probabilistic safety analysis. This last section can be read without reference to the preceding sections.

2   Preliminary Remarks

Safety. Structural safety is not a physical, measurable property. Rather it is a quality one attributes to certain structures or designs for which he has a high confidence that they have been prepared by professionals who are well enough informed about the nature of loads and the behavior of structures to have been sufficiently prudent in their drive to reduce the first cost of the structure. "Sufficiently prudent" implies that they have paid proper respect to the imperfect and incomplete character of all information about loads, materials, and structures.

Probabilistic Methods. The purpose of probabilistic methods is to provide quantitative guidance in achieving structural safety. Probabilities are also not physical, measurable properties. But just as it has helped the gambler and the animal breeder in their professions to *act* as if a coin possessed a probability of coming up heads or a particular pair of cattle a probability of producing a solid brown offspring, so, too, can it help the structural engineer to act as if structural safety can be measured as a probability of satisfactory performance. First, probabilistic methods provide the structural engineering profession with unequivocal means to quantify and transmit among themselves information about the degree of uncertainty in various components of their total problem (see Section 7.2). To be "properly prudent," the designer should be as well informed about the uncertainty as he is about the expected behavior. Secondly, probabilistic methods of structural safety analysis provide the means to operate on this quantitative uncertainty information in a manner which is internally consistent (for example, so that load combinations are treated consistently with individual loads, or so that the reliability of a structural system can be inferred from the information available about the components) (see Sections 7.3, 7.5, 7.6). Finally, decision theoretic probabilistic methods provide means to help the profession or the designer decide what is sufficiently prudent, both in an absolute sense and in a relative sense (that is, for different conditions of the degree of uncertainty or for different consequences of unsatisfactory structural performance, or both—see Section 7.4). In a practical sense, many important aspects of structural safety can, in fact, be quantified with resultant gains in consistency and economy in design.

Probability-Based Design. The goal of probability-based structural design specifications (or formats) is to provide design criteria that are relatively simple to use and that deviate as little as necessary from what a more rigorous, costly reliability analysis would suggest (see Section 7.3). What degree of deviation (to provide appropriate simplicity) is reasonable is a function of the problem at hand. Tall building design, with its higher levels of engineering practice and its more serious consequences (in initial or "expected failure cost") of deviations from the ideal, should not tolerate the simplicity inherent in specifications for lesser design problems (see Section 7.6).

Objectives of this Chapter. It is fully appreciated that "safety" can be improved by more rigid office review of plans, by improved training of construction inspectors, or by literally hundreds of changes in the way a building is designed, constructed, and operated. Specific suggestions of these kinds are the subject of other chapters. Similarly, other chapters will present best the discussions of the potential ways a tall building can "fail" (in a structural or serviceability sense); the critical limit states are compiled in Chapters SB-8 and CB-2.

The function of this chapter has been interpreted as providing background and recommended methodology for improving the way safety is defined, analyzed, and treated in design. Today this purpose implies the introduction of a quantitative (probabilistic) definition of safety together with the requisite forms of information and analysis. In this context, different levels of office plan-checking, quality control, or inspection will, in principle, influence safety through their influence on some component of the uncertainty. Different ways that the structural system might fail represent, in the context of probabilistic safety analysis, different "modes of failure" that must be treated.

3　Present Practice

Uncertainty Reporting. The most common procedures for discussing uncertainty and for providing for it in structural design have severe limitations. These are probably best appreciated by committees or designers charged with coordinating the information provided by individual technical committees or individual specialists into a total set of specifications or a single design. Lacking a single method, the individuals are likely to adopt separate procedures for handling the uncertainty in their particular problems, and different levels of conservatism in presenting their final recommendations. It is a commonly heard complaint in major projects (such as nuclear power plants) that an unknown but large degree of expensive ultra-conservatism has been produced in the final product, simply by the uncontrolled compounding of safety factors that each specialist has used to "protect himself" before transmitting his recommendation upward. It is impossible, for example, to understand how a designer or committee can be expected to coordinate intelligently the use in design of, or the assignment of load factors to, design loads when one technical committee recommends a design load based on a 50-yr return period, another uses the expected lifetime maximum load, and another simply says that "used in conjunction with present design practices, this design load will provide structures which perform satisfactorily." Yet this is effectively the situation in present practice. It is noteworthy, parenthetically, that, while apparently "less scientific," only the last of these three load committee statements recognizes that load and strength committees cannot operate rationally independently of one another. A primary purpose of uncertainty reporting is to permit coordination of these two facets of the total structural design problem.

There is significant room for professional improvement in reporting uncertainty. It is believed that this can be accomplished much more easily now that the profession has reached a stage of maturity in which virtually every technical field has competent specialists who are also trained in probabilistic methods, and in which the appreciation for the advantages of using probabilistic methods to analyze and report engineering problems is more widely spread.

Analysis and Specification of Safety. The analysis of structural safety is an ill-defined process in present conventional practice. The commonly used measure of safety is the safety factor (this is the ratio of yield to allowable stress in working stress design, or the ratio of factored load to design strength in load-factor designs). Under certain circumstances (that is, when enough terms are defined in a common manner) it is possible to rank simple designs with respect to safety by ranking them by the value of their safety factors. The procedure is not valid, however, to compare structures of two even mildly different types: "design strengths" are defined differently for different materials, as are "design loads" for different types of loads; some members are far more sensitive than others to deviations in dimensions from those assumed in analysis; the ratio of dead to live load may influence safety for a fixed safety factor value; "overloads" of a certain percentage are often more likely for earthquake loads than for wind loads; the relationship of structural system safety to cross-section (or component) safety is quite different for ductile, redundant structures from what it is for brittle, determinate structures; etc. The safety factor alone is not a consistent measure of relative safety, much less of absolute safety. There is no guidance given in present literature as to what represents an adequate safety factor, except for that which can be inferred from a general appreciation of past experience with structures built to not dissimilar levels. [We say "general appreciation" because there is, to our knowledge, no systematic documentation, collection, and analysis of observed structural performance (bad or good) under past codes, despite the obvious usefulness such information would have (Lind, 1964).] The safety factor concept only works after the fact; there is no explicit way to extend it into a new situation, which very tall buildings may well represent. These criticisms are true of any procedure of safety analysis or specification which does not include a systematic way to derive safety factors or load factors from information about the degree of uncertainty in the components of the structural design problem.

It is believed that schemes are now available which represent a significant improvement upon present practice (see Section 7.3). These are schemes which coordinate reported information about uncertainty and about structural behavior of members and systems into quantitative measures of structural safety. These procedures employ axiomatic probability theory, which guarantees that the component information is being treated consistently and rigorously to produce system information. Guidance is available, too, as to what absolute levels these safety measures (probabilities) should have. Finally, with respect to implementation, a spectrum of degrees of accuracy (versus simplicity in application) is available, ranging down to the level where the schemes simply provide formulas for specifying how the values of load factors in a CEB/ISO-like format should be selected for a particular limit state, as a function of the component uncertainty levels and the desired safety level (that is, the semiprobabilistic format is retained but a fully probabilistic scheme is used to implement it). It seems appropriate in light of the potential consequences of overconservative or unconservative design of tall buildings that efforts be made to move towards taking advantage of these improvements.

4 Information Needed for Improved Safety Analyses and Specifications

Since in design application these methods need be no more difficult to use than modern present (limit state) methods, the major requirement for application of these improved methods is the availability (in proper form) of the profession's information. This is not to repeat the oft-heard statement that probabilistic methods will not be useful until more statistical data are collected. (Design proceeds now without these data; it must be possible to do at least as well in the future without them.) Rather it is saying that the information available to the profession at any point in time should be reported by appropriate specialists in a way that transmits not only their recommendations as to how to predict some phenomenon, but also the degree of uncertainty one faces when making the prediction. These two items are the total information that is best known by the specialist committees and that is needed by designers and code-coordinating committees.

At any point in time the uncertainty associated with making a prediction is made up of uncertainty both in the values of the independent variables in the prediction algorithm and in the algorithm itself. So, for example, a design recommendation for predicting the maximum (pseudostatic) wind pressures on a tall building contains uncertainty both in the independent variables, such as the maximum (20-min mean) wind velocity that will occur, and in the procedure itself. The procedure or algorithm is the set of assumptions, equations, graphs, definitions, etc., that the designer is to use. Because of man's incomplete understanding of the phenomena involved and because of intentional simplifications in the procedure recommended for design, the procedure for converting wind velocity to pseudostatic pressure is imperfect; the ratio of observed to algorithm-predicted (pseudostatic) wind pressures will not be unity for every building and storm to which the method is applied (given the value of the independent variable, wind velocity), as it would be if the algorithm were perfect. Rather, there will be dispersion in the observations of this ratio. In design, this uncertainty in the algorithm is indistinguishable from that in the wind velocity itself. Both can be investigated, measured, and reported in statistical terms. Estimating the means, standard deviations, and distribution shapes of wind velocities (as a function of geographical location) is no more nor less difficult than estimating similar parameters for the algorithm "error" (as a function, perhaps, of building types)(Vickery, 1971). Data and professional judgment play an important role in both situations; lacking sufficient or satisfactory direct data, it may be necessary to base the parameter estimates largely on professional experience in related situations.

In this context it is perfectly meaningful (and perhaps necessary) to estimate the probability that an airplane will strike a tall building located in Brussels even though our present data are limited to a single incident in New York, nearly 30 years ago. The fact that data are so limited makes the estimate a gross judgment; this fact (this uncertainty) can be expressed by defining the "true" probability as a random variable, of which the "estimate" represents a mean value, and of which the assigned probability distribution represents the degree of uncertainty one has in the probability estimate. So, too, it becomes reasonable to report (without, perhaps, any observations of continuously monitored rooms) that a committee estimates that the expected value (mean) of the maximum lifetime gravity live load in a typical bay of a tall building is 200 kg/m^2 (40 psf), and that this maximum load has Type I Extreme Value distribution with a coefficient of variation of 15%. In addition, they might report that owing to poor information they are uncertain about the true mean; this collective uncertainty can be expressed by assigning the mean itself a distribution [say, normal with expectation 200 kg/m^2(40 psf) and standard deviation 50 kg/m^2(10 psf)]. Similar statements might be made about the coefficient of variation and even the distribution type of the maximum lifetime load. Future data might (or might not) confirm their estimate of the mean, reducing the value 10 to near zero. These statements about the bay to bay ("objective") variability in load and about the committee's present state of ("subjective") uncertainty as to the parameter values in their model of live load represent the state of the profession's information about the subject.

The degree of variability and of professional uncertainty both represent information of value to designers or code committees. The information is, in these ways, reported directly and explicitly without bias. In addition, it is reported in a manner which can be operated on by the simple but consistent rules of axiomatic probability theory in order to learn its implications upon the uncertainty in total structural performance. Axiomatic theory does not distinguish between the "objectivity" or "subjectivity" of the probability assignments; it simply operates on them in a consistent manner.

What is needed both to enhance the completeness of the knowledge available to the profession as a whole, and to implement improved safety analysis methods, then, is not so much more data as more information. In particular, it is needed about the degree of uncertainty faced, where this uncertainty may include the lack of sufficient data. Information about uncertainty is properly expressed by probability assignments, or, at a minimum, by coefficients of variation [that is, as percentages of the best estimate (see Section 7.3)]. The only concept which may be new is the use of probability to quantify uncertainty which cannot be interpreted in relative frequency terms, but only in subjective or "degree-of-belief" terms. It may take time and experience before engineers are as comfortable with this concept as they are now with probabilistic definitions of wind or snow loads, and before appropriate schemes for assessing these probabilities are well developed. In the meantime, "best estimates" and judgments represent a start in the proper direction. In this regard probabilistic approach to safety should be looked upon as a consistent framework that allows the improvement of codes as our estimates of uncertainties are updated. Bayes' influence rules can be used for that purpose. Therefore, usefulness of probabilistic criteria is not limited to immediate changes in design rules: what is important is that a rational basis be provided for the evolution of codes with the ever-growing details of experience.

5   Safety and Serviceability Analyses

Within the discipline of probabilistic structural safety analysis, the need is recognized to identify the various events that might lead to some cost or "disutility" to occupier, owner, or designer (see Section 7.3). Therefore, one must identify carefully the various potential modes of structural behavior with respect to both serviceability and structural failure. Methods of predicting this performance as a function of independent variables such as loads and resistances form the basis for reliability analysis (see Section 7.6). The identification of failure modes and procedures (such as statics, etc.) of predicting performance may not differ in probabilistic analyses from those used in conventional structural design. The former analyses, however, model the independent variables as random variables. The output of the analysis includes estimated probabilities of occurrence of these events. The methods for carrying out these analyses efficiently are by no means fully developed for all building problems, tall or otherwise (Ferry Borges, 1971). Nonetheless it does not appear that any new kinds of reliability analyses or difficulties will arise in tall buildings (see Section 7.6).

The question of scale, however, may suggest that approximate methods of safety analysis which were considered accurate for smaller structures will no longer be appropriate in tall buildings. For example, in certain circumstances the failure probabilities of modes of failure can be added to estimate the failure probability of the structural system. For tall buildings, the number of such modes (that is, critical cross sections) may be so large as to make this sum an inaccurate estimate (even to the point that it exceeds unity). Similarly, neglected modes of failure or simplifications in structural behavior previously assumed in reliability analysis may no longer be adequate approximations for tall buildings, complicating the safety analysis.

Methods of safety specification which have not proved inadequate for simpler structures may prove inappropriate for tall buildings. For example, most load-factor methods emphasize in effect the safety of cross sections or members, as opposed to that of structural systems. It is an elementary principle of reliability engineering (appreciated years ago by the electronics and aerospace industries) that larger systems are less reliable than smaller systems (of equal component or member reliability). This simple conclusion holds without qualification, however, only when the components are not redundant and when the component failure events are not correlated. Neither condition holds in tall ductile frames under environmental loads (see Section 7.6). Intelligent treatment in analysis and in safety specifications of system (versus simply component) reliability may prove both important and relatively difficult.

Another safety issue that present safety specifications often do not reflect, but that is critical in tall buildings, is the difference in consequences of failure that will arise in different failure events. By any reasoning, formal or informal, lower story columns in tall buildings should, for example, be designed more conservatively than upper story columns. Safety specifications that do not distinguish between these two cases are presumably inconsistent (either too conservative in one case or unconservative in the other). The differences in consequences are more extreme the taller the building.

6 Summary

Probabilistic methods can improve upon presently used schemes for safety analysis and specification, without significant change in complexity of application. Such new methods should be considered for more important structures such as tall buildings, as well as more conventional design. The newer methods require more information (but not necessarily more statistical data) from individual committees, namely quantitative measures of uncertainty. This information should be reported about the design procedures recommended as well as about the important design variables. Tall building safety analyses should prove no different in kind from those for conventional design, although the greater structural complexity and the greater extremes in importance of certain members may demand more accurate methods.

7.2 ASSESSING AND REPORTING UNCERTAINTIES

Many seemingly different problems encountered in an assessment of the safety and serviceability of tall buildings are in reality very closely related. By means of established methods of probability theory, a consistent basis for uncertainty analysis can be established.

Perhaps the most elementary problem involving uncertainty is prediction of physical quantities, such as steel yield point or concrete crushing strength. Uncertainty in such cases simply means that repeated measurements have not been identical. As a result one can only state a probability that the design quantity will be equal to each of the several possible numerical values.

A somewhat more complex problem is encountered when the value of a design quantity depends on other uncertain design parameters such as, for example, the ultimate moment capacity of underreinforced concrete beams. In laboratory tests beam depth to reinforcement d, steel yield point f_y, and concrete strength f'_c, are measured and so are known. The relationship between moment capacity and these quantities has been established except for a random experimental or equation error. Moment capacity is then uncertain even under laboratory conditions.

In design all of d, f_y, and f'_c are uncertain or random variables and the uncertainty in moment capacity in a real structure is greater than the uncertainty in laboratory tests. The equation error must be combined with the uncertainties in the basic parameters to establish a statement of the probability of all possible values of real moment capacity.

Structural design would be of limited interest if only such simple uncertainties were involved. Clearly this is not the case since "theoretical results are a vague and approximate image of physical reality. We come nearer to this reality only by adding the results of experiments to the mathematical results, by observing the actual phenomena, by establishing a conceptual basis for these phenomena, and above all by understanding intuitively the static behaviour of our works" (Nervi, 1956).

Paraphrasing this statement in probabilistic terms one can say that there are many uncertainties associated with existing theories of structural response. To evaluate the total uncertainty in structural behavior, a conceptual basis for prediction must be established and judgment must be used to evaluate the uncertainties inherent in analysis.

In this section some basic concepts and methods of uncertainty analysis are represented through simple illustrative examples. In each case the objective of analysis is a measure of the probabilities that each possible value of a design variable will occur or the probability distribution of the variable. Since engineering judgment and a variety of conceptual models are admitted in analysis, unique final statements of uncertainty are not to be expected. The aim of this report is to suggest to those concerned with load, strength, and structural analysis how they might approach a rational analysis of at least some of the uncertainties they encounter.

1   One Variable Problems

As a simple example involving a single random variable, consider the problem of aircraft collisions with a tall building. A reasonable approach is to assume that a collision can occur in any year with probability q and that the probability of more than one collision in any year is negligible. A variety of random variables can be defined for such a problem, but perhaps the most useful is the number of collisions which occur during a specified lifetime of Nyr. Denoting this variable X, it is readily shown that its distribution $p(x)$ is binomial (Benjamin and Cornell, 1970). Thus

$$p(x) = \frac{N!}{x!(N-x)!} q^x (1-q)^{N-x} \tag{7.1}$$

If collisions occur on average once every 50 yr, $q = 0.02$. The probability of, for example, no collisions in 10 yr ($x = 0$) is 0.806. One of the relatively unusual features of this problem is that the uncertainty in the random variable is completely described by a single probability measure q.

A somewhat more difficult problem is prediction of the strength of glass. Repeated measurements of plate glass of a particular thickness and size suggest that the probability $P(g)$ of glass failure at a stress less than any value G can be adequately represented by (Frownfelter, 1959)

$$P(g) = \frac{1}{1865\sqrt{2\pi}} \int_{-\infty}^{g} \exp\left[-\frac{1}{2}\left(\frac{t - 8400}{1865}\right)^2 \right] dt \tag{7.2}$$

Unlike the preceding descrete random variable, the strength variable G is continuous since it can assume any value within an interval.

Eq. 7.2 indicates that the uncertainty in glass strength is completely characterized by a particular mathematical expression involving two constants—8400 psi and 1865 psi. These constants have been estimated from experimental data using conventional statistical methods (Benjamin and Cornell, 1970). In this particular case, the constants correspond to the mean or expected value $E(G)$ and standard deviation $\sigma(G)$. In this case the mean is also the most likely value and the value with a 50% chance of being exceeded. The mean and variance or square of the standard deviation are generally called the first and second moments in safety analysis.

In general, the mean of a random variable is a measure of the central tendency of the variable, while the variance is a measure of the relative probability of values removed from the mean. Thus, for example, in this case, the breaking strength exceeded 95% of the time is equal to 5300 psi. Alternatively the probability of any strength less than g is measured indirectly by the quantity $(g - 8400)/1865$, because if the value of this quantity is known, one can enter a table to find the probability.

Several important points concerning the distribution of Eq. 7.2 should be made. First, the mathematical form of Eq. 7.2, the so-called normal distribution, is used only because it fits the data reasonably well and is mathematically simple. Many other distributions, such as extreme value distributions, should be and are used in other situations. The normal distribution is obviously not completely valid in this case since negative strengths are not physically possible.

More importantly however, it should be noted that the uncertainty in breaking stress cannot be characterized by a single fractile such as the value exceeded 95% of the time. To demonstrate this point, consider two glass types whose strength have means 8500 psi and 9300 psi, and standard deviations 1500 psi and 2000 psi, respectively. In both cases a strength of 6000 psi is exceeded 95% of the time or they have the same 5% fractile.

But, as shown in Fig. 7.1, if these two glass types are subjected to a wind pressure causing a stress below 6000 psi the glass with the smaller mean strength is less likely to fail or is safer. If a stress greater than 6000 psi is applied the other glass type is safer. If a random wind pressure is applied, the probability of failure depends on both the mean and variance of glass strength.

It can be generally concluded that rational uncertainty analysis requires at least two measures for almost every random variable capable of assuming more than two numerical values. The most meaningful and useful uncertainty measures for general use are probably means and variances.

As a final example involving one random variable, consider prediction of the width of a concrete beam in a structure. In this case few data are available and uncertainty must be estimated from judgment. Although procedures have been suggested for assigning complete probability distributions to all possible values of beam width, the numerical precision of individual judgment probably does not justify complex analysis. Estimation of means and variances or means and selected fractiles probably represents the limit of realistic analysis. If only two uncertainties measures are established, statements of the probability of various values of a random variable must be approximate.

Mean values can be realistically estimated since they are approximately most likely values or 50% fractiles of a variable, but estimation of variance is somewhat more difficult. Some guidance can be obtained from the observation that traditional minimum values often have approximately a 1% to 5% chance of not being exceeded. Maximum values have the same order of probability of being exceeded. One convention that has been suggested is to assume that values judged to be very unlikely or to have odds of approximately 50 to 1 of being exceeded be taken as two standard deviations above the mean.

In estimating uncertainty measures, the traditional concept of conservative bias can be adopted in a modified form. In practice, variances can be overestimated and means can be underestimated or overestimated depending on whether small values or large values reduce over-all safety. Alternatively, uncertainty in estimation of moments can be incorporated directly, as shown in the next section.

If only the mean and variance of a variable are known, loads with approximately equal chance of being exceeded are the same number of standard deviations above their means. Similarly, strengths a constant number of standard deviations below the means have approximately the same probability of being exceeded. This consideration has led to the use of so-called characteristic values in the CEB/ISO code format (Ferry Borges and Castanheta, 1971).

2 Two Variable Problems

In the design of tall buildings against wind forces, both wind velocity and direction must be considered. The corresponding random variables must be considered together since the probability distribution of one depends on the value of

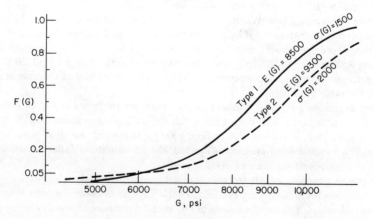

Fig. 7.1 Two glass types with common 5% fractile value but different safety levels at other stresses

the other. A complete uncertainty measure consists of a function $p(V,D)$ assigning a probability to every combination of wind velocity V, and direction D.

Two distributions of each variable arise in such problems: single variable or marginal distributions such as $f_v(v)$, which is the distribution of velocity considered separately, and conditional distributions such as $f_{V|D}(v,d)$, which is the distribution of wind velocity given the wind direction. As well as the usual moments such as $E(V)$, $E(D)$, $Var(V)$, $Var(D)$ there are the expected values and variances of one variable given the other variable, $E(V|D)$, $Var(V|D)$, $E(D|V)$, and $Var(V|D)$. There is also the correlation coefficient $\rho_{V,D}$ which measures the dependence of the two variables. In general, conditional moments such as $D(V|D)$ are functions of the given value of the second variable. At least 5 parameters (2 means, 2 variances, and the correlation coefficient) are required to characterize the uncertainty in two related variables.

The concept of conditional probabilities is of vital importance in uncertainty analysis. Applications include the assessment of uncertainty in real stresses given calculated stresses, real strength given calculated strength, real dimensions given drawing dimensions, and real deflections given calculated effects.

In fact every probability statement is a conditional statement. For example, Eq. 7.1 is the probability of x collisions given the parameter q. Similarly, Eq. 7.2 is the probability of glass strength given the constants 8400 psi and 1865 psi and that the distribution is normal. Recognizing the conditional nature of probability statement such as Eq. 7.2, one can immediately include in analysis uncertainty in the uncertainty measures themselves.

Suppose in the glass strength situation that instead of estimating E_G or μ_G to be exactly equal to 8400, it is assumed that μ_G itself is uncertain with moments $E(\mu_G) = 8400$ psi and $Var(\mu_G) = (500)^2$. It follows from Eq. 7.2 that $E(G|\mu_G) = \mu_G$ and $Var(G|\mu_G) = (1865)^2$. Using the general result in Eq. 7.101 of the Appendix it also follows that $E(X) = 8400$ psi and $Var(X) = (1865)^2 + (500)^2$. The differences between the two variances indicate that uncertainty in μ_G increases the uncertainty in glass strength.

As mentioned previously, conditional operations also provide a procedure for transferring laboratory or theoretical results to conditions in a real structure. Let us suppose, for example, that the drift of a tall structure is calculated using conventional structural analysis with all stiffness properties and the form of the pressure distribution assumed known. The only variable explicitly assumed random is the peak annual wind velocity V. The calculated maximum annual drift D_e is a known (assumed) function of wind speed and the uncertainty parameters $E(D_e)$ and $Var(D_e)$ can be estimated using the methods of the next section. The uncertainty parameters $E(D_r)$ and $Var(D_r)$ of the real maximum annual drift D_r must be estimated.

Suppose now that it is judged that the most likely value of D_r is the calculated value D_e and the coefficient of variation of D_r given D_e is 0.1. The latter statement can be taken to mean that the real drift is the calculated drift plus or minus 20%. Using Eqs. 7.102, the moments of real drift are simply $E(D_r) = E(D_e)$, and $Var(D_r) = 0.01E^2(D_e) + 1.01 \, Var(D_e)$. As expected, the total uncertainty in real drift is greater than that in calculated drift. The probability of any real drift D_r is measured by the difference between D_r and $E(D_r)$ divided by the standard deviation of D_r.

The relative dependence of random variables is also of great importance. To demonstrate this, consider the total yield force of two apparently identical bars in a concrete beam. The total yield force is simply the sum of the yield forces of the two bars (Benjamin and Cornell, 1970). Denoting the total force F and the yield forces of the two bars as F_1 and F_2, consider two cases. In one case the two yield forces are independent random variables, or a knowledge of one force does not affect the uncertainty in the other. Using Eqs. 7.103, the mean and variance of total force are then $E(F) = 2E(F_1) = 2E(F_2)$, and $\text{Var}(F) = 2\text{Var}(F_1) = 2\text{Var}(F_2)$. In the second case, the two yield forces are completely dependent and identical, or if one bar force is known the other is also known. The moments of total force are then $E(F) = 2E(F_1)$, and $\text{Var}(F) = 4\text{Var}(F_1)$. The first case has less variance than the second case and so involves less uncertainty.

In reality one would expect a strong dependence in strength of two bars of the same area in a single beam. However, bar strengths in different structures could be assumed completely independent.

3   Equations and Algorithms—Uncertainties

Most design problems involve a variety of random variables which are related through equations that have been tested experimentally or through analytic procedures or design algorithms. As an example, consider the superposition of stresses in the ground floor columns of an N-story structure due to occupancy loads. The total calculated load effect L_e can be written for a simple case in the form

$$L_e = \sum_{i=1}^{N} L_i \tag{7.3}$$

in which L_i = effect of the load on the ith floor. Load effects depend on geometry and elastic properties, which are usually assumed known, and the intensity of live loading on the ith floor, which is assumed random. Implicit in this formulation is an assumed load pattern.

With the reasonable assumption that live loads on one floor do not affect loads on any other, or that the L_i are independent, the moments of calculated total load effects are, from Eq. 7.103

$$E(L_e) = \sum_{i=1}^{N} E(L_i) \tag{7.4a}$$

$$\text{Var}(L_e) = \sum_{i=1}^{N} \text{Var}(L_i) \tag{7.4b}$$

The moments measure the uncertainty in total calculated load at any particular time during the life of the structure.

An important property of load superposition can be shown by examining a special case in which all $\text{Var}(L_i)$ are equal and the variance of calculated load is thus $N\,\text{Var}(L_i)$. If characteristic or maximum loads are defined to be two standard deviations above the means, maximum values of the individual floor loads are simply

$$\text{Max}(L_i) = E(L_i) + 2\sigma(L_i) \tag{7.5}$$

and the maximum total calculated load effect with the same probability of being exceeded is

$$\text{Max}(L_e) = \sum_{i=1}^{N} E(L_i) + 2\sqrt{N}\,\sigma(L_i) \tag{7.6}$$

If instead total load were computed by adding the effects of maximum floor loads, maximum total load would be estimated by

$$\text{Max}(L_e) = \sum_{i=1}^{N} E(L_i) + 2N\sigma(L_i) \tag{7.7}$$

which is significantly greater than the result of Eq. 7.6. The total load of Eq. 7.7 has a much smaller probability of being exceeded than the maximum floor loads of Eq. 7.6.

As a general rule, one can say that the 95% fractile, for example, of the sum of random variables is less than the sum of the 95% fractiles of the variables. This fact is widely recognized in tall building design and results from the fact that extreme values of all loads are very unlikely to occur at the same time.

Having the parameters of calculated load effects, real load effects L_r can be estimated in several ways. First, conditional operations can be used as in the drift example of the preceding article by estimating $E(L_r|L_e)$ and Var $(L_r|L_e)$ and using Eqs. 7.101 and 7.102. A second approach is to define a new random variable ϕ_1 by the relationship

$$L_r = \phi_1 L_e \tag{7.8}$$

in which the variable ϕ_1 = ratio of real to calculated load effects. In reality one would expect ϕ_1 to depend on L_e because of unknown systematic errors in analytical procedures, material properties, and load idealizations. Since such errors are unknown however, ϕ_1 can be assumed independent of L_e and the parameters of ϕ_1 can be estimated. If the calculated load effect is unbiased, the expected value of ϕ_1 is 1.0. Eqs. 7.104 lead to

$$E(L_r) = E(L_e) = \bar{L}_e \tag{7.9a}$$

$$\text{Var}(L_r) = \bar{L}_e^2 \text{Var}(\phi_1) + \text{Var}(L_e) + \text{Var}(\phi_1)\,\text{Var}(L_e) \tag{7.9b}$$

for the uncertainty parameters of real load effects.

As an alternative to the assumed form of Eq. 7.8, real effects might be estimated by a relationship of the form

$$L_r = L_e + \phi_2 \tag{7.10}$$

The moments of L_r can now be estimated from Eqs. 7.103 after the parameters of ϕ_2 are established.

A different approach to estimating L_e in linear analysis would be to express the real load effect in the form

$$L_e = \sum_{i=1}^{N} \alpha_i L_i \tag{7.11}$$

in which the α_i = uncertain functions of geometry and material properties and the L_i represent the magnitudes of floor loads. The preceding procedures are obtained if all α_i are assumed known to establish L_e, and then the uncertainties in all α_i are considered at once by operating on L_e to obtain L_r. Alternatively, one can introduce the uncertainties in α_i by estimating $E(\alpha_i)$ and $\mathrm{Var}(\alpha_i)$. Assuming α_i and L_i to be independent random variables, L_r is the sum of simple products and so has moments

$$E(L_r) = \sum_{i=1}^{N} E(\alpha_i)\, E(L_i) \tag{7.12a}$$

$$\mathrm{Var}(L_r) = \sum_{i=1}^{N} E^2(\alpha_i)\, \mathrm{Var}(L_i) + \sum_{i=1}^{N} E^2(L_i)\, \mathrm{Var}(\alpha_i) + \sum_{i=1}^{N} \mathrm{Var}(\alpha_i)\, \mathrm{Var}(L_i) \tag{7.12b}$$

from Eqs. 7.104 and 7.103.

A more complex situation arises when time-dependent loads of different types are superimposed. When superimposing wind loads and occupancy loads, for example, the fact that annual maximum loads are unlikely to occur on the same day must be considered. Some preliminary analyses of this problem have been attempted (Ferry Borges and Castanheta, 1971; Turkstra, 1969), but no agreement on procedure has been reached.

In general, design equations are not simple sums, and products and approximate methods must be used to estimate uncertainty parameters. A procedure involving only the first partial derivatives of a general function $F(X_1, X_2, \ldots X_n)$ and the means and variances of the random variables $X_1 \ldots X_n$ is detailed in the Appendix.

As an example, consider the moment capacity M of an underreinforced concrete beam which depends on the variable of the form $Q = A_s F_y / B D F_c$, in which the independent variables are various dimensions and materials strengths. In experimental tests B, D, F_y, and F_c and hence Q are known. The moment capacity M given these parameters can then be written

$$\frac{M}{B, D, F_c, Q} = \phi B D^2 F_c Q (1 - 0.59Q) \tag{7.13}$$

in which ϕ = random variable representing the spread of test results about theoretical values. The mean and standard variation of ϕ are approximately 1.13 and 0.11, respectively (Turkstra, 1969).

In design D, F_y, and F_c as well as ϕ must be considered uncertain with means $E(D)$, $E(F_y)$, $E(F_c)$, $E(\phi)$ and coefficients of variation V_D, V_{F_y}, V_{F_c}, and V_ϕ, respectively. Using the methods of Eq. 7.106, which assumes the variables to be independent, an estimate of the mean of real moment capacity is

$$E(M) = 1.13 B E(D)^2 E(F_c) E(Q)[1 - 0.59E(Q)] \tag{7.14}$$

in which

$$E(Q) = \frac{A_s}{B E(D)} \frac{E(F_y)}{E(F_c)}.$$

The coefficient of variation of real moment capacity is approximately given by

$$V_M^2 = V_\phi^2 + \frac{V_D^2 + [0.59E(Q)V_{F_c}]^2 + \{[1 - 1.18E(Q)]V_{F_y}\}^2}{[1 - 0.59E(Q)]^2} \tag{7.15}$$

The dependence of V_M on $E(Q)$ suggests that in design moment capacity should also depend on $E(Q)$.

A similar analysis has been made by Vickery (1971) to assess the variability of gust loading factors. The mean and variance of nine factors affecting gust loads were considered.

It is important to realize the approximate nature of all such operations. The general result of Eq. 7.105 is completely valid only for relatively flat functions. For other types of functions a consistent but approximate assessment of uncertainty is obtained. If the distributions of all random variables are known, a more reliable estimate of the uncertainty of a function can be obtained from Monte Carlo methods.

4 General Uncertainty Analysis

The preceding examples and the analytical methods summarized in the Appendix are special cases of a general approach to uncertainty assessment which consists of the following steps:

1. All physical variables affecting safety and serviceability are identified and their probability distributions estimated. In the absence of data, only means and variances are estimated. The dependence or independence of all variables should be examined. A rational combination of load and resistance uncertainties to assess over-all safety and serviceability is not possible unless at least two uncertainty measures of every relevant random variable are given.

2. The total uncertainty in calculated design quantities is assessed by combining uncertainties in the variables affecting the design quantity. Rules for computing means and variances of simple sum and product forms are given by Eqs. 7.103 and 7.104. An approximate method for more complex functions is given by Eq. 7.105.

3. Real load effects and strength can be estimated from calculated values by conditional operations Eqs. 7.100, 7.101, 7.102, or by setting up conceptual models such as the simple form of Eq. 7.8 or simple summation form of Eq. 7.104. Such models and the uncertainty measures involved must be established from judgment.

More detailed methods are presently being developed to evaluate the practicality of the suggested procedures in particular problems in tall building design.

7.3   CODE SPECIFICATION OF SAFETY AND SERVICEABILITY

The main purpose of building codes should be the maximization of utility from the standpoint of society. This statement is nearly a tautology. Yet contemporary codes do not seem to fulfill their paramount role, for they deal with optimization in indirect and cryptic ways. Actually the time is not ripe for complete, explicit formats of reliability optimization. Given the restraints, present-day codes do, in general terms, approximately accomplish the stated objective, and there is an evolutionary trend toward the direct attack on optimization. An approach to building code optimization has been advanced by Ravindra and Lind (1971) and Lind (1971a).

In order meaningfully to describe the state of the art it is necessary to examine the shape that a long-range goal of the building code format can take as well as strategies available to reach the goal.

These views on the matter apply to code provisions on the design of buildings in general. Some details to be discussed later pertain chiefly or exclusively to tall buildings.

1   The Goal

It is well to examine the opening sentence of this section.

Code Objectives. It speaks about the *main* purpose of codes because there should be other objectives. The outstanding secondary objectives are: (1) Educational; and (2) the definition of legal and moral responsibilities. Both objectives are closely related to the central purpose.

The educational function of codes tends to simplify their enforcement. In cases when a code is not enforced, this role modifies established practice making it approach the practice that would ensue from systematic code enforcement.

Definition of legal responsibilities increases the efficacy of code enforcement, while definition of moral responsibilities increases the degree to which a code is applied when not enforced.

Society. The word society in that sentence is open to interpretation. The fact that codes are usually issued by municipal governments suggests that society, in this sense, is made up exclusively of the city inhabitants. Yet, in countries where there is a marked difference in the standards of living in the main city and in the rest of the nation, it may not be wise to base the estimate of utility on the sole preferences of those who dwell in the city; and for reasons of ethics as well as of wisdom it is proper to take into account the interests of the entire human race and of future as well as present generations (Churchman, 1968), without unbalancing the issue to the point of making the code seem disloyal to those who expect to be served by it. The same reasoning applies, and more dramatically so, to differences between various quarters of a city that is to be ruled by a single code.

These differences may not be apparent when the question is viewed in the light of traditional building codes, in which required levels of safety have been dogmatically made to look like absolute standards. The matter becomes clear in the framework of optimization. For example, there are indications that the amount society is willing to pay to save an anonymous human life is the present value of the average individual's expected contribution to the gross national product during the rest of his life (Ackoff, undated). Evidently this amount may be quite different depending on the group of people from which the average individual is to be taken and on the time when one is to look at his expected contribution to gross national product, particularly in a country whose per capita product is increasing at an appreciable rate.

Negative Utility Associated with Nonmaterial Losses. The amount that society will pay to save a human life can be rationalized on the ground that society must be willing to give all its resources to save the lives of all its members; under the assumption of a linear relation between expenditure and number of lives saved, one arrives at the figure quoted. However, at least in the range of one to a hundred human lives lost in a single event, society reacts in a markedly nonlinear fashion (Lind and Basler, 1972). There is room for more study to elucidate the relations between the intensity of society's reactions to human losses and how much it is willing to spend in order to prevent them, as well as between the behavior of society and the expected wellbeing of future generations; in other words, to elucidate the relations between what the present generation wishes, what is good for it, and what is ethical.

A vigorous current opposes the treatment of loss of human lives as negative utility and favors the use of a restriction limiting the expected death rate per unit time to values appreciably below those associated with normal activities. Thus one would strive for optimization without counting losses associated with deaths, but introducing as restriction the condition that the risk function not exceed a specified value or that the failure probability over a period of, say, 30 yr not exceed some limit.

Some objections can be raised to this second viewpoint. For example, structural systems are conceivable in which a minor expenditure can bring the expected toll per unit time much below the allowable limit; however, such solutions will not be adopted unless one deals explicitly with the corresponding savings to society. Still, as will be seen, there are other reasons in favor of having the next generation of building codes contain reliability limitations, in the form of design restrictions.

Several of the foregoing considerations can be made is connection with other "intangible" losses, associated with physical injury to human beings, loss of prestige of those participating in the conception and execution of a structure, esthetic questions, architectural functioning, degree of light exposure, and so on.

Building Code Committee. Since social groups other than the voters in the city are to be reckoned with, the adoption of code provisions by direct referendum will not do. It must also be discarded, of course, for reasons of expediency. On the other hand, the advantages of the voting process as a source of information, feedback, and control should not be lightly cast aside. In view of these considerations, practically the only operative scheme seems to lie in the setting up of an interdisciplinary committee formed by specialists elected periodically by popular vote and faced with the possibility of reelection.

It might be argued that the present state of affairs does not differ substantially from the proposed solution. After all, in democratic countries most municipal governments are elected by local inhabitants and usually one of the series of acts whereby these governments are judged concerns the drafting, adoption, and implementation of building codes. But these acts are a minor part of their entire activity. It is no doubt desirable to disengage building code questions from the other, mostly political, actions involved in government.

The committee would include at least an architect, an engineer, an economist, and an urban sociologist, as there is little justification for engineers to be the only authorized interpreters of the wishes of local and distant, present and future communities. Nonengineers would be the interpreters of these wishes while engineers would draft code provisions to attain the corresponding, optimum, degrees of safety; engineers would also be in charge of controlling the application of safety provisions. Each member of the committee holds office for one year, say, with an unlimited number of possible reelections. In a large city the committee's task would be confined to proposing changes in the code, establishing general criteria for its interpretation, and intervening in special instances.

Some countries adopt national rather than municipal building codes. The corresponding committees would obviously have modalities differing somewhat from those described in the foregoing paragraph. Among other tasks the national committees would establish regional differences in code requirements as a function of social, economic, climatic, meterologic, geologic, and geotectonic characteristics.

Ideal Code Format. It is clear that attempts at indirect ways of attaining optimum design require an impractical array of obscure and inaccurate adjustments in design loads, design material strengths, coefficients, and formulas for design. This is true of the use of characteristic values, load factors, design seismic coefficients, and wind pressures, etc. Even formulas that produce approximately optimum results for the design of individual structural members or sections of these members are inadequate for the design of structural systems when the formulas do not deal explicitly with reliability optimization. The code should contain clauses leading to the calculation of the optimum values of design parameters, as this will allow benefiting from the engineer's loyalty to society; by knowing which is society's optimum solution he will often tend to approach it, although it will usually differ from the owner's optimal. The code should also include clauses leading to the calculation of those values of the parameters for which society breaks even between building the project in question and investing in common stock. The ranges between these values of the parameters mark the conditions under which it is worth erecting the building from society's standpoint. There may be an overlap with a similar range for the owner; if and only if this is the case is the building to be erected. These matters are shown schematically in Fig. 7.2.

In contrast with present codes the ideal format should specify upper as well as lower bounds on safety and serviceability. Also, since the range of costs is often wider in architectural items than in structures, the code should set limits on such concepts as luxury. It should include standards on functioning as well. Compared with present formats, this type of specifications will sound excessively restrictive of individual liberties. But in comparison with other measures that tend to protect the economy of capitalist countries, it is not farfetched that codes include provisions tending to limit the amount of money that individuals bury in foundations and building materials. Nevertheless, when the time draws near to the drafting of building codes having the format advocated here, variations in wording will probably be found advisable to fit the political style of different countries.

In the realm of construction tolerances on geometry, strength, and other material properties, the usual practice forbids construction that violates specified limits. This leads to the replacement or strengthening of portions of the structure that do not meet the tolerances, which often works against the interests of owner, contractor, and society. In many cases a more satisfactory solution from all points of view consists in penalizing the price of the defective portions of a structure and, under certain circumstances, adding a (very small) bonus when the quality of a structural portion is above standard. This approach has been worked out, under some simplifying assumptions, for the price of concrete (Rosenblueth et al., 1974). The penalty and bonus are a function of the cylinder strengths and are computed so that the owner's utility is not appreciably affected by failure to meet the specified strength. Of course, when the penalty is very large it is preferable to replace or strengthen the structural portion in question.

A similar approach could be successful in future building codes in connection with serviceability as well as with meeting the specified concrete strength, thus replacing clauses that merely fix bounds.

Valid objections can be raised to this proposal, since the owner may be quite reluctant to accept the bonus and penalty clauses. Yet a solution must be found to this aspect of code optimization for society. The expected quality of fabrication and workmanship will be reflected in the choice of safety factors, safety indices, or other design parameters, and may be regarded as a means for rewarding or penalizing the expected quality, but the actual quality obtained during construction, as evinced in the monitoring and control of construction activities, requires a separate treatment which thus far has only found its way in contract clauses. Building codes will serve the interests of society incompletely if they ignore this issue.

Before proposing a strategy to attain the desired code format it is worth describing the main types of building codes from the viewpoints of safety and serviceability.

2 Existing Types of Building Codes

Serviceability Requirements. It is sometimes stated that a building code should only be concerned with safety. This is based on the premise that serviceability affects only the owner, whereas safety affects society. It is fallacious because the owner is a member of society and so are the tenants and the public at large who frequent a building. The owner's capital, moreover, can be put to a different use, say in works of direct social interest. Perhaps because this situation is generally recognized, most codes contain clauses intended to control serviceability and there is a trend to broaden the spectrum of this type of code requirements.

Allowable Values. Practically all code specifications are expressed in the form of minimum allowable standards. This is consistent with the assumption that the reliability that is optimum for the owner is smaller than the maximum acceptable to society. In the representation of Fig. 7.2 this is the same as the assumption that x_{po} always lies to the left of x_{s2}. This is usually true because the owner is normally interested in returns at shorter time spans than society. However, there are exceptions—owners with an obsessive concern for safety or with a flair for the monumental. To cover these it is advisable to specify upper limits as well, which can best be accomplished by limiting the smallest amount of utility that the building can originate for society.

Use of Safety Factors.   Much discussion has been expended on whether the use of load factors, stress-reduction coefficients, or partial factors of safety is basically the soundest. Suppose first that in the design of a given structure all loads are to be increased by a single factor and all strengths are to be reduced by a single coefficient. In statically determinate structures whatever the constituent materials' stress-strain relations, and in structures of linear behavior whatever their degree of static indeterminacy, the individual values of the load factor and of the stress-reduction factor will be irrelevant; safety will depend only on the ratio of these two numbers, or "safety factor." The same is true of nonlinear, statically indeterminate systems if the stress-reduction coefficient affects equally stresses associated with given strains; otherwise the equivalence is approximate. (The last remark refers only to the approximate equivalence between load factors and the reciprocal of the stress-reduction coefficient in a given structure, as the values of these numbers associated with a given probability of failure may differ considerably between structures, depending on the number of critical sections, on redundancy, on stress-strain relations, and so on.)

The advantages of the use of load factors appear when different groups of loads are affected by different factors. For instance, the design of a rigid block standing on a horizontal surface and subject to gravity and lateral loads is practically unaffected by the choice of the stress-reduction coefficient. It is equally insensitive to the magnitude of the load factor if vertical and horizontal forces are to be multiplied by the same number. However, the probability of its overturning can be controlled if its base dimensions are governed by a design in which vertical loads are affected by one factor and lateral forces by another. (It is important to notice that, although this artifice permits controlling the probability of overturning, it does so in an obscure and indirect manner. It would be more satisfactory to use the margin of safety against overturning as design variable and specify the maximum probability of its being smaller than zero. It would be even better if one dealt with the cost of overturning and with the cost of modifying this probability.)

A special situation arises when one group of loads can reverse the sign of stresses caused by another group of loads. For example, structural members that are

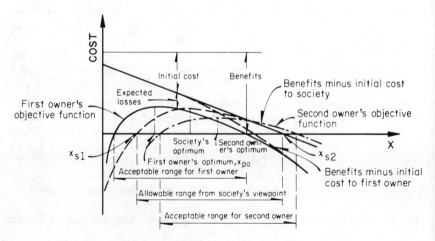

Fig. 7.2 Objective functions for society and two different investors *(Rosenblueth and Esteva, 1971)*

subjected to tension under dead load may, under the combined action of a sufficiently high live or wind load and a sufficiently low dead load, be subjected to compression. Similarly there may be reversals in the sign of torques, shears, and bending moments. Mere selection of working stresses will not protect a structure against many types of failure caused by stress reversal; neither will a choice of load factors greater than unity unless one is willing grossly to overdesign those structural members or portions thereof for which the probability of reversal is negligible. One solution consists in using load factors smaller than one for the first group of loads and greater than one for the second group. The structure, then, is checked for two combinations of load, in one of which the load factor for permanent load is smaller than one. Care must be exerted in choosing the load factors; as shown by Allen (1969), values found in most codes for the latter factor are so large as to lead to high probabilities of failure under stress reversal.

In turn, the usefulness of stress-reduction factors arises when different coefficients are used in designing against different modes of failure (say, shear and flexure), when dimensioning the various constituent materials in composite structures (say, computing the cross-sectional dimensions of concrete and the amount of steel in reinforced concrete members), and when differentiating materials produced under different control standards.

In traditional formats the introduction of partial factors—one for loads and one for strengths—is useful when both sets of conditions are present. The most important asset is economic, for the use of partial factors can do away with some instances of gross overdesign due to the choice of a single safety factor intended to cover the most unfavorable conditions likely to be met in practice. Alternatively to the use of partial factors one may resort to modifications in the design loads and in the design formulas if there is a desire to preserve simplicity in the specification of load factors and stress-reduction factors, respectively. For example, in the usual code format, although design dead loads can be compared with values computed in a conventional fashion, there is no evident standard with which to compare design wind speeds and seismic base shear coefficients; these can be adjusted at will so as to dispense with a set of load factors for lateral loads that would differ from the one used for gravity forces in designing for the combined action of gravity and lateral loads. Other examples of hidden factors include certain specified live loads [such as 4790 Pa (100 psf) on balconies, in which the probability of failure is high from uncertainties about the position of reinforcement or about the conditions at the support, and the consequences of failure can be particularly severe]; and the use of conservative criteria for live-load reduction (which leads to a desirable relative overdesign of the lower-story columns in tall buildings). Also, commonly used methods for the design of slabs or continuous joists in flexure, under vertical loads, rest on coefficients that produce less safe designs than those for the same members when designed against shear failures and less safe than the criteria for design of other structural members; and the difference is justified in view of the lesser consequences of failure associated with the flexural mode in joists and slabs. The moment coefficients usually applied for design of two-way and flat slabs do not satisfy the requirements of statics. This state of affairs is objectionable, among other reasons because it creates confusion among those who apply the coefficients without being fully aware of the implications of such practice; it can cause undesirable features in design of structures whose characteristics differ from those for which the indirect safety provisions have been established; and there is no assurance that even for these structures such provisions lead to the most desirable designs, be it only approximately. It would be preferable to bring the main factors at play into the open so that the designer could judge the situation on its own merits.

Use of Simplified Stress-Strain Relations. No longer is there room for discussion on whether building codes should provide for safety in terms of working stresses or of ultimate strengths. Out of tradition the working stress format is, in general, associated with the assumption of linear behavior and with the use of safety factors that are the reciprocals of stress reduction factors. Ultimate strength design is associated with the assumption of perfectly plastic behavior—supplemented with the specification of ultimate strain in the concrete—and ordinarily with the use of load factors or of partial factors. The universal trend is toward adopting ultimate strength design for safety computations, preserving the assumption of linear behavior for some calculations concerning serviceability. The systematic use of this multiple checking constitutes the essence of the widely advocated limit state design (Allen, 1970a).

The question of using stress reducing coefficients, load factors, or split factors has been discussed. If this is dissociated from that of linear against plastic behavior the latter loses almost all importance. It reduces to choosing between one or the other approximation to the stress-strain curves of building materials. Which approximation one decides to use and which adjustments to make (such as taking the average concrete stress in columns as a fraction of the nominal strength and making this fraction depend on that strength) depends on the accuracy sought. For most computations concerning safety the (slightly adjusted) assumption of perfect plasticity is sufficiently accurate. For most applications to questions of serviceability it is advisable to use linear or pseudolinear theories of material behavior.

There are obvious exceptions to the foregoing remarks about the choice of a theory of material behavior for safety analyses. Exceptions concern design of structures and structural members governed by instability (or, more generally, slenderness effects), loss of support, and so on. In these there is need for a more accurate treatment of stress-strain relations.

Characteristic Values. Loads as well as resistances are random variables. Load factors and stress-reduction coefficients refer to specific values of these variables. Those ("characteristic") values are intended to be functions of the probability density functions of the variables in question. Such is the case with the "minimum guaranteed" yield stress of steel, the specified strength of concrete in compression, and so on. The relationship between these values and the probability distributions of the corresponding variables is obscure. The same is true of "nominal" values (those shown on drawings and in specifications), which may or may not coincide with the characteristic values. The situation encumbers the evaluation of the reliability attained in design, and hence practically closes the door to improvements over blind application of code requirements. At the same time it leads to inconsistent values of structural reliability.

Semiprobabilistic Formats. In an attempt toward consistency in reliabilities, several building codes have come to define characteristic material strengths as those values for which there is a relatively small, fixed probability (say 2% or 5%) of finding a lower strength. They have defined characteristic loads as those values for which there is a similar probability that the structure will be submitted to a larger load during some arbitrary time span (say 30 yr or 100 yr). The ratios of characteristic strengths to characteristic loads are known as characteristic load factors or safety factors.

For reasons of simplicity these codes specify that the characteristic strengths and loads be taken equal to their expected values, respectively minus or plus a certain number of times the corresponding standard deviations. The factor affecting the standard deviations is derived on the assumption that strengths and loads are normally distributed. This approach was suggested earlier by the International Council for Building Research (Torroja et al., 1958). Such simplifications are reasonable provided the characteristic values do not differ excessively from the corresponding expectations and if the distributions are approximately normal; otherwise one can arrive at seriously erroneous results, such as negative characteristic strengths for timber in tension. In what follows it will be assumed that characteristic values are defined in terms of the probabilities of meeting a more unfavorable value of strength or load and that the simplification that fixes the standard deviation will be used only when appropriate.

Essentially the same approach has been advocated by Ang and Amin (1969). In the Ang-Amin proposal the choice of characteristic values is to be based on "objective" probabilities, while that of the characteristic safety factor is to arise from "subjective" probabilities. The two types of probabilities are, respectively, the ones derived from a conceptual or stochastic model of the phenomena at play and those associated with uncertainty about the model parameters or about the model itself.

Use of characteristic values has been extended in some building codes to cross-sectional dimensions (Departamento del Distrito Federal, 1966). For example, on the basis of statistical data on the effective depth of slabs the characteristic effective depth for negative moment is taken equal to the one shown on the drawings minus 20 mm (0.8 in.), while that for positive bending moment is not reduced relative to the one in the drawings.

This format has several assets. By preserving the use of characteristic values it can aid in fixing legal responsibility: if, in the event of failure, it can be shown that material strength or cross-sectional dimensions were smaller than their characteristic values, the builder can be held responsible; the same is true if the dead load exceeds its characteristic value; if the live load exceeded the corresponding characteristic values, the owner or tenants can be held responsible; if the wind or earthquake loads exceeded their design limits, failure can be ascribed to an act of God; and if none of these events holds true, responsibility can be laid on the designer. For these verdicts to be tenable the characteristic values of the loads must correspond to sufficiently rare events and the characteristic strengths and cross-sectional dimensions must not be excessively low in terms of the size of the sample that it is practical to test. The characteristic factor of safety required to produce a given reliability, down to failure probabilities of about 10^{-3}, is far less sensitive to the types of distributions of strengths and loads than the central factor of safety (one relating expected values, modes, or medians of strengths and loads). By using a somewhat different formulation insensitivity of the characteristic safety factor to the types of distributions can be extended to failure probabilities as low as 10^{-6}. Yet the format can be criticized on the following counts.

First, the near independence of the safety factor required to attain a given reliability relative to the probability distribution of loads and strengths is only an apparent advantage of this format (Turkstra, 1970a). The characteristic values are associated with certain probabilities of meeting less favorable values of the variables. Hence, these points of the corresponding probability distribution functions must be known with accuracy in order for the safety factor to give the desired reliability, whether that factor is characteristic or central.

Second, the semiprobabilistic format takes care of randomness in the strength of members due to variability of material strength. Aside from this and from the effects of randomness of cross-sectional dimensions, other random variables sometimes affect the distribution of member strengths. For example, resistance to buckling in the inelastic range is conditioned to a large extent by residual stresses, by eccentricities that are usually not included in analysis ("accidental" eccentricities), and by the stiffnesses of other structural members. It would be inadequately handled by adopting a load factor and a reduction coefficient to be applied to the tangent modulus of elasticity and to material strength, computed in the manner of stress-reduction factors. Similar remarks apply to design of bridge decks against loss of support. The matter of buckling can be taken care of by specifying characteristic eccentricities, whether minimum (ACI, 1971) or additional (Departamento del Distrito Federal, 1966) relative to the computed values, and by adjusting the design formulas, as in most contemporary building codes. Such procedures cannot produce entirely consistent results; they obscure the design process, and they introduce serious difficulties in the recognition of variations in uncertainties about structural parameters.

Third, expected values are additive, whereas characteristic values are not. Thus, if the characteristic live and dead loads are associated with the same probability of exceedence, their sum is associated with a smaller probability that it be exceeded. Similarly for the product of independent variables. Suppose that the characteristic material strength and cross-sectional dimensions correspond to the same probability of meeting a more unfavorable value. Then the shear strength or resisting moment of a cross section, computed from the characteristic values, will correspond to a (usually much) smaller probability of finding a smaller value. These objections suggest using explicitly the probability distributions of the variables involved, or certain parameters of those distributions, such as expectations and variances, rather than characteristic values. The matter can also be taken care of by introducing additional, linearization factors, but the proliferation of factors is objectionable, as discussed below.

Fourth, this format does not provide for calculation of reliabilities. Hence one must ignore the large variation there is from one structure to another in the relation between the reliability of the entire structure and those of its members.

Finally, a rational design criterion should be sensitive to such matters as the consequences of failure and the dependence of initial cost on reliability. The code format under consideration does not allow for a criterion with these traits, for it omits consideration of the economic nature of design problems.

The last two objections can, in principle, be surmounted by introducing additional factors, one to correct for the relation between member and structural reliabilities, and one which might be termed an "importance" factor, to incorporate economic considerations. The latter type of factor would be similar to the one introduced in the Soviet code (USSR State Committee for Construction, 1962).

However, the adoption of a long series of factors, each related cryptically and indirectly with the relevant variables, can only lead to a complicated and confusing building code which cannot be made to cover cases that deviate from those assumed in its drafting. An overt treatment of these variables would be much preferable.

It follows from this critique that it is desirable to develop and adopt other code formats.

3 The Additive $F - 1$ Format

Baker (1956) has advocated a format based on

$$F - 1 = (F_S - 1) + (F_R - 1) \tag{7.16}$$

in which F, F_S, and F_R are respectively the over-all safety factor, the one to be applied to loads assuming that resistances are deterministically equal to their nominal values, and the one to be used with resistances under the assumption that loads are equal to their nominal values, and all of these safety factors are associated with the same probability of failure.

As shown in Fig. 7.3 this criterion gives relatively consistent safety factors for a variety of realistic combinations of probability distributions of load and resistance, at least down to failure probabilities of 10^{-5} and up to coefficients of variation of loads and strengths as high as 0.4. These results apply to the central safety factors. In some instances more favorable results can be expected for the characteristic safety factors, provided the characteristic load and resistance are adequately chosen.

The approach can be generalized to cases in which R and S are each treated as the product of several independent random variables.

In this format the influence of the consequences of failure is taken into account by adding or subtracting certain quantities to F. It can be shown that the approach does not lead to consistent results.

Despite the attractiveness of this format, which stems from its simplicity, it

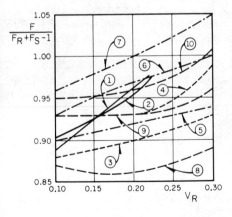

Curve	Load	Strength	Vs	Symbol
1	Normal	Lognormal	0.1	———
2			0.3	
3	Lognormal	Lognormal	0.1	– – – –
4			0.3	
5	Normal truncated	Lognormal	0.1	– · – ·
6			0.3	
7			0.4	
8	Extreme type I	Lognormal	0.1	– –
9			0.3	
10			0.4	

Failure probability $= 10^{-5}$

Fig. 7.3 Split safety factors in Baker's version *(Rosenblueth and Esteva, 1971)*

presents essentially the objections noted above in connection with the semiprobabilistic format.

4 First-Order Second-Moment Format

The format advanced by Cornell (1969a, 1969b) and further developed by Ravindra et al. and by Lind (1969, 1971a, and 1971b) marks an important improvement over the ones described. It has points in common with previous proposals by Soviet researchers, by Basler (1961), and by Tichy and Vorliček (1972). The following is a succinct version of Cornell's format.

Consider a structure having a single mode of failure and subjected to a set of loads proportional to a single random variable W. Let the random variable I denote the influence coefficient of this load in a structural member, at a critical section, or at a point where failure may take place. The corresponding load effect is

$$S = IW \tag{7.17}$$

The value of W is uncertain because it is a future event; that of I is uncertain because of uncertainty in the geometry of the structure, material behavior (in statically indeterminate systems), and error in and conscious simplification of the analysis methods.

The pertinent resistance of the structure is a scalar, R, and it is assumed that failure occurs when $R < S$. The resistance can be written

$$R = A\,M\,Q \tag{7.18}$$

in which A = geometrical property of the structure, such as cross-sectional area or section modulus; M = material strength; and Q = variable reflecting uncertainty in strength calculations. All these quantities are random variables because of the designer's inability to predict them in an exact manner. Coefficients entering the formula may be incorporated in either A, M, or Q.

It is assumed that W, I, A, M, and Q are mutually independent. Cornell's format gives a design procedure based on the expectations and standard deviations of these variables only. It has been shown that this format is unique (Lind, 1971b).

The safety margin is defined as

$$G = R - S \tag{7.19}$$

Two of its distribution parameters are

$$E(G) = E(R) - E(S) \tag{7.20}$$

and

$$\sigma^2(G) = \sigma^2(R) + \sigma^2(S) \tag{7.21}$$

in which $E(\,\cdot\,)$ and $\sigma(\,\cdot\,)$ denote expectation and standard deviation, respectively. Moments of higher order are disregarded. The only measure of reliability is the coefficient of variation

$$V_G = \frac{\sigma(G)}{E(G)} \tag{7.22}$$

Define now the safety index as

$$\beta = \frac{1}{V_G} \tag{7.23}$$

Then

$$\beta = \frac{E(R) - E(S)}{[\sigma^2(R) + \sigma^2(S)]^{1/2}} \tag{7.24}$$

If the probability distribution of G is entirely determined by $E(G)$ and $\sigma(G)$, there is a unique relationship between structural reliability and β.

Let the central safety factor be $F = E(R)/E(S)$. It follows from Eq. 7.24 that

$$\beta^2 = \frac{(F - 1)^2}{F^2 V_R^2 + V_S^2} \tag{7.25}$$

so that F can be obtained from β, V_R, and V_S. Rigorously, F cannot be written as the product of the safety factors F_R and F_S, where each depends only on the statistics of strength and load effect, respectively. Yet this decomposition of F can be accomplished in an approximate way which is satisfactory for many practical purposes. To this end introduce Lind's "linearization function" α of the variables x_0, $x_1, \ldots, x_n$ (Lind, 1971a)

$$\alpha = \frac{(1 + \Sigma x_i^2)^{1/2}}{1 + \Sigma x_i} \tag{7.26}$$

Lind has shown that

$$\frac{1}{\sqrt{1 + n}} \leq \alpha \leq 1 \tag{7.27}$$

When $n = 1$ and $1/3 \leq x \leq 3$, $\alpha = 0.75$ with an error not exceeding 5%. Now let $\alpha = \alpha(F V_R / V_S)$ in Eq. 7.24. It follows that, for most practical conditions

$$(1 - \alpha\beta V_R) E(R) = (1 + \alpha\beta V_S) E(S) \tag{7.28}$$

Finally let

$$F_R = \frac{1}{1 - \alpha\beta V_R} \tag{7.29}$$

and

$$F_S = 1 + \alpha\beta V_S \tag{7.30}$$

which depend only on the statistics of R and of S, respectively. From Eq. 7.28, then

$$F = F_R F_S \tag{7.31}$$

This partial-factor or split-factor formulation coincides with that of CEB and ISO. The manner in which it has been derived facilitates the choice of load factors from Eqs. 7.29 and 7.30 in terms of the desired probability of failure (indirectly of the safety index) and the coefficients of variation of strength and of load effect. Through the use of Eq. 7.26 this analysis can be extended to arrive at

$$F \cong F_W F_I F_A F_M F_Q \tag{7.32}$$

in which each partial load factor depends exclusively on the statistics of the corresponding random variable $W, I, \ldots$ However, according to Eq. 7.27, all that one can say about α is that it will lie between 0.45 and 1, and the error introduced by this decomposition will often be excessive. It is far preferable to revert to the original Eq. 7.23 and compute the coefficient of variation of the safety margin G in terms of the statistics of all the random variables involved. Indeed, this approach is preferable also to the use of split safety factors (Eq. 7.31), for one can then do away with many of the objections raised against other code formats; by dealing directly with V_G one can, for example, unobjectionably combine dead and live loads and also open the way for an explicit treatment of reliabilities without thereby introducing excessive computational difficulties. This approach, at the same time, retains the advantages of the partial-factor format.

Cornell's format provides a means for obtaining approximately consistent reliabilities within a simplified framework where no information is required concerning the shapes of the probability density functions of the variables involved. The probability of survival is specified indirectly, through the safety index β. Other ways of specifying safety are possible, also in terms only of means and variances of loads and strengths. In any case a first-order approximation is used for computing these means and variances which are, in general, nonlinear functions of more elementary parameters, such as load intensity, modulus of elasticity, material strength, and cross-sectional dimensions.

Most of the literature concerned with this format implies the hypothesis that loads and resistances are normally distributed. The assumption is unnecessary and can be seriously in error. This is particularly true for large values of the safety index, since there is a sizable overestimate of the probability that resistance lies in the neighborhood of zero, and negative resistances are assigned finite probabilities. More realistic probability distributions can be adopted. For a variety of combinations of the probability distributions of loads and resistances one obtains

$$F = \exp\left(\beta \sqrt{V_R^2 + V_S^2}\right) \tag{7.33}$$

as an approximate expression for the central safety factor (Esteva and Rosenblueth, 1971). Here β is related with loads and resistances through

$$\beta = \frac{E(lnR - lnS)}{\sigma(lnR - lnS)} \tag{7.34}$$

in which $E(\cdot)$ and $\sigma(\cdot)$, respectively, denote expectation and standard deviation, and with the probability of failure through

$$P_f = 460\, e^{-4.3\,\beta} \qquad\qquad (7.35)$$

Eq. 7.33 is an approximation to the solution that holds exactly when R and S are independent and lognormally distributed.

As shown in Fig. 7.4, Eq. 7.33 provides safety factors in agreement with those derived from a variety of realistic assumptions concerning the types of probability distributions of load and strength. Of the usual types only the curves corresponding to the case in which load and strength are both normally distributed depart from the general trend and from Eq. 7.33.

The format allows recognition of correlations between loads and resistances, for in the calculation of coefficients of variation one can take finite covariances into account. Eq. 7.33 is valid in the special case of zero covariances.

The safety index β is uniquely related to the reliability. Hence, although the format does not provide for explicit consideration of the economic nature of design, it can be referred to a format that deals openly with reliability optimizations as has been done by Mau (1971). It is thus ideally suited as an intermediate step between present formats and a more rational one with explicit reliability optimization.

In the first stages of adoption of this format, the relation between member or section reliability and structural system reliability, the consequences of failure, and the sensitivity of initial cost to the design reliability will have to be taken into account by using correction factors or adjustments in the safety index (Esteva and Rosenblueth, 1971; Moses and Tichy, 1973).

5 Examples of Semiprobabilistic and Probabilistic Design

The foregoing formats will now be illustrated by means of two simple examples. Suppose first that it is desired to design a tension member of a statically determinate truss that supports 74 m² (800 ft²) of office floor. Let $E(D) = 178$ kN (40 kips) and $E(L) = 26.7$ kN (6 kips), in which D and L = dead and live load, respectively, and,

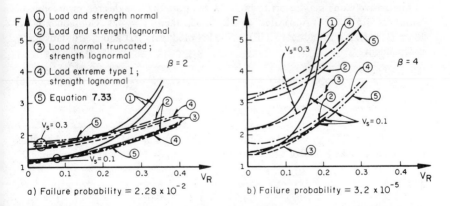

Fig. 7.4 Safety factors as functions of coefficients of variation (*Rosenblueth and Esteva, 1971*)

with reference to the notation in Eqs. 7.17 through 7.32, $E(I) = 0.75$, $E(A) = a$, $E(M) = 276$ MPa (40 ksi), $E(Q) = 1$, $V_L = 0.70$, and $V_D = V_I = V_A = V_M = V_Q = 0.05$. Here a = the unknown specified cross-sectional area of the member. Suppose further that in the ranges of interest all the probability distributions in question can be approximated as normal.

If the maximum effect of live load is calculated under the assumption of space independence of live loads it is found equal to the sum of two terms (Rosenblueth, 1956). The first term is the expected live load, equal to the expected live load per unit area times the influence coefficient and times the tributary area for the structural member or the critical section being considered. The second term is proportional to the standard deviation of the live load effect. The standard deviation is equal to the first term times a coefficient and times the standard deviation of the total live load acting on the tributary area (the latter standard deviation is inversely proportional to the square root of this area). This coefficient can be taken equal to 1.2 for most practical purposes. Accordingly, the coefficient of variation of live load, 0.70, will be multiplied by 1.2.

Using a CEB-type format one would begin by defining critical values of the loads and resistance. If exclusion limits are fixed at the level of 2% probability, these values are approximately equal to the expectations plus or minus twice the corresponding standard deviations. Identifying them by subscript k one would find $D_k = 196$ kN (44 kips), $L_k = 6(1 + 2 \times 1.2 \times 0.70) = 71.5$ kN (16.08 kips), and $M_k = 248$ MPa (36 ksi). Then one would take for I and for A their expected values and for Q the value 1 and would introduce some, relatively small, characteristic safety factors, say $F_S = 1.25$ and $F_R = 1.2$. Accordingly, for a total load of $44 + 16.08 = 60.08$ kips ($196 + 71.5 = 267.5$ kN), one would find a required nominal area

$$a = \frac{1.25 \times 0.75 \times 1.2 \times 60.08}{36} = 1230 \text{ mm}^2 \ (1.88 \text{ sq in.})$$

The same result can be obtained using the Ang-Amin format with a safety factor of 1.5, or with a larger characteristic load, smaller characteristic resistance, and smaller safety factor.

Alternatively one may resort to Eq. 7.32. Suppose that the desired probability of failure is 1.5×10^{-5}. According to Eq. 7.35, then, $\beta = 4.0$. Consequently, if $W = D + L$, it is found that $E(W) = 205$ kN (46 kips). If D and L are statistically independent

$$\sigma(W) = [\sigma^2(D) + 1.2^2\sigma^2(L)]^{1/2} \tag{7.36}$$

$$\sigma(W) = 24.3 \text{ kN (42 kips).}$$

Hence, $V_W = 5.42/46 = 0.118$. From Eq. 7.27, with $n = 4$, $0.45 \leq \alpha \leq 1$. It is reasonable to take $\alpha = 0.6$. Then, from Eq. 7.30, $F_I = 1.120$, while, from Eq. 7.29

$$F_I = F_A = F_M = \frac{1}{1 - 0.6 \times 4.0 \times 0.05} = 1.135$$

Therefore, $F = 1.283 \times 1.120 \times 1.135^3 = 2.10$, and

$$a = \frac{2.10 \times 0.75 \times 46}{40} = 1255 \text{ mm}^2 \text{ (1.81 sq in.)}$$

An alternative approach would use Eqs. 7.29, 7.30, and 7.31 with $\alpha = 0.75$. To this end compute

$$V_S = (V_W^2 + V_I^2)^{1/2} \tag{7.37}$$

$$V_S = 0.128$$

and

$$V_R = (V_Q^2 + V_M^2 + V_A^2)^{1/2} \tag{7.38}$$

$$V_R = 0.0866$$

Accordingly, $F_S = 1.384$, $F_R = 1.350$, $F = 1.87$, and $a = 1065 \text{ mm}^2$ (1.62 sq in.). More directly, F may be computed by solving Eq. 7.25

$$F = \frac{\beta(V_R^2 + V_S^2 - \beta^2 V_R^2 V_S^2)^{1/2}}{1 - \beta^2 V_R^2} \tag{7.39}$$

$$F = 1.775$$

so that $a = 1005 \text{ mm}^2$ (1.53 sq in.).
Compare this last safety factor with the result of applying Eq. 7.16

$$F = 1 + 0.384 + 0.350 = 1.734$$

Finally, consider use of Eq. 7.33 again with a safety index of 4.0

$$F = \exp[4.0(0.128^2 + 0.0866^2)^{1/2}] = 1.853$$

so that $a = 1030 \text{ mm}^2$ (1.61 sq in.).
Now consider a tension member in a joist carrying 4.63 m^2 (50 sq ft) of office area. Assume $E(D) = 11.1$ kN (2.5 kips) and $E(L) = 16.7$ kN (0.375 kips) in proportion to the area supported and to the data for the first example, while $V_L = 2.8$, in proportion to the square root of the area. Take the rest of the data as for the first example.
Using the CEB-type format it is found that $a = 115.5 \text{ mm}^2$ (0.176 sq in.). Designing on the basis of Eq. 7.32, $a = 132.5 \text{ mm}^2$ (0.202 sq in.). From Eqs. 7.29, 7.30, and 7.31, $a = 123.5 \text{ mm}^2$ (0.188 sq in.). From Eq. 7.39, $a = 117.5 \text{ mm}^2$ (0.179 sq in.). And from Eq. 7.33, $a = 211 \text{ mm}^2$ (0.326 sq in.). All of these areas computed for the tension member are appreciably larger than the ratio of areas of office floor, $50/800 = 1/16$, times the corresponding values for the truss member. This is due to the increase in the coefficient of variation of live load.
Differences between results obtained by the different criteria increase with the coefficient of variation for high coefficients of variation. Thus, the ratio of the cross-sectional areas found by the most conservative to the least conservative

criterion is 1.17 for the truss member and 2.08 for the joist member. These discrepancies point to the need for research into the applicable probability distributions and development of corresponding approximate formulas of design.

6 Examples of Reliability Optimization

The following paragraphs illustrate the explicit optimization of reliability in relatively simple cases. The objective function to be maximized is taken to be

$$Z = B - C - J \tag{7.40}$$

in which B = benefits derived from the existence of the structure being designed; C = its initial cost; J = losses due to failure; and all these quantities are expected present values.

Conversion of future into present values will be done by multiplying benefits and losses incurred at time t by the factor $\exp(-\gamma t)$, in which γ = constant. It will be assumed that the benefits derived from the structure's existence, while it exists, are independent of the reliability.

Whether an entire structure or a structural member is being considered, its initial cost will be taken as a linear function of the safety factor, whether central or characteristic. The probability distributions of resistances, normalized with respect to the corresponding expectations, will be assumed independent of these expectations and outside the designer's control.

Two situations will be considered. In one the structure can fail upon completion or not at all. In the other, resistances are time independent and loads constitute a generalized Poisson process. In both, the economic conditions of the problem will be taken as a stationary process. Hence, if the structure was originally worth building it will be worth rebuilding in the event of failure, provided the cost of rebuilding does not exceed the original cost; and it is worth repairing in the event of damage, provided the cost of restoring its original conditions of resistance and serviceability do not exceed the expected loss in present value of rentability (or, more generally, in benefits) caused by the damage.

Structure Having Single Mode of Failure.   Suppose first that the structure can only fail upon completion. If the structure is rebuilt or repaired instantaneously in the event of collapse or damage, then

$$Z = B - c_1 - c_2F - \frac{P_f H}{1 - P_f} \tag{7.41}$$

in which c_1 and c_2 = constants, and H = loss in the event of failure or damage (Rosenblueth and Mendoza, 1971). When the optimum P_f is very small, P_f can be neglected in comparison with one. If, further, H is taken to be independent of F, replacing Eq. 7.35 in Eq. 7.41 gives

$$Z = B - c_1 - c_2e^{\beta V R/S} - 460He^{-4.3\beta} \tag{7.42}$$

Differentiating with respect to β and equating to zero, one obtains

$$\beta_0 = \frac{1}{4.3 + V_{R/S}} \, ln \, \frac{1978H}{c_2 V_{R/S}} \qquad (7.43)$$

and F_0 is obtained by writing β_0 for β in Eq. 7.33.

For example, suppose it is desired to design a prismatic beam of rectangular cross section, subjected to a load W. Suppose that the only pertinent mode of failure is through excessive deflection, which would cause damage in nonstructural elements supported by the beam. If this can only take place within the beam's range of linear behavior, the criterion of failure will be $K < W/\eta$, in which K = beam stiffness and η = random coefficient. On the other hand, K can be written as δbd^3, in which δ = another random coefficient; b = beam width; and d = beam depth. The probability distribution of η must reflect the uncertainty there is about the deflection that would cause the nonstructural damage, while the distribution of δ must correspond to uncertainty in the prediction of the maximum deflection.

The ratio R/S will be taken equal to $K\eta/W$, and the load factor as $K_c E(\eta)/E(W)$, in which K_c, the calculated or nominal value of K, is $E(\delta)E(b)[E(d)]^3$.

Suppose it is decided to make $E(d) = 3E(b)$. The initial cost, which is of the form $c_1' + c_2'E(b)E(d)$, in which c_1' and c_2' = constants, will become $c_1' + 3c_2'[E(b)]^2$. In order to make use of Eq. 7.43, the initial cost will be put in terms of F and linearized, to give $c_1 + c_2F$. The value of c_2 will be taken equal to dC/dF when $F = F_0$, in which F_0 is found by an iteration procedure. Thus, if b_1 denotes the value of $E(b)$ for which $F = 1$, F can be written $[E(b)/b_1]^4$ and C becomes $c_1' + 3c_2'b_1^2F_0'^{1/2}$ so that

$$c_2 = \frac{3b_1^2c_2'}{2F_0'^{1/2}} \qquad (7.44)$$

in which F_0' = tentative value of F_0.

Assume the following data: $\sigma(b) = \sigma(d) = 12.7$ mm (0.5 in.); $V_W = 0.2V_\delta = 0.3$; $V_\eta = 0.5$; and $H = 30b_1^2c_2'$. [The standard deviations of b and d are taken independent of the corresponding nominal values in accordance with available indications to this effect (Johnson, 1953).] A first-order approximation to the squared coefficient of variation of the nth power of any random variable X is

$$V_{X^n}^2 = n^2V_X^2 \qquad (7.45)$$

(Benjamin and Cornell, 1970). Consequently

$$V_{R/S}^2 = V_\delta^2 + V_\eta^2 + V_W^2 + V_b^2 + V_{d^3}^2$$

becomes

$$V_{R/S}^2 \simeq V_\delta^2 + V_\eta^2 + V_W^2 + 2V_b^2$$

If one tentatively takes the optimum $E(b)$, $E_0(b) = 1.5 \, b_1$, $F_0'^{1/2}$ is found to be $1.5^2 = 2.25$, and Eq. 7.44 gives $c_2 = 0.297 \, b_1^2c_2'$. From Eq. 7.43

$$\beta_0 = \frac{1}{4.3 + V_{R/S}} \, ln \, \frac{6670 \times 30}{V_{R/S}}$$

Now, if $E_0(b) = 254$ mm (10 in.), $\beta_0 = 2.56$, from Eq. 7.33, $F_0 = 4.489$, and $E_0(b) = 1.48b_1$. The result is relatively insensitive to the assumed $E_0(b)$.

If failure involves collapse, the cost of rebuilding must be added to the direct losses due to failure. In Eq. 7.44, H must be replaced with $H + c_1 + c_2F_0$; the resulting equation can be solved iteratively. Actually H is a function of the live load acting at the time of failure. A solution is available under the assumption that H is a linear function of this load (Mendoza et al., 1971).

Suppose now that the load constitutes a generalized Poisson process with rate of exceedence $\lambda = \lambda(S)$. The expected present value of the loss incurred when the structure fails for the first time is $HE_R(\lambda/\lambda + \gamma)$, in which $\lambda = \lambda(R)$ and $E_R(\cdot)$ denotes expectation with R as random variable (Rosenblueth and Mendoza, 1971). The expected present value of the loss due to all the failures is

$$J = \frac{HE_R\!\left(\dfrac{\lambda}{\lambda + \gamma}\right)}{1 - E_R\!\left(\dfrac{\lambda}{\lambda + \gamma}\right)} \tag{7.46}$$

For systems having linear behavior and subjected to earthquake the assumption that λ is proportional to S^{-r} (to R^{-r} in Eq. 7.36), where r is a constant, is a satisfactory approximation to the rate of exceedence of seismic response over a wide range of natural periods and degrees of damping (Esteva, 1970). Explicit expressions have been obtained for the optimum resistance under this assumption (Rosenblueth and Mendoza, 1971).

Other Solutions Available.   A closed reliability-optimization solution is available, under assumptions similar to those made above, which permits deciding when a defense-plateau scheme is advisable for relatively simple structures (Rosenblueth and Mendoza, 1971).

An approximate solution has also been obtained for statically determinate structural assemblages (Rosenblueth and Mendoza, 1971). In it, correlation between the strengths of the various structural members is taken into account by assuming that

$$R_i = \chi \xi_i \tag{7.47}$$

in which R_i = strength of the ith member, and χ and the ξ_i's = independent random variables. The same treatment can be extended to structural members having several, correlated, potential modes of failure.

Methods using mathematical programming have been developed for isostatic as well as for perfectly plastic, statically indeterminate structures (Moses and Stevenson, 1969).

It has been shown (Switzky, 1964) that the relative values of the optimum resistances are practically independent of the over-all reliability (and hence of the relation between cost of failure and initial costs) within a very wide range of the latter when the costs of individual members are proportional to the corresponding resistances ($c_1 = 0$). When the costs are linear functions of these resistances ($c_1 \neq 0$) the relative values of the optimum member reliabilities are practically independent of the over-all reliability, provided the individual reliabilities are proportional to negative powers of the corresponding resistances within the ranges of interest (Rosenblueth and Mendoza, 1971).

7   A Strategy

The impatient convert to the ideal format described at the beginning of this section may want to implement it immediately. This would not be a rational decision. [The term rational is here given the contemporary sense: maximum efficiency in modifying the Universe to make it tend towards one's ideal (Rosenblueth, 1970).] It would almost surely be doomed to failure. Before such a step is taken the stage should be prepared (Rosenblueth, 1971) by:

1. Launching an educational and publicity campaign to make the probabilistic and optimization approaches palatable to makers and users of building codes. The process is already under way, through inclusion of probabilities and decision theory as required subjects in many undergraduate curricula, publication of papers dealing with the matters at various levels, and complementary actions. It is worth intensifying and supplementing.

2. Adopting for the next code generation the first-order second-moment format described above, which indirectly deals with section or member reliabilities. Corrections or adjustments would account for the relation between these and system reliabilities, and for variations in desired reliabilities with type of structure. If building code committees are reluctant to adopt this format as the only framework for structural design, it can probably be incorporated as an alternative approach, much as was done in several codes with ultimate strength design which, through an effective escalation, has come to supplant the older methods of conventional design. The latter strategy, although slower, has the advantage of allowing the new format to be tested and improved in the process. There may be some temptation to mend the present split-factor format to make it approach the desired shape, rather than adopt a different format like the one advocated here. That would, however, retard the process by introducing new concepts and additional factors which would later have to be dropped.

3. Introducing explicit reliability optimization procedures as alternates for the design problems most amenable to this approach. Because of lack of familiarity of the profession with the new format there would be need for a specification of minimum allowable safety indices in each case.

4. Developing simple, approximate formulas, graphs, computer programs, and other design aids to facilitate adoption of the ideal format. Of particular benefit would be the development of reliability-oriented and reliability-optimization-oriented computer languages. At the same time data permitting better reliability calculations and assessment of consequences of failure should be gathered and processed.

Even then adoption of the ideal format would proceed gradually. There are many aspects of the theory, the gathering of statistical data, and their interpretation that are far from having reached a satisfactory state. It would be too optimistic to assume that all such aspects will be satisfactorily solved by the time the foregoing steps have been taken.

An apparent objection to the early adoption of the explicit-optimization format is the scarcity of data on the frequency distribution of loads, geometric characteristics of structural members, and material behavior. Actually the same scarcity besets all other code formats but is hidden in the adoption of relatively arbitrary design values and coefficients. By bringing into the open the present state of affairs the format advocated would point out the areas in which observation and research are most urgently needed. While those data are gathered and the research carried out the probability distributions to be used for design will have to be strongly subjective. Bayesian statistics affords the basis for the formulation of these distributions, for their improvement as data become available, and for their use in design (Rosenblueth, 1971). Nevertheless there is sore need for the gathering and processing of statistical data on the in-situ properties of construction materials, discrepancies between the geometry of structures as built and that shown on structural drawings, and loads and imposed deformations; data on the calibration of methods of structural analysis and design; and data on the consequences of failure.

8   Special Features of Tall Buildings

From the viewpoint of building codes, tall buildings present the following special features.

Large Number of Potential Modes of Failure.   For a given number of bays and given member reliabilities, the over-all reliability is a decreasing function of the number of stories. If a code is based on allowable member reliabilities (or safety factors) deemed adequate for buildings having a small number of potential modes of failure, it will err on the unsafe side in tall structures. This is particularly serious under dynamic lateral loading, such as that due to earthquake, since the larger the number of potential modes of failure the higher the likelihood that a major portion of the inelastic energy required for survival will have to be taken in one or a few modes, overtaxing them. The matter is roughly offset in some earthquake resistant provisions by setting a lower limit to the base shear coefficient when this coefficient is expressed as a function of building height, number of stories, or fundamental period of vibration (Anderson et al., 1952); in others, the story shears are not to be taken smaller than some fraction of what a static analysis would indicate, with base shear coefficient independent of the fundamental period (Departamento del Distrito Federal, 1966); in yet other codes, the base shear coefficient is made to decrease with fundamental period at a much slower rate than would be justified for a single-degree system (International Conference of Building Officials, 1971). The latter device is more conservative than it would seem at first sight, since the base shear coefficient of multistory buildings in the linear range should be smaller than that for a single-degree system having the same fundamental period of vibration to achieve the same member reliabilities (Newmark and Rosenblueth, 1971).

Differences in Consequences of Failure.   In a tall building there usually is a spectacular difference between the consequences of failure of penthouse columns and of that of ground story columns. This type of difference should be reflected in allowable reliability formats (and in safety factor formats) by making the minimum reliability (or the safety factor) an increasing function of the number of stories between the elevation considered and the roof.

Progressive Failures. Tall buildings are especially vulnerable to partial collapses that begin at one elevation and propagate upwards and downwards—the so-called progressive failures. A mishap of this nature in London, initiated by an explosion (Griffiths et al., 1968), has initiated a tendency requiring sufficient structural capacity practically to assure that this type of failure will not develop. It is debatable whether occurrence of a single incident of this nature should justify taking conservative measures in the design of all buildings. A cost-benefit analysis is justified before a code is modified on this count.

Distribution of Wind and Earthquake Forces. Approximate rules that are adequate for low and moderately tall buildings may err substantially in the taller structures. For example, the increase of wind pressure with height is not to be ignored and the flexibility of these structures may pose special problems, particularly because of the low damping which characterizes modern tall buildings: inertia forces set up by wind-induced vibrations make wind forces increase more rapidly with height than would be construed from merely examining the variation of wind pressures. Seismic forces may increase more rapidly with height than would be indicated by an elementary analysis using a linear variation of horizontal accelerations; this is particularly noticeable in the more slender buildings and has led to the provision of assuming that a portion of the base shear acts at the roof of buildings having high slenderness ratios (Anderson et al., 1952), but it is also justified in buildings that deform only as shear beams (Bustamante, 1965).

Appendages. The taller a building the higher the likelihood that the fundamental period of its appendages (antenna towers, penthouses, etc.) will coincide with one of the building's natural periods of vibration. This may subject the appendages to very high magnification factors under seismic excitation (Newmark and Rosenblueth, 1971).

Overturning Moments. Sizable overturning moments can be produced in tall buildings under earthquake or wind, calling for difficult and expensive measures in columns, walls, and foundations. Owing partly to this reason, drastic reductions were allowed until recently in many building codes relative to the overturning moments obtained from integration of the seismic story-shear envelope. Some reduction can be justified [up to about 15% (Newmark and Rosenblueth, 1971)] because the maximum shears do not occur all at the same time and with the same sign, and one can argue for an insignificant additional reduction on other bases (Newmark and Rosenblueth, 1971), certainly not for the reductions that used to be customary. The Caracas earthquake of 1966 caused many column failures directly attributable to overturning moments and thereby called attention to this matter. As a consequence, some codes have swung in the opposite direction, omitting all reductions in overturning moments (International Conference of Building Officials, 1971).

Axial Deformations in Columns. It is difficult to have a code specify when axial deformations in columns must be taken into account in analysis. They are almost always significant when analyzing tall buildings under lateral load; they can also be decisive under gravity loads, when some columns are subjected to high static forces and others are not, because of differences in numbers of stories carried by them.

This situation can cause severe secondary bending moments in some beams and should be taken into account either in design or in the construction procedure.

Tilting. The possibility of tilting is often a major source of concern in the design of tall buildings. They may tilt because of eccentricity of gravity loads, overturning moment caused by earthquake or wind, settlement of an adjoining structure, emergence of an adjoining structure (when the latter rests on point-bearing piles and the building in question tends to settle or the ground undergoes subsidence), or differential compressibility of the subsoil. Even when the loads are strictly coincident with the center of gravity of the base, there are no neighboring structures, and the ground is homogeneous, there may be a tendency toward tilting if the base is not doubly symmetric (say, in the case of flatiron buildings). With a doubly symmetric base and a nominally homogeneous subsoil, tendency to tilt may be due to random variations in compressibility. This situation calls for a limitation of the allowable average settlement. The latter problem has been dealt with using cost-benefit analysis (Reséndiz and Herrera, 1969a), and the optimum number of soil specimens to be tested has been calculated using preposterior analysis under certain simplifying assumptions (Rosenblueth, 1969).

9 Summary and Conclusions

The ideal building code format is one of explicit reliability optimization, with some clauses worded in terms of bonuses and penalties rather than prohibitions. It should tend to optimization of design and construction from the viewpoint of society. Its adoption implies structural changes in building departments; there is need for an interdisciplinary committee attached to every building department. Committee members should be elected for a short period of office by popular vote, and they should run for an indefinite number of reelections.

On the other hand, present codes do not go beyond the use of split factors and characteristic values of load and resistance. Yet a drastic change into the ideal format is not advisable. This state of affairs calls for a strategy for evolution comprising steps in education: development of simple formulas, graphs, tables, computer programs, and computer languages oriented toward reliability and reliability optimization, research into the probability distributions of the relevant parameters concerning loads, resistances, and consequences of failure; introduction of a first-order second-moment format; adoption of a few, especially simple, alternate clauses permitting design based on reliability optimization, accompanied by the ideal format as an alternate procedure; and a systematic progression toward its supplanting existing formats.

Absence of satisfactory data on the statistical distributions of many parameters is not a good reason for postponing initiation of this strategy. The sooner code formats are rationalized the earlier present ignorance will become apparent, and it will be possible rationally to establish priorities in research.

Solutions are available for the calculation of member reliabilities and of structural reliabilities and reliability functions, as well as for the optimization of reliabilities, as described in this section; some of these solutions use approximate methods, and some of them are probably ready for incorporation as alternates into the next generation of building codes.

7.4   THE MODELING OF STRUCTURAL ACTIONS

The selection of safety levels in tall building design involves, as does any choice between a set of technical alternatives to solve a socioeconomic problem, the selection of a balance between potential system performance and required investment. Explicit quantitative evaluation has not been made in the past in problems such as the present one, where complex consequences of malperformance (including loss of life) are involved. Nevertheless, a trade-off of costs versus benefits is implicit in any deliberate national decision regulating the use of technology.

Starr (1969) has suggested that a partial answer to the question "How safe is safe enough?" can be obtained historically. His approach does not seek to find what is "best" for society according to a set of philosophical principles; rather it establishes what is "traditionally acceptable" and expresses the development of such tradition with time, assuming that historical records (statistics) are adequate and reveal social preferences sufficiently permanent to permit their use in decision making. Restricting his study to accidental deaths arising from technological developments in public use, he found that the statistical risk of death from disease appears to be a psychological yardstick for the acceptable level of other risks. In a sample application to atomic power plant safety he found the interesting result that the design target risk level determined by purely economic criteria was much lower than the present socially accepted risk for electric power plants. His methodology for revealing existing social preferences provides an insight into the cost-benefit balance on the socioeconomic plane which is a necessary ingredient in a judicious safety level decision.

The goal of this section is to outline a framework of thought sufficiently general that it may form a common basis for all safety level decisions in tall building technology (structural safety, fire safety, etc.). The discussion is limited to a common methodology for establishing target risk levels. The establishment of these levels for the several subsystems is left for the proper context. We shall, however, illustrate the approach by an example, comparing fire risk with risk of window glass breakage. The specific design question of how a particular system is to be engineered to achieve the target risk level is the subject of much study currently; it is an assumption, which we believe is justified, that practical solutions to this problem can be developed within a few years.

Mauch and Schneider (1973) have outlined a system of quantitative concepts as a framework for the selection of target risks for technical activities. The approach has elsewhere been illustrated by the optimization of pipeline location risks and of risks associated with a system of ammunition depots. The framework given in this section is developed from the concepts of Mauch and Schneider.

The proposed rationale is a logical extension of reliability analysis to permit optimization of a socioeconomic system operating partially under public control. Two major objections can be raised against a new conceptual framework of this kind from the viewpoint of practice.

First, it does not represent all known aspects of such systems. For example, the theory encompasses the classical concept of utility, known to conflict with certain aspects of common individual behavior (such as simultaneously gambling and taking out insurance). The theory is therefore not descriptive of reality; it is merely normative. Taking the familiar field of mechanics for comparison, the rationale advanced here does not have the universality of Newton's laws of motion—it is rather like Hooke's law, correct at most for some systems, possibly for none depending on the fidelity demanded of the representation. The usefulness of Hooke's law cannot be judged on the basis of the many aspects of matter it fails to represent; it is an acceptable tool in design because it leads to reliable predictions of material behavior under conditions known in advance. Similarly, the essential aspects of the proposed rationale are consistency and reliability in decision making.

Second, it may be objected that the theory is not useful if we do not have the data necessary to define the risk-cost curves required in the analysis. This objection has little validity, in that efficient data collection is possible only after a suitable conceptual framework has been established. For example, much of the effort that was expended to date on live load measurement has been wasted because a clear concept of the function of the data was not available. Similarly, it would have been unjustified to criticize Hooke's law on the grounds that Young's modulus was unknown—without the conceptual framework of Hooke's law, efficient data collection for the description of elastic behavior would not have been possible. An important aspect of the theory contained in this section is that it defines an approach to efficient collection of the relevant data.

1 Risk

The socioeconomic system is composed of a set of N activities (the precise meaning of this term will be discussed subsequently) A_i, $i = 1,2, \ldots, N$, divided into those in which an individual participates on a "voluntary" basis and those imposed by society. The process of optimization of cost versus benefit is fundamentally the same in both sets of activities; in the former an individual uses his own value system, while in the latter the criteria and options are determined in part by a controlling body. Because of the complexity of large societies (defined as autonomous entities), only the control group (in the present case of interest: the building code authority) is likely to be fully aware of the criteria employed, and the feedback time required to process the experience resulting from the decisions is likely to be long.

Associated with each activity is a risk (a precise meaning will be assigned to this word subsequently) that depends on various possible losses and the probability with which they are incurred. An individual perceives risk on a personal plane. All risks may be divided on legal grounds into: (1) The basic risk (the minimum risk anyone incurs merely by the activity of living in a society) R_0; (2) the personal risk (associated with optional activities wholly or mainly under individual control) R_p; and (3) the culpable risk, R_c, in which a liability is incurred by some other party that can be held responsible. It is difficult to point to any case of a code authority having been held responsible for risks, but it would appear that the authority of a code writing body arises out of a definite responsibility to society; the risks under consideration here would therefore be composed of R_0 and R_c, outside and within liability, respectively. The problem is to determine what level of risk, associated with those activities that are controlled by the code authority, is optimum (in a sense to be defined). Nevertheless, the code authority is properly restricted to operate only within the bounds of the basic risk R_0, since the probability of a code authority being found at fault must be kept negligible if it is to operate as a permanent institution of society.

The way risk is perceived on a personal plane relates to a set of values which may be divided into three modes: (1) Economic (material) values; (2) the value of human life; and (3) cultural-ideal values (including moral values and the "quality of life"). Any loss, for example the loss of a limb, may be evaluated on all three, modally different scales. It is a fundamental premise of societal decision making that personal risks of the members of society can be mapped onto a sociomoral plane where risks have a single-mode (scalar) quality. This mapping may be subject to certain ideal constraints [for example, in a democracy, that it must be independent of the labeling of the individuals (Luce and Raiffa, 1975)], but its exact nature is unknown and reflected only in the intuition of the decision maker. However, the premise from the viewpoint of the decision maker is that personally perceived risks can be compared by the individual as "greater," "equal," or ":smaller," and that this set of values with sufficient fidelity is reflected by similar ordinal risks on an objective socioeconomic plane. The acceptance of social responsibility implies that one has the ability to judge value on behalf of an (average) individual and weigh value between individuals. We are concerned here with optimization only on this public, socioeconomic plane.

Social decision making is not merely a matter of weighing individual preference on a social scale. There are also ethical considerations to be made, and they are important in matters of vital concern such as building safety. What present society wants must be viewed by the decision maker with reservation on behalf of future generations, for example. A building code authority does not just ask what is expedient to satisfy the current desires of a constituency, but asks "What *ought* the code to prescribe," reflecting the ethical aspects of the decision.

The contradiction between social preferences and ethical imperatives is, however, only an apparent one. A decision maker who, motivated by ethical idealism, would disregard the views of present society would violate the principle (Protagoras) that the measure of all things is man, substituting an ideal construct over the best judgment of his contemporaries without objective justification. In the following, we present a viewpoint of safety level decision making which is basically in accord with Starr's formulation without conflicting with the *homo mentor* principle. Any conceivable obligations to future generations, to other entities or ideal constructs, are implicitly accounted for by the presumption of a suitable parental instinct, etc., influencing the value structure of the constituents on whose behalf the code authority is exercised.

The components of total risk $R_0 + R_p + R_c$ are easily estimated. Canada Yearbook (1971) gives for 1967 and 1968 an average total mortality rate of $74 \times 10^{-4} = R_0 + R_p + R_c$. Of this, the component due to disease and suicide equals 68×10^{-4}, whereas the remaining 5.8×10^{-4} are assigned to motor vehicle accidents (2.7×10^{-4}), all other accidents (2.9×10^{-4}), and homicide and war (0.16×10^{-4}). As a rough estimate, in approximately one fourth of all deaths in motor vehicle accidents and in one tenth of all other accidents, a liability can be assigned to another party. The remainder of the accidental deaths and death from homicide and war must be assigned to basic risk R_0 (since suicide is excluded). Thus, we obtain the estimates

$$R_0 \approx (5.8 - 1) \times 10^{-4} \quad \approx 5 \times 10^{-4}$$
$$R_p \approx (74 - 5 - 1) \times 10^{-4} \approx 68 \times 10^{-4}$$
$$R_c \approx \left(\frac{2.7}{4} + \frac{2.9}{10}\right) \times 10^{-4} \approx 1 \times 10^{-4}$$

deaths per individual per year (in Canada). In addition, the total risk $R_0 + R_p + R_c$ encompasses roughly 0.01 to 0.1 injuries and \$100 material loss per individual per year.

Risk plays a central role in the safety level problem of any system (such as tall building technology) that operates partly under public control. It appears expedient to use risks as state variables or as auxiliary variables of fundamental importance. Before assigning a precise meaning to this notion, we observe in passing that the word "risk" has been employed: (1) In decision theory in the context "decision under risk" as opposed to "decision under uncertainty," to distinguish between situations in which probabilities can and cannot be assigned to the unknown states of the adversary or nature (Canada Yearbook, 1971); and (2) in the sense of "probability of failure" in some recent works. The notion of risk does not play a central role in either of these contexts, and case (2) can reasonably be considered as a special case of the use now to be proposed. We define risk as a precise mathematical quantity, as follows.

With each activity A is associated an exposure to several, mutually exclusive, basic loss events e_j with corresponding socioeconomic loss L_j and probability p_j. With each loss event is associated an additive scalar single-valued risk function

$$R_j = R_j(L_j, p_j) \tag{7.48}$$

Since each loss event e_j can be conceived as the component of two mutually exclusive events $e_j' + e_j''$, both with loss L_j, with probabilities p_j' and p_j'' such that $p_j' + p_j'' = p_j$, it follows that the risk function must be linear in the probability. Thus the risk associated with a simple or compound loss event is

$$R = \Sigma R_j = \Sigma p_j \, g(L_j) \tag{7.49}$$

Certain results by Starr (1969) appear superficially to contradict Eq. 7.49. From a plot of accident rate against hourly wage in the mining industries he found that the acceptance of individual risk (in terms of man-days lost per man-hour of exposure) is approximately an exponential function of the wages. However, the accuracy of the data is not sufficient to rule out the anticipated linear relation of risk (in excess of the basic risk value) acceptance as a function of wages. Moreover, any true nonlinearity in the relationship may merely reflect nonlinearity in the utility of a wage increment as function of wage.

The risk function, Eq. 7.49 is clearly not linear in the measure of loss events on the material plane. For example, 200 separate accidents each with one fatality have much less socioeconomic impact than one accident with 200 fatalities. Evidently, $g(\ )$ is monotonic; the terminology "risk" suggests it to be increasing. We may, however, let L_j denote directly the socioeconomic value of the loss, using the value of g for a loss event as the value of $L\,dj$ associated with the event to obtain the risk function in the simplest form

$$R = \Sigma p_j L_j \tag{7.50}$$

We also associate a material-economic value l_j with each loss event e_j. The relation between socioeconomic value and material value of a loss is a monotonic function

$$L_j = g_j(l_j) = \rho_j(l_j)l_j \tag{7.51}$$

in which ρ may be called the "aversion function" (Mauch and Schneider, 1973). For strictly material losses, ρ is a constant. For the particular case of fatalities, Mauch and Schneider have estimated some (relative) values of the aversion function. In English terminology their estimates are roughly described as: approximately unity for "small accidents" (1 fatality), 10 for "large accidents" (approximately 10 fatalities), 100 for "catastrophes" (10 to 30 fatalities), and 1000 for "major catastrophes" ($>$30 fatalities), as illustrated in Fig. 7.5. The aversion function ρ_j may differ with different classes of loss events as indicated by subscript j. For example, 3 fatalities due to structural collapse of a dwelling and 3 fatalities due to fire of the same dwelling have widely different socioeconomic measures. The point of interest here is not the exact values of these equivalents or the methods by which they could be established, but rather that rational (that is, self-consistent with respect to a fixed set of values) decision making on the socioeconomic plane may formally be described in terms of a risk function of the simple form of Eq. 7.50. It is interesting to note in passing that such mappings, while implicit in almost all safety decisions, are employed explicitly in measuring the risk in some fields. Reference is made to an accepted standard describing as a "measure of injury experience" a "disability severity rate" calculated according to a schedule in which a case of death, for example, is charged as 6000 days lost and a loss of one eye is charged as 1800 days (ANSI, 1967).

The formulation is a generalization of classical material-economic decision (making ρ equal to a constant, which may be taken as unity) which, in turn, includes the special case of ordinary reliability analysis when only a single loss event, "failure," is considered. In these special cases, Eq. 7.50 reduces respectively to

$$R = \Sigma p_j l_j \tag{7.52}$$

$$R = \Sigma p_j \tag{7.53}$$

The risk concept is readily extended to a continuous spectrum of loss events, interpreting the summation symbol appropriately in the sense of integration over the loss domain. This is important, for example, in the case of structural losses (in reinforced concrete structures covering the spectrum: cracks, yield, spalling, gross distortion, collapse)—the major part of the total loss is associated with cracks and yield, which are not often thought of as failure and are poorly represented by the discretization "failure/no failure." The occurrence of some of the limit states in this spectrum is "almost certain" in the case of a tall building; this aspect is covered in the present formulation. On the other hand, there may be some difficulties of defining a reasonable cut-off point at the rare events end of the spectrum; it may be debated in some locations whether or not some highly unlikely events such as tornadoes, aircraft collisions, or near nuclear bomb explosions should be taken into account. While not necessary, it would seem justified to disregard some events such as acts of war or "acts of God" in normal design, as is currently the practice.

2 Socioeconomic Optimization

Now, consider only the class **A** of activities, characterized as the set of all activities A_i, $i = 1, \ldots, n$ that contribute to the basic risk and operate under socioeconomic control. The control is exercised through the prescription of a finite set of M control parameters λ_k, $k = 1, \ldots, M$ which may be safety factors, allowable amounts of contaminants of effluent, etc. A set of values of λ_k constitutes a point in the control parameter space Λ and defines a socioeconomic state of total basic risk R and total allocation of resources C invested in the control of risk. These invested resources are formally similar to the risk function if they are taken as losses L_j ($= \rho\, l_j$ in which ρ = the constant socioeconomic equivalent of the material constant investment l_j) incurred with certainty, $p_j = 1$; C and R are therefore commensurate quantities. The generalized loss function $T \equiv C + R$ is a scalar point function in control parameter space Λ representing the total socioeconomic cost associated with the points λ_k, $k = 1, \ldots, M$. The optimal state is the one that minimizes the loss function T.

Assuming that λ_k are continuous variables, and that $T(\lambda_k)$ is continuous with continuous partial derivatives, we may state:

1. A necessary condition for the socioeconomic optimum is that the gradient of T vanishes, that is

$$\text{grad } T \equiv \left(\frac{\partial T}{\partial \lambda_1}, \ldots, \frac{\partial T}{\partial \lambda_M} \right) = 0 \qquad (7.54)$$

If we restrict attention to the states characterized by points on the surface $C = C_0 = $ constant, in which $C_0 = $ total optimum investment, we get:

2. Among all states with a given constant investment, the optimum state minimizes the total basic risk. In the same fashion:

3. Among all states with given total basic risk, the optimum state minimizes the total investment. The total resource allocation C may be decomposed in

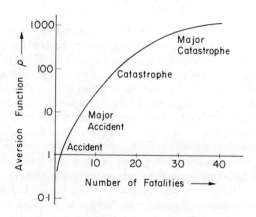

Fig. 7.5 Aversion function (schematic)

several ways, for example as a sum of activity costs C_i, one associated with each activity A_i, $i = 1, \ldots, n$, that is

$$C = \sum_{i=1}^{n} C_i \tag{7.55}$$

At optimum the gradient of R and C are equal and opposite vectors in Λ. Assuming that the number of activities n is less than the number of control parameters M (this can always be effected by lumping of activities), we may use ΔC_i as a parametrization at the optimum point for the risk increment ΔR thus

$$\Delta R = \Delta R(\Delta C_i) \tag{7.56}$$

If we treat the resource allocations ΔC_i as independent parameters, ΔR may be visualized as a scalar point function in an n-dimensional orthogonal Cartesian coordinate system ΔC_i. In this system, the surfaces of constant C are planes with a normal that forms the same angle with the coordinate axes. At the optimum point (the origin) the gradient $\Sigma(\Delta R)$ is alined with the normal. Its projections $\partial \Delta R / \partial \Delta C_i$ on the coordinate axes are therefore all equal. Thus:

4. A necessary condition for socioeconomic optimum is that the rates of change of total risk with respect to individual activity resource allocations are the same for all activities. Alternatively, we may decompose the total risk R into a sum of activity risks R_i and express the total allocation of resources as a function of these risks as

$$\Delta C = \Delta C(\Delta R_i) \tag{7.57}$$

Then, by a similar argument we get:

5. A necessary condition for socioeconomic optimum is that the rates of change of total cost with respect to individual activity risk is the same for all activities. The total activity of class **A** may be decomposed into individual activities A_i in a variety of ways. For some of these decompositions, it may reasonably be assumed that a change in the investment in an individual activity ΔC_i has no influence on the risk associated with another activity ΔR_j ($j \neq 1$). A decomposition of all activities into separate activities of this kind is called "independent." The two preceding propositions then specialize into:

6. A necessary condition for socioeconomic optimum in a system of independent activities is that the rates of change of individual risk as a function of individual resource allocation (and vice versa) are the same for all activities.

The preceding discussion relates to a total optimization of all control parameters of society simultaneously. The results are useful insofar as they characterize the optimum state; however, simultaneous optimization is not a practical possibility in a complex society. In addition, there may be arbitrary bounds that are imposed on the socioeconomic optimum for political reasons. Very often, the amount of funds available is restricted to not exceed a given value C^*, in which case the search for an optimum is restricted to the subdomain $C \leq C^*$. For example, a specified amount may have been made available to produce a specified number of public housing units. Or, conversely, public pressure may dictate a maximum basic risk R_0^* which may not be exceeded at any cost. The problem of safety levels in society then presents itself as one of constrained optimization, but it remains fundamentally the same.

A more realistic and perhaps also more tractable formulation might be to replace absolute constraints with suitable penalty functions representing something less than absolute resistance to transcend a constraint when there are sufficiently strong reasons to do so. For the present purpose there is, however, no need to pursue this formulation.

We assume that society has imposed a maximum on total basic risk and ask how this is best distributed among two activities, say $i = 1$ "tall buildings," and $i = 2$ "other activities in class **A**." Using costs C_1 and C_2 as state variables we may ask how the total risk $R_1 + R_2 = R^*$ is to be distributed between the two. The basic information required for each activity is the state equation (risk-cost curve)

$$R_1 = R_1(C_1) \tag{7.58}$$

$$R_2 = R_2(C_2) \tag{7.59}$$

As before, it may be shown that when the total cost is minimized, we have

$$\frac{dR_1}{dC_1} = \frac{dR_2}{dC_2} \tag{7.60}$$

It should be noted that this formulation does not assume each activity to be internally optimized; it is only required that the state equations (reflecting a particular degree of internal optimization) exist. We conclude:

7. At socioeconomic optimum, the rate of change of risk with cost obtainable for one activity should equal that obtainable for all other socioeconomic activities that contribute to the basic risk and operate under social control. Now, presume that such a balance has been established between "tall buildings" and other activities in class **A**. This balance may be characterized either by its particular total risk for tall buildings R_1^* or by an allowable investment into safety measures C_1^* for tall buildings; other investments that do not contribute to a reduction of the risk are left out of the discussion. We now ask: How are the tall building design parameters $\lambda_1, \lambda_2, \ldots, \lambda_m$ to be selected so as to minimize the total cost while maintaining the assigned risk ceiling R_1^*? At the optimum we may, as before, decompose the cost increment ΔC into a set of specific cost increments ΔC_i, each associated with one of the control parameters. As before, we write the relationships $\Delta C = \Delta C(\lambda_i)$ and $\Delta R_i = \Delta R_i(\lambda_i)$, assumed montonic, and express total cost increment as function of risks

$$\Delta C = \Delta C(\Delta R_i) \qquad (7.61)$$

With a risk ceiling, we have the constraint $\Sigma \Delta R_i = 0$. As before, it may be shown that:

8. The distribution of risks associated with individual design parameters for a given total risk that minimizes total cost is characterized by equal partial rates of change of total cost with respect to changes in individual risks. Because of the duality of cost and risk in this formulation, a dual proposition may be stated for a cost constraint which, however, does not seem of much value in the present context.

3 Activities

"Activity" has been employed in this section as an undefined notion serving to label costs, risks, and control parameters. The term is employed in material economics to denote the interior of a closed accounting surface in a suitable space, conveniently chosen to yield tractable or significant state variables. In the simplest form the division is simply geographic, but usually the terms refer to an abstract organization space reflected, for example in such terms as "private sector," "public sector," etc. Or a firm may be organized into departments, the flow of goods and services into and out of these departments (or subdepartments, or groups of departments as convenient) being state variables. The use in the socioeconomic concept seems to involve an even higher order of interactions. Every individual or organization in a society is effectively exposed to some risk from the activities under public control. If a building safety factor is changed, the influence is by no means confined to the building industry alone—the risk of practically everyone in society is affected. This raises the question: How is the class **A** of publicly controlled risk-producing activities best subdivided for the purposes of analysis? The subdivision will, of course, depend on the aim; in the present case it is to compare costs and risks associated with tall building technology with other costs and risks.

A complete analysis of this problem is outside the scope of this section. It is sufficient to show that a precise meaning can always be assigned for a given decomposition of **A**. It is always possible to label each control parameter by activity index k for the subdivision $\mathbf{A}\,(A_1 \ldots A_k \ldots)$; with each λ_i is associated a generalized loss $L_i = L_i(\lambda_j) \equiv \partial R/\partial \lambda_i$ and a generalized initial cost $C_i = C_i(\lambda_j) = \partial C/\partial \lambda_i$, $j = 1, 2, \ldots, M$ which, through the label, are assigned uniquely to the appropriate activity. Corresponding generalized quantities can then be calculated for each activity in an obvious fashion.

4 Example

Application of the principles presented in this section can be illustrated on a simplified M-parameter system in which two parameters, n and t, are variable. To fix ideas let us consider a 50 000 m² steel frame building, having 50 stories of 25 m × 40 m × 2.50 m each; total height 125 m (Fig. 7.6). The system under study is the totality of individuals and institutions interacting with this building as owner, contractor, tenant or bystander, etc. Let n be the ratio of design fire load to average fire load for the building (fire load is defined as the weight of combustible material), called the fire load design factor (Lie, 1972). The exterior walls of the building are covered with plate glass panels 1 m × 2.5 m of thickness t, simply supported along all four edges. The aim is to find the glass thickness $t = t(n)$ of optimum reliability relative to the fire safety reflected in the fire load design factor n.

For the purpose of this example it is sufficient to use a realistic set of numerical values; in application to a real building code considerable care must be taken to verify the numerical basis of the calculations. Here, the values used by Lie in fire resistance optimization studies are used. Each story of 1000 m² is regarded as a fire resistant compartment; fire resistance is obtained by insulating the steel members and floors at a cost of 1% per unit increase of n; probability of occurrence of fire, p, equals $2 \times 10^{-7}/m^2/yr$; coefficient of variation of fire resistance V_R, equals 0.4, and of fire load V_W equals 0.7; loss of contents and indirect losses, m, equals 3 times the building cost which is $f = \$200/m^2$; cost of repair of fire damage is 5 times the building cost; service life of the building t_D is 50 yr; the interest rate i is 7% (Lie, 1972).

Disregarding the cost of fire protection in comparison with the building cost, and assuming that fire load and fire resistance are normally distributed, Lie (1972) has calculated the capitalized loss expectation as a function of the fire load factor, n. To the relatively small risk to life and limb, this loss expectation may be identified with the risk, yielding the risk versus cost characteristic shown in Fig. 7.7.

The strength of glass is affected by many factors; surface condition, size, age, humidity, etc. For illustration, we neglect these factors and accept the results of 287 tests on 1/4-in. specimens of plate glass sampled from the production of two plants over two years, showing an apparently normal distribution with mean strength of 8400 psi and a coefficient of variation of 0.22 (Frownfelter, 1969).

The wind load is also influenced by a number of factors: direction, location, dynamic response of the panel, etc. Again, we neglect these factors and use the typical distribution of annual extreme pressures published by Davenport (1970).

The reliability of one panel as a function of t is easily calculated by convolution. Assuming that the strength of any panel is statistically independent of the strength

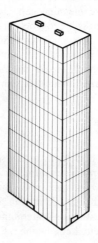

Fig. 7.6 50-story building (example)

of any other panel, the expected number of panel failures in 50 yr is equal to (2000)(50) times the probability of failure of one panel.

The cost of a glass failure is estimated by assuming that one person is lightly injured (calculated at 600 man-days lost production) with probability 0.3; heavily injured (2500 days) with probability 0.25; and killed with probability 0.15 (6000 days lost); whereas no significant damage occurs with probability 0.3; the expected number of man-days lost is then (0.3)(600) + (0.25)(2500) + (0.15)(6000). Assume that a man-day contributes $48 to the Gross National Product (Canada Yearbook, 1971). Then, the expected loss of one glass panel failure is $82 000.

The risk as a function of panel thickness is shown in the risk-cost-curve in Fig. 7.8. Again, the panel thickness may be taken as a function of glass cost, indicated by the double scale along the abscissa in Fig. 7.8. By comparison of slopes between Figs. 7.7 and 7.8, the correspondence between thickness of glass t and fire load factor n is finally established as shown in Fig. 7.9. The result would suggest that no true balancing of risks is possible in this case, since there is no commercially available thickness of glass that falls near the optimum.

The reader is reminded that the assumptions made in this example are not universally valid, so that no general conclusions or particular significance should be attached to the calculated values in this example.

5 Conclusion

The selection of safety levels in tall building technology is presented as a problem of socioeconomic optimization. The formulation does not neglect psychological and moral values, but presumes that these values can be expressed rationally and

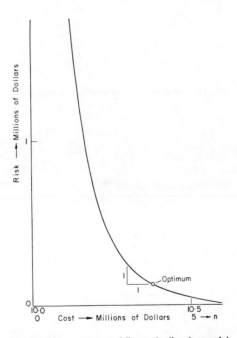

Fig. 7.7 Risk-cost curve of fire protection (example)

objectively on behalf of a society as a whole by the code-writing authority. This includes specifically the influence of past performance on present performance criteria ("People will accept what they have been accustomed to"). The formulation is thus relative to a set of values; it is also relative to a state of knowledge, reflected in the probability measure, and relative to a technology or code format. For example, an optimum may be sought either on the basis that all members have the same safety factor on material strength (as in most design codes currently in operation), or on the basis that safety vary with the structural importance of the

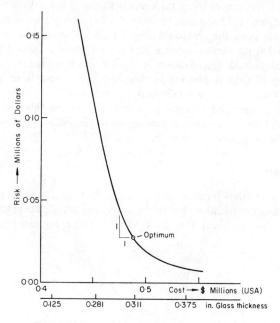

Fig. 7.8 Risk-cost curve for plate glass (example)

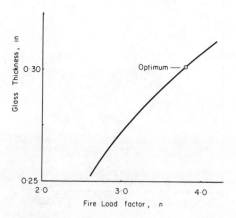

Fig. 7.9 Correspondence between design factors for glass breakage and fire (example)

member (which may be ideal, but too cumbersome for practice); the optimization is performed with respect to a fixed code format. The question of optimal degree of differentiation (number and kind of basic safety factors) or detail in the codes for tall buildings has not been considered here; it is probably best treated empirically in the context of a specific application. With the continuing trend of automation of design calculations, the practically acceptable amount of complication in a code is greatly increased. For example, to have an individual safety factor for each story in tall frameworks would not tax the memory capacity of an automatic computer.

As a generalization of utility and reliability, the notion of risk is introduced as a fundamental quantity in the formulation. It is an additive function over a set of elementary loss events; for mutually exclusive losses it is the sum of the products of socioeconomic loss with the associated probability of loss.

All risks are divided into personal risk, culpable risk, and basic risk; socioeconomic optimization is defined as the minimization of the sum of total basic risk and total investment to reduce basic risk. The state equations, expressing individual risk as a function of investment to reduce risk, for all components of the socioeconomic system or subsystem in question, play a fundamental role in the formulation. These equations contain all the information necessary in the optimization; they characterize the socioeconomic behavior of any system whether or not it is internally optimized. Gross statistics for the socioeconomic system as a whole would therefore suffice to define the operating characteristics of the environment of the system under study (tall building activity), while state equations for the components of the tall building activity may be sought by detailed analysis. If for a particular state of the total code or recommendations, the rate of change of risk with respect to cost associated with all code parameters is known, a better state can be found by a change that tends to equalize these rates. If all rates are equal the code is internally optimized. If the rate for the code as a whole is equal to that for the remainder of the socioeconomic system as a whole, the code is externally optimized.

7.5 LOADS AND LOAD COMBINATIONS

1 Loading and Safety Analysis

The reliability analysis required in structural design has to deal with the risk of damage or unserviceability. This risk is related primarily to mechanical phenomena due to loading. A first, rough definition of loadings arises: a loading is any cause which is able to produce stresses in a structure.

Any possible loading process leads to a definite structural behavior. Structural behavior could be normal (complete serviceability for the whole pre-established service duration) or could involve any degree of unserviceability or damage at any time moment. A structure could be characterized by a set of parameters able to define its behavior under any loading process (examples of parameters: ultimate loadings, stiffnesses, natural periods, etc.). Roughly speaking, engineers should design structures having such values of characteristic parameters that neither damage nor unserviceability is unduly likely to occur during pre-established service life.

Loadings, as well as structural characteristics, are random; that is, different, nominally identical structures would be actually subjected to nonidentical loadings and would be actually characterized by different values of structural parameters. These more or less important differences cannot be controlled at present, thus an inherent, intrinsic randomness of both kinds of parameters has to be accepted. The mass stability of the values of these parameters justifies the use of probabilistic concepts for describing this randomness.

Loading analysis must consider two main aspects of the problem: (1) Analysis of physical aspects, oriented mainly towards defining a coherent deterministic model; and (2) analysis of stochastic aspects, oriented mainly towards developing bases for quantitative safety and serviceability analysis.

Safety analysis for any structure is a result of analysis of: (1) Data on loadings; (2) structural characteristics; and (3) the use of structural mechanics (more accurately, stochastic structural mechanics should be used in this view). One important fact should be noted: theories and techniques of structural mechanics are quite well developed at present (1979), giving in most cases a high degree of reliability to results of analysis if reliable data are used. In contrast, present data on structural characteristics and especially on loadings are affected by a degree of uncertainty which can be high. This uncertainty cannot be reduced by the use of structural mechanics and so it will directly affect the reliability of safety analysis.

Safety analysis is dealt with at present from a probabilistic viewpoint. Nevertheless probabilistic concepts must be used on the basis of accurately defined deterministic models. Some features of loadings from the latter viewpoint must be therefore dealt with primarily. This is the only way to yield satisfactory reliability to subsequent probabilistic analysis.

2   Physical Characteristics of Loadings

A smoother definition of loadings than the definition previously given would be of obvious interest. Nevertheless an accurate definition is difficult. Several problems should be answered in this view. Consider the following questions:

1. How to distinguish in any case loadings from structural characteristics? Are prestressing, shrinkage, etc., loadings or structural characteristics?

2. How to separate mechanical phenomena from other physical phenomena that sometimes seriously influence safety (examples: corrosion, very high or very low temperatures affecting material characteristics)? How to get a reconciliation with the viewpoint of thermodynamics which does not permit independent treatment of mechanical aspects of physical phenomena?

Structural engineers are thus obliged to recognize an existing uncertainty of concept, having an as yet undefined influence on the whole problem of safety analysis and design decision.

The following problems in this paragraph will be dealt with throughout from a deterministic standpoint. Problems will be dealt with for which unanswered questions [such as (1) and (2) above] are not critical. Some criteria, D_i, of loading classification must be taken into account.

Criterion D_1. Loading origin. One could deal with loads that are inherent to a structure (example: dead load), that are due to service (example: live loads), that are due to natural factors (examples: wind, earthquake), or that are due to exceptional events (examples: explosion, failure of some structural member). This classification criterion, on which classical codes are based, is gradually losing its importance, due to its minor significance for the requirements of modern safety analysis.

Criterion D_2.   Action mode. Most loadings could be related to the following cases: (1) Given systems of forces; and (2) imposed strains or support displacements. Nevertheless, these cases are only limiting cases of the general case of interaction between structure and environment. Examples of interaction include: static interaction between a silo and its footing, or between a structure and the ground (interaction can be significant in cases of soil pressure or of differential settlements); dynamic interaction between ground and structure or between water and dam during an earthquake, or dynamic interaction between moving loads and structures. Reduction of the general case of interaction to the limit cases (1) or (2) stated previously is primarily a question of ratio of impedances of structure to environment. High structural impedance involves limit case (1), while low structural impedance involves limit case (2). The action mode of loadings has a capital influence on the nature of limit states to be considered in structural analysis.

Criterion D_3.   Dependence on time and space coordinates. Time dependence permits a classification into static and (various kinds of) dynamic loadings. Of course, the choice of parameters characterizing dynamic loads is a question in itself (examples: sinusoidal forces can be simply characterized by amplitudes and frequencies, while wind or earthquake loadings must be characterized according to more sophisticated concepts, suitable for structural analysis, as power spectral densities, etc.).

Dependence on space coordinates is another important aspect. A tendency to adopt idealized space distributions could lead to omission of analysis of some characteristic, eventually determinant patterns of structural behavior (for example: omission of analysis for nonsymmetrical loading of some shells).

Criterion D_4.   Time dependence upon large time intervals. This criterion relates not to mechanical behavior but to safety analysis. One can deal, from this viewpoint, with permanent loadings, with commonly occurring temporary loadings (service loads, snow, etc.), and with rarely occurring (eventually catastrophic), usually transient loadings (earthquakes, explosions, etc.).

Criterion D_5.   Mutual existential dependency of loads. Loads can be existentially independent (they can occur independently of other loads), existentially dependent (they cannot exist without the existence of a primary load), and existentially exclusive (they cannot exist simultaneously). This criterion is deterministic; we deal with it in solving the load-combinations problems (Tichy, 1974).

Any kind of classification does not automatically answer a basic problem: how to define the primary characteristics of loadings. This problem is important especially in cases when the second criterion cannot lead to a simple limit case. For example: Which is the primary characteristic of a seismic motion—an ideal undisturbed motion, which cannot actually occur at the structure site, or the actual motion, disturbed by the interaction phenomenon? Which is the primary characteristic of wind, especially in case of resonance due to Kármán vortices—mean, undisturbed wind velocity, or amplitude of lateral pressures, defined by the interaction with the structure?

A conclusion of this paragraph: hard work is still to be done in order to define characteristics of loadings, even from a deterministic point of view.

3 Deterministic Representation of Loadings

As stated earlier, structural design involves some comparison between acting (predicted) loadings on one hand, and loadings a structure is able to bear, on the other hand. This can be done only by comparing some scalar parameters of both kinds of factors. A need for quantification is thus raised. More accurately speaking, loadings and structural characteristics should be represented by means of some coordinates, related to some comprehensive reference system. The complexity of the problem is obvious if all the possibilities raised by the classifications of the preceding Article (especially with respect to the second, third, and fourth criteria) are considered.

Loadings S will be considered as systems of given forces or of imposed displacements or strains, or both. A loading, S, being given, its product with a scalar number q (q: real), qS, has obviously the sense of a loading whose components have q times increased intensities. The sum of two loadings, S_1 and S_2, assumed to act possibly on a structure, is also a loading, defined by each of the components of S_1 and each of the components of S_2. (The sense of the difference of two loadings is obvious.) These definitions show that, given a system of loadings S_i, a linear combination of them is also a loading, possibly acting on the same structure. A first general property of loadings which can act on a structure thus becomes obvious.

This is property L_1. The set of loadings $\mathbf{S}$ possibly acting on a given structure is a linear space (the property L_1 is valid for static, as well as for dynamic loadings).

To make a difference between loadings with various kinds of dependence on space or time coordinates, metric properties of the space $\mathbf{S}$ can be put to evidence. Stress and strain tensors corresponding to a loading S_i (assuming linear behavior of the structure) $\sigma_{kl\,(i)}(x_1,x_2,x_3,t)$, and $\epsilon_{kl\,(i)}(x_1,x_2,x_3,t)$, will be considered in this view. A finite, long time interval, of T_0 length, covering the service duration, will also be defined. The scalar product of two loadings S_1 and S_2, $\langle S_1,S_2 \rangle$, will be defined by

$$\langle S_1,S_2 \rangle = \frac{1}{T_0} \int_0^{T_0} \left[\int_V \sum_{k,l}^{1,3} \sigma_{kl\,(1)}(x_1,x_2,x_3,t)\epsilon_{kl\,(2)}(x_1,x_2,x_3,t)\, dV \right] dt \qquad (7.62)$$

or, in the case of static loadings, by the simplified relation

$$\langle S_1,S_2 \rangle = \int_V \sum_{k,l}^{1,3} \sigma_{kl\,(1)}(x_1,x_2,x_3)\epsilon_{kl\,(2)}(x_1,x_2,x_3)\, dV \qquad (7.63)$$

The norm of a loading, $\|S\|$, will be given by

$$\|S\| = \sqrt{\langle S,S \rangle} \qquad (7.64)$$

and the angle between two loadings, α_{12}, by

$$\cos\alpha_{12} = \frac{\langle S_1,S_2 \rangle}{\|S_1\|\,\|S_2\|} \qquad (7.65)$$

The metric properties put to evidence in this way may be stated in the following manner.

For property L_2, the set of loadings $\mathbf{S}$ possibly acting on a structure is a Hilbert space. Any system of n linearly independent loadings, S_i, spans an n-dimensional subspace, S_n, of the space S. In this case, any loading S belonging to the subspace S_n, can be represented as a linear combination of the form

$$S = \sum_i^{1,n} q_i S_i \tag{7.66}$$

in which the parameters q_i play the role of Cartesian coordinates. The scalar product of two loadings, S_1 and S_2, becomes in this case

$$\langle S_1, S_2 \rangle = \sum_{i,j}^{1,n} \langle S_i, S_j \rangle q_{i(1)} q_{j(2)} \tag{7.67}$$

Note that the assumption of linear dependence between stress and strain tensors adopted for defining the scalar product of two loadings is merely a convenient method for introducing a reference system similar to Cartesian coordinates, and does not imply any restriction for the analysis and representation of nonlinear structural behavior.

The space of loadings thus defined permits introducing an accurate language in treating problems of structural safety. The basis of the space is defined in terms of loadings, and not of stresses, internal forces, etc., since the latter parameters do not satisfy the property L_1 (very high stresses or internal forces are not compatible with physical properties, while very strong loadings could be imagined).

The space of loadings, S, also permits representation of structural characteristics. If various kinds of structural behavior (normal behavior with perfectly reversible deformation, occurrence of plastic strain or of a plastic hinge at any time moment, loss of stability at any time moment, collapse, etc.) are considered, these kinds of behavior can be imagined as plotted against the coordinates of loadings producing them. One can speak about several representative domains in the space S (domains of linear behavior, of various degrees of plastic deformation, etc.). Boundaries of such domains represent limit states of structures dealt with.

The space of loadings thus becomes a general tool for the deterministic analysis of loadings and of structural characteristics and behavior. It can be adopted as a basis for stochastic analysis of safety problems too, since it permits accurate definitions of various events and of their probabilities. More or less simplified representations of this kind have been adopted by several authors. Some examples in this view are given by Augusti and Baratta, 1972; Ferry Borges and Castanheta, 1971; and Sandi, 1966a.

The representation adopted is unfortunately very sophisticated for practical purposes, even in the case of relatively simple structural problems. It is therefore necessary to simplify this representation in order to permit performance of computations. The most efficient way in this view is that of adopting for representation a subspace having a minimum reasonable number of dimensions. This way involves primarily a reduction of the number of parameters characterizing loadings. Examples:

1. Snow loading occurring at any time moment on a roof could be characterized by its maximum (with respect to time) intensities at a few points
   (eventually at a single one).

2. Seismic motion in one direction occurring at any time moment at a given site could be characterized by the root mean square of acceleration, by its predominant frequency, and by a measure of the degree of power concentration in the vicinity of predominant frequency. Reduction of the complexity of problems must be carefully dealt with, in order not to neglect some parameters of first importance for structural analysis.

In conclusion, a coherent deterministic representation of the set of loadings possibly acting on a given structure and of structural behavior is a necessary basis for safety analysis. Extensive research is still needed in order to reach a systematic solution for representation problems, to be mathematically correct and also of current practical use.

4 Random Nature of Loadings

Loadings, as well as structural characteristics, have a random nature. One can speak about twofold randomness: (1) Objective (intrinsic, inherent) randomness, which is due to factors beyond actual control possibilities; and (2) subjective randomness, which is due primarily to the actual lack of information on computation data and of analysis concepts and techniques. The two kinds of randomness previously dealt with can interfere. It can be imagined that future increased control possibilities will lead to some decrease of objective randomness.

The sense of objective randomness could be stated as follows:

1. A set **A** of structures built according to identical design solutions, having nominally identical functions, will be considered.

2. Different elements of the set **A** considered will be actually subjected to different loading processes, although any nominal parameter that can be controlled has identical values for all elements. The same fact is valid for parameters representing structural characteristics.

3. Parameters characterizing the loading processes of several elements of the set **A** have different values for different elements, but the relative frequencies of their values are stable.

4. Cases of loadings for which the stability of relative frequencies of the values of characteristic parameters cannot be confirmed or has no sense, can no longer be treated (on probabilistic bases.)

The objective randomness of loadings can be dealt with by probabilistic means, having in view the following steps:

1. Elaboration of a coherent deterministic model for the loading process dealt with (the previous paragraph should be kept in view in this sense).

2. Definition on this basis of characteristic events, of a probabilistic measure of these events, and, eventually, of some characteristic random variables, random functions, or random fields.

The subjective randomness is due to two kinds of factors: (1) Uncertainty related to the actual distributions of random parameters dealt with; and (2) uncertainty generated by insufficiently accurate concepts and techniques of analysis. The uncertainty related to the distributions of parameters can be dealt with by means of concepts and techniques given by mathematical statistics (degree of reliability of statistical data, techniques of estimating parameters characterizing statistical sets). The uncertainty generated by insufficiently accurate concepts and techniques of analysis raises more difficult problems which have not been dealt with as yet under sufficiently general assumptions. Needs for fundamental research are obvious, especially in view of analyzing the latter kind of uncertainty. A comparison of the importance of the latter kinds of uncertainty shows that in almost all cases inaccuracies due to concepts and techniques of analysis are minor and relatively easily remediable. The use of modern computer techniques, as well as of experimental methods, has a considerable role at present in making these inaccuracies of little significance.

5   Probabilistic Representation of Loadings

Once a deterministic model for a kind of loading has been adopted, probability functions or densities can be defined for the characteristic parameters introduced. The type of function to be adopted for representation depends primarily on the deterministic model. The number of possibilities occurring can be easily remarked if all the possibilities introduced by criteria D_3 and D_4 of Article 2 of this section are considered (the criterion D_1 has no significance in this view; what concerns the criterion D_2 should not influence, as a principle, the treatment of loading analysis problems).

Possibilities raised by criterion D_3 could be summarized as follows:

1. With respect to time dependence of loads (considered for brief time intervals, comparable with the natural periods of structures): static loads can be dealt with as random variables for which one-dimensional distributions can be considered, while dynamic loads having simple types of time dependence (example: sinusoidal loads, periodic shocks, etc.) could be dealt with by means of probability densities of amplitudes and frequencies; and randomly varying dynamic loads (wind gusts, seismic accelerations, etc.) have to be dealt with by means of more sophisticated techniques. One way adopted is that of the analysis of distribution of extreme gust intensities or acceleration pulses intensities; a more suitable way appears to be the theory of random functions having continuous spectra (power spectrum densities, etc.), which can be adopted in a natural manner for dynamic analysis of structures.

2. Regarding dependence of loads on space coordinates: concentrated or uniformly distributed loads can be dealt with as random variables; significantly nonuniformly distributed loads (for example, live loads, snow loading) must be treated by more sophisticated means (theoretically, random fields). A suitable way appears to be that of analyzing distribution of values of Fourier coefficients.

With respect to criterion D_3, a general remark can be made: tools adopted for algebraization in deterministic analysis are suitable also for stochastic analysis (examples: Fourier analysis of dependence on space coordinates permits a successful algebraization of random fields, that is of random functions of space coordinates; Fourier or Laplace transforms for time dependence correspond to power spectrum density techniques for stationary or nonstationary random functions).

Possibilities raised by criterion D_4 could be summarized as follows:

1. The main task is that of representing in a most suitable manner the type of random occurrence of various loadings.

2. The problem of defining a reasonable set of parameters characterizing one case of occurrence is basic for formulating the problem of distribution with respect to time.

3. Distributions of various characteristics of loadings must deal especially with extreme values in the case of intensity-type parameters, but with random variation in the vicinity of expected values for frequency-type parameters (for example, in the case of dynamic loads).

4. The interest for intensity-type parameters is oriented mainly towards prediction of extreme values, occurring very seldom, so that statistical data available must be often extrapolated; extrapolation techniques therefore play an important role in this field.

Research in this field has two main tasks: development of satisfactory mathematical models for any type of loading, and deriving actual distributions on the basis of statistical studies. The more difficult task is obviously the latter, since it is related sometimes to considerable efforts for sampling statistical data (provided that sampling is actually possible). Impossibility of sampling statistical data can be compensated in some cases by indirect methods (Bayesian techniques, equivalence between variability in time and among the elements of statistical population, etc.).

Research work accomplished to date does not cover all the possibilities enumerated. Attention has been given mainly to permanent loadings (characterized by one single parameter), to some types of dynamic loadings (wind gusts, seismic ground motions), and to distribution of intensity-type parameters for infrequent loadings (Pearson, Poisson, Gumbel, etc., distributions). Some research has been done with respect to space coordinate dependence of static loadings, of wind gusts, and of earthquake loadings. Several important features have been practically neglected. The main cause of these shortcomings is the difficulty of sampling satisfactory statistical information able to build a support for theoretical developments. Some of the most characteristic and important research work with respect to loading distribution has been done by Kármán, Mitchell and Woodgate, Cornell and Peir for live loads; by Barstein, Davenport, Harris, Pischikov, and Vickery for wind and snow loading; and by Bolotin, Ferry Borges, and Housner for earthquake loading. Extreme values of live loads, their simultaneous occurrence on different floors and buildings, their space variation, and the influence of room size have been dealt with. Distribution of extreme winds, features of power spectrum densities (including space correlation) of wind gusts, influence of rugosity and macrorugosity, and effects of Kármán vortices, aerodynamic coefficients, etc., have been investigated to date. Distributions of extreme earthquake magnitudes and intensities, influence of local geology and of focus depth and epicentral distance on spectral characteristics of ground motion have also been investigated. This research is actually contributing to the gradual refinement of design codes.

Once the deterministic representation of Article 3 is adopted, distributions of loadings should be conceived primarily as probability densities of the coordinates q of loadings with respect to a reference system that has been previously chosen. Nevertheless, obtaining probability densities of this type involves a considerable quantity of information based on sampling work.

6 Simultaneous Occurrence of Different Loads

Structures are subjected as a rule not to a single loading, but to a combination of different loadings. Such combinations are most significant for the risk of damage or unserviceability. Structural analysis must be performed, therefore, having in view the simultaneous effects of various loadings.

In some cases different loadings are stochastically independent. That means, in mathematical terms, that, for some loadings $S_1, S_2, \ldots S_n$ having the coordinates $q_{i(1)}, q_{i(2)}, \ldots q_{i(n)}$, the joint probability-density is a product of probability densities characterizing each of the loadings. One can accept that such independence exists between dead load and snow loading, for example. On the other hand, there exist several other cases when different loadings are not stochastically independent. As an example, the case of simultaneous action of wind and snow could be considered. Strong winds will influence space distributions and intensities of snow loading for various kinds of roofs. The most general and complete manner of treating such cases is that of Bayesian relations. Unfortunately, the determination of conditional probabilities required by such relations is not possible without a quantity of information that is seldom available. Imagine in this view the research needed for determining conditional distributions for parameters of snow and wind loadings, for all possible shapes of roofs! The lack of information on conditional probabilities has led some specialists to analyze correlations between some loadings. This treatment is simple for dead-load type loadings, but involves supplementary definitions for temporary loadings. Imagine again the case of wind and snow loading, where season, area, loading duration, etc., must be simultaneously considered.

The problem of simultaneous occurrence of different loadings has some common features with the problem of loadings that are characterized by several parameters, the joint probability distribution of which is to be dealt with. Imagine in this sense the space distribution of snow or live loads, or the nonsynchronous time dependence of wind gusts at different points of a structure.

The probabilities characterizing simultaneous occurrence of critical values of parameters for various loadings should be always kept in view, since conventional values which are reasonable for loadings considered as isolated from other loadings may become extremely unreasonable for the case of simultaneous effects of different loadings. Some practical remarks given in Article 9 of this section are important in this view.

One can affirm that research performed to date has given many more results for loadings considered one by one than for problems of simultaneous action of different loadings. Research results obtained to date on the latter subject are based rather on theoretical assumptions and analysis, due to sampling difficulties. Recommendations given by codes are rather the result of engineering judgment.

The need for research on load combinations is obvious, if importance of the problem as well as present lack of knowledge are considered.

7 Loading Distribution and Probabilities of Damage

The problem of loading analysis can be kept correctly in view only if it is considered to be a part of the problem of safety analysis. This is valid for theoretical aspects as well as for an approach to practical design.

A simple example can illustrate a general approach to the problem of probabilistic safety analysis. Consider a structure subjected to a load depending on a single parameter Q, the probability density of which is $f_Q(q)$. The structure itself is characterized by some values $R_{(1)}, R_{(2)}, \ldots R_{(n)}$ of the load (these values are assumed to build an increasing sequence); exceeding of each of them produces a qualitative change in structural behavior (occurrence of cracking, development of a first plastic hinge, ..., collapse). Each of the values $R_{(k)}$ is random and is characterized by a probability density $f_{(k)}(r)$ (any probability density will be assumed to vanish for negative values of its argument). Then

$$Q > R_{(k)} \tag{7.68}$$

involves exceeding the kth limit state. The probability of this inequality

$$H_{(k)} = P[Q > R_{(k)}] \tag{7.69}$$

can be determined by means of

$$P[Q > R_{(k)}] = \iint\limits_{Q > R_{(k)}} f_Q(q) f_{(k)}(r) \, dq \, dr =$$

$$\int_0^\infty f_Q(q) \left[\int_0^q f_{(k)}(r) \, dr \right] dq = \int_0^\infty f_Q(q) \, F_{(k)}(q) \, dq \tag{7.70}$$

in which the probability function $F_{(k)}(r)$ is introduced, which denotes the probability of exceeding the kth limit state if the load intensity becomes $Q = r$. One can thus distinguish three kinds of functions:

1. The probability density $f_Q(q)$, which is the basic characteristic of loading.

2. The probability functions $F_{(k)}(r)$, which are strength characteristics of the structure dealt with (probabilities determined by these functions have a sense of conditional probabilities, exceeding a given limit state if the loading has a given intensity).

3. The probabilities $H_{(k)}$, which are characteristics of the structural safety (or better stated, of unsafety).

There exist, of course, some relations between the probabilities $H_{(k)}$. An increasing sequence $R_{(k)}$ leads to a decreasing sequence $H_{(k)}$.

The preceding approach can be extended to the case of n-dimensional distribution of loading. This case occurs (see Article 3 of this section) as an idealization which permits a deterministic representation of structural analysis in an Euclidean space. The values $R_{(k)}$ must be replaced now by the random boundaries of some domains $\Omega_{(k)}$ representing different states of behavior. Then $H_{(k)}$ will represent in this case probabilities of belonging (of the point having random coordinates Q_i) to the complementary domain $\Omega_{(k)}$. Inequalities for the probabilities $H_{(k)}$ will remain valid only if inclusion relations $\Omega_{(1)} \subseteq \Omega_{(2)} \subseteq \ldots \Omega_{(n)}$ are satisfied. The assumption of loading depending on a single parameter leads to the concentration of the load distribution on a straight line intersecting the boundaries of $\Omega_{(k)}$ at abscissas $R_{(k)}$, so that the analysis reduces to Eqs. 7.68 and 7.70.

In some cases a global measure of the state of structural behavior can be useful. This measure can be considered as a damage measure and can have a physical or a nonphysical (for example an economic) sense. Examples of such quantities are the Palmgren-Miner cumulative damage measure in the case of fatigue phenomena and the probable cost of damage and repair. Damage measures D often have a random nature (example: the cost of damage and repair due to exceeding a certain limit state depends on several factors that are external to the structure and, at the same time, beyond control). Expected values $E(D)$ of damage measures D can be often of interest for some evaluations. Assuming the values $E(D)_{(k)}$, corresponding to exceeding the limit states (k), are given, the over-all expected damage measure would become

$$E(D) = [H_{(1)} - H_{(2)}] E(D)_{(1)} + [H_{(2)} - H_{(3)}] E(D)_{(2)} + \ldots + H_{(n)} E(D)_{(n)} \quad (7.71)$$

Eq. 7.71 is valid only in cases when relations $R_{(1)} \leq R_{(2)} \leq \ldots R_{(n)}$, respectively $\Omega_{(1)} \subseteq \Omega_{(2)} \subseteq \ldots \subseteq \Omega_{(n)}$ are satisfied.

Structural design decisions can influence the probability functions $F_{(k)}(r)$ and hence the expected value $E(D)$. Possibilities of optimizing structural solutions by simultaneously considering several limit states are put to evidence in this way. More detailed discussion on this subject has been presented in Section 7.4 of this chapter.

8 Lack of Information on Loadings

Evaluations of structural safety must be based on accurate information on loadings and structural characteristics. This necessity should be understood in probabilistic terms, that is, predicted distributions (or at least their lower-order moments and probabilities of rare values that are significant for the risk of structural damage) must be sufficiently reliable. The lack of data reliability implies a lack of reliability of evaluations on structural safety. Differences between predicted and real distributions have a random nature. Techniques of mathematical statistics, based on the viewpoint that observed relative frequencies vary randomly with respect to real probabilities, may be of interest in analyzing differences between real and predicted distributions of loadings or structural characteristics. Bayesian relations can be also of interest in this field. Nevertheless, the introduction of some concepts and techniques of information theory is interesting for the analysis of lack of information (Pugachov, 1960). The adoption of entropy as a global measure of uncertainty and the additive character of entropy offer a potential tool for measuring the contribution of any step (or shortcoming) of research activity, and of any inaccuracy of structural analysis, to the uncertainty in the evaluation of structural safety. The use of such techniques remains a task of future research on structural safety. Although the manner of using concepts of information theory in this field has not been accurately defined, it is here suggested that speaking in terms of entropy and information quantity could be suggestive for readers.

Information on loadings is generally less reliable than information on structural characteristics. One could say that entropy added by data on loadings is greater than entropy added by data on structural characteristics, or by techniques of structural analysis. The lack of information is important especially for infrequent, high intensity loadings, which are the most significant for the risk to which structures are subjected. Increase of variance of loadings is generally followed by a decreased reliability of data on the actual loading distributions.

Theoretical models of the mechanisms of occurrence of various kinds of loadings have not so far been generally developed. One is thus obliged to assume some theoretical distributions (normal, lognormal, Poisson, etc.) and to prove how these distributions fit with empirical distributions. The absence of theoretical models is unfavorable primarily for extrapolating empirical data in order to predict the features of actual distributions in the range of seldom occurring strong or catastrophic loadings. This aspect of lack of information is compensated in some cases by the fact that structures are not designed, as a rule, to resist catastrophic loadings, so that exact knowledge of the features of such loadings is not required. As a general rule, the effect of research is a quantity of information which results in a decrease of entropy. The efficiency of research could be measured by comparing the quantity of information obtained with its cost. Research strategy should be adopted (or optimized) so as to deal with fields that make a major contribution to the over-all entropy of safety estimate, and where the ratio of quantity of information obtained to research cost is high. These objectives could be achieved after developing concepts and techniques for quantifying entropy and information in the field of structural research.

Some main topics yet to be covered in the field of research on loadings include:

1. Current research in order to refine information on the actual distributions.

2. Development of theoretical models to predict features of distributions in the range where statistical data cannot be practically obtained.

3. Development of techniques of quantifying the reliability of information on factors affecting structural safety.

4. Development of a design philosophy on how to have in view the reliability of data on loadings and structural characteristics in adopting design decisions.

9   Some Aspects Introduced by Tall Buildings

Some synthetic aspects of loadings acting on tall buildings should be underlined in conclusion. These aspects concern the relative importance of various loadings, the simultaneous occurrence of different loadings, the most significant features of some loadings, and some remarks on the damage pattern.

With respect to the relative importance of various loadings, the main influences belong to the building materials and to the over-all dimensions of buildings. Heavy building materials lead, as a rule, to little importance of live loads, while light materials require more accuracy in live load analysis. Lateral loads are, as a rule, of great importance for tall buildings. This importance depends primarily on the total height or on the ratio of total height to horizontal over-all dimensions. Tall buildings are, as a rule, sensitive to catastrophic loadings, such as earthquakes and explosions. Snow loading is, as a rule, of little importance for tall building structures and plays a significant role only for roof members. Loadings due to equipment are, as a rule, of local importance too.

With regard to the simultaneous occurrence of various loadings, the most specific aspects are those involved in live loads applied at different floors. Current (not reduced) design values for live loads are significant for the design of horizontal members (plates, slabs), but not for vertical ones. In the case of multistory buildings, vertical members of lower stories should be designed having in view rather the expected values of intensities of live loads, which are several times less than current design values (code provisions are still quite conservative in this area). Design engineers of multistory buildings should turn their attention also to the case of vanishing live loads and low values of permanent loads, which can be significant for the case of action of lateral loads (column reinforcement, overturning problem).

With respect to the features of loadings, the question arises of whether sophisticated analysis is justified or not. As a rule, live loads can be assumed to be uniformly distributed on any floor. Wind gusts can be assumed to act simultaneously at all points. On the other hand, nonsynchronous seismic ground accelerations can be significant (leading to strong torsional oscillations, or to important influence of the disturbing tilting accelerations). Nonsynchronous ground accelerations could be analyzed only on the basis of stochastic concepts.

With regard to the damage pattern, this can play a major role for structural safety. The case of chain failure due to explosion dislocating prefabricated members is classical at present. Failure due to earthquake could have similar features. As an important example, overstressing of some lateral and vertical members, due to moderate torsional oscillations, could lead, by stiffness decrease, to important additional eccentricities leading to torsional-type collapse. Another characteristic example is that of horizontal members connecting bearing walls of tall buildings. These members are subjected mainly to imposed deformations due to differential settlements and to given forces due to lateral loading. Concepts of analysis and definition of limit states and of damage pattern here raise considerable difficulties. Analysis of possible failure patterns or biographies could be quite sophisticated for tall buildings, but could lead, at the same time, to important conclusions on loadings and on structural safety.

7.6　SAFETY ANALYSIS FOR TALL BUILDINGS

There are unique aspects to reliability analysis in tall buildings that must be considered. To date, reliability analysis has considered examples of the following classes of problems: (1) Small framed structures with relatively few possible collapse failure modes; (2) large truss type structures in which yielding of any of a large number of elements was a failure criterion; and (3) complex aerospace structures in which testing was an integral part of the reliability study to bring out the potential failure modes.

Tall buildings differ from these examples in several important ways. There are in tall buildings many elements with many types of loading, each subjected to wide statistical variability, including gravity, temperature, blast, wind, earthquake, and construction and fabrication loads. Damage can occur at different levels ranging from simple yielding and deflections, causing cracks and broken window panes, to large static and dynamic displacements leading to complete unserviceability and finally collapse which can involve major destruction and loss of life. Each failure level and its associated damage cost and probability of occurrence must be considered in an over-all optimization process for the structure. Finally, because of complexity and cost considerations tests of tall building models to evaluate strength capacity and reliability are not feasible. Since tall buildings are often one of a kind structures, hypothetical models of random structural behavior and loads and their respective statistical variabilities must be developed to allow a complete reliability analysis. This requires close cooperation with research work on the deterministic analysis of structures such as stiffness, stability, and ultimate strength so margins of safety can be modeled probabilistically.

Examples of reliability analysis of some structural behavior models will be given herein, along with several suggested areas requiring future research. The models to be elaborated are applicable in some form to such problems as the prediction of yielding and deflection and the prediction of collapse modes, both on a floor-by-floor basis due to gravity load and sideway collapse due to lateral wind and earthquake load. Some approximate methods are suggested to transform dynamic loadings into equivalent static loads for the reliability analysis. Finally, it should be recognized that for the forseeable future design of elements such as beams and columns in tall buildings will be done on an element-by-element basis rather than using total system criteria. Hence it will be necessary to establish a control factor in going from the over-all desired system reliability for optimal economy and evaluating its necessary influence in the design of the element. It is proposed that an additional "partial" factor of safety be considered for this purpose. This factor would be greater than 1.0 if the system reliability was less than that of the element, such as in a "weakest-link" chain effect of members in series so that if any one fails the entire system fails. The safety factor would be less than 1.0 if the system reliability was greater than the element reliability due to effective load redistribution leading to a "fail-safe" system. Some examples will be given of both "weakest-link" and "fail-safe" systems. An important feature for safety codes is that the partial safety factor is relatively independent of frequency distribution and failure but depends mainly on geometry, correlation coefficients, and mode of failure.

1   Some Further Reliability Problems

It is now generally accepted that the reliability of a structure can be feasibly assured by fulfillment of two fundamental reliability conditions: (1) Ultimate condition; and (2) serviceability condition. Various design methods were developed during past decades which alternatively check either the ultimate limit state or the serviceability limit state, or both simultaneously.

The two groups of reliability conditions are reflected in the development of the reliability theory, separating two distinct groups of problems:

1. High reliability problems (or low failure probability problems), which involve very small or even zero probabilities of failure (yield, brittle fracture, loss of stability, etc.), with corresponding particular types of "load-structure" behavior models used in the reliability analysis.

2. Medium or even unspecified reliability problems (or problems with failure probability greater than, say, $1/10$), which are based on the acceptance of the

achievement of some limit state (such as cracking, local yield, deflection, vibration, etc.), not yet harmful even from the point of view of serviceability.

Both groups apply in tall building design, with the second group having probably relatively greater importance than is usual, due to the increased importance of self-weight, vertical transport of elements during erection, etc.

At present (1979) the techniques for high reliability problems are being developed and sufficient basic knowledge is available for tall building reliability analysis. It is only necessary to elaborate a reasonable theoretical solution leading to practical design and, further, to collect data (particularly on loads) needed for numerical analysis. A survey of existing models of reliability analysis is given later on.

Many medium reliability problems, however, are presently not covered by any reliability theory, although they are frequently of decisive importance in the structural design and its economic impact. To illustrate, a cracking limit state can be briefly discussed.

In a reinforced concrete structure the presence of cracks under working loads is not dangerous. Paradoxically, a high incidence of cracks is preferred since a small number of cracks implies large crack widths. Evidently the probability of crack occurrence in the lifetime of the structure is close to 1.0, the probability of working load occurrence is 0.5 to 1, and maximum crack widths are allowed with probability 1.0 or slightly less, etc. In prestressed structures, according to the present practice, a certain number of cracks is accepted under some specified load levels (even under working loads). Again, high probabilities of occurrence are assumed.

Finally, unspecified reliability concerns cases where the occurrence of a limit state is without any importance, such as when crack widths and deflections are often not limited by any conditions.

2 Models of High Reliability Analysis

In reviewing the structural reliability analysis literature the model that first appears is usually the one member-one load example often called the fundamental case of structural reliability (Cornell, 1967; Ferry Borges, 1971). All of the load variability is lumped into one loading term S and all the strength variability in one term R (resistance). Load and resistance are assumed independent; the failure probability (reliability $= 1 - P_f$) may be evaluated from either of the integrals which give the probability that load exceeds strength, namely:

$$P_f = \int_0^\infty [F_R(x)]f_S(x)dx = 1 - \int_0^\infty [F_S(x)]f_R(x)dx \qquad (7.72)$$

A most comprehensive survey of the results of the evaluation of the integral for P_f has been given by Ferry Borges (1971). The results are in the form of the element safety factor required versus a specified failure probability. Various curves are given for different parameters of the distributions including: (1) Coefficients of variability of both R and S; (2) frequency distribution for R and S such as normal, lognormal, Weibull, extremal, etc.; and (3) definition of the safety factor in terms of ratio of mean (central) and characteristic values (0.05 and 0.005 fractiles).

Except for cases where both frequency distributions are normal or lognormal, the evaluation of P_f usually requires a computer program for the numerical integration.

The results are useful in clarifying the sensitivity of safety factors to parameter assumptions on respective distributions, variabilities, and failure probabilities.

In application to tall buildings the fundamental reliability case (one member-one load) is only of limited application, because of multiple load combinations of both static and dynamic nature and various possible member failures and levels of failure as discussed previously. Some extension to multiload conditions and multimember structural systems will now be given.

"Weakest-Link." An important factor in controlling structural deflections and serviceability is the protection against the onset of damage by yielding or deflections as defined by an elastic structural analysis. The safety factors to guard against such occurrences are usually set at a lower level than the safety factors for collapse because of their respective damage levels. The following paragraph illustrates several problems in reliability analysis for "weakest-link" systems.

One element—m load conditions or repetitions of the same load. Eq. 7.73

$$P_f = 1 - \int_0^\infty \left[\prod_{j=1}^m F_{S_j}(x) \right] f_R(x) dx \tag{7.73}$$

is applicable if a load distribution exists, for example, on a maximum annual basis and failure probability is needed over a period of m years.

Condition of n elements—one load. Eq. 7.74 is applicable

$$P_f = 1 - \int_0^\infty \left\{ \prod_{i=1}^n [1 - F_{R_i}(a_i x)] \right\} f_S(x) dx \tag{7.74}$$

in which a_i relates the force or stress level in element i to the load $S = x$. Eq. 7.74 is a failure probability analysis for a "weakest-link" system under one load application and may also apply to a single member with several modes of failure. It is a weakest-link analysis since the failure of any element is equivalent to failure of the system. A "weakest-link" model is, of course, appropriate for statically determinate structures or subassemblages which have no possibility of load redistribution after first yielding occurs. Eq. 7.74, however, assumes independent strength terms which may not be true if the same strength parameters affect more than one failure mode in a member such as yield and shear failure, or if time effects like corrosion act uniformly on all members. Examples of failure probability for the "weakest-link" model are given in Fig. 7.10 showing the central safety factor versus the number of elements for various coefficients of variation and frequency distributions and a given failure probability. It is assumed for calculation that each element is proportioned with the same safety factor. The curves are normalized by dividing the single element safety factor evaluated by the fundamental reliability case so we can deduce a partial factor of safety for relating system to element safety factors. Thus for example, in a weakest-link system with 100 elements, the central safety factor based on the ratio of mean values would need the variability in Fig. 7.10(b) for normally distributed load (coefficient of variation = 30%) and strength (5%) variables to be increased about 12% to maintain the same failure probability (0.0001) for the system. For parameters typical of building live load Fig. 7.10(a) shows a partial factor of safety of 1.5 for a 100-element system with normally distributed variables. An interesting aspect of Fig. 7.10 is the relative insensitivity of the normalized partial safety factor to frequency distributions and coefficients of variation. Fig. 7.10(b) is more representative for the case where load variability greatly exceeds strength variation, as in wind and earthquake loads.

Condition of *n* members—*m* loads. The extension of the "weakest-link" to multiload combinations leads to major computational difficulties and requires evaluation of multiple integrals for numerical results. It is usually not possible with multiple loads to combine the loads into one frequency distribution since each load may affect the strength element in a different way. In some cases load effects may even cancel. For tall buildings problems the load combination question, therefore, must be approximated in some manner. Cornell (1967) has suggested that each load combination could be treated with only one basic frequency distribution such as: (1) "Average" live load levels with wind load defined by a frequency distribution; or (2) live load defined by a distribution and no wind loading acting. An upper-bound

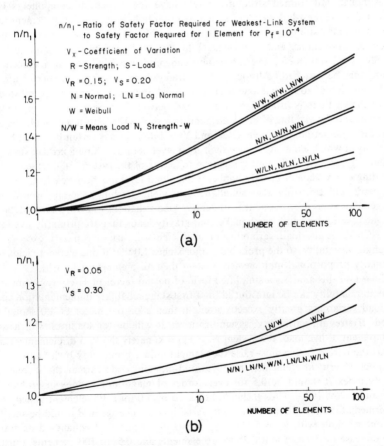

Fig. 7.10 Normalized central safety factor (partial factor of safety) versus number of members, weakest-link structure, $P_f = 10^{-4}$

value for the over-all failure probability of multiload and member combinations has been given by several investigations as

$$P_f \leq \sum_i \sum_j P_{f_{ij}} \tag{7.75}$$

in which $P_{f_{ij}}$ is evaluated as a fundamental case reliability analysis of the ith element due to the jth load condition. The degree of approximation in Eq. 7.75 has been illustrated in cases where there is only one load condition (Moses and Stevenson, 1970a). If the load variability greatly exceeds the strength variability, as in wind or earthquake loading, then the approximation is overly conservative and P_f actually approaches the maximum of any individual element failure probability. If the strength variability is dominant then the approximation is indeed a good one. A better approximation than Eq. 7.75 is to sum over load conditions with each P_f for a given load condition found from an analysis similar to Eq. 7.74.

Although tall framed structures rarely have few structural components constructed as weakest-link systems, so that over-all failure occurs if any element fails, the model may still be useful for controlling the likelihood of serviceability damage such as deflections and cracking. Note that self-equilibrating loads such as temperature, settlement, and fabrication can be disregarded only if a shakedown limit can be reached. Although most frames are statically indeterminate so redistribution of additional load occurs after yielding of any element, several studies have shown there is little difference in load between the onset of yielding in one element and the yielding of many elements in a similarly proportioned multielement statically indeterminate system (Yao and Yeh, 1969). This is certainly true in brittle systems in which elements reduce their load level upon reaching a critical stress, so failure of one element is almost identical to failure of the system. In ductile systems yielding of an element usually implies a high load level has been reached, so other elements will probably also simultaneously yield, leading to large over-all displacements. This may not be true under live load situations but will almost certainly be the case under wind, earthquake, and gravity loads that are primarily live load. In such cases the load variability or coefficient of variation greatly exceeds the strength variability, so the probability approaches 1.0 that if one element yields in a similarly proportional multielement system then all members will yield.

Based on this analysis a simplified form of partial factor of safety for element to system reliability can be introduced for a first stage reliability implementation code. If load variability greatly exceeds strength then a partial factor of 1.0 should be used. If strength variability is significant, as it will be for loadings with a high component of live load, the system P_f is approximately the sum of element values. Thus the partial factor must raise the element failure probability by a factor n, the number of critical elements. In the second-moment code format the increase in safety index β should be 0.5 for every order of magnitude change in probability (Cornell, 1969, 1970). Thus β should be raised by 1.0 for a 100-element system. For intermediate ratios of load to strength variability the change in β would be smaller. In one example with $\gamma_R = 5\%$ and $\gamma_P = 30\%$ for a normal frequency distribution the increase in β was about 0.25 for 10 elements and 0.5 for 100 elements. Further systematic calculations are needed to put the results in proper tabular form for design. It should be kept in mind that γ_R to be used in the partial safety factor evaluation is the variability corresponding to section variability within a single structure and not the variability from structure to structure. This neglects then the variation among various producers, manufacturers, and fabricators.

Collapse Models. In a tall building with ductile or semiductile members, ultimate collapse or maximum equilibrium load usually occurs with at least several elements participating in the failure mode. The element load distribution pattern and even behavior of elements is greatly altered from the yield model discussed previously, in which force distribution could be calculated by elastic structural analysis. Examples include: (1) Collapse of a floor due to gravity load with plastic hinges forming at the ends and the midspan; (2) lateral instability with all columns in a floor having no remaining lateral resistance; (3) sideway collapse failure under lateral (dynamic) or combined vertical and lateral loading; and (4) incremental collapse due to load repetitions. Some failure mechanisms for these cases are illustrated in Fig. 7.11. In general, a convenient reliability expression for the reserve strength of the collapse mode is

$$Z_j = \sum_{i=1}^{P} a_{ji} M_i - \sum_{i=1}^{L} b_{jk} S_k \qquad j = 1, N \qquad (7.76)$$

in which Z_j = reserve strength or margin of safety of the jth collapse mode; M_i = ith strength term resisting in that collapse mode; and S_k = kth load term causing the collapse. The random variables are the M_i and S_k terms. The reliability analysis is to find the probability P_{fj} that the collapse mode occurs, that is

$$P_{fj} = Pr(Z_j < 0) \qquad (7.77)$$

In the case of N potential collapse modes there is statistical correlation between the various Z_j occurrences due to both load and strength terms participating in more than one collapse mode. Such correlation has been evaluated by Stevenson (1967) for two-story frames with up to 51 failure modes. It was concluded that a reasonable approach for the over-all safety is to let P_f of the system equal the sum of the various collapse mode failure probabilities

$$P_f = \sum_{j=1}^{N} P_{fj} \qquad (7.78)$$

Eq. 7.78 has also been tested by Baratta (1973a) for a frame with 220 collapse modes, and it was found to give a good estimate in the range of small failure probabilities. Although exact evaluation of P_{fj} requires multiple integration to be evaluated, approximations using only a single numerical integration analogous to the fundamental reliability problem have been developed and give good approximations (Stevenson and Moses, 1970b). A further factor is that if many random terms are present in the Z_j expression the probability distribution frequency for Z_j approaches a normal frequency distribution by virtue of the central limit theorem. The use of normal distributions also permits the easy inclusion of strength correlation terms in the form of covariances which enter the expression for the standard deviation of Z_j. Other approximate analyses for the collapse problem have been given by Tichy and Vorlicek (1964). A technique for finding bounds or collapse probability has been offered by Augusti and Baratta (1972). One important factor due to the way members participate in the expression for Z_j is that the choice of frequency distribution for M and S is less important than in the fundamental reliability problem, and thus the use of assumed distributions for random terms is more reasonable. A comparision of results for prediction of collapse is shown in Fig. 7.12 for a simple collapse beam model of Fig. 7.11(a). Also Fig. 7.12 shows that the normal distribution is often an upper-bound limit on the various combinations of frequency distribution. This was discovered by Shin (1971) in several examples with numerous combinations of frequency distribution and coefficient of variations. Using the simple example in Fig. 7.11(a) as an illustration for evaluating collapse of systems, the reliability can be evaluated directly for the normal probability case in a simple manner. Assuming strengths as independent variables, the mean and standard deviation of Z are

$$E(Z) = E(M)_1 + 2E(M)_2 + E(M)_3 - \frac{E(S)L}{2} \tag{7.79}$$

and

$$\sigma_Z^2 = \sigma_{M1}^2 + 4\sigma_{M2}^2 + \sigma_{M3}^2 + \sigma_S^2 \frac{L^2}{4} \tag{7.80}$$

Further assuming that strength terms have the same mean and standard deviation leads to

$$P_f = \Phi(\beta) \tag{7.81}$$

for failure probability, in which

$$\beta = \frac{E(Z)}{\sigma_Z} = \frac{F-1}{\left(\frac{3}{8}F^2\gamma_M^2 + \gamma_S^2\right)^{1/2}}$$

$F = 4E(M)/[E(S)L/2]$, the central safety factor; $\gamma_M =$ coefficient of variation of $M = \sigma_M/E(M)$; $\gamma_S =$ coefficient of variation of $S = \sigma_S/E(S)$; and $\Phi(\beta) =$ normal distribution function available in tables as function of β. Thus, for example, a safety factor of 1.67 and $\gamma_M = 0.05$ and $\gamma_S = 0.2$ leads to $P_f = 6.3 \times 10^{-4}$.

In the general case of collapse modes with P strength terms and L load terms we find

$$\sigma_{Z_j}^2 = \sum_{i=1}^{P} a_{ji}^2 \sigma_{M_i}^2 + \sum_{k=1}^{L} b_k^2 \sigma_{S_k}^2 \tag{7.82}$$

and

$$\beta = \frac{E(Z)}{\sigma_Z} = \frac{F-1}{\left\{\frac{\Sigma a_i^2 \sigma_{M_i}^2}{[\Sigma a_i E(M_i)]^2}F^2 + \frac{\Sigma b_k^2 \sigma_{S_k}^2}{[\Sigma b_k E(S_k)]^2}\right\}^{1/2}} \tag{7.83}$$

For illustration consider the case of all a and b equal: the expression for safety level becomes

$$\beta = \frac{F - 1}{(F^2\gamma_M^2 P^{-1} + \gamma_S^2 L^{-1})^{1/2}} \tag{7.84}$$

Using an approach suggested by Lind (1968) to simplify reliability expression gives

$$F = \frac{1 + 0.75\beta\ \dfrac{\gamma_S}{\sqrt{L}}}{1 - 0.75\beta\ \dfrac{\gamma_M}{\sqrt{P}}} \tag{7.85}$$

in which F is now the central safety factor for the collapse mode required to give a

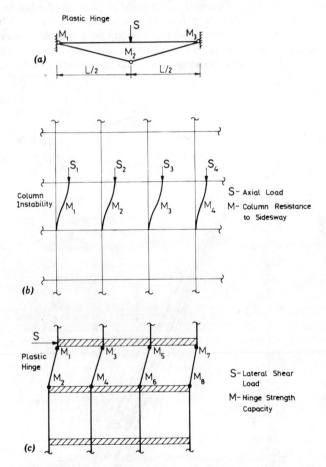

Fig. 7.11(a) Beam collapse mode; (b) Sidesway buckling of floor; (c) Collapse of frame due to lateral load

strength level associated with the normalized safety level β. It should be noted that L and P in Eq. 7.85 refer to the number of uncorrelated terms participating in the collapse mode. If any terms have statistical correlation, then this increases the variance of Z and thus increases the value of F needed for a given failure probability (Cornell, 1967). Expressions similar to Eq. 7.84 can also be derived with Taylor series expansions for the case where the strength terms, M_j, are themselves functions of other random variables, such as reinforced concrete elements which depend on variability of material, fabrication, eccentricity, etc. Such results are useful for inclusion in second-moment code formats.

Eq. 7.85 shows for collapse design problems that the respective load and strength variations should be reduced by a factor proportional to $\sqrt{L}$ or $\sqrt{P}$ whenever more than one independent load or one independent strength term participates in the damage mode. This reduction could be incorporated in a second-moment code format and is analogous to the column load reduction factor currently in use. A conflicting consideration in collapse analysis is the implication of using Eq. 7.78 for the over-all system reliability. In a first stage, reliability format Eq. 7.78 should suffice as it is conservative. Some investigations into both behavior aspects as well as economic implications are needed to prepare charts showing the partial safety factor due to collapse mode correlation, and would be dependent on the number of

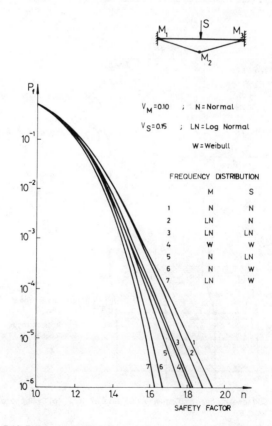

Fig. 7.12 Failure probability due to collapse versus central safety factor

modes and strength margin correlation coefficients. The latter term is easily calculated for linear expressions such as Eq. 7.76 (Stevenson, 1967).

3 Models of Medium Reliability Analysis

Little can be said about this group of models as few systematic researches have been reported. Problems of serviceability limit states have been studied only deterministically (with only some sporadic papers using a stochastic approach), and in many cases empirically. It can be expected, however, that on the whole the "weakest-link" and "fail-safe" system will remain as basic after some adjustments.

Particular attention must be paid to the deformation bounds which theoretically have an analogous position to working loads or ultimate loads, but which are governed by entirely other factors. This is similarly valid for crack widths.

The following research in medium reliability analysis is needed:

1. Establishment of stochastic models for structural resistances such as cracking limit, crack width, and stiffness.

2. Establishment of stochastic models for bounds (allowable deflections).

3. Elaboration of a reliability theory for medium or unspecified reliability.

4. Analysis of the economic impact of serviceability limit states in tall buildings.

4 Discussion

The present state of reliability analysis described covers two models applicable to safety theory for tall buildings. These are the prediction of damage by a "weakest-link" criterion, and the limit or ultimate state failure by collapse. In addition to work described for medium reliability analysis, further research is needed on prediction of intermediate stages of failure, such as inelastic large permanent displacements and cracking of primary and secondary structural supports which may not involve total collapse. These developments require integration of work in deterministic structural analysis and behavior so the resultant margins of safety can be modeled in terms of the random load and strength terms. Some discussion will now be given on the application of the basic prediction models to some problems associated with tall buildings.

Dynamic Loads. Wind and earthquake load distributions over some specified time interval exhibit much higher variability than either gravity or typical strength terms. In order to apply them to a collapse model as shown in Fig. 7.11 suggested by Rosenblueth and Esteva (1971a, 1971b) it would be necessary to transform the dynamic loading into equivalent static effects. Ferry Borges (1971) has described earthquake loads with an assumed response model and has found Type II extremal distributions with coefficients of variations (c.v.) of about 75%. Similar results were obtained by Shin (1971) using a random vibration model to obtain maximum response due to both earthquake and wind loads and the computation of equivalent static structural forces. In both loadings a Type II extremal distribution gave the best fit for the equivalent lateral dynamic response. These results were based on a structural response model which is elastic and needs to be extended to inelastic dynamic behavior response. Such inelastic behavior, however, if the yielding is localized in a tall building, may not affect the over-all dynamic response so the prediction of maximum equivalent loads can be based on a static model. Work by Veletsos also indicated that the maximum response of inelastic multidegree of freedom systems bears a strong resemblance to elastic response under earthquake and pulse type loadings (Veletsos and Vann, 1971). This question requires further research for tall building structures. Since the load variability will be high with c.v. = 75% to 100% for earthquake and c.v. = 30% to 40% for wind (Shin, 1971), the correlation of lateral load terms in a sideway collapse model is important. In fact, a reliability bound which considers the worst collapse mode only in evaluating the failure probability of the system may prove to be adequate. Thus, in a first stage of a probability based code using the second moment format, in calculating P_f for a tall building under primarily lateral loading the c.v. of the reserve strength for each possible collapse mode evaluated on a floor-by-floor basis should be determined. The floor with the large c.v. should give a failure probability close to that for the entire building. Thus partial factors of safety to relate collapse mode to system reliability may not be necessary at this stage. Dynamic loads, especially wind effect, also lead to serviceability problems when the peak dynamic response often reaches large amplitudes. In this case strength variability is not a factor, but rather the building stiffness and damping play a major role. Although stiffness and natural frequency can often be calculated deterministically, the damping ratio may be subject to considerable variation. Since its effect on wind vibration amplitude is important some investigation should be given to the statistical distribution of damping ratios.

Column Instability.   In an unbraced frame each floor must be checked for lateral instability. For lower levels the column loads have many independent sources from the floors above so that strength variability may dominate as indicated by Eq. 7.85. For unbraced buildings the sum of all columns strengths in a plane frame on a given floor contribute to its resistance to lateral instability (Yura, 1971) and thus the collapse model in Eq. 7.76 is quite applicable. For braced frames each column would be analyzed independently and so a model with one element and multiple loads acting simultaneously might be applicable. Rokach (1970) has presented results for estimates of column strength variability and even column-to-column strength correlation. The correlation would be reflected in the $S^{1/2}$ term in Eq. 7.85. In both braced and unbraced column systems the P_f for the entire building system needs to be evaluated from combinations of each failure mode probability. However, the influence of load variability on columns is difficult to model for reliability analysis since many load terms from the upper floor contribute to the column load in any floor. Cornell (1970) has proposed a simplified method for handling load correlation for a given column using a second-moment computation. Specifications have long recognized that design loads should be reduced in lower story columns by introducing a load reduction factor. This is similar to the $L^{1/2}$ reduction factor on γ_S in Eq. 7.85. The more independent terms contributing to the load variance the greater the reduction factor. There is, however, another factor, which is the over-all reliability of the system, and includes column load correlation and floor-by-floor failure correlation. The failure probability of the system will definitely exceed the largest failure probability of any floor instability, but the question of what the partial factor of safety should be in this case requires further investigation.

Gravity Loads (Beam Failure). The effects of gravity loads on beam failure modes is easier to consider since the most important loading effect comes from a single span within the multistory frame. The reliability models described previously can be directly applied to predict either significant displacement, provided a proper shakedown limit is reached, or collapse by formation of plastic hinges. Since there are many potential failure mechanisms in a tall frame due to gravity loads the reliability of the system against this type of occurrence needs to be estimated. A conservative approach is to sum all failure mode probabilities into an over-all estimate for the system. This would necessarily lead to higher specified reliabilities for each potential mode to achieve a desired system reliability or a partial factor of safety for element to system reliabilities greater than 1. An estimate for the necessary partial factor of safety could be made from a curve such as in Fig. 7.12 showing failure probability versus safety factor for a collapse mode. If there were, for example, 100 independent potential failure modes in a system then the partial safety factor would be calculated as the additional safety factor needed to reduce the element failure probability by a factor of 100. It has been shown for two story-two bay frames that usually only one mode of collapse contributes most of the failure probability of the system (Stevenson and Moses, 1970b). This may not be the case, however, for tall buildings with regular arrangements of bays. Load correlation is a factor also in beam failures, since if floor loads are correlated this would reduce the necessary partial factor of safety. Empirical research is needed to determine floor-by-floor correlation of gravity live loads for both column load reduction factors and correlation between beam failure modes. Also it should be noted that strength variability has a component statistically dependent within a given building and another component statistically independent from section to section. Only the latter quantity should be included in computing the partial factor of safety for element to system safety. Another factor may also be the evolution of live loads over the time span of the building. If the function of the building changes, for example from office to warehousing, the live loads are likely to increase on all floors —similarly if there is a style change to heavy furniture or to use of certain types of office equipment. A consistent approach, however, in apportioning reliability levels to individual potential failure elements implies that reduction factors and partial safety factors to relate element to system probabilities are relative factors which still may remain unchanged even if all live load on all floors were to uniformly increase over time.

System Optimization. The tools of reliability analysis can implement a rational approach to choosing safety factors consistent with knowledge of determinate structural phenomena as well as information on random properties of loads and resistances. The design problem is compounded by the need to consider both different levels of damage, ranging from cracking and deflections to ultimate collapse, and the relation between element and system reliability. Even in a first stage reliability implementation code, such as a second-moment format for safety factors including partial safety factors, the matter of optimum proportioning and assigning of element failure levels even without economical considerations of consequences of failures is a major task. Methods of mathematical programming should be useful in this regard, handling the various constraints and design variables (Cohn and Parimi, 1971; Moses, 1968).

7.7 PRESENT AND FUTURE OF PROBABILISTIC METHODS

As stated in Section 7.1, structural safety is measured by the degree of confidence that one has about the satisfactory performance of a given structure, and depends on the uncertainties associated with our knowledge about strengths and internal forces or deformations at different critical sections or portions of the system. Use of probability theory provides a rational method for evaluating uncertainties from different sources, studying their combined effects, and assigning numerical values to safety. Hence, a framework can be established to permit consistent evaluations of safety, to guide designers in their attempts to reach acceptable safety levels, and to guide code writers in their search for ways to define those acceptable safety levels.

The various sections of this chapter concentrate on some operational schemes that can be used for dealing with imperfectly known variables in the process of making design decisions. The scope of those sections covers problems arising in two different stages of this process: specification writing and detailed design. In a manner consistent with present practice, the latter stage involves the individual designer, who bases his decisions on the verification of recommended safety factors, obtained according to prescribed (or generally agreed-on) procedures from specified probabilistic descriptions of the variables in play. The former stage corresponds to the work of committees in charge of recommending proper algorithms and constants.

Decision making being a prime objective of engineering, the formulation presented is not intended as a substitute for engineering judgment and intuition, but rather as a framework where statistical information, conceptual descriptions of phenomena, and intuitive estimates can be assimilated, together with their respective uncertainties. A basic contribution of the proposed approach stems from its ability to translate to a common, precise language, objective and subjective information and to make compatible intuitive estimates produced by code committees and by individual designers. Probabilistic descriptions and evaluations of failure consequences may be left in the hands of bodies of experts when that seems adequate, but, unlike in conventional practice, criteria are clearly stated about handling of unforeseen situations and evaluation of new parameters by the individual designer, in such a way as to produce consistent safety designs.

Safety analysis for tall buildings involves a range of problems much wider than those covered by classical reliability theory. Failure may be the result of statistical variability of loads and strengths or, what is more frequent, it may have its origin in events beyond that variability, such as gross construction errors, application of loads greatly in excess of those specified, or exceptional events. Excitations may originate from a wide number of sources, some of them amenable to control, and others escaping it. Time and space variation of each excitation is complex, but design recommendations have to specify it by a few parameters.

One or several of a large number of potential failure modes, with different consequences and degrees of damage, may occur at different instants. Each mode implies failure of a number of members or critical sections, and some members may participate in more than one failure mode. Increasing safety in a given mode may increase or decrease safety in other modes whose consequences may be smaller or greater than those of the former.

On top of the preceding difficulties, reliability analysis for tall buildings deals with unique systems, for which, as a rule, probabilities cannot be inferred from repeated testing of similar prototypes. This poses some questions open to the liveliest discussion: Why should probability theory be used? And why should probabilities be based on statistical information as well as on subjective judgment?

As a result of problems such as those just described, quantitative evaluation of safety by means of probability theory is only lately finding its way to practical applications. Hence, this section is mostly a look into the future, with enough ground for controversy, rather than a description of accepted practice.

1   Safety Analysis for Tall Buildings

Failure probability in a given mode is defined as the probability that the generalized load action which is critical in that mode exceeds the corresponding strength. As a first step in the safety analysis of a structural system, the modes with the highest expected consequences must be identified and used in the formulation of a reliability-oriented model. Probabilistic models of the significant load actions are then developed, and failure probabilities computed for the relevant modes. Those probabilities are then compared with specified values or, alternatively, some possible solutions are compared in the frame of a cost-benefit analysis, where each solution is characterized by its initial cost, its actualized expected benefits, and its actualized expected consequences of failure, all as functions of failure probabilities in every mode.

In practical design, a detailed analysis such as that just described is only exceptionally applied, and its systematic use by individual designers will probably not be feasible nor justifiable in the next few years. Although that formulation is generally accepted as a worthy long-term goal, opinions diverge as to the ways and means of approaching it.

Even within the limitations of the most conservative tendencies, substantial improvements are contemplated in the methods for assessing and specifying safety. In an immediate stage, the desirable safety level in each mode has to be indirectly attained through application of recommendations about acceptable safety factors or failure probabilities for individual members. The difference from present recommendations will lie in the ability of code writers to base them on system reliability analyses.

The practice of specifying member safety instead of system safety has its counterpart in the application of allowable stress methods, and as the latter have given place to limit states design, the former will have to be substituted with system reliability design criteria. It is often argued that designers are not yet ready for handling those criteria in everyday practice, firstly because of insufficient training in reliability analysis, and secondly because of lack of the necessary parameters of the probability distributions in play. However, as shown later in this section, simplified models are available for evaluating safety of ordinary tall buildings with respect to the most important failure modes, and reasonable estimates of the parameters are within reach of the profession. This should make it feasible for researchers or code writers to improve their recommendations for individual member design and to suggest alternate, refined procedures, according to which designers would perform system reliability analyses for some particular cases in the near future. Buildings possessing exceptional shapes or framing systems would probably not satisfy the conditions necessary for applying either of the two alternative methods described. Assessment of their safety would require formal reliability analyses.

2 Analysis of Uncertainty

Ideally, every variable of interest should be described by its probability density function. In practice, it often happens that neither the statistical information nor the state of knowledge of the physical processes involved suffice for that purpose, and each uncertain variable has to be described by only two or perhaps three parameters (mean, variance, and rate of decay of the tail of the probability density function or of the cumulative or complementary distribution functions in the range of interest). Where the joint distribution of several random variables is important, their probabilistic description should include the mentioned parameters of the single-variable distributions as well as the corresponding covariances or correlation functions. Thus, the probability distribution of the load capacity of an intermediate span of a continuous beam is a function of the joint distribution of the strengths at all sections of the beam span. If the location of the three plastic hinges required for occurrence of a mechanism failure is known, the mean and the variance of the bending load capacity of the beam span can be obtained in terms of the means, variances, and covariances of the bending strengths of the beam at the sections of the potential plastic hinges. Reasonable assumptions have to be made about the location of those hinges, or the uncertainty about their location can be explicitly included in the evaluation of uncertainty about the load capacity under discussion.

Similarly, the variance of the effect at a critical section resulting from the contributions of loads acting on different portions of a structural system can be obtained as a function of the variances and covariances of those contributions.

The uncertainty associated with the variables handled in structural design may stem from different sources. Strength of a critical section is uncertain because the properties of the material at that section are not precisely known, because the actual dimensions of structural members may differ from their nominal values, and because working formulas for predicting member strength from material properties and section dimensions are only approximate descriptions of imperfectly known phenomena. Likewise, forces at critical sections are uncertain because load intensities are uncertain, because their actual space distribution has to be simplified for the purpose of structural analysis, and because of the simplifications included in the methods of structural analysis themselves. In practice, assimilation of the various contributions of uncertainty for loads and strengths can be done as suggested elsewhere (Cornell, 1969; Rosenblueth and Esteva, 1971b).

The fact that the parameters defining uncertainty are uncertain themselves is discussed in Section 7.2, in which a criterion is presented for obtaining the resultant or *marginal* uncertainty, including its *conditional* value given the parameters mentioned above and the uncertainty about those parameters. This is a fundamental problem in structural safety, as well as in many other engineering decision processes, since some of the most relevant variables that enter in such decisions do not lend themselves to estimation of the parameters of their probability distributions according to the methods of conventional statistical theory.

The simple expressions derived in Section 7.2 for obtaining the marginal variance of a variable the parameters of whose probability distribution are uncertain are only particular results of the powerful methods of Bayesian statistical analysis. Unlike conventional statistics, Bayesian analysis does not limit its scope to testing hypotheses for arbitrary significance levels, or to obtaining probabilities that given statistical parameters fall within given confidence intervals. Rather, it permits evaluation of the joint probability distributions of those statistical parameters, and hence of the marginal distributions of the underlying uncertain variables.

A second feature, perhaps more important than the former, of Bayesian analysis, is that it provides efficient tools for assimilation of information from different sources when trying to formulate a probabilistic model for a given variable when the information coming from some of those sources may be significant in comparison with the results of direct observation. This situation occurs, for instance, when dealing with the consequences of gross construction errors, with the action of exceptional events, such as blast or airplane collision, or with some more frequent events, such as intense earthquakes or wind storms, when few or no direct records have been obtained at the construction site. In all these cases, assessment of probabilities will be greatly influenced by intuition or by subjective extrapolation of results from comparable, better known conditions. Here lies the possibility of replacing intuitive specification of safety factors with rational values derived from probability distributions based on subjective and objective information. The formal methods for integrating results from these two sources have been discussed by Cornell (1969c) and Esteva (1969a).

Some methods have been devised for extracting consistent quantitative probabilistic assessments from subjective feelings about uncertainty (Esteva, 1969b). They have been applied in some operations research problems, but no evaluation has been made of their usefulness and justification in the analysis of structural safety. Less sophisticated methods have been used for making subjective probability assessments in the solution of some structural design decision problems (Esteva, 1969b; Sexsmith, 1967). An important task that should be expected in the future from specification writing committees is their quantitative assessment of the uncertainties involved in each piece of information used in design. Achievement of this will be feasible by application of the methods of Bayesian statistics, as described previously.

Section 7.2 also refers to the problem of deriving uncertainty expressions for variables that are obtained as known functions of some basic variables for which means, variances, and perhaps probability distributions are directly defined. The first-order approximations suggested (Eqs. 7.103 to 7.106) have gained acceptance among practically oriented researchers on structural safety. However, improved formulations seem convenient, in view of the evidence about their poor accuracy when applied to strongly nonlinear functions.

3 Actions and Their Models

This Article refers to external forces, such as dead, live and wind loads, to inertia forces, such as those produced by earthquake, and to stresses caused by imposed deformations, modified by interaction with the structure, such as temperature and foundation settlement effects.

Some loads are applied shortly after construction and remain practically constant thereafter. Others have significant time dependent variations. The former can be idealized as simple random variables, and the latter have to be represented by stochastic process models. In general, the instantaneous value of a given action cannot be fully described by a scalar but by a vector of components, which can be stochastically dependent or independent. Evaluation of reliability as a function of time implies the superposition of various multicomponent stochastic processes. A rigorous analysis is at present beyond practical possibilities, but some simplified stochastic models that preserve the essential probabilistic properties of their refined counterparts can be adopted for obtaining reliability estimates in practice.

Section 7.5 contains a discussion about the probabilistic features of the most frequent types of actions that may act on tall buildings, and the problems encountered when trying to obtain reliabilities under their combined action. It also stresses the importance of studying the physical processes involved as a basis for developing conceptual models of each type of action, and then defining their stochastic models and the corresponding parameters. The present summary deals primarily with some examples of the stochastic models that may be used to represent different actions.

Attention is called here to the important problem of assessing the degree of confidence in the stochastic models suggested and in their parameters, as well as to the problem of obtaining marginal uncertainties about loads in terms of their objective (given a model) and subjective (type of model) uncertainties. However, only a simple example is presented regarding this topic in view of the scarcity of related experiences.

Permanent Loads.   Loads designated as permanent suffer important variations in magnitude only during the construction stage. They may undergo slight fluctuations thereafter, but it is reasonable in general to assume them to be random but constant. Uncertainty about them is ordinarily small, and it results usually from discrepancies between actual and nominal dimensions of elements and finishing rather than from material properties. Exceptions occur, for instance, when the degree of wetness of a porous material may influence significantly its unit weight, or when the earth pressure on a retaining wall may vary following the fluctuations of the water table.

Live Loads.   Live load on office and apartment buildings can be separated into its ordinary and exceptional contributions. The former include loads acting during an important fraction of the lifetime of the structure, and result from its normal operation. The latter act only under exceptional circumstances, during a small fraction of the lifetime of the structure. Ordinary live loads may suffer daily variations (number of office personnel and visitors vary with hour), long-term systematic variations (furniture in a given room ordinarily increases gradually), and random concentrated jumps (change of occupancy or destiny). For practical purposes, a model has been suggested (Peir, 1971) according to which the load on a given area remains constant between changes of occupancy, and these changes take place as a simple Poisson process. Thus, the model is specified by the mean rate of change of occupancy (which is a function of the area) and the distribution of the instantaneous load for any occupancy. This distribution is a function of the tributary area and of the number of stories included in it, and depends on the space correlation structure of the live load. Only recently has this correlation structure been investigated using the results of field surveys (Peir, 1971).

The model for ordinary live load suggested provides the basis for determining the distribution of the live load effect at any critical section at an arbitrary instant. The distribution of the maximum effects over a given number of years can be obtained by application of standard methods for analysis of extreme values. Exceptional live loads are more difficult to handle at present. They may occur, for instance, during a party held at a small area in a building, or when a large area is remodeled, and its furniture is packed in a small space, or when a crowd packs corridors and stairways during an emergency. Some building codes cover the possibility of exceptional live loads by specifying very high concentrated and distributed loads to be supposed acting on arbitrary areas. Since these exceptional loads seldom have more than a local effect, and since the probability of exceptional live loads acting simultaneously on more than one separated area of a building is very low, their effect can be modeled by loads of random intensity applied on specified areas or rooms, at instants described by a given stochastic process. No superposition of several contributions on a given critical section at a given instant would have to be considered (with the exception perhaps of columns supporting several levels of corridors and stairways), but the stochastic process of exceptional actions at the section could be obtained as the superposition of the various contributing stochastic processes. The distribution of the maximum combined effect of the ordinary and the exceptional contributions during a given time period may be obtained by a formal superposition of the corresponding stochastic processes or, alternatively, a conservative result can be obtained by assuming that the maximum sum is equal to the sum of the maxima.

Wind. Wind pressures acting on a building are related through pressure coefficients to the velocities of the flow unmodified by the presence of the building. Even though it is a known fact that those coefficients vary with wind turbulence and other factors, their values can be taken as constant and equal to those determined on rigid models subjected to uniform flow in wind tunnels. The fluctuations of wind velocity with respect to space and time can thus be transformed into fluctuations in wind pressure with time and throughout the exposed surface of the building. Instead of making a rigorous analysis of the multiparameter stochastic process that describes the fluctuation of wind pressures during the life of the building, it has been suggested that the maximum instantaneous dynamic response to wind for a given return period (or, equivalently, for a given probability of exceedance during a given time interval) be obtained as the product of the response to the mean velocity that corresponds to that return period and a gust factor. The mean velocities are obtained by averaging velocities over intervals on the order of several minutes to one hour, and their maxima have been shown to conform with the extremal distribution. The gust factor is obtained as the ratio of the mean of the maximum response during the averaging period to the response to the mean velocity during that period (Davenport, 1961). The variance of the maximum instantaneous response during the averaging period is neglected when computing the gust factor, because it is much smaller than the variance of the maximum mean velocity during the intervals of several decades on which design for wind is based. Computation of the gust factor uses as raw data the power spectral density of velocity fluctuations at different locations and their space correlation functions for each frequency component of the excitation. These functions are available for several conditions, but significant deviations are encountered between them and between the resulting gust factors as suggested by different authors (Davenport, 1967; Vellozzi and

Cohen, 1968). Recognition of the fact that the different types of wind storms that may occur at a given place may have different turbulence structures would lead to a more refined formulation, where the process of events giving place to significant wind response would be obtained as the superposition of several stochastic processes, each having different distribution of maximum wind velocities and different turbulence structures.

Practically all the studies available on the dynamic response of structures to wind assume linear behavior. Some recent studies show that reductions of about 20% in response to winds defining the design can be obtained as a result of hysteretic damping produced by nonlinear structural behavior (Wyatt and May, 1971).

Earthquake. Earthquakes are transient phenomena, of very short duration as compared with wind storms, and the intensity and frequency content of the ground motion vary systematically during each event. For these reasons, the distribution of the maximum seismic response for each event cannot be obtained by a simple application of the theory of stationary processes. As for the case of wind action, most of the uncertainty in the response is related to the unknown intensity of each event and not to its detailed characteristics. This justifies the practice that is now gaining acceptance of adopting fairly rough assumptions for obtaining estimates of the distribution of the maximum response for each event of a given intensity, and of then combining that distribution with the distribution of the maximum intensity during a given time interval, in order to obtain the distribution of the maximum structural response during that interval (Esteva, 1969a; Newmark and Rosenblueth, 1971). Again, as for the wind problem, in many cases the variance of the maximum response given an intensity can be neglected in comparison with the variance of the maximum intensity, and only the expected value, and not the complete distribution, has to be estimated for the former variable.

For linear structures, simple approximate expressions have been developed for the distribution of their maximum response to earthquakes idealized as segments of white noise of equivalent duration (Rosenblueth and Bustamante, 1962), and some corrections have been proposed to account for the influence of nonstationarity and actual shape of the power spectrum (Rosenblueth and Elorduy, 1969). For the same class of structures, alternate procedures have been suggested to obtain the distribution of the maximum response of stationary processes of an arbitrary and constant power spectral density and to modify it on account of nonstationarity (Hou, 1968). For nonlinear multidegree systems with arbitrary laws of variation of stiffnesses and yield levels some simulation studies have been undertaken, but they have not been systematic, and hence they have not led to simple (or complicated) rules for estimating the expected value (much less the distribution) of the maximum response from the statistical properties of earthquakes. While the development of those rules is recommended, simulation oriented towards specific structures is suggested as the most practical formulation in the immediate future.

Occurrence of earthquakes of different intensities can be idealized as a generalized Poisson process, or according to more refined models, when time and space correlation of shocks is thought to be significant. In order to obtain the distribution of the maximum response when the distribution of the maximum intensity has been established it is necessary to count with the distribution (or at least with the expected value) of the maximum response for each intensity; but the intensity, understood as a single parameter, does not contain enough information for describing the statistical properties of motions that may influence the response of a wide range of structures. Thus, when a short period structure is analyzed, its maximum response can be related to the maximum ground acceleration, in a manner nearly independent of the frequency content of the motion, while for very long period systems it would be convenient to measure intensity by the maximum ground displacement. Some intermediate period systems are sensitive almost exclusively to maximum ground velocities, but others frequently met in practice fall in the ranges where either acceleration and velocity or velocity and displacement can strongly influence the response. Those cases are sensitive to the frequency content of the motion, which depends in turn on magnitude and focal distance of each earthquake. These cases can be handled, for instance, by treating the occurrence of earthquakes at different potential sources as separate stochastic processes.

Earthquake excitations are modified by some uncertain properties of the structure, such as stiffness, damping, yield level, and dead and live load. The influence that uncertainty about some of them has on the distribution of the maximum response can be analyzed by some available simplified procedures (Rosenblueth and Esteva, 1971b; Hou, 1968), but no clear picture of its relative importance has been established yet.

Evaluation of the distribution of the maximum seismic response of structures is hindered also by the lack of sufficient statistical information about intensities and return periods at given locations. A particular application has been reported of Bayesian analysis to the determination of the marginal probability of exceedance of given intensities when the process of such events is assumed to be a Poisson process whose mean rate is uncertain (Esteva, 1968).

Accidental Loads.   The probability distribution of the effects of some accidental loads (such as blast or airplane collision) can only be assessed by a mixed approach where the frequency of the events is estimated intuitively, on the basis of direct or indirect observations, or by extrapolation of comparable conditions, and the expected effects of each event are based on considerations about the physical processes involved. For very rare events the intuitive probabilities of occurrence would be so low that no further study of the risk implied by them would be required.

Foundation Settlements.   Differential settlements between the bottom ends of different columns depend on the characteristics of the system of discharges and on the soil properties, and are influenced by interaction with the structural stiffnesses. Tilting can be significant in tall buildings founded directly or through friction piles on compressible soil layers, and its magnitude suffers to a lesser extent the influence of the interaction mentioned. The mean and the variance of the average vertical settlement and of the tilting angle of a tall building founded on compressible soil have been obtained under the assumption of statistical independence of the soil properties at any two points beneath the foundation (Reséndiz and Herrera, 1969b). Very small variances are obtained for those displacements, particularly for the tilting angle, since the mentioned assumption assigns a negligible probability to the existence of a wide area, asymetrically located, having compressibility significantly higher or lower than the average. Adequate analyses of this problem will have to include reasonable estimates of the space correlation functions of the soil properties.

Other Effects.   Stresses caused by temperature, erection, shrinkage, and other similar effects, are also amenable to a mixed objective-subjective assessment of probabilities. This is a virgin area for future research.

Load Combinations.   When two or more permanent loads are superposed, the distribution (or at least the mean and the variance of their sum) can be obtained by straightforward application of standard methods of probability theory. When some of the contributions are stochastic processes of time, analysis of the distribution of the maximum of their sum over given time intervals gives place to a complex computational problem for which no general simplified method has been derived. Some particular cases can be discussed in some detail, however.

Suppose accidental loads from n different sources, each represented by a set of random occurrence times and a probability distribution of the magnitude of each event. Suppose also that the probability of more than one load acting simultaneously is negligible. (This happens, for instance, when considering the superposition of extreme wind, exceptional live load, and earthquake.) If $R_i(t)$ represents the reliability function (that is, the probability of survival as a function of time) obtained separately for each type of load, then the over-all reliability function can be obtained as

$$R(t) = \prod_{i=1}^{n} R_i(t)$$

if all the contributions are independent. For small failure probabilities the over-all failure probability, as a function of time, is equal to the sum of the failure probabilities under each contribution.

Superposition of the effects of dead load, ordinary live load, and wind can be approximately handled as though the first two were permanent, while the latter is defined by the distribution of the maximum value as a function of time. For any given time, the probability distribution of maximum effect would be obtained as the distribution of the sum of two independent random variables. The superposition of dead, ordinary, and earthquake load becomes more complicated because of the influence of dead and live loads on earthquake effects. As a first approximation, both vertical loads can be taken equal to their expected values for the purpose of computing the distribution of maximum earthquake effects. The case in which the space of possible magnitudes of live load at the instant of the earthquake can be reduced to a two-valued set (for instance, an auditorium that is assumed to be either empty or full with a deterministic load) has been studied by Mendoza and Rosenblueth (1971).

Measures of the Effects of Loads.   The previous discussion seems to imply that the significance of any load on safety can be measured by the maximum amplitude of some critical stresses, internal forces or deformations. However, tall buildings can also fail as a result of high and low cycle fatigue or of accumulated damage. There is no information, for instance, as to the potential influence of the overstressing undergone by some members during an intense earthquake on the system properties for future shocks. With the exception of some isolated efforts (Kasiraj and Yao, 1968), all the experimental and analytical work in this area, specifically oriented towards tall buildings, is a task waiting to be done.

4 System Reliability

Nature of Problem.   The reliability of a system is measured by the probability that it will perform satisfactorily. Failure may affect one or more of the various functions expected from the system, and it may extend to all or to a portion of it. Hence, different failure modes will have different consequences, and therefore it will be of interest to evaluate reliabilities with respect to various limit states or damage levels. Reaching the yield stress at a given cross section may be called failure with respect to a limit state, but it may be only an intermediate stage in the process leading to another limit state. Some modes take place when at least one member reaches a critical condition, while others require that a group of sections reach a limit state. Since some members participate in several modes, failure events are not independent. Since each mode may have different consequences, the probability of reaching each failure condition is not as significant as the expected cost of the consequences.

In practice, the most significant modes may be identified and their reliability computed by means of simplified models. Due to the correlation between loads and between strengths, adequate safety with respect to some modes is inferred from the safety of those studied in detail. This makes reasonable the practice of specifying a given member reliability when another system reliability is aimed for, and of verifying safety levels for only a few of the numerous potential modes in design problems.

Identification of significant failure modes is not a simple problem in general, nor is it the evaluation of their possible consequences. Yet, rational specification and assessment of safety are based on those two concepts. Take, for instance, one of the simplest conceivable cases: a fixed-end concrete beam. Failure by tension of the reinforcement is called ductile, while flexural compression and diagonal tension are called brittle. However, there is not enough knowledge at present to predict when a beam-span with three plastic hinges or one with both ends cracked by diagonal tension will actually collapse.

Take now a girder that forms part of a tall building frame. Will its failure be strictly local, or will it endanger the stability of a large portion of the frame? Suppose a column that fails in the sense that its maximum compressive capacity is reached. Will it cause the collapse of only the portion of structure directly above it, or will it affect also the neighboring frames? Or, as has often bewildered engineers, will the frame accommodate to the loss of one of its supports? Suppose, finally, a column that settles as a result of foundation failure, or a whole building that tilts. What effect does this have on the stress distribution in the structure, and what additional design effects would it be worth specifying in order to get adequate protection against these eventualities?

Quantitative answers to the preceding questions in everyday design practice seem beyond present possibilities, and perhaps it is not desirable to make safety factors depend on the individual estimates of such vaguely defined failure consequences.

This does not mean acceptance of a status quo concerning use of conventional safety factors, since, despite years of use, all that is known about them is that they are not too unsafe. However, they have been shown to be inconsistent, it is thought that they may be too conservative in some cases, and they do not provide a framework for studying optimum policies for apportioning strength among individual members when system reliabilities are specified. It is the task of researchers on structural safety to develop and to calibrate simplified models for system reliability analysis, and to produce consistent safety recommendations.

Failure Modes. Some modes may refer to collapse, and some others to serviceability conditions. Collapse of a complete building or of a portion of it may result, for instance, from reaching a limit state in one single critical section, a critical instability condition in a subassemblage, or a mechanism condition from successive yielding and stress redistribution at a set of plastic hinges. The first case, which may be exemplified by crushing of a reinforced concrete column, or diagonal tension cracking of a beam of the same material, is known as brittle failure. The third case is designated as ductile failure, and it may occur in simple-span or continuous beams, or in building frames subjected to vertical or to lateral forces. Occasionally, before the mechanism condition is reached, sudden failure at a plastic hinge may occur as a result of excessive yielding, with the corresponding reduction in system capacity. This mixed type of failure predominates in tall frames with shear walls, where lateral strength is obtained from the contributions of the walls and of the neighboring frames. If the set of lateral loads is assumed to increase proportionally, ordinary rigid-plastic analysis may be applied to predict the capacity of the system under the assumption that every plastic hinge can yield as much as required until the plastic mechanism condition is reached. However, hinge rotation demands are so large at some locations of these structures that often brittle behavior at some hinges will prevent the development of perfectly ductile response.

Unstiffened frames provide in general more favorable conditions for the development of perfectly ductile story response to lateral loads. Mixed ductile-brittle behavior in these cases may stem from column crushing or from reaching a critical instability condition at a story, which may take place after some plastic hinges have formed, or before that, under an elastic distribution of stresses. In the latter case, and still under the assumption of proportionally increasing loads, analysis of safety would be similar to that corresponding to reaching a limit state in one single critical section (later described as "weakest-link" systems).

Even when perfectly ductile response and static loading are assumed, evaluation of system reliability with respect to sideways collapse of a story is hindered by the possibility of a large number of potential mechanisms that may lead to the same collapse mode. At least for unstiffened frames, simplified models have been developed which serve to estimate marginal story reliability, correlation between random safety factors in any two stories, and reliability of the whole system. These models do not apply to composite systems made of frames and shear walls, in view of the larger degree of coupling involved among reliabilities in different modes and strengths of members in different stories.

Serviceability failure modes ordinarily cannot be defined in so sharp a manner as collapse failure modes (although, even for these, collapse may mean anything from need to demolish a heavily damaged structure to actual sudden collapse), but rather a continuously varying degree of damage may be used to define the possible states of different portions of the system. Damage may be measured by such parameters as deflections, amplitudes of vibration, crack widths, or differential settlements, or by their equivalent material cost. From the standpoint of practical design, the definition of a set of discrete limit states with respect to which safety factors are specified may be desirable. However, the advantages of the alternate procedure of explicitly basing design decisions on considerations about cost of damage will be stressed later.

Models of System Reliability Analysis.   Most safety problems arising in tall buildings are far more complex than the fundamental reliability case where a load system defined by one single parameter acts on a structure with only one potential failure mode. Although that elementary model may be applied to obtain estimates of system reliability when loads and strengths are each strongly correlated, and when the expected consequences of one failure mode govern the design require-ments, more refined models are necessary to cover a wider scope of problems and to evaluate the range of applicability of their simplified versions. A few models are available that derive system reliabilities rigorously from joint distributions of multiparameter loads and strengths, starting from the premises of structural analysis and probability theory. Conceptually they are very simple, but in practice they may require excessive amounts of numerical work. Their usefulness stems from the fact that they provide the basis for working models derived from the same premises after introduction of more or less drastic assumptions. The models of the latter kind are described in these paragraphs. In all cases a single application of a multicomponent load is assumed. Multiple application of loads and reliability as a function of time are discussed subsequently.

In Section 7.6, system reliability models are grouped into two categories, that assume respectively perfectly brittle and perfectly ductile behavior. Despite their simplicity these models may be extended or adapted to cover a wide range of practical problems, as will be shown.

Weakest-link models owe their name to their assumption that the system fails if any of its members fails. The classical weakest-link system is the statically determinate truss, that will fail in the same mode—collapse—regardless of the critical section where the event originates. This model is seldom directly applicable in its original form for evaluation of tall building safety, either because these structures accept substantial redistribution of stresses, or because failure events starting at different critical sections may damage different portions of the system, and hence may have different consequences. Thus, frame instability may occur at any of the stories of a tall building, each story considered as a potential weakest link, but collapse will probably extend in each case only to the portion of the building above the story where failure started. Many modern tall buildings possess a load bearing system that consists of wall panels resting on a few columns in the ground floor. Often, failure probability under the action of vertical loads is much higher for these columns than for the wall panels in the upper stories. In those cases, each column constitutes a potential weakest link in the total collapse mode. Neither the frame stories in the first example nor the columns in the second example just described are elementary potential weakest links in the classical sense, since a certain degree of stress redistribution is necessary before each subassemblage (story) or member (column) reaches its maximum capacity. However, it offers great practical advantages to assume that those subassemblages and members are equivalent links whose strength distributions and probabilistic correlations are evaluated through application of the "mechanism" or "collapse" models described below.

The equation for the failure probability of a classical weakest-link system with stochastically independent strengths and perfectly correlated load actions at critical sections is given in Section 7.6. It is applied to estimate the influence of some variables on the ratio of the required safety factor for a weakest-link system within critical sections to that for a single mode system such that both have the same failure probability. A plot is given of this ratio for the case where all member strengths possess a probability distribution of the same type, with the same coefficient of variation and the same central safety factor. The results shown correspond to various combinations of probability distribution types for loads and for strengths, and to two pairs of coefficients of variation of these variables. For moderate values of these parameters it is found that the ratio under discussion may be as high as 1.4 and 1.8, respectively, for systems with 10 and with 100 members. For systems with a small coefficient of variation of strength and a moderate coefficient of variation of load, the corresponding ratio may be as high as 1.1 and 1.3. In both cases, the ratios are very sensitive to the type of probability distribution.

These results may be used to provide estimates and upper bounds for over-all failure probabilities of some systems representative of tall buildings subjected to multicomponent loading even when they do not satisfy the assumptions of the basic model. Some studies show that for similarly proportioned multielement statically indeterminate systems, there is little difference in load between the onset of yielding in one element and that of many elements. If, in addition, the load variability greatly exceeds strength variability, yielding of all elements participating in a given failure mode will occur at about the same load level, and hence the simplest form of the weakest-link model will approximately apply. Some additional results are necessary before these comments can be stated in a quantitative manner. In the meantime, it is suggested that the element safety factor for a given system reliability be taken equal to a partial factor multiplied by that required for obtaining the same reliability in a single-mode, single-load system with the same variability of loads and strengths as the average for the members of the system. The partial factor may be taken equal to 1 if load is much more uncertain than strength, and if load components are strongly correlated. If strength variability is significant, or if actions at each critical section are nearly uncorrelated, a conservative solution is proposed: the probability of failure of the system is taken as the sum of the values for all elements. If a second-moment design format is used, this means that the safety index β for the design of each member should be raised by 1 for a 100-element system. Due to the strong dependence of the ratio of required system-to-member safety factor on the type of distribution function, this recommendation is the result of a rough approximation.

The preceding discussion suggests that some models should be developed for safety analysis of weakest-link systems with more general correlation patterns. Rosenblueth and Esteva (1971a, 1971b) deal with the cases where loads and strengths may be expressed as

$$R_i = A_i R_0; i = 1, \ldots, n \tag{7.86}$$

$$S_j = B_j S_0; j = 1, \ldots, n \tag{7.87}$$

in which R_i and S_j = respectively the strength at section i and the load action at section j; n = number of critical sections; and R_0, S_0, A_i and B_j are all mutually independent. Their means and variances may be obtained if means, variances, and covariances of loads and strengths are available (Rosenblueth and Esteva, 1971b, 1971a). The probability that failure take place in precisely the ith mode is

$$p_i = \int F_{Z_i}(u) \prod_{j \neq i} F_{X_j}(u) f_{\mu_i}(u) du \tag{7.88}$$

in which $Z_i = (R_0/S_0)/E(B_i/A_i); X_j = (B_j/A_j) /E(B_i/A_i); \mu_i = (B_i/A_i)/E(B_i/A_i)$; and $E(.)$ means expectation. Regardless of the forms of F_{Z_i}, F_{X_j} and f_{μ_i}, Eq 7.88 lends itself to numerical integration. It may be applied, for instance, to the evaluation of the failure probability in each story of a tall frame subjected to wind load, or to a beam that may fail in bending or in diagonal tension. Other applications are described in the sequel.

Ductile mechanism models assume that stress redistribution takes place each time that the yield limit is reached at a critical section, that a new redistribution occurs again as the load is increased and yielding starts at new critical sections, and that an unlimited capacity of plastic deformation is available at each section. Collapse occurs when the number and location of the yielding sections is such that a mechanism is formed. For a given set of loads and strengths, the potential failure mechanisms can be identified and the corresponding capacity determined by means of a rigid plastic analysis. If the components of the load system were increased proportionally, the critical mode would be that with the lowest safety factor. The model is ordinarily used in connection with limit analysis of continuous frames, but it can be extended to other statically indeterminate structures, such as braced frames and wall-frame systems.

When loads and strengths are uncertain, identification of the governing failure mechanism is possible only when both the load and the strength systems are made each of perfectly correlated components. In general, not only the safety factor, but also the critical failure mechanism will be uncertain. Previous work by Stevenson and Moses (1970) shows that the random safety margin Z_j for the jth potential failure mechanism may be expressed as a linear combination of the load components on the structure and the strengths at the critical sections that yield in that mechanism. When the loads are increased proportionally, failure in precisely the jth mode occurs if $Z_j < 0$ and $Z_j < Z_k$ for any $k \neq j$. Let p_i denote this probability. Then the failure probability P_f (regardless of mode) is obtained as

$$\sum_{j=1}^{n} P_j.$$

Alternatively, P_f may be obtained as $\Sigma P (Z_i < 0, Z_1 > 0, \ldots, Z_{j-1} > 0)$, in which $P(E_1, E_2, \ldots, E_m)$ is the probability of the joint occurrence of $E_1, E_2, \ldots, E_m$. None of these expressions lends itself to practical applications, since they involve numerical evaluation of multiple integrals. Hence, some approximations involving only simple integrals have been derived (Stevenson and Moses, 1970).

Ductile mechanism models can also be analyzed by application of Eqs. 7.86, 7.87, and 7.88. It suffices to take R_i and S_j respectively equal to the strength and load terms in the expression for Z_i, and to evaluate the required means, variances, and covariances by application of elementary statistical equations to the detailed expressions for R_i and S_j. Here lies the analogy between the equivalent links of a ductile system and the actual links of a nonredundant system.

The number of potential failure modes is large. In the deterministic case, detailed analysis of them all is circumvented by application of upper and lower bound theorems for the safety factor. In the probabilistic case, upper and lower bounds for failure probabilities can also be obtained in terms of the solutions for an incomplete set of potential mechanisms (Augusti and Baratta, 1971, 1972). Owing to the regularity of ordinary building frames, simple solutions can be obtained in some particular cases. For instance, lateral strength of a story is proportional to the sum of the moment capacities at the ends of all columns in that story. Each moment capacity is the smallest of the column yield moment and the available capacity of the members joining at its end. Means and variances of all moment capacities can be estimated (Esteva and Rosenblueth, 1971) and used in the computation of the mean and the variance of the lateral strength of the story. This formulation permits reducing the number of mechanisms involving lateral sway to one for each story.

Most structural systems used for tall buildings behave in a mixed ductile-brittle manner, since the capacity of plastic deformation at each yielding section is limited. In some cases, premature collapse may be the result of stress redistribution, when the latter implies not only a change in the portions that the various elements take of a given over-all action, but also a change in the nature of the action. This may be the case, for instance, when yielding of a group of lateral resisting elements at a story during an earthquake may generate excessive story-torsion and, eventually, brittle torsional failure of individual columns (Esteva, 1969c). This poses the question of evaluation of safety with respect to a series of modes in cascade, that is, a succession of modes such that occurrence of one of them would be possible only after occurrence of those before it in the series. At any given load level the probability of a given mode would be obtained recursively as its conditional probability given the occurrence of the previous mode times the probability of the latter. The problem becomes more difficult to handle when the order in which the modes may occur is not fixed, and occurrence of each mode modifies safety with respect to the rest. This represents, for instance, a process of increasing loading where plastic hinges of limited deformation capacity may form in any order, and it is of interest to estimate the distribution of the demand for deformation capacity at various locations in order to design for it. If loads and strengths are strongly correlated, approximate estimates can be obtained by assuming that the order in which the hinges form is the same as that obtained from a deterministic analysis where an increasing load, with components proportional to the means of their final values, acts on a structure with properties equal to the mean values of those of the real system.

Multistory systems composed of interacting frames and shear walls subjected to lateral forces are typical cases whose response has to be modeled by mixed behavior systems: during the initial stages, loading is distributed among frames and shear walls according to a pattern consistent with elastic behavior. As the load increases, the first plastic hinges form, ordinarily at the girder-ends joining shear walls at the uppermost floor levels. This causes a rise in the portion of the total shear force and overturning moment resisted by the shear walls at each story. Further load increases may lead to local deformations in excess of ductile capacity at some hinges, hence to brittle failure of those sections, and hence to a new rise of the portions of shear force and overturning moment taken by the walls. The condition thus reached may imply the development of critical conditions at some sections of the walls or of their foundations that would not be detected from the conventional structural analysis of the system in its original state.

Variation of Reliability with Time.   Loads may vary with time, as described. Strengths may do so as a result of increase of material strength with time, decrease of effective material strength with load duration, and variation of system properties during the construction stage. The problem is practically disregarded in this chapter, since it has only been the object of some isolated quantitative studies. However, the few available results can be applied in the attempts to establish practical recommendations for attaining consistent safety levels.

The superposition of permanent loads and exceptional live loads will probably occur during the first few years after construction, and it will be reasonable to assume, for the purpose of evaluating safety and expected benefits as a function of time, that failure under their combined action could occur only right after construction. The corresponding probability would be obtained under the assumption of a single load application, where the load system would be equal to the superpositon of the mentioned loads, the structural system would coincide with that of the finished construction, and the material strength would correspond to a long duration load applied to a sufficiently aged material. Similarly, consistent assumptions can also be made for the evaluation of safety at given stages in the construction process. This type of analysis would not apply, however, to the reconstruction stages of systems damaged by earthquakes shortly before, since, as a result of the aftershock activity, there would be a significant probability of strong motions during the reconstruction interval.

Evaluation of system reliability under some accidental excitations, such as wind, earthquake, and blast requires explicit dealing with time, since the maximum intensities of these excitations for which it is economical to design occur with return intervals of at least several decades. Under the assumption of constant deterministic strength and vertical loads, the seismic intensity that leads to failure can be computed. If exceedance of that intensity can be represented, as suggested above, by a Poisson or by a renewal stochastic process, the reliability function can be obtained as the probability of no exceedance of the failure intensity during a given time interval, or as the probability that the waiting time for occurrence of that intensity is longer than the given interval. If strength and vertical loads are constant but random, the failure intensity (in other words the seismic strength of the system) is also random, and the reliability function must be obtained by weighing the function obtained for the deterministic strength case with respect to the probability density function of the failure intensity. In practice a number of potential modes or degrees of damage can be expected to occur. For every given intensity it is possible to estimate the probabilities of the various modes and the distribution of the cost of their consequences. The distributions of failure probabilities and of nominal or actualized costs of failure consequences during given time intervals can be obtained by application of elementary concepts of the theories of extreme values and of Poisson and renewal stochastic processes. For structures that may be subjected to accidental loads, studies of this type would provide a basis for making decisions concerning selection of design parameters that may affect safety with respect to more than one mode. These studies are still to be undertaken.

5   Reliability Level Decisions

The objective of engineering design is optimization, that is, attaining a balance between the potential performance of a system and the required investment [see

Section 7.4 and Rosenblueth (1973)]. Traditionally, safety factors have been selected on the basis of intuition, influenced in swinging fashion by the contemporary events of good or ill performance of existing structures. Despite this experience, and the power of engineering judgment, there is evidence that intuitive decisions about reliability levels often fail to produce optimum designs (Esteva, 1968). Inefficiency of pure intuition is accentuated by changing fashions concerning architectural and structural conceptions and hence, possibly, by the vulnerability of the new systems before phenomena that were not significant for old-fashioned structures.

In a modern society of growing demands, allocation of resources to building safe structures is only one of many activities in a system whose performance should be optimized in terms of that society. Hence the suggestion in Section 7.4 of a model based on Mauch and Schneider (1973) where decisions about investments on buildings are interacted by the possibility of investing in other sources of benefits for given communities. The model assumes a system made up of a number of activities that may be subjected to public control. Each activity involves social benefits (not mentioned explicitly in Section 7.4) and risks that vary as a function of the resources allocated to it. The sum of expected costs, benefits, and risks for all activities is to be optimized. Evaluation of benefits and risks implies the development of scales of social preferences, according to which the various modes of response of the social system can be mapped into a scalar function. This is the weakest aspect of the model, owing to the difficulties involved in performing this mapping. However, the model provides a conceptual framework for making semiquantitative decisions and for the efficient collection of relevant data.

The extent to which investment in buildings is to be subjected to public control is a matter of the economic organization of each society, and in some cases it may be closely related to policies covering a wide spectrum, from industrial development to social security and income tax. The possibility of exerting that control as well as its potential significance on a national macroeconomy are obvious—for instance, when applied to making decisions concerning massive construction of low-cost housing units.

Safety is one of the variables affecting the cost-benefit curve of given buildings. Establishing that curve entails treating the building as a system, dividing it into a set of subsystems or activities (structure, foundation, finishes, facilities, piping, etc.) and a set of specifications, or control rules, related to those subsystems (architectural specifications, safety, etc.), and optimizing at the building level. Each activity in the construction of a building produces benefits and risks that may interact with those related to some other activity. Thus, boring the girders may decrease their safety, but it may produce substantial savings in the cost of piping or in the total height of the building. The size of the windows made in a shear wall will influence both the benefits of good lighting and ventilation and the risk of failure. The esthetic considerations supporting the construction of daring structures should be weighed with regard to the implied variation in their optimum safety levels.

The problem of optimizing within a wide-scope framework can be converted into an iterative two-step process: internal optimization is used in the production of curves for specific projects which are later fed into the over-all system. After the latter is optimized, some of its operating restrictions or the consequences of its nonlinearity may become obvious, and may lead to modifications of the preference scale for the various functions of a building and hence of its cost-benefit curve. For instance, a conclusion of the analysis of the macroeconomic system might limit the per capita allocation for building housing units. Both architectural and safety standards would have to be lowered, but the decrease in safety might start to weigh more if it approached a strongly nonlinear range of societal response as related to number of failures. Although practically unexplored at present, application of these concepts in practice is challenging and promising.

In Section 7.4 an optimization model for a system where everything is specified with the exception of the recommended safety level is discussed in some detail (Rosenblueth, 1973). Such analyses should be used in the process of obtaining quantitative expressions for the interaction of safety with all the building systems. Up to now their use has been confined to the suboptimization problem where architectural and other decisions precede formal evaluations of safety, and account for its influence only in a quantitative manner.

There is no agreement as to the validity of making safety decisions on the basis of optimization analyses, without imposing restrictions on the absolute values of acceptable risk levels. It can be argued that the disagreement might be only apparent, since statement of upper bounds for failure probabilities might be made equivalent to a scale of social preferences according to which acceptance of risk would decrease sharply after a given value. Those bounds would probably be relaxed by any decision maker faced with the problem of building as many dwelling units as possible with a limited amount of money, where social pressures so demand. Establishing new bounds that no decision maker would trespass would be equivalent to accepting the existence of risk levels beyond which it would be wiser not to build. But it is not clear how close those bounds would be to some numbers mentioned as acceptable for modern societies (Augusti and Baratta, 1972). Besides, evidence is mentioned of the opposite situation, when the safety levels accepted by society have been lower than those obtained from cost-benefit analyses.

Establishment of mechanisms that will permit assessment of societal preference lies at the basis of any serious attempt for drastic improvements in the practice of safety level selection. The idea described in Section 7.3 (due to Rosenblueth), of setting up interdisciplinary groups of specialists elected by popular vote, is probably too preliminary and not without pitfalls, but it may constitute a hint for an efficient solution.

6 Codified Safety Recommendations

Nature of Safety Prescriptions.   Building codes should serve to maximize utility from the standpoint of society (Rosenblueth, 1973). Ideally, their wording should reflect their purpose, but in practice the latter is concealed behind statements that specify minimum standards and assign legal responsibilities. Codes should also serve to spread new concepts and criteria, but this function is also hindered by lack of clarity in safety specification.

There are some reasons for the inconsistency between objectives and format. In the first place, the tools required for reliability analysis of complex systems and for assessment of the utility functions of their expected performance are not yet sufficiently developed, at least not to the extent that they could be applied in routine design practice.

Even when dealing with systems for which simplified reliability models have been developed, there seems to be a consensus that evaluation of utility functions could be left to individual designers only in some particular instances, which do not include those involving risk to human lives or other losses whose value to society is difficult to quantify. Interdisciplinary building code committees should take up this job.

The only general way of specifying safety in such a manner that individual optimum designs will be obtained under all conceivable circumstances is by writing explicitly in optimization terms. If another format has to be used, code writers should aim for optimization over the population of systems to be designed, subject to the constraint of the given format (Ravindra and Lind, 1972). The wider range of conditions a format can reflect, the closer to their optimum will lie the individual designs, and the closer to its maximum possible value will be the utility of the ensemble. Thus, the optimum design format is characterized by a proper balance between generality and simplicity. Explicit specification of safety in optimization terms is a worthy long-term goal, but given the present state of knowledge and abilities it will have to be preceded by interim codes expressed in less advanced terms. These interim codes should be written in such a manner as to facilitate their evolution towards their ideal form.

Present Trends in Specification of Safety

Traditional design formats.   Traditional formats specify design values of loads and strengths, as well as strength reduction and load factors. Their virtues and faults have been extensively discussed (Rosenblueth and Esteva, 1971a; Rosenblueth, 1973). The faults are summarized by the statements that those formats do not provide any guide as to the safety levels that they imply, nor as to the relations between design values of given variables and their probable range of variation; that they do not show how to handle consistently some situations not covered explicitly by them; and that they make use of unnecessarily cryptic recommendations when trying to cover some particular safety problems.

Semiprobabilistic codes.   Use of semiprobabilistic formats constitutes a step forward, since it includes information about uncertainty in load intensities and material strengths. Characteristic values, that is, values corresponding to given probabilities, are assumed to be accurately defined in terms of mean values plus or minus a given number of standard deviations. Criticism of this format is often based on the sensitivity of the relation between actual and assumed probabilities to the type of family distributions, particularly in the left tail of strength distribution functions, where finite probabilites are assigned to negative values. This problem can be circumvented simply by changing the recommended expression for computing characteristic values. However, there remains the substantial objection that codes in which this format has been adopted do not show schemes generally applicable for combining uncertainties or for handling special cases. Thus, consistent characteristic values for member strengths are specified by placing apparently arbitrary factors before the strength prediction formulas expressed in terms of the characteristic values of material strengths and the nominal values of member dimensions. Similarly, the influence of unknown residual stresses on the buckling capacity of a column is often accounted for by specifying reduced values for the tangent modulus of elasticity of the material. Some other examples of the awkward design rules that have to be derived are discussed in Section 7.3.

Second-moment theories.   The main asset of second-moment-format codes is that they provide consistent safety designs through the use of distribution-free expressions (that is, expressions that are independent of the shapes of the probability distributions) for safety factors. These are the first kind of formulations that permit systematic analysis of a wide range of design problems, as well as proper combination of uncertainties stemming from different sources, with only the limitations of the insensitivity of the required safety factors to the types of probability distribution functions and of the first-order approximation for the computation of means and variances of functions of random variables. Their generality extends, for instance, to cases where the minimum and not the maximum value of a variable is critical (vertical load helping to prevent overturning of a retaining wall), or where the failure condition is expressed in terms of an interaction diagram (members under combined bending and axial load), as well as to those instances where several loads have to be superposed, whether they are independent (dead and live loads) or correlated (live load plus earthquake effects; wind and snow loads). Some special rules are still required, though, for handling those cases where a random variable may adopt positive or negative values with approximately equal probabilities (eccentricity of a nominally concentric load).

Equations that follow serve to specify safety factors when means and variances of loads and strengths related to given failure modes are known. Actual evaluation of these parameters for code practical case is the essential feature of the second-moment codes. Some possible criteria for this evaluation were discussed or suggested when dealing with actions and with system reliability.

The original second-moment format assumes that safety in any given failure mode is measured by the coefficient of variation of the safety margin, $R - S$, in which R = strength and S = load effect. Thus, the required mean strength is related to the mean load effect and to the variances of these two variables through the safety index β as

$$E(R) \geq E(S) + \beta[\text{var}(R) + \text{var}(S)]^{1/2} \tag{7.89}$$

if θ = required central safety factor, that is, the ratio $E(R)/E(S)$, and V_R and V_S = coefficients of variation of strength and load action respectively, then (Cornell, 1969)

$$\theta = \{1 + [\beta^2 V_R^2 + \beta^2 V_S^2(1 - \beta^2 V_R^2)]^{1/2}\} (1 - \beta^2 V_R^2)^{-1/2} \tag{7.90}$$

An alternate second-order expression for the required ratio $E(R)/E(S)$ can be obtained when the safety condition is expressed as (Rosenblueth and Esteva, 1971a, 1971b)

$$E(\ln R) \geq E(\ln S) + \beta[\text{var}(\ln R) + \text{var}(\ln S)]^{1/2} \tag{7.91}$$

in which $E(\ )$ = expected value, and ln stands for natural logarithm. In this case

$$\theta = \frac{(1 + V_R^2)^{1/2}}{(1 + V_S^2)^{1/2}} \exp\{\beta[\ln(1 + V_R^2)(1 + V_S^2)]^{1/2}\} \tag{7.92}$$

Eq. 7.92 can be simplified to give

$$\theta \simeq \exp \beta (V_R^2 + V_S^2)^{1/2} \tag{7.93}$$

Adequacy of Eqs. 7.90, 7.92 and 7.93 to represent the required central safety factors has been studied by comparing their variation in terms of β, V_R and V_S with the required values computed for specified failure probabilities under various assumptions concerning the shapes of the probability distributions of loads and strengths. It was concluded that Eq. 7.90 departs from the general trend when V_R approaches 1, giving place to inadmissibly high results in the vicinity of that value. Eqs. 7.92 and 7.93 give approximately the same results, and predict reasonably well the relative variation (although not necessarily the absolute values) of θ for the most frequent distribution functions and for failure probabilities at least as low as 10^{-5}. Hence, after proper calibration with present practice, Eq. 7.93 can be used in a second-moment-format code.

Even when adopting a distribution free format, it is desirable to be ready for including whatever information is or may become available in the future concerning the distributions of given types of loads or strengths. This can be done, for instance, by replacing V_R and V_S in Eq. 7.93 by $\gamma_R V_R$ and $\gamma_S V_S$, respectively, in which γ_R and γ_S would depend on the type of strength and load action and would be specified in such a manner as to represent the tail of the distribution of interest in the significant range of probabilities.

Second-moment split-factor codes.   Some groups favor adoption of a split factor formulation of the safety condition (Lind, 1969; Ravindra et al., 1969). They base their proposal on the advantages of departing less radically than Eqs. 7.90 and 7.93 from accepted practice, on the necessity of defining characteristic values intended to assign legal and professional responsibilities, and on the need to give more weight to information about the significant tails of distribution functions that is implied by basing decisions on means and variances alone. Derivation of such recommendations from a second-moment analysis of uncertainty is based on the possibility of expressing Eq. 7.89 in the form

$$E(R) \geq E(S) + \beta\alpha\,(\sigma_R + \sigma_S) \qquad (7.94)$$

in which σ = standard deviation and $\alpha = (\sigma_R^2 + \sigma_S^2)^{1/}/(\sigma_R + \sigma_S)$ can be taken equal to 0.75, with an error not exceeding 5% if $1/3 \leq \sigma_R/\sigma_S \leq 3$. The design condition is then expressed as $R^* \geqslant S^*$, in which R^* and S^*, the characteristic values of loads and strengths, are obtained as

$$R^* = E(R)(1 - \beta\alpha V_R), \; S^* = E(S)(1 + \beta\alpha V_S) \qquad (7.95)$$

Again, Eq. 7.95 does not behave adequately in the range of $\beta\alpha V_R$ approaching 1. An alternate split factor formulation is obtained if the expression for α defined above is substituted in Eq. 7.93 to give

$$R^* = E(R) \exp - (\beta\alpha V_R), \; S^* = E(S) \exp (\beta\alpha V_S) \qquad (7.96)$$

Eqs. 7.96 are more sensitive to the split-factors approximation than Eq. 7.95, since small errors in α are amplified when multiplied by β and substituted in the exponential expression. Thus, if $\alpha = 0.75$, $\beta = 5$, $V_S = 0.3$ and $V_R = 0$, then exp $\beta(V_R^2 + V_S^2)^{1/2} = 4.5$, while exp $(\beta\alpha V_R)$ exp $(\beta\alpha V_S) = 3.1$, an error of 31% on the unconservative side, while use of Eq. 7.95 leads to an error due to splitting of only 15%. However, this disadvantage of the exponential form is compensated by its satisfactory performance over the range of all possible values of βV_R. A higher value of α can be adopted, that will produce somewhat conservative results for V_R/V_S near 1, and less unconservative when one of the coefficients of variation predominates.

The expression $\theta = (1 + \beta\alpha V_R)(1 + \beta\alpha V_S)$ seems promising too. When compared with Eqs. 7.90 and 7.93 or with the curves for θ obtained for various combinations of distributions it is seen to fall well below them all. This may not be too serious, since in case it were adopted the applicable values of β should be obtained by calibration with respect to present designs. The problem remains that if it is calibrated with respect to some reasonable probability distributions of relatively large coefficients of variation, it will be unconservative for small values of those parameters.

Whatever the specific second-moment basic equation that is used to implement a split factor format, a systematic procedure has to be devised for obtaining characteristic values of functions of several variables. This has been successfully done for some special cases (Ravindra et al., 1969).

A general procedure has been presented by Paloheimo and Hannus (1974) who deal with the case when the safety margin is expressed as a linear (or linearized) function of a number of random variables.

Extended reliability concept.   Alternate procedures (Ang and Amin, 1969; Ang and Ellingwood, 1971) have been suggested for handling imperfect information about applicable probability distributions of the random variables defining design, as well as uncertainty stemming from sources for which probabilities cannot be inferred from statistical analysis of repeated experiments. The extended reliability concept defines failure as the probability that $R < NS$, in which the distributions of R and S are supposed to be obtained from so-called objective information, and N = arbitrary factor to cover other sources of uncertainty (errors in member dimensions, in estimation of the tails of the probability distributions, or in the computation algorithms, etc.). Then N is also treated as random and the corresponding uncertainty incorporated in the evaluation of the safety factor. The formulation succeeds in obtaining design recommendations which are less sensitive to the shapes of the probability distributions than those derived from the classical reliability concept. However, it does not satisfy the desirable condition of clearly identifying each piece of uncertainty and of thus facilitating more detailed application of engineering judgment.

Invariant formats.   Ditlevsen (1973) has shown that none of the previous formulations of design is invariant in the sense that once a safety index is specified and a set of assumptions is made concerning means and standard deviations (or variation coefficients) of the basic variables the same design is obtained by different, independent designers. In fact, he has shown that it is not possible to find a format of the R versus S type that is invariant with respect to all the possible manners in which R and S can be expressed in a given problem. He also developed the first invariant safety format, which consisted in expressing the failure equation in terms of the (unfavorable) characteristic values of the basic variables, where all these characteristic values were made to depend on the mean and standard deviation of the corresponding distribution and on the safety index β.

Further developments were carried out by Hasofer and Lind (1973), who defined the safety index as the minimum distance from the origin to the failure surface when the latter is represented in the multidimensional space of the random variables $x_i = [X_i - E(X_i)]/\sigma_i$, in which X_i = one of the basic variable in terms of which the design is formulated, and $E(X_i)$and σ_i = its mean and standard deviation, respectively. Esteva (1974) used the basic idea of Hasofer-Lind's formulation, but presented the design criteria in terms of characteristic values, and included a transformation that permits taking into account whatever information may be available concerning the rate of variation of probabilities with values of the basic variables in the relevant ranges of their probability distributions. Finally, Veneziano (1974) generalized the concept of invariance, and presented a comprehensive discussion of the types of invariance that can be preserved under different types of design formats.

Optimum reliability.   Some cases can be envisaged in which design in optimum reliability terms is feasible and advisable in the next generation of codes. For instance, when deflection limitations do not hide any instability problem, some guidelines might be provided to designers in order to let them obtain cost functions associated with deflections or distortions and define optimum acceptable values. Thus, allowable values of beam deflections, differential settlements, and story sidesway could be obtained in each particular case as functions of the type of finishing and contents of a building. The models suggested by Rosenblueth (1973) are simple enough to be considered as possible design formats. Extension to instances involving more complex systems or more uncertain failure is a matter of prescribing utility functions and simplified reliability models.

7 Concluding Remarks

There is general agreement that the time has come for writing design specifications that handle uncertainty in an explicit manner. There are wide divergences, however, as to the form, complexity, and scope of codified recommendations. Some groups favor relatively mild advances, such as defining characteristic values for design in terms of means plus or minus a number of standard deviations of the distributions of the basic variables, while others support adoption of design criteria based on central values and variances of actions and strengths at critical sections, and set approximate rules for deriving the relevant statistical parameters. Others, still, advocate use of cost-benefit analyses at least for some failure modes having consequences easy to quantify, while they accept less advanced criteria for other failure modes. Common preoccupations of all groups are code calibration, writing simple but general design rules, and development of working models and design aids.

The ideal form of specifying safety is through reliability optimization. Writing complete codes explicitly in such terms does not seem feasible at present, but a strategy can be devised to approach that desirable stage in an optimum manner. Besides the required research, this strategy should include educational campaigns, successive generations of gradually advancing codes and development of graphs, computer programs and languages, and other design aids.

Scarcity of statistical data on loads, strengths, dimensions, and consequences of failure is pointed at as a reason for postponing adoption of reliability based codes. However, engineers continue to build structures guided by arbitrary rules that hide the actual problems and offer no help for assessment of safety. They should do at least as well if they used rational methods of uncertainty analysis for interpreting the scanty available information. In the production of methods for evaluating and specifying safety, engineering judgment will continue to play an important role, but a formal framework will guide it as to the quantities to be estimated. If code writers can pull safety factors out of their sleeves they will do a better job if they are allowed to first guess at the probabilities in play.

Only after rational design formats are adopted will the required information become evident, research needs recognized, and efficient data collection started.

7.8 PROBABILISTIC CONCEPTS AND DESIGN PRACTICE

1 Scope

The preceding sections provide a state-of-the-art treatment of probabilistic methods in structural engineering. The present degree of development and calibration of those methods does not warrant their direct application by designers, however desirable it may be. At the code-writing level, however, those concepts are gaining wide recognition and they have been applied to the definition of consistent design values of acting loads, member strengths, and safety factors. Hence, while other chapters in this monograph are oriented towards direct applications by designers of the widely accepted concepts those chapters deal with, our emphasis here is on the general philosophy and the available tools of a new and swiftly developing field. Thus, the purpose of this section is to summarize the importance of probabilistic concepts in the establishment of safety design parameters and to illustrate the manner in which some of those concepts have influenced design practice.

From previous sections it is concluded that the main asset of probabilistic methods is their capability for defining safety in a quantitative manner and for reaching decisions about adequate safety levels. Thus, bases are provided for quantitatively describing uncertainties tied to elementary variables such as load intensities, material strengths, execution imperfections, or equation errors, and for combining those uncertainties in order to estimate uncertainties tied to some transformed variables, such as bending moment at the end of a given beam, seismic overturning moment at a given story, available capacity at either of those sections, or ratio of available to required capacity at a section acted upon by a combination of axial load and bending moment. Failure probabilities or simpler, although less precise, measures of safety can be obtained through adequate processing of probabilistic descriptions of available and required capacities. These safety measures set the ground for the computation of expected consequences of failure that account both for the nominal cost of failure in case it occurs and for its probability of taking place. Optimum safety levels can then be obtained through an analysis that compares initial costs required for attaining given safety levels with the expected benefits and costs of failure corresponding to them. Application of optimization criteria such as those advocated here are hindered, even at the code-writer level, by the existence of many methodological gaps to be filled and of many controversies to be settled. Fruitful applications, however, have been made of the methodology and concepts presented in this chapter and of the basic philosophy underlying them. Some of those applications are the matter of the discussion that follows.

2   Design Parameters and Safety Levels

Design criteria are usually based on the comparison of nominal "maximum probable" forces acting at given critical sections with the corresponding "minimum probable" capacities. The meaning of the terms "maximum probable" and "minimum probable" is vague and may even be misleading unless a measure is attached to the probabilities that values more unfavorable than those maximum and minimum are attained. But the probability distributions of internal forces and section capacities cannot, in general, be directly derived from statistical observations about those variables. They have to be derived, instead, through analytical transformations from the available distributions of other variables. Thus, the internal force produced by live load at a critical section is usually computed through an algorithm that assumes a nominal value of live load intensity throughout the tributary area and applies standard methods of structural analysis. Likewise, in order to determine the distribution of structural capacity of a critical section one must cope with uncertainties in material properties, in fabrication inaccuracies, and in formula-prediction errors.

The methodology for transforming the distributions (or characteristic values of them) of basic variables in order to obtain those corresponding to derived variables is provided by probability theory. Thus, we can answer questions such as the following: What computations should be performed in order to obtain the bending moment at a critical section that will be exceeded with probability of 2% during the life of a structure, starting from the load intensity over a given area that is exceeded with probability 2% at a random instant, a description of the probable fluctuations of load intensity from one point of the tributary area to another, and a measure of the accuracy of structural analysis criteria? How can one estimate the coefficient of variation of bending capacity of a reinforced concrete beam when mean values and coefficients of variation of material properties, fabrication inaccuracies, and formula-prediction errors are available? How should the value of the total load effect at a critical section, corresponding to 2% probability of being exceeded, be obtained from the individual values of dead and live load effects corresponding to the same probabilities?

Procedures for performing these computations are outlined in Section 7.2 of this chapter. Detailed derivations of design values for different limit states and different materials and structural members can be found in several references (Galambos and Ravindra, 1973; Rosenblueth and Esteva, 1971b; Cornell, 1972; Allen, 1970; Sexsmith, 1967; Benjamin and Shah, 1972; Meli, 1976).

Once the probability distributions (or some of their characteristic parameters) are defined for load effect and available strength at a critical section, the problem remains of specifying the relationships that should exist among those distributions when a given safety level is aimed for. According to Section 7.3, those relationships can be expressed as central safety factors—ratios of the mean values of strength and load effect—or as nominal safety factors—ratios between nominal values of minimum probable strength and maximum probable load. Whatever type of relationship is adopted, safety factors are functions of the desired failure probabilities, of the type of probability distributions of the variables at play, and of one or more parameters of those distributions. Because the types of the relevant probability distributions are not always well defined, alternate, although less precise, measures of safety have been proposed. One such measure (see Section 7.3) is the safety index β which is related with the parameters of the distributions of loads and strengths through Eq. 7.34 of Section 7.3, and is approximately related with failure probability through Eq. 7.35.

3 Member and System Reliability

In perfectly brittle structures, reaching the ultimate capacity of a critical section means failure of the system. In perfectly ductile structures where instability effects are not significant, failure of the system does not take place before yielding of critical sections at sufficient locations to allow the formation of a collapse mechanism. None of these extreme conditions actually occurs in reality, but the ductile model often provides a reasonable approximation for practical problems. As shown in Section 7.6, for a given failure mechanism the central safety factor required to attain a given safety decreases significantly with increasing number of critical sections involved in the mechanism, particularly when the corresponding strengths are stochastically independent and, on the average, contribute in approximately equal portions to system strength. Of particular interest in connection with tall buildings is the distribution of story shear capacity, where collapse at a given story implies usually the formation of a large number of plastic hinges, and may be reached through different potential mechanisms. As a consequence of this, and of the existence of positive statistical correlation between strengths of critical sections, the influence of the number of those sections is not as drastic as would be predicted by a model that considers a single failure mode and stochastically independent strengths.

This problem has been recognized, for instance, in the Earthquake Resistant Design chapter of the proposed (1976) Mexico City Building Code, where it is specified that for the design of any structural element that contributes more than 20% to story capacity in shear, twisting, or overturning moment, the load factor should be 20% higher than would be required otherwise.

4 Optimization

The preceding discussion deals with the problem of specifying design values when safety levels have been decided upon. But how safe is safe enough? How should desirable safety levels be established? There is a diversity of opinions in this respect, some of them basically contradictory between themselves, others only apparently so. It is said that desirable safety levels should be established by comparison with other consciously accepted, voluntary risks, such as those connected with flying or with driving an automobile. It is also said that present safety levels, although reached intuitively and lacking over-all consistency, are on the average near optimum, as society automatically optimizes when deciding on the use of resources that can be applied to a wide range of human needs. However debatable this statement may be, it is a fact that formal optimization criteria as advocated in Section 7.4 are still beyond reach in design practice, although they have been applied to a limited extent by code writers. Their use has to be combined with a calibration of the safety levels implied by present design recommendations.

7.9 APPENDIX

1 Distributions and Moments

The probability distribution $f(x)$ of a random variable X assigns a number to every possible value of the variable. If the variable is continuous the mean or first moment is defined by

$$\mu_X = E(X) = \int_x xf(x)dx \qquad (7.97)$$

while the variance or second moment is

$$\mathrm{Var}(X) = \int_x (x - \bar{x})^2 f(x)dx \qquad (7.98)$$

The standard deviation $\sigma(X)$ is the square root of $\mathrm{Var}(X)$. The coefficient of variation is $\sigma(X)/E(X)$. If the variable is discrete, the integrals in Eqs. 7.97 and 7.98 become summations.

The joint distribution $f(x,y)$ of two variables X and Y assigns a relative likelihood to all possible pairs of values. The distribution of either variable considered separately or the marginal distributions can be obtained from

$$f(x) = \int_y f(x,y)dy \qquad (7.99)$$

The conditional distribution of one variable given the value of the other such as $fz)x|y)$ can be found from $f(x)\,f(y|x)$. Conditional moments are defined by

$$E(Y|X) = \int_y yf(y|x)dy \qquad (7.100a)$$

$$\mathrm{Var}\,(Y|X) = \int_y [y - E(Y|X)]^2 f(y|x)dy \qquad (7.100b)$$

The (linear) probabilistic dependence of two variables is measured by their covariance which is defined by

$$\mathrm{Cov}\,(X,Y) = \int_x \int_y (x - \mu_X)(y - \mu_Y)f(x,y)dxdy \qquad (7.101)$$

or their correlation coefficient $\rho(X,Y) = \mathrm{Cov}(X,Y)/\sigma(X)\sigma(Y)$. If the variables are independent their covariance is zero, $f(x|y) = f(x)$, and $f(y|x) = f(y)$.

2 Conditional Moments

The moments of a variable Y can be obtained if the conditional moments

$E(Y|X)$ and Var $(Y|X)$ and the distribution $f(x)$ and known; thus

$$E(Y) = \int_x E(Y|x)f(x)dx \qquad (7.102a)$$

$$\text{Var } (Y) = \int_x \text{Var } (Y|x)f(x)dx + \int_x [E(Y|x) - E(Y)]^2 f(x)dx \qquad (7.102b)$$

Eqs. 7.102 reduce to a simple form if $E(Y|X) = a_1 X$ and Var $(Y|X) = a_2^2$ in which a_1 and a_2 are constants, thus

$$E(Y) = a_1 E(X) \qquad (7.103a)$$

$$\text{Var}(Y) = a_2^2 + a_1^2 \text{Var}(X) \qquad (7.103b)$$

Another simple case arises if $E(Y|X) = a_1 X$ and the coefficient of variation of Y given X is a constant a_3. In this case

$$E(Y) = a_1 E(X) \qquad (7.104a)$$

$$\text{Var}(Y) = a_3^2 a_1^2 E^2(X) + a_1^2 (1 + a_3^2) \text{Var}(X) \qquad (7.104b)$$

3 Moments of Functions

In general, if $Y = F(X)$ the distribution of Y is not of the same type as the distribution of X.

In the special case when $Y = a_1 X_1 + a_2 Y_2 + \ldots a_n X_n$ in which the a_i are constants

$$E(Y) = \sum_i a_i E(X_i) \qquad (7.105a)$$

$$\text{Var}(Y) = \sum_i a_i^2 \text{Var}(X_i) + \sum_{\substack{j=ij=1 \\ i \neq j}}^{n}\sum^{n} a_i a_j \text{Cov}(X_i, X_j) \qquad (7.105b)$$

If the variables are not uncorrelated all covariances must be considered.

In the special case when $Y = X_1 X_2$ and X_1 and X_2 are independent

$$E(Y) = E(X_1)E(X_2) \qquad (7.106a)$$

$$\text{Var}(Y) = \text{Var}(X_1)E^2(X_2) + \text{Var}(X_2)E^2(X_1) + \text{Var}(X_1)\text{Var}(X_2) \quad (7.106b)$$

In general, if $Y = F(X_1, X_2 \ldots X_n)$ approximate moments can be obtained from

$$E(Y) = F(\mu_1, \mu_2 \ldots \mu_n) + \frac{1}{2}\sum_{i=1}^{n}\sum_{j=1}^{n} \alpha_{ij} \text{Cov}(X_i, X_j) \qquad (7.107a)$$

$$\text{Var}(Y) = \sum_{i=1}^{n} \sum_{j=1}^{n} \beta_{ij} \, \text{Cov}(X_i, X_j) \qquad (7.107b)$$

in which

$$\alpha_{ij} = \frac{\partial^2 F}{\partial X_i \partial X_j}$$

evaluated at $X_i = \mu_i$, $(i = 1, 2 \ldots n)$, and

$$\beta_{ij} = \frac{\partial F}{\partial X_i} \frac{\partial F}{\partial X_j}$$

evaluated at $X_i = \mu_i$. The quantities α_{ij} and β_{ij} are constants.
If all X_i are independent, approximate moments are

$$E(Y) = F(\mu_1, \mu_2 \ldots \mu_n) \qquad (7.108a)$$

$$\text{Var}(Y) = \sum_{L=1}^{n} \beta_i^2 \, \text{Var}(X_i) \qquad (7.108b)$$

in which $\beta_i = \partial F / \partial X_i$ evaluated at $X_i = \mu_i$.

Eqs. 7.107 and 7.108 may involve substantial approximations for nonlinear functions.

7.10 CONDENSED REFERENCES/BIBLIOGRAPHY

The following is a condensed bibliography for this chapter. Not only does it include all articles referred to or cited in the text, but it also contains bibliography for further reading. The full citations will be found at the end of the Volume. What is given here should be sufficient information to lead the reader to the correct article: the author, date, and title. In case of multiple authors, only the first named is listed.

ACI 1971, *ACI Standard of Building Code Requirements for Reinforced Concrete*
ANSI 1967, *Method of Recording and Measuring Work Injury Experience*
Allen 1968, *Discussion of Choice of Failure Probabilities*
Allen 1969, *Safety Factors for Stress Reversal*
Allen 1970a, *Limit State Design—A Unified Procedure for the Design of Structures*
Allen 1970b, *Probabilistic Study of Reinforced Concrete in Bending*
Amin 1968, *Non-Stationary Stochastic Model for Earthquake Motions*
Anderson 1952, *Lateral Forces of Earthquake and Wind*
Ang 1968, *A Bibliography on Structural Safety*
Ang 1969, *Safety Factors and Probability in Structural Design*
Ang 1971, *Critical Analysis of Reliability Principles Relative to Design*
Ang 1973, *Towards Risk-Based Design and Performance Criteria*
Augusti 1971, *Limit Analysis of Structures with Stochastic Strength Variations*
Augusti 1972, *Theory of Probability and Limit Analysis of Structures Under Multi-Parameter*

Baker 1956, *The Ultimate-Load Theory Applied to the Design of Reinforced Concrete*
Baratta 1973a, *Improvement in Static Method for Limit Analysis of Structures with Stochastic*
Baratta 1973b, *A Remark on the Probabilistic Analysis of Structural Safety*
Barstein 1959, *Wind Loading on Tall Buildings*
Basler 1961, *Research Concerning Risk Analysis of Building Systems*

Belyaev 1969, *Statistical Method of Determining Standard Stresses for Steel Structures*
Benjamin 1970, *Probability, Statistics, and Decisions for Civil Engineers*
Benjamin 1972, *Information for Probabilistic Code Format*
Benjamin 1973, *Probabilistic Methods*
Bolotin 1962, *On Combinations of Random Loadings Acting on a Structure*
Bolotin 1964, *Modern Problems of Structural Mechanics*
Bolotin 1965, *Statistical Methods in Structural Mechanics*
Bolotin 1971, *Application of Methods of Probability Theory and of Reliability*
Bredsdorff undated, *The Performance of Structural Design by Characteristic Values*
Bustamante 1965, *Seismic Shears and Overturning Moments in Buildings*

CEB 1964, *Recommendations for an International Code of Practice for Reinforced Concrete*
CEB 1969, *General Principles for the Verification of Safety*
CIB 1978, *Report on Structural Safety*
Casciati 1973, *On the Reliability Theory of Structures*
Churchman 1968, *Challenge to Reason*
Cohn 1971, *Multi-Criteria Probabilistic Structural Design*
Cornell 1967, *Bounds on the Reliability of Structural Systems*
Cornell 1969a, *Structural Safety Specifications Based on Second-Moment Reliability Analysis*
Cornell 1969b, *A Probability-Based Structural Code*
Cornell 1969c, *Bayesian Statistical Theory and Reliability-Based Design*
Cornell 1970, *First Order Reliability Theory of Structural Design*
Cornell 1972, *Implementing Probability-Based Structural Codes*
Cornell 1973, *Theme Report: Structural Safety and Probabilistic Methods*
Crandall 1958, *Random Vibration*
Crandall 1963, *Random Vibration*

Davenport 1961, *The Application of Statistical Concepts to the Wind Loading of Structures*
Davenport 1966, *The Treatment of Wind Loading on Tall Buildings*
Davenport 1967, *Gust Loading Factors*
Davenport 1970, *Wind Loading on Tall Buildings*
Departamento del Distrito Federal 1966, *Building Code for the Federal District*
Ditlevsen 1973, *Structural Reliability and the Invariance Problem*
Drozdov 1973, *The Principles of Analysis of Spatial Structures in the USSR*

Esteva 1968, *Basis for the Formulation of Decisions of Seismic Design*
Esteva 1969a, *Seismic Risk and Seismic Design Decisions*
Esteva 1969b, *Seismicity Prediction: A Bayesian Approach*
Esteva 1969c, *Lessons From Some Recent Earthquakes in Latin America*
Esteva 1970, *Practical Considerations in the Bayesian Estimate of Seismic Risk*
Esteva 1971, *Use of Reliability Theory in Building Codes*
Esteva 1973, *Summary Report: Structural Safety and Probabilistic Methods*
Esteva 1974, *Invariant Safety Formats in Practical Design*

Ferry Borges 1968a, *Statistical Estimate of Seismic Loading*
Ferry Borges 1968b, *Dynamic Loading*
Ferry Borges 1969, *General Recommendations Derived From Basic Studies on Structural Safety*
Ferry Borges 1971, *Structural Safety*
Fishburn 1964, *Decision and Value Theory*
Freudenthal 1966, *The Analysis of Structural Safety*
Frownfelter 1969, *Structural Testing on Large Glass Installations*

Galambos 1973, *Tentative Load and Resistance Factor Design Criteria for Steel Buildings*
Griffiths 1968, *Collapse of Flats at Ronan Point, Canning Town*

Harris 1968, *Measurement of Wind Structure at Heights up to 598 ft. Above Ground Level*
Harvancik 1973, *Criteria for Design and Calculation of Load-Bearing Structures of Tall Buildings*
Hasofer 1973, *An Exact and Invariant Second Moment Code Format*
Horacek 1973, *Recent Knowledge on the Solution of the Load-Bearing Wall System*
Horak 1973, *Reliability and Effectiveness of Tall Buildings*
Horak 1974, *Reliability and Effectiveness of Tall Buildings*
Hou 1968, *Earthquake Simulation Models and Their Applications*

Information Canada 1971, *Canada Yearbook*
International Conference of Building Officials 1971, *Uniform Building Code*

Johnson 1953, *Strength, Safety and Economical Dimensions of Structures*

Kasiraj 1968, *Low Cycle Fatigue of Seismic Structures*
König 1973, *German Code Requirements*

Lewicki 1972, *Commentary on Design Safety Margins for Tall Concrete Building*
Lie 1972, *Optimum Fire Resistance of Structures*
Ligtenberg 1969, *Structural Safety and Catastrophic Events*
Ligtenberg 1973, *What Safety Margin is Necessary in a Structure?*
Lind 1964, *Safety, Economy and Reliability in Structural Design*
Lind 1968, *Deterministic Formats for the Probabilistic Design of Structures*
Lind 1969, *Deterministic Formats for the Probabilistic Design of Structures*
Lind 1971a, *The Design of Structural Design Norms*
Lind 1971b, *Consistent Partial Safety Factors*
Lind 1972, *Safety Level Decisions*
Lind 1973, *Safety Level Decisions*
Luce 1975, *Games and Decisions*

Magnusson 1973, *Probabilistic Analysis of Fire Safety*
Manuzio 1973, *Present Trends in Probabilistic Studies of Structural Safety*
Matescu 1963, *Contributions to the Study of Snow Agglomeration on Buildings Under Wind*
Mau 1971, *Optimum Design of Structures with a Minimum Expected Cost Criterion*
Mauch 1973, *The Direct Endangering of the Living Space*
McGuire 1974, *Prevention of Progressive Collapse*
Meli 1976, *Bases for the Standards of Structural Design of Project Regulation of Construction*
Mendoza 1971, *Design Live Load in Auditoriums Subjected to Earthquake*
Mitchell 1969, *Loadings on Buildings*
Moses 1968, *Optimum Design for Structural Safety*
Moses 1969, *Approaches to Structural Reliability and Optimization*
Moses 1970, *Reliability Based Structural Design*
Moses 1973, *Safety Analysis for Tall Buildings*
Murzewski 1972, *Safety of Tall Buildings and Probabilistic Methods*
Murzewski 1972, *A Stochastic Model for Live Loads in Tall Buildings*

Negoita 1970, *Contributions Concerning Probabilistic Aspects of Loads Due to Weather*
Nervi 1956, *Structures*
Newmark 1971, *Fundamentals of Earthquake Engineering*
Nowak 1972, *Some Problems in the Reliability-Based Design of Tall Buildings*

Ott 1969, *Reliability Under Uncertain Parameters, Stochastic Loads and Resistances*

Paloheimo 1974, *Structural Design Based on Weighted Fractiles*
Panggabean 1976, *On the Safety of Tall Buildings*
Peir 1971, *A Stochastic Live Load Model for Buildings*
Pugachov 1960, *Theory of Random Functions and its Application to Problems of Automatic*

Ravindra 1969, *Probabilistic Evaluation of Safety Factors*
Ravindra 1971, *Optimization of a Structural Code*
Reséndiz 1969a, *A Probabilistic Formulation of Settlement-Controlled Design*
Reséndiz 1969b, *Distributions of Foundation Settlements on Compressible Soil*
Rokach 1970, *A Statistical Study of the Strength of Steel Columns*
Rosenblueth 1956, *Theory of Live Loads on Buildings*
Rosenblueth 1962, *Distribution of Structural Response to Earthquakes*
Rosenblueth 1964, *Probabilistic Design to Resist Earthquakes*
Rosenblueth 1969, *Applications of Decision Theory*
Rosenblueth 1969, *Response of Linear Systems to Certain Transient Disturbances*
Rosenblueth 1970, *Ethical Decisions in Engineering*
Rosenblueth 1971, *Decisions Theory in Earthquake Engineering*
Rosenblueth 1971a, *Reliability Basis for Some Mexican Codes*
Rosenblueth 1971b, *Reliability Optimization in Isostatic Structures*
Rosenblueth 1972, *Structural Safety and Probabilistic Methods*
Rosenblueth 1973, *Code Specification of Safety and Serviceability*
Rosenblueth 1974a, *Analysis of Risk*
Rosenblueth 1974b, *Bonus and Penalty in Acceptance Criteria for Concrete*
Rosenblueth 1975a, *Optimum Design in Earthquake Engineering*
Rosenblueth 1975b, *Point Estimates for Probability Moments*
Rosenblueth 1975c, *The Future of Earthquake Engineering*
Rosenblueth 1975d, *Uncertainty in Structural Engineering*
Rzhanitzyn 1969, *It Is Necessary to Improve the Standards of Design of Building Structures*

Sandi 1966a, *Contributions to the Theory of Structural Design*
Sandi 1966b, *Safety of Structures Subjected to Temporary Loadings*
Sandi 1970, *Conventional Seismic Forces Corresponding to Non-Synchronous Ground Motion*
Sandi 1973a, *Failure Model Calculations*
Sandi 1973b, *Loads and Load Combinations*
Schueller 1974, *Reliability of Tall Buildings Under Wind Action*
Schueller 1974, *On the Reliability Assessment of Slender Structures*
Schueller 1974, *Reliability Oriented Design of Tower Like Structures Theoretical Concept*
Sedo 1973,*Practical Application of New Methods of Calculation of Buildings of Large Precast*
Sexsmith 1967, *Reliability Analysis of Concrete Structures*
Shah 1970, *Statistical Evaluation of Load Factors in Structural Design*
Shin 1971, *Studies on Reliability Based Analysis of Structures*
Shinozuka 1969, *Structural Safety and Optimum Proof Load*
Starr 1969, *Social Benefit Versus Technological Risk*
Stevens 1973, *Limit State Philosophy and Application*
Stevenson 1967, *Reliability Analysis and Optimum Design of Structural Systems with Application*
Stevenson 1970, *Reliability Analysis of Frame Structures*
Stone 1970, *Report on Future Building Regulations*
Switzky 1964, *Minimum Weight Design with Structural Reliability*

Tichý 1964, *Safety of Reinforced Concrete Framed Structures*
Tichý 1969, *A Logical System for Partial Safety Factors*
Tichý 1972, *Statistical Theory of Concrete Structures*
Tichý 1974, *A Probabilistic Model for Structural Actions*
Tichý 1974, *Combination of Structural Actions*
Tichý 1974, *Reliability Problems in Structural Theory*
Torroja 1958, *Load Factors*
Turkstra 1969, *A Statistical Investigation of Under-Reinforced Concrete Beam Moment*
Turkstra 1970a, *Discussion of Safety Factors and Probability in Structural Design*
Turkstra 1970b, *Theory of Structural Design Decisions*
Turkstra 1973, *Assessing and Reporting Uncertainties*

USSR State Committee for Construction 1962, *Building Standards and Regulations*

Veletsos 1971, *Response of Ground-Excited Elasto-Plastic Systems*
Vellozzi 1968, *Gust Response Factors*
Veneziano 1974, *Second Moment Reliability*
Vickery 1969, *On the Reliability of Gust Loading Factors*
Vickery 1971, *On the Reliability of Gust Loading Factors*
Vorlicek 1969, *Distribution of Extreme Values in Structural Theory*

Watson 1975, *Safety and List Time of Modern Tall Buildings. Examples of Accidents*
Wiegel 1970, *Earthquake Engineering*
Wu 1974, *Modeling and Simulation of a Fire Protection Probability Decision Tree*
Wittman 1976, *Reliability Oriented Design of Tower Like Structures Experimental Methods*
Wyatt 1971, *The Ultimate Load Behavior of Structures Under Wind Loading*

Yao 1969, *Formulation of Structural Reliability*
Yura 1971, *The Effective Length of Columns in Unbraced Frames*

Current Questions, Problems, and Research Needs

This appendix identifies problem areas for further study and research. It constitutes an update of Council Report No. 5, first issued in 1972, as part of its mission to identify such problems for interested investigators and organizations. The sequence of headings is the same as that used in this volume. Numbers in parentheses refer to the Committee responsible for the topic. Additional suggestions of study areas should be forwarded to Council Headquarters for transmission to the appropriate Committee for possible inclusion in the next revision of the Council's report on the subject.

GRAVITY LOADS AND TEMPERATURE EFFECTS (5)

1. What is a more rational basis for determination of design loads?
2. What should be used for construction loads? Occasionally these are the largest loads a structure will ever support.
3. For what construction configurations and for what story heights must one consider temperature effects?
4. What is the range of variation in floor loads—uncertainty factor (see "Structural Safety")?
5. How can we correlate design loads used in different countries? Equal design load does not mean equal safety (especially) with respect to wind.
6. How does one determine statistically the unusual peak floor loads for which the designer now makes provision by "judgment"?
7. What should be used for mechanical equipment loads?
8. When and how should one consider impact loading due to live loads?
9. How can maintenance personnel be trained to have the knowledge regarding the maximum loading capacity and optimum positions of loads of buildings?
10. Probability of live loads being achieved or exceeded. One effect is design camber of precast concrete elements. Finishing problems occur because of differential camber which is not relieved.

EARTHQUAKE LOADING AND RESPONSE (6)

1. What is the existing earthquake disaster potential in major cities in seismic regions?
2. What are relative merits of different structural systems with regard to earthquake loading?
3. What field observations should be made and how have past measurements influenced earthquake resistant design?
4. Installation of strong motion instruments to obtain worldwide earthquake records.
5. Development of improved strong motion instruments, such as magnetic type analog or digital systems, which can be coupled directly into computer systems.
6. Installation of strong motion instruments in different soil systems, including measurement of motions at different depths.
7. Development of methods for characterizing nonlinear soil properties as required for mathematical modeling.
8. Development of nonlinear finite element soil response analysis procedure.
9. Dynamic, cyclic, and nonlinear tests of structural components.
10. Dynamic, cyclic, and nonlinear tests of large-scale complete building structures.
11. Field tests of typical structures of all types in the elastic range and correlation with analytical results.
12. Development of modeling techniques to represent nonlinear structural performance.
13. Developing means of prescribing seismic input to buildings in terms of energy or ductility requirements as well as strength and stiffness limits.
14. Effect of earthquake on nonstructural aspects of design.
15. Detailed studies of buildings of all types damaged by earthquake, including damage range from slight to total.
16. Develop techniques for minimizing damage to nonstructural elements.
17. Develop guidelines for design which provide for low-cost repairs after major earthquakes.
18. Develop guidelines for design that minimizes the life hazard in case of a very severe earthquake.
19. Nonlinear analysis of tall concrete framed structures subjected to earthquake loading.
20. In-plane effects in floor slabs near openings and discontinuities.
21. Progressive collapse and earthquake resistant design of high-rise masonry and precast concrete bearing wall buildings.
22. What is the actual and required ductile behavior of structural system (including shear walls and braced frames) when subjected to seismic events?

WIND LOADS AND WIND EFFECTS (7)

Structural Response

1. Comparisons of full-scale and wind tunnel model experiments. There is still a need to assess the responses of individual as well as classes of buildings.
2. Systematic wind tunnel studies of different geometric building shapes to determine dynamic and static response factors. Verification of theories.
3. Wind tunnel studies of interference effects between adjacent buildings—the wake buffeting problem. What are the critical factors for augmentation of the response?
4. The characteristics of aerodynamic damping; indications as to when it may be significant.
5. Torsional loads due to wind; determination of the dynamic and static components and methods for their prediction.
6. Response of tall buildings in the postelastic range under the action of dynamic wind loading.
7. Combined torsional and transverse loads; their prediction and effects.

Cladding Loads

8. Comparisons of full-scale and model measurements of exterior pressures on cladding.
9. Estimation of interior pressures on buildings.
10. Systematic wind tunnel study of exterior pressures on cladding. Reduction to design format including full-scale model corrections.
11. Assessment of the glass/wind pressure interactions: the "static fatigue" characteristics of glass.

Environmental and Other Effects

12. Wind climate in pedestrian regions: the aerodynamic causes of strong flows and methods for their alleviation.
13. Effect of wind on mechanical exhausts and inlets. The effect of porosity and wind pressure on stack effects.
14. Aerodynamic noise and its alleviation.
14. Groaning due to sway.
16. Scouring action due to wind-driven rain.
17. Oscillation of elevator cables due to wind sway.

Criteria for Wind Loading

18. Acceptability and tolerance criteria for windiness at street level.
19. Assessment of acceleration levels in tall buildings and criteria for satisfactory performance.
20. Deflection limitations for tall buildings.

Risk and Reliability

21. Risk assessment under wind loading for various limit states. Estimate of uncertainties.
22. Effects of tornadoes and hurricane winds on tall buildings.

FIRE (8A)

1. Improved methods of protecting personnel during fire.
2. Techniques for interrupting "stack effect" in very tall buildings.
3. Incorporation of improved fire detection systems.
4. How does the actual fire development in a building influence the structural protection requirements?
5. Physiological reaction to smoke, toxic gases, and high temperatures; psychological reactions (panic) of humans to such events.
6. Determine the extent of structural damage that can reasonably be admitted in case of fire with regard to the possibilities of repair and to the serviceability after fire (for steel and reinforced concrete).
7. How can earlier fire detection and control be achieved?
8. Mechanism of smoke movement in a tall building.
9. How to increase speed of communication with fire department upon the detection of a fire situation.
10. How can one minimize the damage due to fire initiated during earthquake, flood, or hurricane?
11. Protection of people in adjoining areas and adjoining properties.

12. Standardization, reliability research, and new improved emergency power plant provisions.

13. What fire safety features are necessary for various occupancies rather than prohibiting any particular occupancy?

14. Need to develop a logical and scientific method of utilizing a building's domestic water system to supply the building's sprinkler system.

15. Need to develop methods of assuring positive protection and reliability of elevators to allow their use as legal exits in emergencies.

16. Need to develop the Systems Approach to fire safety for use as a legitimate substitute for present specification-type legal requirements.

17. Facilitate the action of firemen fighting fire inside tall buildings and control idle spectators and the curious.

18. What is the optimum width for an exit stair in a tall building requiring rapid total evacuation in case of fire?

19. What management and human behavioral problems must be dealt with to have occupants of tall buildings *ascend* stairs to reach zones of safety or temporary refuge in case of fire?

20. What are the problems encountered in having people evacuating down one exit stair shift over to another stair to avoid smoke, fire department operations, accident, blockage, etc.?

21. Does some urgency motive become operative in an evacuation situation interpreted by evacuees as a genuine emergency, and does this increase or decrease the crowd density, speed, and flow in the exit stair?

22. What activities should be undertaken during a mass evacuation in a tall building to reduce the risk of smoke movement into exit stairs? (For example, measures could include bottom venting, controlling the number and location of opened doors from floor areas, etc.)

23. What total evacuation time can reasonably be expected to be achieved for various tall building heights, populations, exit capacities, etc.? What are the confidence limits for achieving total evacuation times within ±20% of predicted times, for example?

24. What is a desirable upper limit for time needed to totally evacuate a tall building (e.g., an existing office building of typical construction and occupancy)? Is this limit related to the time needed for the fire department to respond and commence operations in the immediate fire area?

25. To correctly assess the magnitude of the fire safety problem in tall buildings more reasonable information is needed on occupant loads or population than exists today. For example, existing building codes often require use of the figure of one occupant for every 9.3 m² (100 sq ft) of office space, but surveys indicate actual average populations are only one-third to one-half that large. More research is needed to determine realistic population loads not only for fire-safety planning but for planning other building services (e.g., elevators, washrooms—which appear to be overprovided in office buildings) and surrounding urban services (e.g., sidewalks, transit facilities, etc.). Information is needed not only on total numbers of people in tall buildings but on arrival-departure patterns daily, hourly, and in various seasons.

26. Are public address systems used in exit stairs during a crowd evacuation situation effective? Can messages be understood? Are they listened to by evacuees?

27. What are the relative advantages and disadvantages of live messages versus programmed recorded messages over a public address system in a tall building fire?

28. Who should be able to operate fire emergency communication systems in tall buildings? Fire emergency staffs resident in each building, fire department personnel, or both? Here distinction must be made between one-way communication (public address) and two-way communication (telephone).

29. How do occupants of tall buildings interpret alarms and other communication used to initiate an emergency response such as immediate evacuation or movement to a refuge area? Why?

30. How will people respond to a refuge situation in a building fire? What are the building environmental factors, communication requirements, supervisory staff requirements, social factors, etc., to make refuge (or sitting out a fire) a workable approach to tall building fire safety? Consider both office buildings and residential buildings.

31. How should balconies on tall buildings be designed so that they can serve better in fire conditions? Should roof areas be designed so that helicopters could land in case of emergency?

32. How have people's attitudes to their safety in tall buildings changed with the extensive media coverage given to serious tall buildings fires and the hazards of fire in tall buildings? Consider, for example, pre-1970 attitudes with post-1975 attitudes. Have people been sensitized to the hazards or have they become complacent?

33. To what extent will people using buildings be confused by the variety of fire emergency procedures employed in contemporary tall buildings? For example, people may live in, work in, and extensively visit several tall buildings normally, and they may become confused by different precautions and fire safety practices in these different buildings.

34. To what extent do high-rise occupants accept fire drills and participate in them? Does this increase their preparedness for dealing with emergencies or does it deter them from fire safety practices? What forms of fire drill are most effective in terms of occupant acceptance and learning?

35. Survey actual practices in tall buildings regarding holding of evacuation drills, other fire drills, training and instruction of occupants. In other words, find out what fire safety procedures are *actually* implemented rather than merely given lip service.

36. Document test evacuations and other fire safety practices in tall buildings. For example, cross-cultural information is needed and larger samples required for much of the work done in the early 1970s in Canada in documenting evacuation via stairs in tall office buildings.

37. What are the alternatives to sprinklers? More new ideas are needed for fire safety systems.

38. What design solutions are feasible, such as power-operated doors, to overcome differential pressure in stairwells?

39. What should be done with elevators in case of fire? Can practical use be made of elevators during the time one waits for the fire department?

40. Where do fires start in tall buildings? Why? How costly are these fires? More factual data are required on this subject.

41. How can controls be established on the fire loads that are brought into buildings by tenants?

42. Effect on fire spread of pressurization of a building.

43. Can new escape methods be designed? (A parallel with life-boats on ocean liners.) Can high-level bridges to other nearby buildings also fill the role of an escape route in addition to fulfilling their normal access function?

44. What are the best methods for evacuating nonambulatory patients from hospitals?

45. How do weather conditions influence design and fire safety?

46. More information and research are needed on the fire rating of bare steel members as part of a structural system.

ACCIDENTAL LOADING (8B)

1. What is the appropriate design pressure to withstand internal blast effects?

2. Further investigation of the development of pressures in gaseous explosions in intercommunicating rooms typical of those in actual buildings.

3. A general method for predicting pressures in gaseous explosions in terms of room geometry, venting, ventilation, and gas leakage rate as a basis for specifying design pressures (with possible trade-offs for venting and ventilation).

4. Further study of the ability of structural elements and connections to withstand impact and impulsive loads of durations on the order of 0.1 sec and under to assist in specifying "equivalent static" design loads.

5. Further study of the efficacy of alternative means of venting gaseous explosions.

6. The development of more soundly based criteria for structural "robustness" in the event of local damage (including "incremental collapse").

7. Flashover after blast.

8. Develop more practical methods and systems of warning of an explosion potential.

9. In the event of bomb threats, what are the best procedures for evacuation?

QUALITY CRITERIA (9)

1. Extent of variation of mechanical properties of materials.

2. Quality control standards modified by virtue of repetition due to height (so-called "learning curve").

3. The extent and influence of geometric variations of structural shapes.

4. Evaluation of workmanship in the field.

5. During mixing, what technique is available to determine how strong concrete will be after it is in place?

6. Consider replacing the term "yield point" in favor of "yield strength" for all steels.

7. Is "strain hardening" significant in the structural behavior of tall buildings? If so, a compilation of statistical information should be made.

8. Compile information concerning tension test properties over the cross section of member, particularly heavy sections.

9. Can "learning curve" or statistical methods be applied to QC sampling, testing, and inspection procedures during manufacture, fabrication and erection?

10. What are the effects on mechanical properties of steel as a result of fire?

11. Compile information concerning actual straightness and out-of-plumbness of steel columns after erection.

12. List and define "imperfections."

13. Method for early determination of desired concrete quality (as placed) is needed. The "quality" in question may refer to compressive strength, modulus of elasticity, tensile strength, wearability, watertightness, or other property that affects the usefulness of the structure.

14. During mixing, what technique is available to determine how strong concrete will be after it is in place?

15. Compile information concerning actual out-of-plumbness of columns after erection.

16. What is the effect on mechanical properties of reinforced concrete and prestressed concrete as a result of fire?

STRUCTURAL SAFETY AND PROBABILISTIC METHODS (10)

1. How does one incorporate probabilistic methods into ordinary design?

2. What are acceptable risks and (expected) costs of failure as they relate to design specification provisions?

3. What are the relationships between actual failures and the "failure criteria"?

4. What are the quantitative measures of uncertainty: (1) Of the various loads; (2) of the various limits of usefulness?

5. A good deal seems to be known about variation in response. What about the variation in the "loading" function?

6. Develop simple field methods of structural safety analysis.

7. Evaluation and definition of consequences of failure, including costs associated with nonstructural partitions.

8. When should the formal probabilistic approach be used?

9. Combination of loads of different origin and duration (short-term and long-term).

10. Statistical models of all load-kinds and of their simultaneous effect.

11. Further work should be done to make possible the evaluation of safety and serviceability of the entire building as a system, not simply a bare frame.

12. Mass psychology induced by uncertainty of structural safety and safety requirements against rare catastrophic loads (airplane collision, sabotage, blast, great fire, earthquake, flood, ground sliding, tornado, etc.).

Nomenclature

GLOSSARY

Accelerogram. Time-history of acceleration; the record produced by an accelerograph.

Accelerograph. Instrument that records time-histories of ground acceleration.

Accelerometer. Device for measuring acceleration.

Accidental load. Load with a low probability of occurrence at a structurally significant magnitude during the life of a particular building, and whose probability of occurrence cannot be readily assessed on the basis of past experience. In practice such loads are usually caused by explosions or impacts. Earthquake loads are not included.

Aftershock. Shock which follows the primary earthquake.

Air-entraining admixture. A liquid admixture added to concrete mixtures in ratio to weight of cement to achieve microscopic size entrained air bubbles. Air-entraining agent is sometimes added to cement during grinding at the time of manufacture.

Allowable stress design. See Working stress design.

Alloy steel. Steel in which alloying elements are specified to a definite minimum or range, or which have specified maximums greater that 1.65% for manganese, 0.60% for silicon, or 0.60% for copper.

Annealed glass. Glass with residual stresses removed by heating uniformly throughout to the annealing temperature range and then cooling at a controlled rate sufficiently slow to avoid reintroduction of new strains due to cooling.

Annealing point (AP). The temperature at which glass internal stress is relieved in a few minutes as measured by an elongation rate of 0.136 mm/min in a 500 mm (20 in.) long, 0.65 ± 0.10 mm diameter glass fiber suspending a 1000g weight (ASTM C336, 1976).

Annealing range. The temperature range within which stress can be removed from glass at a commercially desirable rate, falling between the annealing point and strain point.

651

Aspect ratio. Term used in design of rectangular lights of glass and obtained by dividing length of long side by length of short side.

Audio/visual warning system. A system designed to operate with the actuation of a fire alarm system within a building and which will provide audio or visual warning, or both.

Automatic sprinkler system. A system of water supplies from pipes and sprinkler heads to automatically detect and instantaneously attack, control, and extinguish a fire with water and sound an alarm. One of the most effective means of combating fires in high-rise buildings.

Batch plant. A plant or installation including material stockpiles, cement storage silo, elevated hoppers for fine and coarse aggregate and cement, accurate weighing means, water source, and admixture dispensers, capable of delivering accurate material proportions to in-plant mixer or rotating drum truck mixers.

Bed joint. Horizontal layer of mortar upon which masonry units are placed (laid).

Bedrock. Continuous, consolidated and/or cemented sedimentary rock, generally of Pliocene age or older, or metaphoric rock, or igneous rock that everywhere underlies top soil or other unconsolidated surficial deposits, and locally forms the earth's surface.

Bite. The amount of glazing overlap on the surface of a light of glass measured to the glass edge.

Black body. A body whose radiation at each wavelength is the maximum possible for any electromagnetic radiator at that temperature; a body that absorbs all light which is incident on it and consequently looks black.

Block cement. Portland cement with interground additives which does not conform to standards for portland cement or air-entraining portland cement, generally due to midrange air content of the test mortar, but which has characteristics suited to manufacturing high-strength concrete masonry units.

Bolsters. Manufactured support devices in continuous lengths for supporting multiple beam or slab reinforcing bars.

Breaking strength. Average breaking stress determined from a significantly large number of specimens, generally 30 or more.

Brick. A masonry unit approximating a rectangular prism in shape and made from burned clay, shale or a mixture of both (a ceramic product).

Calorific values. Amount of heat liberated by the combustion of a unit weight (or if a gas, a unit volume) of fuel.

Capping compound. Thin layer of commercially prepared sulfur compound or high-strength gypsum or other acceptable material molded to fill specimen irregularities and provide true planes normal to specimen vertical axis to allow accurate compression test results.

Carbon steel. Steel without specified minimums for alloying elements except specified copper minimum may be 0.40% or less and specified maximums may not exceed 1.65% for manganese, 0.60% for silicon and 0.60% for copper.

Cavity (cavities). Continuous horizontal and vertical space(s) between wythes of masonry walls with wythes tied together by metal ties.

Cell. Intentionally formed hollow space in concrete masonry unit, building tile, or brick.

(Central) safety factor. Ratio of mean values of strength and load effect.

Central value. A measure of the central tendency of a variable, usually represented by its mean or expected value.

Characteristic burning velocity (of a gas). Velocity of unburnt gas with respect to a steady-state plane combustion wave.

Characteristic strength. The average strength required to produce the required assurance of achievement of the design strength.

Characteristic value. Value of a variable that has an agreed probability of not being attained or not being exceeded, depending on which is the more unfavorable condition; this value corresponds to a particular fractile of the probability distribution of the variable. Alternatively, the mean plus or minus an agreed-upon number of standard deviations.

Coarse aggregate. Natural or manufactured aggregate of specified gradation with particle sizes generally larger than No. 4 sieve (ASTM C136, 1976).

Coefficient of variation. A nondimensional measure of dispersion. It is equal to standard deviation divided by mean.

Color code. A system of individual or multiple color stripes to indicate steel specification and strength grade.

Compressive strength (concrete). Strength determined by testing standard specimens at predetermined age after curing under prescribed conditions as stipulated by controlling code or project specification.

Compressive strength (mortar, grout). Strength determined by testing standard 50-mm (2-in.) cubes under standard testing conditions at predetermined age(s) after curing, all as stipulated by controlling code or specification.

Concentrated load. Point load or load concentrated on a finite area; expressed in terms of force (pound, kgf).

Concrete block. A hollow, prismatic concrete masonry unit.

Concrete brick. A solid concrete masonry unit generally the shape of a rectangular prism.

Concrete masonry unit. Precast unit made from portland cement and suitable aggregates and produced in a variety of modular shapes, sizes, and cross sections.

Concrete pump. A piece of equipment capable of receiving plastic concrete and forcing it through pipe or hose under pressure to the point of discharge, often several stories above the pump receiving hopper.

Construction manager. Party or firm which provides construction management services, commonly a general contractor retained by the owner during the project development stage to provide consultation as well as to manage and direct the construction stage generally performed by trade contractors retained on behalf of the owner by the construction manager.

Control chart. A graphical plot of data accumulated or derived from test results of samples secured from a manufactured material or product.

Core(s). Hollow volumes, generally cylindrical, permitted in solid and hollow brick.

Correlation. The degree of (linear) probabilistic dependency between two jointly distributed random variables; relative large correlations imply that the knowledge of the value of one random variable reduces significantly the uncertainty in the value of the other. Measures of correlation are: for covariance

$$\sigma_{X,Y} = \mathrm{Cov}(X,Y) = E[(x - m_X)(y - m_Y)] = \int_Y \int_X (x - m_X)(y - m_Y)\,dx\,dy$$

and for correlation coefficient (a nondimensional measure of correlation)

$$\rho_{X,Y} = \frac{\mathrm{Cov}(X,Y)}{\sigma_X \sigma_Y}$$

Creep strength. Stress that produces a given rate of movement at a specific temperature.

Cross-sectional area. Area of section taken at right angles to the longitudinal axis.

Crush. Small surface pits with gray or white cast.

Cryogenics. Branch of physics that deals with production and effects of very low temperatures.

Cusum chart. A form of control chart in which the cumulative sum of the deviations from the design mean value of the function under consideration is plotted.

Damping. Resistance to vibration that causes a progressive reduction of motion with time or distance.

Deflagration. Relatively slow combustion of a flammable mixture maintained by processes of heat transfer and diffusion and associated with combustion waves travelling at speeds below that of sound.

Design mix or mix design. Final concrete mixture proportions selected using trial mixture proportions or actual field performance data as a guide.

Detonation. Very rapid combustion of a high explosive or other flammable mixture associated with shock waves sustained by the energy of the chemical reaction and travelling at speeds in excess of that of sound.

Diffraction load. Force on a structure due to the direct and reflected pressure of an air blast as it first envelops the structure.

Discontinuity. Generally internal pipe ruptures, laminations, and nonmetallic inclusions. Surface discontinuities may include blisters, crazing cracks, gouges, laps, seams, pits, scabs, and rolled-in scale.

Double glazing. Two sheets of glass with sealed air space between, glazed into supporting sash or framework.

Dowels. Short reinforcing bars joining two sections of concrete, often lapping with column bars. Smooth dowels with expansion caps are used to prevent relative displacement of adjacent concrete sections in direction normal to dowel axis.

Drag load. Force on a structure due to the high velocity of the air particles in the moving air stream behind the shock or pressure front of a blast wave.

Ductility ratio. Ratio between the maximum displacement or deflection (actual or allowable) of a structure or element and the displacement or deflection at the transition from linearly elastic to perfectly plastic response in a simple idealization of the actual resistance-displacement relationship.

Efflorescence. Staining visible on concrete or masonry surfaces caused by moisture leaching water-soluble salts from within mortar or concrete and depositing the salts on the surface.

Elevator control. See Lift control.

Elongation. Increase in length between reference marks on tensile specimen from original condition to fracture expressed as a percentage of original gage length.

Emergency control center. Compartment in a secure area with efficient communications systems throughout the building, and from which instructions can be given to building occupants to direct them in an emergency.

Emergency power supply. Emergency generator to supply sufficient electrical capacity to meet essential services should power failure take place in a fire.

Empirical performance. Relying or based on experiment or experience of reactions.

Epicenter. Point on earth's surface directly above focus of earthquake.

Exit signs. Fixed illuminated sign indicating emergency exit, including directional signs.

Fail-safe design. A design philosophy that states that if an element is fully loaded to design load, the element will not fail or reach certain prescribed limit state.

Fault. A fracture or fracture zone along which there has been a displacement of the two sides relative to one another parallel to the fracture.

Fine aggregate. Natural or manufactured sand, 95% or more passing No. 4 sieve (ASTM C136, 1976).

Fineness modulus. Index number indicating coarseness of aggregate determined by summing percent coarser than U.S. sieve sizes 3-in., 1-1/2-in., 3/4-in., 3/8-in., No. 4, 8, 16, 30, 50, and 100 and dividing by 100. Larger number indicates coarser material.

Fire alarm system. Manually operated system designed to give warning of fire.

Fire detection system. A system, such as an automatic smoke or heat detector system, designed to detect automatically the presence of smoke, heat, flame or combustion products and give warning, connected directly to fire service control rooms.

Fire loads. Quantity of combustible materials on a specific area of a building; includes floor coverings, finishes on room surfaces, draperies, furniture, and contents.

First-aid fire fighting equipment. Portable equipment in the form of fire extinguishers and hose reel for use by building occupants.

Float glass. Glass produced by flowing molten glass to a uniform thickness over a molten bed of tin and drawing the sheet, first to a cooler area where it solidifies, and then through an annealing lehr (tunnel shaped oven).

Flow. The percentage increase in diameter of a standard mortar specimen on a standardized and calibrated drop table after 25 drops of 12.7 mm (0.5 in.) in 15 seconds.

Focal depth. Depth of earthquake focus below ground surface.

Focus. Point within the earth which marks the origin of the elastic waves of an earthquake; point where the rupture first occurs (hypocenter).

Foreman. Person in charge of a group of workers of a specific trade and who reports to superintendent or other superior.

Foreshock. Earthquake that commonly precedes a larger earthquake or main shock by seconds to weeks, and that originates at or near the focus of the larger earthquake.

Free-field overpressure. Pressure above atmospheric in the unobstructed moving air stream of a blast wave.

Friction velocity. A term expressing the shear stress or surface drag of the planetary wind boundary layer.

Gagging. Cold straightening of steel shapes by bending by point loading in a high capacity press.

Gaussian distribution curve. Normal distribution curve. Shape of curve may be modified by probability density function.

Glazing. Means of holding glass tight in frames or sash while also making installation airtight and watertight.

Gradient height. Height at the top of the planetary wind boundary layer, about 600 m (1975 ft).

Gravel. Coarse aggregate with generally smooth, rounded surfaces resulting from natural erosion of rock.

Green block. Concrete masonry units after ejection from forming equipment but not yet fully cured.

Grout. A fluid mixture of portland cement, sand, water, and possibly lime, used for pouring and working into hollow cells, joints and cavities in masonry construction to embed reinforcing steel and bond units continuously together.

Heat-affected zone. Unmelted portion of base metal in which microstructure has been altered by heat of welding.

Heat number. Identifying designation and marking given to elements produced from a given melt of steel.

Heat-strengthened glass. Glass heated to a temperature above the annealing point and cooled at a sufficiently rapid controlled rate to achieve surface compression above 24 MPa (3500 psi) and edge compression above 38 MPa (5500 psi).

High-strength concrete. Concrete with a design compressive strength equal to or greater than 35 MPa (5000 psi).

High-strength concrete masonry. Masonry units with a net area compressive strength equal to or greater than 24 MPa (3500 psi).

Heat-treated steel. Heating of steel above the transformation range followed by rapid cooling (quenching) or slow cooling (normalizing), prolonged heating within or below the transformation range followed by slow cooling (annealing), or reheating to a temperature below the transformation range and cooling at a controlled rate (tempering).

Hollow brick. Units in which net area in every plane parallel to bearing surface is not less than 60% of gross area on same plane.

Hot-rolled steel. Steel rolled to final shape and thickness in a steel rolling mill starting with billets or slabs preheated to approximately 730°C (1350°F).

Hypocentral distance. Distance from a site on the surface of the earth to the focus, or hypocenter, of an earthquake.

Inclusion. Nonmetallic material included within the base metal. May be widely dispersed globules, or may form stringers or laminar defects if concentrated before rolling.

Insulating glass. Two sheets of glass, often spaced ±5 mm (3/16 in.) apart with fully fused edges with enclosed volume filled with dry air or dry gas.

Intensity (of an earthquake). A measure of earthquake size at a particular place as determined by its effect on persons, structures, and earth materials. The principal scale used in the United States today is the Modified Mercalli Scale, 1956 revision. Intensity is a measure of effects, contrasted with magnitude which is a measure of energy.

Interstitial porosity. The ratio of voids between aggregate particles in concrete masonry units (as opposed to voids in cement-sand matrix due to zero-slump mixture or voids in lightweight aggregate particles).

Isotherm. A line on a map of the earth's surface connecting points having the same mean temperature for a given period.

Isotropic. Possession of uniform properties in all directions.

Lamellar tear. Steplike fracture caused by internal fractures of the steel microstructure connected by nonmetallic inclusions and caused by tension in the thickness direction of the metal.

Lift (Elevator) control. A control system by which all elevators (lifts) are automatically returned to the ground floor in the event of fire, and remain there until otherwise operated.

Light(s) or lite(s). Term used in the glass industry for single pieces of glass or single glass panes in a window sash unit.

Lightweight aggregate. Aggregate for producing lightweight concrete masonry units and structural concrete, generally clay, shale or slate expanded and fused under high heat producing cellular particles with apparent specific gravity of 1.5 to 2.0.

Lightweight structural concrete. Portland cement concrete mixed using lightweight coarse aggregate and sometimes both lightweight coarse and fine aggregate and weighing less than 18 kN/m (115 lb/ft).

Limit state. Condition in which a structure or a part thereof ceases to fulfil one of its functions or to satisfy the conditions for which it was designed. Limit states can be classified in two categories: (1) *Ultimate limit states*, corresponding to the load-carrying capacity of the structure—safety is usually related to these types of limit state; and (2) *serviceability limit states*, related to the criteria governing normal use of the structure.

Liquefaction. Transformation of unconsolidated or poorly consolidated water-saturated granular material (such as silt or sand) into a liquefied state as a consequence of increased pore-water pressures. The increase in pore-water pressure is often caused by earthquake shaking.

Load factor. Factor applied to a load to express probability of not being exceeded; a safety factor.

Loose density. Means of determining acceptability of lightweight structural aggregate (dry loose density) and for comparing moisture contents of aggregate in the stockpile in order to adjust batching weights, preferably using a 0.014 m^3 (0.5-ft^3) bucket and accurate scale.

Low-alloy steel. High-strength steels with yield strengths of 290 MPa to 480 MPa (42 000 psi to 70 000 psi) with specified minimums and maximums for alloying elements but produced with primary emphasis on mechanical properties.

Lower yield point. The minimum stress observed after the drop of the beam or in the autographic stress-strain curve after the upper yield point, if any, has been achieved.

Magnitude/Richter magnitude. A measure of the size of an earthquake which is based on the amount of energy released. Technically it is defined as the logarithm of the maximum amplitude recorded by a particular type of seismograph located 100 km (62 miles) from the epicenter. Magnitude is not the same as intensity (see Intensity).

Master builder. A person fully capable in esthetics, structure, architecture, and all else required to direct the construction of major architectural works.

Mechanical properties. Those properties which describe the elastic and inelastic responses of a material to applied forces (tensile strength, yield strength, impact strength, creep strength, elongation, proportional limit, others).

Membrane behavior. Participation of in-plane stresses in resisting deflection of plates undergoing deflections which are large compared to plate thickness.

Membrane ceiling. Built-up roofing, a weather resistant (flexible or semiflexible) covering consisting of alternate layers of felt and bitumen, fabricated in a continuous covering and surfaced with aggregate or asphaltic material.

Modulus of rupture. Tensile stress at extreme fiber of unreinforced concrete beam specimen or masonry unit plus mortar specimen tested in flexure.

Mortar. A plastic mixture of cementitious materials, sand and water.

Neutral plane. The surface within a beam containing the fibers not strained during bending.

Nondestructive testing. Use of one or more available testing techniques or systems to evaluate the presence or absence of defects or one or more material characteristics without changing or damaging the material tested.

Normal distribution curve. Gaussian distribution curve, symmetrical in form, with the probability density function equal to unity.

Normal weight concrete. Portland cement concrete mixed using both sand and coarse aggregate with specific gravities generally above 2.6 but less than 3.0.

Occupancy. The people, processes, and things confined within the space of the building.

Outline specifications. Skeleton specifications presenting controlling codes and primary material, equipment, and workmanship standards for use during the planning and design development stages of a project.

Over-design factor. A factor used to establish average required strength based on known or predicted standard deviation and allowable number of tests below design strength f'_c in accord with statistical control procedures of ACI 214 (1977).

Partial factors of safety. Factors to be applied separately to loads and strengths in order to provide adequate safety levels; those applied to load are usually called load factors and those applied to strength are called strength reduction factors (coefficients).

Participation factor. Factor defining the extent of participation of a mode of vibration in dynamic analysis.

Peak factor. Number of standard deviations by which the peak value exceeds the mean.

Period. In geology, a major subdivision of an era. In seismology, the interval of time required for completion of a cyclic motion or recurring event, e.g., the time between two consecutive peaks of a wave. In structural engineering, the length of time for a structure to complete one oscillation.

Petrographic examination. Analysis of the constituents of concrete, yielding the approximate cement content.

Poisson distribution curve. A curve representing the probability of occurrence of a given value or values within a given range based upon Poisson's law of small numbers.

Portland cement. Mixture of limestone and clayey materials containing alumina and silica burned into clinker in a rotating kiln at 1480°C to 1650°C (2700°F to 3000°F), then ground into a powder which hardens by chemical reaction when mixed with water.

Portland-pozzolan cement. Hydraulic cement consisting of uniform blend of portland cement and fine pozzolan produced by intergrinding or blending or a combination of intergrinding and blending (see ASTM C595, 1976).

Postheat. Heating of completed weld joint and surrounding base metal to prescribed temperature versus time including reduced cooling rate, if specified.

Power law exponent. Exponent related to velocity profile.

Pozzolan. A finely divided or ground material added to concrete instead of additional cement, which in the presence of water will react with calcium hydroxide to form cementitious compounds.

Preheat. Heating of metal to be joined to a prescribed temperature prior to the beginning of welding.

Pressurization of staircase. System designed to minimize the passage of smoke and hot gas into staircases.

Prism test. A compression test of a masonry assemblage used to establish design stress values for engineered masonry construction, in which the h/d basic ratio is 2.0 for concrete masonry, and 5.0 for brick masonry.

Probability. A quantitative measure of the degree of rational belief in the occurrence of an outcome or on a variable taking a particular value. Uncertainty may be associated with inherent randomness of the phenomenon (objective uncertainty) or with imperfect knowledge of the characteristic of the phenomenon (subjective uncertainty). Mathematically, probability is a real-valued function satisfying three simple axioms.

Probability density function. The expression providing the ordinates for each abscissa on the graphical plot of the probability density curve.

Probability (distribution) functions. Functions that describe the probability law of random variables. Different functions are used: for (cumulative) distribution function

$$F_X(x) = P(X \leq x)$$

in which P = probability that the random variable x takes values equal or less than x; and for (probability) mass function (used for discrete random variables)

$$P_X(x) = P(X = x)$$

for each possible value x of X.

Quality assurance. A formalized program including administrative procedures designed to assure that quality control tests procedures, controls, and personnel effectively achieve the intended quality.

Quality control. A formalized system of procedures and controls used to determine as-produced quality or acceptance quality.

Quality control program. A formal program, generally committed to writing, including acceptance standards, procedures, and personnel qualifications, and stipulating observation, testing, and reporting functions designed to reliably control quality of completed product or component parts or material.

Quasiresonance. Vibration of large amplitude in a system, caused by a relatively small stimulus of the same period as the natural vibration period of the system.

Rabbet. L-shaped recess in sash to receive glass and glazing system. Under certain conditions, rabbet may be U-shaped to receive zip-in glazing gaskets.

Random variable. Numerical variable whose values depend on the outcome of a random experiment and therefore cannot be predicted in advance. Random variables can be discrete or continuous (or mixed).

Reaction to fire. Test to assess the key properties of ignitability, flame spread, rate of heat release, and smoke production in certain situations.

Ready-mix concrete. Concrete manufactured for delivery in the plastic state, generally in concrete mixer trucks.

Reduction of area. The difference between the smallest cross-sectional area of the fractured tensile specimen and the original area, expressed as a percentage of original area.

Reinforced masonry. Masonry in which steel reinforcement is embedded and acts together with the masonry units, mortar and grout, if any, to resist imposed and gravity forces.

Reliability. The probability of survival of a structure; it can be obtained as one minus the probability of reaching a limit state.

Residual stress. Stress locked into steel sections or assemblies due to differential cooling rates and times throughout the volume of metal.

Retarding admixture. An admixture, generally liquid, generally added during concrete batching, which increases the time between adding mixing water and occurrence of initial and final set.

Return period. Average length of time between occurrences of an event.

Risk of ignition. Study of behavior of materials during the early stages of fire.

Safety factor. Coefficient to be applied to loads or strength (or both) in order to attain the desired reliability; ratio between characteristic values of strength and load effect.

Safety glazing. Lights of glass heat-treated, laminated, or containing embedded wire mesh to conform to standards for reducing likelihood of injury due to glass breakage.

Safety index. A parameter that measures the reliability of a structure; usually represented by the number of standard deviations that the mean of the variable defining safety exceeds its critical value.

Safety margin. Difference between mean values of strength and load effect.

Sample variance. A measure of the scatter of individual values of a sample with respect to its average, that is

$$S^2 = \frac{1}{n} \sum_{i=1}^{n} (x_i - \bar{X})^2$$

Sash. Framework holding glass and glazing system.

Screen test. Synonym for sieve test or sieve analysis for gradation of fine or coarse aggregate per ASTM C136 (1976).

Seismicity. Term or parameter which represents the seismic activity within a given area.

Shock wave. Rapidly moving pressure wave characterized by an extremely steep pressure gradient.

Side-on overpressure. Alternative name for free-field overpressure.

Slump. A measurement of the consistency of concrete as-mixed using a slump cone (ASTM C143, 1974).

Softening point (SP). The temperature at which a 0.65 ± 0.10-mm diameter glass fiber 235 mm long elongates at a rate of 1 mm/min when the upper 100 mm length is heated under controlled conditions (ASTM C338, 1973).

Solid brick. A unit with cross-sectional area of 75% or more of total area on every plane parallel to the bearing surface.

Spalling of concrete. Flaking or cracking due to frost, chemical action, or movement of structure.

Stack action. Any structure or part which contains a flue or flues for the discharge of gases; in warm air heating systems a vertical supply duct.

Stack bond. Bonding pattern where masonry units are placed one above the other without overlapping adjacent units above or below.

Standard deviation, σ_x. The square root of the variance.

Steady state heat flow. Heat flow through a material based on equivalent lowest and highest temperatures that do not change with time.

Stirrups. Reinforcing bars formed to enclose longitudinal reinforcement in beams, girders, and joists, and to provide reinforcement against diagonal tension (shear) forces.

Stoichiometric mixture. The highest concentration of a flammable gas in air that allows complete combustion of the gas.

Stone. Coarse aggregate prepared by crushing and selective size screening of natural bed rock, boulders, cobblestones (generally limestone, sandstone, granite, basalt, traprock).

Stone. Crystalline inclusion within glass.

Strain point. The temperature at which glass internal stress is relieved in a few hours.

Strain-gage rosette. Consists of three or more surface lines which pass through or surround a point and represent axes of strain gages applied to determine plane stresses at the subject point.

Stress-relieving. Uniform heating of steel to a temperature sufficiently high to relax internal stresses followed by cooling at a slow and controlled rate.

Strike slip fault. Fault that has had lateral (horizontal) displacement of one side with respect to the other.

Suction. A characteristic of concrete and brick masonry which draws moisture out of mortar and into the surrounding masonry units (also called initial rate of absorption or IRA).

Temperature gradient. A rate of change in a quantity such as temperature or pressure; a curve representing such a rate of change.

Tempered glass. Annealed glass reheated to a temperature near the softening point and rapidly cooled at a controlled rate to produce high surface compression and edge compression stresses. Breakage results in dicing, the formation of innumerable small fragments generally cubical in shape. Tempered glass is 4 or more times stronger than annealed float glass.

Tensile strength. The maximum axial load placed on a tension test specimen prior to failure divided by the original area.

Thermal diffusivity. Thermal conductivity divided by the product of the specific heat and unit weight; an index of the ease with which a material undergoes a change in temperature.

Thermal gradient. Change of temperature through a thickness of material in a specified direction.

Tolerance. Acceptable deviation range from theoretical size or dimension.

Tributary area. Loaded area contributing force to a structural element, such as the portion of a floor supported by a beam.

Tsunami/seismic sea waves. Sea wave produced by displacements of the ocean bottom, often the result of earthquakes, volcanic activity, or landslides.

Turbulence intensity. Expression of the amount of turbulence, or fluctuations in the air flow, relative to the mean wind velocity.

Uniform load. Load distributed uniformly over an area, expressed as force per unit area (in kilopascals, pounds per square foot, or kilograms per square meter).

Unit weight. Weight of material per unit of volume; density.

Universal mill plates. Plates edge rolled to uniform width as well as surface rolled to prescribed thickness.

Upper yield point. The maximum stress observed immediately prior to the drop of the beam or at the peak of the autographic stress-strain diagram when a sharp-kneed stress-strain diagram is obtained.

V-mask. A graphical construction designed such that when placed on the last point in a Cusum plot the preceding points will all fall within the V unless a change in control has occurred.

Variance of a random variable. A measure of the dispersion of the random variable with respect to its mean, that is

$$\sigma_X^2 = \text{Var}\,[X] = \int_X (x - m_X)^2 f_X(x)\,dx$$

Velocity profile. Variation of longitudinal wind velocity with height.

Velocity spectra. Distribution of turbulent wind energy as a function of frequency.

Veneer. Brick used as facing material only without utilizing its load-bearing properties. Brick veneer is usually stabilized by ties to rigid structure.

Ventilation/air-conditioning control systems. System designed to prevent the passage of smoke or combustion products (or both) from compartment to compartment.

Venting (of a gaseous explosion). Reduction of the pressure reached in a confined gaseous explosion by the expulsion of part of the flammable mixture from the enclosure before it burns, either through pre-existing openings or through openings created by the breakage of windows or other light and weak elements by the initial pressure rise.

Volatile component. Substance that passes off easily as a gas or vapor.

Water-cement ratio. Ratio of free water in concrete mix to weight of cement, preferably expressed as a decimal number.

Water-reducing admixture. An admixture, generally liquid, added during concrete batching in ratio to weight of cement, which reduces water demand while maintaining or increasing slump, workability, and cohesiveness of the mix.

Water retention. Ratio by dividing flow of a mortar measured after exposure to vacuum in a standard perforated dish by the initial flow and expressed as a percentage.

Weld zone. The volume of weld metal and melted base metal bounded by the fusion line.

Workability (concrete). Characteristic of flowing readily when vibrated into corners of formwork as well as between and around reinforcing steel without segregation, harshness, or stickiness to provide uniformly compacted, dense concrete.

Workability (grout). Characteristic of fluidity while resisting segregation or separation of ingredients which allows grout to be poured and puddled into masonry voids, completely filling all cavities and cells.

Workability (mortar). Readily trowelable into uniform thickness on masonry adhering to bending surfaces without settling, flowing, or drooping.

Working stress design. A method of proportioning structures for service-load forces, using allowable stresses based on prescribed factors of safety.

Yield point. First stress in a material (less than the ultimate tensile stress) at which strain increases without an increase in stress. This term is intended only for use for materials exhibiting this characteristic.

Yield strength. The stress at which a material exhibits a specified deviation from proportionality between stress and strain. The 0.2% offset value is commonly used.

Yield stress. The load at one of the yield values described divided by the original test specimen area (not a preferred term).

SYMBOLS

The numerals in parentheses refer to the chapters in Volume CL in which the given symbol is used.

A	= area of opening	(4)
A	= glass area	(6)
A	= peak amplitude of seismograph record	(2)
A	= window area	(4)
A_G	= maximum ground acceleration in g units	(2)
A_g	= gross area of an uncut brick	(6)
A_n	= net area of a complete brick	(6)
A_o	= reference value for amplitude	(2)
A_T	= surface area of enclosed walls and ceiling of room	(4)
A_w	= window area	(4)
A_1	= area of lower opening	(4)
A_2	= area of upper opening	(4)
A or B	= accumulated tributary area	(1)
ARL	= average run length	(6)
a	= acceleration	(2)
a	= area of enclosing walls of shaft	(4)
a	= thermal diffusivity of protective material	(4)
B	= benefits	(7)
B	= width of brick specimen	(6)
b	= breadth of building (normal to wind)	(3)
b	= width of specimen	(6)
C	= consequential damage	(4)
C	= constant for computing fundamental natural period of vibration of tall buildings ($C = 0.11$ for steel and $C = 0.07$ for reinforced concrete)	(2)
C	= contaminant concentration in upper half of building	(4)
C	= design lateral force used in earthquake resistant design of building	(2)
C	= initial cost	(7)
C	= seismic base-shear coefficient, determined in consideration of $Z, I, S, K,$ and T	(2)
C_g	= coefficient of variation of glass breaking stress	(6)
C_g	= gross area compressive strength of a brick	(6)

C_{ns}	= average net area compressive strength of brick determined from five cut specimens	(6)
C_o	= contaminant concentration on grade level fire floor	(4)
C_o	= linear change	(2)
C_F, C_M	= force and moment coefficients = $F/q_{ref}A$, $M/q_{ref}A h$ ("ref" will normally be to top of building h; $A = bh$ or $d h$)	(3)
$C_{p\sigma}$	= root-mean-square pressure coefficient ($= \sigma_p/\bar{q}_{ref}$)	(3)
$C_{\bar{p}}$	= mean pressure coefficient $[= (\bar{p} - \bar{p}_{ref})/q_{ref}]$	(3)
$C_{\hat{p}}$	= peak pressure coefficient $[= (\hat{p} - \bar{p}_{ref}/q_{ref}]$	(3)
C_{rb}	= brick strength correction factor	(6)
C_{vp}	= prism strength correction factor	(6)
C_{ρ_a}	= specific heat of steel	(4)
Cov$[X, Y]$	= Covariance	(7)
CUSUM M	= $\sum_{i=1}^{n}$ strength deviations from design mean	(6)
CUSUM SD	= $\sum_{i=1}^{n}$ deviations from design standard deviation	(6)
D	= damage	(7)
D	= dead load	(1)
d	= depth of building (in streamwise direction)	(3)
d	= depth of specimen	(6)
d	= distance to center of energy release	(2)
d	= number of small single doors to shaft	(4)
d	= V-mask design parameter	(6)
d_o	= standard reference distance to center of energy release	(2)
E	= earthquake load	(1)
E	= Young's modulus	(3)
$E[\ ]$	= expectation of function in bracket, for example, the mean $E[X]$	(7)
$E(\cdot)$	= expectation	(7)
e	= base of Naperian (natural) logarithms: 2.718$^+$	(6)
e	= eccentricity	(1)
e	= thickness of protective material	(4)
F	= axial column load	(1)
F	= cumulative probability distribution function (CDF)	(7)
F	= factor which varies with height and the lowest exterior design temperature	(4)
F	= safety factor	(7)
F	= total earthquake force or shear at base of structure	(2)
F_c	= Euler column load	(1)
F_R	= CDF of resistance	(7)
F_S	= CDF of load or load effect	(7)
$F_X(x)$	= cumulative probability distribution (CDF)	(7)
$F_{X,Y}(x,y)$	= joint CDF	(7)
$F_{X/Y}(x,y)$	= conditional CDF	(7)
F. S.	= factor of safety	(6)
f	= character of faulting	(2)
f	= shape factor	(4)
f_c	= individual test strength	(6)

f_{cm}	= design mean strength	(6)
f_{cr}	= required average strength	(6)
f_{cu}	= characteristic strength	(6)
f_i	= lateral seismic force applied to level designated i	(2)
f_{ki}	= design seismic force acting at i in kth vibrational mode	(2)
f_m	= calculated compressive stress in masonry, axial or flexural	(6)
f_t	= calculated flexural tensile stress in masonry	(6)
f_t	= concentrated load at top of slender structure	(2)
$f_X(x)$	= probability density function (PDF)	(7)
$f_{X,Y}(x,y)$	= joint PDF	(7)
$f_{X/Y}(x,y)$	= conditional PDF	(7)
f'_b	= average brick compressive strength	(6)
f'_c	= compressive strength of concrete at 28 days	(6)
f'_m	= specified compressive strength of masonry used in design	(6)
$\underline{fcm}$	= actual mean strength	(6)
G	= gust response factor	(3)
g	= acceleration due to gravity	(3)
g	= as subscript, referenced to gradient height	(3)
g	= gravitational acceleration	(2)
g	= peak factor [for example = $(\hat{x} - \bar{x})/\sigma_x$]	(3)
H	= building height	(2)
H	= height of opening	(4)
$H(n)$	= mechanical admittance function	(4)
h	= as subscript, referenced to top	(3)
h	= height of building	(3)
h	= story height	(2)
h	= window height	(4)
I	= importance of structure as related to its use (importance factor)	(2)
I_C	= column moment of inertia	(2)
I_d	= moment of inertia of supported slab	(4)
I_G	= girder moment of inertia	(2)
J	= failure losses	(7)
K	= cost of structural elements	(4)
K	= heat transfer coefficient	(4)
K	= type of construction, damping, ductility, or energy-absorptive capacity of the structure (construction factor)	(2)
K'	= structural type factor	(2)
k	= coefficient of probability	(1)
k_i	= lateral seismic coefficient assigned to level i, determined in consideration of Z, I, S, K, and T	(2)
k_{ki}	= lateral seismic coefficient assigned to level i in kth vibration mode	(2)
k, c	= constants for Weibull probability distribution	(3)
L	= height of flame tip above base of fire	(4)
L	= length of brick specimen	(6)
L	= live load	(1)
L	= load or loss	(7)
L	= span length of beam	(4)

L	= total weight of fire load	(4)
L	= uniform applied load	(6)
L_C	= column length	(2)
L_G	= girder length	(2)
l	= distance between connections of two successive diagonals of a joint or truss	(4)
$l\,g$	= nature of local geology at seismograph site	(2)
M	= bending moment at working load	(4)
M	= magnitude of earthquake	(2)
M	= moment effect of load	(1)
M	= structural material factor	(2)
M_p	= plastic moment	(4)
M_t	= ultimate moment capacity at normal temperature	(4)
$M_{t\theta}$	= ultimate moment capacity at fire temperature	(4)
N	= value under consideration	(2)
N_i	= other value except N_{max}	(2)
N_{max}	= maximum value among all modes	(2)
n	= damping expressed as fraction of critical damping	(2)
n	= damping ratio	(2)
n	= frequency (n_o natural frequency of first structural mode)	(3)
n	= number of compartments into which fire floor is divided	(4)
n	= number of rearrangements of loads or number of floors	(1)
n	= number of results	(6)
n	= number of tests in sample	(6)
n	= parameter characterizing functional importance of structural elements	(4)
$nL/\bar{u}$	= reduced frequency (L is a reference length requiring definition)	(3)
$\dfrac{nS\,x(n)}{\sigma_x^2}$	= normalized spectra	(3)
o	= as subscript, freestream conditions	(3)
P	= applied test load	(6)
P	= total failure load (glass)	(6)
$P[\ ]$	= probability of event defined within the brackets	(7)
P_f	= probability of failure	(7)
P_f	= probability of reaching limit state	(4)
P_s	= weight of specimen	(6)
P_t	= probability of flashover	(4)
P_u	= failure load	(4)
$P_{(x)}$	= probability density function of x	(3)
$P_{(x>a)}$	= probability distribution function of x exceeding a	(3)
PF	= participation factor	(2)
p	= pressure	(3)
p	= probability	(7)
p	= probability of breakage (glass)	(6)
p	= probability of load occurrence	(1)
p^n	= cumulative probability	(1)
Q_k	= characteristic load	(1)

Q_m	= value of most unfavorable load	(1)
q	= dynamic pressure $(= 1/2\rho\bar{u}^2)$	(3)
q_{cr}	= critical load	(4)
R	= aspect ratio (glass)	(6)
R	= general gas constant	(4)
R	= live load reduction factor, as a percentage	(1)
R	= resistance or risk or reliability	(7)
R	= return period	(3)
R	= risk factor	(2)
R	= structural rigidity with respect to restraining member	(4)
R	= ventilation controlled burning rate	(4)
R_g	= gross area modulus of rupture	(6)
R_n	= net area modulus of rupture	(6)
S	= bending stress	(6)
S	= load or load effect	(7)
S	= size of earthquake	(2)
S	= subsoil condition (soil factor)	(2)
S_A	= acceleration spectrum in g units	(2)
S_a	= absolute acceleration of oscillator mass	(2)
S_d	= relative displacement of oscillator mass	(2)
S_o	= reference size of earthquake	(2)
S_{ps}	= pseudovelocity	(2)
S_v	= relative velocity of oscillator mass	(2)
$Su(n), Sv(n), Sw(n),$		
$Sp(n), SF(n)$	= power spectral density of velocity components, pressure and force	(3)
s	= standard deviation	(6)
s_d	= selected design stress for glass	(6)
s	= actual standard deviation	(6)
$\bar{s}$	= average breaking stress (glass) = MOR	(6)
s/v	= "size and shape" factor, ratio of heated area to volume	(4)
T	= fundamental natural period of vibration of structure in direction under consideration	(2)
T	= loads, forces, and effects due to contraction or expansion resulting from temperature change	(1)
T	= temperature	(4)
T_a	= absolute temperature corresponding to θ_a $(\theta_a + 273)$	(4)
T_f	= absolute temperature corresponding to θ_f $(\theta_f + 273)$	(4)
T_k	= natural period of kth vibration	(2)
T_o	= predominant period of soil	(2)
T_s	= characteristic site period, in seconds	(2)
t	= glass thickness	(6)
t	= standard variable	(6)
t	= thickness of masonry wall	(6)
t	= time	(7)
t_f	= fire resistance as measured in standard test	(4)
u_*	= friction velocity $(= \sqrt{\tau_0/\rho})$	(3)
$\bar{u}/nL$	= reduced velocity (L is a reference length requiring definition)	(3)

$\bar{u}/\bar{u}_g$	= velocity profile	(3)
u, v, w	= as subscripts, reference velocity	(3)
u, v, w	= velocity components in the longitudinal, lateral and vertical directions respectively (meteorological convention) (split into components $u = \bar{u} + u'$)	(3)
V or v	= coefficient of variation	(6)
V_M	= coefficient of variation of M (safety margin)	(7)
V_{max}	= maximum base shear of building	(2)
V_P	= coefficient of variation of load	(7)
V_R	= coefficient of variation of resistance	(7)
V_S	= coefficient of variation of load or load effect	(7)
$V\Delta$	= story shear distortion characteristics	(2)
$V_x = \sigma_x/\mu_x$	= coefficient of variation	(7)
W	= amount of combustible material in fire compartment	(4)
W	= column load or wind load	(1)
W	= gain of weight of brick, in grams	(6)
W	= total vertical load used for seismic calculations	(2)
W	= weight of building	(2)
w	= cusum chart parameter	(6)
w	= window width	(4)
w_i	= portion of W located at or assigned to level i	(2)
$\bar{X}$	= average of n test results	(6)
X_i	= individual test result	(6)
X_N	= response displacement amplitude	(2)
x	= gain of weight of brick due to moisture gain corrected to standard area	(6)
x_{ki}	= deflection at i in kth free vibration	(2)
x, y, z	= as subscripts, reference directions	(3)
x, y, z	= axis system, and displacement in the longitudinal, lateral and vertical direction respectively (meteorological convention)	(3)
Z	= seismicity of the region (seismic zoning factor)	(2)
Z	= time after start of response, in seconds	(2)
Z	= Zener-Holloman parameter (style of Σ_t versus θ curve)	(4)
Z_p	= plastic modulus	(4)
α	= angle of attack	(3)
α	= maximum stress (glass)	(6)
α	= power law exponent	(3)
$\alpha\theta$	= free unitary expansion	(4)
β	= coefficient defining effect of creep	(4)
β	= safety index (Eq. 7.23)	(7)
β	= wind direction (North 0–360°, East 90°)	(3)
γ	= coefficient defining insulation properties of protective material	(4)
ΔH	= energy of activation of creep	(4)
$\Delta\theta_a$	= increase in steel temperature between time t and $t + \Delta t$	(4)
δ	= logarithmic decrement damping ratio ($= \ln x_n/x_{n+1}$)	(3)
δ	= relative mean quadratic deviation of distribution of maximum loading	(1)

$\delta_{\chi Y}$	= correlation coefficient	(7)
ζ	= critical damping ratio ($= \delta/2\pi$)	(3)
θ	= departure from f_{cm} divided by $\underline{s}$	(6)
θ	= temperature	(4)
θ	= time	(4)
θ_r	= critical temperature (θ_{cr})	(4)
$\theta_a(t)$	= temperature at time t	(4)
θ_f	= medium temperature of fire between time t and $t + \Delta t$	(4)
κ	= surface drag coefficient ($= \tau_o/\rho\bar{u}_{\text{ref}}^2$)	(3)
λ	= latitude	(3)
μ	= dynamic viscosity of air	(3)
$\mu_\chi = E(X)$	= mean	(7)
ν	= cycling rate or rate of crossing of mean	

$$= \frac{\int_0^\infty n^2 S(n)\,dn}{\int_0^\infty S(n)\,dn}^{1/2} \tag{3}$$

ξ	= damping expressed as percentage of critical damping	(2)
ρ	= density of air	(3)
ρ	= stiffness index	(2)
ρ_a	= density of steel	(4)
Σ_K	= restrained unitary expansion	(4)
Σ_t	= creep strain	(4)
$\Sigma_{t,o}$	= ordinate at origin of Σ_t versus θ curve	(4)
$\Sigma\theta$	= real unitary expansion	(4)
σ	= standard deviation (or RMS of fluctuating component)	(3)
σ	= stress	(4)
σ_e	= yield stress	(4)
$\sigma_e(\theta_r)$	= σ_e at critical load	(4)
$\sigma_{u_z}/\bar{u}_z$	= turbulence intensity (that is, normalized on local longitudinal velocity)	(3)
$\sigma_\chi, \sigma(\chi)$	= standard deviation	(7)
$\sigma_\chi^2 = \text{Var}(X)$	= variance	(7)
τ_0	= surface shear stress in wind profile equation	(3)
ϕ	= V-mask design parameter	(6)
χ	= probability density function	(6)
$\chi_{(n)}$	= aerodynamic admittance function	(3)
χ, x(typical)	= random variable; specific value of that variable	(7)
$\bar{}$	= as superscript, reference to mean value (usually hourly mean)	(3)
$\hat{}$	= as superscript, reference to peak or maximum value (usually average maximum hourly value for a given probability of occurrence)	(3)
$\dot{}$	= as superscript, reference to first derivative	(3)
$'$	= as superscript, reference to fluctuating component	(3)
$\ddot{}$	= as superscript, reference to second derivative	(3)

ABBREVIATIONS

AAMA	Architectural Aluminum Manufacturers Association, USA
ACI	American Concrete Institute
AIA	American Institute of Architects
AISC	American Institute of Steel Construction
AISI	American Iron and Steel Institute
ANSI	American National Standards Institute
ARL	Average Run Length
ASCE	American Society of Civil Engineers
ASHRAE	American Society of Heating, Refrigerating, and Air Conditioning Engineers
ASME	American Society of Mechanical Engineers
ASNT	American Society for Nondestructive Testing
ASTM	American Society for Testing and Materials
AWS	American Welding Society
BIA	Brick Institute of America
BBC	Basic Building Code, USA
BOCA	Building Officials and Code Administrators International, USA
BRE	Building Research Establishment, Garston, England
BRI	Building Research Institute, USA
BS	British Standard
BSI	British Standards Institution, London
CABO	Council of American Building Officials
CB	Structural Design of Tall Concrete and Masonry Buildings
CEB	Comité Européen du Béton (since 1976 Comité Euro-International du Béton). European Concrete Committee
CIB	Conseil International du Batiment pour la Recherche, l'Etude et la Documentation, International Council for Building Research, Studies, and Documentation
CP	Code of Practice (as in CP: 110), United Kingdom
CSVTA	Czechoslovak Scientific and Technical Association, Bratislava, Czechoslovakia
DC	District of Columbia, USA
DIN	Deutsche Industrie Normen, German Industrial Standards
ECCS	European Coal and Steel Community, Brussels, Belgium
EERI	Earthquake Engineering Research Institute
ESSA	Environmental Science Services Administration
FIP	Fédération Internationale de la Précontrainte, International Federation for Prestressing
GSA	General Services Administration of the U.S. Government
HAZ	Heat-affected zone
HUD	Department of Housing and Urban Development of the U.S. Government
IABSE	International Association of Bridge and Structural Engineers
IAEE	International Association for Earthquake Engineering
ICBO	International Conference of Building Officials, USA
IRA	Initial rate of absorption
ISO	International Organization for Standardization, Geneva, Switzerland

MT	Magnetic particle testing
NBS	National Bureau of Standards (U.S. Department of Commerce)
NDT	Nondestructive testing
NFPA	National Fire Protection Association, USA
NOAA	National Oceanic and Atmospheric Agency
NPL	National Physical Laboratory, Teddington, England
NRCC	National Research Council of Canada, Ottawa, Canada
PC	Planning and Environmental Criteria for Tall Buildings
PCI	Prestressed Concrete Institute, USA
PPG	PPG Industries, Inc., Pittsburgh, USA
PT	Dye penetrant testing
RET	Research Energy Technique
RT	Radiographic testing
SAA	Standards Association of Australia, North Sydney, Australia
SB	Structural Design of Tall Buildings
SBCC	Southern Building Code Congress, USA
SC	Tall Building Systems and Concepts
SSBC	Southern Standard Building Code, USA
UBC	Uniform Building Code, USA
ULI	Underwriters' Laboratories, Inc., USA
USA	United States of America
UT	Ultrasonic testing
VT	Visual evaluation and measurement
WWF	Welded wire fabric (concrete reinforcement)

UNITS

In the table below are given conversion factors for commonly used units. The numerical values have been rounded off to the values shown. The British (Imperial) System of units is the same as the American System except where noted. Le Système International d'Unités (abbreviated "SI") is the name formally given in 1960 to the system of units partly derived from, and replacing, the old metric system.

SI	American	Old Metric
	Length	
1 mm	0.03937 in.	1 mm
1 m	3.28083 ft	1 m
	1.093613 yd	
1 km	0.62137 mile	1 km
	Area	
1 mm^2	0.00155 in.^{2}	1 mm^2
1 m^2	10.76392 ft^2	1 m^2
	1.19599 yd^2	
1 km^2	247.1043 acres	1 km^2
1 hectare	2.471 acres[1]	1 hectare
	Volume	
1 cm^3	0.061023 in.^{3}	1 cc
		1 ml
1 m^3	35.3147 ft^3	1 m^3
	1.30795 yd^3	
	264.172 gal[2] liquid	
	Velocity	
1 m/sec	3.28084 ft/sec	1 m/sec
1 km/hr	0.62137 miles/hr	1 km/hr
	Acceleration	
1 m/sec^2	3.28084 ft/sec^2	1 m/sec^2
	Mass	
1 g	0.035274 oz	1 g
1 kg	2.2046216 lb[3]	1 kg
	Density	
1 kg/m^3	0.062428 lb/ft^3	1 kg/m^3
	Force, Weight	
1 N	0.224809 lbf	0.101972 kgf
1 kN	0.1124045 tons[4]	
1 MN	224.809 kips	
1 kN/m	0.06853 kips/ft	
1 kN/m^2	20.9 lbf/ft^2	
	Torque, Bending Moment	
1 N-m	0.73756 lbf-ft	0.101972 kgf-m
1 kN-m	0.73756 kip-ft	101.972 kgf-m

SI	American	Old Metric
	Pressure, Stress	
$1\ N/m^2 = 1\ Pa$	0.000145038 psi	$0.101972\ kgf/m^2$
$1\ kN/m^2 = 1\ kPa$	20.8855 psf	
$1\ MN/m^2 = 1\ MPa$	0.145038 ksi	
	Viscosity (Dynamic)	
$1\ N\text{-sec}/m^2$	$0.0208854\ lbf\text{-sec}/ft^2$	$0.101972\ kgf\text{-sec}/m^2$
	Viscosity (Kinematic)	
$1\ m^2/sec$	$10.7639\ ft^2/sec$	$1\ m^2/sec$
	Energy, Work	
$1\ J = 1\ N\text{-m}$	0.737562 lbf-ft	0.00027778 w-hr
1 MJ	0.37251 hp-hr	0.27778 kw-hr
	Power	
$1\ W = 1\ J/sec$	0.737562 lbf ft/sec	1 w
1 kW	1.34102 hp	1 kw
	Temperature	
K = 273.15 + °C	°F = (°C × 1.8) + 32	°C = (°F − 32)/1.8
K = 273.15 + 5/9(°F − 32)		
K = 273.15 + 5/9(°R − 491.69)		

(1) Hectare as an alternative for km^2 is restricted to land and water areas.
(2) $1\ m^3 = 219.9693$ Imperial gallons.
(3) 1 kg = 0.068522 slugs.
(4) 1 American ton = 2000 lb.   1 kN = 0.1003612 Imperial ton.   1 Imperial ton = 2240 lb.

Abbreviations for Units

°C	degree Celsius (centigrade)	kW	kilowatt
cc	cubic centimeters	lb	pound
cm	centimeter	lbf	pound force
°F	degree Fahrenheit	MJ	megajoule
ft	foot	MPa	megapascal
g	gram	m	meter
gal	gallon	ml	milliliter
hp	horsepower	mm	millimeter
hr	hour	MN	meganewton
Imp	British Imperial	N	newton
in.	inch	oz	ounce
J	joule	Pa	pascal
K	kelvin	psf	pounds per square foot
kg	kilogram	psi	pounds per square inch
kgf	kilogram-force	°R	degree Rankine
kip	1000 pound force	sec	second
km	kilometer	slug	14.594 kg
kN	kilonewton	W	watt
kPa	kilopascal	yd	yard
ksi	kips per square inch		

CONVERSION TABLE FOR COMMITTEES AND CHAPTERS

The Council maintains an ongoing bibliography organized according to subject areas that are identified by the committee number. For this reason (and also because future editions of the Monograph may have different chapter numbers) the *committee* designations have been retained in the parenthetical information at the end of each bibliographic citation. The following conversion table is supplied for reference as is needed.

Committee	Chapter Number	Chapter Title
5	CL-1	Gravity Loads and Temperature Effects
6	CL-2	Earthquake Loading and Response
7	CL-3	Wind Loading and Wind Effects
8A	CL-4	Fire
8B	CL-5	Accidental Loading
9	CL-6	Quality Criteria
10	CL-7	Structural Safety and Probabilistic Methods

References/Bibliography

The citations that follow include both references and bibliography. The list includes all articles referred to or cited in the text and it also includes bibliography for further reading. The material is arranged alphabetically by author, followed by the year of publication. Since the citation in the text is to author and year, there will be instances in which reference is made to two different articles published in the same year by the same authors. In those instances it has been necessary to affix letters to the year to provide proper identification.

Where articles are published in a language other than English, the translation of the title is given first, followed by the title in the original language.

The numbers in parentheses designate the committee for which the citation is appropriate. (See facing page for committee/chapter conversion table.)

Additional bibliographies are available through the Council.

AAMA, 1971
  ALUMINUM CURTAIN WALLS #4, Architectural Aluminum Manufacturers Association, Chicago, Ill. (9)
ACI, 1971
  ACI STANDARD OF BUILDING CODE REQUIREMENTS FOR REINFORCED CONCRETE, ACI 318-71, American Concrete Institute, Detroit, Mich. (10)
ACI Committee 211, 1969
  RECOMMENDED PRACTICE FOR SELECTING PROPORTIONS FOR STRUCTURAL LIGHTWEIGHT CONCRETE, ACI 211.2-69 (Revised 1977), American Concrete Institute. (9)
ACI Committee 211, 1977
  RECOMMENDED PRACTICE FOR SELECTING PROPORTIONS FOR NORMAL AND HEAVYWEIGHT CONCRETE, ACI 211.1-77, American Concrete Institute. (9)
ACI Committee 213, 1979
  GUIDE FOR STRUCTURAL LIGHTWEIGHT AGGREGATE CONCRETE, *Concrete International*, American Concrete Institute, Vol. 1, No. 2. (9)
ACI Committee 214, 1957
  RECOMMENDED PRACTICE FOR EVALUATION OF COMPRESSION TEST RESULTS OF FIELD CONCRETE, *ACI Journal*, American Concrete Institute, Vol. 29, No. 1, pp. 1-19. (9)
ACI Committee 214, 1965
  RECOMMENDED PRACTICE FOR EVALUATION OF COMPRESSION TEST RESULTS OF FIELD CONCRETE, *ACI Journal*, American Concrete Institute, Vol. 61, No. 9, pp. 1057-1072. (9)

ACI Committee 217, 1977
RECOMMENDED PRACTICE FOR EVALUATION OF STRENGTH TESTS OF CONCRETE (ACI 217-77), American Concrete Institute, Detroit, Mich. (9)
ACI Committee 301, 1975
ACI STANDARD SPECIFICATIONS FOR STRUCTURAL CONCRETE FOR BUILDINGS (ACI 301-72) (Revised 1975), *ACI Journal*, American Concrete Institute, Vol. 72, No. 12. (9)
ACI Committee 305, 1977
HOT WEATHER CONCRETING, *ACI Journal*, American Concrete Institute, Vol. 74, No. 8, pp. 317–332. (9)
ACI Committee 306, 1972
ACI STANDARD—RECOMMENDED PRACTICE FOR COLD WEATHER CONCRETING (ACI 306-66) (Reaffirmed 1972), *ACI Journal*, American Concrete Institute, Vol. 75, No. 5, pp. 161–183. (9)
ACI Committee 308, 1971
ACI STANDARD—RECOMMENDED PRACTICE FOR CURING CONCRETE (ACI 308-71) (Reaffirmed October 1978), *ACI Journal*, American Concrete Institute, Vol. 68, No. 4, pp. 233–243. (9)
ACI Committee 318, 1977a
BUILDING CODE REQUIREMENTS FOR REINFORCED CONCRETE, ACI 318-77, American Concrete Institute. (9)
ACI Committee 318, 1977b
ACI STANDARD BUILDING CODE REQUIREMENTS FOR REINFORCED CONCRETE (ACI 318-77), *ACI Journal*, American Concrete Institute, Vol. 74, No. 12, p. 622. (9)
ACI Committee 318, 1977c
COMMENTARY ON BUILDING CODE REQUIREMENTS FOR REINFORCED CONCRETE (ACI 318-77), American Concrete Institute. (9)
ACI Committee 318, 1977d
PROPOSED REVISIONS: BUILDING CODE REQUIREMENTS FOR REINFORCED CONCRETE (ACI 318-71), *ACI Journal*, American Concrete Institute, Vol. 74, No. 7, Discussion 74-1, pp. 301–308. (9)
ACI Committee 347, 1977
ACI STANDARD RECOMMENDED PRACTICE FOR CONCRETE FORMWORK (ACI 347-78), *ACI Journal*, American Concrete Institute, Vol. 74, No. 9, pp. 397–434; Vol. 75, No. 6, Discussion 74-38, June, 1978, pp. 263–268. (9)
ACI Committee 531, 1970
CONCRETE MASONRY STRUCTURES—DESIGN AND CONSTRUCTION, *ACI Journal*, American Concrete Institute, Vol. 67, Nos. 5 and 6, Titles 67-23a and 67-23b, pp. 380–403 and 442–460. (9)
ACI Committee 531, 1978a
PROPOSED ACI STANDARD BUILDING CODE REQUIREMENTS FOR CONCRETE MASONRY STRUCTURES, *ACI Journal*, American Concrete Institute, Vol. 75, No. 8, Title 75-42, pp. 384–403. (9)
ACI Committee 531, 1978b
COMMENTARY ON BUILDING CODE REQUIREMENTS FOR CONCRETE MASONRY STRUCTURES, *ACI Journal*, American Concrete Institute, Vol. 75, No. 9, Title 75-50, pp. 460–498. (9)
ACI Committee 613, 1954
RECOMMENDED PRACTICE FOR SELECTING PROPORTIONS FOR CONCRETE (ACI 613-54), *ACI Journal*, American Concrete Institute, Vol. 26, No. 1, September; Vol. 51, pp. 49–64. (9)
ACI Committee 613, 1959
RECOMMENDED PRACTICE FOR SELECTING PROPORTIONS FOR STRUCTURAL LIGHTWEIGHT CONCRETE (ACI 613A-59), *ACI Journal*, American Concrete Institute, Vol. 30, No. 3; Vol. 55, September 1958, p. 305. (9)
AISC, 1978
SPECIFICATION FOR THE DESIGN, FABRICATION AND ERECTION OF STRUCTURAL STEEL FOR BUILDINGS with Commentary, effective November, 1978, American Institute of Steel Construction, Chicago, Ill. (9)

AISI, 1965
STRUCTURAL PROPERTIES OF HIGH STRENGTH STEELS AT ELEVATED TEMPERATURE, American Iron and Steel Institute, Washington, D.C. (8A)

ANSI, 1967
METHOD OF RECORDING AND MEASURING WORK INJURY EXPERIENCE, USAS Z16.1, American National Standards Institute, Inc., New York. (10)

ANSI, 1969
OPERATION OF ELEVATORS UNDER FIRE OR OTHER EMERGENCY CONDITIONS, American National Standards Institute, Inc., New York, A17.1 Appendix "E", Supplement C-1969. (8A)

ANSI A41.1, 1953
AMERICAN STANDARD BUILDING CODE REQUIREMENTS FOR MASONRY, American National Standards Institute, Inc., New York (Reaffirmed 1970). (9)

ANSI A41.2, 1960
BUILDING CODE REQUIREMENTS FOR CONCRETE MASONRY, American National Standards Institute, Inc., New York (Reaffirmed 1970). (9)

ANSI A58.1, 1972
AMERICAN NATIONAL STANDARD BUILDING CODE REQUIREMENTS FOR MINIMUM DESIGN LOADS IN BUILDINGS AND OTHER STRUCTURES, American National Standards Institute, Inc., New York. (9)

ANSI Z97.1, 1972
PERFORMANCE SPECIFICATIONS AND METHODS OF TEST FOR SAFETY GLAZING MATERIAL USED IN BUILDINGS, American National Standards Institute, Inc., New York. (9)

ASCE, 1961
DESIGN OF STRUCTURES TO RESIST NUCLEAR WEAPONS EFFECTS, Manual of Engineering Practice No. 42, ASCE, New York. (8B)

ASCE Task Committee on Structural Safety, 1968
A BIBLIOGRAPHY ON STRUCTURAL SAFETY, ASCE Task Committee on Structural Safety, A.H-S. Ang, Chmn.; 3rd draft copy prepared in Dept. of Civil Engineering, University of New Mexico, Albuquerque, N.M. (10)

ASCE-IABSE, 1973
PLANNING AND DESIGN OF TALL BUILDINGS: BIBLIOGRAPHY OF TALL BUILDINGS, ASCE, New York, and IABSE, Zürich, Switzerland. (8A)

ASHRAE, 1972
INFILTRATION AND NATURAL VENTILATION, ASHRAE Handbook of Fundamentals, American Society of Heating, Refrigerating, and Air Conditioning Engineers, New York, Chapter 19. (8A)

ASHRAE, 1973a
FIRE AND SMOKE CONTROL, ASHRAE Handbook, Systems, American Society of Heating, Refrigerating, and Air Conditioning Engineers, New York, Chapter 41, pp. 41.1–41.18. (8A)

ASHRAE, 1973b
SYMPOSIUM ON EXPERIENCE AND APPLICATIONS ON SMOKE AND FIRE CONTROL, ASHRAE Annual Meeting (Louisville, Kentucky, June). (8A)

ASTM, 1971a
STANDARD METHODS OF TENSION TESTING OF METALLIC MATERIALS, E8-69, Annual Book of ASTM Standards, Part 31, American Society for Testing and Materials, Philadelphia, Pa. (9)

ASTM, 1971b
STANDARD SPECIFICATION FOR GENERAL REQUIREMENTS FOR GENERAL REQUIREMENTS FOR DELIVERY OF ROLLED STEEL PLATES, SHAPES, SHEET PILING AND BARS FOR STRUCTURAL USE, AC-70, Annual Book of ASTM Standards, Part 4, American Society for Testing and Materials, Philadelphia, Pa. (9)

ASTM, 1974
STANDARD METHODS OF FIRE TEST OF BUILDING CONSTRUCTION AND MATERIALS, American Society for Testing and Materials, Philadelphia, Pa., No. 119. (8A)

ASTM, 1979
ANNUAL BOOK OF STANDARDS, issued in 48 parts, American Society for Testing and Materials, Philadelphia, Pa. (9)

ASTM A615-78, 1978
STANDARD SPECIFICATION FOR DEFORMED AND PLAIN BILLET-STEEL BARS FOR CONCRETE REINFORCEMENT, American Society for Testing and Materials, Philadelphia, Pa. (9)

ASTM C31-69, 1969
STANDARD METHOD OF MAKING AND CURING CONCRETE TEST SPECIMENS IN THE FIELD, American Society for Testing and Materials, Philadelphia, Pa. (9)

ASTM C33-78, 1978
STANDARD SPECIFICATION FOR CONCRETE AGGREGATES, American Society for Testing and Materials, Philadelphia, Pa. (9)

ASTM C67-78, 1978
STANDARD METHODS OF SAMPLING AND TESTING BRICK AND STRUCTURAL CLAY TILE, American Society for Testing and Materials, Philadelphia, Pa. (9)

ASTM C90-75, 1975
STANDARD SPECIFICATION FOR HOLLOW LOAD-BEARING CONCRETE MASONRY UNITS, American Society for Testing and Materials, Philadelphia, Pa. (9)

ASTM C91-78, 1978
STANDARD SPECIFICATION FOR MASONRY CEMENT, American Society for Testing and Materials, Philadelphia, Pa. (9)

ASTM C109-77, 1977
STANDARD TEST METHOD FOR COMPRESSIVE STRENGTH OF HYDRAULIC CEMENT MORTARS (USING 2-IN OR 50-MM CUBE SPECIMENS), American Society for Testing and Materials, Philadelphia, Pa. (9)

ASTM C136-76, 1976
TEST FOR SIEVE OR SCREEN ANALYSIS OF FINE AND COARSE AGGREGATES, American Society for Testing and Materials, Philadelphia, Pa. (9)

ASTM C140-75, 1975
STANDARD METHODS OF TESTING CONCRETE MASONRY UNITS, American Society for Testing and Materials, Philadelphia, Pa. (9)

ASTM C143-74, 1974
TEST FOR SLUMP OF PORTLAND CEMENT CONCRETE, American Society for Testing and Materials, Philadelphia, Pa. (9)

ASTM C145-75, 1975
STANDARD SPECIFICATION FOR SOLID LOAD-BEARING CONCRETE MASONRY UNITS, American Society for Testing and Materials, Philadelphia, Pa. (9)

ASTM C150-78a, 1978
STANDARD SPECIFICATION FOR PORTLAND CEMENT, American Society for Testing and Materials, Philadelphia, Pa. (9)

ASTM C158-72, 1972
STANDARD METHODS OF FLEXURE TESTING OF GLASS (DETERMINATION OF MODULUS OF RUPTURE), American Society for Testing and Materials, Philadelphia, Pa. (9)

ASTM C173-78, 1978
STANDARD TEST METHOD FOR AIR CONTENT OF FRESHLY MIXED CONCRETE BY THE VOLUMETRIC METHOD, American Society for Testing and Materials, Philadelphia, Pa. (9)

ASTM C270-73, 1973
STANDARD SPECIFICATION FOR MORTAR FOR UNIT MASONRY, American Society for Testing and Materials, Philadelphia, Pa. (9)

ASTM C336-76, 1976
TEST FOR ANNEALING POINT AND STRAIN POINT OF GLASS BY FIBER ELONGATION, American Society for Testing and Materials, Philadelphia, Pa. (9)

ASTM C338-73, 1973
TEST FOR SOFTENING POINT OF GLASS, American Society for Testing and Materials, Philadelphia, Pa. (9)

ASTM C470-76, 1976
  STANDARD SPECIFICATION FOR MOLDS FOR FORMING CONCRETE TEST
  CYLINDERS VERTICALLY, American Society for Testing and Materials, Philadelphia,
  Pa. (9)
ASTM C476-71, 1971
  STANDARD SPECIFICATION FOR MORTAR AND GROUT FOR REINFORCED
  MASONRY, American Society for Testing and Materials, Philadelphia, Pa. (9)
ASTM C542-76, 1976
  STANDARD SPECIFICATION FOR LOCK-STRIP GASKETS, American Society for
  Testing and Materials, Philadelphia, Pa. (9)
ASTM C595-76, 1976
  SPECIFICATION FOR BLENDED HYDRAULIC CEMENTS, American Society for
  Testing and Materials, Philadelphia, Pa. (9)
ASTM C780-74, 1974
  STANDARD METHOD FOR PRECONSTRUCTION AND CONSTRUCTION EVAL-
  UATION OF MORTARS FOR PLAIN AND REINFORCED UNIT MASONRY,
  American Society for Testing and Materials, Philadelphia, Pa. (9)
ASTM E72-77, 1977
  STANDARD METHODS OF CONDUCTING STRENGTH TESTS OF PANELS FOR
  BUILDING CONSTRUCTION, American Society for Testing and Materials, Phila-
  delphia, Pa. (9)
ASTM E149-76, 1976
  STANDARD TEST METHOD FOR BOND STRENGTH OF MORTAR TO MASON-
  RY UNITS, American Society for Testing and Materials, Philadelphia, Pa. (9)
ASTM E330-72, 1972
  STANDARD TEST METHOD FOR STRUCTURAL PERFORMANCE OF EXTE-
  RIOR WINDOWS, CURTAIN WALLS, AND DOORS UNDER THE INFLUENCE
  OF WIND LOADS, American Society for Testing and Materials, Philadelphia, Pa. (9)
ASTM E447-74, 1974
  STANDARD TEST METHODS FOR COMPRESSIVE STRENGTH OF MASONRY
  PRISMS, American Society for Testing and Materials, Philadelphia, Pa. (9)
ASTM E518-76, 1976
  STANDARD TEST METHODS FOR FLEXURAL BOND STRENGTH OF MASON-
  RY, American Society for Testing and Materials, Philadelphia, Pa. (9)
ASTM STP 169-A, 1966
  SIGNIFICANCE OF TESTS AND PROPERTIES OF CONCRETE AND CONCRETE
  MAKING MATERIALS, American Society for Testing and Materials, Philadelphia, Pa.
  (9)
Abraham, C. and Thedié, J., undated
  THE COST OF HUMAN LIFE IN ECONOMIC DECISIONS (Le prix d'une vie humaine
  dans les décisions économiques), French Revue of Research Operations. (8A)
Adams, P. F., 1966
  PLASTIC DESIGN IN HIGH STRENGTH STEEL, Fritz Engineering Laboratory Report
  No. 297.19, Lehigh University, Bethlehem, Pa. (9)
Adams, P. F. and Galambos, T. V., 1969
  MATERIAL CONSIDERATIONS IN PLASTIC DESIGN, Publications of IABSE 29-II,
  IABSE, Zürich, Switzerland, pp. 1–18. (9)
Agarwal, R. K. and Gardiner, N. J., 1974
  FORM AND SHORE REQUIREMENTS FOR MULTISTOREY FLAT SLAB TYPE
  BUILDINGS, ACI Journal, American Concrete Institute, Vol. 71, No. 11, pp. 559–569.
  (5)
Alexander, S. J. and Hambly, E. C., 1970
  THE DESIGN OF STRUCTURES TO WITHSTAND GASEOUS EXPLOSIONS: PART
  2, Concrete, Vol. 4, pp. 107–116. (8B)
Allen, D. E., 1968
  Discussion of CHOICE OF FAILURE PROBABILITIES by C. J. Turkstra, Journal of the
  Structural Division, ASCE, Vol. 94, No. ST9, Proc. Paper 6090, pp. 2169–2173. (10)
Allen, D. E., 1969
  SAFETY FACTORS FOR STRESS REVERSAL, Publications of IABSE 29-II, Zürich,
  Switzerland. (10)

Allen, D. E., 1970a
LIMIT STATE DESIGN—A UNIFIED PROCEDURE FOR THE DESIGN OF STRUC-
TURES, *Engineering Journal*, Vol. 53, No. 2, pp. 18–29. (10)

Allen, D. E., 1970b
PROBABILISTIC STUDY OF REINFORCED CONCRETE IN BENDING, Technical
Paper 311, Division of Building Research, National Research Council of Canada, Ottawa.
(10)

Allen, D. E., 1973
SUMMARY REPORT: GRAVITY LOADS AND TEMPERATURE EFFECTS, Plan-
ning and Design of Tall Buildings, Proceedings of 1972 ASCE-IABSE International
Conference, Vol. 1b, ASCE, New York, pp. 145–150. (5)

Allen, D. E. and Dalgleish, W. A., 1973
DYNAMIC WIND LOADS AND CLADDING DESIGN, IABSE Symposium on
Resistance and Ultimate Deformability of Structures Acted on by Well Defined Repeated
Loads (Lisbon, Portugal), pp. 279–285. (7)

Allen, D. E. and Schriever, W. R., 1972
PROGRESSIVE COLLAPSE, ABNORMAL LOADS, AND BUILDING CODES, Research Paper No. 578, Division of Building Research, Ottawa, Canada. (8B)

Allen, J. P. and Freedman, S., 1964
A REVIEW OF BLOCK CEMENTS—1964, National Concrete Masonry Association,
Herndon, Va. (9)

Allgood, J. R. and Swihart, G. R., 1970
DESIGN OF FLEXURAL MEMBERS FOR STATIC AND BLAST LOADING, ACI
Monograph No. 5, American Concrete Institute/Iowa State University Press, Detroit,
Mich. (8B)

Alpert, R. L., 1972
CALCULATION OF RESPONSE TIME OF CEILING-MOUNTED FIRE DETEC-
TORS, National Fire Protection Association, 76th Annual Meeting, Philadelphia, Pa.
(8A)

Alpsten, G. A., 1967
RESIDUAL STRESSES IN HOT-ROLLED STEEL SHAPES (Egenspänningar i Varm-
valsade Stålprofiler), Division of Structural Engineering and Bridge Building, The Royal
Institute of Technology, Stockholm, Sweden. (9)

Alpsten, G. A., 1968
THERMAL RESIDUAL STRESSES IN HOT-ROLLED STEEL MEMBERS, Fritz
Engineering Laboratory Report No. 337.3, Lehigh University, Bethlehem, Pa. (9)

Alpsten, G. A., 1970a
RESIDUAL STRESSES AND MECHANICAL PROPERTIES OF COLD-STRAIGHT-
ENED H-SHAPES (Egenspänningar och Materialhållfasthet i Kallriktade Bredfläns-
profiler), *Jernkontorets Annaler*, Stockholm, Sweden, Vol. 154, pp. 255–283. (9)

Alpsten, G. A., 1970b
VARIATIONS IN STRENGTH AND CROSS-SECTIONAL DIMENSION OF STRUC-
TURAL SHAPES (Variationer i Materialhållfasthet och tv Ärsnittsdimensioner hos
Konstruktionsprofiler), Proceedings, Stålbyggnad—Nordiska Forskningsdagar, Swedish
Institute of Steel Construction, August, pp. 2:1–2:17. (9)

Alpsten, G. A. 1970c
RESIDUAL STRESSES AND STRAIN-HARDENING EFFECTS IN COLD-
STRAIGHTENED WIDE-FLANGE SHAPES (Egenspänningar och Töjhärdnings-
effekter i Kallriktade Bredflänsprofiler), Proceedings, Stålbyggnad—Nordiska Forskningsdagar, Swedish Institute of Steel Construction, pp. 25:1–25:19. (9)

Alpsten, G. A., 1972
PREDICTION OF RESIDUAL STRESSES IN MEDIUM-SIZE TO HEAVY WELDED
STEEL SHAPES, paper presented at IABSE Congress (Amsterdam, The Netherlands,
May). (9)

Alpsten, G. A., 1973
VARIATIONS IN MECHANICAL AND CROSS-SECTIONAL PROPERTIES OF
STEEL, Planning and Design of Tall Buildings, Proceedings of 1972 ASCE-IABSE Inter-
national Conference, Vol. 1b, ASCE, New York, pp. 755–807. (9)

Alpsten, G. A., undated a
VARIATIONS IN THE STRENGTH OF STRUCTURAL STEEL, Report No. 39.4, Swedish Institute of Steel Construction, Stockholm, Sweden. (9)

Alpsten, G. A., undated b
STATISTICAL INVESTIGATION OF THE STRENGTH OF ROLLED AND WELDED STRUCTURAL STEEL SHAPES, Report 39.5, Swedish Institute of Steel Construction, Stockholm, Sweden. (9)

Alpsten, G. A. and Tall, L., 1970
RESIDUAL STRESSES IN HEAVY WELDED SHAPES, *Welding Journal*, Vol. 49, No. 3, pp. 93-s–105-s. (9)

Amaral, N. A., 1973
COMMENTARIES ON THE PROPOSAL FOR THE REVISION OF THE BRAZILIAN STANDARD FOR THE DESIGN AND CONSTRUCTION OF REINFORCED CONCRETE, South American Regional Conference on Tall Buildings (Porto Alegre, Brazil), Vol. 1. (7)

Amariei, D., Brinzei, A., Diaconu, D., Manolovici, M., Ciongradi, I., Iticovici, M. and Mariniscu, S., 1975
COMPARATIVE ASPECTS WITH REGARD TO EARTHQUAKE RESPONSE OF STRUCTURES OF MONOLITHIC OR PRECAST FRAMES (Aspecte Comparative Privind Raspunsul Seismic al Structurilor din Cadre Monolite si Prefabricate), Reinforced Concrete Tall Buildings, Proceedings of Conference (Iasi, Romania), Vol. 1, Consiliul National al Inginerilor si Technicienilor, Iasi, Romania, pp. 105–120. (6)

Amin, M. and Ang, A. H-S., 1966
A NONSTATIONARY STOCHASTIC MODEL FOR STRONG-MOTION EARTH-QUAKES, University of Illinois, April. (6)

Amin, M. and Ang, A. H-S., 1968
NONSTATIONARY STOCHASTIC MODEL FOR EARTHQUAKE MOTIONS, *Journal of the Engineering Mechanics Division*, ASCE, Vol. 94, No. EM2, Proc. Paper 5906, p. 559. (10)

Amrhein, J. E., 1972
MASONRY DESIGN MANUAL, 2nd Edition, Masonry Industry Advancement Committee, Masonry Institute of America, Los Angeles, Calif. (9)

Amrhein, J. E., 1973
REINFORCED MASONRY ENGINEERING HANDBOOK, CLAY AND CONCRETE MASONRY, 2nd Edition, Masonry Institute of America, Los Angeles, Calif. (9)

Anderson, A. W., Blume, J. A., Degenkolb, H. J., Hammill, H. B., Knapik, E. M., Marchand, H. L., Powers, H. C., Rinne, J. E., Sedgwick, G. A. and Sjoberg, H. O., 1952
LATERAL FORCES OF EARTHQUAKE AND WIND, *Transactions*, ASCE, Vol. 117, pp. 716–754. (10)

Ang, A. H-S., 1973
TOWARDS RISK-BASED DESIGN AND PERFORMANCE CRITERIA, Planning and Design of Tall Buildings, Proceedings of the 1972 ASCE-IABSE International Conference, Vol. 1b, ASCE, New York, pp. 1007–1012. (10)

Ang, A. H-S. and Amin, M., 1969
SAFETY FACTORS AND PROBABILITY IN STRUCTURAL DESIGN, *Journal of the Structural Division*, ASCE, Vol. 95, No. ST7, Proc. Paper 6667, pp. 1389–1405. (10)

Ang, A. H-S. and Amin, M., 1971
FORMULATION OF WIND-RESISTANT DESIGN BASED ON ACCEPTABLE RISK, Proceedings of the 3rd International Conference on Wind Effects on Buildings and Structures (Tokyo, Japan), Part III, pp. 511–520. (7)

Ang, A. H-S. and Ellingwood, B. R., 1971
CRITICAL ANALYSIS OF RELIABILITY PRINCIPLES RELATIVE TO DESIGN, 1st International Conference on Applications of Statistics and Probability to Soil and Structural Engineering (University of Hong Kong, September). (10)

Anthony, K. C., 1970
THE BACKGROUND TO THE STATISTICAL APPROACH, *The Modern Design of Wind Sensitive Structures*, Proceedings of the CIRIA Seminar (London, England), pp. 17–27. (7)

Anthony, K. C., 1974
THE WIND ENVIRONMENT OF BUILDINGS WITH PARTICULAR REFERENCE
TO THE PENANG URBAN CENTRE, Proceedings of the Conference on Tall
Buildings, 25th National/Regional Conference (Kuala Lumpur, Malaysia), pp. 8-12–8-23.
(7)
Anthony, K. C., 1975
WIND ENGINEERING—THE PERSONAL VIEW OF A PRACTISING ENGINEER,
4th International Conference on Wind Effects on Buildings and Structures (London,
England), Cambridge Press, Cambridge, England. (7)
Aoyama, H., Ito, M., Sugano, S. and Nakata, S., 1970
A STUDY ON THE CAUSE OF DAMAGE TO THE HACHINOHE TECHNICAL
COLLEGE DUE TO 1968 TOKACHI-OKI EARTHQUAKE (PART 1), Proceedings of
the 3rd Japan Earthquake Engineering Symposium. (6)
Apeland, K., 1973
REDUCTION OF LIVE LOADS AND COMBINATIONS OF LOADS, Planning and
Design of Tall Buildings, Proceedings of 1972 ASCE-IABSE International Conference,
Vol. 1b, No. 5-5, ASCE, New York. (5)
Apperley, R. and Vickery, B. J., 1974
THE PREDICTION AND EVALUATION OF THE GROUND LEVEL WIND EN-
VIRONMENT, Proceedings, 5th Australasian Conference on Hydraulics and Fluid
Mechanics, University of Canterbury, New Zealand. (7)
Applied Technology Council, 1978
TENTATIVE PROVISIONS FOR THE DEVELOPMENT OF SEISMIC REGULA-
TIONS FOR BUILDINGS, ATC 3-06, U.S. Government Printing Office, Washington,
D.C. (6)
Arakawa, H., 1974
STRONG GUSTS IN THE LOWEST 250-m LAYER OVER THE CITY OF TOKYO,
Proceedings of the 1974 2nd USA/Japan Research Seminar on Wind Effects on
Structures, University of Tokyo Press, Tokyo, Japan. (7)
Arias, A., 1973
RATING OF GROUND MOTION, Planning and Design of Tall Buildings, Proceedings of
the 1972 ASCE-IABSE International Conference, Vol. 1b, ASCE, New York, pp.
320–323. (6)
Armer, G. S. T., 1977a
THE PERFORMANCE OF DAMAGED LARGE PANEL STRUCTURES, BRE Sem-
inar Paper, Building Research Establishment, Garston, England. (8B)
Armer, G. S. T., 1977b
THE RESPONSE OF A MODEL 18-STOREY PANEL STRUCTURE TO IMPACT
AND EXPLOSIVE LOADING, BRE Seminar Paper, Building Research Establishment,
Garston, England. (8B)
Armitt, J. and Counihan, J., 1968
THE SIMULATION OF THE ATMOSPHERIC BOUNDARY LAYER IN A WIND
TUNNEL, Atmospheric Environment, Pergamon Press, Vol. 2, pp. 49–71. (7)
Arnault, P., Ehm, H. and Kruppa, J., 1974
HEATING BEHAVIOR OF EXTERNAL COLUMNS UNDER FIRE EXPOSURE
(Evolution des temperatures dans des póteaux extérieurs soumis à des incendies), CECM,
Vol. 3-74/7f. (8A)
Arnault, P., Ehm, H. and Kruppa, J., 1976
RESISTANCE TO FIRE OF STRUCTURES MADE OF STEEL AND CONCRETE
(Résistance au feu des poutres mixtes, acier-beton), CTICM, Vol. 2.10, 20-4. (8A)
Arya, A. S., 1973
SEISMIC BEHAVIOR AND DESIGN OF MULTI-STORIED STEEL BUILDINGS,
Proceedings of Conference (New Delhi, India, January), Indian National Group of the
IABSE, New Delhi, India, pp. III11–III14. (6)
Ashton, L. A. and Malhotra, H. L., 1964
CURTAIN WALLING AND FIRE PROTECTION, Architects Journal, Vol. 140, No. 19,
pp. 1059–1064. (8A)
Associate Committee on the National Building Code of Canada, 1973
MEASURES FOR FIRE SAFETY IN HIGH BUILDINGS, The Associate Committee on
the National Buildings Code, National Research Council, Ottawa, Canada, NRCC No.
13366. (8A)

Astbury, N. F., West, H. W. and Hodgkinson, H. R., 1973
EXPERIMENTAL GAS EXPLOSIONS—REPORT OF FURTHER TESTS AT POTTERS MARSTON, *Proceedings*, British Ceramic Society, No. 21, April, pp. 195–212. (8B)

Astbury, N. F., West, H. W., Hodgkinson, H. R., Cubbage, P. A. and Clare, R., 1970
GAS EXPLOSIONS IN LOAD-BEARING BRICK STRUCTURES, Special Publication No. 68, British Ceramic Research Association, Stoke-on-Trent, England. (8B)

Augusti, G. and Baratta, A., 1971
LIMIT ANALYSIS OF STRUCTURES WITH STOCHASTIC STRENGTH VARIATIONS, University of Palermo, Italy. (10)

Augusti, G. and Baratta, A., 1972
THEORY OF PROBABILITY AND LIMIT ANALYSIS OF STRUCTURES UNDER MULTI-PARAMETER LOADING, presented at International Symposium on Problems of Plasticity, Warsaw, Poland. (10)

Australian Standardizing Body, 1975
RULES FOR MINIMUM DESIGN LOADS ON STRUCTURES (METRIC UNITS), THE LOADING CODE, Australian Wind Code AS1170, Part 2, Australian Standardizing Body, North Sydney, Australia. (7)

Aycardi, L. G., 1973
STRUCTURAL BEHAVIOR UNDER SEISMIC LOAD (Estudios Sismicos y Comportamiento de las Estructuras), Proceedings of the National Conference on Tall Buildings (Bogotá, Colombia, September), Colombia School of Engineering, Bogotá, Colombia, pp. 17–37. (6)

Aynsley, R. M., 1973
WIND EFFECTS ON HIGH AND LOW RISE HOUSING, *Architectural Science Review*, Vol. 16, No. 3. (7)

Aynsley, R. M., 1974
ENVIRONMENTAL WIND PROBLEMS AROUND BUILDINGS, *Building Forum*, Vol. 6, No. 1. (7)

Aynsley, R. M., Melbourne, W. H. and Vickery, B. J., 1976
ARCHITECTURAL AERODYNAMICS, Applied Science Publishers. (7)

BIA, 1969
BUILDING CODE REQUIREMENTS FOR ENGINEERED BRICK MASONRY, Brick Institute of America, McLean, Va., August 1969 (reprinted March 1976). (9)

BIA, 1972
BIA TECHNICAL NOTES ON BRICK CONSTRUCTION, BIA Technical Note No. 8A, Brick Institute of America, Philadelphia, Pa., October/November. (9)

BOCA, 1973
PROPOSED STANDARD FOR THE DESIGN AND INSTALLATION OF THE SUPPRESSION SYSTEMS FOR LIFE SAFETY, Building Officials and Code Administrators International, Chicago, Ill., No. 13-1973. (8A)

BOCA, 1978
THE BOCA BASIC BUILDING CODE/1978, Building Officials and Code Administrators International, Inc., 7th Ed., Chicago, Ill. (9)

BRI, 1972
STRENGTH OF SENNICHI DEPARTMENT STORE BUILDING AFTER FIRE, unpublished report to Building Research Institute, Washington, D.C., September 27. (8A)

BSI, 1968
PRECAUTIONS AGAINST FIRE: OFFICE BUILDINGS, CP3, British Standards Institution, London, England, Chapter 4, Part 3. (8A)

BSI, 1969
SPECIFICATION FOR WELDABLE STRUCTURAL STEELS, British Standard 4360, Part 2, British Standards Institution, London, England. (9)

BSI, 1970, 1974·
AUTOMATIC FIRE ALARM SYSTEMS IN BUILDINGS, Part 1, Heat-sensitive (point) detectors; Part 2, Heat-sensitive (line) detectors; Part 3, Smoke-sensitive detectors; Part 4, Control and indicating equipment, No. 3116, British Standards Institution, London, England. (8A)

BSI, 1972
CODE OF PRACTICE FOR THE STRUCTURAL USE OF CONCRETE, PART 1, DESIGN MATERIALS AND WORKMANSHIP, CP110:Part 1, British Standards Institution, London, England. (Amended to February 1976). (9)

BSI, 1976
STRUCTURAL RECOMMENDATIONS FOR LOAD BEARING WALLS, British Standard CP111, British Standards Institution, London, England. (9)

BSI, 1978
STRUCTURAL USE OF MASONRY, PART 1: REINFORCED MASONRY. British Standard BS5628, British Standards Institution, London, England. (9)

Badami, G. N., 1973
HI-RISE BUILDING CONSTRUCTION IN INDIA AND PROBLEMS OF FIRE, Proceedings of 8th National/Regional Conference (New Delhi, India, January), Indian National Group of IABSE, New Delhi, India. (8A)

Baines, W. D., 1963
EFFECTS OF VELOCITY DISTRIBUTION ON WIND LOADS AND FLOW PATTERNS ON BUILDINGS, Proceedings of the International Conference on Wind Effects on Buildings and Structures (NPL, Teddington, England), pp. 197–223. (7)

Baker, A. L. L., 1956
THE ULTIMATE-LOAD THEORY APPLIED TO THE DESIGN OF REINFORCED AND PRESTRESSED CONCRETE FRAMES, Concrete Publications Ltd., London, England. (10)

Baker, J. F., Williams, E. L. and Lax, D., 1948
THE DESIGN OF FRAMED BUILDINGS AGAINST HIGH EXPLOSIVE BOMBS, The Civil Engineer in War, Vol. 3, Institution of Civil Engineers, London, England, pp. 80–112. (8B)

Baldwin, R. and Allen, G., 1970
SOME STATISTICS OF DAMAGE TO BUILDINGS IN FIRES, F-R Note 805, Fire Research Station, Borehamwood, England. (8A)

Bandrabur, C., Damien, R., Iahandi, C. and Popescu, M., 1975
AN EXPERIMENTAL STUDY ON THE EFFECT OF WIND IN DETERMINING THE HEAT REQUIREMENT FOR TALL BUILDINGS HEATING SYSTEMS, Proceedings of the 34th National/Regional Conference (Iasi, Romania), Vol. II, pp. 91–106. (7)

Baratta, A., 1973a
AN IMPROVEMENT IN THE STATIC METHOD FOR LIMIT ANALYSIS OF STRUCTURES WITH STOCHASTIC STRENGTH VARIATIONS, Journal of Structural Mechanics, Vol. 1, No. 4. (10)

Baratta, A., 1973b
A REMARK ON THE PROBABILISTIC ANALYSIS OF STRUCTURAL SAFETY, Planning and Design of Tall Buildings, Proceedings of the 1972 ASCE-IABSE International Conference, Vol. 1b, ASCE, New York, pp. 1039–1042. (10)

Barrett, R. E. and Locklin, D. W., 1969
A COMPUTER TECHNIQUE FOR PREDICTING SMOKE MOVEMENT IN TALL BUILDINGS, Fire Technology, Society of Fire Protection Association, Boston, Mass., Vol. 5, No. 4, pp. 299–310. (8A)

Barstein, M. F., 1959
WIND LOADING ON TALL BUILDINGS (in Russian), Stroitel'naya Mekhan. i Raschet Sooruzheniy, USSR, No. 3. (10)

Barstein, M. F., 1971
SOME PROBLEMS OF DESIGN OF TALL STRUCTURES FOR WIND EFFECT, Proceedings of the 3rd International Conference on Wind Effects on Buildings and Structures (Tokyo, Japan), Part III, pp. 609–646. (7)

Basler, E., 1961
RESEARCH CONCERNING RISK ANALYSIS OF BUILDING SYSTEMS (Untersuchungen über den Sicherheits Begriff von Bauwerken), Schweizer Archive (4), Solothurn, Switzerland. (10)

Baynes, C., 1974
THE STATISTICS OF STRONG WINDS FOR ENGINEERING APPLICATIONS, thesis presented to the University of Western Ontario, at London, Ontario, Canada, in 1974, in partial fulfillment of the requirements for the degree of Doctor of Engineering Science.

Bearman, P. W., 1970
WIND LOADS ON STRUCTURES IN TURBULENT FLOW, Proceedings, Seminar at the Institution of Civil Engineers, London, England, pp. 65–82. (7)

Bearman, P. W., 1971
WIND LOADS ON STRUCTURES IN TURBULENT FLOW, The Modern. Design of Wind Sensitive Structures, Proceedings of the CIRIA Seminar (London, England). (7)

Bearman, P. W. and Davies, M. E., 1975
THE FLOW ABOUT OSCILLATING BLUFF STRUCTURES, 4th International Conference on Wind Effects on Buildings and Structures (London, England), University of Cambridge Press, Cambridge, England. (7)

Beckett, H. E., and Godfrey, J. A., 1974
WINDOWS, PERFORMANCE, DESIGN AND INSTALLATION, vanNostrand Reinhold Company, New York. (9)

Beer, G. and Tall, L., 1970
THE STRENGTH OF HEAVY WELDED BOX COLUMNS, Fritz Engineering Laboratory Report No. 337.27, Lehigh University, Bethlehem, Pa. (9)

Belyaev, B. I., 1969
STATISTICAL METHOD OF DETERMINING STANDARD STRESSES FOR STEEL STRUCTURES, Stroitel'naya Promyshennost' (3): 32–37, 1954; translated by D. E. Allen in "A Statistical Method of Design of Building Structures," Technical Translation 1368, National Research Council of Canada, Ottawa, pp. 15–36. (10)

Benjamin, J. R., 1973
PROBABILISTIC METHODS, Planning and Design of Tall Buildings, Proceedings of the 1972 ASCE-IABSE International Conference, Vol. 1b, ASCE, New York, pp. 1013–1016. (10)

Benjamin, J. R. and Cornell, C. A., 1970
PROBABILITY, STATISTICS, AND DECISIONS FOR CIVIL ENGINEERS, McGraw-Hill Book Co., Inc., New York, N.Y. (10)

Benjamin, J. R. and Shah, H. C., 1972
INFORMATION FOR PROBABILISTIC CODE FORMAT, Technical Report 15b, Dept. of Civil Engineering, Stanford University, Calif. (10)

Beresford, F. D., 1964
AN ANALYTICAL EXAMINATION OF PROPPED FLOORS IN MULTI-STOREY FLAT PLATE CONSTRUCTION, Constructional Review, Vol. 37, No. 11, p. 16. (5)

Beresford, F. D., 1971
SHORING AND RESHORING OF FLOORS IN MULTISTOREY BUILDINGS, presented at Symposium on Formwork, Concrete Institute of Australia (Melbourne, Australia, April). (5)

Berg, G. V., 1964a
THE 1963 SKOPJE EARTHQUAKE, Proceedings of the 3rd World Conference on Earthquake Engineering (New Zealand), Vol. III. (6)

Berg, G. V., 1964b
THE SKOPJE, YUGOSLAVIA EARTHQUAKE, JULY 26, 1963, American Iron and Steel Institute, Washington, D.C. (6)

Berg, G. V. and Stratta, J. L., 1964
ANCHORAGE AND THE ALASKA EARTHQUAKE OF MARCH 27, 1964, American Iron and Steel Institute, Washington, D.C. (6)

Bertero, V. V., 1973
DUCTILITY AND SEISMIC RESPONSE, Planning and Design of Tall Buildings, Proceedings of the 1972 ASCE-IABSE International Conference, Vol. 1b, ASCE, New York, pp. 303–309. (6)

Bertero, V. V., Fratessa, P. F., Manin, S. A., Sexton, J. H., Scordelis, A. C., Wilson, E. L., Wyllie, L., Seed, H. and Penzien, J., 1970
SEISMIC ANALYSIS OF THE CHARAIMA BUILDING CARABALLEDA, VENEZUELA, Earthquake Engineering Research Center Report No. 70-4, University of California, Berkeley. (6)

Bessey, G. E., 1950
INVESTIGATION ON BUILDING FIRES: THE VISIBLE CHANGES IN CONCRETE OR MORTAR EXPOSED TO HIGH TEMPERATURE, HMSO, London, England. (8A)

Bielak, J., 1971
  EARTHQUAKE RESPONSE OF BUILDING-FOUNDATION SYSTEMS, Report No.
  EERL 71-04, California Institute of Technology, Pasadena, Calif. (6)
Binder, R. W., 1964
  THE ACAPULCO, MEXICO, EARTHQUAKES OF MAY 11 AND MAY 19, 1962,
  Proceedings of the 3rd World Conference on Earthquake Engineering (New Zealand). (6)
Birkeland, P. W. and Westhoff, L. J., 1971
  DIMENSIONAL TOLERANCES IN A TALL CONCRETE BUILDING, ACI Journal,
  American Concrete Institute, Vol. 68, No. 8, pp. 600–607. (9)
Birkeland, P. W. and Westhoff, L. J., 1973
  DIMENSIONAL TOLERANCE—CONCRETE, Planning and Design of Tall Buildings,
  Proceedings of the 1972 ASCE-IABSE International Conference, Vol. 1b, ASCE, New
  York, pp. 845–850. (9)
Birman, A. E., 1973
  FIRE AND SAFETY (Engenharia de Seguranca em Edificios Altos), Proceedings of South
  American Regional Conference on Tall Buildings (Porto Alegre, Brazil, December),
  Sociedad de Engenharia do Rio Grande do Sul, Porto Alegre, Brazil. (8A)
Bjorhovde, R. and Tall, L., 1970
  SURVEY OF UTILIZATION AND MANUFACTURE OF HEAVY COLUMNS, Report
  No. 337.7, Fritz Engineering Laboratory, Lehigh University, Bethlehem, Pa. (9)
Bjorhovde, R., Brozzetti, J., Alpsten, G. A. and Tall, L., 1972
  RESIDUAL STRESSES IN THICK WELDED PLATES, Welding Journal, Vol. 51, No. 8,
  August, pp. 392-s–405-s. (9)
Bjorhovde, R. and Tall, L., 1970
  SURVEY OF UTILIZATION AND MANUFACTURE OF HEAVY COLUMNS, Fritz
  Engineering Laboratory Report No. 337.7, Lehigh University, Bethlehem, Pa. (9)
Blakey, F. A. and Beresford, F. D., 1965
  STRIPPING OF FORMWORK FOR CONCRETE IN BUILDINGS IN RELATION TO
  STRUCTURAL DESIGN, Civil Engineering Transactions, Institution of Engineers,
  Australia, Vol. CE7, No. 2, October, pp. 16–20. (5)
Bletzacker, E. W., 1966
  EFFECT OF STRUCTURAL RESTRAINT ON THE FIRE RESISTANCE OF
  PROTECTED STEEL BEAMS AND FLOOR AND ROOF ASSEMBLIES, Final
  Report, Building Research Laboratory, Ohio State University, pp. 246–266. (8A)
Blick, R. L., Peterson, F. and Winter, M. E., 1974
  PROPORTIONING AND CONTROLLING HIGH-STRENGTH CONCRETE, Propor-
  tioning Concrete Mixes, SP-46, ACI, Detroit, Mich., pp. 143–163. (9)
Blume, J. A., 1956
  PERIOD DETERMINATIONS AND OTHER EARTHQUAKE STUDIES OF A
  FIFTEEN-STORY BUILDING, Proceedings, 1st World Conference on Earthquake
  Engineering (Berkeley, Calif.). (6)
Blume, J. A., 1960a
  A RESERVE ENERGY TECHNIQUE FOR THE DESIGN AND RATING OF
  STRUCTURES IN THE INELASTIC RANGE, Proceedings, 2nd World Conference on
  Earthquake Engineering (Japan). (6)
Blume, J. A., 1960b
  STRUCTURAL DYNAMICS IN EARTHQUAKE-RESISTANT DESIGN, Journal of the
  Structural Division, ASCE, Vol. 86, No. ST4, Proc. Paper 1695, July 1958 with discussions
  ending September 1959; also in Transactions, ASCE, Vol. 125, pp. 1088–1139. (6)
Blume, J. A., 1967
  A STRUCTURAL-DYNAMIC ANALYSIS OF AN EARTHQUAKE DAMAGED
  FOURTEEN-STORY BUILDING, The Prince William Sound, Alaska, Earthquake of
  1964 and Aftershocks, Vol. II, Part A., U.S. Department of Commerce, Environmental
  Science Services Administration, Publication 10-3. (6)
Blume, J. A., 1968
  DYNAMIC CHARACTERISTICS OF MULTISTORY BUILDINGS, Journal of the
  Structural Division, ASCE, Vol. 94, No. ST2, Proc. Paper 5787, pp. 377–402. (6)

Blume, J. A., 1969a
RESPONSE OF HIGHRISE BUILDINGS TO GROUND MOTION FROM UNDER-GROUND NUCLEAR DETONATIONS, Bulletin, Seismological Society of America, Vol. 59, No. 6, pp. 2343–2370. (6)

Blume, J. A., 1969b
STRUCTURAL DYNAMICS OF CANTILEVER-TYPE BUILDINGS, Proceedings of the 4th World Conference on Earthquake Engineering (Santiago, Chile). (6)

Blume, J. A., 1970
THE MOTION AND DAMPING OF BUILDINGS RELATIVE TO SEISMIC RE-SPONSE SPECTRA, Bulletin, Seismological Society of America, Vol. 60, February, pp. 231–249. (6)

Blume, J. A., 1971
BUILDING COLUMNS UNDER STRONG EARTHQUAKE EXPOSURE, Journal of the Structural Division, ASCE, Vol. 97, No. ST9, Proc. Paper 8398, pp. 2351–2369. (6)

Blume, J. A., 1972
HIGHRISE BUILDING CHARACTERISTICS AND RESPONSES DETERMINED FROM NUCLEAR SEISMOLOGY, Bulletin, Seismological Society of America, Vol. 62. (6)

Blume, J. A., 1973
ELEMENTS OF A DYNAMICS—INELASTIC DESIGN CODE, Proceedings of the 5th World Conference on Earthquake Engineering (Italy). (6)

Blume, J., Newmark, N. and Corning, L. H., 1961
DESIGN OF MULTISTORY REINFORCED CONCRETE BUILDINGS FOR EARTH-QUAKE MOTIONS, Portland Cement Association, Chicago, Ill. (6)

Board of County Commissioners, 1974
THE SOUTH FLORIDA BUILDING CODE, Board of County Commissioners, Dade County, Florida, 1974 Edition, pp. 35-11 and 35-12. (9)

Bob, C., Furdui, C., Minaescu, A. and Rosu, C., 1975
THE QUALITY OF LIGHTWEIGHT AGGREGATES CONCRETE FOR THE WALLS OF BUILDINGS OVER 10 STORIES (Calitatea Betoanelor Usuoare De Granulit Turnate Prin Glisare In Diafragmele Blocurilor De Locuinte Cu P+10 Niveluri), Reinforced Concrete Tall Buildings (Constructii Inalte de Beton Armat), Vols. I & II, (Proceedings of Conference held in Iasi, Romania, October, 1975), Consiliul National al Inginerilor si Tehnicienilor, Iasi, Romania. (9)

Bohac, A., 1968
LIVE LOADS REDUCTION IN THE MAIN ELEMENTS DESIGN OF THE MULTI-STOREY INDUSTRIAL BUILDING (Zmenšování Nahodilého Zatížení Při Naýrhu Hlavních Částí 'Nosné Konstrukce Vícepodlažních Prúmyslových Budov), Building Research Institute, Prague, Czechoslovakia, Stavební Výzkum, No. 1, 2, 3. (5)

Bohac, A., 1971
FLOOR LOADINGS IN RETAIL PREMISES—THE RESULTS OF A SURVEY, CP 15/71, Building Research Establishment, Garston, England, September. (5)

Bohac, A., 1973
THE UNIFORM LIVE LOAD REDUCTION FOR THE DESIGN OF THE MAIN STRUCTURAL ELEMENTS, Proceedings of the National Conference on Tall Buildings (Bratislava, Czechoslovakia, April), Lehigh University, Bethlehem, Pa., pp. 249–256. (5)

Bohac, A., 1976
FLOOR LOADINGS IN DOMESTIC BUILDINGS—THE RESULTS OF A SURVEY, CP -/76, Building Research Establishment, Garston, England. (5)

Bolotin, V. V., 1962
ON COMBINATIONS OF RANDOM LOADINGS ACTING ON A STRUCTURE (in Russian), Stroitel'naya Mekhanika i Raschet Sooruzheniy, USSR, No. 2. (10)

Bolotin, V. V., 1965
STATISTICAL METHODS IN STRUCTURAL MECHANICS (in Russian), 2nd ed., Moscow, USSR. (10)

Bolotin, V. V., 1971
APPLICATION OF METHODS OF PROBABILITY THEORY AND OF RELIABILITY THEORY IN STRUCTURAL DESIGN (in Russian), Stroyizdat, Moscow, USSR. (10)

Bolotin, V. V., Goldenblat, I. I. and Korchinskiy, I. L., 1964
MODERN PROBLEMS OF STRUCTURAL MECHANICS (in Russian), Moscow, USSR. (10)

Boner, E., 1973
FIRE PROTECTION IN TALL BUILDINGS (Brandschutz bei Hochhaüsern), Proceedings of Tall Buildings Conference (Zürich, Switzerland, October), SIA-Fachgruppen für Bruckenbau und Hochbau (FBH) und für Architektur (FGA), Zürich, Switzerland. (8A)

Bongard, W., 1963
BURNING TEST FOR PROTECTED STEEL STRUCTURES (Brandversuche mit Aussenstutzen aus Stahl), Der Stahlbau, May. (8A)

Bono, J. A., 1969
NEW CRITERIA FOR FIRE ENDURANCE TEST, Underwriters Laboratories, Inc., Chicago, Ill. (8A)

Botizan, P., 1971
COMPUTATION BY TAKABEYA METHOD OF IRREGULAR BUILDING FRAMES WITH VARIABLE CROSS-SECTIONAL MEMBERS SUBJECTED TO WIND AND EARTHQUAKE FORCES (Le calcul des cadres étages irreguliers et à barres de section variable soumis à l'action du vent et aux forces sismiques par la méthode Takabeya), 3rd International Conference on Wind Effects on Buildings and Structures (Tokyo, Japan), Part III, pp. 579–588. (7)

Bowes, P. C. and Field, P., 1969
THE ASSESSMENT OF SMOKE PRODUCTION BY BUILDING MATERIALS IN FIRES, Fire Research Note No. 749, Joint Fires Research Organization. (8A)

Bradley, J. W. and McCauley, R. B., 1964
EFFECTS OF POROSITY ON QUENCHED AND TEMPERED STEEL, Welding Journal, Vol. 43, No. 9, pp. 408-s–414-s. (9)

Brearley, A. W. and Brearley, H., 1918
INGOTS AND INGOT MOULDS, Longmans, Green & Co., London, England. (9)

Bredsdorff, P., Spøhr, H. and Feilberg Hansen, K., undated
THE PERFORMANCE OF STRUCTURAL DESIGN BY CHARACTERISTIC VALUES, Danish Building Research Institute, Copenhagen, Denmark. (10)

Briggs, G. A., 1969
PLUME RISE, AEC Critical Review Series, TID-25075, Clearinghouse for Federal Scientific and Technical Information, Springfield, Va., p. 81. (7)

British Fire Protection Systems Association Ltd., 1973
REPORT ON THE PERFORMANCE OF FIRE ALARM SYSTEMS IN BRITAIN, British Fire Protection Systems Association, Ltd., London, England. (8A)

Brode, H. L., 1968
REVIEW OF NUCLEAR WEAPONS EFFECTS, Annual Review of Nuclear Science, Vol. 18, pp. 153–202. (8B)

Brooks, R. R., 1973
A STUDY OF WIND STRUCTURES IN AN URBAN ENVIRONMENT, Meteorological Study No. 27, Australian Bureau of Meteorology. (7)

Brooks, R. R. and Spillane, K. T., 1968
THE EFFECT OF AVERAGING TIME AND SAMPLE DURATION ON ESTIMATION AND MEASUREMENT OF MAXIMUM WIND GUST, Journal of Applied Meteorology, Vol. 7, No. 4, pp. 567–574. (7)

Brown, H. and Maryon, J., 1975
THE TALL BUILDINGS EXPERIENCE: PERCEPTION OF WIND MOVEMENTS, Building Materials, Vol. 18, No. 2. (7)

Brown, W. G., 1969
A LOAD DURATION THEORY FOR GLASS DESIGN, Proceedings of the Annual Meeting of the International Committee on Glass (Toronto, Canada), pp. 75–79 (Research paper 508, Division of Building Research, Ottawa, Canada, 1972). (7)

Brozzetti, J., Alpsten, G. A. and Tall, L., 1970
RESIDUAL STRESSES IN A HEAVY ROLLED SHAPE 14WF730, Fritz Engineering Laboratory Report No. 337.10, Lehigh University, Bethlehem, Pa. (9)

Brozzetti, J., Alpsten, G. A. and Tall, L., 1971
WELDING PARAMETERS, THICK PLATES, AND COLUMN STRENGTH, Welding Journal, Vol. 50, No. 8, pp. 332-s–342-s. (9)

Bubnov, S., 1973
DAMAGE EVALUATION, Planning and Design of Tall Buildings, Proceedings of the 1972 ASCE-IABSE International Conference, Vol. 1b, ASCE, New York, pp. 247–254. (6)

Building Services Engineer, 1971
SMOKE TESTS IN THE PRESSURIZED STAIRS AND LOBBIES OF A 26-STORY
OFFICE BUILDING, *Building Services Engineer*, Vol. 39, December. (8A)

Burdekin, F. M., 1971
LAMELLAR TEARING IN BRIDGE GIRDERS—A CASE HISTORY, *Metal Construction and British Welding Journal*, Vol. 3, No. 5, May, pp. 205–209. (9)

Burnett, E. F. P., Somes, N. F. and Leyendecker, E. V., 1973
RESIDENTIAL BUILDINGS AND GAS-RELATED EXPLOSIONS, NBSIR 73-208,
National Bureau of Standards, Washington, D.C. (8B)

Bustamante, J. I., 1965
SEISMIC SHEARS AND OVERTURNING MOMENTS IN BUILDINGS, Proceedings,
3rd World Conference on Earthquake Engineering (Auckland and Wellington, New
Zealand), pp. 4.144–4.160. (10)

Butcher, E. G. and Hall, M. A., 1971
SMOKE TESTS IN THE LAW COURTS BUILDING, Fire Research Note No. 889, Joint
Fire Research Organization, HMSO, London, England. (8A)

Butcher, E. G., Chitty, T. B. and Ashton, L. A., 1966
THE TEMPERATURE ATTAINED BY STEEL IN BUILDING FIRES, Fire Research
Technical Paper No. 15, HMSO, London, England. (8A)

Butcher, E. G., Fardell, P. J. and Clarke, J. J., 1968
PRESSURISATION AS A MEANS OF CONTROLLING THE MOVEMENT OF
SMOKE AND TOXIC GASES ON ESCAPE ROUTES, Fire Research Note No. 704,
Joint Fires Research Organization, London, England. (8A)

Butcher, E. G., Langdon-Thomas, G. J. and Bedford, G. K., 1968
FIRE AND CAR-PARK BUILDINGS, Fire Note No. 10, HMSO, London, England. (8A)

Butlin, R. N., 1975
A REVIEW OF INFORMATION ON EXPERIMENTS CONCERNING THE VENT-
ING OF GAS EXPLOSIONS IN BUILDINGS, Fire Research Note No. 1026, Fire
Research Station, Borehamwood, England. (8B)

Butlin, R. N. and Tonkin, P. S., 1974
PRESSURES PRODUCED BY GAS EXPLOSIONS IN A VENTED COMPARTMENT,
Fire Research Note No. 1019, Fire Research Station, Borehamwood, England. (8B)

Button, D. A., 1975
CONSIDERATIONS OF ENERGY, ENVIRONMENT AND STRUCTURE IN WIN-
DOW DESIGN, Proceedings of the 35th National/Regional Conference (South Africa,
November). (7)

CABO, 1978
PCI PLANT CERTIFICATION PROGRAM, National Research Board Report No.
NRB-105, prepared by International Conference of Building Officials, Council of
American Building Officials, Washington, D.C. (9)

CCMTC, 1975
RECOMMENDED TESTING PROCEDURES FOR CONCRETE MASONRY UNITS,
PRISMS, GROUT, AND MORTAR, California Concrete Masonry Technical Com-
mittee, Los Angeles, Calif. (9)

CEB, 1964
RECOMMENDATIONS FOR AN INTERNATIONAL CODE OF PRACTICE FOR
REINFORCED CONCRETE, Comité Européen du Béton; translated by American
Concrete Institute, Detroit, Mich., and Cement and Concrete Association, London,
England. (10)

CEB, 1969
GENERAL PRINCIPLES FOR THE VERIFICATION OF SAFETY, Draft for ISO/
TC/90, Comité Européen du Béton, 13th plenary session (Delft, The Netherlands,
September). (10)

CIB, 1978
REPORT ON STRUCTURAL SAFETY, Mémoires C.E.R.E.S., CIB Working Commission
W9, No. 54, Centre d'Etudes de Recherches et d'Essais Scientifiques du Génie Civil,
University of Liége, Belgium. October. (10)

CIDECT, 1970
CONCRETE FILLED HOLLOW SECTION COLUMNS, Monograph No. 1, International
Committee for the Development and Study of Tubular Structures, London, England. (8A)

CIRIA 1971
THE MODERN DESIGN OF WIND SENSITIVE STRUCTURES, Proceedings of the CIRIA Seminar (London, England). (7)

CTICM, 1975
FORECASTING FIRE EFFECTS ON STEEL STRUCTURES (Prévision par le calcul du comportement au feu des structures en acier), CTICM, Puteaux, France, September. (8A)

Cahn, D. S., Phillips, J. C., Ishai, O. and Aroni, S., 1973
DURABILITY OF FIBER GLASS-PORTLAND CEMENT COMPOSITES, *ACI Journal*, American Concrete Institute, Detroit, Mich., Vol. 70, pp. 187–189 (translated into Italian and published in *Il Calcestruzzo Preconfenzionato*, No. 30, July 1974). (9)

Calavera, J., 1975
INFLUENCE OF STRENGTH VARIATIONS OF MATERIALS AND DIMENSION-AL VARIATIONS OF REINFORCED CONCRETE MEMBERS UPON THEIR LOAD BEARING CAPACITY, Monograph No. 324, Instituto Eduardo Torroja, Madrid, Spain. (9)

Calegari, D. D., 1973
ELECTROLYTIC CORROSION IN STEEL FRAMES OF REINFORCED AND PRE-STRESSED CONCRETE (Corrosao Eletrolitica nas Armaduras de Aco dos Concretos Armado e Protendido), South American Regional Conference on Tall Buildings (Porto Alegre, Brazil, December), Vols. I and II, Sociedade de Engenharia do Rio Grande do Sul, Porto Alegre, Brazil, pp. 297–305 (in Portuguese). (9)

California Institute of Technology, 1972
ANALYSIS OF STRONG MOTION EARTHQUAKE ACCELEROGRAMS, EERL 72-80, Vol. III, Part A. (6)

Capacete, J. L. and Martin, I., 1972
PROPOSED REVISION OF ACI605-69: RECOMMENDED PRACTICE FOR HOT WEATHER CONCRETING, *ACI Journal*, American Concrete Institute, Vol. 69, No. 1, discussion 68-45, pp. 70–71. (9)

Carmona, J. S., 1973
EARTHQUAKE EFFECTS ON THE MASONRY OF MULTISTORY BUILDINGS, Planning and Design of Tall Buildings, Proceedings of the 1972 ASCE-IABSE International Conference, Vol. 1b, ASCE, New York, pp. 284–290. (6)

Cartwright, D. W. and Longuet-Higgins, M. S., 1956
THE STATISTICAL DISTRIBUTION OF THE MAXIMA OF A RANDOM FUNCTION, *Proceedings of the Royal Society*, London, England, Vol. A237, pp. 212–232. (7)

Carydis, P. and Ermopoulos, J., 1975
INFLUENCE OF THE DISCONTINUITY ALONG THE HEIGHT OF MULTISTORY FRAMES ON THEIR DYNAMIC AND SEISMIC RESPONSE, Proceedings of Hellenic Conference on Tall Buildings, (Athens, Greece, October) Technical Chamber of Greece, Athens, Greece. (6)

Carydis, P. G. and Sbokos, J. P., 1975
RESPONSE SPECTRA OF GREEK STRONG MOTION, Proceedings of Hellenic Conference on Tall Buildings, (Athens, Greece, October), Technical Chamber of Greece, Athens, Greece. (6)

Casciati, F. and Sacchi, G., 1973
ON THE RELIABILITY THEORY OF THE STRUCTURES, *Meccanica*, Vol. 9, No. 4. (10)

Castellani, A., 1973
OSCILLATIONS OF A TALL BUILDING, DUE TO OUT OF PHASE SEISMIC MOTIONS ALONG ITS FOUNDATIONS, Proceedings of Italian National Conference on Tall Buildings, (Sorrento, Italy, October), Collegio dei Tecnici dell' Acciaio, Milan, Italy, pp. 51–63. (6)

Cavoulakos, N. B., 1975
FIRE PROTECTION OF TALL BUILDINGS, Proceedings of Hellenic Conference on Tall Buildings, (Athens, Greece, October), Technical Chamber of Greece, Athens, Greece. (8A)

Cermak, J. E., 1965
SIMULATION OF ATMOSPHERIC MOTION BY WIND TUNNEL FLOW, Technical Report CER66, Colorado State University, Fort Collins, Colo. (7)

Cermak, J. E., 1970
SEPARATION-INDUCED PRESSURE FLUCTUATIONS ON BUILDINGS, Proceedings, Seminar on Wind Load on Structures, University of Hawaii, pp. 55–70. (7)

Cermak, J. E., 1971a
LABORATORY SIMULATION OF ATMOSPHERIC BOUNDARY LAYER, *Journal*, AIAA, Vol. 9, No. 9. (7)
Cermak, J. E., 1971b
WIND LOADING AND WIND EFFECTS, Proceedings of 5th Regional Conference (Chicago, Ill.), Lehigh University, Bethlehem, Pa., pp. 49–52. (7)
Cermak, J. E., 1975
APPLICATION OF FLUID MECHANICS TO WIND ENGINEERING, Freeman Scholar Lecture, *Journal of Fluid Engineering*, ASME, Vol. 97, No. 1. (7)
Cermak, J. E. and Melbourne, W. H., 1973
WIND EFFECTS ON TALL BUILDINGS—AREAS FOR RESEARCH, Planning and Design of Tall Buildings, Proceedings of the 1972 ASCE-IABSE International Conference, Vol. 1b, ASCE, New York, pp. 435–440. (7)
Cermak, J. E. and Sadeh, W. Z., 1971
PRESSURE FLUCTUATIONS ON BUILDINGS, Proceedings of 3rd International Conference on Wind Effects on Buildings and Structures (Tokyo, Japan), pp. 189–198. (7)
Cermak, J. E., Peterka, J. and Dreher, K. J., 1974
WIND PRESSURES ON A HOUSE ROOF, Proceedings, 2nd USA/Japan Research Seminar on Wind Effects on Structures, University of Tokyo Press, Japan. (7)
Cermak, J. E., Sadeh, W. Z. and Hsi, G., 1969
FLUCTUATING MOMENTS ON TALL BUILDINGS PRODUCED BY WIND LOADING, Proceedings of Technical Meeting on Wind Loads on Buildings and Structures, Buildings Science Series No. 30, National Bureau of Standards, Gaithersburg, Md. (7)
Chakravorty, M. K., Nelson, M. F. and Whitman, R. V., 1971
APPROXIMATE ANALYSIS OF 3-DOF MODEL FOR SOIL-STRUCTURE INTERACTION, Report No. 5, Co-operative Research with the National University of Mexico, Department of Civil Engineering, Massachusetts Institute of Technology, Cambridge, Mass. (6)
Cham, T. S., 1974
WIND TUNNEL INVESTIGATION ON THE FLOOD-LIT TOWER OF THE SINGAPORE NATIONAL STADIUM, Proceedings of the 25th National/Regional Conference on Tall Buildings (Kuala Lumpur, Malaysia), p. 8-1. (7)
Chang, C. C., 1971a
TORNADO WIND EFFECTS ON BUILDINGS AND STRUCTURES WITH LABORATORY SIMULATION, Proceedings of the 3rd International Conference on Wind Effects on Buildings and Structures (Tokyo, Japan), Part II, pp. 231–240. (7)
Chang, C. C., 1971b
WHAT WE LEARNED FROM THE TORNADO OF LUBBOCK, TEXAS, USA, MAY 11, 1970, Proceedings of the 3rd International Conference on Wind Effects on Buildings and Structures (Tokyo, Japan), Part III, pp. 471–480. (7)
Chang, F. K., 1974
SOLUTIONS TO THE WIND MOTION PROBLEM IN TALL BUILDING DESIGN, Proceedings, Regional Conference on Tall Buildings (Bangkok, Thailand), pp. 583–588. (7)
Chapeau, W., 1978
LAMELLAR TEARING, IABSE Surveys S-6/78, IABSE, Zürich, Switzerland, August. (9)
Chen, P. W., 1973
DESIGN DEVELOPMENTS—NORTH AND SOUTH AMERICA, Planning and Design of Tall Buildings, Proceedings of the 1972 ASCE-IASBE International Conference, Vol. 1b, ASCE, New York, pp. 423–430. (7)
Chen, P. W. and Robertson, L. E., 1972
HUMAN PERCEPTION THRESHOLDS OF HORIZONTAL MOTION, *Journal of the Structural Division*, ASCE, Vol. 98, No. ST8, Proc. Paper 9142, pp. 1681–1695. (7)
Chen, W. F. and Mehta, H. C., 1975
STRUCTURAL USE OF SULFUR FOR IMPREGNATION OF BUILDING MATERIALS, Proceedings of Pan-Pacific Tall Buildings Conference, (Honolulu, Hawaii, January), University of Hawaii, Honolulu, Hawaii, pp. 123–135. (9)
Cheng, E. D. H. and Chiu, A. N. L., 1974
TOPOGRAPHICAL EFFECTS ON WIND PATTERNS, Proceedings, 2nd USA/Japan Research Seminar on Wind Effects on Structures, University of Tokyo Press, Japan. (7)

Chiu, A. N. L., 1974
WIND EFFECTS ON TALL BUILDINGS, Proceedings, 25th National/Regional Conference (Kuala Lumpur, Malaysia, December), Institution of Engineers, Kuala Lumpur, Malaysia, pp. 8.6–8.11. (7)

Chiu, A. N. L. and Hongladaromp, T., 1974
WIND FORCES ON HIGH-RISE BUILDINGS AND COMMENTS, Proceedings, 26th Regional Conference on High-Rise Housing Workshop (Singapore, December). (7)

Chiu, A. N. L. and Shimabukuro, M. T., 1974
SIMULATING WIND RECORDS FOR DYNAMIC RESPONSE ANALYSIS, Proceedings, 22nd National/Regional Conference (Bangkok, Thailand), pp. 479–489. (7)

Chiu, A. N. L., Santo, P. T. and Taoka, G. T., 1974
STRUCTURE RESPONSE TO WIND FORCES, Proceedings, 22nd National/Regional Conference on Tall Buildings (Bangkok, Thailand, January), Asian Institute of Technology, Bangkok, Thailand, pp. 589–603. (7)

Choi Cheong Chuen, E., 1971
CORRELATION AND SPECTRAL FUNCTIONS OF ATMOSPHERIC TURBULENCE, Proceedings of the 3rd International Conference on Wind Effects on Buildings and Structures (Tokyo, Japan), Paper 1.5. (7)

Choi Cheong Chuen, E., 1976
ESTIMATION OF DESIGN WIND SPEEDS IN HONG KONG, Proceedings of the 2nd Tall Buildings Conference (Hong Kong, September). (7)

Christian, W. J. and Waterman, T. E., 1970
FIRE BEHAVIOR OF INTERIOR FINISH MATERIALS, Fire Technology, Vol. 6, No. 2, Society of Fire Protection Engineers, Boston, Mass., pp. 165–178. (8A)

Churchman, C. W., 1968
CHALLENGE TO REASON, McGraw-Hill Book Co., Inc., New York, N.Y. (10)

Ciesielski, R., 1972a
DYNAMICAL PROBLEMS IN THE DESIGN OF TALL BUILDINGS, Proceedings of the National Conference on Tall Buildings (Warsaw, Poland, November), Vol. 1, Warsaw Technical University, Polish Group of IABSE, Warsaw, Poland, pp. 313–330. (6, 7)

Ciesielski, R., 1972b
DYNAMIC CHARACTERISTICS OF TALL BUILDINGS AS DETERMINED BY THE MEASUREMENTS OF VIBRATIONS DUE TO WEAK WIND GUSTS, Proceedings of the 7th National/Regional Conference (Warsaw, Poland), pp. 83–96. (7)

Ciongradi, I., Ungureanu, N. and Ciongradi, C., 1975
THE EFFECT OF INTERACTION BETWEEN STRUCTURE, FOUNDATION AND SOIL UPON THE STANDARD EARTHQUAKE RESPONSE OF REINFORCED CONCRETE TALL BUILDINGS (Efectul Conlucrarii Dintre Structura, Fundatie si Teren Asupraraspunsului Seismic Normat al Cladirilor Inalte de Beton Armat), Reinforced Concrete Tall Buildings, Proceedings of Conference (Iasi, Romania, October), Vol. 1, Consiliul National al Inginerilor si Tehnicienilor, Iasi, Romania, pp. 73–83. (6)

Claiborne, G. R., 1971
AUTOMATIC SPRINKLER—IT IS, IT ISN'T, The Building Official and Code Administrator, Building Officials and Code Administrators International, Inc., Chicago, Ill., June. (8A)

Claiborne, G. R. and Wahl, L., 1973
REQUIREMENT FOR FIRE PROTECTION AND SAFETY IN TALL BUILDINGS, Planning and Design of Tall Buildings, Proceedings of the 1972 ASCE-IABSE International Conference, Vol. 1b, ASCE, New York, pp. 541–568. (8A)

Clarkson, B. L. and Mayes, W. H., 1972
SONIC-BOOM-INDUCED BUILDING STRUCTURE RESPONSES INCLUDING DAMAGE, Journal, Acoustic Society of America, Vol. 51, pp. 742–757. (8B)

Clough, R., 1955
ON THE IMPORTANCE OF HIGHER MODES OF VIBRATION IN THE EARTHQUAKE RESPONSE OF A TALL BUILDING, Bulletin, Seismological Society of America, Vol. 45, No. 4. (6)

Clough, R. W. and Chopra, A. A., 1966
EARTHQUAKE STRESS ANALYSIS IN EARTH DAMS, Journal of the Engineering Mechanics Division, ASCE, Vol. 92, No. EM2, Proc. Paper 4793, pp. 197–212. (6)

Clough, R. W., King, I. P. and Wilson, E. L., 1963
LARGE CAPACITY MULTISTORY FRAME ANALYSIS PROGRAMS, *Journal of the Structural Division*, ASCE, Vol. 89, No. ST4, Proc. Paper 3592, pp. 179–204. (6)

Clough, R. W., King, I. P. and Wilson, E. L., 1964
STRUCTURAL ANALYSIS OF MULTISTORY BUILDINGS, *Journal of the Structural Division*, ASCE, Vol. 90, No. ST3, Proc. Paper 3925, pp. 19–34. (6)

Clough, R. W., Rea, D., Tang, D. and Watabe, M., 1973
EARTHQUAKE SIMULATOR TEST OF A THREE STORY STEEL FRAME STRUC-TURE, Proceedings of the 5th World Conference on Earthquake Engineering (Rome, Italy), Vol. I, Edigraf, Rome, Italy. (6)

Coe, R. F., 1971
CONFIDENCE IN WELDED CONSTRUCTION, *Australian Welding Journal*, October, p. 27. (9)

Cohen, E., Vellozzi, J. and Thom, H. C. S., 1967
PROPOSED AMERICAN STANDARD BUILDING CODE REQUIREMENTS FOR MINIMUM DESIGN WIND LOADS, Proceedings of the International Research Seminar on Wind Effects on Buildings and Structures (Ottawa, Canada), pp. 163–166. (7)

Cohn, M. Z. and Parimi, S. R., 1971
MULTI-CRITERIA PROBABILISTIC STRUCTURAL DESIGN, Report No. 84, Solid Mechanics Division, University of Waterloo, Ont., Canada. (10)

Colell, D., 1973
SOME SAFETY MEASURES AGAINST FIRES IN VERY HIGH BUILDINGS (Algunas Medidas de Protection Contra Incendios en Edificios De Gran Altura), Proceedings of Regional Conference on Tall Buildings, (Madrid, Spain, September), Tipografia Artistica, Madrid, Spain. (8A)

Colin, P. E. and D'have, R., 1963
EXECUTION OF TESTS ON MODELS OF BUILDINGS CARRIED OUT IN AN AERODYNAMIC TUNNEL WITH RELATION TO MEASUREMENTS MADE ON REAL STRUCTURES (Execution en tunnel aerodynamique d'essais sur maquettes de bâtiments en rapport avec les mesures faites sur constructions réelles), Proceedings of the International Conference on Wind Effects on Buildings and Structures (NPL, Teddingt-on, England), pp. 255–281. (7)

Concrete and Masonry Industry, 1975
FIRE SAFETY IN HIGH-RISE BUILDINGS, Concrete and Masonry Industry Position Statement, Concrete Industry Board, Inc., New York, October. (8A)

Concrete Construction, 1976
WATER TOWER PLACE—HIGH STRENGTH CONCRETE, *Concrete Construction*, March, pp. 102–104. (9)

Cook, N. J., 1973
ON SIMULATING THE LOWER THIRD OF THE URBAN ADIABATIC BOUND-ARY LAYER IN A WIND TUNNEL, *Atmospheric Environment*, Pergamon Press, London, England, Vol. 7, pp. 691–705. (7)

Cook, N. J., 1975
A BOUNDARY LAYER WIND TUNNEL FOR BUILDING AERODYNAMICS, *Journal of Industrial Aerodynamics*, Vol. 1, No. 1. (7)

Cook, N. J. and Redfearn, D., 1975
CALIBRATION AND USE OF HOT-WIRE PROBE FOR HIGHLY TURBULENT AND REVERSING FLOWS, *Journal of Industrial Aerodynamics*, Vol. 1, No. 3. (7)

Corke, T. C., Nagib, H. M. and Tan-Atichat, J., 1975
FLOW NEAR A MODEL OF A BUILDING IN SIMULATED ATMOSPHERIC SURFACE LAYERS GENERATED BY THE COUNTER-JET TECHNIQUE, Pro-ceedings of the 4th International Conference on Wind Effects on Buildings and Structures (London, England), University of Cambridge Press, Cambridge, England. (7)

Cornell, C. A., 1967
BOUNDS ON THE RELIABILITY OF STRUCTURAL SYSTEMS, *Journal of the Structural Division*, ASCE, Vol. 93, No. ST1, Proc. Paper 5096, p. 171. (10)

Cornell, C. A., 1969a
STRUCTURAL SAFETY SPECIFICATIONS BASED ON SECOND-MOMENT RE-LIABILITY ANALYSIS, presented at IABSE International Symposium on Concepts of Safety of Structures and Methods of Analysis (London, England, September), Vol. 4, pp. 235–245. (10)

Cornell, C. A., 1969b
A PROBABILITY-BASED STRUCTURAL CODE, *ACI Journal*, American Concrete Institute, Vol. 66, No. 12. (8A, 10)

Cornell, C. A., 1969c
BAYESIAN STATISTICAL THEORY AND RELIABILITY-BASED DESIGN, International Conference on Structural Safety and Reliability of Engineering Structures (Washington, D.C.). (10)

Cornell, C. A., 1970a
FIRST ORDER RELIABILITY THEORY OF STRUCTURAL DESIGN, *Structural Reliability and Codified Design*, N. C. Lind, ed., University of Waterloo Press, Waterloo, Ont., Canada. (10)

Cornell, C. A., 1970b
PROBABILISTIC ANALYSIS OF DAMAGE TO STRUCTURES UNDER SEISMIC LOADS, *Dynamic Waves in Civil Engineering*, Proceedings of a Conference (Swansea, Wales, July), John Wiley and Sons, England. (6)

Cornell, C. A., 1972
IMPLEMENTING PROBABILITY-BASED STRUCTURAL CODES, Probabilistic Design of Reinforced Concrete Building, Special Publication 31, American Concrete Institute, Detroit, Mich. (10)

Cornell, C. A., 1973
THEME REPORT: STRUCTURAL SAFETY AND PROBABILISTIC METHODS, Planning and Design of Tall Buildings, Proceedings of the ASCE-IABSE International Conference, Vol. 1b, ASCE, New York, pp. 911–918. (10)

Correale, W. H., DeCicco, P. R. and Cresci, R. J., 1973
STAIR PRESSURIZATION FOR FIRE PROTECTION, *The Military Engineer*, Vol. 65, No. 427, pp. 318–322. (8A)

Coull, A. and Subedi, N. K., 1971
HULL-CORE STRUCTURES SUBJECTED TO LATERAL FORCES, Proceedings of the 3rd International Conference on Wind Effects on Buildings and Structures (Tokyo, Japan), Part III, pp. 569–578. (7)

Counihan, J., 1969
AN IMPROVED METHOD OF SIMULATING AN ATMOSPHERIC BOUNDARY LAYER IN A WIND TUNNEL, *Atmospheric Environment*, Vol. 3, pp. 197–214. (7)

Counihan, J., 1975
ADIABATIC ATMOSPHERIC BOUNDARY LAYERS: A REVIEW AND ANALYSIS OF DATA FROM THE PERIOD 1880–1972, *Atmospheric Environment*, Vol. 9, pp. 871–905.

Coyle, D. C., 1931
MEASURING THE BEHAVIOUR OF TALL BUILDINGS, *Engineering News-Record*, pp. 310–313. (7)

Crandall, S. H., ed., 1958
RANDOM VIBRATION, Vol. 1, Technology Press, Cambridge, Mass. (10)

Crandall, S. H., ed., 1963
RANDOM VIBRATION, Vol. 2, Technology Press, Cambridge, Mass. (10)

Crist, R. A. and Shaver, J. R., 1976
DEFLECTION PERFORMANCE CRITERIA FOR FLOORS, Technical Note 900, National Bureau of Standards, U.S. Department of Commerce, Washington, D.C. (5)

Csanady, G. T., 1973
TURBULENT DIFFUSION IN THE ENVIRONMENT, D. Reidel Publishing Co., p. 248. (7)

Cubbage, P. A. and Marshall, M. R., 1973
PRESSURES GENERATED BY EXPLOSIONS OF GAS-AIR MIXTURES IN VENTED ENCLOSURES, Communication 926, 39th Autumn Research Meeting, Institution of Gas Engineers, London, England. (8B)

Cubbage, P. A. and Simmonds, W. A., 1955
AN INVESTIGATION OF EXPLOSION RELIEFS FOR INDUSTRIAL DRYING OVENS: 1—TOP RELIEFS IN BOX OVENS, Gas Council Research Communication GC23, The Gas Council, London, England. (8B)

Culver, C. C., 1976
SURVEY RESULTS FOR FIRE LOADS AND LIVE LOADS IN OFFICE BUILDINGS, NBS Building Science Series 85, National Bureau of Standards, U.S. Department of Commerce, Washington, D.C., pp. 1–14, 125–126. (5)

DIN, 1973a
STRUCTURAL STEELS—QUALITY SPECIFICATIONS (Allgemeine Baustahle —Gütevorschriften), DIN 17 100, Deutsches Institut für Normung, Berlin, Germany. (9)
DIN, undated a
TENSILE TESTING—CONCEPTS, SYMBOLS (Augversuch-Begriffe, Zeichen), DIN 50 145, Deutsches Institut für Normung, Berlin, Germany. (9)
DIN, 1973b
TESTING OF METALLIC MATERIALS (Prufung Metallischer Verkstoffe), DIN 50 146, Deutsches Institut für Normung, Berlin, Germany. (9)
Daddi, I. and Mazzolani, F. M., 1972
EXPERIMENTAL DETERMINATION OF STRUCTURAL IMPERFECTIONS IN STEEL H-SHAPES (Determinazione Sperimentale delle Imperfezioni Strutturali nei Profilati in Acciaio), *Costruzioni Metalliche*, No. 5, Milan, Italy. (9)
Dahlin, O. and Alpsten, G. A., 1976
DIMENSIONAL DEVIATIONS OF MULTI-STORY STEEL FRAMES (Mattavvikelser vid Flervanings Stalstommar), Proceedings of Nordic Research Conference for Steel Construction (Helsinki, Finland, August). (9)
Dalgliesh, W. A., 1969a
DIGITAL DATA ACQUISITION SYSTEM FOR MEASURING WIND EFFECTS OF TALL BUILDINGS, Special Technical Note 533, March. (7)
Dalgliesh, W. A., 1969b
EXPERIENCE WITH WIND PRESSURE MEASUREMENTS ON A FULL-SCALE BUILDING, Proceedings of the Technical Meeting Concerning Wind Loads on Buildings and Structures (NBS, Gaithersburg, Md.), Building Science Series 30. (7)
Dalgliesh, W. A., 1970
WIND PRESSURE MEASUREMENTS ON FULL SCALE BUILDINGS, Proceedings of the Symposium at Northwestern University (Evanston, Ill.) (7)
Dalgliesh, W. A., 1971
STATISTICAL TREATMENT OF PEAK GUSTS ON CLADDING, *Journal of the Structural Division*, ASCE, Vol. 97, No. ST9, Proc. Paper 8356, pp. 2173–2187. (7)
Dalgliesh, W. A., 1974
WIND LOADS FOR GLASS DESIGN, Proceedings of the 2nd USA/Japan Research Seminar on Wind Effects on Structures, University of Tokyo Press. (7)
Dalgliesh, W. A., 1975
COMPARISON OF MODE/FULL-SCALE WIND PRESSURES ON A HIGH-RISE BUILDING, *Journal of Industrial Aerodynamics*, Vol. 1, No. 1. (7)
Dalgliesh, W. A. and Marshall, R. D., 1973
RESEARCH REVIEW—NORTH AND SOUTH AMERICA, Planning and Design of Tall Buildings, Proceedings of the 1972 ASCE-IABSE International Conference, Vol. 1b, ASCE, New York, pp. 383–392. (7)
Dalgliesh, W. A., Wright, W. and Schriever, W. R., 1967
WIND PRESSURE MEASUREMENTS ON A FULL-SCALE HIGH-RISE OFFICE BUILDING, Proceedings of the International Research Seminar on Wind Effects on Buildings and Structures, (Ottawa, Canada, September), DBR Research Paper No. 379, (NRC 10414). (7)
Da Rocha, A., 1973
ULTIMATE STRENGTH ANALYSIS OF TALL BUILDINGS SUBJECTED TO WIND FORCES (Calculo da acao do vento nos edificios altos pelo metodo de rotura), South American Regional Conference on Tall Buildings (Porto Alegre, Brazil), Vol. II. (7)
Davenport, A. G., 1960
A RATIONALE FOR THE DETERMINATION OF BASIC DESIGN WIND VELOCITIES, *Journal of the Structural Division*, ASCE, Vol. 86, No. ST5, Proc. Paper 2476, pp. 39–68. (7)

Davenport, A. G., 1961a
THE APPLICATION OF STATISTICAL CONCEPTS TO THE WIND LOADING OF
STRUCTURES, *Proceedings*, Institution of Civil Engineers, London, England, Vol. 19,
pp. 449–472. (7, 10)
Davenport, A. G., 1961b
THE SPECTRUM OF HORIZONTAL GUSTINESS NEAR THE GROUND IN HIGH
WINDS, *Quarterly Journal of the Royal Meteorological Society*, Vol. 87, pp. 194–211. (7)
Davenport, A. G., 1962
THE RESPONSE OF SLENDER LINE-LIKE STRUCTURES TO GUSTY WIND,
Proceedings, Institution of Civil Engineers, London, England, Vol. 23, pp. 389–408. (7)
Davenport, A. G., 1963a
THE RELATIONSHIP OF WIND STRUCTURE TO WIND LOADING, Proceedings of
the International Conference on Wind Loads on Buildings and Structures, (NPL,
Teddington, England), pp. 54–111. (7)
Davenport, A. G., 1963b
BUFFET OF STRUCTURES BY GUSTS, Proceedings of the 1st International Symposium
on Wind Effects on Buildings and Structures (London, England), HMSO, London,
England (1965). (7)
Davenport, A. G., 1964
NOTE ON THE DISTRIBUTION OF THE LARGEST VALUE OF A RANDOM
FUNCTION WITH APPLICATION TO GUST LOADING, *Proceedings*, Institution of
Civil Engineers, London, England, Vol. 28, pp. 187–196. (7)
Davenport, A. G., 1966a
ESTIMATION OF REPEATED LOADS ON STRUCTURES WITH APPLICATION TO
WIND INDUCED FATIGUE AND OVERLOAD, Proceedings of the RILEM Inter-
national Symposium on Effects of Repeated Loading of Materials and Structures (Mexico
City, Mexico) (also appears in *Ingineria*, Vol. 38, No. 171, 1968). (7)
Davenport, A. G., 1966b
THE TREATMENT OF WIND LOADING ON TALL BUILDINGS, Symposium on Tall
Buildings (University of Southampton, England), Pergamon Press, Inc., N.Y. (7, 10)
Davenport, A. G., 1967a
THE DEPENDENCE OF WIND LOADS ON METEOROLOGICAL PARAMETERS,
Proceedings of the International Conference on Wind Loads on Buildings and Structures
(Ottawa, Canada), University of Toronto Press, Toronto, Canada, pp. 19–81. (7)
Davenport, A. G., 1967b
GUST LOADING FACTORS, *Journal of the Structural Division*, ASCE, Vol. 93, No. ST3,
Proc. Paper 5255, pp. 11–34. (7, 10)
Davenport, A. G., 1967c
THE APPLICATION OF THE BOUNDARY LAYER WIND TUNNEL TO THE
PREDICTION OF WIND LOADING, Proceedings of the International Seminar on
Wind Effects on Buildings and Structures (Ottawa, Canada). (7)
Davenport, A. G., 1967d
THE RELATIONSHIP OF METEOROLOGICAL FACTORS TO WIND LOADING,
Proceedings of the Symposium on Tall Buildings (University of Southampton, April
1966), A. Coull and B. S. Smith, eds., Pergamon Press, London, England. (7)
Davenport, A. G., 1970a
AN ANALYSIS OF WIND INDUCED BUILDING MOVEMENT AND COLUMN
STRAIN TAKEN AT THE JOHN HANCOCK CENTER (CHICAGO), BLWT-10-70,
University of Western Ontario, Ontario, Canada. (7)
Davenport, A. G., 1970b
WIND LOADING ON TALL BUILDINGS, Proceedings, Chicago Design Symposium on
Wind Effects on High-Rise Buildings (Northwestern University, Evanston, Ill., March), p.
139. (10)
Davenport, A. G., 1971a
ON THE STATISTICAL PREDICTION OF STRUCTURAL PERFORMANCE IN THE
WIND ENVIRONMENT, presented at the ASCE National Structural Engineering
Meeting (Baltimore, Md.), Preprint 1420. (7)
Davenport, A. G., 1971b
WIND LOADING AND WIND EFFECTS, Proceedings of the 3rd Regional Conference
(Tokyo, Japan), pp. 98–100. (7)

Davenport, A. G., 1972a
AN APPROACH TO HUMAN COMFORT CRITERIA FOR ENVIRONMENTAL WIND CONDITIONS, Colloquium on Building Climatology (Stockholm, Sweden). (7)

Davenport, A. G., 1972b
WIND LOADING AND WIND EFFECTS, Proceedings, 6th National/Regional Conference (Delft, The Netherlands), pp. 34–35. (7)

Davenport, A. G., 1972c
STRUCTURAL SAFETY AND RELIABILITY UNDER WIND ACTION, Structural Safety and Reliability, A. Freudenthal, ed., Pergamon Press, New York, pp. 131–145. (7)

Davenport, A. G., 1973
THEME REPORT: WIND LOADING AND WIND EFFECTS, Planning and Design of Tall Buildings, Proceedings of the 1972 ASCE-IABSE International Conference, Vol. 1b, ASCE, New York, pp. 335–364. (7)

Davenport, A. G., 1975a
CRITERIA FOR DESIGN AGAINST WIND ACTION, Proceedings, Conference on Tall Buildings (South Africa, November). (7)

Davenport, A. G., 1975b
PERSPECTIVES ON THE FULL-SCALE MEASUREMENT OF WIND EFFECTS, Journal of Industrial Aerodynamics, Vol. 1, No. 1. (7)

Davenport, A. G., 1975c
THE DESIGN OF TALL BUILDINGS FOR WIND FORCES: INTERNATIONAL DEVELOPMENTS AND THE PRESENT STATE OF THE ART, Proceedings of the 35th National/Regional Conference (South Africa, November). (7)

Davenport, A. G., 1976
Discussion of WIND PRESSURES ON BUILDINGS—PROBABILITY DENSITIES by J. A. Peterka and J. E. Cermak, Journal of the Structural Division, ASCE, Vol. 102, No. ST11, Proc. Paper 12510, pp. 2235–2237. (7)

Davenport, A. G. and Dalgliesh, W. A., 1971
A PRELIMINARY APPRAISAL OF WIND LOADING CONCEPTS OF THE 1970 CANADIAN NATIONAL BUILDING CODE, Proceedings of the 3rd International Conference on Wind Effects on Buildings and Structures, Part III (Tokyo, Japan), pp. 441–450. (7)

Davenport, A. G. and Isyumov, N., 1975
THE GROUND LEVEL WIND ENVIRONMENT IN BUILT-UP AREAS, Proceedings of the 4th International Conference on Wind Effects on Buildings and Structures (London, England). (7)

Davenport, A. G. and Zilch, K., 1973
WIND LOADS AND SAFETY OF TALL BUILDINGS (Windlasten und Sicherheit von Hochlaüsern), Sicherheit von Betonbauten, Deutscher Beton-Verein, Wiesbaden, Germany. (7)

Davenport, A. G., Bowen, C. F. P. and Isyumov, N., 1970
A STUDY OF WIND EFFECTS ON THE COMMERCE COURT PROJECT—PART II, BLWT-3-70, University of Western Ontario, Ontario, Canada. (7)

Davenport, A. G., Isyumov, N. and Jandali, T., 1971
A STUDY OF WIND EFFECTS FOR THE SEARS PROJECT, Report BLWT-5-71, University of Western Ontario, Ontario, Canada. (7)

Davenport, A. G., Isuymov, N., Fader, D. J. and Bowen, C. F. P., 1970a
A STUDY OF WIND EFFECTS FOR THE THEME TOWERS, CENTURY CITY, LOS ANGELES, Report BLWT-7-70, University of Western Ontario, Ontario, Canada. (7)

Davenport, A. G., Isyumov, N., Fader, D. J. and Bowen, C. F. P., 1970b
STUDY OF WIND EFFECTS ON THE WORLD TRADE CENTRE, NEW YORK: EXTERIOR PRESSURE ON PLAZA BUILDINGS—AIR-FLOW IN PLAZA, Engineering Science Research Report BLWT-6-70, University of Western Ontario, Ontario, Canada. (7)

Davenport, A. G., Van Koten, H., Scruton, C., Wyatt, T. A. and Jensen, M., 1971
WIND LOADS, Proceedings, 2nd National/Regional Conference (Bled, Yugoslavia), pp. 28–29. (7)

Deacon, E. L., 1955
GUST VARIATION WITH HEIGHT UP TO 150 M, Quarterly Journal of the Royal Meteorological Society, Vol. 81, pp. 562–573. (7)

De Cicco, P. R., Cresci, R. J. and Correale, W. H., 1972
REPORT OF FIRE TESTS, ANALYSES AND EVALUATION OF STAIR PRESSURI-
ZATION AND EXHAUST IN HIGH-RISE OFFICE BUILDINGS PERFORMED
FOR THE NEW YORK CITY FIRE DEPARTMENT, Brooklyn Polytechnic Institute,
New York. (8A)

Degenkolb, H. J. and Hanson, R. D., 1969
THE JULY 29, 1967, VENEZUELA EARTHQUAKE, LESSONS FOR THE STRUC-
TURAL ENGINEER, Proceedings on the 4th World Conference on Earthquake
Engineering, Vol. III. (6)

Degenkolb, J. G., 1971
SMOKE-PROOF ENCLOSURES, ASHRAE Journal, Vol. 13, No. 4, pp. 33–38. (8A)

Degenkolb, J. G., 1974
THE EVOLUTION OF HIGH RISE FIRE PROTECTION, The Building Official and
Code Administrator International, Inc., Chicago, Ill., September-October. (8A)

Del Corro Gutierrez, J., 1973
CALCULATIONS OF THE EARTHQUAKE ACTION ACCORDING TO THE NTE
ECS-1973 STANDARD OF THE HABITATION MINISTRY (Calculo de la Accion
Sismica Segun la Norma NTE ECS-1973 Del M), Proceedings of Regional Conference on
Tall Buildings, (Madrid, Spain, September) Tipografia Artistica, Madrid, Spain, pp.
83–90. (6)

Department of Employment, 1975
THE FLIXBOROUGH DISASTER: REPORT OF THE COURT OF INQUIRY, HMSO,
London, England. (8B)

Departamento del Distrito Federal, 1966
BUILDING CODE FOR THE FEDERAL DISTRICT (Reglamento de las Construcciones
en el Distrito Federal), Mexico City, Mexico. (10)

Devaty, F., Horina, B. and Reichel, V., 1973
FIREPROOF FLOORS WITH METAL PANELS, 10th Regional Conference Proceedings
(Bratislava, Czechoslovakia, April), CSVTA—Czechoslovak Scientific and Technical
Association, Bratislava, Czechoslovakia. (8A)

Dezfulian, H. and Seed. H. B., 1969a
SEISMIC RESPONSE OF SOIL DEPOSITS UNDERLAIN BY SLOPING ROCK
BOUNDARIES, Earthquake Engineering Research Center Report No. EERC 69-9,
University of California, Berkeley, Calif. (6)

Dezfulian, H. and Seed, H. B., 1969b
RESPONSE OF NON-UNIFORM SOIL DEPOSITS TO TRAVELLING SEISMIC
WAVES, Earthquake Engineering Research Center Report No. EERC 69-13, University
of California, Berkeley, Calif. (6)

Dibaj, M. and Penzien, J., 1969a
NONLINEAR SEISMIC RESPONSE OF EARTH STRUCTURES, Earthquake Engi-
neering Research Center Report No. EERC 69-2, University of California, Berkeley,
Calif. (6)

Dibaj, M. and Penzien, J., 1969b
RESPONSE OF EARTH DAMS TO TRAVELLING SEISMIC WAVES, Journal of the
Soil Mechanics and Foundations Division, ASCE, Vol. 95, No. SM2, Proc. Paper 6453, pp.
541–560. (6)

Dick, J. B. and Thomas, D. A., 1953
AIR INFILTRATION THROUGH GAPS AROUND WINDOWS, Journal of Heating and
Ventilating Engineers, London, England, Vol. 21, p. 85. (8A)

Dickey, W. L., 1973
MASONRY STRESSES BY PRISM TESTING, Masonry Industry, June. (9)

Dietrich, R. and Fürste, W., 1973
METHODS FOR ANALYSING THE LOADING AND LIMITING STRUCTURAL
RESPONSE OF NUCLEAR POWER PLANTS UNDER AIRCRAFT IMPACT AND
EXTERNAL BLAST (Berechnungsmethoden zur Ermittlung von Belastungsbedin-
gungen und Grenztragfahingkeitsverhalten von Kernkraftwerks-Bauwerks-Strukturen bei
aussergewohlichen ausseren Einwirkungen wie Flugzengabsturz und Gasdruckwelle),
Preprints of the 2nd International Conference on Structural Mechanics in Reactor
Technology (Berlin, Germany), Vol. 6B, Paper J 3/1, Commission of the European
Communities, Brussels, Belgium. (8B)

Dimarogonas, P., 1975
A TRANSFER MATRIX APPROACH FOR THE RESEARCH OF TALL BUILDINGS TO REAL EARTHQUAKES, Proceedings of Hellenic Conference on Tall Buildings (Athens, Greece, October), Technical Chamber of Greece, Athens, Greece. (6)

Ditlevsen, O., 1973
STRUCTURAL RELIABILITY AND THE INVARIANCE PROBLEM, Dept. of Civil Engineering, Danish Engineering Academy. (10)

Dorn, J. E., 1962
PROGRESS IN UNDERSTANDING HIGH TEMPERATURE CREEP, Grillet Memorial Lecture, American Society for Testing and Materials, Philadelphia, Pa. (8A)

Dorwick, D. J., 1977
EARTHQUAKE RESISTANT DESIGN, John Wiley and Sons, Inc., London, England. (6)

Dragosavic, M., 1973
STRUCTURAL MEASURES AGAINST NATURAL-GAS EXPLOSIONS IN HIGH-RISE BLOCKS OF FLATS, Heron, Vol. 19, No. 4, pp. 1–51. (8B)

Drakatos, P., 1975
THE NOISE IN TALL BUILDINGS, Proceedings of the Hellenic Conference on Tall Buildings (Athens, Greece, October). (7)

Driskell, J. J., 1968
MEXICO CITY EARTHQUAKE OF 2ND AUGUST, 1968, Proceedings of the Structural Engineers Association of California. (6)

Drozdov, P. F., 1973
THE PRINCIPLES OF ANALYSIS OF SPATIAL STRUCTURES IN THE USSR, 10th Regional Conference Proceedings (Bratislava, Czechoslovakia, April), CSVTA—Czechoslovak Scientifical and Technical Association, Bratislava, Czechoslovakia. (10)

Drysdale, R. G., 1975
PLACEMENT ERRORS FOR REINFORCING IN CONCRETE COLUMNS, ACI Journal, American Concrete Institute, Vol. 72, No. 1, pp. 9–15. (9)

Drysdale, R. G. and Hamid, A. A., 1979
BEHAVIOR OF CONCRETE BLOCK MASONRY UNDER AXIAL COMPRESSION, ACI Journal, American Concrete Institute, Vol. 76, No. 6, Title 76-32, pp. 707–721. (9)

Duchene-Marullaz, P., 1975
FULL SCALE MEASUREMENTS OF ATMOSPHERIC TURBULENCE IN A SUBURBAN AREA, Proceedings of the 4th International Conference on Wind Effects on Buildings and Structures (London, England). (7)

Dufour, R. E., 1963
SURVEY OF AVAILABLE INFORMATION ON THE TOXICITY OF THE COMBUSTION AND THERMAL DECOMPOSITION PRODUCTS OF CERTAIN BUILDING MATERIALS UNDER FIRE CONDITIONS, Bulletin of Research No. 531, U.S. National Board of Fire Underwriters, Underwriters Laboratories, Inc., Chicago, Ill. (8A)

Duke, C. M., Monge, J., Whitman, R. V. and Nakagawa, K., 1973
ECONOMIC AND SOCIAL ASPECTS, Planning and Design of Tall Buildings, Proceedings of the 1972 ASCE-IABSE International Conference, Vol. 1b, ASCE, New York, pp. 255–266. (6)

Duncan, A. J., 1965
QUALITY CONTROL AND INDUSTRIAL STATISTICS, Chapter XXII, Richard D. Irwin, Inc., Homewood, Ill., pp. 411–429. (9)

Dunham, J. W., 1947
DESIGN LIVE LOADS IN BUILDINGS, Transactions, ASCE, Vol. 112, No. 2311, pp. 725–744. (5)

Durgin, F. H. and Tong, P., 1972
THE EFFECT OF TWIST MOTION ON THE DYNAMIC MULTIMODE RESPONSE OF A BUILDING, Proceedings of the IVTAM-IAHR Symposium on Flow Induced Structural Vibrations (Karlsruhe, Germany), Springer-Verlag, Berlin, Germany. (7)

Durst, C. S., 1960
WIND SPEEDS OVER SHORT PERIODS OF TIME, Meteorological Magazine, Vol. 89, Paper No. 1056. (7)

Dutt, A. J., 1974a
AN INVESTIGATION OF THE WIND PRESSURE DISTRIBUTION ON THE M.I.T. TOWERS, SHAH ALAM, Proceedings of the 25th National/Regional Conference (Kuala Lumpur, Malaysia), pp. 8-24-8-28. (7)

Dutt, A. J., 1974b
AN APPROACH TO THE SIMPLIFICATION OF THE DYNAMIC CHARACTER- ISTICS OF WIND LOADING ON TALL BUILDINGS, Proceedings of the 25th National/Regional Conference (Kuala Lumpur, Malaysia), pp. 8-41-8-48. (7)

ECCS, 1974a
RESEARCH INTO THE FIRE RESISTANCE OF STEEL STRUCTURES, European Coal and Steel Community, Brussels, Belgium. (8A)

ECCS, 1974b
FIRE SAFETY IN CONSTRUCTIONAL STEELWORK, CECM-III-74-2E, European Convention for Constructional Steelwork, Brussels, Belgium. (8A)

EERI, 1969-1971
STRONG-MOTION EARTHQUAKE ACCELEROGRAMS, Earthquake Engineering Research Institute, Berkeley, Calif., Vols. 1A, 1B, 1C. (6)

EERI Conference Proceedings, 1973
MANAGUA, NICARAGUA EARTHQUAKE OF DECEMBER 23, 1972, Proceedings of Conference held at Pasadena, Calif., November, Earthquake Engineering Research Institute, Berkeley, Calif. (6)

EERI Reconnaissance Report, 1973
MANAGUA, NICARAGUA, EARTHQUAKE OF DECEMBER 23, 1972, Earthquake Engineering Research Institute, Berkeley, Calif., May. (6)

ESSA, 1969
STUDIES IN SEISMICITY AND EARTHQUAKE DAMAGE STATISTICS, U.S. Department of Commerce, Environmental Science Services Administration, Coast and Geodetic Survey. (6)

Eaton, K. J., 1975
CLADDING AND THE WIND, BRE Current Paper 47-75, HMSO, London, England. (7)

Eaton, K. J. and Mayne, J. R., 1975
THE MEASUREMENT OF WIND PRESSURES ON TWO-STOREY HOUSES AT AYLESBURY, Journal of Industrial Aerodynamics, Vol. 1 No. 1, pp. 67–109. (7)

Ehm, H., 1973
BEHAVIOR OF THE STRUCTURE UNDER FIRE, Planning and Design of Tall Buildings, Proceedings of the 1972 ASCE-IABSE International Conference, Vol. 1b, ASCE, New York, pp. 491–522. (8A)

Elevator World, 1971
EDITORIAL, SPEAKING OF ISSUES, Elevator World, February, pp. 2–5. (8A)

Elliott, W. P., 1958
THE GROWTH OF THE ATMOSPHERIC INTERNAL BOUNDARY LAYER, Trans- actions, American Geophysical Union, Vol. 39, No. 6, pp. 1048–1054. (7)

Ellis, N., 1975
A NEW TECHNIQUE FOR EVALUATING THE FLUCTUATING LIFT AND DRAG FORCE DISTRIBUTION ON BUILDING STRUCTURES, 4th International Con- ference on Wind Effects on Buildings and Structures (London, England), University of Cambridge Press, Cambridge, England. (7)

Emmons, H. W., 1967
FIRE RESEARCH ABROAD, Fire Technology, Vol. 3, No. 3, pp. 225–231. (8A)

Esquillan, N., 1963
THE 1963 FRENCH REGULATIONS DEFINING THE EFFECT OF WIND ON BUILDINGS (Les règles françaises 1963 définissant les effets du vent sur les construc- tions), International Conference on Wind Effects on Buildings and Structures (NPL, Teddington, England). (7)

Esteva, L., 1968
BASIS FOR THE FORMULATION OF DECISIONS ON SEISMIC DESIGN (Bases para la Formulacion de Decisiones de Diseño Sísmico), Institute of Engineering, National University, Mexico. (10)

Esteva, L., 1969a
SEISMIC RISK AND SEISMIC DESIGN DECISIONS, Seminar on the Earthquake Resistant Design of Nuclear Reactors (Massachusetts Institute of Technology, Cambridge, Mass.). (10)
Esteva, L., 1969b
SEISMICITY PREDICTION: A BAYESIAN APPROACH, Proceedings, 4th World Conference on Earthquake Engineering (Santiago, Chile). (10)
Esteva, L., 1970
PRACTICAL CONSIDERATIONS IN THE BAYESIAN ESTIMATE OF SEISMIC RISK (Consideraciones practicas en la Estimacion Bayesiana de Riesgo Sísmico), *Ingenieria*, Vol. 40, No. 2, pp. 209–228. (10)
Esteva, L., 1973
SUMMARY REPORT: STRUCTURAL SAFETY AND PROBABILISTIC METHODS, Planning and Design of Tall Buildings (Proceedings of the 1972 ASCE-IABSE International Conference), Vol. 1b, ASCE, New York, pp. 1043–1066. (10)
Esteva, L., 1974
INVARIANT SAFETY FORMATS IN PRACTICAL DESIGN, International Workshop on the Definition, Classification and Evaluation of Code Formats (LNEC, Lisbon, Portugal). (10)
Esteva, L. and Gutierrez, A., 1969
LESSONS FROM SOME RECENT EARTHQUAKES IN LATIN AMERICA, Proceedings of the 4th World Conference on Earthquake Engineering (Santiago, Chile). (6, 10)
Esteva, L. and Rosenblueth, E., 1971
USE OF RELIABILITY THEORY IN BUILDING CODES, 1st International Conference on Applications of Statistics and Probability to Soil and Structural Engineering (University of Hong Kong, September). (10)
Estuar, F. R., 1966
WELDING RESIDUAL STRESSES AND THE STRENGTH OF HEAVY COLUMN SHAPES, dissertation presented to Lehigh University, at Bethlehem, Pa., in August, in partial fulfillment of the requirements for the degree of Doctor of Philosophy (University Microfilms, Inc., Ann Arbor, Mich.). (9)
Euronorm 34-62, 1962
HOT-ROLLED WIDE-FLANGE H-SHAPES WITH PARALLEL FLANGE SIDES —TOLERANCES (Warmgewaltze Breite I-Träger (I-Breitflanschträger) Mit Parallelen Flanschflächen—Zulässige Abweichungen), Europäische Gemeinschaft fur Kohle und Stahl, Brussels, Belgium, May. (9)

FOC, 1968
RULES FOR AUTOMATIC SPRINKLER INSTALLATION, 29th ed., Fire Offices Committee, December. (8A)
Feld, J., 1964
LESSONS FROM FAILURES OF CONCRETE STRUCTURES, Monograph No. 1, American Concrete Institute, Detroit, Mich. (5)
Ferahian, R. H., 1972
BUILDINGS: DESIGN FOR PREVENTION OF PROGRESSIVE COLLAPSE, *Civil Engineering*, ASCE, Vol. 42, No. 2, pp. 66–69. (8B)
Ferguson, B. J., 1974
THE INTER-RELATIONSHIP OF INTERNATIONAL MATERIAL SPECIFICATIONS AND DESIGN CODES WITH PARTICULAR REFERENCE TO WELDED STEEL WIRE REINFORCING FABRIC, Proceedings, Conference on Tall Buildings (Kuala Lumpur, Malaysia, December), Institution of Engineers, Kuala Lumpur, Malaysia, pp. 7-18–7-28. (9)
Ferrante, A. and Gomes Franco, J. S., 1973
EARTHQUAKE LOADING (Sobre a Aplicacao de Computadores Para Analise de Estructuras Resistentes de Edificios Altos), Proceedings of South American Regional Conference on Tall Buildings, (Porto Alegre, Brazil, December), Vol. II, Sociedad de Engenharia do Rio Grande do Sul, pp. 261–277. (6)
Ferry Borges, J., 1968a
STATISTICAL ESTIMATE OF SEISMIC LOADING, Proceedings, 5th Congress of IABSE. (10)

Ferry Borges, J., 1968b
DYNAMIC LOADING, General Report on Theme VI, Proceedings, 8th Congress of
IABSE. (10)

Ferry Borges, J. and Castanheta, M., 1969
GENERAL RECOMMENDATIONS DERIVED FROM BASIC STUDIES ON STRUC-
TURAL SAFETY, prepared discussion, IABSE Symposium on Concepts of Safety
(London, England). (10)

Ferry Borges, J. and Castanheta, M., 1971
STRUCTURAL SAFETY, LNEC, Lisbon, Portugal, March. (10)

Ferry Borges, J., Castanheta, M. and Borges, A. R. J., 1971
DESIGN CRITERIA FOR WIND LOADS ON STATISTICAL BASIS, 3rd International
Conference on Wind Effects on Buildings and Structures (Tokyo, Japan), Part III, pp.
521–530. (7)

Fichtl, G. H., Kaufman, J. W. and Vaughan, W. W., 1969
THE CHARACTERISTICS OF ATMOSPHERIC TURBULENCE AS RELATED TO
WIND LOADS ON TALL STRUCTURES, Proceedings of the Technical Meeting
Concerning Wind Loads on Buildings and Structures, National Bureau of Standards
(Gaithersburg, Md.), Building Science Series No. 30. (7)

Finn, W. D. L., 1967
STATIC AND SEISMIC ANALYSIS OF SLOPES, Rock Mechanics and Engineering
Geology, Journal of the International Society of Rock Mechanics. (6)

Finn, W. D. L., Emery, J. J. and Reimer, R. B., 1971
THE EFFECT OF FOUNDATION SOILS ON SEISMIC RESPONSE OF STRUC-
TURES, Proceedings of the 1st Canadian Conference on Earthquake Engineering
Research (Vancouver, B.C., Canada). (6)

Fintel, M., Nieves, J. M., Jobse, H. J., Amrhein, J. E. and Griffin, P. G., 1969
PRELIMINARY REPORT—THE BEHAVIOR OF REINFORCED CONCRETE
STRUCTURES IN THE CARACAS, VENEZUELA, EARTHQUAKE OF JULY 29,
1967, Portland Cement Association. (6)

Finzi, L. and Paris, L., 1967
THE NEW ITALIAN REGULATIONS FOR WIND LOADS ON STRUCTURES,
Proceedings of the International Research Seminar on Wind Effects on Buildings and
Structures (Ottawa, Canada). (7)

Fiorato, A. E., 1973a
GEOMETRIC IMPERFECTIONS IN CONCRETE STRUCTURES, Document D5:1973,
National Swedish Institute for Buildings Research, Stockholm, Sweden. (9)

Fiorato, A. E., 1973b
GEOMETRIC VARIATIONS IN THE COLUMNS OF A PRECAST CONCRETE
INDUSTRIAL BUILDING, Journal of the Prestressed Concrete Institute, Chicago, Ill.,
Vol. 18, No. 4. (9)

Fiorato, A. E. and Sahlin, S., 1973
DIMENSIONAL TOLERANCE IN CONCRETE, Planning and Design of Tall Buildings,
(Proceedings of the 1972 ASCE-IABSE International Conference), ASCE, New York,
Vol. 1b, pp. 893–895. (9)

Fire, 1972
INTUMESCENT HONEYCOMB FIRE BARRIERS NOW AVAILABLE, Fire, England,
Vol. 65, September. (8A)

Fishburn, C. C., 1961
EFFECT OF MORTAR PROPERTIES IN STRENGTH OF MASONRY, National
Bureau of Standards (U.S. Department of Commerce) Monograph 36, Washington, D.C.,
November. (9)

Fishburn, P. C., 1964
DECISION AND VALUE THEORY, John Wiley & Sons, New York. (10)

Fitzgerald, J. F., 1973
BUILDING CODE CHANGES AND HI-RISE SAFETY, Actual Specifiying Engineer, Vol.
29, No. 7, pp. 87–89. (8A)

Fitzgerald, J. F., 1976
BIBLIOGRAPHY ON PANIC REACTION, unpublished communication to the Council.
(8A)

Fleming, J. F., 1971
   STRUCTURAL FRAMING FOR DRIFT LIMITATION IN HIGHRISE BUILDINGS,
   3rd International Conference on Wind Effects on Buildings and Structures Part III
   (Tokyo, Japan), pp. 559–568. (7)
Fosca, V. and Gavrilas, I., 1975
   SOME ASPECTS CONCERNING THE EFFECT OF WIND ON THE THERMAL
   CONDITIONS IN TALL BUILDINGS, 34th National/Regional Conference (Iasi,
   Romania), pp. 67–86. (7)
Foy, E. and Harlow, A. F., 1928
   CLOWNING THROUGH LIFE, Dutton, New York, pp. 104–113. (8A)
Franck, N., 1963
   MODEL LAW AND EXPERIMENTAL TECHNIQUES FOR THE DETERMINATION
   OF WIND LOADS ON BUILDINGS, Proceedings, Conference on Wind Effects on
   Buildings and Structures (NPL Teddington, England), HMSO, London, England, pp.
   182–196. (7)
Freeman, G., 1974
   PROBLEMS ASSOCIATED WITH FIRE IN TALL BUILDINGS, Proceedings of
   Conference on Tall Buildings, (Kuala Lumpur, Malaysia, December), Institution of
   Engineers, Kuala Lumpur, Malaysia. (8A)
Freudenthal, A. M., Garrelts, J. M. and Shinozuka, M., 1966
   THE ANALYSIS OF STRUCTURAL SAFETY, *Journal of the Structural Division*, ASCE,
   Vol. 92, No. ST1, Proc. Paper 4682, p. 267. (10)
Fribush, S. L., 1973
   ESTIMATES OF VEHICULAR COLLISIONS WITH MULTISTORY BUILDINGS,
   NBSIR 73-175, National Bureau of Standards, Washington, D.C. (8B)
Frownfelter, C. R., 1969
   STRUCTURAL TESTING ON LARGE GLASS INSTALLATIONS, Special Technical
   Publication No. 251, ASTM Symposium on Testing Window Assemblies, ASTM,
   Philadelphia, Pa., pp. 19–30. (10)
Fry, J. F., 1971
   GAS EXPLOSIONS ATTENDED BY FIRE BRIGADES IN DWELLINGS, *Journal of the
   Institute of Fuel*, Vol. 44, pp. 470–471. (8B)
Fujii, K., Hibi, K. and Kaneko, T., 1974
   WIND PRESSURE MEASUREMENTS ON A TALL BUILDING—FURTHER RE-
   SULTS FROM THE ASAHI-TOKAI BUILDING, Symposium on Full-Scale Meas-
   urements of Wind Effects on Tall Buildings and Other Structures, University of Western
   Ontario, Canada, pp. 23–29. (7)
Fujimoto, M., Ohkuma, T. and Amano, T., 1975
   DYNAMIC MODEL TESTS OF A HIGH-RISE BUILDING IN WIND TUNNEL
   FLOW AND IN NATURAL WINDS, Proceedings, 4th International Conference on
   Wind Effects on Buildings and Structures (London, England), University of Cambridge
   Press, England. (7)
Fujita, K., undated
   CHARACTERISTICS OF FIRE INSIDE A NONCOMBUSTIBLE ROOM AND PRE-
   VENTION OF FIRE DAMAGE, Japanese Ministry of Construction, Building Research
   Institute, Report 1, No. 1, Tokyo, Japan. (8A)
Fujita, T. T., 1974
   RECENT CONCEPTS OF TORNADO WINDS, Proceedings, 2nd USA/Japan Research
   Seminar on Wind Effects on Structures, University of Tokyo Press, Tokyo, Japan. (7)
Funahashi, I., Kinoshita, K. and Aoyama. H., 1969
   VIBRATION TESTS AND TEST TO FAILURE OF A 7 STORIED BUILDING
   SURVIVED A SEVERE EARTHQUAKE, Proceedings of the 4th World Conference on
   Earthquake Engineering (Santiago, Chile). (6)
Funakawa, M. and Umakoshi, R., 1971
   VIBRATION OF A CYLINDER CAUSED BY WAKE FORCE, Proceedings, 3rd
   International Conference on Wind Effects on Buildings and Structures (Tokyo, Japan).
   (7)

GSA, 1971a
PUBLIC BUILDINGS SERVICE INTERNATIONAL CONFERENCE ON FIRE SAFE-
TY IN HIGH-RISE BUILDINGS, Proceedings, Airlie House, Warrenton, Va., General
Services Administration, Washington, D.C. (8A)

GSA, 1971b
RECONVENED INTERNATIONAL CONFERENCE ON FIRE SAFETY IN HIGH-
RISE BUILDINGS, Proceedings of Conference held in Washington, D.C. in October,
General Services Administration, Public Buildings Service. (8A)

GSA, 1974
FIRE SAFETY SYSTEMS—RICHARD B. RUSSELL COURTHOUSE AND FEDERAL
OFFICE BUILDING, ATLANTA, GEORGIA, Status Report, General Services Ad-
ministration, Washington, D.C. (8A)

GSA, 1975
BUILDING FIRE SAFETY CRITERIA, General Services Administration, Washington,
D.C., February. (8A)

GSA, HUD, NBS, NSF, 1973
RESEARCH PRACTICE NEEDS, Conference on Fire Safety for Buildings, Airlie House,
Warrenton, Va., July. (8A)

Gage, M. and Newman, K., 1972
SPECIFICATION AND USE OF READY MIXED CONCRETE, Architectural Press,
London, England, pp. 53–60. (9)

Galambos, T. V. and Ravindra, M. K., 1973a
LOAD FACTOR DESIGN FOR COMBINATION OF LOADS, Preprint No. 1940, ASCE
National Structural Engineering Meeting (San Francisco, Calif., April), ASCE, New
York. (5)

Galambos, T. V. and Ravindra, M. K., 1973b
TENTATIVE LOAD AND RESISTANCE FACTOR DESIGN CRITERIA FOR STEEL
BUILDINGS, Civil and Environmental Engineering Dept., Washington University
School of Engineering and Applied Science, St. Louis, Mo. (10)

Galambos, T. V., Gould, P. L., Ravindra, M. K., Suryoutomo, H., and Crist, R. A., 1973
STRUCTURAL DEFLECTIONS—A LITERATURE AND STATE-OF-THE-ART SUR-
VEY, Building Science Series 47, U.S. Dept. of Commerce, National Bureau of Standards,
Gaithersburg, Md, October. (7)

Galbreath, M., 1968a
FIRE IN HIGH BUILDINGS, Fire Study 21, NRC 10081, National Research Council of
Canada, Ottawa. (8A)

Galbreath, M., 1968b
A SURVEY OF EXIT FACILITIES IN HIGH OFFICE BUILDINGS, British Research
Note 64, Boston Spa, England, October. (8A)

Galbreath, M., 1969
TIME OF EVACUATION BY STAIRS IN HIGH BUILDINGS, reprint from *Fire
Fighting in Canada*, FR Note 8, February. (8A)

Gandemer, J., 1975
WIND ENVIRONMENT AROUND BUILDINGS: AERODYNAMIC CONCEPTS,
Proceedings, 4th International Conference on Wind Effects on Buildings and Structures
(London, England), University of Cambridge Press, England. (7)

Garofolo, E., Molenock, P. R. and Smith, G. V., 1952
THE INFLUENCE OF TEMPERATURE ON THE ELASTIC CONSTANTS OF SOME
COMMERCIAL STEELS, Determination of Elastic Constants, STP-129, American
Society for Testing and Materials, Philadelphia, Pa. (8A)

Geiger, W., 1974
GENERATION AND PROPAGATION OF PRESSURE WAVES DUE TO UNCON-
FINED CHEMICAL EXPLOSIONS AND THEIR IMPACT ON NUCLEAR POWER
PLANT STRUCTURES, *Nuclear Engineering and Design*, Vol. 27, pp. 189–198. (8B)

Gellert, M. and Gluck, J., 1972
THE INFLUENCE OF AXIAL LOAD ON EIGEN-FREQUENCIES OF A VIBRAT-
ING LATERAL RESTRAINT CANTILEVER, *International Journal of Mechanical
Science*, Vol. 14, Pergamon Press, England, pp. 723–728. (6)

Gewain, R. G., 1974
FIRE EXPERIENCE AND FIRE TESTS IN AUTOMOBILE PARKING STRUC-
TURES, *Fire Journal*, Vol. 67, No. 4, July. (8A)

Giangreco, E. and Ramasco, R., 1974
ON THE SEISMIC BEHAVIOR OF TALL BUILDINGS AND OTHER RELATED
STRUCTURAL TYPES, Proceedings of the Regional Conference on Tall Buildings
(Bangkok, Thailand, January), Asian Institute of Technology, Bangkok, Thailand, pp.
683–706. (6)

Gibson, L. and Packham, D. R., 1972
A VERY EARLY WARNING SMOKE DETECTOR, Australian Patent No. PA-9230-72,
Patent Office, Canberra, Australia. (8A)

Gill, G. C., 1969
GUIDELINES IN SELECTING WIND MEASURING INSTRUMENTS AND THEIR
LOCATIONS FOR WIND LOADING STUDIES, Proceedings, Technical Meeting
concerning Wind Loads on Buildings and Structures (NBS, Gaithersburg, Md.), Building
Science Series No. 30. (7)

Gilling, D., Miller, P. O. and Whitbread, R. E., 1971
THE INFLUENCE OF A WIND-TUNNEL STUDY ON THE DESIGN FOR THE
QANTAS CENTRE, SYDNEY, AUSTRALIA, Proceedings, 3rd International Con-
ference on Wind Effects on Buildings and Structures (Tokyo, Japan). (7)

Givoni, B. and Paciuk, M., 1972
AIR FLOW AROUND HIGH RISE BUILDINGS, Proceedings, CIB/RILEM Sympo-
sium, Teaching the Teachers on Building Climatology, Swedish Institute of Building
Research, Stockholm, Sweden. (7)

Glass, A. J., 1969
MASS PSYCHOLOGY—THE DETERMINANTS OF BEHAVIOR UNDER EMER-
GENCY CONDITIONS, Proceedings of Workshop on Mass Burns, National Academy
of Science, Washington, D.C., pp. 11–24. (8A)

Glasstone, S., Ed., 1962
THE EFFECTS OF NUCLEAR WEAPONS, U.S. Atomic Energy Commission, Washington, D.C., Revised Edition, p. 163; and Revised Edition, 1964. (8A, 8B)

Glauser, E., 1973
LOADINGS (Erdrebenbeanspruchung von Hochhausern), Proceedings on the National
Conference on Tall Buildings, (Zürich, Switzerland, October), SIA-Fachgruppen für
Bruckenbau und Hochbau (FBH) und für Architektur (FGA), Zürich, Switzerland, pp.
85–108. (5)
TORSIONAL-FLEXURAL VIBRATION OF MULTI-STORY STRUCTURES, Planning
and Design of Tall Buildings, Proceedings of the 1972 ASCE-IABSE International
Conference, Vol. 1b, ASCE, New York, p. 298. (6)

Godfrey, G. B. and Reese, R. C., 1971
GRAVITY LOADS AND TEMPERATURE EFFECTS, Proceedings of the National
Conference on Tall Buildings, (Bled, Yugoslavia, May), Lehigh University, Bethlehem,
Pa., p. 25. (5)

Goldbeck, A. T. and Gray, J. E., 1942
A METHOD OF PROPORTIONING CONCRETE FOR STRENGTH, WORKABIL-
ITY, AND DURABILITY, Engineering Bulletin No. 11, National Crushed Stone
Association, Washington, D.C. (9)

Goldman, J. L., 1974
TIME-DEPENDENT VARIATIONS OF VERTICAL STORM WIND PROFILES,
Proceedings, 2nd USA/Japan Research Seminar on Wind Effects on Buildings and
Structures, University Of Tokyo Press, Tokyo, Japan. (7)

Gomes, L. and Vickery, B. J., 1974
ON THE PREDICTION OF EXTREME WIND SPEEDS FROM THE PARENT
DISTRIBUTION, Proceedings, Conference on the Application of Probability Theory to
Structural Design (Melbourne, Australia), Institution of Engineers of Australia. (7)

Gomes, L. and Vickery, B. J., 1976a
ON THUNDERSTORM WIND GUSTS IN AUSTRALIA, Research Report No. R277,
School of Civil Engineering, University of Sydney, Australia. (7)

Gomes, L. and Vickery, B. J., 1976b
ON THE PREDICTION OF TROPICAL CYCLONE GUST SPEEDS ALONG THE NORTHERN AUSTRALIAN COAST, Research Report R278, School of Civil Engineering, University of Sydney, Australia. (7)

Gorove, A. and Cermak, J. E., 1967
DYNAMIC RESPONSE OF PRESSURE TRANSMISSION LINES TO PULSE INPUT, Technical Report. (7).

Goschy, B., 1974
GEOMETRIC IMPERFECTIONS, unpublished communication to the Joint Committee, May. (9)

Goto, T., 1975
RESEARCH ON VIBRATION CRITERIA FROM THE VIEWPOINT OF PEOPLE LIVING IN HIGH-RISE BUILDINGS (PART 1): VARIOUS RESPONSES OF HUMANS TO MOTION, Transactions of AIJ, Japan, 237 (11): 109–118; Technical Translation 1881, National Research Council of Canada. (7)

Gramolin, I. V., 1972
QUALITY CONTROL CRITERIA, 6th Regional Conference Proceedings (Delft, The Netherlands, May), Lehigh University, Bethlehem, Pa., pp. 39–40. (9)

Granstrom, S. A., 1956
LOADING CHARACTERISTICS OF AIR BLASTS FROM DETONATING CHARGES, Transactions, Royal Institute of Technology, Stockholm, Sweden, No. 100. (8B)

Granstrom, S. A., 1971
STABILITY OF BUILDINGS AFTER ACCIDENTAL DAMAGE (Byggnaders Stabilitet efter Katastrofskador), Report R20: 1971, National Swedish Institute for Building Research, Stockholm, Sweden. (8B)

Granstrom, S. A. and Carlsson, M., 1974
THE BEHAVIOR OF BUILDINGS UNDER EXTREME LOADS (Byggnaders Beteende vid Overpaverkningar), Report T3: 1974, National Swedish Institute for Building Research, Stockholm, Sweden. (8B)

Granstrom, S. A. and Carlsson, M., 1976
TERRORIST EXPLOSION IN THE GERMAN EMBASSY, STOCKHOLM, 1975, AN EXAMPLE OF EXTREME LOADING IN AN OFFICE BUILDING (Sprangningen i Vasttyska Ambassaden i Stockholm 1975, ett Exempel pa Overpaverkan i Kontorshus), Report T16: 1976, National Swedish Institute for Building Research, Stockholm, Sweden. (8B)

Greco, C., 1973
TRENDS IN THE MODERN CODE (Orientamenti nella Moderna Normativa Sismica), Report 349, Instituto di Tecnica della Costruzioni, University of Naples, Naples, Italy. (6)

Greco, C. and Ramesco, R., 1972
THE SEISMIC RESPONSE OF PLANE FRAMED STRUCTURES OF ANY SHAPE (La Risposta Sismica di Strutture Intelaiate di Forma Qualsiasi), Giornale del Genio Civile, Rome, Italy, Nos. 4, 5, 6, p. 127. (6)

Green, J. K., 1971
REINSTATEMENT OF CONCRETE STRUCTURES AFTER FIRE, Architects Journal, July, pp. 93–99, 151–155. (8A)

Green, J. K. and Long, W. B., 1971
UNIT REPAIRS TO FIRE DAMAGED CONCRETE STRUCTURES, Architects Journal, April, pp. 118–122. (8A)

Green, W. L., Hamad, M. F. and McCauley, R. B., 1958
THE EFFECTS OF POROSITY ON MILD STEEL WELDS, Welding Journal, Vol. 37, No. 5, pp. 206-s–209-s. (9)

Greene, W. E., Jr., 1973
STOCHASTIC MODELS AND LIVE LOAD SURVEYS, Planning and Design of Tall Buildings, Proceedings of 1972 ASCE-IABSE International Conference, Vol. 1b, No. 5-2B, ASCE, New York, pp. 35–58. (5)

Griffith, A. A., 1920
THE PHENOMENA OF RUPTURE AND FLOW IN SOLIDS, Philosophical Transactions of the Royal Society, Vol. A221, London, England, pp. 163–198. (9)

Griffiths, H., Pugsley, A. and Saunders, O., 1968
REPORT OF THE INQUIRY INTO THE COLLAPSE OF FLATS AT RONAN POINT, CANNING TOWN, LONDON, HMSO, London, England. (8B, 10)

Gross, D. J., 1962
EXPERIMENTS ON BURNING OF CROSS PILES OF WOOD, Journal of Research, National Bureau of Standards, Vol. 66C, No. 2, April–June, pp. 99–105. (8A)

Gross, D. and Robertson, A. F., 1965
EXPERIMENTAL FIRE IN ENCLOSURES, 10th Symposium (International) on Combustion, Combustion Institute, Pittsburgh, Pa. (8A)

Gross, D. J., Loftus, J. J. and Robertson, A. F., 1967
STP 422, American Society for Testing and Materials, Philadelphia, Pa., p. 166. (8A)

Group for Dynamic Tests of High-Rise Buildings, 1969
SUMMARIZED REPORT ON DYNAMIC TESTS OF HIGH-RISE BUILDINGS AND COOPERATIVE PLAN FOR LARGE-SCALE VIBRATION TESTS, Proceedings of the 4th World Conference on Earthquake Engineering (Santiago, Chile). (6)

Grundy, P. and Kabaila, A., 1963
CONSTRUCTION LOADS ON SLABS WITH SHORED FORMWORK IN MULTI-STORY BUILDINGS, ACI Journal, American Concrete Institute, Vol. 60, No. 12. (5)

Gumbel, E. J., 1954
STATISTICAL THEORY OF EXTREME VALUES AND SOME PRACTICAL APPLICATIONS, Applied Mathematics, NBS, Gaithersburg, Md. (7)

Gustaferro, A. H. and Scott, N. L., 1975
HOW FIRE CONSIDERATIONS AFFECT THE DESIGN OF TALL BUILDINGS, Pan-Pacific Tall Buildings Conference Proceedings (Honolulu, Hawaii, January), University of Hawaii, Honolulu, Hawaii. (8A)

Gutenberg, B. and Richter, C. F., 1954
SEISMICITY OF THE EARTH, Hafner Publications, Inc., New York. (6)

Guttero, M. M., 1970
PROVISIONAL PROPOSAL CONCERNING OVERLOADS IN OFFICES (Propuesta Provisoria de Sobrecargas en Oficinas), Symposium on Behavior of Structures, Tucumán, Argentina. (5)

Guttero, M. M., 1971a
STUDY OF OVERLOADS IN OFFICES DONE IN 1960 (Estudio de Sobrecarga en Oficina, Realizado en el año 1960), XIV Jornades Sudamericanas de Ingeniería Estructural y IV S.P.E. (Buenos Aires, Argentina), Vol. IV. (5)

Guttero, M. M., 1971b
PILOT INVESTIGATION OF OVERLOADS IN GARAGES (Investigación Piloto de Sobrecargas en Garaje), XV Jornadas Sudamericanas de Ingenieria Estructual, Porto Alegre, Brazil. (5)

Guttero, M. M., 1975
PILOT INVESTIGATION OF OVERLOADS IN PROPOSED HALLS (Investigación Piloto de Sobrecargas en Salas de Estar), XVII Jornadas Sudamericanas de Ingeniería Estructural y V S.P.E., Caracas, Venezuela. (5)

Halitsky, J., 1965
EXTENSIONS ON STACK HEIGHT REQUIRED TO LIMIT CONTAMINATION OF BUILDING AIR INTAKES, Journal, American Industrial Hygiene Association, Vol. 26, pp. 106–116. (7)

Halpin, B. M., 1973
AN IN DEPTH FIRE CASUALTY STUDY, 1st European Fire Conference, National Fire Protection Association, October. (8A)

Hamzah, M., 1974
FIRE PROTECTION OF HIGH RISE BUILDINGS IN KUALA LUMPUR, Proceedings of Conference on Tall Buildings (Kuala Lumpur, Malaysia, December), Institution of Engineers, Kuala Lumpur, Malaysia. (8A)

Hanafusa, T., 1976
STRUCTURE OF THE PLANETARY BOUNDARY LAYER IN HIGH WINDS OBSERVED FROM A 0.5-km TV TOWER, Proceedings of the 1974 2nd USA/Japan Research Seminar on Wind Effects on Structures, University of Tokyo Press, Tokyo, Japan. (7)

Hansen, R. J., Reed, J. W. and Vanmarcke, E., 1973
HUMAN RESPONSE TO WIND INDUCED MOTIONS OF BUILDINGS, *Journal of the Structural Division*, ASCE, Vol. 99, No. ST7, Proc. Paper 9868, pp. 1589–1605. (7)

Hanson, R. D. and Degenkolb, H. J., 1967
THE VENEZUELA EARTHQUAKE, JULY 29, 1967, American Iron and Steel Institute, Washington, D.C. (6)

Haris, A. A. K., 1972
MINIMUM ECCENTRICITY REQUIREMENTS IN THE DESIGN OF REINFORCED CONCRETE COLUMNS, CESRL Dissertation No. 72-1, University of Texas, Austin, Tex., March. (9)

Harmathy, T. Z., 1967
DEFLECTION AND FAILURE OF STEEL SUPPORTED FLOORS AND BEAMS IN FIRE, Symposium on Fire Test Methods, STP 422, American Society for Testing and Materials, Philadelphia, Pa. (8A)

Harmathy, T. Z., 1968
DETERMINING THE TEMPERATURE HISTORY OF CONCRETE CONSTRUCTION DURING FIRE EXPOSURE, *ACI Journal*, American Concrete Institute, Vol. 65, No. 11, pp. 954–964. (8A)

Harmathy, T. Z. and Stanzak, W. W., 1970
ELEVATED TEMPERATURE TENSILE AND CREEP PROPERTIES OF SOME STRUCTURAL AND PRESTRESSING STEELS, Research Paper No. 424, Division of Building Research, Ottawa, Canada. (8A)

Harris, R. I., 1963
THE RESPONSE OF STRUCTURES TO GUSTS, Proceedings of the International Conference on Wind Effects on Buildings and Structures (NPL, Teddington, England). (7)

Harris, R. I., 1968a
MEASUREMENT OF WIND STRUCTURE AT HEIGHTS UP TO 598 FT ABOVE GROUND LEVEL, Symposium on Wind Effects on Buildings and Structures, Loughborough University, England. (10)

Harris, R. I., 1968b
ON THE SPECTRUM AND AUTOCORRELATION FUNCTION OF GUSTINESS IN HIGH WINDS, Electrical Research Association Report No. 5273. (7)

Harris, R. I., 1971
THE NATURE OF THE WIND, *The Modern Design of Wind Sensitive Structures*, Proceedings of the CIRIA Seminar, London, England. (7)

Harris, R. I., 1975
THE RELEVANCE OF WIND STRUCTURE TO DESIGN, Proceedings of the 4th International Conference on Wind Effects on Buildings and Structures (London, England), University of Cambridge Press, Cambridge, England. (7)

Harrison, G. A., 1974
THE HIGH-RISE FIRE PROBLEM, CRC Critical Reviews in Environmental Control, Chemical Rubber Co., Cleveland, Ohio, October. (8A)

Hart, G. C., 1969
COMBINING A WIND TUNNEL ANALYSIS WITH A THREE-DIMENSIONAL ANALYTIC BUILDING ANALYSIS, Proceedings of the Technical Meeting Concerning Wind Loads on Buildings and Structures (NBS, Gaithersburg, Md.), Building Science Series 30. (7)

Hart, G. C., DiJulio, R. M., Jr. and Lew, M., 1974
HIGH-RISE BUILDING RESPONSE: DAMPING AND PERIOD NONLINEARITIES, Proceedings of the 5th World Conference on Earthquake Engineering (Rome, Italy, April). (6)

Hart, G. C., DiJulio, R. M., Jr. and Lew, M., 1975
TORSIONAL RESPONSE AND DESIGN OF BUILDINGS, *Journal of the Structural Division*, ASCE, Vol. 101, No. ST2, Proc. Paper 11126, pp. 397–416. (6)

Harvancik, J., 1973
CRITERIA FOR DESIGN AND CALCULATION OF LOAD-BEARING STRUCTURES OF TALL BUILDINGS, 10th Regional Conference Proceedings (Bratislava, Czechoslovakia, April), CSVTA-Czechoslovak Scientific and Technical Association, Bratislava, Czechoslovakia. (10)

Hasofer, A. M. and Lind, N. C., 1973
AN EXACT AND INVARIANT SECOND MOMENT CODE FORMAT, University of
Waterloo, Ont., Canada. (10)

Herrera, I. and Rosenblueth, E., 1965
RESPONSE SPECTRA ON STRATIFIED SOIL, Proceedings of the 3rd World Conference on Earthquake Engineering (New Zealand). (6)

Heselden, A. J. M., 1968
PARAMETERS DETERMINING THE SEVERITY OF FIRE, Paper in Symposium No.
2—Behaviour of Structural Steel in Fire, 1967, HMSO, London, England. (8A)

Heselden, A. J. M., 1971
FIRE PROBLEMS OF PEDESTRIAN PRECINCTS, PART I: THE SMOKE PRO-
DUCTION OF VARIOUS MATERIALS, Joint Fire Research Organization, Fire
Research Note No. 856. (8A)

Heuschkel, J., 1971
ANISOTROPY AND WELDABILITY, *Welding Journal*, Vol. 60, No. 3, pp. 111-s–126-s.
(9)

Higashi, Y. and Hirosawa, M., 1974
SYNTHETIC RESEARCH ON EARTHQUAKE RESISTANT CHARACTERISTICS
OF REINFORCED CONCRETE COLUMNS, Proceedings of the National Conference
on Tall Buildings (Tokyo, Japan, August), Architectural Institute of Japan, Tokyo, Japan,
pp. 43–44. (6)

Hinkle, J. E., 1963
AN EVALUATION OF WELD QUALITY AS A COST FACTOR, *Welding Journal*, Vol.
42, No. 1, pp. 23–28. (9)

Hino, M., 1964
ON THE GUST FACTOR-RELATIONSHIP BETWEEN THE INSTANTANEOUS
MAXIMA AND AVERAGING AND SAMPLING TIMES, Proceedings of the 14th
Japan National Congress for Applied Mechanics, pp. 132–139. (7)

Hino, M., 1971
SPECTRUM OF GUSTY WIND, Proceedings of the Conference on Wind Effects on
Buildings and Structures (Tokyo, Japan), pp. 68–78. (7)

Hirsch, G. and Ruschewyh, H., 1971
NEWER INVESTIGATIONS OF NON-STEADY WIND LOADINGS AND THE
DYNAMIC RESPONSE OF TALL BUILDINGS AND OTHER CONSTRUCTIONS,
Proceedings of the 3rd International Conference on Wind Effects on Buildings and
Structures (Tokyo, Japan). (7)

Hirsch, G. and Ruscheweyh, H., 1975
VIBRATION MEASUREMENTS ON A CABLE-STAYED BRIDGE UNDER CON-
STRUCTION, *Journal of Industrial Aerodynamics*, Vol. 1, No. 3, pp. 297–300. (7)

Hisada, T., 1971a
EARTHQUAKE LOADING AND RESPONSE CRITERIA, 3rd Regional Conference
Proceedings (Tokyo, Japan, September), Muto Institute of Structural Mechanics, Tokyo,
Japan, pp. 63–78. (6)

Hisada, T., 1971b
EARTHQUAKE LOADING AND RESPONSE CRITERIA, 2nd Regional Conference
Proceedings (Bled, Yugoslavia, May), Lehigh University, Bethlehem, Pa., p. 28. (6)

Hisada, T., 1971c
EARTHQUAKE RESISTANT DESIGN OF HIGH-RISE BUILDINGS IN JAPAN, 3rd
Regional Conference Proceedings (Tokyo, Japan, September), Muto Institute of Struc-
tural Mechanics, Tokyo, Japan, pp. 90–98. (6)

Hisada, T., 1973
LOADING AND RESPONSE CRITERIA AND CODE REQUIREMENTS, Planning
and Design of Tall Buildings, Proceedings of the 1972 ASCE-IABSE International
Conference, Vol. 1b, ASCE, New York, pp. 267–278. (6)

Hobsen, V. J. and Steward, L. J., 1972
PRESSURIZATION OF ESCAPE ROUTES IN BUILDINGS, Fire Research Note No.
958, Fire Research Station, Borehamwood, Herts., England. (8A)

Hoecker, W. H., 1961
WIND SPEED AND AIR FLOW PATTERNS IN THE DALLAS TORNADO OF
APRIL 2, 1957, *Monthly Weather Review*, No. 88, No. 5, pp. 167–180. (7)

Holley, W. L. and Banister, J. R., 1975
USE OF DYNAMICALLY RESPONDING MANOMETERS TO MONITOR STRUC-
TURAL WIND PRESSURE LOADS, Journal of Industrial Aerodynamics, Vol. 1, No. 7,
pp. 139–166. (7)

Hollister, S. C., 1969
THE ENGINEERING INTERPRETATION OF WEATHER BUREAU RECORDS
FOR WIND LOADING ON STRUCTURES, Proceedings of the Technical Meeting
Concerning Wind Loads on Buildings and Structures, National Bureau of Standards
(Gaithersburg, Md.), Building Science Series 30. (7)

Holm, T. A., 1972
ENGINEERED MASONRY WITH HIGH STRENGTH LIGHTWEIGHT CONCRETE
MASONRY UNITS, Concrete Facts, Expanded Shale Institute, Vol. 17, No. 2,
September. (9)

Holm, T. A., 1976
BLOCK CONCRETE IS A STRUCTURAL MATERIAL, Journal of Testing and Evaluation, American Society for Testing and Materials, Vol. 4, No. 4, pp. 293–299. (9)

Holm, T. A., undated
UNPUBLISHED DATA FROM EXPERIMENTAL BLOCK RUNS, private commu-
nication to E. J. White, Jr., Skilling, Helle, Christiansen, Robertson, P. C., New York. (9)

Holm, T. and Chilress, L. K., 1973
TENSION TESTING OF BUILDING UNITS, United States Patent No. 3 792 608. (9)

Holmes, J. D., 1973
WIND PRESSURE FLUCTUATIONS ON A LARGE BUILDING, thesis presented to
Monash University, Australia, in partial fulfillment of the requirements for the degree of
Doctor of Philosophy. (7)

Holmes, J. D., 1975
PRESSURE FLUCTUATIONS ON A LARGE BUILDING AND ALONG-WIND
STRUCTURAL LOADING, Journal of Industrial Aerodynamics, Vol. 1, No. 1, pp.
249–278. (7)

Horacek, E., 1973
RECENT KNOWLEDGE ON THE THEORETICAL AND EXPERIMENTAL SO-
LUTION OF THE LOAD-BEARING WALL SYSTEM OF HIGH-RISE BUILDINGS,
10th Regional Conference Proceedings (Bratislava, Czechoslovakia, April), CSVTA-
Czechoslovak Scientific and Technical Association, Bratislava, Czechoslovakia. (10)

Horak, V., 1973
RELIABILITY AND EFFECTIVENESS OF TALL BUILDINGS, 10th Regional Conference Proceedings (Bratislava, Czechoslovakia, April), CSTVA-Czechoslovak Scientific
and Technical Association, Bratislava, Czechoslovakia. (10)

Horak, V., 1974
RELIABILITY AND EFFECTIVENESS OF TALL BUILDINGS, Proceedings of the
Regional Conference on Tall Buildings (Bangkok, Thailand, January), Asian Institute of
Technology, Bangkok, Thailand. (10)

Hou, S., 1968
EARTHQUAKE SIMULATION MODELS AND THEIR APPLICATIONS, Report
R68-17, Dept. of Civil Engineering, Massachusetts Institute of Technology, Cambridge,
Mass. (10)

Housner, G. W., 1947
CHARACTERISTICS OF STRONG MOTION EARTHQUAKES, Bulletin, Seismological
Society of America, Vol. 31, No. 1. (6)

Housner, G. W., 1956
LIMIT DESIGN OF STRUCTURES TO RESIST EARTHQUAKES, Proceedings of the
1st World Conference on Earthquake Engineering, Berkeley, Calif. (6)

Housner, G. W., 1963
U.S. ATOMIC ENERGY COMMISSION REPORT TID-7024, U.S. Atomic Energy
Commission, Washington, D.C., August. (6)

Housner, G. W., 1973
EARTHQUAKE GROUND MOTION, Planning and Design of Tall Buildings, Proceedings of the 1972 ASCE-IABSE International Conference, Vol. 1b, ASCE, New York,
pp. 159–176. (6)

Housner, G. W. and Brady, A. G., 1963
NATURAL PERIODS OF VIBRATION OF BUILDINGS, *Journal of the Engineering Mechanics Division*, ASCE, Vol. 89, No. EM4, Proc. Paper 3613, pp. 31–65. (6)

Housner, G. W. and Jennings, P. C., 1964
GENERATION OF ARTIFICIAL EARTHQUAKES, *Journal of the Engineering Mechanics Division*, ASCE, Vol. 90, EM1, Proc. Paper 3806, pp. 113–150. (6)

Huang, L. Y., 1973
TEMPERATURE LOADS, Planning and Design of Tall Buildings, Proceedings of the 1972 ASCE-IABSE International Conference, Vol. 1b, No. 5-6, ASCE, New York, pp. 97–120. (5)

Hudson, D. E., 1971
STRONG MOTION INSTRUMENTAL DATA ON THE SAN FERNANDO EARTH-QUAKE OF FEBRUARY 9, 1971, California Institute of Technology, Pasadena, Calif. (6)

Hudson, D. E., Alford, J. L. and Housner, G. W., 1954
MEASURED RESPONSE OF A STRUCTURE TO AN EXPLOSIVE-GENERATED GROUND SHOCK, *Bulletin*, Seismological Society of America, Vol. 44, No. 3. (6)

Huh, C. K., 1971
THE BEHAVIOUR OF LIFT FLUCTUATIONS ON THE SQUARE CYLINDERS IN THE WIND TUNNEL TEST, 3rd International Conference on Wind Effects on Buildings and Structures (Tokyo, Japan). (7)

Humphreys, W. Y., 1973
THE ALARMING PROBLEM, *Fire Journal*, Vol. 67, No. 5, National Fire Protection Association, Boston, Mass. (8A)

Hunt, J. C. R., 1975a
WIND TUNNEL SIMULATION OF ATMOSPHERIC BOUNDARY LAYER: A REPORT ON EUROMECH 50, *Journal of Fluid Mechanics*, Vol. 70, Part 3, pp. 543–559. (7)

Hunt, J. C. R., 1975b
TURBULENT VELOCITIES NEAR AND FLUCTUATING SURFACE PRESSURES ON STRUCTURES IN TURBULENT WINDS, Proceedings of the 4th International Conference on Wind Effects on Buildings and Structures (London, England), University of Cambridge Press, Cambridge, England. (7)

Hunt, J. C. R., Poulton, E. C. and Mumford, J. C., 1976
THE EFFECTS OF WIND ON PEOPLE; NEW CRITERIA BASED ON WIND TUNNEL EXPERIMENTS, *Building and Environment*, Pergamon Press, London, England, Vol. 2, pp. 15–28. (7)

Husid, R. and Sanchez, J., 1974
EARTHQUAKE RESPONSE REDUCTION IN BUILDINGS WITH AN ELASTO-PLASTIC STORY, Proceedings of the Regional Conference on Tall Buildings (Porto Alegre, Brazil, December), Asian Institute of Technology, Bangkok, Thailand, pp. 671–682. (6)

Hutcheon, N. B. and Shorter, G. W., 1968
SMOKE PROBLEMS IN HIGH-RISE BUILDINGS, *ASHRAE Journal*, Vol. 10, No. 9. (8A)

IAEE, 1960
PROCEEDINGS OF SECOND WORLD CONFERENCE ON EARTHQUAKE EN-GINEERING, International Association for Earthquake Engineering (Tokyo, Japan). (6)

IAEE, 1965
PROCEEDINGS OF THIRD WORLD CONFERENCE ON EARTHQUAKE ENGI-NEERING, International Association for Earthquake Engineering (New Zealand). (6)

IAEE, 1969
PROCEEDINGS OF FOURTH WORLD CONFERENCE ON EARTHQUAKE EN-GINEERING, International Association for Earthquake Engineering (Santiago, Chile). (6)

IAEE, 1973
EARTHQUAKE RESISTANT REGULATIONS—A WORLD LIST, International Association for Earthquake Engineering, April; and its supplement, 1976. (6)

ICBO, 1970
UNIFORM BUILDING CODE, 1970 Edition, International Conference of Building Officials, Whittier, Calif. (6)
ICBO, 1971
UNIFORM BUILDING CODE, International Conference of Building Officials, Whittier, Calif. (10)
ICBO, 1976
UNIFORM BUILDING CODE, International Conference of Building Officials, Whittier, Calif. (6)
ICBO, 1979
UNIFORM BUILDING CODE, 1979 Edition, International Conference of Building Officials, Whittier, Calif. (9)
IHVE, 1973
RECOMMENDATIONS RELATING THE DESIGN OF AIR-HANDLING SYSTEMS TO FIRE AND SMOKE CONTROL IN BUILDINGS, IHVE Technical Memoranda 1, The Institution of Heating and Ventilating Engineers, London, England. (8A)
ISE, 1969
THE IMPLICATIONS OF THE REPORT OF THE INQUIRY INTO THE COLLAPSE OF FLATS AT RONAN POINT, CANNING TOWN, Report of an Open Discussion Meeting, *Structural Engineer*, Vol. 47, pp. 255–284, 387–389. (8B)
ISO, 1970
METHODS OF EVALUATING DESIGN EARTHQUAKE FORCES ON STRUC-TURES, prepared by WG 1, ISO/TC 98, International Organization for Standardization, Geneva, Switzerland. (6)
ISO, 1974
FIRE RESISTANCE TESTS ON DOOR AND SHUTTER ASSEMBLIES, DIS 3008, International Organization for Standardization, Geneva, Switzerland. (8A)
ISO, 1975
FIRE RESISTANCE TEST OF STRUCTURES, ISO/R834, International Organization for Standardization, Geneva, Switzerland. (8A)
ISO, 1976
FIRE RESISTANCE TEST ON DOOR AND SHUTTER ASSEMBLIES, DIS 3008-1976E, (Revised), International Organization for Standardization, Geneva, Switzerland. (8A)
Iberall, A. S., 1950
ATTENUATION OF OSCILLATORY PRESSURES IN INSTRUMENT LINES, Research Paper RP 2115, U.S. National Bureau of Standards; ASME *Transactions*. (7)
Idriss, I. M. and Seed, H. B., 1967
RESPONSE OF EARTH BANKS DURING EARTHQUAKES, *Journal of the Soil Mechanics and Foundations Division*, ASCE, Vol. 93, No. SM3, Proc. Paper 5232, pp. 61–82. (6)
Idriss, I. M. and Seed, H. B., 1968a
SEISMIC RESPONSE OF HORIZONTAL SOIL LAYERS, *Journal of the Soil Mechanics and Foundations Division*, ASCE, Vol. 94, No. SM4, Proc. Paper 6043, pp. 1003–1031. (6)
Idriss, I. M. and Seed, H. B., 1968b
AN ANALYSIS OF GROUND MOTIONS DURING THE 1957 SAN FRANCISCO EARTHQUAKE, *Bulletin*, Seismological Society of America, Vol. 58, No. 6, pp. 2013–2032. (6)
Idriss, I. M. and Seed, H. B., 1970
SEISMIC RESPONSE OF SOIL DEPOSITS, *Journal of the Soil Mechanics and Foundations Division*, ASCE, Vol. 96, No. SM2, Proc. Paper 7175, pp. 631–638. (6)
Idriss, I. M., Dezfulian, H. and Seed, H. B., 1969
COMPUTER PROGRAMS FOR EVALUATING THE SEISMIC RESPONSE OF SOIL DEPOSITS WITH NONLINEAR CHARACTERISTICS USING EQUIVALENT LIN-EAR PROCEDURES, Geotechnical Engineering Research Report, University of California, Berkeley, Calif. (6)
Information Canada, 1971
CANADA YEARBOOK 1971, Information Canada, Ottawa, Canada. (10)

Ingberg, S. H., 1928
TESTS OF THE SEVERITY OF BUILDING FIRES, *National Fire Protection Association Quarterly*, Vol. 22, No. 1, pp. 43–61. (8A)
International Conference of Building Officials, 1971
See ICBO, 1971. (10)
Isberner, A. W., 1974
PROPERTIES OF MASONRY CEMENT MORTARS, Research and Development Bulletin RDO 19.01 M, Portland Cement Association, Skokie, Ill. (9)
Ishizaki, H., 1967
EFFECTS OF WIND PRESSURE FLUCTUATIONS ON STRUCTURES, International Conference on Wind Effects on Buildings and Structures (NPL, Teddington, England). (7)
Ishizaki, H., 1971a
STORM FREQUENCIES AND WIND LOAD PROBLEMS, International Conference on Wind Effects on Buildings and Structures (Tokyo, Japan). (7)
Ishizaki, H., 1971b
CURRENT STUDIES ON WIND LOADS IN JAPAN, 3rd National/Regional Conference (Tokyo, Japan), pp. 101–106. (7)
Ishizaki, H., 1973
RESEARCH REVIEW—ASIA AND AUSTRALIA, Planning and Design of Tall Buildings, Proceedings of the 1972 ASCE-IABSE Conference, Vol. 1b, ASCE, New York, pp. 365–374. (7)
Ishizaki, H., 1974
ON THE WIND RESISTANT DESIGN OF EXTERIOR CLADDING, Proceedings of the 14th National/Regional Conference on Tall Buildings (Tokyo, Japan), pp. 85–86. (7)
Ishizaki, H., 1975
ON THE DESIGN OF GLASS PANE AGAINST WIND LOADING, Proceedings of the 4th International Conference on Wind Effects on Buildings and Structures (London, England), University of Cambridge Press, Cambridge, England. (7)
Ishizaki, H., 1976
PROBLEMS IN DESIGNING WINDOW GLASS AGAINST WIND PRESSURE, Proceedings of the 1974 2nd USA/Japan Research Seminar on Wind Effects on Structures, University of Tokyo Press, Tokyo, Japan. (7)
Ishizaki, H. and Sung, I. W., 1971
INFLUENCE OF ADJACENT BUILDINGS TO WIND, Proceedings, 3rd International Conference on Wind Effects on Buildings and Structures (Tokyo, Japan). (7)
Ishizaki, H., Miyoshi, S. and Miura, T., 1977
ON THE DESIGN OF GLASS PANE AGAINST WIND LOADING, Proceedings of the 4th International Conference on Wind Effects on Buildings and Structures (London, England), Cambridge University Press, Cambridge, England, pp. 605–611. (9)
Isyumov, N. and Brignall, J., 1975
SOME FULL SCALE MEASUREMENTS OF WIND INDUCED RESPONSE OF THE CN TOWER, TORONTO, *Journal of Industrial Aerodynamics*, Vol. 1, No. 2, pp. 213–219. (7)
Isyumov, N. and Davenport, A. G., 1975a
THE GROUND LEVEL WIND ENVIRONMENT IN BUILT-UP AREAS, Proceedings of the 4th International Conference on Buildings and Structures (London, England), University of Cambridge Press, Cambridge, England. (7)
Isyumov, N. and Davenport, A. G., 1975b
COMPARISON OF FULL SCALE AND WIND TUNNEL WIND SPEED MEASUREMENTS IN THE COMMERCE COURT PLAZA, *Journal of Industrial Aerodynamics*, Vol. 1, No. 2, pp. 201–202. (7)
Isyumov, N., Jandali, T. and Davenport, A. G., 1974
MODEL STUDIES AND THE PREDICTION OF FULL SCALE LEVELS OF STACK GAS CONCENTRATION, 67 APCA Meeting (Denver, Colo.), Paper No. 74-162. (7)
Izumi, M., 1971
IMPACT AND DYNAMIC LOAD EFFECTS, 3rd Regional Conference Proceedings (Tokyo, Japan, September), Muto Institute of Structural Mechanics, Tokyo, Japan, pp. 36–43. (6)

Izumi, M., 1973
    IMPACT AND DYNAMIC LOAD EFFECTS, Planning and Design of Tall Buildings,
    Proceedings of 1972 ASCE-IABSE International Conference, Vol. 1b, No. 5-4, ASCE,
    New York, pp. 77–84. (5)

JFRO, 1969
    MOVEMENT OF SMOKE ON ESCAPE ROUTES IN BUILDINGS, Symposium No. 4,
    Joint Fire Research Organisation, United Kingdom, April. (8A)
Jackson, N., 1973
    CONCRETE QUALITY, Planning and Design of Tall Buildings, Proceedings of the 1972
    ASCE-IABSE International Conference, Vol. 1b, ASCE, New York, p. 896. (9)
Jackson, N., 1974
    CONCRETE QUALITY CONTROL, Proceedings of the Regional Conference on Tall
    Buildings (Bangkok, Thailand, January), Asian Institute of Technology, Bangkok,
    Thailand, pp. 213–227. (9)
Jackson, P. S., 1975
    A THEORY FOR WIND FLOW OVER ESCARPMENTS, Proceedings of the 4th
    International Conference on Wind Effects on Buildings and Structures (London,
    England), University of Cambridge Press, Cambridge, England. (7)
Jacobsen, L. S., 1939
    NATURAL PERIODS OF UNIFORM CANTILEVER BEAMS, Transactions, ASCE,
    Vol. 104, Paper No. 2025, p. 402. (6)
Jain, O. P. and Palaniswamy, S. P., 1973
    EFFECT OF CONSTRUCTION STAGES ON THE STRESSES IN MULTI-STORIED
    FRAMES, Proceedings of National Conference on Tall Buildings, (New Delhi, India,
    January) Indian National Group of IABSE, New Delhi, India, pp. V1–V8. (5)
Janele, J., 1973
    THE CHECK OF ALIGNMENT OF PLANE VERTICAL ELEVATION WALLS, 10th
    Regional Conference Proceedings, (Bratislava, Czechoslovakia, April), Vols. I and II,
    CSVTA—Czechoslovak Scientific and Technical Association, Bratislava, Czechoslovakia
    (two editions: English and Czech), pp. 326–332. (9)
Japan National Committee of IAEE, 1965
    NIIGATA EARTHQUAKE OF 1964, Proceedings of the 3rd World Conference on
    Earthquake Engineering (New Zealand), Vol. III. (6)
Japan National Committee of IAEE, 1968
    SOME RECENT EARTHQUAKE ENGINEERING RESEARCH AND PRACTICE IN
    JAPAN, December. (6)
Japanese Association of Fire Science and Engineering, 1972
    KASAI (Fire), Magazine, Tokyo, Japan. (8A)
Japanese Association of Fire Science and Engineering, 1974
    OCCASIONAL REPORT NO. 1, Tokyo, Japan. (8A)
Jennings, P. C., Ed., 1971
    ENGINEERING FEATURES OF THE SAN FERNANDO EARTHQUAKE, FEB-
    RUARY 9, 1971, EERL No. 71-02 Earthquake Engineering Research Laboratory,
    California Institute of Technology. (6)
Jennings, P. C., Housner, G. W. and Tsau, N. C., 1969
    EARTHQUAKE MOTIONS FOR DESIGN PURPOSES, Proceedings of the 4th World
    Conference on Earthquake Engineering (Santiago, Chile). (6)
Jensen, M., 1958
    THE MODEL LAW FOR PHENOMENA IN THE NATURAL WIND, Ingeniores, Int.
    Ed. 2. (7)
Jensen, M., 1967
    SOME LESSONS LEARNED IN BUILDING AERODYNAMICS RESEARCH, Special
    Introductory Lecture, Proceedings, International Research Seminar on Wind Effects on
    Buildings and Structures (Ottawa, Canada). (7)
Jensen, M. and Franck, N., 1963
    PROPOSED CODE OF PRACTICE FOR WIND LOADS FOR DENMARK, Pro-
    ceedings of the International Conference on Wind Effects on Buildings and Structures
    (NPL, Teddington, England). (7)

Jensen, M. and Franck, N., 1965
    MODEL SCALE TESTS IN TURBULENT WIND, Parts I and II, Danish Technical Press, Copenhagen, Denmark. (7)
Jensen, M. and Franck, N., 1967
    MAXIMUM WIND VELOCITIES IN DENMARK, Proceedings, International Research Seminar on Wind Effects on Buildings and Structures (Ottawa, Canada). (7)
Jensen, R., 1973
    MEANS OF FIRE FIGHTING AND SAFETY DEVICES, Planning and Design of Tall Buildings, Proceedings of the 1972 ASCE-IABSE International Conference, Vol. 1b, ASCE, New York, pp. 523–540. (8A)
Jerus, G., 1972
    FIRE SAFETY IN TALL BUILDINGS, 6th Regional Conference Proceedings (Delft, The Netherlands, May), Lehigh University, Bethlehem, Pa. (8A)
Johansson, A. and Warris, B., 1969
    DEVIATIONS OF THE LOCATION OF REINFORCEMENT, Proceedings No. 40, Swedish Cement and Concrete Research Institute, Stockholm, Sweden. (9)
Johnson, A. I., 1953
    STRENGTH, SAFETY AND ECONOMICAL DIMENSIONS OF STRUCTURES, Bulletin 12, Div. of Building Statics and Structural Engineering, Royal Institute of Technology, Stockholm, Sweden. (10)
Johnson, A. I., 1971
    STRENGTH, SAFETY AND ECONOMICAL DIMENSIONS OF STRUCTURES, Document D7: 1979, Statens Institute for Byggnadsforskning, Stockholm, Sweden. (9)
Johnson, S. M., 1973
    DEAD, LIVE AND CONSTRUCTION LOADS, Planning and Design of Tall Buildings, Proceedings of 1972 ASCE-IABSE International Conference, Vol. 1b, No. 5-3, ASCE, New York, pp. 59–76. (5)
Joubert, P. N., Perry, A. E. and Stevens, L. K., 1971
    DRAG OF A BLUFF BODY IMMERSED IN A ROUGHWALL BOUNDARY LAYER, Proceedings, 3rd International Conference on Wind Effects on Buildings and Structures (Tokyo, Japan). (7)
Joubert, P. N., Stevens, L. K., Good, M. C., Hoffmann, E. R. and Perry, A. E., 1967
    THE DRAG OF BLUFF BODIES IMMERSED IN A TURBULENT BOUNDARY LAYER, Proceedings, International Research Seminar on Wind Effects on Buildings and Structures (Ottawa, Canada). (7)
Juhasova, E., 1973
    DYNAMIC PROPERTIES OF SOME TYPES OF FRAMED TALL BUILDINGS, 10th Regional Conference Proceedings (Bratislava, Czechoslovakia, April), CSVTA-Czechoslovak Scientific and Technical Association, Bratislava, Czechoslovakia, pp. 286–293. (6, 7)
Juillerat, E. E., 1962
    THE HARTFORD HOSPITAL FIRE, *National Fire Protection Association Quarterly*, Vol. 55, No. 3, pp. 295–303. (8A)
Juillerat, E. E. and Gaudet, R. E., 1967
    FIRE AT DALE'S PENTHOUSE RESTAURANT, *Fire Journal*, High-Rise Building Fires and Fire Safety, National Fire Protection Association, Boston, Mass., pp. 52–56 (reprint). (8A)

Kajfasz, S., 1973
    EXTERNAL BLAST, Planning and Design of Tall Buildings, Proceedings of the 1972 ASCE-IABSE International Conference, Vol. 1b, No. 8-D6, ASCE, New York, pp. 717–718. (8B)
Kamei, I. and Motai, H., 1971
    APPLICATION TO DESIGN OF RESEARCH ON TALL BUILDING WIND EFFECTS, Proceedings, 3rd International Conference on Wind Effects on Buildings and Structures (Tokyo, Japan). (7)
Kanai, K., 1951
    RELATION BETWEEN THE NATURE OF SURFACE LAYER AND THE AMPLITUDES OF EARTHQUAKE MOTIONS, *Bulletin*, Earthquake Research Institute, Berkeley, Calif. (6)

Kármán, T., 1966
INVESTIGATIONS OF OCCUPANCY LOADINGS ON FLOORS OF DWELLINGS (in German), *Österreichischer Ingenieur-Zeitschrift*, Vol. 9, No. 4, pp. 119–123. (5)

Kármán, T., 1969
STATISTICAL INVESTIGATIONS ON LIVE LOADS ON FLOORS, Committee W23, Conseil International du Bâtiment. (5)

Kasiraj, I. and Yao, J. T. P., 1968
LOW CYCLE FATIGUE FAILURE OF SEISMIC STRUCTURES, University of New Mexico, Albuquerque, N.M. (10)

Kato, B. and Akiyama, H., 1974
EXPERIMENTAL STUDY ON BUFFETING VIBRATIONS OF TALL BUILDINGS, Proceedings, 2nd USA/Japan Research Seminar on Wind Effects on Structures, University of Tokyo Press, Japan. (7)

Kato, B., Akiyama, H. and Okada, H., 1976
WIND LOADING STUDIES ON TALL BUILDINGS AT MODEL SCALE, Proceedings, 2nd Tall Buildings Conference (Hong Kong, September). (7)

Kato, B., Akiyama, H., Kawabata, S. and Kanda, J., 1971
WIND TUNNEL TEST FOR DYNAMIC RESPONSE OF TALL BUILDING, Proceedings, 3rd International Conference on Wind Effects on Buildings and Structures (Tokyo, Japan). (7)

Katsura, J., 1974
FLUCTUATING WIND PRESSURE ON THE SIDE SURFACES ON MODELS WITH LONG RECTANGULAR SECTIONS, Proceedings, 2nd USA/Japan Research Seminar on Wind Effects on Structures, University of Tokyo, Japan. (7)

Kavanagh, T. C., 1971
QUALITY CONTROL, 5th Regional Conference Proceedings (Chicago, Ill., November/December), Lehigh University, Bethlehem, Pa., pp. 57–59. (9)

Kavyrchine, M. and Struck, W., 1975
THE EFFECT OF IMPACT LOADING ON BUILDING: PART 6: PRACTICAL APPLICATION TO TESTING, DESIGN AND RESEARCH, *Matériaux et Construction*, Vol. 8, pp. 125–129. (8B)

Kawagoe, K., 1967
ESTIMATION OF FIRE TEMPERATURE-TIME CURVE IN ROOMS, Building Research Institute Research Paper No. 29, Tokyo, Japan, October. (8A)

Kawagoe, K., 1971
FACTORS INFLUENCING NATURAL FIRES AND THEIR DEVELOPMENT, Proceedings of the 3rd Regional Conference (Tokyo, Japan, September), Muto Institute of Structural Mechanics, Tokyo, Japan. (8A)

Kawagoe, K., 1973
SYSTEM DESIGN FOR FIRE SAFETY, Planning and Design of Tall Buildings, Proceedings of the 1972 ASCE-IABSE International Conference, Vol. 1b, ASCE, New York, pp. 569–584. (8A)

Kawagoe, K. and Sekine, T., 1963
ESTIMATION OF FIRE TEMPERATURE-TIME CURVE IN ROOMS, BRI Occasional Report No. 11. (8A)

Kawai, H. and Ishizaki, H., 1975
ON THE RELATION BETWEEN THE FLUCTUATIONS OF WIND SPEED AND PRESSURE ON THE WINDWARD SURFACE, Proceedings, Pan-Pacific Tall Buildings Conference (Honolulu, Hawaii), pp. 267–278. (7)

Kawai, H. and Ishikazi, H., 1976
LOCAL WIND PRESSURE CHARACTERISTICS ON A FULL-SCALE TALL BUILDING, Proceedings, 2nd Tall Buildings Conference (Hong Kong, September). (7)

Kawasumi, H., Morimoto, R., Umemura, H., Okamoto, S. and Kubo, K., 1968
GENERAL REPORT ON THE NIIGATA EARTHQUAKE OF JUNE 16, 1964, Electrical Engineering College Press, Chiyoda-ku, Tokyo, Japan. (6)

Kawatani, Y., Cermak, J. E. and Meroney, R. H., 1971
CHARACTERISTICS OF THE MEAN FLOW OVER A SIMULATED URBAN AREA, Proceedings, 3rd International Conference on Wind Effects on Buildings and Structures (Tokyo, Japan). (7)

Kebo, V., 1973
SOME EXPERIENCE ACQUIRED BY ASSEMBLY OF STEEL STRUCTURES OF MULTI-STORY BUILDINGS, 10th Regional Conference Proceedings (Bratislava, Czechoslovakia, April), Vols. I and II, CSVTA-Czechoslovak Scientific and Technical Association, Bratislava, Czechoslovakia (two editions: English and Czech), pp. 177–186. (9)

Keintzel, E., 1975
DUCTILITY AND SAFETY OF SHEAR WALL TALL BUILDINGS IN SEISMIC REGIONS (Zahigkeit und Sicherheit von Wandscheiben-Hochhausern in Erdbebengebieten), Reinforced Concrete Tall Buildings (Proceedings of Conference held in Iasi, Romania, October), Vol. 1, Consiliul National al Inginerilor si Tehnicienilor, Iasi, Romania, pp. 415–425. (6)

Kenya Government Ministry of Works, 1973
CODE OF PRACTICE FOR THE DESIGN AND CONSTRUCTION OF BUILDINGS AND OTHER STRUCTURES IN RELATION TO EARTHQUAKES, Kenya Government Ministry of Works, Kenya. (6)

Kesler, C. E., 1959
EFFECT ON LENGTH TO DIAMETER RATIO ON COMPRESSIVE STRENGTH —AN ASTM COOPERATIVE INVESTIGATION, Proceedings, American Society for Testing and Materials, Philadelphia, Pa., Vol. 59, pp. 1216–1229. (9)

Khan, F. R. and Parmelee, R. A., 1971
SERVICE CRITERIA FOR TALL BUILDINGS FOR WIND LOADING, Proceedings, 3rd International Conference on Wind Effects on Buildings and Structures (Tokyo, Japan). (7)

Kihara, H., 1960
RELATION BETWEEN RESULTS OF NONDESTRUCTIVE TESTING OF MATERIALS AND THEIR MECHANICAL STRENGTH, University of Tokyo, Japan. (9)

Kimura, H., 1957
BASIC THEORY OF BUILDING PLAN, Equipments, Kyoritsu Publisher, Tokyo, Japan. (8A)

Kingman, F. E. T., Coleman, E. H. and Rasbash, D. J., 1953
THE PRODUCTS OF COMBUSTION IN BURNING BUILDINGS, Journal of Applied Chemistry, Vol. 3, pp. 463–468. (8A)

Kinney, C. F., 1962
EXPLOSIVE SHOCKS IN AIR, The Macmillan Co., New York. (8B)

Kishima, Y., Alpsten, G. A. and Tall, L., 1969
RESIDUAL STRESSES IN WELDED SHAPES OF FLAME-CUT PLATES IN ASTM A572 (50) STEEL, Fritz Engineering Laboratory Report No. 321.2, Lehigh University, Bethlehem, Pa., June. (9)

Kobayashi, H. and Kagami, H., 1966
A NUMERICAL ANALYSIS OF THE PROPAGATION OF SHEAR WAVES IN MULTI-LAYERED GROUND, Proceedings, Japan Earthquake Engineering Symposium (Tokyo, Japan), pp. 15–20. (6)

Kobayashi, S. and Yoshida, M., 1971
MEASUREMENT AND ANALYSIS OF VIBRATION OF HIGH-RISE BUILDING IN STRONG WIND, Proceedings, 3rd International Conference on Wind Effects on Buildings and Structures (Tokyo, Japan). (7)

Kochle, R., 1974
MEASURING THE OSCILLATIONS OF TALL BUILDINGS WITH A LASER-INTERFEROMETER, Proceedings, Conference on Tall Buildings (Kuala Lumpur, Malaysia), pp. 8.29–8.40. (7)

Kolousek, V. and Naprstek, J. et al., 1973
VIBRATION OF STRUCTURES OF TALL BUILDINGS, Proceedings, 10th Regional Conference (Bratislava, Czechoslovakia), pp. 267–285. (7)

Kolousek, V. and Pirner, M., 1975
WIND EFFECTS ON TALL BUILDINGS, Proceedings, 4th International Conference on Wind Effects on Buildings and Structures (London, England), Cambridge University Press, Cambridge, England. (7)

König, G., 1973
GERMAN CODE REQUIREMENTS, Planning and Design of Tall Buildings, Proceedings of the 1972 ASCE-IABSE International Conference, Vol. 1b, ASCE, New York, pp. 1027–1031. (10)

König, G. and Zilch, K., 1970
A CONTRIBUTION TO THE ANALYSIS IN A GUSTY WIND (Ein Beitrag Zur
Berechnung von Bauwerken im Goeigen Wind), Ernst und Sohn, Berlin, Germany. (7)
Koppes, W. F., 1969
DESIGN WIND LOADS FOR BUILDING WALL ELEMENTS, Proceedings, Technical
Meeting Concerning Wind Loads on Buildings and Structures (NBS, Gaithersburg, Md.),
Building Science Series 30. (7)
Kordina, K. and Krampf, L., 1976
AN EXAMINATION OF THE EFFECTS OF A BIG FIRE IN SOME CONCRETE
BUILDINGS (in German), Beton- und Stahlbetonbau, Vol. 67, No. 5, pp. 108–113 and No.
6, pp. 129–134; Fire Prevention Science and Technology, No. 14, Fire Protection
Association, London, England, pp. 4–17 (in English). (8A)
Korenev, R. G., 1971
SOME PROBLEMS OF DYNAMIC DESIGN OF ELASTIC STRUCTURES EQUIP-
PED WITH DAMPERS FOR WIND EFFECT, Proceedings, 3rd International Con-
ference on Wind Effects on Buildings and Structures (Tokyo, Japan). (7)
Korenev, R. G., 1973
DYNAMICAL VIBRATION ABSORBERS OF TALL BUILDINGS AND TOWERS,
10th Regional Conference Proceedings (Bratislava, Czechoslovakia, April), CSVTA
—Czechoslovak Scientific and Technical Association, Bratislava, Czechoslovakia, pp.
294–297. (6, 7)
Korenev, R. G., 1975
ON DAMPING WIND INDUCED VIBRATIONS OF FLEXIBLE STRUCTURES,
Proceedings, 4th International Conference on Wind Effects on Buildings and Structures
(London, England), Cambridge University Press, Cambridge, England. (7)
Kostem, C. N., 1972
THERMAL STRESSES AND DEFORMATIONS IN PNEUMATIC CUSHION ROOFS,
Proceedings of the International Association for Shell and Spatial Structures Symposium
on Pneumatic Structures, Vol. 2, Delft, The Netherlands. (5)
Kostem, C. N., 1976
LOAD CARRYING CAPACITY OF RIBBED PRESTRESSED CONCRETE ROOF
PANELS, Proceedings of the International Association for Shell and Spatial Structures'
World Congress on Space Enclosures (Montréal, Canada). (5)
Kotze, F. W. C., 1975
FIRE FIGHTING, EDUCATION AND EVACUATION PROBLEMS IN TALL
BUILDINGS, Proceedings of the South African Conference on Tall Buildings (Joha-
nnesburg, South Africa, November), Hortors Printers, Johannesburg, South Africa. (8A)
Kovacs, W. D., Seed, H. B. and Idriss, I. M., 1971
STUDIES OF SEISMIC RESPONSE OF CLAY BANKS, Journal of the Soil Mechanics and
Foundations Division, ASCE, Vol. 97, No. SM2, Proc. Paper 7878, pp. 441–456. (6)
Kozak, J., 1971
STATICAL SYSTEMS OF TALL BUILDINGS WITH CORE STRUCTURES, Pro-
ceedings, 4th Regional Conference (Prague, Czechoslovakia), pp. 21–36. (7)
Krishna, J., 1973
ASEISMIC DESIGN OF BUILDINGS, Planning and Design of Tall Buildings, Pro-
ceedings of the 1972 ASCE-IABSE International Conference, Vol. 1b, ASCE, New York,
pp. 299–302. (6)
Krishna, J. and Chandrasekaran, A. R., 1973
SUITABILITY OF TALL BUILDINGS IN SEISMIC ZONES, Proceedings of National
Conference on Tall Buildings (New Delhi, India, January), Indian National Group of
IABSE, New Delhi, India, pp. III51–III56. (6)
Krishnaswamy, A. K., Rao, G. N. V., Rao, A. K. and Durvasula, S., 1971
RECENT WIND TUNNEL INVESTIGATIONS ON THE AERODYNAMIC STABIL-
ITY OF ENGINEERING STRUCTURES IN INDIA, Proceedings, 3rd International
Conference on Wind Effects on Buildings and Structures (Tokyo, Japan). (7)
Kruppa, J., 1975
DETERMINATION OF THE CRITICAL TEMPERATURE OF A STATICALLY
INDETERMINATE STRUCTURE (Détermination de la Température de Ruine d'une
Structure Hyperstatique), Symposium, Structures of Steel and Various Materials Used
—Report of Steel Construction, AIPC, Dresden, Germany. (8A)

Kruppa, J., 1976
  STUDY OF TEMPERATURES AND CRITERIA OF STEEL STRUCTURES (Calcul
  des Températures Critiques de Structures Métalliques), *Revue de Construction Metallique*,
  CTICM, No. 3. (8A)
Kulkarni, A. S., 1973
  FIRE PROTECTION IN HIGH-RISE BUILDINGS, Proceedings of the National
  Conference on Tall Buildings, (New Delhi, India, January), Indian National Group of
  IABSE, New Delhi, India. (8A)
Kulkarni, S. R. and Roy, S., 1973
  EFFECTS OF WINDS ON TALL BUILDINGS, Proceedings, National Conference on
  Tall Buildings (New Delhi, India), pp. II.125–II.140. (7)
Kunze, W. E., Sbarounis, J. A. and Amrhein, J. E., 1965
  THE MARCH 27, 1964, ALASKAN EARTHQUAKE, Portland Cement Association,
  Skokie, Ill. (6)
Kus, S., Lacki, T. and Zuranski, J. A., 1971
  THE NEW POLISH CODE OF PRACTICE FOR WIND LOADS IN COMPARISON
  WITH OTHER ACTUAL STANDARDS, Proceedings, 3rd International Conference on
  Wind Loads on Buildings and Structures (Tokyo, Japan). (7)
Kwiatkowski, J. and Ostrowski, B., 1974
  LOAD DISTRIBUTION ON VERTICAL BRACES IN A MULTI-STOREY FRAME
  INCLUDING THE INFLUENCE OF VERTICAL FORCES, *Proceedings*, Institution of
  Civil Engineers, Part 2, Vol. 57, December, pp. 707–716. (5)

Lalwani, C. K., 1973
  DESIGN ASSUMPTIONS, Planning and Design of Tall Buildings, Proceedings of the 1972
  ASCE-IABSE International Conference, Vol. 1b, No. 5-D2, ASCE, New York. (5)
Lam, R. P., 1973
  WIND EFFECTS ON TALL BUILDINGS IN HONG KONG, Proceedings, Regional
  Conference on Tall Buildings (Hong Kong), pp. 99–104. (7)
Lam, R. P. and Lam, L. C., 1975
  WIND LOAD FOR CLADDING DESIGN, Proceedings, 4th International Conference on
  Wind Effects on Buildings and Structures (London, England), Cambridge University
  Press, Cambridge, England. (7)
Laneville, A. and Parkinson, G. V., 1971
  EFFECTS OF TURBULENCE ON GALLOPING OF BLUFF CYLINDERS, Pro-
  ceedings, 3rd International Conference on Wind Effects on Buildings and Structures
  (Tokyo, Japan). (7)
Laneville, A., Gartshore, I. S. and Parkinson, G. V., 1975
  AN EXPLANATION OF SOME EFFECTS OF TURBULENCE ON BLUFF BODIES,
  Proceedings, 4th International Conference on Wind Effects on Buildings and Structures
  (London, England), Cambridge University Press, Cambridge, England. (7)
Lange, L. and Laue, H., 1973
  DYNAMIC LOADING OF A REACTOR BUILDING BY AN AIRPLANE CRASH
  (Dynamische Belastung Eines Reaktorgebaues Infolge Flugzeugabsturz), Preprints of the
  2nd International Conference on Structural Mechanics in Reactor Technology (Berlin,
  Germany), Vol. 6B, Paper J 3/2, Commission of the European Communities, Brussels,
  Belgium. (8B)
Langhaar, H. L., 1951
  DIMENSIONAL ANALYSIS AND THEORY OF MODELS, John Wiley & Sons, Inc.,
  New York. (7)
Lathrop, J. K., 1977
  300 FIRE FIGHTERS SAVE LOS ANGELES HIGH-RISE OFFICE BUILDING, *Fire
  Journal*, NFPA, Boston, Mass., September. (8A)
Lathrop, J. K., et al., 1975
  IN OSCEOLA, A MATTER OF CONTENTS, *Fire Journal*, Vol. 69, No. 3, National Fire
  Protection Association, Boston, Mass., May, pp. 20–26. (8A)
Laurie, J. A. P., 1975
  DESIGN LOADS FOR TALL BUILDINGS, Proceedings of the National Conference on
  Tall Buildings (Johannesburg, South Africa, November), Hortors Printers, Johannesburg,
  South Africa. (5, 7)

Law, M., 1963
HEAT RADIATION FROM FIRES AND BUILDING SEPARATION, Fire Research Technical Paper No. 5, HMSO, London, England. (8A)

Law, M., 1968
RADIATION FROM FIRES IN A COMPARTMENT, Fire Research Technical Paper No. 20, HMSO, London, England. (8A)

Law, M., 1972
NOMOGRAMS FOR THE FIRE PROTECTION OF STRUCTURAL STEELWORK, Fire Protection Science and Technology, No. 3, November. (8A)

Law, M., 1973
THE PREDICTION OF FIRE RESISTANCE, Symposium No. 5, 1971, Fire Resistance Requirements for Buildings: A New Approach, HMSO, London, England. (8A)

Law, M., 1974
FIRE—THE RISKS AND THE PRECAUTIONS, Proceedings of the Conference on Tall Buildings and People, (Oxford, England, September), The Institution of Structural Engineers, London, England. (8A)

Law, M. and Arnault, P., 1973
FIRE LOADS, NATURAL FIRES AND STANDARD FIRES, State-of-the-Art Report No. 1, Technical Committee 8, Proceedings of the 1972 ASCE-IABSE International Conference, ASCE, New York. (8A)

Lawson, T. V., 1973
THE WIND ENVIRONMENT OF BUILDINGS: A LOGICAL APPROACH TO THE ESTABLISHMENT OF CRITERIA, TVL/7301, Dept. of Aeronautical Engineering, University of Bristol, England. (7)

Lawson, T. V., 1974
THE MEASUREMENT OF SHORT TERM AVERAGE PRESSURES IN A WIND TUNNEL INVESTIGATION, Journal of Industrial Aerodynamics, Vol. 1, No. 3, pp. 233–238. (7)

Lawson, T. V. and Penwarden, A. D., 1975
THE EFFECTS OF WIND ON PEOPLE IN THE VICINITY OF BUILDINGS, Proceedings, 4th International Conference on Wind Effects on Buildings and Structures (London, England), Cambridge University Press, Cambridge, England. (7)

Lay, M. G., 1973
A RATIONAL APPROACH TO FIRE RESISTANT DESIGN, Proceedings of the 12th Regional Conference (Sydney, Australia, August), Lehigh University, Bethlehem, Pa. (8A)

Lea, F. C. and Crowther, O. H., 1914
THE CHANGE OF THE MODULUS OF ELASTICITY AND OF OTHER PROPERTIES OF METAL WITH TEMPERATURE, Engineering, Vol. 98. (8A)

Leach, S. J. and Bloomfield, D. P., 1973
VENTILATION IN RELATION TO TOXIC AND FLAMMABLE GASES IN BUILDINGS, Building Science, Vol. 8, pp. 289–310; also Current Paper CP 36/74, Building Research Establishment, Garston, England, 1974. (8B)

Leadon, B. M. and Doddington, H. W., 1974
TERRAIN AND WIND CLIMATE DESCRIPTION AND WIND PROFILE INSTRUMENTATION FOR THE INDEPENDENT LIFE TOWER STUDY, Proceedings, 2nd USA/Japan Research Seminar on Wind Effects on Structures, University of Tokyo Press, Japan. (7)

Leutheusser, H. J., 1969
INFLUENCE OF ARCHITECTURAL FEATURES ON THE STATIC WIND LOADING OF BUILDINGS, Proceedings, Technical Meeting Concerning Wind Loads on Buildings and Structures (NBS, Gaithersburg, Md.), Building Science Series 30. (7)

Levelius, W. H. and Alpsten, G. A., 1971
QUALITY CONTROL, 2nd Regional Conference Proceedings (Bled, Yugoslavia, May), Lehigh University, Bethlehem, Pa., pp. 31–32. (9)

Lew, H. S., 1976
SAFETY DURING CONSTRUCTION OF CONCRETE BUILDINGS—A STATUS REPORT, BSS 80, National Bureau of Standards, U.S. Department of Commerce, Washington, D.C., January. (5)

Lew, H. S., Leyendecker, E. V. and Dikkers, R. D., 1971
ENGINEERING ASPECTS OF THE 1971 SAN FERNANDO EARTHQUAKE, U.S. Department of Commerce, National Bureau of Standards, Building Science Series 40. (6)

Lewicki, B., Kukulski, W. and Pawlikowski, J., 1972
COMMENTARY ON DESIGN SAFETY MARGINS FOR TALL CONCRETE BUILD-ING, Proceedings of the Regional Conference on the Planning and Design of Tall Buildings (Warsaw, Poland, November), Vol. I, Warsaw Technical University, Polish Group of IABSE, Warsaw, Poland. (10)

Lewis, B. and von Elbe, G., 1961
COMBUSTION, FLAMES AND EXPLOSIONS OF GASES, Academic Press, New York, 2nd ed. (8B)

Leyendecker, E. V. and Fattal, S. G., 1973
INVESTIGATION OF THE SKYLINE PLAZA COLLAPSE IN FAIRFAX COUNTY, VIRGINIA, NBSIR 73-222, National Bureau of Standards, U.S. Dept. of Commerce, Washington, D.C. (8B)

Leyendecker, E. V., Breen, J. E., Somes, N. F. and Swatta, M., 1976
ABNORMAL LOADS ON BUILDINGS AND PROGRESSIVE COLLAPSE: AN ANNOTATED BIBLIOGRAPHY, Building Science Series 67, National Bureau of Standards, U.S. Dept. of Commerce, Washington, D.C. (8B)

Lie, T. T., 1972a
FIRE AND BUILDINGS, Applied Science Publishers, Ltd., London, England. (8A)

Lie, T. T., 1972b
OPTIMUM FIRE RESISTANCE OF STRUCTURES, *Journal of the Structural Division*, ASCE, Vol. 98, No. ST1, Proc. Paper 8638, January, pp. 215–232. (10)

Lie, T. T. and Allen, D. E., 1974
FIRE RESISTANCE ON REINFORCED CONCRETE COLUMNS, IABSE Symposium on Design and Safety of Reinforced Concrete Composite Members, Quebec, Canada, Preliminary Publication, Reports of the Working Commissions, Vol. 16. (8A)

Lie, T. T. and McGuire, J. H., 1975
CONTROL OF SMOKE IN HIGH-RISE BUILDINGS, *Fire Technology*, Vol. 11, No. 1, February, pp. 5–14. (8A)

Lie, T. T. and Stanzak, W. W., 1974
EMPIRICAL METHOD FOR CALCULATING FIRE RESISTANCE OF STEEL COLUMNS, *Engineering Journal*, Vol. 57, No. 5/6. (8A)

Ligtenberg, F. K., 1969
STRUCTURAL SAFETY AND CATASTROPHIC EVENTS, Symposium on Concepts of Safety and Structures and Methods of Design (London, England), Final Report, IABSE, Zürich, Switzerland, pp. 25–33. (8B, 10)

Ligtenberg, F. K., 1971
WHAT SAFETY MARGIN IS NECESSARY IN A STRUCTURE? Report No. BI-71-22, Organization for Industrial Research TNO, Institute TNO for Building Materials and Building Structures, The Netherlands, April. (8A)

Ligtenberg, F. K., 1973
WHAT SAFETY MARGIN IS NECESSARY IN A STRUCTURE? Planning and Design of Tall Buildings, Proceedings of the 1972 ASCE-IABSE International Conference, Vol. 1b, ASCE, New York, pp. 1032–1037. (10)

Lin, Y. K., 1967
PROBABILISTIC THEORY OF STRUCTURAL DYNAMICS, McGraw-Hill Book Co., Inc., New York. (7)

Lind, N. C., 1968
DETERMINISTIC FORMATS FOR THE PROBABILISTIC DESIGN OF STRUC-TURES, Seminar on Structural Optimization, Division of Solid Mechanics, University of Waterloo Press, Waterloo, Ontario, Canada, November. (10)

Lind, N. C., 1971a
THE DESIGN OF STRUCTURAL DESIGN NORMS, SM Report 89, Solid Mechanics Division, University of Waterloo, Waterloo, Ontario, Canada, August. (10)

Lind, N. C., 1971b
CONSISTENT PARTIAL SAFETY FACTORS, *Journal of the Structural Division*, ASCE, Vol. 97, No. ST6, Proc. Paper 8166, pp. 1651–1669. (10)

Lind, N. C. and Basler, E., 1973
SAFETY LEVEL DECISIONS, Planning and Design of Tall Buildings, Proceedings of the
1972 ASCE-IABSE International Conference, Vol. 1b, ASCE, New York, pp. 961–972.
(10)
Lind, N. C., Turkstra, C. J. and Wright, D. T., 1964
SAFETY, ECONOMY AND RELIABILITY IN STRUCTURAL DESIGN, presented at
the 7th Congress of IABSE, held at Rio de Janeiro, Brazil. (10)
Lishamer, J. A., 1977
PRESTRESSED CONCRETE INSTITUTE PLANT CERTIFICATION PROGRAM,
Modern Concrete, Prestressed Concrete Institute, Vol. 41, No. 4. (9)
Little, A. D., 1967
PUBLIC SAFETY AND GAS DISTRIBUTION, Survey for the American Gas Associ-
ation. (8B)
Lord, J., 1973
INELASTIC DYNAMIC BEHAVIOR OF TALL BUILDINGS, Planning and Design of
Tall Buildings, Proceedings of the 1972 ASCE-IABSE International Conference, Vol. 1b,
ASCE, New York, pp. 291–297. (6)
Lorensten, A. M., 1971
CONSIDERATION OF IMPERFECTIONS IN THE DESIGN OF PREFABRICATED
BUILDINGS (Berakningsmassig Hansyn Till Imperfektioner I Montagebyggen), Tek-
niska Nrs 25, Halmstads Jarnverks AB, Sweden. (9)
Lowman, G. L., 1973
PROBLEMS OF FIRE PREVENTION AND MEANS OF ESCAPE IN THE CASE OF
FIRE IN HONG KONG BUILDINGS, Proceedings of the Conference on Tall Buildings
(Hong Kong, August), Lehigh University, Bethlehem, Pa. (8A)
Luce, R. D. and Raiffa, H., 1975
GAMES AND DECISIONS, John Wiley and Sons, Inc., New York, N.Y. (10)
Lumley, J. L., and Panofsky, H. A., 1964
THE STRUCTURE OF ATMOSPHERIC TURBULENCE, Interscience Publishers, New
York. (7)
Lyalin, I. M., 1973
STRUCTURAL FIRE PRECAUTIONS IN THE SOVIET UNION, Proceedings of the
12th Regional Conference (Sydney, Australia, August), Lehigh University, Bethlehem, Pa.
(8A)
Lysmer, J., Seed, H. B. and Schnabel, P. B., 1971
INFLUENCE OF BASE-ROCK CHARACTERISTICS ON GROUND RESPONSE,
Bulletin, Seismological Society of America, Vol. 61, No. 5, pp. 1213–1232. (6)

Macdonald, A. J. and Morgan, J., 1971
A METHOD FOR CALCULATING THE VIBRATION AMPLITUDES OF SLENDER
STRUCTURES IN TURBULENT WINDS, Proceedings, 3rd International Conference
on Wind Effects on Buildings and Structures (Tokyo, Japan). (7)
MacGregor, J., 1971
WHY THE WIND HOWLS AROUND THOSE PLAZAS CLOSE TO SKYSCRAPERS,
The Wall Street Journal, Dow Jones & Co., Inc. (7)
Mackey, S., 1973
SUMMARY REPORT: WIND LOADING AND WIND EFFECTS, Planning and Design
of Tall Buildings, Proceedings of the 1972 ASCE-IABSE International Conference, Vol.
1b, ASCE, New York, pp. 445–462. (7)
Mackey, S., 1975
SOME ASPECTS OF HIGH RISE, HIGH DENSITY URBAN DEVELOPMENT IN
HONG KONG, Proceedings, Pan-Pacific Tall Buildings Conference (Honolulu, Hawaii),
pp. 64–75. (7)
Mackey, S. and Ko., P., 1975
SPATIAL CONFIGURATION OF GUSTS, Proceedings of the 4th International Con-
ference on Wind Effects on Buildings and Structures (London, England), University of
Cambridge Press, Cambridge, England. (7)
Mackey, S., Lam, R. P. and Lam, L. C. H., 1974
A FULL SCALE AND WIND TUNNEL STUDY OF WIND LOADING ON A
BUILDING, Proceedings, Regional Conference on Tall Buildings (Bangkok, Thailand),
pp. 535–551. (7)

Magnusson, S. E., 1973a
PROBABILISTIC ANALYSIS OF FIRE SAFETY, paper presented at the April 9–13 ASCE National Structural Engineering Meeting (San Francisco, Calif.). (8A)

Magnusson, S. E., 1973b
PROBABILISTIC ANALYSIS OF FIRE SAFETY, Planning and Design of Tall Buildings, Proceedings of the 1972 ASCE-IABSE International Conference, Vol. 1B, ASCE, New York, pp. 1016–1026. (10)

Magnusson, S. E. and Pettersson, O. A., 1969a
A QUALIFIED FIRE PROTECTION DESIGN OF STRUCTURAL STEEL MEMBERS, Byggmastaren, No. 9, Stockholm, Sweden. (8A)

Magnusson, S. E. and Pettersson, O. A., 1969b
FIRE ENGINEERING DIMENSIONING OF INSULATED STEEL STRUCTURES HAVING LOAD-BEARING OR SEPARATING FUNCTIONS, Vag-och Vattenbyg Aren, No. 4, pp. 197–213. (8A)

Magnusson, S. E. and Thelandersson, S., 1971
COMMENTS ON THE RATE OF GAS FLOW AND RATE OF BURNING FOR FIRES IN ENCLOSURES, Lund Institute of Technology Division of Structural Mechanics and Concrete Construction, Bulletin No. 19, Lund, Sweden. (8A)

Mainstone, R. J., 1960
STUDIES IN COMPOSITE CONSTRUCTION, PART III—TESTS ON NEW GOVERNMENT OFFICES, Research Paper No. 28, Department of Scientific and Industrial Research, London, England. (5)

Mainstone, R. J., 1966
STRUCTURAL TESTS ON AN EXPERIMENTAL HELICOPTER PLATFORM, Proceedings, Institution of Civil Engineers, Vol. 33, pp. 65–91. (8B)

Mainstone, R. J., 1971
THE BREAKAGE OF GLASS WINDOWS BY GAS EXPLOSIONS, Current Paper CP 26/71, Building Research Station, Garston, England. (8B)

Mainstone, R., 1973
INTERNAL BLAST, Planning and Design of Tall Buildings, Proceedings of the 1972 ASCE-IABSE International Conference, Vol. 1b, No. 8-6, ASCE, New York, pp. 643–660. (8B)

Mainstone, R. J., 1974a
THE HAZARDS OF EXPLOSION, IMPACT, AND OTHER LOADINGS ON TALL BUILDINGS, Tall Buildings and People, IABSE/ISE Conference (Oxford, England), pp. 122–129; Institution of Structural Engineers, London, England; Current Paper CP 64/64, Building Research Establishment, Garston, England. (8B)

Mainstone, R. J., ed., 1974b
BUILDINGS AND THE HAZARD OF EXPLOSION, Proceedings of a Symposium at the Building Research Establishment (Garston, England, October 18, 1972). (8B)

Mainstone, R. J., 1975
THE EFFECT OF IMPACT LOADING ON BUILDING: PART 4: PROPERTIES OF MATERIALS AT HIGH RATES OF STRAINING OR LOADING, Matériaux et Construction, Vol. 8, pp. 102–116; Current Paper CP 62/75, Building Research Establishment, Garston, England. (8B)

Mainstone, R. J., 1976
THE RESPONSE OF BUILDINGS TO ACCIDENTAL EXPLOSIONS, Conference on Performance of Building Structures (Glasgow, Scotland), Pentech Press, London, England, Vol. 1, pp. 173–188; Current Paper CP 24/76, Building Research Establishment, Garston, England. (8B)

Mainstone, R. J., 1978
ACCIDENTAL EXPLOSIONS AND IMPACTS: SOME LESSONS FROM RECENT INCIDENTS, ISE Symposium on stability of low-rise buildings of hybrid construction (London, England, July), Institution of Structural Engineers, London, pp. 13–23. (8B)

Mainstone, R. J. and Butlin, R. N., 1976
REPORT ON AN EXPLOSION AT MERSEY HOUSE, BOOTLE, LANCS., Current Paper CP 34/76, Building Research Establishment, Garston, England. (8B)

Mainstone, R. J., Nicholson, H. G. and Alexander, S. J., 1978
STRUCTURAL DAMAGE IN BUILDINGS CAUSED BY GASEOUS EXPLOSIONS AND OTHER ACCIDENTAL LOADINGS 1971–76, Current Paper CP —/77, Building Research Establishment, Garston, England. (8B)

Mak, C. K., 1975
ULTIMATE STRENGTH DESIGN OF MULTI-STORY STEEL BUILDING COL-
UMNS FOR FIRE AND MECHANICAL LOADS, Proceedings of the Pan-Pacific
Conference (Honolulu, Hawaii, January), University of Hawaii, Honolulu, Hawaii. (8A)

Makino, M., Nakahara, M. and Sato, T., 1971
SOME FIELD TEST RESULTS OF WIND PRESSURES ON A TALL BUILDING,
Proceedings of the 3rd International Conference on Wind Effects on Buildings and
Structures (Tokyo, Japan). (7)

Malhotra, H. L., 1974
DETERMINATION OF FLAME SPREAD AND FIRE RESISTANCE, Proceedings of
the 1st European Fire Conference (October 15–17, 1973, Geneva, Switzerland); Building
Research Establishment Current Paper CP 72/74, Borehamwood, England. (8A)

Malhotra, H. L. and Milbank, N., 1964
MOVEMENT OF SMOKE IN ESCAPE ROUTES AND EFFECT OF PRESSURIZA-
TION, Results of Some Tests Performed in a New Jersey Department Store, JFRO Fire
Research Note No. 566. (8A)

Malinowski, H. K., 1971
WIND EFFECTS ON THE AIR MOVEMENT INSIDE BUILDING, Proceedings of the
3rd International Conference on Wind Effects on Buildings and Structures (Tokyo,
Japan). (7)

Manuzio, C., 1973
PRESENT TRENDS IN PROBABILISTIC STUDIES OF STRUCTURAL SAFETY,
Proceedings of the Italian National Conference on Tall Buildings (Sorrento, Italy,
October), Collegio dei Tecnici dell' Acciaio, Milan, Italy. (10)

Margarido, A. F., 1974
THE FIRE AND RESTORATION OF THE "EDIFICIO ANDRAUS" IN SAÕ PAULO,
BRAZIL, unpublished communication to the Council. (8A)

Marosszeky, M., 1972
CONSTRUCTION LOADS IMPOSED IN MULTI-STOREY STRUCTURES, Civil
Engineering Transactions, Institution of Engineers, Sydney, Australia, Vol. CE 14, No. 1,
pp. 91–93. (5)

Marryatt, H. W., 1971
AUTOMATIC SPRINKLER PERFORMANCE IN AUSTRALIA AND NEW ZEA-
LAND, Australian Fire Protection Association, Melbourne, Australia. (8A)

Marryatt, H. W., 1974
SIGNIFICANT FIRE CASES IN AUSTRALIA, unpublished communication to the
Council. (8A)

Marshall, R. D., 1975
A STUDY OF WIND PRESSURES ON A SINGLE FAMILY DWELLING IN MODEL
AND FULL SCALE, Journal of Industrial Aerodynamics, Vol. 1, No. 2, pp. 177–199. (7)

Martin, C. R. and Soong, T. T., 1976
MODAL CONTROL OF MULTISTORY STRUCTURES, Journal of the Engineering
Mechanics Division, ASCE, Vol. 102, No. EM4, Proc. Paper 12321, pp. 613–623. (7)

Martin, S. B., 1965
DIFFUSION CONTROLLED IGNITION OF CELLULOSIC MATERIALS BY IN-
TENSE RADIANT ENERGY, 10th International Symposium on Combustion, (Pitts-
burgh, Pa.) Combustion Institute, pp. 877–896. (8A)

Massie, C. W., 1971
IF YOU HAVE GOOD CONCRETE YOU CAN PUMP IT, reprint from Concrete Construction, Concrete Construction Publications, Addison, Ill., pp. 227–230. (9)

Matcescu, C., 1963
CONTRIBUTIONS TO THE STUDY OF SNOW AGGLOMERATION ON BUILD-
INGS UNDER WIND ACTION, Studies and Research in Applied Mechanics, Vol. 3 (in
Romanian). (10)

Matsumoto, M. P., 1975
THE SENSITIVITY OF RESPONSE SPECTRA FOR DYNAMIC ANALYSES OF
TALL BUILDINGS, Pan-Pacific Tall Buildings Conference Proceedings (Honolulu,
Hawaii, January), University of Hawaii, Honolulu, Hawaii, pp. 25–39. (6)

Matthiesen, R. B., Duke, C. M., Leeds, D. J. and Fraser, J. C., 1964
SITE CHARACTERISTICS OF SOUTHERN CALIFORNIA STRONG-MOTION EARTHQUAKE STATIONS, PART TWO, Report No. 64015, Department of Engineering, University of California, Los Angeles, Calif. (6)

Mau, S.-T., 1971
OPTIMUM DESIGN OF STRUCTURES WITH A MINIMUM EXPECTED COST CRITERION, Dept. of Structural Engineering, Cornell University, Ithaca, N.Y. (10)

Mauch, S. P. and Schneider, T., 1973
THE DIRECT ENDANGERING OF THE LIVING SPACE (Die unmittelbare Gefahrdung unseres Lebensraumes), *Schweizer Archiv*, 37; National Research Council, Ottawa, Canada. (10)

Maugh, L. C., 1969
DESIGN AND CONSTRUCTION FOR WHAT WIND LOADS AND WHY, Proceedings of the Technical Meeting Concerning Wind Loads on Buildings and Structures (NBS Gaithersburg, Md.), Building Science Series 30. (7)

Mayne, J. R. and Walker, G. R., 1976
THE RESPONSE OF GLAZING TO WIND PRESSURE, Building Research Establishment Current Paper CP44/76, Building Research Station, Garston, England. (9)

Mazilu, P., 1973
ASEISMIC DESIGN IN ROMANIA, Planning and Design of Tall Buildings, Proceedings of the 1972 ASCE-IABSE International Conference, Vol. 1b, ASCE, New York, pp. 279–283. (6)

McCormick, E. J., 1957
HUMAN ENGINEER, McGraw-Hill Book Co., Inc., New York. (8A)

McCormick, R. A., 1971
AIR POLLUTION IN THE LOCALITY OF BUILDINGS, *Philosophical Transactions*, Royal Society, London, England, Series A, Vol. 269, pp. 515–526. (7)

McDonald, J. R., 1970
STRUCTURAL RESPONSE OF A TWENTY STORY BUILDING TO THE LUBBOCK TORNADO, Texas Technical University Storm Research Report No. 01, Lubbock, Tex., October. (7)

McGuire, J. H., 1965
FIRE AND THE SPATIAL SEPARATION OF BUILDINGS, *Fire Technology*, Vol. 1, No. 4, pp. 278–287. (8A)

McGuire, J. H. and Tamura, G. T., 1971a
SMOKE CONTROL IN HIGH-RISE BUILDINGS, National Research Council of Canada, Division of Building Research, Canadian Building Digest No. 133, January. (8A)

McGuire, J. H. and Tamura, G. T., 1971b
SMOKE CONTROL IN HIGH-RISE BUILDINGS, National Research Council of Canada, Division of Building Research, Canadian Building Digest No. 134, February. (8A)

McGuire, J. H. and Tamura, G. T., 1975
SIMPLE ANALYSIS OF SMOKE-FLOW PROBLEMS IN HIGH BUILDINGS, *Fire Technology*, Vol. 11, No. 1, pp. 15–22. (8A)

McGuire, J. H., Tamura, G. T. and Wilson, A. G., 1970
FACTORS IN CONTROLLING SMOKE IN HIGH BUILDINGS, *Fire Hazards in Buildings*, ASHRAE Symposium Bulletin (San Francisco, Calif.); Division of Building Research Technical Paper No. 342 (NRC 12016), January. (8A)

McGuire, W., 1974
PREVENTION OF PROGRESSIVE COLLAPSE, Proceedings of the Regional Conference on Tall Buildings (Bangkok, Thailand, January), Asian Institute of Technology, Bangkok, Thailand. (10)

McHale, E. T., 1974
LIFE SUPPORT WITHOUT COMBUSTION HAZARDS, *Fire Technology*, Vol. 10, No. 1, pp. 15–24. (8A)

McKaïg, T. H., 1962
BUILDING FAILURES: CASE STUDIES IN CONSTRUCTION AND DESIGN, McGraw-Hill Book Co., Inc., New York. (8B)

McKeon, R. J. and Melbourne, W. H., 1971
WIND TUNNEL BLOCKAGE EFFECTS AND DRAG ON BLUFF BODIES IN A ROUGH WALL BOUNDARY LAYER, Proceedings, 3rd International Conference on Wind Effects on Buildings and Structures (Tokyo, Japan). (7)

McVehil, G. E., Ludwig, G. R. and Sundram, R. T., 1967
ON THE FEASIBILITY OF MODELLING SMALL SCALE ATMOSPHERIC MOTIONS, Report 2B-2328-p-1 Cornell Aero. Laboratory. (7)

Mehta, K. C., McDonald, J. R. and Minor, J. E., 1974
TORNADIC LOADS ON STRUCTURES, Proceedings of the 1974 2nd USA/Japan Research Seminar on Wind Effects on Structures, University of Tokyo Press, Tokyo, Japan. (7)

Meisen, W. A. and Reinsel, R. E., 1977
EMERGENCIES IN TALL BUILDINGS: THE DESIGNERS RESPOND TO HUMAN RESPONSE, Proceedings of the Conference on Human Response To Tall Buildings (Chicago, Ill., July), Dowden, Hutchison, & Ross, Inc., Stroudsburg, Pa. (8A)

Meister, R. I., 1937
THE PHYSIOLOGICAL EVALUATION OF VIBRATION MEASUREMENT (Die Physiologische Wertung von Erschütterungsmessungen), *Akustische Zeitschrift*, Vol. 2, pp. 1–10. (6)

Melbourne, W. H., 1968
WIND TUNNEL MODELLING OF BUOYANT CHIMNEY PLUMES, Proceedings of the 3rd Australian Conference on Hydraulics and Fluid Mechanics, Institution of Engineers of Australia, Sydney, Australia. (7)

Melbourne, W. H., 1971a
GROUND LEVEL WINDS CAUSED BY LARGE BUILDINGS, Monash University, Department of Mechanical Engineering, MMER 4, Australia (also Melbourne and Joubert, Proceedings of the International Conference on Wind Effects on Buildings and Structures, Tokyo, Japan, p. 165). (7)

Melbourne, W. H., 1971b
COMPARISON OF PRESSURE MEASUREMENTS MADE ON A LARGE ISOLATED BUILDING IN FULL AND MODEL SCALE, Proceedings of the 3rd International Conference on Wind Effects on Buildings and Structures (Tokyo, Japan). (7)

Melbourne, W. H., 1972
MODELLING OF STRUCTURES TO MEASURE WIND EFFECTS, Proceedings of the Conference on Structural Models (Sydney, Australia), Cement and Concrete Assoc. of Australia in conjunction with Dept. of Architectural Science, University of Sydney, and Institution of Engineers, Australia, N.S.W. Division. (7)

Melbourne, W. H., 1973a
WEST GATE BRIDGE TUNNEL TESTS, Proprietary Report. (7)

Melbourne, W. H., 1973b
WIND TUNNEL TEST EXPECTATIONS, Planning and Design of Tall Buildings, Proceedings of the 1972 ASCE-IABSE International Conference, Vol. 1b, ASCE, New York, pp. 441–444. (7)

Melbourne, W. H., 1974
PEAK FACTORS FOR STRUCTURES OSCILLATING UNDER WIND ACTION, Proceedings of the Conference on the Application of Probability Theory to Structural Design, Institution of Engineers, Australia, pp. 34–44. (7)

Melbourne, W. H., 1975a
CROSS-WIND RESPONSE OF STRUCTURES TO WIND ACTION, Proceedings of the 4th International Conference on Wind Effects on Buildings and Structures (London, England) University of Cambridge Press, Cambridge, England. (7)

Melbourne, W. H., 1975b
THE RELEVANCE OF CODIFICATION TO DESIGN, Proceedings of the 4th International Conference on Wind Effects on Buildings and Structures (London, England), University of Cambridge Press, Cambridge, England. (7)

Melbourne, W. H., 1975c
PROBABILITY DISTRIBUTIONS OF RESPONSE OF BHP HOUSE TO WIND ACTION AND MODEL COMPARISONS, presented at the International Conference on Full Scale Measurement of the Effect of Wind on Tall Buildings and Other Structures (University of Western Ontario, Canada), *Journal of Industrial Aerodynamics*, Vol. 1, No. 2, pp. 167–175. (7)

Melbourne, W. H., 1975d
DISCUSSION ON SESSION 7—PRACTICAL APPLICATION, 4th International Conference on Wind Effects on Buildings and Structures, (London, England) University of Cambridge Press, Cambridge, England, p. 663. (7)

Melbourne, W. H., 1977
PROBABILITY DISTRIBUTIONS ASSOCIATED WITH THE WIND LOADING OF STRUCTURES, Australian Civil Engineering *Transactions*, Institution of Engineers, pp. 58–67. (7)

Melbourne, W. H. and Gartshore, I. S., 1975
A WIND TUNNEL MODEL STUDY OF AIR CONDITIONING CONTAMINATION BY INTAKE OF FLUE GAS, International Congress on Instrumentation in Aerospace Simluation Facilities, IEEE Publication 75 CHO 993-6 AES. (7)

Melbourne, W. H. and Joubert, P. N., 1971
PROBLEMS OF WIND FLOW AT THE BASE OF TALL BUILDINGS, Proceedings of the International Conference on Wind Effects on Buildings and Structures (Tokyo, Japan). (7)

Melbourne, W. H. and Sharp, D. B., 1976
EFFECTS OF UPWIND BUILDINGS ON THE RESPONSE OF TALL BUILDINGS, 2nd Tall Buildings Conference (Hong Kong, September). (7)

Meli, R., 1976
BASES FOR THE STANDARDS OF STRUCTURAL DESIGN OF PROJECT REGULATION OF CONSTRUCTION FOR THE FEDERAL DISTRICT (Bases para los criterios de diseño estructural del proyecto de reglamento de contrucciones para el Distrito Federal), *Ingeniería*, Vol. 46, No. 2. (10)

Melinek, S. J., 1972
A METHOD OF EVALUATING HUMAN LIFE FOR ECONOMIC PURPOSES, Fire Research Note No. 950, Fire Research Establishment, Garston, England, November. (8A)

Melinek, S. J., 1975
CIB SYMPOSIUM ON THE CONTROL OF SMOKE MOVEMENT IN BUILDING FIRES, Paper No. 5, Fire Research Establishment, Garston, England, November. (8A)

Mendoza, E., Rosenblueth, E. and Bretón, A., 1971
DESIGN LIVE LOAD IN AUDITORIUMS SUBJECTED TO EARTHQUAKE (Carga Viva de Diseño en Auditorios Subjetos a Temblor), Congreso Nacional de Ingeniería Sísmica, Acapulco, Mexico. (10)

Merritt, R. G. and Housner, G. W., 1954
EFFECT OF FOUNDATION COMPLIANCE ON EARTHQUAKE STRESSES IN MULTISTORY BUILDINGS, *Bulletin*, Seismological Society of America, Vol. 44, No. 4. (6)

Mihalache, A. and Popp, T., 1975
SOME ASPECTS CONCERNING THE DYNAMIC RESPONSE OF TALL BUILDINGS TO THE EFFECT OF WIND, Proceedings of the 34th National/Regional Conference (Iasi, Romania), pp. 265–282. (7)

Miki, S., Ohba, H. and Kamei, T., 1971
QUALITY ASSURANCE SYSTEM IN STEEL FRAME FABRICATION OF TALL BUILDING, 3rd Regional Conference Proceedings (Tokyo, Japan, September), Muto Institute of Structural Mechanics, Tokyo, Japan, pp. 116–121. (9)

Miller, P. O., 1972
MODEL ANALYSIS OF THE QANTAS CENTRE, Conference on Structural Models, (Sydney, Australia) Cement and Concrete Association of Australia in conjunction with the Department of Architectural Science, University of Sydney and Institution of Civil Engineers, Australia, NSW Division. (7)

Miller, P. O., 1973
QANTAS CENTRE, SYDNEY, DESIGN AND CONSTRUCTION PLANNING, Proceedings of the 12th National/Regional Conference (Sydney, Australia), pp. 410–423. (7)

Milner, R. M. and Thorgood, R. P., 1971
ACCURACY AND ITS STRUCTURAL IMPLICATIONS FOR LOAD-BEARING BRICK CONSTRUCTION, Building Research Establishment, Building Research Station, Garston, England, November. (9)

Minami, K., Sakarai, J. and Katanama, 1970
SOME EFFECTS OF SUBSTRUCTURE PROPORTIONS AND ADJACENT SOIL INTERACTION ON THE SEISMIC RESPONSE OF BUILDINGS, 3rd Japanese Earthquake Engineering Symposium. (6)
Ministry of Labour, 1965
GUIDE TO THE USE OF FLAME ARRESTERS AND EXPLOSION RELIEFS, Ministry of Labour, Safety, Health, and Welfare Series No. 34, HMSO, London, England. (8A)
Minor, J. E., 1974
WINDOW GLASS IN WINDSTORMS , Civil Engineering Report Series CE 74-01, Department of Civil Engineering, Texas Tech University, Lubbock, Tex., May. (7, 9)
Mitchell, G. R., 1969
LOADINGS ON BUILDINGS, IABSE Symposium on Concepts of Safety, London, England. (10)
Mitchell, G. R., 1973
LOADINGS ON BUILDINGS, Planning and Design of Tall Buildings, Proceedings of the 1972 ASCE-IABSE International Conference, Vol. 1b, No. 5-2A, ASCE, New York. (5)
Mitchell, G. R. and Woodgate, R. W., 1971a
FLOOR LOADINGS IN OFFICE BUILDINGS—THE RESULTS OF A SURVEY, Current Paper CP 3/71, Building Research Establishment, Garston, England. (5)
Mitchell, G. R. and Woodgate, R. W., 1971b
FLOOR LOADING IN RETAIL PREMISES—THE RESULTS OF A SURVEY, Current Paper 25/71, Building Research Establishment, Garston, England. (5)
Mitchell, G. R. and Woodgate, R. W., 1977
FLOOR LOADINGS IN DOMESTIC BUILDINGS—THE RESULTS OF A SURVEY, Current Paper 2/77, Building Research Establishment, Garston, England. (5)
Mitsuta, Y., 1976
PRELIMINARY RESULTS OF TYPHOON WIND OBSERVATION AT TARAMA ISLAND, OKINAWA, Proceedings of the 1974, 2nd USA/Japan Research Seminar on Wind Effects on Structures, University of Tokyo Press, Tokyo, Japan. (7)
Miyoshi, S., Ida, M. and Miura, T., 1971
WIND PRESSURE COEFFICIENTS ON EXTERIOR WALL ELEMENTS OF TALL BUILDINGS, Proceedings of the 3rd International Conference on Wind Effects on Buildings and Structures (Tokyo, Japan). (7)
Mori, T., 1976
WIND TUNNEL STUDIES OF WIND EXCITED OSCILLATIONS OF TALL BUILD-INGS, Proceedings of the 1974 2nd USA/Japan Research Seminar on Wind Effects on Structures, University of Tokyo Press, Tokyo, Japan. (7)
Morris, J. and van Aardt, J. H. P., 1975
TALL BUILDINGS: CONSIDERATIONS GOVERNING THE CHOICE OF MATE-RIALS AND FINISHES, South African Conference on Tall Buildings Proceedings, (Johannesburg, South Africa, November), Paper 10, National Building Research Institute, Pretoria, South Africa. (9)
Morris, W. A. and Hopkinson, J., 1974
FIRE RESEARCH NOTE NO. 995, Fire Research Establishment, England. (8A)
Morton, F., 1970
REPORT OF THE INQUIRY INTO THE SAFETY OF NATURAL GAS AS A FUEL, HMSO, London, England. (8B)
Morton, J., Davies, S. R. and Hendry, A. W., 1971
THE STABILITY OF LOAD-BEARING BRICKWORK STRUCTURES FOLLOWING ACCIDENTAL DAMAGE TO A MAJOR BEARING WALL OR PIER, SIBMAC Proceedings, British Ceramic Research Association, Stoke-on-Trent, England, pp. 276–281. (8B)
Moses, F., 1968
OPTIMUM DESIGN FOR STRUCTURAL SAFETY, Final Report, 8th IABSE Congress, New York, September, p. 163. (10)
Moses, F. and Stevenson, J. D., 1969
APPROACHES TO STRUCTURAL RELIABILITY AND OPTIMIZATION, SM Study 1, Solid Mechanics Division, University of Waterloo, Ont., Canada, pp. 81–210. (10)

Moses, F. and Stevenson, J. D., 1970
RELIABILITY-BASED STRUCTURAL DESIGN, *Journal of the Structural Division*, ASCE, Vol. 96, No. ST2, Proc. Paper 7072, p. 221. (10)
Moses, F. and Tichy, M., 1973
SAFETY ANALYSIS FOR TALL BUILDINGS, Proceedings of the 1972 ASCE-IABSE International Conference, Vol. 1b, ASCE, New York, pp. 993–1006. (10)
Motta, F., 1973
COMPLEMENTARY AND PROTECTION WORKS IN STEEL STRUCTURES (Opere di Finitura e Protezione nelle Costruzioni in Acciaio), *Tecnica e Ricostruzione*, Catania, Italy. (8A)
Moulen, A. W., 1973
CONTROL OF SMOKE FROM FIRE IN AN AIR-CONDITIONED BUILDING, TR 44/153/140, Experimental Building Station, Australia, September. (8A)
Muller, F. P. and Nieser, H., 1975
MEASUREMENTS OF WIND-INDUCED VIBRATIONS ON A CONCRETE CHIMNEY, *Journal of Industrial Aerodynamics*, Vol. 1, No. 3, pp. 239–248. (7)
Murakami, S., Shoda, T. and Kobayashi, N., 1975
WIND EFFECTS ON AIR FLOWS IN HALF ENCLOSED SPACES, Proceedings of the 4th International Conference on Wind Effects on Buildings and Structures (London, England), University of Cambridge Press, Cambridge, England. (7)
Murota, T., 1976
AN EXPERIMENTAL STUDY ON THE DRAG COEFFICIENT OF SCREENS FOR BUILDING USE, Proceedings of the 1974, 2nd USA/Japan Research Seminar on Wind Effects on Structures, University of Tokyo Press, Tokyo, Japan. (7)
Murphy, L. M., 1973
SAN FERNANDO, CALIFORNIA, EARTHQUAKE OF FEBRUARY 9, 1971, 3 vols., National Oceanic and Atmospheric Administration and Earthquake Engineering Research Institute. (6)
Murzewski, J., 1972
SAFETY OF TALL BUILDINGS AND PROBABILISTIC METHODS, Proceedings of the Regional Conference on the Planning and Design of Tall Buildings (Warsaw, Poland, November), Vol. I, Warsaw Technical University, Polish Group of IABSE, Warsaw, Poland. (10)
Murzewski, J. and Ucisko, L., 1972
MAXIMUM WIND LOAD FOR A PRESCRIBED SITUATION OF A BUILDING, Proceedings of the National Conference on Tall Buildings (Warsaw, Poland), pp. 159–166. (7)
Murzewski, J. and Winiarz, A., 1972
A STOCHASTIC MODEL FOR LIVE LOADS IN TALL BUILDINGS, Proceedings of the Regional Conference on the Planning and Design of Tall Buildings (Warsaw, Poland, November), Vol. I, Warsaw Technical University, Polish Group of IABSE, Warsaw, Poland. (5, 10)
Muto, K., 1971a
FLUTTERING DESIGN OF KEIO PLAZA HOTEL, Proceedings of the 3rd Regional Conference (Tokyo, Japan), pp. 107–110. (7)
Muto, K., 1971b
STRONG MOTION RECORDS AND SIMULATION ANALYSIS OF KII BUILDING IN SAN FERNANDO EARTHQUAKE, Muto Report 71-2-1, Muto Institute of Structural Mechanics, Tokyo, Japan. (6)
Muto, K., 1974
ASEISMIC DESIGN AND POST CONSTRUCTION STUDY, Proceedings of the National Conference on Tall Buildings, (Tokyo, Japan, August), Architectural Institute of Japan, Tokyo, Japan, pp. 31–40. (6)
Muto, K. and Nagata, M., 1974
THE EARTHQUAKE RESISTANT INSTALLING METHOD OF TELECOMMUNICATION INSTRUMENTS IN HIGH-RISE BUILDING, Proceedings of the National Conference on Tall Buildings (Tokyo, Japan, August), Architectural Institute of Japan, Tokyo, Japan, pp. 83–84. (6)

Muto, K., Hisada, T., Yamamoto, M., Tsugawa, T. and Bessno, S., 1974
ASEISMIC DESIGN AND STUDY OF TALL REINFORCED CONCRETE BUILD-INGS, Proceedings of the National Conference on Tall Buildings (Tokyo, Japan, August) Architectural Institute of Japan, Tokyo, Japan, pp. 37–42. (6)

NCMA, 1966
MOISTURE CONTENT VS. COMPRESSIVE STRENGTH OF CONCRETE BLOCK, (Technical), National Concrete Masonry Association, Herndon, Va. (9)
NCMA, 1968
SPECIFICATION FOR THE DESIGN AND CONSTRUCTION OF LOAD BEARING CONCRETE MASONRY, National Concrete Masonry Association, Herndon, Va. (8th printing May, 1978 includes updating of reference standards and editorial revisions). (9)
NCMA, 1971
SPECIAL CONSIDERATIONS FOR MANUFACTURING HIGH STRENGTH CON-CRETE MASONRY UNITS, National Concrete Masonry Association, Herndon, Va. (9)
NFPA, 1967
LIFE SAFETY CODE, NFPA 101-1067, Appendix "A", Item A-5-113, National Fire Protection Association, Boston, Mass. (8A)
NFPA, 1971
INSTALLATION OF SPRINKLER SYSTEMS, NFPA No. 13-1971, National Fire Protection Association, Boston, Mass., August. (8A)
NFPA, 1972
FIRE JOURNAL, National Fire Protection Association, Boston, Mass., June. (8A)
NFPA, 1973a
CODE FOR SAFETY TO LIFE FROM FIRE IN BUILDINGS AND STRUCTURES, NFPA 101-1973, National Fire Protection Association, Boston, Mass., May. (8A)
NFPA, 1973b
LIFE SAFETY CODE, NFPA 101, ANSI 9.1-1973, National Fire Protection Association, Boston, Mass. (8A)
NFPA, 1974a
STANDARD FOR AUTOMATIC FIRE DETECTORS, NFPA No. 72E-1974, National Fire Protection Association, Boston, Mass. (8A)
NFPA, 1974b
TAIYO DEPARTMENT STORE FIRE, DUMAMOTO, JAPAN, Fire Journal reprint, Fires in High-Rise Buildings, National Fire Protection Association, Boston, Mass., pp. 20–21. (8A)
NFPA, 1975a
STANDARD FOR INSTALLATION OF SPRINKLER SYSTEMS, NFPA 13-1975, National Fire Protection Association, Boston, Mass., May. (8A)
NFPA, 1975b
STANDARD FOR THE INSTALLATION, MAINTENANCE AND USE OF PORT-ABLE FIRE EXTINGUISHERS, NFPA No. 10-1975, National Fire Protection Association, Boston, Mass. (8A)
NFPA, 1975c
STANDARD FOR FIRE DOORS AND WINDOWS, NFPA 80-1975, National Fire Protection Association, Boston, Mass., November. (8A)
NOAA, 1928–1977
UNITED STATES EARTHQUAKES (ANNUAL PUBLICATION), National Oceanic and Atmospheric Agency, U.S. Superintendent of Documents, Washington, D.C. (6)
NZS, 1976
NEW ZEALAND STANDARD CODE OF PRACTICE FOR GENERAL STRUC-TURAL DESIGN AND DESIGN LOADINGS FOR BUILDINGS, NZS 4203. (6)
Nagaraja Rao, N. R. and Tall, L., 1961
RESIDUAL STRESSES IN WELDED PLATES, Welding Journal, Vol. 40, No. 10, pp. 468-s–480-s. (9)
Nakagawa, K., 1964
SIMPLE CONSIDERATION ON HUMAN PANIC PROBLEM IN CASE OF SMALL EARTHQUAKE IN THE TOP PART OF HIGHRISE BUILDING (in Japanese), Studies on Design Standards of Highrise Buildings, Vol. 2, Building, Building Contractors Society. (6)

Nakayama, H., Matsumoto, M. and Inagaki, M., 1970
    RESTRAINT FORCES ON WELDING JOINTS ON STEEL FRAME FABRICATION,
    Architectural Institute of Japan annual report, Tokyo, Japan. (9)
Napper, L. A., 1973
    INSPECTION PRACTICES FOR TALL BUILDINGS, Planning and Design of Tall
    Buildings, Proceedings of the 1972 ASCE-IABSE International Conference, Vol. 1b,
    ASCE, New York, pp. 898–899. (9)
Narita, H. and Yokoyama, F., 1974
    THE STRUCTURAL DESIGN OF KAIJO BUILDING (TOKYO MARINE AND FIRE
    INSURANCE BUILDING), Proceedings of the National Conference on Tall Buildings
    (Tokyo, Japan, August), Architectural Institute of Japan, Tokyo, Japan, pp. 93–98. (6)
National Research Center for Disaster Prevention, 1970
    STRONG-MOTION EARTHQUAKE RECORDS IN JAPAN, Vols. 1–21, Earthquake
    Research Institute, University of Tokyo, Tokyo, Japan. (6)
National Research Council Committee on the Alaska Earthquake, 1973
    THE GREAT ALASKA EARTHQUAKE OF 1964, NAS-NRC Publication Nos. 1601–
    1608, Washington, D.C. (6)
Naudascher, H., ed., 1974
    FLUID-INDUCED STRUCTURAL VIBRATIONS, J. Springer-Verlag, New York. (7)
Navaratnarajah, V., 1974
    A COMPARATIVE STUDY OF CODES OF PRACTICE IN DESIGN OF TALL
    BUILDINGS, Proceedings of the National Conference on Tall Buildings (Kuala Lumpur,
    Malaysia, December), Institution of Engineers, Kuala Lumpur, Malaysia, p. 7-1. (5)
Negoita, A. and Iancau, V., 1970
    CONTRIBUTIONS CONCERNING PROBABILISTIC ASPECTS OF LOADS DUE TO
    WEATHER CONDITIONS AND STRUCTURAL SAFETY (in Romanian), Studies
    and Research of Applied Mechanics, 4. (10)
Negoita, A. and Pop, I., 1975
    FRAMED TALL BUILDINGS SUBJECTED TO LATERAL FORCES, Proceedings of
    the 34th National/Regional Conference (Iasi, Romania), pp. 283–296. (7)
Nejman, T. J., Radwanowski, L. and Sieczkowski, J., 1974
    GRAVI-STABILITY OF TALL BUILDINGS, Proceedings of the Regional Conference on
    Tall Buildings, (Bangkok, Thailand, January), Asian Institute of Technology, Bangkok,
    Thailand, pp. 665–669. (6, 7)
Nemoto, S., 1968
    SIMILARITY BETWEEN NATURAL LOCAL WIND IN THE ATMOSPHERE AND
    MODEL WIND IN A WIND TUNNEL, Meteorology and Geophysics, Vol. XIX, No. 2.
    (7)
Nervi, P. L., 1956
    STRUCTURES, F. W. Dodge Co., New York. (10)
New York City, 1975
    BUILDING CODE OF THE CITY OF NEW YORK, Title C, Part II, New York Building
    Code, Article 10, Section 1011.0 Glass Panels, pp. 10-23–10-25. (9)
Newberry, C. W., 1963
    THE MEASUREMENT OF WIND PRESSURES ON TALL BUILDINGS, Proceedings
    of the International Conference on Wind Effects on Buildings and Structures (NPL,
    Teddington, England). (7)
Newberry, C. W. and Eaton, K. J., 1974
    WIND LOADING HANDBOOK, BRE Report, HMSO, London, England. (7)
Newberry, C. W., Eaton, K. J. and Mayne, J. R., 1967
    THE NATURE OF GUST LOADING ON TALL BUILDINGS, Proceedings of the
    International Research Seminar on Wind Effects on Buildings and Structures (Ottawa,
    Canada). (7)
Newberry, C. W., Eaton, K. J. and Mayne, J. R., 1971
    WIND PRESSURES ON THE POST OFFICE TOWER, LONDON, Proceedings of the
    International Conference on Wind Effects on Buildings and Structures (Tokyo, Japan)
    (also BRE Current Paper CP 37/71). (7)
Newberry, C. W., Eaton, K. J. and Mayne, J. R., 1973a
    WIND LOADING ON TALL BUILDINGS—FURTHER RESULTS FROM ROYEX
    HOUSE, Industrial Aerodynamics Abstracts, Vol. 4, No. 4 (also BRE Current Paper CP
    29/73). (7)

Newberry, C. W., Eaton, K. J. and Mayne, J. R., 1973b
WIND PRESSURES AND STRAIN MEASUREMENTS AT THE POST OFFICE
TOWER, BRE Current Paper CP 30/73, Garston, England. (7)

Newman, R. P., 1959
EFFECTS ON FATIGUE STRENGTH OF INTERNAL DEFECTS IN WELDED JOINTS,
British Welding Journal, Vol. 6, No. 2, pp. 59–64. (9)

Newman, R. P. and Dawes, M. G., 1965
EXPLORATORY FATIGUE TESTS ON TRANSVERSE BUTT WELDS CONTAIN-
ING LACK OF PENETRATION, BWRA Report, British Welding Research Associ-
ation, Cambridge, England, June-July. (9)

Newmark, N. M., 1956
AN ENGINEERING APPROACH TO BLAST RESISTANT DESIGN, *Transactions*,
ASCE, Vol. 121, pp. 45–64. (8B)

Newmark, N. M., 1963
DESIGN OF STRUCTURES FOR DYNAMIC LOADS INCLUDING THE EFFECTS
OF VIBRATION AND GROUND SHOCK, Symposium on Scientific Problems of
Protective Construction, Swiss Federal Institute of Technology, Zürich, Switzerland, pp.
148–248. (8B)

Newmark, N. M., 1966
RELATION BETWEEN WIND AND EARTHQUAKE RESPONSE OF TALL BUILD-
INGS, Proceedings of the Illinois Structural Engineering Conference (University of
Illinois, Urbana, Ill.), pp. 137–156. (8B)

Newmark, N. M., 1969
TORSION IN SYMMETRICAL BUILDINGS, Proceedings of the 4th World Conference
on Earthquake Engineering (Santiago, Chile). (6)

Newmark, N., 1973
EXTERNAL BLAST, Planning and Design of Tall Buildings, Proceedings of the 1972
ASCE-IABSE International Conference, Vol. 1b-8, ASCE, New York, pp. 661–676. (8B)

Newmark, N. M. and Rosenblueth, E., 1971
FUNDAMENTALS OF EARTHQUAKE ENGINEERING, Prentice-Hall, Inc., Englewood Cliffs, N.J. (6, 8B, 10)

Newsweek, 1942
CATASTROPHE: COCONUT GROVE, BOSTON'S OLDEST NIGHTCLUB, *Newsweek*,
December 7, New York, pp. 42–43. (8A)

Nichols, J. R., 1940
TOLERANCES IN BUILDING CONSTRUCTION, *ACI Journal*, American Concrete
Institute, Vol. 36, No. 4, pp. 493–496. (9)

Nikai, S., 1971
METHOD OF FIREPROOFING THE STEEL FRAMED BUILDING IN JAPAN,
Proceedings of the 3rd Regional Conference (Tokyo, Japan, September), Muto Institute
of Structural Mechanics, Tokyo, Japan. (8A)

Nilsson, L., 1971
THE EFFECT OF POROSITY AND AIR FLOW FACTOR ON THE RATE OF
BURNING FOR FIRE IN ENCLOSED SPACE, Statens Institut for Byggnadsfors-
kning, Rapport R22, Stockholm, Sweden. (8A)

Norris, C. H., Hansen, R. J., Holley, M. J., Biggs, J. M., Namyet, S. and Minami, J. K., 1959
STRUCTURAL DESIGN FOR DYNAMIC LOADS, McGraw-Hill Book Co., Inc., New
York. (8B)

Novak, M., 1971
GALLOPING AND VORTEX INDUCED OSCILLATIONS OF STRUCTURES, Pro-
ceedings of the 3rd International Conference on Wind Effects on Buildings and Structures
(Tokyo, Japan). (7)

Novak, O., 1971
INFORMATION ON RESEARCH OF WIND EFFECT ON HIGH BUILDINGS AND
STRUCTURES IN THE CZECHOSLOVAK SOCIALIST REPUBLIC, Proceedings of
the 4th National/Regional Conference (Prague, Czechoslovakia), pp. 59–61. (7)

Nowak, A. S., 1972
SOME PROBLEMS IN THE RELIABILITY-BASED DESIGN OF TALL BUILDINGS,
Proceedings of the Regional Conference on the Planning and Design of Tall Buildings
(Warsaw, Poland, November), Vol. II, Warsaw Technical University, Polish Group of
IABSE, Warsaw, Poland. (10)

Nutt, J., 1973
SUPERIMPOSED LOADS, Proceedings of the National Conference on Tall Buildings
(Sydney, Australia, August), Joint Committee on Tall Buildings, Lehigh University,
Bethlehem, Pa., pp. 203–217. (5)

OTUA, 1975
DATA ON SOME CURRENTLY USED STEELS (Données Physiques sur Quelques
Aciers D'Utilisation Courante), Technical Office for Utilization of Steel, Neuilly, France,
April. (8A)
O'Bryne, K., 1974
WIND LOADING IN NAIROBI—PLAN—EAST AFRICA, British Standards Institution,
London, England, November/December. (7)
Odar, E., Nishino, F. and Tall, L., 1967
RESIDUAL STRESSES IN ROLLED HEAT-TREATED "T-1" SHAPES, Bulletin 121,
Welding Research Council, New York. (9)
Odgaard, A. and Olesen, S. O., 1972
LOCAL FAILURE IN PANEL BUILDINGS: A DISCUSSION ILLUSTRATED BY A
MODEL TEST, Report No. 017, Danish Centre for Building Technology and Construc-
tion Research, Lyngby, Denmark. (8B)
Ogura, K. and Hirosawa, M., 1971
PART 1: SHEAR DESIGN IN NEW RECOMMENDATION OF AIJ FOR STRUC-
TURAL DESIGN OF REINFORCED CONCRETE, 3rd Regional Conference Pro-
ceedings (Tokyo, Japan, September), Muto Institute of Structural Mechanics, Tokyo,
Japan, pp. 208–211. (6)
O'Hagan, J. T., 1972
NEW YORK FIRE DEPARTMENT CONDUCTS FIRE TESTS IN HIGH-RISE, Fire
Engineering, Journal of Fire Protection Profession, New York, Vol. 125, No. 9, pp. 26–28.
(8A)
Ohba, H. and Kamei, T., 1971
A NEW CONCEPT OF BUILDING FRAME PRODUCTION SYSTEM INTENDED
FOR MASS PRODUCTION SYSTEM STRUCTURE, ASCE-IABSE Joint Committee
Report, Prague, Czechoslovakia. (9)
Ohba, H., Yamauchi, K. and Murata, Y., 1968
AUTOMATION OF MANUFACTURING PROCESS FOR STEEL STRUCTURE,
Welding Technique, Sanpo, Tokyo, Japan. (9)
Ohsaki, Y., 1966
NIIGATA EARTHQUAKES, 1964 BUILDING DAMAGE AND SOIL CONDITION,
Soil and Foundation, Vol. VI, No. 2, pp. 14–37. (6)
Ohsawa, Y., 1971a
EXPERIMENTAL STUDY OF STRUCTURAL BEHAVIOR, 2nd Regional Conference
Proceedings, (Bled, Yugoslavia, May), Lehigh University, Bethlehem, Pa., p. 27. (6)
Ohsawa, Y., 1971b
OBSERVATION OF STRUCTURAL BEHAVIOR, 3rd Regional Conference Proceedings
(Tokyo, Japan, September), Muto Institute of Structural Mechanics, Tokyo, Japan, pp.
56–62. (6)
Ohsawa, Y., Murakami, M., Nishikawa, T. and Aoyama, H., 1969
EARTHQUAKE MEASUREMENTS IN AND AROUND A REINFORCED CON-
CRETE BUILDING, Proceedings of the 4th World Conference on Earthquake Engi-
neering (Santiago, Chile). (6)
Ohshima, M., 1953
VIBRATION AND HUMAN BEINGS (in Japanese), Tekko Rodo Eisei (Steel Labour
Health), Vol. 2-1, 2, 3, 4. (6)
Olmer, J., 1973
MEASUREMENTS OF TALL BUILDINGS OSCILLATIONS, Proceedings of the 10th
National/Regional Conference (Bratislava, Czechoslovakia), pp. 300–304. (7)
Omote, Y., Takeda, T., Moritaka, I. and Yoshiora, K., 1970
EXPERIMENT AND RESEARCH ON THE RESPONSE OF THE MODEL STRUC-
TURE UNDER IMPACT LOADING (PART 1), Proceedings of the 3rd Japan
Earthquake Engineering Symposium (Tokyo, Japan). (6)

O'Rourke, M. J. and Parmelee, R. A., 1975
SERVICEABILITY ANALYSIS FOR WIND LOADS ON BUILDINGS, Proceedings of the 4th International Conference on Wind Effects on Buildings and Structures (London, England), University of Cambridge Press, Cambridge, England. (7)

Orczykowski, A., Korycki, S., Kwiecinski, B., Rymkiewicz, A. and Wadowski, A., 1972
THE PROBLEMS OF TALL CONCRETE BUILDINGS REALIZATION, Proceedings of the National Conference on Tall Buildings (Warsaw, Poland), pp. 283–290. (7)

Ostrowski, J. S., Marshall, J. S. and Cermak, J. E., 1967
VORTEX FORMATION AND PRESSURE FLUCTUATIONS ON BUILDINGS, Proceedings of the International Seminar on Wind Effects on Buildings and Structures, Ottawa, Canada, pp. 459–484. (7)

Otsuki, Y., Washizu, K., Fujii, K., Ito, T., Tomizawa, H. and Yoshida, M., 1971
WIND EXCITED VIBRATIONS OF A TOWER OF NEARLY SQUARE CROSS SECTION, Proceedings of the 3rd International Conference on Wind Effects on Buildings and Structures (Tokyo, Japan), Saikon Shuppan Co., Ltd., Tokyo, Japan. (7)

Ott, K. S. and Shah, H. C., 1969
RELIABILITY UNDER CERTAIN PARAMETERS, STOCHASTIC LOADS AND RESISTANCES, discussion prepared for IABSE Symposium on Concepts of Safety (London, England). (10)

PCA, 1974
REPORT OF TASK 1—LOADING CONDITIONS, Study of Large Panel Concrete Structures, U.S. Dept. of Housing and Urban Development, Washington, D.C. (5)

PCI, 1977a
MANUAL FOR QUALITY CONTROL FOR PLANTS AND PRODUCTION OF PRECAST PRESTRESSED CONCRETE PRODUCTS, MNL-116-77, Prestressed Concrete Institute, Chicago, Ill. (9)

PCI, 1977b
MANUAL FOR QUALITY CONTROL FOR PLANTS AND PRODUCTION OF ARCHITECTURAL PRECAST CONCRETE PRODUCTS, MNL-117-77, Prestressed Concrete Institute, Chicago, Ill. (9)

PPG, 1979
GLASS THICKNESS RECOMMENDATIONS TO MEET ARCHITECTS' SPECIFIED 1-MINUTE WIND LOADING, PPG Industries, Pittsburgh, Pa., April. (9)

PPG TSR 104C, undated a
INSTALLATION RECOMMENDATIONS—WINDOW, PPG Industries, Pittsburgh, Pa. (9)

PPG TSR 104D, undated b
INSTALLATION RECOMMENDATIONS—TINTED GLASS, PPG Industries, Pittsburgh, Pa. (9)

Page, J. K., 1974
FIVE METEOROLOGICAL FACETS OF THE DESIGN OF TALL BUILDINGS, Proceedings of the 23rd National/Regional Conference (Oxford, England), Institution of Structural Engineers, pp. 103–111. (7)

Palmer, K. N., 1973
DUST EXPLOSIONS AND FIRES, Chapman and Hall, London, England. (8B)

Palmer, K. N. and Taylor, W., 1974
FIRE HAZARDS OF PLASTICS IN FURNITURE AND FURNISHINGS: IGNITION STUDIES, Current Paper CP18/74, Building Research Establishment, Borehamwood, England. (8A)

Paloheimo, E. and Hannus, M., 1974
STRUCTURAL DESIGN BASED ON WEIGHTED FRACTILES, Journal of the Structural Division, ASCE, Vol. 100, No. ST7, Proc. Paper 10663, p. 1367. (10)

Panggabean, H. and Schueller, G. I., 1976
ON THE SAFETY OF TALL BUILDINGS, Beiträge zur Anwendung der Aeroelastik im Bauwesen, Technical Report No. 8, Munich, Germany, November. (8A, 10)

Panggabean, H. and Wittmann, F. H., 1976
ON THE DEPENDENCE OF FREQUENCY DENSITY OF THE WIND ON THE HEIGHT ABOVE THE GROUND, THE AVERAGE WIND VELOCITY AND THE

SURFACE ROUGHNESS (Uber die Abhangigkeit der Frequenzdichte des Windes von der Hohe, der mittleren Windgeschwindigkeit und der Bodenrauhigkeit), Proceedings of the 2nd Kolloquium Industrieaerodyn., FHS-Aachen, Germany, pp. 19–34. (7)

Panggabean, H., Schueller, G. I. and Wittmann, F. H., 1975
RELIABILITY BASED DESIGN OF SLENDER STRUCTURES UNDER WIND ACTION, Proceedings of the 4th International Conference on Wind Effects on Buildings and Structures (London, England), University of Cambridge Press, Cambridge, England. (7)

Panggabean, H., Schneider, F. X., Wittman, F. H. and Schueller, G. I., 1974
A CONTRIBUTION TO THE STATISTICAL ANALYSIS OF THE DESIGN WIND VELOCITY, (Beitrag zur statistischen Analyse der Windeschwindigkeit), Proceedings of the 1st Kolloquium Industrieaerodyn., FHS-Aachen, Germany, pp. 19–36. (7)

Pankhurst, R. C., 1964
DIMENSIONAL ANALYSIS AND SCALE FACTORS, Chapman and Hall, London, England. (7)

Pasquill, F., 1972
SOME ASPECTS OF BOUNDARY LAYER DESCRIPTION, Quarterly Journal of the Royal Meteorological Society, Vol. 98, No. 417, pp. 469–494. (7)

Patton, R. M., 1971
LIFE SAFETY SYSTEM, Fire Journal, Vol. 65, National Fire Protection Association, Boston, Mass., January. (8A)

Pauls, J. L., 1958
EVACUATION AND OTHER FIRE SAFETY MEASURES IN HIGH BUILDINGS, Transactions, ASHRAE, Vol. 81, Part 1. (8A)

Pauls, J. L., 1975
MOVEMENT OF PEOPLE IN BUILDINGS, Division of Building Research, National Research Council of Canada, Ottawa, Canada. (8A)

Peir, J. C., 1971
A STOCHASTIC LIVE LOAD MODEL FOR BUILDINGS, Report R71-35, Department of Civil Engineering, Massachusetts Institute of Technology, Cambridge, Mass. (10)

Penwarden, A. D., 1972
WIND ENVIRONMENT AROUND TALL BUILDINGS, Building Research Digest, No. 141. (7)

Penwarden, A. D., 1973
ACCEPTABLE WIND SPEEDS IN TOWNS, Building Science, Vol. 8, No. 3. (7)

Penwarden, A. D. and Wise, A. F. E., 1975
WIND ENVIRONMENT AROUND BUILDINGS, HMSO, London, England (also, Honolulu Magnetic and Seismological Observatory, Honolulu, Hawaii). (7)

Penzien, J., Scheffey, C. F. and Parmelee, R. A., 1964
SEISMIC ANALYSIS OF BRIDGES ON LONG PILES, Journal of the Engineering Mechanics Division, ASCE, Vol. 90, No. EM3, Proc. Paper 3953, pp. 223–254. (6)

Peterka, J. A. and Cermak, J. E., 1974
PROBABILITY DISTRIBUTIONS OF WIND PRESSURE FLUCTUATIONS ON BUILDINGS, presented at the ASCE Speciality Conference on Probabilistic Methods in Engineering, (Stanford University, Stanford, Calif.), p. 15. (7)

Peterka, J. A. and Cermak, J. E., 1975a
WIND PRESSURES ON BUILDINGS–PROBABILITY DENSITIES, Journal of the Structural Division, ASCE, Vol. 101, No. ST6, Proc. Paper 11373, pp. 1255–1267. (7)

Peterka, J. A. and Cermak, J. E., 1975b
TURBULENCE IN BUILDING WAKES, Proceedings of the 4th International Conference on Wind Effects on Buildings and Structures (London, England), University of Cambridge Press, Cambridge, England. (7)

Peterka, J. A. and Cermak, J. E., 1976
PEAK PRESSURE DURATION IN SEPARATED REGIONS ON A STRUCTURE, Proceedings of the 1974 2nd USA/Japan Research Seminar on Wind Effects on Structures, University of Tokyo Press, Tokyo, Japan. (7)

Peterson, C. E., 1969
  OHIO STATE UNIVERSITY FIRES....*Fire Journal*, High-Rise Building Fires and Safety, National Fire Protection Association, pp. 66–70 (reprint). (8A)
Pettersson, O., 1973
  FIRE ENGINEERING DESIGN OF TALL BUILDINGS, Planning and Design of Tall Buildings, Proceedings of the 1972 ASCE-IABSE International Conference, Vol. 1b, ASCE, New York, pp. 585–642. (8A)
Pettersson, O., Magnusson, S. V. and Thor, J., 1976
  FIRE ENGINEERING DESIGN OF STEEL STRUCTURES, Publication 50, Swedish Institute of Steel Construction, Stockholm, Sweden. (8A)
Peyrot, A. H., Saul, W. E., Jayachandran, P. and Tantichaiboriboon, 1974
  MULTI-DEGREE DYNAMIC ANALYSIS OF TALL BUILDINGS SUBJECTED TO WIND AS A STOCHASTIC PROCESS, Proceedings of the Regional Conference on Tall Buildings (Bangkok, Thailand), pp. 555–569. (7)
Pielke, R. A. and Panofsky, H. A., 1970
  TURBULENCE CHARACTERISTICS ALONG SEVERAL TOWERS, *Boundary Layer Meteorology*, Vol. 1, pp. 115–130. (7)
Pinkham, C. W., 1973
  EVALUATION OF EARTHQUAKE DAMAGE, Planning and Design of Tall Buildings, Proceedings of the 1972 ASCE-IABSE International Conference, Vol. 1b, ASCE, New York, pp. 229–246. (6)
Pirner, M., 1973
  THE VERIFICATION OF DYNAMIC RESPONSE OF TALL BUILDINGS UNDER WIND LOADING, Proceedings of the 10th National/Regional Conference (Bratislava, Czechoslovakia), pp. 257–266. (7)
Pittsburgh Plate Glass Company, 1965
  See PPG TSR 101, 1965. (7)
Plate, E. J., 1971
  AERODYNAMIC CHARACTERISTICS OF ATMOSPHERIC BOUNDARY LAYERS, U.S. Atomic Energy Commission Critical Review Series. (7)
Plummer, H. C. and Blume, J. A., 1953
  REINFORCED BRICK MASONRY AND LATERAL FORCE DESIGN, Structural Clay Products Institute, Washington, D.C. (9)
Poestkoke, R., Van Lindert, F. X. C. M., Van Nunen, J. W. G. and Conrads, L. A., 1976
  COMPARISON OF FULL SCALE WIND CLIMATE AROUND A HIGH-RISE BUILDING WITH WIND TUNNEL TESTS ON A MODEL, NLR MP 76009 U, National Aerospace Laboratory. (7)
Polyakov, S. V., Denison, B. E., Zhunusov, T. Zh., Konovodchenko, V. I. and Cherkashin, A. V., 1969
  INVESTIGATIONS INTO EARTHQUAKE RESISTANCE OF LARGE-PANEL BUILDINGS, Proceedings of the 4th World Conference on Earthquake Engineering (Santiago, Chile, January), Vol. I, University of Chile. (6)
Popp, C., 1965
  INVESTIGATIONS ON THE IMPACT OF VEHICLES ON REINFORCED CONCRETE COLUMNS AND FRAMES (Untersuchungen über den Stossverlauf beim Aufprall von Kraftfahrzeugen auf Stutzen und Rahmenstiele aus Stahlbeton), *Deutscher Ausschuss für Stahlbeton*, No. 172. (8B)
Popplewell, N., 1975
  THE RESPONSE OF BOX-LIKE STRUCTURES TO WEAK EXPLOSIONS, *Journal of Sound and Vibration*, Vol. 42, pp. 65–84. (8B)
Port and Harbor Research Institute, 1978
  ANNUAL REPORT ON STRONG-MOTION EARTHQUAKE RECORDS IN JAPANESE PORTS, Ministry of Transport, Japan. (6)
Powers, W. R., 1971a
  NEW YORK OFFICE BUILDING FIRE, *Fire Journal*, National Fire Protection Association, Boston, Mass., January. (8A)
Powers, W. R., 1971b
  OFFICE BUILDING FIRE, 919 THIRD AVENUE, NEW YORK CITY, *Fire Journal* reprint, National Fire Protection Association, Boston, Mass., March. (8A)

Prabhu, K. S., Gopalacharyulu, S. and Johns, D. J., 1975
  DESIGN CRITERIA FOR STABILITY OF CYLINDRICAL SHELLS SUBJECTED TO
  WIND LOADING, Proceedings of the 4th International Conference on Wind Effects on
  Buildings and Structures (London, England), University of Cambridge Press, Cambridge,
  England. (7)
Pris, R., 1963a
  DETERMINATION OF THE ACTION OF TURBULENT WIND ON BUILDINGS
  AND STRUCTURES (Détermination de l'action d'un vent turbulent sur les bâtiments et
  constructions), Proceedings of the International Conference on Wind Effects on Buildings
  and Structures (NPL, Teddington, England). (7)
Pris, R., 1963b
  PREPARATION OF TESTS ON MODELS OF BUILDINGS IN AERODYNAMICS
  LABORATORY AND THE APPLICATION TO THE TRUE HEIGHT (Préparation
  des essais sur maquettes de bâtiments au laboratoire aerodynamique et applications a la
  vraie grandeur), Proceedings of the International Conference on Wind Effects on
  Buildings and Structures (NPL, Teddington, England). (7)
Pugachov, V. S., 1960
  THEORY OF RANDOM FUNCTIONS AND ITS APPLICATION TO PROBLEMS OF
  AUTOMATIC CONTROL 2nd ed., Moscow, USSR (in Russian). (10)

QMC-IMR, 1973
  SMOKE FROM BURNING PLASTICS, A Micro-Symposium Organized by the Industrial
  Materials Research Unit, Queen Mary College, February. (8A)
Quarantelli, E. L., 1977
  PANIC BEHAVIOR: SOME EMPIRICAL OBSERVATIONS, Proceedings of the Con-
  ference on Human Response to Tall Buildings (Chicago, Ill., July), Dowden, Hutchison &
  Ross, Inc., Stroudsburg, Pa.; also Disaster Research Center, Columbus, Ohio. (8A)

Rainer, J. H., 1971
  DYNAMIC GROUND COMPLIANCE IN MULTI-STORY BUILDINGS, Journal of
  Sound and Vibration, Vol. 16, No. 4, pp. 615–622. (6)
Ramesh, C. K. and Limaya, S. D., 1973
  WIND FORCES ON TALL BUILDINGS—EVALUATION TO DESIGN, Proceedings of
  the National Conference on Tall Buildings (New Delhi, India), pp. iiii03–iiii31. (7)
Randall, F. A., Jr. and Panarese, W. C., 1976
  CONCRETE MASONRY HANDBOOK FOR ARCHITECTS, ENGINEERS, BUILDERS,
  Portland Cement Association, Skokie, Ill. (9)
Ranga Raju, K. G. and Singh, V., 1975
  BLOCKAGE EFFECTS ON DRAG OF SHARP-EDGED BODIES, Journal of Industrial
  Aerodynamics, Vol. 1, No. 3, pp. 301–310. (7)
Rao, V. V. S. and Srivastava, O. S., 1974
  STABILITY OF FOUNDATIONS OF TALL STRUCTURES UNDER EARTH-
  QUAKES—A CASE STUDY, Proceedings of the Regional Conference on Tall Buildings
  (Bangkok, Thailand, January), Asian Institute of Technology, Bangkok, Thailand, pp.
  755–764. (6)
Rasbash, D. J., 1967
  SMOKE AND TOXIC PRODUCTS PRODUCED AT FIRES, Transactions, Journal of the
  Plastics Institute, Cons. Suppl. No. 2, pp. 55–62. (8A)
Rasbash, D. J., 1969
  EXPLOSIONS IN DOMESTIC STRUCTURES, Part 1: THE RELIEF OF GAS AND
  VAPOUR EXPLOSIONS IN DOMESTIC STRUCTURES, Structural Engineer, Vol. 47,
  pp. 404–408. (8B)
Rasbash, D. J., 1970
  GAS EXPLOSIONS IN MULTIPLE COMPARTMENTS, Fire Research Note No. 847,
  Fire Research Station, Borehamwood, England; reissued, Dept. of the Environment,
  London, England, 1971. (8B)
Rasbash, D. J. and Stark, G. W. V., 1966
  THE GENERATION OF CARBON MONOXIDE BY FIRES IN COMPARTMENT,
  Fire Research Note No. 614, Fire Research Station, Borehamwood, England. (8A)
Rathbun, J. C., 1940
  WIND FORCES ON TALL BUILDINGS, Transactions, ASCE, Vol. 105, Paper No. 2056,
  pp. 1–41. (7)

Ravindra, M. K. and Lind, N. C., 1971
OPTIMIZATION OF A STRUCTURAL CODE, SM Report 72, Solid Mechanics Division, University of Waterloo, Waterloo, Ont., Canada, January. (10)

Ravindra, M. K., Heany, A. C. and Lind, N. C., 1969
PROBABILISTIC EVALUATION OF SAFETY FACTORS, IABSE Symposium on Concepts of Safety of Structures and Methods of Design, Final Report, London, England, Vol. 4, pp. 35–46. (10)

Reardon, F. G., 1973
BRISBANE WIND STORM, Division of Building Research, Report 33, CSIRO, Australia. (7)

Reese, R. C., 1973
THEME REPORT: GRAVITY LOADS AND TEMPERATURE EFFECTS, Planning and Design of Tall Buildings, Proceedings of the 1972 ASCE-IABSE International Conference, Vol. 1b, No. TC-5, ASCE, New York. (5)

Reese, R. T. and Kostem, C. N., 1973
A METHOD TO DETERMINE THE SENSITIVITY OF MATHEMATICAL MODELS IN DETERMINISTIC STRUCTURAL DYNAMICS, Fritz Engineering Laboratory Report No. 400.9, Lehigh University, Bethlehem, Pa. (7)

Reeves, P. M., Campbell, G. S., Ganzer, V. M. and Joppa, R. G., 1974
DEVELOPMENT AND APPLICATION OF A NON-GAUSSIAN ATMOSPHERIC TURBULENCE MODEL FOR USE IN FLIGHT SIMULATORS, NASA Contractor Report 2451, September. (7)

Reichel, V., 1973
FIRE SAFETY PROBLEMS IN TALL BUILDINGS, Proceedings of the 10th Regional Conference (Bratislava, Czechslovakia, April), CSVTA, Czechoslovak Scientific and Technical Association, Bratislava, Czechoslovakia. (8A)

Reséndiz, D. and Herrera, I., 1969a
A PROBABILISTIC FORMULATION OF SETTLEMENT CONTROLLED DESIGN, Proceedings of the 7th International Conference on Soil Mechanics and Foundation Engineering (Mexico City, Mexico), Vol. 2, pp. 239–245. (10)

Reséndiz, D. and Herrera, I., 1969b
DISTRIBUTIONS OF FOUNDATION SETTLEMENTS ON COMPRESSIBLE SOIL, Proceedings of the 7th International Conference on Soil Mechanics and Foundation Engineering (Mexico City, Mexico). (10)

Rice, S. O., 1944
MATHEMATICAL ANALYSIS OF RANDOM NOISE, Bell Technical Journal, Vol. 18, 282 (1944) and 19, 46 (1945). (7)

Richter, C. F., 1958
ELEMENTARY SEISMOLOGY, W. H. Freeman, Inc., San Francisco, Calif. (6)

Riera, J. D., 1968
ON THE STRESS ANALYSIS OF STRUCTURES SUBJECTED TO AIRCRAFT IMPACT FORCES, Nuclear Engineering and Design, Vol. 8, pp. 415–426. (8B)

Riera, J. D., Reimundin, J. C. and Cudmani, R., 1973
DIRECT WIND, South American Regional Conference on Tall Buildings (Porto Alegre, Brazil), pp. 53–74. (7)

Roberts, A. F., 1974
THE BEHAVIOUR OF POLYURETHANE FOAM IN FIRE, Insulation, November/December, pp. 10–16. (8A)

Roberts, J. J., 1973
THE EFFECT OF DIFFERENT TEST PROCEDURES UPON THE INDICATED STRENGTH OF CONCRETE BLOCKS IN COMPRESSION, Magazine of Concrete Research, Vol. 25, No. 83, June. (9)

Robertson, A. F. and Ryan, J. V., 1959
PROPOSED CRITERIA FOR DEFINING LOAD FAILURE OF BEAMS, FLOORS AND ROOF CONSTRUCTIONS DURING FIRE TESTS, Journal of Research, National Bureau of Standards, Vol. 63C. (8A)

Robertson, L. E., 1973a
LIMITATIONS ON SWAYING MOTION OF TALL BUILDINGS IMPOSED BY HUMAN RESPONSE FACTORS, Proceedings of the Australian Conference on Planning and Design of Tall Buildings (University of Sydney, August, 1972), Sydney, Australia. (7)

Robertson, L. E., 1973b
DESIGN CRITERIA FOR VERY TALL BUILDINGS, Proceedings of the Australian Conference on Planning and Design of Tall Buildings (University of Sydney, August, 1972), Sydney, Australia, pp. 171–180. (7)

Robertson, L. E., 1976
Private communication to the Council (January 8, 1976). (5)

Robertson, L. E. and Chen, P. W., 1967
APPLICATION TO DESIGN OF RESEARCH ON WIND EFFECTS, International Seminar on Wind Effects on Buildings and Structures (Ottawa, Canada), University of Toronto Press. (7)

Robertson, L. E. and Chen, P. W., 1969
THE TREATMENT OF WIND IN THE DESIGN OF VERY TALL BUILDINGS, Proceedings of the Technology Meeting Concerning Wind Loads on Buildings and Structures (NBS, Gaithersburg, Md.), Building Science Series 30. (7)

Rodin, J. and Chanon, C., 1969
SAFETY IN LARGE PANEL CONSTRUCTION, Symposium on Concepts of Safety of Structures and Methods of Design (London, England), Final Report, IABSE, Zürich, Switzerland, pp. 1–12. (8B)

Roesset, J. M. and Whitman, R. V., 1969
THEORETICAL BACKGROUND FOR AMPLIFICATION STUDIES, Research Report No. R69-15, Soils Publication No. 231, M.I.T. Inter-American Program in Civil Engineering, Department of Civil Engineering, Massachusetts Institute of Technology, Cambridge, Mass. (6)

Rokach, A. J., 1970
A STATISTICAL STUDY OF THE STRENGTH OF STEEL COLUMNS, R70-60, Department of Civil Engineering, Massachusetts Institute of Technology, Cambridge, Mass., September. (10)

Rosenblueth, E., 1956
THEORY OF LIVE LOADS ON BUILDINGS (Teoría de la Carga Viva en Edificios), Ingeniería, Vol. 29, No. 4, pp. 51–72. (10)

Rosenblueth, E., 1960
THE EARTHQUAKE OF 28 JULY 1957, IN MEXICO CITY, Proceedings of the 2nd World Conference on Earthquake Engineering (Tokyo, Japan). (6)

Rosenblueth, E., 1964
PROBABILISTIC DESIGN TO RESIST EARTHQUAKES, Journal of the Engineering Mechanics Division, ASCE, Vol. 90, No. EM5, Proc. Paper 4090, October, pp. 189–220. (10)

Rosenblueth, E., 1969
APPLICATIONS OF DECISION THEORY, Proceedings of the 7th International Conference on Soil Mechanics and Foundation Engineering (Mexico City, Mexico), Vol. 3, pp. 230–233. (10)

Rosenblueth, E., 1970
ETHICAL DECISIONS IN ENGINEERING (Decisiones Éticas en Ingeniería), Ingeniería, Vol. 40, No. 4, pp. 383–396. (10)

Rosenblueth, E., 1971
DECISIONS THEORY IN EARTHQUAKE ENGINEERING, 1st National Conference on Earthquake Engineering (Wellington, New Zealand). (10)

Rosenblueth, E., 1972
STRUCTURAL SAFETY AND PROBABILISTIC METHODS, Proceedings of the 6th Regional Conference (Delft, The Netherlands, May), Lehigh University, Bethlehem, Pa. (10)

Rosenblueth, E., 1973a
CODE SPECIFICATION OF SAFETY AND SERVICEABILITY, Planning and Design of Tall Buildings, Proceedings of the 1972 ASCE-IABSE International Conference, Vol. 1b, ASCE, New York, pp. 931–960. (10)

Rosenblueth, E., 1973b
FLOOR LOADS, Planning and Design of Tall Buildings, Proceedings of the 1972 ASCE-IABSE International Conference, Vol. 1b, No. 5-D1, ASCE, New York. (5)

Rosenblueth, E., 1974
ANALYSIS OF RISK, Proceedings of 5th World Conference on Earthquake Engineering, (Rome, Italy), Vol. 2, pp. CIL–CLVIII. (10)

Rosenblueth, E., 1975a
OPTIMUM DESIGN IN EARTHQUAKE ENGINEERING (Diseño Optimo En Ingeniera Sismica), *Ingeniera*, Vol. 45, No. 3, pp. 275–295. (10)
Rosenblueth, E., 1975b
POINT ESTIMATES FOR PROBABILITY MOMENTS, Proceedings of National Academy of Sciences, Vol. 72, No. 10, October, pp. 2812–2814. (10)
Rosenblueth, E., 1975c
THE FUTURE OF EARTHQUAKE ENGINEERING (El Futuro de la Ingenieria Sismica), Revista IMCYC, Mexico City, Mexico, Vol. 13, March/April, pp. 9–16. (10)
Rosenblueth, E., 1975d
UNCERTAINTY IN STRUCTURAL ENGINEERING, Boletia del Instituto Mexicana de Planeacion y Operacion de Sistemas, Vol. 27, January/February, pp. 1–37. (10)
Rosenblueth, E. and Bustamante, J. I., 1962
DISTRIBUTION OF STRUCTURAL RESPONSE TO EARTHQUAKES, *Journal of the Engineering Mechanics Division*, ASCE, Vol. 88, No. EM3, Proc. Paper 3177, June, pp. 75–106. (10)
Rosenblueth, E. and Elorduy, J., 1969
RESPONSE OF LINEAR SYSTEMS TO CERTAIN TRANSIENT DISTURBANCES, Proceedings of the 4th World Conference on Earthquake Engineering (Santiago, Chile). (6, 10)
Rosenblueth, E. and Esteva, L., 1971
RELIABILITY BASIS FOR SOME MEXICAN CODES, ACI Symposium on Structural Reliability (Denver, Colo.) (10)
Rosenblueth, E. and Mendoza, E., 1971
RELIABILITY OPTIMIZATION IN ISOSTATIC STRUCTURES, *Journal of the Engineering Mechanics Division*, ASCE, Vol. 97, No. EM6, Proc. Paper 8584, p. 1625. (10)
Rosenblueth, E., Esteva, L. and Damy, J. E., 1974
BONUS AND PENALTY IN ACCEPTANCE CRITERIA FOR CONCRETE, *ACI Journal*, American Concrete Institute, Vol. 71, No. 9, pp. 466–472. (10)
Rothé, J. P., 1969
THE SEISMICITY OF THE EARTH, UNESCO. (6)
Rozlivka, L. and Horina, B., 1973
MAIN PROBLEMS OF NEW STEELS WITH INCREASED RESISTANCE AGAINST CORROSION IN BUILDING STRUCTURES, 10th Regional Conference Proceedings (Bratislava, Czechoslovakia, April), Vols. I and II, CSVTA—Czechoslovak Scientific and Technical Association, Bratislava, Czechoslovakia (two editions: English and Czech), pp. 427–432. (9)
Rubin, A., and Cohen, A., 1974
OCCUPANT BEHAVIOR IN BUILDING FIRES, NBS Technical Note 818, U.S. Dept. of Commerce, National Bureau of Standards, Gaithersburg, Md. (8A)
Rubinstein, M. F., 1964
EFFECT OF AXIAL DEFORMATION ON THE PERIODS OF A TALL BUILDING, *Bulletin*, Seismological Society of America, Vol. 54, No. 1. (6)
Ruiz, P. and Penzien, J., 1969
PROBABILISTIC STUDY OF THE BEHAVIOR OF STRUCTURES DURING EARTHQUAKES, Report 69-3, Earthquake Engineering Research Center, University of California, Berkeley, Calif. (6)
Rummerfield, P. S., Cholak, J. and Kereiakes, J., 1967
ESTIMATION OF LOCAL DIFFUSION OF POLLUTANTS FROM A CHIMNEY: A PROTOTYPE STUDY EMPLOYING AN ACTIVATED TRACER, *Journal*, American Industrial Hygiene Association, Vol. 28, pp. 171–180. (7)
Ruscheweyh, H., 1973
EMPIRICAL VALUES OF NATURAL FREQUENCIES OF TALL BUILDINGS, 10th Regional Conference Proceedings (Bratislava, Czechoslovakia, April), CSVTA—Czechoslovak Scientific and Technical Association, Bratislava, Czechoslovakia, pp. 298–299. (6, 7)
Russell, L. R., 1971
PROBABILITY DISTRIBUTION OF HURRICANE EFFECTS, *Journal of the Waterways, Harbors and Coastal Engineering Division*, ASCE, Vol. 97, No. WW1, Proc. Paper 7886, pp. 139–154. (7)

Rzhanitzyn, A. R., 1969
IT IS NECESSARY TO IMPROVE THE STANDARDS OF DESIGN OF BUILDING STRUCTURES (Neobkodimo Sovershenstvovat' Normy Rascieta Stroitel' Nykk Konstructsii), *Stroitel' naya Promyshennost'*, Vol. 8, 1957, pp. 29–32; translated by D. E. Allen in "A Statistical Method of Design of Building Structures," National Research Council of Canada, Technical Translation 1360, Ottawa, Canada, 1969, pp. 1–14. (10)

SAA, 1971
CODE FOR AUTOMATIC SPRINKLER INSTALLATIONS, CA16-1971, Standards Association of Australia, North Sydney, Australia. (8A)
SAA, 1971
METHOD OF MEASUREMENT OF CIVIL ENGINEERING QUANTITIES (METRIC UNITS), AS1181-1971, Standards Association of Australia, North Sydney, Australia. (9)
SAA, 1971–1975
RULES FOR MINIMUM DESIGN LOADS ON STRUCTURES (METRIC UNITS) —DEAD AND LIVE LOADS, Standards Association of Australia, AS1170, Part 1. (5)
SAA, 1972a
PREFERRED SIZES OF BUILDING COMPONENTS (METRIC UNITS), AS1224-1972, Standards Association of Australia, North Sydney, Australia. (9)
SAA, 1972b
USE OF LIFTS IN EMERGENCIES, MP24-1972, Standards Association of Australia, North Sydney, Australia. (8A)
SAA, 1973
CODE OF PRACTICE FOR INSTALLATION OF GLASS IN BUILDINGS, AS1288-1973, Standards Association of Australia, North Sydney, Australia. (9)
SAA, 1973–1975
METHODS FOR FIRE TESTS ON BUILDING MATERIALS AND STRUCTURES, AS1530, Standards Association of Australia, North Sydney, Australia. (8A)
SAA, 1974a
RULES FOR BRICKWORK IN BUILDINGS (METRIC UNITS), (known as SAA Brickwork Code—Metric), AS1640, Standards Association of Australia, North Sydney, Australia. (9)
SAA, 1974b
RULES FOR THE DESIGN AND APPLICATION OF METAL ARC WELDING IN STEEL BUILDING CONSTRUCTION (known as the SAA Code for Welding in Buildings), AS1554-1974, (3 parts), Standards Association of Australia, North Sydney, Australia. (9)
SAA, 1974c
AUSTRALIAN SPECIFICATION FOR FIRE DAMPERS, AS 1682-1974, Standards Association of Australia, North Sydney, Australia. (8A)
SAA, 1974d
SAA MECHANICAL VENTILATION AND AIR CONDITIONING CODE, Part I—Fire Precautions in Buildings with Air-Handling Systems, Standards Association of Australia, North Sydney, Australia. (8A)
SAA, 1974e
RULES FOR AUTOMATIC FIRE ALARM INSTALLATIONS, AS1670-1974, Standards Association of Australia, North Sydney, Australia. (8A)
SAA, 1976
FIRE DOOR CODE: FIRE DOORS, AS 1905, Part 1-1976, Standards Association of Australia, North Sydney, Australia. (8A)
SNiP II-6-74, 1976
DESIGN LOADS, Chapter 6 of Part II (Design Specifications), SNiP II-6-74, Building Code and Rules (Design Specifications for Buildings), Gosstroi, Moscow, USSR. (5)
Sadeh, W. Z. and Cermak, J. E., 1972
TURBULENCE EFFECTS ON WALL PRESSURE FLUCTUATIONS, *Journal of the Engineering Mechanics Division*, ASCE, Vol. 98, No. EM6, Proc. Paper 9445, pp. 1365–1379. (7)
Sae-Ung, S., 1976
ACTIVE CONTROL OF BUILDING STRUCTURES SUBJECTED TO WIND LOADS, dissertation presented to the School of Civil Engineering, Purdue University, at West Lafayette, Ind., in May 1976, in partial fulfillment of the requirements for the degree of Doctor of Philosophy. (7)

Sae-Ung, S. and Yao, J. T. P., 1975
ACTIVE CONTROL OF BUILDING STRUCTURES SUBJECTED TO WIND LOADS,
Technical Report No. CE-STR-75-2, School of Civil Engineering, Purdue University,
Lafayette, Ind., October. (7)

Saffir, H. S., 1974
EFFECTS OF HIGH WIND ON GLAZING AND CURTAIN WALLS, AND RA-
TIONAL DESIGN METHODS FOR GLAZING AND CURTAIN WALLS, Pro-
ceedings of the 1974 2nd USA/Japan Research Seminar on Wind Effects on Structures,
University of Tokyo Press, Tokyo, Japan. (7)

Saffir, H. S., 1975
GLASS AND CURTAIN WALL EFFECTS OF HIGH WINDS: REQUIRED DESIGN
CRITERIA, Proceedings of the 4th International Conference on Wind Effects on
Buildings and Structures (London, England), University of Cambridge Press, Cambridge,
England. (7)

Sahlin, S. A., 1971a
IMPERFECTIONS IN STRUCTURES CONSTRUCTED WITH PREFABRICATED
CONCRETE ELEMENTS (Imperfektioner Vid Montagebyggande Med Betongelement),
Tekniska Meddelanden Nr. 25, Halmstads Jarnverks AB, Sweden. (8B, 9)

Sahlin, S. A., 1971b
STRUCTURAL MASONRY, Prentice-Hall, Inc., Englewood Cliffs, N.J. (8B, 9)

Sahlin, S. and Nilsson, L., 1975
THE EFFECT OF IMPACT LOADING ON BUILDING: PART 3, THEORETICAL
ANALYSIS OF STRESS AND STRAIN PROPAGATION DURING IMPACT,
Matériaux et Construction, Vol. 8, pp. 88–101. (8B)

Sakaguchi, Y., Nakamura, K. and Yoshida, T., 1971
EFFECT OF WELD THERMAL CYCLES AND STRESS ON FRICTION BOLTS AND
SURFACES IN CASE OF FRICTION BOLT JOINTS WITH WELDING APPLIED
LATER. Architectural Institution of Japan annual report, Tokyo, Japan. (9)

Salleras, J. M., 1971
PILOT INVESTIGATION OF OVERLOADS ON DWELLINGS (Investigación Piloto de
Sobrecargas en Viviendas), XIV Jornadas Sudamericanas de Ingeniería Estructural y IV
S.P.E.-VI.VIII (Buenos Aires, Argentina). (5)

Salleras, J. M., 1974
INVESTIGATION OF OVERLOADS IN DORMITORIES (Investigación de Sobrecargas
en Dormitorios), XVI Jornadas Sudamericanas de Ingeniería Estructural (Buenos Aires,
Argentina). (5)

Salleras, J. M., 1975
DETERMINATION OF OVERLOADS EQUIVALENTS IN DORMITORIES (Determi-
nación de Sobrecargas equivalentes en Dormitorios), XVII Jornadas Sudamericanas de
Ingeniería Estructural y V S.P.E., Caracas, Venezuela. (5)

Sampson, A. F., 1972
THE GENERAL SERVICES ADMINISTRATION'S SYSTEMS APPROACH TO LIFE
SAFETY IN STRUCTURES, presented at the 1972 NFPA Annual Meeting (Phila-
delphia, Pa.), Fire Journal reprint, High Rise Building Fires and Fire Safety, NFPA,
Boston, Mass., pp. 77–79. (8A)

Sander, D. M. and Tamura, G. T., 1973
A FORTRAN IV PROGRAM TO SIMULATE AIR MOVEMENT IN MULTI-STOREY
BUILDINGS, National Research Council of Canada, Division of Building Research,
Computer Program No. 35, March. (8A)

Sandi, H., 1966a
CONTRIBUTIONS TO THE THEORY OF STRUCTURAL DESIGN (in Romanian),
thesis presented to the Institute of Civil Engineering, Bucharest, Romania. (10)

Sandi, H., 1966b
SAFETY OF STRUCTURES SUBJECTED TO TEMPORARY LOADINGS, Studies and
Research of Applied Mechanics, 5. (10)

Sandi, H., 1970
CONVENTIONAL SEISMIC FORCES CORRESPONDING TO NON-SYNCHRO-
NOUS GROUND MOTION, 3rd European Symposium on Earthquake Engineering
(Sofia, Bulgaria). (10)

Sandi, H., 1973a
FAILURE MODEL CALCULATIONS, Planning and Design of Tall Buildings, Proceedings of the 1972 ASCE-IABSE International Conference, Vol. 1b, ASCE, New York, pp. 1038. (10)

Sandi, H., 1973b
LOADS AND LOAD COMBINATIONS, Planning and Design of Tall Buildings, Proceedings of the 1972 ASCE-IABSE International Conference, Vol. 1b, ASCE, New York, pp. 973–992. (10)

Sandi, H., 1973c
NON-SYNCHRONOUS GROUND MOTION, Planning and Design of Tall Buildings, Proceedings of the 1972 ASCE-IABSE International Conference, Vol. 1b, ASCE, New York, pp. 325–326. (6)

Sara, G., 1972
DIMENSIONING OF FRAMED STRUCTURE FOR REINFORCED CONCRETE BUILDINGS IN SEISMIC AREA (Sul Dimensionamento Dell' Intelaiatura Degli Edifici in Cemento Armato in Zona Sismica), Rondazione Politecnica per il Mezzogiorno d'Italia, No. 68. (6)

Saragoni, G. R., 1973
A NEW KIND OF GROUND MOTION, Planning and Design of Tall Buildings, Proceedings of the 1972 ASCE-IABSE International Conference, Vol. 1b, ASCE, New York, pp. 323–324. (6)

Saragoni, G. R. and Hart, G. C., 1972
NONSTATIONARY ANALYSIS AND SIMULATION OF EARTHQUAKE GROUND MOTION, No. UCLA-ENG-7238, UCLA Technical Report, Los Angeles, Calif. (6)

Saragoni, G. R. and Hart, G. C., 1974
SIMULATION OF ARTIFICIAL EARTHQUAKES, Earthquake Engineering and Structural Dynamics, Vol. 2, John Wiley & Sons, Ltd., Chichester, England. (6)

Sarria Molina, A., 1973
SEISMIC HISTORY AND RESEARCH, (Historia Sismica Colombiana y del Compartamiento Estructural), National Seminar on Tall Buildings, Proceedings of Conference (Bogotá, Colombia, September), Colombia School of Engineering, Bogotá, Colombia, pp. 115–136. (6)

Sarto, H., 1966
BEHAVIOR OF END RESTRAINED STEEL MEMBERS UNDER FIRE, Bulletin, Fire Prevention Society of Japan, Vol. 15, No. 1. (8A)

Sasaki, J. R. and Wilson, A. G., 1965
AIR LEAKAGE VALUE FOR RESIDENTIAL WINDOWS, ASHRAE Journal, Vol. 71, Part 2, pp. 81–88. (Reprint available from National Research Council of Canada, NRCC 9786.) (8A)

Saul, W. E., Jayachandran, P. and Tantichaiboriboon, V., 1974
EFFECT AND CALCULATION OF DAMPING ON THE RESPONSE OF TALL BUILDINGS, Proceedings of the Regional Conference on Tall Buildings (Bangkok, Thailand), pp. 571–581. (7)

Saunders, J. W., 1971
FLUTTER INSTABILITY OF RECTANGULAR BUILDINGS, Proceedings of the 4th Australasian Conference on Hydraulics and Fluid Mechanics (Monash University, Australia). (7)

Saunders, J. W. and Melbourne, W. H., 1975
TALL RECTANGULAR BUILDING RESPONSE TO CROSS-WIND EXCITATION, Proceedings of the 4th International Conference on Wind Effects on Buildings and Structures (London, England), University of Cambridge Press, Cambridge, England. (7)

Sawyer, H. A., 1973
ECONOMIC BASIS FOR SEISMIC RESISTANCE, Planning and Design of Tall Buildings, Proceedings of the 1972 ASCE-IABSE International Conference, Vol. 1b, ASCE, New York, p. 319. (6)

Scanlon, R. H., 1977
FLOW-INDUCED VIBRATIONS OF CIVIL STRUCTURES, Advances in Civil Engineering Through Engineering Mechanics, ASCE 2nd Annual Engineering Mechanics Division Specialty Conference, (Raleigh, N.C., May), ASCE, New York, pp. 339–341. (7)

Schiff, A. J., 1974
A MEASURING SYSTEM FOR DETERMINING WIND LOADS AND THE RE-
SULTING RESPONSE OF LARGE STRUCTURES, Proceedings of 1974 2nd USA/
Japan Research Seminar on Wind Effects on Structures, University of Tokyo Press,
Tokyo, Japan. (7)

Schmitt, F. E., 1926
THE FLORIDA HURRICANE AND SOME OF ITS EFFECTS, Engineering News-
Record, Vol. 97, pp. 586–591 and 624–627 October 7–14. (7)

Schnabel, P. B. and Seed, H. B., 1972
ACCELERATIONS IN ROCK FOR EARTHQUAKES IN THE WESTERN UNITED
STATES, Report No. EERC 72-2, Earthquake Engineering Research Center, University
of California, Berkeley, Calif. (6)

Schneider, F. X., 1975
WIND AND STRESS MEASUREMENTS AT THE MUNICH OLYMPIC TOWER
(Wind-und-Betonspannungsmessungen am Olympiaturm München), Beitrage zur Aero-
elastik im Bauwesen, Technical Report No. 1, January. (7)

Schneider, F. X. and Wittmann, F. H., 1975
AN INVESTIGATION OF WIND EXCITED TRANSVERSAL OSCILLATIONS OF
SLENDER STRUCTURES, Proceedings of the 4th International Conference on Wind
Effects on Buildings and Structures (London, England), University of Cambridge Press,
Cambridge, England. (7)

Schneider, F. X. and Wittmann, F. H., 1976
ON THE CALCULATION OF THE PROBABILITY OF FAILURE OF SLENDER
STRUCTURES USING THE MONTE CARLO SIMULATION METHOD (Zur
Berechnung der Versagens-Wahrscheinlichkeit schwindgender Bauwerke unter Verwen-
dung der Monte Carlo Methode), Proceedings of the 2nd Kolloquium Industrieaerodyn
(FHS-Aachen, Germany), pp. 233–250. (7)

Scholes, S. R., 1975
MODERN GLASS PRACTICE, Cahners Books, Boston, Mass., 7th Revised Edition,
revised and enlarged by Charles H. Greene, Ph.D. (9)

Schriever, W. R., 1976
GROUND LEVEL WINDS AROUND TALL BUILDINGS, CBD 174, February. (7)

Schriever, W. R. and Dalgliesh, W. A., 1968
RECENT RESEARCH ON WIND FORCES ON TALL BUILDINGS, Proceedings of
Canadian Structural Engineering Conference, DBR Technical Paper No. 298 (NRC
10682), Canadian Steel Industrial Construction Council, Ont., Canada. (7)

Schueller, G. I., 1974a
RELIABILITY OF TALL BUILDINGS UNDER WIND ACTION, Proceedings of the
ASCE-IABSE Conference on Tall Buildings (Bangkok, Thailand), pp. 521–533. (7, 10)

Schueller, G. I., 1974b
SOME ASPECTS OF RELIABILITY ASSESSMENTS OF STRUCTURES UNDER
WIND ACTION, presented at the ASCE-EMD Specialty Conference on Probabilistic
Methods and Concepts in Engineering (Stanford University, Stanford, Calif.). (7)

Schueller, G. I., 1976
RELIABILITY ORIENTED DESIGN OF TOWER LIKE STRUCTURES—THEORE-
TICAL CONCEPT (Zuverlässigkeitsorientierte Bemessung turmartiger Tragwerke
—theoretisches Konzept), Neuere Erkenntnisse über Schwingungen von Bauwerken im
Wind, Haus der Technik, Vortragsveröffentlichungen, Report No. 347, Vulkan Verlag,
Essen, Germany, pp. 61–92. (10)

Schueller, G. I. and Panggabean, H., 1974
ON THE RELIABILITY ASSESSMENT OF SLENDER STRUCTURES (Uber die
Zuverlässigkeitsbeurteilung von schlanken Tragwerken), Proceedings, 1st Kolloquium
Industrieaerodyn, FHS-Aachen, Germany, pp. 63–74. (10)

Schueller, G. I. and Panggabean, H., 1975
THE CALCULATION OF THE DESIGN WIND VELOCITY BASED ON A RELI-
ABILITY CONCEPT (Ermittlung der Bemessungsgeschwindigkeit unter Zugrundelegung
eines Zuverlässigkeitskonzeptes), Beiträge zur Anwendung der Aeroelastik im Bauwesen,
Technical Report No. 2, Munich, Germany, April. (7)

Schueller, G. I. and Panggabean, H., 1976
PROBABILISTIC DETERMINATION OF DESIGN WIND VELOCITY IN GERMANY, *Proceedings*, Institution of Civil Engineers, London, England, Part 2, Vol. 61. (7)

Schueller, G. I. and Wittmann, F. H., 1976
RELIABILITY CONSIDERATIONS BASED ON MEASUREMENTS OF WIND EFFECTS TAKEN AT THE MUNICH T.V. TOWER, Technical Note, *Journal of Industrial Aerodynamics*, Vol. 1, No. 4. (7)

Schueller, G. I., Panggabean, H. and Wittmann, F. H., 1975
SPECTRAL AND TIME HISTORY APPROACH FOR THE PREDICTION OF THE BEHAVIOUR OF SLENDER STRUCTURES UNDER WIND LOAD—A COMPARATIVE STUDY (Beitrage zur Anwendung der Aeroelastik im Bauwesen), Technical Report No. 6 (Munich, Germany). (7)

Schultz, D. P., 1964
PANIC BEHAVIOR: DISCUSSION AND READINGS, Mary Washington College, University of Virginia, Random House, New York. (8A)

Scruton, C., 1963
ON THE WIND-EXCITED OSCILLATIONS OF STACKS, TOWERS AND MASTS, Proceedings of the International Conference on Wind Effects on Buildings and Structures (NPL, Teddington, England). (7)

Scruton, C., 1967
AERODYNAMICS OF STRUCTURES, Proceedings of the International Seminar on Wind Effects on Buildings and Structures (Ottawa, Canada), Theme Paper. (7)

Sedo, V., 1973
PRACTICAL APPLICATION OF NEW METHODS OF CALCULATION OF BUILDINGS OF LARGE PRECAST CONCRETE PANELS IN EXISTING DESIGN PRACTICE, 10th Regional Conference Proceedings (Bratislava, Czechoslovakia, April), CSVTA—Czechoslovak Scientific and Technological Association, Bratislava, Czechoslovakia. (10)

Seed, H. B., 1969
THE INFLUENCE OF LOCAL SOIL CONDITIONS ON EARTHQUAKE DAMAGE, Proceedings of Specialty Session 2, 7th International Conference on Soil Mechanics and Foundation Engineering (Mexico City, Mexico). (6)

Seed, H. B. and Idriss, I. M., 1969
INFLUENCE OF SOIL CONDITIONS ON GROUND MOTIONS DURING EARTHQUAKES, *Journal of the Soil Mechanics and Foundations Division*, ASCE, Vol. 95, No. SM1, Proc. Paper 6347, pp. 99–137. (6)

Seed, H. B. and Idriss, I. M., 1970a
ANALYSES OF GROUND MOTIONS AT UNION BAY, SEATTLE DURING EARTHQUAKES AND DISTANT NUCLEAR BLASTS, *Bulletin*, Seismological Society of America, February. (6)

Seed, H. B. and Idriss, I. M., 1970b
RELATIONSHIPS BETWEEN SOIL CONDITIONS AND BUILDING DAMAGE IN CARACAS EARTHQUAKE OF JULY 29, 1967, University of California, EERC 70-2. (6)

Seed, H. B. and Wilson, S. D., 1967
THE TURNAGAIN HEIGHTS LANDSLIDE, ANCHORAGE, ALASKA, *Journal of the Soil Mechanics and Foundations Division*, ASCE, Vol. 93, No. SM4, Proc. Paper 5320, pp. 325–353. (6)

Seed, H. B., Idriss, I. M. and Kiefer, F. W., 1969
CHARACTERISTICS OF ROCK MOTIONS DURING EARTHQUAKES, *Journal of the Soil Mechanics and Foundations Division*, ASCE, Vol. 95, No. SM5, Proc. Paper 6783, pp. 1199–1218. (6)

Seed, H. B., Ugas, C. and Lysmer, J., 1974
SITE DEPENDENT SPECTRA FOR EARTHQUAKE-RESISTANT DESIGN, Report No. EERC 74-12, Earthquake Engineering Research Center, University of California, Berkeley, Calif. (6)

Seed, H. B., Muraka, R., Lysmer, J. and Idriss, I. M., 1975
RELATIONSHIPS BETWEEN MAXIMUM ACCELERATION, MAXIMUM VELOCITY DISTANCE FROM SOURCE AND LOCAL SITE CONDITIONS FOR MODERATELY STRONG EARTHQUAKES, Report No. EERC 75-17, Earthquake Engineering Research Center, University of California, Berkeley, Calif. (6)

Seigel, L. G., 1969
THE PROJECTION OF FLAMES FROM BURNING BUILDINGS, *Fire Technology*, Vol. 5, No. 1. (8A)

Seismology Committee of the Structural Engineers Association of California, 1975
RECOMMENDED LATERAL FORCE REQUIREMENTS AND COMMENTARY. (6)

Self, M. W., 1975
STRUCTURAL PROPERTIES OF LOAD BEARING CONCRETE MASONRY, ASTM STP 589, American Society for Testing and Materials, Philadelphia, Pa. (9)

Selvaraj, J. S. and Sharma, S. P., 1974
INFLUENCE OF CONSTRUCTION SEQUENCE ON THE STRESSES IN TALL BUILDING FRAMES, Proceedings of the National Conference on Tall Buildings (Bangkok, Thailand, January), Asian Institute of Technology, Bangkok, Thailand, pp. 197–211. (5)

Sexsmith, R. G., 1967
RELIABILITY ANALYSIS OF CONCRETE STRUCTURES, Technical Report No. 83, Dept. of Civil Engineering, Stanford University, Calif. (10)

Sfintesco, D., 1971
FIRE AND BLAST, 5th Regional Conference Proceedings, (Chicago, Ill., November/December), Lehigh University, Bethlehem, Pa. (8A)

Sfintesco, D., 1973a
FIRE AND BLAST, Proceedings of the Regional Conference on Tall Buildings (Hong Kong, August), Lehigh University, Bethlehem, Pa. (8A)

Sfintesco, D., 1973b
FIRE SAFETY CRITERIA FOR THE DESIGN OF TALL BUILDINGS, Proceedings of Conference held in Sydney, Australia (August), Lehigh University, Bethlehem, Pa. (8A)

Sfintesco, D., 1973c
THEME REPORT: FIRE AND BLAST, Planning and Design of Tall Buildings, Proceedings of the 1972 ASCE-IABSE International Conference, Vol. 1b, ASCE, New York, pp. 463–474. (8A)

Sfintesco, D., 1976
TOWERING HAVEN—CONDENSED STORY OF A FIRE, unpublished communication to the Council. (8A)

Sfintesco, D. and Wyatt, T. A., 1975
A PROPOSED EUROPEAN CODE OF PRACTICE: CURRENT WORK OF THE ECCS TOWARDS SPECIFICATION OF THE EFFECT OF WIND ON STRUCTURES, Proceedings, 4th International Conference on Wind Effects on Buildings and Structures (London, England), Cambridge University Press, Cambridge, England. (7)

Sfintesco, D., Claiborne, G. R., Ehm, H. and Mainstone, R., 1971
FIRE AND BLAST, 2nd Regional Conference Proceedings, (Bled, Yugoslavia, May), Lehigh University, Bethlehem, Pa. (8A)

Shah, H. C., 1970
STATISTICAL EVALUATION OF LOAD FACTORS IN STRUCTURAL DESIGN, Study No. 3, *Structural Reliability and Codified Design*, N. C. Lind, ed., University of Waterloo, Ont., Canada. (10)

Shand, E. B., 1958
GLASS ENGINEERING HANDBOOK, 2nd ed., McGraw-Hill Book Co., Inc., New York. (9)

Sharpe, R. L. and Kost, G., 1971
STRUCTURAL RESPONSE TO SONIC BOOMS, *Journal of the Structural Division*, ASCE, Vol. 97, No. ST4, Proc. Paper 8063, pp. 1157–1174. (8B)

Sharry, J. A., 1973
AN ATRIUM FIRE, *Fire Journal* reprint, Fires in High-Rise Buildings, NFPA, Boston, Mass., pp. 41–43. (8A)

Sharry, J. A., 1974
SOUTH AMERICA BURNING, *Fire Journal* reprint, Fires in High-Rise Buildings, NFPA, Boston, Mass., pp. 9–19. (8A)

Sharry, J. A., 1975
HIGH-RISE HOTEL FIRE, VIRGINIA BEACH, *Fire Journal*, Vol. 69, No. 1, pp. 20–22. (8A)

Shaver, J. R., 1976
CORRELATION OF FLOOR VIBRATION TO HUMAN RESPONSE, Technical Note 904, National Bureau of Standards, U.S. Department of Commerce, Washington, D.C., May. (5)

Shaw, C. Y. and Tamura, G. T., 1973
FORTRAN IV PROGRAMS FOR CALCULATING SIZES AND VENTING CAPACITIES OF SMOKE SHAFTS, National Research Council of Canada, Division of Building Research, Computer Program No. 36, August. (8A)

Shaw, C. Y. and Tamura, G. T., 1974
PROGRAM TO SIMULATE STAIR-SHAFT PRESSURIZATION SYSTEM IN MULTI-STOREY BUILDINGS, National Research Council of Canada, Division of Building Research, Computer Program No. 38, December. (8A)

Shaw, C. Y., Sander, D. M. and Tamura, G. T., 1973
AIR LEAKAGE MEASUREMENTS OF THE EXTERIOR WALLS OF TALL BUILDINGS, *ASHRAE Transactions*, Vol. 79, Part 2, ASHRAE, New York, pp. 40–48. (Reprint available from National Research Council of Canada, NRCC 13951.) (8A)

Shears, M., 1970
PROBLEMS IN THE APPLICATION OF STATISTICAL DESIGN METHODS, The Modern Design of Wind Sensitive Structures, Proceedings of the CIRIA Seminar (London, England). (7)

Shears, M., 1975
REPORT ON WIND VIBRATION MEASUREMENTS TAKEN AT THE EMLEY MOOR TELEVISION TOWER, *Journal of Industrial Aerodynamics*, Vol. 1, No. 2, pp. 113–125. (7)

Shellard, H. C., 1963
THE ESTIMATION OF DESIGN WIND SPEEDS, Proceedings of Conference (NPL, Teddington, England), Vol. 1, pp. 29–52. (7)

Shellard, H. C., 1967
RESULTS OF SOME RECENT SPECIAL MEASUREMENTS IN THE UNITED KINGDOM RELEVANT TO WIND LOADING PROBLEMS, Proceedings, International Research Seminar on Wind Effects on Buildings and Structures (Ottawa, Canada). (7)

Shepherd, R., 1973
NEW ZEALAND EARTHQUAKE PROVISIONS, Proceedings of the 12th Regional Conference (Sydney, Australia, August), Lehigh University, Bethlehem, Pa., pp. 82–95. (6)

Shewhart, W. A., 1926
QUALITY CONTROL CHARTS, *Bell System Technical Journal*, October, pp. 593–603. (9)

Shibata, H., Fujii, S., Iguchi, M., Sato, H. and Akino, K., 1969
OBSERVATION OF DAMAGES OF INDUSTRIAL FIRMS IN NIIGATA EARTHQUAKE, Proceedings of the 4th World Conference on Earthquake Engineering (Santiago, Chile), Vol. 3. (6)

Shiga, T. and Ogawa, J., 1969
THE EXPERIMENTAL STUDY ON THE DYNAMIC BEHAVIOR OF REINFORCED CONCRETE FRAMES, Proceedings of the 4th World Conference on Earthquake Engineering (Santiago, Chile). (6)

Shin, Y. S., 1971
STUDIES ON RELIABILITY BASED ANALYSIS OF STRUCTURES, thesis presented to Case Western Reserve University, at Cleveland, Ohio, in September, in partial fulfillment of the requirements for the degree of Doctor of Philosophy. (10)

Shinozuka, M., 1969
STRUCTURAL SAFETY AND OPTIMUM PROOF LOAD, prepared discussion for IABSE Symposium on Concepts of Safety (London, England). (10)

Shinozuka, M. and Yao, J. T. P., 1977
ACTIVE/PASSIVE CONTROL OF CIVIL ENGINEERING STRUCTURES, Advances in Civil Engineering Through Engineering Mechanics, ASCE 2nd Annual Engineering Mechanics Division Specialty Conference (Raleigh, N.C., May), ASCE, New York, pp. 113–115. (7)

Shiotani, M. and Arai, H., 1967
LATERAL STRUCTURES OF GUSTS IN HIGH WINDS, Proceedings, International Research Seminar on Wind Effects on Buildings and Structures (Ottawa, Canada). (7)

Shiotani, M. and Iwatani, Y., 1971
  CORRELATIONS OF WIND VELOCITIES IN RELATION TO GUST LOADINGS,
  Proceedings, International Conference on Wind Effects on Buildings and Structures
  (Tokyo, Japan), Paper 1.6. (7)
Shiotani, M. and Iwatani, Y., 1974
  A STUDY OF WIND FLOW AT THE BASE OF BUILDINGS, Proceedings, 2nd
  USA/Japan Research Seminar on Wind Effects on Structures, University of Tokyo Press,
  Japan. (7)
Shorter, G. W., 1967
  FIRE IN TALL BUILDINGS, reprint from *Fire Fighting in Canada*, FR Note 7, October.
  (8A)
Shorter, G. W., McGuire, J. H., Hutcheon, N. B. and Legget, R. F., 1960
  THE ST. LAWRENCE BURNS, *NFPA Quarterly*, Vol. 53, No. 4, Boston, Mass., pp.
  300–316. (8A)
Simha, D. A., 1973
  WIND EFFECT ON BUILDINGS, Proceedings, National Conference on Tall Buildings
  (New Delhi, India), pp. 11.141–11.149. (7)
Simha, D. A., 1973
  FIRE SAFETY IN TALL BUILDINGS, Proceedings of National Conference on Tall
  Buildings (New Delhi, India, January), Indian National Group of the IABSE, New Delhi,
  India. (8A)
Simiu, E., 1973a
  LOGARITHMIC PROFILES AND DESIGN WIND SPEEDS, *Journal of the Engineering
  Mechanics Division*, ASCE, Vol. 99, No. EM5, Proc. Paper 10100, pp. 1073–1083. (7)
Simiu, E., 1973b
  GUST FACTORS AND ALONGWIND PRESSURE CORRELATIONS, *Journal of the
  Structural Division*, ASCE, Vol. 100, No. ST9, Proc. Paper 9686, pp. 773–783. (7)
Simiu, E., 1974
  IMPROVED METHODS FOR DETERMINING WIND PROFILES AND DYNAMIC
  STRUCTURAL RESPONSE TO WIND, Proceedings, Regional Conference on Tall
  Buildings (Bangkok, Thailand), pp. 491–503. (7)
Simiu, E., 1975
  EQUIVALENT STATIC WIND LOADS FOR TALL BUILDING DESIGN, Proceedings,
  4th International Conference on Wind Effects on Buildings and Structures (London,
  England), Cambridge University Press, Cambridge, England. (7)
Simiu, E. and Filliben, J. J., 1975
  PROBABILISTIC MODELS OF EXTREME WIND SPEEDS: UNCERTAINTIES AND
  LIMITATIONS, Proceedings, 4th International Conference on Wind Effects on Build-
  ings and Structures (London, England), Cambridge University Press, Cambridge,
  England. (7)
Simiu, E. and Lozier, D. W., 1975
  THE BUFFETING OF TALL STRUCTURES BY STRONG WINDS, Building Science
  Series 74, NBS, Gaithersburg, Md., October. (7)
Simms, D. L., 1960
  IGNITION OF CELLULOSIC MATERIALS BY RADIATION, *Combustion and Flame*,
  Vol. 4, No. 4, pp. 293–300. (8A)
Singer, I. A. and Smith, M. E., 1969
  THE ADEQUACY OF EXISTING METEOROLOGICAL DATA FOR EVALUATING
  STRUCTURAL PROBLEMS, Proceedings, Technical Meeting Concerning Wind Loads
  on Buildings and Structures (NBS, Gaithersburg, Md.), Building Science Series 30. (7)
Singer, I. A., Busch, N. E. and Frizzola, J. A., 1967
  THE MICROMETEOROLOGY OF THE TURBULENT FLOW FIELD IN THE
  ATMOSPHERIC SURFACE BOUNDARY LAYER, Proceedings, International Sem-
  inar on Wind Effects on Buildings and Structures (Ottawa, Canada). (7)
Sinha, B. P. and Hendry, A. W., 1970
  THE STABILITY OF A FIVE-STOREY BRICKWORK CROSS-WALL STRUCTURE
  FOLLOWING THE REMOVAL OF A SECTION OF A MAIN LOAD-BEARING
  WALL, Technical Note No. 165, British Ceramic Research Association, Stoke-on-Trent,
  England. (8B)

Slack, J. H., 1971
EXPLOSIONS IN BUILDINGS—THE BEHAVIOUR OF REINFORCED CONCRETE FRAMES, *Concrete*, Vol. 5, pp. 109–114. (8B)

Smart, H. R., Stevens, L. K. and Joubert, P. N., 1967
DYNAMIC STRUCTURAL RESPONSE TO NATURAL WIND, Proceedings, International Research Seminar on Wind Effects on Buildings and Structures (Ottawa, Canada). (7)

Smith, P. G. and Thomas, P. H., 1970
THE RATE OF BURNING WOOD CRIBS, *Fire Technology*, Vol. 6, No. 1, pp. 29–38. (8A)

Snyder, W. H., 1972
SIMILARITY CRITERIA FOR THE APPLICATION OF FLUID MODELS TO THE STUDY OF AIR POLLUTION METEOROLOGY, *Boundary Layer Meteorology*, 3. (7)

Society of Steel Construction of Japan, 1975
WIND RESISTANT DESIGN REGULATIONS—A WORLD LIST 1975: Australia, Austria, Belgium, Brazil, Canada, Chile, Czechoslovakia, Denmark, France, Germany (East), Germany (West), India, Israel, Italy, Japan, Netherlands, New Zealand, Norway, Poland, Portugal, Romania, Spain, Sweden, Switzerland, Turkey, United Kingdom, Uruguay, U.S.A., U.S.S.R., compiled by the Japanese Organizing Committee of the 3rd International Conference on Wind Effects on Buildings and Structures and the Committee of Wind Loading, Society of Steel Construction of Japan. (6)

Somes, N. F., 1973a
ABNORMAL LOADING ON BUILDINGS AND PROGRESSIVE COLLAPSE, NBSIR 73-221, National Bureau of Standards, Gaithersburg, Md. (8B)

Somes, N. F., 1973b
PROGRESSIVE COLLAPSE RISK, Planning and Design of Tall Buildings, Proceedings of the 1972 ASCE-IABSE International Conference, Vol. 1b, ASCE, New York, p. 727. (8B)

Somes, N. F., Dikkers, R. D. and Boone, T. H., 1971
LUBBOCK TORNADO: A SURVEY OF BUILDING DAMAGE IN AN URBAN AREA, NBS Technical Note 558, Building Research Div., Institute for Applied Technology, NBS, Gaithersburg, Md. (7)

Soon, C. T., 1974
WIND TUNNEL INVESTIGATION ON THE FLOODLIT TOWER OF THE SINGAPORE NATIONAL STADIUM, Proceedings, Conference on Tall Buildings (Kuala Lumpur, Malaysia), pp. 8.1–8.5. (7)

Sozen, M. A. and Matthiesen, R. B., 1975
ENGINEERING REPORT ON THE MANAGUA EARTHQUAKE OF 23 DECEMBER 1972, National Academy of Sciences. (6)

Sozen, M. A., Jennings, P. C., Matthiesen, R. B., Housner, G. W. and Newmark, N. M., 1968
ENGINEERING REPORT ON THE CARACAS EARTHQUAKE OF 29 JULY 1967, National Academy of Sciences. (6)

Springfield, J., 1973
CODES AND MODEL TESTING, Planning and Design of Tall Buildings, Proceedings of the 1972 ASCE-IABSE International Conference, Vol. 1b, ASCE, New York, pp. 431–434. (7)

Standen, N. M., Dalgliesh, W. A. and Templin, R. J., 1971
A WIND TUNNEL AND FULL-SCALE STUDY OF TURBULENT WIND PRESSURES ON A TALL BUILDING, Proceedings, 3rd International Conference on Wind Effects on Buildings and Structures (Tokyo, Japan). (7)

Stansby, P. K. and Wootton, L. R., 1975
THE VALUE OF WIND RESEARCH TO CIVIL ENGINEERING, Proceedings, 4th International Conference on Wind Effects on Buildings and Structures (London, England), Cambridge University Press, Cambridge, England. (7)

Stark, G. W. V., 1972
SMOKE AND TOXIC GASES FROM BURNING PLASTICS, presented at The Prevention and Control of Fires in Ships Symposium, Royal Institute of Naval Architects, Institute of Marine Engineers, June. (8A)

Starr, C., 1969
SOCIAL BENEFIT VERSUS TECHNOLOGICAL RISK, *Science*, Vol. 165, September, pp. 1232–1283. (10)

Steele, W. A., Bowser, D. and Chapman, R. E., 1973
THE INCIDENCE OF HAZARDOUS MATERIAL ACCIDENTS DURING TRANS-PORTATION AND STORAGE, NBSIR 73–412, National Bureau of Standards, Gaithersburg, Md. (8B)

Steffens, R. J., 1974
STRUCTURAL VIBRATION AND DAMAGE, Building Research Establishment, Garston, England. (5)

Steinbrugge, K. V. and Flores, R., 1963
A STRUCTURAL ENGINEERING VIEWPOINT (Chilean Earthquakes of May 1960), Bulletin, Seismology Society of America, February. (6)

Steinbrugge, K. V., Clous, W. K. and Scott, N. H., 1969
THE SANTA ROSA, CALIFORNIA, EARTHQUAKES OF OCTOBER 1, 1969, Environmental Sciences Services Administration, U.S. Department of Commerce. (6)

Steinbrugge, K. V., Schader, E. E., Bigglestone, H. C. and Weers, C. A., 1971
SAN FERNANDO EARTHQUAKE, FEBRUARY 9, 1971, Pacific Fire Rating Bureau, San Francisco, Calif. (6)

Stevens, L. K., 1967
ELASTIC STABILITY OF PRACTICAL MULTI-STOREY FRAMES, Proceedings, Institution of Civil Engineers, London, England, Vol. 36, pp. 99–117. (7)

Stevens, L. K., 1973a
DESIGN DEVELOPMENTS—ASIA AND AUSTRALASIA, Planning and Design of Tall Buildings, Proceedings of the 1972 ASCE-IABSE International Conference, Vol. 1b, ASCE, New York, pp. 399–406. (7)

Stevens, L. K., 1973b
LIMIT STATE PHILOSOPHY AND APPLICATION, Proceedings of Conference held in Sydney, Australia (August), Lehigh University, Bethlehem. Pa. (10)

Stevenson, J. D., 1967
RELIABILITY ANALYSIS AND OPTIMUM DESIGN OF STRUCTURAL SYSTEMS WITH APPLICATION TO RIGID FRAMES, Report No. 14, Division of Solid Mechanics, Case Western Reserve University, November. (10)

Stevenson, J. D. and Moses, F., 1970
RELIABILITY ANALYSIS OF FRAME STRUCTURES, Journal of the Structural Division, ASCE, Vol. 96, No. ST11, Proc. Paper 7692, pp. 2409–2427. (10)

Stiller, M., 1973
QUALITY CONTROL OF CONCRETE IN GERMANY, Planning and Design of Tall Buildings, Proceedings of the 1972 ASCE-IABSE International Conference, Vol. 1b, ASCE, New York, p. 897. (9)

Stockridge, J. G., 1969
QUALITY CONTROL METHODS FOR MASONRY STRENGTH, Construction Specifications Institute, Specifier, February. (9)

Stone, C. B., et al., 1971
REPORT ON FUTURE BUILDING REGULATIONS, The Structural Engineer, Vol. 49, No. 9, pp. 430–432. (10)

Stone, W. R., 1974
OFFICE BUILDING, Fire Journal reprint, Fires in High-Rise Buildings, NFPA, Boston, Mass., pp. 35–36. (8A)

Stramdahl, I., 1973
THE TRANAS FIRE TESTS, Document D3, National Swedish Institute for Building Research, Stockholm, Sweden. (8A)

Strehlow, R. A., 1973
UNCONFINED VAPOR-CLOUD EXPLOSIONS—AN OVERVIEW, Proceedings, 14th International Symposium on Combustion (Pennsylvania State Univ., 1972), The Combustion Institute, Pittsburgh, Pa., pp. 1189–1200. (8B)

Struck, W. and Voggenreiter, W., 1975
THE EFFECT OF IMPACT LOADING ON BUILDING: PART 2, EXAMPLES OF IMPACT AND IMPULSIVE LOADING IN THE FIELD OF CIVIL ENGINEERING, Matériaux et Construction, Vol. 8, pp. 81–87. (8B)

Struck, W., Limburger, E. and Eifler, H., 1973
PROBLEMS AND GAPS OF KNOWLEDGE IN THE ASSESSMENT OF THE RESPONSE OF REINFORCED CONCRETE STRUCTURES UNDER IMPACT

LOADING (Probleme und Kenntnislucken bei der Beurteilung des Widerstandes von Stahlbetonbauteilen gegenüber stossartiger Belastung), Preprints of the 2nd International Conference on Structural Mechanics in Reactor Technology (Berlin, Germany), Vol. 4, paper J 3/4, Commission of the European Communities, Brussels, Belgium. (8B)

Structural Engineers Association of Southern California, 1972
POST EARTHQUAKE ANALYSIS OF THE DEPARTMENT OF WATER AND POWER BUILDINGS, LOS ANGELES, CALIFORNIA, February. (6)

Structural Standard Committee, 1959
DESIGN STANDARD VALUE ON VIBRATION ELIMINATION OF BUILDING (Draft) (in Japanese), *Journal of Architecture and Building Science*, Architectural Institute of Japan, Vol. 74, No. 875. (6)

Surry, D., 1967
TURBULENCE IN A WIND TUNNEL AND ITS USE IN STUDYING THE TURBULENCE EFFECTS ON THE AERODYNAMICS OF A RIGID CIRCULAR CYLINDER, Proceedings, International Research Seminar on Wind Effects on Buildings and Structures (Ottawa, Canada). (7)

Surry, D. and Tryggvason, B. V., 1975
FLUCTUATING PRESSURES ON TALL BUILDINGS, 2nd U.S. National Conference on Wind Engineering Research, Colorado State University. (7)

Suzuki, F., Minikami, T., Morimoto, R., Oquea, K., Okamoto, S., Suwa, A. and Umemura, H., 1971
GENERAL REPORT ON THE TOKACHI-OKI EARTHQUAKE OF 1968, Keigaku Publishing Company, Chiyoda-ku, Tokyo, Japan. (6)

Swayne, L. H., 1975
FIRE PROTECTION AT THE NATIONAL ARCHIVES, *Fire Journal*, Vol. 69, No. 1, pp. 65–67. (8A)

Swedish FPA, 1969
INTERNATIONAL SYMPOSIUM: PLASTIC-FIRE-CORROSION, Swedish Fire Protection Association, *Skydd*, Stockholm, Sweden. (8A)

Switzky, H., 1964
MINIMUM WEIGHT DESIGN WITH STRUCTURAL RELIABILITY, AIAA 5th Annual Structures and Materials Conference, American Institute of Aeronautics, New York, pp. 316–322. (10)

Szoke, D., 1973
QUALITY CONTROL OF BUILDINGS OF LARGE PRECAST CONCRETE PANELS, 10th Regional Conference Proceedings, (Bratislava, Czechoslovakia, April), Vols. I and II, CSVTA-Czechoslovak Scientific and Technical Association, Bratislava, Czechoslovakia (two editions: English and Czech), pp. 333–342. (9)

Tajimi, H., 1974
ASEISMIC PROBLEMS ON A TALL BUILDING ERECTED AT A SITE UNDERLAIN BY AN INCLINED BASE ROCK, Proceedings of the National Conference on Tall Buildings, (Conference held in Tokyo, Japan, August), Architectural Institute of Japan, Tokyo, Japan, pp. 9–10. (6)

Tajimi, H., Ichino, I. and Gotoh, H., 1966 .
NEW TYPE TWO AXES ELECTROHYDRAULIC SHAKING TABLE BY SEROMECHANISM AND EARTHQUAKE ENGINEERING, October. (6)

Takahashi, K., 1971
A STUDY OF THE RETURN PERIOD AND DESIGN LOAD BY MEANS OF THE MONTE CARLO METHOD, Proceedings, 3rd International Conference on Wind Effects on Buildings and Structures (Tokyo, Japan). (7)

Takeda, T., Suzen, M. A. and Nielsen, N. N., 1970
REINFORCED CONCRETE RESPONSE TO SIMULATED EARTHQUAKES, *Journal of the Structural Division*, ASCE, Vol. 96, No. ST12, Proc. Paper 7759, pp. 2557–2573. (6)

Takeuchi, M., Matsui, G., Nagai, R. and Kazama, S., 1971
ACTUAL FLUCTUATING WIND PRESSURE ON A TALL BUILDING AND ITS RESPONSE, Proceedings, 3rd International Conference on Wind Effects on Buildings and Structures (Tokyo, Japan). (7)

Tall, L., 1961
RESIDUAL STRESSES IN WELDED PLATES: A THEORETICAL STUDY, *Welding Journal*, Vol. 43, January. (8A)

Tamboli, A. R., 1973
SOIL-STRUCTURE SYSTEMS, Planning and Design of Tall Buildings, (Proceedings of Conference held at Lehigh University, August, 1972), Vol. 1b, ASCE, New York, p. 318. (6)

Tamura, G. T., 1969
COMPUTER ANALYSIS OF SMOKE MOVEMENT IN TALL BUILDINGS, *Transactions*, ASHRAE, Vol. 75, Part II; DBR Research Paper No. 452, (NRC 11542). (8A)

Tamura, G. T., 1970
ANALYSIS OF SMOKE SHAFTS FOR CONTROL OF SMOKE MOVEMENT IN BUILDINGS, *Transactions*, ASHRAE, Vol. 76, Part II, pp. 290–297. (Reprint available from National Research Council of Canada, NRCC 12356.) (8A)

Tamura, G. T., 1972
COMPUTER ANALYSIS OF SMOKE CONTROL WITH BUILDING AIR HANDLING SYSTEM, *ASHRAE Journal*, Vol. 14, No. 8, pp. 46–54. (Reprint available from National Research Council of Canada, Ottawa, Canada, NRCC 12809.) (8A)

Tamura, G. T., 1974
EXPERIMENTAL STUDIES ON PRESSURIZED ESCAPE ROUTES, *Transactions*, ASHRAE, Vol. 80, Part II. (8A)

Tamura, G. T. and McGuire, J. H., 1971
SMOKE MOVEMENT IN HIGH-RISE BUILDINGS, *Canadian Building Digest*, No. 133, National Research Council of Canada, Division of Building Research, Ottawa, Canada. (8A)

Tamura, G. T. and McGuire, J. H., 1973
THE PRESSURIZED BUILDING METHOD OF CONTROLLING SMOKE IN HIGH-RISE BUILDINGS, Technical Paper No. 394, NRCC 13365, National Research Council of Canada, Division of Building Research, September. (8A)

Tamura, G. T. and Shaw, C. Y., 1973
BASIS FOR THE DESIGN OF SMOKE SHAFTS, *Fire Technology*, Vol. 9, No. 3, pp. 209–222. (8A)

Tamura, G. T. and Wilson, A. G., 1968
PRESSURE DIFFERENCES CAUSED BY WIND ON TWO TALL BUILDINGS, *ASHRAE Transactions*, Vol. 74, Part II; DBR Research Paper No. 393 (NRC 10628). (7)

Tamura, G. T. and Wilson, A. G., 1970
NATURAL VENTING TO CONTROL SMOKE MOVEMENT IN BUILDINGS VIA VERTICAL SHAFTS, *Transactions*, ASHRAE, Vol. 76, Part II, pp. 279–289. (Reprint available from National Research Council of Canada, Ottawa, Canada, NRCC 12357.) (8A)

Tanaka, H., 1971
VIBRATIONS OF BLUFF-SECTIONAL STRUCTURES UNDER WIND ACTION, Proceedings of the 3rd International Conference on Wind Effects on Buildings and Structures (Tokyo, Japan). (7)

Tanaka, T. et al., 1969
PERIOD AND DAMPING OF VIBRATIONS IN ACTUAL BUILDING DURING EARTHQUAKES, Bulletin of the Earthquake Research Institute, University of Tokyo, Japan, Vol. 147, November. (6)

Tanaka, M., 1970
HOW TO MAKE PRODUCTION SYSTEM EFFECTIVE, Sangyo-Nouritsu Tanki-Daigaku, Tokyo, Japan, April. (9)

Taneja, C. A. and Jindal, B. K., 1973
DEVELOPMENT OF LIGHT WEIGHT CONCRETE FOR MULTI-STORIED CONSTRUCTION, National Conference on Tall Buildings (New Delhi, India, January), Indian National Group of the IABSE, New Delhi, India, pp. V9–V16. (9)

Taoka, G. T. and Chiu, A. N. L., 1974
VIBRATIONS OF TALL REINFORCED CONCRETE BUILDINGS TO WIND FORCES, Proceedings of the 1974 2nd USA/Japan Research Seminar on Wind Effects on Structures, University of Tokyo Press, Tokyo, Japan. (7)

Task Group 5, CRC, 1971
CLASSIFICATION OF STEEL FOR STRUCTURES, *Engineering Journal*, AISC, July, pp. 99–109. (9)

Taylor, A., 1970
THE RELEVANCE TO A CONSTRUCTOR, Proceedings of CIRIA Seminar (London, England). (7)

Taylor, E. E. F., 1974
JOINTS IN MULTI-STORY STEEL FRAMED BUILDINGS, Proceedings of the Regional Conference on Tall Buildings (Bangkok, Thailand, January), Asian Institute of Technology, Bangkok, Thailand, pp. 829–842. (9)

Taylor, P. J., 1967
EFFECTS OF FORMWORK STRIPPING TIME ON DEFLECTIONS OF FLAT SLABS AND PLATES, Australian Civil Engineering and Construction, Melbourne, Australia, February 6, pp. 31–35. (5)

Templin, J., 1969
INTERIM PROGRESS NOTE ON SIMULATION OF EARTH'S SURFACE WINDS BY ARTIFICIALLY THICKENED WIND TUNNEL BOUNDARY LAYERS, LTR-LA-22, National Aeronautical Establishment, Ottawa, Canada. (7)

Teunissen, H. W., 1975
SIMULATION OF THE PLANETARY BOUNDARY LAYER IN A MULTIPLE-JET WIND TUNNEL, *Atmospheric Environment*, Vol. 9, Pergamon Press, pp. 145–179. (7)

Tewerson, A., 1971
SOME OBSERVATIONS ON EXPERIMENTAL FIRES IN ENCLOSURES, PART I: CELLULOSIC MATERIALS, Technical Report No. 18305, Factory Mutual Research Corporation. (8A)

Theobald, C. R. and Heselden, A. J. M., 1968
FULLY DEVELOPED FIRES WITH FURNITURE IN A COMPARTMENT, Fire Research Note No. 718, Joint Fire Research Organization, Borehamwood, England. (8A)

Thom, H. C. S., 1963
TORNADO PROBABILITIES U.S.A., *Monthly Weather Review*, pp. 730–736. (7)

Thom, H. C. S., 1967
TOWARD A UNIVERSAL CLIMATOLOGICAL EXTREME DISTRIBUTION, Proceedings of the International Seminar on Wind Effects on Buildings and Structures (Ottawa, Canada). (7)

Thomann, H., 1973
WIND ACTION ON TALL BUILDINGS, Report 1 Tall Buildings, Proceedings of the 17th National/Regional Conference (Zurich, Switzerland), pp. 109–115. (7)

Thomas, B. F., 1972
MOUNTING OF ANEMOMETERS IN THE VICTORIA DOCK AREA, BHP Melbourne Research Laboratories, Report MRL 16/5, Melbourne, Australia, March. (7)

Thomas, B., 1973
MEASUREMENT OF GLASS TEMPERATURES AT LEVEL 42 OF BHP HOUSE, MRL 16/7, Melbourne Research Laboratories, The Broken Hill Proprietary Company Ltd., Melbourne, Australia, March. (5)

Thomas, B. F., 1973
THE STRUCTURAL INSTRUMENTATION OF BHP HOUSE, Australian ISC Conference on Steel Developments, Newcastle, Australian Institute of Steel Construction. (7)

Thomas, P. H., 1967
THEORETICAL CONSIDERATIONS OF THE GROWTH TO FLASHOVER OF COMPARTMENT FIRES, Fire Research Note No. 663. (8A)

Thomas, P. H., 1973
EFFECTS OF FUEL GEOMETRY IN FIRES, Summer School on Heat Transfer in Fires, Trogir, Yugoslavia, Building Research Establishment Current Paper CP29/74, Borehamwood, England. (8A)

Thomas, P. H., 1974
FIRES IN MODEL ROOMS: CIB RESEARCH PROGRAMMES 4th International Fire Protection Seminar (Zurich, Switzerland, October 1973), Building Research Establishment Current Paper CP32/74, Borehamwood, England. (8A)

Thomas, P. H. and Baldwin, R., 1971
SOME COMMENTS ON THE CHOICE OF FAILURE PROBABILITIES IN FIRES, Response paper for CIB Colloquium on Safety of Structures in Fire, June. (8A)

Thomas, P. H. and Law, M., 1974
THE PROJECTION OF FLAMES FROM BUILDINGS ON FIRE, Fire Prevention Science and Technology No. 10, December, pp. 19–26. (8A)

Thomas, P. H., Heselden, A. J. M. and Law, M., 1967
FULLY DEVELOPED COMPARTMENT FIRES—TWO KINDS OF BEHAVIOUR, Fire Research Technical Paper No. 18, HMSO, London, England. (8A)

Thomas, P. H., Heselden, A. J. M. and Law, M., 1970
BURNING RATE OF VENTILATION CONTROLLED FIRES IN COMPARTMENTS, Fire Technology, Vol. 6, No. 2, pp. 123–125. (8A)

Thompson, R. J., et al., 1975
THE DECISION TREE FOR FIRE SAFETY SYSTEMS ANALYSIS: WHAT IT IS AND HOW TO USE IT, Fire Journal, July, September, and November (3 parts). (8A)

Thor, J., 1973
DEFORMATIONS AND CRITICAL LOADS OF STEEL BEAMS UNDER FIRE EXPOSURE CONDITIONS, Document D 16, National Swedish Building Research, Stockholm, Sweden. (8A)

Tichý, M., 1969
A LOGICAL SYSTEM FOR PARTIAL SAFETY FACTORS, prepared discussion, IABSE Symposium on Concepts of Safety (London, England). (10)

Tichý, M., 1974a
COMBINATIONS OF STRUCTURAL ACTIONS (LEVEL I APPROACH), Acta Technica ČSAV, No. 2, Czechoslovakia. (5, 7, 8A, 10)

Tichý, M., 1974b
A PROBABILISTIC MODEL FOR STRUCTURAL ACTIONS, Acta Technica ČSAV, No. 5, Czechoslovakia. (5, 7, 8A, 10)

Tichý, M., 1974c
RELIABILITY PROBLEMS IN THE STRUCTURAL THEORY (Problemy Spolehlivosti v Teorii Stavebnich Konstrukci), Stavebnicky Časopis, No. 12 (English translation available from Author). (10, 8A)

Tichý, M. and Vorliček, M., 1964
SAFETY OF REINFORCED CONCRETE FRAMED STRUCTURES, International Symposium on the Flexural Mechanics of Reinforced Concrete (Miami, Fla., November). (10)

Tichý, M. and Vorliček, M., 1972
STATISTICAL THEORY OF CONCRETE STRUCTURES, Irish University Press, Shannon, Ireland. (10)

Timoshenko, S., 1940
THEORY OF PLATES AND SHELLS, McGraw-Hill Book Co., Inc., New York. (9)

Tomii, M., 1971
SHEAR WALLS, Proceedings of the 3rd Regional Conference on Planning and Design of Tall Buildings (Tokyo, Japan, September). (8B)

Tomii, M., 1973
SHEAR WALLS, State of Art Report No. 4 of Technical Committee No. 21 of the International Conference on Tall Buildings, Lehigh University, Bethlehem, Pa., August. (8B)

Tomonaga, K., 1971
ACTUALLY MEASURED ERRORS IN FABRICATION OF KASUMIGASEKI BUILDING, 3rd Regional Conference Proceedings (Tokyo, Japan, September), Muto Institute of Structural Mechanics, Tokyo, Japan, pp. 122–133. (9)

Tooley, Fay V., 1974
THE HANDBOOK OF GLASS MANUFACTURE, (Vol. I & II), Books for Industry, Inc., New York. (9)

Torroja, E., Esquillan, N., Mazure, J. P., Rinaldi, G., Rüsch, H. and Thomas, E. G., 1958
LOAD FACTORS, ACI Journal, American Concrete Institute, Vol. 55, pp. 567–572. (10)

Towsend, W. H., 1972
THE INELASTIC BEHAVIOUR OF REINFORCED CONCRETE BEAM-COLUMN CONNECTIONS, thesis presented to the University of Michigan, at Ann Arbor, Mich. in partial fulfillment of the requirements for the degree of Doctor of Philosophy. (8B)

Trigario, I., 1973
SOME OF THE PROBLEMS FACED IN THE DESIGN OF A MULTI-FLOOR BUILDING, Italian National Conference on Tall Buildings, (Proceedings of Conference

held in Sorrento, Italy, October), Collegio dei Tecnici dell Acciaio, Milan, Italy, pp. 87–98. (6, 7)

Tryggvason, B. V., Surry, D. and Davenport, A. G., 1975
ON THE PREDICTION OF DESIGN PRESSURES FOR GLASS AND CLADDING WITH PARTICULAR REFERENCE TO HURRICANE REGIONS, Proceedings of the ASCE National Structural Engineering Convention (New Orleans, La.). (7)

Tsai, C. R. and Stewart, R. A., 1976
STRESS ANALYSIS OF LARGE DEFLECTION GLASS PLATES BY THE FINITE ELEMENT METHOD, *Journal of the American Ceramic Society*, Vol. 59, Nos. 9–10, pp. 445–448. (9)

Turkstra, C. J., 1969
A STATISTICAL INVESTIGATION OF UNDERREINFORCED CONCRETE BEAM MOMENT CAPACITY, Structural Concrete Series No. 6, Dept. of Civil Engineering and Applied Mechanics, McGill University, Montréal, Canada. (10)

Turkstra, C. J., 1970a
Discussion of SAFETY FACTORS AND PROBABILITY IN STRUCTURAL DESIGN by A. H-S. Ang and M. Amin, *Journal of the Structural Division*, ASCE, Vol. 96, No. ST5, Proc. Paper 7250, pp. 986–988. (10)

Turkstra, C. J., 1970b
THEORY OF STRUCTURAL DESIGN DECISIONS, SM Study No. 2, Solid Mechanics Division, University of Waterloo, Ont., Canada. (10)

Turkstra, C. J. and Shah, H. C., 1973
ASSESSING AND REPORTING UNCERTAINTIES, Planning and Design of Tall Buildings, Proceedings of the 1972 ASCE-IABSE International Conference, Vol. 1b, ASCE, New York, pp. 919–930. (10)

U.S. Army, Navy, and Air Force, 1969
STRUCTURES TO RESIST THE EFFECTS OF ACCIDENTAL EXPLOSIONS, TM5-1300/NAVFAC P-397/AFM 88-22, U.S. Government Printing Office, Washington, D.C.

U.S. Department of Commerce, NOAA and EERI, 1973
SAN FERNANDO, CALIFORNIA EARTHQUAKES OF FEBRUARY 9, 1971, 3 Vols., United States Government Printing Office, Washington, D.C. (6)

U.S. National Transport Safety Board, 1969
A STUDY OF SAFETY CONSIDERATIONS IN THE UTILIZATION OF AIRSPACE OVER AND UNDER FEDERALLY AIDED HIGHWAYS, Report No. SB60-34, National Transport Safety Board. (8B)

USA Federal Safety Standard 16 CFR 1201, 1977
ARCHITECTURAL GLAZING MATERIALS, Federal Register Vol. 42, No. 4, Part V, Consumer Product Safety Commission, Establishment of Safety Standards, January, pp. 1428–1450. (9)

USSR State Committee for Construction, 1962
BUILDING STANDARDS AND REGULATIONS (Stroitel'nie Normi i Pravila), Gosy-darstvenni Komitet Soveta Ministrov SSSR po Delan Stroitelstva, Moscow, USSR. (10)

Ueda, C., 1969
STUDY ON THE LARGE SCALE DISPLACEMENT VIBRATION TEST FOR THE 1/25 SCALE MODEL OF THE 17-STORIED BUILDING, J.N.R., Proceedings of the 4th World Conference on Earthquake Engineering (Santiago, Chile). (6)

Umemura, H., 1970
EARTHQUAKE RESISTANT DESIGN OF STRUCTURES, University of Tokyo, Tokyo, Japan. (8B)

Underwriters Laboratories, Inc., 1971
SMOKE DETECTORS, PHOTOELECTRIC TYPE, FOR FIRE-PROTECTIVE SIG-NALING SYSTEMS, Underwriters Laboratories, Inc., Chicago, Ill. (8A)

Underwriters Laboratories, Inc., 1974a
SMOKE DETECTORS, COMBUSTION PRODUCTS TYPE, FOR FIRE-PROTECTIVE SIGNALING SYSTEMS, Underwriters Laboratories, Inc., Chicago, Ill. (8A)

Underwriters Laboratories, Inc., 1974b
THERMOSTATS, FIRE DETECTION, Underwriters Laboratories, Inc., Chicago, Ill. (8A)

Underwriters Laboratories, Inc., 1978
FIRE RESISTANCE DIRECTORY, Underwriters Laboratories, Inc., Chicago, Ill. (9) (8B)

Urbano, C., 1973
LOAD TESTS (GRAVITY LOADS) ON BUILDINGS, Italian National Conference on Tall Buildings (Sorrento, Italy, October), Collegio dei Tecnici dell' Acciaio, Milan, Italy. (9)
Uribe, J. U., 1973
THE AVIANCA FIRE (Efectos del Fuego Sobre la Estructura del Edificio Avianca), Proceedings of the National Conference on Tall Buildings (Bogotá, Colombia, September), Colombian School of Engineering, Bogotá, Colombia. (8A)
Utne, V., 1971
EXPLOSION DISASTER, STORE SLETTE, GREENLAND (Eksplosionsulykken, Store Slette, Grønland), report of inspection. (8B)

Valera, J. E., 1968
SEISMIC INTERACTION OF GRANULAR SOILS AND RIGID RETAINING STRUCTURES, thesis presented to the University of California, at Berkeley, Calif., in partial fulfillment of the requirements for the degree of Doctor of Philosophy. (6)
Van Der Hoven, I., 1957
POWER SPECTRUM OF HORIZONTAL WIND SPEED IN THE FREQUENCY RANGE FROM 0.0007 TO 900 CYCLES PER HOUR, International Meteorology, Vol. 4, pp. 160–164. (7)
Van Dobben De Bruyn, C. S., 1968
CUMULATIVE SUM TESTS: THEORY AND PRACTICE, Griffins Statistical Monographs and Courses No. 24, Griffin, London, England. (9)
Van Koten, H., 1967
WIND MEASUREMENTS ON HIGH BUILDINGS IN THE NETHERLANDS, Proceedings of the 2nd International Conference on Wind Effects on Buildings and Structures (Ottawa, Canada), University of Toronto Press, Toronto, Canada. (7)
Van Koten, H., 1971
THE COMPARISON OF MEASURED AND CALCULATED AMPLITUDES OF SOME BUILDINGS, AND DETERMINATION OF THE DAMPING EFFECTS OF THE BUILDINGS, Proceedings of the 3rd International Conference on Wind Effects on Buildings and Structures (Tokyo, Japan). (7)
Van Koten, H., 1973
RESEARCH REVIEW—EUROPE AND AFRICA, Planning and Design of Tall Buildings, Proceedings of the 1972 ASCE-IABSE International Conference. Vol. 1b, ASCE, New York, pp. 375–382. (7)
Vanmarcke, E. H., 1972
PROPERTIES OF SPECIAL MOMENTS WITH APPLICATION TO RANDOM VIBRATION, Journal of the Engineering Mechanics Division, ASCE, Vol. 98, No. EM2, Proc. Paper 8822, pp. 425–446. (6)
van Uchelen, O. and Menzel, C., 1973
NATURAL GAS EXPLOSIONS AND BUILDING CONSTRUCTION (Aardgasexplosies en Bouwkundige Constructies), Gas, Vol. 93, pp. 144–173. (8B)
Veletsos, A. S. and Vann, W. P., 1971
RESPONSE OF GROUND-EXCITED ELASTOPLASTIC SYSTEMS, Journal of the Structural Division, ASCE, Vol. 97, No. ST4, Proc. Paper 8075, p. 1257. (10)
Velozzi, J. and Cohen, E., 1968
GUST RESPONSE FACTORS, Journal of the Structural Division, ASCE, Vol. 94, No. ST6, Proc. Paper 5980, June, pp. 1295–1313. (7, 10)
Veneziano, D., 1974
SECOND MOMENT RELIABILITY, ASCE-EMD Specialty Conference on Probabilistic Methods in Civil Engineering (Stanford University, Calif.). (10)
Versé, G., 1935
THE ELASTIC PROPERTIES OF STEEL AT HIGH TEMPERATURES, Transactions, ASME, Vol. 57, pp. 1–4. (8A)
Vickery, B. J., 1966
ON THE ASSESSMENT OF WIND EFFECTS ON ELASTIC STRUCTURE, Civil Engineering Transactions, Institution of Engineers, Australia, pp. 183−192. (7)
Vickery, B. J., 1969
ON THE RELIABILITY OF GUST LOADING FACTORS, NBS Building Science Series 30, U.S. Department of Commerce, Washington, D.C. (7)

Vickery, B. J., 1970
WIND ACTION ON SINGLE YIELDING STRUCTURES, *Journal of the Engineering Mechanics Division*, ASCE, Vol. 96, No. EM2, Proc. Paper 7204, pp. 107–120. (7)

Vickery, B. J., 1971a
ON THE ASSESSMENT OF WIND EFFECTS ON ELASTIC STRUCTURES, Civil Engineering Transactions, Institution of Engineers, Australia, pp. 183–192. (7)

Vickery, B. J., 1971b
WIND INDUCED VIBRATIONS OF TOWERS, STACKS AND MASTS, Proceedings of the 3rd International Conference on Wind Effects on Buildings and Structures (Tokyo, Japan). (7)

Vickery, B. J., 1971c
ON THE RELIABILITY OF GUST LOADING FACTORS, Paper No. 2918, *Civil Engineering Transactions*, Institution of Engineers, Australia, April. (10)

Vickery, B. J., 1972
ON THE AEROELASTIC MODELLING OF STRUCTURES IN WIND, Proceedings of the Conference on Structural Models (Sydney, Australia), Cement and Concrete Assoc. of Australia in conjunction with Dept. of Architectural Science, University of Sydney, and Institution of Engineers, Australia, N.S.W. Division. (7)

Vickery, B. J., 1973a
NOTES ON WIND FORCES ON TALL BUILDINGS, Proceedings of the Conference on Planning and Design of Tall Buildings (Sydney University, Sydney, Australia). (7)

Vickery, B. J., 1973b
ON THE PROVISIONS AND LIMITATIONS OF THE AUSTRALIAN WIND LOADING CODE, Proceedings of the Conference on Planning and Design of Tall Buildings (Sydney University, Sydney, Australia). (7)

Vickery, B. J., 1973c
ON THE USE OF BALLOON DATA TO DEFINE WIND SPEEDS FOR TALL BUILDINGS, Civil Engineering Report R226, University of Sydney, Sydney, Australia. (7)

Vickery, B. J., 1976
THE DESIGN AND PERFORMANCE OF A LOW-COST BOUNDARY LAYER WIND TUNNEL, Proceedings of the 1974 2nd USA/Japan Research Seminar on Wind Effects on Structures, University of Tokyo Press, Tokyo, Japan. (7)

Vickery, B. J. and Apperley, L. W., 1973
ON THE PREDICTION OF THE GROUND LEVEL WIND ENVIRONMENT, Civil Engineering Report R227, University of Sydney, Sydney, Australia. (7)

Vickery, B. J. and Davenport, A. G., 1967
A COMPARISON OF THEORETICAL AND EXPERIMENTAL DETERMINATION OF THE RESPONSE OF ELASTIC STRUCTURES TO TURBULENT FLOW, Proceedings of the International Conference on Wind Effects on Buildings and Structures (Ottawa, Canada), University of Toronto Press, Toronto, Canada. (7)

Vickery, B. J. and Davenport, A. G., 1970
AN INVESTIGATION OF THE BEHAVIOUR IN WIND OF THE PROPOSED CENTRE POINT TOWER, SYDNEY, AUSTRALIA, Report BLWT-1-70, University of Western Ontario, Ontario, Canada. (7)

Vickery, B. J., Melbourne, W. A. and Davenport, A. G., 1974
THE STRUCTURAL AND ENVIRONMENTAL EFFECTS OF WIND ON BUILD-INGS AND STRUCTURES, unpublished course notes, University of Sydney, Australia, and Monash University, Australia. (7)

Vinnakota, S., 1974
FIRE RESISTANCE OF STEEL STRUCTURES, Report No. 10, ICOM, Swiss Federal Institute of Technology, Lausanne, Switzerland, October. (8A)

Vinnakota, S., 1975
BEHAVIOR OF STEEL STRUCTURES IN FIRE (Comportement des Structures Métalliques en Cas d'Incendie), *Construction Métallique*, Paris, France, Vol. 12, No. 3. (8A)

Vorliček, M., 1969
DISTRIBUTION OF EXTREME VALUES IN STRUCTURAL THEORY, *Acta Technica*, ČSAV, No. 6, Czechoslovakia. (5, 7, 8A, 10)

Vorliček, M., 1974
THEORETICAL MODELS OF YEARLY SNOW LOAD MAXIMA (Teoretické Modely Ročhních Maxim Tíhy Snehu), *Stavebnicky Casopis*, No. 12. (7)

Vorliček, M. and Holický, M., 1976
STATISTICAL DESIGN OF TOLERANCES OF ASSEMBLED STRUCTURES (Statistický Výpočet Tolerancí Montovaných Konstrukcí), CVUT Academia, Prague, Czechoslovakia. (9)

Wagner, J. P., 1972
SURVEY OF TOXIC SPECIES EVOLVED IN THE PYROLYSIS AND COMBUSTION OF POLYMERS, Fire Research Abstracts and Reviews No. 1, 14. (8A)
Wakabayashi, M. and Yagui, T., 1973
CORE DESIGN, (Nucleos Resistentes de Edificios Elevados), South American Regional Conference on Tall Buildings, (Proceedings of Conference held in Porto Alegre, Brazil, December), Vol. 1, Sociedade de Engenharia do Rio Grande do Sul, Porto Alegre, Brazil, pp. 157–170. (6)
Wakamatsu, T., 1969
FIELD EXPERIMENT ON SMOKE CONTROL (Smoke Stopping Experiment by Pressurization of Staircase), Report of Conference on Buildings, August. (8A)
Wakamatsu, T., 1971
CALCULATION OF SMOKE MOVEMENT IN BUILDINGS (1st Report), BRI Research Paper No. 33 (1968), (2nd Report), BRI Research Paper No. 46. (8A)
Wakamatsu, T., 1972
DESIGN OF FIRE COVER ON STEEL STRUCTURE, BRI Research Paper No. 54, May; Ministry of Construction, Japanese Government. (8A)
Wakamatsu, T. and Yamana, T., 1969
CALCULATION OF SMOKE MOVEMENT AND MEASURES CONTROLLING SMOKE., Annual Report, Building Research Institute, Tokyo, Japan (in Japanese). (8A)
Walker, G. R., 1975
INVESTIGATIONS OF WIND DESIGN CRITERIA USING A STATISTICAL SIMULATION MODEL, Proceedings of the 4th International Conference on Wind Effects on Buildings and Structures (London, England), University of Cambridge Press, Cambridge, England. (7)
Ward, H. S. and Rainer, J. H., 1972
EXPERIMENTAL DETERMINATION OF STRUCTURE AND FOUNDATION PARAMETERS USING WIND-INDUCED VIBRATIONS, Proceedings of the Institution of Civil Engineers, London, England, Part 2, Vol. 53, Sept., pp. 305–321. (7)
Wardlaw, R. L., 1972
WIND TUNNEL INVESTIGATIONS IN INDUSTRIAL AERODYNAMICS, Canadian Aeronautics and Space Journal, Vol. 18, No. 3, pp. 53–59. (7)
Wargon, A., 1973
CENTERPOINT PROJECT, SYDNEY, Proceedings of the 12 National/Regional Conference (Sydney, Australia), pp. 445–477. (7)
Wargon, A., 1975a
APPLICATION OF POST-TENSIONING TECHNIQUES AND OTHER USES OF CABLES IN HIGH RISE STRUCTURES, Pan-Pacific Tall Buildings Conference Proceedings (Honolulu, Hawaii, January), University of Hawaii, Honolulu, Hawaii, pp. 111–122. (6, 7)
Wargon, A., 1975b
APPLICATION OF POST-TENSIONING TECHNIQUES AND OTHER USES OF CABLES IN HIGH RISE STRUCTURES, Pan-Pacific Tall Buildings Conference (Honolulu, Hawaii), pp. 111–122. (7)
Warren, C. H. E., 1972
RECENT SONIC BANG STUDIES IN THE UNITED KINGDOM, Journal of the Acoustical Society of America, Vol. 51, pp. 783–789. (8B)
Watabe, M., 1975
SEISMIC LOADING AND RESPONSE OF TALL BUILDINGS, Hellenic Conference on Tall Buildings (Athens, Greece, October), Technical Chamber of Greece, Athens, Greece. (6)
Watrous, L. D., 1969
FIRE IN HIGH-RISE APARTMENT BUILDING; HAWTHORNE HOUSE, CHICAGO,

Fire Journal Reprint, High-Rise Building Fires and Fire Safety, National Fire Protection
Association, Boston, Mass., May, pp. 45–51. (8A)

Watrous, L. D., 1973
HIGH-RISE FIRE IN NEW ORLEANS, *Fire Journal* Reprint, Fire in High-Rise Buildings,
NFPA, Boston, Mass., pp. 22–25. (8A)

Watson, V., 1975
SAFETY AND LIST TIME OF MODERN TALL BUILDINGS: EXAMPLES OF
ACCIDENTS IN BUILDINGS, Questions Concerning Unusual and Outstanding
Aspects of Tall, Multi-Story Buildings (Proceedings of Conference held in Budapest,
Hungary, May), Dr. Gabos Gyorgy, 200 Ivterjedelem 20, 25/A/5/IV, Budapest, Hungary.
(10)

Wen, Y. K. and Ang, A. H-S, 1975
TORNADO RISK AND WIND EFFECT ON STRUCTURES, Proceedings of the 4th
International Conference on Wind Effects on Buildings and Structures (London,
England), University of Cambridge Press, Cambridge, England. (7)

Wen, Y. K. and Shinozuka, M., 1971
MONTE CARLO SOLUTION OF STRUCTURAL RESPONSE TO WIND LOAD,
Proceedings of the 3rd International Conference on Wind Effects on Buildings and
Structures (Tokyo, Japan). (7)

Wheatley, P., 1973
FIRE TEMPERATURE AND TOXIC EFFECTS ON STRUCTURES AND OCCU-
PANTS, Proceedings of the Regional Conference on Tall Buildings (Hong Kong,
August), Lehigh University, Bethlehem, Pa. (8A)

Wheatley, R. A., 1974
FIRE AND SMOKE PROBLEMS IN TALL BUILDINGS, unpublished communication
to the Council. (8A)

Wheen, R. J., 1973a
POSITIVE CONTROL OF CONSTRUCTION FLOOR LOADS IN MULTI-STOREY
CONCRETE BUILDINGS, Civil Engineering Report R.212, University of Sydney,
Sydney, Australia. (5)

Wheen, R. J., 1973b
POSITIVE CONTROL OF CONSTRUCTION FLOOR LOADS, *Building Materials*, Vol.
16, No. 3, Sydney, Australia. (5)

Wheen, R. J., 1974
PRACTICAL ASPECTS OF THE CONTROL OF CONSTRUCTION LOADS IN TALL
BUILDINGS, Building Materials, MLC Centre, Sydney, Australia, Vol. 16, No. 6,
April/May. (5)

Whitbread, R. E., 1963
MODEL SIMULATION OF WIND EFFECTS ON STRUCTURES, Proceedings of the
International Conference on Wind Effects on Buildings and Structures (NPL, Tedding-
ton, England. (7)

Whitbread, R. E., 1974
WIND LOAD AND ENVIRONMENTAL STUDIES FOR THE 183 m NATIONAL
WESTMINSTER BANK BUILDING, NPL Report Man. Science R114. (7)

Whitbread, R. E., 1975
THE MEASUREMENT OF NON-STEADY WIND FORCES ON SMALL-SCALE
BUILDING MODELS, Proceedings of the 4th International Conference on Wind Effects
on Buildings and Structures (London, England), University of Cambridge Press,
Cambridge, England. (7)

Whitman, R. V., 1969
EFFECT OF SOIL CONDITIONS UPON DAMAGE TO STRUCTURES: CARACAS
EARTHQUAKE OF 29 JULY 1967, Unpublished Report to the Presidential Commis-
sion for Study of the the Earthquake, Caracas, Venezuela. (6)

Whitman, R. V., Biggs, J. M., Brennan, J. E., Cornell, C. A., Neufille de, R. L. and Vanmarcke,
E. H., 1975
SEISMIC DESIGN DECISION ANALYSIS, *Journal of the Structural Division*, ASCE, Vol.
101, No. ST5, Proc. Paper 11309, pp. 1067–1084. (6)

Wianecki, J., 1971
AERODYNAMIC STUDIES ON AEROELASTIC MODELS OF TOWERS AND TALL BUILDINGS REALIZED RECENTLY AT C.E.B.T.P. IN PARIS, Proceedings of the 3rd International Conference on Wind Effects on Buildings and Structures (Tokyo, Japan). (7)

Wiegel, R. L., ed., 1970
EARTHQUAKE ENGINEERING, Prentice-Hall, Inc., Englewood Cliffs, N.J. (6, 10)

Wiggins, J. H. and Moran, D. F., 1971
EARTHQUAKE SAFETY IN THE CITY OF LONG BEACH BASED ON THE CONCEPT OF "BALANCED RISK," J. H. Wiggins Company, Palos Verdes Estates, Calif. (6)

Wilford, M. J. and Yu, C. W., 1973
CATENARY ACTION IN DAMAGED STRUCTURES, DOE/CIRIA Seminar Paper, CIRIA, London, England. (8B)

Willey, A. E., 1972a
TAE YON KAK HOTEL FIRE, SEOUL, KOREA, Fire Journal, National Fire Protection Association, Boston, Mass., May, pp. 25–33. (8A)

Willey, A. E., 1972b
HIGH-RISE BUILDING FIRE, SAÕ PAULO, BRAZIL, Fire Journal, National Fire Protection Association, Boston, Mass., July, pp. 4–15. (8A)

Willey, A. E., 1973
BAPTIST TOWERS HOUSING FOR THE ELDERLY, ATLANTA, GEORGIA, Fire Journal Reprint, Fires in High-Rise Buildings, NFPA, Boston, Mass., pp 28–34, 36. (8A)

Wilson, A. G. and Shorter, G. W., 1970
FIRE AND HIGH BUILDINGS, Fire Technology, Vol. 6, No. 4; DBR Technical Paper No. 333 (NRC 11789), November. (8A)

Wilson, A. G. and Shorter, G. W., 1971
THE SMOKE PROBLEM AND ITS CONTROL IN HIGH-RISE BUILDINGS, Research into Practice: The Challenge of Application, 5th CIB Congress, Versailles; DBR Technical Paper 365, (NRC 12580), June. (8A)

Wilson, A. G. and Tamura, G. T., 1968a
STACK EFFECT IN BUILDINGS, Canadian Building Digest No. 104, National Research Council of Canada, Division of Building Research, Ottawa, Canada, August. (8A)

Wilson, A. G. and Tamura, G. T., 1968b
STACK EFFECT AND BUILDING DESIGN, Canadian Building Digest No. 107, National Research Council of Canada, Division of Building Research, Ottawa, Canada. (8A)

Wiren, B. G., 1975
A WIND TUNNEL STUDY OF WIND VELOCITIES IN PASSAGE BETWEEN AND THROUGH BUILDINGS, Proceedings of the 4th International Conference on Wind Effects on Buildings and Structures (London, England), University of Cambridge Press, Cambridge, England. (7)

Wise, A. F. E., Sexton, D. E. and Lillywhite, M. S. T., 1965
STUDIES OF AIR FLOW AROUND BUILDINGS, Architects Journal, Vol. 141. (7)

Wise, A. F. E., 1971
EFFECTS DUE TO GROUPS OF BUILDINGS, A Discussion on Architectural Aerodynamics, Philosophical Transactions, The Royal Society of London, Mathematics and Physical Sciences, Vol. 269, pp. 469–483. (7)

Withey, S. B., 1962
REACTION TO UNCERTAIN THREAT, Man and Society in Disaster, C. W. Baker and N. Y. Chapman, eds., Basic Books. (8A)

Witteveen, J., 1966
FIRE RESISTANT CONSTRUCTION IN STEEL BUILDINGS (Brandveilighed Stanconstruction Centram Bowen in Staal), Rotterdam, The Netherlands. (8A)

Witteveen, J., 1969
BASIC PRINCIPLES OF FIRE PREVENTION IN BUILDINGS AND THE THEORETICAL DETERMINATION OF THE LOAD BEARING CAPACITY [Grondslagen Voor de Brandpreventie van Gebouwen en de Berekening van Dragemde Constructie bij Brand (2)], Bouw No. 33/34, 16/23-8-1969. (8A)

Witteveen, J., 1972
FIRE AND BLAST, Proceedings of the 6th Regional Conference (Delft, The Netherlands, May), Lehigh University, Bethlehem, Pa. (8A)

Witteveen, J. and Twilt, L., 1971
BASIC PRINCIPLES OF FIRE PREVENTION, CIB Colloquium on Fire Engineering, Paris, France, April. (8A)

Wittmann, F. H., 1976
RELIABILITY ORIENTED DESIGN OF TOWER LIKE STRUCTURES—EXPERIMENTAL METHODS (Zuverlässigkeitsorientierte Bemussung Turmartiger Tragwerke —Experimentelle Methoden), Neuere Erkenntnisse über Schwingungen von Bauwerken im Wind, Haus der Technik, Vortragsveröffentlichugen, Report No. 347, Vulkan Verlag, Essen, pp. 52–60. (10, 8A)

Wittmann, F. H. and Birmoser, H., 1976
ON THE DAMPING OF SLENDER REINFORCED CONCRETE STRUCTURES (Zur dampfund schlanker konstruktionen aus stahlbeton), Proceedings of the 2nd Kolloquium Industiraerodyn, FHS-Aachen, Germany, pp. 279–292. (7)

Wolovits, F., 1975
TECHNICAL AND ECONOMIC CONSIDERATIONS CONCERNING THE INFLUENCE OF CONCRETE QUALITY IN CALCULATING THE COLUMNS OF TALL STRUCTURES (Consideratii Tehnico-Economice Privind Influenta Marcii de Beton Asupra Dimensionarii Stilpilor Constructiilor Etajate), Reinforced Concrete Tall Buildings (Constructii Inalte de Beton Armat), Vols. I & II, (Proceedings of Conference held in Iasi, Romania, October), Consiliul National al Inginerilor si Tehnicienilor, Iasi, Romania, pp. 363–372. (9)

Wong, R. T. and Cooper, R. S., 1974
EVALUATION OF SETTLEMENT UNDER EARTHQUAKE LOADING CONDITIONS OF BUILDINGS FOUNDED IN GRANULAR SOILS, Proceedings of the Regional Conference, (Conference held in Bangkok, Thailand, January), Asian Institute of Technology, Bangkok, Thailand, pp. 739–753. (6)

Wood, F. J., ed., 1967
THE PRINCE WILLIAM SOUND, ALASKA, EARTHQUAKE OF 1964 AND AFTERSHOCKS, VOLUMES I, II, AND III, Environmental Science Services Administration, U.S. Department of Commerce. (6)

Wood, P. G., 1972
THE BEHAVIOR OF PEOPLE IN FIRES, Joint Fire Research Organization Fire Research Note No. 953. (8A)

Woodward, R. H. and Goldsmith, P. L., 1964
CUMULATIVE SUM TECHNIQUES, I. C. I. Monograph, No. 3, Oliver and Boyd, Edinburgh, Scotland. (9)

Woolley, W. D., 1972
NITROGEN-CONTAINING PRODUCTS FROM THE THERMAL DECOMPOSITION OF FLEXIBLE POLYURETHANE FOAMS, British Polymer Journal, Vol. 4, No. 1, pp. 27–43. (8A)

Woolley, W. D. and Wadley, A., 1970
THE THERMAL DECOMPOSITION PRODUCTS OF PHENOFORMALDEHYDE LAMINATES, F-R Note 852, Fire Research Station, Borehamwood, England. (8A)

Wootton, L. R. and Scruton, C., 1971
AERODYNAMIC STABILITY, The Modern Design of Wind Sensitive Structures, Proceedings of the CIRIA Seminar (London, England). (7)

Wright, R. H. and Kramer, S., 1973
BUILDING PERFORMANCE IN THE 1972 MANAGUA EARTHQUAKE, NBS Technical Note 807, Institute for Applied Technology, National Bureau of Standards. (6)

Wright, R. N., 1973
SURVEY OF FIRE AND LIVE LOADS, Planning and Design of Tall Buildings, Proceedings of the 1972 ASCE-IABSE International Conference, Vol. 1b, No. 5-D3, ASCE, New York. (5)

Wu, C., 1974
MODELING AND SIMULATION OF A FIRE PROTECTION PROBABILITY DECISION TREE ON TALL BUILDINGS, Proceedings of the Regional Conference on Tall Buildings (Bangkok, Thailand, January), Asian Institute of Technology, Bangkok, Thailand. (8A, 10)

Wyatt, T. A., 1971a
THE CALCULATION OF STRUCTURAL RESPONSE, The Modern Design of Wind Sensitive Structures, Proceedings of the CIRIA Seminar (London, England), pp. 17–27. (7)

Wyatt, T. A., 1971b
A REVIEW OF WIND LOADING SPECIFICATIONS, *Structural Engineering*, London, England. (7)

Wyatt, T. A., 1975a
A PROPOSED EUROPEAN CODE OF PRACTICE, Proceedings of the 4th International Conference on Wind Effects on Buildings and Structures (London, England), Cambridge Press, Cambridge, England. (7)

Wyatt, T. A., 1975b
THE RELEVANCE OF PROBABILISTIC ANALYSIS TO DESIGN, Proceedings of the 4th International Conference on Wind Effects on Buildings and Structures (London, England), University of Cambridge Press, Cambridge, England. (7)

Wyatt, T. A. and May, H. I., 1971
THE ULTIMATE LOAD BEHAVIOUR OF STRUCTURES UNDER WIND LOADING, Proceedings of the 3rd International Conference on Wind Effects on Buildings and Structures (Tokyo, Japan). (7, 10)

Yamada, M., 1971
EFFECT OF CYCLIC LOADING ON BUILDINGS, 3rd Regional Conference Proceedings (Tokyo, Japan, September) Muto Institute of Structural Mechanics, Tokyo, Japan, pp. 194–195. (6)

Yamada, M. and Goto, T., 1969
HUMAN FEELING FOR LONG PERIOD VIBRATIONS (in Japanese), *Kenchiku Gijjutsu (Building Engineering)*, No. 212, April. (6)

Yamada, M. and Goto, T., 1975
CRITERIA FOR MOTION IN TALL BUILDINGS, Proceedings of the Chicago Conference on Human Response of Tall Buildings, Vol. 1, pp. 46–61. (7)

Yamada, M. and Kawamura, H., 1974
ASEISMIC SAFETY OF REINFORCED CONCRETE BUILDINGS, Proceedings of the National Conference on Tall Buildings (Tokyo, Japan, August), Architectural Institute of Japan, Tokyo, Japan, pp. 45–46. (6)

Yamada, M. and Yagi, S., 1973
SHEAR EXPLOSION OF REINFORCED CONCRETE SHORT COLUMNS FOR THE BASIS TO ESTABLISH A NEW ASEISMIC DESIGN OF REINFORCED CONCRETE STRUCTURES, Proceedings, 5th World Conference on Earthquake Engineering (Rome, Italy), Vol. 2D, No. 90. (8B)

Yamauchi, K. and Kamei, T., 1968
FUTURE PROSPECTS FOR STEEL SKELETON FABRICATION, Architectural Materials, Kenchiku gizyutsu-sha, February. (9)

Yang, J. N., 1975
APPLICATION OF OPTIMAL CONTROL THEORY TO CIVIL ENGINEERING STRUCTURES, *Journal of the Engineering Mechanics Division*, ASCE, Vol. 101, No. EM6, pp. 819–838. (7)

Yang, J. N. and Gianopulos, F., 1977
ACTIVE TENDON CONTROL OF SLENDER STRUCTURES, Advances in Civil Engineering Through Engineering Mechanics, ASCE 2nd Annual Engineering Mechanics Division Specialty Conference (Raleigh, N.C., May), ASCE, New York, pp. 339–341. (7)

Yao, J. T. P. and Yeh, H. Y., 1969
FORMULATION OF STRUCTURAL RELIABILITY, *Journal of the Structural Division*, ASCE, Vol. 95, No. ST12, Proc. Paper 6939, p. 2611. (10)

Yao, 1973
EXPLOSION VENTING OF LOW STRENGTH EQUIPMENT AND STRUCTURES, 8th Symposium on Loss Prevention in the Process Industries (Philadelphia, Pa.), AIChE, New York, pp. 1–9. (8B)

Yerlici, V. A., 1974
A COMPARISON OF EARTHQUAKE LOADS FOR A TALL BUILDING DETER-MINED BY DIFFERENT METHODS, Proceedings of the Regional Conference on Tall Buildings (Bangkok, Thailand, January), Asian Institute of Technology, Bangkok, Thailand, pp. 607–619. (6)

Yokel, F. Y., Mathey, R. G. and Dikkers, R. D., 1971
STRENGTH OF MASONRY WALLS UNDER COMPRESSIVE AND TRANSVERSE LOADS, National Bureau of Standards, Building Science Series No. 34, Washington, D.C., March. (9)

Yokoi, S., 1960
STUDY ON THE PREVENTION OF FIRE-SPREAD BY HOT UPWARD CURRENT, Building Research Institute Report No. 34, Tokyo, Japan. (8A)

Yoshikawa, Y. and Ishizaki, H., 1974
ON THE WIND PRESSURE AND THE WIND FLOW AROUND A TALL BUILD-ING, Proceedings of the Regional Conference on Tall Buildings (Bangkok, Thailand), pp. 505–519. (7)

Yu, C. W., 1974
RESEARCH ON HORIZONTAL JOINTS IN LARGE PANEL CONSTRUCTION, Report to Department of the Environment by Imperial College of Science and Technology, London, England. (8B)

Yuill, C. H., 1975
FIRE SAFETY IN TALL BUILDINGS—DESIGN FACTORS, Proceedings of the South African Conference on Tall Buildings (Johannesburg, South Africa, November), Hortors Printer, Johannesburg, South Africa. (8A)

Yura, J., 1971
THE EFFECTIVE LENGTH OF COLUMNS IN UNBRACED FRAMES, *Engineering Journal*, AISC, April. (10)

Zeevaert, A., 1957
LATINO AMERICANA BUILDING, Proceedings of the Structural Engineers Association of California. (6)

Zeller, E. and Puebe, J. L., 1971
WIND-INDUCED VIBRATION OF REAL BUILDING AND AERODYNAMIC PRES-SURE ACTING ON IT, Proceedings of the 3rd International Conference on Wind Effects on Buildings and Structures (Tokyo, Japan). (7)

Zilch, K., 1974
DESIGN OF STRUCTURES FOR EARTHQUAKE LOADS—A STATE OF THE ART REPORT (Bemessung von Bauwerken Gegen Erdebenbelastungen—Ein Bericht zum Stand der Forschung und Praxis), Die Bautechnik 51 Berlin, pp. 145–155. (6)

Zuk, W., 1968
KINECTIC STRUCTURES, *Civil Engineering*, ASCE, Vol. 38, No. 12, pp. 62–64. (7)

Zuk, W. and Clark, R. H., 1970
KINECTIC ARCHITECTURE, Van Nostrand-Reinhold Co., New York. (7)

Contributors

The following list identifies those who have contributed material specifically for possible use in Volume CL. The names, affiliations, and countries are given, together with the chapter(s) to which a contribution was made. The committee chairmen and editors were given quite complete latitude in the use of material, and frequently length limitations prevented the inclusion of much valuable material. Thus, every contributor is listed, whether or not the material was used in the final version. The effort here is to recognize and acknowledge the contributions.

Some of the material came to Headquarters directly, some came from the Proceedings of the First International Conference, some was stimulated at the special sessions held at the regional conferences, and some came directly to the committee leaders. The bibliography contains all contributions, and most of the unpublished documents are in the Council data base.

Allen, D.E., National Research Council, Ottawa, CDN (1, 4)
Alpsten, G.A., Stalbyggnadskontroll AB, Saltsjobaden, S (6)
Anderson, A.A., A.B.A.M. Engineers Inc., Tacoma, WA, USA (6)
Ang, A. H-S, University of Illinois, Urbana, IL, USA (7)
Anzalone, V., Tishman Realty & Construction Co., Bayside, NY, USA (6)

Apeland, K., Multiconsult A.S., Oslo, N (1)
Arias, A., Universidad de Chile, Santiago, RCH (2)
Arnault III, P., CTICM, Puteaux, F (4)
Au, L-T, Consulting Engineer, Los Angeles, CA, USA (R)*
Aycardi, L.G., Aycardi Ingenieria, Bogota, CO (R)

Baratta, A., University of Naples, Naples, I (7)
Barthelemy, B., Lehigh University, Bethlehem, PA, USA (4)
Basler, E., Basler & Hofmann, Zurich, CH (7)
Batanero, J.G., Ciudad Universitaria, Madrid, E (R)
Benjamin, J.R., EDAC, Palo Alto, CA, USA (7)

Beresford, F.D., CSIRO, Highett, Victoria, AUS (1)
Bertero, V.V., University of California, Berkeley, CA, USA (2)
Birkeland, P.W., A.B.A.M. Engineers Inc., Tacoma, WA, USA (6)
Biskup, J.T., Canadian Welding Bureau, Toronto, CDN (6)
Bitterice, M.G., PPG Industries, Inc., Pittsburgh, PA (6)
Bizri, H., Rock Springs, WY, USA (4)

*Designates organizer of National/Regional Conference

Blakey, F.A., CSIRO, Highett, Victoria, AUS (1)
Blessmann, J., Federal University of Rio Grande do Sul, Porto Alegre, BR (3) (R)
Blick, R.L., Material Service Corp., Chicago, IL (6)
Blume, J.A., John A. Blume & Associates, Engineers, San Francisco, CA, USA (2)
Bresler, B., Wiss, Janney, Elstner & Associates, Inc., Emeryville, CA, USA (4)

Bruinette, K.E., Bruinette, Kruger, Stoffberg & Hugo, Pretoria, ZA (R)
Bubnov, S., Yugoslav Association—Earthquake Engineering, Ljubljana, YU (2) (R)
Calegari, D.D., Federal University of Rio Grande Do Sul, Porto Alegre, BR (6)
Carmona, J.S., Universidad Nacional de Cuyo, San Juan, RA (2)
Cermak, J.E., Colorado State University, Fort Collins, CO, USA (3)

Chen, P.W., Consulting Engineer, Englewood Cliffs, NJ, USA (3)
Cheng, H.K., H.K. Cheng & Associates, Hong Kong, HK (R)
Chiu, A., University of Hawaii, Honolulu, HI, USA (R)
Claiborne, G.R., Grinnell Corp., Los Angeles, CA, USA (4)
Clough, R.W., University of California, Berkeley, CA, USA (2)

Conway, D., Arkisyst, UNESCO, Paris, F (R)
Cornell, C.A., Massachusetts Institute of Technology, Cambridge, MA, USA (7)
Coroneos, D., Consulting Engineer, Athens, GR (R)
Cowan, H.J., The University of Sydney, Sydney, AUS (R)
Crist, R.A., ASCE, New York, NY, USA (1)

Dalgliesh, W.A., National Research Council of Canada, Ottawa, CDN (3)
Davenport, A.G., University of Western Ontario, London, CDN (3)
De Buen, O., National University of Mexico, Mexico City, MEX (R)
Degenkolb, J.G., Fire Protection Consulting Engineer, Glendale, CA, USA (4)
Dore, E., Cement & Concrete Association, London, GB (4)

Duke, C.M., University of California, Los Angeles, CA, USA (2)
Eaton, K.J., Building Research Station, Watford, GB (3)
Ehm, H., Technischen Universität Braunschweig, Braunschweig, BRD (4)
El-Demirdash, I.A., Cairo University, Giza, ET (R)
Elstner, R.C., Wiss, Janney, Elstner & Associates, Inc., Northbrook, IL, USA (4)

Esteva, L., Ciudad Universitaria, Mexico City, MEX (7)
Faltus, F., Technical University, Prague, CS (R)
Ferguson, B.J., A.R.C. Industries, Ltd., Melbourne, AUS (6)
Finzi, L., University of Milan, Milan, I (R)
Fiorato, A.E., Portland Cement Association, Skokie, IL, USA (6)

Fitzgerald, J.F., Chicago Department of Buildings, Chicago, IL, USA (4)
Freeman, G., Fire Services Headquarters, North Point, HK (4)
Fuller, G.R., HUD, Washington, D.C., USA (1)
Galambos, T.V., Washington University, St. Louis, MO, USA (1,2)
Galbreath, M., National Research Council of Canada, Ottawa, CDN (4)

Gaylord, E., University of Illinois, Urbana, IL, USA
Gellert, M., Technion Israel, Haifa, IL (2)
Glück, J., Technion Israel, Haifa, IL (2)
Godfrey, G.B., CONSTRADO, Croydon, GB (1)
Golden, F., Concrete Industry Board of New York, New York, NY, USA (6)

Goschy, B., Geotechnical Institution, Budapest, H (6) (R)
Gramolin, I., GOSSTROY, Moscow, SU (6) (R)
Granstrom, S., Sven Tyren AB, Stockholm, S (5)
Greene, Jr., W.E., National Bureau of Standards, Washington, D.C., USA (1)
Grundy, P., Monash University, Victoria, AUS (1)

Gustaferro, A.H., Consulting Engineers Group Inc., Glenview, IL, USA (4)
Guttero, M.M., Facultad de Arquitectura Y Urbanismo, Buenos Aires, RA (1)
Halasz, O., Technical University, Budapest, H (R)
Harrison, G.A., National Bureau of Standards, Washington, D.C., USA (4)
Hart, G.C., University of California, Los Angeles, CA, USA (2)

Henderson, W., University of Edinburgh, Edinburgh, Scotland (R)
Heun, R.C., New York Concrete Institute, New York, NY (6)
Hisada, T., Kajima Institute of Construction Technology, Tokyo, J (2)
Holm, T.A., Solite Corporation, West New York, NJ, USA (6)
Hongladaromp, T., Expressway & Rapid Transit Authority, Bangkok, T (R)

Housner, G.W., California Institute of Technology, Pasadena, CA, USA (2)
Huang, L.Y., Smith, Hinchman & Grolls Assoc. Inc., Detroit, MI, USA (1)
Ishizaki, H., Kyoto University, Kyoto, J (3)
Ito, M., University of Tokyo, Tokyo, J (3)
Izumi, M., Ministry of Construction, Tokyo, J (1)

Jackson, F., Institution of Fire Engineers, Hong Kong Branch, North Point, HK (4)
Jackson, N., University of Dundee, Dundee, GB (6)
Jaunet, Cdt., Paris Fire Brigade, Paris, F (4)
Jensen, R.H., Rolf Jensen & Associates, Inc., Deerfield, IL, USA (4)
Johnson, S.M., URS/Madigan-Praeger, Inc., New York, NY, USA (1)

Kabaila, A.P., University of New South Wales, Kensington, AUS (1)
Kaddah, H., Hamed Kaddah & Partners, Cairo, ET (R)
Kajfasz, S., Polish Academy of Sciences, Warsaw, PL (4, 5)
Kamei, T., Kawasaki Heavy Industries, Ltd., Noda, J (6)
Karthardja, A., Directorate of Building Research, Bandung, RI (R)

Kawagoe, K., Science University of Tokyo, Noda-shi, J (4)
Keough, J.J., Experimental Building Station, Chatswood, AUS (4)
Kill, R.F., Chicago Building Department, Chicago, IL, USA (4)
Knight, D., BHP Melbourne Research Labs, Clayton, AUS (4)
König, G.F., König und Heunisch, Frankfurt Am Main, BRD (1, 7)

Kordina, K., Technischen Universität Braunschweig, Braunschweig, BRD (4)
Kotze, F.W.C., Fire Department, Johannesburg, ZA (4)
Kowalczyk, R.M., Polish Academy of Sciences, Warsaw, PL
Kozak, J., Vitkovice Design Office, Floglova, CS (R)
Krishna, J., University of Roorkee, Roorkee, IND (2)

Kruppa, J., CTICM, Puteaux, F (4)
Ku, J., Institution of Structural Engineers, Hong Kong, HK (R)
Lalwani, C.L., Barber & Hoffman, Inc., Cleveland, OH, USA (1)
Laurie, J.A.P., South African Council for Scientific & Industrial Research, Pretoria, ZA (1)
Law, M., Ove Arup & Partners, London, GB (4)

Lay, M.G., Australian Road Research Board, Victoria, AUS (4)
Lee, S.L., University of Singapore, Singapore, SGP (R)
Levelius, W.H., Pittsburgh Testing Laboratory, Pittsburgh, PA, USA (6)
Lew, H.S., National Bureau of Standards, Washington, D.C., USA (1)
L'Hermite, R., Union Technique Interprofessionelle, Paris, F (6)

Lie, T.T., National Research Council, Ottawa, CDN (4)
Liebenberg, A.C., Liebenberg & Stander, Capetown, ZA (7)
Ligtenberg, F.K., Institut T.N.O., Delft, NL (7)
Lim, B., University of Singapore, Singapore, SGP (R)
Lind, N.C., University of Waterloo, Waterloo, CDN (7)

Lord, J., Seismic Engineering Association, Ltd., Los Angeles, CA, USA (2)
Lu, L.W., Lehigh University, Bethlehem, PA, USA (R)
Lubinski, M., Politechnika Warszawska, Warsaw, PL (R)
Mackey, S., Consulting Engineer, Hong Kong, HK (3) (R)
Magnusson, S.E., Lund Institute of Technology, Lund, S (7)

Mainstone, R.J., Building Research Station, Watford, GB (1, 4, 5)
Mandy, S.N., Carlton Center, Ltd., Johannesburg, ZA (5)
Margarido, A.F., Figueindo Ferraz Ltda., Sao Paulo, BR (4)
Marincek, M., University of Ljubljana, Ljubljana, YU (R)
Marosszeky, M., Civil & Civic Pty., Ltd., Sydney, AUS (1)

Marryatt, H.W., Foundation Chairman & Life Member of the Australian Fire Protection Association, Wangaratta, AUS (4)
Marshall, R.D., National Bureau of Standards, Washington, D.C., USA (3)
Martin, I., Capacete-Martin & Associates, San Juan, PR (6)
Massie, C.W., Jetway, Ogden, UT (6)
Mayes, R.L., Applied Technology Council, Palo Alto, CA (2)

Mayne, J.R., Building Research Station, Watford, GB (3)
Mazilu, P., Institute of Civil Engineers, Bucarest, R (2) (R)
McGuire, J.H., National Research Council of Canada, Ottawa, CDN (4)
Melbourne, W.H., Monash University, Victoria, AUS (3)
Meli, R., Ciudad Universitaria, Mexico City, MEX (7)

Miki, S., Kawasaki Heavy Industries, Ltd., Hyogo, J (6)
Millen, J.A., affiliation not available, Pittsburgh, PA, USA (6)
Milner, J., London Fire Brigade, London, GB (4)
Mitchell, G.R., Building Research Station, Watford, GB (1)
Moharram, A., Arab Consulting Engineers, Cairo, ET (R)

Monge, J.E., University of Chile, Santiago, RCH (2)
Morris, J., National Building Research Institute, Pretoria, ZA (6)
Moses, F., Case Western Reserve University, Cleveland, OH, USA (7)
Moyer, J.I., Lehigh University, Bethlehem, PA, USA
Muto, K., Muto Institute of Structural Mechanics, Inc., Tokyo, J (1, 2) (R)

Naka, T., University of Tokyo, Tokyo, J (R)
Nakagawa, K., Ohbayashi-Gumi, Ltd., Tokyo, J (2)
Napper, L.A., Bethlehem Steel Company, Bethlehem, PA, USA (6)
Nassar, G., Arab Consulting Engineers, Cairo, ET (R)
Navaratnarajah, V., University of Malaya, Kuala Lumpur, PTM (1)

Nelson, H.E., National Bureau of Standards, Washington, D.C., USA (4)
Newmark, N.M., University of Illinois, Urbana, IL, USA (5)
Oba, H., Kawasaki Heavy Industries, Ltd., Noda, J (6)
Osawa, Y., University of Tokyo, Tokyo, J (2)
Penzien, J., University of California, Berkeley, CA, USA (2)

Pettersson, O., Lund Institute of Technology, Lund, S (4)
Pinkham, C.W., S.B. Barnes & Associates, Los Angeles, CA, USA (2)
Preece, F.R., Testing Engineers, Inc., San Francisco, CA, USA (6)
Prendergast, E., Chicago Fire Department, Chicago, IL, USA (4)
Principe, F.J., Principe-Danna, Inc., Long Island City, NY, USA (6)

Quasebarth, W., Atlas Machine & Iron Works, Inc., Gainesville, VA, USA (6)
Rahulan, G., Sepakat Setia Perunding, Kuala Lumpur, PTM (R)
Rasbash, D.J., Department of Fire Safety Engineering, Edinburgh, Scotland (4)
Ravindra, M.K., Sargent & Lundy, Chicago, IL, USA (1)
Reese, R.C., Raymond Reese Associates, Toledo, OH, USA (1)

Reinitzhuber, F., Consulting Engineer, Duisburg-Rheinhausen, BRD (R)
Reznik, S., Central Research & Design Institute for Dwellings, Moscow, SU (6)
Robertson, L.E., Skilling, Helle, Christiansen, Robertson, New York, NY, USA
Roosseno, R., Professor, Jakarta, RI (R)
Rosenblueth, E., Ciudad Universitaria, Mexico City, MEX (1, 7)

Rubanenko, B., Research and Design Institute for Dwellings, Moscow, SU (R)
Sahlin, S., Chalmers University of Technology, Goteborg, S (6)
Saillard, Y., CEB, Paris, F (1)
Sandberg, H.R., Alfred Bensch & Company, Chicago, IL, USA (R)
Sandi, H., Building Research Institute, Bucarest, R (2, 7)

Saragoni, G.R., University of Chile, Santiago, RCH (2)
Sawyer, Jr., H.A., Consulting Engineer, Gainesville, FL, USA (2)
Schneider, L.M., Experimental Building Station, Chatswood, AUS (1)
Schriever, W.R., National Research Council of Canada, Ottawa, CDN (1, 4)
Schulz, G., Universität Innsbruck, Innsbruck, A (R)

Scruton, C., Industrial Aerodynamics Consultant, Hayling Island, GB (3)
Seed, H.B., University of California, Berkeley, CA, USA (2)
Seigel, L.G., U.S. Steel Corporation, Monroeville, PA, USA (4)
Sfintesco, D., CTICM, Paris, F (4) (R)
Shah, H.C., Stanford University, Stanford, CA, USA (7)

Shaver, J.R., National Bureau of Standards, Gaithersburg, MD, USA (1)
Shepherd, R., University of Auckland, Auckland, NZ (2) (R)
Somes, N.F., National Bureau of Standards, Washington, D.C., USA (4, 5)
Spratt, B.H., Cement & Concrete Association, Bucks., GB (1)
Springfield, J., C.D. Carruthers & Wallace, Consultants, Rexdale, CDN (3)

Spyropoulos, C., U.S. Department of Housing & Urban Development, Washington, D.C., USA (3)
Stevens, L.K., University of Melbourne, Parkville, AUS (3)
Stiller, M., Deutscher Beton-Verein, Wiesbaden, BRD (6)
Tamboli, A.R., Consulting Engineer, Verona, NJ, USA (2)
Taylor, P.J., Peter Taylor & Associates, North Sydney, AUS (1)

Contributors

Thomas, B.F., BHP Melbourne Research Labs, Clayton, AUS (1, 3)
Thomas, P.K., Ministry of Shipping & Transport, New Delhi, IND (R)
Thompson, R.J., National Fire Protection Association, Boston, MA, USA (4)
Thürlimann, B., Swiss Federal Institute of Technology, Zurich, CH (R)
Tichy, M., Building Research Institute, Prague, CS (7)

Tomonaga, K., Yokogawa Bridge Works, Ltd., Tokyo, J (6)
Turkstra, C.J., McGill University, Montreal, CDN (7)
Urbano, C., Technical University of Milan, Milano, I (6)
Uribe, J., Escuela Colombiana de Ingeniera, Bogota, CO (4)
Van Aardt, J.H.P., National Building Research Institute, Pretoria, ZA (6)

Van Douwen, A., Technical University of Delft, Delft, NL (R)
van Koten, H., Institute TNO for Building Material & Building Structures, Rijswijk, NL (3)
Vavaroutas, B.A., B.A. Vavaroutas Consulting Engineers, Athens, GR (R)
Vickery, B.J., University of Western Ontario, London, CDN (3)
Volkamer, C.W., International Association of Fire Chiefs, Washington, D.C., USA (4)

Wahl, L., CTICM, Puteaux, F (4)
Wakabayashi, M., Kyoto University, Uji City, J (1) (R)
Westhoff, L.J., Baugh Construction Company, Seattle, WA, USA (6)
Wheatley, R.A., Fire Prevention Bureau, Hong Kong, HK (4)
Wheen, R.J., The University of Sydney, Sydney, AUS (1)

Whitbread, R.E., National Maritime Institute, Teddington, GB (3)
White, Jr., E.J., Skilling, Helle, Christiansen, & Robertson, New York, NY, USA (6)
Whitman, R.V., Massachusetts Institute of Technology, Cambridge, MA, USA (2)
Wildt, R.H., Bethlehem Steel Corp., Bethlehem, PA, USA (4)
Witteveen, J., Institute TNO for Building Materials & Building Structures, Rijswijk, NL (4)

Woodgate, R.W., Building Research Station, Watford, GB (1)
Wright, R.N., National Bureau of Standards, Washington, D.C., USA (1)
Wyatt, T.A., Imperial College, London, GB (3)
Yuill, C.H., Southwest Research Institute (Retired), San Antonio, TX, USA (4)

Building Index

The following index enables the reader to identify the page number on which a particular building is mentioned. Numbers in italics designate page numbers for figures. Numbers in italics that follow cities refer to panoramic photographic views.

771

Name Index

The following list cites the page numbers on which the indicated names are mentioned. The list includes the authors as well as other individuals or organizations named in the text.

Names followed by years refer to bibliographic citations that are included in the appendix entitled "References/Bibliography." When the name is followed by initials, the designated page shows membership in one of the committes of the Council.

Subject Index

292, 294
neutral stability 173
neutrally stable atmospheric wind 214
Nevada Testing Ground 73
new building 23, 294
new building project 444
new code approach 239
new concrete 341
new fireproof building 350
New Orleans, Louisiana 353, 370
new standardized procedure 273
New York Fire Brigade 315
New York, N.Y., USA 42, 152, 166, 167,
    168, 370, 422, 423, 541
New York skyscraper 146
New York State 42
New Zealand 137
New Zealand Standard Code of Practice
    132
Newton's law of motion 576
next code generation 571
nightclub 370
Niigata earthquake, 1964 70, 113
Niigata, Japan 70
nitrogen 276, 277
noise 21, 157, 310, 318
noise level 229
nominal area 566
nominal cost of failure 635
nominal damage 342
nominal dead load 5
nominal gradient wind speed 161
nominal safety factor 636
nominal size 5
nominal strength 455, 558
nominally concentric load 631
nominally homogeneous subsoil 573
nomogram 401
non-uniform thickness 503
nonadaptive behavior 302
noncombustible material 255, 306, 309
noncombustible wall 308
noncombustible wall surface 253
noncompliance 332
nondestructive testing 445, 464
nondestructive testing of glass 528
nondimensional scaling parameter 214
nonengineer 554
nonidentical loading 587
nonindustrial building 407, 408
nonlinear analysis 50, 529
nonlinear dynamic analysis 51
nonlinear function 640
nonlinear material 81
nonlinear multidegree system 618

nonlinear, statically indeterminate sys-
    tem 556
nonlinear strain effect 101
nonlinear stress-deformation 81
nonlinear stress-strain characteristic 79
nonlinear structural behavior 591, 618
nonloadbearing interior partition 29
nonmaterial loss 553
nonmechanical property 273
nonrational aspect 297
nonrational behavior 298
nonredundant system 625
nonreinforced masonry 505
nonresidential use 407, 408
nonseismic load 120, 121
nonsocial activity 298
nonsocial aspect 297, 298
nonsocial behavior 298
nonstandard field method 507
nonstationarity 618
nonstationary random function 594
nonstructural cladding 89
nonstructural damage 119, 120, 569
nonstructural element 29, 110, 113, 115,
    129, 427, 569
nonstructural infill wall 116
nonstructural item 118
nonstructural measure 430
nonstructural protection 275
nonsymmetrical loading 589
nonsynchronous seismic ground accel-
    eration 599
nonsynchronous time dependence 595
nonuniform cap thickness 504
nonuniform load 8, 505
nonuniform thermal stress distribution
    28
nonuniformly distributed load 593
nonwelded plate 459
normal aggregate 6
normal aging 523
normal behavior 591
normal design 579
normal distribution 232, 545, 584, 605,
    606
normal distribution curve 471
normal door 312
normal ductile shear failure 465
normal exit sign 304
normal frequency distribution 468, 604,
    605
normal insulation 27
normal lighting system 314
normal live load 20
normal load 394